BUSINESS AND COMPANY LEGISLATION

BUSINESS AND COMPANY LEGISLATION

Jason Ellis

Published by
College of Law Publishing,
Braboeuf Manor, Portsmouth Road, St Catherines, Guildford GU3 1HA

British Library Cataloging-in-Publication Data
A catalogue record for this book is available from the British Library.

ISBN 978 1 915469 80 9

Typeset by Style Photosetting Ltd, Mayfield, East Sussex

Contents

Note: The text of the legislation incorporates amendments and repeals to 6 April 2024. Repeals and omissions are indicated by an ellipsis. Prospective repeals and legislation not yet brought into force are printed in italics; legislation remaining in force but to be amended is noted to this effect.

However, although the amendments made by the Economic Crime and Corporate Transparency Act 2023 that are in force as at 6 April 2024 have been incorporated into the text, amendments by the 2023 Act that remain prospective as at that date have not been included or noted. As such, amendments to legislation contained within this book may have been made by the 2023 Act since publication. Readers are, therefore, advised to confirm the up to date position when referring to this book.

This text is for student reference only. It should not be relied upon either as a complete or accurate statement or representation of the law nor in the formulation or provision of advice.

Financial Services and Securities Regulation

Companies Act 2006

Arrangement of sections

Companies Act 2006

2006 c. 46

An Act to reform company law and restate the greater part of the enactments relating to companies; to make other provision relating to companies and other forms of business organisation; to make provision about directors' disqualification, business names, auditors and actuaries; to amend Part 9 of the Enterprise Act 2002; and for connected purposes. [8th November 2006]

PART 1
GENERAL INTRODUCTORY PROVISIONS

Companies and Companies Acts

1   Companies

(1)   In the Companies Acts, unless the context otherwise requires—
"company" means a company formed and registered under this Act, that is—
    (a)   a company so formed and registered after the commencement of this Part, or
    (b)   a company that immediately before the commencement of this Part—
        (i)   was formed and registered under the Companies Act 1985 or the Companies (Northern Ireland) Order 1986, or
        (ii)   was an existing company for the purposes of that Act or that Order,
    (which is to be treated on commencement as if formed and registered under this Act).

(2)   Certain provisions of the Companies Acts apply to—
    (a)   companies registered, but not formed, under this Act (see Chapter 1 of Part 33), and
    (b)   bodies incorporated in the United Kingdom but not registered under this Act (see Chapter 2 of that Part).

(3)   For provisions applying to companies incorporated outside the United Kingdom, see Part 34 (overseas companies).

2   The Companies Acts

(1)   In this Act "the Companies Acts" means—
    (a)   the company law provisions of this Act,
    (b)   Part 2 of the Companies (Audit, Investigations and Community Enterprise) Act 2004 (community interest companies), and
    (c)   the provisions of the Companies Act 1985 and the Companies Consolidation (Consequential Provisions) Act 1985 that remain in force.

(2)   The company law provisions of this Act are—
    (a)   the provisions of Parts 1 to 39 of this Act, and
    (b)   the provisions of Parts 45 to 47 of this Act so far as they apply for the purposes of those Parts.

Types of company

3   Limited and unlimited companies

(1)   A company is a "limited company" if the liability of its members is limited by its constitution.
It may be limited by shares or limited by guarantee.

(2)   If their liability is limited to the amount, if any, unpaid on the shares held by them, the company is "limited by shares".

(3)   If their liability is limited to such amount as the members undertake to contribute to the assets of the company in the event of its being wound up, the company is "limited by guarantee".

(4)   If there is no limit on the liability of its members, the company is an "unlimited company".

4   Private and public companies

(1)   A "private company" is any company that is not a public company.

(2)   A "public company" is a company limited by shares or limited by guarantee and having a share capital—

   (a)   whose certificate of incorporation states that it is a public company, and

   (b)   in relation to which the requirements of this Act, or the former Companies Acts, as to registration or re-registration as a public company have been complied with on or after the relevant date.

(3)   For the purposes of subsection (2)(b) the relevant date is—

   (a)   in relation to registration or re-registration in Great Britain, 22nd December 1980;

   (b)   in relation to registration or re-registration in Northern Ireland, 1st July 1983.

(4)   For the two major differences between private and public companies, see Part 20.

5   Companies limited by guarantee and having share capital

(1)   A company cannot be formed as, or become, a company limited by guarantee with a share capital.

(2)   Provision to this effect has been in force—

   (a)   in Great Britain since 22nd December 1980, and

   (b)   in Northern Ireland since 1st July 1983.

(3)   Any provision in the constitution of a company limited by guarantee that purports to divide the company's undertaking into shares or interests is a provision for a share capital.

   This applies whether or not the nominal value or number of the shares or interests is specified by the provision.

6   Community interest companies

(1)   In accordance with Part 2 of the Companies (Audit, Investigations and Community Enterprise) Act 2004—

   (a)   a company limited by shares or a company limited by guarantee and not having a share capital may be formed as or become a community interest company, and

   (b)   a company limited by guarantee and having a share capital may become a community interest company.

(2)   The other provisions of the Companies Acts have effect subject to that Part.

PART 2

COMPANY FORMATION

General

7   Method of forming company

(1)   A company is formed under this Act by one or more persons—

   (a)   subscribing their names to a memorandum of association (see section 8), and

   (b)   complying with the requirements of this Act as to registration (see sections 9 to 13).

(2)   A company may not be so formed for an unlawful purpose.

8   Memorandum of association

(1)   A memorandum of association is a memorandum stating that the subscribers—

   (a)   wish to form a company under this Act, and

   (b)   agree to become members of the company and, in the case of a company that is to have a share capital, to take at least one share each.

(2)   The memorandum must be in the prescribed form and must be authenticated by each subscriber.

Requirements for registration

9   Registration documents

(1)   The memorandum of association must be delivered to the registrar together with an application for registration of the company, the documents required by this section and a statement of compliance.

(2)   The application for registration must state—

(a)   the company's proposed name,

(b)   whether the company's registered office is to be situated in England and Wales (or in Wales), in Scotland or in Northern Ireland,

(c)   whether the liability of the members of the company is to be limited, and if so whether it is to be limited by shares or by guarantee, …

(d)   whether the company is to be a private or a public company, and

(e)   that the subscribers wish to form the company for lawful purposes.

(3)   If the application is delivered by a person as agent for the subscribers to the memorandum of association, it must state his name and address.

(4)   The application must contain—

(a)   in the case of a company that is to have a share capital, a statement of capital and initial shareholdings (see section 10);

(b)   in the case of a company that is to be limited by guarantee, a statement of guarantee (see section 11);

(c)   a statement of the company's proposed officers (see section 12);

(d)   a statement of initial significant control (see section 12A).

(5)   The application must also contain—

(a)   a statement of the intended address of the company's registered office, which must be an appropriate address within the meaning given by section 86(2); …

(aa)   a statement of the intended registered email address of the company, which must be an appropriate email address within the meaning given by section 88A(2);

(b)   a copy of any proposed articles of association (to the extent that these are not supplied by the default application of model articles: see section 20); and

(c)   a statement of the type of company it is to be and its intended principal business activities.

(5A)   The information as to the company's type must be given by reference to the classification scheme prescribed for the purposes of this section.

(5B)   The information as to the company's intended principal business activities may be given by reference to one or more categories of any prescribed system of classifying business activities.

(6)   The application must be delivered—

(a)   to the registrar of companies for England and Wales, if the registered office of the company is to be situated in England and Wales (or in Wales);

(b)   to the registrar of companies for Scotland, if the registered office of the company is to be situated in Scotland;

(c)   to the registrar of companies for Northern Ireland, if the registered office of the company is to be situated in Northern Ireland.

10   Statement of capital and initial shareholdings

(1)   The statement of capital and initial shareholdings required to be delivered in the case of a company that is to have a share capital must comply with this section.

(2)   It must state—

(a)   the total number of shares of the company to be taken on formation by the subscribers to the memorandum of association,

(b)   the aggregate nominal value of those shares,

(ba)   the aggregate amount (if any) to be unpaid on those shares (whether on account of their nominal value or by way of premium), and

(c)   for each class of shares—

    (i) prescribed particulars of the rights attached to the shares,

    (ii) the total number of shares of that class, and

    (iii) the aggregate nominal value of shares of that class, ...

  (d) ...

(3) It must contain such information as may be prescribed for the purpose of identifying the subscribers to the memorandum of association.

(4) It must state, with respect to each subscriber to the memorandum—

  (a) the number, nominal value (of each share) and class of shares to be taken by him on formation, and

  (b) the amount to be paid up and the amount (if any) to be unpaid on each share (whether on account of the nominal value of the share or by way of premium).

(5) Where a subscriber to the memorandum is to take shares of more than one class, the information required under subsection (4) (a) is required for each class.

11 Statement of guarantee

(1) The statement of guarantee required to be delivered in the case of a company that is to be limited by guarantee must comply with this section.

(2) It must contain such information as may be prescribed for the purpose of identifying the subscribers to the memorandum of association.

(3) It must state that each member undertakes that, if the company is wound up while he is a member, or within one year after he ceases to be a member, he will contribute to the assets of the company such amount as may be required for—

  (a) payment of the debts and liabilities of the company contracted before he ceases to be a member,

  (b) payment of the costs, charges and expenses of winding up, and

  (c) adjustment of the rights of the contributories among themselves, not exceeding a specified amount.

12 Statement of proposed officers

(1) The statement of the company's proposed officers required to be delivered to the registrar must contain the required particulars of—

  (a) the person who is, or persons who are, to be the first director or directors of the company;

  (b) in the case of a company that is to be a private company, any person who is (or any persons who are) to be the first secretary (or joint secretaries) of the company;

  (c) in the case of a company that is to be a public company, the person who is (or the persons who are) to be the first secretary (or joint secretaries) of the company.

(2) The required particulars are the particulars that will be required (or, in the absence of an election under section 167A or 279A, would be required) to be stated—

  (a) in the case of a director, in the company's register of directors and register of directors' residential addresses (see sections 162 to 166);

  (b) in the case of a secretary, in the company's register of secretaries (see sections 277 to 279).

(3) The statement must also include a statement by the subscribers to the memorandum of association that each of the persons named as a director, as secretary or as one of the joint secretaries has consented to act in the relevant capacity.

  If all the partners in a firm are to be joint secretaries, consent may be given by one partner on behalf of all of them.

12A Statement of initial significant control

(1) The statement of initial significant control required to be delivered to the registrar must—

  (a) state whether, on incorporation, there will be anyone who will count for the purposes of section 790M (register of people with significant control over a company) as either a registrable person or a registrable relevant legal entity in relation to the company,

  (b) include the required particulars of anyone who will count as such, and

(c)   include any other matters that on incorporation will be required (or, in the absence of an election under section 790X, would be required) to be entered in the company's PSC register by virtue of section 790M.

(2)   It is not necessary to include under subsection (1)(b) the date on which someone becomes a registrable person or a registrable relevant legal entity in relation to the company.

(3)   If the statement includes required particulars of an individual, it must also contain a statement that those particulars are included with the knowledge of that individual.

(4)   "Registrable person", "registrable relevant legal entity" and "required particulars" have the meanings given in Part 21A (see sections 790C and 790K).

13   Statement of compliance

(1)   The statement of compliance required to be delivered to the registrar is a statement that the requirements of this Act as to registration have been complied with.

(2)   The registrar may accept the statement of compliance as sufficient evidence of compliance.

Registration and its effect

14   Registration

If the registrar is satisfied that the requirements of this Act as to registration are complied with, he shall register the documents delivered to him.

15   Issue of certificate of incorporation

(1)   On the registration of a company, the registrar of companies shall give a certificate that the company is incorporated.

(2)   The certificate must state—
(a)   the name and registered number of the company,
(b)   the date of its incorporation,
(c)   whether it is a limited or unlimited company, and if it is limited whether it is limited by shares or limited by guarantee,
(d)   whether it is a private or a public company, and
(e)   whether the company's registered office is situated in England and Wales (or in Wales), in Scotland or in Northern Ireland.

(3)   The certificate must be signed by the registrar or authenticated by the registrar's official seal.

(4)   The certificate is conclusive evidence that the requirements of this Act as to registration have been complied with and that the company is duly registered under this Act.

16   Effect of registration

(1)   The registration of a company has the following effects as from the date of incorporation.

(2)   The subscribers to the memorandum, together with such other persons as may from time to time become members of the company, are a body corporate by the name stated in the certificate of incorporation.

(3)   That body corporate is capable of exercising all the functions of an incorporated company.

(4)   The status, registered email address and registered office of the company are as stated in, or in connection with, the application for registration.

(5)   In the case of a company having a share capital, the subscribers to the memorandum become holders of the shares specified in the statement of capital and initial shareholdings.

(6)   The persons named in the statement of proposed officers—
(a)   as director, or
(b)   as secretary or joint secretary of the company,
are deemed to have been appointed to that office.

PART 3
A COMPANY'S CONSTITUTION

CHAPTER 1
INTRODUCTORY

17   A company's constitution

Unless the context otherwise requires, references in the Companies Acts to a company's constitution include—

(a)   the company's articles, and

(b)   any resolutions and agreements to which Chapter 3 applies (see section 29).

CHAPTER 2
ARTICLES OF ASSOCIATION

General

18   Articles of association

(1)   A company must have articles of association prescribing regulations for the company.

(2)   Unless it is a company to which model articles apply by virtue of section 20 (default application of model articles in case of limited company), it must register articles of association.

(3)   Articles of association registered by a company must—

(a)   be contained in a single document, and

(b)   be divided into paragraphs numbered consecutively.

(4)   References in the Companies Acts to a company's "articles" are to its articles of association.

19   Power of Secretary of State to prescribe model articles

(1)   The Secretary of State may by regulations prescribe model articles of association for companies.

(2)   Different model articles may be prescribed for different descriptions of company.

(3)   A company may adopt all or any of the provisions of model articles.

(4)   Any amendment of model articles by regulations under this section does not affect a company registered before the amendment takes effect. "Amendment" here includes addition, alteration or repeal.

(5)   Regulations under this section are subject to negative resolution procedure.

20   Default application of model articles

(1)   On the formation of a limited company—

(a)   if articles are not registered, or

(b)   if articles are registered, in so far as they do not exclude or modify the relevant model articles,

the relevant model articles (so far as applicable) form part of the company's articles in the same manner and to the same extent as if articles in the form of those articles had been duly registered.

(2)   The "relevant model articles" means the model articles prescribed for a company of that description as in force at the date on which the company is registered.

Alteration of articles

21   Amendment of articles

(1)   A company may amend its articles by special resolution.

(2)   In the case of a company that is a charity, this is subject to—

(a)   in England and Wales, sections 197 and 198 of the Charities Act 2011;

(b)   in Northern Ireland, *Article 9 of the Charities (Northern Ireland) Order 1987*.

(3)   In the case of a company that is registered in the Scottish Charity Register, this is subject to—

(a)   section 112 of the Companies Act 1989, and

(b)   section 16 of the Charities and Trustee Investment (Scotland) Act 2005.

Note. The italicized words in subsection (2)(b) are substituted by the words "section 96 of the Charities Act (Northern Ireland) 2008" by the Charities Act (Northern Ireland) 2008, s. 183, Sch. 8, para. 13(1), as from a day to be appointed.

22   Entrenched provisions of the articles

(1)   A company's articles may contain provision ("provision for entrenchment") to the effect that specified provisions of the articles may be amended or repealed only if conditions are met, or procedures are complied with, that are more restrictive than those applicable in the case of a special resolution.

(2)   Provision for entrenchment may only be made—
   (a)   in the company's articles on formation, or
   (b)   by an amendment of the company's articles agreed to by all the members of the company.

(3)   Provision for entrenchment does not prevent amendment of the company's articles—
   (a)   by agreement of all the members of the company, or
   (b)   by order of a court or other authority having power to alter the company's articles.

(4)   Nothing in this section affects any power of a court or other authority to alter a company's articles.

23   Notice to registrar of existence of restriction on amendment of articles

(1)   Where a company's articles—
   (a)   on formation contain provision for entrenchment,
   (b)   are amended so as to include such provision, or
   (c)   are altered by order of a court or other authority so as to restrict or exclude the power of the company to amend its articles,
the company must give notice of that fact to the registrar.

(2)   Where a company's articles—
   (a)   are amended so as to remove provision for entrenchment, or
   (b)   are altered by order of a court or other authority—
       (i)   so as to remove such provision, or
       (ii)   so as to remove any other restriction on, or any exclusion of, the power of the company to amend its articles,
the company must give notice of that fact to the registrar.

24   Statement of compliance where amendment of articles restricted

(1)   This section applies where a company's articles are subject—
   (a)   to provision for entrenchment, or
   (b)   to an order of a court or other authority restricting or excluding the company's power to amend the articles.

(2)   If the company—
   (a)   amends its articles, and
   (b)   is required to send to the registrar a document making or evidencing the amendment,
the company must deliver with that document a statement of compliance.

(3)   The statement of compliance required is a statement certifying that the amendment has been made in accordance with the company's articles and, where relevant, any applicable order of a court or other authority.

(4)   The registrar may rely on the statement of compliance as sufficient evidence of the matters stated in it.

25   Effect of alteration of articles on company's members

(1)   A member of a company is not bound by an alteration to its articles after the date on which he became a member, if and so far as the alteration—
   (a)   requires him to take or subscribe for more shares than the number held by him at the date on which the alteration is made, or

(b)   in any way increases his liability as at that date to contribute to the company's share capital or otherwise to pay money to the company.

(2)   Subsection (1) does not apply in a case where the member agrees in writing, either before or after the alteration is made, to be bound by the alteration.

26   Registrar to be sent copy of amended articles

(1)   Where a company amends its articles it must send to the registrar a copy of the articles as amended not later than 15 days after the amendment takes effect.

(2)   This section does not require a company to set out in its articles any provisions of model articles that—

(a)   are applied by the articles, or

(b)   apply by virtue of section 20 (default application of model articles).

(3)   If a company fails to comply with this section an offence is committed by—

(a)   the company, and

(b)   every officer of the company who is in default.

(4)   A person guilty of an offence under this section is liable on summary conviction to a fine not exceeding level 3 on the standard scale and, for continued contravention, a daily default fine not exceeding one-tenth of level 3 on the standard scale.

27   Registrar's notice to comply in case of failure with respect to amended articles

(1)   If it appears to the registrar that a company has failed to comply with any enactment requiring it—

(a)   to send to the registrar a document making or evidencing an alteration in the company's articles, or

(b)   to send to the registrar a copy of the company's articles as amended, the registrar may give notice to the company requiring it to comply.

(2)   The notice must—

(a)   state the date on which it is issued, and

(b)   require the company to comply within 28 days from that date.

(3)   If the company complies with the notice within the specified time, no criminal proceedings may be brought in respect of the failure to comply with the enactment mentioned in subsection (1).

(4)   If the company does not comply with the notice within the specified time, it is liable to a civil penalty of £200.

This is in addition to any liability to criminal proceedings in respect of the failure mentioned in subsection (1).

(5)   The penalty may be recovered by the registrar and is to be paid into the Consolidated Fund.

Supplementary

28   Existing companies: provisions of memorandum treated as provisions of articles

(1)   Provisions that immediately before the commencement of this Part were contained in a company's memorandum but are not provisions of the kind mentioned in section 8 (provisions of new-style memorandum) are to be treated after the commencement of this Part as provisions of the company's articles.

(2)   This applies not only to substantive provisions but also to provision for entrenchment (as defined in section 22).

(3)   The provisions of this Part about provision for entrenchment apply to such provision as they apply to provision made on the company's formation, except that the duty under section 23(1)(a) to give notice to the registrar does not apply.

CHAPTER 3
RESOLUTIONS AND AGREEMENTS AFFECTING A COMPANY'S CONSTITUTION

29   Resolutions and agreements affecting a company's constitution

(1)   This Chapter applies to—

(a)   any special resolution;

(b)   any resolution or agreement agreed to by all the members of a company that, if not so agreed to, would not have been effective for its purpose unless passed as a special resolution;

(c)   any resolution or agreement agreed to by all the members of a class of shareholders that, if not so agreed to, would not have been effective for its purpose unless passed by some particular majority or otherwise in some particular manner;

(d)   any resolution or agreement that effectively binds all members of a class of shareholders though not agreed to by all those members;

(e)   any other resolution or agreement to which this Chapter applies by virtue of any enactment.

(2)   References in subsection (1) to a member of a company, or of a class of members of a company, do not include the company itself where it is such a member by virtue only of its holding shares as treasury shares.

30   Copies of resolutions or agreements to be forwarded to registrar

(1)   A copy of every resolution or agreement to which this Chapter applies, or (in the case of a resolution or agreement that is not in writing) a written memorandum setting out its terms, must be forwarded to the registrar within 15 days after it is passed or made.

(2)   If a company fails to comply with this section, an offence is committed by—

(a)   the company, and

(b)   every officer of it who is in default.

(3)   A person guilty of an offence under this section is liable on summary conviction to a fine not exceeding level 3 on the standard scale and, for continued contravention, a daily default fine not exceeding one-tenth of level 3 on the standard scale.

(4)   For the purposes of this section, a liquidator of the company is treated as an officer of it.

CHAPTER 4

MISCELLANEOUS AND SUPPLEMENTARY PROVISIONS

Statement of company's objects

31   Statement of company's objects

(1)   Unless a company's articles specifically restrict the objects of the company, its objects are unrestricted.

(2)   Where a company amends its articles so as to add, remove or alter a statement of the company's objects—

(a)   it must give notice to the registrar,

(b)   on receipt of the notice, the registrar shall register it, and

(c)   the amendment is not effective until entry of that notice on the register.

(3)   Any such amendment does not affect any rights or obligations of the company or render defective any legal proceedings by or against it.

(4)   In the case of a company that is a charity, the provisions of this section have effect subject to—

(a)   in England and Wales, sections 197 and 198 of the Charities Act 2011;

(b)   in Northern Ireland, section 96 of the Charities Act (Northern Ireland) 2008.

(5)   In the case of a company that is entered in the Scottish Charity Register, the provisions of this section have effect subject to the provisions of the Charities and Trustee Investment (Scotland) Act 2005.

Other provisions with respect to a company's constitution

32   Constitutional documents to be provided to members

(1)   A company must, on request by any member, send to him the following documents—

(a)   an up-to-date copy of the company's articles;

(b)   a copy of any resolution or agreement relating to the company to which Chapter 3 applies (resolutions and agreements affecting a company's constitution) and that is for the time being in force;

(c)   a copy of any document required to be sent to the registrar under—

    (i)   section 34(2) (notice where company's constitution altered by enactment), or

    (ii)   section 35(2)(a) (notice where order of court or other authority alters company's constitution);

(d)   a copy of any court order under section 899 (order sanctioning compromise or arrangement) or section 900 (order facilitating reconstruction or amalgamation);

(da)   a copy of any court order under section 901F (order sanctioning compromise or arrangement for company in financial difficulty) or section 901J (order facilitating reconstruction or amalgamation);

(e)   a copy of any court order under section 996 (protection of members against unfair prejudice: powers of the court) that alters the company's constitution;

(f)   a copy of the company's current certificate of incorporation, and of any past certificates of incorporation;

(g)   in the case of a company with a share capital, a current statement of capital;

(h)   in the case of a company limited by guarantee, a copy of the statement of guarantee.

(2)   The statement of capital required by subsection (1)(g) is a statement of—

(a)   the total number of shares of the company,

(b)   the aggregate nominal value of those shares,

(ba)   the aggregate amount (if any) unpaid on those shares (whether on account of their nominal value or by way of premium), and

(c)   for each class of shares—

    (i)   prescribed particulars of the rights attached to the shares,

    (ii)   the total number of shares of that class, and

    (iii)   the aggregate nominal value of shares of that class, ...

(d)   ...

(3)   If a company makes default in complying with this section, an offence is committed by every officer of the company who is in default.

(4)   A person guilty of an offence under this section is liable on summary conviction to a fine not exceeding level 3 on the standard scale.

33   Effect of company's constitution

(1)   The provisions of a company's constitution bind the company and its members to the same extent as if there were covenants on the part of the company and of each member to observe those provisions.

(2)   Money payable by a member to the company under its constitution is a debt due from him to the company.

In England and Wales and Northern Ireland it is of the nature of an ordinary contract debt.

34   Notice to registrar where company's constitution altered by enactment

(1)   This section applies where a company's constitution is altered by an enactment, other than an enactment amending the general law.

(2)   The company must give notice of the alteration to the registrar, specifying the enactment, not later than 15 days after the enactment comes into force. In the case of a special enactment the notice must be accompanied by a copy of the enactment.

(3)   If the enactment amends—

(a)   the company's articles, or

(b)   a resolution or agreement to which Chapter 3 applies (resolutions and agreements affecting a company's constitution),

the notice must be accompanied by a copy of the company's articles, or the resolution or agreement in question, as amended.

(4)   A "special enactment" means an enactment that is not a public general enactment, and includes—

(a)   an Act for confirming a provisional order,

(b)   any provision of a public general Act in relation to the passing of which any of the standing orders of the House of Lords or the House of Commons relating to Private Business applied, or

(c)   any enactment to the extent that it is incorporated in or applied for the purposes of a special enactment.

(5)   If a company fails to comply with this section an offence is committed by—

(a)   the company, and

(b)   every officer of the company who is in default.

(6)   A person guilty of an offence under this section is liable on summary conviction to a fine not exceeding level 3 on the standard scale and, for continued contravention, a daily default fine not exceeding one-tenth of level 3 on the standard scale.

35   Notice to registrar where company's constitution altered by order

(1)   Where a company's constitution is altered by an order of a court or other authority, the company must give notice to the registrar of the alteration not later than 15 days after the alteration takes effect.

(2)   The notice must be accompanied by—

(a)   a copy of the order, and

(b)   if the order amends—

(i)   the company's articles, or

(ii)   a resolution or agreement to which Chapter 3 applies (resolutions and agreements affecting the company's constitution),

a copy of the company's articles, or the resolution or agreement in question, as amended.

(3)   If a company fails to comply with this section an offence is committed by—

(a)   the company, and

(b)   every officer of the company who is in default.

(4)   A person guilty of an offence under this section is liable on summary conviction to a fine not exceeding level 3 on the standard scale and, for continued contravention, a daily default fine not exceeding one-tenth of level 3 on the standard scale.

(5)   This section does not apply where provision is made by another enactment for the delivery to the registrar of a copy of the order in question.

36   Documents to be incorporated in or accompany copies of articles issued by company

(1)   Every copy of a company's articles issued by the company must be accompanied by—

(a)   a copy of any resolution or agreement relating to the company to which Chapter 3 applies (resolutions and agreements affecting a company's constitution),

(b)   where the company has been required to give notice to the registrar under section 34(2) (notice where company's constitution altered by enactment), a statement that the enactment in question alters the effect of the company's constitution,

(c)   where the company's constitution is altered by a special enactment (see section 34(4)), a copy of the enactment, and

(d)   a copy of any order required to be sent to the registrar under section 35(2)(a) (order of court or other authority altering company's constitution).

(2)   This does not require the articles to be accompanied by a copy of a document or by a statement if—

(a)   the effect of the resolution, agreement, enactment or order (as the case may be) on the company's constitution has been incorporated into the articles by amendment, or

(b)   the resolution, agreement, enactment or order (as the case may be) is not for the time being in force.

(3)   If the company fails to comply with this section, an offence is committed by every officer of the company who is in default.

(4)   A person guilty of an offence under this section is liable on summary conviction to a fine not exceeding level 3 on the standard scale for each occasion on which copies are issued, or, as the case may be, requested.

(5)   For the purposes of this section, a liquidator of the company is treated as an officer of it.

Supplementary provisions

37   Right to participate in profits otherwise than as member void

In the case of a company limited by guarantee and not having a share capital any provision in the company's articles, or in any resolution of the company, purporting to give a person a right to participate in the divisible profits of the company otherwise than as a member is void.

38   Application to single member companies of enactments and rules of law

Any enactment or rule of law applicable to companies formed by two or more persons or having two or more members applies with any necessary modification in relation to a company formed by one person or having only one person as a member.

PART 4
A COMPANY'S CAPACITY AND RELATED MATTERS

Capacity of company and power of directors to bind it

39   A company's capacity

(1)   The validity of an act done by a company shall not be called into question on the ground of lack of capacity by reason of anything in the company's constitution.

(2)   This section has effect subject to section 42 (companies that are charities).

40   Power of directors to bind the company

(1)   In favour of a person dealing with a company in good faith, the power of the directors to bind the company, or authorise others to do so, is deemed to be free of any limitation under the company's constitution.

(2)   For this purpose—
    (a)   a person "deals with" a company if he is a party to any transaction or other act to which the company is a party,
    (b)   a person dealing with a company—
        (i)   is not bound to enquire as to any limitation on the powers of the directors to bind the company or authorise others to do so,
        (ii)   is presumed to have acted in good faith unless the contrary is proved, and
        (iii)   is not to be regarded as acting in bad faith by reason only of his knowing that an act is beyond the powers of the directors under the company's constitution.

(3)   The references above to limitations on the directors' powers under the company's constitution include limitations deriving—
    (a)   from a resolution of the company or of any class of shareholders, or
    (b)   from any agreement between the members of the company or of any class of shareholders.

(4)   This section does not affect any right of a member of the company to bring proceedings to restrain the doing of an action that is beyond the powers of the directors.

But no such proceedings lie in respect of an act to be done in fulfilment of a legal obligation arising from a previous act of the company.

(5)   This section does not affect any liability incurred by the directors, or any other person, by reason of the directors' exceeding their powers.

(6)   This section has effect subject to—
section 41 (transactions with directors or their associates), and
section 42 (companies that are charities).

41   Constitutional limitations: transactions involving directors or their associates

(1)   This section applies to a transaction if or to the extent that its validity depends on section 40 (power of directors deemed to be free of limitations under company's constitution in favour of person dealing with company in good faith).

Nothing in this section shall be read as excluding the operation of any other enactment or rule of law by virtue of which the transaction may be called in question or any liability to the company may arise.

(2)   Where—

(a)   a company enters into such a transaction, and

(b)   the parties to the transaction include—

(i)   a director of the company or of its holding company, or

(ii)   a person connected with any such director,

the transaction is voidable at the instance of the company.

(3)   Whether or not it is avoided, any such party to the transaction as is mentioned in subsection (2)(b)(i) or (ii), and any director of the company who authorised the transaction, is liable—

(a)   to account to the company for any gain he has made directly or indirectly by the transaction, and

(b)   to indemnify the company for any loss or damage resulting from the transaction.

(4)   The transaction ceases to be voidable if—

(a)   restitution of any money or other asset which was the subject matter of the transaction is no longer possible, or

(b)   the company is indemnified for any loss or damage resulting from the transaction, or

(c)   rights acquired bona fide for value and without actual notice of the directors' exceeding their powers by a person who is not party to the transaction would be affected by the avoidance, or

(d)   the transaction is affirmed by the company.

(5)   A person other than a director of the company is not liable under subsection (3) if he shows that at the time the transaction was entered into he did not know that the directors were exceeding their powers.

(6)   Nothing in the preceding provisions of this section affects the rights of any party to the transaction not within subsection (2)(b)(i) or (ii).

But the court may, on the application of the company or any such party, make an order affirming, severing or setting aside the transaction on such terms as appear to the court to be just.

(7)   In this section—

(a)   "transaction" includes any act; and

(b)   the reference to a person connected with a director has the same meaning as in Part 10 (company directors).

42   Constitutional limitations: companies that are charities

(1)   Sections 39 and 40 (company's capacity and power of directors to bind company) do not apply to the acts of a company that is a charity except in favour of a person who—

(a)   does not know at the time the act is done that the company is a charity, or

(b)   gives full consideration in money or money's worth in relation to the act in question and does not know (as the case may be)—

(i)   that the act is not permitted by the company's constitution, or

(ii))   that the act is beyond the powers of the directors.

(2)   Where a company that is a charity purports to transfer or grant an interest in property, the fact that (as the case may be)—

(a)   the act was not permitted by the company's constitution, or

(b)   the directors in connection with the act exceeded any limitation on their powers under the company's constitution, does not affect the title of a person who subsequently acquires the property or any interest in it for full consideration without actual notice of any such circumstances affecting the validity of the company's act.

(3)   In any proceedings arising out of subsection (1) or (2) the burden of proving—

          (a)   that a person knew that the company was a charity, or

          (b)   that a person knew that an act was not permitted by the company's constitution or was beyond the powers of the directors,

      lies on the person asserting that fact.

(4)   In the case of a company that is a charity the affirmation of a transaction to which section 41 applies (transactions with directors or their associates) is ineffective without the prior written consent of—

          (a)   in England and Wales, the Charity Commission;

          (b)   in Northern Ireland, the Department for Social Development.

(5)   This section does not extend to Scotland (but see section 112 of the Companies Act 1989).

Formalities of doing business under the law of England and Wales or Northern Ireland

43   Company contracts

(1)   Under the law of England and Wales or Northern Ireland a contract may be made—

          (a)   by a company, by writing under its common seal, or

          (b)   on behalf of a company, by a person acting under its authority, express or implied.

(2)   Any formalities required by law in the case of a contract made by an individual also apply, unless a contrary intention appears, to a contract made by or on behalf of a company.

44   Execution of documents

(1)   Under the law of England and Wales or Northern Ireland a document is executed by a company—

          (a)   by the affixing of its common seal, or

          (b)   by signature in accordance with the following provisions.

(2)   A document is validly executed by a company if it is signed on behalf of the company—

          (a)   by two authorised signatories, or

          (b)   by a director of the company in the presence of a witness who attests the signature.

(3)   The following are "authorised signatories" for the purposes of subsection (2)—

          (a)   every director of the company, and

          (b)   in the case of a private company with a secretary or a public company, the secretary (or any joint secretary) of the company.

(4)   A document signed in accordance with subsection (2) and expressed, in whatever words, to be executed by the company has the same effect as if executed under the common seal of the company.

(5)   In favour of a purchaser a document is deemed to have been duly executed by a company if it purports to be signed in accordance with subsection (2).

      A "purchaser" means a purchaser in good faith for valuable consideration and includes a lessee, mortgagee or other person who for valuable consideration acquires an interest in property.

(6)   Where a document is to be signed by a person on behalf of more than one company, it is not duly signed by that person for the purposes of this section unless he signs it separately in each capacity.

(7)   References in this section to a document being (or purporting to be) signed by a director or secretary are to be read, in a case where that office is held by a firm, as references to its being (or purporting to be) signed by an individual authorised by the firm to sign on its behalf.

(8)   This section applies to a document that is (or purports to be) executed by a company in the name of or on behalf of another person whether or not that person is also a company.

45   Common seal

(1)   A company may have a common seal, but need not have one.

(2)   A company which has a common seal shall have its name engraved in legible characters on the seal.

(3)   If a company fails to comply with subsection (2) an offence is committed by—

    (a)   the company, and

    (b)   every officer of the company who is in default.

(4)   An officer of a company, or a person acting on behalf of a company, commits an offence if he uses, or authorises the use of, a seal purporting to be a seal of the company on which its name is not engraved as required by subsection (2).

(5)   A person guilty of an offence under this section is liable on summary conviction to a fine not exceeding level 3 on the standard scale.

(6)   This section does not form part of the law of Scotland.

46   Execution of deeds

(1)   A document is validly executed by a company as a deed for the purposes of section 1(2)(b) of the Law of Property (Miscellaneous Provisions) Act 1989 and for the purposes of the law of Northern Ireland if, and only if—

    (a)   it is duly executed by the company, and

    (b)   it is delivered as a deed.

(2)   For the purposes of subsection (1)(b) a document is presumed to be delivered upon its being executed, unless a contrary intention is proved.

47   Execution of deeds or other documents by attorney

(1)   Under the law of England and Wales or Northern Ireland a company may, by instrument executed as a deed, empower a person, either generally or in respect of specified matters, as its attorney to execute deeds or other documents on its behalf.

(2)   A deed or other document so executed, whether in the United Kingdom or elsewhere, has effect as if executed by the company.

Formalities of doing business under the law of Scotland

48   Execution of documents by companies

(1)   The following provisions form part of the law of Scotland only.

(2)   Notwithstanding the provisions of any enactment, a company need not have a company seal.

(3)   For the purposes of any enactment—

    (a)   providing for a document to be executed by a company by affixing its common seal, or

    (b)   referring (in whatever terms) to a document so executed,

    a document signed or subscribed (or, in the case of an electronic document, authenticated) by or on behalf of the company in accordance with the provisions of the Requirements of Writing (Scotland) Act 1995 has effect as if so executed.

Other matters

49   Official seal for use abroad

(1)   A company that has a common seal may have an official seal for use outside the United Kingdom.

(2)   The official seal must be a facsimile of the company's common seal, with the addition on its face of the place or places where it is to be used.

(3)   The official seal when duly affixed to a document has the same effect as the company's common seal.

    This subsection does not extend to Scotland.

(4)   A company having an official seal for use outside the United Kingdom may—

    (a)   by writing under its common seal, or

    (b)   as respects Scotland, by writing subscribed or authenticated in accordance with the Requirements of Writing (Scotland) Act 1995,

    authorise any person appointed for the purpose to affix the official seal to any deed or other document to which the company is party.

(5)   As between the company and a person dealing with such an agent, the agent's authority continues—

(a) during the period mentioned in the instrument conferring the authority, or

(b) if no period is mentioned, until notice of the revocation or termination of the agent's authority has been given to the person dealing with him.

(6) The person affixing the official seal must certify in writing on the deed or other document to which the seal is affixed the date on which, and place at which, it is affixed.

50 Official seal for share certificates etc

(1) A company that has a common seal may have an official seal for use—

(a) for sealing securities issued by the company, or

(b) for sealing documents creating or evidencing securities so issued.

(2) The official seal—

(a) must be a facsimile of the company's common seal, with the addition on its face of the word "Securities", and

(b) when duly affixed to the document has the same effect as the company's common seal.

51 Pre-incorporation contracts, deeds and obligations

(1) A contract that purports to be made by or on behalf of a company at a time when the company has not been formed has effect, subject to any agreement to the contrary, as one made with the person purporting to act for the company or as agent for it, and he is personally liable on the contract accordingly.

(2) Subsection (1) applies—

(a) to the making of a deed under the law of England and Wales or Northern Ireland, and

(b) to the undertaking of an obligation under the law of Scotland,

as it applies to the making of a contract.

52 Bills of exchange and promissory notes

A bill of exchange or promissory note is deemed to have been made, accepted or endorsed on behalf of a company if made, accepted or endorsed in the name of, or by or on behalf or on account of, the company by a person acting under its authority.

PART 5
A COMPANY'S NAME

CHAPTER 1
GENERAL REQUIREMENTS

Prohibited names

53 Prohibited names

A company must not be registered under this Act by a name if, in the opinion of the Secretary of State—

(a) its use by the company would constitute an offence, or

(b) it is offensive.

53A Names for criminal purposes

A company must not be registered under this Act by a name if, in the opinion of the Secretary of State, the registration of the company by that name is intended to facilitate—

(a) the commission of an offence involving dishonesty or deception, or

(b) the carrying out of conduct that, if carried out in any part of the United Kingdom, would amount to such an offence.

Sensitive words and expressions

54 Names suggesting connection with government or public authority

(1) The approval of the Secretary of State is required for a company to be registered under this Act by a name that would be likely to give the impression that the company is connected with—

    (a)   Her Majesty's Government, any part of the Scottish administration, the Welsh Assembly Government or Her Majesty's Government in Northern Ireland,

    (b)   a local authority, or

    (c)   any public authority specified for the purposes of this section by regulations made by the Secretary of State.

(2)   For the purposes of this section—

"local authority" means—

    (a)   a local authority within the meaning of the Local Government Act 1972, the Common Council of the City of London or the Council of the Isles of Scilly,

    (b)   a council constituted under section 2 of the Local Government etc. (Scotland) Act 1994, or

    (c)   a district council in Northern Ireland;

"public authority" includes any person or body having functions of a public nature.

(3)   Regulations under this section are subject to affirmative resolution procedure.

55   **Other sensitive words or expressions**

(1)   The approval of the Secretary of State is required for a company to be registered under this Act by a name that includes a word or expression for the time being specified in regulations made by the Secretary of State under this section.

(2)   Regulations under this section are subject to approval after being made.

56   **Duty to seek comments of government department or other specified body**

(1)   The Secretary of State may by regulations under—

    (a)   section 54 (name suggesting connection with government or public authority), or

    (b)   section 55 (other sensitive words or expressions),

require that, in connection with an application for the approval of the Secretary of State under that section, the applicant must seek the view of a specified Government department or other body.

(2)   Where such a requirement applies, the applicant must request the specified department or other body (in writing) to indicate whether (and if so why) it has any objections to the proposed name.

(3)   Where a request under this section is made in connection with an application for the registration of a company under this Act, the application must—

    (a)   include a statement that a request under this section has been made, and

    (b)   be accompanied by a copy of any response received.

(4)   Where a request under this section is made in connection with a change in a company's name, the notice of the change sent to the registrar must be accompanied by—

    (a)   a statement by a director or secretary of the company that a request under this section has been made, and

    (b)   a copy of any response received.

(5)   In this section "specified" means specified in the regulations.

56A   **Names suggesting connection with foreign governments etc**

A company must not be registered under this Act by a name that, in the opinion of the Secretary of State, would be likely to give the false impression that the company is connected with—

    (a)   a foreign government or an agency or authority of a foreign government, or

    (b)   an international organisation whose members include two or more countries or territories (or their governments).

Permitted characters etc

57   **Permitted characters etc**

(1)   The Secretary of State may make provision by regulations—

    (a)   as to the letters or other characters, signs or symbols (including accents and other diacritical marks) and punctuation that may be used in the name of a company registered under this Act; and

(b)   specifying a standard style or format for the name of a company for the purposes of registration.

(2)   The regulations may prohibit the use of specified characters, signs or symbols when appearing in a specified position (in particular, at the beginning of a name).

(3)   A company may not be registered under this Act by a name that consists of or includes anything that is not permitted in accordance with regulations under this section.

(4)   Regulations under this section are subject to negative resolution procedure.

(5)   In this section "specified" means specified in the regulations.

Computer code

57A   Names containing computer code

A company must not be registered under this Act by a name that, in the opinion of the Secretary of State, consists of or includes computer code.

Prohibitions where a company has been required to change a name

57B   Prohibition on re-registering name following direction

(1)   Where a company's name has at any time been changed following a direction under section 67, 75, 76, 76A or 76B, or an order under section 73, the company must not subsequently be registered under this Act by the original name or a name that is similar to it.

(2)   But subsection (1) does not prevent the registration of the company by any name approved by the Secretary of State.

(3)   In subsection (1)—

(a)   the reference to the name of a company being changed following a direction under a particular section includes a case where a new name is determined for the company under section 76D because of its failure to comply with the direction;

(b)   the reference to the name of a company being changed following an order under section 73 includes a case where a new name is determined for the company under section 73(4) because of its failure to comply with an order.

57C   Name that another company has been directed to change

(1)   Where a company has at any time been directed under section 67, 75, 76, 76A or 76B, or ordered under section 73, to change its name, no other company may be registered under this Act by that name or a name that is similar if—

(a)   that company is an existing company and there is a person who has, or has had, a relevant relationship with both companies, or

(b)   an application has been made for the registration of that company and, if it is registered, there will on its incorporation be a person who has, or has had, a relevant relationship with both companies.

(2)   But subsection (1) does not prevent the registration of the company by any name approved by the Secretary of State.

(3)   For the purposes of subsection (1) it is irrelevant whether the person has, or has had, a relevant relationship with both companies at the same time.

(4)   For the purposes of this section a person has a "relevant relationship" with a company if the person is—

(a)   an officer, or

(b)   a member or former member.

(5)   In subsection (1)—

(a)   the reference to the name of a company being changed following a direction under a particular section includes a case where a new name is determined for the company under section 76D because of its failure to comply with the direction;

(b) the reference to the name of a company being changed following an order under section 73 includes a case where a new name is determined for the company under section 73(4) because of its failure to comply with an order.

CHAPTER 2
INDICATIONS OF COMPANY TYPE OR LEGAL FORM

Required indications for limited companies

58 Public limited companies

(1) The name of a limited company that is a public company must end with "public limited company" or "p.l.c.".

(2) In the case of a Welsh company, its name may instead end with "cwmni cyfyngedig cyhoeddus" or "c.c.c.".

(3) This section does not apply to community interest companies (but see section 33(3) and (4) of the Companies (Audit, Investigations and Community Enterprise) Act 2004).

59 Private limited companies

(1) The name of a limited company that is a private company must end with "limited" or "ltd.".

(2) In the case of a Welsh company, its name may instead end with "cyfyngedig" or "cyf.".

(3) Certain companies are exempt from this requirement (see section 60).

(4) This section does not apply to community interest companies (but see section 33(1) and (2) of the Companies (Audit, Investigations and Community Enterprise) Act 2004).

60 Exemption from requirement as to use of "limited"

(1) A private company is exempt from section 59 (requirement to have name ending with "limited" or permitted alternative) if—
   (a) it is a charity,
   (b) it is exempted from the requirement of that section by regulations made by the Secretary of State, or
   (c) it meets the conditions specified in—
       section 61 (continuation of existing exemption: companies limited by shares), or
       section 62 (continuation of existing exemption: companies limited by guarantee).

(2) The registrar may refuse to register a private limited company by a name that does not include the word "limited" (or a permitted alternative) unless a statement has been delivered to him that the company meets the conditions for exemption.

(3) The registrar may accept the statement as sufficient evidence of the matters stated in it.

(4) Regulations under this section are subject to negative resolution procedure.

61 Continuation of existing exemption: companies limited by shares

(1) This section applies to a private company limited by shares—
   (a) that on 25th February 1982—
       (i) was registered in Great Britain, and
       (ii) had a name that, by virtue of a licence under section 19 of the Companies Act 1948 (or corresponding earlier legislation), did not include the word "limited" or any of the permitted alternatives, or
   (b) that on 30th June 1983—
       (i) was registered in Northern Ireland, and
       (ii) had a name that, by virtue of a licence under section 19 of the Companies Act (Northern Ireland) 1960 (or corresponding earlier legislation), did not include the word "limited" or any of the permitted alternatives.

(2) A company to which this section applies is exempt from section 59 (requirement to have name ending with "limited" or permitted alternative) so long as—
   (a) it continues to meet the following two conditions, and

(b)   it does not change its name.

(3)   The first condition is that the objects of the company are the promotion of commerce, art, science, education, religion, charity or any profession, and anything incidental or conducive to any of those objects.

(4)   The second condition is that the company's articles—

(a)   require its income to be applied in promoting its objects,

(b)   prohibit the payment of dividends, or any return of capital, to its members, and

(c)   require all the assets that would otherwise be available to its members generally to be transferred on its winding up either—

(i)   to another body with objects similar to its own, or

(ii)   to another body the objects of which are the promotion of charity and anything incidental or conducive thereto,

(whether or not the body is a member of the company).

62   Continuation of existing exemption: companies limited by guarantee

(1)   A private company limited by guarantee that immediately before the commencement of this Part—

(a)   was exempt by virtue of section 30 of the Companies Act 1985 or Article 40 of the Companies (Northern Ireland) Order 1986 from the requirement to have a name including the word "limited" or a permitted alternative, and

(b)   had a name that did not include the word "limited" or any of the permitted alternatives,

is exempt from section 59 (requirement to have name ending with "limited" or permitted alternative) so long as it continues to meet the following two conditions and does not change its name.

(2)   The first condition is that the objects of the company are the promotion of commerce, art, science, education, religion, charity or any profession, and anything incidental or conducive to any of those objects.

(3)   The second condition is that the company's articles—

(a)   require its income to be applied in promoting its objects,

(b)   prohibit the payment of dividends to its members, and

(c)   require all the assets that would otherwise be available to its members generally to be transferred on its winding up either—

(i)   to another body with objects similar to its own, or

(ii)   to another body the objects of which are the promotion of charity and anything incidental or conducive thereto,

(whether or not the body is a member of the company).

63   Exempt company: restriction on amendment of articles

(1)   A private company—

(a)   that is exempt under section 61 or 62 from the requirement to use "limited" (or a permitted alternative) as part of its name, and

(b)   whose name does not include "limited" or any of the permitted alternatives,

must not amend its articles so that it ceases to comply with the conditions for exemption under that section.

(2)   If subsection (1) above is contravened an offence is committed by—

(a)   the company, and

(b)   every officer of the company who is in default.

For this purpose a shadow director is treated as an officer of the company.

(3)   A person guilty of an offence under this section is liable on summary conviction to a fine not exceeding level 5 on the standard scale and, for continued contravention, a daily default fine not exceeding one-tenth of the greater of £5,000 or level 4 on the standard scale.

(4)   Where immediately before the commencement of this section—

(a)   a company was exempt by virtue of section 30 of the Companies Act 1985 or Article 40 of the Companies (Northern Ireland) Order 1986 from the requirement to have a name including the word "limited" (or a permitted alternative), and

(b)   the company's memorandum or articles contained provision preventing an alteration of them without the approval of—

    (i)   the Board of Trade or a Northern Ireland department (or any other department or Minister), or

    (ii)   the Charity Commission,

that provision, and any condition of any such licence as is mentioned in section 61(1)(a)(ii) or (b)(ii) requiring such provision, shall cease to have effect. This does not apply if, or to the extent that, the provision is required by or under any other enactment.

(5)   It is hereby declared that any such provision as is mentioned in subsection (4)(b) formerly contained in a company's memorandum was at all material times capable, with the appropriate approval, of being altered or removed under section 17 of the Companies Act 1985 or Article 28 of the Companies (Northern Ireland) Order 1986 (or corresponding earlier enactments).

64   Power to direct change of name in case of company ceasing to be entitled to exemption

(1)   If it appears to the Secretary of State that a company whose name does not include "limited" or any of the permitted alternatives—

(a)   has ceased to be entitled to exemption under section 60(1)(a) or (b), or

(b)   in the case of a company within section 61 or 62 (which impose conditions as to the objects and articles of the company)—

    (i)   has carried on any business other than the promotion of any of the objects mentioned in subsection (3) of section 61 or, as the case may be, subsection (2) of section 62, or

    (ii)   has acted inconsistently with the provision required by subsection (4)(a) or (b) of section 61 or, as the case may be, subsection (3)(a) or (b) of section 62,

the Secretary of State may direct the company to change its name so that it ends with "limited" or one of the permitted alternatives.

(2)   The direction must be in writing and must specify the period within which the company is to change its name.

(2A)   The period must be a period of at least 28 days beginning with the date of the direction.

(2B)   The Secretary of State may by further direction in writing extend the period.

Any such direction must be given before the end of the period for the time being specified.

(3)   A change of name in order to comply with a direction under this section may be made by resolution of the directors.

This is without prejudice to any other method of changing the company's name.

(4)   Where a resolution of the directors is passed in accordance with subsection (3), the company must give notice to the registrar of the change.

Sections 80 and 81 apply as regards the registration and effect of the change.

(5)   If the company fails to comply with a direction under this section an offence is committed by—

(a)   the company, and

(b)   every officer of the company who is in default.

(6)   A person guilty of an offence under this section is liable on summary conviction to a fine not exceeding level 5 on the standard scale and, for continued contravention, a daily default fine not exceeding one-tenth of the greater of £5,000 or level 4 on the standard scale.

(6A)   Where a direction is given under subsection (1), the registrar may omit from the material on the register that is available for public inspection any mention of the name to which the direction relates.

(7)   A company that has been directed to change its name under this section may not, without the approval of the Secretary of State, subsequently change its name so that it does not include "limited" or one of the permitted alternatives.

This does not apply to a change of name on re-registration or on conversion to a community interest company.

Inappropriate use of indications of company type or legal form

65   Inappropriate use of indications of company type or legal form

(1)   The Secretary of State may make provision by regulations prohibiting the use in a company name of specified words, expressions or other indications—
         (a)   that are associated with a particular type of company or form of organisation, or
         (b)   that are similar to words, expressions or other indications associated with a particular type of company or form of organisation.

(2)   The regulations may prohibit the use of words, expressions or other indications—
         (a)   in a specified part, or otherwise than in a specified part, of a company's name;
         (b)   in conjunction with, or otherwise than in conjunction with, such other words, expressions or indications as may be specified.

(3)   A company must not be registered under this Act by a name that consists of or includes anything prohibited by regulations under this section.

(4)   In this section "specified" means specified in the regulations.

(5)   Regulations under this section are subject to negative resolution procedure.

CHAPTER 3
SIMILARITY TO OTHER NAMES

Similarity to other name on registrar's index

66   Name not to be the same as another in the index

(1)   A company must not be registered under this Act by a name that is the same as another name appearing in the registrar's index of company names.

(2)   The Secretary of State may make provision by regulations supplementing this section.

(3)   The regulations may make provision—
         (a)   as to matters that are to be disregarded, and
         (b)   as to words, expressions, signs or symbols that are, or are not, to be regarded as the same, for the purposes of this section.

(4)   The regulations may provide—
         (a)   that registration by a name that would otherwise be prohibited under this section is permitted—
                (i)   in specified circumstances, or
                (ii)   with specified consent, and
         (b)   that if those circumstances obtain or that consent is given at the time a company is registered by a name, a subsequent change of circumstances or withdrawal of consent does not affect the registration.

(5)   Regulations under this section are subject to negative resolution procedure.

(6)   In this section "specified" means specified in the regulations.

67   Power to direct change of name in case of similarity to existing name

(1)   The Secretary of State may direct a company to change its name if it has been registered in a name that is the same as or, in the opinion of the Secretary of State, too like—
         (a)   a name appearing at the time of the registration in the registrar's index of company names, or
         (b)   a name that should have appeared in that index at that time.

(1A)   Where a direction is given under subsection (1), the registrar may omit from the material on the register that is available for public inspection any mention of the name to which the direction relates (so far as it relates to the company to which the direction is given).

(2)   The Secretary of State may make provision by regulations supplementing this section.

(3)   The regulations may make provision—

(a) as to matters that are to be disregarded, and

(b) as to words, expressions, signs or symbols that are, or are not, to be regarded as the same,

for the purposes of this section.

(4) The regulations may provide—

    (a) that no direction is to be given under this section in respect of a name—

        (i) in specified circumstances, or

        (ii) if specified consent is given, and

    (b) that a subsequent change of circumstances or withdrawal of consent does not give rise to grounds for a direction under this section.

(5) Regulations under this section are subject to negative resolution procedure.

(6) In this section "specified" means specified in the regulations.

68 Direction to change name: supplementary provisions

(1) The following provisions have effect in relation to a direction under section 67 (power to direct change of name in case of similarity to existing name).

(2) Any such direction—

    (a) must be given within twelve months of the company's registration by the name in question, and

    (b) must specify the period within which the company is to change its name.

(2A) The period must be a period of at least 28 days beginning with the date of the direction.

(3) The Secretary of State may by a further direction extend that period.

Any such direction must be given before the end of the period for the time being specified.

(4) A direction under section 67 or this section must be in writing.

(5) If a company fails to comply with the direction, an offence is committed by—

    (a) the company, and

    (b) every officer of the company who is in default.

For this purpose a shadow director is treated as an officer of the company.

(6) A person guilty of an offence under this section is liable on summary conviction to a fine not exceeding level 3 on the standard scale and, for continued contravention, a daily default fine not exceeding one-tenth of level 3 on the standard scale.

Similarity to other name in which person has goodwill

69 Objection to company's registered name

(1) A person ("the applicant") may object to a company's registered name on the ground—

    (a) that it is the same as a name associated with the applicant in which he has goodwill, or

    (b) that it is sufficiently similar to such a name that its use in the United Kingdom or elsewhere would be likely to mislead members of the public in the United Kingdom or elsewhere by suggesting a connection between the company and the applicant.

(2) The objection must be made by application to a company names adjudicator (see section 70).

(3) The company concerned shall be the primary respondent to the application. Any of the following may be joined as respondents—

    (a) any member or person who was a member at the time at which the name was registered;

    (b) any director or person who was a director at the time at which the name was registered.

(4) If the ground specified in subsection (1)(a) or (b) is established, it is for the respondents to show—

    (a) that the name was registered before the commencement of the activities on which the applicant relies to show goodwill; or

    (b) ...

    (c) that the name was registered in the ordinary course of a company formation business and the company is available for sale to the applicant on the standard terms of that business; or

    (d) that the name was adopted in good faith; or

    (e) that the interests of the applicant are not adversely affected to any significant extent.

If none of those is shown, the objection shall be upheld.

(5)   If the facts mentioned in subsection (4)(a) ... or (c) are established, the objection shall nevertheless be upheld if the applicant shows that the main purpose of the respondents (or any of them) in registering the name was to obtain money (or other consideration) from the applicant or prevent him from registering the name.

(6)   If the objection is not upheld under subsection (4) or (5), it shall be dismissed.

(7)   In this section "goodwill" includes reputation of any description.

70   Company names adjudicators

(1)   The Secretary of State shall appoint persons to be company names adjudicators.

(2)   The persons appointed must have such legal or other experience as, in the Secretary of State's opinion, makes them suitable for appointment.

(3)   An adjudicator—
       (a)   holds office in accordance with the terms of his appointment,
       (b)   is eligible for re-appointment when his term of office ends,
       (c)   may resign at any time by notice in writing given to the Secretary of State, and
       (d)   may be dismissed by the Secretary of State on the ground of incapacity or misconduct.

(4)   One of the adjudicators shall be appointed Chief Adjudicator.
He shall perform such functions as the Secretary of State may assign to him.

(5)   The other adjudicators shall undertake such duties as the Chief Adjudicator may determine.

(6)   The Secretary of State may—
       (a)   appoint staff for the adjudicators;
       (b)   pay remuneration and expenses to the adjudicators and their staff;
       (c)   defray other costs arising in relation to the performance by the adjudicators of their functions;
       (d)   compensate persons for ceasing to be adjudicators.

71   Procedural rules

(1)   The Secretary of State may make rules about proceedings before a company names adjudicator.

(2)   The rules may, in particular, make provision—
       (a)   as to how an application is to be made and the form and content of an application or other documents;
       (b)   for fees to be charged;
       (c)   about the service of documents and the consequences of failure to serve them;
       (d)   as to the form and manner in which evidence is to be given;
       (e)   for circumstances in which hearings are required and those in which they are not;
       (f)   for cases to be heard by more than one adjudicator;
       (g)   setting time limits for anything required to be done in connection with the proceedings (and allowing for such limits to be extended, even if they have expired);
       (h)   enabling the adjudicator to strike out an application, or any defence, in whole or in part—
             (i)   on the ground that it is vexatious, has no reasonable prospect of success or is otherwise misconceived, or
             (ii)   for failure to comply with the requirements of the rules;
       (i)   conferring power to order security for costs (in Scotland, caution for expenses);
       (j)   as to how far proceedings are to be held in public;
       (k)   requiring one party to bear the costs (in Scotland, expenses) of another and as to the taxing (or settling) the amount of such costs (or expenses).

(3)   The rules may confer on the Chief Adjudicator power to determine any matter that could be the subject of provision in the rules.

(4)   Rules under this section shall be made by statutory instrument which shall be subject to annulment in pursuance of a resolution of either House of Parliament.

72   Decision of adjudicator to be made available to public

(1)   A company names adjudicator must, within 90 days of determining an application under section 69, make his decision and his reasons for it available to the public.

(2)   He may do so by means of a website or by such other means as appear to him to be appropriate.

73   Order requiring name to be changed

(1)   If an application under section 69 is upheld, the adjudicator shall make an order—

    (a)   requiring the respondent company to change its name to one that is not an offending name, and

    (b)   requiring all the respondents—

        (i)   to take all such steps as are within their power to make, or facilitate the making, of that change, and

        (ii)   not to cause or permit any steps to be taken calculated to result in another company being registered with a name that is an offending name.

(2)   An "offending name" means a name that, by reason of its similarity to the name associated with the applicant in which he claims goodwill, would be likely—

    (a)   to be the subject of a direction under section 67 (power of Secretary of State to direct change of name), or

    (b)   to give rise to a further application under section 69.

(3)   The order must specify a date by which the respondent company's name is to be changed and may be enforced—

    (a)   in England and Wales or Northern Ireland, in the same way as an order of the High Court;

    (b)   in Scotland, in the same way as a decree of the Court of Session.

(4)   If the respondent company's name is not changed in accordance with the order by the specified date, the adjudicator may determine a new name for the company.

(5)   If the adjudicator determines a new name for the respondent company he must give notice of his determination—

    (a)   to the applicant,

    (b)   to the respondents, and

    (c)   to the registrar.

(6)   For the purposes of this section a company's name is changed when the change takes effect in accordance with section 81(1) (on the issue of the new certification of incorporation).

(7)   Where an order is made under subsection (1), the registrar may omit from the material on the register that is available for public inspection any mention of the name to which the order relates.

74   Appeal from adjudicator's decision

(1)   An appeal lies to the court from any decision of a company names adjudicator to uphold or dismiss an application under section 69.

(2)   Notice of appeal against a decision upholding an application must be given before the date specified in the adjudicator's order by which the respondent company's name is to be changed.

(3)   If notice of appeal is given against a decision upholding an application, the effect of the adjudicator's order is suspended.

(4)   If on appeal the court—

    (a)   affirms the decision of the adjudicator to uphold the application, or

    (b)   reverses the decision of the adjudicator to dismiss the application,

the court may (as the case may require) specify the date by which the adjudicator's order is to be complied with, remit the matter to the adjudicator or make any order or determination that the adjudicator might have made.

(5)   If the court determines a new name for the company it must give notice of the determination—

    (a)   to the parties to the appeal, and

    (b)   to the registrar.

CHAPTER 4
OTHER POWERS OF THE SECRETARY OF STATE AND THE REGISTRAR

Provision of misleading information

75   Provision of misleading information etc

(1)   If it appears to the Secretary of State—

(a)   that misleading information has been given for the purposes of a company's registration by a particular name, or

(b)   that an undertaking or assurance has been given for that purpose and has not been fulfilled,

the Secretary of State may direct the company to change its name.

(2)   Any such direction—

(a)   must be given within five years of the company's registration by that name, and

(b)   must specify the period within which the company is to change its name.

(2A)   The period must be at least 28 days beginning with the date of the direction.

(3)   The Secretary of State may by a further direction extend the period within which the company is to change its name.

Any such direction must be given before the end of the period for the time being specified.

(4)   A direction under this section must be in writing.

(4A)   Where a direction is given under subsection (1), the registrar may omit from the material on the register that is available for public inspection any mention of the name to which the direction relates.

(5)   If a company fails to comply with a direction under this section, an offence is committed by—

(a)   the company, and

(b)   every officer of the company who is in default.

For this purpose a shadow director is treated as an officer of the company.

(6)   A person guilty of an offence under this section is liable on summary conviction to a fine not exceeding level 3 on the standard scale and, for continued contravention, a daily default fine not exceeding one-tenth of level 3 on the standard scale.

Misleading indication of activities and names used for criminal purposes

76   Misleading indication of activities

(1)   If in the opinion of the Secretary of State the name by which a company is registered gives so misleading an indication of the nature of its activities as to pose a risk of harm to the public in the United Kingdom or elsewhere, the Secretary of State may direct the company to change its name.

(2)   The direction must be in writing and must specify the period within which the company is to change its name.

(3)   The period must be a period of at least 28 days beginning with the date of the direction.

(3A)   The Secretary of State may by further direction in writing extend the period.

Any such direction must be given before the end of the period for the time being specified.

(4)   A company may apply to the court to set aside a direction under subsection (1).

(4A)   Any application under subsection (4) must be made within the period of three weeks beginning with the date of the direction.

(5)   The court may set the direction aside or confirm it.

If the direction is confirmed, the court shall specify the period within which the direction is to be complied with.

(5A)   If a company applies to the court under subsection (4) to set aside a direction, it is not required to comply with the direction while the proceedings are ongoing.

(5B)   Where a direction is given under subsection (1), the registrar may omit from the material on the register that is available for public inspection any mention of the name to which the direction relates.

(6)   If a company fails to comply with a direction under subsection (1), an offence is committed by—

(a)   the company, and

(b)　every officer of the company who is in default.

For this purpose a shadow director is treated as an officer of the company.

(7)　A person guilty of an offence under this section is liable on summary conviction to a fine not exceeding level 3 on the standard scale and, for continued contravention, a daily default fine not exceeding one-tenth of level 3 on the standard scale.

76A　Power to direct change of name used for criminal purposes

(1)　The Secretary of State may direct a company to change its name if it appears to the Secretary of State that the name has been used, or is intended to be used, by the company to facilitate—

(a)　the commission of an offence involving dishonesty or deception, or

(b)　the carrying out of conduct that, if carried out in any part of the United Kingdom, would amount to such an offence.

(2)　The direction must be in writing and must specify the period within which the company is to change its name.

(3)　The period must be a period of at least 28 days beginning with the date of the direction.

(4)　The Secretary of State may by further direction in writing extend the period.

Any such direction must be given before the end of the period for the time being specified.

(5)　A company may apply to the court to set aside a direction under subsection (1).

(6)　Any application under subsection (5) must be made within the period of three weeks beginning with the date of the direction.

(7)　On an application under subsection (5) the court may set the direction aside or confirm it.

(8)　If on an application under subsection (5) the direction is confirmed, the court must specify the period within which the direction is to be complied with.

(9)　Where a direction is given under subsection (1), the registrar may omit from the material on the register that is available for public inspection any mention of the name to which the direction relates.

(10)　If a company applies to the court under subsection (5) to set aside a direction, the company is not required to comply with the direction while the proceedings are ongoing.

(11)　If a company fails to comply with a direction under subsection (1), an offence is committed by—

(a)　the company, and

(b)　every officer of the company who is in default.

For this purpose a shadow director is treated as an officer of the company.

(12)　A person guilty of an offence under this section is liable on summary conviction to a fine not exceeding level 3 on the standard scale and, for continued contravention, a daily default fine not exceeding one-tenth of level 3 on the standard scale.

Direction to change name wrongly registered

76B　Direction to change name wrongly registered

(1)　The Secretary of State may direct a company to change its name if—

(a)　it appears to the Secretary of State that the company's registration by that name was in contravention of any requirement imposed by this Part, or

(b)　the Secretary of State did not, at the time at which the name was registered, form the opinion mentioned in section 53, 56A or 57A, but had proper grounds for doing so.

(2)　The direction must be in writing and must specify the period within which the company is to change its name.

(3)　The period must be a period of at least 28 days beginning with the date of the direction.

(4)　The Secretary of State may by further direction in writing extend the period.

Any such direction must be given before the end of the period for the time being specified.

(5)　A company may apply to the court to set aside a direction under subsection (1).

(6)　Any application under subsection (5) must be made within the period of three weeks beginning with the date of the direction.

(7)　On an application under subsection (5) the court may set the direction aside or confirm it.

(8)   If on an application under subsection (5) the direction is confirmed, the court must specify the period within which the direction is to be complied with.

(9)   Where a direction is given under subsection (1), the registrar may omit from the material on the register that is available for public inspection any mention of the name to which the direction relates.

(10)   If a company applies to the court under subsection (5) to set aside a direction, the company is not required to comply with the direction while the proceedings are ongoing.

(11)   If a company fails to comply with a direction under subsection (1), an offence is committed by—
        (a) the company, and
        (b) every officer of the company who is in default.
        For this purpose a shadow director is treated as an officer of the company.

(12)   A person guilty of an offence under this section is liable on summary conviction to a fine not exceeding level 3 on the standard scale and, for continued contravention, a daily default fine not exceeding one-tenth of level 3 on the standard scale.

Registrar's powers to change names

76C   Registrar's power to change name containing computer code

(1)   Where, in the opinion of the registrar, a company's registered name consists of or includes computer code, the registrar may—
        (a) determine a new name for the company, and
        (b) remove from the register any reference to the company's old name.

(2)   If the registrar determines a new name for a company under this section, the registrar must—
        (a) give the company notice of the determination, and
        (b) place a note of the determination in the register.

(3)   Where a company is given a direction under section 76B to change its name—
        (a) that does not affect the registrar's power to act under subsection (1), but
        (b) if the registrar does so, the direction lapses.

76D   Registrar's power to change name for failure to comply with direction

(1)   Where a company fails to comply with a direction to change its name, the registrar may determine a new name for the company.

(2)   The reference in subsection (1) to a direction to change a company's name is to a direction under section 64, 67, 75, 76, 76A or 76B.

(3)   If the registrar determines a new name for a company under this section, the registrar must—
        (a) give the company notice of the determination, and
        (b) place a note of the determination in the register.

CHAPTER 4A
EXCEPTIONS

76E   Exceptions based on national security etc

(1)   Nothing in this Part prevents the registration of a company under this Act by a name if the Secretary of State is satisfied that the registration of the company by that name is necessary—
        (a) in the interests of national security, or
        (b) for the purposes of preventing or detecting serious crime.

(2)   For the purposes of subsection (1)(b)—
        (a) "crime" means conduct which—
             (i)   constitutes a criminal offence, or
             (ii)   is, or corresponds to, any conduct which, if it all took place in any one part of the United Kingdom, would constitute a criminal offence, and
        (b) crime is "serious" if—

(i)   the offence which is or would be constituted by the conduct is an offence for which the maximum sentence (in any part of the United Kingdom) is imprisonment for 3 years or more, or

(ii)   the conduct involves the use of violence, results in substantial financial gain or is conduct by a large number of persons in pursuit of a common purpose.

CHAPTER 5
CHANGE OF NAME

77   Change of name

(1)   A company may change its name—

    (a)   by special resolution (see section 78), or

    (b)   by other means provided for by the company's articles (see section 79).

(2)   The name of a company may also be changed—

    (a)   by resolution of the directors acting under section 64 (change of name to comply with direction of Secretary of State under that section);

    (b)   on the determination of a new name by a company names adjudicator under section 73 (powers of adjudicator on upholding objection to company name);

    (c)   on the determination of a new name by the court under section 74 (appeal against decision of company names adjudicator);

    (d)   under section 1033 (company's name on restoration to the register);

    (e)   by resolution of the directors acting under section 45(3) of the Charities Act 2011 (change of name to comply with direction of Charity Commission).

78   Change of name by special resolution

(1)   Where a change of name has been agreed to by a company by special resolution, the company must give notice to the registrar.

This is in addition to the obligation to forward a copy of the resolution to the registrar.

(2)   Where a change of name by special resolution is conditional on the occurrence of an event, the notice given to the registrar of the change must—

    (a)   specify that the change is conditional, and

    (b)   state whether the event has occurred.

(3)   If the notice states that the event has not occurred—

    (a)   the registrar is not required to act under section 80 (registration and issue of new certificate of incorporation) until further notice,

    (b)   when the event occurs, the company must give notice to the registrar stating that it has occurred, and

    (c)   the registrar may rely on the statement as sufficient evidence of the matters stated in it.

79   Change of name by means provided for in company's articles

(1)   Where a change of a company's name has been made by other means provided for by its articles—

    (a)   the company must give notice to the registrar, and

    (b)   the notice must be accompanied by a statement that the change of name has been made by means provided for by the company's articles.

(2)   The registrar may rely on the statement as sufficient evidence of the matters stated in it.

80   Change of name: registration and issue of new certificate of incorporation

(1)   This section applies where—

    (a)   the registrar receives notice of a change of a company's name and is satisfied—

        (i)   that the new name complies with the requirements of this Part, and

        (ii)   that the requirements of the Companies Acts, and any relevant requirements of the company's articles, with respect to a change of name are complied with, or

    (b)   the registrar determines a new name for a company under section 76C or 76D.

(2)   The registrar must enter the new name on the register in place of the former name.

(3)   On the registration of the new name, the registrar must issue a certificate of incorporation altered to meet the circumstances of the case.

81   Change of name: effect

(1)   A change of a company's name has effect from the date on which the new certificate of incorporation is issued.

(2)   The change does not affect any rights or obligations of the company or render defective any legal proceedings by or against it.

(3)   Any legal proceedings that might have been continued or commenced against it by its former name may be continued or commenced against it by its new name.

CHAPTER 6
TRADING DISCLOSURES

82   Requirement to disclose company name etc

(1)   The Secretary of State may by regulations make provision requiring companies—
   (a)   to display specified information in specified locations,
   (b)   to state specified information in specified descriptions of document or communication, and
   (c)   to provide specified information on request to those they deal with in the course of their business.

(2)   The regulations—
   (a)   must in every case require disclosure of the name of the company, and
   (b)   may make provision as to the manner in which any specified information is to be displayed, stated or provided.

(3)   The regulations may provide that, for the purposes of any requirement to disclose a company's name, any variation between a word or words required to be part of the name and a permitted abbreviation of that word or those words (or vice versa) shall be disregarded.

(4)   In this section "specified" means specified in the regulations.

(5)   Regulations under this section are subject to affirmative resolution procedure.

83   Civil consequences of failure to make required disclosure

(1)   This section applies to any legal proceedings brought by a company to which section 82 applies (requirement to disclose company name etc) to enforce a right arising out of a contract made in the course of a business in respect of which the company was, at the time the contract was made, in breach of regulations under that section.

(2)   The proceedings shall be dismissed if the defendant (in Scotland, the defender) to the proceedings shows—
   (a)   that he has a claim against the claimant (pursuer) arising out of the contract that he has been unable to pursue by reason of the latter's breach of the regulations, or
   (b)   that he has suffered some financial loss in connection with the contract by reason of the claimant's (pursuer's) breach of the regulations,
unless the court before which the proceedings are brought is satisfied that it is just and equitable to permit the proceedings to continue.

(3)   This section does not affect the right of any person to enforce such rights as he may have against another person in any proceedings brought by that person.

84   Criminal consequences of failure to make required disclosures

(1)   Regulations under section 82 may provide—
   (a)   that where a company fails, without reasonable excuse, to comply with any specified requirement of regulations under that section an offence is committed by—
      (i)   the company, and
      (ii)   every officer of the company who is in default;

    (b)   that a person guilty of such an offence is liable on summary conviction to a fine not exceeding level 3 on the standard scale and, for continued contravention, a daily default fine not exceeding one-tenth of level 3 on the standard scale.

(2)   The regulations may provide that, for the purposes of any provision made under subsection (1), a shadow director of the company is to be treated as an officer of the company.

(3)   In subsection (1)(a) "specified" means specified in the regulations.

85   Minor variations in form of name to be left out of account

(1)   For the purposes of this Chapter, in considering a company's name no account is to be taken of—
    (a)whether upper or lower case characters (or a combination of the two) are used,
    (b)   whether diacritical marks or punctuation are present or absent,
    (c)   whether the name is in the same format or style as is specified under section 57(1)(b) for the purposes of registration,
    provided there is no real likelihood of names differing only in those respects being taken to be different names.

(2)   This does not affect the operation of regulations under section 57(1)(a) permitting only specified characters, diacritical marks or punctuation.

PART 6

A COMPANY'S REGISTERED OFFICE AND EMAIL ADDRESS

General

86   Duty to ensure registered office at appropriate address

(1)   A company must ensure that its registered office is at all times at an appropriate address.

(2)   An address is an "appropriate address" if, in the ordinary course of events—
    (a)   a document addressed to the company, and delivered there by hand or by post, would be expected to come to the attention of a person acting on behalf of the company, and
    (b)   the delivery of documents there is capable of being recorded by the obtaining of an acknowledgement of delivery.

(3)   If a company fails, without reasonable excuse, to comply with this section an offence is committed by—
    (a)   the company, and
    (b)   every officer of the company who is in default.

(4)   A person guilty of an offence under this section is liable on summary conviction—
    (a)   in England and Wales, to a fine;
    (b)   in Scotland or Northern Ireland, to a fine not exceeding level 5 on the standard scale and, for continued contravention, a daily default fine not exceeding one-tenth of level 5 on the standard scale.

(5)   Subsection (1) does not apply in relation to a company during any period for which the address of its registered office is a default address nominated by virtue of section 1097A(3)(h).

87   Change of address of registered office

(1)   A company may change the address of its registered office by giving notice to the registrar.

(1A)   The notice must include a statement that the new address is an appropriate address within the meaning given by section 86(2).

(2)   The change takes effect upon the notice being registered by the registrar, but until the end of the period of 14 days beginning with the date on which it is registered a person may validly serve any document on the company at the address previously registered.

(3)   For the purposes of any duty of a company—
    (a)   to keep available for inspection at its registered office any register, index or other document, or
    (b)   to mention the address of its registered office in any document,

a company that has given notice to the registrar of a change in the address of its registered office may act on the change as from such date, not more than 14 days after the notice is given, as it may determine.

(4)   Where a company unavoidably ceases to perform at its registered office any such duty as is mentioned in subsection (3)(a) in circumstances in which it was not practicable to give prior notice to the registrar of a change in the address of its registered office, but—
    (a)   resumes performance of that duty at other premises as soon as practicable, and
    (b)   gives notice accordingly to the registrar of a change in the situation of its registered office within 14 days of doing so,
it is not to be treated as having failed to comply with that duty.

Welsh companies

88   Welsh companies

(1)   In the Companies Acts a "Welsh company" means a company as to which it is stated in the register that its registered office is to be situated in Wales.

(2)   A company—
    (a)   whose registered office is in Wales, and
    (b)   as to which it is stated in the register that its registered office is to be situated in England and Wales,
may by special resolution require the register to be amended so that it states that the company's registered office is to be situated in Wales.

(3)   A company—
    (a)   whose registered office is in Wales, and
    (b)   as to which it is stated in the register that its registered office is to be situated in Wales,
may by special resolution require the register to be amended so that it states that the company's registered office is to be situated in England and Wales.

(4)   Where a company passes a resolution under this section it must give notice to the registrar, who shall—
    (a)   amend the register accordingly, and
    (b)   issue a new certificate of incorporation altered to meet the circumstances of the case.

Registered email address

88A   Duty to maintain a registered email address

(1)   A company must ensure that its registered email address is at all times an appropriate email address.

(2)   An email address is an "appropriate email address" if, in the ordinary course of events, emails sent to it by the registrar would be expected to come to the attention of a person acting on behalf of the company.

(3)   If a company fails, without reasonable excuse, to comply with this section an offence is committed by—
    (a)   the company, and
    (b)   every officer of the company who is in default.

(4)   A person guilty of an offence under this section is liable on summary conviction—
    (a)   in England and Wales, to a fine;
    (b)   in Scotland or Northern Ireland, to a fine not exceeding level 5 on the standard scale and, for continued contravention, a daily default fine not exceeding one-tenth of level 5 on the standard scale.

88B   Change of registered email address

(1)   A company may change its registered email address by giving notice to the registrar.

(2)   The notice must include a statement that the new address is an appropriate email address within the meaning given by section 88A(2).

(3)   The change takes effect upon the notice being registered by the registrar.

PART 7
RE-REGISTRATION AS A MEANS OF ALTERING A COMPANY'S STATUS

Introductory

89 Alteration of status by re-registration

A company may by re-registration under this Part alter its status—

(a)   from a private company to a public company (see sections 90 to 96);

(b)   from a public company to a private company (see sections 97 to 101);

(c)   from a private limited company to an unlimited company (see sections 102 to 104);

(d)   from an unlimited private company to a limited company (see sections 105 to 108);

(e)   from a public company to an unlimited private company (see sections 109 to 111).

Private company becoming public

90 Re-registration of private company as public

(1)   A private company (whether limited or unlimited) may be re-registered as a public company limited by shares if—

(a)   a special resolution that it should be so re-registered is passed,

(b)   the conditions specified below are met, and

(c)   an application for re-registration is delivered to the registrar in accordance with section 94, together with—

    (i)   the other documents required by that section, and

    (ii)   a statement of compliance.

(2)   The conditions are—

(a)   that the company has a share capital;

(b)   that the requirements of section 91 are met as regards its share capital;

(c)   that the requirements of section 92 are met as regards its net assets;

(d)   if section 93 applies (recent allotment of shares for non-cash consideration), that the requirements of that section are met; and

(e)   that the company has not previously been re-registered as unlimited.

(3)   The company must make such changes—

(a)   in its name, and

(b)   in its articles,

as are necessary in connection with its becoming a public company.

(4)   If the company is unlimited it must also make such changes in its articles as are necessary in connection with its becoming a company limited by shares.

91 Requirements as to share capital

(1)   The following requirements must be met at the time the special resolution is passed that the company should be re-registered as a public company—

(a)   the nominal value of the company's allotted share capital must be not less than the authorised minimum;

(b)   each of the company's allotted shares must be paid up at least as to one-quarter of the nominal value of that share and the whole of any premium on it;

(c)   if any shares in the company or any premium on them have been fully or partly paid up by an undertaking given by any person that he or another should do work or perform services (whether for the company or any other person), the undertaking must have been performed or otherwise discharged;

(d)   if shares have been allotted as fully or partly paid up as to their nominal value or any premium on them otherwise than in cash, and the consideration for the allotment consists of or includes an undertaking to the company (other than one to which paragraph (c) applies), then either—

    (i)   the undertaking must have been performed or otherwise discharged, or

(ii)   there must be a contract between the company and some person pursuant to which the undertaking is to be performed within five years from the time the special resolution is passed.

(2)   For the purpose of determining whether the requirements in subsection (1)(b), (c) and (d) are met, the following may be disregarded—

(a)   shares allotted—

    (i)   before 22nd June 1982 in the case of a company then registered in Great Britain, or

    (ii)   before 31st December 1984 in the case of a company then registered in Northern Ireland;

(b)   shares allotted in pursuance of an employees' share scheme by reason of which the company would, but for this subsection, be precluded under subsection (1)(b) (but not otherwise) from being re-registered as a public company.

(3)   No more than one-tenth of the nominal value of the company's allotted share capital is to be disregarded under subsection (2)(a).

For this purpose the allotted share capital is treated as not including shares disregarded under subsection (2)(b).

(4)   Shares disregarded under subsection (2) are treated as not forming part of the allotted share capital for the purposes of subsection (1)(a).

(5)   A company must not be re-registered as a public company if it appears to the registrar that—

(a)   the company has resolved to reduce its share capital,

(b)   the reduction—

    (i)   is made under section 626 (reduction in connection with redenomination of share capital),

    (iii)   is supported by a solvency statement in accordance with section 643, or

    (iii)   has been confirmed by an order of the court under section 648, and

(c)   the effect of the reduction is, or will be, that the nominal value of the company's allotted share capital is below the authorised minimum.

92   Requirements as to net assets

(1)   A company applying to re-register as a public company must obtain—

(a)   a balance sheet prepared as at a date not more than seven months before the date on which the application is delivered to the registrar,

(b)   an unqualified report by the company's auditor on that balance sheet, and

(c)   a written statement by the company's auditor that in his opinion at the balance sheet date the amount of the company's net assets was not less than the aggregate of its called-up share capital and undistributable reserves.

(2)   Between the balance sheet date and the date on which the application for re-registration is delivered to the registrar, there must be no change in the company's financial position that results in the amount of its net assets becoming less than the aggregate of its called-up share capital and undistributable reserves.

(3)   In subsection (1)(b) an "unqualified report" means—

(a)   if the balance sheet was prepared for a financial year of the company, a report stating without material qualification the auditor's opinion that the balance sheet has been properly prepared in accordance with the requirements of this Act;

(b)   if the balance sheet was not prepared for a financial year of the company, a report stating without material qualification the auditor's opinion that the balance sheet has been properly prepared in accordance with the provisions of this Act which would have applied if it had been prepared for a financial year of the company.

(4)   For the purposes of an auditor's report on a balance sheet that was not prepared for a financial year of the company, the provisions of this Act apply with such modifications as are necessary by reason of that fact.

(5)   For the purposes of subsection (3) a qualification is material unless the auditor states in his report that the matter giving rise to the qualification is not material for the purpose of determining (by

reference to the company's balance sheet) whether at the balance sheet date the amount of the company's net assets was not less than the aggregate of its called-up share capital and undistributable reserves.

(6)   In this Part "net assets" and "undistributable reserves" have the same meaning as in section 831 (net asset restriction on distributions by public companies).

93   Recent allotment of shares for non-cash consideration

(1)   This section applies where—

     (a)   shares are allotted by the company in the period between the date as at which the balance sheet required by section 92 is prepared and the passing of the resolution that the company should re-register as a public company, and

     (b)   the shares are allotted as fully or partly paid up as to their nominal value or any premium on them otherwise than in cash.

(2)   The registrar shall not entertain an application by the company for re-registration as a public company unless—

     (a)   the requirements of section 593(1)(a) and (b) have been complied with (independent valuation of non-cash consideration; valuer's report to company not more than six months before allotment), or

     (b)   the allotment is in connection with—

         (i)   a share exchange (see subsections (3) to (5) below), or

         (ii)   a proposed merger with another company (see subsection (6) below).

(3)   An allotment is in connection with a share exchange if—

     (a)   the shares are allotted in connection with an arrangement under which the whole or part of the consideration for the shares allotted is provided by—

         (i)   the transfer to the company allotting the shares of shares (or shares of a particular class) in another company, or

         (ii)   the cancellation of shares (or shares of a particular class) in another company; and

     (b)   the allotment is open to all the holders of the shares of the other company in question (or, where the arrangement applies only to shares of a particular class, to all the holders of the company's shares of that class) to take part in the arrangement in connection with which the shares are allotted.

(4)   In determining whether a person is a holder of shares for the purposes of subsection (3), there shall be disregarded—

     (a)   shares held by, or by a nominee of, the company allotting the shares;

     (b)   shares held by, or by a nominee of—

         (i)   the holding company of the company allotting the shares,

         (ii)   a subsidiary of the company allotting the shares, or

         (iii)   a subsidiary of the holding company of the company allotting the shares.

(5)   It is immaterial, for the purposes of deciding whether an allotment is in connection with a share exchange, whether or not the arrangement in connection with which the shares are allotted involves the issue to the company allotting the shares of shares (or shares of a particular class) in the other company.

(6)   There is a proposed merger with another company if one of the companies concerned proposes to acquire all the assets and liabilities of the other in exchange for the issue of its shares or other securities to shareholders of the other (whether or not accompanied by a cash payment).

     "Another company" includes any body corporate.

(7)   For the purposes of this section—

     (a)   the consideration for an allotment does not include any amount standing to the credit of any of the company's reserve accounts, or of its profit and loss account, that has been applied in paying up (to any extent) any of the shares allotted or any premium on those shares; and

     (b)   "arrangement" means any agreement, scheme or arrangement, (including an arrangement sanctioned in accordance with—

         (i)   Part 26 or 26A of this Act (arrangements and reconstructions), or

         (ii)   section 110 of the Insolvency Act 1986 or Article 96 of the Insolvency (Northern Ireland) Order 1989 (liquidator in winding up accepting shares as consideration for sale of company's property)).

94 Application and accompanying documents

(1) An application for re-registration as a public company must contain—
  (a) a statement of the company's proposed name on re-registration; and
  (b) in the case of a company without a secretary, a statement of the company's proposed secretary (see section 95).

(2) The application must be accompanied by—
  (a) a copy of the special resolution that the company should re-register as a public company (unless a copy has already been forwarded to the registrar under Chapter 3 of Part 3);
  (b) a copy of the company's articles as proposed to be amended;
  (c) a copy of the balance sheet and other documents referred to in section 92(1); ...
  (d) if section 93 applies (recent allotment of shares for non-cash consideration), a copy of the valuation report (if any) under subsection (2) (a) of that section; and
  (e) a statement of the aggregate amount paid up on the shares of the company on account of their nominal value.

(3) The statement of compliance required to be delivered together with the application is a statement that the requirements of this Part as to re-registration as a public company have been complied with.

(4) The registrar may accept the statement of compliance as sufficient evidence that the company is entitled to be re-registered as a public company.

95 Statement of proposed secretary

(1) The statement of the company's proposed secretary must contain the required particulars of the person who is or the persons who are to be the secretary or joint secretaries of the company.

(2) The required particulars are the particulars that will be required to be stated in the company's register of secretaries (see sections 277 to 279).

(3) The statement must also include a statement by the company that the person named as secretary, or each of the persons named as joint secretaries, has consented to act in the relevant capacity. If all the partners in a firm are to be joint secretaries, consent may be given by one partner on behalf of all of them.

96 Issue of certificate of incorporation on re-registration

(1) If on an application for re-registration as a public company the registrar is satisfied that the company is entitled to be so re-registered, the company shall be re-registered accordingly.

(2) The registrar must issue a certificate of incorporation altered to meet the circumstances of the case.

(3) The certificate must state that it is issued on re-registration and the date on which it is issued.

(4) On the issue of the certificate—
  (a) the company by virtue of the issue of the certificate becomes a public company,
  (b) the changes in the company's name and articles take effect, and
  (c) where the application contained a statement under section 95 (statement of proposed secretary), the person or persons named in the statement as secretary or joint secretary of the company are deemed to have been appointed to that office.

(5) The certificate is conclusive evidence that the requirements of this Act as to re-registration have been complied with.

Public company becoming private

97 Re-registration of public company as private limited company

(1) A public company may be re-registered as a private limited company if—
  (a) a special resolution that it should be so re-registered is passed,

(b)   the conditions specified below are met, and

(c)   an application for re-registration is delivered to the registrar in accordance with section 100, together with—

    (i)   the other documents required by that section, and

    (ii)   a statement of compliance.

(2)   The conditions are that—

(a)   where no application under section 98 for cancellation of the resolution has been made—

    (i)   having regard to the number of members who consented to or voted in favour of the resolution, no such application may be made, or

    (ii)   the period within which such an application could be made has expired, or

(b)   where such an application has been made—

    (i)   the application has been withdrawn, or

    (ii)   an order has been made confirming the resolution and a copy of that order has been delivered to the registrar.

(3)   The company must make such changes—

(a)   in its name, and

(b)   in its articles,

as are necessary in connection with its becoming a private company limited by shares or, as the case may be, by guarantee.

98   Application to court to cancel resolution

(1)   Where a special resolution by a public company to be re-registered as a private limited company has been passed, an application to the court for the cancellation of the resolution may be made—

(a)   by the holders of not less in the aggregate than 5% in nominal value of the company's issued share capital or any class of the company's issued share capital (disregarding any shares held by the company as treasury shares);

(b)   if the company is not limited by shares, by not less than 5% of its members; or

(c)   by not less than 50 of the company's members;

but not by a person who has consented to or voted in favour of the resolution.

(2)   The application must be made within 28 days after the passing of the resolution and may be made on behalf of the persons entitled to make it by such one or more of their number as they may appoint for the purpose.

(3)   On the hearing of the application the court shall make an order either cancelling or confirming the resolution.

(4)   The court may—

(a)   make that order on such terms and conditions as it thinks fit,

(b)   if it thinks fit adjourn the proceedings in order that an arrangement may be made to the satisfaction of the court for the purchase of the interests of dissentient members, and

(c)   give such directions, and make such orders, as it thinks expedient for facilitating or carrying into effect any such arrangement.

(5)   The court's order may, if the court thinks fit—

(a)   provide for the purchase by the company of the shares of any of its members and for the reduction accordingly of the company's capital; and

(b)   make such alteration in the company's articles as may be required in consequence of that provision.

(6)   The court's order may, if the court thinks fit, require the company not to make any, or any specified, amendments to its articles without the leave of the court.

(7)   In this section and section 99(3) "the court", in England and Wales, means the High Court.

99   Notice to registrar of court application or order

(1)   On making an application under section 98 (application to court to cancel resolution) the applicants, or the person making the application on their behalf, must immediately give notice to the registrar.

This is without prejudice to any provision of rules of court as to service of notice of the application.

(2)   On being served with notice of any such application, the company must immediately give notice to the registrar.

(3)   Within 15 days of the making of the court's order on the application, or such longer period as the court may at any time direct, the company must deliver to the registrar a copy of the order.

(4)   If a company fails to comply with subsection (2) or (3) an offence is committed by—

(a)   the company, and

(b)   every officer of the company who is in default.

(5)   A person guilty of an offence under this section is liable on summary conviction to a fine not exceeding level 3 on the standard scale and, for continued contravention, a daily default fine not exceeding one-tenth of level 3 on the standard scale.

100   Application and accompanying documents

(1)   An application for re-registration as a private limited company must contain a statement of the company's proposed name on re-registration.

(2)   The application must be accompanied by—

(a)   a copy of the resolution that the company should re-register as a private limited company (unless a copy has already been forwarded to the registrar under Chapter 3 of Part 3); and

(b)   a copy of the company's articles as proposed to be amended.

(3)   The statement of compliance required to be delivered together with the application is a statement that the requirements of this Part as to re-registration as a private limited company have been complied with.

(4)   The registrar may accept the statement of compliance as sufficient evidence that the company is entitled to be re-registered as a private limited company.

101   Issue of certificate of incorporation on re-registration

(1)   If on an application for re-registration as a private limited company the registrar is satisfied that the company is entitled to be so re-registered, the company shall be re-registered accordingly.

(2)   The registrar must issue a certificate of incorporation altered to meet the circumstances of the case.

(3)   The certificate must state that it is issued on re-registration and the date on which it is issued.

(4)   On the issue of the certificate—

(a)   the company by virtue of the issue of the certificate becomes a private limited company, and

(b)   the changes in the company's name and articles take effect.

(5)   The certificate is conclusive evidence that the requirements of this Act as to re-registration have been complied with.

Private limited company becoming unlimited

102   Re-registration of private limited company as unlimited

(1)   A private limited company may be re-registered as an unlimited company if—

(a)   all the members of the company have assented to its being so re-registered,

(b)   the condition specified below is met, and

(c)   an application for re-registration is delivered to the registrar in accordance with section 103, together with—

(i)   the other documents required by that section, and

(ii)   a statement of compliance.

(2)   The condition is that the company has not previously been re-registered as limited.

(3)   The company must make such changes in its name and its articles—

(a)   as are necessary in connection with its becoming an unlimited company; and

(b)   if it is to have a share capital, as are necessary in connection with its becoming an unlimited company having a share capital.

(4)   For the purposes of this section—

(a)   a trustee in bankruptcy of a member of the company is entitled, to the exclusion of the member, to assent to the company's becoming unlimited; and

(b)   the personal representative of a deceased member of the company may assent on behalf of the deceased.

(5)   In subsection (4)(a), "a trustee in bankruptcy of a member of the company" includes—

(a)   a trustee or interim trustee in the sequestration under the Bankruptcy (Scotland) Act 2016 of the estate of a member of the company;

(b)   a trustee under a protected trustee deed (within the meaning of the Bankruptcy (Scotland) Act 2016) granted by a member of the company.

103   Application and accompanying documents

(1)   An application for re-registration as an unlimited company must contain a statement of the company's proposed name on re-registration.

(2)   The application must be accompanied by—

(a)   the prescribed form of assent to the company's being registered as an unlimited company, authenticated by or on behalf of all the members of the company;

(b)   a copy of the company's articles as proposed to be amended.

(3)   The statement of compliance required to be delivered together with the application is a statement that the requirements of this Part as to re-registration as an unlimited company have been complied with.

(4)   The statement must contain a statement by the directors of the company—

(a)   that the persons by whom or on whose behalf the form of assent is authenticated constitute the whole membership of the company, and

(b)   if any of the members have not authenticated that form themselves, that the directors have taken all reasonable steps to satisfy themselves that each person who authenticated it on behalf of a member was lawfully empowered to do so.

(5)   The registrar may accept the statement of compliance as sufficient evidence that the company is entitled to be re-registered as an unlimited company.

104   Issue of certificate of incorporation on re-registration

(1)   If on an application for re-registration of a private limited company as an unlimited company the registrar is satisfied that the company is entitled to be so re-registered, the company shall be re-registered accordingly.

(2)   The registrar must issue a certificate of incorporation altered to meet the circumstances of the case.

(3)   The certificate must state that it is issued on re-registration and the date on which it is issued.

(4)   On the issue of the certificate—

(a)   the company by virtue of the issue of the certificate becomes an unlimited company, and

(b)   the changes in the company's name and articles take effect.

(5)   The certificate is conclusive evidence that the requirements of this Act as to re-registration have been complied with.

Unlimited private company becoming limited

105   Re-registration of unlimited company as limited

(1)   An unlimited company may be re-registered as a private limited company if—

(a)   a special resolution that it should be so re-registered is passed,

(b)   the condition specified below is met, and

(c)   an application for re-registration is delivered to the registrar in accordance with section 106, together with—

(i)   the other documents required by that section, and

(ii)   a statement of compliance.

(2)   The condition is that the company has not previously been re-registered as unlimited.

(3)   The special resolution must state whether the company is to be limited by shares or by guarantee.

(4)   The company must make such changes—
        (a)   in its name, and
        (b)   in its articles,
        as are necessary in connection with its becoming a company limited by shares or, as the case may
        be, by guarantee.

106   Application and accompanying documents

(1)   An application for re-registration as a limited company must contain a statement of the
        company's proposed name on re-registration.
(2)   The application must be accompanied by—
        (a)   a copy of the resolution that the company should re-register as a private limited company
                (unless a copy has already been forwarded to the registrar under Chapter 3 of Part 3);
        (b)   if the company is to be limited by guarantee, a statement of guarantee;
        (c)   a copy of the company's articles as proposed to be amended.
(3)   The statement of guarantee required to be delivered in the case of a company that is to be limited
        by guarantee must state that each member undertakes that, if the company is wound up while he is
        a member, or within one year after he ceases to be a member, he will contribute to the assets of the
        company such amount as may be required for—
        (a)   payment of the debts and liabilities of the company contracted before he ceases to be a
                member,
        (b)   payment of the costs, charges and expenses of winding up, and
        (c)   adjustment of the rights of the contributories among themselves,
        not exceeding a specified amount.
(4)   The statement of compliance required to be delivered together with the application is a statement
        that the requirements of this Part as to re-registration as a limited company have been complied
        with.
(5)   The registrar may accept the statement of compliance as sufficient evidence that the company is
        entitled to be re-registered as a limited company.

107   Issue of certificate of incorporation on re-registration

(1)   If on an application for re-registration of an unlimited company as a limited company the registrar
        is satisfied that the company is entitled to be so re-registered, the company shall be re-registered
        accordingly.
(2)   The registrar must issue a certificate of incorporation altered to meet the circumstances of the
        case.
(3)   The certificate must state that it is issued on re-registration and the date on which it is so issued.
(4)   On the issue of the certificate—
        (a)   the company by virtue of the issue of the certificate becomes a limited company, and
        (b)   the changes in the company's name and articles take effect.
(5)   The certificate is conclusive evidence that the requirements of this Act as to re-registration have
        been complied with.

108   Statement of capital required where company already has share capital

(1)   A company which on re-registration under section 107 already has allotted share capital must
        within 15 days after the re-registration deliver a statement of capital to the registrar.
(2)   This does not apply if the information which would be included in the statement has already been
        sent to the registrar in—
        (a)   a statement of capital and initial shareholdings (see section 10), or
        (b)   (if different) the last statement of capital sent by the company.
(3)   The statement of capital must state with respect to the company's share capital on re-
        registration—
        (a)   the total number of shares of the company,
        (b)   the aggregate nominal value of those shares,

(ba) the aggregate amount (if any) unpaid on those shares (whether on account of their nominal value or by way of premium), and

(c) for each class of shares—

    (i)   prescribed particulars of the rights attached to the shares,

    (ii)   the total number of shares of that class, and

    (iii)   the aggregate nominal value of shares of that class, …

(d) …

(4)   If default is made in complying with this section, an offence is committed by—

(a) the company, and

(b) every officer of the company who is in default.

(5)   A person guilty of an offence under this section is liable on summary conviction to a fine not exceeding level 3 on the standard scale and, for continued contravention, a daily default fine not exceeding one-tenth of level 3 on the standard scale.

Public company becoming private and unlimited

109   **Re-registration of public company as private and unlimited**

(1)   A public company limited by shares may be re-registered as an unlimited private company with a share capital if—

(a) all the members of the company have assented to its being so re-registered,

(b) the condition specified below is met, and

(c) an application for re-registration is delivered to the registrar in accordance with section 110, together with—

    (i)   the other documents required by that section, and

    (ii)   a statement of compliance.

(2)   The condition is that the company has not previously been re-registered—

(a) as limited, or

(b) as unlimited.

(3)   The company must make such changes—

(a) in its name, and

(b) in its articles,

as are necessary in connection with its becoming an unlimited private company.

(4)   For the purposes of this section—

(a) a trustee in bankruptcy of a member of the company is entitled, to the exclusion of the member, to assent to the company's re-registration; and

(b) the personal representative of a deceased member of the company may assent on behalf of the deceased.

(5)   In subsection (4)(a), "a trustee in bankruptcy of a member of the company" includes—

(a) a trustee or interim trustee in the sequestration under the Bankruptcy (Scotland) Act 2016 of the estate of a member of the company;

(b) a trustee under a protected trustee deed (within the meaning of the Bankruptcy (Scotland) Act 2016) granted by a member of the company.

110   **Application and accompanying documents**

(1)   An application for re-registration of a public company as an unlimited private company must contain a statement of the company's proposed name on re-registration.

(2)   The application must be accompanied by—

(a) the prescribed form of assent to the company's being registered as an unlimited company, authenticated by or on behalf of all the members of the company, and

(b) a copy of the company's articles as proposed to be amended.

(3)   The statement of compliance required to be delivered together with the application is a statement that the requirements of this Part as to re-registration as an unlimited private company have been complied with.

(4)   The statement must contain a statement by the directors of the company—

(a)   that the persons by whom or on whose behalf the form of assent is authenticated constitute the whole membership of the company, and

(b)   if any of the members have not authenticated that form themselves, that the directors have taken all reasonable steps to satisfy themselves that each person who authenticated it on behalf of a member was lawfully empowered to do so.

(5)   The registrar may accept the statement of compliance as sufficient evidence that the company is entitled to be re-registered as an unlimited private company.

111   Issue of certificate of incorporation on re-registration

(1)   If on an application for re-registration of a public company as an unlimited private company the registrar is satisfied that the company is entitled to be so re-registered, the company shall be re-registered accordingly.

(2)   The registrar must issue a certificate of incorporation altered to meet the circumstances of the case.

(3)   The certificate must state that it is issued on re-registration and the date on which it is so issued.

(4)   On the issue of the certificate—

(a)   the company by virtue of the issue of the certificate becomes an unlimited private company, and

(b)   the changes in the company's name and articles take effect.

(5)   The certificate is conclusive evidence that the requirements of this Act as to re-registration have been complied with.

PART 8
A COMPANY'S MEMBERS

CHAPTER 1
THE MEMBERS OF A COMPANY

112   The members of a company

(1)   The subscribers of a company's memorandum are deemed to have agreed to become members of the company, and on its registration become members and must be entered as such in its register of members.

(2)   Every other person who agrees to become a member of a company, and whose name is entered in its register of members, is a member of the company.

(3)   Where an election under section 128B is in force in respect of a company—

(a)   the requirement in subsection (1) to enter particulars of members in the company's register of members does not apply, and

(b)   subsection (2) has effect as if the reference to a person whose name is entered in the company's register of members were a reference to a person with respect to whom the following steps have been taken—

(i)   the person's name has been delivered to the registrar under section 128E, and

(ii)   the document containing that information has been registered by the registrar.

CHAPTER 2
REGISTER OF MEMBERS

General

112A   Alternative method of record-keeping

This Chapter must be read with Chapter 2A (which allows for an alternative method of record-keeping in the case of private companies).

113   Register of members

(1)   Every company must keep a register of its members.

(2)   There must be entered in the register—

(a) the names and addresses of the members,

(b) the date on which each person was registered as a member, and

(c) the date at which any person ceased to be a member.

(3) In the case of a company having a share capital, there must be entered in the register, with the names and addresses of the members, a statement of—

(a) the shares held by each member, distinguishing each share—

    (i) by its number (so long as the share has a number), and

    (ii) where the company has more than one class of issued shares, by its class, and

(b) the amount paid or agreed to be considered as paid on the shares of each member.

(4) If the company has converted any of its shares into stock, and given notice of the conversion to the registrar, the register of members must show the amount and class of stock held by each member instead of the amount of shares and the particulars relating to shares specified above.

(5) In the case of joint holders of shares or stock in a company, the company's register of members must state the names of each joint holder.

In other respects joint holders are regarded for the purposes of this Chapter as a single member (so that the register must show a single address).

(6) In the case of a company that does not have a share capital but has more than one class of members, there must be entered in the register, with the names and addresses of the members, a statement of the class to which each member belongs.

(7) If a company makes default in complying with this section an offence is committed by—

(a) the company, and

(b) every officer of the company who is in default.

(8) A person guilty of an offence under this section is liable on summary conviction to a fine not exceeding level 3 on the standard scale and, for continued contravention, a daily default fine not exceeding one-tenth of level 3 on the standard scale.

114 Register to be kept available for inspection

(1) A company's register of members must be kept available for inspection—

(a) at its registered office, or

(b) at a place specified in regulations under section 1136.

This is subject to any restriction imposed by regulations under section 120A (protected material).

(2) A company must give notice to the registrar of the place where its register of members is kept available for inspection and of any change in that place.

(3) No such notice is required if the register has, at all times since it came into existence (or, in the case of a register in existence on the relevant date, at all times since then) been kept available for inspection at the company's registered office.

(4) The relevant date for the purposes of subsection (3) is—

(a) 1st July 1948 in the case of a company registered in Great Britain, and

(b) 1st April 1961 in the case of a company registered in Northern Ireland.

(5) If a company makes default for 14 days in complying with subsection (2), an offence is committed by—

(a) the company, and

(b) every officer of the company who is in default.

(6) A person guilty of an offence under this section is liable on summary conviction to a fine not exceeding level 3 on the standard scale and, for continued contravention, a daily default fine not exceeding one-tenth of level 3 on the standard scale.

115 Index of members

(1) Every company having more than 50 members must keep an index of the names of the members of the company, unless the register of members is in such a form as to constitute in itself an index.

(2) The company must make any necessary alteration in the index within 14 days after the date on which any alteration is made in the register of members.

(3)   The index must contain, in respect of each member, a sufficient indication to enable the account of that member in the register to be readily found.

(4)   The index must be at all times kept available for inspection at the same place as the register of members.

(4A)   Subsection (4) is subject to any restriction imposed by regulations under section 120A (protected material).

(5)   If default is made in complying with this section, an offence is committed by—
        (a)   the company, and
        (b)   every officer of the company who is in default.

(6)   A person guilty of an offence under this section is liable on summary conviction to a fine not exceeding level 3 on the standard scale and, for continued contravention, a daily default fine not exceeding one-tenth of level 3 on the standard scale.

116   Rights to inspect and require copies

(1)   The register and the index of members' names must be open to the inspection—
        (a)   of any member of the company without charge, and
        (b)   of any other person on payment of such fee as may be prescribed.

(2)   Any person may require a copy of a company's register of members, or of any part of it, on payment of such fee as may be prescribed.

(2A)   Subsections (1) and (2) are subject to any restriction imposed by regulations under section 120A (protected material).

(3)   A person seeking to exercise either of the rights conferred by this section must make a request to the company to that effect.

(4)   The request must contain the following information—
        (a)   in the case of an individual, his name and address;
        (b)   in the case of an organisation, the name and address of an individual responsible for making the request on behalf of the organisation;
        (c)   the purpose for which the information is to be used; and
        (d)   whether the information will be disclosed to any other person, and if so—
              (i)   where that person is an individual, his name and address,
              (ii)   where that person is an organisation, the name and address of an individual responsible for receiving the information on its behalf, and
              (iii)   the purpose for which the information is to be used by that person.

117   Register of members: response to request for inspection or copy

(1)   Where a company receives a request under section 116 (register of members: right to inspect and require copy), it must within five working days either—
        (a)   comply with the request, or
        (b)   apply to the court.

(2)   If it applies to the court it must notify the person making the request.

(3)   If on an application under this section the court is satisfied that the inspection or copy is not sought for a proper purpose—
        (a)   it shall direct the company not to comply with the request, and
        (b)   it may further order that the company's costs (in Scotland, expenses) on the application be paid in whole or in part by the person who made the request, even if he is not a party to the application.

(4)   If the court makes such a direction and it appears to the court that the company is or may be subject to other requests made for a similar purpose (whether made by the same person or different persons), it may direct that the company is not to comply with any such request.
        The order must contain such provision as appears to the court appropriate to identify the requests to which it applies.

(5)   If on an application under this section the court does not direct the company not to comply with the request, the company must comply with the request immediately upon the court giving its decision or, as the case may be, the proceedings being discontinued.

118   Register of members: refusal of inspection or default in providing copy

(1)   If an inspection required under section 116 (register of members: right to inspect and require copy) is refused or default is made in providing a copy required under that section, otherwise than in accordance with an order of the court, an offence is committed by—
        (a)   the company, and
        (b)   every officer of the company who is in default.

(2)   A person guilty of an offence under this section is liable on summary conviction to a fine not exceeding level 3 on the standard scale and, for continued contravention, a daily default fine not exceeding one-tenth of level 3 on the standard scale.

(3)   In the case of any such refusal or default the court may by order compel an immediate inspection or, as the case may be, direct that the copy required be sent to the person requesting it.

119   Register of members: offences in connection with request for or disclosure of information

(1)   It is an offence for a person knowingly or recklessly to make in a request under section 116 (register of members: right to inspect or require copy) a statement that is misleading, false or deceptive in a material particular.

(2)   It is an offence for a person in possession of information obtained by exercise of either of the rights conferred by that section—
        (a)   to do anything that results in the information being disclosed to another person, or
        (b)   to fail to do anything with the result that the information is disclosed to another person,
        knowing, or having reason to suspect, that person may use the information for a purpose that is not a proper purpose.

(3)   A person guilty of an offence under this section is liable—
        (a)   on conviction on indictment, to imprisonment for a term not exceeding two years or a fine (or both);
        (b)   on summary conviction—
               (i)   in England and Wales, to imprisonment for a term not exceeding twelve months or to a fine not exceeding the statutory maximum (or both);
               (ii)   in Scotland or Northern Ireland, to imprisonment for a term not exceeding six months, or to a fine not exceeding the statutory maximum (or both).

120   Information as to state of register and index

(1)   When a person inspects the register, or the company provides him with a copy of the register or any part of it, the company must inform him of the most recent date (if any) on which alterations were made to the register and whether there are further alterations to be made.

(2)   When a person inspects the index of members' names, the company must inform him whether there is any alteration to the register that is not reflected in the index.

(2A)   Subsections (1) and (2) do not apply to an alteration that relates to information that the company is required to refrain from disclosing by virtue of regulations under section 120A (protected material).

(3)   If a company fails to provide the information required under subsection (1) or (2), an offence is committed by—
        (a)   the company, and
        (b)   every officer of the company who is in default.

(4)   A person guilty of an offence under this section is liable on summary conviction to a fine not exceeding level 3 on the standard scale.

120A   Power to make regulations protecting material

(1)   The Secretary of State may by regulations—

      (a)   require a company to refrain from using, or refrain from disclosing, individual membership information except in circumstances specified in the regulations;

      (b)   confer power on the registrar, on application, to make an order requiring a company to refrain from using, or refrain from disclosing, individual membership information except in circumstances specified in the regulations.

(2)   "Individual membership information" means information that—

      (a)   relates to an individual who is a member or former member of the company, and

      (b)   is required to be entered in the company's register of members or index of members' names.

(3)   Regulations under subsection (1)(b) may make provision as to—

      (a)   who may make an application;

      (b)   the grounds on which an application may be made;

      (c)   the information to be included in and documents to accompany an application;

      (d)   how an application is to be determined;

      (e)   the notice to be given of an application and its outcome;

      (f)   the duration of and procedures for revoking the restrictions on use and disclosure.

(4)   Provision under subsection (3) may in particular—

      (a)   confer a discretion on the registrar;

      (b)   provide for a question to be referred to a person other than the registrar for the purposes of determining the application or revoking the restrictions.

(5)   Regulations under this section are subject to affirmative resolution procedure.

(6)   Nothing in this section or in regulations made under it affects the use or disclosure of information about a person in any other capacity (for example, the use or disclosure of information about a person in that person's capacity as an officer of the company).

120B   Offence of failing to comply with regulations under section 120A

(1)   If a company contravenes a restriction on the use or disclosure of information imposed by virtue of regulations under section 120A, an offence is committed by—

      (a)   the company, and

      (b)   every officer of the company who is in default.

(2)   A person guilty of an offence under this section is liable on summary conviction—

      (a)   in England and Wales, to a fine;

      (b)   in Scotland or Northern Ireland, to a fine not exceeding level 5 on the standard scale and, for continued contravention, a daily default fine not exceeding one-tenth of level 5 on the standard scale.

121   Removal of entries relating to former members

An entry relating to a former member of the company may be removed from the register after the expiration of ten years from the date on which he ceased to be a member.

Special cases

122   Share warrants

(1)   Until a share warrant issued by a company is surrendered the following are deemed to be the particulars required to be entered in the register of members in respect of the warrant—

      (a)   the fact of the issue of the warrant,

      (b)   a statement of the shares included in the warrant, distinguishing each share by its number so long as the share has a number, and

      (c)   the date of the issue of the warrant.

(2)   ...

(3)   The bearer of a share warrant may, if the articles of the company so provide, be deemed a member of the company within the meaning of this Act, either to the full extent or for any purposes defined in the articles.

(4)   ...

(5)   The company is responsible for any loss incurred by any person by reason of the company entering in the register the name of a bearer of a share warrant in respect of the shares specified in it without the warrant being surrendered and cancelled.

(6)   On the surrender of a share warrant, the date of the surrender must be entered in the register.

123   Single member companies

(1)   If a limited company is formed under this Act with only one member there shall be entered in the company's register of members, with the name and address of the sole member, a statement that the company has only one member.

(2)   If the number of members of a limited company falls to one, or if an unlimited company with only one member becomes a limited company on re-registration, there shall upon the occurrence of that event be entered in the company's register of members, with the name and address of the sole member—
        (a)   a statement that the company has only one member, and
        (b)   the date on which the company became a company having only one member.

(3)   If the membership of a limited company increases from one to two or more members, there shall upon the occurrence of that event be entered in the company's register of members, with the name and address of the person who was formerly the sole member—
        (a)   a statement that the company has ceased to have only one member, and
        (b)   the date on which that event occurred.

(4)   If a company makes default in complying with this section, an offence is committed by—
        (a)   the company, and
        (b)   every officer of the company who is in default.

(5)   A person guilty of an offence under this section is liable on summary conviction to a fine not exceeding level 3 on the standard scale and, for continued contravention, a daily default fine not exceeding one-tenth of level 3 on the standard scale.

124   Company holding its own shares as treasury shares

(1)   Where a company purchases its own shares in circumstances in which section 724 (treasury shares) applies—
        (a)   the requirements of section 113 (register of members) need not be complied with if the company cancels all of the shares forthwith after the purchase, and
        (b)   if the company does not cancel all of the shares forthwith after the purchase, any share that is so cancelled shall be disregarded for the purposes of that section.

(2)   Subject to subsection (1), where a company holds shares as treasury shares the company must be entered in the register as the member holding those shares.

Supplementary

125   Power of court to rectify register

(1)   If a company's register of members—
        (a)   does not include information that it is required to include, or
        (b)   includes information that it is not required to include,
        the person aggrieved, or any member of the company, or the company, may apply to the court for rectification of the register.

(2)   The court may either refuse the application or may order rectification of the register and payment by the company of any damages sustained by any party aggrieved.

(3)   On such an application the court may decide any question relating to the title of a person who is a party to the application to have his name entered in or omitted from the register, whether the question arises between members or alleged members, or between members or alleged members on the one hand and the company on the other hand, and generally may decide any question necessary or expedient to be decided for rectification of the register.

(4)   In the case of a company required by this Act to send a list of its members to the registrar of companies, the court, when making an order for rectification of the register, shall by its order direct notice of the rectification to be given to the registrar.

126   Trusts not to be entered on register

No notice of any trust, expressed, implied or constructive, shall be entered on the register of members of a company registered in England and Wales or Northern Ireland, or be receivable by the registrar.

127   Register to be evidence

The register of members is prima facie evidence of any matters which are by this Act directed or authorised to be inserted in it, except for any matters of which the central register is prima facie evidence by virtue of section 128H.

128   Time limit for claims arising from entry in register

(1)   Liability incurred by a company—
    (a)   from the making or deletion of an entry in the register of members, or
    (b)   from a failure to make or delete any such entry,
    is not enforceable more than ten years after the date on which the entry was made or deleted or, as the case may be, the failure first occurred.

(2)   This is without prejudice to any lesser period of limitation (and, in Scotland, to any rule that the obligation giving rise to the liability prescribes before the expiry of that period).

CHAPTER 2A
OPTION TO KEEP INFORMATION ON CENTRAL REGISTER

128A   Introduction

(1)   This Chapter sets out rules allowing private companies to keep information on the register kept by the registrar instead of entering it in their register of members.

(2)   The register kept by the registrar (see section 1080) is referred to in this Chapter as "the central register".

128B   Right to make an election

(1)   An election may be made under this section—
    (a)   by the subscribers wishing to form a private company under this Act, or
    (b)   by the private company itself once it is formed and registered.

(2)   In the latter case, the election is of no effect unless, before it is made—
    (a)   all the members of the company have assented to the making of the election, and
    (b)   any overseas branch registers that the company was keeping under Chapter 3 have been discontinued and all the entries in those registers transferred to the company's register of members in accordance with section 135.

(3)   An election under this section is made by giving notice of election to the registrar.

(4)   If the notice is given by subscribers wishing to form a private company--
    (a)   it must be given when the documents required to be delivered under section 9 are delivered to the registrar, and
    (b)   it must be accompanied by a statement containing all the information that—
        (i)   would be required (in the absence of the notice) to be entered in the company's register of members on incorporation of the company, and
        (ii)   is not otherwise included in the documents delivered under section 9.

(5)   If the notice is given by the company, it must be accompanied by—
    (a)   a statement by the company—
        (i)   that all the members of the company have assented to the making of the election, and

        (ii)   if the company was keeping any overseas branch registers, that all such registers have been discontinued and all the entries in them transferred to the company's register of members in accordance with section 135, and

    (b)   a statement containing all the information that is required to be contained in the company's register of members as at the date of the notice in respect of matters that are current as at that date.

(6)   The company must where necessary update the statement sent under subsection (5)(b) to ensure that the final version delivered to the registrar contains all the information that is required to be contained in the company's register of members as at the time immediately before the election takes effect (see section 128C) in respect of matters that are current as at that time.

(7)   The obligation in subsection (6) to update the statement includes an obligation to rectify it (where necessary) in consequence of the company's register of members being rectified (whether before or after the election takes effect).

(8)   If default is made in complying with subsection (6), an offence is committed by—

    (a)   the company, and

    (b)   every officer of the company who is in default.

For this purpose a shadow director is treated as an officer of the company.

(9)   A person guilty of an offence under this section is liable on summary conviction to a fine not exceeding level 3 on the standard scale and, for continued contravention, a daily default fine not exceeding one-tenth of level 3 on the standard scale.

(10)   A reference in this Chapter to matters that are current as at a given date or time is a reference to—

    (a)   persons who are members of the company as at that date or time, and

    (b)   any other matters that are current as at that date or time.

128C   Effective date of election

(1)   An election made under section 128B takes effect when the notice of election is registered by the registrar.

(2)   The election remains in force until either—

    (a)   the company ceases to be a private company, or

    (b)   a notice of withdrawal sent by the company under section 128J is registered by the registrar, whichever occurs first.

128D   Effect of election on obligations under Chapter 2

(1)   The effect of an election under section 128B on a company's obligations under Chapter 2 is as follows.

(2)   The company's obligation to maintain a register of members does not apply with respect to the period when the election is in force.

(3)   This means that, during that period—

    (a)   the company must continue to keep a register of members in accordance with Chapter 2 (a "historic" register) containing all the information that was required to be stated in that register as at the time immediately before the election took effect, but

    (b)   the company does not have to update that register to reflect any changes that occur after that time.

(4)   Subsections (2) and (3) apply to the index of members (if the company is obliged to keep an index of members) as they apply to the register of members.

(5)   The provisions of Chapter 2 (including the rights to inspect or require copies of the register and to inspect the index) continue to apply to the historic register and, if applicable, the historic index during the period when the election is in force.

(6)   The company must place a note in its historic register—

    (a)   stating that an election under section 128B is in force,

    (b)   recording when that election took effect, and

    (c)   indicating that up-to-date information about its members is available for public inspection on the central register.

(7)   Subsections (7) and (8) of section 113 apply if a company makes default in complying with subsection (6) as they apply if a company makes default in complying with that section.

(8)   The obligations under this section with respect to a historic register and historic index do not apply in a case where the election was made by subscribers wishing to form a private company.

128E   Duty to notify registrar of changes

(1)   The duty under subsection (2) applies during the period when an election under section 128B is in force.

(2)   The company must deliver to the registrar any relevant information that the company would during that period have been obliged under this Act to enter in its register of members, had the election not been in force.

(3)   "Relevant information" means information other than—

(a)   the date mentioned in section 113(2)(b) (date when person registered as member),

(b)   the date mentioned in section 123(3)(b) (date when membership of limited company increases from one to two or more members), and

(c)   the dates mentioned in the following provisions, but only in cases where the date to be recorded in the central register is to be the date on which the document containing information of the relevant change is registered by the registrar—

(i)   section 113(2)(c) (date when person ceases to be member),

(ii)   section 123(2)(b) (date when company becomes single member company).

(4)   The relevant information must be delivered as soon as reasonably practicable after the company becomes aware of it and, in any event, no later than the time by which the company would have been required to enter the information in its register of members.

(5)   In a case of the kind described in subsection (3)(c), the company must, when it delivers information under subsection (2) of the relevant change, indicate to the registrar that, in accordance with section 1081(1A), the date to be recorded in the central register is to be the date on which the document containing that information is registered by the registrar.

(6)   If default is made in complying with this section, an offence is committed by—

(a)   the company, and

(b)   every officer of the company who is in default.

For this purpose a shadow director is treated as an officer of the company.

(7)   A person guilty of an offence under this section is liable on summary conviction to a fine not exceeding level 3 on the standard scale and, for continued contravention, a daily default fine not exceeding one-tenth of level 3 on the standard scale.

128F   Information as to state of central register

(1)   When a person inspects or requests a copy of material on the central register relating to a company in respect of which an election under section 128B is in force, the person may ask the company to confirm that all information that the company is required to deliver to the registrar under this Chapter has been delivered.

(2)   If a company fails to respond to a request under subsection (1), an offence is committed by—

(a)   the company, and

(b)   every officer of the company who is in default.

(3)   A person guilty of an offence under this section is liable on summary conviction to a fine not exceeding level 3 on the standard scale.

128G   Power of court to order company to remedy default or delay

(1)   This section applies if—

(a)   the name of a person is without sufficient cause included in, or omitted from, information that a company delivers to the registrar under this Chapter concerning its members, or

(b)   default is made or unnecessary delay takes place in informing the registrar under this Chapter of—

(i)   the name of a person who is to be a member of the company, or

(ii)   the fact that a person has ceased or is to cease to be a member of the company.

(2)   The person aggrieved, or any member of the company, or the company, may apply to the court for an order—
    (a)   requiring the company to deliver to the registrar the information (or statements) necessary to rectify the position, and
    (b)   where applicable, requiring the registrar to record under section 1081(1A) the date determined by the court.

(3)   The court may either refuse the application or may make the order and order the company to pay any damages sustained by any party aggrieved.

(4)   On such an application the court may decide—
    (a)   any question relating to the title of a person who is a party to the application to have the person's name included in or omitted from information delivered to the registrar under this Chapter about the company's members, whether the question arises between members or alleged members, or between members or alleged members on the one hand and the company on the other hand, and
    (b)   any question necessary or expedient to be decided for rectifying the position.

(5)   Nothing in this section affects a person's rights under section 1095 or 1096 (rectification of register on application to registrar or under court order).

128H   Central register to be evidence

(1)   The central register is prima facie evidence of any matters about which a company is required to deliver information to the registrar under this Chapter.

(2)   Subsection (1) does not apply to information to be included in a statement under section 128B(5)(b) or in any updated statement under section 128B(6).

128I   Time limits for claims arising from delivery to registrar

(1)   Liability incurred by a company—
    (a)   from the delivery to the registrar of information under this Chapter, or
    (b)   from a failure to deliver any such information,
is not enforceable more than 10 years after the date on which the information was delivered or, as the case may be, the failure first occurred.

(2)   This is without prejudice to any lesser period of limitation (and, in Scotland, to any rule that the obligation giving rise to the liability prescribes before the expiry of that period).

128J   Withdrawing the election

(1)   A company may withdraw an election made by or in respect of it under section 128B.

(2)   Withdrawal is achieved by giving notice of withdrawal to the registrar.

(3)   The withdrawal takes effect when the notice is registered by the registrar.

(4)   The effect of withdrawal is that the company's obligation under Chapter 2 to maintain a register of members applies from then on with respect to the period going forward.

(5)   This means that, when the withdrawal takes effect—
    (a)   the company must enter in its register of members all the information that is required to be contained in that register in respect of matters that are current as at that time,
    (b)   the company must also retain in its register all the information that it was required under section 128D(3)(a) to keep in a historic register while the election was in force, but
    (c)   the company is not required to enter in its register information relating to the period when the election was in force that is no longer current.

(6)   The company must place a note in its register of members—
    (a)   stating that the election under section 128B has been withdrawn,
    (b)   recording when that withdrawal took effect, and
    (c)   indicating that information about its members relating to the period when the election was in force that is no longer current is available for public inspection on the central register.

(7)   Subsections (7) and (8) of section 113 apply if a company makes default in complying with subsection (6) as they apply if a company makes default in complying with that section.

128K   Power to extend option to public companies

(1)   The Secretary of State may by regulations amend this Act—

    (a)   to extend sections 128A to 128J (with or without modification) to public companies or public companies of a class specified in the regulations, and

    (b)   to make such other amendments as the Secretary of State thinks fit in consequence of that extension.

(2)   Regulations under this section are subject to affirmative resolution procedure.

CHAPTER 3
OVERSEAS BRANCH REGISTERS

129   Overseas branch registers

(1)   A company having a share capital may, if it transacts business in a country or territory to which this Chapter applies, cause to be kept there a branch register of members resident there (an "overseas branch register").

(2)   This Chapter applies to—

    (a)   any part of Her Majesty's dominions outside the United Kingdom, the Channel Islands and the Isle of Man, and

    (b)   the countries or territories listed below.

Bangladesh	Malaysia
Cyprus	Malta
Dominica	Nigeria
The Gambia	Pakistan
Ghana	Seychelles
Guyana	Sierra Leone
The Hong Kong Special Administrative Region of the People's Republic of China	Singapore
India	South Africa
Ireland	Sri Lanka
Kenya	Swaziland
Kiribati	Trinidad and Tobago
Lesotho	Uganda
Malawi	Zimbabwe

(3)   The Secretary of State may make provision by regulations as to the circumstances in which a company is to be regarded as keeping a register in a particular country or territory.

(4)   Regulations under this section are subject to negative resolution procedure.

(5)   References—

    (a)   in any Act or instrument (including, in particular, a company's articles) to a dominion register, or

    (b)   in articles registered before 1st November 1929 to a colonial register,

    are to be read (unless the context otherwise requires) as a reference to an overseas branch register kept under this section.

(6)   A company's right under subsection (1) to keep an overseas branch register does not apply during or with respect to any period when an election is in force in respect of the company under section 128B.

130   Notice of opening of overseas branch register

(1)   A company that begins to keep an overseas branch register must give notice to the registrar within 14 days of doing so, stating the country or territory in which the register is kept.

(2)   If default is made in complying with subsection (1), an offence is committed by—

    (a)   the company, and

    (b)   every officer of the company who is in default.

(3)   A person guilty of an offence under subsection (2) is liable on summary conviction to a fine not exceeding level 3 on the standard scale and, for continued contravention, a daily default fine not exceeding one-tenth of level 3 on the standard scale.

131   Keeping of overseas branch register

(1)   An overseas branch register is regarded as part of the company's register of members ("the main register").

(2)   The Secretary of State may make provision by regulations modifying any provision of Chapter 2 (register of members) as it applies in relation to an overseas branch register.

(3)   Regulations under this section are subject to negative resolution procedure.

(4)   Subject to the provisions of this Act, a company may by its articles make such provision as it thinks fit as to the keeping of overseas branch registers.

132   Register or duplicate to be kept available for inspection in UK

(1)   A company that keeps an overseas branch register must keep available for inspection—
        (a)   the register, or
        (b)   a duplicate of the register duly entered up from time to time,
        at the place in the United Kingdom where the company's main register is kept available for inspection.

(2)   Any such duplicate is treated for all purposes of this Act as part of the main register.

(3)   If default is made in complying with subsection (1), an offence is committed by—
        (a)   the company, and
        (b)   every officer of the company who is in default.

(4)   A person guilty of an offence under subsection (3) is liable on summary conviction to a fine not exceeding level 3 on the standard scale and, for continued contravention, a daily default fine not exceeding one-tenth of level 3 on the standard scale.

133   Transactions in shares registered in overseas branch register

(1)   Shares registered in an overseas branch register must be distinguished from those registered in the main register.

(2)   No transaction with respect to shares registered in an overseas branch register may be registered in any other register.

(3)   An instrument of transfer of a share registered in an overseas branch register—
        (a)   is regarded as a transfer of property situated outside the United Kingdom, and
        (b)   unless executed in a part of the United Kingdom, is exempt from stamp duty.

134   Jurisdiction of local courts

(1)   A competent court in a country or territory where an overseas branch register is kept may exercise the same jurisdiction as is exercisable by a court in the United Kingdom—
        (a)   to rectify the register (see section 125), or
        (b)   in relation to a request for inspection or a copy of the register (see section 117).

(2)   The offences—
        (a)   of refusing inspection or failing to provide a copy of the register (see section 118), and
        (b)   of making a false, misleading or deceptive statement in a request for inspection or a copy (see section 119),
        may be prosecuted summarily before any tribunal having summary criminal jurisdiction in the country or territory where the register is kept.

(3)   This section extends only to those countries and territories to which paragraph 3 of Schedule 14 to the Companies Act 1985 (which made similar provision) extended immediately before the coming into force of this Chapter.

135   Discontinuance of overseas branch register

(1)   A company may discontinue an overseas branch register.

(2)   If it does so all the entries in that register must be transferred—

(a)   to some other overseas branch register kept in the same country or territory, or

(b)   to the main register.

(3)   The company must give notice to the registrar within 14 days of the discontinuance.

(4)   If default is made in complying with subsection (3), an offence is committed by—

(a)   the company, and

(b)   every officer of the company who is in default.

(5)   A person guilty of an offence under subsection (4) is liable on summary conviction to a fine not exceeding level 3 on the standard scale and, for continued contravention, a daily default fine not exceeding one-tenth of level 3 on the standard scale.

CHAPTER 4
PROHIBITION ON SUBSIDIARY BEING MEMBER OF ITS HOLDING COMPANY

General prohibition

136   Prohibition on subsidiary being a member of its holding company

(1)   Except as provided by this Chapter—

(a)   a body corporate cannot be a member of a company that is its holding company, and

(b)   any allotment or transfer of shares in a company to its subsidiary is void.

(2)   The exceptions are provided for in—

section 138 (subsidiary acting as personal representative or trustee), and

section 141 (subsidiary acting as authorised dealer in securities).

137   Shares acquired before prohibition became applicable

(1)   Where a body corporate became a holder of shares in a company—

(a)   before the relevant date, or

(b)   on or after that date and before the commencement of this Chapter in circumstances in which the prohibition in section 23(1) of the Companies Act 1985 or Article 33(1) of the Companies (Northern Ireland) Order 1986 (or any corresponding earlier enactment), as it then had effect, did not apply, or

(c)   on or after the commencement of this Chapter in circumstances in which the prohibition in section 136 did not apply,

it may continue to be a member of the company.

(2)   The relevant date for the purposes of subsection (1)(a) is—

(a)   1st July 1948 in the case of a company registered in Great Britain, and

(b)   1st April 1961 in the case of a company registered in Northern Ireland.

(3)   So long as it is permitted to continue as a member of a company by virtue of this section, an allotment to it of fully paid shares in the company may be validly made by way of capitalisation of reserves of the company.

(4)   But, so long as the prohibition in section 136 would (apart from this section) apply, it has no right to vote in respect of the shares mentioned in subsection (1) above, or any shares allotted as mentioned in subsection (3) above, on a written resolution or at meetings of the company or of any class of its members.

Subsidiary acting as personal representative or trustee

138   Subsidiary acting as personal representative or trustee

(1)   The prohibition in section 136 (prohibition on subsidiary being a member of its holding company) does not apply where the subsidiary is concerned only—

(a)   as personal representative, or

(b)   as trustee,

unless, in the latter case, the holding company or a subsidiary of it is beneficially interested under the trust.

(2)   For the purpose of ascertaining whether the holding company or a subsidiary is so interested, there shall be disregarded—

(a)   any interest held only by way of security for the purposes of a transaction entered into by the holding company or subsidiary in the ordinary course of a business that includes the lending of money;

(b)   any interest within—

section 139 (interests to be disregarded: residual interest under pension scheme or employees' share scheme), or

section 140 (interests to be disregarded: employer's rights of recovery under pension scheme or employees' share scheme);

(c)   any rights that the company or subsidiary has in its capacity as trustee, including in particular—

(i)   any right to recover its expenses or be remunerated out of the trust property, and

(ii)   any right to be indemnified out of the trust property for any liability incurred by reason of any act or omission in the performance of its duties as trustee.

139   Interests to be disregarded: residual interest under pension scheme or employees' share scheme

(1)   Where shares in a company are held on trust for the purposes of a pension scheme or employees' share scheme, there shall be disregarded for the purposes of section 138 any residual interest that has not vested in possession.

(2)   A "residual interest" means a right of the company or subsidiary ("the residual beneficiary") to receive any of the trust property in the event of—

(a)   all the liabilities arising under the scheme having been satisfied or provided for, or

(b)   the residual beneficiary ceasing to participate in the scheme, or

(c)   the trust property at any time exceeding what is necessary for satisfying the liabilities arising or expected to arise under the scheme.

(3)   In subsection (2)—

(a)   the reference to a right includes a right dependent on the exercise of a discretion vested by the scheme in the trustee or another person, and

(b)   the reference to liabilities arising under a scheme includes liabilities that have resulted, or may result, from the exercise of any such discretion.

(4)   For the purposes of this section a residual interest vests in possession—

(a)   in a case within subsection (2)(a), on the occurrence of the event mentioned there (whether or not the amount of the property receivable pursuant to the right is ascertained);

(b)   in a case within subsection (2)(b) or (c), when the residual beneficiary becomes entitled to require the trustee to transfer to him any of the property receivable pursuant to the right.

(5)   In this section "pension scheme" means a scheme for the provision of benefits consisting of or including relevant benefits for or in respect of employees or former employees.

(6)   In subsection (5)—

(a)   "relevant benefits" means any pension, lump sum, gratuity or other like benefit given or to be given on retirement or on death or in anticipation of retirement or, in connection with past service, after retirement or death; and

(b)   "employee" shall be read as if a director of a company were employed by it.

140   Interests to be disregarded: employer's rights of recovery under pension scheme or employees' share scheme

(1)   Where shares in a company are held on trust for the purposes of a pension scheme or employees' share scheme, there shall be disregarded for the purposes of section 138 any charge or lien on, or set-off against, any benefit or other right or interest under the scheme for the purpose of enabling the employer or former employer of a member of the scheme to obtain the discharge of a monetary obligation due to him from the member.

(2)   In the case of a trust for the purposes of a pension scheme there shall also be disregarded any right to receive from the trustee of the scheme, or as trustee of the scheme to retain, an amount that can be recovered or retained, under … section 57 of the Pension Schemes (Northern Ireland) Act 1993

(deduction of contributions equivalent premium from refund of scheme contributions) or otherwise, as reimbursement or partial reimbursement for any contributions equivalent premium paid in connection with the scheme under Part 3 of that Act.

(3)   In this section "pension scheme" means a scheme for the provision of benefits consisting of or including relevant benefits for or in respect of employees or former employees.

"Relevant benefits" here means any pension, lump sum, gratuity or other like benefit given or to be given on retirement or on death or in anticipation of retirement or, in connection with past service, after retirement or death.

(4)   In this section "employer" and "employee" shall be read as if a director of a company were employed by it.

Subsidiary acting as dealer in securities

141   Subsidiary acting as authorised dealer in securities

(1)   The prohibition in section 136 (prohibition on subsidiary being a member of its holding company) does not apply where the shares are held by the subsidiary in the ordinary course of its business as an intermediary.

(2)   For this purpose a person is an intermediary if he—
   (a)   carries on a bona fide business of dealing in securities,
   (b)   is a member of or has access to a UK regulated market, and
   (c)   does not carry on an excluded business.

(3)   The following are excluded businesses—
   (a)   a business that consists wholly or mainly in the making or managing of investments;
   (b)   a business that consists wholly or mainly in, or is carried on wholly or mainly for the purposes of, providing services to persons who are connected with the person carrying on the business;
   (c)   a business that consists in insurance business;
   (d)   a business that consists in managing or acting as trustee in relation to a pension scheme, or that is carried on by the manager or trustee of such a scheme in connection with or for the purposes of the scheme;
   (e)   a business that consists in operating or acting as trustee in relation to a collective investment scheme, or that is carried on by the operator or trustee of such a scheme in connection with and for the purposes of the scheme.

(4)   For the purposes of this section—
   (a)   the question whether a person is connected with another shall be determined in accordance with section 1122 of the Corporation Tax Act 2010;
   (b)   "'collective investment scheme" has the meaning given in section 235 of the Financial Services and Markets Act 2000;
   (c)   "insurance business" means business that consists in the effecting or carrying out of contracts of insurance;
   (d)   "securities" includes—
        (i)   options,
        (ii)   futures, and
        (iii)   contracts for differences,
        and rights or interests in those investments;
   (e)   "trustee" and "the operator" in relation to a collective investment scheme shall be construed in accordance with section 237(2) of the Financial Services and Markets Act 2000.

(5)   Expressions used in this section that are also used in the provisions regulating activities under the Financial Services and Markets Act 2000 have the same meaning here as they do in those provisions.

See section 22 of that Act, orders made under that section and Schedule 2 to that Act.

142   Protection of third parties in other cases where subsidiary acting as dealer in securities

(1)   This section applies where—

(a)   a subsidiary that is a dealer in securities has purportedly acquired shares in its holding company in contravention of the prohibition in section 136, and

(b)   a person acting in good faith has agreed, for value and without notice of the contravention, to acquire shares in the holding company—

    (i)   from the subsidiary, or

    (ii)   from someone who has purportedly acquired the shares after their disposal by the subsidiary.

(2)   A transfer to that person of the shares mentioned in subsection (1)(a) has the same effect as it would have had if their original acquisition by the subsidiary had not been in contravention of the prohibition.

Supplementary

143   Application of provisions to companies not limited by shares

In relation to a company other than a company limited by shares, the references in this Chapter to shares shall be read as references to the interest of its members as such, whatever the form of that interest.

144   Application of provisions to nominees

The provisions of this Chapter apply to a nominee acting on behalf of a subsidiary as to the subsidiary itself.

PART 9
EXERCISE OF MEMBERS' RIGHTS

Effect of provisions in company's articles

145   Effect of provisions of articles as to enjoyment or exercise of members' rights

(1)   This section applies where provision is made by a company's articles enabling a member to nominate another person or persons as entitled to enjoy or exercise all or any specified rights of the member in relation to the company.

(2)   So far as is necessary to give effect to that provision, anything required or authorised by any provision of the Companies Acts to be done by or in relation to the member shall instead be done, or (as the case may be) may instead be done, by or in relation to the nominated person (or each of them) as if he were a member of the company.

(3)   This applies, in particular, to the rights conferred by—

(a)   sections 291 and 293 (right to be sent proposed written resolution);

(b)   section 292 (right to require circulation of written resolution);

(c)   section 303 (right to require directors to call general meeting);

(d)   section 310 (right to notice of general meetings);

(e)   section 314 (right to require circulation of a statement);

(ea)   section 319A (right to ask question at meeting of traded company);

(f)   section 324 (right to appoint proxy to act at meeting);

(g)   section 338 (right to require circulation of resolution for AGM of public company); and

(ga)   section 338A (traded companies: members' power to include matters in business dealt with at AGM);

(gb)   360AA (traded companies: confirmation of receipt of electronic voting);

(gc)   360BA (traded companies: right to confirmation of vote after a general meeting);

(h)   section 423 (right to be sent a copy of annual accounts and reports).

(4)   This section and any such provision as is mentioned in subsection (1)—

(a)   do not confer rights enforceable against the company by anyone other than the member, and

(b)   do not affect the requirements for an effective transfer or other disposition of the whole or part of a member's interest in the company.

Information rights

146   Traded companies: nomination of persons to enjoy information rights

(1)   This section applies to a company whose shares are admitted to trading on a UK regulated market or an EU regulated market.

(2)   A member of such a company who holds shares on behalf of another person may nominate that person to enjoy information rights.

(3)   "Information rights" means—

    (a)   the right to receive a copy of all communications that the company sends to its members generally or to any class of its members that includes the person making the nomination, and

    (b)   the rights conferred by—

        (i)   section 431 or 432 (right to require copies of accounts and reports), and

        (ii)   section 1145 (right to require hard copy version of document or information provided in another form).

(4)   The reference in subsection (3) (a) to communications that a company sends to its members generally includes the company's annual accounts and reports. For the application of section 426 (option to provide strategic report with supplementary material) in relation to a person nominated to enjoy information rights, see subsection (5) of that section.

(5)   A company need not act on a nomination purporting to relate to certain information rights only.

147   Information rights: form in which copies to be provided

(1)   This section applies as regards the form in which copies are to be provided to a person nominated under section 146 (nomination of person to enjoy information rights).

(2)   If the person to be nominated wishes to receive hard copy communications, he must—

    (a)   request the person making the nomination to notify the company of that fact, and

    (b)   provide an address to which such copies may be sent.

    This must be done before the nomination is made.

(3)   If having received such a request the person making the nomination—

    (a)   notifies the company that the nominated person wishes to receive hard copy communications, and

    (b)   provides the company with that address,

    the right of the nominated person is to receive hard copy communications accordingly.

(4)   This is subject to the provisions of Parts 3 and 4 of Schedule 5 (communications by company) under which the company may take steps to enable it to communicate in electronic form or by means of a website.

(5)   If no such notification is given (or no address is provided), the nominated person is taken to have agreed that documents or information may be sent or supplied to him by the company by means of a website.

(6)   That agreement—

    (a)   may be revoked by the nominated person, and

    (b)   does not affect his right under section 1145 to require a hard copy version of a document or information provided in any other form.

148   Termination or suspension of nomination

(1)   The following provisions have effect in relation to a nomination under section 146 (nomination of person to enjoy information rights).

(2)   The nomination may be terminated at the request of the member or of the nominated person.

(3)   The nomination ceases to have effect on the occurrence in relation to the member or the nominated person of any of the following—

    (a)   in the case of an individual, death or bankruptcy;

    (b)   in the case of a body corporate, dissolution or the making of an order for the winding up of the body otherwise than for the purposes of reconstruction.

(4)   In subsection (3)—

    (a)   the reference to bankruptcy includes—

        (i)   the sequestration of a person's estate, and

        (ii)   a person's estate being the subject of a protected trust deed (within the meaning of the Bankruptcy (Scotland) Act 2016); and

   (b)   the reference to the making of an order for winding up is to—

        (i)   the making of such an order under the Insolvency Act 1986 or the Insolvency (Northern Ireland) Order 1989, or

        (ii)   any corresponding proceeding under the law of a country or territory outside the United Kingdom.

(5)   The effect of any nominations made by a member is suspended at any time when there are more nominated persons than the member has shares in the company.

(6)   Where—

   (a)   the member holds different classes of shares with different information rights, and

   (b)   there are more nominated persons than he has shares conferring a particular right,

the effect of any nominations made by him is suspended to the extent that they confer that right.

(7)   Where the company—

   (a)   enquires of a nominated person whether he wishes to retain information rights, and

   (b)   does not receive a response within the period of 28 days beginning with the date on which the company's enquiry was sent,

the nomination ceases to have effect at the end of that period.

Such an enquiry is not to be made of a person more than once in any twelve-month period.

(8)   The termination or suspension of a nomination means that the company is not required to act on it.

It does not prevent the company from continuing to do so, to such extent or for such period as it thinks fit.

149   Information as to possible rights in relation to voting

(1)   This section applies where a company sends a copy of a notice of a meeting to a person nominated under section 146 (nomination of person to enjoy information rights)

(2)   The copy of the notice must be accompanied by a statement that—

   (a)   he may have a right under an agreement between him and the member by whom he was nominated to be appointed, or to have someone else appointed, as a proxy for the meeting, and

   (b)   if he has no such right or does not wish to exercise it, he may have a right under such an agreement to give instructions to the member as to the exercise of voting rights.

(3)   Section 325 (notice of meeting to contain statement of member's rights in relation to appointment of proxy) does not apply to the copy, and the company must either—

   (a)   omit the notice required by that section, or

   (b)   include it but state that it does not apply to the nominated person.

150   Information rights: status of rights

(1)   This section has effect as regards the rights conferred by a nomination under section 146 (nomination of person to enjoy information rights).

(2)   Enjoyment by the nominated person of the rights conferred by the nomination is enforceable against the company by the member as if they were rights conferred by the company's articles.

(3)   Any enactment, and any provision of the company's articles, having effect in relation to communications with members has a corresponding effect (subject to any necessary adaptations) in relation to communications with the nominated person.

(4)   In particular—

   (a)   where under any enactment, or any provision of the company's articles, the members of a company entitled to receive a document or information are determined as at a date or time before it is sent or supplied, the company need not send or supply it to a nominated person—

        (i)   whose nomination was received by the company after that date or time, or

        (ii)   if that date or time falls in a period of suspension of his nomination; and

(b)   where under any enactment, or any provision of the company's articles, the right of a member to receive a document or information depends on the company having a current address for him, the same applies to any person nominated by him.

(5)   The rights conferred by the nomination—
(a)   are in addition to the rights of the member himself, and
(b)   do not affect any rights exercisable by virtue of any such provision as is mentioned in section 145 (provisions of company's articles as to enjoyment or exercise of members' rights).

(6)   A failure to give effect to the rights conferred by the nomination does not affect the validity of anything done by or on behalf of the company.

(7)   References in this section to the rights conferred by the nomination are to—
(a)   the rights referred to in section 146(3) (information rights), and
(b)   where applicable, the rights conferred by section 147(3) (right to hard copy communications) and section 149 (information as to possible voting rights).

151   Information rights: power to amend

(1)   The Secretary of State may by regulations amend the provisions of sections 146 to 150 (information rights) so as to—
(a)   extend or restrict the classes of companies to which section 146 applies,
(b)   make other provision as to the circumstances in which a nomination may be made under that section, or
(c)   extend or restrict the rights conferred by such a nomination.

(2)   The regulations may make such consequential modifications of any other provisions of this Part, or of any other enactment, as appear to the Secretary of State to be necessary.

(3)   Regulations under this section are subject to affirmative resolution procedure.

Exercise of rights where shares held on behalf of others

152   Exercise of rights where shares held on behalf of others: exercise in different ways

(1)   Where a member holds shares in a company on behalf of more than one person—
(a)   rights attached to the shares, and
(b)   rights under any enactment exercisable by virtue of holding the shares,
need not all be exercised, and if exercised, need not all be exercised in the same way.

(2)   A member who exercises such rights but does not exercise all his rights, must inform the company to what extent he is exercising the rights.

(3)   A member who exercises such rights in different ways must inform the company of the ways in which he is exercising them and to what extent they are exercised in each way.

(4)   If a member exercises such rights without informing the company—
(a)   that he is not exercising all his rights, or
(b)   that he is exercising his rights in different ways,
the company is entitled to assume that he is exercising all his rights and is exercising them in the same way.

153   Exercise of rights where shares held on behalf of others: members' requests

(1)   This section applies for the purposes of—
(a)   section 314 (power to require circulation of statement),
(b)   section 338 (public companies: power to require circulation of resolution for AGM),
(ba) section 338A (traded companies: members' power to include matters in business dealt with at AGM),
(c)   section 342 (power to require independent report on poll), and
(d)   section 527 (power to require website publication of audit concerns).

(2)   A company is required to act under any of those sections if it receives a request in relation to which the following conditions are met—
(a)   it is made by at least 100 persons;
(b)   it is authenticated by all the persons making it;

(c)   in the case of any of those persons who is not a member of the company, it is accompanied by a statement—

    (i)   of the full name and address of a person ("the member") who is a member of the company and holds shares on behalf of that person,

    (ii)   that the member is holding those shares on behalf of that person in the course of a business,

    (iii)   of the number of shares in the company that the member holds on behalf of that person,

    (iv)   of the total amount paid up on those shares,

    (v)   that those shares are not held on behalf of anyone else or, if they are, that the other person or persons are not among the other persons making the request,

    (vi)   that some or all of those shares confer voting rights that are relevant for the purposes of making a request under the section in question, and

    (vii)   that the person has the right to instruct the member how to exercise those rights;

(d)   in the case of any of those persons who is a member of the company, it is accompanied by a statement—

    (i)   that he holds shares otherwise than on behalf of another person, or

    (ii)   that he holds shares on behalf of one or more other persons but those persons are not among the other persons making the request;

(e)   it is accompanied by such evidence as the company may reasonably require of the matters mentioned in paragraph (c) and (d);

(f)   the total amount of the sums paid up on—

    (i)   shares held as mentioned in paragraph (c), and

    (ii)   shares held as mentioned in paragraph (d),

    divided by the number of persons making the request, is not less than £100;

(g)   the request complies with any other requirements of the section in question as to contents, timing and otherwise.

PART 10
A COMPANY'S DIRECTORS

CHAPTER 1
APPOINTMENT AND REMOVAL OF DIRECTORS

Requirement to have directors

154   Companies required to have directors

(1)   A private company must have at least one director.

(2)   A public company must have at least two directors.

155   *Companies required to have at least one director who is a natural person*

(1)   A company must have at least one director who is a natural person.

(2)   This requirement is met if the office of director is held by a natural person as a corporation sole or otherwise by virtue of an office.

Note. This section is repealed by the Small Business, Enterprise and Employment Act 2015, s. 87(1), (2), as from a day to be appointed.

156   Direction requiring company to make appointment

(1)   If it appears to the Secretary of State that a company is in breach of—

section 154 (requirements as to number of directors), or

section 155 (requirement to have at least one director who is a natural person),

the Secretary of State may give the company a direction under this section.

(2)   The direction must specify—

(a)   the statutory requirement the company appears to be in breach of,

(b)   what the company must do in order to comply with the direction, and

(c) the period within which it must do so.

That period must be not less than one month or more than three months after the date on which the direction is given.

(3)   The direction must also inform the company of the consequences of failing to comply.

(4)   Where the company is in breach of section 154 or 155 it must comply with the direction by—

(a) making the necessary appointment or appointments, and

(b) giving notice of them under section 167,

before the end of the period specified in the direction.

(5)   If the company has already made the necessary appointment or appointments (or so far as it has done so), it must comply with the direction by giving notice of them under section 167 before the end of the period specified in the direction.

(6)   If a company fails to comply with a direction under this section, an offence is committed by—

(a) the company, and

(b) every officer of the company who is in default.

For this purpose a shadow director is treated as an officer of the company.

(7)   A person guilty of an offence under this section is liable on summary conviction to a fine not exceeding level 5 on the standard scale and, for continued contravention, a daily default fine not exceeding one-tenth of the greater of £5,000 or level 4 on the standard scale.

Note. This section is amended by the Small Business, Enterprise and Employment Act 2015, s. 87(1), (3), as from a day to be appointed.

Appointment

156A   *Each director to be a natural person*

(1)   A person may not be appointed a director of a company unless the person is a natural person.

(2)   Subsection (1) does not prohibit the holding of the office of director by a natural person as a corporation sole or otherwise by virtue of an office.

(3)   An appointment made in contravention of this section is void.

(4)   Nothing in this section affects any liability of a person under any provision of the Companies Acts or any other enactment if the person—

(a) purports to act as director, or

(b) acts as shadow director,

although the person could not, by virtue of this section, be validly appointed as a director.

(5)   This section has effect subject to section 156B (power to provide for exceptions from requirement that each director be a natural person).

(6)   If a purported appointment is made in contravention of this section, an offence is committed by—

(a) the company purporting to make the appointment,

(b) where the purported appointment is of a body corporate or a firm that is a legal person under the law by which it is governed, that body corporate or firm, and

(c) every officer of a person falling within paragraph (a) or (b) who is in default.

For this purpose a shadow director is treated as an officer of a company.

(7)   A person guilty of an offence under this section is liable on summary conviction—

(a) in England and Wales, to a fine;

(b) in Scotland or Northern Ireland, to a fine not exceeding level 5 on the standard scale.

Note. This section is inserted by the Small Business, Enterprise and Employment Act 2015, s. 87(1), (4), as from a day to be appointed (save for certain purposes).

156B   Power to provide for exceptions from requirement that each director be a natural person

(1)   The Secretary of State may make provision by regulations for cases in which a person who is not a natural person may be appointed a director of a company.

(2)   The regulations must specify the circumstances in which, and any conditions subject to which, the appointment may be made.

(3)   Provision made by virtue of subsection (2) may in particular include provision that an appointment may be made only with the approval of a regulatory body specified in the regulations.

(4)   The regulations must include provision that a company must have at least one director who is a natural person (and for this purpose the requirement is met if the office of director is held by a natural person as a corporation sole or otherwise by virtue of an office).

(5)   Regulations under this section may amend section 164 so as to require particulars relating to exceptions to be contained in a company's register of directors.

(6)   The regulations may make different provision for different parts of the United Kingdom.
        This is without prejudice to the general power to make different provision for different cases.

(7)   Regulations under this section are subject to affirmative resolution procedure.

156C   ***Existing director who is not a natural person***

(1)   In this section "the relevant day" is the day after the end of the period of 12 months beginning with the day on which section 156A comes into force.

(2)   Where—

(a)   a person appointed a director of a company before section 156A comes into force is not a natural person, and

(b)   the case is not one excepted from that section by regulations under section 156B,

that person ceases to hold office by virtue of that appointment on the relevant day.

(2A)   Nothing in this section affects any liability of a person under any provision of the Companies Acts or any other enactment, if, having ceased to hold office by virtue of subsection (2), the person—

(a)   purports to act as director, or

(b)   acts as shadow director.

(3)   The company must—

(a)   make the necessary consequential alteration in its register of directors, and

(b)   give notice to the registrar of the change in accordance with section 167.

(4)   If an election is in force under section 167A in respect of the company, the company must, in place of doing the things required by subsection (3), deliver to the registrar in accordance with section 167D the information of which the company would otherwise have been obliged to give notice under subsection (3).

(5)   If it appears to the registrar that—

(a)   a notice should have, but has not, been given in accordance with subsection (3)(b), or

(b)   information should have, but has not, been delivered in accordance with subsection (4),

the registrar must place a note in the register recording the fact.

Note. This section is inserted by the Small Business, Enterprise and Employment Act 2015, s. 87(1), (4), as from a day to be appointed (save for certain purposes).

157   **Minimum age for appointment as director**

(1)   A person may not be appointed a director of a company unless he has attained the age of 16 years.

(2)   This does not affect the validity of an appointment that is not to take effect until the person appointed attains that age.

(3)   Where the office of director of a company is held by a corporation sole, or otherwise by virtue of another office, the appointment to that other office of a person who has not attained the age of 16 years is not effective also to make him a director of the company until he attains the age of 16 years.

(4)   An appointment made in contravention of this section is void.

(5)   Nothing in this section affects any liability of a person under any provision of the Companies Acts if he—

(a)   purports to act as director, or

(b)   acts as a shadow director,

although he could not, by virtue of this section, be validly appointed as a director.

(6)   This section has effect subject to section 158 (power to provide for exceptions from minimum age requirement).

158   Power to provide for exceptions from minimum age requirement

(1)   The Secretary of State may make provision by regulations for cases in which a person who has not attained the age of 16 years may be appointed a director of a company.

(2)   The regulations must specify the circumstances in which, and any conditions subject to which, the appointment may be made.

(3)   If the specified circumstances cease to obtain, or any specified conditions cease to be met, a person who was appointed by virtue of the regulations and who has not since attained the age of 16 years ceases to hold office by virtue of that appointment

(3A)   Nothing in subsection (3) affects any liability of a person under any provision of the Companies Acts or any other enactment, if, having ceased to hold office by virtue of that subsection, the person—

(a)   purports to act as director, or

(b)   acts as shadow director.

(4)   The regulations may make different provision for different parts of the United Kingdom.
        This is without prejudice to the general power to make different provision for different cases.

(5)   Regulations under this section are subject to negative resolution procedure.

159   ...

159A   Disqualified person not to be appointed as director

(1)   A person may not be appointed a director of a company if the person is disqualified under the directors disqualification legislation (see subsection (2)).

(2)   In the table—

(a)   Part 1 defines "disqualified under the directors disqualification legislation" for the purposes of provisions of this Act so far as relating to—

(i)   a company registered in England and Wales or Scotland, or

(ii)   the delivery of a document to the registrar of companies for England and Wales or Scotland or a statement contained in such a document;

(b)   Part 2 defines "disqualified under the directors disqualification legislation" for the purposes of provisions of this Act so far as relating to—

(i)   a company registered in Northern Ireland, or

(ii)   the delivery of a document to the registrar of companies for Northern Ireland or a statement contained in such a document.

For those purposes a person (P) is disqualified under the directors disqualification legislation if:	Except in the application of the provision in relation to P acting in a capacity, or doing anything, for which P has the permission of a court or the authority of a licence, or in respect of which an exception applies, by virtue of:
Part 1: England and Wales and Scotland	
P is subject to a disqualification order or undertaking under the Company Directors Disqualification Act 1986.	Section 1(1), 1A(1) or 9B(4) of the 1986 Act.
Any of the circumstances mentioned in section 11 of the Company Directors Disqualification Act 1986 (bankruptcy etc) apply to P.	Section 11 of the 1986 Act.

P is subject to director disqualification sanctions within the meaning of section 11A of the Company Directors Disqualification Act 1986.	Section 15(3A) of the Sanctions and Anti-Money Laundering Act 2018 (exceptions and licences).
Section 12 of the Company Directors Disqualification Act 1986 (disabilities on revocation of administration order against an individual) applies to P.	Section 12 of the 1986 Act.
P is subject to a disqualification order or undertaking mentioned in section 12A or 12B of the Company Directors Disqualification Act 1986 (recognition of Northern Ireland disqualification orders and undertakings).	Section 12A or 12B of the 1986 Act.
P is disqualified as mentioned in section 1184(2)(a) or (b) or is subject to a disqualification undertaking under section 1184(3).	Section 1184(5).
Part 2: Northern Ireland	
P is subject to a disqualification order or undertaking under the Company Directors Disqualification (Northern Ireland) Order 2002 (SI 2002/3150 (NI 4)).	Article 3(1), 4(1) or 13B(4) of the 2002 Order.
Any of the circumstances mentioned in Article 15 of the Company Directors Disqualification (Northern Ireland) Order 2002 (bankruptcy etc) apply to P.	Article 15 of the 2002 Order.
P is subject to director disqualification sanctions within the meaning of Article 15A of the Company Directors Disqualification (Northern Ireland) Order 2002.	Section 15(3A) of the Sanctions and Anti-Money Laundering Act 2018 (exceptions and licences).
Article 16 of the Company Directors Disqualification (Northern Ireland) Order 2002 (disabilities on revocation of administration order against an individual) applies to P.	Article 16 of the 2002 Order.
P is subject to a disqualification order or undertaking mentioned in Article 17 of the Company Directors Disqualification (Northern Ireland) Order 2002 (recognition of GB disqualification orders and undertakings).	Article 17 of the 2002 Order.
P is disqualified as mentioned in section 1184(2)(a) or (b) or is subject to a disqualification undertaking under section 1184(3).	Section 1184(5).

(3) An appointment made in contravention of this section is void.

(4) Nothing in this section affects any liability of a person under any provision of the Companies Acts or any other enactment if the person—

(a) purports to act as director, or

(b) acts as shadow director,

although the person could not, by virtue of this section, be validly appointed as a director.

160 Appointment of directors of public company to be voted on individually

(1) At a general meeting of a public company a motion for the appointment of two or more persons as directors of the company by a single resolution must not be made unless a resolution that it should be so made has first been agreed to by the meeting without any vote being given against it.

(2)   A resolution moved in contravention of this section is void, whether or not its being so moved was objected to at the time.

But where a resolution so moved is passed, no provision for the automatic reappointment of retiring directors in default of another appointment applies.

(3)   For the purposes of this section a motion for approving a person's appointment, or for nominating a person for appointment, is treated as a motion for his appointment.

(4)   Nothing in this section applies to a resolution amending the company's articles.

161   Validity of acts of directors

(1)   The acts of a person acting as a director are valid notwithstanding that it is afterwards discovered—

(a)   that there was a defect in his appointment;

(b)   that he was disqualified from holding office;

(c)   that he had ceased to hold office;

(d)   that he was not entitled to vote on the matter in question.

(2)   This applies even if the resolution for his appointment is void under section 160 (appointment of directors of public company to be voted on individually).

Register of directors, etc

161A   Alternative method of record-keeping

Sections 162 to 167 must be read with sections 167A to 167E (which allow for an alternative method of record-keeping in the case of private companies).

162   Register of directors

(1)   Every company must keep a register of its directors.

(2)   The register must contain the required particulars (see sections 163, 164 and 166) of each person who is a director of the company.

(3)   The register must be kept available for inspection—

(a)   at the company's registered office, or

(b)   at a place specified in regulations under section 1136.

(4)   The company must give notice to the registrar—

(a)   of the place at which the register is kept available for inspection, and

(b)   of any change in that place,

unless it has at all times been kept at the company's registered office.

(5)   The register must be open to the inspection—

(a)   of any member of the company without charge, and

(b)   of any other person on payment of such fee as may be prescribed.

(6)   If default is made in complying with subsection (1), (2) or (3) or if default is made for 14 days in complying with subsection (4), or if an inspection required under subsection (5) is refused, an offence is committed by—

(a)   the company, and

(b)   every officer of the company who is in default.

For this purpose a shadow director is treated as an officer of the company.

(7)   A person guilty of an offence under this section is liable on summary conviction to a fine not exceeding level 5 on the standard scale and, for continued contravention, a daily default fine not exceeding one-tenth of the greater of £5,000 or level 4 on the standard scale.

(8)   In the case of a refusal of inspection of the register, the court may by order compel an immediate inspection of it.

163   Particulars of directors to be registered: individuals

(1)   A company's register of directors must contain the following particulars in the case of an individual—

(a)   name and any former name;

(b)   a service address;

(c)   the country or state (or part of the United Kingdom) in which he is usually resident;

(d)   nationality;

(e)   business occupation (if any);

(f)   date of birth.

(2)   For the purposes of this section "name" means a person's Christian name (or other forename) and surname, except that in the case of—

(a)   a peer, or

(b)   an individual usually known by a title,

the title may be stated instead of his Christian name (or other forename) and surname or in addition to either or both of them.

(3)   For the purposes of this section a "former name" means a name by which the individual was formerly known for business purposes.

Where a person is or was formerly known by more than one such name, each of them must be stated.

(4)   It is not necessary for the register to contain particulars of a former name in the following cases—

(a)   in the case of a peer or an individual normally known by a British title, where the name is one by which the person was known previous to the adoption of or succession to the title;

(b)   in the case of any person, where the former name—

(i)   was changed or disused before the person attained the age of 16 years, or

(ii)   has been changed or disused for 20 years or more.

(5)   A person's service address may be stated to be "The company's registered office".

164   **Particulars of directors to be registered: corporate directors and firms**

A company's register of directors must contain the following particulars in the case of a body corporate, or a firm that is a legal person under the law by which it is governed—

(a)   corporate or firm name;

(b)   registered or principal office;

(c)   in the case of a limited company that is a UK-registered company, the registered number;

(d)   in any other case, particulars of—

(i)   the legal form of the company or firm and the law by which it is governed, and

(ii)   if applicable, the register in which it is entered (including details of the state) and its registration number in that register.

165   **Register of directors' residential addresses**

(1)   Every company must keep a register of directors' residential addresses.

(2)   The register must state the usual residential address of each of the company's directors.

(3)   If a director's usual residential address is the same as his service address (as stated in the company's register of directors), the register of directors' residential addresses need only contain an entry to that effect.

This does not apply if his service address is stated to be "The company's registered office".

(4)   If default is made in complying with this section, an offence is committed by—

(a)   the company, and

(b)   every officer of the company who is in default.

For this purpose a shadow director is treated as an officer of the company.

(5)   A person guilty of an offence under this section is liable on summary conviction to a fine not exceeding level 5 on the standard scale and, for continued contravention, a daily default fine not exceeding one-tenth of the greater of £5,000 or level 4 on the standard scale.

(6)   This section applies only to directors who are individuals, not where the director is a body corporate or a firm that is a legal person under the law by which it is governed.

166   **Particulars of directors to be registered: power to make regulations**

(1)   The Secretary of State may make provision by regulations amending—

section 163 (particulars of directors to be registered: individuals), section 164 (particulars of directors to be registered: corporate directors and firms), or

section 165 (register of directors' residential addresses),

so as to add to or remove items from the particulars required to be contained in a company's register of directors or register of directors' residential addresses.

(2)   Regulations under this section are subject to affirmative resolution procedure.

167   Duty to notify registrar of changes

(1)   A company must, within the period of 14 days from—

    (a)   a person becoming or ceasing to be a director, or

    (b)   the occurrence of any change in the particulars contained in its register of directors or its register of directors' residential addresses,

give notice to the registrar of the change and of the date on which it occurred.

(2)   Notice of a person having become a director of the company must—

    (a)   contain a statement of the particulars of the new director that are required to be included in the company's register of directors and its register of directors' residential addresses, and

    (b)   be accompanied by a statement by the company that the person has consented to act in that capacity.

(3)   Where—

    (a)   a company gives notice of a change of a director's service address as stated in the company's register of directors, and

    (b)   the notice is not accompanied by notice of any resulting change in the particulars contained in the company's register of directors' residential addresses,

the notice must be accompanied by a statement that no such change is required.

(4)   If default is made in complying with this section, an offence is committed by—

    (a)   the company, and

    (b)   every officer of the company who is in default.

For this purpose a shadow director is treated as an officer of the company.

(5)   A person guilty of an offence under this section is liable on summary conviction to a fine not exceeding level 5 on the standard scale and, for continued contravention, a daily default fine not exceeding one-tenth of the greater of £5,000 or level 4 on the standard scale.

Option to keep information on the central register

167A   Right to make an election

(1)   An election may be made under this section in respect of a register of directors or a register of directors' residential addresses (or both).

(2)   The election may be made—

    (a)   by the subscribers wishing to form a private company under this Act, or

    (b)   by the private company itself once it is formed and registered.

(3)   The election is made by giving notice of election to the registrar.

(4)   If the notice is given by subscribers wishing to form a private company, it must be given when the documents required to be delivered under section 9 are delivered to the registrar.

167B   Effective date of election

(1)   An election made under section 167A takes effect when the notice of election is registered by the registrar.

(2)   The election remains in force until either—

    (a)   the company ceases to be a private company, or

    (b)   a notice of withdrawal sent by the company under section 167E is registered by the registrar, whichever occurs first.

167C   Effect of election on obligations under sections 162 to 167

(1)   If an election is in force under section 167A with respect to a company, the company's obligations under sections 162 to 167—

(a)   to keep and maintain a register of the relevant kind, and

(b)   to notify the registrar of changes to it,

do not apply with respect to the period when the election is in force.

(2)   The reference in subsection (1) to a register "of the relevant kind" is to a register (whether a register of directors or a register of directors' residential addresses) of the kind in respect of which the election is made.

167D   Duty to notify registrar of changes

(1)   The duty under subsection (2) applies during the period when an election under section 167A is in force.

(2)   The company must deliver to the registrar—

(a)   any information of which the company would during that period have been obliged to give notice under section 167, had the election not been in force, and

(b)   any statement that would have had to accompany such a notice.

(3)   The information (and any accompanying statement) must be delivered as soon as reasonably practicable after the company becomes aware of the information and, in any event, no later than the time by which the company would have been required under section 167 to give notice of the information.

(4)   If default is made in complying with this section, an offence is committed by—

(a)   the company, and

(b)   every officer of the company who is in default.

For this purpose a shadow director is treated as an officer of the company.

(5)   A person guilty of an offence under this section is liable on summary conviction—

(a)   in England and Wales, to a fine and, for continued contravention, a daily default fine not exceeding the greater of £500 and one-tenth of level 4 on the standard scale;

(b)   in Scotland or Northern Ireland, to a fine not exceeding level 5 on the standard scale and, for continued contravention, a daily default fine not exceeding one-tenth of level 5 on the standard scale.

167E   Withdrawing the election

(1)   A company may withdraw an election made by or in respect of it under section 167A.

(2)   Withdrawal is achieved by giving notice of withdrawal to the registrar.

(3)   The withdrawal takes effect when the notice is registered by the registrar.

(4)   The effect of withdrawal is that the company's obligation under section 162 or (as the case may be) 165 to keep and maintain a register of the relevant kind, and its obligation under section 167 to notify the registrar of changes to that register, apply from then on with respect to the period going forward.

(5)   This means that, when the withdrawal takes effect—

(a)   the company must enter in that register all the information that is required to be contained in that register in respect of matters that are current as at that time, but

(b)   the company is not required to enter in its register information relating to the period when the election was in force that is no longer current.

167F   Power to extend option to public companies

(1)   The Secretary of State may by regulations amend this Act

(a)   to extend sections 167A to 167E (with or without modification) to public companies or public companies of a class specified in the regulations, and

(b)   to make such other amendments as the Secretary of State thinks fit in consequence of that extension.

(2)   Regulations under this section are subject to affirmative resolution procedure.

Removal

168   Resolution to remove director

(1)   A company may by ordinary resolution at a meeting remove a director before the expiration of his period of office, notwithstanding anything in any agreement between it and him.

(2)   Special notice is required of a resolution to remove a director under this section or to appoint somebody instead of a director so removed at the meeting at which he is removed.

(3)   A vacancy created by the removal of a director under this section, if not filled at the meeting at which he is removed, may be filled as a casual vacancy.

(4)   A person appointed director in place of a person removed under this section is treated, for the purpose of determining the time at which he or any other director is to retire, as if he had become director on the day on which the person in whose place he is appointed was last appointed a director.

(5)   This section is not to be taken—

(a)   as depriving a person removed under it of compensation or damages payable to him in respect of the termination of his appointment as director or of any appointment terminating with that as director, or

(b)   as derogating from any power to remove a director that may exist apart from this section.

169   Director's right to protest against removal

(1)   On receipt of notice of an intended resolution to remove a director under section 168, the company must forthwith send a copy of the notice to the director concerned.

(2)   The director (whether or not a member of the company) is entitled to be heard on the resolution at the meeting.

(3)   Where notice is given of an intended resolution to remove a director under that section, and the director concerned makes with respect to it representations in writing to the company (not exceeding a reasonable length) and requests their notification to members of the company, the company shall, unless the representations are received by it too late for it to do so—

(a)   in any notice of the resolution given to members of the company state the fact of the representations having been made; and

(b)   send a copy of the representations to every member of the company to whom notice of the meeting is sent (whether before or after receipt of the representations by the company).

(4)   If a copy of the representations is not sent as required by subsection (3) because received too late or because of the company's default, the director may (without prejudice to his right to be heard orally) require that the representations shall be read out at the meeting.

(5)   Copies of the representations need not be sent out and the representations need not be read out at the meeting if, on the application either of the company or of any other person who claims to be aggrieved, the court is satisfied that the rights conferred by this section are being abused.

(6)   The court may order the company's costs (in Scotland, expenses) on an application under subsection (5) to be paid in whole or in part by the director, notwithstanding that he is not a party to the application.

169A   Removal from office of disqualified directors

(1)   A person who has been appointed as a director of a company ceases to hold office by virtue of that appointment if the person becomes disqualified under the directors disqualification legislation (see section 159A(2)).

(2)   Nothing in this section affects any liability of a person under any provision of the Companies Acts or any other enactment, if, having ceased to hold office by virtue of subsection (1), the person—

(a)   purports to act as director, or

(b)   acts as shadow director.

(3)   In relation to a person appointed as a director of a company before the time when this section comes into force, the reference in subsection (1) to a person who becomes disqualified includes a reference to a person who, at that time, is already disqualified.

CHAPTER 2
GENERAL DUTIES OF DIRECTORS

Introductory

170 Scope and nature of general duties

(1) The general duties specified in sections 171 to 177 are owed by a director of a company to the company.

(2) A person who ceases to be a director continues to be subject—

(a) to the duty in section 175 (duty to avoid conflicts of interest) as regards the exploitation of any property, information or opportunity of which he became aware at a time when he was a director, and

(b) to the duty in section 176 (duty not to accept benefits from third parties) as regards things done or omitted by him before he ceased to be a director.

To that extent those duties apply to a former director as to a director, subject to any necessary adaptations.

(3) The general duties are based on certain common law rules and equitable principles as they apply in relation to directors and have effect in place of those rules and principles as regards the duties owed to a company by a director.

(4) The general duties shall be interpreted and applied in the same way as common law rules or equitable principles, and regard shall be had to the corresponding common law rules and equitable principles in interpreting and applying the general duties.

(5) The general duties apply to a shadow director of a company where and to the extent that they are capable of so applying.

The general duties

171 Duty to act within powers

A director of a company must—

(a) act in accordance with the company's constitution, and

(b) only exercise powers for the purposes for which they are conferred.

172 Duty to promote the success of the company

(1) A director of a company must act in the way he considers, in good faith, would be most likely to promote the success of the company for the benefit of its members as a whole, and in doing so have regard (amongst other matters) to—

(a) the likely consequences of any decision in the long term,

(b) the interests of the company's employees,

(c) the need to foster the company's business relationships with suppliers, customers and others,

(d) the impact of the company's operations on the community and the environment,

(e) the desirability of the company maintaining a reputation for high standards of business conduct, and

(f) the need to act fairly as between members of the company.

(2) Where or to the extent that the purposes of the company consist of or include purposes other than the benefit of its members, subsection (1) has effect as if the reference to promoting the success of the company for the benefit of its members were to achieving those purposes.

(3) The duty imposed by this section has effect subject to any enactment or rule of law requiring directors, in certain circumstances, to consider or act in the interests of creditors of the company.

173 Duty to exercise independent judgment

(1) A director of a company must exercise independent judgment.

(2) This duty is not infringed by his acting—

(a) in accordance with an agreement duly entered into by the company that restricts the future exercise of discretion by its directors, or

(b)   in a way authorised by the company's constitution.

174   Duty to exercise reasonable care, skill and diligence

(1)   A director of a company must exercise reasonable care, skill and diligence.

(2)   This means the care, skill and diligence that would be exercised by a reasonably diligent person with—

(a)   the general knowledge, skill and experience that may reasonably be expected of a person carrying out the functions carried out by the director in relation to the company, and

(b)   the general knowledge, skill and experience that the director has.

175   Duty to avoid conflicts of interest

(1)   A director of a company must avoid a situation in which he has, or can have, a direct or indirect interest that conflicts, or possibly may conflict, with the interests of the company.

(2)   This applies in particular to the exploitation of any property, information or opportunity (and it is immaterial whether the company could take advantage of the property, information or opportunity).

(3)   This duty does not apply to a conflict of interest arising in relation to a transaction or arrangement with the company.

(4)   This duty is not infringed—

(a)   if the situation cannot reasonably be regarded as likely to give rise to a conflict of interest; or

(b)   if the matter has been authorised by the directors.

(5)   Authorisation may be given by the directors—

(a)   where the company is a private company and nothing in the company's constitution invalidates such authorisation, by the matter being proposed to and authorised by the directors; or

(b)   where the company is a public company and its constitution includes provision enabling the directors to authorise the matter, by the matter being proposed to and authorised by them in accordance with the constitution.

(6)   The authorisation is effective only if—

(a)   any requirement as to the quorum at the meeting at which the matter is considered is met without counting the director in question or any other interested director, and

(b)   the matter was agreed to without their voting or would have been agreed to if their votes had not been counted.

(7)   Any reference in this section to a conflict of interest includes a conflict of interest and duty and a conflict of duties.

176   Duty not to accept benefits from third parties

(1)   A director of a company must not accept a benefit from a third party conferred by reason of—

(a)   his being a director, or

(b)   his doing (or not doing) anything as director.

(2)   A "third party" means a person other than the company, an associated body corporate or a person acting on behalf of the company or an associated body corporate.

(3)   Benefits received by a director from a person by whom his services (as a director or otherwise) are provided to the company are not regarded as conferred by a third party.

(4)   This duty is not infringed if the acceptance of the benefit cannot reasonably be regarded as likely to give rise to a conflict of interest.

(5)   Any reference in this section to a conflict of interest includes a conflict of interest and duty and a conflict of duties.

177   Duty to declare interest in proposed transaction or arrangement

(1)   If a director of a company is in any way, directly or indirectly, interested in a proposed transaction or arrangement with the company, he must declare the nature and extent of that interest to the other directors.

(2)   The declaration may (but need not) be made—
        (a)   at a meeting of the directors, or
        (b)   by notice to the directors in accordance with—
              (i)   section 184 (notice in writing), or
              (ii)   section 185 (general notice).

(3)   If a declaration of interest under this section proves to be, or becomes, inaccurate or incomplete, a further declaration must be made.

(4)   Any declaration required by this section must be made before the company enters into the transaction or arrangement.

(5)   This section does not require a declaration of an interest of which the director is not aware or where the director is not aware of the transaction or arrangement in question.
        For this purpose a director is treated as being aware of matters of which he ought reasonably to be aware.

(6)   A director need not declare an interest—
        (a)   if it cannot reasonably be regarded as likely to give rise to a conflict of interest;
        (b)   if, or to the extent that, the other directors are already aware of it (and for this purpose the other directors are treated as aware of anything of which they ought reasonably to be aware); or
        (c)   if, or to the extent that, it concerns terms of his service contract that have been or are to be considered—
              (i)   by a meeting of the directors, or
              (ii)   by a committee of the directors appointed for the purpose under the company's constitution.

Supplementary provisions

178   Civil consequences of breach of general duties

(1)   The consequences of breach (or threatened breach) of sections 171 to 177 are the same as would apply if the corresponding common law rule or equitable principle applied.

(2)   The duties in those sections (with the exception of section 174 (duty to exercise reasonable care, skill and diligence)) are, accordingly, enforceable in the same way as any other fiduciary duty owed to a company by its directors.

179   Cases within more than one of the general duties

Except as otherwise provided, more than one of the general duties may apply in any given case.

180   Consent, approval or authorisation by members

(1)   In a case where—
        (a)   section 175 (duty to avoid conflicts of interest) is complied with by authorisation by the directors, or
        (b)   section 177 (duty to declare interest in proposed transaction or arrangement) is complied with,
        the transaction or arrangement is not liable to be set aside by virtue of any common law rule or equitable principle requiring the consent or approval of the members of the company.
        This is without prejudice to any enactment, or provision of the company's constitution, requiring such consent or approval.

(2)   The application of the general duties is not affected by the fact that the case also falls within Chapter 4 or 4A (transactions requiring approval of members), except that where either of those Chapters applies and—
        (a)   approval is given under the Chapter concerned, or
        (b)   the matter is one as to which it is provided that approval is not needed,
        it is not necessary also to comply with section 175 (duty to avoid conflicts of interest) or section 176 (duty not to accept benefits from third parties).

(3)   Compliance with the general duties does not remove the need for approval under any applicable provision of Chapter 4 or 4A (transactions requiring approval of members).

(4)   The general duties—

    (a)   have effect subject to any rule of law enabling the company to give authority, specifically or generally, for anything to be done (or omitted) by the directors, or any of them, that would otherwise be a breach of duty, and

    (b)   where the company's articles contain provisions for dealing with conflicts of interest, are not infringed by anything done (or omitted) by the directors, or any of them, in accordance with those provisions.

(5)   Otherwise, the general duties have effect (except as otherwise provided or the context otherwise requires) notwithstanding any enactment or rule of law.

181   Modification of provisions in relation to charitable companies

(1)   In their application to a company that is a charity, the provisions of this Chapter have effect subject to this section.

(2)   Section 175 (duty to avoid conflicts of interest) has effect as if—

    (a)   for subsection (3) (which disapplies the duty to avoid conflicts of interest in the case of a transaction or arrangement with the company) there were substituted—

        "(3)   This duty does not apply to a conflict of interest arising in relation to a transaction or arrangement with the company if or to the extent that the company's articles allow that duty to be so disapplied, which they may do only in relation to descriptions of transaction or arrangement specified in the company's articles.";

    (b)   for subsection (5) (which specifies how directors of a company may give authority under that section for a transaction or arrangement) there were substituted—

        "(5)   Authorisation may be given by the directors where the company's constitution includes provision enabling them to authorise the matter, by the matter being proposed to and authorised by them in accordance with the constitution.".

(3)   Section 180(2)(b) (which disapplies certain duties under this Chapter in relation to cases excepted from requirement to obtain approval by members under Chapter 4) applies only if or to the extent that the company's articles allow those duties to be so disapplied, which they may do only in relation to descriptions of transaction or arrangement specified in the company's articles.

(4)   ...

(5)   This section does not extend to Scotland.

CHAPTER 3
DECLARATION OF INTEREST IN EXISTING TRANSACTION OR ARRANGEMENT

182   Declaration of interest in existing transaction or arrangement

(1)   Where a director of a company is in any way, directly or indirectly, interested in a transaction or arrangement that has been entered into by the company, he must declare the nature and extent of the interest to the other directors in accordance with this section.

    This section does not apply if or to the extent that the interest has been declared under section 177 (duty to declare interest in proposed transaction or arrangement).

(2)   The declaration must be made—

    (a)   at a meeting of the directors, or

    (b)   by notice in writing (see section 184), or

    (c)   by general notice (see section 185).

(3)   If a declaration of interest under this section proves to be, or becomes, inaccurate or incomplete, a further declaration must be made.

(4)   Any declaration required by this section must be made as soon as is reasonably practicable.

    Failure to comply with this requirement does not affect the underlying duty to make the declaration.

(5)   This section does not require a declaration of an interest of which the director is not aware or where the director is not aware of the transaction or arrangement in question.

For this purpose a director is treated as being aware of matters of which he ought reasonably to be aware.

(6)   A director need not declare an interest under this section—

(a)   if it cannot reasonably be regarded as likely to give rise to a conflict of interest;

(b)   if, or to the extent that, the other directors are already aware of it (and for this purpose the other directors are treated as aware of anything of which they ought reasonably to be aware); or

(c)   if, or to the extent that, it concerns terms of his service contract that have been or are to be considered—

(i)   by a meeting of the directors, or

(ii)   by a committee of the directors appointed for the purpose under the company's constitution.

183   Offence of failure to declare interest

(1)   A director who fails to comply with the requirements of section 182 (declaration of interest in existing transaction or arrangement) commits an offence.

(2)   A person guilty of an offence under this section is liable—

(a)   on conviction on indictment, to a fine;

(b)   on summary conviction, to a fine not exceeding the statutory maximum.

184   Declaration made by notice in writing

(1)   This section applies to a declaration of interest made by notice in writing.

(2)   The director must send the notice to the other directors.

(3)   The notice may be sent in hard copy form or, if the recipient has agreed to receive it in electronic form, in an agreed electronic form.

(4)   The notice may be sent—

(a)   by hand or by post, or

(b)   if the recipient has agreed to receive it by electronic means, by agreed electronic means.

(5)   Where a director declares an interest by notice in writing in accordance with this section—

(a)   the making of the declaration is deemed to form part of the proceedings at the next meeting of the directors after the notice is given, and

(b)   the provisions of section 248 (minutes of meetings of directors) apply as if the declaration had been made at that meeting.

185   General notice treated as sufficient declaration

(1)   General notice in accordance with this section is a sufficient declaration of interest in relation to the matters to which it relates.

(2)   General notice is notice given to the directors of a company to the effect that the director—

(a)   has an interest (as member, officer, employee or otherwise) in a specified body corporate or firm and is to be regarded as interested in any transaction or arrangement that may, after the date of the notice, be made with that body corporate or firm, or

(b)   is connected with a specified person (other than a body corporate or firm) and is to be regarded as interested in any transaction or arrangement that may, after the date of the notice, be made with that person.

(3)   The notice must state the nature and extent of the director's interest in the body corporate or firm or, as the case may be, the nature of his connection with the person.

(4)   General notice is not effective unless—

(a)   it is given at a meeting of the directors, or

(b)   the director takes reasonable steps to secure that it is brought up and read at the next meeting of the directors after it is given.

186   Declaration of interest in case of company with sole director

(1)   Where a declaration of interest under section 182 (duty to declare interest in existing transaction or arrangement) is required of a sole director of a company that is required to have more than one director—

     (a)   the declaration must be recorded in writing,

     (b)   the making of the declaration is deemed to form part of the proceedings at the next meeting of the directors after the notice is given, and

     (c)   the provisions of section 248 (minutes of meetings of directors) apply as if the declaration had been made at that meeting.

(2)   Nothing in this section affects the operation of section 231 (contract with sole member who is also a director: terms to be set out in writing or recorded in minutes).

187   Declaration of interest in existing transaction by shadow director

(1)   The provisions of this Chapter relating to the duty under section 182 (duty to declare interest in existing transaction or arrangement) apply to a shadow director as to a director, but with the following adaptations.

(2)   Subsection (2)(a) of that section (declaration at meeting of directors) does not apply.

(3)   In section 185 (general notice treated as sufficient declaration), subsection (4) (notice to be given at or brought up and read at meeting of directors) does not apply.

(4)   General notice by a shadow director is not effective unless given by notice in writing in accordance with section 184.

CHAPTER 4

TRANSACTIONS WITH DIRECTORS REQUIRING APPROVAL OF MEMBERS

Service contracts

188   Directors' long-term service contracts: requirement of members' approval

(1)   This section applies to provision under which the guaranteed term of a director's employment—

     (a)   with the company of which he is a director, or

     (b)   where he is the director of a holding company, within the group consisting of that company and its subsidiaries,

is, or may be, longer than two years.

(2)   A company may not agree to such provision unless it has been approved—

     (a)   by resolution of the members of the company, and

     (b)   in the case of a director of a holding company, by resolution of the members of that company.

(3)   The guaranteed term of a director's employment is—

     (a)   the period (if any) during which the director's employment—

         (i)   is to continue, or may be continued otherwise than at the instance of the company (whether under the original agreement or under a new agreement entered into in pursuance of it), and

         (ii)   cannot be terminated by the company by notice, or can be so terminated only in specified circumstances, or

     (b)   in the case of employment terminable by the company by notice, the period of notice required to be given,

or, in the case of employment having a period within paragraph (a) and a period within paragraph (b), the aggregate of those periods.

(4)   If more than six months before the end of the guaranteed term of a director's employment the company enters into a further service contract (otherwise than in pursuance of a right conferred, by or under the original contract, on the other party to it), this section applies as if there were added to the guaranteed term of the new contract the unexpired period of the guaranteed term of the original contract.

(5)   A resolution approving provision to which this section applies must not be passed unless a memorandum setting out the proposed contract incorporating the provision is made available to members—

(a)   in the case of a written resolution, by being sent or submitted to every eligible member at or before the time at which the proposed resolution is sent or submitted to him;

(b)   in the case of a resolution at a meeting, by being made available for inspection by members of the company both—

(i)   at the company's registered office for not less than 15 days ending with the date of the meeting, and

(ii)   at the meeting itself.

(6)   No approval is required under this section on the part of the members of a body corporate that—

(a)   is not a UK-registered company, or

(b)   is a wholly-owned subsidiary of another body corporate.

(7)   In this section "employment" means any employment under a director's service contract.

189   Directors' long-term service contracts: civil consequences of contravention

If a company agrees to provision in contravention of section 188 (directors' long-term service contracts: requirement of members' approval)—

(a)   the provision is void, to the extent of the contravention, and

(b)   the contract is deemed to contain a term entitling the company to terminate it at any time by the giving of reasonable notice.

Substantial property transactions

190   Substantial property transactions: requirement of members' approval

(1)   A company may not enter into an arrangement under which—

(a)   a director of the company or of its holding company, or a person connected with such a director, acquires or is to acquire from the company (directly or indirectly) a substantial non-cash asset, or

(b)   the company acquires or is to acquire a substantial non-cash asset (directly or indirectly) from such a director or a person so connected,

unless the arrangement has been approved by a resolution of the members of the company or is conditional on such approval being obtained.

For the meaning of "substantial non-cash asset" see section 191.

(2)   If the director or connected person is a director of the company's holding company or a person connected with such a director, the arrangement must also have been approved by a resolution of the members of the holding company or be conditional on such approval being obtained.

(3)   A company shall not be subject to any liability by reason of a failure to obtain approval required by this section.

(4)   No approval is required under this section on the part of the members of a body corporate that—

(a)   is not a UK-registered company, or

(b)   is a wholly-owned subsidiary of another body corporate.

(5)   For the purposes of this section—

(a)   an arrangement involving more than one non-cash asset, or

(b)   an arrangement that is one of a series involving non-cash assets,

shall be treated as if they involved a non-cash asset of a value equal to the aggregate value of all the non-cash assets involved in the arrangement or, as the case may be, the series.

(6)   This section does not apply to a transaction so far as it relates—

(a)   to anything to which a director of a company is entitled under his service contract, or

(b)   to payment for loss of office as defined in section 215 (payments to which the requirements of Chapter 4 or 4A apply).

191   Meaning of "substantial"

(1)   This section explains what is meant in section 190 (requirement of approval for substantial property transactions) by a "substantial" non-cash asset.

(2)   An asset is a substantial asset in relation to a company if its value—

    (a)   exceeds 10% of the company's asset value and is more than £5,000, or

    (b)   exceeds £100,000.

(3)   For this purpose a company's "asset value" at any time is—

    (a)   the value of the company's net assets determined by reference to its most recent statutory accounts, or

    (b)   if no statutory accounts have been prepared, the amount of the company's called-up share capital.

(4)   A company's "statutory accounts" means its annual accounts prepared in accordance with Part 15, and its "most recent" statutory accounts means those in relation to which the time for sending them out to members (see section 424) is most recent.

(5)   Whether an asset is a substantial asset shall be determined as at the time the arrangement is entered into.

192   Exception for transactions with members or other group companies

Approval is not required under section 190 (requirement of members' approval for substantial property transactions)—

    (a)   for a transaction between a company and a person in his character as a member of that company, or

    (b)   for a transaction between—

        (i)   a holding company and its wholly-owned subsidiary, or

        (ii)   two wholly-owned subsidiaries of the same holding company.

193   Exception in case of company in winding up or administration

(1)   This section applies to a company—

    (a)   that is being wound up (unless the winding up is a members' voluntary winding up), or

    (b)   that is in administration within the meaning of Schedule B1 to the Insolvency Act 1986 or the Insolvency (Northern Ireland) Order 1989.

(2)   Approval is not required under section 190 (requirement of members' approval for substantial property transactions)—

    (a)   on the part of the members of a company to which this section applies, or

    (b)   for an arrangement entered into by a company to which this section applies.

194   Exception for transactions on recognised investment exchange

(1)   Approval is not required under section 190 (requirement of members' approval for substantial property transactions) for a transaction on a recognised investment exchange effected by a director, or a person connected with him, through the agency of a person who in relation to the transaction acts as an independent broker.

(2)   For this purpose—

    (a)   "independent broker" means a person who, independently of the director or any person connected with him, selects the person with whom the transaction is to be effected; and

    (b)   "recognised investment exchange" has the same meaning as in Part 18 of the Financial Services and Markets Act 2000.

195   Property transactions: civil consequences of contravention

(1)   This section applies where a company enters into an arrangement in contravention of section 190 (requirement of members' approval for substantial property transactions).

(2)   The arrangement, and any transaction entered into in pursuance of the arrangement (whether by the company or any other person), is voidable at the instance of the company, unless—

    (a)   restitution of any money or other asset that was the subject matter of the arrangement or transaction is no longer possible,

(b)   the company has been indemnified in pursuance of this section by any other persons for the loss or damage suffered by it, or

(c)   rights acquired in good faith, for value and without actual notice of the contravention by a person who is not a party to the arrangement or transaction would be affected by the avoidance.

(3)   Whether or not the arrangement or any such transaction has been avoided, each of the persons specified in subsection (4) is liable—

(a)   to account to the company for any gain that he has made directly or indirectly by the arrangement or transaction, and

(b)   (jointly and severally with any other person so liable under this section) to indemnify the company for any loss or damage resulting from the arrangement or transaction.

(4)   The persons so liable are—

(a)   any director of the company or of its holding company with whom the company entered into the arrangement in contravention of section 190,

(b)   any person with whom the company entered into the arrangement in contravention of that section who is connected with a director of the company or of its holding company,

(c)   the director of the company or of its holding company with whom any such person is connected, and

(d)   any other director of the company who authorised the arrangement or any transaction entered into in pursuance of such an arrangement.

(5)   Subsections (3) and (4) are subject to the following two subsections.

(6)   In the case of an arrangement entered into by a company in contravention of section 190 with a person connected with a director of the company or of its holding company, that director is not liable by virtue of subsection (4)(c) if he shows that he took all reasonable steps to secure the company's compliance with that section.

(7)   In any case—

(a)   a person so connected is not liable by virtue of subsection (4)(b), and

(b)   a director is not liable by virtue of subsection (4)(d),

if he shows that, at the time the arrangement was entered into, he did not know the relevant circumstances constituting the contravention.

(8)   Nothing in this section shall be read as excluding the operation of any other enactment or rule of law by virtue of which the arrangement or transaction may be called in question or any liability to the company may arise.

196   Property transactions: effect of subsequent affirmation

Where a transaction or arrangement is entered into by a company in contravention of section 190 (requirement of members' approval) but, within a reasonable period, it is affirmed—

(a)   in the case of a contravention of subsection (1) of that section, by resolution of the members of the company, and

(b)   in the case of a contravention of subsection (2) of that section, by resolution of the members of the holding company,

the transaction or arrangement may no longer be avoided under section 195.

Loans, quasi-loans and credit transactions

197   Loans to directors: requirement of members' approval

(1)   A company may not—

(a)   make a loan to a director of the company or of its holding company, or

(b)   give a guarantee or provide security in connection with a loan made by any person to such a director,

unless the transaction has been approved by a resolution of the members of the company.

(2)   If the director is a director of the company's holding company, the transaction must also have been approved by a resolution of the members of the holding company.

(3)   A resolution approving a transaction to which this section applies must not be passed unless a memorandum setting out the matters mentioned in subsection (4) is made available to members—
    (a)   in the case of a written resolution, by being sent or submitted to every eligible member at or before the time at which the proposed resolution is sent or submitted to him;
    (b)   in the case of a resolution at a meeting, by being made available for inspection by members of the company both—
        (i)   at the company's registered office for not less than 15 days ending with the date of the meeting, and
        (ii)   at the meeting itself.
(4)   The matters to be disclosed are—
    (a)   the nature of the transaction,
    (b)   the amount of the loan and the purpose for which it is required, and
    (c)   the extent of the company's liability under any transaction connected with the loan.
(5)   No approval is required under this section on the part of the members of a body corporate that—
    (a)   is not a UK-registered company, or
    (b)   is a wholly-owned subsidiary of another body corporate.

198   Quasi-loans to directors: requirement of members' approval

(1)   This section applies to a company if it is—
    (a)   a public company, or
    (b)   a company associated with a public company.
(2)   A company to which this section applies may not—
    (a)   make a quasi-loan to a director of the company or of its holding company, or
    (b)   give a guarantee or provide security in connection with a quasi-loan made by any person to such a director,
unless the transaction has been approved by a resolution of the members of the company.
(3)   If the director is a director of the company's holding company, the transaction must also have been approved by a resolution of the members of the holding company.
(4)   A resolution approving a transaction to which this section applies must not be passed unless a memorandum setting out the matters mentioned in subsection (5) is made available to members—
    (a)   in the case of a written resolution, by being sent or submitted to every eligible member at or before the time at which the proposed resolution is sent or submitted to him;
    (b)   in the case of a resolution at a meeting, by being made available for inspection by members of the company both—
        (i)   at the company's registered office for not less than 15 days ending with the date of the meeting, and
        (ii)   at the meeting itself.
(5)   The matters to be disclosed are—
    (a)   the nature of the transaction,
    (b)   the amount of the quasi-loan and the purpose for which it is required, and
    (c)   the extent of the company's liability under any transaction connected with the quasi-loan.
(6)   No approval is required under this section on the part of the members of a body corporate that—
    (a)   is not a UK-registered company, or
    (b)   is a wholly-owned subsidiary of another body corporate.

199   Meaning of "quasi-loan" and related expressions

(1)   A "quasi-loan" is a transaction under which one party ("the creditor") agrees to pay, or pays otherwise than in pursuance of an agreement, a sum for another ("the borrower") or agrees to reimburse, or reimburses otherwise than in pursuance of an agreement, expenditure incurred by another party for another ("the borrower")—
    (a)   on terms that the borrower (or a person on his behalf) will reimburse the creditor; or
    (b)   in circumstances giving rise to a liability on the borrower to reimburse the creditor.
(2)   Any reference to the person to whom a quasi-loan is made is a reference to the borrower.

(3)   The liabilities of the borrower under a quasi-loan include the liabilities of any person who has agreed to reimburse the creditor on behalf of the borrower.

200   Loans or quasi-loans to persons connected with directors: requirement of members' approval

(1)   This section applies to a company if it is—
  (a)   a public company, or
  (b)   a company associated with a public company.

(2)   A company to which this section applies may not—
  (a)   make a loan or quasi-loan to a person connected with a director of the company or of its holding company, or
  (b)   give a guarantee or provide security in connection with a loan or quasi-loan made by any person to a person connected with such a director,
        unless the transaction has been approved by a resolution of the members of the company.

(3)   If the connected person is a person connected with a director of the company's holding company, the transaction must also have been approved by a resolution of the members of the holding company.

(4)   A resolution approving a transaction to which this section applies must not be passed unless a memorandum setting out the matters mentioned in subsection (5) is made available to members—
  (a)   in the case of a written resolution, by being sent or submitted to every eligible member at or before the time at which the proposed resolution is sent or submitted to him;
  (b)   in the case of a resolution at a meeting, by being made available for inspection by members of the company both—
        (i)   at the company's registered office for not less than 15 days ending with the date of the meeting, and
        (ii)   at the meeting itself.

(5)   The matters to be disclosed are—
  (a)   the nature of the transaction,
  (b)   the amount of the loan or quasi-loan and the purpose for which it is required, and
  (c)   the extent of the company's liability under any transaction connected with the loan or quasi-loan.

(6)   No approval is required under this section on the part of the members of a body corporate that—
  (a)   is not a UK-registered company, or
  (b)   is a wholly-owned subsidiary of another body corporate.

201   Credit transactions: requirement of members' approval

(1)   This section applies to a company if it is—
  (a)   a public company, or
  (b)   a company associated with a public company.

(2)   A company to which this section applies may not—
  (a)   enter into a credit transaction as creditor for the benefit of a director of the company or of its holding company, or a person connected with such a director, or
  (b)   give a guarantee or provide security in connection with a credit transaction entered into by any person for the benefit of such a director, or a person connected with such a director,
        unless the transaction (that is, the credit transaction, the giving of the guarantee or the provision of security, as the case may be) has been approved by a resolution of the members of the company.

(3)   If the director or connected person is a director of its holding company or a person connected with such a director, the transaction must also have been approved by a resolution of the members of the holding company.

(4)   A resolution approving a transaction to which this section applies must not be passed unless a memorandum setting out the matters mentioned in subsection (5) is made available to members—

(a)   in the case of a written resolution, by being sent or submitted to every eligible member at or before the time at which the proposed resolution is sent or submitted to him;

(b)   in the case of a resolution at a meeting, by being made available for inspection by members of the company both—

(i)   at the company's registered office for not less than 15 days ending with the date of the meeting, and

(ii)   at the meeting itself.

(5)   The matters to be disclosed are—

(a)   the nature of the transaction,

(b)   the value of the credit transaction and the purpose for which the land, goods or services sold or otherwise disposed of, leased, hired or supplied under the credit transaction are required, and

(c)   the extent of the company's liability under any transaction connected with the credit transaction.

(6)   No approval is required under this section on the part of the members of a body corporate that—

(a)   is not a UK-registered company, or

(b)   is a wholly-owned subsidiary of another body corporate.

202   Meaning of "credit transaction"

(1)   A "credit transaction" is a transaction under which one party ("the creditor")—

(a)   supplies any goods or sells any land under a hire-purchase agreement or a conditional sale agreement,

(b)   leases or hires any land or goods in return for periodical payments, or

(c)   otherwise disposes of land or supplies goods or services on the understanding that payment (whether in a lump sum or instalments or by way of periodical payments or otherwise) is to be deferred.

(2)   Any reference to the person for whose benefit a credit transaction is entered into is to the person to whom goods, land or services are supplied, sold, leased, hired or otherwise disposed of under the transaction.

(3)   In this section—

"conditional sale agreement" has the same meaning as in the Consumer Credit Act 1974; and "services" means anything other than goods or land.

203   Related arrangements: requirement of members' approval

(1)   A company may not—

(a)   take part in an arrangement under which—

(i)   another person enters into a transaction that, if it had been entered into by the company, would have required approval under section 197, 198, 200 or 201, and

(ii)   that person, in pursuance of the arrangement, obtains a benefit from the company or a body corporate associated with it, or

(b)   arrange for the assignment to it, or assumption by it, of any rights, obligations or liabilities under a transaction that, if it had been entered into by the company, would have required such approval,

unless the arrangement in question has been approved by a resolution of the members of the company.

(2)   If the director or connected person for whom the transaction is entered into is a director of its holding company or a person connected with such a director, the arrangement must also have been approved by a resolution of the members of the holding company.

(3)   A resolution approving an arrangement to which this section applies must not be passed unless a memorandum setting out the matters mentioned in subsection (4) is made available to members—

(a)   in the case of a written resolution, by being sent or submitted to every eligible member at or before the time at which the proposed resolution is sent or submitted to him;

    (b)   in the case of a resolution at a meeting, by being made available for inspection by members of the company both—

        (i)   at the company's registered office for not less than 15 days ending with the date of the meeting, and

        (ii)   at the meeting itself.

(4)   The matters to be disclosed are—

    (a)   the matters that would have to be disclosed if the company were seeking approval of the transaction to which the arrangement relates,

    (b)   the nature of the arrangement, and

    (c)   the extent of the company's liability under the arrangement or any transaction connected with it.

(5)   No approval is required under this section on the part of the members of a body corporate that—

    (a)   is not a UK-registered company, or

    (b)   is a wholly-owned subsidiary of another body corporate.

(6)   In determining for the purposes of this section whether a transaction is one that would have required approval under section 197, 198, 200 or 201 if it had been entered into by the company, the transaction shall be treated as having been entered into on the date of the arrangement.

204   Exception for expenditure on company business

(1)   Approval is not required under section 197, 198, 200 or 201 (requirement of members' approval for loans etc) for anything done by a company—

    (a)   to provide a director of the company or of its holding company, or a person connected with any such director, with funds to meet expenditure incurred or to be incurred by him—

        (i)   for the purposes of the company, or

        (ii)   for the purpose of enabling him properly to perform his duties as an officer of the company, or

    (b)   to enable any such person to avoid incurring such expenditure.

(2)   This section does not authorise a company to enter into a transaction if the aggregate of—

    (a)   the value of the transaction in question, and

    (b)   the value of any other relevant transactions or arrangements, exceeds £50,000.

205   Exception for expenditure on defending proceedings etc

(1)   Approval is not required under section 197, 198, 200 or 201 (requirement of members' approval for loans etc) for anything done by a company—

    (a)   to provide a director of the company or of its holding company with funds to meet expenditure incurred or to be incurred by him—

        (i)   in defending any criminal or civil proceedings in connection with any alleged negligence, default, breach of duty or breach of trust by him in relation to the company or an associated company, or

        (ii)   in connection with an application for relief (see subsection (5)), or

    (b)   to enable any such director to avoid incurring such expenditure, if it is done on the following terms.

(2)   The terms are—

    (a)   that the loan is to be repaid, or (as the case may be) any liability of the company incurred under any transaction connected with the thing done is to be discharged, in the event of—

        (i)   the director being convicted in the proceedings,

        (ii)   judgment being given against him in the proceedings, or

        (iii) the court refusing to grant him relief on the application; and

    (b)   that it is to be so repaid or discharged not later than—

        (i)   the date when the conviction becomes final,

        (ii)   the date when the judgment becomes final, or

        (iii) the date when the refusal of relief becomes final.

(3)   For this purpose a conviction, judgment or refusal of relief becomes final—

(a)   if not appealed against, at the end of the period for bringing an appeal;

(b)   if appealed against, when the appeal (or any further appeal) is disposed of.

(4)   An appeal is disposed of—

(a)   if it is determined and the period for bringing any further appeal has ended, or

(b)   if it is abandoned or otherwise ceases to have effect.

(5)   The reference in subsection (1)(a)(ii) to an application for relief is to an application for relief under—

section 661(3) or (4) (power of court to grant relief in case of acquisition of shares by innocent nominee), or

section 1157 (general power of court to grant relief in case of honest and reasonable conduct).

206   Exception for expenditure in connection with regulatory action or investigation

Approval is not required under section 197, 198, 200 or 201 (requirement of members' approval for loans etc) for anything done by a company—

(a)   to provide a director of the company or of its holding company with funds to meet expenditure incurred or to be incurred by him in defending himself—

(i)   in an investigation by a regulatory authority, or

(ii)   against action proposed to be taken by a regulatory authority,

in connection with any alleged negligence, default, breach of duty or breach of trust by him in relation to the company or an associated company, or

(b)   to enable any such director to avoid incurring such expenditure.

207   Exceptions for minor and business transactions

(1)   Approval is not required under section 197, 198 or 200 for a company to make a loan or quasi-loan, or to give a guarantee or provide security in connection with a loan or quasi-loan, if the aggregate of—

(a)   the value of the transaction, and

(b)   the value of any other relevant transactions or arrangements, does not exceed £10,000.

(2)   Approval is not required under section 201 for a company to enter into a credit transaction, or to give a guarantee or provide security in connection with a credit transaction, if the aggregate of—

(a)   the value of the transaction (that is, of the credit transaction, guarantee or security), and

(b)   the value of any other relevant transactions or arrangements,

does not exceed £15,000.

(3)   Approval is not required under section 201 for a company to enter into a credit transaction, or to give a guarantee or provide security in connection with a credit transaction, if—

(a)   the transaction is entered into by the company in the ordinary course of the company's business, and

(b)   the value of the transaction is not greater, and the terms on which it is entered into are not more favourable, than it is reasonable to expect the company would have offered to, or in respect of, a person of the same financial standing but unconnected with the company.

208   Exceptions for intra-group transactions

(1)   Approval is not required under section 197, 198 or 200 for—

(a)   the making of a loan or quasi-loan to an associated body corporate, or

(b)   the giving of a guarantee or provision of security in connection with a loan or quasi-loan made to an associated body corporate.

(2)   Approval is not required under section 201—

(a)   to enter into a credit transaction as creditor for the benefit of an associated body corporate, or

(b)   to give a guarantee or provide security in connection with a credit transaction entered into by any person for the benefit of an associated body corporate.

209 **Exceptions for money-lending companies**

(1) Approval is not required under section 197, 198 or 200 for the making of a loan or quasi-loan, or the giving of a guarantee or provision of security in connection with a loan or quasi-loan, by a money-lending company if—

(a) the transaction (that is, the loan, quasi-loan, guarantee or security) is entered into by the company in the ordinary course of the company's business, and

(b) the value of the transaction is not greater, and its terms are not more favourable, than it is reasonable to expect the company would have offered to a person of the same financial standing but unconnected with the company.

(2) A "money-lending company" means a company whose ordinary business includes the making of loans or quasi-loans, or the giving of guarantees or provision of security in connection with loans or quasi-loans.

(3) The condition specified in subsection (1)(b) does not of itself prevent a company from making a home loan—

(a) to a director of the company or of its holding company, or

(b) to an employee of the company,

if loans of that description are ordinarily made by the company to its employees and the terms of the loan in question are no more favourable than those on which such loans are ordinarily made.

(4) For the purposes of subsection (3) a "home loan" means a loan—

(a) for the purpose of facilitating the purchase, for use as the only or main residence of the person to whom the loan is made, of the whole or part of any dwelling-house together with any land to be occupied and enjoyed with it,

(b) for the purpose of improving a dwelling-house or part of a dwelling-house so used or any land occupied and enjoyed with it, or

(c) in substitution for any loan made by any person and falling within paragraph (a) or (b).

210 **Other relevant transactions or arrangements**

(1) This section has effect for determining what are "other relevant transactions or arrangements" for the purposes of any exception to section 197, 198, 200 or 201. In the following provisions "the relevant exception" means the exception for the purposes of which that falls to be determined.

(2) Other relevant transactions or arrangements are those previously entered into, or entered into at the same time as the transaction or arrangement in question in relation to which the following conditions are met.

(3) Where the transaction or arrangement in question is entered into—

(a) for a director of the company entering into it, or

(b) for a person connected with such a director,

the conditions are that the transaction or arrangement was (or is) entered into for that director, or a person connected with him, by virtue of the relevant exception by that company or by any of its subsidiaries.

(4) Where the transaction or arrangement in question is entered into—

(a) for a director of the holding company of the company entering into it, or

(b) for a person connected with such a director,

the conditions are that the transaction or arrangement was (or is) entered into for that director, or a person connected with him, by virtue of the relevant exception by the holding company or by any of its subsidiaries.

(5) A transaction or arrangement entered into by a company that at the time it was entered into—

(a) was a subsidiary of the company entering into the transaction or arrangement in question, or

(b) was a subsidiary of that company's holding company,

is not a relevant transaction or arrangement if, at the time the question arises whether the transaction or arrangement in question falls within a relevant exception, it is no longer such a subsidiary.

211   The value of transactions and arrangements

(1)   For the purposes of sections 197 to 214 (loans etc)—

    (a)   the value of a transaction or arrangement is determined as follows, and

    (b)   the value of any other relevant transaction or arrangement is taken to be the value so determined reduced by any amount by which the liabilities of the person for whom the transaction or arrangement was made have been reduced.

(2)   The value of a loan is the amount of its principal.

(3)   The value of a quasi-loan is the amount, or maximum amount, that the person to whom the quasi-loan is made is liable to reimburse the creditor.

(4)   The value of a credit transaction is the price that it is reasonable to expect could be obtained for the goods, services or land to which the transaction relates if they had been supplied (at the time the transaction is entered into) in the ordinary course of business and on the same terms (apart from price) as they have been supplied, or are to be supplied, under the transaction in question.

(5)   The value of a guarantee or security is the amount guaranteed or secured.

(6)   The value of an arrangement to which section 203 (related arrangements) applies is the value of the transaction to which the arrangement relates.

(7)   If the value of a transaction or arrangement is not capable of being expressed as a specific sum of money—

    (a)   whether because the amount of any liability arising under the transaction or arrangement is unascertainable, or for any other reason, and

    (b)   whether or not any liability under the transaction or arrangement has been reduced,

    its value is deemed to exceed £50,000.

212   The person for whom a transaction or arrangement is entered into

For the purposes of sections 197 to 214 (loans etc) the person for whom a transaction or arrangement is entered into is—

    (a)   in the case of a loan or quasi-loan, the person to whom it is made;

    (b)   in the case of a credit transaction, the person to whom goods, land or services are supplied, sold, hired, leased or otherwise disposed of under the transaction;

    (c)   in the case of a guarantee or security, the person for whom the transaction is made in connection with which the guarantee or security is entered into;

    (d)   in the case of an arrangement within section 203 (related arrangements), the person for whom the transaction is made to which the arrangement relates.

213   Loans etc: civil consequences of contravention

(1)   This section applies where a company enters into a transaction or arrangement in contravention of section 197, 198, 200, 201 or 203 (requirement of members' approval for loans etc).

(2)   The transaction or arrangement is voidable at the instance of the company, unless—

    (a)   restitution of any money or other asset that was the subject matter of the transaction or arrangement is no longer possible,

    (b)   the company has been indemnified for any loss or damage resulting from the transaction or arrangement, or

    (c)   rights acquired in good faith, for value and without actual notice of the contravention by a person who is not a party to the transaction or arrangement would be affected by the avoidance.

(3)   Whether or not the transaction or arrangement has been avoided, each of the persons specified in subsection (4) is liable—

    (a)   to account to the company for any gain that he has made directly or indirectly by the transaction or arrangement, and

    (b)   (jointly and severally with any other person so liable under this section) to indemnify the company for any loss or damage resulting from the transaction or arrangement.

(4)   The persons so liable are—

(a) any director of the company or of its holding company with whom the company entered into the transaction or arrangement in contravention of section 197, 198, 201 or 203,

(b) any person with whom the company entered into the transaction or arrangement in contravention of any of those sections who is connected with a director of the company or of its holding company,

(c) the director of the company or of its holding company with whom any such person is connected, and

(d) any other director of the company who authorised the transaction or arrangement.

(5) Subsections (3) and (4) are subject to the following two subsections.

(6) In the case of a transaction or arrangement entered into by a company in contravention of section 200, 201 or 203 with a person connected with a director of the company or of its holding company, that director is not liable by virtue of subsection (4)(c) if he shows that he took all reasonable steps to secure the company's compliance with the section concerned.

(7) In any case—

(a) a person so connected is not liable by virtue of subsection (4)(b), and

(b) a director is not liable by virtue of subsection (4)(d),

if he shows that, at the time the transaction or arrangement was entered into, he did not know the relevant circumstances constituting the contravention.

(8) Nothing in this section shall be read as excluding the operation of any other enactment or rule of law by virtue of which the transaction or arrangement may be called in question or any liability to the company may arise.

214 Loans etc: effect of subsequent affirmation

(1) Where a transaction or arrangement is entered into by a company in contravention of section 197, 198, 200, 201 or 203 (requirement of members' approval for loans etc) but, within a reasonable period, it is affirmed—

(a) in the case of a contravention of the requirement for a resolution of the members of the company, by a resolution of the members of the company, and

(b) in the case of a contravention of the requirement for a resolution of the members of the company's holding company, by a resolution of the members of the holding company,

the transaction or arrangement may no longer be avoided under section 213.

Payments for loss of office

215 Payments for loss of office

(1) In this Chapter a "payment for loss of office" means a payment made to a director or past director of a company—

(a) by way of compensation for loss of office as director of the company,

(b) by way of compensation for loss, while director of the company or in connection with his ceasing to be a director of it, of—

(i) any other office or employment in connection with the management of the affairs of the company, or

(ii) any office (as director or otherwise) or employment in connection with the management of the affairs of any subsidiary undertaking of the company,

(c) as consideration for or in connection with his retirement from his office as director of the company, or

(d) as consideration for or in connection with his retirement, while director of the company or in connection with his ceasing to be a director of it, from—

(i) any other office or employment in connection with the management of the affairs of the company, or

(ii) any office (as director or otherwise) or employment in connection with the management of the affairs of any subsidiary undertaking of the company.

(2) The references to compensation and consideration include benefits otherwise than in cash and references in this Chapter to payment have a corresponding meaning.

(3)   For the purposes of sections 217 to 221 (payments requiring members' approval)—
        (a)   payment to a person connected with a director, or
        (b)   payment to any person at the direction of, or for the benefit of, a director or a person connected with him,
        is treated as payment to the director.

(4)   References in those sections to payment by a person include payment by another person at the direction of, or on behalf of, the person referred to.

(5)   Nothing in this section or sections 216 to 222 applies in relation to a payment for loss of office to a director of a quoted company or unquoted traded company other than a payment to which section 226C does not apply by virtue of section 226D(6).

(6)   "Unquoted traded company" means a traded company (as defined by section 360C) that is not a quoted company.

216   Amounts taken to be payments for loss of office

(1)   This section applies where in connection with any such transfer as is mentioned in section 218 or 219 (payment in connection with transfer of undertaking, property or shares) a director of the company—
        (a)   is to cease to hold office, or
        (b)   is to cease to be the holder of—
                (i)   any other office or employment in connection with the management of the affairs of the company, or
                (ii)   any office (as director or otherwise) or employment in connection with the management of the affairs of any subsidiary undertaking of the company.

(2)   If in connection with any such transfer—
        (a)   the price to be paid to the director for any shares in the company held by him is in excess of the price which could at the time have been obtained by other holders of like shares, or
        (b)   any valuable consideration is given to the director by a person other than the company,
        the excess or, as the case may be, the money value of the consideration is taken for the purposes of those sections to have been a payment for loss of office.

217   Payment by company: requirement of members' approval

(1)   A company may not make a payment for loss of office to a director of the company unless the payment has been approved by a resolution of the members of the company.

(2)   A company may not make a payment for loss of office to a director of its holding company unless the payment has been approved by a resolution of the members of each of those companies.

(3)   A resolution approving a payment to which this section applies must not be passed unless a memorandum setting out particulars of the proposed payment (including its amount) is made available to the members of the company whose approval is sought—
        (a)   in the case of a written resolution, by being sent or submitted to every eligible member at or before the time at which the proposed resolution is sent or submitted to him;
        (b)   in the case of a resolution at a meeting, by being made available for inspection by the members both—
                (i)   at the company's registered office for not less than 15 days ending with the date of the meeting, and
                (ii)   at the meeting itself.

(4)   No approval is required under this section on the part of the members of a body corporate that—
        (a)   is not a UK-registered company, or
        (b)   is a wholly-owned subsidiary of another body corporate.

218   Payment in connection with transfer of undertaking etc: requirement of members' approval

(1)   No payment for loss of office may be made by any person to a director of a company in connection with the transfer of the whole or any part of the undertaking or property of the company unless the payment has been approved by a resolution of the members of the company.

(2) No payment for loss of office may be made by any person to a director of a company in connection with the transfer of the whole or any part of the undertaking or property of a subsidiary of the company unless the payment has been approved by a resolution of the members of each of the companies.

(3) A resolution approving a payment to which this section applies must not be passed unless a memorandum setting out particulars of the proposed payment (including its amount) is made available to the members of the company whose approval is sought—

    (a) in the case of a written resolution, by being sent or submitted to every eligible member at or before the time at which the proposed resolution is sent or submitted to him;

    (b) in the case of a resolution at a meeting, by being made available for inspection by the members both—

        (i) at the company's registered office for not less than 15 days ending with the date of the meeting, and

        (ii) at the meeting itself.

(4) No approval is required under this section on the part of the members of a body corporate that—

    (a) is not a UK-registered company, or

    (b) is a wholly-owned subsidiary of another body corporate.

(5) A payment made in pursuance of an arrangement—

    (a) entered into as part of the agreement for the transfer in question, or within one year before or two years after that agreement, and

    (b) to which the company whose undertaking or property is transferred, or any person to whom the transfer is made, is privy,

is presumed, except in so far as the contrary is shown, to be a payment to which this section applies.

219 Payment in connection with share transfer: requirement of members' approval

(1) No payment for loss of office may be made by any person to a director of a company in connection with a transfer of shares in the company, or in a subsidiary of the company, resulting from a takeover bid unless the payment has been approved by a resolution of the relevant shareholders.

(2) The relevant shareholders are the holders of the shares to which the bid relates and any holders of shares of the same class as any of those shares.

(3) A resolution approving a payment to which this section applies must not be passed unless a memorandum setting out particulars of the proposed payment (including its amount) is made available to the members of the company whose approval is sought—

    (a) in the case of a written resolution, by being sent or submitted to every eligible member at or before the time at which the proposed resolution is sent or submitted to him;

    (b) in the case of a resolution at a meeting, by being made available for inspection by the members both—

        (i) at the company's registered office for not less than 15 days ending with the date of the meeting, and

        (ii) at the meeting itself.

(4) Neither the person making the offer, nor any associate of his (as defined in section 988), is entitled to vote on the resolution, but—

    (a) where the resolution is proposed as a written resolution, they are entitled (if they would otherwise be so entitled) to be sent a copy of it, and

    (b) at any meeting to consider the resolution they are entitled (if they would otherwise be so entitled) to be given notice of the meeting, to attend and speak and if present (in person or by proxy) to count towards the quorum.

(5) If at a meeting to consider the resolution a quorum is not present, and after the meeting has been adjourned to a later date a quorum is again not present, the payment is (for the purposes of this section) deemed to have been approved.

(6) No approval is required under this section on the part of shareholders in a body corporate that—

(a)   is not a UK-registered company, or

(b)   is a wholly-owned subsidiary of another body corporate.

(7)   A payment made in pursuance of an arrangement—

(a)   entered into as part of the agreement for the transfer in question, or within one year before or two years after that agreement, and

(b)   to which the company whose shares are the subject of the bid, or any person to whom the transfer is made, is privy,

is presumed, except in so far as the contrary is shown, to be a payment to which this section applies.

220   Exception for payments in discharge of legal obligations etc

(1)   Approval is not required under section 217, 218 or 219 (payments requiring members' approval) for a payment made in good faith—

(a)   in discharge of an existing legal obligation (as defined below),

(b)   by way of damages for breach of such an obligation,

(c)   by way of settlement or compromise of any claim arising in connection with the termination of a person's office or employment, or

(d)   by way of pension in respect of past services.

(2)   In relation to a payment within section 217 (payment by company) an existing legal obligation means an obligation of the company, or any body corporate associated with it, that was not entered into in connection with, or in consequence of, the event giving rise to the payment for loss of office.

(3)   In relation to a payment within section 218 or 219 (payment in connection with transfer of undertaking, property or shares) an existing legal obligation means an obligation of the person making the payment that was not entered into for the purposes of, in connection with or in consequence of, the transfer in question.

(4)   In the case of a payment within both section 217 and section 218, or within both section 217 and section 219, subsection (2) above applies and not subsection (3).

(5)   A payment part of which falls within subsection (1) above and part of which does not is treated as if the parts were separate payments.

221   Exception for small payments

(1)   Approval is not required under section 217, 218 or 219 (payments requiring members' approval) if—

(a)   the payment in question is made by the company or any of its subsidiaries, and

(b)   the amount or value of the payment, together with the amount or value of any other relevant payments, does not exceed £200.

(2)   For this purpose "other relevant payments" are payments for loss of office in relation to which the following conditions are met.

(3)   Where the payment in question is one to which section 217 (payment by company) applies, the conditions are that the other payment was or is paid—

(a)   by the company making the payment in question or any of its subsidiaries,

(b)   to the director to whom that payment is made, and

(c)   in connection with the same event.

(4)   Where the payment in question is one to which section 218 or 219 applies (payment in connection with transfer of undertaking, property or shares), the conditions are that the other payment was (or is) paid in connection with the same transfer—

(a)   to the director to whom the payment in question was made, and

(b)   by the company making the payment or any of its subsidiaries.

222   Payments made without approval: civil consequences

(1)   If a payment is made in contravention of section 217 (payment by company)—

(a)   it is held by the recipient on trust for the company making the payment, and

(b) any director who authorised the payment is jointly and severally liable to indemnify the company that made the payment for any loss resulting from it.

(2) If a payment is made in contravention of section 218 (payment in connection with transfer of undertaking etc), it is held by the recipient on trust for the company whose undertaking or property is or is proposed to be transferred.

(3) If a payment is made in contravention of section 219 (payment in connection with share transfer)—

(a) it is held by the recipient on trust for persons who have sold their shares as a result of the offer made, and

(b) the expenses incurred by the recipient in distributing that sum amongst those persons shall be borne by him and not retained out of that sum.

(4) If a payment is in contravention of section 217 and section 218, subsection (2) of this section applies rather than subsection (1).

(5) If a payment is in contravention of section 217 and section 219, subsection (3) of this section applies rather than subsection (1), unless the court directs otherwise.

Supplementary

223 Transactions requiring members' approval: application of provisions to shadow directors

(1) For the purposes of—

(a) sections 188 and 189 (directors' service contracts),

(b) sections 190 to 196 (property transactions),

(c) sections 197 to 214 (loans etc), and

(d) sections 215 to 222 (payments for loss of office),

a shadow director is treated as a director.

(2) Any reference in those provisions to loss of office as a director does not apply in relation to loss of a person's status as a shadow director.

224 Approval by written resolution: accidental failure to send memorandum

(1) Where—

(a) approval under this Chapter is sought by written resolution, and

(b) a memorandum is required under this Chapter to be sent or submitted to every eligible member before the resolution is passed,

any accidental failure to send or submit the memorandum to one or more members shall be disregarded for the purpose of determining whether the requirement has been met.

(2) Subsection (1) has effect subject to any provision of the company's articles.

225 Cases where approval is required under more than one provision

(1) Approval may be required under more than one provision of this Chapter.

(2) If so, the requirements of each applicable provision must be met.

(3) This does not require a separate resolution for the purposes of each provision.

226 ...

CHAPTER 4A

DIRECTORS OF QUOTED COMPANIES AND TRADED COMPANIES: SPECIAL PROVISION

Interpretation

226A Key definitions

(1) In this Chapter—

"directors' remuneration policy" means the policy of a quoted company, or of an unquoted traded company, with respect to the making of remuneration payments and payments for loss of office;

"quoted company" has the same meaning as in Part 15 of this Act;

"remuneration payment" means any form of payment or other benefit made to or otherwise conferred on a person as consideration for the person—

(a)   holding, agreeing to hold or having held office as director of a company, or

(b)   holding, agreeing to hold or having held, during a period when the person is or was such a director—

    (i)   any other office or employment in connection with the management of the affairs of the company, or

    (ii)   any office (as director or otherwise) or employment in connection with the management of the affairs of any subsidiary undertaking of the company,

other than a payment for loss of office;

"payment for loss of office" has the same meaning as in Chapter 4 of this Part;

"unquoted traded company" means a traded company (as defined by section 360C) that is not a quoted company.

(2)   Subsection (3) applies where, in connection with a relevant transfer, a director of a quoted company or unquoted traded company is—

(a)   to cease to hold office as director, or

(b)   to cease to be the holder of—

    (i)   any other office or employment in connection with the management of the affairs of the company, or

    (ii)   any office (as director or otherwise) or employment in connection with the management of the affairs of any subsidiary undertaking of the company.

(3)   If in connection with the transfer—

(a)   the price to be paid to the director for any shares in the company held by the director is in excess of the price which could at the time have been obtained by other holders of like shares, or

(b)   any valuable consideration is given to the director by a person other than the company,

the excess or, as the case may be, the money value of the consideration is taken for the purposes of section 226C to have been a payment for loss of office.

(4)   In subsection (2), "relevant transfer" means—

(a)   a transfer of the whole or any part of the undertaking or property of the company or a subsidiary of the company;

(b)   a transfer of shares in the company, or in a subsidiary of the company, resulting from a takeover bid.

(5)   References in this Chapter to the making of a remuneration payment or to the making of a payment for loss of office are to be read in accordance with this section.

(6)   References in this Chapter to a payment by a company include a payment by another person at the direction of, or on behalf of, the company.

(7)   References in this Chapter to a payment to a person ("B") who is, has been or is to be a director of a company include—

(a)   a payment to a person connected with B, or

(b)   a payment to a person at the direction of, or for the benefit of, B or a person connected with B.

(8)   Section 252 applies for the purposes of determining whether a person is connected with a person who has been, or is to be, a director of a company as it applies for the purposes of determining whether a person is connected with a director.

(9)   References in this Chapter to a director include a shadow director but references to loss of office as a director do not include loss of a person's status as a shadow director.

(10)   References in this Chapter (other than sections 226E(2)(b) and (5)) to a director of a company include a person who is not a director of the company but who is—

(a)   its chief executive officer (however described), or

(b)   where such a function exists in the company, its deputy chief executive officer (however described).

Restrictions relating to remuneration or loss of office payments

226B   Remuneration payments

(1)   A quoted company or unquoted traded company may not make a remuneration payment to a person who is, or is to be or has been, a director of the company unless—

(a)   the payment is consistent with the approved directors' remuneration policy, or

(b)   an amendment to that policy authorising the company to make the payment has been approved by resolution of the members of the company.

(2)   The approved directors' remuneration policy is the most recent remuneration policy to have been approved by a resolution passed by the members of the company in general meeting.

226C   Loss of office payments

(1)   No payment for loss of office may be made by any person to a person who is, or has been, a director of a quoted company or of an unquoted traded company unless—

(a)   the payment is consistent with the approved directors' remuneration policy, or

(b)   an amendment to that policy authorising the company to make the payment has been approved by resolution of the members of the company.

(2)   The approved directors' remuneration policy is the most recent remuneration policy to have been approved by a resolution passed by the members of the company in general meeting.

226D   Sections 226B and 226C: supplementary

(1)   A resolution approving an amendment for the purposes of section 226B(1)(b) or 226C(1)(b) must not be passed unless a memorandum setting out particulars of the proposed payment to which the amendment relates (including its amount) is made available for inspection by the members of the company—

(a)   at the company's registered office for not less than 15 days ending with the date of the meeting at which the resolution is to be considered, and

(b)   at that meeting itself.

(2)   The memorandum must explain the ways in which the payment would be inconsistent with the approved directors' remuneration policy (within the meaning of the section in question) but for the amendment.

(3)   The company must ensure that the memorandum is made available on the company's website from the first day on which the memorandum is made available for inspection under subsection (1) until its next accounts meeting.

(4)   Failure to comply with subsection (3) does not affect the validity of the meeting at which a resolution is passed approving the amendment to which the memorandum relates or the validity of anything done at the meeting.

(5)   Nothing in section 226B or 226C authorises the making of a remuneration payment or (as the case may be) a payment for loss of office in contravention of the articles of the company concerned.

(6)   Nothing in section 226B or 226C applies in relation to a remuneration payment or (as the case may be) a payment for loss of office made to a person who is, or is to be or has been, a director of a quoted company or of an unquoted traded company before the earlier of—

(a)   the end of the first financial year of the company to begin on or after the day on which it becomes a quoted company or (as the case may be) an unquoted traded company, and

(b)   the date from which the company's first directors' remuneration policy to be approved under section 439A takes effect.

(7)   In this section the "company's website" is the website on which the company makes material available under section 430.

Supplementary

226E   Payments made without approval: civil consequences

(1)   An obligation (however arising) to make a payment which would be in contravention of section 226B or 226C has no effect.

(2)   If a payment is made in contravention of section 226B or 226C—
    (a)   it is held by the recipient on trust for the company or other person making the payment, and
    (b)   in the case of a payment by a company, any director who authorised the payment is jointly and severally liable to indemnify the company that made the payment for any loss resulting from it.

(3)   If a payment for loss of office is made in contravention of section 226C to a director of a quoted company or of an unquoted traded company in connection with the transfer of the whole or any part of the undertaking or property of the company or a subsidiary of the company—
    (a)   subsection (2) does not apply, and
    (b)   the payment is held by the recipient on trust for the company whose undertaking or property is or is proposed to be transferred.

(4)   If a payment for loss of office is made in contravention of section 226C to a director of a quoted company or of an unquoted traded company in connection with a transfer of shares in the company, or in a subsidiary of the company, resulting from a takeover bid—
    (a)   subsection (2) does not apply,
    (b)   the payment is held by the recipient on trust for persons who have sold their shares as a result of the offer made, and
    (c)   the expenses incurred by the recipient in distributing that sum amongst those persons shall be borne by the recipient and not retained out of that sum.

(5)   If in proceedings against a director for the enforcement of a liability under subsection (2)(b)—
    (a)   the director shows that he or she has acted honestly and reasonably, and
    (b)   the court considers that, having regard to all the circumstances of the case, the director ought to be relieved of liability,
the court may relieve the director, either wholly or in part, from liability on such terms as the court thinks fit.

226F   Relationship with requirements under Chapter 4

(1)   This Chapter does not affect any requirement for approval by a resolution of the members of a company which applies in relation to the company under Chapter 4.

(2)   Where the making of a payment to which section 226B or 226C applies requires approval by a resolution of the members of the company concerned under Chapter 4, approval obtained for the purposes of that Chapter is to be treated as satisfying the requirements of section 226B(1)(b) or (as the case may be) 226C(1)(b).

CHAPTER 5
DIRECTORS' SERVICE CONTRACTS

227   Directors' service contracts

(1)   For the purposes of this Part a director's "service contract", in relation to a company, means a contract under which—
    (a)   a director of the company undertakes personally to perform services (as director or otherwise) for the company, or for a subsidiary of the company, or
    (b)   services (as director or otherwise) that a director of the company undertakes personally to perform are made available by a third party to the company, or to a subsidiary of the company.

(2)   The provisions of this Part relating to directors' service contracts apply to the terms of a person's appointment as a director of a company.
They are not restricted to contracts for the performance of services outside the scope of the ordinary duties of a director.

228   Copy of contract or memorandum of terms to be available for inspection

(1)   A company must keep available for inspection—
    (a)   a copy of every director's service contract with the company or with a subsidiary of the company, or

(b)   if the contract is not in writing, a written memorandum setting out the terms of the contract.

(2)   All the copies and memoranda must be kept available for inspection at—

(a)   the company's registered office, or

(b)   a place specified in regulations under section 1136.

(3)   The copies and memoranda must be retained by the company for at least one year from the date of termination or expiry of the contract and must be kept available for inspection during that time.

(4)   The company must give notice to the registrar—

(a)   of the place at which the copies and memoranda are kept available for inspection, and

(b)   of any change in that place,

unless they have at all times been kept at the company's registered office.

(5)   If default is made in complying with subsection (1), (2) or (3), or default is made for 14 days in complying with subsection (4), an offence is committed by every officer of the company who is in default.

(6)   A person guilty of an offence under this section is liable on summary conviction to a fine not exceeding level 3 on the standard scale and, for continued contravention, a daily default fine not exceeding one-tenth of level 3 on the standard scale.

(7)   The provisions of this section apply to a variation of a director's service contract as they apply to the original contract.

229   Right of member to inspect and request copy

(1)   Every copy or memorandum required to be kept under section 228 must be open to inspection by any member of the company without charge.

(2)   Any member of the company is entitled, on request and on payment of such fee as may be prescribed, to be provided with a copy of any such copy or memorandum.

The copy must be provided within seven days after the request is received by the company.

(3)   If an inspection required under subsection (1) is refused, or default is made in complying with subsection (2), an offence is committed by every officer of the company who is in default.

(4)   A person guilty of an offence under this section is liable on summary conviction to a fine not exceeding level 3 on the standard scale and, for continued contravention, a daily default fine not exceeding one-tenth of level 3 on the standard scale.

(5)   In the case of any such refusal or default the court may by order compel an immediate inspection or, as the case may be, direct that the copy required be sent to the person requiring it.

230   Directors' service contracts: application of provisions to shadow directors

A shadow director is treated as a director for the purposes of the provisions of this Chapter.

CHAPTER 6
CONTRACTS WITH SOLE MEMBERS WHO ARE DIRECTORS

231   Contract with sole member who is also a director

(1)   This section applies where—

(a)   a limited company having only one member enters into a contract with the sole member,

(b)   the sole member is also a director of the company, and

(c)   the contract is not entered into in the ordinary course of the company's business.

(2)   The company must, unless the contract is in writing, ensure that the terms of the contract are either—

(a)   set out in a written memorandum, or

(b)   recorded in the minutes of the first meeting of the directors of the company following the making of the contract.

(3)   If a company fails to comply with this section an offence is committed by every officer of the company who is in default.

(4)   A person guilty of an offence under this section is liable on summary conviction to a fine not exceeding level 5 on the standard scale.

(5)   For the purposes of this section a shadow director is treated as a director.

(6)   Failure to comply with this section in relation to a contract does not affect the validity of the contract.

(7)   Nothing in this section shall be read as excluding the operation of any other enactment or rule of law applying to contracts between a company and a director of the company.

CHAPTER 7
DIRECTORS' LIABILITIES

Provision protecting directors from liability

232   Provisions protecting directors from liability

(1)   Any provision that purports to exempt a director of a company (to any extent) from any liability that would otherwise attach to him in connection with any negligence, default, breach of duty or breach of trust in relation to the company is void.

(2)   Any provision by which a company directly or indirectly provides an indemnity (to any extent) for a director of the company, or of an associated company, against any liability attaching to him in connection with any negligence, default, breach of duty or breach of trust in relation to the company of which he is a director is void, except as permitted by—
   (a)   section 233 (provision of insurance),
   (b)   section 234 (qualifying third party indemnity provision), or
   (c)   section 235 (qualifying pension scheme indemnity provision).

(3)   This section applies to any provision, whether contained in a company's articles or in any contract with the company or otherwise.

(4)   Nothing in this section prevents a company's articles from making such provision as has previously been lawful for dealing with conflicts of interest.

233   Provision of insurance

Section 232(2) (voidness of provisions for indemnifying directors) does not prevent a company from purchasing and maintaining for a director of the company, or of an associated company, insurance against any such liability as is mentioned in that subsection.

234   Qualifying third party indemnity provision

(1)   Section 232(2) (voidness of provisions for indemnifying directors) does not apply to qualifying third party indemnity provision.

(2)   Third party indemnity provision means provision for indemnity against liability incurred by the director to a person other than the company or an associated company.
Such provision is qualifying third party indemnity provision if the following requirements are met.

(3)   The provision must not provide any indemnity against—
   (a)   any liability of the director to pay—
        (i)   a fine imposed in criminal proceedings, or
        (ii)   a sum payable to a regulatory authority by way of a penalty in respect of non-compliance with any requirement of a regulatory nature (however arising); or
   (b)   any liability incurred by the director—
        (i)   in defending criminal proceedings in which he is convicted, or
        (ii)   in defending civil proceedings brought by the company, or an associated company, in which judgment is given against him, or
        (iii) in connection with an application for relief (see subsection (6)) in which the court refuses to grant him relief.

(4)   The references in subsection (3)(b) to a conviction, judgment or refusal of relief are to the final decision in the proceedings.

(5)   For this purpose—
   (a)   a conviction, judgment or refusal of relief becomes final—
        (i)   if not appealed against, at the end of the period for bringing an appeal, or

          (ii)   if appealed against, at the time when the appeal (or any further appeal) is disposed of; and

    (b)   an appeal is disposed of—

          (i)   if it is determined and the period for bringing any further appeal has ended, or

          (ii)   if it is abandoned or otherwise ceases to have effect.

(6)   The reference in subsection (3)(b)(iii) to an application for relief is to an application for relief under—

section 661(3) or (4) (power of court to grant relief in case of acquisition of shares by innocent nominee), or

section 1157 (general power of court to grant relief in case of honest and reasonable conduct).

235 Qualifying pension scheme indemnity provision

(1)   Section 232(2) (voidness of provisions for indemnifying directors) does not apply to qualifying pension scheme indemnity provision.

(2)   Pension scheme indemnity provision means provision indemnifying a director of a company that is a trustee of an occupational pension scheme against liability incurred in connection with the company's activities as trustee of the scheme.

Such provision is qualifying pension scheme indemnity provision if the following requirements are met.

(3)   The provision must not provide any indemnity against—

    (a)   any liability of the director to pay—

          (i)   a fine imposed in criminal proceedings, or

          (ii)   a sum payable to a regulatory authority by way of a penalty in respect of non-compliance with any requirement of a regulatory nature (however arising); or

    (b)   any liability incurred by the director in defending criminal proceedings in which he is convicted.

(4)   The reference in subsection (3)(b) to a conviction is to the final decision in the proceedings.

(5)   For this purpose—

    (a)   a conviction becomes final—

          (i)   if not appealed against, at the end of the period for bringing an appeal, or

          (ii)   if appealed against, at the time when the appeal (or any further appeal) is disposed of; and

    (b)   an appeal is disposed of—

          (i)   if it is determined and the period for bringing any further appeal has ended, or

          (ii)   if it is abandoned or otherwise ceases to have effect.

(6)   In this section "occupational pension scheme" means an occupational pension scheme as defined in section 150(5) of the Finance Act 2004 that is established under a trust.

236 Qualifying indemnity provision to be disclosed in directors' report

(1)   This section requires disclosure in the directors' report of—

    (a)   qualifying third party indemnity provision, and

    (b)   qualifying pension scheme indemnity provision.

Such provision is referred to in this section as "qualifying indemnity provision".

(2)   If when a directors' report is approved any qualifying indemnity provision (whether made by the company or otherwise) is in force for the benefit of one or more directors of the company, the report must state that such provision is in force.

(3)   If at any time during the financial year to which a directors' report relates any such provision was in force for the benefit of one or more persons who were then directors of the company, the report must state that such provision was in force.

(4)   If when a directors' report is approved qualifying indemnity provision made by the company is in force for the benefit of one or more directors of an associated company, the report must state that such provision is in force.

(5)   If at any time during the financial year to which a directors' report relates any such provision was in force for the benefit of one or more persons who were then directors of an associated company, the report must state that such provision was in force.

237   Copy of qualifying indemnity provision to be available for inspection

(1)   This section has effect where qualifying indemnity provision is made for a director of a company, and applies—

    (a)   to the company of which he is a director (whether the provision is made by that company or an associated company), and

    (b)   where the provision is made by an associated company, to that company.

(2)   That company or, as the case may be, each of them must keep available for inspection—

    (a)   a copy of the qualifying indemnity provision, or

    (b)   if the provision is not in writing, a written memorandum setting out its terms.

(3)   The copy or memorandum must be kept available for inspection at—

    (a)   the company's registered office, or

    (b)   a place specified in regulations under section 1136.

(4)   The copy or memorandum must be retained by the company for at least one year from the date of termination or expiry of the provision and must be kept available for inspection during that time.

(5)   The company must give notice to the registrar—

    (a)   of the place at which the copy or memorandum is kept available for inspection, and

    (b)   of any change in that place,

unless it has at all times been kept at the company's registered office.

(6)   If default is made in complying with subsection (2), (3) or (4), or default is made for 14 days in complying with subsection (5), an offence is committed by every officer of the company who is in default.

(7)   A person guilty of an offence under this section is liable on summary conviction to a fine not exceeding level 3 on the standard scale and, for continued contravention, a daily default fine not exceeding one-tenth of level 3 on the standard scale.

(8)   The provisions of this section apply to a variation of a qualifying indemnity provision as they apply to the original provision.

(9)   In this section "qualifying indemnity provision" means—

    (a)   qualifying third party indemnity provision, and

    (b)   qualifying pension scheme indemnity provision.

238   Right of member to inspect and request copy

(1)   Every copy or memorandum required to be kept by a company under section 237 must be open to inspection by any member of the company without charge.

(2)   Any member of the company is entitled, on request and on payment of such fee as may be prescribed, to be provided with a copy of any such copy or memorandum.

The copy must be provided within seven days after the request is received by the company.

(3)   If an inspection required under subsection (1) is refused, or default is made in complying with subsection (2), an offence is committed by every officer of the company who is in default.

(4)   A person guilty of an offence under this section is liable on summary conviction to a fine not exceeding level 3 on the standard scale and, for continued contravention, a daily default fine not exceeding one-tenth of level 3 on the standard scale.

(5)   In the case of any such refusal or default the court may by order compel an immediate inspection or, as the case may be, direct that the copy required be sent to the person requiring it.

Ratification of acts giving rise to liability

239   Ratification of acts of directors

(1)   This section applies to the ratification by a company of conduct by a director amounting to negligence, default, breach of duty or breach of trust in relation to the company.

(2)   The decision of the company to ratify such conduct must be made by resolution of the members of the company.

(3)   Where the resolution is proposed as a written resolution neither the director (if a member of the company) nor any member connected with him is an eligible member.

(4)   Where the resolution is proposed at a meeting, it is passed only if the necessary majority is obtained disregarding votes in favour of the resolution by the director (if a member of the company) and any member connected with him.

This does not prevent the director or any such member from attending, being counted towards the quorum and taking part in the proceedings at any meeting at which the decision is considered.

(5)   For the purposes of this section—

    (a)   "conduct" includes acts and omissions;

    (b)   "director" includes a former director;

    (c)   a shadow director is treated as a director; and

    (d)   in section 252 (meaning of "connected person"), subsection (3) does not apply (exclusion of person who is himself a director).

(6)   Nothing in this section affects—

    (a)   the validity of a decision taken by unanimous consent of the members of the company, or

    (b)   any power of the directors to agree not to sue, or to settle or release a claim made by them on behalf of the company.

(7)   This section does not affect any other enactment or rule of law imposing additional requirements for valid ratification or any rule of law as to acts that are incapable of being ratified by the company.

CHAPTER 8
DIRECTORS' RESIDENTIAL ADDRESSES: PROTECTION FROM DISCLOSURE

240   Protected information

(1)   This Chapter makes provision for protecting, in the case of a company director who is an individual—

    (a)   information as to his usual residential address;

    (b)   the information that his service address is his usual residential address.

(2)   That information is referred to in this Chapter as "protected information".

(3)   Information does not cease to be protected information on the individual ceasing to be a director of the company.

References in this Chapter to a director include, to that extent, a former director.

241   Protected information: restriction on use or disclosure by company

(1)   A company must not use or disclose protected information about any of its directors, except—

    (a)   for communicating with the director concerned,

    (b)   in order to comply with any requirement of the Companies Acts as to particulars to be sent to the registrar, or

    (c)   in accordance with section 244 (disclosure under court order).

(2)   Subsection (1) does not prohibit any use or disclosure of protected information with the consent of the director concerned.

(3)   If a company uses or discloses information in contravention of subsection (1), an offence is committed by—

    (a)   the company, and

    (b)   every officer of the company who is in default.

(4)   A person guilty of an offence under this section is liable on summary conviction—

    (a)   in England and Wales, to a fine;

    (b)   in Scotland or Northern Ireland, to a fine not exceeding level 5 on the standard scale and, for continued contravention, a daily default fine not exceeding one-tenth of level 5 on the standard scale.

242   Protected information: restriction on ... disclosure by registrar

(1)   The registrar must omit protected information from the material on the register that is available for inspection where—

    (a)   it is contained in a document delivered to him in which such information is required to be stated, and

    (b)   in the case of a document having more than one part, it is contained in a part of the document in which such information is required to be stated.

(2)   The registrar is not obliged—

    (a)   to check other documents or (as the case may be) other parts of the document to ensure the absence of protected information, or

    (b)   to omit from the material that is available for public inspection anything registered before this Chapter comes into force.

(3)   The registrar must not ... disclose protected information except—

    (a)   as permitted by section 243 (permitted ... disclosure by registrar), ...

    (b)   in accordance with section 244 (disclosure under court order), or

    (c)   as permitted by section 1110F (general powers of disclosure by the registrar).

243   Permitted ... disclosure by the registrar

(1)   ...

(2)   The registrar may disclose protected information to a credit reference agency.

(3)   The Secretary of State may make provision by regulations—

    (a)   specifying conditions for the disclosure of protected information in accordance with this section, and

    (b)   providing for the charging of fees.

(4)   The Secretary of State may make provision by regulations requiring the registrar, on application, to refrain from disclosing protected information relating to a director to a credit reference agency.

(5)   Regulations under subsection (4) may make provision as to—

    (a)   who may make an application,

    (b)   the grounds on which an application may be made,

    (c)   the information to be included in and documents to accompany an application, and

    (d)   how an application is to be determined.

(6)   Regulations under subsection (4) may in particular confer a discretion on the registrar.

(6A)   Provision under subsection (5)(d) may in particular provide for a question to be referred to a person other than the registrar for the purposes of determining the application.

(7)   In this section—

"credit reference agency" means a person carrying on a business comprising the furnishing of information relevant to the financial standing of individuals, being information collected by the agency for that purpose; ...

...

(8)   Regulations under this section are subject to negative resolution procedure.

244   Disclosure under court order

(1)   The court may make an order for the disclosure of protected information by the company or by the registrar if—

    (a)   there is evidence that service of documents at a service address other than the director's usual residential address is not effective to bring them to the notice of the director, or

    (b)   it is necessary or expedient for the information to be provided in connection with the enforcement of an order or decree of the court,

and the court is otherwise satisfied that it is appropriate to make the order.

(2)   An order for disclosure by the registrar is to be made only if the company—

    (a)   does not have the director's usual residential address, or

    (b)   has been dissolved.

(3) The order may be made on the application of a liquidator, creditor or member of the company, or any other person appearing to the court to have a sufficient interest.

(4) The order must specify the persons to whom, and purposes for which, disclosure is authorised.

245 Circumstances in which registrar may put address on the public record

(1) The registrar may put a director's usual residential address on the public record if—

    (a) communications sent by the registrar to the director and requiring a response within a specified period remain unanswered, or

    (b) there is evidence that service of documents at a service address provided in place of the director's usual residential address is not effective to bring them to the notice of the director.

(2) The registrar must give notice of the proposal—

    (a) to the director, and

    (b) to every company of which the registrar has been notified that the individual is a director.

(3) The notice must—

    (a) state the grounds on which it is proposed to put the director's usual residential address on the public record, and

    (b) specify a period within which representations may be made before that is done.

(4) It must be sent to the director at his usual residential address, unless it appears to the registrar that service at that address may be ineffective to bring it to the individual's notice, in which case it may be sent to any service address provided in place of that address.

(5) The registrar must take account of any representations received within the specified period.

(6) What is meant by putting the address on the public record is explained in section 246.

246 Putting the address on the public record

(1) If the registrar decides in accordance with section 245 that a director's usual residential address is to be put on the public record, the registrar must proceed as if each relevant company had given notice under section 167H—

    (a) stating a change in the director's service address, and

    (b) stating the director's usual residential address as their new service address.

(2) The registrar must give notice of having done so—

    (a) to the director, and

    (b) to every relevant company.

(3) The notice must state the date of the registrar's decision to put the director's usual residential address on the public record.

(4) Where a director's usual residential address has been put on the public record by the registrar under this section, for the period of five years beginning with the date of the registrar's decision no service address may be registered for the director other than their usual residential address (but see subsection (5)).

(5) Subsection (4)—

    (a) does not limit the service address that may be registered for the director under regulations under section 1097B (rectification of register), and

    (b) ceases to apply in relation to the director if a new service address is registered for the director under those regulations.

(6) In this section "relevant company" means each company given notice under section 245(2)(b).

CHAPTER 9
SUPPLEMENTARY PROVISIONS

Provision for employees on cessation or transfer of business

247 Power to make provision for employees on cessation or transfer of business

(1) The powers of the directors of a company include (if they would not otherwise do so) power to make provision for the benefit of persons employed or formerly employed by the company, or any

of its subsidiaries, in connection with the cessation or the transfer to any person of the whole or part of the undertaking of the company or that subsidiary.

(2)   This power is exercisable notwithstanding the general duty imposed by section 172 (duty to promote the success of the company).

(3)   In the case of a company that is a charity it is exercisable notwithstanding any restrictions on the directors' powers (or the company's capacity) flowing from the objects of the company.

(4)   The power may only be exercised if sanctioned—
        (a)   by a resolution of the company, or
        (b)   by a resolution of the directors,
        in accordance with the following provisions.

(5)   A resolution of the directors—
        (a)   must be authorised by the company's articles, and
        (b)   is not sufficient sanction for payments to or for the benefit of directors, former directors or shadow directors.

(6)   Any other requirements of the company's articles as to the exercise of the power conferred by this section must be complied with.

(7)   Any payment under this section must be made—
        (a)   before the commencement of any winding up of the company, and
        (b)   out of profits of the company that are available for dividend.

Records of meetings of directors

248   Minutes of directors' meetings

(1)   Every company must cause minutes of all proceedings at meetings of its directors to be recorded.

(2)   The records must be kept for at least ten years from the date of the meeting.

(3)   If a company fails to comply with this section, an offence is committed by every officer of the company who is in default.

(4)   A person guilty of an offence under this section is liable on summary conviction to a fine not exceeding level 3 on the standard scale and, for continued contravention, a daily default fine not exceeding one-tenth of level 3 on the standard scale.

249   Minutes as evidence

(1)   Minutes recorded in accordance with section 248, if purporting to be authenticated by the chairman of the meeting or by the chairman of the next directors' meeting, are evidence (in Scotland, sufficient evidence) of the proceedings at the meeting.

(2)   Where minutes have been made in accordance with that section of the proceedings of a meeting of directors, then, until the contrary is proved—
        (a)   the meeting is deemed duly held and convened,
        (b)   all proceedings at the meeting are deemed to have duly taken place, and
        (c)   all appointments at the meeting are deemed valid.

Meaning of 'director' and 'shadow director'

250   "Director"

In the Companies Acts "director" includes any person occupying the position of director, by whatever name called.

251   "Shadow director"

(1)   In the Companies Acts "shadow director", in relation to a company, means a person in accordance with whose directions or instructions the directors of the company are accustomed to act.

(2)   A person is not to be regarded as a shadow director by reason only that the directors act—
        (a)   on advice given by that person in a professional capacity;
        (b)   in accordance with instructions, a direction, guidance or advice given by that person in the exercise of a function conferred by or under an enactment;

(c)   in accordance with guidance or advice given by that person in that person's capacity as a Minister of the Crown (within the meaning of the Ministers of the Crown Act 1975).

(3)   A body corporate is not to be regarded as a shadow director of any of its subsidiary companies for the purposes of—

Chapter 2 (general duties of directors),

Chapter 4 (transactions requiring members' approval), or

Chapter 6 (contract with sole member who is also a director),

by reason only that the directors of the subsidiary are accustomed to act in accordance with its directions or instructions.

Other definitions

252   Persons connected with a director

(1)   This section defines what is meant by references in this Part to a person being "connected" with a director of a company (or a director being "connected" with a person).

(2)   The following persons (and only those persons) are connected with a director of a company—

   (a)   members of the director's family (see section 253);

   (b)   a body corporate with which the director is connected (as defined in section 254);

   (c)   a person acting in his capacity as trustee of a trust—

      (i)   the beneficiaries of which include the director or a person who by virtue of paragraph (a) or (b) is connected with him, or

      (ii)   the terms of which confer a power on the trustees that may be exercised for the benefit of the director or any such person,

   other than a trust for the purposes of an employees' share scheme or a pension scheme;

   (d)   a person acting in his capacity as partner—

      (i)   of the director, or

      (ii)   of a person who, by virtue of paragraph (a), (b) or (c), is connected with that director;

   (e)   a firm that is a legal person under the law by which it is governed and in which—

      (i)   the director is a partner,

      (ii)   a partner is a person who, by virtue of paragraph (a), (b) or (c) is connected with the director, or

      (iii)   a partner is a firm in which the director is a partner or in which there is a partner who, by virtue of paragraph (a), (b) or (c), is connected with the director.

(3)   References in this Part to a person connected with a director of a company do not include a person who is himself a director of the company.

253   Members of a director's family

(1)   This section defines what is meant by references in this Part to members of a director's family.

(2)   For the purposes of this Part the members of a director's family are—

   (a)   the director's spouse or civil partner;

   (b)   any other person (whether of a different sex or the same sex) with whom the director lives as partner in an enduring family relationship;

   (c)   the director's children or step-children;

   (d)   any children or step-children of a person within paragraph (b) (and who are not children or step-children of the director) who live with the director and have not attained the age of 18;

   (e)   the director's parents.

(3)   Subsection (2)(b) does not apply if the other person is the director's grandparent or grandchild, sister, brother, aunt or uncle, or nephew or niece.

254   Director "connected with" a body corporate

(1)   This section defines what is meant by references in this Part to a director being "connected with" a body corporate.

(2)   A director is connected with a body corporate if, but only if, he and the persons connected with
        him together—
        (a)   are interested in shares comprised in the equity share capital of that body corporate of a
              nominal value equal to at least 20% of that share capital, or
        (b)   are entitled to exercise or control the exercise of more than 20% of the voting power at any
              general meeting of that body.
(3)   The rules set out in Schedule 1 (references to interest in shares or debentures) apply for the
        purposes of this section.
(4)   References in this section to voting power the exercise of which is controlled by a director include
        voting power whose exercise is controlled by a body corporate controlled by him.
(5)   Shares in a company held as treasury shares, and any voting rights attached to such shares, are
        disregarded for the purposes of this section.
(6)   For the avoidance of circularity in the application of section 252 (meaning of "connected
        person")—
        (a)   a body corporate with which a director is connected is not treated for the purposes of this
              section as connected with him unless it is also connected with him by virtue of subsection
              (2)(c) or (d) of that section (connection as trustee or partner); and
        (b)   a trustee of a trust the beneficiaries of which include (or may include) a body corporate with
              which a director is connected is not treated for the purposes of this section as connected with
              a director by reason only of that fact.

255   Director "controlling" a body corporate

(1)   This section defines what is meant by references in this Part to a director "controlling" a body
        corporate.
(2)   A director of a company is taken to control a body corporate if, but only if—
        (a)   he or any person connected with him—
              (i)   is interested in any part of the equity share capital of that body, or
              (ii)   is entitled to exercise or control the exercise of any part of the voting power at any
                      general meeting of that body, and
        (b)   he, the persons connected with him and the other directors of that company, together—
              (i)   are interested in more than 50% of that share capital, or
              (ii)   are entitled to exercise or control the exercise of more than 50% of that voting
                      power.
(3)   The rules set out in Schedule 1 (references to interest in shares or debentures) apply for the
        purposes of this section.
(4)   References in this section to voting power the exercise of which is controlled by a director include
        voting power whose exercise is controlled by a body corporate controlled by him.
(5)   Shares in a company held as treasury shares, and any voting rights attached to such shares, are
        disregarded for the purposes of this section.
(6)   For the avoidance of circularity in the application of section 252 (meaning of "connected person")—
        (a)   a body corporate with which a director is connected is not treated for the purposes of this
              section as connected with him unless it is also connected with him by virtue of subsection
              (2)(c) or (d) of that section (connection as trustee or partner); and
        (b)   a trustee of a trust the beneficiaries of which include (or may include) a body corporate with
              which a director is connected is not treated for the purposes of this section as connected with
              a director by reason only of that fact.

256   Associated bodies corporate

        For the purposes of this Part—
        (a)   bodies corporate are associated if one is a subsidiary of the other or both are subsidiaries of
              the same body corporate, and
        (b)   companies are associated if one is a subsidiary of the other or both are subsidiaries of the
              same body corporate.

257 References to company's constitution

(1) References in this Part to a company's constitution include—

    (a) any resolution or other decision come to in accordance with the constitution, and

    (b) any decision by the members of the company, or a class of members, that is treated by virtue of any enactment or rule of law as equivalent to a decision by the company.

(2) This is in addition to the matters mentioned in section 17 (general provision as to matters contained in company's constitution).

General

258 Power to increase financial limits

(1) The Secretary of State may by order substitute for any sum of money specified in this Part a larger sum specified in the order.

(2) An order under this section is subject to negative resolution procedure.

(3) An order does not have effect in relation to anything done or not done before it comes into force. Accordingly, proceedings in respect of any liability incurred before that time may be continued or instituted as if the order had not been made.

259 Transactions under foreign law

For the purposes of this Part it is immaterial whether the law that (apart from this Act) governs an arrangement or transaction is the law of the United Kingdom, or a part of it, or not.

PART 11
DERIVATIVE CLAIMS AND PROCEEDINGS BY MEMBERS

CHAPTER 1
DERIVATIVE CLAIMS IN ENGLAND AND WALES OR NORTHERN IRELAND

260 Derivative claims

(1) This Chapter applies to proceedings in England and Wales or Northern Ireland by a member of a company—

    (a) in respect of a cause of action vested in the company, and

    (b) seeking relief on behalf of the company.

This is referred to in this Chapter as a "derivative claim".

(2) A derivative claim may only be brought—

    (a) under this Chapter, or

    (b) in pursuance of an order of the court in proceedings under section 994 (proceedings for protection of members against unfair prejudice).

(3) A derivative claim under this Chapter may be brought only in respect of a cause of action arising from an actual or proposed act or omission involving negligence, default, breach of duty or breach of trust by a director of the company.

The cause of action may be against the director or another person (or both).

(4) It is immaterial whether the cause of action arose before or after the person seeking to bring or continue the derivative claim became a member of the company.

(5) For the purposes of this Chapter—

    (a) "director" includes a former director;

    (b) a shadow director is treated as a director; and

    (c) references to a member of a company include a person who is not a member but to whom shares in the company have been transferred or transmitted by operation of law.

261 Application for permission to continue derivative claim

(1) A member of a company who brings a derivative claim under this Chapter must apply to the court for permission (in Northern Ireland, leave) to continue it.

(2) If it appears to the court that the application and the evidence filed by the applicant in support of it do not disclose a prima facie case for giving permission (or leave), the court—

       (a)   must dismiss the application, and

       (b)   may make any consequential order it considers appropriate.

(3)   If the application is not dismissed under subsection (2), the court—

       (a)   may give directions as to the evidence to be provided by the company, and

       (b)   may adjourn the proceedings to enable the evidence to be obtained.

(4)   On hearing the application, the court may—

       (a)   give permission (or leave) to continue the claim on such terms as it thinks fit,

       (b)   refuse permission (or leave) and dismiss the claim, or

       (c)   adjourn the proceedings on the application and give such directions as it thinks fit.

262   Application for permission to continue claim as a derivative claim

(1)   This section applies where—

       (a)   a company has brought a claim, and

       (b)   the cause of action on which the claim is based could be pursued as a derivative claim under this Chapter.

(2)   A member of the company may apply to the court for permission (in Northern Ireland, leave) to continue the claim as a derivative claim on the ground that—

       (a)   the manner in which the company commenced or continued the claim amounts to an abuse of the process of the court,

       (b)   the company has failed to prosecute the claim diligently, and

       (c)   it is appropriate for the member to continue the claim as a derivative claim.

(3)   If it appears to the court that the application and the evidence filed by the applicant in support of it do not disclose a prima facie case for giving permission (or leave), the court—

       (a)   must dismiss the application, and

       (b)   may make any consequential order it considers appropriate.

(4)   If the application is not dismissed under subsection (3), the court—

       (a)   may give directions as to the evidence to be provided by the company, and

       (b)   may adjourn the proceedings to enable the evidence to be obtained.

(5)   On hearing the application, the court may—

       (a)   give permission (or leave) to continue the claim as a derivative claim on such terms as it thinks fit,

       (b)   refuse permission (or leave) and dismiss the application, or

       (c)   adjourn the proceedings on the application and give such directions as it thinks fit.

263   Whether permission to be given

(1)   The following provisions have effect where a member of a company applies for permission (in Northern Ireland, leave) under section 261 or 262.

(2)   Permission (or leave) must be refused if the court is satisfied—

       (a)   that a person acting in accordance with section 172 (duty to promote the success of the company) would not seek to continue the claim, or

       (b)   where the cause of action arises from an act or omission that is yet to occur, that the act or omission has been authorised by the company, or

       (c)   where the cause of action arises from an act or omission that has already occurred, that the act or omission—

           (i)   was authorised by the company before it occurred, or

           (ii)   has been ratified by the company since it occurred.

(3)   In considering whether to give permission (or leave) the court must take into account, in particular—

       (a)   whether the member is acting in good faith in seeking to continue the claim;

       (b)   the importance that a person acting in accordance with section 172 (duty to promote the success of the company) would attach to continuing it;

       (c)   where the cause of action results from an act or omission that is yet to occur, whether the act or omission could be, and in the circumstances would be likely to be—

        (i)   authorised by the company before it occurs, or

        (ii)   ratified by the company after it occurs;

    (d)   where the cause of action arises from an act or omission that has already occurred, whether the act or omission could be, and in the circumstances would be likely to be, ratified by the company;

    (e)   whether the company has decided not to pursue the claim;

    (f)   whether the act or omission in respect of which the claim is brought gives rise to a cause of action that the member could pursue in his own right rather than on behalf of the company.

(4)   In considering whether to give permission (or leave) the court shall have particular regard to any evidence before it as to the views of members of the company who have no personal interest, direct or indirect, in the matter.

(5)   The Secretary of State may by regulations—

    (a)   amend subsection (2) so as to alter or add to the circumstances in which permission (or leave) is to be refused;

    (b)   amend subsection (3) so as to alter or add to the matters that the court is required to take into account in considering whether to give permission (or leave).

(6)   Before making any such regulations the Secretary of State shall consult such persons as he considers appropriate.

(7)   Regulations under this section are subject to affirmative resolution procedure.

264   Application for permission to continue derivative claim brought by another member

(1)   This section applies where a member of a company ("the claimant")—

    (a)   has brought a derivative claim,

    (b)   has continued as a derivative claim a claim brought by the company, or

    (c)   has continued a derivative claim under this section.

(2)   Another member of the company ("the applicant") may apply to the court for permission (in Northern Ireland, leave) to continue the claim on the ground that—

    (a)   the manner in which the proceedings have been commenced or continued by the claimant amounts to an abuse of the process of the court,

    (b)   the claimant has failed to prosecute the claim diligently, and

    (c)   it is appropriate for the applicant to continue the claim as a derivative claim.

(3)   If it appears to the court that the application and the evidence filed by the applicant in support of it do not disclose a prima facie case for giving permission (or leave), the court—

    (a)   must dismiss the application, and

    (b)   may make any consequential order it considers appropriate.

(4)   If the application is not dismissed under subsection (3), the court—

    (a)   may give directions as to the evidence to be provided by the company, and

    (b)   may adjourn the proceedings to enable the evidence to be obtained.

(5)   On hearing the application, the court may—

    (a)   give permission (or leave) to continue the claim on such terms as it thinks fit,

    (b)   refuse permission (or leave) and dismiss the application, or

    (c)   adjourn the proceedings on the application and give such directions as it thinks fit.

CHAPTER 2
DERIVATIVE PROCEEDINGS IN SCOTLAND

265   Derivative proceedings

(1)   In Scotland, a member of a company may raise proceedings in respect of an act or omission specified in subsection (3) in order to protect the interests of the company and obtain a remedy on its behalf.

(2)   A member of a company may raise such proceedings only under subsection (1).

(3)   The act or omission referred to in subsection (1) is any actual or proposed act or omission involving negligence, default, breach of duty or breach of trust by a director of the company.

(4)   Proceedings may be raised under subsection (1) against (either or both)—
    (a)   the director referred to in subsection (3), or
    (b)   another person.

(5)   It is immaterial whether the act or omission in respect of which the proceedings are to be raised or, in the case of continuing proceedings under section 267 or 269, are raised, arose before or after the person seeking to raise or continue them became a member of the company.

(6)   This section does not affect—
    (a)   any right of a member of a company to raise proceedings in respect of an act or omission specified in subsection (3) in order to protect his own interests and obtain a remedy on his own behalf, or
    (b)   the court's power to make an order under section 996(2)(c) or anything done under such an order.

(7)   In this Chapter—
    (a)   proceedings raised under subsection (1) are referred to as "derivative proceedings",
    (b)   the act or omission in respect of which they are raised is referred to as the "cause of action",
    (c)   "director" includes a former director,
    (d)   references to a director include a shadow director, and
    (e)   references to a member of a company include a person who is not a member but to whom shares in the company have been transferred or transmitted by operation of law.

266   Requirement for leave and notice

(1)   Derivative proceedings may be raised by a member of a company only with the leave of the court.

(2)   An application for leave must—
    (a)   specify the cause of action, and
    (b)   summarise the facts on which the derivative proceedings are to be based.

(3)   If it appears to the court that the application and the evidence produced by the applicant in support of it do not disclose a prima facie case for granting it, the court—
    (a)   must refuse the application, and
    (b)   may make any consequential order it considers appropriate.

(4)   If the application is not refused under subsection (3)—
    (a)   the applicant must serve the application on the company,
    (b)   the court—
        (i)   may make an order requiring evidence to be produced by the company, and
        (ii)   may adjourn the proceedings on the application to enable the evidence to be obtained, and
    (c)   the company is entitled to take part in the further proceedings on the application.

(5)   On hearing the application, the court may—
    (a)   grant the application on such terms as it thinks fit,
    (b)   refuse the application, or
    (c)   adjourn the proceedings on the application and make such order as to further procedure as it thinks fit.

267   Application to continue proceedings as derivative proceedings

(1)   This section applies where—
    (a)   a company has raised proceedings, and
    (b)   the proceedings are in respect of an act or omission which could be the basis for derivative proceedings.

(2)   A member of the company may apply to the court to be substituted for the company in the proceedings, and for the proceedings to continue in consequence as derivative proceedings, on the ground that—
    (a)   the manner in which the company commenced or continued the proceedings amounts to an abuse of the process of the court,
    (b)   the company has failed to prosecute the proceedings diligently, and

(c)   it is appropriate for the member to be substituted for the company in the proceedings.

(3)   If it appears to the court that the application and the evidence produced by the applicant in support of it do not disclose a prima facie case for granting it, the court—

(a)   must refuse the application, and

(b)   may make any consequential order it considers appropriate.

(4)   If the application is not refused under subsection (3)—

(a)   the applicant must serve the application on the company,

(b)   the court—

(i)   may make an order requiring evidence to be produced by the company, and

(ii)   may adjourn the proceedings on the application to enable the evidence to be obtained, and

(c)   the company is entitled to take part in the further proceedings on the application.

(5)   On hearing the application, the court may—

(a)   grant the application on such terms as it thinks fit,

(b)   refuse the application, or

(c)   adjourn the proceedings on the application and make such order as to further procedure as it thinks fit.

268   Granting of leave

(1)   The court must refuse leave to raise derivative proceedings or an application under section 267 if satisfied—

(a)   that a person acting in accordance with section 172 (duty to promote the success of the company) would not seek to raise or continue the proceedings (as the case may be), or

(b)   where the cause of action is an act or omission that is yet to occur, that the act or omission has been authorised by the company, or

(c)   where the cause of action is an act or omission that has already occurred, that the act or omission—

(i)   was authorised by the company before it occurred, or

(ii)   has been ratified by the company since it occurred.

(2)   In considering whether to grant leave to raise derivative proceedings or an application under section 267, the court must take into account, in particular—

(a)   whether the member is acting in good faith in seeking to raise or continue the proceedings (as the case may be),

(b)   the importance that a person acting in accordance with section 172 (duty to promote the success of the company) would attach to raising or continuing them (as the case may be),

(c)   where the cause of action is an act or omission that is yet to occur, whether the act or omission could be, and in the circumstances would be likely to be—

(i)   authorised by the company before it occurs, or

(ii)   ratified by the company after it occurs,

(d)   where the cause of action is an act or omission that has already occurred, whether the act or omission could be, and in the circumstances would be likely to be, ratified by the company,

(e)   whether the company has decided not to raise proceedings in respect of the same cause of action or to persist in the proceedings (as the case may be),

(f)   whether the cause of action is one which the member could pursue in his own right rather than on behalf of the company.

(3)   In considering whether to grant leave to raise derivative proceedings or an application under section 267, the court shall have particular regard to any evidence before it as to the views of members of the company who have no personal interest, direct or indirect, in the matter.

(4)   The Secretary of State may by regulations—

(a)   amend subsection (1) so as to alter or add to the circumstances in which leave or an application is to be refused,

(b)   amend subsection (2) so as to alter or add to the matters that the court is required to take into account in considering whether to grant leave or an application.

(5)   Before making any such regulations the Secretary of State shall consult such persons as he considers appropriate.

(6)   Regulations under this section are subject to affirmative resolution procedure.

269   Application by member to be substituted for member pursuing derivative proceedings

(1)   This section applies where a member of a company ("the claimant")—

     (a)   has raised derivative proceedings,

     (b)   has continued as derivative proceedings raised by the company, or

     (c)   has continued derivative proceedings under this section.

(2)   Another member of the company ("the applicant") may apply to the court to be substituted for the claimant in the action on the ground that—

     (a)   the manner in which the proceedings have been commenced or continued by the claimant amounts to an abuse of the process of the court,

     (b)   the claimant has failed to prosecute the proceedings diligently, and

     (c)   it is appropriate for the applicant to be substituted for the claimant in the proceedings.

(3)   If it appears to the court that the application and the evidence produced by the applicant in support of it do not disclose a prima facie case for granting it, the court—

     (a)   must refuse the application, and

     (b)   may make any consequential order it considers appropriate.

(4)   If the application is not refused under subsection (3)—

     (a)   the applicant must serve the application on the company,

     (b)   the court—

         (i)   may make an order requiring evidence to be produced by the company, and

         (ii)   may adjourn the proceedings on the application to enable the evidence to be obtained, and

     (c)   the company is entitled to take part in the further proceedings on the application.

(5)   On hearing the application, the court may—

     (a)   grant the application on such terms as it thinks fit,

     (b)   refuse the application, or

     (c)   adjourn the proceedings on the application and make such order as to further procedure as it thinks fit.

PART 12

COMPANY SECRETARIES

Private companies

270   Private company not required to have secretary

(1)   A private company is not required to have a secretary.

(2)   References in the Companies Acts to a private company "without a secretary" are to a private company that for the time being is taking advantage of the exemption in subsection (1); and references to a private company "with a secretary" shall be construed accordingly.

(3)   In the case of a private company without a secretary—

     (a)   anything authorised or required to be given or sent to, or served on, the company by being sent to its secretary—

         (i)   may be given or sent to, or served on, the company itself, and

         (ii)   if addressed to the secretary shall be treated as addressed to the company; and

     (b)   anything else required or authorised to be done by or to the secretary of the company may be done by or to—

         (i)   a director, or

         (ii)   a person authorised generally or specifically in that behalf by the directors.

Public companies

271   Public company required to have secretary

A public company must have a secretary.

272   Direction requiring public company to appoint secretary

(1)   If it appears to the Secretary of State that a public company is in breach of section 271 (requirement to have secretary), the Secretary of State may give the company a direction under this section.

(2)   The direction must state that the company appears to be in breach of that section and specify—

(a)   what the company must do in order to comply with the direction, and

(b)   the period within which it must do so.

That period must be not less than one month or more than three months after the date on which the direction is given.

(3)   The direction must also inform the company of the consequences of failing to comply.

(4)   Where the company is in breach of section 271 it must comply with the direction by—

(a)   making the necessary appointment, and

(b)   giving notice of it under section 276,

before the end of the period specified in the direction.

(5)   If the company has already made the necessary appointment, it must comply with the direction by giving notice of it under section 276 before the end of the period specified in the direction.

(6)   If a company fails to comply with a direction under this section, an offence is committed by—

(a)   the company, and

(b)   every officer of the company who is in default.

For this purpose a shadow director is treated as an officer of the company.

(7)   A person guilty of an offence under this section is liable on summary conviction to a fine not exceeding level 5 on the standard scale and, for continued contravention, a daily default fine not exceeding one-tenth of the greater of £5,000 or level 4 on the standard scale.

273   Qualifications of secretaries of public companies

(1)   It is the duty of the directors of a public company to take all reasonable steps to secure that the secretary (or each joint secretary) of the company—

(a)   is a person who appears to them to have the requisite knowledge and experience to discharge the functions of secretary of the company, and

(b)   has one or more of the following qualifications.

(2)   The qualifications are—

(a)   that he has held the office of secretary of a public company for at least three of the five years immediately preceding his appointment as secretary;

(b)   that he is a member of any of the bodies specified in subsection (3);

(c)   that he is a barrister, advocate or solicitor called or admitted in any part of the United Kingdom;

(d)   that he is a person who, by virtue of his holding or having held any other position or his being a member of any other body, appears to the directors to be capable of discharging the functions of secretary of the company.

(3)   The bodies referred to in subsection (2)(b) are—

(a)   the Institute of Chartered Accountants in England and Wales;

(b)   the Institute of Chartered Accountants of Scotland;

(c)   the Association of Chartered Certified Accountants;

(d)   the Institute of Chartered Accountants in Ireland;

(e)   the Institute of Chartered Secretaries and Administrators;

(f)   the Chartered Institute of Management Accountants;

(g)   the Chartered Institute of Public Finance and Accountancy.

Provisions applying to private companies with a secretary and to public companies

274   Discharge of functions where office vacant or secretary unable to act

Where in the case of any company the office of secretary is vacant, or there is for any other reason no secretary capable of acting, anything required or authorised to be done by or to the secretary may be done—

(a)   by or to an assistant or deputy secretary (if any), or

(b)   if there is no assistant or deputy secretary or none capable of acting, by or to any person authorised generally or specifically in that behalf by the directors.

274A   Alternative method of record-keeping

Sections 275 and 276 must be read with sections 279A to 279E (which allow for an alternative method of record-keeping in the case of private companies).

275   Duty to keep register of secretaries

(1)   A company must keep a register of its secretaries.

(2)   The register must contain the required particulars (see sections 277 to 279) of the person who is, or persons who are, the secretary or joint secretaries of the company.

(3)   The register must be kept available for inspection—

(a)   at the company's registered office, or

(b)   at a place specified in regulations under section 1136.

(4)   The company must give notice to the registrar—

(a)   of the place at which the register is kept available for inspection, and

(b)   of any change in that place,

unless it has at all times been kept at the company's registered office.

(5)   The register must be open to the inspection—

(a)   of any member of the company without charge, and

(b)   of any other person on payment of such fee as may be prescribed.

(6)   If default is made in complying with subsection (1), (2) or (3), or if default is made for 14 days in complying with subsection (4), or if an inspection required under subsection (5) is refused, an offence is committed by—

(a)   the company, and

(b)   every officer of the company who is in default.

For this purpose a shadow director is treated as an officer of the company.

(7)   A person guilty of an offence under this section is liable on summary conviction to a fine not exceeding level 5 on the standard scale and, for continued contravention, a daily default fine not exceeding one-tenth of the greater of £5,000 or level 4 on the standard scale.

(8)   In the case of a refusal of inspection of the register, the court may by order compel an immediate inspection of it.

276   Duty to notify registrar of changes

(1)   A company must, within the period of 14 days from—

(a)   a person becoming or ceasing to be its secretary or one of its joint secretaries, or

(b)   the occurrence of any change in the particulars contained in its register of secretaries,

give notice to the registrar of the change and of the date on which it occurred.

(2)   Notice of a person having become secretary, or one of joint secretaries, of the company must be accompanied by a statement by the company that the person has consented to act in the relevant capacity.

(3)   If default is made in complying with this section, an offence is committed by every officer of the company who is in default.

For this purpose a shadow director is treated as an officer of the company.

(4)   A person guilty of an offence under this section is liable on summary conviction to a fine not exceeding level 5 on the standard scale and, for continued contravention, a daily default fine not exceeding one-tenth of the greater of £5,000 or level 4 on the standard scale.

277 Particulars of secretaries to be registered: individuals

(1) A company's register of secretaries must contain the following particulars in the case of an individual—

(a) name and any former name;

(b) address.

(2) For the purposes of this section "name" means a person's Christian name (or other forename) and surname, except that in the case of—

(a) a peer, or

(b) an individual usually known by a title,

the title may be stated instead of his Christian name (or other forename) and surname or in addition to either or both of them.

(3) For the purposes of this section a "former name" means a name by which the individual was formerly known for business purposes.

Where a person is or was formerly known by more than one such name, each of them must be stated.

(4) It is not necessary for the register to contain particulars of a former name in the following cases—

(a) in the case of a peer or an individual normally known by a British title, where the name is one by which the person was known previous to the adoption of or succession to the title;

(b) in the case of any person, where the former name—

(i) was changed or disused before the person attained the age of 16 years, or

(ii) has been changed or disused for 20 years or more.

(5) The address required to be stated in the register is a service address. This may be stated to be "The company's registered office".

278 Particulars of secretaries to be registered: corporate secretaries and firms

(1) A company's register of secretaries must contain the following particulars in the case of a body corporate, or a firm that is a legal person under the law by which it is governed—

(a) corporate or firm name;

(b) registered or principal office;

(c) in the case of a limited company that is a UK-registered company, the registered number;

(d) in any other case, particulars of—

(i) the legal form of the company or firm and the law by which it is governed, and

(ii) if applicable, the register in which it is entered (including details of the state) and its registration number in that register.

(2) If all the partners in a firm are joint secretaries it is sufficient to state the particulars that would be required if the firm were a legal person and the firm had been appointed secretary.

279 Particulars of secretaries to be registered: power to make regulations

(1) The Secretary of State may make provision by regulations amending—

section 277 (particulars of secretaries to be registered: individuals), or

section 278 (particulars of secretaries to be registered: corporate secretaries and firms),

so as to add to or remove items from the particulars required to be contained in a company's register of secretaries.

(2) Regulations under this section are subject to affirmative resolution procedure.

Option to keep information on the central register

279A Right to make an election

(1) An election may be made under this section—

(a) by the subscribers wishing to form a private company under this Act, or

(b) by the private company itself once it is formed and registered.

(2) The election is made by giving notice of election to the registrar.

(3) If the notice is given by subscribers wishing to form a private company, it must be given when the documents required to be delivered under section 9 are delivered to the registrar.

279B   Effective date of election

(1)   An election made under section 279A takes effect when the notice of election is registered by the registrar.

(2)   The election remains in force until either—

(a)   the company ceases to be a private company, or

(b)   a notice of withdrawal sent by the company under section 279E is registered by the registrar,

whichever occurs first.

279C   Effect of election on obligations under sections 275 and 276

If an election is in force under section 279A in respect of a company, the company's obligations—

(a)   to keep and maintain a register of secretaries under section 275, and

(b)   to notify the registrar of changes to it under section 276,

do not apply with respect to the period when the election is in force.

279D   Duty to notify registrar of changes

(1)   The duty under subsection (2) applies during the period when an election under section 279A is in force.

(2)   The company must deliver to the registrar—

(a)   any information of which the company would during that period have been obliged to give notice under section 276, had the election not been in force, and

(b)   any statement that would have had to accompany such a notice.

(3)   The information (and any accompanying statement) must be delivered as soon as reasonably practicable after the company becomes aware of the information and, in any event, no later than the time by which the company would have been obliged under section 276 to give notice of the information.

(4)   If default is made in complying with this section, an offence is committed by—

(a)   the company, and

(b)   every officer of the company who is in default.

For this purpose a shadow director is treated as an officer of the company.

(5)   A person guilty of an offence under this section is liable on summary conviction—

(a)   in England and Wales, to a fine and, for continued contravention, a daily default fine not exceeding the greater of £500 and one-tenth of level 4 on the standard scale;

(b)   in Scotland or Northern Ireland, to a fine not exceeding level 5 on the standard scale and, for continued contravention, a daily default fine not exceeding one-tenth of level 5 on the standard scale.

279E   Withdrawing the election

(1)   A company may withdraw an election made by or in respect of it under section 279A.

(2)   Withdrawal is achieved by giving notice of withdrawal to the registrar.

(3)   The withdrawal takes effect when the notice is registered by the registrar.

(4)   The effect of withdrawal is that the company's obligation under section 275 to keep and maintain a register of secretaries, and its obligation under section 276 to notify the registrar of changes to that register, apply from then on with respect to the period going forward.

(5)   This means that, when the withdrawal takes effect—

(a)   the company must enter in its register of secretaries all the information that is required to be contained in that register in respect of matters that are current as at that time, but

(b)   the company is not required to enter in its register information relating to the period when the election was in force that is no longer current.

279F   Power to extend option to public companies

(1)   The Secretary of State may by regulations amend this Act—

(a)   to extend sections 279A to 279E (with or without modification) to public companies or public companies of a class specified in the regulations, and

(b)   to make such other amendments as the Secretary of State thinks fit in consequence of that extension.

(2)   Regulations under this section are subject to affirmative resolution procedure.

280   Acts done by person in dual capacity

A provision requiring or authorising a thing to be done by or to a director and the secretary of a company is not satisfied by its being done by or to the same person acting both as director and as, or in place of, the secretary.

PART 13
RESOLUTIONS AND MEETINGS

CHAPTER 1
GENERAL PROVISIONS ABOUT RESOLUTIONS

281   Resolutions

(1)   A resolution of the members (or of a class of members) of a private company must be passed—
(a)   as a written resolution in accordance with Chapter 2, or
(b)   at a meeting of the members (to which the provisions of Chapter 3 apply).

(2)   A resolution of the members (or of a class of members) of a public company must be passed at a meeting of the members (to which the provisions of Chapter 3 and, where relevant, Chapter 4 apply).

(3)   Where a provision of the Companies Acts—
(a)   requires a resolution of a company, or of the members (or a class of members) of a company, and
(b)   does not specify what kind of resolution is required,
what is required is an ordinary resolution unless the company's articles require a higher majority (or unanimity).

(4)   Nothing in this Part affects any enactment or rule of law as to—
(a)   things done otherwise than by passing a resolution,
(b)   circumstances in which a resolution is or is not treated as having been passed, or
(c)   cases in which a person is precluded from alleging that a resolution has not been duly passed.

282   Ordinary resolutions

(1)   An ordinary resolution of the members (or of a class of members) of a company means a resolution that is passed by a simple majority.

(2)   A written resolution is passed by a simple majority if it is passed by members representing a simple majority of the total voting rights of eligible members (see Chapter 2).

(3)   A resolution passed at a meeting on a show of hands is passed by a simple majority if it is passed by a simple majority of the votes cast by those entitled to vote.

(4)   A resolution passed on a poll taken at a meeting is passed by a simple majority if it is passed by members representing a simple majority of the total voting rights of members who (being entitled to do so) vote in person, by proxy or in advance (see section 322A) on the resolution.

(5)   Anything that may be done by ordinary resolution may also be done by special resolution.

283   Special resolutions

(1)   A special resolution of the members (or of a class of members) of a company means a resolution passed by a majority of not less than 75%.

(2)   A written resolution is passed by a majority of not less than 75% if it is passed by members representing not less than 75% of the total voting rights of eligible members (see Chapter 2).

(3)   Where a resolution of a private company is passed as a written resolution—
(a)   the resolution is not a special resolution unless it stated that it was proposed as a special resolution, and

(b)   if the resolution so stated, it may only be passed as a special resolution.

(4)   A resolution passed at a meeting on a show of hands is passed by a majority of not less than 75% if it is passed by not less than 75% of the votes cast by those entitled to vote.

(5)   A resolution passed on a poll taken at a meeting is passed by a majority of not less than 75% if it is passed by members representing not less than 75% of the total voting rights of the members who (being entitled to do so) vote in person, by proxy or in advance (see section 322A) on the resolution.

(6)   Where a resolution is passed at a meeting—

(a)   the resolution is not a special resolution unless the notice of the meeting included the text of the resolution and specified the intention to propose the resolution as a special resolution, and

(b)   if the notice of the meeting so specified, the resolution may only be passed as a special resolution.

284   Votes: general rules

(1)   On a vote on a written resolution—

(a)   in the case of a company having a share capital, every member has one vote in respect of each share or each £10 of stock held by him, and

(b)   in any other case, every member has one vote.

(2)   On a vote on a resolution on a show of hands at a meeting, each member present in person has one vote.

(3)   On a vote on a resolution on a poll taken at a meeting—

(a)   in the case of a company having a share capital, every member has one vote in respect of each share or each £10 of stock held by him, and

(b)   in any other case, every member has one vote.

(4)   The provisions of this section have effect subject to any provision of the company's articles.

(5)   Nothing in this section is to be read as restricting the effect of—

section 152 (exercise of rights by nominees),

section 285 (voting by proxy),

section 322 (exercise of voting rights on poll),

section 322A (voting on a poll: votes cast in advance), or

section 323 (representation of corporations at meetings).

285   Voting by proxy

(1)   On a vote on a resolution on a show of hands at a meeting, every proxy present who has been duly appointed by one or more members entitled to vote on the resolution has one vote.

This is subject to subsection (2).

(2)   On a vote on a resolution on a show of hands at a meeting, a proxy has one vote for and one vote against the resolution if—

(a)   the proxy has been duly appointed by more than one member entitled to vote on the resolution, and

(b)   the proxy has been instructed by one or more of those members to vote for the resolution and by one or more other of those members to vote against it.

(3)   On a poll taken at a meeting of a company all or any of the voting rights of a member may be exercised by one or more duly appointed proxies.

(4)   Where a member appoints more than one proxy, subsection (3) does not authorise the exercise by the proxies taken together of more extensive voting rights than could be exercised by the member in person.

(5)   Subsections (1) and (2) have effect subject to any provision of the company's articles.

285A   Voting rights on poll or written resolution

In relation to a resolution required or authorised by an enactment, if a private company's articles provide that a member has a different number of votes in relation to a resolution when it is passed as a written resolution and when it is passed on a poll taken at a meeting—

    (a)   the provision about how many votes a member has in relation to the resolution passed on a poll is void, and

    (b)   a member has the same number of votes in relation to the resolution when it is passed on a poll as the member has when it is passed as a written resolution.

286   Votes of joint holders of shares

(1)   In the case of joint holders of shares of a company, only the vote of the senior holder who votes (and any proxies duly authorised by him) may be counted by the company.

(2)   For the purposes of this section, the senior holder of a share is determined by the order in which the names of the joint holders appear in the register of members (or, if an election under section 128B is in force in respect of the company, in the register kept by the registrar under section 1080).

(3)   Subsections (1) and (2) have effect subject to any provision of the company's articles.

287   Saving for provisions of articles as to determination of entitlement to vote

Nothing in this Chapter affects—

    (a)   any provision of a company's articles—

        (i)   requiring an objection to a person's entitlement to vote on a resolution to be made in accordance with the articles, and

        (ii)   for the determination of any such objection to be final and conclusive, or

    (b)   the grounds on which such a determination may be questioned in legal proceedings.

CHAPTER 2
WRITTEN RESOLUTIONS

General provisions about written resolutions

288   Written resolutions of private companies

(1)   In the Companies Acts a "written resolution" means a resolution of a private company proposed and passed in accordance with this Chapter.

(2)   The following may not be passed as a written resolution—

    (a)   a resolution under section 168 removing a director before the expiration of his period of office;

    (b)   a resolution under section 510 removing an auditor before the expiration of his term of office.

(3)   A resolution may be proposed as a written resolution—

    (a)   by the directors of a private company (see section 291), or

    (b)   by the members of a private company (see sections 292 to 295).

(4)   References in enactments passed or made before this Chapter comes into force to—

    (a)   a resolution of a company in general meeting, or

    (b)   a resolution of a meeting of a class of members of the company,

have effect as if they included references to a written resolution of the members, or of a class of members, of a private company (as appropriate).

(5)   A written resolution of a private company has effect as if passed (as the case may be)—

    (a)   by the company in general meeting, or

    (b)   by a meeting of a class of members of the company,

and references in enactments passed or made before this section comes into force to a meeting at which a resolution is passed or to members voting in favour of a resolution shall be construed accordingly.

289   Eligible members

(1)   In relation to a resolution proposed as a written resolution of a private company, the eligible members are the members who would have been entitled to vote on the resolution on the circulation date of the resolution (see section 290).

(2)   If the persons entitled to vote on a written resolution change during the course of the day that is the circulation date of the resolution, the eligible members are the persons entitled to vote on the resolution at the time that the first copy of the resolution is sent or submitted to a member for his agreement.

Circulation of written resolutions

290   Circulation date

References in this Part to the circulation date of a written resolution are to the date on which copies of it are sent or submitted to members in accordance with this Chapter (or if copies are sent or submitted to members on different days, to the first of those days).

291   Circulation of written resolutions proposed by directors

(1)   This section applies to a resolution proposed as a written resolution by the directors of the company.

(2)   The company must send or submit a copy of the resolution to every eligible member.

(3)   The company must do so—

    (a)   by sending copies at the same time (so far as reasonably practicable) to all eligible members in hard copy form, in electronic form or by means of a website, or

    (b)   if it is possible to do so without undue delay, by submitting the same copy to each eligible member in turn (or different copies to each of a number of eligible members in turn),

    or by sending copies to some members in accordance with paragraph (a) and submitting a copy or copies to other members in accordance with paragraph (b).

(4)   The copy of the resolution must be accompanied by a statement informing the member—

    (a)   how to signify agreement to the resolution (see section 296), and

    (b)   as to the date by which the resolution must be passed if it is not to lapse (see section 297).

(5)   In the event of default in complying with this section, an offence is committed by every officer of the company who is in default.

(6)   A person guilty of an offence under this section is liable—

    (a)   on conviction on indictment, to a fine;

    (b)   on summary conviction, to a fine not exceeding the statutory maximum.

(7)   The validity of the resolution, if passed, is not affected by a failure to comply with this section.

292   Members' power to require circulation of written resolution

(1)   The members of a private company may require the company to circulate a resolution that may properly be moved and is proposed to be moved as a written resolution.

(2)   Any resolution may properly be moved as a written resolution unless—

    (a)   it would, if passed, be ineffective (whether by reason of inconsistency with any enactment or the company's constitution or otherwise),

    (b)   it is defamatory of any person, or

    (c)   it is frivolous or vexatious.

(3)   Where the members require a company to circulate a resolution they may require the company to circulate with it a statement of not more than 1,000 words on the subject matter of the resolution.

(4)   A company is required to circulate the resolution and any accompanying statement once it has received requests that it do so from members representing not less than the requisite percentage of the total voting rights of all members entitled to vote on the resolution.

(5)   The "requisite percentage" is 5% or such lower percentage as is specified for this purpose in the company's articles.

(6)   A request—

    (a)   may be in hard copy form or in electronic form,

    (b)   must identify the resolution and any accompanying statement, and

    (c)   must be authenticated by the person or persons making it.

293 Circulation of written resolution proposed by members

(1) A company that is required under section 292 to circulate a resolution must send or submit to every eligible member—

(a) a copy of the resolution, and

(b) a copy of any accompanying statement.

This is subject to section 294(2) (deposit or tender of sum in respect of expenses of circulation) and section 295 (application not to circulate members' statement).

(2) The company must do so—

(a) by sending copies at the same time (so far as reasonably practicable) to all eligible members in hard copy form, in electronic form or by means of a website, or

(b) if it is possible to do so without undue delay, by submitting the same copy to each eligible member in turn (or different copies to each of a number of eligible members in turn),

or by sending copies to some members in accordance with paragraph (a) and submitting a copy or copies to other members in accordance with paragraph (b).

(3) The company must send or submit the copies (or, if copies are sent or submitted to members on different days, the first of those copies) not more than 21 days after it becomes subject to the requirement under section 292 to circulate the resolution.

(4) The copy of the resolution must be accompanied by guidance as to—

(a) how to signify agreement to the resolution (see section 296), and

(b) the date by which the resolution must be passed if it is not to lapse (see section 297).

(5) In the event of default in complying with this section, an offence is committed by every officer of the company who is in default.

(6) A person guilty of an offence under this section is liable—

(a) on conviction on indictment, to a fine;

(b) on summary conviction, to a fine not exceeding the statutory maximum.

(7) The validity of the resolution, if passed, is not affected by a failure to comply with this section.

294 Expenses of circulation

(1) The expenses of the company in complying with section 293 must be paid by the members who requested the circulation of the resolution unless the company resolves otherwise.

(2) Unless the company has previously so resolved, it is not bound to comply with that section unless there is deposited with or tendered to it a sum reasonably sufficient to meet its expenses in doing so.

295 Application not to circulate members' statement

(1) A company is not required to circulate a members' statement under section 293 if, on an application by the company or another person who claims to be aggrieved, the court is satisfied that the rights conferred by section 292 and that section are being abused.

(2) The court may order the members who requested the circulation of the statement to pay the whole or part of the company's costs (in Scotland, expenses) on such an application, even if they are not parties to the application.

Agreeing to written resolutions

296 Procedure for signifying agreement to written resolution

(1) A member signifies his agreement to a proposed written resolution when the company receives from him (or from someone acting on his behalf) an authenticated document—

(a) identifying the resolution to which it relates, and

(b) indicating his agreement to the resolution.

(2) The document must be sent to the company in hard copy form or in electronic form.

(3) A member's agreement to a written resolution, once signified, may not be revoked.

(4) A written resolution is passed when the required majority of eligible members have signified their agreement to it.

297   Period for agreeing to written resolution

(1)   A proposed written resolution lapses if it is not passed before the end of—

    (a)   the period specified for this purpose in the company's articles, or

    (b)   if none is specified, the period of 28 days beginning with the circulation date.

(2)   The agreement of a member to a written resolution is ineffective if signified after the expiry of that period.

Supplementary

298   Sending documents relating to written resolutions by electronic means

(1)   Where a company has given an electronic address in any document containing or accompanying a proposed written resolution, it is deemed to have agreed that any document or information relating to that resolution may be sent by electronic means to that address (subject to any conditions or limitations specified in the document).

(2)   In this section "electronic address" means any address or number used for the purposes of sending or receiving documents or information by electronic means.

299   Publication of written resolution on website

(1)   This section applies where a company sends—

    (a)   a written resolution, or

    (b)   a statement relating to a written resolution,

to a person by means of a website.

(2)   The resolution or statement is not validly sent for the purposes of this Chapter unless the resolution is available on the website throughout the period beginning with the circulation date and ending on the date on which the resolution lapses under section 297.

300   Relationship between this Chapter and provisions of company's articles

A provision of the articles of a private company is void in so far as it would have the effect that a resolution that is required by or otherwise provided for in an enactment could not be proposed and passed as a written resolution.

CHAPTER 3
RESOLUTIONS AT MEETINGS

General provisions about resolutions at meetings

301   Resolutions at general meetings

A resolution of the members of a company is validly passed at a general meeting if—

    (a)   notice of the meeting and of the resolution is given, and

    (b)   the meeting is held and conducted,

in accordance with the provisions of this Chapter (and, where relevant, Chapter 4) and the company's articles.

Calling meetings

302   Directors' power to call general meetings

The directors of a company may call a general meeting of the company.

303   Members' power to require directors to call general meeting

(1)   The members of a company may require the directors to call a general meeting of the company.

(2)   The directors are required to call a general meeting once the company has received requests to do so from—

    (a)   members representing at least 5% of such of the paid-up capital of the company as carries the right of voting at general meetings of the company (excluding any paid-up capital held as treasury shares); or

(b)   in the case of a company not having a share capital, members who represent at least 5% of the total voting rights of all the members having a right to vote at general meetings.

(3)   …

(4)   A request—

(a)   must state the general nature of the business to be dealt with at the meeting, and

(b)   may include the text of a resolution that may properly be moved and is intended to be moved at the meeting.

(5)   A resolution may properly be moved at a meeting unless—

(a)   it would, if passed, be ineffective (whether by reason of inconsistency with any enactment or the company's constitution or otherwise),

(b)   it is defamatory of any person, or

(c)   it is frivolous or vexatious.

(6)   A request—

(a)   may be in hard copy form or in electronic form, and

(b)   must be authenticated by the person or persons making it.

304   Directors' duty to call meetings required by members

(1)   Directors required under section 303 to call a general meeting of the company must call a meeting—

(a)   within 21 days from the date on which they become subject to the requirement, and

(b)   to be held on a date not more than 28 days after the date of the notice convening the meeting.

(2)   If the requests received by the company identify a resolution intended to be moved at the meeting, the notice of the meeting must include notice of the resolution.

(3)   The business that may be dealt with at the meeting includes a resolution of which notice is given in accordance with this section.

(4)   If the resolution is to be proposed as a special resolution, the directors are treated as not having duly called the meeting if they do not give the required notice of the resolution in accordance with section 283.

305   Power of members to call meeting at company's expense

(1)   If the directors—

(a)   are required under section 303 to call a meeting, and

(b)   do not do so in accordance with section 304,

the members who requested the meeting, or any of them representing more than one half of the total voting rights of all of them, may themselves call a general meeting.

(2)   Where the requests received by the company included the text of a resolution intended to be moved at the meeting, the notice of the meeting must include notice of the resolution.

(3)   The meeting must be called for a date not more than three months after the date on which the directors become subject to the requirement to call a meeting.

(4)   The meeting must be called in the same manner, as nearly as possible, as that in which meetings are required to be called by directors of the company.

(5)   The business which may be dealt with at the meeting includes a resolution of which notice is given in accordance with this section.

(6)   Any reasonable expenses incurred by the members requesting the meeting by reason of the failure of the directors duly to call a meeting must be reimbursed by the company.

(7)   Any sum so reimbursed shall be retained by the company out of any sums due or to become due from the company by way of fees or other remuneration in respect of the services of such of the directors as were in default.

306   Power of court to order meeting

(1)   This section applies if for any reason it is impracticable—

(a)   to call a meeting of a company in any manner in which meetings of that company may be called, or

(b)   to conduct the meeting in the manner prescribed by the company's articles or this Act.

(2)   The court may, either of its own motion or on the application—
- (a)   of a director of the company, or
- (b)   of a member of the company who would be entitled to vote at the meeting,

order a meeting to be called, held and conducted in any manner the court thinks fit.

(3)   Where such an order is made, the court may give such ancillary or consequential directions as it thinks expedient.

(4)   Such directions may include a direction that one member of the company present at the meeting be deemed to constitute a quorum.

(5)   A meeting called, held and conducted in accordance with an order under this section is deemed for all purposes to be a meeting of the company duly called, held and conducted.

Notice of meetings

307   Notice required of general meeting

(A1)   This section applies to—
- (a)   a general meeting of a company that is not a traded company; and
- (b)   a general meeting of a traded company that is an opted-in company (as defined by section 971(1)), where—
  - (i)   the meeting is held to decide whether to take any action that might result in the frustration of a takeover bid for the company; or
  - (ii)   the meeting is held by virtue of section 969 (power of offeror to require general meeting to be held).

(A2)   For corresponding provision in relation to general meetings of traded companies (other than meetings within subsection (A1)(b)), see section 307A.

(1)   A general meeting of a private company (other than an adjourned meeting) must be called by notice of at least 14 days.

(2)   A general meeting of a public company (other than an adjourned meeting) must be called by notice of—
- (a)   in the case of an annual general meeting, at least 21 days, and
- (b)   in any other case, at least 14 days.

(3)   The company's articles may require a longer period of notice than that specified in subsection (1) or (2).

(4)   A general meeting may be called by shorter notice than that otherwise required if shorter notice is agreed by the members.

(5)   The shorter notice must be agreed to by a majority in number of the members having a right to attend and vote at the meeting, being a majority who—
- (a)   together hold not less than the requisite percentage in nominal value of the shares giving a right to attend and vote at the meeting (excluding any shares in the company held as treasury shares), or
- (b)   in the case of a company not having a share capital, together represent not less than the requisite percentage of the total voting rights at that meeting of all the members.

(6)   The requisite percentage is—
- (a)   in the case of a private company, 90% or such higher percentage (not exceeding 95%) as may be specified in the company's articles;
- (b)   in the case of a public company, 95%.

(7)   Subsections (5) and (6) do not apply to an annual general meeting of a public company (see instead section 337(2)).

307A   Notice required of general meeting: certain meetings of traded companies

(1)   A general meeting of a traded company must be called by notice of—
- (a)   in a case where conditions A to C (set out below) are met, at least 14 days;
- (b)   in any other case, at least 21 days.

(2)   Condition A is that the general meeting is not an annual general meeting.

(3) Condition B is that the company offers the facility for members to vote by electronic means accessible to all members who hold shares that carry rights to vote at general meetings.

This condition is met if there is a facility, offered by the company and accessible to all such members, to appoint a proxy by means of a website.

(4) Condition C is that a special resolution reducing the period of notice to not less than 14 days has been passed—

(a) at the immediately preceding annual general meeting, or

(b) at a general meeting held since that annual general meeting.

(5) In the case of a company which has not yet held an annual general meeting, condition C is that a special resolution reducing the period of notice to not less than 14 days has been passed at a general meeting.

(6) The company's articles may require a longer period of notice than that specified in subsection (1).

(7) Where a general meeting is adjourned, the adjourned meeting may be called by shorter notice than required by subsection (1).

But in the case of an adjournment for lack of a quorum this subsection applies only if—

(a) no business is to be dealt with at the adjourned meeting the general nature of which was not stated in the notice of the original meeting, and

(b) the adjourned meeting is to be held at least 10 days after the original meeting.

(8) Nothing in this section applies in relation to a general meeting of a kind mentioned in section 307(A1)(b) (certain meetings regarding takeover of opted-in company).

308 Manner in which notice to be given

Notice of a general meeting of a company must be given—

(a) in hard copy form,

(b) in electronic form, or

(c) by means of a website (see section 309),

or partly by one such means and partly by another.

309 Publication of notice of meeting on website

(1) Notice of a meeting is not validly given by a company by means of a website unless it is given in accordance with this section.

(2) When the company notifies a member of the presence of the notice on the website the notification must—

(a) state that it concerns a notice of a company meeting,

(b) specify the place, date and time of the meeting, and

(c) in the case of a public company, state whether the meeting will be an annual general meeting.

(3) The notice must be available on the website throughout the period beginning with the date of that notification and ending with the conclusion of the meeting.

310 Persons entitled to receive notice of meetings

(1) Notice of a general meeting of a company must be sent to—

(a) every member of the company, and

(b) every director.

(2) In subsection (1), the reference to members includes any person who is entitled to a share in consequence of the death or bankruptcy of a member, if the company has been notified of their entitlement.

(3) In subsection (2), the reference to the bankruptcy of a member includes—

(a) the sequestration of the estate of a member;

(b) a member's estate being the subject of a protected trust deed (within the meaning of the Bankruptcy (Scotland) Act 2016).

(4) This section has effect subject to—

(a) any enactment, and

(b) any provision of the company's articles.

311   Contents of notices of meetings

(1)   Notice of a general meeting of a company must state—

    (a)   the time and date of the meeting, and

    (b)   the place of the meeting.

(2)   Notice of a general meeting of a company must state the general nature of the business to be dealt with at the meeting.

In relation to a company other than a traded company, this subsection has effect subject to any provision of the company's articles.

(3)   Notice of a general meeting of a traded company must also include—

    (a)   a statement giving the address of the website on which the information required by section 311A (traded companies: publication of information in advance of general meeting) is published;

    (b)   a statement—

        (i)   that the right to vote at the meeting is determined by reference to the register of members (or, if an election under section 128B is in force in respect of the company, by reference to the register kept by the registrar under section 1080), and

        (ii)   of the time when that right will be determined in accordance with section 360B(2) (traded companies: share dealings before general meetings);

    (c)   a statement of the procedures with which members must comply in order to be able to attend and vote at the meeting (including the date by which they must comply);

    (d)   a statement giving details of any forms to be used for the appointment of a proxy;

    (e)   where the company offers the facility for members to vote in advance (see section 322A) or by electronic means (see section 360A), a statement of the procedure for doing so (including the date by which it must be done, and details of any forms to be used); and

    (f)   a statement of the right of members to ask questions in accordance with section 319A (traded companies: questions at meetings).

311A   Traded companies: publication of information in advance of general meeting

(1)   A traded company must ensure that the following information relating to a general meeting of the company is made available on a website—

    (a)   the matters set out in the notice of the meeting;

    (b)   the total numbers of—

        (i)   shares in the company, and

        (ii)   shares of each class,

    in respect of which members are entitled to exercise voting rights at the meeting;

    (c)   the totals of the voting rights that members are entitled to exercise at the meeting in respect of the shares of each class;

    (d)   members' statements, members' resolutions and members' matters of business received by the company after the first date on which notice of the meeting is given.

(2)   The information must be made available on a website that—

    (a)   is maintained by or on behalf of the company, and

    (b)   identifies the company.

(3)   Access to the information on the website, and the ability to obtain a hard copy of the information from the website, must not be conditional on payment of a fee or otherwise restricted.

(4)   The information—

    (a)   must be made available—

        (i)   in the case of information required by subsection (1)(a) to (c), on or before the first date on which notice of the meeting is given, and

        (ii)   in the case of information required by subsection (1)(d), as soon as reasonably practicable, and

    (b)   must be kept available throughout the period of two years beginning with the date on which it is first made available on a website in accordance with this section.

(5)   A failure to make information available throughout the period specified in subsection (4)(b) is disregarded if—
        (a)   the information is made available on the website for part of that period, and
        (b)   the failure is wholly attributable to circumstances that it would not be reasonable to have expected the company to prevent or avoid.

(6)   The amounts mentioned in subsection (1)(b) and (c) must be ascertained at the latest practicable time before the first date on which notice of the meeting is given.

(7)   Failure to comply with this section does not affect the validity of the meeting or of anything done at the meeting.

(8)   If this section is not complied with as respects any meeting, an offence is committed by every officer of the company who is in default.

(9)   A person guilty of an offence under this section is liable on summary conviction to a fine not exceeding level 3 on the standard scale.

312   Resolution requiring special notice

(1)   Where by any provision of the Companies Acts special notice is required of a resolution, the resolution is not effective unless notice of the intention to move it has been given to the company at least 28 days before the meeting at which it is moved.

(2)   The company must, where practicable, give its members notice of any such resolution in the same manner and at the same time as it gives notice of the meeting.

(3)   Where that is not practicable, the company must give its members notice at least 14 days before the meeting—
        (a)   by advertisement in a newspaper having an appropriate circulation, or
        (b)   in any other manner allowed by the company's articles.

(4)   If, after notice of the intention to move such a resolution has been given to the company, a meeting is called for a date 28 days or less after the notice has been given, the notice is deemed to have been properly given, though not given within the time required.

313   Accidental failure to give notice of resolution or meeting

(1)   Where a company gives notice of—
        (a)   a general meeting, or
        (b)   a resolution intended to be moved at a general meeting,
        any accidental failure to give notice to one or more persons shall be disregarded for the purpose of determining whether notice of the meeting or resolution (as the case may be) is duly given.

(2)   Except in relation to notice given under—
        (a)   section 304 (notice of meetings required by members),
        (b)   section 305 (notice of meetings called by members), or
        (c)   section 339 (notice of resolutions at AGMs proposed by members),
        subsection (1) has effect subject to any provision of the company's articles.

Members' statements

314   Members' power to require circulation of statements

(1)   The members of a company may require the company to circulate, to members of the company entitled to receive notice of a general meeting, a statement of not more than 1,000 words with respect to—
        (a)   a matter referred to in a proposed resolution to be dealt with at that meeting, or
        (b)   other business to be dealt with at that meeting.

(2)   A company is required to circulate a statement once it has received requests to do so from—
        (a)   members representing at least 5% of the total voting rights of all the members who have a relevant right to vote (excluding any voting rights attached to any shares in the company held as treasury shares), or
        (b)   at least 100 members who have a relevant right to vote and hold shares in the company on which there has been paid up an average sum, per member, of at least £100.

See also section 153 (exercise of rights where shares held on behalf of others).

(3)   In subsection (2), a "relevant right to vote" means—

      (a)   in relation to a statement with respect to a matter referred to in a proposed resolution, a right to vote on that resolution at the meeting to which the requests relate, and

      (b)   in relation to any other statement, a right to vote at the meeting to which the requests relate.

(4)   A request—

      (a)   may be in hard copy form or in electronic form,

      (b)   must identify the statement to be circulated,

      (c)   must be authenticated by the person or persons making it, and

      (d)   must be received by the company at least one week before the meeting to which it relates.

315   Company's duty to circulate members' statement

(1)   A company that is required under section 314, to circulate a statement must send a copy of it to each member of the company entitled to receive notice of the meeting—

      (a)   in the same manner as the notice of the meeting, and

      (b)   at the same time as, or as soon as reasonably practicable after, it gives notice of the meeting.

(2)   Subsection (1) has effect subject to section 316(2) (deposit or tender of sum in respect of expenses of circulation) and section 317 (application not to circulate members' statement).

(3)   In the event of default in complying with this section, an offence is committed by every officer of the company who is in default.

(4)   A person guilty of an offence under this section is liable—

      (a)   on conviction on indictment, to a fine;

      (b)   on summary conviction, to a fine not exceeding the statutory maximum.

316   Expenses of circulating members' statement

(1)   The expenses of the company in complying with section 315 need not be paid by the members who requested the circulation of the statement if—

      (a)   the meeting to which the requests relate is an annual general meeting of a public company, and

      (b)   requests sufficient to require the company to circulate the statement are received before the end of the financial year preceding the meeting.

(2)   Otherwise—

      (a)   the expenses of the company in complying with that section must be paid by the members who requested the circulation of the statement unless the company resolves otherwise, and

      (b)   unless the company has previously so resolved, it is not bound to comply with that section unless there is deposited with or tendered to it, not later than one week before the meeting, a sum reasonably sufficient to meet its expenses in doing so.

317   Application not to circulate members' statement

(1)   A company is not required to circulate a members' statement under section 315 if, on an application by the company or another person who claims to be aggrieved, the court is satisfied that the rights conferred by section 314 and that section are being abused.

(2)   The court may order the members who requested the circulation of the statement to pay the whole or part of the company's costs (in Scotland, expenses) on such an application, even if they are not parties to the application.

Procedure at meetings

318   Quorum at meetings

(1)   In the case of a company limited by shares or guarantee and having only one member, one qualifying person present at a meeting is a quorum.

(2)   In any other case, subject to the provisions of the company's articles, two qualifying persons present at a meeting are a quorum, unless—

(a)   each is a qualifying person only because he is authorised under section 323 to act as the representative of a corporation in relation to the meeting, and they are representatives of the same corporation; or

(b)   each is a qualifying person only because he is appointed as proxy of a member in relation to the meeting, and they are proxies of the same member.

(3)   For the purposes of this section a "qualifying person" means—

(a)   an individual who is a member of the company,

(b)   a person authorised under section 323 (representation of corporations at meetings) to act as the representative of a corporation in relation to the meeting, or

(c)   a person appointed as proxy of a member in relation to the meeting.

319   Chairman of meeting

(1)   A member may be elected to be the chairman of a general meeting by a resolution of the company passed at the meeting.

(2)   Subsection (1) is subject to any provision of the company's articles that states who may or may not be chairman.

319A   Traded companies: questions at meetings

(1)   At a general meeting of a traded company, the company must cause to be answered any question relating to the business being dealt with at the meeting put by a member attending the meeting.

(2)   No such answer need be given—

(a)   if to do so would—

(i)   interfere unduly with the preparation for the meeting, or

(ii)   involve the disclosure of confidential information;

(b)   if the answer has already been given on a website in the form of an answer to a question; or

(c)   if it is undesirable in the interests of the company or the good order of the meeting that the question be answered.

320   Declaration by chairman on a show of hands

(1)   On a vote on a resolution at a meeting on a show of hands, a declaration by the chairman that the resolution—

(a)   has or has not been passed, or

(b)   passed with a particular majority,

is conclusive evidence of that fact without proof of the number or proportion of the votes recorded in favour of or against the resolution.

(2)   An entry in respect of such a declaration in minutes of the meeting recorded in accordance with section 355 is also conclusive evidence of that fact without such proof.

(3)   This section does not have effect if a poll is demanded in respect of the resolution (and the demand is not subsequently withdrawn).

321   Right to demand a poll

(1)   A provision of a company's articles is void in so far as it would have the effect of excluding the right to demand a poll at a general meeting on any question other than—

(a)   the election of the chairman of the meeting, or

(b)   the adjournment of the meeting.

(2)   A provision of a company's articles is void in so far as it would have the effect of making ineffective a demand for a poll on any such question which is made—

(a)   by not less than 5 members having the right to vote on the resolution; or

(b)   by a member or members representing not less than 10% of the total voting rights of all the members having the right to vote on the resolution (excluding any voting rights attached to any shares in the company held as treasury shares); or

(c)   by a member or members holding shares in the company conferring a right to vote on the resolution, being shares on which an aggregate sum has been paid up equal to not less than

10% of the total sum paid up on all the shares conferring that right (excluding shares in the company conferring a right to vote on the resolution which are held as treasury shares).

322   Voting on a poll

On a poll taken at a general meeting of a company, a member entitled to more than one vote need not, if he votes, use all his votes or cast all the votes he uses in the same way.

322A   Voting on a poll: votes cast in advance

(1)   A company's articles may contain provision to the effect that on a vote on a resolution on a poll taken at a meeting, the votes may include votes cast in advance.

(2)   In the case of a traded company any such provision in relation to voting at a general meeting may be made subject only to such requirements and restrictions as are—

(a)   necessary to ensure the identification of the person voting, and

(b)   proportionate to the achievement of that objective.

Nothing in this subsection affects any power of a company to require reasonable evidence of the entitlement of any person who is not a member to vote.

(3)   Any provision of a company's articles is void in so far as it would have the effect of requiring any document casting a vote in advance to be received by the company or another person earlier than the following time—

(a)   in the case of a poll taken more than 48 hours after it was demanded, 24 hours before the time appointed for the taking of the poll;

(b)   in the case of any other poll, 48 hours before the time for holding the meeting or adjourned meeting.

(4)   In calculating the periods mentioned in subsection (3), no account is to be taken of any part of a day that is not a working day.

323   Representation of corporations at meetings

(1)   If a corporation (whether or not a company within the meaning of this Act) is a member of a company, it may by resolution of its directors or other governing body authorise a person or persons to act as its representative or representatives at any meeting of the company.

(2)   A person authorised by a corporation is entitled to exercise (on behalf of the corporation) the same powers as the corporation could exercise if it were an individual member of the company.

Where a corporation authorises more than one person, this subsection is subject to subsections (3) and (4).

(3)   On a vote on a resolution on a show of hands at a meeting of the company, each authorised person has the same voting rights as the corporation would be entitled to.

(4)   Where subsection (3) does not apply and more than one authorised person purport to exercise a power under subsection (2) in respect of the same shares—

(a)   if they purport to exercise the power in the same way as each other, the power is treated as exercised in that way;

(b)   if they do not purport to exercise the power in the same way as each other, the power is treated as not exercised.

Proxies

324   Rights to appoint proxies

(1)   A member of a company is entitled to appoint another person as his proxy to exercise all or any of his rights to attend and to speak and vote at a meeting of the company.

(2)   In the case of a company having a share capital, a member may appoint more than one proxy in relation to a meeting, provided that each proxy is appointed to exercise the rights attached to a different share or shares held by him, or (as the case may be) to a different £10, or multiple of £10, of stock held by him.

324A   Obligation of proxy to vote in accordance with instructions

A proxy must vote in accordance with any instructions given by the member by whom the proxy is appointed.

325   Notice of meeting to contain statement of rights

(1)   In every notice calling a meeting of a company there must appear, with reasonable prominence, a statement informing the member of—

    (a)   his rights under section 324, and

    (b)   any more extensive rights conferred by the company's articles to appoint more than one proxy.

(2)   Failure to comply with this section does not affect the validity of the meeting or of anything done at the meeting.

(3)   If this section is not complied with as respects any meeting, an offence is committed by every officer of the company who is in default.

(4)   A person guilty of an offence under this section is liable on summary conviction to a fine not exceeding level 3 on the standard scale.

326   Company-sponsored invitations to appoint proxies

(1)   If for the purposes of a meeting there are issued at the company's expense invitations to members to appoint as proxy a specified person or a number of specified persons, the invitations must be issued to all members entitled to vote at the meeting.

(2)   Subsection (1) is not contravened if—

    (a)   there is issued to a member at his request a form of appointment naming the proxy or a list of persons willing to act as proxy, and

    (b)   the form or list is available on request to all members entitled to vote at the meeting.

(3)   If subsection (1) is contravened as respects a meeting, an offence is committed by every officer of the company who is in default.

(4)   A person guilty of an offence under this section is liable on summary conviction to a fine not exceeding level 3 on the standard scale.

327   Notice required of appointment of proxy etc

(A1)   In the case of a traded company—

    (a)   the appointment of a person as proxy for a member must be notified to the company in writing;

    (b)   where such an appointment is made, the company may require reasonable evidence of—

        (i)   the identity of the member and of the proxy,

        (ii)   the member's instructions (if any) as to how the proxy is to vote, and

        (iii)   where the proxy is appointed by a person acting on behalf of the member, authority of that person to make the appointment;

    but may not require to be provided with anything else relating to the appointment.

(1)   The following provisions apply in the case of traded companies and other companies as regards—

    (a)   the appointment of a proxy, and

    (b)   any document necessary to show the validity of, or otherwise relating to, the appointment of a proxy.

(2)   Any provision of the company's articles is void in so far as it would have the effect of requiring any such appointment or document to be received by the company or another person earlier than the following time—

    (a)   in the case of a meeting or adjourned meeting, 48 hours before the time for holding the meeting or adjourned meeting;

    (b)   in the case of a poll taken more than 48 hours after it was demanded, 24 hours before the time appointed for the taking of the poll;

    (c)   ...

(3)   In calculating the periods mentioned in subsection (2) no account shall be taken of any part of a day that is not a working day.

328   Chairing meetings

(1)   A proxy may be elected to be the chairman of a general meeting by a resolution of the company passed at the meeting.

(2)   Subsection (1) is subject to any provision of the company's articles that states who may or who may not be chairman.

329   Right of proxy to demand a poll

(1)   The appointment of a proxy to vote on a matter at a meeting of a company authorises the proxy to demand, or join in demanding, a poll on that matter.

(2)   In applying the provisions of section 321(2) (requirements for effective demand), a demand by a proxy counts—

(a)   for the purposes of paragraph (a), as a demand by the member;

(b)   for the purposes of paragraph (b), as a demand by a member representing the voting rights that the proxy is authorised to exercise;

(c)   for the purposes of paragraph (c), as a demand by a member holding the shares to which those rights are attached.

330   Notice required of termination of proxy's authority

(A1)   In the case of a traded company the termination of the authority of a person to act as proxy must be notified to the company in writing.

(1)   The following provisions apply in the case of traded companies and other companies as regards notice that the authority of a person to act as proxy is terminated ("notice of termination").

(2)   The termination of the authority of a person to act as proxy does not affect—

(a)   whether he counts in deciding whether there is a quorum at a meeting,

(b)   the validity of anything he does as chairman of a meeting, or

(c)   the validity of a poll demanded by him at a meeting,

unless the company receives notice of the termination before the commencement of the meeting.

(3)   The termination of the authority of a person to act as proxy does not affect the validity of a vote given by that person unless the company receives notice of the termination—

(a)   before the commencement of the meeting or adjourned meeting at which the vote is given, or

(b)   in the case of a poll taken more than 48 hours after it is demanded, before the time appointed for taking the poll.

(4)   If the company's articles require or permit members to give notice of termination to a person other than the company, the references above to the company receiving notice have effect as if they were or (as the case may be) included a reference to that person.

(5)   Subsections (2) and (3) have effect subject to any provision of the company's articles which has the effect of requiring notice of termination to be received by the company or another person at a time earlier than that specified in those subsections.

This is subject to subsection (6).

(6)   Any provision of the company's articles is void in so far as it would have the effect of requiring notice of termination to be received by the company or another person earlier than the following time—

(a)   in the case of a meeting or adjourned meeting, 48 hours before the time for holding the meeting or adjourned meeting;

(b)   in the case of a poll taken more than 48 hours after it was demanded, 24 hours before the time appointed for the taking of the poll;

(c)   ...

(7)   In calculating the periods mentioned in subsections (3)(b) and (6) no account shall be taken of any part of a day that is not a working day.

331 Saving for more extensive rights conferred by articles

Nothing in sections 324 to 330 (proxies) prevents a company's articles from conferring more extensive rights on members or proxies than are conferred by those sections.

Adjourned meetings

332 Resolution passed at adjourned meeting

Where a resolution is passed at an adjourned meeting of a company, the resolution is for all purposes to be treated as having been passed on the date on which it was in fact passed, and is not to be deemed passed on any earlier date.

Electronic communications

333 Sending documents relating to meetings etc in electronic form

(1) Where a company has given an electronic address in a notice calling a meeting, it is deemed to have agreed that any document or information relating to proceedings at the meeting may be sent by electronic means to that address (subject to any conditions or limitations specified in the notice).

(2) Where a company has given an electronic address—

(a) in an instrument of proxy sent out by the company in relation to the meeting, or

(b) in an invitation to appoint a proxy issued by the company in relation to the meeting,

it is deemed to have agreed that any document or information relating to proxies for that meeting may be sent by electronic means to that address (subject to any conditions or limitations specified in the notice).

(3) In subsection (2), documents relating to proxies include—

(a) the appointment of a proxy in relation to a meeting,

(b) any document necessary to show the validity of, or otherwise relating to, the appointment of a proxy, and

(c) notice of the termination of the authority of a proxy.

(4) In this section "electronic address" means any address or number used for the purposes of sending or receiving documents or information by electronic means.

333A Traded company: duty to provide electronic address for receipt of proxies etc

(1) A traded company must provide an electronic address for the receipt of any document or information relating to proxies for a general meeting.

(2) The company must provide the address either—

(a) by giving it when sending out an instrument of proxy for the purposes of the meeting or issuing an invitation to appoint a proxy for those purposes; or

(b) by ensuring that it is made available, throughout the period beginning with the first date on which notice of the meeting is given and ending with the conclusion of the meeting, on the website on which the information required by section 311A(1) is made available.

(3) The company is deemed to have agreed that any document or information relating to proxies for the meeting may be sent by electronic means to the address provided (subject to any limitations specified by the company when providing the address).

(4) In this section—

(a) documents relating to proxies include—

(i) the appointment of a proxy for a meeting,

(ii) any document necessary to show the validity of, or otherwise relating to, the appointment of a proxy, and

(iii) notice of the termination of the authority of a proxy;

(b) "electronic address" has the meaning given by section 333(4).

334   Application to class meetings

(1)   The provisions of this Chapter apply (with necessary modifications) in relation to a meeting of holders of a class of shares as they apply in relation to a general meeting.

This is subject to subsections (2) to (3).

(2)   The following provisions of this Chapter do not apply in relation to a meeting of holders of a class of shares—

(a)   sections 303 to 305 (members' power to require directors to call general meeting), ...

(b)   section 306 (power of court to order meeting), and

(c)   sections 311(3), 311A, 319A, 327(A1), 330(A1) and 333A (additional requirements relating to traded companies).

(2A)   Section 307(1) to (6) apply in relation to a meeting of holders of a class of shares in a traded company as they apply in relation to a meeting of holders of a class of shares in a company other than a traded company (and, accordingly, section 307A does not apply in relation to such a meeting).

(3)   The following provisions (in addition to those mentioned in subsection (2)) do not apply in relation to a meeting in connection with the variation of rights attached to a class of shares (a "variation of class rights meeting")—

(a)   section 318 (quorum), and

(b)   section 321 (right to demand a poll).

(4)   The quorum for a variation of class rights meeting is—

(a)   for a meeting other than an adjourned meeting, two persons present holding at least one-third in nominal value of the issued shares of the class in question (excluding any shares of that class held as treasury shares);

(b)   for an adjourned meeting, one person present holding shares of the class in question.

(5)   For the purposes of subsection (4), where a person is present by proxy or proxies, he is treated as holding only the shares in respect of which those proxies are authorised to exercise voting rights.

(6)   At a variation of class rights meeting, any holder of shares of the class in question present may demand a poll.

(7)   For the purposes of this section—

(a)   any amendment of a provision contained in a company's articles for the variation of the rights attached to a class of shares, or the insertion of any such provision into the articles, is itself to be treated as a variation of those rights, and

(b)   references to the variation of rights attached to a class of shares include references to their abrogation.

335   Application to class meetings: companies without a share capital

(1)   The provisions of this Chapter apply (with necessary modifications) in relation to a meeting of a class of members of a company without a share capital as they apply in relation to a general meeting.

This is subject to subsections (2) and (3).

(2)   The following provisions of this Chapter do not apply in relation to a meeting of a class of members—

(a)   sections 303 to 305 (members' power to require directors to call general meeting), and

(b)   section 306 (power of court to order meeting).

(3)   The following provisions (in addition to those mentioned in subsection (2)) do not apply in relation to a meeting in connection with the variation of the rights of a class of members (a "variation of class rights meeting")—

(a)   section 318 (quorum), and

(b)   section 321 (right to demand a poll).

(4)   The quorum for a variation of class rights meeting is—

(a)   for a meeting other than an adjourned meeting, two members of the class present (in person or by proxy) who together represent at least one-third of the voting rights of the class;

(b)   for an adjourned meeting, one member of the class present (in person or by proxy).

(5)   At a variation of class rights meeting, any member present (in person or by proxy) may demand a poll.

(6)   For the purposes of this section—

(a)   any amendment of a provision contained in a company's articles for the variation of the rights of a class of members, or the insertion of any such provision into the articles, is itself to be treated as a variation of those rights, and

(b)   references to the variation of rights of a class of members include references to their abrogation.

CHAPTER 4
PUBLIC COMPANIES AND TRADED COMPANIES: ADDITIONAL REQUIREMENTS
FOR AGMS

336   Public companies and traded companies: annual general meeting

(1)   Every public company must hold a general meeting as its annual general meeting in each period of 6 months beginning with the day following its accounting reference date (in addition to any other meetings held during that period).

(1A)   Every private company that is a traded company must hold a general meeting as its annual general meeting in each period of 9 months beginning with the day following its accounting reference date (in addition to any other meetings held during that period).

(2)   A company that fails to comply with subsection (1) or (1A) as a result of giving notice under section 392 (alteration of accounting reference date)—

(a)   specifying a new accounting reference date, and

(b)   stating that the current accounting reference period or the previous accounting reference period is to be shortened,

shall be treated as if it had complied with subsection (1) or (1A) if it holds a general meeting as its annual general meeting within 3 months of giving that notice.

(3)   If a company fails to comply with subsection (1) or (1A), an offence is committed by every officer of the company who is in default.

(4)   A person guilty of an offence under this section is liable—

(a)   on conviction on indictment, to a fine;

(b)   on summary conviction, to a fine not exceeding the statutory maximum.

337   Public companies and traded companies: notice of AGM

(1)   A notice calling an annual general meeting of a public company or a private company that is a traded company must state that the meeting is an annual general meeting.

(2)   An annual general meeting of a public company that is not a traded company may be called by shorter notice than that required by section 307(2) or by the company's articles (as the case may be), if all the members entitled to attend and vote at the meeting agree to the shorter notice.

(3)   Where a notice calling an annual general meeting of a traded company is given more than 6 weeks before the meeting, the notice must include—

(a)   if the company is a public company, a statement of the right under section 338 to require the company to give notice of a resolution to be moved at the meeting, and

(b)   whether or not the company is a public company, a statement of the right under section 338A to require the company to include a matter in the business to be dealt with at the meeting.

338   Public companies: members' power to require circulation of resolutions for AGMs

(1)   The members of a public company may require the company to give, to members of the company entitled to receive notice of the next annual general meeting, notice of a resolution which may properly be moved and is intended to be moved at that meeting.

(2)   A resolution may properly be moved at an annual general meeting unless—

    (a)   it would, if passed, be ineffective (whether by reason of inconsistency with any enactment or the company's constitution or otherwise),

    (b)   it is defamatory of any person, or

    (c)   it is frivolous or vexatious.

(3)   A company is required to give notice of a resolution once it has received requests that it do so from—

    (a)   members representing at least 5% of the total voting rights of all the members who have a right to vote on the resolution at the annual general meeting to which the requests relate (excluding any voting rights attached to any shares in the company held as treasury shares), or

    (b)   at least 100 members who have a right to vote on the resolution at the annual general meeting to which the requests relate and hold shares in the company on which there has been paid up an average sum, per member, of at least £100.

See also section 153 (exercise of rights where shares held on behalf of others).

(4)   A request—

    (a)   may be in hard copy form or in electronic form,

    (b)   must identify the resolution of which notice is to be given,

    (c)   must be authenticated by the person or persons making it, and

    (d)   must be received by the company not later than—

        (i)   6 weeks before the annual general meeting to which the requests relate, or

        (ii)   if later, the time at which notice is given of that meeting.

338A   Traded companies: members' power to include other matters in business dealt with at AGM

(1)   The members of a traded company may request the company to include in the business to be dealt with at an annual general meeting any matter (other than a proposed resolution) which may properly be included in the business.

(2)   A matter may properly be included in the business at an annual general meeting unless—

    (a)   it is defamatory of any person, or

    (b)   it is frivolous or vexatious.

(3)   A company is required to include such a matter once it has received requests that it do so from—

    (a)   members representing at least 5% of the total voting rights of all the members who have a right to vote at the meeting, or

    (b)   at least 100 members who have a right to vote at the meeting and hold shares in the company on which there has been paid up an average sum, per member, of at least £100.

See also section 153 (exercise of rights where shares held on behalf of others).

(4)   A request—

    (a)   may be in hard copy form or in electronic form,

    (b)   must identify the matter to be included in the business,

    (c)   must be accompanied by a statement setting out the grounds for the request, and

    (d)   must be authenticated by the person or persons making it.

(5)   A request must be received by the company not later than—

    (a)   6 weeks before the meeting, or

    (b)   if later, the time at which notice is given of the meeting.

339   Public companies: company's duty to circulate members' resolutions for AGMs

(1)   A company that is required under section 338 to give notice of a resolution must send a copy of it to each member of the company entitled to receive notice of the annual general meeting—

    (a)   in the same manner as notice of the meeting, and

    (b)   at the same time as, or as soon as reasonably practicable after, it gives notice of the meeting.

(2)   Subsection (1) has effect subject to section 340(2) (deposit or tender of sum in respect of expenses of circulation).

(3)   The business which may be dealt with at an annual general meeting includes a resolution of which notice is given in accordance with this section.

(4)   In the event of default in complying with this section, an offence is committed by every officer of the company who is in default.

(5)   A person guilty of an offence under this section is liable—

    (a)   on conviction on indictment, to a fine;

    (b)   on summary conviction, to a fine not exceeding the statutory maximum.

340   Public companies: expenses of circulating members' resolutions for AGM

(1)   The expenses of the company in complying with section 339 need not be paid by the members who requested the circulation of the resolution if requests sufficient to require the company to circulate it are received before the end of the financial year preceding the meeting.

(2)   Otherwise—

    (a)   the expenses of the company in complying with that section must be paid by the members who requested the circulation of the resolution unless the company resolves otherwise, and

    (b)   unless the company has previously so resolved, it is not bound to comply with that section unless there is deposited with or tendered to it, not later than—

        (i)   six weeks before the annual general meeting to which the requests relate, or

        (ii)   if later, the time at which notice is given of that meeting,

    a sum reasonably sufficient to meet its expenses in complying with that section.

340A   Traded companies: duty to circulate members' matters for AGM

(1)   A company that is required under section 338A to include any matter in the business to be dealt with at an annual general meeting must—

    (a)   give notice of it to each member of the company entitled to receive notice of the annual general meeting—

        (i)   in the same manner as notice of the meeting, and

        (ii)   at the same time as, or as soon as reasonably practicable after, it gives notice of the meeting, and

    (b)   publish it on the same website as that on which the company published the information required by section 311A.

(2)   Subsection (1) has effect subject to section 340B(2) (deposit or tender of sum in respect of expenses of circulation).

(3)   In the event of default in complying with this section, an offence is committed by every officer of the company who is in default.

(4)   A person guilty of an offence under this section is liable—

    (a)   on conviction on indictment, to a fine;

    (b)   on summary conviction, to a fine not exceeding the statutory maximum.

340B   Traded companies: expenses of circulating members' matters to be dealt with at AGM

(1)   The expenses of the company in complying with section 340A need not be paid by the members who requested the inclusion of the matter in the business to be dealt with at the annual general meeting if requests sufficient to require the company to include the matter are received before the end of the financial year preceding the meeting.

(2)   Otherwise—

    (a)   the expenses of the company in complying with that section must be paid by the members who requested the inclusion of the matter unless the company resolves otherwise, and

    (b)   unless the company has previously so resolved, it is not bound to comply with that section unless there is deposited with or tendered to it, not later than—

        (i)   six weeks before the annual general meeting to which the requests relate, or

        (ii)   if later, the time at which notice is given of that meeting,

    a sum reasonably sufficient to meet its expenses in complying with that section.

CHAPTER 5
ADDITIONAL REQUIREMENTS FOR QUOTED COMPANIES AND TRADED COMPANIES

Website publication of poll results

341   Results of poll to be made available on website

(1)   Where a poll is taken at a general meeting of a quoted company that is not a traded company, the company must ensure that the following information is made available on a website—

    (a)   the date of the meeting,

    (b)   the text of the resolution or, as the case may be, a description of the subject matter of the poll,

    (c)   the number of votes cast in favour, and

    (d)   the number of votes cast against.

(1A)   Where a poll is taken at a general meeting of a traded company, the company must ensure that the following information is made available on a website—

    (a)   the date of the meeting,

    (b)   the text of the resolution or, as the case may be, a description of the subject matter of the poll,

    (c)   the number of votes validly cast,

    (d)   the proportion of the company's issued share capital (determined at the time at which the right to vote is determined under section 360B(2)) represented by those votes,

    (e)   the number of votes cast in favour,

    (f)   the number of votes cast against, and

    (g)   the number of abstentions (if counted).

(1B)   A traded company must comply with subsection (1A) by—

    (a)   the end of 16 days beginning with the day of the meeting, or

    (b)   if later, the end of the first working day after the day on which the result of the poll is declared.

(2)   The provisions of section 353 (requirements as to website availability) apply.

(3)   In the event of default in complying with this section (or with the requirements of section 353 as it applies for the purposes of this section), an offence is committed by every officer of the company who is in default.

(4)   A person guilty of an offence under subsection (3) is liable on summary conviction to a fine not exceeding level 3 on the standard scale.

(5)   Failure to comply with this section (or the requirements of section 353) does not affect the validity of—

    (a)   the poll, or

    (b)   the resolution or other business (if passed or agreed to) to which the poll relates.

(6)   This section only applies to polls taken after this section comes into force.

Independent report on poll

342   Members' power to require independent report on poll

(1)   The members of a quoted company may require the directors to obtain an independent report on any poll taken, or to be taken, at a general meeting of the company.

(2)   The directors are required to obtain an independent report if they receive requests to do so from—

    (a)   members representing not less than 5% of the total voting rights of all the members who have a right to vote on the matter to which the poll relates (excluding any voting rights attached to any shares in the company held as treasury shares), or

    (b)   not less than 100 members who have a right to vote on the matter to which the poll relates and hold shares in the company on which there has been paid up an average sum, per member, of not less than £100.

See also section 153 (exercise of rights where shares held on behalf of others).

(3)   Where the requests relate to more than one poll, subsection (2) must be satisfied in relation to each of them.

(4)   A request—

    (a)   may be in hard copy form or in electronic form,

    (b)   must identify the poll or polls to which it relates,

    (c)   must be authenticated by the person or persons making it, and

    (d)   must be received by the company not later than one week after the date on which the poll is taken.

343   Appointment of independent assessor

(1)   Directors who are required under section 342 to obtain an independent report on a poll or polls must appoint a person they consider to be appropriate (an "independent assessor") to prepare a report for the company on it or them.

(2)   The appointment must be made within one week after the company being required to obtain the report.

(3)   The directors must not appoint a person who—

    (a)   does not meet the independence requirement in section 344, or

    (b)   has another role in relation to any poll on which he is to report (including, in particular, a role in connection with collecting or counting votes or with the appointment of proxies).

(4)   In the event of default in complying with this section, an offence is committed by every officer of the company who is in default.

(5)   A person guilty of an offence under this section is liable on summary conviction to a fine not exceeding level 5 on the standard scale.

(6)   If at the meeting no poll on which a report is required is taken—

    (a)   the directors are not required to obtain a report from the independent assessor, and

    (b)   his appointment ceases (but without prejudice to any right to be paid for work done before the appointment ceased).

344   Independence requirement

(1)   A person may not be appointed as an independent assessor—

    (a)   if he is—

        (i)   an officer or employee of the company, or

        (ii)   a partner or employee of such a person, or a partnership of which such a person is a partner;

    (b)   if he is—

        (i)   an officer or employee of an associated undertaking of the company, or

        (ii)   a partner or employee of such a person, or a partnership of which such a person is a partner;

    (c)   if there exists between—

        (i)   the person or an associate of his, and

        (ii)   the company or an associated undertaking of the company, a connection of any such description as may be specified by regulations made by the Secretary of State.

(2)   An auditor of the company is not regarded as an officer or employee of the company for this purpose.

(3)   In this section—

"associated undertaking" means—

    (a)   a parent undertaking or subsidiary undertaking of the company, or

    (b)   a subsidiary undertaking of a parent undertaking of the company; and

"associate" has the meaning given by section 345.

(4)   Regulations under this section are subject to negative resolution procedure.

345   Meaning of "associate"

(1)   This section defines "associate" for the purposes of section 344 (independence requirement).

(2)   In relation to an individual, "associate" means—

  (a)   that individual's spouse or civil partner or minor child or step-child,
  (b)   any body corporate of which that individual is a director, and
  (c)   any employee or partner of that individual.
(3)   In relation to a body corporate, "associate" means—
  (a)   any body corporate of which that body is a director,
  (b)   any body corporate in the same group as that body, and
  (c)   any employee or partner of that body or of any body corporate in the same group.
(4)   In relation to a partnership that is a legal person under the law by which it is governed, "associate" means—
  (a)   any body corporate of which that partnership is a director,
  (b)   any employee of or partner in that partnership, and
  (c)   any person who is an associate of a partner in that partnership.
(5)   In relation to a partnership that is not a legal person under the law by which it is governed, "associate" means any person who is an associate of any of the partners.
(6)   In this section, in relation to a limited liability partnership, for "director" read "member".

346   Effect of appointment of a partnership
(1)   This section applies where a partnership that is not a legal person under the law by which it is governed is appointed as an independent assessor.
(2)   Unless a contrary intention appears, the appointment is of the partnership as such and not of the partners.
(3)   Where the partnership ceases, the appointment is to be treated as extending to—
  (a)   any partnership that succeeds to the practice of that partnership, or
  (b)   any other person who succeeds to that practice having previously carried it on in partnership.
(4)   For the purposes of subsection (3)—
  (a)   a partnership is regarded as succeeding to the practice of another partnership only if the members of the successor partnership are substantially the same as those of the former partnership, and
  (b)   a partnership or other person is regarded as succeeding to the practice of a partnership only if it or he succeeds to the whole or substantially the whole of the business of the former partnership.
(5)   Where the partnership ceases and the appointment is not treated under subsection (3) as extending to any partnership or other person, the appointment may with the consent of the company be treated as extending to a partnership, or other person, who succeeds to—
  (a)   the business of the former partnership, or
  (b)   such part of it as is agreed by the company is to be treated as comprising the appointment.

347   The independent assessor's report
(1)   The report of the independent assessor must state his opinion whether—
  (a)   the procedures adopted in connection with the poll or polls were adequate;
  (b)   the votes cast (including proxy votes) were fairly and accurately recorded and counted;
  (c)   the validity of members' appointments of proxies was fairly assessed;
  (d)   the notice of the meeting complied with section 325 (notice of meeting to contain statement of rights to appoint proxy);
  (e)   section 326 (company-sponsored invitations to appoint proxies) was complied with in relation to the meeting.
(2)   The report must give his reasons for the opinions stated.
(3)   If he is unable to form an opinion on any of those matters, the report must record that fact and state the reasons for it.
(4)   The report must state the name of the independent assessor.

348   Rights of independent assessor: right to attend meeting etc
(1)   Where an independent assessor has been appointed to report on a poll, he is entitled to attend—

      (a)   the meeting at which the poll may be taken, and

      (b)   any subsequent proceedings in connection with the poll.

(2)   He is also entitled to be provided by the company with a copy of—

      (a)   the notice of the meeting, and

      (b)   any other communication provided by the company in connection with the meeting to persons who have a right to vote on the matter to which the poll relates.

(3)   The rights conferred by this section are only to be exercised to the extent that the independent assessor considers necessary for the preparation of his report.

(4)   If the independent assessor is a firm, the right under subsection (1) to attend the meeting and any subsequent proceedings in connection with the poll is exercisable by an individual authorised by the firm in writing to act as its representative for that purpose.

349   Rights of independent assessor: right to information

(1)   The independent assessor is entitled to access to the company's records relating to—

      (a)   any poll on which he is to report;

      (b)   the meeting at which the poll or polls may be, or were, taken.

(2)   The independent assessor may require anyone who at any material time was—

      (a)   a director or secretary of the company,

      (b)   an employee of the company,

      (c)   a person holding or accountable for any of the company's records,

      (d)   a member of the company, or

      (e)   an agent of the company,

     to provide him with information or explanations for the purpose of preparing his report.

(3)   For this purpose "agent" includes the company's bankers, solicitors and auditor.

(4)   A statement made by a person in response to a requirement under this section may not be used in evidence against him in criminal proceedings except proceedings for an offence under section 350 (offences relating to provision of information).

(5)   A person is not required by this section to disclose information in respect of which a claim to legal professional privilege (in Scotland, to confidentiality of communications) could be maintained in legal proceedings.

350   Offences relating to provision of information

(1)   A person who fails to comply with a requirement under section 349 without delay commits an offence unless it was not reasonably practicable for him to provide the required information or explanation.

(2)   A person guilty of an offence under subsection (1) is liable on summary conviction to a fine not exceeding level 3 on the standard scale.

(3)   A person commits an offence who knowingly or recklessly makes to an independent assessor a statement (oral or written) that—

      (a)   conveys or purports to convey any information or explanations which the independent assessor requires, or is entitled to require, under section 349, and

      (b)   is misleading, false or deceptive in a material particular.

(4)   A person guilty of an offence under subsection (3) is liable—

      (a)   on conviction on indictment, to imprisonment for a term not exceeding two years or a fine (or both);

      (b)   on summary conviction—

         (i)   in England and Wales, to imprisonment for a term not exceeding twelve months or to a fine not exceeding the statutory maximum (or both);

         (ii)   in Scotland or Northern Ireland, to imprisonment for a term not exceeding six months, or to a fine not exceeding the statutory maximum (or both).

(5)   Nothing in this section affects any right of an independent assessor to apply for an injunction (in Scotland, an interdict or an order for specific performance) to enforce any of his rights under section 348 or 349.

351   Information to be made available on website

(1)   Where an independent assessor has been appointed to report on a poll, the company must ensure
         that the following information is made available on a website—
         (a)   the fact of his appointment,
         (b)   his identity,
         (c)   the text of the resolution or, as the case may be, a description of the subject matter of the
               poll to which his appointment relates, and
         (d)   a copy of a report by him which complies with section 347.

(2)   The provisions of section 353 (requirements as to website availability) apply.

(3)   In the event of default in complying with this section (or with the requirements of section 353 as
         it applies for the purposes of this section), an offence is committed by every officer of the
         company who is in default.

(4)   A person guilty of an offence under subsection (3) is liable on summary conviction to a fine not
         exceeding level 3 on the standard scale.

(5)   Failure to comply with this section (or the requirements of section 353) does not affect the
         validity of—
         (a)   the poll, or
         (b)   the resolution or other business (if passed or agreed to) to which the poll relates.

Supplementary

352   Application of provisions to class meetings

(1)   The provisions of section 341 (results of poll to be made available on website) apply (with any
         necessary modifications) in relation to a meeting of holders of a class of shares of a quoted
         company or traded company in connection with the variation of the rights attached to such shares
         as they apply in relation to a general meeting of the company.

(1A)   The provisions of section 342 to 351 (independent report on poll) apply (with any necessary
         modifications) in relation to a meeting of holders of a class of shares of a quoted company in
         connection with the variation of the rights attached to such shares as they apply in relation to a
         general meeting of the company.

(2)   For the purposes of this section—
         (a)   any amendment of a provision contained in a company's articles for the variation of the
               rights attached to a class of shares, or the insertion of any such provision into the articles, is
               itself to be treated as a variation of those rights, and
         (b)   references to the variation of rights attached to a class of shares include references to their
               abrogation.

353   Requirements as to website availability

(1)   The following provisions apply for the purposes of—
         section 341 (results of poll to be made available on website), and
         section 351 (report of independent observer to be made available on website).

(2)   The information must be made available on a website that—
         (a)   is maintained by or on behalf of the company, and
         (b)   identifies the company in question.

(3)   Access to the information on the website, and the ability to obtain a hard copy of the information
         from the website, must not be conditional on the payment of a fee or otherwise restricted.

(4)   The information—
         (a)   must be made available as soon as reasonably practicable, and
         (b)   must be kept available throughout the period of two years beginning with the date on which
               it is first made available on a website in accordance with this section.

(5)   A failure to make information available on a website throughout the period specified in
         subsection (4)(b) is disregarded if—
         (a)   the information is made available on the website for part of that period, and

(b)   the failure is wholly attributable to circumstances that it would not be reasonable to have expected the company to prevent or avoid.

354   Power to limit or extend the types of company to which provisions of this Chapter apply

(1)   The Secretary of State may by regulations—
(a)   limit the types of company to which some or all of the provisions of this Chapter apply, or
(b)   extend some or all of the provisions of this Chapter to additional types of company.

(2)   Regulations under this section extending the application of any provision of this Chapter are subject to affirmative resolution procedure.

(3)   Any other regulations under this section are subject to negative resolution procedure.

(4)   Regulations under this section may—
(a)   amend the provisions of this Chapter (apart from this section);
(b)   repeal and re-enact provisions of this Chapter with modifications of form or arrangement, whether or not they are modified in substance;
(c)   contain such consequential, incidental and supplementary provisions (including provisions amending, repealing or revoking enactments) as the Secretary of State thinks fit.

CHAPTER 6
RECORDS OF RESOLUTIONS AND MEETINGS

355   Records of resolutions and meetings etc

(1)   Every company must keep records comprising—
(a)   copies of all resolutions of members passed otherwise than at general meetings,
(b)   minutes of all proceedings of general meetings, and
(c)   details provided to the company in accordance with section 357 (decisions of sole member).

(2)   The records must be kept for at least ten years from the date of the resolution, meeting or decision (as appropriate).

(3)   If a company fails to comply with this section, an offence is committed by every officer of the company who is in default.

(4)   A person guilty of an offence under this section is liable on summary conviction to a fine not exceeding level 3 on the standard scale and, for continued contravention, a daily default fine not exceeding one-tenth of level 3 on the standard scale.

356   Records as evidence of resolutions etc

(1)   This section applies to the records kept in accordance with section 355.

(2)   The record of a resolution passed otherwise than at a general meeting, if purporting to be signed by a director of the company or by the company secretary, is evidence (in Scotland, sufficient evidence) of the passing of the resolution.

(3)   Where there is a record of a written resolution of a private company, the requirements of this Act with respect to the passing of the resolution are deemed to be complied with unless the contrary is proved.

(4)   The minutes of proceedings of a general meeting, if purporting to be signed by the chairman of that meeting or by the chairman of the next general meeting, are evidence (in Scotland, sufficient evidence) of the proceedings at the meeting.

(5)   Where there is a record of proceedings of a general meeting of a company, then, until the contrary is proved—
(a)   the meeting is deemed duly held and convened,
(b)   all proceedings at the meeting are deemed to have duly taken place, and
(c)   all appointments at the meeting are deemed valid.

357   Records of decisions by sole member

(1)   This section applies to a company limited by shares or by guarantee that has only one member.

(2)   Where the member takes any decision that—
(a)   may be taken by the company in general meeting, and

(b) has effect as if agreed by the company in general meeting, he must (unless that decision is taken by way of a written resolution) provide the company with details of that decision.

(3) If a person fails to comply with this section he commits an offence.

(4) A person guilty of an offence under this section is liable on summary conviction to a fine not exceeding level 2 on the standard scale.

(5) Failure to comply with this section does not affect the validity of any decision referred to in subsection (2).

358 Inspection of records of resolutions and meetings

(1) The records referred to in section 355 (records of resolutions etc) relating to the previous ten years must be kept available for inspection—
(a) at the company's registered office, or
(b) at a place specified in regulations under section 1136.

(2) The company must give notice to the registrar—
(a) of the place at which the records are kept available for inspection, and
(b) of any change in that place,
unless they have at all times been kept at the company's registered office.

(3) The records must be open to the inspection of any member of the company without charge.

(4) Any member may require a copy of any of the records on payment of such fee as may be prescribed.

(5) If default is made for 14 days in complying with subsection (2) or an inspection required under subsection (3) is refused, or a copy requested under subsection (4) is not sent, an offence is committed by every officer of the company who is in default.

(6) A person guilty of an offence under this section is liable on summary conviction to a fine not exceeding level 3 on the standard scale and, for continued contravention, a daily default fine not exceeding one-tenth of level 3 on the standard scale.

(7) In a case in which an inspection required under subsection (3) is refused or a copy requested under subsection (4) is not sent, the court may by order compel an immediate inspection of the records or direct that the copies required be sent to the persons who requested them.

359 Records of resolutions and meetings of class of members

The provisions of this Chapter apply (with necessary modifications) in relation to resolutions and meetings of—
(a) holders of a class of shares, and
(b) in the case of a company without a share capital, a class of members, as they apply in relation to resolutions of members generally and to general meetings.

CHAPTER 7
SUPPLEMENTARY PROVISIONS

360 Computation of periods of notice etc: clear day rule

(1) This section applies for the purposes of the following provisions of this Part—
section 307(1) and (2) (notice required of general meeting),
section 307A(1), (4), (5) and (7)(b) (notice required of general meeting of traded company),
section 312(1) and (3) (resolution requiring special notice),
section 314(4)(d) (request to circulate members' statement),
section 316(2)(b) (expenses of circulating statement to be deposited or tendered before meeting),
section 337(3) (contents of notice of AGM of traded company),
section 338(4)(d)(i) (request to circulate member's resolution at AGM of public company), ...
section 338A(5) (request to include matter in the business to be dealt with at AGM of traded company),
section 340(2)(b)(i) (expenses of circulating statement to be deposited or tendered before meeting), and
section 340B(2)(b) (traded companies: duty to circulate members' matters for AGM).

(2)   Any reference in those provisions to a period of notice, or to a period before a meeting by which a request must be received or sum deposited or tendered, is to a period of the specified length excluding—
(a)   the day of the meeting, and
(b)   the day on which the notice is given, the request received or the sum deposited or tendered.

360A   Electronic meetings and voting

(1)   Nothing in this Part is to be taken to preclude the holding and conducting of a meeting in such a way that persons who are not present together at the same place may by electronic means attend and speak and vote at it.

(2)   In the case of a traded company the use of electronic means for the purpose of enabling members to participate in a general meeting may be made subject only to such requirements and restrictions as are—
(a)   necessary to ensure the identification of those taking part and the security of the electronic communication, and
(b)   proportionate to the achievement of those objectives.

(3)   Nothing in subsection (2) affects any power of a company to require reasonable evidence of the entitlement of any person who is not a member to participate in the meeting.

360AA   Traded companies: confirmation of receipt of electronic voting

(1)   In the case of a traded company, where a vote is cast on a poll by electronic means the company must ensure that, as soon as reasonably practicable after the vote has been received, confirmation of receipt of the vote is sent by electronic means to—
(a)   the member, where that person cast the vote,
(b)   the proxy, where the vote was cast by proxy, or
(c)   the representative, where the vote was cast by a person authorised to act as a representative of a corporation in accordance with section 323(1).

(2)   A vote under subsection (1) includes any vote cast—
(a)   at a meeting;
(b)   at an electronic meeting conducted in accordance with section 360A;
(c)   in advance of a meeting or electronic meeting (see section 322A).

360B   Traded companies: requirements for participating in and voting at general meetings

(1)   Any provision of a traded company's articles is void in so far as it would have the effect of—
(a)   imposing a restriction on a right of a member to participate in and vote at a general meeting of the company unless the member's shares have (after having been acquired by the member and before the meeting) been deposited with, or transferred to, or registered in the name of another person, or
(b)   imposing a restriction on the right of a member to transfer shares in the company during the period of 48 hours before the time for the holding of a general meeting of the company if that right would not otherwise be subject to that restriction.

(2)   A traded company must determine the right to vote at a general meeting of the company by reference to the register of members as at a time (determined by the company) that is not more than 48 hours before the time for the holding of the meeting.

(3)   In calculating the period mentioned in subsection (1)(b) or (2), no account is to be taken of any part of a day that is not a working day.

(4)   Nothing in this section affects—
(a)   the operation of—
(i)   Part 22 of this Act (information about interests in a company's shares),
(ii)   Part 15 of the Companies Act 1985 (orders imposing restrictions on shares), or
(iii)   any provision in a company's articles relating to the application of any provision of either of those Parts; or
(b)   the validity of articles prescribed, or to the same effect as articles prescribed, under section 19 of this Act (power of Secretary of State to prescribe model articles).

(5)   If an election is in force under section 128B in respect of a company, the reference in subsection
       (2) to the register of members is to be read as a reference to the register kept by the registrar under
       section 1080.

360BA Traded companies: right to confirmation of vote after a general meeting

(1)   Where the conditions in subsection (2) are met, a traded company must provide information to a
       member which enables the member to confirm that their vote on a resolution at a general meeting
       where a poll has been taken has been validly recorded and counted.

(2)   The conditions are that—
       (a)   the member makes a request for the information, which request is received by the company
              no later than 30 days from the date of that general meeting, and
       (b)   the member does not have any other reasonable means by which to determine that their vote
              has been validly recorded and counted by the company.

(3)   The information under subsection (1) must be provided to the member as soon as reasonably
       practicable and in any event by the end of the period of 15 days beginning with whichever is the
       later of the first working day after the day on which—
       (a)   the result of the poll is declared for that resolution; or
       (b)   the request for information under subsection (2)(a) is received by the company.

360C   Meaning of "traded company"

       In this Part, "traded company" means a company any shares of which—
       (a)   carry rights to vote at general meetings, and
       (b)   are admitted to trading on a UK regulated market or an EU regulated market by or with the
              consent of the company.

361   Meaning of "quoted company"

       In this Part "quoted company" has the same meaning as in Part 15 of this Act.

...

PART 15
ACCOUNTS AND REPORTS

CHAPTER 1
INTRODUCTION

General

380   Scheme of this Part

(1)   The requirements of this Part as to accounts and reports apply in relation to each financial year of
       a company.

(2)   In certain respects different provisions apply to different kinds of company.

(3), (4) ...

(4)   In this Part, where provisions do not apply to all kinds of company—
       (a)   provisions applying to companies subject to the small companies regime appear before the
              provisions applying to other companies,
       (b)   provisions applying to private companies appear before the provisions applying to public
              companies, and
       (c)   provisions applying to quoted companies appear after the provisions applying to other
              companies.

Companies subject to the small companies regime

381   Companies subject to the small companies regime

       The small companies regime ... applies to a company for a financial year in relation to which the
       company—

(a)   qualifies as small (see sections 382 and 383), and

(b)   is not excluded from the regime (see section 384).

382   Companies qualifying as small: general

(1)   A company qualifies as small in relation to its first financial year if the qualifying conditions are met in that year.

(1A)   Subject to subsection (2), a company qualifies as small in relation to a subsequent financial year if the qualifying conditions are met in that year.

(2)   In relation to a subsequent financial year, where on its balance sheet date a company meets or ceases to meet the qualifying conditions, that affects its qualification as a small company only if it occurs in two consecutive financial years.

(3)   The qualifying conditions are met by a company in a year in which it satisfies two or more of the following requirements—

1.	Turnover	Not more than £10.2 million
2.	Balance sheet total	Not more than £5.1 million
3.	Number of employees	Not more than 50

(4)   For a period that is a company's financial year but not in fact a year the maximum figures for turnover must be proportionately adjusted.

(5)   The balance sheet total means the aggregate of the amounts shown as assets in the company's balance sheet.

(6)   The number of employees means the average number of persons employed by the company in the year, determined as follows—

(a)   find for each month in the financial year the number of persons employed under contracts of service by the company in that month (whether throughout the month or not),

(b)   add together the monthly totals, and

(c)   divide by the number of months in the financial year.

(7)   This section is subject to section 383 (companies qualifying as small: parent companies).

383   Companies qualifying as small: parent companies

(1)   A parent company qualifies as a small company in relation to a financial year only if the group headed by it qualifies as a small group.

(2)   A group qualifies as small in relation to the parent company's first financial year if the qualifying conditions are met in that year.

(2A)   Subject to subsection (3), a group qualifies as small in relation to a subsequent financial year of the parent company if the qualifying conditions are met in that year.

(3)   In relation to a subsequent financial year of the parent company, where on the parent company's balance sheet date the group meets or ceases to meet the qualifying conditions, that affects the group's qualification as a small group only if it occurs in two consecutive financial years.

(4)   The qualifying conditions are met by a group in a year in which it satisfies two or more of the following requirements—

1.	Aggregate turnover	Not more than £10.2 million net (or £12.2 million gross)
2.	Aggregate balance sheet total	Not more than £5.1 million net (or £6.1 million gross)
3.	Aggregate number of employees	Not more than 50

(5)   The aggregate figures are ascertained by aggregating the relevant figures determined in accordance with section 382 for each member of the group.

(6)   In relation to the aggregate figures for turnover and balance sheet total—

"net" means after any set-offs and other adjustments made to eliminate group transactions—

(a)   in the case of Companies Act accounts, in accordance with regulations under section 404,

(b)   in the case of IAS accounts, in accordance with UK-adopted international accounting standards; and

"gross" means without those set-offs and other adjustments.

A company may satisfy any relevant requirement on the basis of either the net or the gross figure.

(7)   The figures for each subsidiary undertaking shall be those included in its individual accounts for the relevant financial year, that is—

    (a) if its financial year ends with that of the parent company, that financial year, and

    (b) if not, its financial year ending last before the end of the financial year of the parent company.

    If those figures cannot be obtained without disproportionate expense or undue delay, the latest available figures shall be taken.

384   Companies excluded from the small companies regime

(1)   The small companies regime does not apply to a company that ... was at any time within the financial year to which the accounts relate—

    (a) a public company,

    (b) a company that—

        (i)   is an authorised insurance company, a banking company, an e-money issuer, a MiFID investment firm or a UCITS management company, ...

        (ii)   carries on insurance market activity, or

        (iii) is a scheme funder of a Master Trust scheme within the meanings given by section 39(1) of the Pension Schemes Act 2017 (interpretation of Part 1), or

    (c) a member of an ineligible group.

(2)   A group is ineligible if any of its members is—

    (a) a traded company,

    (b) a body corporate (other than a company) whose shares are admitted to trading on a UK regulated market,

    (c) a person (other than a small company) who has permission under Part 4A of the Financial Services and Markets Act 2000 to carry on a regulated activity,

    (ca) an e-money issuer,

    (d) a small company that is an authorised insurance company, a banking company, ... a MiFID investment firm or a UCITS management company, ...

    (e) a person who carries on insurance market activity, or

    (f) a scheme funder of a Master Trust scheme within the meanings given by section 39(1) of the Pension Schemes Act 2017 (interpretation of Part 1).

(3)   A company is a small company for the purposes of subsection (2) if it qualified as small in relation to its last financial year ending on or before the end of the financial year to which the accounts relate.

384A   Companies qualifying as micro-entities

(1)   A company qualifies as a micro-entity in relation to its first financial year if the qualifying conditions are met in that year.

(2)   Subject to subsection (3), a company qualifies as a micro-entity in relation to a subsequent financial year if the qualifying conditions are met in that year.

(3)   In relation to a subsequent financial year, where on its balance sheet date a company meets or ceases to meet the qualifying conditions, that affects its qualification as a micro-entity only if it occurs in two consecutive financial years.

(4)   The qualifying conditions are met by a company in a year in which it satisfies two or more of the following requirements—

1.	Turnover	Not more than £632,000
2.	Balance sheet total	Not more than £316,000
3.	Number of employees	Not more than 10

(5)   For a period that is a company's financial year but not in fact a year the maximum figures for turnover must be proportionately adjusted.

(6)   The balance sheet total means the aggregate of the amounts shown as assets in the company's balance sheet.

(7) The number of employees means the average number of persons employed by the company in the year, determined as follows—

    (a) find for each month in the financial year the number of persons employed under contracts of service by the company in that month (whether throughout the month or not),

    (b) add together the monthly totals, and

    (c) divide by the number of months in the financial year.

(8) In the case of a company which is a parent company, the company qualifies as a micro-entity in relation to a financial year only if—

    (a) the company qualifies as a micro-entity in relation to that year, as determined by subsections (1) to (7), and

    (b) the group headed by the company qualifies as a small group, as determined by section 383(2) to (7).

384B Companies excluded from being treated as micro-entities

(1) The micro-entity provisions do not apply in relation to a company's accounts for a particular financial year if the company … at any time within that year—

    (a) was a company excluded from the small companies regime by virtue of section 384,

    (b) would have been an investment undertaking as defined in Article 2(14) of Directive 2013/34/EU of 26 June 2013 on the annual financial statements etc of certain types of undertakings were the United Kingdom a member State,

    (c) would have been a financial holding undertaking as defined in Article 2(15) of that Directive were the United Kingdom a member State,

    (d) a credit institution within the meaning given by Article 4(1)(1) of Regulation (EU) No. 575/2013 of the European Parliament and of the Council, which is a CRR firm within the meaning of Article 4(1)(2A) of that Regulation,

    (e) would have been an insurance undertaking as defined in Article 2(1) of Council Directive 91/674/EEC of 19 December 1991 on the annual accounts of insurance undertakings were the United Kingdom a member State, or

    (f) was a charity.

(2) The micro-entity provisions also do not apply in relation to a company's accounts for a financial year if—

    (a) the company is a parent company which prepares group accounts for that year as permitted by section 399(4), or

    (b) the company is not a parent company but its accounts are included in consolidated group accounts for that year.

Quoted and unquoted companies

385 Quoted and unquoted companies

(1) For the purposes of this Part a company is a quoted company in relation to a financial year if it is a quoted company immediately before the end of the accounting reference period by reference to which that financial year was determined.

(2) A "quoted company" means a company whose equity share capital—

    (a) has been included in the official list in accordance with the provisions of Part 6 of the Financial Services and Markets Act 2000, or

    (b) is officially listed in an EEA State, or

    (c) is admitted to dealing on either the New York Stock Exchange or the exchange known as Nasdaq.

In paragraph (a) "the official list" has the meaning given by section 103(1) of the Financial Services and Markets Act 2000.

(3) An "unquoted company" means a company that is not a quoted company.

(4) The Secretary of State may by regulations amend or replace the provisions of subsections (1) to (2) so as to limit or extend the application of some or all of the provisions of this Part that are expressed to apply to quoted companies.

(5)   Regulations under this section extending the application of any such provision of this Part are subject to affirmative resolution procedure.

(6)   Any other regulations under this section are subject to negative resolution procedure.

CHAPTER 2
ACCOUNTING RECORDS

386   Duty to keep accounting records

(1)   Every company must keep adequate accounting records.

(2)   Adequate accounting records means records that are sufficient—

   (a)   to show and explain the company's transactions,

   (b)   to disclose with reasonable accuracy, at any time, the financial position of the company at that time, and

   (c)   to enable the directors to ensure that any accounts required to be prepared comply with the requirements of this Act ....

(3)   Accounting records must, in particular, contain—

   (a)   entries from day to day of all sums of money received and expended by the company and the matters in respect of which the receipt and expenditure takes place, and

   (b)   a record of the assets and liabilities of the company.

(4)   If the company's business involves dealing in goods, the accounting records must contain—

   (a)   statements of stock held by the company at the end of each financial year of the company,

   (b)   all statements of stocktakings from which any statement of stock as is mentioned in paragraph (a) has been or is to be prepared, and

   (c)   except in the case of goods sold by way of ordinary retail trade, statements of all goods sold and purchased, showing the goods and the buyers and sellers in sufficient detail to enable all these to be identified.

(5)   A parent company that has a subsidiary undertaking in relation to which the above requirements do not apply must take reasonable steps to secure that the undertaking keeps such accounting records as to enable the directors of the parent company to ensure that any accounts required to be prepared under this Part comply with the requirements of this Act ....

387   Duty to keep accounting records: offence

(1)   If a company fails to comply with any provision of section 386 (duty to keep accounting records), an offence is committed by every officer of the company who is in default.

(2)   It is a defence for a person charged with such an offence to show that he acted honestly and that in the circumstances in which the company's business was carried on the default was excusable.

(3)   A person guilty of an offence under this section is liable—

   (a)   on conviction on indictment, to imprisonment for a term not exceeding two years or a fine (or both);

   (b)   on summary conviction—

       (i)   in England and Wales, to imprisonment for a term not exceeding twelve months or to a fine not exceeding the statutory maximum (or both);

       (ii)   in Scotland or Northern Ireland, to imprisonment for a term not exceeding six months, or to a fine not exceeding the statutory maximum (or both).

388   Where and for how long records to be kept

(1)   A company's accounting records—

   (a)   must be kept at its registered office or such other place as the directors think fit, and

   (b)   must at all times be open to inspection by the company's officers.

(2)   If accounting records are kept at a place outside the United Kingdom, accounts and returns with respect to the business dealt with in the accounting records so kept must be sent to, and kept at, a place in the United Kingdom, and must at all times be open to such inspection.

(3)   The accounts and returns to be sent to the United Kingdom must be such as to—

(a) disclose with reasonable accuracy the financial position of the business in question at intervals of not more than six months, and

(b) enable the directors to ensure that the accounts required to be prepared under this Part comply with the requirements of this Act ...

(4) Accounting records that a company is required by section 386 to keep must be preserved by it—

(a) in the case of a private company, for three years from the date on which they are made;

(b) in the case of a public company, for six years from the date on which they are made.

(5) Subsection (4) is subject to any provision contained in rules made under section 411 of the Insolvency Act 1986 (company insolvency rules) or Article 359 of the Insolvency (Northern Ireland) Order 1989.

389 Where and for how long records to be kept: offences

(1) If a company fails to comply with any provision of subsections (1) to (3) of section 388 (requirements as to keeping of accounting records), an offence is committed by every officer of the company who is in default.

(2) It is a defence for a person charged with such an offence to show that he acted honestly and that in the circumstances in which the company's business was carried on the default was excusable.

(3) An officer of a company commits an offence if he—

(a) fails to take all reasonable steps for securing compliance by the company with subsection (4) of that section (period for which records to be preserved), or

(b) intentionally causes any default by the company under that subsection.

(4) A person guilty of an offence under this section is liable—

(a) on conviction on indictment, to imprisonment for a term not exceeding two years or a fine (or both);

(b) on summary conviction—

(i) in England and Wales, to imprisonment for a term not exceeding twelve months or to a fine not exceeding the statutory maximum (or both);

(ii) in Scotland or Northern Ireland, to imprisonment for a term not exceeding six months, or to a fine not exceeding the statutory maximum (or both).

CHAPTER 3
A COMPANY'S FINANCIAL YEAR

390 A company's financial year

(1) A company's financial year is determined as follows.

(2) Its first financial year—

(a) begins with the first day of its first accounting reference period, and

(b) ends with the last day of that period or such other date, not more than seven days before or after the end of that period, as the directors may determine.

(3) Subsequent financial years—

(a) begin with the day immediately following the end of the company's previous financial year, and

(b) end with the last day of its next accounting reference period or such other date, not more than seven days before or after the end of that period, as the directors may determine.

(4) In relation to an undertaking that is not a company, references in this Act to its financial year are to any period in respect of which a profit and loss account of the undertaking is required to be made up (by its constitution or by the law under which it is established), whether that period is a year or not.

(5) The directors of a parent company must secure that, except where in their opinion there are good reasons against it, the financial year of each of its subsidiary undertakings coincides with the company's own financial year.

391   Accounting reference periods and accounting reference date

(1)   A company's accounting reference periods are determined according to its accounting reference date in each calendar year.

(2)   The accounting reference date of a company incorporated in Great Britain before 1st April 1996 is—

    (a)   the date specified by notice to the registrar in accordance with section 224(2) of the Companies Act 1985 (notice specifying accounting reference date given within nine months of incorporation), or

    (b)   failing such notice—

        (i)   in the case of a company incorporated before 1st April 1990, 31st March, and

        (ii)   in the case of a company incorporated on or after 1st April 1990, the last day of the month in which the anniversary of its incorporation falls.

(3)   The accounting reference date of a company incorporated in Northern Ireland before 22nd August 1997 is—

    (a)   the date specified by notice to the registrar in accordance with article 232(2) of the Companies (Northern Ireland) Order 1986 (notice specifying accounting reference date given within nine months of incorporation), or

    (b)   failing such notice—

        (i)   in the case of a company incorporated before the coming into operation of Article 5 of the Companies (Northern Ireland) Order 1990, 31st March, and

        (ii)   in the case of a company incorporated after the coming into operation of that Article, the last day of the month in which the anniversary of its incorporation falls.

(4)   The accounting reference date of a company incorporated—

    (a)   in Great Britain on or after 1st April 1996 and before the commencement of this Act,

    (b)   in Northern Ireland on or after 22nd August 1997 and before the commencement of this Act, or

    (c)   after the commencement of this Act,

    is the last day of the month in which the anniversary of its incorporation falls.

(5)   A company's first accounting reference period is the period of more than six months, but not more than 18 months, beginning with the date of its incorporation and ending with its accounting reference date.

(6)   Its subsequent accounting reference periods are successive periods of twelve months beginning immediately after the end of the previous accounting reference period and ending with its accounting reference date.

(7)   This section has effect subject to the provisions of section 392 (alteration of accounting reference date).

392   Alteration of accounting reference date

(1)   A company may by notice given to the registrar specify a new accounting reference date having effect in relation to—

    (a)   the company's current accounting reference period and subsequent periods, or

    (b)   the company's previous accounting reference period and subsequent periods.

    A company's "previous accounting reference period" means the one immediately preceding its current accounting reference period.

(2)   The notice must state whether the current or previous accounting reference period—

    (a)   is to be shortened, so as to come to an end on the first occasion on which the new accounting reference date falls or fell after the beginning of the period, or

    (b)   is to be extended, so as to come to an end on the second occasion on which that date falls or fell after the beginning of the period.

(3)   A notice extending a company's current or previous accounting reference period is not effective if given less than five years after the end of an earlier accounting reference period of the company that was extended under this section.

    This does not apply—

(a) to a notice given by a company that is a subsidiary undertaking or parent undertaking of another UK undertaking if the new accounting reference date coincides with that of the other UK undertaking or, where that undertaking is not a company, with the last day of its financial year, or

(b) where the company is in administration under Part 2 of the Insolvency Act 1986 or Part 3 of the Insolvency (Northern Ireland) Order 1989, or

(c) where the Secretary of State directs that it should not apply, which he may do with respect to a notice that has been given or that may be given.

(4) A notice under this section may not be given in respect of a previous accounting reference period if the period for filing accounts and reports for the financial year determined by reference to that accounting reference period has already expired.

(5) An accounting reference period may not be extended so as to exceed 18 months and a notice under this section is ineffective if the current or previous accounting reference period as extended in accordance with the notice would exceed that limit.

This does not apply where the company is in administration under Part 2 of the Insolvency Act 1986 or Part 3 of the Insolvency (Northern Ireland) Order 1989.

(6) In this section "UK undertaking" means an undertaking established under the law of any part of the United Kingdom ....

CHAPTER 4
ANNUAL ACCOUNTS

General

393 Accounts to give true and fair view

(1) The directors of a company must not approve accounts for the purposes of this Chapter unless they are satisfied that they give a true and fair view of the assets, liabilities, financial position and profit or loss—

(a) in the case of the company's individual accounts, of the company;

(b) in the case of the company's group accounts, of the undertakings included in the consolidation as a whole, so far as concerns members of the company.

(1A) The following provisions apply to the directors of a company which qualifies as a micro-entity in relation to a financial year (see sections 384A and 384B) in their consideration of whether the Companies Act individual accounts of the company for that year give a true and fair view as required by subsection (1)(a)—

(a) where the accounts comprise only micro-entity minimum accounting items, the directors must disregard any provision of an accounting standard which would require the accounts to contain information additional to those items,

(b) in relation to a micro-entity minimum accounting item contained in the accounts, the directors must disregard any provision of an accounting standard which would require the accounts to contain further information in relation to that item, and

(c) where the accounts contain an item of information additional to the micro-entity minimum accounting items, the directors must have regard to any provision of an accounting standard which relates to that item.

(2) The auditor of a company in carrying out his functions under this Act in relation to the company's annual accounts must have regard to the directors' duty under subsection (1).

Individual accounts

394 Duty to prepare individual accounts

The directors of every company must prepare accounts for the company for each of its financial years unless the company is exempt from that requirement under section 394A.

Those accounts are referred to as the company's "individual accounts".

394A Individual accounts: exemption for dormant subsidiaries

(1) A company is exempt from the requirement to prepare individual accounts for a financial year if—

 (a) it is itself a subsidiary undertaking,

 (b) it has been dormant throughout the whole of that year, and

 (c) its parent undertaking is established under the law of any part of the United Kingdom.

(2) Exemption is conditional upon compliance with all of the following conditions—

 (a) all members of the company must agree to the exemption in respect of the financial year in question,

 (b) the parent undertaking must give a guarantee under section 394C in respect of that year,

 (c) the company must be included in the consolidated accounts drawn up for that year or to an earlier date in that year by the parent undertaking in accordance with—

  (i) if the undertaking is a company, the requirements of this Part of this Act, or, if the undertaking is not a company, the legal requirements which apply to the drawing up of consolidated accounts for that undertaking, or

  (ii) UK-adopted international accounting standards,

 (d) the parent undertaking must disclose in the notes to the consolidated accounts that the company is exempt from the requirement to prepare individual accounts by virtue of this section, and

 (e) the directors of the company must deliver to the registrar within the period for filing the company's accounts and reports for that year—

  (i) a written notice of the agreement referred to in subsection (2)(a),

  (ii) the statement referred to in section 394C(1),

  (iii) a copy of the consolidated accounts referred to in subsection (2)(c),

  (iv) a copy of the auditor's report on those accounts, and

  (v) a copy of the consolidated annual report drawn up by the parent undertaking.

394B Companies excluded from the dormant subsidiaries exemption

A company is not entitled to the exemption conferred by section 394A (dormant subsidiaries) if it was at any time within the financial year in question—

(a) a traded company,

(b) a company that—

 (i) is an authorised insurance company, a banking company, an e-money issuer, a MiFID investment firm or a UCITS management company, or

 (ii) carries on insurance market activity, or

(c) a special register body as defined in section 117(1) of the Trade Union and Labour Relations (Consolidation) Act 1992 (c 52) or an employers' association as defined in section 122 of that Act or Article 4 of the Industrial Relations (Northern Ireland) Order 1992 (SI 1992/807) (NI 5).

394C Dormant subsidiaries exemption: parent undertaking declaration of guarantee

(1) A guarantee is given by a parent undertaking under this section when the directors of the subsidiary company deliver to the registrar a statement by the parent undertaking that it guarantees the subsidiary company under this section.

(2) The statement under subsection (1) must be authenticated by the parent undertaking and must specify—

 (a) the name of the parent undertaking,

 (b) the registered number (if any) of the parent undertaking,

 (c) ...

 (d) the name and registered number of the subsidiary company in respect of which the guarantee is being given,

 (e) the date of the statement, and

 (f) the financial year to which the guarantee relates.

(3)   A guarantee given under this section has the effect that—

    (a)   the parent undertaking guarantees all outstanding liabilities to which the subsidiary company is subject at the end of the financial year to which the guarantee relates, until they are satisfied in full, and

    (b)   the guarantee is enforceable against the parent undertaking by any person to whom the subsidiary company is liable in respect of those liabilities.

395   Individual accounts: applicable accounting framework

(1)   A company's individual accounts may be prepared—

    (a)   in accordance with section 396 ("Companies Act individual accounts"), or

    (b)   in accordance with UK-adopted international accounting standards ("IAS individual accounts").

This is subject to the following provisions of this section and to section 407 (consistency of financial reporting within group).

(2)   The individual accounts of a company that is a charity must be Companies Act individual accounts.

(3)   After the first financial year in which the directors of a company prepare IAS individual accounts ("the first IAS year"), all subsequent individual accounts of the company must be prepared in accordance with UK-adopted international accounting standards unless there is a relevant change of circumstance.

This is subject to subsection (4A).

(4)   There is a relevant change of circumstance if, at any time during or after the first IAS year—

    (a)   the company becomes a subsidiary undertaking of another undertaking that does not prepare IAS individual accounts,

    (aa) the company ceases to be a subsidiary undertaking,

    (b)   the company ceases to be a company with securities admitted to trading on a UK regulated market, or

    (c)   a parent undertaking of the company ceases to be an undertaking with securities admitted to trading on a UK regulated market.

(4A)   After a financial year in which the directors of a company prepare IAS individual accounts for the company, the directors may change to preparing Companies Act individual accounts for a reason other than a relevant change of circumstance provided they have not changed to Companies Act individual accounts in the period of five years preceding the first day of that financial year.

(4B)   In calculating the five year period for the purpose of subsection (4A), no account should be taken of a change due to a relevant change of circumstance.

(5)   If, having changed to preparing Companies Act individual accounts ..., the directors again prepare IAS individual accounts for the company, subsections (3) and (4) apply again as if the first financial year for which such accounts are again prepared were the first IAS year.

396   Companies Act individual accounts

(A1)   Companies Act individual accounts must state—

    (a)   the part of the United Kingdom in which the company is registered,

    (b)   the company's registered number,

    (c)   whether the company is a public or a private company and whether it is limited by shares or by guarantee,

    (d)   the address of the company's registered office, and

    (e)   where appropriate, the fact that the company is being wound-up.

(1)   Companies Act individual accounts must comprise—

    (a)   a balance sheet as at the last day of the financial year, and

    (b)   a profit and loss account.

(2)   The accounts must—

    (a)   in the case of the balance sheet, give a true and fair view of the state of affairs of the company as at the end of the financial year, and

(b)   in the case of the profit and loss account, give a true and fair view of the profit or loss of the company for the financial year.

(2A)   In the case of the individual accounts of a company which qualifies as a micro-entity in relation to the financial year (see sections 384A and 384B), the micro-entity minimum accounting items included in the company's accounts for the year are presumed to give the true and fair view required by subsection (2).

(3)   The accounts must comply with provision made by the Secretary of State by regulations as to—
(a)   the form and content of the balance sheet and profit and loss account, and
(b)   additional information to be provided by way of notes to the accounts.

(4)   If compliance with the regulations, and any other provision made by or under this Act as to the matters to be included in a company's individual accounts or in notes to those accounts, would not be sufficient to give a true and fair view, the necessary additional information must be given in the accounts or in a note to them.

(5)   If in special circumstances compliance with any of those provisions is inconsistent with the requirement to give a true and fair view, the directors must depart from that provision to the extent necessary to give a true and fair view.

Particulars of any such departure, the reasons for it and its effect must be given in a note to the accounts.

(6)   Subsections (4) and (5) do not apply in relation to the micro-entity minimum accounting items included in the individual accounts of a company for a financial year in relation to which the company qualifies as a micro-entity.

397   IAS individual accounts

(1)   IAS individual accounts must state—
(a)   the part of the United Kingdom in which the company is registered,
(b)   the company's registered number,
(c)   whether the company is a public or a private company and whether it is limited by shares or by guarantee,
(d)   the address of the company's registered office, and
(e)   where appropriate, the fact that the company is being wound-up.

(2)   The notes to the accounts must state that the accounts have been prepared in accordance with UK-adopted international accounting standards.

398   ...

Group accounts: other companies

399   Duty to prepare group accounts

(1)   ...

(2)   If at the end of a financial year a company is a parent company the directors, as well as preparing individual accounts for the year, must prepare group accounts for the year unless the company is exempt from that requirement.

(2A)   A company is exempt from the requirement to prepare group accounts if—
(a)   at the end of the financial year, the company—
(i)   is subject to the small companies regime, or
(ii)   would be subject to the small companies regime but for being a public company, and
(b)   is not a member of a group which, at any time during the financial year, has an undertaking falling within subsection (2B) as a member.

(2B)   An undertaking falls within this subsection if—
(a)   it is established under the law of any part of the United Kingdom,
(b)   it has to prepare accounts in accordance with the requirements of this Part of this Act, and
(c)   it—

(i)   is an undertaking whose transferable securities are admitted to trading on a UK regulated market,

(ii)   is a credit institution within the meaning given by Article 4(1)(1) of Regulation (EU) No. 575/2013 of the European Parliament and of the Council, which is a CRR firm within the meaning of Article 4(1)(2A) of that Regulation, or

(iii) would be an insurance undertaking within the meaning given by Article 2(1) of Council Directive 91/674/EEC of the European Parliament and of the Council on the annual accounts of insurance undertakings were the United Kingdom a member State.

(3)   There are further exemptions under—

section 400 (company included in UK accounts of larger group),

section 401 (company included in non-UK accounts of larger group), and section 402 (company none of whose subsidiary undertakings need be included in the consolidation).

(4)   A company … which is exempt from the requirement to prepare group accounts, may do so.

400   Exemption for company included in UK group accounts of larger group

(1)   A company is exempt from the requirement to prepare group accounts if it is itself a subsidiary undertaking and its immediate parent undertaking is established under the law of any part of the United Kingdom, in the following cases—

(a)   where the company is a wholly-owned subsidiary of that parent undertaking;

(b)   where that parent undertaking holds 90% or more of the allotted shares in the company and the remaining shareholders have approved the exemption;

(c)   where that parent undertaking holds more than 50% (but less than 90%) of the allotted shares in the company and notice requesting the preparation of group accounts has not been served on the company by the shareholders holding in aggregate at least 5% of the allotted shares in the company.

Such notice must be served at least six months before the end of the financial year to which it relates.

(2)   Exemption is conditional upon compliance with all of the following conditions—

(a)   the company must be included in consolidated accounts for a larger group drawn up to the same date, or to an earlier date in the same financial year, by a parent undertaking established under the law of any part of the United Kingdom;

(b)   those accounts must be drawn up and audited, and that parent undertaking's annual report must be drawn up …—

(i)   if the undertaking is a company, in accordance with the requirements of this Part of this Act, or, if the undertaking is not a company, the legal requirements which apply to the drawing up of consolidated accounts for that undertaking, or

(ii)   in accordance with UK-adopted international accounting standards;

(c)   the company must disclose in the notes to its individual accounts that it is exempt from the obligation to prepare and deliver group accounts;

(d)   the company must state in its individual accounts the name of the parent undertaking that draws up the group accounts referred to above and—

(i)   the address of the undertaking's registered office …, or

(ii)   if it is unincorporated, the address of its principal place of business;

(e)   the company must deliver to the registrar, within the period for filing its accounts and reports for the financial year in question, copies of—

(i)   those group accounts, and

(ii)   the parent undertaking's annual report,

together with the auditor's report on them;

(f)   any requirement of Part 35 of this Act as to the delivery to the registrar of a certified translation into English must be met in relation to any document comprised in the accounts and reports delivered in accordance with paragraph (e).

(3)   For the purposes of subsection (1)(b) and (c) shares held by a wholly-owned subsidiary of the parent undertaking, or held on behalf of the parent undertaking or a wholly-owned subsidiary, shall be attributed to the parent undertaking.

(4)   The exemption does not apply to a company which is a traded company.

(5)   Shares held by directors of a company for the purpose of complying with any share qualification requirement shall be disregarded in determining for the purposes of this section whether the company is a wholly-owned subsidiary.

(6)   ...

401   Exemption for company included in non-UK group accounts of larger group

(1)   A company is exempt from the requirement to prepare group accounts if it is itself a subsidiary undertaking and its parent undertaking is not established under the law of any part of the United Kingdom, in the following cases—

   (a)   where the company is a wholly-owned subsidiary of that parent undertaking;

   (b)   where that parent undertaking holds 90% or more of the allotted shares in the company and the remaining shareholders have approved the exemption; or

   (c)   where that parent undertaking holds more than 50% (but less than 90%) of the allotted shares in the company and notice requesting the preparation of group accounts has not been served on the company by the shareholders holding in aggregate at least 5% of the allotted shares in the company.

   Such notice must be served at least six months before the end of the financial year to which it relates.

(2)   Exemption is conditional upon compliance with all of the following conditions—

   (a)   the company and all of its subsidiary undertakings must be included in consolidated accounts for a larger group drawn up to the same date, or to an earlier date in the same financial year, by a parent undertaking;

   (b)   those accounts and, where appropriate, the group's annual report, must be drawn up—

      (i)   ...

      (ii)   in a manner equivalent to consolidated accounts and consolidated reports drawn up in accordance with the requirements of this Part of this Act,

      (iii)   in accordance with UK-adopted international accounting standards, or

      (iv)   in accordance with accounting standards which are equivalent to such international accounting standards, as determined pursuant to Commission Regulation (EC) No. 1569/2007(a) of 21 December 2007 establishing a mechanism for the determination of equivalence of accounting standards applied by third country issuers of securities pursuant to Directives 2003/71/EC and 2004/109/EC of the European Parliament and of the Council;

   (c)   the group accounts must be audited by one or more persons authorised to audit accounts under the law under which the parent undertaking which draws them up is established;

   (d)   the company must disclose in its individual accounts that it is exempt from the obligation to prepare and deliver group accounts;

   (e)   the company must state in its individual accounts the name of the parent undertaking which draws up the group accounts referred to above and—

      (i)   the address of the undertaking's registered office (whether in or outside the United Kingdom), or;

      (ii)   if it is unincorporated, the address of its principal place of business;

   (f)   the company must deliver to the registrar, within the period for filing its accounts and reports for the financial year in question, copies of—

      (i)   the group accounts, and

      (ii)   where appropriate, the consolidated annual report,

      together with the auditor's report on them;

(g) any requirement of Part 35 of this Act as to the delivery to the registrar of a certified translation into English must be met in relation to any document comprised in the accounts and reports delivered in accordance with paragraph (f).

(3) For the purposes of subsection (1)(b) and (c), shares held by a wholly-owned subsidiary of the parent undertaking, or held on behalf of the parent undertaking or a wholly-owned subsidiary, are attributed to the parent undertaking.

(4) The exemption does not apply to a company which is a traded company.

(5) Shares held by directors of a company for the purpose of complying with any share qualification requirement shall be disregarded in determining for the purposes of this section whether the company is a wholly-owned subsidiary.

(6) ...

402 Exemption if no subsidiary undertakings need be included in the consolidation

A parent company is exempt from the requirement to prepare group accounts if under section 405 all of its subsidiary undertakings could be excluded from consolidation in Companies Act group accounts.

Group accounts: general

403 Group accounts: applicable accounting framework

(1) The group accounts of a parent company whose securities are, on its balance sheet date, admitted to trading on a UK regulated market must be prepared in accordance with UK-adopted international accounting standards ("IAS group accounts").

(2) The group accounts of other companies may be prepared—
(a) in accordance with section 404 ("Companies Act group accounts"), or
(b) in accordance with UK-adopted international accounting standards ("IAS group accounts").
This is subject to the following provisions of this section.

(3) The group accounts of a parent company that is a charity must be Companies Act group accounts.

(4) After the first financial year in which the directors of a parent company prepare IAS group accounts ("the first IAS year"), all subsequent group accounts of the company must be prepared in accordance with UK-adopted international accounting standards unless there is a relevant change of circumstance.
This is subject to subsection (5A).

(5) There is a relevant change of circumstance if, at any time during or after the first IAS year—
(a) the company becomes a subsidiary undertaking of another undertaking that does not prepare IAS group accounts,
(b) the company ceases to be a company with securities admitted to trading on a UK regulated market, or
(c) a parent undertaking of the company ceases to be an undertaking with securities admitted to trading on a UK regulated market.

(5A) After a financial year in which the directors of a parent company prepare IAS group accounts for the company, the directors may change to preparing Companies Act group accounts for a reason other than a relevant change of circumstance provided they have not changed to Companies Act group accounts in the period of five years preceding the first day of that financial year.

(5B) In calculating the five year period for the purpose of subsection (5A), no account should be taken of a change due to a relevant change of circumstance.

(6) If, having changed to preparing Companies Act group accounts ..., the directors again prepare IAS group accounts for the company, subsections (4) and (5) apply again as if the first financial year for which such accounts are again prepared were the first IAS year.

404 Companies Act group accounts

(A1) Companies Act group accounts must state, in respect of the parent company—
(a) the part of the United Kingdom in which the company is registered,
(b) the company's registered number,

     (c)   whether the company is a public or a private company and whether it is limited by shares or by guarantee,

     (d)   the address of the company's registered office, and

     (e)   where appropriate, the fact that the company is being wound-up.

(1)   Companies Act group accounts must comprise—

     (a)   a consolidated balance sheet dealing with the state of affairs of the parent company and its subsidiary undertakings, and

     (b)   a consolidated profit and loss account dealing with the profit or loss of the parent company and its subsidiary undertakings.

(2)   The accounts must give a true and fair view of the state of affairs as at the end of the financial year, and the profit or loss for the financial year, of the undertakings included in the consolidation as a whole, so far as concerns members of the company.

(3)   The accounts must comply with provision made by the Secretary of State by regulations as to—

     (a)   the form and content of the consolidated balance sheet and consolidated profit and loss account, and

     (b)   additional information to be provided by way of notes to the accounts.

(4)   If compliance with the regulations, and any other provision made by or under this Act as to the matters to be included in a company's group accounts or in notes to those accounts, would not be sufficient to give a true and fair view, the necessary additional information must be given in the accounts or in a note to them.

(5)   If in special circumstances compliance with any of those provisions is inconsistent with the requirement to give a true and fair view, the directors must depart from that provision to the extent necessary to give a true and fair view.

     Particulars of any such departure, the reasons for it and its effect must be given in a note to the accounts.

405   Companies Act group accounts: subsidiary undertakings included in the consolidation

(1)   Where a parent company prepares Companies Act group accounts, all the subsidiary undertakings of the company must be included in the consolidation, subject to the following exceptions.

(2)   A subsidiary undertaking may be excluded from consolidation if its inclusion is not material for the purpose of giving a true and fair view (but two or more undertakings may be excluded only if they are not material taken together).

(3)   A subsidiary undertaking may be excluded from consolidation where—

     (a)   severe long-term restrictions substantially hinder the exercise of the rights of the parent company over the assets or management of that undertaking, or

     (b)   extremely rare circumstances mean that the information necessary for the preparation of group accounts cannot be obtained without disproportionate expense or undue delay, or

     (c)   the interest of the parent company is held exclusively with a view to subsequent resale.

(4)   The reference in subsection (3)(a) to the rights of the parent company and the reference in subsection (3)(c) to the interest of the parent company are, respectively, to rights and interests held by or attributed to the company for the purposes of the definition of "parent undertaking" (see section 1162) in the absence of which it would not be the parent company.

406   IAS group accounts

(1)   IAS group accounts must state—

     (a)   the part of the United Kingdom in which the company is registered,

     (b)   the company's registered number,

     (c)   whether the company is a public or a private company and whether it is limited by shares or by guarantee,

     (d)   the address of the company's registered office, and

     (e)   where appropriate, the fact that the company is being wound-up.

(2)   The notes to the accounts must state that the accounts have been prepared in accordance with UK-adopted international accounting standards.

407   Consistency of financial reporting within group

(1)   The directors of a parent company must secure that the individual accounts of—

(a)   the parent company, and

(b)   each of its subsidiary undertakings,

are all prepared using the same financial reporting framework, except to the extent that in their opinion there are good reasons for not doing so.

(2)   Subsection (1) does not apply if the directors do not prepare group accounts for the parent company.

(3)   Subsection (1) only applies to accounts of subsidiary undertakings that are required to be prepared under this Part.

(4)   Subsection (1) does not require accounts of undertakings that are charities to be prepared using the same financial reporting framework as accounts of undertakings which are not charities.

(5)   Subsection (1)(a) does not apply where the directors of a parent company prepare IAS group accounts and IAS individual accounts.

408   Individual profit and loss account where group accounts prepared

(1)   This section applies where—

(a)   a company prepares group accounts in accordance with this Act, and

(b)   the company's individual balance sheet shows the company's profit and loss for the financial year determined in accordance with this Act.

(2)   ...

(3)   The company's individual profit and loss account must be approved in accordance with section 414(1) (approval by directors) but may be omitted from the company's annual accounts for the purposes of the other provisions of the Companies Acts.

(4)   The exemption conferred by this section is conditional upon its being disclosed in the company's annual accounts that the exemption applies.

Information to be given in notes to the accounts

409   Information about related undertakings

(1)   The Secretary of State may make provision by regulations requiring information about related undertakings to be given in notes to a company's annual accounts.

(2)   The regulations—

(a)   may make different provision according to whether or not the company prepares group accounts, and

(b)   may specify the descriptions of undertaking in relation to which they apply, and make different provision in relation to different descriptions of related undertaking.

(3)   The regulations may provide that information need not be disclosed with respect to an undertaking that—

(a)   is established under the law of a country outside the United Kingdom, or

(b)   carries on business outside the United Kingdom,

if the following conditions are met.

(4)   The conditions are—

(a)   that in the opinion of the directors of the company the disclosure would be seriously prejudicial to the business of—

(i)   that undertaking,

(ii)   the company,

(iii)   any of the company's subsidiary undertakings, or

(iv)   any other undertaking which is included in the consolidation;

(b)   that the Secretary of State agrees that the information need not be disclosed.

(5)   Where advantage is taken of any such exemption, that fact must be stated in a note to the company's annual accounts.

410   ...

410A   Information about off-balance sheet arrangements

(1)   If in any financial year—
    (a)   a company is or has been party to arrangements that are not reflected in its balance sheet, and
    (b)   at the balance sheet date the risks or benefits arising from those arrangements are material, the information required by this section must be given in the notes to the company's annual accounts.

(2)   The information required is—
    (a)   the nature and business purpose of the arrangements, and
    (b)   the financial impact of the arrangements on the company.

(3)   The information need only be given to the extent necessary for enabling the financial position of the company to be assessed.

(4)   If the company is subject to the small companies regime in relation to the financial year (see section 381), it need not comply with subsection (2)(b).

(5)   This section applies in relation to group accounts as if the undertakings included in the consolidation were a single company.

411   Information about employee numbers and costs

(1)   The notes to a company's annual accounts must disclose the average number of persons employed by the company in the financial year.

(1A)   In the case of a company not subject to the small companies regime, the notes to the company's accounts must also disclose the average number of persons within each category of persons so employed.

(2)   The categories by reference to which the number required to be disclosed by subsection (1A) is to be determined must be such as the directors may select having regard to the manner in which the company's activities are organised.

(3)   The average number required by subsection (1) or (1A) is determined by dividing the relevant annual number by the number of months in the financial year.

(4)   The relevant annual number is determined by ascertaining for each month in the financial year—
    (a)   for the purposes of subsection (1), the number of persons employed under contracts of service by the company in that month (whether throughout the month or not);
    (b)   for the purposes of subsection (1A), the number of persons in the category in question of persons so employed;
and adding together all the monthly numbers.

(5)   Except in the case of a company subject to the small companies regime, the notes to the company's annual accounts or the profit and loss account must disclose, with reference to all persons employed by the company during the financial year, the total staff costs of the company relating to the financial year broken down between—
    (a)   wages and salaries paid or payable in respect of that year to those persons,
    (b)   social security costs incurred by the company on their behalf, and
    (c)   other pension costs so incurred.

(6)   In subsection (5)—
"pension costs" includes any costs incurred by the company in respect of—
    (a)   any pension scheme established for the purpose of providing pensions for persons currently or formerly employed by the company,
    (b)   any sums set aside for the future payment of pensions directly by the company to current or former employees, and
    (c)   any pensions paid directly to such persons without having first been set aside;
"social security costs" means any contributions by the company to any state social security or pension scheme, fund or arrangement.

(7)   This section applies in relation to group accounts as if the undertakings included in the consolidation were a single company.

412   Information about directors' benefits: remuneration

(1)   The Secretary of State may make provision by regulations requiring information to be given in notes to a company's annual accounts about directors' remuneration.

(2)   The matters about which information may be required include—

    (a)   gains made by directors on the exercise of share options;

    (b)   benefits received or receivable by directors under long-term incentive schemes;

    (c)   payments for loss of office (as defined in section 215);

    (d)   benefits receivable, and contributions for the purpose of providing benefits, in respect of past services of a person as director or in any other capacity while director;

    (e)   consideration paid to or receivable by third parties for making available the services of a person as director or in any other capacity while director.

(3)   Without prejudice to the generality of subsection (1), regulations under this section may make any such provision as was made immediately before the commencement of this Part by Part 1 of Schedule 6 to the Companies Act 1985.

(4)   For the purposes of this section, and regulations made under it, amounts paid to or receivable by—

    (a)   a person connected with a director, or

    (b)   a body corporate controlled by a director,

are treated as paid to or receivable by the director.

The expressions "connected with" and "controlled by" in this subsection have the same meaning as in Part 10 (company directors).

(5)   It is the duty of—

    (a)   any director of a company, and

    (b)   any person who is or has at any time in the preceding five years been a director of the company,

to give notice to the company of such matters relating to himself as may be necessary for the purposes of regulations under this section.

(6)   A person who makes default in complying with subsection (5) commits an offence and is liable on summary conviction to a fine not exceeding level 3 on the standard scale.

413   Information about directors' benefits: advances, credit and guarantees

(1)   In the case of a company that does not prepare group accounts, details of—

    (a)   advances and credits granted by the company to its directors, and

    (b)   guarantees of any kind entered into by the company on behalf of its directors,

must be shown in the notes to its individual accounts.

(2)   In the case of a parent company that prepares group accounts, details of—

    (a)   advances and credits granted to the directors of the parent company, by that company or by any of its subsidiary undertakings, and

    (b)   guarantees of any kind entered into on behalf of the directors of the parent company, by that company or by any of its subsidiary undertakings,

must be shown in the notes to the group accounts.

(3)   The details required of an advance or credit are—

    (a)   its amount,

    (b)   an indication of the interest rate,

    (c)   its main conditions, …

    (d)   any amounts repaid,

    (e)   any amounts written off, and

    (f)   any amounts waived.

(4)   The details required of a guarantee are—

    (a)   its main terms,

    (b)   the amount of the maximum liability that may be incurred by the company (or its subsidiary), and

(c)   any amount paid and any liability incurred by the company (or its subsidiary) for the purpose of fulfilling the guarantee (including any loss incurred by reason of enforcement of the guarantee).

(5)   There must also be stated in the notes to the accounts the totals—

      (a)   of amounts stated under subsection (3)(a),

      (b)   of amounts stated under subsection (3)(d),

      (ba) of amounts stated under subsection 3(e),

      (bb) of amounts stated under subsection 3(f),

      (c)   of amounts stated under subsection (4)(b), and

      (d)   of amounts stated under subsection (4)(c).

(6)   References in this section to the directors of a company are to the persons who were directors at any time in the financial year to which the accounts relate.

(7)   The requirements of this section apply in relation to every advance, credit or guarantee subsisting at any time in the financial year to which the accounts relate—

      (a)   whenever it was entered into,

      (b)   whether or not the person concerned was a director of the company in question at the time it was entered into, and

      (c)   in the case of an advance, credit or guarantee involving a subsidiary undertaking of that company, whether or not that undertaking was such a subsidiary undertaking at the time it was entered into.

(8)   Banking companies and the holding companies of credit institutions need only state the details required by subsection (5)(a) and (c).

Approval and signing of accounts

414   Approval and signing of accounts

(1)   A company's annual accounts must be approved by the board of directors and signed on behalf of the board by a director of the company.

(2)   The signature must be on the company's balance sheet.

(3)   If the accounts are prepared in accordance with the small companies regime, the balance sheet must contain, in a prominent position above the signature—

      (a)   in the case of individual accounts prepared in accordance with the micro-entity provisions, a statement to that effect, or

      (b)   in the case of accounts not prepared as mentioned in paragraph (a), a statement to the effect that the accounts have been prepared in accordance with the provisions applicable to companies subject to the small companies regime.

(4)   If annual accounts are approved that do not comply with the requirements of this Act ..., every director of the company who—

      (a)   knew that they did not comply, or was reckless as to whether they complied, and

      (b)   failed to take reasonable steps to secure compliance with those requirements or, as the case may be, to prevent the accounts from being approved,

commits an offence.

(5)   A person guilty of an offence under this section is liable—

      (a)   on conviction on indictment, to a fine;

      (b)   on summary conviction, to a fine not exceeding the statutory maximum.

CHAPTER 4A
STRATEGIC REPORT

414A   Duty to prepare strategic report

(1)   The directors of a company must prepare a strategic report for each financial year of the company.

(2)   Subsection (1) does not apply if the company is entitled to the small companies exemption.

(3)   For a financial year in which—

      (a)   the company is a parent company, and

(b) the directors of the company prepare group accounts,

the strategic report must be a consolidated report (a "group strategic report") relating to the undertakings included in the consolidation.

(4) A group strategic report may, where appropriate, give greater emphasis to the matters that are significant to the undertakings included in the consolidation, taken as a whole.

(5) In the case of failure to comply with the requirement to prepare a strategic report, an offence is committed by every person who—

(a) was a director of the company immediately before the end of the period for filing accounts and reports for the financial year in question, and

(b) failed to take all reasonable steps for securing compliance with that requirement.

(6) A person guilty of an offence under this section is liable—

(a) on conviction on indictment, to a fine;

(b) on summary conviction, to a fine not exceeding the statutory maximum.

414B Strategic report: small companies exemption

A company is entitled to the small companies exemption in relation to the strategic report for a financial year if—

(a) it is entitled to prepare accounts for the year in accordance with the small companies regime, or

(b) it would be so entitled but for being or having been a member of an ineligible group.

414C Contents of strategic report

(1) The purpose of the strategic report is to inform members of the company and help them assess how the directors have performed their duty under section 172 (duty to promote the success of the company).

(2) The strategic report must contain—

(a) a fair review of the company's business, and

(b) a description of the principal risks and uncertainties facing the company.

Section 414CZA (section 172(1) statement) and sections 414CA and 414CB (non-financial and sustainability information statement) make further provision about the contents of a strategic report.

(3) The review required is a balanced and comprehensive analysis of—

(a) the development and performance of the company's business during the financial year, and

(b) the position of the company's business at the end of that year,

consistent with the size and complexity of the business.

(4) The review must, to the extent necessary for an understanding of the development, performance or position of the company's business, include—

(a) analysis using financial key performance indicators, and

(b) where appropriate, analysis using other key performance indicators, including information relating to environmental matters and employee matters.

(5) In subsection (4), "key performance indicators" means factors by reference to which the development, performance or position of the company's business can be measured effectively.

(6) Where a company qualifies as medium-sized in relation to a financial year (see sections 465 to 467), the review for the year need not comply with the requirements of subsection (4) so far as they relate to non-financial information.

(7) In the case of a quoted company the strategic report must, to the extent necessary for an understanding of the development, performance or position of the company's business, include—

(a) the main trends and factors likely to affect the future development, performance and position of the company's business, and

(b) information about—

(i) environmental matters (including the impact of the company's business on the environment),

(ii) the company's employees, and

(iii)   social, community and human rights issues,

including information about any policies of the company in relation to those matters and the effectiveness of those policies.

If the report does not contain information of each kind mentioned in paragraphs (b)(i), (ii) and (iii), it must state which of those kinds of information it does not contain.

(8)   In the case of a quoted company the strategic report must include—

    (a)   a description of the company's strategy,

    (b)   a description of the company's business model,

    (c)   a breakdown showing at the end of the financial year—

        (i)   the number of persons of each sex who were directors of the company;

        (ii)   the number of persons of each sex who were senior managers of the company (other than persons falling within sub-paragraph (i)); and

        (iii)   the number of persons of each sex who were employees of the company.

(9)   In subsection (8), "senior manager" means a person who—

    (a)   has responsibility for planning, directing or controlling the activities of the company, or a strategically significant part of the company, and

    (b)   is an employee of the company.

(10)   In relation to a group strategic report—

    (a)   the reference to the company in subsection (8)(c)(i) is to the parent company; and

    (b)   the breakdown required by subsection (8)(c)(ii) must include the number of persons of each sex who were the directors of the undertakings included in the consolidation.

(11)   The strategic report may also contain such of the matters otherwise required by regulations made under section 416(4) to be disclosed in the directors' report as the directors consider are of strategic importance to the company.

(12)   The report must, where appropriate, include references to, and additional explanations of, amounts included in the company's annual accounts.

(13)   Subject to paragraph (10), in relation to a group strategic report this section has effect as if the references to the company were references to the undertakings included in the consolidation.

(14)   Nothing in this section requires the disclosure of information about impending developments or matters in the course of negotiation if the disclosure would, in the opinion of the directors, be seriously prejudicial to the interests of the company.

414CZA Section 172(1) statement

(1)   A strategic report for a financial year of a company must include a statement (a "section 172(1) statement") which describes how the directors have had regard to the matters set out in section 172(1)(a) to (f) when performing their duty under section 172.

(2)   Subsection (1) does not apply if the company qualifies as medium-sized in relation to that financial year (see sections 465 to 467).

414CA Non-financial and sustainability information statement

(A1)   A strategic report of a company to which this subsection applies must include a non-financial and sustainability information statement.

(1)   Subsection (A1) applies to a company if it was at any time within the financial year to which the report relates—

    (a)   a traded company,

    (b)   a banking company,

    (c)   an authorised insurance company, ...

    (d)   a company carrying on insurance market activity, or

    (e)   a company any securities of which are admitted to trading on the market known as the Alternative Investment Market.

(1A)   Subsection (A1) also applies to a company if it was a high turnover company in relation to that financial year.

(1B)   Subsections (1) and (1A) are subject to subsections (3) to (7).

(2) If the company's strategic report is a group strategic report, the non-financial and sustainability information statement to be included in the report under subsection (A1) must be a consolidated statement (a "group non-financial and sustainability information statement") relating to the undertakings included in the consolidation.

(2A) A company is a "high turnover company" in relation to a financial year—

    (a) where the company was not a parent company in that financial year, if in that year the company's turnover was more than £500 million;

    (b) where the company was a parent company at any time within that financial year, if in that year a group headed by the company had an aggregate turnover of more than £500 million net.

(2B) For a period that is a company's financial year but not in fact a year the figures for turnover given by subsection (2A) must be proportionately adjusted.

(2C) For the purposes of subsection (2A)(b)—

    (a) aggregate turnover is ascertained by aggregating the relevant figures determined for each member of the group;

    (b) "net", in relation to aggregate turnover, is to be interpreted in accordance with section 383(6).

(2D) Section 383(7) applies for the purposes of subsection (2A)(b) of this section as it applies for the purposes of section 383.

(3) Subsection (A1) does not apply to a company if—

    (a) the company is subject to the small companies regime in relation to that financial year (see sections 382 to 384), or

    (b) the company qualifies as medium-sized in relation to that financial year (see sections 465 to 467).

(4) Subsection (A1) does not apply—

    (a) to a company which was not a parent company in that financial year, if the company had no more than 500 employees in that financial year, or

    (b) to a company which was a parent company at any time within that financial year, if the aggregate number of employees for a group headed by that company in that financial year was no more than 500.

(5) The number of employees means the average number of persons employed by the company in the year, determined as follows—

    (a) find for each month in the financial year the number of persons employed under contracts of service by the company in that month (whether throughout the month or not),

    (b) add together the monthly totals, and

    (c) divide by the number of months in the financial year.

(6) The aggregate number of employees for a group is ascertained by aggregating the relevant figures determined in accordance with subsection (5) for each member of the group.

(7) Subsection (A1) does not apply to a company if the company is a subsidiary undertaking at the end of that financial year and is included in—

    (a) a group strategic report of a parent undertaking of the company that satisfies the requirements in subsection (8), …

    (b) …

(8) The requirements in this subsection are that—

    (a) the group strategic report relates to undertakings that include the company and its subsidiary undertakings (if any),

    (b) the report is prepared for a financial year of the parent undertaking that ends at the same time as, or before the end of, the company's financial year, and

    (c) the report includes a group non-financial and sustainability information statement in respect of all the undertakings included in the consolidation.

(9) …

(10)   A company to which subsection (A1) does not apply may include a non-financial and
         sustainability information statement in its strategic report or, as the case may be, a group non-
         financial and sustainability information statement in its group strategic report.

414CB Contents of non-financial and sustainability information statement

(A1)   The non-financial and sustainability information statement must contain the climate-related
         financial disclosures of the company.

(1)   If the company is of a kind described in section 414CA(1)(a), (b), (c) or (d), the non-financial and
         sustainability information statement must contain information, to the extent necessary for an
         understanding of the company's development, performance and position and the impact of its
         activity, relating to, as a minimum—
         (a) environmental matters (including the impact of the company's business on the
              environment),
         (b) the company's employees,
         (c) social matters,
         (d) respect for human rights, and
         (e) anti-corruption and anti-bribery matters.

(2)   The information required by subsection (1) must include—
         (a) a brief description of the company's business model,
         (b) a description of the policies pursued by the company in relation to the matters mentioned in
              subsection (1)(a) to (e) and any due diligence processes implemented by the company in
              pursuance of those policies,
         (c) a description of the outcome of those policies,
         (d) a description of the principal risks relating to the matters mentioned in subsection (1)(a) to
              (e) arising in connection with the company's operations and, where relevant and
              proportionate—
              (i)   a description of its business relationships, products and services which are likely to
                     cause adverse impacts in those areas of risk, and
              (ii)   a description of how it manages the principal risks, and
         (e) a description of the non-financial key performance indicators relevant to the company's
              business.

(2A)   In this section, "climate-related financial disclosures" mean—
         (a) a description of the company's governance arrangements in relation to assessing and
              managing climate-related risks and opportunities;
         (b) a description of how the company identifies, assesses, and manages climate-related risks
              and opportunities;
         (c) a description of how processes for identifying, assessing, and managing climate-related
              risks are integrated into the company's overall risk management process;
         (d) a description of—
              (i)   the principal climate-related risks and opportunities arising in connection with the
                     company's operations, and
              (ii)   the time periods by reference to which those risks and opportunities are assessed;
         (e) a description of the actual and potential impacts of the principal climate-related risks and
              opportunities on the company's business model and strategy;
         (f) an analysis of the resilience of the company's business model and strategy, taking into
              consideration different climate-related scenarios;
         (g) a description of the targets used by the company to manage climate-related risks and to
              realise climate-related opportunities and of performance against those targets; and
         (h) a description of the key performance indicators used to assess progress against targets used
              to manage climate-related risks and realise climate-related opportunities and of the
              calculations on which those key performance indicators are based.

(3)   In subsection (2)(e), "key performance indicators" means factors by reference to which the development, performance or position of the company's business, or the impact of the company's activity, can be measured effectively.

(4)   If the company does not pursue policies in relation to one or more of the matters mentioned in subsection (1)(a) to (e), the statement must provide a clear and reasoned explanation for the company's not doing so.

(4A)   Where the directors of a company reasonably believe that, having regard to the nature of the company's business, and the manner in which it is carried on, the whole or a part of a climate-related financial disclosure required by subsection (2A)(e), (f), (g) or (h) is not necessary for an understanding of the company's business, the directors may omit the whole or (as the case requires) the relevant part of that climate-related financial disclosure.

(4B)   Where the directors omit the whole or part of a climate-related financial disclosure in reliance on subsection (4A) the non-financial and sustainability information statement must provide a clear and reasoned explanation of the directors' reasonable belief mentioned in that subsection.

(5)   The statement must, where appropriate, include references to, and additional explanations of, amounts included in the company's annual accounts.

(6)   If information required by subsections (1) to (5) to be included in the statement is published by the company by means of a national, EU-based or international reporting framework, the statement must specify the framework or frameworks used, instead of including that information.

(7)   If a non-financial and sustainability information statement complies with subsections (1) to (6), the strategic report of which it is part is to be treated as complying with the requirements in—

    (a)   section 414C(4)(b),

    (b)   section 414C(7), except as it relates to community issues,

    (c)   section 414C(8)(b), and

    (d)   section 414C(12), so far as relating to the provisions mentioned in paragraphs (a) to (c).

(8)   In relation to a group non-financial and sustainability information statement, this section has effect as if the references to the company were references to the undertakings included in the consolidation.

(9)   Nothing in this section requires the disclosure of information about impending developments or matters in the course of negotiation if the disclosure would, in the opinion of the directors, be seriously prejudicial to the commercial interests of the company, provided that the non-disclosure does not prevent a fair and balanced understanding of the company's development, performance or position or the impact of the company's activity.

(10)   The Secretary of State may issue guidance on the climate-related financial disclosures, which are described in subsection (2A), and otherwise in connection with the requirements of this section and section 414CA.

414D   Approval and signing of strategic report

(1)   The strategic report must be approved by the board of directors and signed on behalf of the board by a director or the secretary of the company.

(2)   If a strategic report is approved that does not comply with the requirements of this Act, every director of the company who—

    (a)   knew that it did not comply, or was reckless as to whether it complied, and

    (b)   failed to take reasonable steps to secure compliance with those requirements or, as the case may be, to prevent the report from being approved, commits an offence.

(3)   A person guilty of an offence under this section is liable—

    (a)   on conviction on indictment, to a fine;

    (b)   on summary conviction, to a fine not exceeding the statutory maximum.

CHAPTER 5
DIRECTORS' REPORT

Directors' report

415   Duty to prepare directors' report

(1)   The directors of a company must prepare a directors' report for each financial year of the company.

(1A)   Subsection (1) does not apply if the company qualifies as a micro-entity (see sections 384A and 384B).

(2)   For a financial year in which—
        (a)   the company is a parent company, and
        (b)   the directors of the company prepare group accounts,
        the directors' report must be a consolidated report (a "group directors' report") relating to the undertakings included in the consolidation.

(3)   A group directors' report may, where appropriate, give greater emphasis to the matters that are significant to the undertakings included in the consolidation, taken as a whole.

(4)   In the case of failure to comply with the requirement to prepare a directors' report, an offence is committed by every person who—
        (a)   was a director of the company immediately before the end of the period for filing accounts and reports for the financial year in question, and
        (b)   failed to take all reasonable steps for securing compliance with that requirement.

(5)   A person guilty of an offence under this section is liable—
        (a)   on conviction on indictment, to a fine;
        (b)   on summary conviction, to a fine not exceeding the statutory maximum.

415A Directors' report: small companies exemption

(1)   A company is entitled to small companies exemption in relation to the directors' report for a financial year if—
        (a)   it is entitled to prepare accounts for the year in accordance with the small companies regime, or
        (b)   it would be so entitled but for being or having been a member of an ineligible group.

(2)   The exemption is relevant to—
        section 416(3) (contents of report: statement of amount recommended by way of dividend), and
        …
        sections 444 to 446 (filing obligations of different descriptions of company).

416   Contents of directors' report: general

(1)   The directors' report for a financial year must state—
        (a)   the names of the persons who, at any time during the financial year, were directors of the company, …
        (b)   …

(2)   …

(3)   Except in the case of a company entitled to the small companies exemption, the report must state the amount (if any) that the directors recommend should be paid by way of dividend.

(4)   The Secretary of State may make provision by regulations as to other matters that must be disclosed in a directors' report.
        Without prejudice to the generality of this power, the regulations may make any such provision as was formerly made by Schedule 7 to the Companies Act 1985.

417   …

418   Contents of directors' report: statement as to disclosure to auditors

(1)   This section applies to a company unless—

    (a)   it is exempt for the financial year in question from the requirements of Part 16 as to audit of accounts, and

    (b)   the directors take advantage of that exemption.

(2)   The directors' report must contain a statement to the effect that, in the case of each of the persons who are directors at the time the report is approved—

    (a)   so far as the director is aware, there is no relevant audit information of which the company's auditor is unaware, and

    (b)   he has taken all the steps that he ought to have taken as a director in order to make himself aware of any relevant audit information and to establish that the company's auditor is aware of that information.

(3)   "Relevant audit information" means information needed by the company's auditor in connection with preparing his report.

(4)   A director is regarded as having taken all the steps that he ought to have taken as a director in order to do the things mentioned in subsection (2)(b) if he has—

    (a)   made such enquiries of his fellow directors and of the company's auditors for that purpose, and

    (b)   taken such other steps (if any) for that purpose,

as are required by his duty as a director of the company to exercise reasonable care, skill and diligence.

(5)   Where a directors' report containing the statement required by this section is approved but the statement is false, every director of the company who—

    (a)   knew that the statement was false, or was reckless as to whether it was false, and

    (b)   failed to take reasonable steps to prevent the report from being approved,

commits an offence.

(6)   A person guilty of an offence under subsection (5) is liable—

    (a)   on conviction on indictment, to imprisonment for a term not exceeding two years or a fine (or both);

    (b)   on summary conviction—

        (i)   in England and Wales, to imprisonment for a term not exceeding twelve months or to a fine not exceeding the statutory maximum (or both);

        (ii)   in Scotland or Northern Ireland, to imprisonment for a term not exceeding six months, or to a fine not exceeding the statutory maximum (or both).

419   Approval and signing of directors' report

(1)   The directors' report must be approved by the board of directors and signed on behalf of the board by a director or the secretary of the company.

(2)   If in preparing the report advantage is taken of the small companies exemption, it must contain a statement to that effect in a prominent position above the signature.

(3)   If a directors' report is approved that does not comply with the requirements of this Act, every director of the company who—

    (a)   knew that it did not comply, or was reckless as to whether it complied, and

    (b)   failed to take reasonable steps to secure compliance with those requirements or, as the case may be, to prevent the report from being approved,

commits an offence.

(4)   A person guilty of an offence under this section is liable—

    (a)   on conviction on indictment, to a fine;

    (b)   on summary conviction, to a fine not exceeding the statutory maximum.

419A   Approval and signing of separate corporate governance statement

Any separate corporate governance statement must be approved by the board of directors and signed on behalf of the board by a director or the secretary of the company.

CHAPTER 6
QUOTED COMPANIES AND TRADED COMPANIES: DIRECTORS' REMUNERATION REPORT

420   Duty to prepare directors' remuneration report

(1)   The directors of a quoted company, or of a traded company (as defined by section 360C) that is not a quoted company, must prepare a directors' remuneration report for each financial year of the company.

(2)   In the case of failure to comply with the requirement to prepare a directors' remuneration report, every person who—

(a)   was a director of the company immediately before the end of the period for filing accounts and reports for the financial year in question, and

(b)   failed to take all reasonable steps for securing compliance with that requirement,

commits an offence.

(3)   A person guilty of an offence under this section is liable—

(a)   on conviction on indictment, to a fine;

(b)   on summary conviction, to a fine not exceeding the statutory maximum.

421   Contents of directors' remuneration report

(1)   The Secretary of State may make provision by regulations as to—

(a)   the information that must be contained in a directors' remuneration report,

(b)   how information is to be set out in the report, and

(c)   what is to be the auditable part of the report.

(2)   Without prejudice to the generality of this power, the regulations may make any such provision as was made, immediately before the commencement of this Part, by Schedule 7A to the Companies Act 1985.

(2A)   The regulations must provide that any information required to be included in the report as to the policy of the company with respect to the making of remuneration payments and payments for loss of office (within the meaning of Chapter 4A of Part 10) is to be set out in a separate part of the report.

(3)   It is the duty of—

(a)   any director of a company, and

(b)   any person who is or has at any time in the preceding five years been a director of the company,

to give notice to the company of such matters relating to himself as may be necessary for the purposes of regulations under this section.

(4)   A person who makes default in complying with subsection (3) commits an offence and is liable on summary conviction to a fine not exceeding level 3 on the standard scale.

422   Approval and signing of directors' remuneration report

(1)   The directors' remuneration report must be approved by the board of directors and signed on behalf of the board by a director or the secretary of the company.

(2)   If a directors' remuneration report is approved that does not comply with the requirements of this Act, every director of the company who—

(a)   knew that it did not comply, or was reckless as to whether it complied, and

(b)   failed to take reasonable steps to secure compliance with those requirements or, as the case may be, to prevent the report from being approved,

commits an offence.

(3)   A person guilty of an offence under this section is liable—

(a)   on conviction on indictment, to a fine;

(b)   on summary conviction, to a fine not exceeding the statutory maximum.

422A   Revisions to directors' remuneration policy

(1)   The directors' remuneration policy contained in a company's directors' remuneration report may be revised.

(2)   Any such revision must be approved by the board of directors.

(3)   The policy as so revised must be set out in a document signed on behalf of the board by a director or the secretary of the company.

(4)   Regulations under section 421(1) may make provision as to—

    (a)   the information that must be contained in a document setting out a revised directors' remuneration policy, and

    (b)   how information is to be set out in the document.

(5)   Sections 422(2) and (3), 454, 456 and 463 apply in relation to such a document as they apply in relation to a directors' remuneration report.

(6)   In this section, "directors' remuneration policy" means the policy of a company with respect to the matters mentioned in section 421(2A).

CHAPTER 7

PUBLICATION OF ACCOUNTS AND REPORTS

Duty to circulate copies of accounts and reports

423   Duty to circulate copies of annual accounts and reports

(1)   Every company must send a copy of its annual accounts and reports for each financial year to—

    (a)   every member of the company,

    (b)   every holder of the company's debentures, and

    (c)   every person who is entitled to receive notice of general meetings.

(2)   Copies need not be sent to a person for whom the company does not have a current address.

(3)   A company has a "current address" for a person if—

    (a)   an address has been notified to the company by the person as one at which documents may be sent to him, and

    (b)   the company has no reason to believe that documents sent to him at that address will not reach him.

(4)   In the case of a company not having a share capital, copies need not be sent to anyone who is not entitled to receive notices of general meetings of the company.

(5)   Where copies are sent out over a period of days, references in the Companies Acts to the day on which copies are sent out shall be read as references to the last day of that period.

(6)   This section has effect subject to section 426 (option to provide strategic report with supplementary material).

424   Time allowed for sending out copies of accounts and reports

(1)   The time allowed for sending out copies of the company's annual accounts and reports is as follows.

(2)   A private company must comply with section 423 not later than—

    (a)   the end of the period for filing accounts and reports, or

    (b)   if earlier, the date on which it actually delivers its accounts and reports to the registrar.

(3)   A public company must comply with section 423 at least 21 days before the date of the relevant accounts meeting.

(4)   If in the case of a public company copies are sent out later than is required by subsection (3), they shall, despite that, be deemed to have been duly sent if it is so agreed by all the members entitled to attend and vote at the relevant accounts meeting.

(5)   Whether the time allowed is that for a private company or a public company is determined by reference to the company's status immediately before the end of the accounting reference period by reference to which the financial year for the accounts in question was determined.

(6)   In this section the "relevant accounts meeting" means the accounts meeting of the company at which the accounts and reports in question are to be laid.

425   Default in sending out copies of accounts and reports: offences

(1)   If default is made in complying with section 423 or 424, an offence is committed by—
    (a)   the company, and
    (b)   every officer of the company who is in default.

(2)   A person guilty of an offence under this section is liable—
    (a)   on conviction on indictment, to a fine;
    (b)   on summary conviction, to a fine not exceeding the statutory maximum.

Option to provide strategic report with supplementary material

426   Option to provide strategic report with supplementary material

(1)   A company may—
    (a)   in such cases as may be specified by regulations made by the Secretary of State, and
    (b)   provided any conditions so specified are complied with,
    provide a copy of the strategic report together with the supplementary material described in section 426A instead of copies of the accounts and reports required to be sent out in accordance with section 423.

(2)   Copies of those accounts and reports must, however, be sent to any person entitled to be sent them in accordance with that section and who wishes to receive them.

(3)   The Secretary of State may make provision by regulations as to the manner in which it is to be ascertained, whether before or after a person becomes entitled to be sent a copy of those accounts and reports, whether he wishes to receive them.

(4)   ...

(5)   This section applies to copies of accounts and reports required to be sent out by virtue of section 146 to a person nominated to enjoy information rights as it applies to copies of accounts and reports required to be sent out in accordance with section 423 to a member of the company.

(6)   Regulations under this section are subject to negative resolution procedure.

426A   Supplementary material

(1)   The supplementary material referred to in section 426 must be prepared in accordance with this section.

(2)   The supplementary material must—
    (a)   contain a statement that the strategic report is only part of the company's annual accounts and reports;
    (b)   state how a person entitled to them can obtain a full copy of the company's annual accounts and reports;
    (c)   state whether the auditor's report on the annual accounts was unqualified or qualified and, if it was qualified, set out the report in full together with any further material needed to understand the qualification;
    (d)   state whether, in that report, the auditor's statement under section 496 (whether strategic report and directors' report consistent with the accounts) was unqualified or qualified and, if it was qualified, set out the qualified statement in full together with any further material needed to understand the qualification;
    (e)   in the case of a quoted company or of a traded company (as defined by section 360C) that is not a quoted company, contain a copy of that part of the directors' remuneration report which sets out the single total figure table in respect of the company's directors' remuneration in accordance with the requirements of Schedule 8 to the Large and Medium-sized Companies (Accounts and Reports) Regulations 2008 (SI 2008/410).

Section 172(1) statement: requirements as to website publication

426B   Section 172(1) statement to be made available on website

(1)   This section applies if—

(a)   a company is required by section 414CZA to include a section 172(1) statement in its strategic report for a financial year, and

(b)   the company is an unquoted company in relation to that financial year.

(2)   The company must ensure that the section 172(1) statement—

(a)   is made available on a website, and

(b)   remains so available until—

    (i)   the section 172(1) statement for the company's next financial year is made available in accordance with this section, or

    (ii)   if the obligation under this section to make a section 172(1) statement available does not arise in relation to the company's next financial year, the end of the company's next financial year.

(3)   The section 172(1) statement must be made available on a website that—

(a)   is maintained by or on behalf of the company, and

(b)   identifies the company in question.

(4)   Access to the section 172(1) statement made available on the website under subsection (2), and the ability to obtain a hard copy of the statement from the website, must not be—

(a)   conditional on the payment of a fee, or

(b)   otherwise restricted, except so far as necessary to comply with any enactment or regulatory requirement (in the United Kingdom or elsewhere).

(5)   The section 172(1) statement—

(a)   must be made available on a website as soon as reasonably practicable, and

(b)   must be kept available throughout the period specified in subsection (2)(b)(i) or (as the case may be) (ii).

(6)   A failure to make the section 172(1) statement available on a website throughout the period specified in subsection (2)(b)(i) or (as the case may be) (ii) is disregarded if—

(a)   the statement is made available on the website for part of that period, and

(b)   the failure is wholly attributable to circumstances that it would not be reasonable to have expected the company to prevent or avoid.

(7)   In the event of default in complying with this section, an offence is committed by every officer of the company who is in default.

(8)   A person guilty of an offence under subsection (7) is liable on summary conviction to a fine not exceeding level 3 on the standard scale.

427–9   ...

Quoted companies: requirements as to website publication

430   **Quoted companies and traded companies: annual accounts and reports to be made available on website**

(1)   A quoted company or unquoted traded company must ensure that its annual accounts and reports—

(a)   are made available on a website, and

(b)   subject to subsection (4ZA), remain so available until the annual accounts and reports for the company's next financial year are made available in accordance with this section.

(2)   The annual accounts and reports must be made available on a website that—

(a)   is maintained by or on behalf of the company, and

(b)   identifies the company in question.

(2A)   If the directors' remuneration policy of a quoted company or unquoted traded company is revised in accordance with section 422A, or amended as mentioned in section 226B(1)(b) or section 226C(1)(b), the company must ensure that the revised or amended policy is made available on the website on which its annual accounts and reports are made available.

(2B)   If a person ceases to be a director of a quoted company or of an unquoted traded company, the company must ensure that the following information is made available on the website on which its annual accounts and reports are made available—

        (a)   the name of the person concerned,

        (b)   particulars of any remuneration payment (within the meaning of Chapter 4A of Part 10) made or to be made to the person after ceasing to be a director, including its amount and how it was calculated, and

        (c)   particulars of any payment for loss of office (within the meaning of that Chapter) made or to be made to the person, including its amount and how it was calculated.

(2C)   Where the members of a quoted company or of an unquoted traded company have passed a resolution approving the relevant directors' remuneration policy (within the meaning of section 439A(7))—

        (a)   the company must ensure that the following information is made available on the website on which its remuneration policy is made available as soon as reasonably practicable, and kept available for as long as that information is applicable—

             (i)   the date of the resolution,

             (ii)   the number of votes validly cast,

             (iii)   the proportion of the company's issued share capital represented by those votes,

             (iv)   the number of votes cast in favour,

             (v)   the number of votes cast against, and

             (vi)   the number of abstentions; and

        (b)   for the purposes of paragraph (a)(iii), the proportion of the issued share capital must be determined by reference to the register of members as at a time (determined by the company) that is not more than 48 hours before the time for the holding of the meeting at which the resolution was passed.

(3)   Access to the material made available on the website under subsections (1) to (2C), and the ability to obtain a hard copy of such material from the website, must not be—

        (a)   conditional on the payment of a fee, or

        (b)   otherwise restricted, except so far as necessary to comply with any enactment or regulatory requirement (in the United Kingdom or elsewhere).

(4)   The annual accounts and reports—

        (a)   must be made available as soon as reasonably practicable, and

        (b)   subject to subsection (4ZA), must be kept available throughout the period specified in subsection (1)(b).

(4ZA) The directors' remuneration report—

        (a)   must be kept available for a period of ten years beginning with the date it is first made available in accordance with this section, and

        (b)   may be kept available for a longer period if it does not contain personal data within the meaning of the Data Protection Act 2018 (see section 3(2) of that Act).

(4A)   Where subsection (2A) or (2B) applies, the material in question—

        (a)   must be made available as soon as reasonably practicable, ...

        (b)   must be kept available until the next directors' remuneration report of the company is made available on the website, and

        (c)   in a subsection (2A) case, must be kept available for at least as long as it is applicable.

(5)   A failure to make material available on a website throughout the period mentioned in subsection (4) or (as the case may be) (4ZA) or (4A) is disregarded if—

        (a)   the material is made available on the website for part of that period, and

        (b)   the failure is wholly attributable to circumstances that it would not be reasonable to have expected the company to prevent or avoid.

(6)   In the event of default in complying with this section, an offence is committed by every officer of the company who is in default.

(7)   A person guilty of an offence under subsection (6) is liable on summary conviction to a fine not exceeding level 3 on the standard scale.

(8)   In this section "unquoted traded company" means a traded company (as defined by section 360C) that is not a quoted company.

Right of member or debenture holder to demand copies of accounts and reports

431   Right of member or debenture holder to copies of accounts and reports: unquoted companies

(1)   A member of, or holder of debentures of, an unquoted company is entitled to be provided, on demand and without charge, with a copy of—

(a)   the company's last annual accounts,

(aa)   the strategic report (if any) for the last financial year,

(b)   the last directors' report, ...

(ba)   the last directors' remuneration report (if any), and

(c)   the auditor's report on those accounts (including the statement on that report and (where applicable) on the strategic report and on the directors' remuneration report).

(2)   The entitlement under this section is to a single copy of those documents, but that is in addition to any copy to which a person may be entitled under section 423.

(3)   If a demand made under this section is not complied with within seven days of receipt by the company, an offence is committed by—

(a)   the company, and

(b)   every officer of the company who is in default.

(4)   A person guilty of an offence under this section is liable on summary conviction to a fine not exceeding level 3 on the standard scale and, for continued contravention, a daily default fine not exceeding one-tenth of level 3 on the standard scale.

432   Right of member or debenture holder to copies of accounts and reports: quoted companies

(1)   A member of, or holder of debentures of, a quoted company is entitled to be provided, on demand and without charge, with a copy of—

(a)   the company's last annual accounts,

(b)   the last directors' remuneration report,

(ba)   the strategic report (if any) for the last financial year,

(c)   the last directors' report, and

(d)   the auditor's report on those accounts (including the report on the directors' remuneration report, on the strategic report (where this is covered by the auditor's report) and on the directors' report).

(2)   The entitlement under this section is to a single copy of those documents, but that is in addition to any copy to which a person may be entitled under section 423.

(3)   If a demand made under this section is not complied with within seven days of receipt by the company, an offence is committed by—

(a)   the company, and

(b)   every officer of the company who is in default.

(4)   A person guilty of an offence under this section is liable on summary conviction to a fine not exceeding level 3 on the standard scale and, for continued contravention, a daily default fine not exceeding one-tenth of level 3 on the standard scale.

Requirements in connection with publication of accounts and reports

433   Name of signatory to be stated in published copies of accounts and reports

(1)   Every copy of a document to which this section applies that is published by or on behalf of the company must state the name of the person who signed it on behalf of the board.

(2)   In the case of an unquoted company that is not a traded company, this section applies to copies of—

(a)   the company's balance sheet, ...

(aa)   the strategic report, and

(b)   the directors' report.

(3)   In the case of a quoted company or of a traded company (as defined by section 360C) that is not a quoted company, this section applies to copies of—

(a)   the company's balance sheet,
(b)   the directors' remuneration report, ...
(ba) the strategic report, and
(c)   the directors' report.

(4)   If a copy is published without the required statement of the signatory's name, an offence is committed by—
(a)   the company, and
(b)   every officer of the company who is in default.

(5)   A person guilty of an offence under this section is liable on summary conviction to a fine not exceeding level 3 on the standard scale.

434   Requirements in connection with publication of statutory accounts

(1)   If a company publishes any of its statutory accounts, they must be accompanied by the auditor's report on those accounts (unless the company is exempt from audit and the directors have taken advantage of that exemption).

(2)   A company that prepares statutory group accounts for a financial year must not publish its statutory individual accounts for that year without also publishing with them its statutory group accounts.

(3)   A company's "statutory accounts" are its accounts for a financial year as required to be delivered to the registrar under section 441.

(4)   If a company contravenes any provision of this section, an offence is committed by—
(a)   the company, and
(b)   every officer of the company who is in default.

(5)   A person guilty of an offence under this section is liable on summary conviction to a fine not exceeding level 3 on the standard scale.

(6)   ...

435   Requirements in connection with publication of non-statutory accounts

(1)   If a company publishes non-statutory accounts, it must publish with them a statement indicating—
(a)   that they are not the company's statutory accounts,
(b)   whether statutory accounts dealing with any financial year with which the non-statutory accounts purport to deal have been delivered to the registrar, and
(c)   whether an auditor's report has been made on the company's statutory accounts for any such financial year, and if so whether the report—
    (i)   was qualified or unqualified, or included a reference to any matters to which the auditor drew attention by way of emphasis without qualifying the report, or
    (ii)   contained a statement under section 498(2) (accounting records or returns inadequate or accounts or directors' remuneration report not agreeing with records and returns), or section 498(3) (failure to obtain necessary information and explanations).

(2)   The company must not publish with non-statutory accounts the auditor's report on the company's statutory accounts.

(3)   References in this section to the publication by a company of "non-statutory accounts" are to the publication of—
(a)   any balance sheet or profit and loss account relating to, or purporting to deal with, a financial year of the company, or
(b)   an account in any form purporting to be a balance sheet or profit and loss account for a group headed by the company relating to, or purporting to deal with, a financial year of the company, otherwise than as part of the company's statutory accounts.

(4)   In subsection (3)(b) "a group headed by the company" means a group consisting of the company and any other undertaking (regardless of whether it is a subsidiary undertaking of the company) other than a parent undertaking of the company.

(5)   If a company contravenes any provision of this section, an offence is committed by—
        (a)   the company, and
        (b)   every officer of the company who is in default.

(6)   A person guilty of an offence under this section is liable on summary conviction to a fine not exceeding level 3 on the standard scale.

(7)   ...

436   Meaning of "publication" in relation to accounts and reports

(1)   This section has effect for the purposes of—
        section 433 (name of signatory to be stated in published copies of accounts and reports),
        section 434 (requirements in connection with publication of statutory accounts), and
        section 435 (requirements in connection with publication of non-statutory accounts).

(2)   For the purposes of those sections a company is regarded as publishing a document if it publishes, issues or circulates it or otherwise makes it available for public inspection in a manner calculated to invite members of the public generally, or any class of members of the public, to read it.

CHAPTER 8
PUBLIC COMPANIES: LAYING OF ACCOUNTS AND REPORTS
BEFORE GENERAL MEETING

437   Public companies: laying of accounts and reports before general meeting

(1)   The directors of a public company must lay before the company in general meeting copies of its annual accounts and reports.

(2)   This section must be complied with not later than the end of the period for filing the accounts and reports in question.

(3)   In the Companies Acts "accounts meeting", in relation to a public company, means a general meeting of the company at which the company's annual accounts and reports are (or are to be) laid in accordance with this section.

438   Public companies: offence of failure to lay accounts and reports

(1)   If the requirements of section 437 (public companies: laying of accounts and reports before general meeting) are not complied with before the end of the period allowed, every person who immediately before the end of that period was a director of the company commits an offence.

(2)   It is a defence for a person charged with such an offence to prove that he took all reasonable steps for securing that those requirements would be complied with before the end of that period.

(3)   It is not a defence to prove that the documents in question were not in fact prepared as required by this Part.

(4)   A person guilty of an offence under this section is liable on summary conviction to a fine not exceeding level 5 on the standard scale and, for continued contravention, a daily default fine not exceeding one-tenth of the greater of £5,000 or level 4 on the standard scale.

CHAPTER 9
QUOTED COMPANIES AND TRADED COMPANIES: MEMBERS' APPROVAL OF
DIRECTORS' REMUNERATION REPORT

439   Quoted companies and traded companies: members' approval of directors' remuneration report

(1)   A company to which this section applies must, prior to the accounts meeting, give to the members of the company entitled to be sent notice of the meeting notice of the intention to move at the meeting, as an ordinary resolution, a resolution approving the directors' remuneration report for the financial year other than the part containing the directors' remuneration policy (as to which see section 439A).

(1A)   This section applies to—
        (a)   a quoted company, and

(b)   a traded company (as defined by section 360C) that is not a quoted company.

(2)   The notice may be given in any manner permitted for the service on the member of notice of the meeting.

(3)   The business that may be dealt with at the accounts meeting includes the resolution.

This is so notwithstanding any default in complying with subsection (1) or (2).

(4)   The existing directors must ensure that the resolution is put to the vote of the meeting.

(5)   No entitlement of a person to remuneration is made conditional on the resolution being passed by reason only of the provision made by this section.

(6)   In this section—

"the accounts meeting" means the general meeting of the company before which the company's annual accounts for the financial year are to be laid; and

"existing director" means a person who is a director of the company immediately before that meeting.

439A   Quoted companies and traded companies: members' approval of directors' remuneration policy

(1)   A quoted company or unquoted traded company must give notice of the intention to move, as an ordinary resolution, a resolution approving the relevant directors' remuneration policy—

(a)   at the accounts meeting held in the first financial year which begins on or after the day on which the company becomes a quoted company or (as the case may be) an unquoted traded company, and

(b)   at an accounts or other general meeting held no later than the end of the period of three financial years beginning with the first financial year after the last accounts or other general meeting in relation to which notice is given under this subsection.

(2)   A quoted company or unquoted traded company must give notice of the intention to move at an accounts meeting, as an ordinary resolution, a resolution approving the relevant directors' remuneration policy if—

(a)   a resolution required to be put to the vote under section 439 was not passed at the last accounts meeting of the company, and

(b)   no notice under this section was given in relation to that meeting or any other general meeting held before the next accounts meeting.

(2A)   A quoted company or unquoted traded company must give notice of the intention to move at an accounts or other general meeting, as an ordinary resolution, a resolution approving the relevant directors' remuneration policy if—

(a)   a resolution required to be put to the vote under subsection (1) or (2) or this subsection was not passed at the last accounts or other general meeting of the company, and

(b)   no notice under this section was given in relation to any other general meeting held before the next accounts meeting.

(3)   Subsection (2) does not apply in relation to a quoted company or unquoted traded company before the first meeting in relation to which it gives notice under subsection (1).

(4)   A notice given under subsection (2) or (2A) is to be treated as given under subsection (1) for the purpose of determining the period within which the next notice under subsection (1) must be given.

(5)   Notice of the intention to move a resolution to which this section applies must be given, prior to the meeting in question, to the members of the company entitled to be sent notice of the meeting.

(6)   Subsections (2) to (4) of section 439 apply for the purposes of a resolution to which this section applies as they apply for the purposes of a resolution to which section 439 applies, with the modification that, for the purposes of a resolution relating to a general meeting other than an accounts meeting, subsection (3) applies as if for "accounts meeting" there were substituted "general meeting".

(7)   For the purposes of this section, the relevant directors' remuneration policy is—

    (a)   in a case where notice is given in relation to an accounts meeting, the remuneration policy contained in the directors' remuneration report in respect of which a resolution under section 439 is required to be put to the vote at that accounts meeting;

    (b)   in a case where notice is given in relation to a general meeting other than an accounts meeting—

        (i)   the remuneration policy contained in the directors' remuneration report in respect of which such a resolution was required to be put to the vote at the last accounts meeting to be held before that other general meeting, or

        (ii)   where that policy has been revised in accordance with section 422A, the policy as so revised.

(8)   In this section—

    (a)   "accounts meeting" means a general meeting of the company before which the company's annual accounts for a financial year are to be laid;

    (b)   "directors' remuneration policy" means the policy of the company with respect to the matters mentioned in section 421(2A);

    (c)   "unquoted traded company" means a traded company (as defined by section 360C) that is not a quoted company.

440   Quoted companies and traded companies: offences in connection with procedure for approval

(1)   In the event of default in complying with section 439(1) or 439A(1), (2) or (2A) (notice to be given of resolution for approval of directors' remuneration report or policy), an offence is committed by every officer of the company who is in default.

(2)   If the resolution is not put to the vote of the meeting to which it relates, an offence is committed by each existing director.

(3)   It is a defence for a person charged with an offence under subsection (2) to prove that he took all reasonable steps for securing that the resolution was put to the vote of the meeting.

(4)   A person guilty of an offence under this section is liable on summary conviction to a fine not exceeding level 3 on the standard scale.

(5)   In this section—

    …

"existing director" means a person who is a director of the company immediately before that meeting.

CHAPTER 10
FILING OF ACCOUNTS AND REPORTS

Duty to file accounts and reports

441   Duty to file accounts and reports with the registrar

(1)   The directors of a company must deliver to the registrar for each financial year the accounts and reports required by—

section 444 (filing obligations of companies subject to small companies regime),

section 444A (filing obligations of companies entitled to small companies exemption in relation to directors' report),

section 445 (filing obligations of medium-sized companies),

section 446 (filing obligations of unquoted companies), or

section 447 (filing obligations of quoted companies).

(2)   This is subject to—

section 448 (unlimited companies exempt from filing obligations), and

section 448A (dormant subsidiaries exempt from filing obligations).

442   Period allowed for filing accounts

(1)   This section specifies the period allowed for the directors of a company to comply with their obligation under section 441 to deliver accounts and reports for a financial year to the registrar. This is referred to in the Companies Acts as the "period for filing" those accounts and reports.

(2)   The period is—

(a)   for a private company, nine months after the end of the relevant accounting reference period, and

(b)   for a public company, six months after the end of that period. This is subject to the following provisions of this section.

(3)   If the relevant accounting reference period is the company's first and is a period of more than twelve months, the period is—

(a)   nine months or six months, as the case may be, from the first anniversary of the incorporation of the company, or

(b)   three months after the end of the accounting reference period,

whichever last expires.

(4)   If the relevant accounting reference period is treated as shortened by virtue of a notice given by the company under section 392 (alteration of accounting reference date), the period is—

(a)   that applicable in accordance with the above provisions, or

(b)   three months from the date of the notice under that section, whichever last expires.

(5)   Subject to subsection (5A), if for any special reason the Secretary of State thinks fit he may, on an application made before the expiry of the period otherwise allowed, by notice in writing to a company extend that period by such further period as may be specified in the notice.

(5A)   Any such extension must not have the effect of extending the period for filing to more than twelve months after the end of the relevant accounting reference period.

(6)   Whether the period allowed is that for a private company or a public company is determined by reference to the company's status immediately before the end of the relevant accounting reference period.

(7)   In this section "the relevant accounting reference period" means the accounting reference period by reference to which the financial year for the accounts in question was determined.

443   Calculation of period allowed

(1)   This section applies for the purposes of calculating the period for filing a company's accounts and reports which is expressed as a specified number of months from a specified date or after the end of a specified previous period.

(2)   Subject to the following provisions, the period ends with the date in the appropriate month corresponding to the specified date or the last day of the specified previous period.

(3)   If the specified date, or the last day of the specified previous period, is the last day of a month, the period ends with the last day of the appropriate month (whether or not that is the corresponding date).

(4)   If—

(a)   the specified date, or the last day of the specified previous period, is not the last day of a month but is the 29th or 30th, and

(b)   the appropriate month is February,

the period ends with the last day of February.

(5)   "The appropriate month" means the month that is the specified number of months after the month in which the specified date, or the end of the specified previous period, falls.

Filing obligations of different descriptions of company

444   Filing obligations of companies subject to small companies regime

(1)   The directors of a company subject to the small companies regime—

(a)   must deliver to the registrar for each financial year a copy of the balance sheet drawn up as at the last day of that year, and

(b)   may also deliver to the registrar—
      (i)   a copy of the company's profit and loss account for that year, and
      (ii)   a copy of the directors' report for that year.

(2)   Where the directors deliver to the registrar a copy of the company's profit and loss account under subsection (1)(b)(i), the directors must also deliver to the registrar a copy of the auditor's report on the accounts (and any directors' report) that it delivers.

This does not apply if the company is exempt from audit and the directors have taken advantage of that exemption.

(2A)   Where the balance sheet or profit and loss account is abridged pursuant to paragraph 1A of Schedule 1 to the Small Companies and Groups (Accounts and Directors' Report) Regulations, the directors must also deliver to the registrar a statement by the company that all the members of the company have consented to the abridgement.

(3)   … the copies of accounts and reports delivered to the registrar must be copies of the company's annual accounts and reports.

(3A), (3B), (4) …

(5)   Where the directors of a company subject to the small companies regime …—
     (a)   do not deliver to the registrar a copy of the company's profit and loss account, or
     (b)   do not deliver to the registrar a copy of the directors' report,
the copy of the balance sheet delivered to the registrar must contain in a prominent position a statement that the company's annual accounts and reports have been delivered in accordance with the provisions applicable to companies subject to the small companies regime.

(5A)   Subject to subsection (5C), where the directors of a company subject to the small companies regime do not deliver to the registrar a copy of the company's profit and loss account—
     (a)   the copy of the balance sheet delivered to the registrar must disclose that fact, and
     (b)   unless the company is exempt from audit and the directors have taken advantage of that exemption, the notes to the balance sheet delivered must satisfy the requirements in subsection (5B).

(5B)   Those requirements are that the notes to the balance sheet must—
     (a)   state whether the auditor's report was qualified or unqualified,
     (b)   where that report was qualified, disclose the basis of the qualification (reproducing any statement under section 498(2)(a) or (b) or section 498(3), if applicable),
     (c)   where that report was unqualified, include a reference to any matters to which the auditor drew attention by way of emphasis, and
     (d)   state—
         (i)   the name of the auditor and (where the auditor is a firm) the name of the person who signed the auditor's report as senior statutory auditor, or
         (ii)   if the conditions in section 506 (circumstances in which names may be omitted) are met, that a resolution has been passed and notified to the Secretary of State in accordance with that section.

(5C)   Subsection (5A) does not apply in relation to a company if—
     (a)   the company qualifies as a micro-entity (see sections 384A and 384B) in relation to a financial year, and
     (b)   the company's accounts are prepared for that year in accordance with any of the micro-entity provisions.

(6)   The copies of the balance sheet and any directors' report delivered to the registrar under this section must state the name of the person who signed it on behalf of the board.

(7)   The copy of the auditor's report delivered to the registrar under this section must—
     (a)   state the name of the auditor and (where the auditor is a firm) the name of the person who signed it as senior statutory auditor, or
     (b)   if the conditions in section 506 (circumstances in which names may be omitted) are met, state that a resolution has been passed and notified to the Secretary of State in accordance with that section.

(8)   If more than one person is appointed as auditor, the references in subsections (5B)(d)(i) and (7)(a) to the name of the auditor are to be read as references to the names of all the auditors.

444A   Filing obligations of companies entitled to small companies exemption in relation to directors' report

(1)   The directors of a company that is entitled to small companies exemption in relation to the directors' report for a financial year—
         (a)   must deliver to the registrar a copy of the company's annual accounts for that year, and
         (b)   may also deliver to the registrar a copy of the directors' report.

(2)   The directors must also deliver to the registrar a copy of the auditor's report on the accounts (and any directors' report) that it delivers.
         This does not apply if the company is exempt from audit and the directors have taken advantage of that exception.

(3)   The copies of the balance sheet and directors' report delivered to the registrar under this section must state the name of the person who signed it on behalf of the board.

(4)   The copy of the auditor's report delivered to the registrar under this section must—
         (a)   state the name of the auditor and (where the auditor is a firm) the name of the person who signed it as senior statutory auditor, or
         (b)   if the conditions in section 506 (circumstances in which names may be omitted) are met, state that a resolution has been passed and notified to the Secretary of State in accordance with that section.

(4A)   If more than one person is appointed as auditor, the reference in subsection (4)(a) to the name of the auditor is to be read as a reference to the names of all the auditors.

(5)   This section does not apply to companies within section 444 (filing obligations of companies subject to the small companies regime).

445   Filing obligations of medium-sized companies

(1)   The directors of a company that qualifies as a medium-sized company in relation to a financial year (see sections 465 to 467) must deliver to the registrar a copy of—
         (a)   the company's annual accounts, …
         (aa) the strategic report, and
         (b)   the directors' report.

(2)   They must also deliver to the registrar a copy of the auditor's report on those accounts (and on the strategic report and the directors' report).
         This does not apply if the company is exempt from audit and the directors have taken advantage of that exemption.

(3), (4) …

(5)   The copies of the balance sheet, strategic report and directors' report delivered to the registrar under this section must state the name of the person who signed it on behalf of the board.

(6)   The copy of the auditor's report delivered to the registrar under this section must—
         (a)   state the name of the auditor and (where the auditor is a firm) the name of the person who signed it as senior statutory auditor, or
         (b)   if the conditions in section 506 (circumstances in which names may be omitted) are met, state that a resolution has been passed and notified to the Secretary of State in accordance with that section.

(6A)   If more than one person is appointed as auditor, the reference in subsection (6)(a) to the name of the auditor is to be read as a reference to the names of all the auditors.

(7)   This section does not apply to companies within—
         (a)   section 444 (filing obligations of companies subject to the small companies regime), or
         (b)   section 444A (filing obligations of companies entitled to small companies exemption in relation to directors' report).

446 **Filing obligations of unquoted companies**

(1) The directors of an unquoted company must deliver to the registrar for each financial year of the company a copy of—

    (a) the company's annual accounts, …

    (aa) the strategic report,

    (b) the directors' report, …

    (ba) any directors' remuneration report, and

    (c) any separate corporate governance statement.

(2) The directors must also deliver to the registrar a copy of the auditor's report on those accounts (and the strategic report (where this is covered by the auditor's report), the directors' report, any directors' remuneration report and any separate corporate governance statement).

This does not apply if the company is exempt from audit and the directors have taken advantage of that exemption.

(3) The copies of the balance sheet, strategic report and directors' report, any directors' remuneration report delivered to the registrar under this section must state the name of the person who signed it on behalf of the board.

(4) The copy of the auditor's report delivered to the registrar under this section must—

    (a) state the name of the auditor and (where the auditor is a firm) the name of the person who signed it as senior statutory auditor, or

    (b) if the conditions in section 506 (circumstances in which names may be omitted) are met, state that a resolution has been passed and notified to the Secretary of State in accordance with that section.

(4A) If more than one person is appointed as auditor, the reference in subsection (4)(a) to the name of the auditor is to be read as a reference to the names of all the auditors.

(5) This section does not apply to companies within—

    (a) section 444 (filing obligations of companies subject to the small companies regime), …

    (aa) section 444A (filing obligations of companies entitled to small companies exemption in relation to directors' report), or

    (b) section 445 (filing obligations of medium-sized companies).

447 **Filing obligations of quoted companies**

(1) The directors of a quoted company must deliver to the registrar for each financial year of the company a copy of—

    (a) the company's annual accounts,

    (b) the directors' remuneration report, …

    (ba) the strategic report,

    (c) the directors' report, and

    (d) any separate corporate governance statement.

(2) They must also deliver a copy of the auditor's report on those accounts (and on the directors' remuneration report, the strategic report (where this is covered by the auditor's report), the directors' report and any separate corporate governance statement).

(3) The copies of the balance sheet, the directors' remuneration report, the strategic report and the directors' report delivered to the registrar under this section must state the name of the person who signed it on behalf of the board.

(4) The copy of the auditor's report delivered to the registrar under this section must—

    (a) state the name of the auditor and (where the auditor is a firm) the name of the person who signed it as senior statutory auditor, or

    (b) if the conditions in section 506 (circumstances in which names may be omitted) are met, state that a resolution has been passed and notified to the Secretary of State in accordance with that section.

(5) If more than one person is appointed as auditor, the reference in subsection (4)(a) to the name of the auditor is to be read as a reference to the names of all the auditors.

448   Unlimited companies exempt from obligation to file accounts

(1)   The directors of an unlimited company are not required to deliver accounts and reports to the registrar in respect of a financial year if the following conditions are met.

(2)   The conditions are that at no time during the relevant accounting reference period—

    (a)   has the company been, to its knowledge, a subsidiary undertaking of an undertaking which was then limited, or

    (b)   have there been, to its knowledge, exercisable by or on behalf of two or more undertakings which were then limited, rights which if exercisable by one of them would have made the company a subsidiary undertaking of it, or

    (c)   has the company been a parent company of an undertaking which was then limited.

The references above to an undertaking being limited at a particular time are to an undertaking (under whatever law established) the liability of whose members is at that time limited.

(3)   The exemption conferred by this section does not apply if—

    (a)   the company is a banking or insurance company or the parent company of a banking or insurance group, or

    (b)   each of the members of the company is—

        (i)   a limited company,

        (ii)   another unlimited company each of whose members is a limited company, …

        (iii)   a Scottish partnership which is not a limited partnership, each of whose members is a limited company, or

        (iv)   a Scottish partnership which is a limited partnership, each of whose general partners is a limited company.

The references in paragraph (b) to a limited company, another unlimited company, a Scottish partnership which is not a limited partnership or a Scottish partnership which is a limited partnership include a comparable undertaking incorporated in or formed under the law of a country or territory outside the United Kingdom.

(4)   Where a company is exempt by virtue of this section from the obligation to deliver accounts—

    (a)   section 434(3) (requirements in connection with publication of statutory accounts: meaning of "statutory accounts") has effect with the substitution for the words "as required to be delivered to the registrar under section 441" of the words "as prepared in accordance with this Part and approved by the board of directors"; and

    (b)   section 435(1)(b) (requirements in connection with publication of non-statutory accounts: statement whether statutory accounts delivered) has effect with the substitution for the words from "whether statutory accounts" to "have been delivered to the registrar" of the words "that the company is exempt from the requirement to deliver statutory accounts".

(5)   In this section—

"general partner" means—

    (a)   in relation to a Scottish partnership which is a limited partnership, a person who is a general partner within the meaning of the Limited Partnerships Act 1907; and

    (b)   in relation to an undertaking incorporated in or formed under the law of any country or territory outside the United Kingdom and which is comparable to a Scottish partnership which is a limited partnership, a person comparable to such a general partner;

"limited partnership" means a partnership registered under the Limited Partnerships Act 1907; and

the "relevant accounting reference period", in relation to a financial year, means the accounting reference period by reference to which that financial year was determined.

448A   Dormant subsidiaries exempt from obligation to file accounts

(1)   The directors of a company are not required to deliver a copy of the company's individual accounts to the registrar in respect of a financial year if—

    (a)   the company is a subsidiary undertaking,

    (b)   it has been dormant throughout the whole of that year, and

    (c)   its parent undertaking is established under the law of any part of the United Kingdom.

(2)   Exemption is conditional upon compliance with all of the following conditions—

    (a)   all members of the company must agree to the exemption in respect of the financial year in question,

    (b)   the parent undertaking must give a guarantee under section 448C in respect of that year,

    (c)   the company must be included in the consolidated accounts drawn up for that year or to an earlier date in that year by the parent undertaking in accordance with—

        (i)   if the undertaking is a company, the requirements of this Part of this Act, or, if the undertaking is not a company, the legal requirements which apply to the drawing up of consolidated accounts for that undertaking, or

        (ii)   UK-adopted international accounting standards,

    (d)   the parent undertaking must disclose in the notes to the consolidated accounts that the directors of the company are exempt from the requirement to deliver a copy of the company's individual accounts to the registrar by virtue of this section, and

    (e)   the directors of the company must deliver to the registrar within the period for filing the company's accounts and reports for that year—

        (i)   a written notice of the agreement referred to in subsection (2)(a),

        (ii)   the statement referred to in section 448C(1),

        (iii)   a copy of the consolidated accounts referred to in subsection (2)(c),

        (iv)   a copy of the auditor's report on those accounts, and

        (v)   a copy of the consolidated annual report drawn up by the parent undertaking.

448B   Companies excluded from the dormant subsidiaries exemption

The directors of a company are not entitled to the exemption conferred by section 448A (dormant subsidiaries) if the company was at any time within the financial year in question—

(a)   a traded company,

(b)   a company that—

    (i)   is an authorised insurance company, a banking company, an e-Money issuer, a MiFID investment firm or a UCITS management company, or

    (ii)   carries on insurance market activity, or

(c)   a special register body as defined in section 117(1) of the Trade Union and Labour Relations (Consolidation) Act 1992 (c 52) or an employers' association as defined in section 122 of that Act or Article 4 of the Industrial Relations (Northern Ireland) Order 1992 (SI 1992/807) (NI 5).

448C   Dormant subsidiaries filing exemption: parent undertaking declaration of guarantee

(1)   A guarantee is given by a parent undertaking under this section when the directors of the subsidiary company deliver to the registrar a statement by the parent undertaking that it guarantees the subsidiary company under this section.

(2)   The statement under subsection (1) must be authenticated by the parent undertaking and must specify—

    (a)   the name of the parent undertaking,

    (b)   the registered number (if any) of the parent undertaking,

    (c)   ...

    (d)   the name and registered number of the subsidiary company in respect of which the guarantee is being given,

    (e)   the date of the statement, and

    (f)   the financial year to which the guarantee relates.

(3)   A guarantee given under this section has the effect that—

    (a)   the parent undertaking guarantees all outstanding liabilities to which the subsidiary company is subject at the end of the financial year to which the guarantee relates, until they are satisfied in full, and

    (b)   the guarantee is enforceable against the parent undertaking by any person to whom the subsidiary company is liable in respect of those liabilities.

Failure to file accounts and reports

451   Default in filing accounts and reports: offences

(1)   If the requirements of section 441 (duty to file accounts and reports) are not complied with in relation to a company's accounts and reports for a financial year before the end of the period for filing those accounts and reports, every person who immediately before the end of that period was a director of the company commits an offence.

(2)   It is a defence for a person charged with such an offence to prove that he took all reasonable steps for securing that those requirements would be complied with before the end of that period.

(3)   It is not a defence to prove that the documents in question were not in fact prepared as required by this Part.

(4)   A person guilty of an offence under this section is liable on summary conviction to a fine not exceeding level 5 on the standard scale and, for continued contravention, a daily default fine not exceeding one-tenth of the greater of £5,000 or level 4 on the standard scale.

452   Default in filing accounts and reports: court order

(1)   If—

   (a)   the requirements of section 441 (duty to file accounts and reports) are not complied with in relation to a company's accounts and reports for a financial year before the end of the period for filing those accounts and reports, and

   (b)   the directors of the company fail to make good the default within 14 days after the service of a notice on them requiring compliance,

   the court may, on the application of any member or creditor of the company or of the registrar, make an order directing the directors (or any of them) to make good the default within such time as may be specified in the order.

(2)   The court's order may provide that all costs (in Scotland, expenses) of and incidental to the application are to be borne by the directors.

453   Civil penalty for failure to file accounts and reports

(1)   Where the requirements of section 441 are not complied with in relation to a company's accounts and reports for a financial year before the end of the period for filing those accounts and reports, the company is liable to a civil penalty.
   This is in addition to any liability of the directors under section 451.

(2)   The amount of the penalty shall be determined in accordance with regulations made by the Secretary of State by reference to—

   (a)   the length of the period between the end of the period for filing the accounts and reports in question and the day on which the requirements are complied with, and

   (b)   whether the company is a private or public company.

(3)   The penalty may be recovered by the registrar and is to be paid into the Consolidated Fund.

(4)   It is not a defence in proceedings under this section to prove that the
   documents in question were not in fact prepared as required by this Part.

(5)   Regulations under this section having the effect of increasing the penalty payable in any case are subject to affirmative resolution procedure. Otherwise, the regulations are subject to negative resolution procedure.

CHAPTER 11
REVISION OF DEFECTIVE ACCOUNTS AND REPORTS

Voluntary revision

454   Voluntary revision of accounts etc

(1)   If it appears to the directors of a company that—

   (a)   the company's annual accounts,

    (b)   the directors' remuneration report or the directors' report, or

    (c)   a strategic report of the company,

did not comply with the requirements of this Act ..., they may prepare revised accounts or a revised report or statement.

(2)   Where copies of the previous accounts or report have been sent out to members, delivered to the registrar or (in the case of a public company) laid before the company in general meeting, the revisions must be confined to—

    (a)   the correction of those respects in which the previous accounts or report did not comply with the requirements of this Act ..., and

    (b)   the making of any necessary consequential alterations.

(3)   The Secretary of State may make provision by regulations as to the application of the provisions of this Act in relation to

    (a)   revised annual accounts,

    (b)   a revised directors' remuneration report or directors' report, or

    (c)   a revised strategic report of the company.

(4)   The regulations may, in particular—

    (a)   make different provision according to whether the previous accounts or report are replaced or are supplemented by a document indicating the corrections to be made;

    (b)   make provision with respect to the functions of the company's auditor in relation to the revised accounts or report;

    (c)   require the directors to take such steps as may be specified in the regulations where the previous accounts or report have been—

        (i)   sent out to members and others under section 423,

        (ii)   laid before the company in general meeting, or

        (iii)   delivered to the registrar,

        or where a strategic report and supplementary material containing information derived from the previous accounts or report have been sent to members under section 426;

    (d)   apply the provisions of this Act (including those creating criminal offences) subject to such additions, exceptions and modifications as are specified in the regulations.

(5)   Regulations under this section are subject to negative resolution procedure.

Secretary of State's notice

455   Secretary of State's notice in respect of accounts or reports

(1)   This section applies where—

    (a)   copies of a company's annual accounts, strategic report or directors' report have been sent out under section 423, or

    (b)   a copy of a company's annual accounts, strategic report or directors' report has been delivered to the registrar or (in the case of a public company) laid before the company in general meeting,

and it appears to the Secretary of State that there is, or may be, a question whether the accounts or report comply with the requirements of this Act ....

(2)   The Secretary of State may give notice to the directors of the company indicating the respects in which it appears that such a question arises or may arise.

(3)   The notice must specify a period of not less than one month for the directors to give an explanation of the accounts or report or prepare revised accounts or a revised report.

(4)   If at the end of the specified period, or such longer period as the Secretary of State may allow, it appears to the Secretary of State that the directors have not—

    (a)   given a satisfactory explanation of the accounts or report, or

    (b)   revised the accounts or report so as to comply with the requirements of this Act ...,

the Secretary of State may apply to the court.

(5)   The provisions of this section apply equally to revised annual accounts, revised strategic reports
         and revised directors' reports, in which case they have effect as if the references to revised
         accounts or reports were references to further revised accounts or reports.

Application to court

456   Application to court in respect of defective accounts or reports

(1)   An application may be made to the court—
         (a)   by the Secretary of State, after having complied with section 455, or
         (b)   by a person authorised by the Secretary of State for the purposes of this section,
         for a declaration (in Scotland, a declarator) that the annual accounts of a company do not comply,
         or a strategic report or a directors' report does not comply, with the requirements of this Act ...
         and for an order requiring the directors of the company to prepare revised accounts or a revised
         report.

(2)   Notice of the application, together with a general statement of the matters at issue in the
         proceedings, shall be given by the applicant to the registrar for registration.

(3)   If the court orders the preparation of revised accounts, it may give directions as to—
         (a)   the auditing of the accounts,
         (b)   the revision of any directors' remuneration report, strategic report and supplementary
               material or directors' report ..., and
         (c)   the taking of steps by the directors to bring the making of the order to the notice of persons
               likely to rely on the previous accounts, and such other matters as the court thinks fit.

(4)   If the court orders the preparation of a revised strategic report or directors' report it may give
         directions as to—
         (a)   the review of the report by the auditors,
         (b)   ...
         (c)   the taking of steps by the directors to bring the making of the order to the notice of persons
               likely to rely on the previous report, and
         (d)   such other matters as the court thinks fit.

(5)   If the court finds that the accounts or report did not comply with the requirements of this Act ... it
         may order that all or part of—
         (a)   the costs (in Scotland, expenses) of and incidental to the application, and
         (b)   any reasonable expenses incurred by the company in connection with or in consequence of
               the preparation of revised accounts or a revised report,
         are to be borne by such of the directors as were party to the approval of the defective accounts or
         report.
         For this purpose every director of the company at the time of the approval of the accounts or
         report shall be taken to have been a party to the approval unless he shows that he took all
         reasonable steps to prevent that approval.

(6)   Where the court makes an order under subsection (5) it shall have regard to whether the directors
         party to the approval of the defective accounts or report knew or ought to have known that the
         accounts or report did not comply with the requirements of this Act ..., and it may exclude one or
         more directors from the order or order the payment of different amounts by different directors.

(7)   On the conclusion of proceedings on an application under this section, the applicant must send to
         the registrar for registration a copy of the court order or, as the case may be, give notice to the
         registrar that the application has failed or been withdrawn.

(8)   The provisions of this section apply equally to revised annual accounts, revised strategic reports
         and revised directors' reports, in which case they have effect as if the references to revised
         accounts or reports were references to further revised accounts or reports.

457   Other persons authorised to apply to the court

(1)   The Secretary of State may by order (an "authorisation order") authorise for the purposes of
         section 456 any person appearing to him—

    (a)   to have an interest in, and to have satisfactory procedures directed to securing, compliance by companies with the requirements of this Act ... relating to accounts, strategic reports and directors' reports,

    (b)   to have satisfactory procedures for receiving and investigating complaints about companies' annual accounts, strategic reports and directors' reports, and

    (c)   otherwise to be a fit and proper person to be authorised.

(2)   A person may be authorised generally or in respect of particular classes of case, and different persons may be authorised in respect of different classes of case.

(3)   The Secretary of State may refuse to authorise a person if he considers that his authorisation is unnecessary having regard to the fact that there are one or more other persons who have been or are likely to be authorised.

(4)   If the authorised person is an unincorporated association, proceedings brought in, or in connection with, the exercise of any function by the association as an authorised person may be brought by or against the association in the name of a body corporate whose constitution provides for the establishment of the association.

(5)   An authorisation order may contain such requirements or other provisions relating to the exercise of functions by the authorised person as appear to the Secretary of State to be appropriate.

No such order is to be made unless it appears to the Secretary of State that the person would, if authorised, exercise his functions as an authorised person in accordance with the provisions proposed.

(6)   Where authorisation is revoked, the revoking order may make such provision as the Secretary of State thinks fit with respect to pending proceedings.

(7)   An order under this section is subject to negative resolution procedure.

458   Disclosure of information by tax authorities

(1)   The Commissioners for Her Majesty's Revenue and Customs may disclose information to a person authorised under section 457 for the purpose of facilitating—

    (a)   the taking of steps by that person to discover whether there are grounds for an application to the court under section 456 (application in respect of defective accounts etc), or

    (b)   a decision by the authorised person whether to make such an application.

(2)   This section applies despite any statutory or other restriction on the disclosure of information.

Provided that, in the case of personal data within the meaning of Parts 5 to 7 of the Data Protection Act 2018 (see section 3(2) and (14) of that Act), information is not to be disclosed in contravention of the data protection legislation.

(3)   Information disclosed to an authorised person under this section—

    (a)   may not be used except in or in connection with—

        (i)   taking steps to discover whether there are grounds for an application to the court under section 456, or

        (ii)   deciding whether or not to make such an application,

    or in, or in connection with, proceedings on such an application; and

    (b)   must not be further disclosed except—

        (i)   to the person to whom the information relates, or

        (ii)   in, or in connection with, proceedings on any such application to the court.

(4)   A person who contravenes subsection (3) commits an offence unless—

    (a)   he did not know, and had no reason to suspect, that the information had been disclosed under this section, or

    (b)   he took all reasonable steps and exercised all due diligence to avoid the commission of the offence.

(5)   A person guilty of an offence under subsection (4) is liable—

    (a)   on conviction on indictment, to imprisonment for a term not exceeding two years or a fine (or both);

    (b)   on summary conviction—

        (i)   in England and Wales, to imprisonment for a term not exceeding twelve months or to a fine not exceeding the statutory maximum (or both);

        (ii)   in Scotland or Northern Ireland, to imprisonment for a term not exceeding six months, or to a fine not exceeding the statutory maximum (or both).

(6)   Where an offence under this section is committed by a body corporate, every officer of the body who is in default also commits the offence.

For this purpose—

(a)   any person who purports to act as director, manager or secretary of the body is treated as an officer of the body, and

(b)   if the body is a company, any shadow director is treated as an officer of the company.

Power of authorised person to require documents etc

459   Power of authorised person to require documents, information and explanations

(1)   This section applies where it appears to a person who is authorised under section 457 that there is, or may be, a question whether a company's annual accounts, strategic report or directors' report complies with the requirements of this Act ....

(2)   The authorised person may require any of the persons mentioned in subsection (3) to produce any document, or to provide him with any information or explanations, that he may reasonably require for the purpose of—

(a)   discovering whether there are grounds for an application to the court under section 456, or

(b)   deciding whether to make such an application.

(3)   Those persons are—

(a)   the company;

(b)   any officer, employee, or auditor of the company;

(c)   any persons who fell within paragraph (b) at a time to which the document or information required by the authorised person relates.

(4)   If a person fails to comply with such a requirement, the authorised person may apply to the court.

(5)   If it appears to the court that the person has failed to comply with a requirement under subsection (2), it may order the person to take such steps as it directs for securing that the documents are produced or the information or explanations are provided.

(6)   A statement made by a person in response to a requirement under subsection (2) or an order under subsection (5) may not be used in evidence against him in any criminal proceedings.

(7)   Nothing in this section compels any person to disclose documents or information in respect of which a claim to legal professional privilege (in Scotland, to confidentiality of communications) could be maintained in legal proceedings.

(8)   In this section "document" includes information recorded in any form.

460   Restrictions on disclosure of information obtained under compulsory powers

(1)   This section applies to information (in whatever form) obtained in pursuance of a requirement or order under section 459 (power of authorised person to require documents etc) that relates to the private affairs of an individual or to any particular business.

(2)   No such information may, during the lifetime of that individual or so long as that business continues to be carried on, be disclosed without the consent of that individual or the person for the time being carrying on that business.

(3)   This does not apply—

(a)   to disclosure permitted by section 461 (permitted disclosure of information obtained under compulsory powers), or

(b)   to the disclosure of information that is or has been available to the public from another source.

(4)   A person who discloses information in contravention of this section commits an offence, unless—

(a)   he did not know, and had no reason to suspect, that the information had been disclosed under section 459, or

(b) he took all reasonable steps and exercised all due diligence to avoid the commission of the offence.

(5) A person guilty of an offence under this section is liable—

    (a) on conviction on indictment, to imprisonment for a term not exceeding two years or a fine (or both);

    (b) on summary conviction—

        (i) in England and Wales or Scotland, to imprisonment for a term not exceeding twelve months or to a fine not exceeding the statutory maximum (or both);

        (ii) in … Northern Ireland, to imprisonment for a term not exceeding six months, or to a fine not exceeding the statutory maximum (or both).

(6) Where an offence under this section is committed by a body corporate, every officer of the body who is in default also commits the offence.

For this purpose—

    (a) any person who purports to act as director, manager or secretary of the body is treated as an officer of the body, and

    (b) if the body is a company, any shadow director is treated as an officer of the company.

461 Permitted disclosure of information obtained under compulsory powers

(1) The prohibition in section 460 of the disclosure of information obtained in pursuance of a requirement or order under section 459 (power of authorised person to require documents etc) that relates to the private affairs of an individual or to any particular business has effect subject to the following exceptions.

(2) It does not apply to the disclosure of information for the purpose of facilitating the carrying out by the authorised person of his functions under section 456.

(3) It does not apply to disclosure to—

    (a) the Secretary of State,

    (b) the Department of Enterprise, Trade and Investment for Northern Ireland,

    (c) the Treasury,

    (d) the Bank of England,

    (e) the Financial Conduct Authority,

    (ea) the Prudential Regulation Authority, or

    (f) the Commissioners for Her Majesty's Revenue and Customs.

(4) It does not apply to disclosure—

    (a) for the purpose of assisting a body designated by an order under section 1252 (delegation of functions of the Secretary of State) to exercise its functions under Part 42;

    (aa) for the purpose of assisting the competent authority to exercise its functions under the Statutory Auditors and Third Country Auditors Regulations 2016 and under the Audit Regulation;

    (b) with a view to the institution of, or otherwise for the purposes of, disciplinary proceedings relating to the performance by an accountant or auditor of his professional duties;

    (c) for the purpose of enabling or assisting the Secretary of State or the Treasury to exercise any of their functions under any of the following—

        (i) the Companies Acts,

        (ii) Part 5 of the Criminal Justice Act 1993 (insider dealing),

        (iii) the Insolvency Act 1986 or the Insolvency (Northern Ireland) Order 1989,

        (iv) the Company Directors Disqualification Act 1986 or the Company Directors Disqualification (Northern Ireland) Order 2002,

        (v) the Financial Services and Markets Act 2000;

    (d) for the purpose of enabling or assisting the Department of Enterprise, Trade and Investment for Northern Ireland to exercise any powers conferred on it by the enactments relating to companies, directors' disqualification or insolvency;

    (e) for the purpose of enabling or assisting the Bank of England to exercise its functions;

(f)   for the purpose of enabling or assisting the Commissioners for Her Majesty's Revenue and Customs to exercise their functions;

(g)   for the purpose of enabling or assisting the Financial Conduct Authority or the Prudential Regulation Authority to exercise its functions under any of the following—

  (i)   the legislation relating to friendly societies …,

  (ia)   the Credit Unions Act 1979,

  (ii)   the Building Societies Act 1986,

  (iii) Part 7 of the Companies Act 1989,

  (iv)   the Financial Services and Markets Act 2000,

  (v)   the Co-operative and Community Benefit Societies Act 2014; or

(h)   in pursuance of any assimilated obligation.

(5)   It does not apply to disclosure to a body exercising functions of a public nature under legislation in any country or territory outside the United Kingdom that appear to the authorised person to be similar to his functions under section 456 for the purpose of enabling or assisting that body to exercise those functions.

(6)   In determining whether to disclose information to a body in accordance with subsection (5), the authorised person must have regard to the following considerations—

(a)   whether the use which the body is likely to make of the information is sufficiently important to justify making the disclosure;

(b)   whether the body has adequate arrangements to prevent the information from being used or further disclosed other than—

  (i)   for the purposes of carrying out the functions mentioned in that subsection, or

  (ii)   for other purposes substantially similar to those for which information disclosed to the authorised person could be used or further disclosed.

(7)   Nothing in this section authorises the making of a disclosure in contravention of the data protection legislation.

462   Power to amend categories of permitted disclosure

(1)   The Secretary of State may by order amend section 461(3), (4) and (5).

(2)   An order under this section must not—

(a)   amend subsection (3) of that section (UK public authorities) by specifying a person unless the person exercises functions of a public nature (whether or not he exercises any other function);

(b)   amend subsection (4) of that section (purposes for which disclosure permitted) by adding or modifying a description of disclosure unless the purpose for which the disclosure is permitted is likely to facilitate the exercise of a function of a public nature;

(c)   amend subsection (5) of that section (overseas regulatory authorities) so as to have the effect of permitting disclosures to be made to a body other than one that exercises functions of a public nature in a country or territory outside the United Kingdom.

(3)   An order under this section is subject to negative resolution procedure.

CHAPTER 12
SUPPLEMENTARY PROVISIONS

Liability for false or misleading statements in reports and statements

463   Liability for false or misleading statements in reports and statements

(1)   The reports and statements to which this section applies are—

(za) the strategic report,

(a)   the directors' report,

(b)   the directors' remuneration report, …

(c)   …

(d)   any separate corporate governance statement.

(2)   A director of a company is liable to compensate the company for any loss suffered by it as a result of—

      (a)   any untrue or misleading statement in a report or statement to which this section applies, or

      (b)   the omission from a report or statement to which this section applies of anything required to be included in it.

(3)   He is so liable only if—

      (a)   he knew the statement to be untrue or misleading or was reckless as to whether it was untrue or misleading, or

      (b)   he knew the omission to be dishonest concealment of a material fact.

(4)   No person shall be subject to any liability to a person other than the company resulting from reliance, by that person or another, on information in a report or statement to which this section applies.

(5)   The reference in subsection (4) to a person being subject to a liability includes a reference to another person being entitled as against him to be granted any civil remedy or to rescind or repudiate an agreement.

(6)   This section does not affect—

      (a)   liability for a civil penalty, or

      (b)   liability for a criminal offence.

Accounting and reporting standards

464 Accounting standards

(1)   In this Part "accounting standards" means statements of standard accounting practice issued by such body or bodies as may be prescribed by regulations.

(2)   References in this Part to accounting standards applicable to a company's annual accounts are to such standards as are, in accordance with their terms, relevant to the company's circumstances and to the accounts.

(3)   Regulations under this section may contain such transitional and other supplementary and incidental provisions as appear to the Secretary of State to be appropriate.

Companies qualifying as medium-sized

465 Companies qualifying as medium-sized: general

(1)   A company qualifies as medium-sized in relation to its first financial year if the qualifying conditions are met in that year.

(2)   A company qualifies as medium-sized in relation to a subsequent financial year—

      (a)   if the qualifying conditions are met in that year and the preceding financial year;

      (b)   if the qualifying conditions are met in that year and the company qualified as medium-sized in relation to the preceding financial year;

      (c)   if the qualifying conditions were met in the preceding financial year and the company qualified as medium-sized in relation to that year.

(3)   The qualifying conditions are met by a company in a year in which it satisfies two or more of the following requirements—

1.	Turnover	Not more than £36 million
2.	Balance sheet total	Not more than £18 million
3.	Number of employees	Not more than 250

(4)   For a period that is a company's financial year but not in fact a year the maximum figures for turnover must be proportionately adjusted.

(5)   The balance sheet total means the aggregate of the amounts shown as assets in the company's balance sheet.

(6)   The number of employees means the average number of persons employed by the company in the year, determined as follows—

      (a)   find for each month in the financial year the number of persons employed under contracts of service by the company in that month (whether throughout the month or not),

(b)   add together the monthly totals, and

(c)   divide by the number of months in the financial year.

(7)   This section is subject to section 466 (companies qualifying as medium-sized: parent companies).

466   Companies qualifying as medium-sized: parent companies

(1)   A parent company qualifies as a medium-sized company in relation to a financial year only if the group headed by it qualifies as a medium-sized group.

(2)   A group qualifies as medium-sized in relation to the parent company's first financial year if the qualifying conditions are met in that year.

(3)   A group qualifies as medium-sized in relation to a subsequent financial year of the parent company—

(a)   if the qualifying conditions are met in that year and the preceding financial year;

(b)   if the qualifying conditions are met in that year and the group qualified as medium-sized in relation to the preceding financial year;

(c)   if the qualifying conditions were met in the preceding financial year and the group qualified as medium-sized in relation to that year.

(4)   The qualifying conditions are met by a group in a year in which it satisfies two or more of the following requirements—

1.	Aggregate turnover	Not more than £36 million net (or £43.2 million gross)
2.	Aggregate balance sheet total	Not more than £18 million net (or £21.6 million gross)
3.	Aggregate number of employees	Not more than 250

(5)   The aggregate figures are ascertained by aggregating the relevant figures determined in accordance with section 465 for each member of the group.

(6)   In relation to the aggregate figures for turnover and balance sheet total—

"net" means after any set-offs and other adjustments made to eliminate group transactions—

(a)   in the case of Companies Act accounts, in accordance with regulations under section 404,

(b)   in the case of IAS accounts, in accordance with UK-adopted international accounting standards; and

"gross" means without those set-offs and other adjustments.

A company may satisfy any relevant requirement on the basis of either the net or the gross figure.

(7)   The figures for each subsidiary undertaking shall be those included in its individual accounts for the relevant financial year, that is—

(a)   if its financial year ends with that of the parent company, that financial year, and

(b)   if not, its financial year ending last before the end of the financial year of the parent company.

If those figures cannot be obtained without disproportionate expense or undue delay, the latest available figures shall be taken.

467   Companies excluded from being treated as medium-sized

(1)   A company is not entitled to take advantage of any of the provisions of this Part relating to companies qualifying as medium-sized if it was at any time within the financial year in question—

(a)   a public company,

(b)   a company that—

(i)   has permission under Part 4A of the Financial Services and Markets Act 2000 to carry on a regulated activity, ...

(ii)   carries on insurance market activity, or

(iii) is a scheme funder of a Master Trust scheme within the meanings given by section 39(1) of the Pension Schemes Act 2017 (interpretation of Part 1), or

(ba) an e-money issuer, or

(c)   a member of an ineligible group.

(2)   A group is ineligible if any of its members is—

(a)   a traded company,

  (b) a body corporate (other than a company) whose shares are admitted to trading on a UK regulated market,

  (c) a person (other than a small company) who has permission under Part 4A of the Financial Services and Markets Act 2000 to carry on a regulated activity,

  (ca) an e-money issuer,

  (d) a small company that is an authorised insurance company, a banking company, ... a MiFID investment firm or a UCITS management company, ...

  (e) a person who carries on insurance market activity, or

  (f) a scheme funder of a Master Trust scheme within the meanings given by section 39(1) of the Pension Schemes Act 2017 (interpretation of Part 1).

(3) A company is a small company for the purposes of subsection (2) if it qualified as small in relation to its last financial year ending on or before the end of the financial year in question.

(4) This section does not prevent a company from taking advantage of section 417(7) (business review: non-financial information) by reason only of its having been a member of an ineligible group at any time within the financial year in question.

General power to make further provision about accounts and reports

468 General power to make further provision about accounts and reports

(1) The Secretary of State may make provision by regulations about—

  (a) the accounts and reports that companies are required to prepare;

  (b) the categories of companies required to prepare accounts and reports of any description;

  (c) the form and content of the accounts and reports that companies are required to prepare;

  (d) the obligations of companies and others as regards—

    (i) the approval of accounts and reports,

    (ii) the sending of accounts and reports to members and others,

    (iii) the laying of accounts and reports before the company in general meeting,

    (iv) the delivery of copies of accounts and reports to the registrar, and

    (v) the publication of accounts and reports.

(2) The regulations may amend this Part by adding, altering or repealing provisions.

(3) But they must not amend (other than consequentially)—

(a) section 393 (accounts to give true and fair view), or

(b) the provisions of Chapter 11 (revision of defective accounts and reports).

(4) The regulations may create criminal offences in cases corresponding to those in which an offence is created by an existing provision of this Part. The maximum penalty for any such offence may not be greater than is provided in relation to an offence under the existing provision.

(5) The regulations may provide for civil penalties in circumstances corresponding to those within section 453(1) (civil penalty for failure to file accounts and reports).

The provisions of section 453(2) to (5) apply in relation to any such penalty.

Other supplementary provisions

469 Preparation and filing of accounts in euros

(1) The amounts set out in the annual accounts of a company may also be shown in the same accounts translated into euros.

(2) When complying with section 441 (duty to file accounts and reports), the directors of a company may deliver to the registrar an additional copy of the company's annual accounts in which the amounts have been translated into euros.

(3) In both cases—

  (a) the amounts must have been translated at the exchange rate prevailing on the date to which the balance sheet is made up, and

  (b) that rate must be disclosed in the notes to the accounts.

(3A) Subsection (3)(b) does not apply to the Companies Act individual accounts of a company for a financial year in which the company qualifies as a micro-entity (see sections 384A and 384B).

(4)   For the purposes of sections 434 and 435 (requirements in connection with published accounts) any additional copy of the company's annual accounts delivered to the registrar under subsection (2) above shall be treated as statutory accounts of the company.

In the case of such a copy, references in those sections to the auditor's report on the company's annual accounts shall be read as references to the auditor's report on the annual accounts of which it is a copy.

470   Power to apply provisions to banking partnerships

(1)   The Secretary of State may by regulations apply to banking partnerships, subject to such exceptions, adaptations and modifications as he considers appropriate, the provisions of this Part (and of regulations made under this Part) applying to banking companies.

(2)   A "banking partnership" means a partnership which has permission under Part 4A of the Financial Services and Markets Act 2000.

But a partnership is not a banking partnership if it has permission to accept deposits only for the purpose of carrying on another regulated activity in accordance with that permission.

(3)   Expressions used in this section that are also used in the provisions regulating activities under the Financial Services and Markets Act 2000 have the same meaning here as they do in those provisions.

See section 22 of that Act, orders made under that section and Schedule 2 to that Act.

(4)   Regulations under this section are subject to affirmative resolution procedure.

471   Meaning of "annual accounts" and related expressions

(1)   In this Part a company's "annual accounts", in relation to a financial year, means—
        (a)   any individual accounts prepared by the company for that year (see section 394), and
        (b)   any group accounts prepared by the company for that year (see section 399).

This is subject to section 408 (option to omit individual profit and loss account from annual accounts where information given in notes to the individual balance sheet).

(2)   In the case of an unquoted company, its "annual accounts and reports" for a financial year are—
        (a)   its annual accounts,
        (aa)   the strategic report (if any),
        (ab)   the directors' remuneration report (if any),
        (b)   the directors' report, and
        (c)   the auditor's report on those accounts, the strategic report (where this is covered by the auditor's report) and the directors' report (unless the company is exempt from audit).

(3)   In the case of a quoted company, its "annual accounts and reports" for a financial year are—
        (a)   its annual accounts,
        (b)   the directors' remuneration report,
        (ba)   the strategic report (if any),
        (c)   the directors' report, and
        (d)   the auditor's report on those accounts, on the auditable part of the directors' remuneration report, on the strategic report (where this is covered by the auditor's report) and on the directors' report.

472   Notes to the accounts

(1)   ...

(1A)   ... in the case of a company which qualifies as a micro-entity in relation to a financial year (see sections 384A and 384B), the notes to the accounts for that year required by section 413 of this Act and regulation 5A of, and paragraph 57 of Part 3 of Schedule 1 to, the Small Companies and Groups (Accounts and Directors' Report) Regulations 2008 (SI 2008/409) must be included at the foot of the balance sheet.

(2)   References in this Part to a company's annual accounts, or to a balance sheet or profit and loss account, include notes to the accounts giving information which is required by any provision of this Act or UK-adopted international accounting standards, and required or allowed by any such provision to be given in a note to company accounts.

472A   **Meaning of "corporate governance statement" etc**

(1)   In this Part "corporate governance statement" means the statement required by rules 7.2.1 to 7.2.11 in the Disclosure Rules and Transparency Rules sourcebook made by the Financial Conduct Authority.

(2)   Those rules were inserted by Annex C of the Disclosure Rules and Transparency Rules Sourcebook (Corporate Governance Rules) Instrument 2008 made by the Authority on 26th June 2008 (FSA 2008/32).

(3)   A "separate" corporate governance statement means one that is not included in the directors' report.

473   **Parliamentary procedure for certain regulations under this Part**

(1)   This section applies to regulations under the following provisions of this Part—
        section 396 (Companies Act individual accounts),
        section 404 (Companies Act group accounts),
        section 409 (information about related undertakings),
        section 412 (information about directors' benefits: remuneration, pensions and compensation for loss of office),
        section 416 (contents of directors' report: general),
        section 421 (contents of directors' remuneration report),
        section 444 (filing obligations of companies subject to small companies regime),
        section 445 (filing obligations of medium-sized companies),
        section 468 (general power to make further provision about accounts and reports).

(2)   Any such regulations may make consequential amendments or repeals in other provisions of this Act, or in other enactments.

(3)   Regulations that—
        (a)   restrict the classes of company which have the benefit of any exemption, exception or special provision,
        (b)   require additional matter to be included in a document of any class, or
        (c)   otherwise render the requirements of this Part more onerous, are subject to affirmative resolution procedure.

(4)   Otherwise, the regulations are subject to negative resolution procedure.

474   **Minor definitions**

(1)   In this Part—
        "e-money issuer" means—
        (a)   an electronic money institution, within the meaning of the Electronic Money Regulations 2011 (SI 2011/99), or
        (b)   a person who has permission under Part 4A of the Financial Services and Markets Act 2000 (c 8) to carry on the activity of issuing electronic money within the meaning of article 9B of the Financial Services and Markets Act 2000 (Regulated Activities) Order 2001 (SI 2001/544);
        "group" means a parent undertaking and its subsidiary undertakings; ...
        ...
        "included in the consolidation", in relation to group accounts, or "included in consolidated group accounts", means that the undertaking is included in the accounts by the method of full (and not proportional) consolidation, and references to an undertaking excluded from consolidation shall be construed accordingly;
        "international accounting standards" means the international accounting standards, within the meaning of Article 2 of Regulation (EC) No. 1606/2002 of the European Parliament and of the Council of 19 July 2002 on the application of international accounting standards;
        "micro-entity minimum accounting item" means an item of information required by this Part or by regulations under this Part to be contained in the Companies Act individual accounts of a

company for a financial year in relation to which it qualifies as a micro-entity (see sections 384A and 384B);

"micro-entity provisions" means any provisions of this Part, Part 16 or regulations under this Part relating specifically to the individual accounts of a company which qualifies as a micro-entity;

...

"MiFID investment firm" means an investment firm within the meaning of Article 2.1A of Regulation (EU) No. 600/2014 of the European Parliament and of the Council of 15 May 2014 on markets in financial instruments, other than—

(a)   a company which is exempted from the definition of "investment firm" by Schedule 3 to the Financial Services and Markets Act 2000 (Regulated Activities) Order 2001 (S.I. 2001/544),

(b)   a company which is an exempt investment firm as defined by regulation 8 (meaning of "exempt investment firm") of the Financial Services and Markets Act 2000 (Markets in Financial Instruments) Regulations 2017 (S.I. 2017/701), and

(c)   any other company which fulfils all the requirements set out in regulation 6(3) of those Regulations;

"profit and loss account", in relation to a company that prepares IAS accounts, includes an income statement or other equivalent financial statement required to be prepared by UK-adopted international accounting standards;

"qualified", in relation to an auditor's report, means that the report does not state the auditor's unqualified opinion that the accounts have been properly prepared in accordance with this Act;

"regulated activity" has the meaning given in section 22 of the Financial Services and Markets Act 2000, except that it does not include activities of the kind specified in any of the following provisions of the Financial Services and Markets Act 2000 (Regulated Activities) Order 2001—

(a)   article 25A (arranging regulated mortgage contracts),

(b)   article 25B (arranging regulated home reversion plans),

(c)   article 25C (arranging regulated home purchase plans),

(ca) article 25E (arranging regulated sale and rent back agreements),

(d)   article 39A (assisting administration and performance of a contract of insurance),

(e)   article 53A (advising on regulated mortgage contracts),

(f)   article 53B (advising on regulated home reversion plans),

(g)   article 53C (advising on regulated home purchase plans),

(ga) article 53D (advising on regulated sale and rent back agreements),

(h)   article 21 (dealing as agent), article 25 (arranging deals in investments) or article 53 (advising on investments) where the activity concerns relevant investments that are not contractually based investments (within the meaning of article 3 of that Order), or

(i)   article 64 (agreeing to carry on a regulated activity of the kind mentioned in paragraphs (a) to (h));

"traded company", unless the context otherwise requires, means a company any of whose transferable securities are admitted to trading on a UK regulated market;

"turnover", in relation to a company, means the amounts derived from the provision of goods and services ..., after deduction of—

(a)   trade discounts,

(b)   value added tax, and

(c)   any other taxes based on the amounts so derived;

"UCITS management company" has the meaning given by the Glossary forming part of the Handbook made by the Financial Conduct Authority under the Financial Services and Markets Act 2000.

"UK-adopted international accounting standards" means the international accounting standards which are adopted for use within the United Kingdom by virtue of Chapter 2 or 3 of Part 2 of the International Accounting Standards and European Public Limited-Liability Company (Amendment etc) (EU Exit) Regulations 2019.

(2)   In the case of an undertaking not trading for profit, any reference in this Part to a profit and loss account is to an income and expenditure account. References to profit and loss and, in relation to group accounts, to a consolidated profit and loss account shall be construed accordingly.

Note. This section is amended by S.I. 2024/105, reg. 47(a), Sch. 3, Pt. 1, para. 24, as from a day to be appointed (save for certain purposes).

PART 16
AUDIT

CHAPTER 1
REQUIREMENT FOR AUDITED ACCOUNTS

Requirement for audited accounts

475   Requirement for audited accounts

(1)   A company's annual accounts for a financial year must be audited in accordance with this Part unless the company—

    (a)   is exempt from audit under—

        section 477 (small companies),

        section 479A (subsidiary companies), or

        section 480 (dormant companies);

        or

    (b)   is exempt from the requirements of this Part under section 482 (non-profit-making companies subject to public sector audit).

(2)   A company is not entitled to any such exemption unless its balance sheet contains a statement by the directors to that effect.

(3)   A company is not entitled to exemption under any of the provisions mentioned in subsection (1)(a) unless its balance sheet contains a statement by the directors to the effect that—

    (a)   the members have not required the company to obtain an audit of its accounts for the year in question in accordance with section 476, and

    (b)   the directors acknowledge their responsibilities for complying with the requirements of this Act with respect to accounting records and the preparation of accounts.

(4)   The statement required by subsection (2) or (3) must appear on the balance sheet above the signature required by section 414.

476   Right of members to require audit

(1)   The members of a company that would otherwise be entitled to exemption from audit under any of the provisions mentioned in section 475(1)(a) may by notice under this section require it to obtain an audit of its accounts for a financial year.

(2)   The notice must be given by—

    (a)   members representing not less in total than 10% in nominal value of the company's issued share capital, or any class of it, or

    (b)   if the company does not have a share capital, not less than 10% in number of the members of the company.

(3)   The notice may not be given before the financial year to which it relates and must be given not later than one month before the end of that year.

Exemption from audit: small companies

477   Small companies: conditions for exemption from audit

(1)   A company that qualifies as a small company in relation to a financial year is exempt from the requirements of this Act relating to the audit of accounts for that year.

(2), (3) ...

(4)   For the purposes of this section—

(a)   whether a company qualifies as a small company shall be determined in accordance with section 382(1) to (6), ...

(b)   ...

(5)   This section has effect subject to—

section 475(2) and (3) (requirements as to statements to be contained in balance sheet),

section 476 (right of members to require audit),

section 478 (companies excluded from small companies exemption), and

section 479 (availability of small companies exemption in case of group company).

478   Companies excluded from small companies exemption

A company is not entitled to the exemption conferred by section 477 (small companies) if it was at any time within the financial year in question—

(a)   a public company,

(b)   a company that—

(i)   is an authorised insurance company, a banking company, an e-money issuer, a MiFID investment firm or a UCITS management company, ...

(ii)   carries on insurance market activity, or

(iii)   is a scheme funder of a Master Trust scheme within the meanings given by section 39(1) of the Pension Schemes Act 2017 (interpretation of Part 1), or

(c)   a special register body as defined in section 117(1) of the Trade Union and Labour Relations (Consolidation) Act 1992 or an employers' association as defined in section 122 of that Act or Article 4 of the Industrial Relations (Northern Ireland) Order 1992.

479   Availability of small companies exemption in case of group company

(1)   A company is not entitled to the exemption conferred by section 477 (small companies) in respect of a financial year during any part of which it was a group company unless—

(a)   the group—

(i)   qualifies as a small group in relation to that financial year, and

(ii)   was not at any time in that year an ineligible group, or

(b)   subsection (3) applies.

(2)   ...

(3)   A company is not excluded by subsection (1) if, throughout the whole of the period or periods during the financial year when it was a group company, it was both a subsidiary undertaking and dormant.

(4)   In this section—

(a)   "group company" means a company that is a parent company or a subsidiary undertaking, and

(b)   "the group", in relation to a group company, means that company together with all its associated undertakings.

For this purpose undertakings are associated if one is a subsidiary undertaking of the other or both are subsidiary undertakings of a third undertaking.

(5)   For the purposes of this section—

(a)   whether a group qualifies as small shall be determined in accordance with section 383 (companies qualifying as small: parent companies);

(b)   "ineligible group" has the meaning given by section 384(2) and (3);

(c)–(e) ...

(6)   The provisions mentioned in subsection (5) apply for the purposes of this section as if all the bodies corporate in the group were companies.

Exemption from audit: qualifying subsidiaries

479A   Subsidiary companies: conditions for exemption from audit

(1)   A company is exempt from the requirements of this Act relating to the audit of individual accounts for a financial year if—

(a)   it is itself a subsidiary undertaking, and

(b)   its parent undertaking is established under the law of any part of the United Kingdom.

(2)   Exemption is conditional upon compliance with all of the following conditions—

(a)   all members of the company must agree to the exemption in respect of the financial year in question,

(b)   the parent undertaking must give a guarantee under section 479C in respect of that year,

(c)   the company must be included in the consolidated accounts drawn up for that year or to an earlier date in that year by the parent undertaking in accordance with—

(i)   if the undertaking is a company, the requirements of Part 15 of this Act, or, if the undertaking is not a company, the legal requirements which apply to the drawing up of consolidated accounts for that undertaking, or

(ii)   UK-adopted international accounting standards (within the meaning given by section 474(1)),

(d)   the parent undertaking must disclose in the notes to the consolidated accounts that the company is exempt from the requirements of this Act relating to the audit of individual accounts by virtue of this section, and

(e)   the directors of the company must deliver to the registrar on or before the date that they file the accounts for that year—

(i)   a written notice of the agreement referred to in subsection (2)(a),

(ii)   the statement referred to in section 479C(1),

(iii)   a copy of the consolidated accounts referred to in subsection (2)(c),

(iv)   a copy of the auditor's report on those accounts, and

(v)   a copy of the consolidated annual report drawn up by the parent undertaking.

(3)   This section has effect subject to—

section 475(2) and (3) (requirements as to statements contained in balance sheet), and

section 476 (right of members to require audit).

479B   Companies excluded from the subsidiary companies audit exemption

A company is not entitled to the exemption conferred by section 479A (subsidiary companies) if it was at any time within the financial year in question—

(a)   a traded company as defined in section 474(1),

(b)   a company that—

(i)   is an authorised insurance company, a banking company, an e-money issuer, a MiFID investment firm or a UCITS management company, ...

(ii)   carries on insurance market activity, or

(iii)   is a scheme funder of a Master Trust scheme within the meanings given by section 39(1) of the Pension Schemes Act 2017 (interpretation of Part 1), or

(c)   a special register body as defined in section 117(1) of the Trade Union and Labour Relations (Consolidation) Act 1992 (c 52) or an employers' association as defined in section 122 of that Act or Article 4 of the Industrial Relations (Northern Ireland) Order 1992 (SI 1992/807) (NI 5).

479C   Subsidiary companies audit exemption: parent undertaking declaration of guarantee

(1)   A guarantee is given by a parent undertaking under this section when the directors of the subsidiary company deliver to the registrar a statement by the parent undertaking that it guarantees the subsidiary company under this section.

(2)   The statement under subsection (1) must be authenticated by the parent undertaking and must specify—

(a)   the name of the parent undertaking,

(b)   the registered number (if any) of the parent undertaking,

(c)   ...

(d)   the name and registered number of the subsidiary company in respect of which the guarantee is being given,

(e)   the date of the statement, and

(f)   the financial year to which the guarantee relates.

(3)   A guarantee given under this section has the effect that—

(a)   the parent undertaking guarantees all outstanding liabilities to which the subsidiary company is subject at the end of the financial year to which the guarantee relates, until they are satisfied in full, and

(b)   the guarantee is enforceable against the parent undertaking by any person to whom the subsidiary company is liable in respect of those liabilities.

Exemption from audit: dormant companies

480   Dormant companies: conditions for exemption from audit

(1)   A company is exempt from the requirements of this Act relating to the audit of accounts in respect of a financial year if—

(a)   it has been dormant since its formation, or

(b)   it has been dormant since the end of the previous financial year and the following conditions are met.

(2)   The conditions are that the company—

(a)   as regards its individual accounts for the financial year in question—

(i)   is entitled to prepare accounts in accordance with the small companies regime (see sections 381 to 384), or

(ii)   would be so entitled but for having been a public company or a member of an ineligible group, and

(b)   is not required to prepare group accounts for that year.

(3)   This section has effect subject to—

section 475(2) and (3) (requirements as to statements to be contained in balance sheet),

section 476 (right of members to require audit), and

section 481 (companies excluded from dormant companies exemption).

481   Companies excluded from dormant companies exemption

A company is not entitled to the exemption conferred by section 480 (dormant companies) if it was at any time within the financial year in question a company that—

(za) is a traded company as defined in section 474(1),

(a)   is an authorised insurance company, a banking company, an e-money issuer, a MiFID investment firm or a UCITS management company, or

(b)   carries on insurance market activity.

Companies subject to public sector audit

482   Non-profit-making companies subject to public sector audit

(1)   The requirements of this Part as to audit of accounts do not apply to a company for a financial year if it is non-profit-making and its accounts—

(a)   are subject to audit by the Comptroller and Auditor General by virtue of an order under section 25(6) of the Government Resources and Accounts Act 2000;

(ab) are subject to audit by the Auditor General for Wales by virtue of—

(i)   an order under section 144 of the Government of Wales Act 1998, or

(ii)   paragraph 18 of Schedule 8 to the Government of Wales Act 2006;

(b)   are accounts—

(i)   in relation to which section 21 of the Public Finance and Accountability (Scotland) Act 2000 (asp 1) (audit of accounts: Auditor General for Scotland) applies, or

(ii)   that are subject to audit by the Auditor General for Scotland by virtue of an order under section 483 (Scottish public sector companies: audit by Auditor General for Scotland); or

(c) are subject to audit by the Comptroller and Auditor General for Northern Ireland by virtue of an order under Article 5(3) of the Audit and Accountability (Northern Ireland) Order 2003.

(2) In the case of a company that is a parent company or a subsidiary undertaking, subsection (1) applies only if every group undertaking is non-profit-making.

(3) In this section "non-profit-making" has the same meaning as in Article 54 of the Treaty on the Functioning of the European Union.

(4) This section has effect subject to section 475(2) (balance sheet to contain statement that company entitled to exemption under this section).

483 Scottish public sector companies: audit by Auditor General for Scotland

(1) The Scottish Ministers may by order provide for the accounts of a company having its registered office in Scotland to be audited by the Auditor General for Scotland.

(2) An order under subsection (1) may be made in relation to a company only if it appears to the Scottish Ministers that the company—

(a) exercises in or as regards Scotland functions of a public nature none of which relate to reserved matters (within the meaning of the Scotland Act 1998), or

(b) is entirely or substantially funded from a body having accounts falling within paragraph (a) or (b) of subsection (3).

(3) Those accounts are—

(a) accounts in relation to which section 21 of the Public Finance and Accountability (Scotland) Act 2000 (asp 1) (audit of accounts: Auditor General for Scotland) applies,

(b) accounts which are subject to audit by the Auditor General for Scotland by virtue of an order under this section.

(4) An order under subsection (1) may make such supplementary or consequential provision (including provision amending an enactment) as the Scottish Ministers think expedient.

(5) An order under subsection (1) shall not be made unless a draft of the statutory instrument containing it has been laid before, and approved by resolution of, the Scottish Parliament.

General power of amendment by regulations

484 General power of amendment by regulations

(1) The Secretary of State may by regulations amend this Chapter or section 539 (minor definitions) so far as applying to this Chapter by adding, altering or repealing provisions.

(2) The regulations may make consequential amendments or repeals in other provisions of this Act, or in other enactments.

(3) Regulations under this section imposing new requirements, or rendering existing requirements more onerous, are subject to affirmative resolution procedure.

(4) Other regulations under this section are subject to negative resolution procedure.

CHAPTER 2
APPOINTMENT OF AUDITORS

Private companies

485 Appointment of auditors of private company: general

(1) An auditor or auditors of a private company must be appointed for each financial year of the company, unless the directors reasonably resolve otherwise on the ground that audited accounts are unlikely to be required.

(2) For each financial year for which an auditor or auditors is or are to be appointed (other than the company's first financial year), the appointment must be made before the end of the period of 28 days beginning with—

(a) the end of the time allowed for sending out copies of the company's annual accounts and reports for the previous financial year (see section 424), or

(b) if earlier, the day on which copies of the company's annual accounts and reports for the previous financial year are sent out under section 423.

This is the "period for appointing auditors".

(3)   The directors may appoint an auditor or auditors of the company—

    (a)   at any time before the company's first period for appointing auditors,

    (b)   following a period during which the company (being exempt from audit) did not have any auditor, at any time before the company's next period for appointing auditors, or

    (c)   to fill a casual vacancy in the office of auditor.

(4)   The members may appoint an auditor or auditors by ordinary resolution—

    (a)   during a period for appointing auditors,

    (b)   if the company should have appointed an auditor or auditors during a period for appointing auditors but failed to do so, or

    (c)   where the directors had power to appoint under subsection (3) but have failed to make an appointment.

(5)   An auditor or auditors of a private company may only be appointed—

    (a)   in accordance with this section, or

    (b)   in accordance with section 486 or 486A (default power of Secretary of State).

This is without prejudice to any deemed re-appointment under section 487.

485A   Appointment of auditors of private company: additional requirements for public interest entities with audit committees

(1)   This section applies to the appointment under section 485(4) of an auditor or auditors of a private company—

    (a)   which is also a public interest entity; and

    (b)   which has an audit committee.

(2)   But it does not apply to the appointment of an Auditor General as auditor or one of the auditors of the company.

(3)   Before an appointment to which this section applies is made—

    (a)   the audit committee of the company must make a recommendation to the directors in connection with the appointment, and

    (b)   the directors must propose an auditor or auditors for appointment. …

(4)   Before the audit committee makes a recommendation or the directors make a proposal under subsection (3), the committee … must carry out a selection procedure in accordance with Article 16(3) of the Audit Regulation, unless the company is a small or medium sized enterprise within the meaning in Article 2(1)(f) of Directive 2003/71/EC.

(5)   The audit committee must in its recommendation—

    (a)   identify its first and second choice candidates for appointment, drawn from those auditors who have participated in a selection procedure under subsection (4),

    (b)   give reasons for the choices so identified,

    (c)   state that—

        (i)   the recommendation is free from influence by a third party, and

        (ii)   no contractual term of the kind mentioned in Article 16(6) of the Audit Regulation has been imposed on the company.

(6)   The directors must include in their proposal—

    (a)   the recommendation made by the audit committee in connection with the appointment, and

    (b)   if the proposal of the directors departs from the preference of the audit committee—

        (i)   a recommendation for a candidate or candidates for appointment drawn from those auditors who have participated in a selection procedure under subsection (4), and

        (ii)   the reasons for not following the audit committee's recommendation.

(7)   Where the audit committee recommends re-appointment of the company's existing auditor or auditors, and the directors are in agreement, subsections (4) and (5)(a) and (b) do not apply.

485B   Appointment of auditors of private company: additional requirements for public interest entities without audit committees

(1)   This section applies to the appointment under section 485(4) of an auditor or auditors of a private company—

(a)   which is also a public interest entity; and

(b)   which does not have an audit committee.

(2)   But it does not apply to the appointment of an Auditor General as auditor or one of the auditors of the company.

(3)   Before an appointment to which this section applies is made the directors must propose an auditor or auditors for appointment.

(4)   Before the directors make a proposal under subsection (3), they must carry out a selection procedure in accordance with Article 16(3) of the Audit Regulation, from which their proposed auditor or auditors must be drawn, unless the company is a small or medium sized enterprise within the meaning in Article 2(1)(f) of Directive 2003/71/EC.

(5)   Subsection (4) does not apply in relation to a proposal to re-appoint the company's existing auditor or auditors.

485C   Restriction on appointment of auditor of private company which is a public interest entity

(1)   A person who has been, or will have been, auditor of a private company which is a public interest entity for every financial year comprised in the maximum engagement period (see section 494ZA) may not be appointed as auditor of the company for any financial year which begins within the period of 4 years beginning with the day after the last day of the last financial year of the maximum engagement period.

(2)   A person who is a member of the same network as the auditor mentioned in subsection (1) may not be appointed as auditor of the company for any financial year which begins within the period of 4 years mentioned in that subsection.

(3)   This section does not apply in relation to an Auditor General.

486   Appointment of auditors of private company: default power of Secretary of State

(1)   If a private company fails to appoint an auditor or auditors in accordance with section 485 ... the Secretary of State may appoint one or more persons to fill the vacancy.

(2)   Where subsection (2) of section 485 applies and the company fails to make the necessary appointment before the end of the period for appointing auditors, the company must within one week of the end of that period give notice to the Secretary of State of his power having become exercisable.

(3)   If a company fails to give the notice required by this section, an offence is committed by—

(a)   the company, and

(b)   every officer of the company who is in default.

(4)   A person guilty of an offence under this section is liable on summary conviction to a fine not exceeding level 3 on the standard scale and, for continued contravention, a daily default fine not exceeding one-tenth of level 3 on the standard scale.

486A   Defective appointments: default power of Secretary of State

(1)   If—

(a)   a private company appoints, or purports to appoint, an auditor or auditors, and

(b)   the appointment or purported appointment is made in breach of section 485A, 485B or 485C (requirements applying to appointment of auditors by public interest entities),

the Secretary of State may appoint another auditor or auditors in place of the auditor or auditors referred to in paragraph (a).

(2)   The breach of section 485A, 485B or 485C does not invalidate any report made under Chapter 3 of this Part by the auditor or auditors on the company's annual reports or accounts before the auditor or auditors are replaced under subsection (1) of this section.

(3)   But where the breach in question is a breach of section 485C, sections 1248 and 1249 (Secretary of State's power to require second audit) apply as if the auditor was not an appropriate person, or the auditors were not appropriate persons, for the period during which the audit was conducted.

(4)   Within one week of becoming aware of the breach of section 485A, 485B or 485C, the company must give notice to the Secretary of State that the power under subsection (1) of this section has become exercisable.

(5)   If the company fails to give the notice required by subsection (4), an offence is committed by—
        (a)   the company, and
        (b)   every officer of the company who is in default.

(6)   A person guilty of an offence under this section is liable on summary conviction to a fine not exceeding level 3 on the standard scale and, for continued contravention, a daily default fine not exceeding one-tenth of level 3 on the standard scale.

487   Term of office of auditors of private company

(1)   An auditor or auditors of a private company hold office in accordance with the terms of their appointment, subject to the requirements that—
        (a)   they do not take office until any previous auditor or auditors cease to hold office, and
        (b)   they cease to hold office at the end of the next period for appointing auditors unless re-appointed.

(1A)–(1E) ...

(2)   Where no auditor has been appointed by the end of the next period for appointing auditors, any auditor in office immediately before that time is deemed to be re-appointed at that time, unless—
        (a)   he was appointed by the directors, or
        (b)   the company's articles require actual re-appointment, or
        (c)   the deemed re-appointment is prevented by the members under section 488, or
        (d)   the members have resolved that he should not be re-appointed, or
        (e)   the directors have resolved that no auditor or auditors should be appointed for the financial year in question, or
        (f)   the auditor's appointment would be in breach of section 485C.

(3)   This is without prejudice to the provisions of this Part as to removal and resignation of auditors.

(4)   No account shall be taken of any loss of the opportunity of deemed re-appointment under this section in ascertaining the amount of any compensation or damages payable to an auditor on his ceasing to hold office for any reason.

487A   ...

488   Prevention by members of deemed re-appointment of auditor

(1)   An auditor of a private company is not deemed to be re-appointed under section 487(2) if the company has received notices under this section from members representing at least the requisite percentage of the total voting rights of all members who would be entitled to vote on a resolution that the auditor should not be re-appointed.

(2)   The "requisite percentage" is 5%, or such lower percentage as is specified for this purpose in the company's articles.

(3)   A notice under this section—
        (a)   may be in hard copy or electronic form,
        (b)   must be authenticated by the person or persons giving it, and
        (c)   must be received by the company before the end of the accounting reference period immediately preceding the time when the deemed re-appointment would have effect.

Public companies

489   Appointment of auditors of public company: general

(1)   An auditor or auditors of a public company must be appointed for each financial year of the company, unless the directors reasonably resolve otherwise on the ground that audited accounts are unlikely to be required.

(2)   For each financial year for which an auditor or auditors is or are to be appointed (other than the company's first financial year), the appointment must be made before the end of the accounts meeting of the company at which the company's annual accounts and reports for the previous financial year are laid.

(3)   The directors may appoint an auditor or auditors of the company—
        (a)   at any time before the company's first accounts meeting;

(b)   following a period during which the company (being exempt from audit) did not have any auditor, at any time before the company's next accounts meeting;

(c)   to fill a casual vacancy in the office of auditor.

(4)   The members may appoint an auditor or auditors by ordinary resolution—

(a)   at an accounts meeting;

(b)   if the company should have appointed an auditor or auditors at an accounts meeting but failed to do so;

(c)   where the directors had power to appoint under subsection (3) but have failed to make an appointment.

(5)   An auditor or auditors of a public company may only be appointed—

(a)   in accordance with this section, or

(b)   in accordance with section 490 or 490A (default power of Secretary of State).

489A   Appointment of auditors of public company: additional requirements for public interest entities with audit committees

(1)   This section applies to the appointment under section 489(4) of an auditor or auditors of a public company—

(a)   which is also a public interest entity; and

(b)   which has an audit committee.

(2)   But it does not apply to the appointment of an Auditor General as auditor or one of the auditors of the company.

(3)   Before an appointment to which this section applies is made—

(a)   the audit committee of the company must make a recommendation to the directors in connection with the appointment, and

(b)   the directors must propose an auditor or auditors for appointment …

(4)   Before the audit committee makes a recommendation or the directors make a proposal under subsection (3), the committee … must carry out a selection procedure in accordance with Article 16(3) of the Audit Regulation, unless the company is—

(a)   a small or medium sized enterprise within the meaning in Article 2(1)(f) of Directive 2003/71/EC; or

(b)   a company with reduced market capitalisation within the meaning in Article 2(1)(t) of that Directive.

(5)   The audit committee must in its recommendation—

(a)   identify its first and second choice candidates for appointment, drawn from those auditors who have participated in a selection procedure under subsection (4),

(b)   give reasons for the choices so identified,

(c)   state that—

(i)   the recommendation is free from influence by a third party, and

(ii)   no contractual term of the kind mentioned in Article 16(6) of the Audit Regulation has been imposed on the company.

(6)   The directors must include in their proposal—

(a)   the recommendation made by the audit committee in connection with the appointment, and

(b)   if the proposal of the directors departs from the preference of the audit committee—

(i)   a recommendation for a candidate or candidates for appointment drawn from those auditors who have participated in a selection procedure under subsection (4), and

(ii)   the reasons for not following the audit committee's recommendation.

(7)   Where the audit committee recommends re-appointment of the company's existing auditor or auditors, and the directors are in agreement, subsections (4) and (5)(a) and (b) do not apply.

489B   Appointment of auditors of public company: additional requirements for public interest entities without audit committees

(1)   This section applies to the appointment under section 489(4) of an auditor or auditors of a public company—

(a)   which is also a public interest entity; and

(b)   which does not have an audit committee.

(2)   But it does not apply to the appointment of an Auditor General as auditor or one of the auditors of the company.

(3)   Before an appointment to which this section applies is made the directors must propose an auditor or auditors for appointment.

(4)   Before the directors make a proposal under subsection (3), the directors must carry out a selection procedure in accordance with Article 16(3) of the Audit Regulation, from which their proposed auditor or auditors must be drawn, unless the company is—

(a)   a small or medium sized enterprise within the meaning in Article 2(1)(f) of Directive 2003/71/EU; or

(b)   a company with reduced market capitalisation within the meaning in Article 2(1)(t) of that Directive.

(5)   Subsection (4) does not apply in relation to a proposal to re-appoint the company's existing auditor or auditors.

489C   **Restriction on appointment of auditor of public company which is a public interest entity**

(1)   A person who has been, or will have been, auditor of a public company which is a public interest entity for every financial year comprised in the maximum engagement period (see section 494ZA) may not be appointed as auditor of the company for any financial year which begins within the period of 4 years beginning with the day after the last day of the last financial year of the maximum engagement period.

(2)   A person who is a member of the same network as the auditor mentioned in subsection (1) may not be appointed as auditor of the company for any financial year which begins within the period of 4 years mentioned in that subsection.

(3)   This section does not apply in relation to an Auditor General.

490   **Appointment of auditors of public company: default power of Secretary of State**

(1)   If a public company fails to appoint an auditor or auditors in accordance with section 489 … the Secretary of State may appoint one or more persons to fill the vacancy.

(2)   Where subsection (2) of section 489 applies and the company fails to make the necessary appointment before the end of the accounts meeting, the company must within one week of the end of that meeting give notice to the Secretary of State of his power having become exercisable.

(3)   If a company fails to give the notice required by this section, an offence is committed by—

(a)   the company, and

(b)   every officer of the company who is in default.

(4)   A person guilty of an offence under this section is liable on summary conviction to a fine not exceeding level 3 on the standard scale and, for continued contravention, a daily default fine not exceeding one-tenth of level 3 on the standard scale.

490A   **Defective appointments: default power of Secretary of State**

(1)   If—

(a)   a public company appoints, or purports to appoint, an auditor or auditors, and

(b)   the appointment or purported appointment is made in breach of section 489A, 489B or 489C (requirements applying to appointment of auditors by public interest entities),

the Secretary of State may appoint another auditor or auditors in place of the auditor or auditors referred to in paragraph (a).

(2)   The breach of section 489A, 489B or 489C does not invalidate any report made under Chapter 3 of this Part by the auditor or auditors on the company's annual reports or accounts before the auditor or auditors are replaced under subsection (1) of this section.

(3)   But where the breach in question is a breach of section 489C, sections 1248 and 1249 (Secretary of State's power to require second audit) apply as if the auditor was not an appropriate person, or the auditors were not appropriate persons, for the period during which the audit was conducted.

(4)   Within one week of becoming aware of the breach of section 489A, 489B or 489C, the company must give notice to the Secretary of State that the power under subsection (1) of this section has become exercisable.

(5)   If the company fails to give the notice required by subsection (4), an offence is committed by—
       (a)   the company, and
       (b)   every officer of the company who is in default.

(6)   A person guilty of an offence under this section is liable on summary conviction to a fine not exceeding level 3 on the standard scale and, for continued contravention, a daily default fine not exceeding one-tenth of level 3 on the standard scale.

491   Term of office of auditors of public company

(1)   The auditor or auditors of a public company hold office in accordance with the terms of their appointment, subject to the requirements that—
       (a)   they do not take office until the previous auditor or auditors have ceased to hold office, and
       (b)   they cease to hold office at the conclusion of the accounts meeting next following their appointment, unless re-appointed.

(1A)–(1E) ...

(2)   This is without prejudice to the provisions of this Part as to removal and resignation of auditors.

491A   ...

General provisions

492   Fixing of auditor's remuneration

(1)   The remuneration of an auditor appointed by the members of a company must be fixed by the members by ordinary resolution or in such manner as the members may by ordinary resolution determine.

(2)   The remuneration of an auditor appointed by the directors of a company must be fixed by the directors.

(3)   The remuneration of an auditor appointed by the Secretary of State must be fixed by the Secretary of State.

(4)   For the purposes of this section "remuneration" includes sums paid in respect of expenses.

(5)   This section applies in relation to benefits in kind as to payments of money.

493   Disclosure of terms of audit appointment

(1)   The Secretary of State may make provision by regulations for securing the disclosure of the terms on which a company's auditor is appointed, remunerated or performs his duties.
       Nothing in the following provisions of this section affects the generality of this power.

(2)   The regulations may—
       (a)   require disclosure of—
              (i)   a copy of any terms that are in writing, and
              (ii)   a written memorandum setting out any terms that are not in writing;
       (b)   require disclosure to be at such times, in such places and by such means as are specified in the regulations;
       (c)   require the place and means of disclosure to be stated—
              (i)   in a note to the company's annual accounts (in the case of its individual accounts) or in such manner as is specified in the regulations (in the case of group accounts),
              (ii)   in the strategic report or the directors' report, or
              (iii)   in the auditor's report on the company's annual accounts.

(3)   The provisions of this section apply to a variation of the terms mentioned in subsection (1) as they apply to the original terms.

(4)   Regulations under this section are subject to affirmative resolution procedure.

494   Disclosure of services provided by auditor or associates and related remuneration

(1)   The Secretary of State may make provision by regulations for securing the disclosure of—

     (a)   the nature of any services provided for a company by the company's auditor (whether in his capacity as auditor or otherwise) or by his associates;

     (b)   the amount of any remuneration received or receivable by a company's auditor, or his associates, in respect of any such services.

     Nothing in the following provisions of this section affects the generality of this power.

(2)   The regulations may provide—

     (a)   for disclosure of the nature of any services provided to be made by reference to any class or description of services specified in the regulations (or any combination of services, however described);

     (b)   for the disclosure of amounts of remuneration received or receivable in respect of services of any class or description specified in the regulations (or any combination of services, however described);

     (c)   for the disclosure of separate amounts so received or receivable by the company's auditor or any of his associates, or of aggregate amounts so received or receivable by all or any of those persons.

(3)   The regulations may—

     (a)   provide that "remuneration" includes sums paid in respect of expenses;

     (b)   apply to benefits in kind as well as to payments of money, and require the disclosure of the nature of any such benefits and their estimated money value;

     (c)   apply to services provided for associates of a company as well as to those provided for a company;

     (d)   define "associate" in relation to an auditor and a company respectively.

(4)   The regulations may provide that any disclosure required by the regulations is to be made—

     (a)   in a note to the company's annual accounts (in the case of its individual accounts) or in such manner as is specified in the regulations (in the case of group accounts),

     (b)   in the strategic report or the directors' report, or

     (c)   in the auditor's report on the company's annual accounts.

(5)   If the regulations provide that any such disclosure is to be made as mentioned in subsection (4)(a) or (b), the regulations may require the auditor to supply the directors of the company with any information necessary to enable the disclosure to be made.

(6)   Regulations under this section are subject to negative resolution procedure.

494ZA The maximum engagement period

(1)   Where a person is auditor of a company for consecutive financial years, the maximum engagement period of the person as auditor of the company—

     (a)   begins with the first of those years (see the appropriate entry in the first column of the following Table), and

     (b)   ends with the financial year specified in the corresponding entry in the second column of the Table:

First financial year of the maximum engagement period	Last financial year of the maximum engagement period
A financial year of the company beginning before 17 June 1994	The last financial year of the company to begin before 17 June 2020.
A financial year of the company beginning— (a) on or after 17 June 1994, and (b) before 17 June 2003	The last financial year of the company to begin before 17 June 2023.

First financial year of the maximum engagement period	Last financial year of the maximum engagement period
A financial year of the company beginning— (a) on or after 17 June 2003, and (b) before 17 June 2016	*No qualifying selection procedure* Where neither the first financial year of the maximum engagement period nor any subsequent financial year is one for which the auditor has been appointed following the carrying out of a qualifying selection procedure, the later of— (a) the last financial year of the company to begin before 17 June 2016, and (b) the last financial year of the company to begin within the period of 10 years beginning with the first day of the first financial year of the maximum engagement period.
	No qualifying selection procedure within 10 years Where the last day of the last financial year of the company to begin within the period of 10 years beginning with the first day of the last financial year of the company for which the auditor was appointed following a qualifying selection procedure is before 17 June 2016— (a) the last financial year of the company to begin before 17 June 2016, unless (b) the auditor is appointed following a qualifying selection procedure for the first financial year of the company to begin on or after 17 June 2016, in which case it is the last financial year of the company to begin within the period of 20 years beginning with the first day of the first financial year of the maximum engagement period.
	Qualifying selection procedure within 10 years In any other case, the earlier of— (a) the last financial year of the company to begin within the period of 10 years beginning with the first day of the last financial year of the company for which the auditor was appointed following a qualifying selection procedure, and (b) the last financial year of the company to begin within the period of 20 years beginning with the first day of the first financial year of the maximum engagement period.
A financial year of the company beginning on or after 17 June 2016	The earlier of— (a) the last financial year of the company to begin within the period of 10 years beginning with the first day of the last financial year of the company for which the auditor was appointed following a qualifying selection procedure, and (b) the last financial year of the company to begin within the period of 20 years beginning with the first day of the first financial year of the maximum engagement period.

(2)   Where the first financial year of the maximum engagement period begins on or after 17 June 2003, the maximum engagement period may be extended by a period of no more than 2 years with the approval of the competent authority.

(3)   Such approval may be given by the competent authority only if it is satisfied that exceptional circumstances exist.

(4)   Where the competent authority gives its approval as mentioned in subsection (2)—

    (a)   the second column of the Table in subsection (1) has effect with the necessary modifications, and

    (b)   the first appointment to be made after the end of the period as so extended must be made following a qualifying selection procedure.

(5)   In this section "qualifying selection procedure" means—

    (a)   in the case of an appointment for a financial year beginning on or after 17 June 2016 made after the Statutory Auditors and Third Country Auditors Regulations 2017 come into force—

        (i)   if the company is a private company and has an audit committee, a selection procedure that complies with the requirements of section 485A(4) and (5)(a) and (b),

        (ii)   if the company is a public company and has an audit committee, a selection procedure that complies with the requirements of subsections 489A(4) and (5)(a) and (b), ...

        (iii)   if the company is a private company and does not have an audit committee, a selection procedure that complies with the requirements of section 485B(4),

        (iv)   if the company is a public company and does not have an audit committee, a selection procedure that complies with the requirements of section 489B(4),

    (b)   in any other case, a selection procedure that substantially meets the requirements of Article 16(2) to (5) of the Audit Regulation as it had effect immediately before IP completion day, having regard to the circumstances at the time (including whether the company had an audit committee).

494A   Interpretation

In this Chapter—

        "audit committee" means a body which performs—

    (a)   the functions referred to in—

        (i)   rule 7.1.3 of the Disclosure Guidance and Transparency Rules sourcebook made by the Financial Conduct Authority (audit committees and their functions) under the Financial Services and Markets Act 2000, or

        (ii)   rule 2.4 of the Audit Committee Part of the Rulebook made by the Prudential Regulation Authority (audit committee) under that Act,

        as they have effect on IP completion day, or

    (b)   equivalent functions;

    ...

        "Auditor General" means—

    (a)   the Comptroller and Auditor General,

    (b)   the Auditor General for Scotland,

    (c)   the Auditor General for Wales, or

    (d)   the Comptroller and Auditor General for Northern Ireland;

        "issuer" has the same meaning as in Part 6 of the Financial Services and Markets Act 2000 (see section 102A(6));

        "network" means an association of persons other than a firm co-operating in audit work by way of—

    (a)   profit-sharing;

    (b)   cost sharing;

    (c)   common ownership, control or management;

(d)   common quality control policies and procedures;

(e)   common business strategy; or

(f)   use of a common name;

"public interest entity" means—

(a)   an issuer whose transferable securities are admitted to trading on a UK regulated market;

(b)   a credit institution within the meaning given by Article 4(1)(1) of Regulation (EU) No 575/2013 of the European Parliament and of the Council, which is a CRR firm within the meaning of Article 4(1)(2A) of that Regulation;

(c)   a person who would be an insurance undertaking as defined in Article 2(1) of Council Directive 91/674/EEC of 19 December 1991 of the European Parliament and of the Council on the annual accounts and consolidated accounts of insurance undertakings as that Article had effect immediately before IP completion day, were the United Kingdom a member State;

…

CHAPTER 3
FUNCTIONS OF AUDITOR

Auditor's report

495   Auditor's report on company's annual accounts

(1)   A company's auditor must make a report to the company's members on all annual accounts of the company of which copies are, during his tenure of office—

(a)   in the case of a private company, to be sent out to members under section 423;

(b)   in the case of a public company, to be laid before the company in general meeting under section 437.

(2)   The auditor's report must include—

(a)   the identity of the company whose annual accounts are the subject of the audit,

(b)   a description of the annual accounts that are the subject of the audit (including the period covered by those accounts),

(c)   a description of the financial reporting framework that has been applied in the preparation of those accounts, and

(d)   a description of the scope of the audit identifying the auditing standards in accordance with which the audit was conducted.

(3)   The report must state clearly whether, in the auditor's opinion, the annual accounts—

(a)   give a true and fair view—

(i)   in the case of an individual balance sheet, of the state of affairs of the company as at the end of the financial year,

(ii)   in the case of an individual profit and loss account, of the profit or loss of the company for the financial year,

(iii)   in the case of group accounts, of the state of affairs as at the end of the financial year and of the profit or loss for the financial year of the undertakings included in the consolidation as a whole, so far as concerns members of the company;

(b)   have been properly prepared in accordance with the relevant financial reporting framework; and

(c)   have been prepared in accordance with the requirements of this Act ....

Expressions used in this subsection or subsection (3A) that are defined for the purposes of Part 15 (see sections 464, 471 and 474) have the same meaning as in that Part.

(3A)   The following provisions apply to the auditors of a company which qualifies as a micro-entity in relation to a financial year (see sections 384A and 384B) in their consideration of whether the Companies Act individual accounts of the company for that year give a true and fair view as mentioned in subsection (3)(a)—

(a) where the accounts comprise only micro-entity minimum accounting items, the auditors must disregard any provision of an accounting standard which would require the accounts to contain information additional to those items,

(b) in relation to a micro-entity minimum accounting item contained in the accounts, the auditors must disregard any provision of an accounting standard which would require the accounts to contain further information in relation to that item, and

(c) where the accounts contain an item of information additional to the micro-entity minimum accounting items, the auditors must have regard to any provision of an accounting standard which relates to that item.

(4) The auditor's report—

(a) must be either unqualified or qualified,

(b) must include a reference to any matters to which the auditor wishes to draw attention by way of emphasis without qualifying the report,

(c) must include a statement on any material uncertainty relating to events or conditions that may cast significant doubt about the company's ability to continue to adopt the going concern basis of accounting, and

(d) must identify the auditor's place of establishment.

(5) Where more than one person is appointed as an auditor—

(a) all the persons appointed must jointly make a report under this section and the report must include a statement as to whether all the persons appointed agree on the matters contained in the report, and

(b) if all the persons appointed cannot agree on the matters contained in the report, the report must include the opinions of each person appointed and give reasons for the disagreement.

496 Auditor's report on strategic report and directors' report

(1) In his report on the company's annual accounts, the auditor must—

(a) state whether, in his opinion, based on the work undertaken in the course of the audit—

(i) the information given in the strategic report (if any) and the directors' report for the financial year for which the accounts are prepared is consistent with those accounts, and

(ii) any such strategic report and the directors' report have been prepared in accordance with applicable legal requirements,

(b) state whether, in the light of the knowledge and understanding of the company and its environment obtained in the course of the audit, he has identified material misstatements in the strategic report (if any) and the directors' report, and

(c) if applicable, give an indication of the nature of each of the misstatements referred to in paragraph (b).

(2) Where more than one person is appointed as auditor, the report must include a statement as to whether all the persons appointed agree on the statements and indications given under subsection (1) and, if they cannot agree on those statements and indications, the report must include the opinions of each person appointed and give reasons for the disagreement.

497 Auditor's report on auditable part of directors' remuneration report

(1) If the company is a quoted company or unquoted traded company, the auditor, in his report on the company's annual accounts for the financial year, must—

(a) report to the company's members on the auditable part of the directors' remuneration report, and

(b) state whether in his opinion that part of the directors' remuneration report has been properly prepared in accordance with this Act.

(2) For the purposes of this Part, "the auditable part" of a directors' remuneration report is the part identified as such by regulations under section 421.

(3) In this section "unquoted traded company" means a traded company (as defined by section 360C) that is not a quoted company.

497A **Auditor's report on separate corporate governance statement**

(1) Where the company prepares a separate corporate governance statement in respect of a financial year, the auditor must, in his report of the company's annual accounts for that year—

    (a) state whether, in his opinion, based on the work undertaken in the course of the audit, the information given in the statement in compliance with rules 7.2.5 and 7.2.6 in the Disclosure Rules and Transparency Rules sourcebook made by the Financial Conduct Authority (information about internal control and risk management systems in relation to financial reporting processes and about share capital structures)—

        (i) is consistent with those accounts, and

        (ii) has been prepared in accordance with applicable legal requirements,

    (b) state whether, in the light of the knowledge and understanding of the company and its environment obtained in the course of the audit, he has identified material misstatements in the information in the statement referred to in paragraph (a),

    (c) if applicable, give an indication of the nature of each of the misstatements referred to in paragraph (b), and

    (d) state whether, in his opinion, based on the work undertaken in the course of the audit, rules 7.2.2, 7.2.3 and 7.2.7 in the Disclosure Rules and Transparency Rules sourcebook made by the Financial Conduct Authority (information about the company's corporate governance code and practices and about its administrative, management and supervisory bodies and their committees) have been complied with, if applicable.

(2) Where more than one person is appointed as auditor, the report must include a statement as to whether all the persons appointed agree on the statements and indications given under subsection (1) and, if they cannot agree on those statements and indications, the report must include the opinions of each person appointed and give reasons for the disagreement.

Duties and rights of auditors

498 **Duties of auditor**

(1) A company's auditor, in preparing his report, must carry out such investigations as will enable him to form an opinion as to—

    (a) whether adequate accounting records have been kept by the company and returns adequate for their audit have been received from branches not visited by him, and

    (b) whether the company's individual accounts are in agreement with the accounting records and returns, and

    (c) in the case of a quoted company or unquoted traded company, whether the auditable part of the company's directors' remuneration report is in agreement with the accounting records and returns.

(2) If the auditor is of the opinion—

    (a) that adequate accounting records have not been kept, or that returns adequate for their audit have not been received from branches not visited by him, or

    (b) that the company's individual accounts are not in agreement with the accounting records and returns, or

    (c) in the case of a quoted company or unquoted traded company, that the auditable part of its directors' remuneration report is not in agreement with the accounting records and returns,

the auditor shall state that fact in his report.

(3) If the auditor fails to obtain all the information and explanations which, to the best of his knowledge and belief, are necessary for the purposes of his audit, he shall state that fact in his report.

(4) If—

    (a) the requirements of regulations under section 412 (disclosure of directors' benefits: remuneration, pensions and compensation for loss of office) are not complied with in the annual accounts, or

(b)   in the case of a quoted company, the requirements of regulations under section 421 as to information forming the auditable part of the directors' remuneration report are not complied with in that report,

the auditor must include in his report, so far as he is reasonably able to do so, a statement giving the required particulars.

(5)   If the directors of the company—
   (a)   have prepared accounts in accordance with the small companies regime, or
   (b)   have taken advantage of small companies exemption from the requirement to prepare a strategic report or in preparing the directors' report,

and in the auditor's opinion they were not entitled to do so, the auditor shall state that fact in his report.

(6)   Where more than one person is appointed as auditor, the report must include a statement as to whether all the persons appointed agree on the statements given under subsections (2) to (5) and, if they cannot agree on those statements, the report must include the opinions of each person appointed and give reasons for the disagreement.

(7)   In this section "unquoted traded company" means a traded company (as defined by section 360C) that is not a quoted company.

498A   Auditor's duties in relation to separate corporate governance statement

Where the company is required to prepare a corporate governance statement in respect of a financial year and no such statement is included in the directors' report—
   (a)   the company's auditor, in preparing his report on the company's annual accounts for that year, must ascertain whether a corporate governance statement has been prepared, and
   (b)   if it appears to the auditor that no such statement has been prepared, he must state that fact in his report.

499   Auditor's general right to information

(1)   An auditor of a company—
   (a)   has a right of access at all times to the company's books, accounts and vouchers (in whatever form they are held), and
   (b)   may require any of the following persons to provide him with such information or explanations as he thinks necessary for the performance of his duties as auditor.

(2)   Those persons are—
   (a)   any officer or employee of the company;
   (b)   any person holding or accountable for any of the company's books, accounts or vouchers;
   (c)   any subsidiary undertaking of the company which is a body corporate incorporated in the United Kingdom;
   (d)   any officer, employee or auditor of any such subsidiary undertaking or any person holding or accountable for any books, accounts or vouchers of any such subsidiary undertaking;
   (e)   any person who fell within any of paragraphs (a) to (d) at a time to which the information or explanations required by the auditor relates or relate.

(3)   A statement made by a person in response to a requirement under this section may not be used in evidence against him in criminal proceedings except proceedings for an offence under section 501.

(4)   Nothing in this section compels a person to disclose information in respect of which a claim to legal professional privilege (in Scotland, to confidentiality of communications) could be maintained in legal proceedings.

500   Auditor's right to information from overseas subsidiaries

(1)   Where a parent company has a subsidiary undertaking that is not a body corporate incorporated in the United Kingdom, the auditor of the parent company may require it to obtain from any of the following persons such information or explanations as he may reasonably require for the purposes of his duties as auditor.

(2)   Those persons are—

(a)   the undertaking;

(b)   any officer, employee or auditor of the undertaking;

(c)   any person holding or accountable for any of the undertaking's books, accounts or vouchers;

(d)   any person who fell within paragraph (b) or (c) at a time to which the information or explanations relates or relate.

(3)   If so required, the parent company must take all such steps as are reasonably open to it to obtain the information or explanations from the person concerned.

(4)   A statement made by a person in response to a requirement under this section may not be used in evidence against him in criminal proceedings except proceedings for an offence under section 501.

(5)   Nothing in this section compels a person to disclose information in respect of which a claim to legal professional privilege (in Scotland, to confidentiality of communications) could be maintained in legal proceedings.

501   Auditor's rights to information: offences

(1)   A person commits an offence who knowingly or recklessly makes to an auditor of a company a statement (oral or written) that—

(a)   conveys or purports to convey any information or explanations which the auditor requires, or is entitled to require, under section 499, and

(b)   is misleading, false or deceptive in a material particular.

(2)   A person guilty of an offence under subsection (1) is liable—

(a)   on conviction on indictment, to imprisonment for a term not exceeding two years or a fine (or both);

(b)   on summary conviction—

(i)   in England and Wales, to imprisonment for a term not exceeding twelve months or to a fine not exceeding the statutory maximum (or both);

(ii)   in Scotland or Northern Ireland, to imprisonment for a term not exceeding six months or to a fine not exceeding the statutory maximum (or both).

(3)   A person who fails to comply with a requirement under section 499 without delay commits an offence unless it was not reasonably practicable for him to provide the required information or explanations.

(4)   If a parent company fails to comply with section 500, an offence is committed by—

(a)   the company, and

(b)   every officer of the company who is in default.

(5)   A person guilty of an offence under subsection (3) or (4) is liable on summary conviction to a fine not exceeding level 3 on the standard scale.

(6)   Nothing in this section affects any right of an auditor to apply for an injunction (in Scotland, an interdict or an order for specific performance) to enforce any of his rights under section 499 or 500.

502   Auditor's rights in relation to resolutions and meetings

(1)   In relation to a written resolution proposed to be agreed to by a private company, the company's auditor is entitled to receive all such communications relating to the resolution as, by virtue of any provision of Chapter 2 of Part 13 of this Act, are required to be supplied to a member of the company.

(2)   A company's auditor is entitled—

(a)   to receive all notices of, and other communications relating to, any general meeting which a member of the company is entitled to receive,

(b)   to attend any general meeting of the company, and

(c)   to be heard at any general meeting which he attends on any part of the business of the meeting which concerns him as auditor.

(3)   Where the auditor is a firm, the right to attend or be heard at a meeting is exercisable by an individual authorised by the firm in writing to act as its representative at the meeting.

Signature of auditor's report

503   Signature of auditor's report

(1)   The auditor's report must state the name of the auditor and be signed and dated.

(2)   Where the auditor is an individual, the report must be signed by him.

(3)   Where the auditor is a firm, the report must be signed by the senior statutory auditor in his own name, for and on behalf of the auditor.

(4)   Where more than one person is appointed as auditor, the report must be signed by all those appointed.

504   Senior statutory auditor

(1)   The senior statutory auditor means the individual identified by the firm as senior statutory auditor in relation to the audit in accordance with—

    (a)   ...

    (b)   ... any relevant guidance issued by—

        (i)   the Secretary of State, or

        (ii)   a body appointed by order of the Secretary of State.

(2)   The person identified as senior statutory auditor must be eligible for appointment as auditor of the company in question (see Chapter 2 of Part 42 of this Act).

(3)   The senior statutory auditor is not, by reason of being named or identified as senior statutory auditor or by reason of his having signed the auditor's report, subject to any civil liability to which he would not otherwise be subject.

(4)   An order appointing a body for the purpose of subsection (1)(b)(ii) is subject to negative resolution procedure.

505   Names to be stated in published copies of auditor's report

(1)   Every copy of the auditor's report that is published by or on behalf of the company must—

    (a)   state the name of the auditor and (where the auditor is a firm) the name of the person who signed it as senior statutory auditor, or

    (b)   if the conditions in section 506 (circumstances in which names may be omitted) are met, state that a resolution has been passed and notified to the Secretary of State in accordance with that section.

(1A)   If more than one person is appointed as auditor, the reference in subsection (1)(a) to the name of the auditor is to be read as a reference to the names of all the auditors.

(2)   For the purposes of this section a company is regarded as publishing the report if it publishes, issues or circulates it or otherwise makes it available for public inspection in a manner calculated to invite members of the public generally, or any class of members of the public, to read it.

(3)   If a copy of the auditor's report is published without the statement required by this section, an offence is committed by—

    (a)   the company, and

    (b)   every officer of the company who is in default.

(4)   A person guilty of an offence under this section is liable on summary conviction to a fine not exceeding level 3 on the standard scale.

506   Circumstances in which names may be omitted

(1)   An auditor's name and, where the auditor is a firm, the name of the person who signed the report as senior statutory auditor, may be omitted from—

    (a)   published copies of the report, and

    (b)   the copy of the report delivered to the registrar under Chapter 10 of Part 15 (filing of accounts and reports),

    if the following conditions are met.

(2)   The conditions are that the company—

(a)   considering on reasonable grounds that statement of the name would create or be likely to create a serious risk that the auditor or senior statutory auditor, or any other person, would be subject to violence or intimidation, has resolved that the name should not be stated, and

(b)   has given notice of the resolution to the Secretary of State, stating—

    (i)   the name and registered number of the company,

    (ii)   the financial year of the company to which the report relates, and

    (iii) the name of the auditor and (where the auditor is a firm) the name of the person who signed the report as senior statutory auditor.

Offences in connection with auditor's report

507   Offences in connection with auditor's report

(1)   A person to whom this section applies commits an offence if he knowingly or recklessly causes a report under section 495 (auditor's report on company's annual accounts) to include any matter that is misleading, false or deceptive in a material particular.

(2)   A person to whom this section applies commits an offence if he knowingly or recklessly causes such a report to omit a statement required by—

(a)   section 498(2)(b) (statement that company's accounts do not agree with accounting records and returns),

(b)   section 498(3) (statement that necessary information and explanations not obtained), or

(c)   section 498(5) (statement that directors wrongly took advantage of exemption from obligation to prepare group accounts).

(3)   This section applies to—

(a)   where the auditor is an individual, that individual and any employee or agent of his who is eligible for appointment as auditor of the company;

(b)   where the auditor is a firm, any director, member, employee or agent of the firm who is eligible for appointment as auditor of the company.

(4)   A person guilty of an offence under this section is liable—

(a)   on conviction on indictment, to a fine;

(b)   on summary conviction, to a fine not exceeding the statutory maximum.

508   Guidance for regulatory and prosecuting authorities: England, Wales and Northern Ireland

(1)   The Secretary of State may issue guidance for the purpose of helping relevant regulatory and prosecuting authorities to determine how they should carry out their functions in cases where behaviour occurs that—

(a)   appears to involve the commission of an offence under section 507 (offences in connection with auditor's report), and

(b)   has been, is being or may be investigated—

    (i)   pursuant to arrangements under paragraph 15 of Schedule 10 (investigation of complaints against auditors and supervisory bodies), or

    (ii)   by the competent authority under the Statutory Auditors and Third Country Auditors Regulations 2016.

(2)   The Secretary of State must obtain the consent of the Attorney General before issuing any such guidance.

(3)   In this section "relevant regulatory and prosecuting authorities" means—

(a)   supervisory bodies within the meaning of Part 42 of this Act,

(b)   bodies to which the Secretary of State may make grants under section 16(1) of the Companies (Audit, Investigations and Community Enterprise) Act 2004 (bodies concerned with accounting standards etc),

(c)   the Director of the Serious Fraud Office,

(d)   the Director of Public Prosecutions or the Director of Public Prosecutions for Northern Ireland, and

(e)   the Secretary of State.

(4)   This section does not apply to Scotland.

509 Guidance for regulatory authorities: Scotland

(1) The Lord Advocate may issue guidance for the purpose of helping relevant regulatory authorities to determine how they should carry out their functions in cases where behaviour occurs that—
 (a) appears to involve the commission of an offence under section 507 (offences in connection with auditor's report), and
 (b) has been, is being or may be investigated—
  (i) pursuant to arrangements under paragraph 15 of Schedule 10 (investigation of complaints against auditors and supervisory bodies), or
  (ii) by the competent authority under the Statutory Auditors and Third Country Auditors Regulations 2016.

(2) The Lord Advocate must consult the Secretary of State before issuing any such guidance.

(3) In this section "relevant regulatory authorities" means—
 (a) supervisory bodies within the meaning of Part 42 of this Act,
 (b) bodies to which the Secretary of State may make grants under section 16(1) of the Companies (Audit, Investigations and Community Enterprise) Act 2004 (bodies concerned with accounting standards etc), and
 (c) the Secretary of State.

(4) This section applies only to Scotland.

CHAPTER 4
REMOVAL, RESIGNATION, ETC OF AUDITORS

Removal of auditor

510 Resolution removing auditor from office

(1) The members of a company may remove an auditor from office at any time.

(2) This power is exercisable only—
 (a) by ordinary resolution at a meeting, and
 (b) in accordance with section 511 (special notice of resolution to remove auditor).

(3) Nothing in this section is to be taken as depriving the person removed of compensation or damages payable to him in respect of the termination—
 (a) of his appointment as auditor, or
 (b) of any appointment terminating with that as auditor.

(4) An auditor may not be removed from office before the expiration of his term of office except—
 (a) by resolution under this section, or
 (b) in accordance with section 511A.

511 Special notice required for resolution removing auditor from office

(1) Special notice is required for a resolution at a general meeting of a company removing an auditor from office.

(2) On receipt of notice of such an intended resolution the company must immediately send a copy of it to the auditor proposed to be removed.

(3) The auditor proposed to be removed may make with respect to the intended resolution representations in writing to the company (not exceeding a reasonable length) and request their notification to members of the company.

(4) The company must (unless the representations are received by it too late for it to do so)—
 (a) in any notice of the resolution given to members of the company, state the fact of the representations having been made, and
 (b) send a copy of the representations to every member of the company to whom notice of the meeting is or has been sent.

(5) If a copy of any such representations is not sent out as required because received too late or because of the company's default, the auditor may (without prejudice to his right to be heard orally) require that the representations be read out at the meeting.

(6)   Copies of the representations need not be sent out and the representations need not be read at the meeting if, on the application either of the company or of any other person claiming to be aggrieved, the court is satisfied that the auditor is using the provisions of this section to secure needless publicity for defamatory matter.

The court may order the company's costs (in Scotland, expenses) on the application to be paid in whole or in part by the auditor, notwithstanding that he is not a party to the application.

511A   Public interest companies: application to court to remove auditor from office

(1)   This section applies only to a public interest company.

(2)   The competent authority may apply to the court for an order removing an auditor of a company from office if the authority considers that there are proper grounds for removing the auditor from office.

(3)   The members of a company may apply to the court for an order removing an auditor of the company from office if the applicant or applicants consider that there are proper grounds for removing the auditor from office.

(4)   If the court is satisfied, on hearing an application under subsection (2), that there are proper grounds for removing the auditor from office, it may make an order removing the auditor from office.

(5)   If the court is satisfied, on hearing an application under subsection (3), that—

  (a)   the applicants represent in total—

    (i)   not less than 5% of the voting rights of all the members having a right to vote at a general meeting of the company, or

    (ii)   not less than 5% in nominal value of the company's share capital, and

  (b)   there are proper grounds for removing the auditor from office,

the court may make an order removing the auditor from office.

(6)   For the purposes of this section, divergence of opinions on accounting treatments or audit procedures are not to be taken to be proper grounds for removing an auditor from office.

(7)   ...

512   ...

513   Rights of auditor who has been removed from office

(1)   An auditor who has been removed by resolution under section 510 or by order of the court under section 511A has, notwithstanding his removal, the rights conferred by section 502(2) in relation to any general meeting of the company—

  (a)   at which his term of office would otherwise have expired, or

  (b)   at which it is proposed to fill the vacancy caused by his removal.

(2)   In such a case the references in that section to matters concerning the auditor as auditor shall be construed as references to matters concerning him as a former auditor.

Failure to re-appoint auditor

514   Failure to re-appoint auditor: special procedure required for written resolution

(1)   This section applies where a resolution is proposed as a written resolution of a private company whose effect would be to appoint a person as auditor in place of a person (the "outgoing auditor") who, at the time the resolution is proposed, is an auditor of the company and who is to cease to hold office at the end of a period for appointing auditors.

But this section does not apply if the auditor is to cease to hold office by virtue of section 510, 511A or 516.

(2)   This section also applies where a resolution is proposed as a written resolution of a private company whose effect would be to appoint a person as auditor where, at the time the resolution is proposed, the company does not have an auditor and the person proposed to be appointed is not a person (the "outgoing auditor") who was an auditor of the company when the company last had an auditor.

But this is subject to subsection (2A).

(2A)   This section does not apply (by virtue of subsection (2)) if—
    (a)   a period for appointing auditors has ended since the outgoing auditor ceased to hold office,
    (b)   the outgoing auditor ceased to hold office by virtue of section 510, 511A or 516, or
    (c)   the outgoing auditor has previously had the opportunity to make representations with respect to a proposed resolution under subsection (4) of this section or an intended resolution under section 515(4).

(3)   Where this section applies, the company must send a copy of the proposed resolution to the person proposed to be appointed and to the outgoing auditor.

(4)   The outgoing auditor may, within 14 days after receiving the notice, make with respect to the proposed resolution representations in writing to the company (not exceeding a reasonable length) and request their circulation to members of the company.

(5)   The company must circulate the representations together with the copy or copies of the resolution circulated in accordance with section 291 (resolution proposed by directors) or section 293 (resolution proposed by members).

(6)   Where subsection (5) applies—
    (a)   the period allowed under section 293(3) for service of copies of the proposed resolution is 28 days instead of 21 days, and
    (b)   the provisions of section 293(5) and (6) (offences) apply in relation to a failure to comply with that subsection as in relation to a default in complying with that section.

(7)   Copies of the representations need not be circulated if, on the application either of the company or of any other person claiming to be aggrieved, the court is satisfied that the auditor is using the provisions of this section to secure needless publicity for defamatory matter.
    The court may order the company's costs (in Scotland, expenses) on the application to be paid in whole or in part by the auditor, notwithstanding that he is not a party to the application.

(8)   If any requirement of this section is not complied with, the resolution is ineffective.

515   Failure to re-appoint auditor: special notice required for resolution at general meeting

(1)   Special notice is required for a resolution at a general meeting of a private company whose effect would be to appoint a person as auditor in place of a person (the "outgoing auditor") who, at the time the notice is given, is an auditor of the company and who is to cease to hold office at the end of a period for appointing auditors.
    But special notice is not required under this subsection if the auditor is to cease to hold office by virtue of section 510, 511A or 516.

(1A)   Special notice is required for a resolution at a general meeting of a public company whose effect would be to appoint a person as auditor in place of a person (the "outgoing auditor") who, at the time the notice is given, is an auditor of the company and who is to cease to hold office at the end of an accounts meeting.
    But special notice is not required under this subsection if the auditor is to cease to hold office by virtue of section 510, 511A or 516.

(2)   Special notice is required for a resolution at a general meeting of a company whose effect would be to appoint a person as auditor where, at the time the notice is given, the company does not have an auditor and the person proposed to be appointed is not a person (the "outgoing auditor") who was an auditor of the company when the company last had an auditor.
    But this is subject to subsection (2A).

(2A)   Special notice is not required under subsection (2) if—
    (a)   a period for appointing auditors has ended or (as the case may be) an accounts meeting of the company has been held since the outgoing auditor ceased to hold office,
    (b)   the outgoing auditor ceased to hold office by virtue of section 510, 511A or 516, or
    (c)   the outgoing auditor has previously had the opportunity to make representations with respect to an intended resolution under subsection (4) of this section or a proposed resolution under section 514(4).

(3)   On receipt of notice of ... an intended resolution mentioned in subsection (1), (1A) or (2) the company shall forthwith send a copy of it to the person proposed to be appointed and to the outgoing auditor.

(4)   The outgoing auditor may make with respect to the intended resolution representations in writing to the company (not exceeding a reasonable length) and request their notification to members of the company.

(5)   The company must (unless the representations are received by it too late for it to do so)—
(a)   in any notice of the resolution given to members of the company, state the fact of the representations having been made, and
(b)   send a copy of the representations to every member of the company to whom notice of the meeting is or has been sent.

(6)   If a copy of any such representations is not sent out as required because received too late or because of the company's default, the outgoing auditor may (without prejudice to his right to be heard orally) require that the representations be read out at the meeting.

(7)   Copies of the representations need not be sent out and the representations need not be read at the meeting if, on the application either of the company or of any other person claiming to be aggrieved, the court is satisfied that the auditor is using the provisions of this section to secure needless publicity for defamatory matter.
       The court may order the company's costs (in Scotland, expenses) on the application to be paid in whole or in part by the outgoing auditor, notwithstanding that he is not a party to the application.

Resignation of auditor

516   Resignation of auditor

(1)   An auditor of a company may resign his office by sending a notice to that effect to the company.

(2)   Where the company is a public interest company, the notice is not effective unless it is accompanied by the statement required by section 519.

(3)   An effective notice of resignation operates to bring the auditor's term of office to an end as of the date on which the notice is received or on such later date as may be specified in it.

517   ...

518   Rights of resigning auditor

(1)   This section applies where an auditor's (A's) notice of resignation is accompanied by a statement under section 519 except where—
(a)   the company is a non-public interest company, and
(b)   the statement includes a statement to the effect that A considers that none of the reasons for A's ceasing to hold office, and no matters (if any) connected with A's ceasing to hold office, need to be brought to the attention of members or creditors of the company (as required by section 519(3B)).

(2)   He may send with the notice an authenticated requisition calling on the directors of the company forthwith duly to convene a general meeting of the company for the purpose of receiving and considering such explanation of the reasons for, and matters connected with, his resignation as he may wish to place before the meeting.

(3)   He may request the company to circulate to its members—
(a)   before the meeting convened on his requisition, or
(b)   before any general meeting at which his term of office would otherwise have expired or at which it is proposed to fill the vacancy caused by his resignation,
a statement in writing (not exceeding a reasonable length) of the reasons for, and matters connected with, his resignation.

(4)   The company must (unless the statement is received too late for it to comply)—
(a)   in any notice of the meeting given to members of the company, state the fact of the statement having been made, and

(b)   send a copy of the statement to every member of the company to whom notice of the meeting is or has been sent.

(5)   The directors must within 21 days from the date on which the company receives a requisition under this section proceed duly to convene a meeting for a day not more than 28 days after the date on which the notice convening the meeting is given.

(6)   If default is made in complying with subsection (5), every director who failed to take all reasonable steps to secure that a meeting was convened commits an offence.

(7)   A person guilty of an offence under this section is liable—
        (a)   on conviction on indictment, to a fine;
        (b)   on summary conviction to a fine not exceeding the statutory maximum.

(8)   If a copy of the statement mentioned above is not sent out as required because received too late or because of the company's default, the auditor may (without prejudice to his right to be heard orally) require that the statement be read out at the meeting.

(9)   Copies of a statement need not be sent out and the statement need not be read out at the meeting if, on the application either of the company or of any other person who claims to be aggrieved, the court is satisfied that the auditor is using the provisions of this section to secure needless publicity for defamatory matter.

        The court may order the company's costs (in Scotland, expenses) on such an application to be paid in whole or in part by the auditor, notwithstanding that he is not a party to the application.

(10)   An auditor who has resigned has, notwithstanding his resignation, the rights conferred by section 502(2) in relation to any such general meeting of the company as is mentioned in subsection (3) (a) or (b) above.

        In such a case the references in that section to matters concerning the auditor as auditor shall be construed as references to matters concerning him as a former auditor.

Statement by auditor on ceasing to hold office

519   Statement by auditor to be sent to company

(1)   An auditor of a public interest company who is ceasing to hold office (at any time and for any reason) must send to the company a statement of the reasons for doing so.

(2)   An auditor ("A") of a non-public interest company who is ceasing to hold office must send to the company a statement of the reasons for doing so unless A satisfies the first or second condition.

(2A)   The first condition is that A is ceasing to hold office—
        (a)   in the case of a private company, at the end of a period for appointing auditors;
        (b)   in the case of a public company, at the end of an accounts meeting.

(2B)   The second condition is that—
        (a)   A's reasons for ceasing to hold office are all exempt reasons (as to which see section 519A(3)), and
        (b)   there are no matters connected with A's ceasing to hold office that A considers need to be brought to the attention of members or creditors of the company.

(3)   A statement under this section must include—
        (a)   the auditor's name and address;
        (b)   the number allocated to the auditor on being entered in the register of auditors kept under section 1239;
        (c)   the company's name and registered number.

(3A)   Where there are matters connected with an auditor's ceasing to hold office that the auditor considers need to be brought to the attention of members or creditors of the company, the statement under this section must include details of those matters.

(3B)   Where—
        (a)   an auditor ("A") of a non-public interest company is required by subsection (2) to send a statement, and

(b)   A considers that none of the reasons for A's ceasing to hold office, and no matters (if any) connected with A's ceasing to hold office, need to be brought to the attention of members or creditors of the company,

A's statement under this section must include a statement to that effect.

(4)   A statement under this section must be sent—

(a)   in the case of resignation, along with the notice of resignation;

(b)   in the case of failure to seek re-appointment, not less than 14 days before the end of the time allowed for next appointing an auditor;

(c)   in any other case, not later than the end of the period of 14 days beginning with the date on which he ceases to hold office.

(5)   A person ceasing to hold office as auditor who fails to comply with this section commits an offence.

(6)   In proceedings for such an offence it is a defence for the person charged to show that he took all reasonable steps and exercised all due diligence to avoid the commission of the offence.

(7)   A person guilty of an offence under this section is liable—

(a)   on conviction on indictment, to a fine;

(b)   on summary conviction, to a fine not exceeding the statutory maximum.

(8)   Where an offence under this section is committed by a body corporate, every officer of the body who is in default also commits the offence.

For this purpose—

(a)   any person who purports to act as director, manager or secretary of the body is treated as an officer of the body, and

(b)   if the body is a company, any shadow director is treated as an officer of the company.

519A   Meaning of "public interest company", "non-public interest company" and "exempt reasons"

(1)   In this Chapter—

"public interest company" means a company which is—

(a)   an issuer whose transferable securities are admitted to trading on a UK regulated market;

(b)   a credit institution within the meaning given by Article 4(1)(1) of Regulation (EU) No 575/2013 of the European Parliament and of the Council, which is a CRR firm within the meaning of Article 4(1)(2A) of that Regulation; or

(c)   a person who would be an insurance undertaking as defined in Article 2(1) of Council Directive 91/674/EEC of 19 December 1991 of the European Parliament and of the Council on the annual accounts and consolidated accounts of insurance undertakings as that Article had effect immediately before IP completion day, were the United Kingdom a member State;

"non-public interest company" means a company that is not a public interest company.

(2)   For the purposes of the definition of "public interest company"—

"issuer" has the same meaning as in Part 6 of the Financial Services and Markets Act 2000 (see section 102A(6));

…

(3)   In the application of this Chapter to an auditor ("A") of a company ceasing to hold office, the following are "exempt reasons"—

(a)   A is no longer to carry out statutory audit work within the meaning of Part 42 (see section 1210(1));

(b)   the company is, or is to become, exempt from audit under section 477, 479A or 480, or from the requirements of this Part under section 482, and intends to include in its balance sheet a statement of the type described in section 475(2);

(c)   the company is a subsidiary undertaking of a parent undertaking that is incorporated in the United Kingdom and—

(i)   the parent undertaking prepares group accounts, and

        (ii)   A is being replaced as auditor of the company by the auditor who is conducting, or is to conduct, an audit of the group accounts;

(d)   the company is being wound up under Part 4 of the Insolvency Act 1986 or Part 5 of the Insolvency (Northern Ireland) Order 1989 (S.I. 1989/2405 (N.I. 19)), whether voluntarily or by the court, or a petition under Part 4 of that Act or Part 5 of that Order for the winding up of the company has been presented and not finally dealt with or withdrawn.

(4)   But the reason described in subsection (3)(c) is only an exempt reason if the auditor who is conducting, or is to conduct, an audit of the group accounts is also conducting, or is also to conduct, the audit (if any) of the accounts of each of the subsidiary undertakings (of the parent undertaking) that is incorporated in the United Kingdom and included in the consolidation.

(5)   The Secretary of State may by order amend the definition of "public interest company" in subsection (1).

(6)   An order under subsection (5) is subject to negative resolution procedure.

520   Company's duties in relation to statement

(1)   This section applies where a company receives from an auditor ("A") who is ceasing to hold office a statement under section 519 except where—

(a)   the company is a non-public interest company, and

(b)   the statement includes a statement to the effect that A considers that none of the reasons for A's ceasing to hold office, and no matters (if any) connected with A's ceasing to hold office, need to be brought to the attention of members or creditors of the company (as required by section 519(3B)).

(2)   Where this section applies, the company must within 14 days of the receipt of the statement either—

(a)   send a copy of it to every person who under section 423 is entitled to be sent copies of the accounts, or

(b)   apply to the court.

(3)   If it applies to the court, the company must notify the auditor of the application.

(4)   If the court is satisfied that the auditor is using the provisions of section 519 to secure needless publicity for defamatory matter—

(a)   it shall direct that copies of the statement need not be sent out, and

(b)   it may further order the company's costs (in Scotland, expenses) on the application to be paid in whole or in part by the auditor, even if he is not a party to the application.

The company must within 14 days of the court's decision send to the persons mentioned in subsection (2)(a) a statement setting out the effect of the order.

(5)   If no such direction is made the company must send copies of the statement to the persons mentioned in subsection (2) (a) within 14 days of the court's decision or, as the case may be, of the discontinuance of the proceedings.

(6)   In the event of default in complying with this section an offence is committed by every officer of the company who is in default.

(7)   In proceedings for such an offence it is a defence for the person charged to show that he took all reasonable steps and exercised all due diligence to avoid the commission of the offence.

(8)   A person guilty of an offence under this section is liable—

(a)   on conviction on indictment, to a fine;

(b)   on summary conviction, to a fine not exceeding the statutory maximum.

521   Copy of statement to be sent to registrar

(A1)   This section applies where an auditor ("A") of a company sends a statement to the company under section 519 except where—

(a)   the company is a non-public interest company, and

(b)   the statement includes a statement to the effect that A considers that none of the reasons for A's ceasing to hold office, and no matters (if any) connected with A's ceasing to hold office, need to be brought to the attention of members or creditors of the company (as required by section 519(3B)).

(1)   Where this section applies, unless within 21 days beginning with the day on which he sent the statement under section 519 the auditor receives notice of an application to the court under section 520, he must within a further seven days send a copy of the statement to the registrar.

(2)   If an application to the court is made under section 520 and the auditor subsequently receives notice under subsection (5) of that section, he must within seven days of receiving the notice send a copy of the statement to the registrar.

(3)   An auditor who fails to comply with subsection (1) or (2) commits an offence.

(4)   In proceedings for such an offence it is a defence for the person charged to show that he took all reasonable steps and exercised all due diligence to avoid the commission of the offence.

(5)   A person guilty of an offence under this section is liable—

(a)   on conviction on indictment, to a fine;

(b)   on summary conviction, to a fine not exceeding the statutory maximum.

(6)   Where an offence under this section is committed by a body corporate, every officer of the body who is in default also commits the offence.

For this purpose—

(a)   any person who purports to act as director, manager or secretary of the body is treated as an officer of the body, and

(b)   if the body is a company, any shadow director is treated as an officer of the company.

522   Duty of auditor to send statement to appropriate audit authority

(1)   Where an auditor of a company sends a statement under section 519, the auditor must at the same time send a copy of the statement to the appropriate audit authority.

(2)–(4) ...

(5)   A person ceasing to hold office as auditor who fails to comply with this section commits an offence.

(6)   If that person is a firm an offence is committed by—

(a)   the firm, and

(b)   every officer of the firm who is in default.

(7)   In proceedings for an offence under this section it is a defence for the person charged to show that he took all reasonable steps and exercised all due diligence to avoid the commission of the offence.

(8)   A person guilty of an offence under this section is liable—

(a)   on conviction on indictment, to a fine;

(b)   on summary conviction, to a fine not exceeding the statutory maximum.

523   Duty of company to notify appropriate audit authority

(1)   This section applies if an auditor is ceasing to hold office—

(a)   in the case of a private company, at any time other than at the end of a period for appointing auditors;

(b)   in the case of a public company, at any time other than at the end of an accounts meeting.

(1A)   But this section does not apply if the company reasonably believes that the only reasons for the auditor's ceasing to hold office are exempt reasons (as to which see section 519A(3)).

(2)   Where this section applies, the company must give notice to the appropriate audit authority that the auditor is ceasing to hold office.

(2A)   The notice is to take the form of a statement by the company of what the company believes to be the reasons for the auditor's ceasing to hold office and must include the information listed in section 519(3).

This is subject to subsection (2C).

(2B)   Subsection (2C) applies where—

(a)   the company receives a statement from the auditor under section 519,

(b)   the statement is sent at the time required by section 519(4), and

(c)   the company agrees with the contents of the statement.

(2C) Where this subsection applies, the notice may instead take the form of a copy of the statement endorsed by the company to the effect that it agrees with the contents of the statement.

(3)   A notice under this section must be given within the period of 28 days beginning with the day on which the auditor ceases to hold office.

(4)   If a company fails to comply with this section, an offence is committed by—
      (a)   the company, and
      (b)   every officer of the company who is in default.

(5)   In proceedings for such an offence it is a defence for the person charged to show that he took all reasonable steps and exercised all due diligence to avoid the commission of the offence.

(6)   A person guilty of an offence under this section is liable—
      (a)   on conviction on indictment, to a fine;
      (b)   on summary conviction, to a fine not exceeding the statutory maximum.

524   Provision of information to accounting authorities

(1)   Where the appropriate audit authority receives a statement under section 522 or a notice under section 523, the authority may forward to the accounting authorities—
      (a)   a copy of the statement or notice, and
      (b)   any other information the authority has received from the auditor or the company concerned in connection with the auditor's ceasing to hold office.

(2)   The accounting authorities are—
      (a)   the Secretary of State, and
      (b)   any person authorised by the Secretary of State for the purposes of section 456 (revision of defective accounts: persons authorised to apply to court).

(3)   ...

(4)   If the court has made an order under section 520(4) directing that copies of the statement need not be sent out by the company, sections 460 and 461 (restriction on further disclosure) apply in relation to the copies sent to the accounting authorities as they apply to information obtained under section 459 (power to require documents etc).

525   Meaning of "appropriate audit authority" ...

(1)   In sections 522, 523 and 524 "appropriate audit authority" means—
      (a)   in relation to an auditor of a public interest company (other than an Auditor General)—
            (i)   the Secretary of State, or
            (ii)   if the Secretary of State has delegated functions under section 1252 to a body whose functions include receiving the statement or notice in question, that body;
      (b)   in relation to an auditor of a non-public interest company (other than an Auditor General), the relevant supervisory body;
      (c)   in relation to an Auditor General, the Independent Supervisor.
      "Supervisory body" and "Independent Supervisor" have the same meaning as in Part 42 (statutory auditors) (see sections 1217 and 1228).

(2), (3)   ...

Supplementary

526   Effect of casual vacancies

      If an auditor ceases to hold office for any reason, any surviving or continuing auditor or auditors may continue to act.

CHAPTER 5
QUOTED COMPANIES: RIGHT OF MEMBERS TO RAISE AUDIT
CONCERNS AT ACCOUNTS MEETING

527   Members' power to require website publication of audit concerns

(1)   The members of a quoted company may require the company to publish on a website a statement setting out any matter relating to—

(a) the audit of the company's accounts (including the auditor's report and the conduct of the audit) that are to be laid before the next accounts meeting, or

(b) any circumstances connected with an auditor of the company ceasing to hold office since the previous accounts meeting,

that the members propose to raise at the next accounts meeting of the company.

(2) A company is required to do so once it has received requests to that effect from—

(a) members representing at least 5% of the total voting rights of all the members who have a relevant right to vote (excluding any voting rights attached to any shares in the company held as treasury shares), or

(b) at least 100 members who have a relevant right to vote and hold shares in the company on which there has been paid up an average sum, per member, of at least £100.

See also section 153 (exercise of rights where shares held on behalf of others).

(3) In subsection (2) a "relevant right to vote" means a right to vote at the accounts meeting.

(4) A request—

(a) may be sent to the company in hard copy or electronic form,

(b) must identify the statement to which it relates,

(c) must be authenticated by the person or persons making it, and

(d) must be received by the company at least one week before the meeting to which it relates.

(5) A quoted company is not required to place on a website a statement under this section if, on an application by the company or another person who claims to be aggrieved, the court is satisfied that the rights conferred by this section are being abused.

(6) The court may order the members requesting website publication to pay the whole or part of the company's costs (in Scotland, expenses) on such an application, even if they are not parties to the application.

528 Requirements as to website availability

(1) The following provisions apply for the purposes of section 527 (website publication of members' statement of audit concerns).

(2) The information must be made available on a website that—

(a) is maintained by or on behalf of the company, and

(b) identifies the company in question.

(3) Access to the information on the website, and the ability to obtain a hard copy of the information from the website, must not be conditional on the payment of a fee or otherwise restricted.

(4) The statement—

(a) must be made available within three working days of the company being required to publish it on a website, and

(b) must be kept available until after the meeting to which it relates.

(5) A failure to make information available on a website throughout the period specified in subsection (4)(b) is disregarded if—

(a) the information is made available on the website for part of that period, and

(b) the failure is wholly attributable to circumstances that it would not be reasonable to have expected the company to prevent or avoid.

529 Website publication: company's supplementary duties

(1) A quoted company must in the notice it gives of the accounts meeting draw attention to—

(a) the possibility of a statement being placed on a website in pursuance of members' requests under section 527, and

(b) the effect of the following provisions of this section.

(2) A company may not require the members requesting website publication to pay its expenses in complying with that section or section 528 (requirements in connection with website publication).

(3) Where a company is required to place a statement on a website under section 527 it must forward the statement to the company's auditor not later than the time when it makes the statement available on the website.

(4)   The business which may be dealt with at the accounts meeting includes any statement that the company has been required under section 527 to publish on a website.

530   Website publication: offences

(1)   In the event of default in complying with
        (a)   section 528 (requirements as to website publication), or
        (b)   section 529 (companies' supplementary duties in relation to request for website publication),
        an offence is committed by every officer of the company who is in default.

(2)   A person guilty of an offence under this section is liable—
        (a)   on conviction on indictment, to a fine;
        (b)   on summary conviction, to a fine not exceeding the statutory maximum.

531   Meaning of "quoted company"

(1)   For the purposes of this Chapter a company is a quoted company if it is a quoted company in accordance with section 385 (quoted and unquoted companies for the purposes of Part 15) in relation to the financial year to which the accounts to be laid at the next accounts meeting relate.

(2)   The provisions of subsections (4) to (6) of that section (power to amend definition by regulations) apply in relation to the provisions of this Chapter as in relation to the provisions of that Part.

CHAPTER 6
AUDITORS' LIABILITY

Voidness of provisions protecting auditors from liability

532   Voidness of provisions protecting auditors from liability

(1)   This section applies to any provision—
        (a)   for exempting an auditor of a company (to any extent) from any liability that would otherwise attach to him in connection with any negligence, default, breach of duty or breach of trust in relation to the company occurring in the course of the audit of accounts, or
        (b)   by which a company directly or indirectly provides an indemnity (to any extent) for an auditor of the company, or of an associated company, against any liability attaching to him in connection with any negligence, default, breach of duty or breach of trust in relation to the company of which he is auditor occurring in the course of the audit of accounts.

(2)   Any such provision is void, except as permitted by—
        (a)   section 533 (indemnity for costs of successfully defending proceedings), or
        (b)   sections 534 to 536 (liability limitation agreements).

(3)   This section applies to any provision, whether contained in a company's articles or in any contract with the company or otherwise.

(4)   For the purposes of this section companies are associated if one is a subsidiary of the other or both are subsidiaries of the same body corporate.

Indemnity for costs of defending proceedings

533   Indemnity for costs of successfully defending proceedings

        Section 532 (general voidness of provisions protecting auditors from liability) does not prevent a company from indemnifying an auditor against any liability incurred by him—
        (a)   in defending proceedings (whether civil or criminal) in which judgment is given in his favour or he is acquitted, or
        (b)   in connection with an application under section 1157 (power of court to grant relief in case of honest and reasonable conduct) in which relief is granted to him by the court.

Liability limitation agreements

534   Liability limitation agreements

(1)   A "liability limitation agreement" is an agreement that purports to limit the amount of a liability owed to a company by its auditor in respect of any negligence, default, breach of duty or breach

of trust, occurring in the course of the audit of accounts, of which the auditor may be guilty in relation to the company.

(2)   Section 532 (general voidness of provisions protecting auditors from liability) does not affect the validity of a liability limitation agreement that—

(a)   complies with section 535 (terms of liability limitation agreement) and of any regulations under that section, and

(b)   is authorised by the members of the company (see section 536).

(3)   Such an agreement—

(a)   is effective to the extent provided by section 537, and

(b)   is not subject—

(i)   in England and Wales or Northern Ireland, to section 2(2) or 3(2)(a) of the Unfair Contract Terms Act 1977;

(ii)   in Scotland, to section 16(1)(b) or 17(1)(a) of that Act.

535   Terms of liability limitation agreement

(1)   A liability limitation agreement—

(a)   must not apply in respect of acts or omissions occurring in the course of the audit of accounts for more than one financial year, and

(b)   must specify the financial year in relation to which it applies.

(2)   The Secretary of State may by regulations—

(a)   require liability limitation agreements to contain specified provisions or provisions of a specified description;

(b)   prohibit liability limitation agreements from containing specified provisions or provisions of a specified description.

"Specified" here means specified in the regulations.

(3)   Without prejudice to the generality of the power conferred by subsection (2), that power may be exercised with a view to preventing adverse effects on competition.

(4)   Subject to the preceding provisions of this section, it is immaterial how a liability limitation agreement is framed.

In particular, the limit on the amount of the auditor's liability need not be a sum of money, or a formula, specified in the agreement.

(5)   Regulations under this section are subject to negative resolution procedure.

536   Authorisation of agreement by members of the company

(1)   A liability limitation agreement is authorised by the members of the company if it has been authorised under this section and that authorisation has not been withdrawn.

(2)   A liability limitation agreement between a private company and its auditor may be authorised—

(a)   by the company passing a resolution, before it enters into the agreement, waiving the need for approval,

(b)   by the company passing a resolution, before it enters into the agreement, approving the agreement's principal terms, or

(c)   by the company passing a resolution, after it enters into the agreement, approving the agreement.

(3)   A liability limitation agreement between a public company and its auditor may be authorised—

(a)   by the company passing a resolution in general meeting, before it enters into the agreement, approving the agreement's principal terms, or

(b)   by the company passing a resolution in general meeting, after it enters into the agreement, approving the agreement.

(4)   The "principal terms" of an agreement are terms specifying, or relevant to the determination of—

(a)   the kind (or kinds) of acts or omissions covered,

(b)   the financial year to which the agreement relates, or

(c)   the limit to which the auditor's liability is subject.

(5)   Authorisation under this section may be withdrawn by the company passing an ordinary resolution to that effect—

    (a)   at any time before the company enters into the agreement, or

    (b)   if the company has already entered into the agreement, before the beginning of the financial year to which the agreement relates. Paragraph (b) has effect notwithstanding anything in the agreement.

537   Effect of liability limitation agreement

(1)   A liability limitation agreement is not effective to limit the auditor's liability to less than such amount as is fair and reasonable in all the circumstances of the case having regard (in particular) to—

    (a)   the auditor's responsibilities under this Part,

    (b)   the nature and purpose of the auditor's contractual obligations to the company, and

    (c)   the professional standards expected of him.

(2)   A liability limitation agreement that purports to limit the auditor's liability to less than the amount mentioned in subsection (1) shall have effect as if it limited his liability to that amount.

(3)   In determining what is fair and reasonable in all the circumstances of the case no account is to be taken of—

    (a)   matters arising after the loss or damage in question has been incurred, or

    (b)   matters (whenever arising) affecting the possibility of recovering compensation from other persons liable in respect of the same loss or damage.

538   Disclosure of agreement by company

(1)   A company which has entered into a liability limitation agreement must make such disclosure in connection with the agreement as the Secretary of State may require by regulations.

(2)   The regulations may provide, in particular, that any disclosure required by the regulations shall be made—

    (a)   in a note to the company's annual accounts (in the case of its individual accounts) or in such manner as is specified in the regulations (in the case of group accounts), or

    (b)   in the directors' report.

(3)   Regulations under this section are subject to negative resolution procedure.

CHAPTER 7

SUPPLEMENTARY PROVISIONS

538A   Meaning of "corporate governance statement" etc

(1)   In this Part "corporate governance statement" means the statement required by rules 7.2.1 to 7.2.11 in the Disclosure Rules and Transparency Rules sourcebook made by the Financial Conduct Authority.

(2)   ...

(3)   A "separate" corporate governance statement means one that is not included in the directors' report.

539   Minor definitions

In this Part—

"e-money issuer" means—

    (a)   an electronic money institution, within the meaning of the Electronic Money Regulations 2011 (SI 2011/99), or

    (b)   a person who has permission under Part 4A of the Financial Services and Markets Act 2000 (c 8) to carry on the activity of issuing electronic money within the meaning of article 9B of the Financial Services and Markets Act 2000 (Regulated Activities) Order 2001 (SI 2001/544);

    ...

"MiFID investment firm" means an investment firm within the meaning of Article 2(1A) of Regulation (EU) No 600/2014 of the European Parliament and of the Council of 15 May 2014 on markets in financial instruments and amending Regulation (EU) No 648/2012, other than—

(a) a company which is exempted from the definition of "investment firm" by Schedule 3 to the Financial Services and Markets Act 2000 (Regulated Activities) Order 2001 (S.I. 2001/544), ...

(b) a company which is an exempt investment firm as defined by regulation 8 (Meaning of "exempt investment firm" in Chapter 1) of the Financial Services and Markets Act 2000 (Markets in Financial Instruments) Regulations 2017 (S.I. 2017/701);

(c) any other company which fulfils all the requirements set out in regulation 6(3) of those Regulations;

"qualified", in relation to an auditor's report (or a statement contained in an auditor's report), means that the report or statement does not state the auditor's unqualified opinion that the accounts have been properly prepared in accordance with this Act or, in the case of an undertaking not required to prepare accounts in accordance with this Act, under any corresponding legislation under which it is required to prepare accounts;

"turnover", in relation to a company, means the amounts derived from the provision of goods and services falling within the company's ordinary activities, after deduction of—

(a) trade discounts,

(b) value added tax, and

(c) any other taxes based on the amounts so derived;

"UCITS management company" has the meaning given by the Glossary forming part of the Handbook made by the Financial Conduct Authority under the Financial Services and Markets Act 2000.

PART 17
A COMPANY'S SHARE CAPITAL

CHAPTER 1
SHARES AND SHARE CAPITAL OF A COMPANY

Shares

540 Shares

(1) In the Companies Acts "share", in relation to a company, means share in the company's share capital.

(2) A company's shares may no longer be converted into stock.

(3) Stock created before the commencement of this Part may be reconverted into shares in accordance with section 620.

(4) In the Companies Acts—

(a) references to shares include stock except where a distinction between share and stock is express or implied, and

(b) references to a number of shares include an amount of stock where the context admits of the reference to shares being read as including stock.

541 Nature of shares

The shares or other interest of a member in a company are personal property (or, in Scotland, moveable property) and are not in the nature of real estate (or heritage).

542 Nominal value of shares

(1) Shares in a limited company having a share capital must each have a fixed nominal value.

(2) An allotment of a share that does not have a fixed nominal value is void.

(3) Shares in a limited company having a share capital may be denominated in any currency, and different classes of shares may be denominated in different currencies.

But see section 765 (initial authorised minimum share capital requirement for public company to be met by reference to share capital denominated in sterling or euros).

(4)   If a company purports to allot shares in contravention of this section, an offence is committed by every officer of the company who is in default.

(5)   A person guilty of an offence under this section is liable—

     (a)   on conviction on indictment, to a fine;

     (b)   on summary conviction, to a fine not exceeding the statutory maximum.

543   Numbering of shares

(1)   Each share in a company having a share capital must be distinguished by its appropriate number, except in the following circumstances.

(2)   If at any time—

     (a)   all the issued shares in a company are fully paid up and rank *pari passu* for all purposes, or

     (b)   all the issued shares of a particular class in a company are fully paid up and rank *pari passu* for all purposes,

none of those shares need thereafter have a distinguishing number so long as it remains fully paid up and ranks *pari passu* for all purposes with all shares of the same class for the time being issued and fully paid up.

544   Transferability of shares

(1)   The shares or other interest of any member in a company are transferable in accordance with the company's articles.

(2)   This is subject to—

     (a)   the Stock Transfer Act 1963 or the Stock Transfer Act (Northern Ireland) 1963 (which enables securities of certain descriptions to be transferred by a simplified process), and

     (b)   regulations under Chapter 2 of Part 21 of this Act (which enable title to securities to be evidenced and transferred without a written instrument).

(3)   See Part 21 of this Act generally as regards share transfers.

545   Companies having a share capital

References in the Companies Acts to a company having a share capital are to a company that has power under its constitution to issue shares.

546   Issued and allotted share capital

(1)   References in the Companies Acts—

     (a)   to "issued share capital" are to shares of a company that have been issued;

     (b)   to "allotted share capital" are to shares of a company that have been allotted.

(2)   References in the Companies Acts to issued or allotted shares, or to issued or allotted share capital, include shares taken on the formation of the company by the subscribers to the company's memorandum.

Share capital

547   Called-up share capital

In the Companies Acts—

"called-up share capital", in relation to a company, means so much of its share capital as equals the aggregate amount of the calls made on its shares (whether or not those calls have been paid), together with—

     (a)   any share capital paid up without being called, and

     (b)   any share capital to be paid on a specified future date under the articles, the terms of allotment of the relevant shares or any other arrangements for payment of those shares; and

"uncalled share capital" is to be construed accordingly.

548   Equity share capital

In the Companies Acts "equity share capital", in relation to a company, means its issued share capital excluding any part of that capital that, neither as respects dividends nor as respects capital, carries any right to participate beyond a specified amount in a distribution.

CHAPTER 2
ALLOTMENT OF SHARES: GENERAL PROVISIONS

Power of directors to allot shares

549   Exercise by directors of power to allot shares etc

(1)   The directors of a company must not exercise any power of the company—
    (a)   to allot shares in the company, or
    (b)   to grant rights to subscribe for, or to convert any security into, shares in the company,
    except in accordance with section 550 (private company with single class of shares) or section 551 (authorisation by company).

(2)   Subsection (1) does not apply—
    (a)   to the allotment of shares in pursuance of an employees' share scheme, or
    (b)   to the grant of a right to subscribe for, or to convert any security into, shares so allotted.

(3)   Subsection (1) does not apply to the allotment of shares pursuant to a right to subscribe for, or to convert any security into, shares in the company.

(3A)   Subsection (1) does not apply to anything done for the purposes of a compromise or arrangement sanctioned in accordance with Part 26A (arrangements and reconstructions: companies in financial difficulty).

(4)   A director who knowingly contravenes, or permits or authorises a contravention of, this section commits an offence.

(5)   A person guilty of an offence under this section is liable—
    (a)   on conviction on indictment, to a fine;
    (b)   on summary conviction, to a fine not exceeding the statutory maximum.

(6)   Nothing in this section affects the validity of an allotment or other transaction.

550   Power of directors to allot shares etc: private company with only one class of shares

Where a private company has only one class of shares, the directors may exercise any power of the company—
    (a)   to allot shares of that class, or
    (b)   to grant rights to subscribe for or to convert any security into such shares,
    except to the extent that they are prohibited from doing so by the company's articles.

551   Power of directors to allot shares etc: authorisation by company

(1)   The directors of a company may exercise a power of the company—
    (a)   to allot shares in the company, or
    (b)   to grant rights to subscribe for or to convert any security into shares in the company,
    if they are authorised to do so by the company's articles or by resolution of the company.

(2)   Authorisation may be given for a particular exercise of the power or for its exercise generally, and may be unconditional or subject to conditions.

(3)   Authorisation must—
    (a)   state the maximum amount of shares that may be allotted under it, and
    (b)   specify the date on which it will expire, which must be not more than five years from—
        (i)   in the case of authorisation contained in the company's articles at the time of its original incorporation, the date of that incorporation;
        (ii)   in any other case, the date on which the resolution is passed by virtue of which the authorisation is given.

(4)   Authorisation may—

        (a)   be renewed or further renewed by resolution of the company for a further period not exceeding five years, and

        (b)   be revoked or varied at any time by resolution of the company.

(5)   A resolution renewing authorisation must—

        (a)   state (or restate) the maximum amount of shares that may be allotted under the authorisation or, as the case may be, the amount remaining to be allotted under it, and

        (b)   specify the date on which the renewed authorisation will expire.

(6)   In relation to rights to subscribe for or to convert any security into shares in the company, references in this section to the maximum amount of shares that may be allotted under the authorisation are to the maximum amount of shares that may be allotted pursuant to the rights.

(7)   The directors may allot shares, or grant rights to subscribe for or to convert any security into shares, after authorisation has expired if—

        (a)   the shares are allotted, or the rights are granted, in pursuance of an offer or agreement made by the company before the authorisation expired, and

        (b)   the authorisation allowed the company to make an offer or agreement which would or might require shares to be allotted, or rights to be granted, after the authorisation had expired.

(8)   A resolution of a company to give, vary, revoke or renew authorisation under this section may be an ordinary resolution, even though it amends the company's articles.

(9)   Chapter 3 of Part 3 (resolutions affecting a company's constitution) applies to a resolution under this section.

Prohibition of commissions, discounts and allowances

552   General prohibition of commissions, discounts and allowances

(1)   Except as permitted by section 553 (permitted commission), a company must not apply any of its shares or capital money, either directly or indirectly, in payment of any commission, discount or allowance to any person in consideration of his—

        (a)   subscribing or agreeing to subscribe (whether absolutely or conditionally) for shares in the company, or

        (b)   procuring or agreeing to procure subscriptions (whether absolute or conditional) for shares in the company.

(2)   It is immaterial how the shares or money are so applied, whether by being added to the purchase money of property acquired by the company or to the contract price of work to be executed for the company, or being paid out of the nominal purchase money or contract price, or otherwise.

(3)   Nothing in this section affects the payment of such brokerage as has previously been lawful.

553   Permitted commission

(1)   A company may, if the following conditions are satisfied, pay a commission to a person in consideration of his subscribing or agreeing to subscribe (whether absolutely or conditionally) for shares in the company, or procuring or agreeing to procure subscriptions (whether absolute or conditional) for shares in the company.

(2)   The conditions are that—

        (a)   the payment of the commission is authorised by the company's articles; and

        (b)   the commission paid or agreed to be paid does not exceed—

            (i)   10% of the price at which the shares are issued, or

            (ii)   the amount or rate authorised by the articles,

        whichever is the less.

(3)   A vendor to, or promoter of, or other person who receives payment in money or shares from, a company may apply any part of the money or shares so received in payment of any commission the payment of which directly by the company would be permitted by this section.

Registration of allotment

554 Registration of allotment

(1) A company must register an allotment of shares as soon as practicable and in any event within two months after the date of the allotment.

(2) This does not apply if the company has issued a share warrant in respect of the shares (see section 779).

(2A) If an election is in force under Chapter 2A of Part 8, the obligation under subsection (1) to register the allotment of shares is replaced by an obligation to deliver particulars of the allotment of shares to the registrar in accordance with that Chapter.

(3) If a company fails to comply with this section, an offence is committed by—
    (a) the company, and
    (b) every officer of the company who is in default.

(4) A person guilty of an offence under this section is liable on summary conviction to a fine not exceeding level 3 on the standard scale and, for continued contravention, a daily default fine not exceeding one-tenth of level 3 on the standard scale.

(5) For the company's duties as to the issue of share certificates etc, see Part 21 (certification and transfer of securities).

Return of allotment

555 Return of allotment by limited company

(1) This section applies to a company limited by shares and to a company limited by guarantee and having a share capital.

(2) The company must, within one month of making an allotment of shares, deliver to the registrar for registration a return of the allotment.

(3) The return must—
    (a) contain the prescribed information, and
    (b) be accompanied by a statement of capital.

(4) The statement of capital must state with respect to the company's share capital at the date to which the return is made up—
    (a) the total number of shares of the company,
    (b) the aggregate nominal value of those shares,
    (ba) the aggregate amount (if any) unpaid on those shares (whether on account of their nominal value or by way of premium), and
    (c) for each class of shares—
        (i) prescribed particulars of the rights attached to the shares,
        (ii) the total number of shares of that class, and
        (iii) the aggregate nominal value of shares of that class, ...
    (d) ...

556 Return of allotment by unlimited company allotting new class of shares

(1) This section applies to an unlimited company that allots shares of a class with rights that are not in all respects uniform with shares previously allotted.

(2) The company must, within one month of making such an allotment, deliver to the registrar for registration a return of the allotment.

(3) The return must contain the prescribed particulars of the rights attached to the shares.

(4) For the purposes of this section shares are not to be treated as different from shares previously allotted by reason only that the former do not carry the same rights to dividends as the latter during the twelve months immediately following the former's allotment.

557 Offence of failure to make return

(1) If a company makes default in complying with—

section 555 (return of allotment of shares by limited company), or section 556 (return of allotment of new class of shares by unlimited company),

an offence is committed by every officer of the company who is in default.

(2)   A person guilty of an offence under this section is liable—

    (a)   on conviction on indictment, to a fine;

    (b)   on summary conviction, to a fine not exceeding the statutory maximum and, for continued contravention, a daily default fine not exceeding one-tenth of the greater of £5,000 or the amount corresponding to level 4 on the standard scale for summary offences.

(3)   In the case of default in delivering to the registrar within one month after the allotment the return required by section 555 or 556—

    (a)   any person liable for the default may apply to the court for relief, and

    (b)   the court, if satisfied—

        (i)   that the omission to deliver the document was accidental or due to inadvertence, or

        (ii)   that it is just and equitable to grant relief,

    may make an order extending the time for delivery of the document for such period as the court thinks proper.

Supplementary provisions

558   When shares are allotted

For the purposes of the Companies Acts shares in a company are taken to be allotted when a person acquires the unconditional right to be included in the company's register of members (or, as the case may be, to have the person's name and other particulars delivered to the registrar under Chapter 2A of Part 8 and registered by the registrar) in respect of the shares.

559   Provisions about allotment not applicable to shares taken on formation

The provisions of this Chapter have no application in relation to the taking of shares by the subscribers to the memorandum on the formation of the company.

CHAPTER 3

ALLOTMENT OF EQUITY SECURITIES: EXISTING SHAREHOLDERS' RIGHT OF PRE-EMPTION

Introductory

560   Meaning of "equity securities" and related expressions

(1)   In this Chapter—

"equity securities" means—

    (a)   ordinary shares in the company, or

    (b)   rights to subscribe for, or to convert securities into, ordinary shares in the company;

"ordinary shares" means shares other than shares that as respects dividends and capital carry a right to participate only up to a specified amount in a distribution.

(2)   References in this Chapter to the allotment of equity securities—

    (a)   include the grant of a right to subscribe for, or to convert any securities into, ordinary shares in the company, and

    (b)   do not include the allotment of shares pursuant to such a right.

(3)   References in this Chapter to the allotment of equity securities include the sale of ordinary shares in the company that immediately before the sale were held by the company as treasury shares.

Existing shareholders' right of pre-emption

561   Existing shareholders' right of pre-emption

(1)   A company must not allot equity securities to a person on any terms unless—

    (a)   it has made an offer to each person who holds ordinary shares in the company to allot to him on the same or more favourable terms a proportion of those securities that is as nearly as practicable equal to the proportion in nominal value held by him of the ordinary share capital of the company, and

    (b)   the period during which any such offer may be accepted has expired or the company has received notice of the acceptance or refusal of every offer so made.

(2)   Securities that a company has offered to allot to a holder of ordinary shares may be allotted to him, or anyone in whose favour he has renounced his right to their allotment, without contravening subsection (1)(b).

(3)   ...

(4)   Shares held by the company as treasury shares are disregarded for the purposes of this section, so that—

    (a)   the company is not treated as a person who holds ordinary shares, and

    (b)   the shares are not treated as forming part of the ordinary share capital of the company.

(5)   This section is subject to—

    (a)   sections 564 to 566A (exceptions to pre-emption right),

    (b)   sections 567 and 568 (exclusion of rights of pre-emption),

    (c)   sections 569 to 573 (disapplication of pre-emption rights), and

    (d)   section 576 (saving for certain older pre-emption procedures).

562   Communication of pre-emption offers to shareholders

(1)   This section has effect as to the manner in which offers required by section 561 are to be made to holders of a company's shares.

(2)   The offer may be made in hard copy or electronic form.

(3)   If the holder—

    (a)   has no registered address in the United Kingdom or an EEA State and has not given to the company an address in the United Kingdom or an EEA State for the service of notices on him, or

    (b)   is the holder of a share warrant,

the offer may be made by causing it, or a notice specifying where a copy of it can be obtained or inspected, to be published in the Gazette.

(4)   The offer must state a period during which it may be accepted and the offer shall not be withdrawn before the end of that period.

(5)   The period must be a period of at least 14 days beginning—

    (a)   in the case of an offer made in hard copy form, with the date on which the offer is sent or supplied;

    (b)   in the case of an offer made in electronic form, with the date on which the offer is sent;

    (c)   in the case of an offer made by publication in the Gazette, with the date of publication.

(6)   The Secretary of State may by regulations made by statutory instrument—

    (a)   reduce the period specified in subsection (5) (but not to less than 14 days), or

    (b)   increase that period.

(7)   A statutory instrument containing regulations made under subsection (6) is subject to affirmative resolution procedure.

563   Liability of company and officers in case of contravention

(1)   This section applies where there is a contravention of—

section 561 (existing shareholders' right of pre-emption), or

section 562 (communication of pre-emption offers to shareholders).

(2)   The company and every officer of it who knowingly authorised or permitted the contravention are jointly and severally liable to compensate any person to whom an offer should have been made in accordance with those provisions for any loss, damage, costs or expenses which the person has sustained or incurred by reason of the contravention.

(3)   No proceedings to recover any such loss, damage, costs or expenses shall be commenced after the expiration of two years—

    (a)   from the delivery to the registrar of companies of the return of allotment, or

(b)   where equity securities other than shares are granted, from the date of the grant.

Exceptions to right of pre-emption

564   Exception to pre-emption right: bonus shares

Section 561(1) (existing shareholders' right of pre-emption) does not apply in relation to the allotment of bonus shares.

565   Exception to pre-emption right: issue for non-cash consideration

Section 561(1) (existing shareholders' right of pre-emption) does not apply to a particular allotment of equity securities if these are, or are to be, wholly or partly paid up otherwise than in cash.

566   Exceptions to pre-emption right: employees' share schemes

Section 561 (existing shareholders' right of pre-emption) does not apply to the allotment of equity securities that would, apart from any renunciation or assignment of the right to their allotment, be held under or allotted or transferred pursuant to an employees' share scheme.

566A   Exception to pre-emption right: companies in financial difficulty

Section 561(1) (existing shareholders' right of pre-emption) does not apply to an allotment of equity securities that is carried out as part of a compromise or arrangement sanctioned in accordance with Part 26A (arrangements and reconstructions: companies in financial difficulty).

Exclusion of right of pre-emption

567   Exclusion of requirements by private companies

(1)   All or any of the requirements of—
       (a)   section 561 (existing shareholders' right of pre-emption), or
       (b)   section 562 (communication of pre-emption offers to shareholders)
       may be excluded by provision contained in the articles of a private company.

(2)   They may be excluded—
       (a)   generally in relation to the allotment by the company of equity securities, or
       (b)   in relation to allotments of a particular description.

(3)   Any requirement or authorisation contained in the articles of a private company that is inconsistent with either of those sections is treated for the purposes of this section as a provision excluding that section.

(4)   A provision to which section 568 applies (exclusion of pre-emption right: corresponding right conferred by articles) is not to be treated as inconsistent with section 561.

568   Exclusion of pre-emption right: articles conferring corresponding right

(1)   The provisions of this section apply where, in a case in which section 561 (existing shareholders' right of pre-emption) would otherwise apply—
       (a)   a company's articles contain provision ("pre-emption provision") prohibiting the company from allotting ordinary shares of a particular class unless it has complied with the condition that it makes such an offer as is described in section 561(1) to each person who holds ordinary shares of that class, and
       (b)   in accordance with that provision—
              (i)   the company makes an offer to allot shares to such a holder, and
              (ii)   he or anyone in whose favour he has renounced his right to their allotment accepts the offer.

(2)   In that case, section 561 does not apply to the allotment of those shares and the company may allot them accordingly.

(3)   The provisions of section 562 (communication of pre-emption offers to shareholders) apply in relation to offers made in pursuance of the pre-emption provision of the company's articles. This is subject to section 567 (exclusion of requirements by private companies).

(4)   If there is a contravention of the pre-emption provision of the company's articles, the company, and every officer of it who knowingly authorised or permitted the contravention, are jointly and severally liable to compensate any person to whom an offer should have been made under the provision for any loss, damage, costs or expenses which the person has sustained or incurred by reason of the contravention.

(5)   No proceedings to recover any such loss, damage, costs or expenses may be commenced after the expiration of two years—
   (a)   from the delivery to the registrar of companies of the return of allotment, or
   (b)   where equity securities other than shares are granted, from the date of the grant.

Disapplication of pre-emption rights

569   Disapplication of pre-emption rights: private company with only one class of shares

(1)   The directors of a private company that has only one class of shares may be given power by the articles, or by a special resolution of the company, to allot equity securities of that class as if section 561 (existing shareholders' right of pre-emption)—
   (a)   did not apply to the allotment, or
   (b)   applied to the allotment with such modifications as the directors may determine.

(2)   Where the directors make an allotment under this section, the provisions of this Chapter have effect accordingly.

570   Disapplication of pre-emption rights: directors acting under general authorisation

(1)   Where the directors of a company are generally authorised for the purposes of section 551 (power of directors to allot shares etc: authorisation by company), they may be given power by the articles, or by a special resolution of the company, to allot equity securities pursuant to that authorisation as if section 561 (existing shareholders' right of pre-emption)—
   (a)   did not apply to the allotment, or
   (b)   applied to the allotment with such modifications as the directors may determine.

(2)   Where the directors make an allotment under this section, the provisions of this Chapter have effect accordingly.

(3)   The power conferred by this section ceases to have effect when the authorisation to which it relates—
   (a)   is revoked, or
   (b)   would (if not renewed) expire.
   But if the authorisation is renewed the power may also be renewed, for a period not longer than that for which the authorisation is renewed, by a special resolution of the company.

(4)   Notwithstanding that the power conferred by this section has expired, the directors may allot equity securities in pursuance of an offer or agreement previously made by the company if the power enabled the company to make an offer or agreement that would or might require equity securities to be allotted after it expired.

571   Disapplication of pre-emption rights by special resolution

(1)   Where the directors of a company are authorised for the purposes of section 551 (power of directors to allot shares etc: authorisation by company), whether generally or otherwise, the company may by special resolution resolve that section 561 (existing shareholders' right of pre-emption)—
   (a)   does not apply to a specified allotment of equity securities to be made pursuant to that authorisation, or
   (b)   applies to such an allotment with such modifications as may be specified in the resolution.

(2)   Where such a resolution is passed the provisions of this Chapter have effect accordingly.

(3)   A special resolution under this section ceases to have effect when the authorisation to which it relates—
   (a)   is revoked, or
   (b)   would (if not renewed) expire.

But if the authorisation is renewed the resolution may also be renewed, for a period not longer than that for which the authorisation is renewed, by a special resolution of the company.

(4)   Notwithstanding that any such resolution has expired, the directors may allot equity securities in pursuance of an offer or agreement previously made by the company if the resolution enabled the company to make an offer or agreement that would or might require equity securities to be allotted after it expired.

(5)   A special resolution under this section, or a special resolution to renew such a resolution, must not be proposed unless—

    (a)   it is recommended by the directors, and

    (b)   the directors have complied with the following provisions.

(6)   Before such a resolution is proposed, the directors must make a written statement setting out—

    (a)   their reasons for making the recommendation,

    (b)   the amount to be paid to the company in respect of the equity securities to be allotted, and

    (c)   the directors' justification of that amount.

(7)   The directors' statement must—

    (a)   if the resolution is proposed as a written resolution, be sent or submitted to every eligible member at or before the time at which the proposed resolution is sent or submitted to him;

    (b)   if the resolution is proposed at a general meeting, be circulated to the members entitled to notice of the meeting with that notice.

572 Liability for false statement in directors' statement

(1)   This section applies in relation to a directors' statement under section 571 (special resolution disapplying pre-emption rights) that is sent, submitted or circulated under subsection (7) of that section.

(2)   A person who knowingly or recklessly authorises or permits the inclusion of any matter that is misleading, false or deceptive in a material particular in such a statement commits an offence.

(3)   A person guilty of an offence under this section is liable—

    (a)   on conviction on indictment, to imprisonment for a term not exceeding two years or a fine (or both);

    (b)   on summary conviction—

        (i)   in England and Wales, to imprisonment for a term not exceeding twelve months or to a fine not exceeding the statutory maximum (or both);

        (ii)   in Scotland or Northern Ireland, to imprisonment for a term not exceeding six months, or to a fine not exceeding the statutory maximum (or both).

573 Disapplication of pre-emption rights: sale of treasury shares

(1)   This section applies in relation to a sale of shares that is an allotment of equity securities by virtue of section 560(3) (sale of shares held by company as treasury shares).

(2)   The directors of a company may be given power by the articles, or by a special resolution of the company, to allot equity securities as if section 561 (existing shareholders' right of pre-emption)—

    (a)   did not apply to the allotment, or

    (b)   applied to the allotment with such modifications as the directors may determine.

(3)   The provisions of section 570(2) and (4) apply in that case as they apply to a case within subsection (1) of that section.

(4)   The company may by special resolution resolve that section 561—

    (a)   shall not apply to a specified allotment of securities, or

    (b)   shall apply to the allotment with such modifications as may be specified in the resolution.

(5)   The provisions of section 571(2) and (4) to (7) apply in that case as they apply to a case within subsection (1) of that section.

Supplementary

574 References to holder of shares in relation to offer

(1)   In this Chapter, in relation to an offer to allot securities required by—

(a)   section 561 (existing shareholders' right of pre-emption), or

(b)   any provision to which section 568 applies (articles conferring corresponding right),

a reference (however expressed) to the holder of shares of any description is to whoever was the holder of shares of that description at the close of business on a date to be specified in the offer.

(2)   The specified date must fall within the period of 28 days immediately before the date of the offer.

575   Saving for other restrictions on offer or allotment

(1)   The provisions of this Chapter are without prejudice to any other enactment by virtue of which a company is prohibited (whether generally or in specified circumstances) from offering or allotting equity securities to any person.

(2)   Where a company cannot by virtue of such an enactment offer or allot equity securities to a holder of ordinary shares of the company, those shares are disregarded for the purposes of section 561 (existing shareholders' right of pre-emption), so that—

(a)   the person is not treated as a person who holds ordinary shares, and

(b)   the shares are not treated as forming part of the ordinary share capital of the company.

576   Saving for certain older pre-emption requirements

(1)   In the case of a public company the provisions of this Chapter do not apply to an allotment of equity securities that are subject to a pre-emption requirement in relation to which section 96(1) of the Companies Act 1985 or Article 106(1) of the Companies (Northern Ireland) Order 1986 applied immediately before the commencement of this Chapter.

(2)   In the case of a private company a pre-emption requirement to which section 96(3) of the Companies Act 1985 or Article 106(3) of the Companies (Northern Ireland) Order 1986 applied immediately before the commencement of this Chapter shall have effect, so long as the company remains a private company, as if it were contained in the company's articles.

(3)   A pre-emption requirement to which section 96(4) of the Companies Act 1985 or Article 106(4) of the Companies (Northern Ireland) Order 1986 applied immediately before the commencement of this section shall be treated for the purposes of this Chapter as if it were contained in the company's articles.

577   Provisions about pre-emption not applicable to shares taken on formation

The provisions of this Chapter have no application in relation to the taking of shares by the subscribers to the memorandum on the formation of the company.

CHAPTER 4
PUBLIC COMPANIES: ALLOTMENT WHERE ISSUE NOT FULLY SUBSCRIBED

578   Public companies: allotment where issue not fully subscribed

(1)   No allotment shall be made of shares of a public company offered for subscription unless—

(a)   the issue is subscribed for in full, or

(b)   the offer is made on terms that the shares subscribed for may be allotted—

(i)   in any event, or

(ii)   if specified conditions are met (and those conditions are met).

(2)   If shares are prohibited from being allotted by subsection (1) and 40 days have elapsed after the first making of the offer, all money received from applicants for shares must be repaid to them forthwith, without interest.

(3)   If any of the money is not repaid within 48 days after the first making of the offer, the directors of the company are jointly and severally liable to repay it, with interest at the rate for the time being specified under section 17 of the Judgments Act 1838 from the expiration of the 48th day.

A director is not so liable if he proves that the default in the repayment of the money was not due to any misconduct or negligence on his part.

(4)   This section applies in the case of shares offered as wholly or partly payable otherwise than in cash as it applies in the case of shares offered for subscription.

(5)   In that case—

(a)   the references in subsection (1) to subscription shall be construed accordingly;

(b)   references in subsections (2) and (3) to the repayment of money received from applicants for shares include—

    (i)   the return of any other consideration so received (including, if the case so requires, the release of the applicant from any undertaking), or

    (ii)   if it is not reasonably practicable to return the consideration, the payment of money equal to its value at the time it was so received;

(c)   references to interest apply accordingly.

(6)   Any condition requiring or binding an applicant for shares to waive compliance with any requirement of this section is void.

579   Public companies: effect of irregular allotment where issue not fully subscribed

(1)   An allotment made by a public company to an applicant in contravention of section 578 (public companies: allotment where issue not fully subscribed) is voidable at the instance of the applicant within one month after the date of the allotment, and not later.

(2)   It is so voidable even if the company is in the course of being wound up.

(3)   A director of a public company who knowingly contravenes, or permits or authorises the contravention of, any provision of section 578 with respect to allotment is liable to compensate the company and the allottee respectively for any loss, damages, costs or expenses that the company or allottee may have sustained or incurred by the contravention.

(4)   Proceedings to recover any such loss, damages, costs or expenses may not be brought more than two years after the date of the allotment.

CHAPTER 5
PAYMENT FOR SHARES

General rules

580   Shares not to be allotted at a discount

(1)   A company's shares must not be allotted at a discount.

(2)   If shares are allotted in contravention of this section, the allottee is liable to pay the company an amount equal to the amount of the discount, with interest at the appropriate rate.

581   Provision for different amounts to be paid on shares

A company, if so authorised by its articles, may—

(a)   make arrangements on the issue of shares for a difference between the shareholders in the amounts and times of payment of calls on their shares;

(b)   accept from any member the whole or part of the amount remaining unpaid on any shares held by him, although no part of that amount has been called up;

(c)   pay a dividend in proportion to the amount paid up on each share where a larger amount is paid up on some shares than on others.

582   General rule as to means of payment

(1)   Shares allotted by a company, and any premium on them, may be paid up in money or money's worth (including goodwill and know-how).

(2)   This section does not prevent a company—

(a)   from allotting bonus shares to its members, or

(b)   from paying up, with sums available for the purpose, any amounts for the time being unpaid on any of its shares (whether on account of the nominal value of the shares or by way of premium).

(3)   This section has effect subject to the following provisions of this Chapter (additional rules for public companies).

583   Meaning of payment in cash

(1)   The following provisions have effect for the purposes of the Companies Acts.

(2)   A share in a company is deemed paid up (as to its nominal value or any premium on it) in cash, or allotted for cash, if the consideration received for the allotment or payment up is a cash consideration.

(3)   A "cash consideration" means—

    (a)   cash received by the company,

    (b)   a cheque received by the company in good faith that the directors have no reason for suspecting will not be paid,

    (c)   a release of a liability of the company for a liquidated sum,

    (d)   an undertaking to pay cash to the company at a future date, or

    (e)   payment by any other means giving rise to a present or future entitlement (of the company or a person acting on the company's behalf) to a payment, or credit equivalent to payment, in cash.

(4)   The Secretary of State may by order provide that particular means of payment specified in the order are to be regarded as falling within subsection (3)(e).

(5)   In relation to the allotment or payment up of shares in a company—

    (a)   the payment of cash to a person other than the company, or

    (b)   an undertaking to pay cash to a person other than the company, counts as consideration other than cash.

    This does not apply for the purposes of Chapter 3 (allotment of equity securities: existing shareholders' right of pre-emption).

(6)   For the purpose of determining whether a share is or is to be allotted for cash, or paid up in cash, "cash" includes foreign currency.

(7)   An order under this section is subject to negative resolution procedure.

Additional rules for public companies

584   Public companies: shares taken by subscribers of memorandum

Shares taken by a subscriber to the memorandum of a public company in pursuance of an undertaking of his in the memorandum, and any premium on the shares, must be paid up in cash.

585   Public companies: must not accept undertaking to do work or perform services

(1)   A public company must not accept at any time, in payment up of its shares or any premium on them, an undertaking given by any person that he or another should do work or perform services for the company or any other person.

(2)   If a public company accepts such an undertaking in payment up of its shares or any premium on them, the holder of the shares when they or the premium are treated as paid up (in whole or in part) by the undertaking is liable—

    (a)   to pay the company in respect of those shares an amount equal to their nominal value, together with the whole of any premium or, if the case so requires, such proportion of that amount as is treated as paid up by the undertaking; and

    (b)   to pay interest at the appropriate rate on the amount payable under paragraph (a).

(3)   The reference in subsection (2) to the holder of shares includes a person who has an unconditional right—

    (a)   to be included in the company's register of members in respect of those shares, or

    (b)   to have an instrument of transfer of them executed in his favour.

586   Public companies: shares must be at least one-quarter paid up

(1)   A public company must not allot a share except as paid up at least as to one-quarter of its nominal value and the whole of any premium on it.

(2)   This does not apply to shares allotted in pursuance of an employees' share scheme.

(3)   If a company allots a share in contravention of this section—

    (a)   the share is to be treated as if one-quarter of its nominal value, together with the whole of any premium on it, had been received, and

(b)   the allottee is liable to pay the company the minimum amount which should have been received in respect of the share under subsection (1) (less the value of any consideration actually applied in payment up, to any extent, of the share and any premium on it), with interest at the appropriate rate.

(4)   Subsection (3) does not apply to the allotment of bonus shares, unless the allottee knew or ought to have known the shares were allotted in contravention of this section.

587   Public companies: payment by long-term undertaking

(1)   A public company must not allot shares as fully or partly paid up (as to their nominal value or any premium on them) otherwise than in cash if the consideration for the allotment is or includes an undertaking which is to be, or may be, performed more than five years after the date of the allotment.

(2)   If a company allots shares in contravention of subsection (1), the allottee is liable to pay the company an amount equal to the aggregate of their nominal value and the whole of any premium (or, if the case so requires, so much of that aggregate as is treated as paid up by the undertaking), with interest at the appropriate rate.

(3)   Where a contract for the allotment of shares does not contravene subsection (1), any variation of the contract that has the effect that the contract would have contravened the subsection, if the terms of the contract as varied had been its original terms, is void.
       This applies also to the variation by a public company of the terms of a contract entered into before the company was re-registered as a public company.

(4)   Where—
       (a)   a public company allots shares for a consideration which consists of or includes (in accordance with subsection (1)) an undertaking that is to be performed within five years of the allotment, and
       (b)   the undertaking is not performed within the period allowed by the contract for the allotment of the shares,
       the allottee is liable to pay the company, at the end of the period so allowed, an amount equal to the aggregate of the nominal value of the shares and the whole of any premium (or, if the case so requires, so much of that aggregate as is treated as paid up by the undertaking), with interest at the appropriate rate.

(5)   References in this section to a contract for the allotment of shares include an ancillary contract relating to payment in respect of them.

Supplementary provisions

588   Liability of subsequent holders of shares

(1)   If a person becomes a holder of shares in respect of which—
       (a)   there has been a contravention of any provision of this Chapter, and
       (b)   by virtue of that contravention another is liable to pay any amount under the provision contravened,
       that person is also liable to pay that amount (jointly and severally with any other person so liable), subject as follows.

(2)   A person otherwise liable under subsection (1) is exempted from that liability if either—
       (a)   he is a purchaser for value and, at the time of the purchase, he did not have actual notice of the contravention concerned, or
       (b)   he derived title to the shares (directly or indirectly) from a person who became a holder of them after the contravention and was not liable under subsection (1).

(3)   References in this section to a holder, in relation to shares in a company, include any person who has an unconditional right—
       (a)   to be included in the company's register of members (or, as the case may be, to have his name and other particulars delivered to the registrar under Chapter 2A of Part 8 and registered by the registrar) in respect of those shares, or
       (b)   to have an instrument of transfer of the shares executed in his favour.

(4)   This section applies in relation to a failure to carry out a term of a contract as mentioned in section 587(4) (public companies: payment by long-term undertaking) as it applies in relation to a contravention of a provision of this Chapter.

589   Power of court to grant relief

(1)   This section applies in relation to liability under—

section 585(2) (liability of allottee in case of breach by public company of prohibition on accepting undertaking to do work or perform services), section 587(2) or (4) (liability of allottee in case of breach by public company of prohibition on payment by long-term undertaking), or section 588 (liability of subsequent holders of shares),

as it applies in relation to a contravention of those sections.

(2)   A person who—

(a)   is subject to any such liability to a company in relation to payment in respect of shares in the company, or

(b)   is subject to any such liability to a company by virtue of an undertaking given to it in, or in connection with, payment for shares in the company,

may apply to the court to be exempted in whole or in part from the liability.

(3)   In the case of a liability within subsection (2)(a), the court may exempt the applicant from the liability only if and to the extent that it appears to the court just and equitable to do so having regard to—

(a)   whether the applicant has paid, or is liable to pay, any amount in respect of—

(i)   any other liability arising in relation to those shares under any provision of this Chapter or Chapter 6, or

(ii)   any liability arising by virtue of any undertaking given in or in connection with payment for those shares;

(b)   whether any person other than the applicant has paid or is likely to pay, whether in pursuance of any order of the court or otherwise, any such amount;

(c)   whether the applicant or any other person—

(i)   has performed in whole or in part, or is likely so to perform any such undertaking, or

(ii)   has done or is likely to do any other thing in payment or part payment for the shares.

(4)   In the case of a liability within subsection (2)(b), the court may exempt the applicant from the liability only if and to the extent that it appears to the court just and equitable to do so having regard to—

(a)   whether the applicant has paid or is liable to pay any amount in respect of liability arising in relation to the shares under any provision of this Chapter or Chapter 6;

(b)   whether any person other than the applicant has paid or is likely to pay, whether in pursuance of any order of the court or otherwise, any such amount.

(5)   In determining whether it should exempt the applicant in whole or in part from any liability, the court must have regard to the following overriding principles—

(a)   a company that has allotted shares should receive money or money's worth at least equal in value to the aggregate of the nominal value of those shares and the whole of any premium or, if the case so requires, so much of that aggregate as is treated as paid up;

(b)   subject to that, where a company would, if the court did not grant the exemption, have more than one remedy against a particular person, it should be for the company to decide which remedy it should remain entitled to pursue.

(6)   If a person brings proceedings against another ("the contributor") for a contribution in respect of liability to a company arising under any provision of this Chapter or Chapter 6 and it appears to the court that the contributor is liable to make such a contribution, the court may, if and to the extent that it appears to it just and equitable to do so having regard to the respective culpability (in respect of the liability to the company) of the contributor and the person bringing the proceedings—

(a)   exempt the contributor in whole or in part from his liability to make such a contribution, or

(b)   order the contributor to make a larger contribution than, but for this subsection, he would be liable to make.

590   Penalty for contravention of this Chapter

(1)   If a company contravenes any of the provisions of this Chapter, an offence is committed by—

(a)   the company, and

(b)   every officer of the company who is in default.

(2)   A person guilty of an offence under this section is liable—

(a)   on conviction on indictment, to a fine;

(b)   on summary conviction, to a fine not exceeding the statutory maximum.

591   Enforceability of undertakings to do work etc

(1)   An undertaking given by any person, in or in connection with payment for shares in a company, to do work or perform services or to do any other thing, if it is enforceable by the company apart from this Chapter, is so enforceable notwithstanding that there has been a contravention in relation to it of a provision of this Chapter or Chapter 6.

(2)   This is without prejudice to section 589 (power of court to grant relief etc in respect of liabilities).

592   The appropriate rate of interest

(1)   For the purposes of this Chapter the "appropriate rate" of interest is 5% per annum or such other rate as may be specified by order made by the Secretary of State.

(2)   An order under this section is subject to negative resolution procedure.

CHAPTER 6
PUBLIC COMPANIES: INDEPENDENT VALUATION OF NON-CASH CONSIDERATION

Non-cash consideration for shares

593   Public company: valuation of non-cash consideration for shares

(1)   A public company must not allot shares as fully or partly paid up (as to their nominal value or any premium on them) otherwise than in cash unless—

(a)   the consideration for the allotment has been independently valued in accordance with the provisions of this Chapter,

(b)   the valuer's report has been made to the company during the six months immediately preceding the allotment of the shares, and

(c)   a copy of the report has been sent to the proposed allottee.

(2)   For this purpose the application of an amount standing to the credit of—

(a)   any of a company's reserve accounts, or

(b)   its profit and loss account,

in paying up (to any extent) shares allotted to members of the company, or premiums on shares so allotted, does not count as consideration for the allotment.

Accordingly, subsection (1) does not apply in that case.

(3)   If a company allots shares in contravention of subsection (1) and either—

(a)   the allottee has not received the valuer's report required to be sent to him, or

(b)   there has been some other contravention of the requirements of this section or section 596 that the allottee knew or ought to have known amounted to a contravention,

the allottee is liable to pay the company an amount equal to the aggregate of the nominal value of the shares and the whole of any premium (or, if the case so requires, so much of that aggregate as is treated as paid up by the consideration), with interest at the appropriate rate.

(4)   This section has effect subject to—

section 594 (exception to valuation requirement: arrangement with another company), and

section 595 (exception to valuation requirement: merger or division).

594 Exception to valuation requirement: arrangement with another company

(1) Section 593 (valuation of non-cash consideration) does not apply to the allotment of shares by a company ("company A") in connection with an arrangement to which this section applies.

(2) This section applies to an arrangement for the allotment of shares in company A on terms that the whole or part of the consideration for the shares allotted is to be provided by—

(a) the transfer to that company, or

(b) the cancellation,

of all or some of the shares, or of all or some of the shares of a particular class, in another company ("company B").

(3) It is immaterial whether the arrangement provides for the issue to company A of shares, or shares of any particular class, in company B.

(4) This section applies to an arrangement only if under the arrangement it is open to all the holders of the shares in company B (or, where the arrangement applies only to shares of a particular class, to all the holders of shares of that class) to take part in the arrangement.

(5) In determining whether that is the case, the following shall be disregarded—

(a) shares held by or by a nominee of company A;

(b) shares held by or by a nominee of a company which is—

(i) the holding company, or a subsidiary, of company A, or

(ii) a subsidiary of such a holding company;

(c) shares held as treasury shares by company B.

(6) In this section—

(a) "arrangement" means any agreement, scheme or arrangement (including an arrangement sanctioned in accordance with—

(i) Part 26 or 26A (arrangements and reconstructions), or

(ii) section 110 of the Insolvency Act 1986 or Article 96 of the Insolvency (Northern Ireland) Order 1989 (liquidator in winding up accepting shares as consideration for sale of company property)), and

(b) "company", except in reference to company A, includes any body corporate.

595 Exception to valuation requirement: merger or division

(1) Section 593 (valuation of non-cash consideration) does not apply to the allotment of shares by a company as part of a scheme to which Part 27 (mergers and divisions of public companies) applies if—

(a) in the case of a scheme involving a merger, an expert's report is drawn up as required by section 909, or

(b) in the case of a scheme involving a division, an expert's report is drawn up as required by section 924.

(2), (3) …

596 Non-cash consideration for shares: requirements as to valuation and report

(1) The provisions of sections 1150 to 1153 (general provisions as to independent valuation and report) apply to the valuation and report required by section 593 (public company: valuation of non-cash consideration for shares).

(2) The valuer's report must state—

(a) the nominal value of the shares to be wholly or partly paid for by the consideration in question;

(b) the amount of any premium payable on the shares;

(c) the description of the consideration and, as respects so much of the consideration as he himself has valued, a description of that part of the consideration, the method used to value it and the date of the valuation;

(d) the extent to which the nominal value of the shares and any premium are to be treated as paid up—

(i) by the consideration;

        (ii)   in cash.

(3)   The valuer's report must contain or be accompanied by a note by him—

      (a)   in the case of a valuation made by a person other than himself, that it appeared to himself reasonable to arrange for it to be so made or to accept a valuation so made,

      (b)   whoever made the valuation, that the method of valuation was reasonable in all the circumstances,

      (c)   that it appears to the valuer that there has been no material change in the value of the consideration in question since the valuation, and

      (d)   that, on the basis of the valuation, the value of the consideration, together with any cash by which the nominal value of the shares or any premium payable on them is to be paid up, is not less than so much of the aggregate of the nominal value and the whole of any such premium as is treated as paid up by the consideration and any such cash.

(4)   Where the consideration to be valued is accepted partly in payment up of the nominal value of the shares and any premium and partly for some other consideration given by the company, section 593 and the preceding provisions of this section apply as if references to the consideration accepted by the company included the proportion of that consideration that is properly attributable to the payment up of that value and any premium.

(5)   In such a case—

      (a)   the valuer must carry out, or arrange for, such other valuations as will enable him to determine that proportion, and

      (b)   his report must state what valuations have been made under this subsection and also the reason for, and method and date of, any such valuation and any other matters which may be relevant to that determination.

597   Copy of report to be delivered to registrar

(1)   A company to which a report is made under section 593 as to the value of any consideration for which, or partly for which, it proposes to allot shares must deliver a copy of the report to the registrar for registration.

(2)   The copy must be delivered at the same time that the company files the return of the allotment of those shares under section 555 (return of allotment by limited company).

(3)   If default is made in complying with subsection (1) or (2), an offence is committed by every officer of the company who is in default.

(4)   A person guilty of an offence under this section is liable—

      (a)   on conviction on indictment, to a fine;

      (b)   on summary conviction, to a fine not exceeding the statutory maximum and, for continued contravention, a daily default fine not exceeding one-tenth of the greater of £5,000 or the amount corresponding to level 4 on the standard scale for summary offences.

(5)   In the case of default in delivering to the registrar any document as required by this section, any person liable for the default may apply to the court for relief.

(6)   The court, if satisfied—

      (a)   that the omission to deliver the document was accidental or due to inadvertence, or

      (b)   that it is just and equitable to grant relief,

may make an order extending the time for delivery of the document for such period as the court thinks proper.

Transfer of non-cash asset in initial period

598   Public company: agreement for transfer of non-cash asset in initial period

(1)   A public company formed as such must not enter into an agreement—

      (a)   with a person who is a subscriber to the company's memorandum,

      (b)   for the transfer by him to the company, or another, before the end of the company's initial period of one or more non-cash assets, and

      (c)   under which the consideration for the transfer to be given by the company is at the time of the agreement equal in value to one-tenth or more of the company's issued share capital, unless the conditions referred to below have been complied with.

(2)   The company's "initial period" means the period of two years beginning with the date of the company being issued with a certificate under section 761 (trading certificate).

(3)   The conditions are those specified in—

section 599 (requirement of independent valuation), and

section 601 (requirement of approval by members).

(4)   This section does not apply where—

(a)   it is part of the company's ordinary business to acquire, or arrange for other persons to acquire, assets of a particular description, and

(b)   the agreement is entered into by the company in the ordinary course of that business.

(5)   This section does not apply to an agreement entered into by the company under the supervision of the court or of an officer authorised by the court for the purpose.

599   Agreement for transfer of non-cash asset: requirement of independent valuation

(1)   The following conditions must have been complied with—

(a)   the consideration to be received by the company, and any consideration other than cash to be given by the company, must have been independently valued in accordance with the provisions of this Chapter,

(b)   the valuer's report must have been made to the company during the six months immediately preceding the date of the agreement, and

(c)   a copy of the report must have been sent to the other party to the proposed agreement not later than the date on which copies have to be circulated to members under section 601(3).

(2)   The reference in subsection (1)(a) to the consideration to be received by the company is to the asset to be transferred to it or, as the case may be, to the advantage to the company of the asset's transfer to another person.

(3)   The reference in subsection (1)(c) to the other party to the proposed agreement is to the person referred to in section 598(1)(a).

If he has received a copy of the report under section 601 in his capacity as a member of the company, it is not necessary to send another copy under this section.

(4)   This section does not affect any requirement to value any consideration for purposes of section 593 (valuation of non-cash consideration for shares).

600   Agreement for transfer of non-cash asset: requirements as to valuation and report

(1)   The provisions of sections 1150 to 1153 (general provisions as to independent valuation and report) apply to the valuation and report required by section 599 (public company: transfer of non-cash asset).

(2)   The valuer's report must state—

(a)   the consideration to be received by the company, describing the asset in question (specifying the amount to be received in cash) and the consideration to be given by the company (specifying the amount to be given in cash), and

(b)   the method and date of valuation.

(3)   The valuer's report must contain or be accompanied by a note by him—

(a)   in the case of a valuation made by a person other than himself, that it appeared to himself reasonable to arrange for it to be so made or to accept a valuation so made,

(b)   whoever made the valuation, that the method of valuation was reasonable in all the circumstances,

(c)   that it appears to the valuer that there has been no material change in the value of the consideration in question since the valuation, and

(d)   that, on the basis of the valuation, the value of the consideration to be received by the company is not less than the value of the consideration to be given by it.

(4)   Any reference in section 599 or this section to consideration given for the transfer of an asset includes consideration given partly for its transfer.

(5)   In such a case—

(a)   the value of any consideration partly so given is to be taken as the proportion of the consideration properly attributable to its transfer,

(b)   the valuer must carry out or arrange for such valuations of anything else as will enable him to determine that proportion, and

(c)   his report must state what valuations have been made for that purpose and also the reason for and method and date of any such valuation and any other matters which may be relevant to that determination.

601   Agreement for transfer of non-cash asset: requirement of approval by members

(1)   The following conditions must have been complied with—

(a)   the terms of the agreement must have been approved by an ordinary resolution of the company,

(b)   copies of the valuer's report must have been circulated to the members entitled to notice of the meeting at which the resolution is proposed, not later than the date on which notice of the meeting is given, and

(c)   a copy of the proposed resolution must have been sent to the other party to the proposed agreement.

(2)   The reference in subsection (1)(c) to the other party to the proposed agreement is to the person referred to in section 598(1)(a).

(3)   ...

602   Copy of resolution to be delivered to registrar

(1)   A company that has passed a resolution under section 601 with respect to the transfer of an asset must, within 15 days of doing so, deliver to the registrar a copy of the resolution together with the valuer's report required by that section.

(2)   If a company fails to comply with subsection (1), an offence is committed by—

(a)   the company, and

(b)   every officer of the company who is in default.

(3)   A person guilty of an offence under this section is liable on summary conviction to a fine not exceeding level 3 on the standard scale and, for continued contravention, to a daily default fine not exceeding one-tenth of level 3 on the standard scale.

603   Adaptation of provisions in relation to company re-registering as public

The provisions of sections 598 to 602 (public companies: transfer of non-cash assets) apply with the following adaptations in relation to a company re-registered as a public company—

(a)   the reference in section 598(1)(a) to a person who is a subscriber to the company's memorandum shall be read as a reference to a person who is a member of the company on the date of re-registration;

(b)   the reference in section 598(2) to the date of the company being issued with a certificate under section 761 (trading certificate) shall be read as a reference to the date of re-registration.

604   Agreement for transfer of non-cash asset: effect of contravention

(1)   This section applies where a public company enters into an agreement in contravention of section 598 and either—

(a)   the other party to the agreement has not received the valuer's report required to be sent to him, or

(b)   there has been some other contravention of the requirements of this Chapter that the other party to the agreement knew or ought to have known amounted to a contravention.

(2)   In those circumstances—

(a)   the company is entitled to recover from that person any consideration given by it under the agreement, or an amount equal to the value of the consideration at the time of the agreement, and

(b)   the agreement, so far as not carried out, is void.

(3)   If the agreement is or includes an agreement for the allotment of shares in the company, then—

   (a)   whether or not the agreement also contravenes section 593 (valuation of non-cash consideration for shares), this section does not apply to it in so far as it is for the allotment of shares, and

   (b)   the allottee is liable to pay the company an amount equal to the aggregate of the nominal value of the shares and the whole of any premium (or, if the case so requires, so much of that aggregate as is treated as paid up by the consideration), with interest at the appropriate rate.

Supplementary provisions

605   Liability of subsequent holders of shares

(1)   If a person becomes a holder of shares in respect of which—

   (a)   there has been a contravention of section 593 (public company: valuation of non-cash consideration for shares), and

   (b)   by virtue of that contravention another is liable to pay any amount under the provision contravened,

   that person is also liable to pay that amount (jointly and severally with any other person so liable), unless he is exempted from liability under subsection (3) below.

(2)   If a company enters into an agreement in contravention of section 598 (public company: agreement for transfer of non-cash asset in initial period) and—

   (a)   the agreement is or includes an agreement for the allotment of shares in the company,

   (b)   a person becomes a holder of shares allotted under the agreement, and

   (c)   by virtue of the agreement and allotment under it another person is liable to pay an amount under section 604,

   the person who becomes the holder of the shares is also liable to pay that amount (jointly and severally with any other person so liable), unless he is exempted from liability under subsection (3) below.

   This applies whether or not the agreement also contravenes section 593.

(3)   A person otherwise liable under subsection (1) or (2) is exempted from that liability if either—

   (a)   he is a purchaser for value and, at the time of the purchase, he did not have actual notice of the contravention concerned, or

   (b)   he derived title to the shares (directly or indirectly) from a person who became a holder of them after the contravention and was not liable under subsection (1) or (2).

(4)   References in this section to a holder, in relation to shares in a company, include any person who has an unconditional right—

   (a)   to be included in the company's register of members (or, as the case may be, to have his name and other particulars delivered to the registrar under Chapter 2A of Part 8 and registered by the registrar) in respect of those shares, or

   (b)   to have an instrument of transfer of the shares executed in his favour.

606   Power of court to grant relief

(1)   A person who—

   (a)   is liable to a company under any provision of this Chapter in relation to payment in respect of any shares in the company, or

   (b)   is liable to a company by virtue of an undertaking given to it in, or in connection with, payment for any shares in the company,

   may apply to the court to be exempted in whole or in part from the liability.

(2)   In the case of a liability within subsection (1)(a), the court may exempt the applicant from the liability only if and to the extent that it appears to the court just and equitable to do so having regard to—

   (a)   whether the applicant has paid, or is liable to pay, any amount in respect of—

      (i) any other liability arising in relation to those shares under any provision of this Chapter or Chapter 5, or (ii)	any liability arising by virtue of any undertaking given in or in connection with payment for those shares;

(b)	whether any person other than the applicant has paid or is likely to pay, whether in pursuance of any order of the court or otherwise, any such amount;

(c)	whether the applicant or any other person—

(i)	has performed in whole or in part, or is likely so to perform any such undertaking, or

(ii)	has done or is likely to do any other thing in payment or part payment for the shares.

(3)	In the case of a liability within subsection (1)(b), the court may exempt the applicant from the liability only if and to the extent that it appears to the court just and equitable to do so having regard to—

(a)	whether the applicant has paid or is liable to pay any amount in respect of liability arising in relation to the shares under any provision of this Chapter or Chapter 5;

(b)	whether any person other than the applicant has paid or is likely to pay, whether in pursuance of any order of the court or otherwise, any such amount.

(4)	In determining whether it should exempt the applicant in whole or in part from any liability, the court must have regard to the following overriding principles—

(a)	that a company that has allotted shares should receive money or money's worth at least equal in value to the aggregate of the nominal value of those shares and the whole of any premium or, if the case so requires, so much of that aggregate as is treated as paid up;

(b)	subject to this, that where such a company would, if the court did not grant the exemption, have more than one remedy against a particular person, it should be for the company to decide which remedy it should remain entitled to pursue.

(5)	If a person brings proceedings against another ("the contributor") for a contribution in respect of liability to a company arising under any provision of this Chapter or Chapter 5 and it appears to the court that the contributor is liable to make such a contribution, the court may, if and to the extent that it appears to it, just and equitable to do so having regard to the respective culpability (in respect of the liability to the company) of the contributor and the person bringing the proceedings—

(a)	exempt the contributor in whole or in part from his liability to make such a contribution, or

(b)	order the contributor to make a larger contribution than, but for this subsection, he would be liable to make.

(6)	Where a person is liable to a company under section 604(2) (agreement for transfer of non-cash asset: effect of contravention), the court may, on application, exempt him in whole or in part from that liability if and to the extent that it appears to the court to be just and equitable to do so having regard to any benefit accruing to the company by virtue of anything done by him towards the carrying out of the agreement mentioned in that subsection.

**607	Penalty for contravention of this Chapter**

(1)	This section applies where a company contravenes—

section 593 (public company allotting shares for non-cash consideration), or

section 598 (public company entering into agreement for transfer of non-cash asset).

(2)	An offence is committed by—

(a)	the company, and

(b)	every officer of the company who is in default.

(3)	A person guilty of an offence under this section is liable—

(a)	on conviction on indictment, to a fine;

(b)	on summary conviction, to a fine not exceeding the statutory maximum.

**608	Enforceability of undertakings to do work etc**

(1)	An undertaking given by any person, in or in connection with payment for shares in a company, to do work or perform services or to do any other thing, if it is enforceable by the company apart

(2)   from this Chapter, is so enforceable notwithstanding that there has been a contravention in relation to it of a provision of this Chapter or Chapter 5.

(2)   This is without prejudice to section 606 (power of court to grant relief etc in respect of liabilities).

609   The appropriate rate of interest

(1)   For the purposes of this Chapter the "appropriate rate" of interest is 5% per annum or such other rate as may be specified by order made by the Secretary of State.

(2)   An order under this section is subject to negative resolution procedure.

CHAPTER 7

SHARE PREMIUMS

The share premium account

610   Application of share premiums

(1)   If a company issues shares at a premium, whether for cash or otherwise, a sum equal to the aggregate amount or value of the premiums on those shares must be transferred to an account called "the share premium account".

(2)   Where, on issuing shares, a company has transferred a sum to the share premium account, it may use that sum to write off—

     (a)   the expenses of the issue of those shares;

     (b)   any commission paid on the issue of those shares.

(3)   The company may use the share premium account to pay up new shares to be allotted to members as fully paid bonus shares.

(4)   Subject to subsections (2) and (3), the provisions of the Companies Acts relating to the reduction of a company's share capital apply as if the share premium account were part of its paid up share capital.

(5)   This section has effect subject to—

     section 611 (group reconstruction relief);

     section 612 (merger relief);

     section 614 (power to make further provisions by regulations).

(6)   In this Chapter "the issuing company" means the company issuing shares as mentioned in subsection (1) above.

Relief from requirements as to share premiums

611   Group reconstruction relief

(1)   This section applies where the issuing company—

     (a)   is a wholly-owned subsidiary of another company ("the holding company"), and

     (b)   allots shares—

          (i)   to the holding company, or

          (ii)   to another wholly-owned subsidiary of the holding company,

          in consideration for the transfer to the issuing company of non-cash assets of a company ("the transferor company") that is a member of the group of companies that comprises the holding company and all its wholly-owned subsidiaries.

(2)   Where the shares in the issuing company allotted in consideration for the transfer are issued at a premium, the issuing company is not required by section 610 to transfer any amount in excess of the minimum premium value to the share premium account.

(3)   The minimum premium value means the amount (if any) by which the base value of the consideration for the shares allotted exceeds the aggregate nominal value of the shares.

(4)   The base value of the consideration for the shares allotted is the amount by which the base value of the assets transferred exceeds the base value of any liabilities of the transferor company assumed by the issuing company as part of the consideration for the assets transferred.

(5)   For the purposes of this section—

     (a)   the base value of assets transferred is taken as—

(i)   the cost of those assets to the transferor company, or

(ii)   if less, the amount at which those assets are stated in the transferor company's accounting records immediately before the transfer;

(b)   the base value of the liabilities assumed is taken as the amount at which they are stated in the transferor company's accounting records immediately before the transfer.

612   Merger relief

(1)   This section applies where the issuing company has secured at least a 90% equity holding in another company in pursuance of an arrangement providing for the allotment of equity shares in the issuing company on terms that the consideration for the shares allotted is to be provided—

(a)   by the issue or transfer to the issuing company of equity shares in the other company, or

(b)   by the cancellation of any such shares not held by the issuing company.

(2)   If the equity shares in the issuing company allotted in pursuance of the arrangement in consideration for the acquisition or cancellation of equity shares in the other company are issued at a premium, section 610 does not apply to the premiums on those shares.

(3)   Where the arrangement also provides for the allotment of any shares in the issuing company on terms that the consideration for those shares is to be provided—

(a)   by the issue or transfer to the issuing company of non-equity shares in the other company, or

(b)   by the cancellation of any such shares in that company not held by the issuing company,

relief under subsection (2) extends to any shares in the issuing company allotted on those terms in pursuance of the arrangement.

(4)   This section does not apply in a case falling within section 611 (group reconstruction relief).

613   Merger relief: meaning of 90% equity holding

(1)   The following provisions have effect to determine for the purposes of section 612 (merger relief) whether a company ("company A") has secured at least a 90% equity holding in another company ("company B") in pursuance of such an arrangement as is mentioned in subsection (1) of that section.

(2)   Company A has secured at least a 90% equity holding in company B if in consequence of an acquisition or cancellation of equity shares in company B (in pursuance of that arrangement) it holds equity shares in company B of an aggregate amount equal to 90% or more of the nominal value of that company's equity share capital.

(3)   For this purpose—

(a)   it is immaterial whether any of those shares were acquired in pursuance of the arrangement; and

(b)   shares in company B held by the company as treasury shares are excluded in determining the nominal value of company B's share capital.

(4)   Where the equity share capital of company B is divided into different classes of shares, company A is not regarded as having secured at least a 90% equity holding in company B unless the requirements of subsection (2) are met in relation to each of those classes of shares taken separately.

(5)   For the purposes of this section shares held by—

(a)   a company that is company A's holding company or subsidiary, or

(b)   a subsidiary of company A's holding company, or

(c)   its or their nominees,

are treated as held by company A.

614   Power to make further provision by regulations

(1)   The Secretary of State may by regulations make such provision as he thinks appropriate—

(a)   for relieving companies from the requirements of section 610 (application of share premiums) in relation to premiums other than cash premiums;

(b)   for restricting or otherwise modifying any relief from those requirements provided by this Chapter.

(2)   Regulations under this section are subject to affirmative resolution procedure.

615   Relief may be reflected in company's balance sheet

An amount corresponding to the amount representing the premiums, or part of the premiums, on shares issued by a company that by virtue of any relief under this Chapter is not included in the company's share premium account may also be disregarded in determining the amount at which any shares or other consideration provided for the shares issued is to be included in the company's balance sheet.

Supplementary provisions

616   Interpretation of this Chapter

(1)   In this Chapter—

"arrangement" means any agreement, scheme or arrangement (including an arrangement sanctioned in accordance with—

(a)   Part 26 or 26A (arrangements and reconstructions), or

(b)   section 110 of the Insolvency Act 1986 or Article 96 of the Insolvency (Northern Ireland) Order 1989 (liquidator in winding up accepting shares as consideration for sale of company property));

"company", except in reference to the issuing company, includes any body corporate;

"equity shares" means shares comprised in a company's equity share capital, and "non-equity shares" means shares (of any class) that are not so comprised;

"the issuing company" has the meaning given by section 610(6).

(2)   References in this Chapter (however expressed) to—

(a)   the acquisition by a company of shares in another company, and

(b)   the issue or allotment of shares to, or the transfer of shares to or by, a company,

include (respectively) the acquisition of shares by, and the issue or allotment or transfer of shares to or by, a nominee of that company.

The reference in section 611 to the transferor company shall be read accordingly.

(3)   References in this Chapter to the transfer of shares in a company include the transfer of a right to be included in the company's register of members (or, as the case may be, have your name and other particulars delivered to the registrar under Chapter 2A of Part 8 and registered by the registrar) in respect of those shares.

CHAPTER 8

ALTERATION OF SHARE CAPITAL

How share capital may be altered

617   Alteration of share capital of limited company

(1)   A limited company having a share capital may not alter its share capital except in the following ways.

(2)   The company may—

(a)   increase its share capital by allotting new shares in accordance with this Part, or

(b)   reduce its share capital in accordance with Chapter 10.

(3)   The company may—

(a)   sub-divide or consolidate all or any of its share capital in accordance with section 618, or

(b)   reconvert stock into shares in accordance with section 620.

(4)   The company may redenominate all or any of its shares in accordance with section 622, and may reduce its share capital in accordance with section 626 in connection with such a redenomination.

(5)   Nothing in this section affects—

(a)   the power of a company to purchase its own shares, or to redeem shares, in accordance with Part 18;

(b)   the power of a company to purchase its own shares in pursuance of an order of the court under—

(i)   section 98 (application to court to cancel resolution for re-registration as a private company),

(ii)   section 721(6) (powers of court on objection to redemption or purchase of shares out of capital),

(iii)   section 759 (remedial order in case of breach of prohibition of public offers by private company), or

(iv)   Part 30 (protection of members against unfair prejudice);

(c)   the forfeiture of shares, or the acceptance of shares surrendered in lieu, in pursuance of the company's articles, for failure to pay any sum payable in respect of the shares;

(d)   the cancellation of shares under section 662 (duty to cancel shares held by or for a public company);

(e)   the power of a company—

     (i)   to enter into a compromise or arrangement in accordance with Part 26 or 26A (arrangements and reconstructions), or

     (ii)   to do anything required to comply with an order of the court on an application under that Part;

(f)   the cancellation of a share warrant issued by the company and of the shares specified in it by a cancellation order or suspended cancellation order made under paragraph 6 of Schedule 4 to the Small Business, Enterprise and Employment Act 2015 (cancellation where share warrants not surrendered in accordance with that Schedule);

(g)   the cancellation of a share warrant issued by the company and of the shares specified in it pursuant to section 1028A(2) or 1032A(2) (cancellation of share warrants on restoration of a company).

Subdivision or consolidation of shares

618   Sub-division or consolidation of shares

(1)   A limited company having a share capital may—

(a)   sub-divide its shares, or any of them, into shares of a smaller nominal amount than its existing shares, or

(b)   consolidate and divide all or any of its share capital into shares of a larger nominal amount than its existing shares.

(2)   In any sub-division, consolidation or division of shares under this section, the proportion between the amount paid and the amount (if any) unpaid on each resulting share must be the same as it was in the case of the share from which that share is derived.

(3)   A company may exercise a power conferred by this section only if its members have passed a resolution authorising it to do so.

(4)   A resolution under subsection (3) may authorise a company—

(a)   to exercise more than one of the powers conferred by this section;

(b)   to exercise a power on more than one occasion;

(c)   to exercise a power at a specified time or in specified circumstances.

(5)   The company's articles may exclude or restrict the exercise of any power conferred by this section.

619   Notice to registrar of sub-division or consolidation

(1)   If a company exercises the power conferred by section 618 (sub-division or consolidation of shares) it must within one month after doing so give notice to the registrar, specifying the shares affected.

(2)   The notice must be accompanied by a statement of capital.

(3)   The statement of capital must state with respect to the company's share capital immediately following the exercise of the power—

(a)   the total number of shares of the company,

(b)   the aggregate nominal value of those shares,

(ba) the aggregate amount (if any) unpaid on those shares (whether on account of their nominal value or by way of premium), and

(c)   for each class of shares—

(i)   prescribed particulars of the rights attached to the shares,

(ii)   the total number of shares of that class, and

(iii)   the aggregate nominal value of shares of that class, ...

(d)   ...

(4)   If default is made in complying with this section, an offence is committed by—

(a)   the company, and

(b)   every officer of the company who is in default.

(5)   A person guilty of an offence under this section is liable on summary conviction to a fine not exceeding level 3 on the standard scale and, for continued contravention, a daily default fine not exceeding one-tenth of level 3 on the standard scale.

Reconversion of stock into shares

620   Reconversion of stock into shares

(1)   A limited company that has converted paid-up shares into stock (before the repeal by this Act of the power to do so) may reconvert that stock into paid-up shares of any nominal value.

(2)   A company may exercise the power conferred by this section only if its members have passed an ordinary resolution authorising it to do so.

(3)   A resolution under subsection (2) may authorise a company to exercise the power conferred by this section—

(a)   on more than one occasion;

(b)   at a specified time or in specified circumstances.

621   Notice to registrar of reconversion of stock into shares

(1)   If a company exercises a power conferred by section 620 (reconversion of stock into shares) it must within one month after doing so give notice to the registrar, specifying the stock affected.

(2)   The notice must be accompanied by a statement of capital.

(3)   The statement of capital must state with respect to the company's share capital immediately following the exercise of the power—

(a)   the total number of shares of the company,

(b)   the aggregate nominal value of those shares,

(ba) the aggregate amount (if any) unpaid on those shares (whether on account of their nominal value or by way of premium), and

(c)   for each class of shares—

(i)   prescribed particulars of the rights attached to the shares,

(ii)   the total number of shares of that class, and

(iii)   the aggregate nominal value of shares of that class, ...

(d)   ...

(4)   If default is made in complying with this section, an offence is committed by—

(a)   the company, and

(b)   every officer of the company who is in default.

(5)   A person guilty of an offence under this section is liable on summary conviction to a fine not exceeding level 3 on the standard scale and, for continued contravention, a daily default fine not exceeding one-tenth of level 3 on the standard scale.

Redenomination of share capital

622   Redenomination of share capital

(1)   A limited company having a share capital may by resolution redenominate its share capital or any class of its share capital.

"Redenominate" means convert shares from having a fixed nominal value in one currency to having a fixed nominal value in another currency.

(2)   The conversion must be made at an appropriate spot rate of exchange specified in the resolution.

(3)   The rate must be either—

(a)   a rate prevailing on a day specified in the resolution, or

(b)   a rate determined by taking the average of rates prevailing on each consecutive day of a period specified in the resolution.

The day or period specified for the purposes of paragraph (a) or (b) must be within the period of 28 days ending on the day before the resolution is passed.

(4)   A resolution under this section may specify conditions which must be met before the redenomination takes effect.

(5)   Redenomination in accordance with a resolution under this section takes effect—

(a)   on the day on which the resolution is passed, or

(b)   on such later day as may be determined in accordance with the resolution.

(6)   A resolution under this section lapses if the redenomination for which it provides has not taken effect at the end of the period of 28 days beginning on the date on which it is passed.

(7)   A company's articles may prohibit or restrict the exercise of the power conferred by this section.

(8)   Chapter 3 of Part 3 (resolutions affecting a company's constitution) applies to a resolution under this section.

623   Calculation of new nominal values

For each class of share the new nominal value of each share is calculated as follows:

Step One

Take the aggregate of the old nominal values of all the shares of that class.

Step Two

Translate that amount into the new currency at the rate of exchange specified in the resolution.

Step Three

Divide that amount by the number of shares in the class.

624   Effect of redenomination

(1)   The redenomination of shares does not affect any rights or obligations of members under the company's constitution, or any restrictions affecting members under the company's constitution. In particular, it does not affect entitlement to dividends (including entitlement to dividends in a particular currency), voting rights or any liability in respect of amounts unpaid on shares.

(2)   For this purpose the company's constitution includes the terms on which any shares of the company are allotted or held.

(3)   Subject to subsection (1), references to the old nominal value of the shares in any agreement or statement, or in any deed, instrument or document, shall (unless the context otherwise requires) be read after the resolution takes effect as references to the new nominal value of the shares.

625   Notice to registrar of redenomination

(1)   If a limited company having a share capital redenominates any of its share capital, it must within one month after doing so give notice to the registrar, specifying the shares redenominated.

(2)   The notice must—

(a)   state the date on which the resolution was passed, and

(b)   be accompanied by a statement of capital.

(3)   The statement of capital must state with respect to the company's share capital as redenominated by the resolution—

(a)   the total number of shares of the company,

(b)   the aggregate nominal value of those shares,

(ba)   the aggregate amount (if any) unpaid on those shares (whether on account of their nominal value or by way of premium), and

(c)   for each class of shares—

(i)   prescribed particulars of the rights attached to the shares,

      (ii)   the total number of shares of that class, and

      (iii)   the aggregate nominal value of shares of that class, ...

  (d) ...

(4)   If default is made in complying with this section, an offence is committed by—

  (a)   the company, and

  (b)   every officer of the company who is in default.

(5)   A person guilty of an offence under this section is liable on summary conviction to a fine not exceeding level 3 on the standard scale and, for continued contravention, a daily default fine not exceeding one-tenth of level 3 on the standard scale.

626   Reduction of capital in connection with redenomination

(1)   A limited company that passes a resolution redenominating some or all of its shares may, for the purpose of adjusting the nominal values of the redenominated shares to obtain values that are, in the opinion of the company, more suitable, reduce its share capital under this section.

(2)   A reduction of capital under this section requires a special resolution of the company.

(3)   Any such resolution must be passed within three months of the resolution effecting the redenomination.

(4)   The amount by which a company's share capital is reduced under this section must not exceed 10% of the nominal value of the company's allotted share capital immediately after the reduction.

(5)   A reduction of capital under this section does not extinguish or reduce any liability in respect of share capital not paid up.

(6)   Nothing in Chapter 10 applies to a reduction of capital under this section.

627   Notice to registrar of reduction of capital in connection with redenomination

(1)   A company that passes a resolution under section 626 (reduction of capital in connection with redenomination) must within 15 days after the resolution is passed give notice to the registrar stating—

  (a)   the date of the resolution, and

  (b)   the date of the resolution under section 622 in connection with which it was passed.

This is in addition to the copies of the resolutions themselves that are required to be delivered to the registrar under Chapter 3 of Part 3.

(2)   The notice must be accompanied by a statement of capital.

(3)   The statement of capital must state with respect to the company's share capital as reduced by the resolution—

  (a)   the total number of shares of the company,

  (b)   the aggregate nominal value of those shares,

  (ba) the aggregate amount (if any) unpaid on those shares (whether on account of their nominal value or by way of premium), and

  (c)   for each class of shares—

      (i)   prescribed particulars of the rights attached to the shares,

      (ii)   the total number of shares of that class, and

      (iii)   the aggregate nominal value of shares of that class, ...

  (d) ...

(4)   The registrar must register the notice and the statement on receipt.

(5)   The reduction of capital is not effective until those documents are registered.

(6)   The company must also deliver to the registrar, within 15 days after the resolution is passed, a statement by the directors confirming that the reduction in share capital is in accordance with section 626(4) (reduction of capital not to exceed 10% of nominal value of allotted shares immediately after reduction).

(7)   If default is made in complying with this section, an offence is committed by—

  (a)   the company, and

  (b)   every officer of the company who is in default.

(8)   A person guilty of an offence under this section is liable—

   (a)   on conviction on indictment to a fine, and

   (b)   on summary conviction to a fine not exceeding the statutory maximum.

628   Redenomination reserve

(1)   The amount by which a company's share capital is reduced under section 626 (reduction of capital in connection with redenomination) must be transferred to a reserve, called "the redenomination reserve".

(2)   The redenomination reserve may be applied by the company in paying up shares to be allotted to members as fully paid bonus shares.

(3)   Subject to that, the provisions of the Companies Acts relating to the reduction of a company's share capital apply as if the redenomination reserve were paid-up share capital of the company.

CHAPTER 9

CLASSES OF SHARE AND CLASS RIGHTS

Introductory

629   Classes of shares

(1)   For the purposes of the Companies Acts shares are of one class if the rights attached to them are in all respects uniform.

(2)   For this purpose the rights attached to shares are not regarded as different from those attached to other shares by reason only that they do not carry the same rights to dividends in the twelve months immediately following their allotment.

Variation of class rights

630   Variation of class rights: companies having a share capital

(1)   This section is concerned with the variation of the rights attached to a class of shares in a company having a share capital.

(2)   Rights attached to a class of a company's shares may only be varied—

   (a)   in accordance with provision in the company's articles for the variation of those rights, or

   (b)   where the company's articles contain no such provision, if the holders of shares of that class consent to the variation in accordance with this section.

(3)   This is without prejudice to any other restrictions on the variation of the rights.

(4)   The consent required for the purposes of this section on the part of the holders of a class of a company's shares is—

   (a)   consent in writing from the holders of at least three-quarters in nominal value of the issued shares of that class (excluding any shares held as treasury shares), or

   (b)   a special resolution passed at a separate general meeting of the holders of that class sanctioning the variation.

(5)   Any amendment of a provision contained in a company's articles for the variation of the rights attached to a class of shares, or the insertion of any such provision into the articles, is itself to be treated as a variation of those rights.

(6)   In this section, and (except where the context otherwise requires) in any provision in a company's articles for the variation of the rights attached to a class of shares, references to the variation of those rights include references to their abrogation.

631   Variation of class rights: companies without a share capital

(1)   This section is concerned with the variation of the rights of a class of members of a company where the company does not have a share capital.

(2)   Rights of a class of members may only be varied—

   (a)   in accordance with provision in the company's articles for the variation of those rights, or

   (b)   where the company's articles contain no such provision, if the members of that class consent to the variation in accordance with this section.

(3)   This is without prejudice to any other restrictions on the variation of the rights.

(4)   The consent required for the purposes of this section on the part of the members of a class is—

    (a)   consent in writing from at least three-quarters of the members of the class, or

    (b)   a special resolution passed at a separate general meeting of the members of that class sanctioning the variation.

(5)   Any amendment of a provision contained in a company's articles for the variation of the rights of a class of members, or the insertion of any such provision into the articles, is itself to be treated as a variation of those rights.

(6)   In this section, and (except where the context otherwise requires) in any provision in a company's articles for the variation of the rights of a class of members, references to the variation of those rights include references to their abrogation.

632   Variation of class rights: saving for court's powers under other provisions

Nothing in section 630 or 631 (variation of class rights) affects the power of the court under—

section 98 (application to cancel resolution for public company to be re-registered as private),

Part 26 (arrangements and reconstructions: general),

Part 26A (arrangements and reconstructions: companies in financial difficulty), or

Part 30 (protection of members against unfair prejudice).

633   Right to object to variation: companies having a share capital

(1)   This section applies where the rights attached to any class of shares in a company are varied under section 630 (variation of class rights: companies having a share capital).

(1)   The holders of not less in the aggregate than 15% of the issued shares of the class in question (being persons who did not consent to or vote in favour of the resolution for the variation) may apply to the court to have the variation cancelled.

For this purpose any of the company's share capital held as treasury shares is disregarded.

(3)   If such an application is made, the variation has no effect unless and until it is confirmed by the court.

(4)   Application to the court—

    (a)   must be made within 21 days after the date on which the consent was given or the resolution was passed (as the case may be), and

    (b)   may be made on behalf of the shareholders entitled to make the application by such one or more of their number as they may appoint in writing for the purpose.

(5)   The court, after hearing the applicant and any other persons who apply to the court to be heard and appear to the court to be interested in the application, may, if satisfied having regard to all the circumstances of the case that the variation would unfairly prejudice the shareholders of the class represented by the applicant, disallow the variation, and shall if not so satisfied confirm it. The decision of the court on any such application is final.

(6)   References in this section to the variation of the rights of holders of a class of shares include references to their abrogation.

634   Right to object to variation: companies without a share capital

(1)   This section applies where the rights of any class of members of a company are varied under section 631 (variation of class rights: companies without a share capital).

(2)   Members amounting to not less than 15% of the members of the class in question (being persons who did not consent to or vote in favour of the resolution for the variation) may apply to the court to have the variation cancelled.

(3)   If such an application is made, the variation has no effect unless and until it is confirmed by the court.

(4)   Application to the court must be made within 21 days after the date on which the consent was given or the resolution was passed (as the case may be) and may be made on behalf of the members entitled to make the application by such one or more of their number as they may appoint in writing for the purpose.

(5)   The court, after hearing the applicant and any other persons who apply to the court to be heard and appear to the court to be interested in the application, may, if satisfied having regard to all the

circumstances of the case that the variation would unfairly prejudice the members of the class represented by the applicant, disallow the variation, and shall if not so satisfied confirm it. The decision of the court on any such application is final.

(6) References in this section to the variation of the rights of a class of members include references to their abrogation.

635 Copy of court order to be forwarded to the registrar

(1) The company must within 15 days after the making of an order by the court on an application under section 633 or 634 (objection to variation of class rights) forward a copy of the order to the registrar.

(2) If default is made in complying with this section an offence is committed by—

(a) the company, and

(b) every officer of the company who is in default.

(3) A person guilty of an offence under this section is liable on summary conviction to a fine not exceeding level 3 on the standard scale and, for continued contravention, a daily default fine not exceeding one-tenth of level 3 on the standard scale.

Matters to be notified to the registrar

636 Notice of name or other designation of class of shares

(1) Where a company assigns a name or other designation, or a new name or other designation, to any class or description of its shares, it must within one month from doing so deliver to the registrar a notice giving particulars of the name or designation so assigned.

(2) If default is made in complying with this section, an offence is committed by—

(a) the company, and

(b) every officer of the company who is in default.

(3) A person guilty of an offence under this section is liable on summary conviction to a fine not exceeding level 3 on the standard scale and, for continued contravention, a daily default fine not exceeding one-tenth of level 3 on the standard scale.

637 Notice of particulars of variation of rights attached to shares

(1) Where the rights attached to any shares of a company are varied, the company must within one month from the date on which the variation is made deliver to the registrar a notice giving particulars of the variation.

(2) If default is made in complying with this section, an offence is committed by—

(a) the company, and

(b) every officer of the company who is in default.

(3) A person guilty of an offence under this section is liable on summary conviction to a fine not exceeding level 3 on the standard scale and, for continued contravention, a daily default fine not exceeding one-tenth of level 3 on the standard scale.

638 Notice of new class of members

(1) If a company not having a share capital creates a new class of members, the company must within one month from the date on which the new class is created deliver to the registrar a notice containing particulars of the rights attached to that class.

(2) If default is made in complying with this section, an offence is committed by—

(a) the company, and

(b) every officer of the company who is in default.

(3) A person guilty of an offence under this section is liable on summary conviction to a fine not exceeding level 3 on the standard scale and, for continued contravention, a daily default fine not exceeding one-tenth of level 3 on the standard scale.

639 Notice of name or other designation of class of members

(1) Where a company not having a share capital assigns a name or other designation, or a new name or other designation, to any class of its members, it must within one month from doing so deliver to the registrar a notice giving particulars of the name or designation so assigned.

(2) If default is made in complying with this section, an offence is committed by—
(a) the company, and
(b) every officer of the company who is in default.

(3) A person guilty of an offence under this section is liable on summary conviction to a fine not exceeding level 3 on the standard scale and, for continued contravention, a daily default fine not exceeding one-tenth of level 3 on the standard scale.

640 Notice of particulars of variation of class rights

(1) If the rights of any class of members of a company not having a share capital are varied, the company must within one month from the date on which the variation is made deliver to the registrar a notice containing particulars of the variation.

(2) If default is made in complying with this section, an offence is committed by—
(a) the company, and
(b) every officer of the company who is in default.

(3) A person guilty of an offence under this section is liable on summary conviction to a fine not exceeding level 3 on the standard scale and, for continued contravention, a daily default fine not exceeding one-tenth of level 3 on the standard scale.

CHAPTER 10
REDUCTION OF SHARE CAPITAL

Introductory

641 Circumstances in which a company may reduce its share capital

(1) A limited company having a share capital may reduce its share capital—
(a) in the case of a private company limited by shares, by special resolution supported by a solvency statement (see sections 642 to 644);
(b) in any case, by special resolution confirmed by the court (see sections 645 to 651).

(2) A company may not reduce its capital under subsection (1)(a) if as a result of the reduction there would no longer be any member of the company holding shares other than redeemable shares.

(2A) A company may not reduce its share capital under subsection (1)(a) or (b) as part of a scheme by virtue of which a person, or a person together with its associates, is to acquire all the shares in the company or (where there is more than one class of shares in a company) all the shares of one or more classes, in each case other than shares that are already held by that person or its associates.

(2B) Subsection (2A) does not apply to a scheme under which—
(a) the company is to have a new parent undertaking,
(b) all or substantially all of the members of the company become members of the parent undertaking, and
(c) the members of the company are to hold proportions of the equity share capital of the parent undertaking in the same or substantially the same proportions as they hold the equity share capital of the company.

(2C) In this section—
"associate" has the meaning given by section 988 (meaning of "associate"), reading references in that section to an offeror as references to the person acquiring the shares in the company;
"scheme" means a compromise or arrangement sanctioned by the court under Part 26 or 26A (arrangements and reconstructions).

(3) Subject to subsections (2) to (2B), a company may reduce its share capital under this section in any way.

(4) In particular, a company may—

       (a)   extinguish or reduce the liability on any of its shares in respect of share capital not paid up, or

       (b)   either with or without extinguishing or reducing liability on any of its shares—

           (i)   cancel any paid-up share capital that is lost or unrepresented by available assets, or

           (ii)   repay any paid-up share capital in excess of the company's wants.

(5)   A special resolution under this section may not provide for a reduction of share capital to take effect later than the date on which the resolution has effect in accordance with this Chapter.

(6)   This Chapter (apart from subsection (5) above) has effect subject to any provision of the company's articles restricting or prohibiting the reduction of the company's share capital.

(7)   In subsection (1)(b), section 91(5)(b)(iii), sections 645 to 651 (except in the phrases "sanctioned by the court under Part 26" and "sanctioned by the court under Part 26A") and 653(1) "the court" means, in England and Wales, the High Court.

Private companies: reduction of capital supported by solvency statement

642   Reduction of capital supported by solvency statement

(1)   A resolution for reducing share capital of a private company limited by shares is supported by a solvency statement if—

       (a)   the directors of the company make a statement of the solvency of the company in accordance with section 643 (a "solvency statement") not more than 15 days before the date on which the resolution is passed, and

       (b)   the resolution and solvency statement are registered in accordance with section 644.

(2)   Where the resolution is proposed as a written resolution, a copy of the solvency statement must be sent or submitted to every eligible member at or before the time at which the proposed resolution is sent or submitted to him.

(3)   Where the resolution is proposed at a general meeting, a copy of the solvency statement must be made available for inspection by members of the company throughout that meeting.

(4)   The validity of a resolution is not affected by a failure to comply with subsection (2) or (3).

643   Solvency statement

(1)   A solvency statement is a statement that each of the directors—

       (a)   has formed the opinion, as regards the company's situation at the date of the statement, that there is no ground on which the company could then be found to be unable to pay (or otherwise discharge) its debts; and

       (b)   has also formed the opinion—

           (i)   if it is intended to commence the winding up of the company within twelve months of that date, that the company will be able to pay (or otherwise discharge) its debts in full within twelve months of the commencement of the winding up; or

           (ii)   in any other case, that the company will be able to pay (or otherwise discharge) its debts as they fall due during the year immediately following that date.

(2)   In forming those opinions, the directors must take into account all of the company's liabilities (including any contingent or prospective liabilities).

(3)   The solvency statement must be in the prescribed form and must state—

       (a)   the date on which it is made, and

       (b)   the name of each director of the company.

(4)   If the directors make a solvency statement without having reasonable grounds for the opinions expressed in it, and the statement is delivered to the registrar, an offence is committed by every director who is in default.

(5)   A person guilty of an offence under subsection (4) is liable—

       (a)   on conviction on indictment, to imprisonment for a term not exceeding two years or a fine (or both);

       (b)   on summary conviction—

           (i)   in England and Wales, to imprisonment for a term not exceeding twelve months or to a fine not exceeding the statutory maximum (or both);

        (ii)   in Scotland or Northern Ireland, to imprisonment for a term not exceeding six months, or to a fine not exceeding the statutory maximum (or both).

644 Registration of resolution and supporting documents

(1) Within 15 days after the resolution for reducing share capital is passed the company must deliver to the registrar—

    (a)   a copy of the solvency statement, and

    (b)   a statement of capital.

This is in addition to the copy of the resolution itself that is required to be delivered to the registrar under Chapter 3 of Part 3.

(2) The statement of capital must state with respect to the company's share capital as reduced by the resolution—

    (a)   the total number of shares of the company,

    (b)   the aggregate nominal value of those shares,

    (ba) the aggregate amount (if any) unpaid on those shares (whether on account of their nominal value or by way of premium), and

    (c)   for each class of shares—

        (i)   prescribed particulars of the rights attached to the shares,

        (ii)   the total number of shares of that class, and

        (iii)   the aggregate nominal value of shares of that class, …

    (d)   …

(3) The registrar must register the documents delivered to him under subsection (1) on receipt.

(4) The resolution does not take effect until those documents are registered.

(5) The company must also deliver to the registrar, within 15 days after the resolution is passed, a statement by the directors confirming that the solvency statement was—

    (a)   made not more than 15 days before the date on which the resolution was passed, and

    (b)   provided to members in accordance with section 642(2) or (3).

(6) The validity of a resolution is not affected by—

    (a)   a failure to deliver the documents required to be delivered to the registrar under subsection (1) within the time specified in that subsection, or

    (b)   a failure to comply with subsection (5).

(7) If the company delivers to the registrar a solvency statement that was not provided to members in accordance with section 642(2) or (3), an offence is committed by every officer of the company who is in default.

(8) If default is made in complying with this section, an offence is committed by—

    (a)   the company, and

    (b)   every officer of the company who is in default.

(9) A person guilty of an offence under subsection (7) or (8) is liable—

    (a)   on conviction on indictment, to a fine;

    (b)   on summary conviction, to a fine not exceeding the statutory maximum.

Reduction of capital confirmed by the court

645 Application to court for order of confirmation

(1) Where a company has passed a resolution for reducing share capital, it may apply to the court for an order confirming the reduction.

(2) If the proposed reduction of capital involves either—

    (a)   diminution of liability in respect of unpaid share capital, or

    (b)   the payment to a shareholder of any paid-up share capital,

section 646 (creditors entitled to object to reduction) applies unless the court directs otherwise.

(3) The court may, if having regard to any special circumstances of the case it thinks proper to do so, direct that section 646 is not to apply as regards any class or classes of creditors.

(4) The court may direct that section 646 is to apply in any other case.

646   Creditors entitled to object to reduction

(1)   Where this section applies (see section 645(2) and (4)), every creditor of the company who—

    (a)   at the date fixed by the court is entitled to any debt or claim that, if that date were the commencement of the winding up of the company would be admissible in proof against the company, and

    (b)   can show that there is a real likelihood that the reduction would result in the company being unable to discharge his debt or claim when it fell due,

    is entitled to object to the reduction of capital.

(2)   The court shall settle a list of creditors entitled to object.

(3)   For that purpose the court—

    (a)   shall ascertain, as far as possible without requiring an application from any creditor, the names of those creditors and the nature and amount of their debts or claims, and

    (b)   may publish notices fixing a day or days within which creditors not entered on the list are to claim to be so entered or are to be excluded from the right of objecting to the reduction of capital.

(4)   If a creditor entered on the list whose debt or claim is not discharged or has not determined does not consent to the reduction, the court may, if it thinks fit, dispense with the consent of that creditor on the company securing payment of his debt or claim.

(5)   For this purpose the debt or claim must be secured by appropriating (as the court may direct) the following amount—

    (a)   if the company admits the full amount of the debt or claim or, though not admitting it, is willing to provide for it, the full amount of the debt or claim;

    (b)   if the company does not admit, and is not willing to provide for, the full amount of the debt or claim, or if the amount is contingent or not ascertained, an amount fixed by the court after the like enquiry and adjudication as if the company were being wound up by the court.

647   Offences in connection with list of creditors

(1)   If an officer of the company—

    (a)   intentionally or recklessly—

        (i)   conceals the name of a creditor entitled to object to the reduction of capital, or

        (ii)   misrepresents the nature or amount of the debt or claim of a creditor, or

    (b)   is knowingly concerned in any such concealment or misrepresentation, he commits an offence.

(2)   A person guilty of an offence under this section is liable—

    (a)   on conviction on indictment, to a fine;

    (b)   on summary conviction, to a fine not exceeding the statutory maximum.

648   Court order confirming reduction

(1)   The court may make an order confirming the reduction of capital on such terms and conditions as it thinks fit.

(2)   The court must not confirm the reduction unless it is satisfied, with respect to every creditor of the company who is entitled to object to the reduction of capital that either—

    (a)   his consent to the reduction has been obtained, or

    (b)   his debt or claim has been discharged, or has determined or has been secured.

(3)   Where the court confirms the reduction, it may order the company to publish (as the court directs) the reasons for reduction of capital, or such other information in regard to it as the court thinks expedient with a view to giving proper information to the public, and (if the court thinks fit) the causes that led to the reduction.

(4)   The court may, if for any special reason it thinks proper to do so, make an order directing that the company must, during such period (commencing on or at any time after the date of the order) as is specified in the order, add to its name as its last words the words "and reduced".

    If such an order is made, those words are, until the end of the period specified in the order, deemed to be part of the company's name.

649 Registration of order and statement of capital

(1) The registrar, on the delivery of a copy of a court order confirming the reduction of a company's share capital and of a statement of capital (approved by the court), shall register the order and statement.

This is subject to section 650 (public company reducing capital below authorised minimum).

(2) The statement of capital must state with respect to the company's share capital as altered by the order—

(a) the total number of shares of the company,

(b) the aggregate nominal value of those shares,

(ba) the aggregate amount (if any) unpaid on those shares (whether on account of their nominal value or by way of premium), and

(c) for each class of shares—

    (i) prescribed particulars of the rights attached to the shares,

    (ii) the total number of shares of that class, and

    (iii) the aggregate nominal value of shares of that class, …

(d) …

(3) The resolution for reducing share capital, as confirmed by the court's order, takes effect—

(a) in the case of a reduction of share capital that forms part of a compromise or arrangement sanctioned by the court under Part 26 (arrangements and reconstructions: general)—

    (i) on delivery of the order and statement of capital to the registrar, or

    (ii) if the court so orders, on the registration of the order and statement of capital;

(aa) in the case of a reduction of share capital that forms part of a compromise or arrangement sanctioned by the court under Part 26A (arrangements and reconstructions: companies in financial difficulty)—

    (i) in the case of any company other than one to which sub-paragraph (ii) applies, on delivery of the order and statement of capital to the registrar;

    (ii) in the case of an overseas company that is not required to register particulars under section 1046, on publication of the order and statement of capital in the Gazette;

    (iii) in either case, if the court so orders, on the registration of the order and statement of capital;

(b) in any case not falling within paragraph (a) or (aa), on the registration of the order and statement of capital.

(4) Notice of the registration of the order and statement of capital must be published in such manner as the court may direct.

(5) The registrar must certify the registration of the order and statement of capital.

(6) The certificate—

(a) must be signed by the registrar or authenticated by the registrar's official seal, and

(b) is conclusive evidence—

    (i) that the requirements of this Act with respect to the reduction of share capital have been complied with, and

    (ii) that the company's share capital is as stated in the statement of capital.

Public company reducing capital below authorised minimum

650 Public company reducing capital below authorised minimum

(1) This section applies where the court makes an order confirming a reduction of a public company's capital that has the effect of bringing the nominal value of its allotted share capital below the authorised minimum.

(2) The registrar must not register the order unless either—

(a) the court so directs, or

(b) the company is first re-registered as a private company.

(3) Section 651 provides an expedited procedure for re-registration in these circumstances.

651   Expedited procedure for re-registration as a private company

(1)   The court may authorise the company to be re-registered as a private company without its having passed the special resolution required by section 97.

(2)   If it does so, the court must specify in the order the changes to the company's name and articles to be made in connection with the re-registration.

(3)   The company may then be re-registered as a private company if an application to that effect is delivered to the registrar together with—

    (a)   a copy of the court's order, and

    (b)   notice of the company's name, and a copy of the company's articles, as altered by the court's order.

(4)   On receipt of such an application the registrar must issue a certificate of incorporation altered to meet the circumstances of the case.

(5)   The certificate must state that it is issued on re-registration and the date on which it is issued.

(6)   On the issue of the certificate—

    (a)   the company by virtue of the issue of the certificate becomes a private company, and

    (b)   the changes in the company's name and articles take effect.

(7)   The certificate is conclusive evidence that the requirements of this Act as to re-registration have been complied with.

Effect of reduction of capital

652   Liability of members following reduction of capital

(1)   Where a company's share capital is reduced a member of the company (past or present) is not liable in respect of any share to any call or contribution exceeding in amount the difference (if any) between—

    (a)   the nominal amount of the share as notified to the registrar in the statement of capital delivered under section 644, 649, 1028A or 1032A of this Act or paragraph 7 of Schedule 4 to the Small Business, Enterprise and Employment Act 2015, and

    (b)   the amount paid on the share or the reduced amount (if any) which is deemed to have been paid on it, as the case may be.

(2)   This is subject to section 653 (liability to creditor in case of omission from list).

(3)   Nothing in this section affects the rights of the contributories among themselves.

653   Liability to creditor in case of omission from list of creditors

(1)   This section applies where, in the case of a reduction of capital confirmed by the court—

    (a)   a creditor entitled to object to the reduction of share capital is by reason of his ignorance—

        (i)   of the proceedings for reduction of share capital, or

        (ii)   of their nature and effect with respect to his debt or claim, not entered on the list of creditors, and

    (b)   after the reduction of capital the company is unable to pay the amount of his debt or claim.

(2)   Every person who was a member of the company at the date on which the resolution for reducing capital took effect under section 649(3) is liable to contribute for the payment of the debt or claim an amount not exceeding that which he would have been liable to contribute if the company had commenced to be wound up on the day before that date.

(3)   If the company is wound up, the court on the application of the creditor in question, and proof of ignorance as mentioned in subsection (1)(a), may if it thinks fit—

    (a)   settle accordingly a list of persons liable to contribute under this section, and

    (b)   make and enforce calls and orders on them as if they were ordinary contributories in a winding up.

(4)   The reference in subsection (1)(b) to a company being unable to pay the amount of a debt or claim has the same meaning as in section 123 of the Insolvency Act 1986 or Article 103 of the Insolvency (Northern Ireland) Order 1989.

CHAPTER 11
MISCELLANEOUS AND SUPPLEMENTARY PROVISIONS

654   Treatment of reserve arising from reduction of capital

(1)   A reserve arising from the reduction of a company's share capital is not distributable, subject to any provision made by order under this section.

(2)   The Secretary of State may by order specify cases in which—

(a)   the prohibition in subsection (1) does not apply, and

(b)   the reserve is to be treated for the purposes of Part 23 (distributions) as a realised profit.

(3)   An order under this section is subject to affirmative resolution procedure.

655   Shares no bar to damages against company

A person is not debarred from obtaining damages or other compensation from a company by reason only of his holding or having held shares in the company or any right to apply or subscribe for shares or to be included in the company's register of members (or have his name and other particulars delivered to the registrar under Chapter 2A of Part 8 and registered by the registrar) in respect of shares.

656   Public companies: duty of directors to call meeting on serious loss of capital

(1)   Where the net assets of a public company are half or less of its called-up share capital, the directors must call a general meeting of the company to consider whether any, and if so what, steps should be taken to deal with the situation.

(2)   They must do so not later than 28 days from the earliest day on which that fact is known to a director of the company.

(3)   The meeting must be convened for a date not later than 56 days from that day.

(4)   If there is a failure to convene a meeting as required by this section, each of the directors of the company who—

(a)   knowingly authorises or permits the failure, or

(b)   after the period during which the meeting should have been convened, knowingly authorises or permits the failure to continue,

commits an offence.

(5)   A person guilty of an offence under this section is liable—

(a)   on conviction on indictment, to a fine;

(b)   on summary conviction, to a fine not exceeding the statutory maximum.

(6)   Nothing in this section authorises the consideration at a meeting convened in pursuance of subsection (1) of any matter that could not have been considered at that meeting apart from this section.

657   General power to make further provision by regulations

(1)   The Secretary of State may by regulations modify the following provisions of this Part—

sections 552 and 553 (prohibited commissions, discounts and allowances),

Chapter 5 (payment for shares),

Chapter 6 (public companies: independent valuation of non-cash consideration),

Chapter 7 (share premiums),

sections 622 to 628 (redenomination of share capital),

Chapter 10 (reduction of capital), and

section 656 (public companies: duty of directors to call meeting on serious loss of capital).

(2)   The regulations may—

(a)   amend or repeal any of those provisions, or

(b)   make such other provision as appears to the Secretary of State appropriate in place of any of those provisions.

(3)   Regulations under this section may make consequential amendments or repeals in other provisions of this Act, or in other enactments.

(4)   Regulations under this section are subject to affirmative resolution procedure.

PART 18

ACQUISITION BY LIMITED COMPANY OF ITS OWN SHARES

CHAPTER 1
GENERAL PROVISIONS

Introductory

658 General rule against limited company acquiring its own shares

(1) A limited company must not acquire its own shares, whether by purchase, subscription or otherwise, except in accordance with the provisions of this Part.

(2) If a company purports to act in contravention of this section—

  (a) an offence is committed by—

    (i) the company, and

    (i) every officer of the company who is in default, and

  (b) the purported acquisition is void.

(3) A person guilty of an offence under this section is liable—

  (a) on conviction on indictment, to imprisonment for a term not exceeding two years or a fine (or both);

  (b) on summary conviction—

    (i) in England and Wales, to imprisonment for a term not exceeding twelve months or a fine not exceeding the statutory maximum (or both);

    (ii) in Scotland or Northern Ireland, to imprisonment for a term not exceeding six months or a fine not exceeding the statutory maximum (or both).

659 Exceptions to general rule

(1) A limited company may acquire any of its own fully paid shares otherwise than for valuable consideration.

(2) Section 658 does not prohibit—

  (a) the acquisition of shares in a reduction of capital duly made;

  (b) the purchase of shares in pursuance of an order of the court under—

    (i) section 98 (application to court to cancel resolution for re-registration as a private company),

    (ii) section 721(6) (powers of court on objection to redemption or purchase of shares out of capital),

    (iii) section 759 (remedial order in case of breach of prohibition of public offers by private company), or

    (iv) Part 30 (protection of members against unfair prejudice);

  (c) the forfeiture of shares, or the acceptance of shares surrendered in lieu, in pursuance of the company's articles, for failure to pay any sum payable in respect of the shares.

Shares held by company's nominee

660 Treatment of shares held by nominee

(1) This section applies where shares in a limited company—

  (a) are taken by a subscriber to the memorandum as nominee of the company,

  (b) are issued to a nominee of the company, or

  (c) are acquired by a nominee of the company, partly paid up, from a third person.

(2) For all purposes—

  (a) the shares are to be treated as held by the nominee on his own account, and

  (b) the company is to be regarded as having no beneficial interest in them.

(3) This section does not apply—

  (a) to shares acquired otherwise than by subscription by a nominee of a public company, where—

        (i)   a person acquires shares in the company with financial assistance given to him, directly or indirectly, by the company for the purpose of or in connection with the acquisition, and

        (ii)   the company has a beneficial interest in the shares;

(b) to shares acquired by a nominee of the company when the company has no beneficial interest in the shares.

661 Liability of others where nominee fails to make payment in respect of shares

(1) This section applies where shares in a limited company—

    (a) are taken by a subscriber to the memorandum as nominee of the company,

    (b) are issued to a nominee of the company, or

    (c) are acquired by a nominee of the company, partly paid up, from a third person.

(2) If the nominee, having been called on to pay any amount for the purposes of paying up, or paying any premium on, the shares, fails to pay that amount within 21 days from being called on to do so, then—

    (a) in the case of shares that he agreed to take as subscriber to the memorandum, the other subscribers to the memorandum, and

    (b) in any other case, the directors of the company when the shares were issued to or acquired by him,

are jointly and severally liable with him to pay that amount.

(3) If in proceedings for the recovery of an amount under subsection (2) it appears to the court that the subscriber or director—

    (a) has acted honestly and reasonably, and

    (b) having regard to all the circumstances of the case, ought fairly to be relieved from liability,

the court may relieve him, either wholly or in part, from his liability on such terms as the court thinks fit.

(4) If a subscriber to a company's memorandum or a director of a company has reason to apprehend that a claim will or might be made for the recovery of any such amount from him—

    (a) he may apply to the court for relief, and

    (b) the court has the same power to relieve him as it would have had in proceedings for recovery of that amount.

(5) This section does not apply to shares acquired by a nominee of the company when the company has no beneficial interest in the shares.

Shares held by or for public company

662 Duty to cancel shares in public company held by or for the company

(1) This section applies in the case of a public company—

    (a) where shares in the company are forfeited, or surrendered to the company in lieu of forfeiture, in pursuance of the articles, for failure to pay any sum payable in respect of the shares;

    (b) where shares in the company are surrendered to the company in pursuance of section 102C(1)(b) of the Building Societies Act 1986;

    (c) where shares in the company are acquired by it (otherwise than in accordance with this Part or Part 30 (protection of members against unfair prejudice)) and the company has a beneficial interest in the shares;

    (d) where a nominee of the company acquires shares in the company from a third party without financial assistance being given directly or indirectly by the company and the company has a beneficial interest in the shares; or

    (e) where a person acquires shares in the company, with financial assistance given to him, directly or indirectly, by the company for the purpose of or in connection with the acquisition, and the company has a beneficial interest in the shares.

(2) Unless the shares or any interest of the company in them are previously disposed of, the company must—

(a) cancel the shares and diminish the amount of the company's share capital by the nominal value of the shares cancelled, and

(b) where the effect is that the nominal value of the company's allotted share capital is brought below the authorised minimum, apply for re-registration as a private company, stating the effect of the cancellation.

(3) It must do so no later than—

(a) in a case within subsection (1)(a) or (b), three years from the date of the forfeiture or surrender;

(b) in a case within subsection (1)(c) or (d), three years from the date of the acquisition;

(c) in a case within subsection (1)(e), one year from the date of the acquisition.

(4) The directors of the company may take any steps necessary to enable the company to comply with this section, and may do so without complying with the provisions of Chapter 10 of Part 17 (reduction of capital).

See also section 664 (re-registration as private company in consequence of cancellation).

(5) Neither the company nor, in a case within subsection (1)(d) or (e), the nominee or other shareholder may exercise any voting rights in respect of the shares.

(6) Any purported exercise of those rights is void.

663 Notice of cancellation of shares

(1) Where a company cancels shares in order to comply with section 662, it must within one month after the shares are cancelled give notice to the registrar, specifying the shares cancelled.

(2) The notice must be accompanied by a statement of capital.

(3) The statement of capital must state with respect to the company's share capital immediately following the cancellation—

(a) the total number of shares of the company,

(b) the aggregate nominal value of those shares,

(ba) the aggregate amount (if any) unpaid on those shares (whether on account of their nominal value or by way of premium), and

(c) for each class of shares—

(i) prescribed particulars of the rights attached to the shares,

(ii) the total number of shares of that class, and

(iii) the aggregate nominal value of shares of that class, ...

(d) ...

(4) If default is made in complying with this section, an offence is committed by—

(a) the company, and

(b) every officer of the company who is in default.

(5) A person guilty of an offence under this section is liable on summary conviction to a fine not exceeding level 3 on the standard scale and, for continued contravention, a daily default fine not exceeding one-tenth of level 3 on the standard scale.

664 Re-registration as private company in consequence of cancellation

(1) Where a company is obliged to re-register as a private company to comply with section 662, the directors may resolve that the company should be so re-registered.

Chapter 3 of Part 3 (resolutions affecting a company's constitution) applies to any such resolution.

(2) The resolution may make such changes—

(a) in the company's name, and

(b) in the company's articles,

as are necessary in connection with its becoming a private company.

(3) The application for re-registration must contain a statement of the company's proposed name on re-registration.

(4) The application must be accompanied by—

(a) a copy of the resolution (unless a copy has already been forwarded under Chapter 3 of Part 3),

(b)   a copy of the company's articles as amended by the resolution, and

(c)   a statement of compliance.

(5)   The statement of compliance required is a statement that the requirements of this section as to re-registration as a private company have been complied with.

(6)   The registrar may accept the statement of compliance as sufficient evidence that the company is entitled to be re-registered as a private company.

665   Issue of certificate of incorporation on re-registration

(1)   If on an application under section 664 the registrar is satisfied that the company is entitled to be re-registered as a private company, the company shall be re-registered accordingly.

(2)   The registrar must issue a certificate of incorporation altered to meet the circumstances of the case.

(3)   The certificate must state that it is issued on re-registration and the date on which it is issued.

(4)   On the issue of the certificate—

(a)   the company by virtue of the issue of the certificate becomes a private company, and

(b)   the changes in the company's name and articles take effect.

(5)   The certificate is conclusive evidence that the requirements of this Act as to re-registration have been complied with.

666   Effect of failure to re-register

(1)   If a public company that is required by section 662 to apply to be re-registered as a private company fails to do so before the end of the period specified in subsection (3) of that section, Chapter 1 of Part 20 (prohibition of public offers by private company) applies to it as if it were a private company.

(2)   Subject to that, the company continues to be treated as a public company until it is so re-registered.

667   Offence in case of failure to cancel shares or re-register

(1)   This section applies where a company, when required to do by section 662—

(a)   fails to cancel any shares, or

(b)   fails to make an application for re-registration as a private company, within the time specified in subsection (3) of that section.

(2)   An offence is committed by—

(a)   the company, and

(b)   every officer of the company who is in default.

(3)   A person guilty of an offence under this section is liable on summary conviction to a fine not exceeding level 3 on the standard scale and, for continued contravention, a daily default fine not exceeding one-tenth of level 3 on the standard scale.

668   Application of provisions to company re-registering as public company

(1)   This section applies where, after shares in a private company—

(a)   are forfeited in pursuance of the company's articles or are surrendered to the company in lieu of forfeiture,

(b)   are acquired by the company (otherwise than by any of the methods permitted by this Part or Part 30 (protection of members against unfair prejudice)), the company having a beneficial interest in the shares,

(c)   are acquired by a nominee of the company from a third party without financial assistance being given directly or indirectly by the company, the company having a beneficial interest in the shares, or

(d)   are acquired by a person with financial assistance given to him, directly or indirectly, by the company for the purpose of or in connection with the acquisition, the company having a beneficial interest in the shares,

the company is re-registered as a public company.

(2)   In that case the provisions of sections 662 to 667 apply to the company as if it had been a public company at the time of the forfeiture, surrender or acquisition, subject to the following modification.

(3)   The modification is that the period specified in section 662(3)(a), (b) or (c) (period for complying with obligations under that section) runs from the date of the re-registration of the company as a public company.

669   Transfer to reserve on acquisition of shares by public company or nominee

(1)   Where—

(a)   a public company, or a nominee of a public company, acquires shares in the company, and

(b)   those shares are shown in a balance sheet of the company as an asset, an amount equal to the value of the shares must be transferred out of profits available for dividend to a reserve fund and is not then available for distribution.

(2)   Subsection (1) applies to an interest in shares as it applies to shares.

As it so applies the reference to the value of the shares shall be read as a reference to the value to the company of its interest in the shares.

Charges of public company on own shares

670   Public companies: general rule against lien or charge on own shares

(1)   A lien or other charge of a public company on its own shares (whether taken expressly or otherwise) is void, except as permitted by this section.

(2)   In the case of any description of company, a charge is permitted if the shares are not fully paid up and the charge is for an amount payable in respect of the shares.

(3)   In the case of a company whose ordinary business—

(a)   includes the lending of money, or

(b)   consists of the provision of credit or the bailment (in Scotland, hiring) of goods under a hire-purchase agreement, or both,

a charge is permitted (whether the shares are fully paid or not) if it arises in connection with a transaction entered into by the company in the ordinary course of that business.

(4)   In the case of a company that has been re-registered as a public company, a charge is permitted if it was in existence immediately before the application for re-registration.

Supplementary provisions

671   Interests to be disregarded in determining whether company has beneficial interest

In determining for the purposes of this Chapter whether a company has a beneficial interest in shares, there shall be disregarded any such interest as is mentioned in—

section 672 (residual interest under pension scheme or employees' share scheme),

section 673 (employer's charges and other rights of recovery), or section 674 (rights as personal representative or trustee).

672   Residual interest under pension scheme or employees' share scheme

(1)   Where the shares are held on trust for the purposes of a pension scheme or employees' share scheme, there shall be disregarded any residual interest of the company that has not vested in possession.

(2)   A "residual interest" means a right of the company to receive any of the trust property in the event of—

(a)   all the liabilities arising under the scheme having been satisfied or provided for, or

(b)   the company ceasing to participate in the scheme, or

(c)   the trust property at any time exceeding what is necessary for satisfying the liabilities arising or expected to arise under the scheme.

(3)   In subsection (2)—

(a)   the reference to a right includes a right dependent on the exercise of a discretion vested by the scheme in the trustee or another person, and

      (b)   the reference to liabilities arising under a scheme includes liabilities that have resulted, or may result, from the exercise of any such discretion.

(4)   For the purposes of this section a residual interest vests in possession—

      (a)   in a case within subsection (2)(a), on the occurrence of the event mentioned there (whether or not the amount of the property receivable pursuant to the right is ascertained);

      (b)   in a case within subsection (2)(b) or (c), when the company becomes entitled to require the trustee to transfer to it any of the property receivable pursuant to that right.

(5)   Where by virtue of this section shares are exempt from section 660 or 661 (shares held by company's nominee) at the time they are taken, issued or acquired but the residual interest in question vests in possession before they are disposed of or fully paid up, those sections apply to the shares as if they had been taken, issued or acquired on the date on which that interest vests in possession.

(6)   Where by virtue of this section shares are exempt from sections 662 to 668 (shares held by or for public company) at the time they are acquired but the residual interest in question vests in possession before they are disposed of, those sections apply to the shares as if they had been acquired on the date on which the interest vests in possession.

673   Employer's charges and other rights of recovery

(1)   Where the shares are held on trust for the purposes of a pension scheme there shall be disregarded—

      (a)   any charge or lien on, or set-off against, any benefit or other right or interest under the scheme for the purpose of enabling the employer or former employer of a member of the scheme to obtain the discharge of a monetary obligation due to him from the member;

      (b)   any right to receive from the trustee of the scheme, or as trustee of the scheme to retain, an amount that can be recovered or retained—

            (i)   ...

            (ii)   under section 57 of the Pension Schemes (Northern Ireland) Act 1993, or otherwise, as reimbursement or partial reimbursement for any contributions equivalent premium paid in connection with the scheme under Part 3 of that Act.

(2)   Where the shares are held on trust for the purposes of an employees' share scheme, there shall be disregarded any charge or lien on, or set-off against, any benefit or other right or interest under the scheme for the purpose of enabling the employer or former employer of a member of the scheme to obtain the discharge of a monetary obligation due to him from the member.

674   Rights as personal representative or trustee

Where the company is a personal representative or trustee, there shall be disregarded any rights that the company has in that capacity including, in particular—

      (a)   any right to recover its expenses or be remunerated out of the estate or trust property, and

      (b)   any right to be indemnified out of that property for any liability incurred by reason of any act or omission of the company in the performance of its duties as personal representative or trustee.

675   Meaning of "pension scheme"

(1)   In this Chapter "pension scheme" means a scheme for the provision of benefits consisting of or including relevant benefits for or in respect of employees or former employees.

(2)   In subsection (1) "relevant benefits" means any pension, lump sum, gratuity or other like benefit given or to be given on retirement or on death or in anticipation of retirement or, in connection with past service, after retirement or death.

676   Application of provisions to directors

For the purposes of this Chapter references to "employer" and "employee", in the context of a pension scheme or employees' share scheme, shall be read as if a director of a company were employed by it.

CHAPTER 2
FINANCIAL ASSISTANCE FOR PURCHASE OF OWN SHARES

Introductory

677   Meaning of "financial assistance"

(1)   In this Chapter "financial assistance" means—
  (a)   financial assistance given by way of gift,
  (b)   financial assistance given—
    (i)   by way of guarantee, security or indemnity (other than an indemnity in respect of the indemnifier's own neglect or default), or
    (ii)   by way of release or waiver,
  (c)   financial assistance given—
    (i)   by way of a loan or any other agreement under which any of the obligations of the person giving the assistance are to be fulfilled at a time when in accordance with the agreement any obligation of another party to the agreement remains unfulfilled, or
    (ii)   by way of the novation of, or the assignment (in Scotland, assignation) of rights arising under, a loan or such other agreement, or
  (d)   any other financial assistance given by a company where—
    (i)   the net assets of the company are reduced to a material extent by the giving of the assistance, or
    (ii)   the company has no net assets.

(2)   "Net assets" here means the aggregate amount of the company's assets less the aggregate amount of its liabilities.

(3)   For this purpose a company's liabilities include—
  (a)   where the company draws up Companies Act individual accounts, any provision of a kind specified for the purposes of this subsection by regulations under section 396, and
  (b)   where the company draws up IAS individual accounts, any provision made in those accounts.

Circumstances in which financial assistance prohibited

678   Assistance for acquisition of shares in public company

(1)   Where a person is acquiring or proposing to acquire shares in a public company, it is not lawful for that company, or a company that is a subsidiary of that company, to give financial assistance directly or indirectly for the purpose of the acquisition before or at the same time as the acquisition takes place.

(2)   Subsection (1) does not prohibit a company from giving financial assistance for the acquisition of shares in it or its holding company if—
  (a)   the company's principal purpose in giving the assistance is not to give it for the purpose of any such acquisition, or
  (b)   the giving of the assistance for that purpose is only an incidental part of some larger purpose of the company,
  and the assistance is given in good faith in the interests of the company.

(3)   Where—
  (a)   a person has acquired shares in a company, and
  (b)   a liability has been incurred (by that or another person) for the purpose of the acquisition,
  it is not lawful for that company, or a company that is a subsidiary of that company, to give financial assistance directly or indirectly for the purpose of reducing or discharging the liability if, at the time the assistance is given, the company in which the shares were acquired is a public company.

(4)   Subsection (3) does not prohibit a company from giving financial assistance if—

(a)   the company's principal purpose in giving the assistance is not to reduce or discharge any liability incurred by a person for the purpose of the acquisition of shares in the company or its holding company, or

(b)   the reduction or discharge of any such liability is only an incidental part of some larger purpose of the company,

and the assistance is given in good faith in the interests of the company.

(5)   This section has effect subject to sections 681 and 682 (unconditional and conditional exceptions to prohibition).

679   Assistance by public company for acquisition of shares in its private holding company

(1)   Where a person is acquiring or proposing to acquire shares in a private company, it is not lawful for a public company that is a subsidiary of that company to give financial assistance directly or indirectly for the purpose of the acquisition before or at the same time as the acquisition takes place.

(2)   Subsection (1) does not prohibit a company from giving financial assistance for the acquisition of shares in its holding company if—

(a)   the company's principal purpose in giving the assistance is not to give it for the purpose of any such acquisition, or

(b)   the giving of the assistance for that purpose is only an incidental part of some larger purpose of the company,

and the assistance is given in good faith in the interests of the company.

(3)   Where—

(a)   a person has acquired shares in a private company, and

(b)   a liability has been incurred (by that or another person) for the purpose of the acquisition,

it is not lawful for a public company that is a subsidiary of that company to give financial assistance directly or indirectly for the purpose of reducing or discharging the liability.

(4)   Subsection (3) does not prohibit a company from giving financial assistance if—

(a)   the company's principal purpose in giving the assistance is not to reduce or discharge any liability incurred by a person for the purpose of the acquisition of shares in its holding company, or

(b)   the reduction or discharge of any such liability is only an incidental part of some larger purpose of the company,

and the assistance is given in good faith in the interests of the company.

(5)   This section has effect subject to sections 681 and 682 (unconditional and conditional exceptions to prohibition).

680   Prohibited financial assistance an offence

(1)   If a company contravenes section 678(1) or (3) or section 679(1) or (3) (prohibited financial assistance) an offence is committed by—

(a)   the company, and

(b)   every officer of the company who is in default.

(2)   A person guilty of an offence under this section is liable—

(a)   on conviction on indictment, to imprisonment for a term not exceeding two years or a fine (or both);

(b)   on summary conviction

(i)   in England and Wales, to imprisonment for a term not exceeding twelve months or to a fine not exceeding the statutory maximum (or both);

(ii)   in Scotland or Northern Ireland, to imprisonment for a term not exceeding six months, or to a fine not exceeding the statutory maximum (or both).

Exceptions from prohibition

681   Unconditional exceptions

(1)   Neither section 678 nor section 679 prohibits a transaction to which this section applies.

(2)   Those transactions are—

      (a)   a distribution of the company's assets by way of—

          (i)   dividend lawfully made, or

          (ii)   distribution in the course of a company's winding up;

      (b)   an allotment of bonus shares;

      (c)   a reduction of capital under Chapter 10 of Part 17;

      (d)   a redemption of shares under Chapter 3 or a purchase of shares under Chapter 4 of this Part;

      (e)   anything done in pursuance of an order of the court under Part 26 or 26A (order sanctioning compromise or arrangement with members or creditors);

      (f)   anything done under an arrangement made in pursuance of section 110 of the Insolvency Act 1986 or Article 96 of the Insolvency (Northern Ireland) Order 1989 (liquidator in winding up accepting shares as consideration for sale of company's property);

      (g)   anything done under an arrangement made between a company and its creditors that is binding on the creditors by virtue of Part 1 of the Insolvency Act 1986 or Part 2 of the Insolvency (Northern Ireland) Order 1989.

682   Conditional exceptions

(1)   Neither section 678 nor section 679 prohibits a transaction to which this section applies—

      (a)   if the company giving the assistance is a private company, or

      (b)   if the company giving the assistance is a public company and—

          (i)   the company has net assets that are not reduced by the giving of the assistance, or

          (ii)   to the extent that those assets are so reduced, the assistance is provided out of distributable profits.

(2)   The transactions to which this section applies are—

      (a)   where the lending of money is part of the ordinary business of the company, the lending of money in the ordinary course of the company's business;

      (b)   the provision by the company, in good faith in the interests of the company or its holding company, of financial assistance for the purposes of an employees' share scheme;

      (c)   the provision of financial assistance by the company for the purposes of or in connection with anything done by the company (or another company in the same group) for the purpose of enabling or facilitating transactions in shares in the first-mentioned company or its holding company between, and involving the acquisition of beneficial ownership of those shares by—

          (i)   bona fide employees or former employees of that company (or another company in the same group), or

          (ii)   spouses or civil partners, widows, widowers or surviving civil partners, or minor children or step-children of any such employees or former employees;

      (d)   the making by the company of loans to persons (other than directors) employed in good faith by the company with a view to enabling those persons to acquire fully paid shares in the company or its holding company to be held by them by way of beneficial ownership.

(3)   The references in this section to "net assets" are to the amount by which the aggregate of the company's assets exceeds the aggregate of its liabilities.

(4)   For this purpose—

      (a)   the amount of both assets and liabilities shall be taken to be as stated in the company's accounting records immediately before the financial assistance is given, and

      (b)   "liabilities" includes any amount retained as reasonably necessary for the purpose of providing for a liability the nature of which is clearly defined and that is either likely to be incurred or certain to be incurred but uncertain as to amount or as to the date on which it will arise.

(5)   For the purposes of subsection (2)(c) a company is in the same group as another company if it is a holding company or subsidiary of that company or a subsidiary of a holding company of that company.

Supplementary

683 Definitions for this Chapter

(1) In this Chapter—

"distributable profits", in relation to the giving of any financial assistance—

(a) means those profits out of which the company could lawfully make a distribution equal in value to that assistance, and

(b) includes, in a case where the financial assistance consists of or includes, or is treated as arising in consequence of, the sale, transfer or other disposition of a non-cash asset, any profit that, if the company were to make a distribution of that character would be available for that purpose (see section 846); and

"distribution" has the same meaning as in Part 23 (distributions) (see section 829).

(2) In this Chapter—

(a) a reference to a person incurring a liability includes his changing his financial position by making an agreement or arrangement (whether enforceable or unenforceable, and whether made on his own account or with any other person) or by any other means, and

(b) a reference to a company giving financial assistance for the purposes of reducing or discharging a liability incurred by a person for the purpose of the acquisition of shares includes its giving such assistance for the purpose of wholly or partly restoring his financial position to what it was before the acquisition took place.

CHAPTER 3
REDEEMABLE SHARES

684 Power of limited company to issue redeemable shares

(1) A limited company having a share capital may issue shares that are to be redeemed or are liable to be redeemed at the option of the company or the shareholder ("redeemable shares"), subject to the following provisions.

(2) The articles of a private limited company may exclude or restrict the issue of redeemable shares.

(3) A public limited company may only issue redeemable shares if it is authorised to do so by its articles.

(4) No redeemable shares may be issued at a time when there are no issued shares of the company that are not redeemable.

685 Terms and manner of redemption

(1) The directors of a limited company may determine the terms, conditions and manner of redemption of shares if they are authorised to do so—

(a) by the company's articles, or

(b) by a resolution of the company.

(2) A resolution under subsection (1)(b) may be an ordinary resolution, even though it amends the company's articles.

(3) Where the directors are authorised under subsection (1) to determine the terms, conditions and manner of redemption of shares—

(a) they must do so before the shares are allotted, and

(b) any obligation of the company to state in a statement of capital the rights attached to the shares extends to the terms, conditions and manner of redemption.

(4) Where the directors are not so authorised, the terms, conditions and manner of redemption of any redeemable shares must be stated in the company's articles.

686 Payment for redeemable shares

(1) Redeemable shares in a limited company may not be redeemed unless they are fully paid.

(2) The terms of redemption of shares in a limited company may provide that the amount payable on redemption may, by agreement between the company and the holder of the shares, be paid on a date later than the redemption date.

(3)   Unless redeemed in accordance with a provision authorised by subsection (2), the shares must be paid for on redemption.

687   Financing of redemption

(1)   A private limited company may redeem redeemable shares out of capital in accordance with Chapter 5.

(2)   Subject to that, redeemable shares in a limited company may only be redeemed out of—
         (a)   distributable profits of the company, or
         (b)   the proceeds of a fresh issue of shares made for the purposes of the redemption.

(3)   Any premium payable on redemption of shares in a limited company must be paid out of distributable profits of the company, subject to the following provision.

(4)   If the redeemable shares were issued at a premium, any premium payable on their redemption may be paid out of the proceeds of a fresh issue of shares made for the purposes of the redemption, up to an amount equal to—
         (a)   the aggregate of the premiums received by the company on the issue of the shares redeemed, or
         (b)   the current amount of the company's share premium account (including any sum transferred to that account in respect of premiums on the new shares),
         whichever is the less.

(5)   The amount of the company's share premium account is reduced by a sum corresponding (or by sums in the aggregate corresponding) to the amount of any payment made under subsection (4).

(6)   This section is subject to section 735(4) (terms of redemption enforceable in a winding up).

688   Redeemed shares treated as cancelled

Where shares in a limited company are redeemed—
         (a)   the shares are treated as cancelled, and
         (b)   the amount of the company's issued share capital is diminished accordingly by the nominal value of the shares redeemed.

689   Notice to registrar of redemption

(1)   If a limited company redeems any redeemable shares it must within one month after doing so give notice to the registrar, specifying the shares redeemed.

(2)   The notice must be accompanied by a statement of capital.

(3)   The statement of capital must state with respect to the company's share capital immediately following the redemption—
         (a)   the total number of shares of the company,
         (b)   the aggregate nominal value of those shares,
         (ba)   the aggregate amount (if any) unpaid on those shares (whether on account of their nominal value or by way of premium), and
         (c)   for each class of shares—
                (i)   prescribed particulars of the rights attached to the shares,
                (ii)   the total number of shares of that class, and
                (iii)   the aggregate nominal value of shares of that class, ...
         (d)   ...

(4)   If default is made in complying with this section, an offence is committed by—
         (a)   the company, and
         (b)   every officer of the company who is in default.

(5)   A person guilty of an offence under this section is liable on summary conviction to a fine not exceeding level 3 on the standard scale and, for continued contravention, a daily default fine not exceeding one-tenth of level 3 on the standard scale.

CHAPTER 4
PURCHASE OF OWN SHARES

General provisions

690 Power of limited company to purchase own shares

(1) A limited company having a share capital may purchase its own shares (including any redeemable shares), subject to—

(a) the following provisions of this Chapter, and

(b) any restriction or prohibition in the company's articles.

(2) A limited company may not purchase its own shares if as a result of the purchase there would no longer be any issued shares of the company other than redeemable shares or shares held as treasury shares.

691 Payment for purchase of own shares

(1) A limited company may not purchase its own shares unless they are fully paid.

(2) Where a limited company purchases its own shares, the shares must be paid for on purchase.

(3) But subsection (2) does not apply in a case where a private limited company is purchasing shares for the purposes of or pursuant to an employees' share scheme.

692 Financing of purchase of own shares

(1) A private limited company may purchase its own shares out of capital in accordance with Chapter 5.

(1ZA) If authorised to do so by its articles, a private limited company may purchase its own shares out of capital otherwise than in accordance with Chapter 5, up to an aggregate purchase price in a financial year of the lower of—

(a) £15,000, or

(b) the nominal value of 5% of its fully paid share capital as at the beginning of the financial year.

(1A) If the share capital of the company is not denominated in sterling, the value in sterling of the share capital shall be calculated for the purposes of subsection (1ZA)(b) at an appropriate spot rate of exchange.

(1B) The rate must be a rate prevailing on a day specified in the resolution authorising the purchase of the shares.

(2) Subject to subsections (1) and (1ZA)—

(a) a limited company may only purchase its own shares out of—

(i) distributable profits of the company, or

(ii) the proceeds of a fresh issue of shares made for the purpose of financing the purchase, and

(b) any premium payable on the purchase by a limited company of its own shares must be paid out of distributable profits of the company, subject to subsection (3).

(3) If the shares to be purchased were issued at a premium, any premium payable on their purchase by the company may be paid out of the proceeds of a fresh issue of shares made for the purpose of financing the purchase, up to an amount equal to—

(a) the aggregate of the premiums received by the company on the issue of the shares purchased, or

(b) the current amount of the company's share premium account (including any sum transferred to that account in respect of premiums on the new shares),

whichever is the less.

(4) The amount of the company's share premium account is reduced by a sum corresponding (or by sums in the aggregate corresponding) to the amount of any payment made under subsection (3).

(5) This section has effect subject to section 735(4) (terms of purchase enforceable in a winding up).

Authority for purchase of own shares

693   Authority for purchase of own shares

(1)   A limited company may only purchase its own shares—

   (a)   by an off-market purchase, authorised in accordance with section 693A or in pursuance of a contract approved in advance in accordance with section 694;

   (b)   by a market purchase, authorised in accordance with section 701.

(2)   A purchase is "off-market" if the shares either—

   (a)   are purchased otherwise than on a recognised investment exchange, or

   (b)   are purchased on a recognised investment exchange but are not subject to a marketing arrangement on the exchange.

(3)   For this purpose a company's shares are subject to a marketing arrangement on a recognised investment exchange if—

   (a)   they are listed under Part 6 of the Financial Services and Markets Act 2000, or

   (b)   the company has been afforded facilities for dealings in the shares to take place on the exchange—

      (i)   without prior permission for individual transactions from the authority governing that investment exchange, and

      (ii)   without limit as to the time during which those facilities are to be available.

(4)   A purchase is a "market purchase" if it is made on a recognised investment exchange and is not an off-market purchase by virtue of subsection (2)(b).

(5)   In this section "recognised investment exchange" means a recognised investment exchange (within the meaning of Part 18 of the Financial Services and Markets Act 2000) other than an overseas exchange (within the meaning of that Part).

693A   Authority for off-market purchase for the purposes of or pursuant to an employees' share scheme

(1)   A company may make an off-market purchase of its own shares for the purposes of or pursuant to an employees' share scheme if the purchase has first been authorised by a resolution of the company under this section.

(2)   That authority—

   (a)   may be general or limited to the purchase of shares of a particular class or description, and

   (b)   may be unconditional or subject to conditions.

(3)   The authority must—

   (a)   specify the maximum number of shares authorised to be acquired, and

   (b)   determine both the maximum and minimum prices that may be paid for the shares.

(4)   The authority may be varied, revoked or from time to time renewed by a resolution of the company.

(5)   A resolution conferring, varying or renewing authority must specify a date on which it is to expire, which must not be later than five years after the date on which the resolution is passed.

(6)   A company may make a purchase of its own shares after the expiry of the time limit specified if—

   (a)   the contract of purchase was concluded before the authority expired, and

   (b)   the terms of the authority permitted the company to make a contract of purchase that would or might be executed wholly or partly after its expiration.

(7)   A resolution to confer or vary authority under this section may determine the maximum or minimum price for purchase by—

   (a)   specifying a particular sum, or

   (b)   providing a basis or formula for calculating the amount of the price (but without reference to any person's discretion or opinion).

(8)   Chapter 3 of Part 3 (resolutions affecting a company's constitution) applies to a resolution under this section.

Authority for off-market purchase

694 Authority for off-market purchase

(1) Subject to section 693A, a company may only make an off-market purchase of its own shares in pursuance of a contract approved prior to the purchase in accordance with this section.

(2) Either—

(a) the terms of the contract must be authorised by a ... resolution of the company before the contract is entered into, or

(b) the contract must provide that no shares may be purchased in pursuance of the contract until its terms have been authorised by a ... resolution of the company.

(3) The contract may be a contract, entered into by the company and relating to shares in the company, that does not amount to a contract to purchase the shares but under which the company may (subject to any conditions) become entitled or obliged to purchase the shares.

(4) The authority conferred by a resolution under this section may be varied, revoked or from time to time renewed by a ... resolution of the company.

(5) In the case of a public company a resolution conferring, varying or renewing authority must specify a date on which the authority is to expire, which must not be later than five years after the date on which the resolution is passed.

(6) A resolution conferring, varying, revoking or renewing authority under this section is subject to—

section 695 (exercise of voting rights), and

section 696 (disclosure of details of contract).

695 Resolution authorising off-market purchase: exercise of voting rights

(1) This section applies to a resolution to confer, vary, revoke or renew authority for the purposes of section 694 (authority for off-market purchase of own shares).

(2) Where the resolution is proposed as a written resolution, a member who holds shares to which the resolution relates is not an eligible member.

(3) Where the resolution is proposed at a meeting of the company, it is not effective if—

(a) any member of the company holding shares to which the resolution relates exercises the voting rights carried by any of those shares in voting on the resolution, and

(b) the resolution would not have been passed if he had not done so.

(4) For this purpose—

(a) a member who holds shares to which the resolution relates is regarded as exercising the voting rights carried by those shares not only if he votes in respect of them on a poll on the question whether the resolution shall be passed, but also if he votes on the resolution otherwise than on a poll;

(b) any member of the company may demand a poll on that question;

(c) a vote and a demand for a poll by a person as proxy for a member are the same respectively as a vote and a demand by the member.

696 Resolution authorising off-market purchase: disclosure of details of contract

(1) This section applies in relation to a resolution to confer, vary, revoke or renew authority for the purposes of section 694 (authority for off-market purchase of own shares).

(2) A copy of the contract (if it is in writing) or a memorandum setting out its terms (if it is not) must be made available to members—

(a) in the case of a written resolution, by being sent or submitted to every eligible member at or before the time at which the proposed resolution is sent or submitted to him;

(b) in the case of a resolution at a meeting, by being made available for inspection by members of the company both—

(i) at the company's registered office for not less than 15 days ending with the date of the meeting, and

(ii) at the meeting itself.

(3) A memorandum of contract terms so made available must include the names of the members holding shares to which the contract relates.

(4)   A copy of the contract so made available must have annexed to it a written memorandum specifying such of those names as do not appear in the contract itself.

(5)   The resolution is not validly passed if the requirements of this section are not complied with

697   Variation of contract for off-market purchase

(1)   A company may only agree to a variation of a contract authorised under section 694 (authority for off-market purchase) if the variation is approved in advance in accordance with this section.

(2)   The terms of the variation must be authorised by a … resolution of the company before it is agreed to.

(3)   That authority may be varied, revoked or from time to time renewed by a … resolution of the company.

(4)   In the case of a public company a resolution conferring, varying or renewing authority must specify a date on which the authority is to expire, which must not be later than five years after the date on which the resolution is passed.

(5)   A resolution conferring, varying, revoking or renewing authority under this section is subject to—
        section 698 (exercise of voting rights), and
        section 699 (disclosure of details of variation).

698   Resolution authorising variation: exercise of voting rights

(1)   This section applies to a resolution to confer, vary, revoke or renew authority for the purposes of section 697 (variation of contract for off-market purchase of own shares).

(2)   Where the resolution is proposed as a written resolution, a member who holds shares to which the resolution relates is not an eligible member.

(3)   Where the resolution is proposed at a meeting of the company, it is not effective if—
        (a)   any member of the company holding shares to which the resolution relates exercises the voting rights carried by any of those shares in voting on the resolution, and
        (b)   the resolution would not have been passed if he had not done so.

(4)   For this purpose—
        (a)   a member who holds shares to which the resolution relates is regarded as exercising the voting rights carried by those shares not only if he votes in respect of them on a poll on the question whether the resolution shall be passed, but also if he votes on the resolution otherwise than on a poll;
        (b)   any member of the company may demand a poll on that question;
        (c)   a vote and a demand for a poll by a person as proxy for a member are the same respectively as a vote and a demand by the member.

699   Resolution authorising variation: disclosure of details of variation

(1)   This section applies in relation to a resolution under section 697 (variation of contract for off-market purchase of own shares).

(2)   A copy of the proposed variation (if it is in writing) or a written memorandum giving details of the proposed variation (if it is not) must be made available to members—
        (a)   in the case of a written resolution, by being sent or submitted to every eligible member at or before the time at which the proposed resolution is sent or submitted to him;
        (b)   in the case of a resolution at a meeting, by being made available for inspection by members of the company both—
                (i)   at the company's registered office for not less than 15 days ending with the date of the meeting, and
                (ii)   at the meeting itself.

(3)   There must also be made available as mentioned in subsection (2) a copy of the original contract or, as the case may be, a memorandum of its terms, together with any variations previously made.

(4)   A memorandum of the proposed variation so made available must include the names of the members holding shares to which the variation relates.

(5)   A copy of the proposed variation so made available must have annexed to it a written memorandum specifying such of those names as do not appear in the variation itself.

(6)   The resolution is not validly passed if the requirements of this section are not complied with.

700   Release of company's rights under contract for off-market purchase

(1)   An agreement by a company to release its rights under a contract approved under section 694 (authorisation of off-market purchase) is void unless the terms of the release agreement are approved in advance in accordance with this section.

(2)   The terms of the proposed agreement must be authorised by a ... resolution of the company before the agreement is entered into.

(3)   That authority may be varied, revoked or from time to time renewed by a ... resolution of the company.

(4)   In the case of a public company a resolution conferring, varying or renewing authority must specify a date on which the authority is to expire, which must not be later than five years after the date on which the resolution is passed.

(5)   The provisions of—
section 698 (exercise of voting rights), and
section 699 (disclosure of details of variation),
apply to a resolution authorising a proposed release agreement as they apply to a resolution authorising a proposed variation.

Authority for market purchase

701   Authority for market purchase

(1)   A company may only make a market purchase of its own shares if the purchase has first been authorised by a resolution of the company.

(2)   That authority—
(a)   may be general or limited to the purchase of shares of a particular class or description, and
(b)   may be unconditional or subject to conditions.

(3)   The authority must—
(a)   specify the maximum number of shares authorised to be acquired, and
(b)   determine both the maximum and minimum prices that may be paid for the shares.

(4)   The authority may be varied, revoked or from time to time renewed by a resolution of the company.

(5)   A resolution conferring, varying or renewing authority must specify a date on which it is to expire, which must not be later than five years after the date on which the resolution is passed.

(6)   A company may make a purchase of its own shares after the expiry of the time limit specified if—
(a)   the contract of purchase was concluded before the authority expired, and
(b)   the terms of the authority permitted the company to make a contract of purchase that would or might be executed wholly or partly after its expiration.

(7)   A resolution to confer or vary authority under this section may determine either or both the maximum and minimum price for purchase by—
(a)   specifying a particular sum, or
(b)   providing a basis or formula for calculating the amount of the price (but without reference to any person's discretion or opinion).

(8)   Chapter 3 of Part 3 (resolutions affecting a company's constitution) applies to a resolution under this section.

Supplementary provisions

702   Copy of contract or memorandum to be available for inspection

(1)   This section applies where a company has entered into—
(a)   a contract approved under section 694 (authorisation of contract for off-market purchase), or
(b)   a contract for a purchase authorised under section 701 (authorisation of market purchase).

(2)   The company must keep available for inspection—
(a)   a copy of the contract, or

        (b)   if the contract is not in writing, a written memorandum setting out its terms.

(3)   The copy or memorandum must be kept available for inspection from the conclusion of the contract until the end of the period of ten years beginning with—

        (a)   the date on which the purchase of all the shares in pursuance of the contract is completed, or

        (b)   the date on which the contract otherwise determines.

(4)   The copy or memorandum must be kept available for inspection—

        (a)   at the company's registered office, or

        (b)   at a place specified in regulations under section 1136.

(5)   The company must give notice to the registrar—

        (a)   of the place at which the copy or memorandum is kept available for inspection, and

        (b)   of any change in that place,

     unless it has at all times been kept at the company's registered office.

(6)   Every copy or memorandum required to be kept under this section must be kept open to inspection without charge—

        (a)   by any member of the company, and

        (b)   in the case of a public company, by any other person.

(7)   The provisions of this section apply to a variation of a contract as they apply to the original contract.

703   Enforcement of right to inspect copy or memorandum

(1)   If default is made in complying with section 702(2), (3) or (4) or default is made for 14 days in complying with section 702(5), or an inspection required under section 702(6) is refused, an offence is committed by—

        (a)   the company, and

        (b)   every officer of the company who is in default.

(2)   A person guilty of an offence under this section is liable on summary conviction to a fine not exceeding level 3 on the standard scale and, for continued contravention, a daily default fine not exceeding one-tenth of level 3 on the standard scale.

(3)   In the case of refusal of an inspection required under section 702(6) the court may by order compel an immediate inspection.

704   No assignment of company's right to purchase own shares

     The rights of a company under a contract authorised under—

        (za)   section 693A (authority for off-market purchase for the purposes of or pursuant to an employees' share scheme),

        (a)   section 694 (authority for off-market purchase), or

        (b)   section 701 (authority for market purchase)

     are not capable of being assigned.

705   Payments apart from purchase price to be made out of distributable profits

(1)   A payment made by a company in consideration of—

        (a)   acquiring any right with respect to the purchase of its own shares in pursuance of a contingent purchase contract approved under section 694 (authorisation of off-market purchase),

        (b)   the variation of any contract approved under that section, or

        (c)   the release of any of the company's obligations with respect to the purchase of any of its own shares under a contract—

            (i)   approved under section 694, or

            (ii)   authorised under section 701 (authorisation of market purchase),

     must be made out of the company's distributable profits.

(2)   If this requirement is not met in relation to a contract, then—

        (a)   in a case within subsection (1)(a), no purchase by the company of its own shares in pursuance of that contract may be made under this Chapter;

(b) in a case within subsection (1)(b), no such purchase following the variation may be made under this Chapter;

(c) in a case within subsection (1)(c), the purported release is void.

706 Treatment of shares purchased

Where a limited company makes a purchase of its own shares in accordance with this Chapter, then—

(a) if section 724 (treasury shares) applies, the shares may be held and dealt with in accordance with Chapter 6;

(b) if that section does not apply—

    (i) the shares are treated as cancelled, and

    (ii) the amount of the company's issued share capital is diminished accordingly by the nominal value of the shares cancelled.

707 Return to registrar of purchase of own shares

(1) Where a company purchases shares under this Chapter, it must deliver a return to the registrar within the period of 28 days beginning with the date on which the shares are delivered to it.

(2) The return must distinguish—

(a) shares in relation to which section 724 (treasury shares) applies and shares in relation to which that section does not apply, and

(b) shares in relation to which that section applies—

    (i) that are cancelled forthwith (under section 729 (cancellation of treasury shares)), and

    (ii) that are not so cancelled.

(3) The return must state, with respect to shares of each class purchased—

(a) the number and nominal value of the shares, and

(b) the date on which they were delivered to the company.

(4) In the case of a public company the return must also state—

(a) the aggregate amount paid by the company for the shares, and

(b) the maximum and minimum prices paid in respect of shares of each class purchased.

(5) Particulars of shares delivered to the company on different dates and under different contracts may be included in a single return.

In such a case the amount required to be stated under subsection (4)(a) is the aggregate amount paid by the company for all the shares to which the return relates.

(6) If default is made in complying with this section an offence is committed by every officer of the company who is in default.

(7) A person guilty of an offence under this section is liable—

(a) on conviction on indictment, to a fine;

(b) on summary conviction to a fine not exceeding the statutory maximum and, for continued contravention, a daily default fine not exceeding one-tenth of the greater of £5,000 or the amount corresponding to level 4 on the standard scale for summary offences.

708 Notice to registrar of cancellation of shares

(1) If on the purchase by a company of any of its own shares in accordance with this Part—

(a) section 724 (treasury shares) does not apply (so that the shares are treated as cancelled), or

(b) that section applies but the shares are cancelled forthwith (under section 729 (cancellation of treasury shares)),

the company must give notice of cancellation to the registrar, within the period of 28 days beginning with the date on which the shares are delivered to it, specifying the shares cancelled.

(2) The notice must be accompanied by a statement of capital, except where the statement of capital would be the same as a statement of capital that is required to be delivered to the registrar under section 720B(1).

(3) The statement of capital must state with respect to the company's share capital immediately following the cancellation—

(a) the total number of shares of the company,

(b) the aggregate nominal value of those shares,

(ba) the aggregate amount (if any) unpaid on those shares (whether on account of their nominal value or by way of premium), and

(c) for each class of shares—

    (i) prescribed particulars of the rights attached to the shares,

    (ii) the total number of shares of that class, and

    (iii) the aggregate nominal value of shares of that class, ...

(d) ...

(4) If default is made in complying with this section, an offence is committed by—

(a) the company, and

(b) every officer of the company who is in default.

(5) A person guilty of an offence under this section is liable on summary conviction to a fine not exceeding level 3 on the standard scale and, for continued contravention, a daily default fine not exceeding one-tenth of level 3 on the standard scale.

CHAPTER 5
REDEMPTION OR PURCHASE BY PRIVATE COMPANY OUT OF CAPITAL

Introductory

709   Power of private limited company to redeem or purchase own shares out of capital

(1) A private limited company may in accordance with this Chapter, but subject to any restriction or prohibition in the company's articles, make a payment in respect of the redemption or purchase of its own shares otherwise than out of distributable profits or the proceeds of a fresh issue of shares.

(2) References below in this Chapter to payment out of capital are to any payment so made, whether or not it would be regarded apart from this section as a payment out of capital.

(3) This Chapter is subject to section 692(1ZA) (purchase of own shares up to annual limit).

The permissible capital payment

710   The permissible capital payment

(1) The payment that may, in accordance with this Chapter, be made by a company out of capital in respect of the redemption or purchase of its own shares is such amount as, after applying for that purpose—

(a) any available profits of the company, and

(b) the proceeds of any fresh issue of shares made for the purposes of the redemption or purchase,

is required to meet the price of redemption or purchase.

(2) That is referred to below in this Chapter as "the permissible capital payment" for the shares.

711   Available profits

(1) For the purposes of this Chapter the available profits of the company, in relation to the redemption or purchase of any shares, are the profits of the company that are available for distribution (within the meaning of Part 23).

(2) But the question whether a company has any profits so available, and the amount of any such profits, shall be determined in accordance with section 712 instead of in accordance with sections 836 to 842 in that Part.

712   Determination of available profits

(1) The available profits of the company are determined as follows.

(2) First, determine the profits of the company by reference to the following items as stated in the relevant accounts—

(a) profits, losses, assets and liabilities,

(b) provisions of the following kinds—

        (i)   where the relevant accounts are Companies Act accounts, provisions of a kind specified for the purposes of this subsection by regulations under section 396;

        (ii)   where the relevant accounts are IAS accounts, provisions of any kind;

    (c)   share capital and reserves (including undistributable reserves).

(3)   Second, reduce the amount so determined by the amount of—

    (a)   any distribution lawfully made by the company, and

    (b)   any other relevant payment lawfully made by the company out of distributable profits,

after the date of the relevant accounts and before the end of the relevant period.

(4)   For this purpose "other relevant payment lawfully made" includes—

    (a)   financial assistance lawfully given out of distributable profits in accordance with Chapter 2,

    (b)   payments lawfully made out of distributable profits in respect of the purchase by the company of any shares in the company, and

    (c)   payments of any description specified in section 705 (payments other than purchase price to be made out of distributable profits) lawfully made by the company.

(5)   The resulting figure is the amount of available profits.

(6)   For the purposes of this section "the relevant accounts" are any accounts that—

    (a)   are prepared as at a date within the relevant period, and

    (b)   are such as to enable a reasonable judgment to be made as to the amounts of the items mentioned in subsection (2).

(7)   In this section "the relevant period" means the period of three months ending with the date on which the solvency statement is made in accordance with section 720A or the directors' statement is made in accordance with section 714.

Requirements for payment out of capital

713   Requirements for payment out of capital

(1)   A payment out of capital by a private company for the redemption or purchase of its own shares is not lawful unless the requirements of the following sections are met—

section 714 (directors' statement and auditor's report);

section 716 (approval by special resolution);

section 719 (public notice of proposed payment);

section 720 (directors' statement and auditor's report to be available for inspection).

(2)   This is subject to section 720A and to any order of the court under section 721 (power of court to extend period for compliance on application by persons objecting to payment).

714   Directors' statement and auditor's report

(1)   The company's directors must make a statement in accordance with this section.

(2)   The statement must specify the amount of the permissible capital payment for the shares in question.

(3)   It must state that, having made full inquiry into the affairs and prospects of the company, the directors have formed the opinion—

    (a)   as regards its initial situation immediately following the date on which the payment out of capital is proposed to be made, that there will be no grounds on which the company could then be found unable to pay its debts, and

    (b)   as regards its prospects for the year immediately following that date, that having regard to—

        (i)   their intentions with respect to the management of the company's business during that year, and

        (ii)   the amount and character of the financial resources that will in their view be available to the company during that year,

the company will be able to continue to carry on business as a going concern (and will accordingly be able to pay its debts as they fall due) throughout that year.

(4)   In forming their opinion for the purposes of subsection (3)(a), the directors must take into account all of the company's liabilities (including any contingent or prospective liabilities).

(5)   The directors' statement must be in the prescribed form and must contain such information with respect to the nature of the company's business as may be prescribed.

(6)   It must in addition have annexed to it a report addressed to the directors by the company's auditor stating that—

     (a)   he has inquired into the company's state of affairs,

     (b)   the amount specified in the statement as the permissible capital payment for the shares in question is in his view properly determined in accordance with sections 710 to 712, and

     (c)   he is not aware of anything to indicate that the opinion expressed by the directors in their statement as to any of the matters mentioned in subsection (3) above is unreasonable in all the circumstances.

715   Directors' statement: offence if no reasonable grounds for opinion

(1)   If the directors make a statement under section 714 without having reasonable grounds for the opinion expressed in it, an offence is committed by every director who is in default.

(2)   A person guilty of an offence under this section is liable—

     (a)   on conviction on indictment, to imprisonment for a term not exceeding two years or a fine (or both);

     (b)   on summary conviction—

         (i)   in England and Wales, to imprisonment for a term not exceeding twelve months or a fine not exceeding the statutory maximum (or both);

         (ii)   in Scotland or Northern Ireland, to imprisonment for a term not exceeding six months or a fine not exceeding the statutory maximum (or both).

716   Payment to be approved by special resolution

(1)   The payment out of capital must be approved by a special resolution of the company.

(2)   The resolution must be passed on, or within the week immediately following, the date on which the directors make the statement required by section 714.

(3)   A resolution under this section is subject to—

section 717 (exercise of voting rights), and

section 718 (disclosure of directors' statement and auditors' report).

717   Resolution authorising payment: exercise of voting rights

(1)   This section applies to a resolution under section 716 (authority for payment out of capital for redemption or purchase of own shares).

(2)   Where the resolution is proposed as a written resolution, a member who holds shares to which the resolution relates is not an eligible member.

(3)   Where the resolution is proposed at a meeting of the company, it is not effective if—

     (a)   any member of the company holding shares to which the resolution relates exercises the voting rights carried by any of those shares in voting on the resolution, and

     (b)   the resolution would not have been passed if he had not done so.

(4)   For this purpose—

     (a)   a member who holds shares to which the resolution relates is regarded as exercising the voting rights carried by those shares not only if he votes in respect of them on a poll on the question whether the resolution shall be passed, but also if he votes on the resolution otherwise than on a poll;

     (b)   any member of the company may demand a poll on that question;

     (c)   a vote and a demand for a poll by a person as proxy for a member are the same respectively as a vote and a demand by the member.

718   Resolution authorising payment: disclosure of directors' statement and auditor's report

(1)   This section applies to a resolution under section 716 (resolution authorising payment out of capital for redemption or purchase of own shares).

(2)   A copy of the directors' statement and auditor's report under section 714 must be made available to members—

(a) in the case of a written resolution, by being sent or submitted to every eligible member at or before the time at which the proposed resolution is sent or submitted to him;

(b) in the case of a resolution at a meeting, by being made available for inspection by members of the company at the meeting.

(3) The resolution is ineffective if this requirement is not complied with.

719 Public notice of proposed payment

(1) Within the week immediately following the date of the resolution under section 716 the company must cause to be published in the Gazette a notice—

(a) stating that the company has approved a payment out of capital for the purpose of acquiring its own shares by redemption or purchase or both (as the case may be),

(b) specifying—

(i) the amount of the permissible capital payment for the shares in question, and

(ii) the date of the resolution,

(c) stating where the directors' statement and auditor's report required by section 714 are available for inspection, and

(d) stating that any creditor of the company may at any time within the five weeks immediately following the date of the resolution apply to the court under section 721 for an order preventing the payment.

(2) Within the week immediately following the date of the resolution the company must also either—

(a) cause a notice to the same effect as that required by subsection (1) to be published in an appropriate national newspaper, or

(b) give notice in writing to that effect to each of its creditors.

(3) "An appropriate national newspaper" means a newspaper circulating throughout the part of the United Kingdom in which the company is registered.

(4) Not later than the day on which the company—

(a) first publishes the notice required by subsection (1), or

(b) if earlier, first publishes or gives the notice required by subsection (2),

the company must deliver to the registrar a copy of the directors' statement and auditor's report required by section 714.

720 Directors' statement and auditor's report to be available for inspection

(1) The directors' statement and auditor's report must be kept available for inspection throughout the period—

(a) beginning with the day on which the company—

(i) first publishes the notice required by section 719(1), or

(ii) if earlier, first publishes or gives the notice required by section 719(2), and

(b) ending five weeks after the date of the resolution for payment out of capital.

(2) They must be kept available for inspection—

(a) at the company's registered office, or

(b) at a place specified in regulations under section 1136.

(3) The company must give notice to the registrar—

(a) of the place at which the statement and report are kept available for inspection, and

(b) of any change in that place,

unless they have at all times been kept at the company's registered office.

(4) They must be open to the inspection of any member or creditor of the company without charge.

(5) If default is made for 14 days in complying with subsection (3), or an inspection under subsection (4) is refused, an offence is committed by—

(a) the company, and

(b) every officer of the company who is in default.

(6) A person guilty of an offence under this section is liable on summary conviction to a fine not exceeding level 3 on the standard scale and, for continued contravention, a daily default fine not exceeding one-tenth of level 3 on the standard scale.

(7)   In the case of a refusal of an inspection required by subsection (4), the court may by order compel an immediate inspection.

Requirements for payment out of capital: employees' share schemes

720A   Reduced requirements for payment out of capital for purchase of own shares for the purposes of or pursuant to an employees' share scheme

(1)   Section 713(1) does not apply to the purchase out of capital by a private company of its own shares for the purposes of or pursuant to an employees' share scheme when approved by special resolution supported by a solvency statement.

(2)   For the purposes of this section a resolution is supported by a solvency statement if—
       (a)   the directors of the company make a solvency statement (see section 643) not more than 15 days before the date on which the resolution is passed, and
       (b)   the resolution and solvency statement are registered in accordance with section 720B.

(3)   Where the resolution is proposed as a written resolution, a copy of the solvency statement must be sent or submitted to every eligible member at or before the time at which the proposed resolution is sent or submitted to the member.

(4)   Where the resolution is proposed at a general meeting, a copy of the solvency statement must be made available for inspection by members of the company throughout that meeting.

(5)   The validity of a resolution is not affected by a failure to comply with subsection (3) or (4).

(6)   Section 717 (resolution authorising payment: exercise of voting rights) applies to a resolution under this section as it applies to a resolution under section 716.

720B   Registration of resolution and supporting documents for purchase of own shares for the purposes of or pursuant to an employees' share scheme

(1)   Within 15 days after the passing of the resolution for a payment out of capital by a private company for the purchase of its own shares for the purposes of or pursuant to an employees' share scheme the company must deliver to the registrar—
       (a)   a copy of the solvency statement,
       (b)   a copy of the resolution, and
       (c)   a statement of capital.

(2)   The statement of capital must state with respect to the company's share capital as reduced by the resolution—
       (a)   the total number of shares of the company,
       (b)   the aggregate nominal value of those shares,
       (ba)   the aggregate amount (if any) unpaid on those shares (whether on account of their nominal value or by way of premium), and
       (c)   for each class of shares—
            (i)   prescribed particulars of the rights attached to the shares,
            (ii)   the total number of shares of that class, and
            (iii)   the aggregate nominal value of shares of that class, ...
       (d)   ...

(3)   The registrar must register the documents delivered to him under subsection (1) on receipt.

(4)   The resolution does not take effect until those documents are registered.

(5)   The company must also deliver to the registrar, within 15 days after the resolution is passed, a statement by the directors confirming that the solvency statement was—
       (a)   made not more than 15 days before the date on which the resolution was passed, and
       (b)   provided to members in accordance with section 720A(3) or (4).

(6)   The validity of a resolution is not affected by—
       (a)   a failure to deliver the documents required to be delivered to the registrar under subsection (1) within the time specified in that subsection, or
       (b)   a failure to comply with subsection (5).

(7)   If the company delivers to the registrar a solvency statement that was not provided to members in accordance with section 720A(3) or (4), an offence is committed by every officer of the company who is in default.

(8)   If default is made in complying with this section, an offence is committed by—
  (a)   the company, and
  (b)   every officer of the company who is in default.

(9)   A person guilty of an offence under subsection (7) or (8) is liable—
  (a)   on conviction on indictment, to a fine;
  (b)   on summary conviction, to a fine not exceeding the statutory maximum.

Objection to payment by members or creditors

721   Application to court to cancel resolution

(1)   Where a private company passes a special resolution approving a payment out of capital for the redemption or purchase of any of its shares—
  (a)   any member of the company (other than one who consented to or voted in favour of the resolution), and
  (b)   any creditor of the company,
  may apply to the court for the cancellation of the resolution.

(2)   The application—
  (a)   must be made within five weeks after the passing of the resolution, and
  (b)   may be made on behalf of the persons entitled to make it by such one or more of their number as they may appoint in writing for the purpose.

(3)   On an application under this section the court may if it thinks fit—
  (a)   adjourn the proceedings in order that an arrangement may be made to the satisfaction of the court—
    (i)   for the purchase of the interests of dissentient members, or
    (ii)   for the protection of dissentient creditors, and
  (b)   give such directions and make such orders as it thinks expedient for facilitating or carrying into effect any such arrangement.

(4)   Subject to that, the court must make an order either cancelling or confirming the resolution, and may do so on such terms and conditions as it thinks fit.

(5)   If the court confirms the resolution, it may by order alter or extend any date or period of time specified—
  (a)   in the resolution, or
  (b)   in any provision of this Chapter applying to the redemption or purchase to which the resolution relates.

(6)   The court's order may, if the court thinks fit—
  (a)   provide for the purchase by the company of the shares of any of its members and for the reduction accordingly of the company's capital, and
  (b)   make any alteration in the company's articles that may be required in consequence of that provision.

(7)   The court's order may, if the court thinks fit, require the company not to make any, or any specified, amendments of its articles without the leave of the court.

722   Notice to registrar of court application or order

(1)   On making an application under section 721 (application to court to cancel resolution) the applicants, or the person making the application on their behalf, must immediately give notice to the registrar.
  This is without prejudice to any provision of rules of court as to service of notice of the application.

(2)   On being served with notice of any such application, the company must immediately give notice to the registrar.

(3)   Within 15 days of the making of the court's order on the application, or such longer period as the court may at any time direct, the company must deliver to the registrar a copy of the order.

(4)   If a company fails to comply with subsection (2) or (3) an offence is committed by—
        (a)   the company, and
        (b)   every officer of the company who is in default.

(5)   A person guilty of an offence under this section is liable on summary conviction to a fine not exceeding level 3 on the standard scale and, for continued contravention, a daily default fine not exceeding one-tenth of level 3 on the standard scale.

Supplementary provisions

723   Time when payment out of capital to be made or shares to be surrendered

(1)   The payment out of capital, if made in accordance with a resolution under section 716 must be made—
        (a)   no earlier than five weeks after the date on which the resolution under section 716 is passed, and
        (b)   no more than seven weeks after that date.

(1A)   Shares to be purchased in accordance with a resolution under section 720A must be surrendered—
        (a)   no earlier than five weeks after the date on which the resolution under section 720A is passed, and
        (b)   no later than seven weeks after that date.

(2)   This is subject to any exercise of the court's powers under section 721(5) (power to alter or extend time where resolution confirmed after objection).

CHAPTER 6
TREASURY SHARES

724   Treasury shares

(1)   This section applies where—
        (a)   a limited company makes a purchase of its own shares in accordance with Chapter 4, and
        (b)   the purchase is made out of distributable profits.

(2)   ...

(3)   Where this section applies the company may—
        (a)   hold the shares (or any of them), or
        (b)   deal with any of them, at any time, in accordance with section 727 or 729.

(4)   Where shares are held by the company, the company must be entered in its register of members (or, as the case may be, the company's name must be delivered to the registrar under Chapter 2A of Part 8) as the member holding the shares.

(5)   In the Companies Acts references to a company holding shares as treasury shares are to the company holding shares that—
        (a)   were (or are treated as having been) purchased by it in circumstances in which this section applies, and
        (b)   have been held by the company continuously since they were so purchased (or treated as purchased).

725   ...

726   Treasury shares: exercise of rights

(1)   This section applies where shares are held by a company as treasury shares.

(2)   The company must not exercise any right in respect of the treasury shares, and any purported exercise of such a right is void.
        This applies, in particular, to any right to attend or vote at meetings.

(3)   No dividend may be paid, and no other distribution (whether in cash or otherwise) of the company's assets (including any distribution of assets to members on a winding up) may be made to the company, in respect of the treasury shares.

(4)   Nothing in this section prevents—

   (a)   an allotment of shares as fully paid bonus shares in respect of the treasury shares, or

   (b)   the payment of any amount payable on the redemption of the treasury shares (if they are redeemable shares).

(5)   Shares allotted as fully paid bonus shares in respect of the treasury shares are treated as if purchased by the company, at the time they were allotted, in circumstances in which section 724(1) (treasury shares) applied.

727   Treasury shares: disposal

(1)   Where shares are held as treasury shares, the company may at any time—

   (a)   sell the shares (or any of them) for a cash consideration, or

   (b)   transfer the shares (or any of them) for the purposes of or pursuant to an employees' share scheme.

(2)   In subsection (1)(a) "cash consideration" means—

   (a)   cash received by the company, or

   (b)   a cheque received by the company in good faith that the directors have no reason for suspecting will not be paid, or

   (c)   a release of a liability of the company for a liquidated sum, or

   (d)   an undertaking to pay cash to the company on or before a date not more than 90 days after the date on which the company agrees to sell the shares, or

   (e)   payment by any other means giving rise to a present or future entitlement (of the company or a person acting on the company's behalf) to a payment, or credit equivalent to payment, in cash.

   For this purpose "cash" includes foreign currency.

(3)   The Secretary of State may by order provide that particular means of payment specified in the order are to be regarded as falling within subsection (2)(e).

(4)   If the company receives a notice under section 979 (takeover offers: right of offeror to buy out minority shareholders) that a person desires to acquire shares held by the company as treasury shares, the company must not sell or transfer the shares to which the notice relates except to that person.

(5)   An order under this section is subject to negative resolution procedure.

728   Treasury shares: notice of disposal

(1)   Where shares held by a company as treasury shares—

   (a)   are sold, or

   (b)   are transferred for the purposes of an employees' share scheme,

   the company must deliver a return to the registrar not later than 28 days after the shares are disposed of.

(2)   The return must state with respect to shares of each class disposed of—

   (a)   the number and nominal value of the shares, and

   (b)   the date on which they were disposed of.

(3)   Particulars of shares disposed of on different dates may be included in a single return.

(4)   If default is made in complying with this section an offence is committed by every officer of the company who is in default.

(5)   A person guilty of an offence under this section is liable—

   (a)   on conviction on indictment, to a fine;

   (b)   on summary conviction, to a fine not exceeding the statutory maximum and, for continued contravention, a daily default fine not exceeding one-tenth of the greater of £5,000 or the amount corresponding to level 4 on the standard scale for summary offences.

729   Treasury shares: cancellation

(1)   Where shares are held as treasury shares, the company may at any time cancel the shares (or any of them).

(2), (3) ...

(4)   If company cancels shares held as treasury shares, the amount of the company's share capital is reduced accordingly by the nominal amount of the shares cancelled.

(5)   The directors may take any steps required to enable the company to cancel its shares under this section without complying with the provisions of Chapter 10 of Part 17 (reduction of share capital).

730   Treasury shares: notice of cancellation

(1)   Where shares held by a company as treasury shares are cancelled, the company must deliver a return to the registrar not later than 28 days after the shares are cancelled.
This does not apply to shares that are cancelled forthwith on their acquisition by the company (see section 708).

(2)   The return must state with respect to shares of each class cancelled—
    (a)   the number and nominal value of the shares, and
    (b)   the date on which they were cancelled.

(3)   Particulars of shares cancelled on different dates may be included in a single return.

(4)   The notice must be accompanied by a statement of capital.

(5)   The statement of capital must state with respect to the company's share capital immediately following the cancellation—
    (a)   the total number of shares of the company,
    (b)   the aggregate nominal value of those shares,
    (ba) the aggregate amount (if any) unpaid on those shares (whether on account of their nominal value or by way of premium), and
    (c)   for each class of shares—
        (i)   prescribed particulars of the rights attached to the shares,
        (ii)   the total number of shares of that class, and
        (iii)   the aggregate nominal value of shares of that class, ...
    (d)   ...

(6)   If default is made in complying with this section, an offence is committed by—
    (a)   the company, and
    (b)   every officer of the company who is in default.

(7)   A person guilty of an offence under this section is liable on summary conviction to a fine not exceeding level 3 on the standard scale and, for continued contravention, a daily default fine not exceeding one-tenth of level 3 on the standard scale.

731   Treasury shares: treatment of proceeds of sale

(1)   Where shares held as treasury shares are sold, the proceeds of sale must be dealt with in accordance with this section.

(2)   If the proceeds of sale are equal to or less than the purchase price paid by the company for the shares, the proceeds are treated for the purposes of Part 23 (distributions) as a realised profit of the company.

(3)   If the proceeds of sale exceed the purchase price paid by the company—
    (a)   an amount equal to the purchase price paid is treated as a realised profit of the company for the purposes of that Part, and
    (b)   the excess must be transferred to the company's share premium account.

(4)   For the purposes of this section—
    (a)   the purchase price paid by the company must be determined by the application of a weighted average price method, and
    (b)   if the shares were allotted to the company as fully paid bonus shares, the purchase price paid for them is treated as nil.

732 **Treasury shares: offences**

(1)   If a company contravenes any of the provisions of this Chapter (except section 730 (notice of cancellation)), an offence is committed by—

(a)   the company, and

(b)   every officer of the company who is in default.

(2)   A person guilty of an offence under this section is liable—

(a)   on conviction on indictment, to a fine;

(b)   on summary conviction to a fine not exceeding the statutory maximum.

CHAPTER 7

SUPPLEMENTARY PROVISIONS

733 **The capital redemption reserve**

(1)   In the following circumstances a company must transfer amounts to a reserve, called the "capital redemption reserve".

(2)   Where under this Part shares of a limited company are redeemed or purchased wholly out of the company's profits, the amount by which the company's issued share capital is diminished in accordance with—

(a)   section 688(b) (on the cancellation of shares redeemed), or

(b)   section 706(b)(ii) (on the cancellation of shares purchased), must be transferred to the capital redemption reserve.

(3)   If—

(a)   the shares are redeemed or purchased wholly or partly out of the proceeds of a fresh issue, and

(b)   the aggregate amount of the proceeds is less than the aggregate nominal value of the shares redeemed or purchased,

the amount of the difference must be transferred to the capital redemption reserve.

This does not apply in the case of a private company if, in addition to the proceeds of the fresh issue, the company applies a payment out of capital under Chapter 5 or under section 692(1ZA) in making the redemption or purchase.

(4)   The amount by which a company's share capital is diminished in accordance with section 729(4) (on the cancellation of shares held as treasury shares) must be transferred to the capital redemption reserve.

(5)   The company may use the capital redemption reserve to pay up new shares to be allotted to members as fully paid bonus shares.

(6)   Subject to that, the provisions of the Companies Acts relating to the reduction of a company's share capital apply as if the capital redemption reserve were part of its paid up share capital.

734 **Accounting consequences of payment out of capital**

(1)   This section applies where a payment out of capital is made in accordance with Chapter 5 or under section 692(1ZA) (redemption or purchase of own shares by private company out of capital).

(1A)   In relation to a payment under section 692(1ZA) references to the permissible capital payment are to the purchase price of the shares or (if less) the part of it met out of the payment under section 692(1ZA) and any proceeds of a fresh issue used to make the purchase.

(2)   If the permissible capital payment is less than the nominal amount of the shares redeemed or purchased, the amount of the difference must be transferred to the company's capital redemption reserve.

(3)   If the permissible capital payment is greater than the nominal amount of the shares redeemed or purchased—

(a)   the amount of any capital redemption reserve, share premium account or fully paid share capital of the company, and

(b)   any amount representing unrealised profits of the company for the time being standing to the credit of any revaluation reserve maintained by the company,

may be reduced by a sum not exceeding (or by sums not in total exceeding) the amount by which the permissible capital payment exceeds the nominal amount of the shares.

(4)   Where the proceeds of a fresh issue are applied by the company in making a redemption or purchase of its own shares in addition to a payment out of capital under Chapter 5, the references in subsections (2) and (3) to the permissible capital payment are to be read as referring to the aggregate of that payment and those proceeds.

735   Effect of company's failure to redeem or purchase

(1)   This section applies where a company—
(a)   issues shares on terms that they are or are liable to be redeemed, or
(b)   agrees to purchase any of its shares.

(2)   The company is not liable in damages in respect of any failure on its part to redeem or purchase any of the shares.
This is without prejudice to any right of the holder of the shares other than his right to sue the company for damages in respect of its failure.

(3)   The court shall not grant an order for specific performance of the terms of redemption or purchase if the company shows that it is unable to meet the costs of redeeming or purchasing the shares in question out of distributable profits.

(4)   If the company is wound up and at the commencement of the winding up any of the shares have not been redeemed or purchased, the terms of redemption or purchase may be enforced against the company.
When shares are redeemed or purchased under this subsection, they are treated as cancelled.

(5)   Subsection (4) does not apply if—
(a)   the terms provided for the redemption or purchase to take place at a date later than that of the commencement of the winding up, or
(b)   during the period—
(i)   beginning with the date on which the redemption or purchase was to have taken place, and
(ii)   ending with the commencement of the winding up,
the company could not at any time have lawfully made a distribution equal in value to the price at which the shares were to have been redeemed or purchased.

(6)   There shall be paid in priority to any amount that the company is liable under subsection (4) to pay in respect of any shares—
(a)   all other debts and liabilities of the company (other than any due to members in their character as such), and
(b)   if other shares carry rights (whether as to capital or as to income) that are preferred to the rights as to capital attaching to the first-mentioned shares, any amount due in satisfaction of those preferred rights.
Subject to that, any such amount shall be paid in priority to any amounts due to members in satisfaction of their rights (whether as to capital or income) as members.

736   Meaning of "distributable profits"

In this Part (except in Chapter 2 (financial assistance): see section 683) "distributable profits", in relation to the making of any payment by a company, means profits out of which the company could lawfully make a distribution (within the meaning given by section 830) equal in value to the payment.

737   General power to make further provision by regulations

(1)   The Secretary of State may by regulations modify the provisions of this Part.

(2)   The regulations may—
(a)   amend or repeal any of the provisions of this Part, or

(b) make such other provision as appears to the Secretary of State appropriate in place of any of the provisions of this Part.

(3) Regulations under this section may make consequential amendments or repeals in other provisions of this Act, or in other enactments.

(4) Regulations under this section are subject to affirmative resolution procedure.

PART 19
DEBENTURES

General provisions

738   Meaning of "debenture"

In the Companies Acts "debenture" includes debenture stock, bonds and any other securities of a company, whether or not constituting a charge on the assets of the company.

739   Perpetual debentures

(1) A condition contained in debentures, or in a deed for securing debentures, is not invalid by reason only that the debentures are made—
   (a) irredeemable, or
   (b) redeemable only—
      (i) on the happening of a contingency (however remote), or
      (ii) on the expiration of a period (however long),
any rule of equity to the contrary notwithstanding.

(2) Subsection (1) applies to debentures whenever issued and to deeds whenever executed.

740   Enforcement of contract to subscribe for debentures

A contract with a company to take up and pay for debentures of the company may be enforced by an order for specific performance.

741   Registration of allotment of debentures

(1) A company must register an allotment of debentures as soon as practicable and in any event within two months after the date of the allotment.

(2) If a company fails to comply with this section, an offence is committed by—
   (a) the company, and
   (b) every officer of the company who is in default.

(3) A person guilty of an offence under this section is liable on summary conviction to a fine not exceeding level 3 on the standard scale and, for continued contravention, a daily default fine not exceeding one-tenth of level 3 on the standard scale.

(4) For the duties of the company as to the issue of the debentures, or certificates of debenture stock, see Part 21 (certification and transfer of securities)

742   Debentures to bearer (Scotland)

Notwithstanding anything in the statute of the Scots Parliament of 1696, chapter 25, debentures to bearer issued in Scotland are valid and binding according to their terms.

Register of debenture holders

743   Register of debenture holders

(1) Any register of debenture holders of a company that is kept by the company must be kept available for inspection—
   (a) at the company's registered office, or
   (b) at a place specified in regulations under section 1136.

(2) A company must give notice to the registrar of the place where any such register is kept available for inspection and of any change in that place.

(3) No such notice is required if the register has, at all times since it came into existence, been kept available for inspection at the company's registered office.

(4)   If a company makes default for 14 days in complying with subsection (2), an offence is committed by—

    (a)   the company, and

    (b)   every officer of the company who is in default.

(5)   A person guilty of an offence under this section is liable on summary conviction to a fine not exceeding level 3 on the standard scale and, for continued contravention, a daily default fine not exceeding one-tenth of level 3 on the standard scale.

(6)   References in this section to a register of debenture holders include a duplicate—

    (a)   of a register of debenture holders that is kept outside the United Kingdom, or

    (b)   of any part of such a register.

744   Register of debenture holders: right to inspect and require copy

(1)   Every register of debenture holders of a company must, except when duly closed, be open to the inspection—

    (a)   of the registered holder of any such debentures, or any holder of shares in the company, without charge, and

    (b)   of any other person on payment of such fee as may be prescribed.

(2)   Any person may require a copy of the register, or any part of it, on payment of such fee as may be prescribed.

(3)   A person seeking to exercise either of the rights conferred by this section must make a request to the company to that effect.

(4)   The request must contain the following information—

    (a)   in the case of an individual, his name and address;

    (b)   in the case of an organisation, the name and address of an individual responsible for making the request on behalf of the organisation;

    (c)   the purpose for which the information is to be used; and

    (d)   whether the information will be disclosed to any other person, and if so—

        (i)   where that person is an individual, his name and address,

        (ii)   where that person is an organisation, the name and address of an individual responsible for receiving the information on its behalf, and

        (iii)   the purpose for which the information is to be used by that person.

(5)   For the purposes of this section a register is "duly closed" if it is closed in accordance with provision contained—

    (a)   in the articles or in the debentures,

    (b)   in the case of debenture stock in the stock certificates, or

    (c)   in the trust deed or other document securing the debentures or debenture stock.

The total period for which a register is closed in any year must not exceed 30 days.

(6)   References in this section to a register of debenture holders include a duplicate—

    (a)   of a register of debenture holders that is kept outside the United Kingdom, or

    (b)   of any part of such a register.

745   Register of debenture holders: response to request for inspection or copy

(1)   Where a company receives a request under section 744 (register of debenture holders: right to inspect and require copy), it must within five working days either—

    (a)   comply with the request, or

    (b)   apply to the court.

(2)   If it applies to the court it must notify the person making the request.

(3)   If on an application under this section the court is satisfied that the inspection or copy is not sought for a proper purpose—

    (a)   it shall direct the company not to comply with the request, and

    (b)   it may further order that the company's costs (in Scotland, expenses) on the application be paid in whole or in part by the person who made the request, even if he is not a party to the application.

(4)   If the court makes such a direction and it appears to the court that the company is or may be subject to other requests made for a similar purpose (whether made by the same person or different persons), it may direct that the company is not to comply with any such request.

The order must contain such provision as appears to the court appropriate to identify the requests to which it applies.

(5)   If on an application under this section the court does not direct the company not to comply with the request, the company must comply with the request immediately upon the court giving its decision or, as the case may be, the proceedings being discontinued.

746   Register of debenture holders: refusal of inspection or default in providing copy

(1)   If an inspection required under section 744 (register of debenture holders: right to inspect and require copy) is refused or default is made in providing a copy required under that section, otherwise than in accordance with an order of the court, an offence is committed by—
        (a)   the company, and
        (b)   every officer of the company who is in default.

(2)   A person guilty of an offence under this section is liable on summary conviction to a fine not exceeding level 3 on the standard scale and, for continued contravention, a daily default fine not exceeding one-tenth of level 3 on the standard scale.

(3)   In the case of any such refusal or default the court may by order compel an immediate inspection or, as the case may be, direct that the copy required be sent to the person requesting it.

747   Register of debenture holders: offences in connection with request for or disclosure of information

(1)   It is an offence for a person knowingly or recklessly to make in a request under section 744 (register of debenture holders: right to inspect and require copy) a statement that is misleading, false or deceptive in a material particular.

(2)   It is an offence for a person in possession of information obtained by exercise of either of the rights conferred by that section—
        (a)   to do anything that results in the information being disclosed to another person, or
        (b)   to fail to do anything with the result that the information is disclosed to another person,
        knowing, or having reason to suspect, that person may use the information for a purpose that is not a proper purpose.

(3)   A person guilty of an offence under this section is liable—
        (a)   on conviction on indictment, to imprisonment for a term not exceeding two years or a fine (or both);
        (b)   on summary conviction—
                (i)   in England and Wales, to imprisonment for a term not exceeding twelve months or to a fine not exceeding the statutory maximum (or both);
                (ii)   in Scotland or Northern Ireland, to imprisonment for a term not exceeding six months, or to a fine not exceeding the statutory maximum (or both).

748   Time limit for claims arising from entry in register

(1)   Liability incurred by a company—
        (a)   from the making or deletion of an entry in the register of debenture holders, or
        (b)   from a failure to make or delete any such entry,
        is not enforceable more than ten years after the date on which the entry was made or deleted or, as the case may be, the failure first occurred.

(2)   This is without prejudice to any lesser period of limitation (and, in Scotland, to any rule that the obligation giving rise to the liability prescribes before the expiry of that period).

Supplementary provisions

749   Right of debenture holder to copy of deed

(1)   Any holder of debentures of a company is entitled, on request and on payment of such fee as may be prescribed, to be provided with a copy of any trust deed for securing the debentures.

(2)   If default is made in complying with this section, an offence is committed by every officer of the company who is in default.

(3)   A person guilty of an offence under this section is liable on summary conviction to a fine not exceeding level 3 on the standard scale and, for continued contravention, a daily default fine not exceeding one-tenth of level 3 on the standard scale.

(4)   In the case of any such default the court may direct that the copy required be sent to the person requiring it.

750   Liability of trustees of debentures

(1)   Any provision contained in—
  (a)   a trust deed for securing an issue of debentures, or
  (b)   any contract with the holders of debentures secured by a trust deed,
  is void in so far as it would have the effect of exempting a trustee of the deed from, or indemnifying him against, liability for breach of trust where he fails to show the degree of care and diligence required of him as trustee, having regard to the provisions of the trust deed conferring on him any powers, authorities or discretions.

(2)   Subsection (1) does not invalidate—
  (a)   a release otherwise validly given in respect of anything done or omitted to be done by a trustee before the giving of the release;
  (b)   any provision enabling such a release to be given—
    (i)   on being agreed to by a majority of not less than 75% in value of the debenture holders present and voting in person or, where proxies are permitted, by proxy at a meeting summoned for the purpose, and
    (ii)   either with respect to specific acts or omissions or on the trustee dying or ceasing to act.

(3)   This section is subject to section 751 (saving for certain older provisions).

751   Liability of trustees of debentures: saving for certain older provisions

(1)   Section 750 (liability of trustees of debentures) does not operate—
  (a)   to invalidate any provision in force on the relevant date so long as any person—
    (i)   then entitled to the benefit of the provision, or
    (ii)   afterwards given the benefit of the provision under subsection (3) below,
    remains a trustee of the deed in question, or
  (b)   to deprive any person of any exemption or right to be indemnified in respect of anything done or omitted to be done by him while any such provision was in force.

(2)   The relevant date for this purpose is—
  (a)   1st July 1948 in a case where section 192 of the Companies Act 1985 applied immediately before the commencement of this section;
  (b)   1st July 1961 in a case where Article 201 of the Companies (Northern Ireland) Order 1986 then applied.

(3)   While any trustee of a trust deed remains entitled to the benefit of a provision saved by subsection (1) above the benefit of that provision may be given either—
  (a)   to all trustees of the deed, present and future, or
  (b)   to any named trustees or proposed trustees of it,
  by a resolution passed by a majority of not less than 75% in value of the debenture holders present in person or, where proxies are permitted, by proxy at a meeting summoned for the purpose.

(4)   A meeting for that purpose must be summoned in accordance with the provisions of the deed or, if the deed makes no provision for summoning meetings, in a manner approved by the court.

752   Power to re-issue redeemed debentures

(1)   Where a company has redeemed debentures previously issued, then unless—
  (a)   provision to the contrary (express or implied) is contained in the company's articles or in any contract made by the company, or

(b)   the company has, by passing a resolution to that effect or by some other act, manifested its intention that the debentures shall be cancelled,

the company may re-issue the debentures, either by re-issuing the same debentures or by issuing new debentures in their place.

This subsection is deemed always to have had effect.

(2)   On a re-issue of redeemed debentures the person entitled to the debentures has (and is deemed always to have had) the same priorities as if the debentures had never been redeemed.

(3)   The re-issue of a debenture or the issue of another debenture in its place under this section is treated as the issue of a new debenture for the purposes of stamp duty.

It is not so treated for the purposes of any provision limiting the amount or number of debentures to be issued.

(4)   A person lending money on the security of a debenture re-issued under this section which appears to be duly stamped may give the debenture in evidence in any proceedings for enforcing his security without payment of the stamp duty or any penalty in respect of it, unless he had notice (or, but for his negligence, might have discovered) that the debenture was not duly stamped. In that case the company is liable to pay the proper stamp duty and penalty.

753   Deposit of debentures to secure advances

Where a company has deposited any of its debentures to secure advances from time to time on current account or otherwise, the debentures are not treated as redeemed by reason only of the company's account having ceased to be in debit while the debentures remained so deposited.

754   Priorities where debentures secured by floating charge

(1)   This section applies where debentures of a company registered in England and Wales or Northern Ireland are secured by a charge that, as created, was a floating charge.

(2)   If possession is taken, by or on behalf of the holders of the debentures, of any property comprised in or subject to the charge, and the company is not at that time in the course of being wound up, the company's preferential debts shall be paid out of assets coming to the hands of the persons taking possession in priority to any claims for principal or interest in respect of the debentures.

(3)   "Preferential debts" means the categories of debts listed in Schedule 6 to the Insolvency Act 1986 or Schedule 4 to the Insolvency (Northern Ireland) Order 1989.

For the purposes of those Schedules "the relevant date" is the date of possession being taken as mentioned in subsection (2).

(4)   Payments under this section shall be recouped, as far as may be, out of the assets of the company available for payment of general creditors.

PART 20

PRIVATE AND PUBLIC COMPANIES

CHAPTER 1

PROHIBITION OF PUBLIC OFFERS BY PRIVATE COMPANIES

755   Prohibition of public offers by private company

(1)   A private company limited by shares or limited by guarantee and having a share capital must not—

(a)   offer to the public any securities of the company, or

(b)   allot or agree to allot any securities of the company with a view to their being offered to the public.

(2)   Unless the contrary is proved, an allotment or agreement to allot securities is presumed to be made with a view to their being offered to the public if an offer of the securities (or any of them) to the public is made—

(a)   within six months after the allotment or agreement to allot, or

(b)   before the receipt by the company of the whole of the consideration to be received by it in respect of the securities.

(3)   A company does not contravene this section if—

      (a)   it acts in good faith in pursuance of arrangements under which it is to re-register as a public company before the securities are allotted, or

      (b)   as part of the terms of the offer it undertakes to re-register as a public company within a specified period, and that undertaking is complied with.

(4)   The specified period for the purposes of subsection (3)(b) must be a period ending not later than six months after the day on which the offer is made (or, in the case of an offer made on different days, first made).

(5)   In this Chapter "securities" means shares or debentures.

756   Meaning of "offer to the public"

(1)   This section explains what is meant in this Chapter by an offer of securities to the public.

(2)   An offer to the public includes an offer to any section of the public, however selected.

(3)   An offer is not regarded as an offer to the public if it can properly be regarded, in all the circumstances, as—

      (a)   not being calculated to result, directly or indirectly, in securities of the company becoming available to persons other than those receiving the offer, or

      (b)   otherwise being a private concern of the person receiving it and the person making it.

(4)   An offer is to be regarded (unless the contrary is proved) as being a private concern of the person receiving it and the person making it if—

      (a)   it is made to a person already connected with the company and, where it is made on terms allowing that person to renounce his rights, the rights may only be renounced in favour of another person already connected with the company; or

      (b)   it is an offer to subscribe for securities to be held under an employees' share scheme and, where it is made on terms allowing that person to renounce his rights, the rights may only be renounced in favour of—

          (i)   another person entitled to hold securities under the scheme, or

          (ii)   a person already connected with the company.

(5)   For the purposes of this section "person already connected with the company" means—

      (a)   an existing member or employee of the company,

      (b)   a member of the family of a person who is or was a member or employee of the company,

      (c)   the widow or widower, or surviving civil partner, of a person who was a member or employee of the company,

      (d)   an existing debenture holder of the company, or

      (e)   a trustee (acting in his capacity as such) of a trust of which the principal beneficiary is a person within any of paragraphs (a) to (d).

(6)   For the purposes of subsection (5)(b) the members of a person's family are the person's spouse or civil partner and children (including step-children) and their descendants.

757   Enforcement of prohibition: order restraining proposed contravention

(1)   If it appears to the court—

      (a)   on an application under this section, or

      (b)   in proceedings under Part 30 (protection of members against unfair prejudice),

    that a company is proposing to act in contravention of section 755 (prohibition of public offers by private companies), the court shall make an order under this section.

(2)   An order under this section is an order restraining the company from contravening that section.

(3)   An application for an order under this section may be made by—

      (a)   a member or creditor of the company, or

      (b)   the Secretary of State.

758   Enforcement of prohibition: orders available to the court after contravention

(1)   This section applies if it appears to the court—

      (a)   on an application under this section, or

      (b)   in proceedings under Part 30 (protection of members against unfair prejudice), that a company has acted in contravention of section 755 (prohibition of public offers by private companies).

(2)   The court must make an order requiring the company to re-register as a public company unless it appears to the court—

    (a)   that the company does not meet the requirements for re-registration as a public company, and

    (b)   that it is impractical or undesirable to require it to take steps to do so.

(3)   If it does not make an order for re-registration, the court may make either or both of the following—

    (a)   a remedial order (see section 759), or

    (b)   an order for the compulsory winding up of the company.

(4)   An application under this section may be made by—

    (a)   a member of the company who—

        (i)   was a member at the time the offer was made (or, if the offer was made over a period, at any time during that period), or

        (ii)   became a member as a result of the offer,

    (b)   a creditor of the company who was a creditor at the time the offer was made (or, if the offer was made over a period, at any time during that period), or

    (c)   the Secretary of State.

759   Enforcement of prohibition: remedial order

(1)   A "remedial order" is an order for the purpose of putting a person affected by anything done in contravention of section 755 (prohibition of public offers by private company) in the position he would have been in if it had not been done.

(2)   The following provisions are without prejudice to the generality of the power to make such an order.

(3)   Where a private company has—

    (a)   allotted securities pursuant to an offer to the public, or

    (b)   allotted or agreed to allot securities with a view to their being offered to the public,

a remedial order may require any person knowingly concerned in the contravention of section 755 to offer to purchase any of those securities at such price and on such other terms as the court thinks fit.

(4)   A remedial order may be made—

    (a)   against any person knowingly concerned in the contravention, whether or not an officer of the company;

    (b)   notwithstanding anything in the company's constitution (which includes, for this purpose, the terms on which any securities of the company are allotted or held);

    (c)   whether or not the holder of the securities subject to the order is the person to whom the company allotted or agreed to allot them.

(5)   Where a remedial order is made against the company itself, the court may provide for the reduction of the company's capital accordingly.

760   Validity of allotment etc not affected

Nothing in this Chapter affects the validity of any allotment or sale of securities or of any agreement to allot or sell securities.

CHAPTER 2
MINIMUM SHARE CAPITAL REQUIREMENT FOR PUBLIC COMPANIES

761   Public company: requirement as to minimum share capital

(1)   A company that is a public company (otherwise than by virtue of re-registration as a public company) must not do business or exercise any borrowing powers unless the registrar has issued it with a certificate under this section (a "trading certificate").

(2)   The registrar shall issue a trading certificate if, on an application made in accordance with section 762, he is satisfied that the nominal value of the company's allotted share capital is not less than the authorised minimum.

(3)   For this purpose a share allotted in pursuance of an employees' share scheme shall not be taken into account unless paid up as to—
         (a)   at least one-quarter of the nominal value of the share, and
         (b)   the whole of any premium on the share.

(4)   A trading certificate has effect from the date on which it is issued and is conclusive evidence that the company is entitled to do business and exercise any borrowing powers.

762   Procedure for obtaining certificate

(1)   An application for a certificate under section 761 must—
         (a)   state that the nominal value of the company's allotted share capital is not less than the authorised minimum,
         (b)   specify the amount, or estimated amount, of the company's preliminary expenses,
         (c)   specify any amount or benefit paid or given, or intended to be paid or given, to any promoter of the company, and the consideration for the payment or benefit, ...
         (d)   be accompanied by a statement of compliance, and
         (e)   be accompanied by a statement of the aggregate amount paid up on the shares of the company on account of their nominal value.

(2)   The statement of compliance is a statement that the company meets the requirements for the issue of a certificate under section 761.

(3)   The registrar may accept the statement of compliance as sufficient evidence of the matters stated in it.

763   The authorised minimum

(1)   "The authorised minimum", in relation to the nominal value of a public company's allotted share capital is—
         (a)   £50,000, or
         (b)   the prescribed euro equivalent.

(2)   The Secretary of State may by order prescribe the amount in euros that is for the time being to be treated as equivalent to the sterling amount of the authorised minimum.

(3)   This power may be exercised from time to time as appears to the Secretary of State to be appropriate.

(4)   The amount prescribed shall be determined by applying an appropriate spot rate of exchange to the sterling amount and rounding to the nearest 100 euros.

(5)   An order under this section is subject to negative resolution procedure.

(6)   This section has effect subject to any exercise of the power conferred by section 764 (power to alter authorised minimum).

764   Power to alter authorised minimum

(1)   The Secretary of State may by order—
         (a)   alter the sterling amount of the authorised minimum, and
         (b)   make a corresponding alteration of the prescribed euro equivalent.

(2)   The amount of the prescribed euro equivalent shall be determined by applying an appropriate spot rate of exchange to the sterling amount and rounding to the nearest 100 euros.

(3)   An order under this section that increases the authorised minimum may—
         (a)   require a public company having an allotted share capital of which the nominal value is less than the amount specified in the order to—
                (i)   increase that value to not less than that amount, or
                (ii)   re-register as a private company;
         (b)   make provision in connection with any such requirement for any of the matters for which provision is made by this Act relating to—
                (i)   a company's registration, re-registration or change of name,

(ii)   payment for shares comprised in a company's share capital, and

(iii)   offers to the public of shares in or debentures of a company,

including provision as to the consequences (in criminal law or otherwise) of a failure to comply with any requirement of the order;

(c)   provide for any provision of the order to come into force on different days for different purposes.

(4)   An order under this section is subject to affirmative resolution procedure.

765   Authorised minimum: application of initial requirement

(1)   The initial requirement for a public company to have allotted share capital of a nominal value not less than the authorised minimum, that is—

(a)   the requirement in section 761(2) for the issue of a trading certificate, or

(b)   the requirement in section 91(1)(a) for re-registration as a public company,

must be met either by reference to allotted share capital denominated in sterling or by reference to allotted share capital denominated in euros (but not partly in one and partly in the other).

(2)   Whether the requirement is met is determined in the first case by reference to the sterling amount and in the second case by reference to the prescribed euro equivalent.

(3)   No account is to be taken of any allotted share capital of the company denominated in a currency other than sterling or, as the case may be, euros.

(4)   If the company could meet the requirement either by reference to share capital denominated in sterling or by reference to share capital denominated in euros, it must elect in its application for a trading certificate or, as the case may be, for re-registration as a public company which is to be the currency by reference to which the matter is determined.

766   Authorised minimum: application where shares denominated in different currencies etc

(1)   The Secretary of State may make provision by regulations as to the application of the authorised minimum in relation to a public company that—

(a)   has shares denominated—

(i)   in more than one currency, or

(ii)   in a currency other than sterling or euros,

(b)   redenominates the whole or part of its allotted share capital, or

(c)   allots new shares.

(2)   The regulations may make provision as to the currencies, exchange rates and dates by reference to which it is to be determined whether the nominal value of the company's allotted share capital is less than the authorised minimum.

(3)   The regulations may provide that where—

(a)   a company has redenominated the whole or part of its allotted share capital, and

(b)   the effect of the redenomination is that the nominal value of the company's allotted share capital is less than the authorised minimum,

the company must re-register as a private company.

(4)   Regulations under subsection (3) may make provision corresponding to any provision made by sections 664 to 667 (re-registration as private company in consequence of cancellation of shares).

(5)   Any regulations under this section have effect subject to section 765 (authorised minimum: application of initial requirement).

(6)   Regulations under this section are subject to negative resolution procedure.

767   Consequences of doing business etc without a trading certificate

(1)   If a company does business or exercises any borrowing powers in contravention of section 761, an offence is committed by—

(a)   the company, and

(b)   every officer of the company who is in default.

(2)   A person guilty of an offence under subsection (1) is liable—

(a)   on conviction on indictment, to a fine;

(b)   on summary conviction, to a fine not exceeding the statutory maximum.

(3)   A contravention of section 761 does not affect the validity of a transaction entered into by the company, but if a company—
    (a)   enters into a transaction in contravention of that section, and
    (b)   fails to comply with its obligations in connection with the transaction within 21 days from being called on to do so,
    the directors of the company are jointly and severally liable to indemnify any other party to the transaction in respect of any loss or damage suffered by him by reason of the company's failure to comply with its obligations.

(4)   The directors who are so liable are those who were directors at the time the company entered into the transaction.

PART 21

CERTIFICATION AND TRANSFER OF SECURITIES

CHAPTER 1

CERTIFICATION AND TRANSFER OF SECURITIES: GENERAL

Share certificates

768   Share certificate to be evidence of title

(1)   In the case of a company registered in England and Wales or Northern Ireland, a certificate under the common seal of the company specifying any shares held by a member is prima facie evidence of his title to the shares.

(2)   In the case of a company registered in Scotland—
    (a)   a certificate under the common seal of the company specifying any shares held by a member, or
    (b)   a certificate specifying any shares held by a member and subscribed by the company in accordance with the Requirements of Writing (Scotland) Act 1995,
    is sufficient evidence, unless the contrary is shown, of his title to the shares.

Issue of certificates etc on allotment

769   Duty of company as to issue of certificates etc on allotment

(1)   A company must, within two months after the allotment of any of its shares, debentures or debenture stock, complete and have ready for delivery—
    (a)   the certificates of the shares allotted,
    (b)   the debentures allotted, or
    (c)   the certificates of the debenture stock allotted.

(2)   Subsection (1) does not apply—
    (a)   if the conditions of issue of the shares, debentures or debenture stock provide otherwise,
    (b)   in the case of allotment to a financial institution (see section 778), or
    (c)   in the case of an allotment of shares if, following the allotment, the company has issued a share warrant in respect of the shares (see section 779).

(3)   If default is made in complying with subsection (1) an offence is committed by every officer of the company who is in default.

(4)   A person guilty of an offence under subsection (3) is liable on summary conviction to a fine not exceeding level 3 on the standard scale and, for continued contravention, a daily default fine not exceeding one-tenth of level 3 on the standard scale.

Transfer of securities

770   Registration of transfer

(1)   A company may not register a transfer of shares in or debentures of the company unless—
    (a)   a proper instrument of transfer has been delivered to it, or
    (b)   the transfer—
        (i)   is an exempt transfer within the Stock Transfer Act 1982, or

(ii)   is in accordance with regulations under Chapter 2 of this Part.

(2)   Subsection (1) does not affect any power of the company to register as shareholder or debenture holder a person to whom the right to any shares in or debentures of the company has been transmitted by operation of law.

(3)   If an election under Chapter 2A of Part 8 is in force in respect of the company, references in this section to registering a transfer (or a person) are to be read as references to delivering particulars of that transfer (or person) to the registrar under that Chapter.

771   Procedure on transfer being lodged

(1)   When a transfer of shares in or debentures of a company has been lodged with the company, the company must either—

(a)   register the transfer, or

(b)   give the transferee notice of refusal to register the transfer, together with its reasons for the refusal,

as soon as practicable and in any event within two months after the date on which the transfer is lodged with it.

(2)   If the company refuses to register the transfer, it must provide the transferee with such further information about the reasons for the refusal as the transferee may reasonably request.

This does not include copies of minutes of meetings of directors.

(2A)   If an election is in force under Chapter 2A of Part 8 in respect of the company, references in this section to registering the transfer are to be read as references to delivering particulars of the transfer to the registrar in accordance with that Chapter.

(3)   If a company fails to comply with this section, an offence is committed by—

(a)   the company, and

(b)   every officer of the company who is in default.

(4)   A person guilty of an offence under this section is liable on summary conviction to a fine not exceeding level 3 on the standard scale and, for continued contravention, a daily default fine not exceeding one-tenth of level 3 on the standard scale.

(5)   This section does not apply—

(a)   in relation to a transfer of shares if the company has issued a share warrant in respect of the shares (see section 779);

(b)   in relation to the transmission of shares or debentures by operation of law.

772   Transfer of shares on application of transferor

On the application of the transferor of any share or interest in a company, the company shall enter in its register of members the name of the transferee (or, as the case may be, deliver the name of the transferee to the registrar under Chapter 2A of Part 8) in the same manner and subject to the same conditions as if the application for the entry (or delivery) were made by the transferee.

773   Execution of share transfer by personal representative

An instrument of transfer of the share or other interest of a deceased member of a company—

(a)   may be made by his personal representative although the personal representative is not himself a member of the company, and

(b)   is as effective as if the personal representative had been such a member at the time of the execution of the instrument.

774   Evidence of grant of probate etc

The production to a company of any document that is by law sufficient evidence of the grant of—

(a)   probate of the will of a deceased person,

(b)   letters of administration of the estate of a deceased person, or

(c)   confirmation as executor of a deceased person,

shall be accepted by the company as sufficient evidence of the grant.

775   Certification of instrument of transfer

(1)   The certification by a company of an instrument of transfer of any shares in, or debentures of, the company is to be taken as a representation by the company to any person acting on the faith of the certification that there have been produced to the company such documents as on their face show a prima facie title to the shares or debentures in the transferor named in the instrument.

(2)   The certification is not to be taken as a representation that the transferor has any title to the shares or debentures.

(3)   Where a person acts on the faith of a false certification by a company made negligently, the company is under the same liability to him as if the certification had been made fraudulently.

(4)   For the purposes of this section—

    (a)   an instrument of transfer is certificated if it bears the words "certificate lodged" (or words to the like effect);

    (b)   the certification of an instrument of transfer is made by a company if—

        (i)   the person issuing the instrument is a person authorised to issue certificated instruments of transfer on the company's behalf, and

        (ii)   the certification is signed by a person authorised to certificate transfers on the company's behalf or by an officer or employee either of the company or of a body corporate so authorised;

    (c)   a certification is treated as signed by a person if—

        (i)   it purports to be authenticated by his signature or initials (whether handwritten or not), and

        (ii)   it is not shown that the signature or initials was or were placed there neither by himself nor by a person authorised to use the signature or initials for the purpose of certificating transfers on the company's behalf.

Issue of certificates etc on transfer

776   Duty of company as to issue of certificates etc on transfer

(1)   A company must, within two months after the date on which a transfer of any of its shares, debentures or debenture stock is lodged with the company, complete and have ready for delivery—

    (a)   the certificates of the shares transferred,

    (b)   the debentures transferred, or

    (c)   the certificates of the debenture stock transferred.

(2)   For this purpose a "transfer" means—

    (a)   a transfer duly stamped and otherwise valid, or

    (b)   an exempt transfer within the Stock Transfer Act 1982,

but does not include a transfer that the company is for any reason entitled to refuse to register and does not register.

(3)   Subsection (1) does not apply—

    (a)   if the conditions of issue of the shares, debentures or debenture stock provide otherwise,

    (b)   in the case of a transfer to a financial institution (see section 778), or

    (c)   in the case of a transfer of shares if, following the transfer, the company has issued a share warrant in respect of the shares (see section 779).

(4)   Subsection (1) has effect subject to section 777 (cases where the Stock Transfer Act 1982 applies).

(5)   If default is made in complying with subsection (1) an offence is committed by every officer of the company who is in default.

(6)   A person guilty of an offence under this section is liable on summary conviction to a fine not exceeding level 3 on the standard scale and, for continued contravention, a daily default fine not exceeding one-tenth of level 3 on the standard scale.

777 Issue of certificates etc: cases within the Stock Transfer Act 1982

(1) Section 776(1) (duty of company as to issue of certificates etc on transfer) does not apply in the case of a transfer to a person where, by virtue of regulations under section 3 of the Stock Transfer Act 1982, he is not entitled to a certificate or other document of or evidencing title in respect of the securities transferred.

(2) But if in such a case the transferee—

    (a) subsequently becomes entitled to such a certificate or other document by virtue of any provision of those regulations, and

    (b) gives notice in writing of that fact to the company,

section 776 (duty to company as to issue of certificates etc) has effect as if the reference in subsection (1) of that section to the date of the lodging of the transfer were a reference to the date of the notice.

Issue of certificates etc on allotment or transfer to financial institution

778 Issue of certificates etc: allotment or transfer to financial institution

(1) A company—

    (a) of which shares or debentures are allotted to a financial institution,

    (b) of which debenture stock is allotted to a financial institution, or

    (c) with which a transfer for transferring shares, debentures or debenture stock to a financial institution is lodged,

is not required in consequence of that allotment or transfer to comply with section 769(1) or 776(1) (duty of company as to issue of certificates etc).

(2) A "financial institution" means—

    (a) a recognised clearing house or a recognised CSD acting in relation to a recognised investment exchange, or

    (b) a nominee of—

        (i) a recognised clearing house or a recognised CSD acting in that way, or

        (ii) a recognised investment exchange,

    designated for the purposes of this section in the rules of the recognised investment exchange in question.

(3) Expressions used in subsection (2) have the same meaning as in Part 18 of the Financial Services and Markets Act 2000.

Share warrants

779 Prohibition on issue of new share warrants and effect of existing share warrants

(1) A company limited by shares may, if so authorised by its articles, issue with respect to any fully paid shares a warrant (a "share warrant") stating that the bearer of the warrant is entitled to the shares specified in it.

(2) A share warrant issued under the company's common seal or (in the case of a company registered in Scotland) subscribed in accordance with the Requirements of Writing (Scotland) Act 1995 entitles the bearer to the shares specified in it and the shares may be transferred by delivery of the warrant.

(3) A company that issues a share warrant may, if so authorised by its articles, provide (by coupons or otherwise) for the payment of the future dividends on the shares included in the warrant.

(4) No share warrant may be issued by a company (irrespective of whether its articles purport to authorise it to do so) on or after the day on which section 84 of the Small Business, Enterprise and Employment Act 2015 comes into force.

780 ...

781 Offences in connection with share warrants (Scotland)

(1) If in Scotland a person—

    (a)   with intent to defraud, forges or alters, or offers, utters, disposes of, or puts off, knowing the same to be forged or altered, any share warrant or coupon, or any document purporting to be a share warrant or coupon issued in pursuance of this Act, or

    (b)   by means of any such forged or altered share warrant, coupon or document—

        (i)   demands or endeavours to obtain or receive any share or interest in a company under this Act, or

        (ii)   demands or endeavours to receive any dividend or money payment in respect of any such share or interest,

    knowing the warrant, coupon or document to be forged or altered,

he commits an offence.

(2)   If in Scotland a person without lawful authority or excuse (of which proof lies on him)—

    (a)   engraves or makes on any plate, wood, stone, or other material, any share warrant or coupon purporting to be—

        (i)   a share warrant or coupon issued or made by any particular company in pursuance of this Act, or

        (ii)   a blank share warrant or coupon so issued or made, or

        (iii)   a part of such a share warrant or coupon, or

    (b)   uses any such plate, wood, stone, or other material, for the making or printing of any such share warrant or coupon, or of any such blank share warrant or coupon or of any part of such a share warrant or coupon, or

    (c)   knowingly has in his custody or possession any such plate, wood, stone, or other material, he commits an offence.

(3)   A person guilty of an offence under subsection (1) is liable on summary conviction to imprisonment for a term not exceeding six months or to a fine not exceeding level 5 on the standard scale (or both).

(4)   A person guilty of an offence under subsection (2) is liable—

    (a)   on conviction on indictment, to imprisonment for a term not exceeding seven years or a fine (or both);

    (b)   on summary conviction, to imprisonment for a term not exceeding six months or a fine not exceeding the statutory maximum (or both).

Supplementary provisions

782   Issue of certificates etc: court order to make good default

(1)   If a company on which a notice has been served requiring it to make good any default in complying with—

    (a)   section 769(1) (duty of company as to issue of certificates etc on allotment),

    (b)   section 776(1) (duty of company as to issue of certificates etc on transfer), or

    (c)   section 780(1) (duty of company as to issue of certificates etc on surrender of share warrant),

fails to make good the default within ten days after service of the notice, the person entitled to have the certificates or the debentures delivered to him may apply to the court.

(2)   The court may on such an application make an order directing the company and any officer of it to make good the default within such time as may be specified in the order.

(3)   The order may provide that all costs (in Scotland, expenses) of and incidental to the application are to be borne by the company or by an officer of it responsible for the default.

CHAPTER 2
EVIDENCING AND TRANSFER OF TITLE TO SECURITIES
WITHOUT WRITTEN INSTRUMENT

Introductory

783 Scope of this Chapter

In this Chapter—

(a) "securities" means shares, debentures, debenture stock, loan stock, bonds, units of a collective investment scheme within the meaning of the Financial Services and Markets Act 2000 and other securities of any description;

(b) references to title to securities include any legal or equitable interest in securities;

(c) references to a transfer of title include a transfer by way of security;

(d) references to transfer without a written instrument include, in relation to bearer securities, transfer without delivery.

784 Power to make regulations

(1) The power to make regulations under this Chapter is exercisable by the Treasury and the Secretary of State, either jointly or concurrently.

(2) References in this Chapter to the authority having power to make regulations shall accordingly be read as references to both or either of them, as the case may require.

(3) Regulations under this Chapter are subject to affirmative resolution procedure.

Powers exercisable

785 Provision enabling procedures for evidencing and transferring title

(1) Provision may be made by regulations for enabling title to securities to be evidenced and transferred without a written instrument.

(2) The regulations may make provision—

(a) for procedures for recording and transferring title to securities, and

(b) for the regulation of those procedures and the persons responsible for or involved in their operation.

(3) The regulations must contain such safeguards as appear to the authority making the regulations appropriate for the protection of investors and for ensuring that competition is not restricted, distorted or prevented.

(4) The regulations may, for the purpose of enabling or facilitating the operation of the procedures provided for by the regulations, make provision with respect to the rights and obligations of persons in relation to securities dealt with under the procedures.

(5) The regulations may include provision for the purpose of giving effect to—

(a) the transmission of title to securities by operation of law;

(b) any restriction on the transfer of title to securities arising by virtue of the provisions of any enactment or instrument, court order or agreement;

(c) any power conferred by any such provision on a person to deal with securities on behalf of the person entitled.

(6) The regulations may make provision with respect to the persons responsible for the operation of the procedures provided for by the regulations—

(a) as to the consequences of their insolvency or incapacity, or

(b) as to the transfer from them to other persons of their functions in relation to those procedures.

(7) The regulations may confer functions on any person, including—

(a) the function of giving guidance or issuing a code of practice in relation to any provision made by the regulations, and

(b) the function of making rules for the purposes of any provision made by the regulations.

(8) The regulations may, in prescribed cases, confer immunity from liability in damages.

786   Provision enabling or requiring arrangements to be adopted

(1)   Regulations under this Chapter may make provision—

    (a)   enabling the members of a company or of any designated class of companies to adopt, by ordinary resolution, arrangements under which title to securities is required to be evidenced or transferred (or both) without a written instrument; or

    (b)   requiring companies, or any designated class of companies, to adopt such arrangements.

(2)   The regulations may make such provision—

    (a)   in respect of all securities issued by a company, or

    (b)   in respect of all securities of a specified description.

(3)   The arrangements provided for by regulations making such provision as is mentioned in subsection (1)—

    (a)   must not be such that a person who but for the arrangements would be entitled to have his name entered in the company's register of members (or, as the case may be, delivered to the registrar under Chapter 2A of Part 8) ceases to be so entitled, and

    (b)   must be such that a person who but for the arrangements would be entitled to exercise any rights in respect of the securities continues to be able effectively to control the exercise of those rights.

(4)   The regulations may—

    (a)   prohibit the issue of any certificate by the company in respect of the issue or transfer of securities,

    (b)   require the provision by the company to holders of securities of statements (at specified intervals or on specified occasions) of the securities held in their name, and

    (c)   make provision as to the matters of which any such certificate or statement is, or is not, evidence.

(5)   In this section—

    (a)   references to a designated class of companies are to a class designated in the regulations or by order under section 787; and

    (b)   "specified" means specified in the regulations.

787   Provision enabling or requiring arrangements to be adopted: order-making powers

(1)   The authority having power to make regulations under this Chapter may by order—

    (a)   designate classes of companies for the purposes of section 786 (provision enabling or requiring arrangements to be adopted);

    (b)   provide that, in relation to securities of a specified description—

        (i)   in a designated class of companies, or

        (ii)   in a specified company or class of companies,

    specified provisions of regulations made under this Chapter by virtue of that section either do not apply or apply subject to specified modifications.

(2)   In subsection (1) "specified" means specified in the order.

(3)   An order under this section is subject to negative resolution procedure.

Supplementary

788   Provision that may be included in regulations

Regulations under this Chapter may—

    (a)   modify or exclude any provision of any enactment or instrument, or any rule of law;

    (b)   apply, with such modifications as may be appropriate, the provisions of any enactment or instrument (including provisions creating criminal offences);

    (c)   require the payment of fees, or enable persons to require the payment of fees, of such amounts as may be specified in the regulations or determined in accordance with them;

    (d)   empower the authority making the regulations to delegate to any person willing and able to discharge them any functions of the authority under the regulations.

789   Duty to consult

Before making—

(a)　regulations under this Chapter, or

(b)　any order under section 787,

the authority having power to make regulations under this Chapter must carry out such consultation as appears to it to be appropriate.

790　**Resolutions to be forwarded to registrar**

Chapter 3 of Part 3 (resolutions affecting a company's constitution) applies to a resolution passed by virtue of regulations under this Chapter.

PART 21A
INFORMATION ABOUT PEOPLE WITH SIGNIFICANT CONTROL

CHAPTER 1
INTRODUCTION

790A　**Overview**

This Part is arranged as follows—

(a)　the remaining provisions of this Chapter identify the companies to which this Part applies and explain some key terms, including what it means to have "significant control" over a company,

(b)　Chapter 2 imposes duties on companies to gather information, and on others to supply information, to enable companies to keep the register required by Chapter 3,

(c)　Chapter 3 requires companies to keep a register, referred to as a register of people with significant control over the company, and to make the register available to the public,

(d)　Chapter 4 gives private companies the option of using an alternative method of record-keeping, and

(e)　Chapter 5 makes provision for excluding certain material from the information available to the public.

790B　**Companies to which this Part applies**

(1)　This Part applies to companies other than—

(a)　companies with voting shares admitted to trading on a UK regulated market or an EU regulated market, and

(b)　companies of any description specified by the Secretary of State by regulations.

(2)　In deciding whether to specify a description of company, the Secretary of State is to have regard to the extent to which companies of that description are bound by disclosure and transparency rules (in the United Kingdom or elsewhere) which are contained in international standards and are equivalent to those applicable to companies referred to in subsection (1)(a).

(3)　...

(4)　Regulations under this section are subject to affirmative resolution procedure.

(5)　In this section—

"voting shares" means shares carrying voting rights;

"voting rights" means rights to vote at general meetings of the company in question, including rights that arise only in certain circumstances.

790C　**Key terms**

(1)　This section explains some key terms used in this Part.

(2)　References to a person with (or having) "significant control" over a company are to an individual who meets one or more of the specified conditions in relation to the company.

(3)　The "specified conditions" are those specified in Part 1 of Schedule 1A.

(4)　Individuals with significant control over a company are either "registrable" or "non-registrable" in relation to the company—

(a)　they are "non-registrable" if they do not hold any interest in the company except through one or more legal entities over each of which they have significant control and—

      (i)   as respects any shares or right in the company which they hold indirectly as described in paragraph 9(1)(b)(i) of Schedule 1A, the legal entity through which the shares or right are held is a relevant legal entity in relation to the company; and

      (ii)   as respects any shares or right in the company which they hold indirectly as described in paragraph 9(1)(b)(ii) of Schedule 1A, at least one of the legal entities in the chain is a relevant legal entity in relation to the company;

(b)   otherwise, they are "registrable",

and references to a "registrable person" in relation to a company are to an individual with significant control over the company who is registrable in relation to that company.

(5)   A "legal entity" is a body corporate or a firm that is a legal person under the law by which it is governed.

(6)   In relation to a company, a legal entity is a "relevant legal entity" if—

    (a)   it would have come within the definition of a person with significant control over the company if it had been an individual, and

    (b)   it is subject to its own disclosure requirements.

(7)   A legal entity is "subject to its own disclosure requirements" if—

    (a)   this Part applies to it (whether by virtue of section 790B or another enactment that extends the application of this Part),

   (aa) it is an eligible Scottish partnership within the meaning of regulation 3(2) of the Scottish Partnerships (Register of People with Significant Control) Regulations 2017,

    (b)   it has voting shares admitted to trading on a UK regulated market or an EU regulated market,

    (c)   it is of a description specified in regulations under section 790B (or that section as extended), or

    (d)   it is of a description specified by the Secretary of State by regulations made under this paragraph.

(8)   A relevant legal entity is either "registrable" or "non-registrable" in relation to a company—

    (a)   it is "non-registrable" if it does not hold any interest in the company except through one or more other legal entities over each of which it has significant control and—

      (i)   as respects any shares or right in the company which it holds indirectly as described in paragraph 9(1)(b)(i) of Schedule 1A, the legal entity through which the shares or right are held is also a relevant legal entity in relation to the company; and

      (ii)   as respects any shares or right in the company which it holds indirectly as described in paragraph 9(1)(b)(ii) of Schedule 1A, at least one of the legal entities in the chain is also a relevant legal entity in relation to the company;

    (b)   otherwise, it is "registrable",

and references to a "registrable relevant legal entity" in relation to a company are to a relevant legal entity which is registrable in relation to that company.

(9)   For the purposes of subsections (4) and (8)—

    (a)   whether someone—

      (i)   holds an interest in a company, or

      (ii)   holds that interest through another legal entity,

is to be determined in accordance with Part 2 of Schedule 1A;

    (b)   whether someone has significant control over that other legal entity is to be determined in accordance with subsections (2) and (3) and Part 1 of Schedule 1A, reading references in those provisions to the company as references to that other entity.

(10)   The register that a company is required to keep under section 790M (register of people with significant control over a company) is referred to as the company's "PSC register".

(11)   In deciding whether to specify a description of legal entity under paragraph (d) of subsection (7), the Secretary of State is to have regard to the extent to which entities of that description are bound by disclosure and transparency rules (in the United Kingdom or elsewhere) equivalent to the ones applying to an entity falling within any other paragraph of that subsection.

(12) Subject to express provision in this Part and to any modification prescribed by regulations under this subsection, this Part is to be read and have effect as if each of the following were an individual, even if they are legal persons under the laws by which they are governed—

    (a) a corporation sole,

    (b) a government or government department of a country or territory or a part of a country or territory,

    (c) an international organisation whose members include two or more countries or territories (or their governments),

    (d) a local authority or local government body in the United Kingdom or elsewhere.

(13) Regulations under subsection (7)(d) are subject to affirmative resolution procedure.

(14) Subject to subsection (13), regulations under this section are subject to negative resolution procedure.

(15) In this section "voting shares" has the same meaning as in section 790B.

CHAPTER 2

INFORMATION-GATHERING

Duty on companies

790D Company's duty to investigate and obtain information

(1) A company to which this Part applies must take reasonable steps—

    (a) to find out if there is anyone who is a registrable person or a registrable relevant legal entity in relation to the company, and

    (b) if so, to identify them.

(2) Without limiting subsection (1), a company to which this Part applies must give notice to anyone whom it knows or has reasonable cause to believe to be a registrable person or a registrable relevant legal entity in relation to it.

(3) The notice, if addressed to an individual, must require the addressee—

    (a) to state whether or not he or she is a registrable person in relation to the company (within the meaning of this Part), and

    (b) if so, to confirm or correct any particulars of his or hers that are included in the notice, and supply any that are missing.

(4) The notice, if addressed to a legal entity, must require the addressee—

    (a) to state whether or not it is a registrable relevant legal entity in relation to the company (within the meaning of this Part), and

    (b) if so, to confirm or correct any of its particulars that are included in the notice, and supply any that are missing.

(5) A company to which this Part applies may also give notice to a person under this section if it knows or has reasonable cause to believe that the person—

    (a) knows the identity of someone who falls within subsection (6), or

    (b) knows the identity of someone likely to have that knowledge.

(6) The persons who fall within this subsection are—

    (a) any registrable person in relation to the company;

    (b) any relevant legal entity in relation to the company;

    (c) any entity which would be a relevant legal entity in relation to the company but for the fact that section 790C(6)(b) does not apply in respect of it.

(7) A notice under subsection (5) may require the addressee—

    (a) to state whether or not the addressee knows the identity of—

        (i) any person who falls within subsection (6), or

        (ii) any person likely to have that knowledge, and

    (b) if so, to supply any particulars of theirs that are within the addressee's knowledge, and state whether or not the particulars are being supplied with the knowledge of each of the persons concerned.

(8)		A notice under this section must state that the addressee is to comply with the notice by no later than the end of the period of one month beginning with the date of the notice.

(9)		The Secretary of State may by regulations make further provision about the giving of notices under this section, including the form and content of any such notices and the manner in which they must be given.

(10)		Regulations under subsection (9) are subject to negative resolution procedure.

(11)		A company is not required to take steps or give notice under this section with respect to a registrable person or registrable relevant legal entity if—
		(a)		the company has already been informed of the person's status as a registrable person or registrable relevant legal entity in relation to it, and been supplied with all the particulars, and
		(b)		in the case of a registrable person, the information and particulars were provided either by the person concerned or with his or her knowledge.

(12)		A person to whom a notice under subsection (5) is given is not required by that notice to disclose any information in respect of which a claim to legal professional privilege (in Scotland, to confidentiality of communications) could be maintained in legal proceedings.

(13)		In this section—
		(a)		a reference to knowing the identity of a person includes knowing information from which that person can be identified, and
		(b)		"particulars" means—
				(i)		in the case of a registrable person or a registrable relevant legal entity, the required particulars (see section 790K), and
				(ii)		in any other case, any particulars that will allow the person to be contacted by the company.

**790E		Company's duty to keep information up-to-date**

(1)		This section applies if particulars of a registrable person or registrable relevant legal entity are stated in a company's PSC register.

(2)		The company must give notice to the person or entity if the company knows or has reasonable cause to believe that a relevant change has occurred.

(3)		In the case of a registrable person, a "relevant change" occurs if—
		(a)		the person ceases to be a registrable person in relation to the company, or
		(b)		any other change occurs as a result of which the particulars stated for the person in the PSC register are incorrect or incomplete.

(4)		In the case of a registrable relevant legal entity, a "relevant change" occurs if—
		(a)		the entity ceases to be a registrable relevant legal entity in relation to the company, or
		(b)		any other change occurs as a result of which the particulars stated for the entity in the PSC register are incorrect or incomplete.

(5)		The company must give the notice—
		(a)		as soon as reasonably practicable, and
		(b)		in any event before the end of the period of 14 days beginning with the earlier of the day after it learns of the change and the day after it first has reasonable cause to believe that the change has occurred.

(6)		The notice must require the addressee—
		(a)		to confirm whether or not the change has occurred, and
		(b)		if so—
				(i)		to state the date of the change, and
				(ii)		to confirm or correct the particulars included in the notice, and supply any that are missing from the notice.

(7)		Subsections (8) to (10) of section 790D apply to notices under this section as to notices under that section.

(8)		A company is not required to give notice under this section if—
		(a)		the company has already been informed of the relevant change, and

(b)   in the case of a registrable person, that information was provided either by the person concerned or with his or her knowledge.

790F   Failure by company to comply with information duties

(1)   If a company fails to comply with a duty under section 790D or 790E to take steps or give notice, an offence is committed by—

(a)   the company, and

(b)   every officer of the company who is in default.

(2)   A person guilty of an offence under this section is liable—

(a)   on conviction on indictment, to imprisonment for a term not exceeding two years or a fine (or both);

(b)   on summary conviction—

    (i)   in England and Wales, to imprisonment for a term not exceeding twelve months or a fine (or both);

    (ii)   in Scotland, to imprisonment for a term not exceeding twelve months or to a fine not exceeding the statutory maximum (or both);

    (iii)   in Northern Ireland, to imprisonment for a term not exceeding six months or to a fine not exceeding the statutory maximum (or both).

Duty on others

790G   Duty to supply information

(1)   This section applies to a person if—

(a)   the person is a registrable person or a registrable relevant legal entity in relation to a company,

(b)   the person knows that to be the case or ought reasonably to do so,

(c)   the required particulars of the person are not stated in the company's PSC register,

(d)   the person has not received notice from the company under section 790D(2), and

(e)   the circumstances described in paragraphs (a) to (d) have continued for a period of at least one month.

(2)   The person must—

(a)   notify the company of the person's status (as a registrable person or registrable relevant legal entity) in relation to the company,

(b)   state the date, to the best of the person's knowledge, on which the person acquired that status, and

(c)   give the company the required particulars (see section 790K).

(3)   The duty under subsection (2) must be complied with by the end of the period of one month beginning with the day on which all the conditions in subsection (1)(a) to (e) were first met with respect to the person.

790H   Duty to update information

(1)   This section applies to a person if—

(a)   the required particulars of the person (whether a registrable person or a registrable relevant legal entity) are stated in a company's PSC register,

(b)   a relevant change occurs,

(c)   the person knows of the change or ought reasonably to do so,

(d)   the company's PSC register has not been altered to reflect the change, and

(e)   the person has not received notice from the company under section 790E by the end of the period of one month beginning with the day on which the change occurred.

(2)   The person must—

(a)   notify the company of the change,

(b)   state the date on which it occurred, and

(c)   give the company any information needed to update the PSC register.

(3)   The duty under subsection (2) must be complied with by the later of—

    (a)   the end of the period of 2 months beginning with the day on which the change occurred, and

    (b)   the end of the period of one month beginning with the day on which the person discovered the change.

(4)   "Relevant change" has the same meaning as in section 790E.

Compliance

790I   Enforcement of disclosure requirements

Schedule 1B contains provisions for when a person (whether an individual or a legal entity) fails to comply with a notice under section 790D or 790E or a duty under section 790G or 790H.

Exemption from information and registration requirements

790J   Power to make exemptions

(1)   The Secretary of State may exempt a person (whether an individual or a legal entity) under this section.

(2)   The effect of an exemption is—

    (a)   the person is not required to comply with any notice under section 790D(2) or 790E (but if a notice is received, the person must bring the existence of the exemption to the attention of the company that sent it),

    (b)   companies are not obliged to take steps or give notice under those sections to or with respect to that person,

    (c)   notices under section 790D(5) do not require anyone else to give any information about that person,

    (d)   the duties imposed by sections 790G and 790H do not apply to that person, and

    (e)   the person does not count for the purposes of section 790M as a registrable person or, as the case may be, a registrable relevant legal entity in relation to any company.

(3)   The Secretary of State must not grant an exemption under this section unless the Secretary of State is satisfied that, having regard to any undertaking given by the person to be exempted, there are special reasons why that person should be exempted.

Required particulars

790K   Required particulars

(1)   The "required particulars" of an individual who is a registrable person are—

    (a)   name,

    (b)   a service address,

    (c)   the country or state (or part of the United Kingdom) in which the individual is usually resident,

    (d)   nationality,

    (e)   date of birth,

    (f)   usual residential address,

    (g)   the date on which the individual became a registrable person in relation to the company in question,

    (h)   the nature of his or her control over that company (see Schedule 1A), and

    (i)   if, in relation to that company, restrictions on using or disclosing any of the individual's PSC particulars are in force under regulations under section 790ZG, that fact.

(2)   In the case of a person in relation to which this Part has effect by virtue of section 790C(12) as if the person were an individual, the "required particulars" are—

    (a)   name,

    (b)   principal office,

    (c)   the legal form of the person and the law by which it is governed,

    (d)   the date on which it became a registrable person in relation to the company in question, and

    (e)   the nature of its control over the company (see Schedule 1A).

(3) The "required particulars" of a registrable relevant legal entity are—

    (a) corporate or firm name,

    (b) registered or principal office,

    (c) the legal form of the entity and the law by which it is governed,

    (d) if applicable, the register of companies in which it is entered (including details of the state) and its registration number in that register,

    (e) the date on which it became a registrable relevant legal entity in relation to the company in question, and

    (f) the nature of its control over that company (see Schedule 1A).

(4) Section 163(2) (particulars of directors to be registered: individuals) applies for the purposes of subsection (1).

(5) The Secretary of State may by regulations make further provision about the particulars required by subsections (1)(h), (2)(e) and (3)(f).

(6) Regulations under subsection (5) are subject to negative resolution procedure.

790L Required particulars: power to amend

(1) The Secretary of State may by regulations amend section 790K so as to add to or remove from any of the lists of required particulars.

(2) Regulations under this section are subject to affirmative resolution procedure.

CHAPTER 3
REGISTER OF PEOPLE WITH SIGNIFICANT CONTROL

790M Duty to keep register

(1) A company to which this Part applies must keep a register of people with significant control over the company.

(2) The required particulars of any individual with significant control over the company who is "registrable" in relation to the company must be entered in the register before the end of the period of 14 days beginning with the day after all the required particulars of that individual are first confirmed.

(3) The company must not enter any of the individual's particulars in the register until they have all been confirmed.

(4) Particulars of any individual with significant control over the company who is "non-registrable" in relation to the company must not be entered in the register.

(5) The required particulars of any entity that is a registrable relevant legal entity in relation to the company must be entered in the register before the end of the period of 14 days beginning with the day after the company first has all the required particulars of that entity.

(6) If the company becomes aware of a relevant change (within the meaning of section 790E) with respect to a registrable person … whose particulars are stated in the register, the company must enter in the register—

    (a) the changes to the required particulars resulting from the relevant change, and

    (b) the date on which the relevant change occurred,

before the end of the period of 14 days beginning with the day after all of those changes and that date are first confirmed.

(6A) If the company becomes aware of a relevant change (within the meaning of section 790E) with respect to a registrable relevant legal entity whose particulars are stated in the register, the company must enter in the register—

    (a) the changes to the required particulars resulting from the relevant change, and

    (b) the date on which the relevant change occurred,

before the end of the period of 14 days beginning with the day after the company first has details of all of those changes and that date.

(7)   The Secretary of State may by regulations require additional matters to be noted in a company's PSC register.

(7A)   If a company is required by regulations made under subsection (7) to note an additional matter in its PSC register, the company must note the additional matter before the end of the period of 14 days beginning with the day after the requirement arises.

(8)   Regulations under subsection (7) are subject to affirmative resolution procedure.

(9)   A person's required particulars, a change to such particulars and the date of any relevant change with respect to a person, are considered for the purposes of this section to have been "confirmed" if—
   (a) the person supplied or confirmed them to the company (whether voluntarily, pursuant to a duty imposed by this Part or otherwise),
   (b) another person did so but with that person's knowledge, or
   (c) they were included in a statement of initial significant control delivered to the registrar under section 9 by subscribers wishing to form the company.

(10)   In the case of someone who was a registrable person or a registrable relevant legal entity in relation to the company on its incorporation—
   (a) the date to be entered in the register as the date on which the individual became a registrable person, or the entity became a registrable relevant legal entity, is to be the date of incorporation, and
   (b) in the case of a registrable person, that particular is deemed to have been "confirmed".

(11)   For the purposes of this section—
   (a) if a person's usual residential address is the same as his or her service address, the entry for him or her in the register may state that fact instead of repeating the address (but this does not apply in a case where the service address is stated to be "The company's registered office");
   (b) nothing in section 126 (trusts not to be entered on register) affects what may be entered in a company's PSC register or is receivable by the registrar in relation to people with significant control over a company (even if they are members of the company);
   (c) see section 790J (exemptions) for cases where a person does not count as a registrable person or a registrable relevant legal entity.

(12)   If a company makes default in complying with this section, an offence is committed by—
   (a) the company, and
   (b) every officer of the company who is in default.

(13)   A person guilty of an offence under this section is liable on summary conviction to a fine not exceeding level 3 on the standard scale and, for continued contravention, a daily default fine not exceeding one-tenth of level 3 on the standard scale.

(14)   A company to which this Part applies is not by virtue of anything done for the purposes of this section affected with notice of, or put upon inquiry as to, the rights of any person in relation to any shares or rights in or with respect to the company.

790N Register to be kept available for inspection

(1)   A company's PSC register must be kept available for inspection—
   (a) at its registered office, or
   (b) at a place specified in regulations under section 1136.

(2)   A company must give notice to the registrar of the place where its PSC register is kept available for inspection and of any change in that place.

(3)   No such notice is required if the register has, at all times since it came into existence, been kept available for inspection at the company's registered office.

(4)   If a company makes default for 14 days in complying with subsection (2), an offence is committed by—
   (a) the company, and
   (b) every officer of the company who is in default.

(5)   A person guilty of an offence under this section is liable on summary conviction to a fine not exceeding level 3 on the standard scale and, for continued contravention, a daily default fine not exceeding one-tenth of level 3 on the standard scale.

790O   Rights to inspect and require copies

(1)   A company's PSC register must be open to the inspection of any person without charge.

(2)   Any person may require a copy of a company's PSC register, or any part of it, on payment of such fee as may be prescribed.

(3)   A person seeking to exercise either of the rights conferred by this section must make a request to the company to that effect.

(4)   The request must contain the following information—

    (a)   in the case of an individual, his or her name and address,

    (b)   in the case of an organisation, the name and address of an individual responsible for making the request on behalf of the organisation, and

    (c)   the purpose for which the information is to be used.

790P   PSC register: response to request for inspection or copy

(1)   Where a company receives a request under section 790O, it must within 5 working days either—

    (a)   comply with the request, or

    (b)   apply to the court.

(2)   If it applies to the court, it must notify the person making the request.

(3)   If on an application under this section the court is satisfied that the inspection or copy is not sought for a proper purpose—

    (a)   it must direct the company not to comply with the request, and

    (b)   it may further order that the company's costs (in Scotland, expenses) on the application be paid in whole or in part by the person who made the request, even if that person is not a party to the application.

(4)   If the court makes such a direction and it appears to the court that the company is or may be subject to other requests made for a similar purpose (whether made by the same person or different persons), it may direct that the company is not to comply with any such request. The order must contain such provision as appears to the court appropriate to identify the requests to which it applies.

(5)   If on an application under this section the court does not direct the company not to comply with the request, the company must comply with the request immediately upon the court giving its decision or, as the case may be, the proceedings being discontinued.

790Q   PSC register: refusal of inspection or default in providing copy

(1)   If an inspection required under section 790O is refused or default is made in providing a copy required under that section, otherwise than in accordance with an order of the court, an offence is committed by—

    (a)   the company, and

    (b)   every officer of the company who is in default.

(2)   A person guilty of an offence under this section is liable on summary conviction to a fine not exceeding level 3 on the standard scale and, for continued contravention, a daily default fine not exceeding one-tenth of level 3 on the standard scale.

(3)   In the case of any such refusal or default the court may by order compel an immediate inspection or, as the case may be, direct that the copy required be sent to the person requesting it.

790R   PSC register: offences in connection with request for or disclosure of information

(1)   It is an offence for a person knowingly or recklessly to make in a request under section 790O a statement that is misleading, false or deceptive in a material particular.

(2)   It is an offence for a person in possession of information obtained by exercise of either of the rights conferred by that section—

(a) to do anything that results in the information being disclosed to another person, or

(b) to fail to do anything with the result that the information is disclosed to another person,

knowing, or having reason to suspect, that person may use the information for a purpose that is not a proper purpose.

(3) A person guilty of an offence under this section is liable—

(a) on conviction on indictment, to imprisonment for a term not exceeding two years or a fine (or both);

(b) on summary conviction—

(i) in England and Wales, to imprisonment for a term not exceeding twelve months or to a fine (or both);

(ii) in Scotland, to imprisonment for a term not exceeding twelve months or to a fine not exceeding the statutory maximum (or both);

(iii) in Northern Ireland, to imprisonment for a term not exceeding six months or to a fine not exceeding the statutory maximum (or both).

790S   Information as to state of register

(1) Where a person inspects the PSC register, or the company provides a person with a copy of the register or any part of it, the company must inform the person of the most recent date (if any) on which alterations were made to the register and whether there are further alterations to be made.

(2) If a company fails to provide the information required under subsection (1), an offence is committed by—

(a) the company, and

(b) every officer of the company who is in default.

(3) A person guilty of an offence under this section is liable on summary conviction to a fine not exceeding level 3 on the standard scale.

790T   Protected information

(1) Section 790N and subsections (1) and (2) of section 790O are subject to—

(a) section 790ZF (protection of information as to usual residential address), and

(b) any provision of regulations made under section 790ZG (protection of material).

(2) Subsection (1) is not to be taken to affect the generality of the power conferred by virtue of section 790ZG(3)(f).

790U   Removal of entries from the register

(1) An entry relating to an individual who used to be a registrable person may be removed from the company's PSC register after the expiration of 10 years from the date on which the individual ceased to be a registrable person in relation to the company.

(2) An entry relating to an entity that used to be a registrable relevant legal entity may be removed from the company's PSC register after the expiration of 10 years from the date on which the entity ceased to be a registrable relevant legal entity in relation to the company.

790V   Power of court to rectify register

(1) If—

(a) the name of any person is, without sufficient cause, entered in or omitted from a company's PSC register as a registrable person or registrable relevant legal entity, or

(b) default is made or unnecessary delay takes place in entering on the PSC register the fact that a person has ceased to be a registrable person or registrable relevant legal entity,

the person aggrieved or any other interested party may apply to the court for rectification of the register.

(2) The court may either refuse the application or may order rectification of the register and payment by the company of any damages sustained by any party aggrieved.

(3) On such an application, the court may—

(a) decide any question as to whether the name of any person who is a party to the application should or should not be entered in or omitted from the register, and

(b) more generally, decide any question necessary or expedient to be decided for rectification of the register.

(4) In the case of a company required by this Act to send information stated in its PSC register to the registrar of companies, the court, when making an order for rectification of the register, must by its order direct notice of the rectification to be given to the registrar.

(5) The reference in this section to "any other interested party" is to—

(a) any member of the company, and

(b) any other person who is a registrable person or a registrable relevant legal entity in relation to the company.

790VA Notification of changes to the registrar

(1) Subsection (2) applies where a company—

(a) enters required particulars in its PSC register,

(b) alters required particulars in its PSC register, or

(c) notes in its PSC register an additional matter that is required to be noted by regulations under section 790M(7).

(2) The company must give notice to the registrar of the change made to its PSC register, and the date on which the change was made, before the end of the period of 14 days beginning with the day after it makes the change.

(3) If default is made in complying with this section, an offence is committed by—

(a) the company, and

(b) every officer of the company who is in default.

(4) For the purpose of subsection (3) a shadow director is treated as an officer of the company.

(5) A person guilty of an offence under this section is liable on summary conviction to a fine not exceeding level 3 on the standard scale and, for continued contravention, a daily default fine not exceeding one-tenth of level 3 on the standard scale.

CHAPTER 4
ALTERNATIVE METHOD OF RECORD-KEEPING

790W Introductory

(1) This Chapter sets out rules allowing private companies to keep information on the register kept by the registrar instead of entering it in their PSC register.

(2) The register kept by the registrar (see section 1080) is referred to in this Chapter as "the central register".

(3) Chapter 3 must be read with this Chapter.

(4) Nothing in this Chapter affects the duties imposed by Chapter 2.

(5) Where an election under section 790X is in force in respect of a company, references in Chapter 2 to the company's PSC register are to be read as references to the central register.

790X Right to make an election

(1) An election may be made under this section—

(a) by the subscribers wishing to form a private company under this Act, or

(b) by the private company itself once it is formed and registered.

(2) The election is of no effect unless—

(a) notice of the intention to make the election was given to each eligible person at least 14 days before the day on which the election was made, and

(b) no objection was received by the subscribers or, as the case may be, the company from any eligible person within that notice period.

(3) A person is an "eligible person" if—

(a) in a case of an election by the subscribers wishing to form a private company, the person's particulars would, but for the election, be required to be entered in the company's PSC register on its incorporation, and

(b) in the case of an election by the company itself—

> (i)   the person is a registrable person or a registrable relevant legal entity in relation to the company, and
>
> (ii)   the person's particulars are stated in the company's PSC register.

(4)   An election under this section is made by giving notice of election to the registrar.

(5)   If the notice is given by subscribers wishing to form a private company—

    (a)   it must be given when the documents required to be delivered under section 9 are delivered to the registrar, and

    (b)   it must be accompanied by a statement confirming that no objection was received as mentioned in subsection (2).

(6)   If the notice is given by the company, it must be accompanied by—

    (a)   a statement confirming that no objection was received as mentioned in subsection (2), and

    (b)   a statement containing all the information that is required to be contained in the company's PSC register as at the date of the notice in respect of matters that are current as at that date.

(7)   The company must where necessary update the statement sent under subsection (6)(b) to ensure that the final version delivered to the registrar contains all the information that is required to be contained in the company's PSC register as at the time immediately before the election takes effect (see section 790Y) in respect of matters that are current as at that time.

(8)   The obligation in subsection (7) to update the statement includes an obligation to rectify it (where necessary) in consequence of the company's PSC register being rectified (whether before or after the election takes effect).

(9)   If default is made in complying with subsection (7), an offence is committed by—

    (a)   the company, and

    (b)   every officer of the company who is in default.

For this purpose a shadow director is treated as an officer of the company.

(10)   A person guilty of an offence under this section is liable on summary conviction to a fine not exceeding level 3 on the standard scale and, for continued contravention, a daily default fine not exceeding one-tenth of level 3 on the standard scale.

(11)   A reference in this Chapter to matters that are current as at a given date or time is a reference to—

    (a)   persons who are a registrable person or registrable relevant legal entity in relation to the company as at that date or time and whose particulars are required to be contained in the company's PSC register as at that date or time, and

    (b)   any other matters that are current as at that date or time.

790Y   Effective date of election

(1)   An election made under section 790X takes effect when the notice of election is registered by the registrar.

(2)   The election remains in force until either—

    (a)   the company ceases to be a private company, or

    (b)   a notice of withdrawal sent by the company under section 790ZD is registered by the registrar, whichever occurs first.

790Z   Effect of election on obligations under Chapter 3

(1)   The effect of an election under section 790X on a company's obligations under Chapter 3 is as follows.

(2)   The company's obligation to maintain a PSC register does not apply with respect to the period when the election is in force.

(3)   This means that, during that period—

    (a)   the company must continue to keep a PSC register in accordance with Chapter 3 (a "historic" register) containing all the information that was required to be stated in that register as at the time immediately before the election took effect, but

    (b)   the company does not have to update that register to reflect any changes that occur after that time.

(4)   The provisions of Chapter 3 (including the rights to inspect or require copies of the PSC register) continue to apply to the historic register during the period when the election is in force.

(5)   The company must place a note in its historic register—

    (a)   stating that an election under section 790X is in force,

    (b)   recording when that election took effect, and

    (c)   indicating that up-to-date information about people with significant control over the company is available for public inspection on the central register.

(6)   Subsections (12) and (13) of section 790M apply if a company makes default in complying with subsection (5) as they apply if a company makes default in complying with that section.

(7)   The obligations under this section with respect to a historic register do not apply in a case where the election was made by subscribers wishing to form a private company.

790ZA Duty to notify registrar of changes

(1)   The duty under subsection (2) applies during the period when an election under section 790X is in force.

(2)   The company must deliver to the registrar any information that the company would during that period have been obliged under Chapter 3 to enter in its PSC register, had the election not been in force.

(3)   The information must be delivered as soon as reasonably practicable after the company becomes aware of it and, in any event, no later than the time by which the company would have been required to enter the information in its PSC register.

(4)   If default is made in complying with this section, an offence is committed by—

    (a)   the company, and

    (b)   every officer of the company who is in default.

    For this purpose a shadow director is treated as an officer of the company.

(5)   A person guilty of an offence under this section is liable on summary conviction to a fine not exceeding level 3 on the standard scale and, for continued contravention, a daily default fine not exceeding one-tenth of level 3 on the standard scale.

790ZB Information as to state of central register

(1)   When a person inspects or requests a copy of material on the central register relating to a company in respect of which an election under section 790X is in force, the person may ask the company to confirm that all information that the company is required to deliver to the registrar under this Chapter has been delivered.

(2)   If a company fails to respond to a request under subsection (1), an offence is committed by—

    (a)   the company, and

    (b)   every officer of the company who is in default.

(3)   A person guilty of an offence under this section is liable on summary conviction to a fine not exceeding level 3 on the standard scale.

790ZC Power of court to order company to remedy default or delay

(1)   This section applies if—

    (a)   the name of a person is without sufficient cause included in, or omitted from, information that a company delivers to the registrar under this Chapter concerning persons who are a registrable person or a registrable relevant legal entity in relation to the company, or

    (b)   default is made or unnecessary delay takes place in informing the registrar under this Chapter that a person—

        (i)   has become a registrable person or a registrable relevant legal entity in relation to the company, or

        (ii)   has ceased to be a registrable person or a registrable relevant legal entity in relation to it.

(2)   The person aggrieved, or any other interested party, may apply to the court for an order requiring the company to deliver to the registrar the information (or statements)necessary to rectify the position.

(3)   The court may either refuse the application or may make the order and order the company to pay any damages sustained by any party aggrieved.

(4)   On such an application the court may decide—

(a)   any question as to whether the name of any person who is a party to the application should or should not be included in or omitted from information delivered to the registrar under this Chapter about persons who are a registrable person or a registrable relevant legal entity in relation to the company, and

(b)   any question necessary or expedient to be decided for rectifying the position.

(5)   Nothing in this section affects a person's rights under section 1095 or 1096 (rectification of register on application to registrar or under court order).

(6)   The reference in this section to "any other interested party" is to—

(a)   any member of the company, and

(b)   any other person who is a registrable person or a registrable relevant legal entity in relation to the company.

790ZD Withdrawing the election

(1)   A company may withdraw an election made by or in respect of it under section 790X.

(2)   Withdrawal is achieved by giving notice of withdrawal to the registrar.

(3)   The withdrawal takes effect when the notice is registered by the registrar.

(4)   The effect of withdrawal is that the company's obligation under Chapter 3 to maintain a PSC register applies from then on with respect to the period going forward.

(5)   This means that, when the withdrawal takes effect—

(a)   the company must enter in its PSC register all the information that is required to be contained in that register in respect of matters that are current as at that time,

(b)   the company must also retain in its register all the information that it was required under section 790Z(3)(a) to keep in a historic register while the election was in force, but

(c)   the company is not required to enter in its register information relating to the period when the election was in force that is no longer current.

(6)   The company must place a note in its PSC register—

(a)   stating that the election under section 790X has been withdrawn,

(b)   recording when that withdrawal took effect, and

(c)   indicating that information about people with significant control over the company relating to the period when the election was in force that is no longer current is available for public inspection on the central register.

(7)   Subsections (12) and (13) of section 790M apply if a company makes default in complying with subsection (6) as they apply if a company makes default in complying with that section.

790ZE Power to extend option to public companies

(1)   The Secretary of State may by regulations amend this Act—

(a)   to extend this Chapter (with or without modification) to public companies or public companies of a class specified in the regulations, and

(b)   to make such other amendments as the Secretary of State thinks fit in consequence of that extension.

(2)   Regulations under this section are subject to affirmative resolution procedure.

CHAPTER 5
PROTECTION FROM DISCLOSURE

790ZF Protection of information as to usual residential address

(1)   The provisions of sections 240 to 244 (directors' residential addresses: protection from disclosure) apply to information within subsection (2) as to protected information within the meaning of those sections.

(2)   The information within this subsection is—

    (a)   information as to the usual residential address of a person with significant control over a company, and

    (b)   the information that such a person's service address is his or her usual residential address.

(3)   ...

790ZG Power to make regulations protecting material

(1)   The Secretary of State may by regulations—

    (a)   require a company to refrain from using, or refrain from disclosing, relevant PSC particulars except in circumstances specified in the regulations;

    (b)   confer power on the registrar, on application, to make an order requiring a company to refrain from using, or refrain from disclosing, relevant PSC particulars except in circumstances specified in the regulations.

(2)   "Relevant PSC particulars" means such particulars of a person with significant control over the company as may be prescribed.

(3)   The reference in subsection (2) to a person with significant control over the company—

    (a)   includes a person who used to be such a person, but

    (b)   does not include any person in relation to which this Part has effect by virtue of section 790C(12) as if the person were an individual.

(4)   Regulations under subsection (1)(b) may make provision as to—

    (a)   who may make an application;

    (b)   the grounds on which an application may be made;

    (c)   the information to be included in and documents to accompany an application;

    (d)   how an application is to be determined;

    (e)   the notice to be given of an application and its outcome;

    (f)   the duration of and procedures for revoking the restrictions on use and disclosure.

(5)   Provision under subsection (4) may in particular—

    (a)   confer a discretion on the registrar;

    (b)   provide for a question to be referred to a person other than the registrar for the purposes of determining the application or revoking the restrictions.

(6)   Regulations under this section are subject to affirmative resolution procedure.

(7)   Nothing in this section or in regulations made under it affects the use or disclosure of particulars of a person in any other capacity (for example, the use or disclosure of particulars of a person in that person's capacity as a member or director of the company).

790ZH Offence of failing to comply with regulations under section 790ZG

(1)   If a company contravenes a restriction on the use or disclosure of information imposed by virtue of regulations under subsection 790ZG, an offence is committed by—

    (a)   the company, and

    (b)   every officer of the company who is in default.

(2)   A person guilty of an offence under this section is liable on summary conviction—

    (a)   in England and Wales, to a fine;

    (b)   in Scotland or Northern Ireland, to a fine not exceeding level 5 on the standard scale and, for continued contravention, a daily default fine not exceeding one-tenth of level 5 on the standard scale.

PART 22

INFORMATION ABOUT INTERESTS IN A COMPANY'S SHARES

Introductory

791   Companies to which this Part applies

This Part applies only to public companies.

792   Shares to which this Part applies

(1)   References in this Part to a company's shares are to the company's issued shares of a class carrying rights to vote in all circumstances at general meetings of the company (including any shares held as treasury shares).

(2)   The temporary suspension of voting rights in respect of any shares does not affect the application of this Part in relation to interests in those or any other shares.

Notice requiring information about interests in shares

793   Notice by company requiring information about interests in its shares

(1)   A public company may give notice under this section to any person whom the company knows or has reasonable cause to believe—

    (a)   to be interested in the company's shares, or

    (b)   to have been so interested at any time during the three years immediately preceding the date on which the notice is issued.

(2)   The notice may require the person—

    (a)   to confirm that fact or (as the case may be) to state whether or not it is the case, and

    (b)   if he holds, or has during that time held, any such interest, to give such further information as may be required in accordance with the following provisions of this section.

(3)   The notice may require the person to whom it is addressed to give particulars of his own present or past interest in the company's shares (held by him at any time during the three year period mentioned in subsection (1)(b)).

(4)   The notice may require the person to whom it is addressed, where—

    (a)   his interest is a present interest and another interest in the shares subsists, or

    (b)   another interest in the shares subsisted during that three year period at a time when his interest subsisted,

to give, so far as lies within his knowledge, such particulars with respect to that other interest as may be required by the notice.

(5)   The particulars referred to in subsections (3) and (4) include—

    (a)   the identity of persons interested in the shares in question, and

    (b)   whether persons interested in the same shares are or were parties to—

        (i)   an agreement to which section 824 applies (certain share acquisition agreements), or

        (ii)   an agreement or arrangement relating to the exercise of any rights conferred by the holding of the shares.

(6)   The notice may require the person to whom it is addressed, where his interest is a past interest, to give (so far as lies within his knowledge) particulars of the identity of the person who held that interest immediately upon his ceasing to hold it.

(7)   The information required by the notice must be given within such reasonable time as may be specified in the notice.

794   Notice requiring information: order imposing restrictions on shares

(1)   Where—

    (a)   a notice under section 793 (notice requiring information about interests in company's shares) is served by a company on a person who is or was interested in shares in the company, and

    (b)   that person fails to give the company the information required by the notice within the time specified in it,

the company may apply to the court for an order directing that the shares in question be subject to restrictions.

For the effect of such an order see section 797.

(2)   If the court is satisfied that such an order may unfairly affect the rights of third parties in respect of the shares, the court may, for the purpose of protecting those rights and subject to such terms as

it thinks fit, direct that such acts by such persons or descriptions of persons and for such purposes as may be set out in the order shall not constitute a breach of the restrictions.

(3) On an application under this section the court may make an interim order. Any such order may be made unconditionally or on such terms as the court thinks fit.

(4) Sections 798 to 802 make further provision about orders under this section.

795 Notice requiring information: offences

(1) A person who—

    (a) fails to comply with a notice under section 793 (notice requiring information about interests in company's shares), or

    (b) in purported compliance with such a notice—

        (i) makes a statement that he knows to be false in a material particular, or

        (ii) recklessly makes a statement that is false in a material particular,

commits an offence.

(2) A person does not commit an offence under subsection (1)(a) if he proves that the requirement to give information was frivolous or vexatious.

(3) A person guilty of an offence under this section is liable—

    (a) on conviction on indictment, to imprisonment for a term not exceeding two years or a fine (or both);

    (b) on summary conviction—

        (i) in England and Wales, to imprisonment for a term not exceeding twelve months or to a fine not exceeding the statutory maximum (or both);

        (ii) in Scotland or Northern Ireland, to imprisonment for a term not exceeding six months, or to a fine not exceeding the statutory maximum (or both).

796 Notice requiring information: persons exempted from obligation to comply

(1) A person is not obliged to comply with a notice under section 793 (notice requiring information about interests in company's shares) if he is for the time being exempted by the Secretary of State from the operation of that section.

(2) The Secretary of State must not grant any such exemption unless—

    (a) he has consulted the Governor of the Bank of England, and

    (b) he (the Secretary of State) is satisfied that, having regard to any undertaking given by the person in question with respect to any interest held or to be held by him in any shares, there are special reasons why that person should not be subject to the obligations imposed by that section.

Orders imposing restrictions on shares

797 Consequences of order imposing restrictions

(1) The effect of an order under section 794 that shares are subject to restrictions is as follows—

    (a) any transfer of the shares is void;

    (b) no voting rights are exercisable in respect of the shares;

    (c) no further shares may be issued in right of the shares or in pursuance of an offer made to their holder;

    (d) except in a liquidation, no payment may be made of sums due from the company on the shares, whether in respect of capital or otherwise.

(2) Where shares are subject to the restriction in subsection (1)(a), an agreement to transfer the shares is void.

This does not apply to an agreement to transfer the shares on the making of an order under section 800 made by virtue of subsection (3)(b) (removal of restrictions in case of court-approved transfer).

(3) Where shares are subject to the restriction in subsection (1)(c) or (d), an agreement to transfer any right to be issued with other shares in right of those shares, or to receive any payment on them (otherwise than in a liquidation), is void.

This does not apply to an agreement to transfer any such right on the making of an order under section 800 made by virtue of subsection (3)(b) (removal of restrictions in case of court-approved transfer).

(4) The provisions of this section are subject—

    (a) to any directions under section 794(2) or section 799(3) (directions for protection of third parties), and

    (b) in the case of an interim order under section 794(3), to the terms of the order.

798 Penalty for attempted evasion of restrictions

(1) This section applies where shares are subject to restrictions by virtue of an order under section 794.

(2) A person commits an offence if he—

    (a) exercises or purports to exercise any right—

        (i) to dispose of shares that to his knowledge, are for the time being subject to restrictions, or

        (ii) to dispose of any right to be issued with any such shares, or

    (b) votes in respect of any such shares (whether as holder or proxy), or appoints a proxy to vote in respect of them, or

    (c) being the holder of any such shares, fails to notify of their being subject to those restrictions a person whom he does not know to be aware of that fact but does know to be entitled (apart from the restrictions) to vote in respect of those shares whether as holder or as proxy, or

    (d) being the holder of any such shares, or being entitled to a right to be issued with other shares in right of them, or to receive any payment on them (otherwise than in a liquidation), enters into an agreement which is void under section 797(2) or (3).

(3) If shares in a company are issued in contravention of the restrictions, an offence is committed by—

    (a) the company, and

    (b) every officer of the company who is in default.

(4) A person guilty of an offence under this section is liable—

    (a) on conviction on indictment, to a fine;

    (b) on summary conviction, to a fine not exceeding the statutory maximum.

(5) The provisions of this section are subject—

    (a) to any directions under—

        section 794(2) (directions for protection of third parties), or

        section 799 or 800 (relaxation or removal of restrictions), and

    (b) in the case of an interim order under section 794(3), to the terms of the order.

799 Relaxation of restrictions

(1) An application may be made to the court on the ground that an order directing that shares shall be subject to restrictions unfairly affects the rights of third parties in respect of the shares.

(2) An application for an order under this section may be made by the company or by any person aggrieved.

(3) If the court is satisfied that the application is well-founded, it may, for the purpose of protecting the rights of third parties in respect of the shares, and subject to such terms as it thinks fit, direct that such acts by such persons or descriptions of persons and for such purposes as may be set out in the order do not constitute a breach of the restrictions.

800 Removal of restrictions

(1) An application may be made to the court for an order directing that the shares shall cease to be subject to restrictions.

(2) An application for an order under this section may be made by the company or by any person aggrieved.

(3) The court must not make an order under this section unless—

    (a)   it is satisfied that the relevant facts about the shares have been disclosed to the company and no unfair advantage has accrued to any person as a result of the earlier failure to make that disclosure, or

    (b)   the shares are to be transferred for valuable consideration and the court approves the transfer.

(4)   An order under this section made by virtue of subsection (3)(b) may continue, in whole or in part, the restrictions mentioned in section 797(1)(c) and (d) (restrictions on issue of further shares or making of payments) so far as they relate to a right acquired or offer made before the transfer.

(5)   Where any restrictions continue in force under subsection (4)—

    (a)   an application may be made under this section for an order directing that the shares shall cease to be subject to those restrictions, and

    (b)   subsection (3) does not apply in relation to the making of such an order.

801 Order for sale of shares

(1)   The court may order that the shares subject to restrictions be sold, subject to the court's approval as to the sale.

(2)   An application for an order under subsection (1) may only be made by the company.

(3)   Where the court has made an order under this section, it may make such further order relating to the sale or transfer of the shares as it thinks fit.

(4)   An application for an order under subsection (3) may be made—

    (a)   by the company,

    (b)   by the person appointed by or in pursuance of the order to effect the sale, or

    (c)   by any person interested in the shares.

(5)   On making an order under subsection (1) or (3) the court may order that the applicant's costs (in Scotland, expenses) be paid out of the proceeds of sale.

802 Application of proceeds of sale under court order

(1)   Where shares are sold in pursuance of an order of the court under section 801, the proceeds of the sale, less the costs of the sale, must be paid into court for the benefit of the persons who are beneficially interested in the shares.

(2)   A person who is beneficially interested in the shares may apply to the court for the whole or part of those proceeds to be paid to him.

(3)   On such an application the court shall order the payment to the applicant of—

    (a)   the whole of the proceeds of sale together with any interest on them, or

    (b)   if another person had a beneficial interest in the shares at the time of their sale, such proportion of the proceeds and interest as the value of the applicant's interest in the shares bears to the total value of the shares.

    This is subject to the following qualification.

(4)   If the court has ordered under section 801(5) that the costs (in Scotland, expenses) of an applicant under that section are to be paid out of the proceeds of sale, the applicant is entitled to payment of his costs (or expenses) out of those proceeds before any person interested in the shares receives any part of those proceeds.

Power of members to require company to act

803 Power of members to require company to act

(1)   The members of a company may require it to exercise its powers under section 793 (notice requiring information about interests in shares).

(2)   A company is required to do so once it has received requests (to the same effect) from members of the company holding at least 10% of such of the paid-up capital of the company as carries a right to vote at general meetings of the company (excluding any voting rights attached to any shares in the company held as treasury shares).

(3)   A request—

    (a)   may be in hard copy form or in electronic form,

(b) must—
    (i)   state that the company is requested to exercise its powers under section 793,
    (ii)   specify the manner in which the company is requested to act, and
    (iii)   give reasonable grounds for requiring the company to exercise those powers in the manner specified, and
(c)   must be authenticated by the person or persons making it.

804   Duty of company to comply with requirement

(1)   A company that is required under section 803 to exercise its powers under section 793 (notice requiring information about interests in company's shares) must exercise those powers in the manner specified in the requests.

(2)   If default is made in complying with subsection (1) an offence is committed by every officer of the company who is in default.

(3)   A person guilty of an offence under this section is liable—
    (a)   on conviction on indictment, to a fine;
    (b)   on summary conviction, to a fine not exceeding the statutory maximum.

805   Report to members on outcome of investigation

(1)   On the conclusion of an investigation carried out by a company in pursuance of a requirement under section 803 the company must cause a report of the information received in pursuance of the investigation to be prepared.
The report must be made available for inspection within a reasonable period (not more than 15 days) after the conclusion of the investigation.

(2)   Where—
    (a)   a company undertakes an investigation in pursuance of a requirement under section 803, and
    (b)   the investigation is not concluded within three months after the date on which the company became subject to the requirement,
the company must cause to be prepared in respect of that period, and in respect of each succeeding period of three months ending before the conclusion of the investigation, an interim report of the information received during that period in pursuance of the investigation.

(3)   Each such report must be made available for inspection within a reasonable period (not more than 15 days) after the end of the period to which it relates.

(4)   The reports must be retained by the company for at least six years from the date on which they are first made available for inspection and must be kept available for inspection during that time—
    (a)   at the company's registered office, or
    (b)   at a place specified in regulations under section 1136.

(5)   The company must give notice to the registrar—
    (a)   of the place at which the reports are kept available for inspection, and
    (b)   of any change in that place,
unless they have at all times been kept at the company's registered office.

(6)   The company must within three days of making any report prepared under this section available for inspection, notify the members who made the requests under section 803 where the report is so available.

(7)   For the purposes of this section an investigation carried out by a company in pursuance of a requirement under section 803 is concluded when—
    (a)   the company has made all such inquiries as are necessary or expedient for the purposes of the requirement, and
    (b)   in the case of each such inquiry—
        (i)   a response has been received by the company, or
        (ii)   the time allowed for a response has elapsed.

806   Report to members: offences

(1)   If default is made for 14 days in complying with section 805(5) (notice to registrar of place at which reports made available for inspection) an offence is committed by—

(a)   the company, and

(b)   every officer of the company who is in default.

(2)   A person guilty of an offence under subsection (1) is liable on summary conviction to a fine not exceeding level 3 on the standard scale and, for continued contravention, a daily default fine not exceeding one-tenth of level 3 on the standard scale.

(3)   If default is made in complying with any other provision of section 805 (report to members on outcome of investigation), an offence is committed by every officer of the company who is in default.

(4)   A person guilty of an offence under subsection (3) is liable—

(a)   on conviction on indictment, to a fine;

(b)   on summary conviction, to a fine not exceeding the statutory maximum.

807   Right to inspect and request copy of reports

(1)   Any report prepared under section 805 must be open to inspection by any person without charge.

(2)   Any person is entitled, on request and on payment of such fee as may be prescribed, to be provided with a copy of any such report or any part of it. The copy must be provided within ten days after the request is received by the company.

(3)   If an inspection required under subsection (1) is refused, or default is made in complying with subsection (2), an offence is committed by—

(a)   the company, and

(b)   every officer of the company who is in default.

(4)   A person guilty of an offence under this section is liable on summary conviction to a fine not exceeding level 3 on the standard scale and, for continued contravention, a daily default fine not exceeding one-tenth of level 3 on the standard scale.

(5)   In the case of any such refusal or default the court may by order compel an immediate inspection or, as the case may be, direct that the copy required be sent to the person requiring it.

Register of interests disclosed

808   Register of interests disclosed

(1)   The company must keep a register of information received by it in pursuance of a requirement imposed under section 793 (notice requiring information about interests in company's shares).

(2)   A company which receives any such information must, within three days of the receipt, enter in the register—

(a)   the fact that the requirement was imposed and the date on which it was imposed, and

(b)   the information received in pursuance of the requirement.

(3)   The information must be entered against the name of the present holder of the shares in question or, if there is no present holder or the present holder is not known, against the name of the person holding the interest.

(4)   The register must be made up so that the entries against the names entered in it appear in chronological order.

(5)   If default is made in complying with this section an offence is committed by—

(a)   the company, and

(b)   every officer of the company who is in default.

(6)   A person guilty of an offence under this section is liable on summary conviction to a fine not exceeding level 3 on the standard scale and, for continued contravention, a daily default fine not exceeding one-tenth of level 3 on the standard scale.

(7)   The company is not by virtue of anything done for the purposes of this section affected with notice of, or put upon inquiry as to, the rights of any person in relation to any shares.

809   Register to be kept available for inspection

(1)   The register kept under section 808 (register of interests disclosed) must be kept available for inspection—

    (a)   at the company's registered office, or

    (b)   at a place specified in regulations under section 1136.

(2)   A company must give notice to the registrar of companies of the place where the register is kept available for inspection and of any change in that place.

(3)   No such notice is required if the register has at all times been kept available for inspection at the company's registered office.

(4)   If default is made in complying with subsection (1), or a company makes default for 14 days in complying with subsection (2), an offence is committed by—

    (a)   the company, and

    (b)   every officer of the company who is in default.

(5)   A person guilty of an offence under this section is liable on summary conviction to a fine not exceeding level 3 on the standard scale and, for continued contravention, a daily default fine not exceeding one-tenth of level 3 on the standard scale.

810   Associated index

(1)   Unless the register kept under section 808 (register of interests disclosed) is kept in such a form as itself to constitute an index, the company must keep an index of the names entered in it.

(2)   The company must make any necessary entry or alteration in the index within ten days after the date on which any entry or alteration is made in the register.

(3)   The index must contain, in respect of each name, a sufficient indication to enable the information entered against it to be readily found.

(4)   The index must be at all times kept available for inspection at the same place as the register.

(5)   If default is made in complying with this section, an offence is committed by—

    (a)   the company, and

    (b)   every officer of the company who is in default.

(6)   A person guilty of an offence under this section is liable on summary conviction to a fine not exceeding level 3 on the standard scale and, for continued contravention, a daily default fine not exceeding one-tenth of level 3 on the standard scale.

811   Rights to inspect and require copy of entries

(1)   The register required to be kept under section 808 (register of interests disclosed), and any associated index, must be open to inspection by any person without charge.

(2)   Any person is entitled, on request and on payment of such fee as may be prescribed, to be provided with a copy of any entry in the register.

(3)   A person seeking to exercise either of the rights conferred by this section must make a request to the company to that effect.

(4)   The request must contain the following information—

    (a)   in the case of an individual, his name and address;

    (b)   in the case of an organisation, the name and address of an individual responsible for making the request on behalf of the organisation;

    (c)   the purpose for which the information is to be used; and

    (d)   whether the information will be disclosed to any other person, and if so—

        (i)   where that person is an individual, his name and address,

        (ii)   where that person is an organisation, the name and address of an individual responsible for receiving the information on its behalf, and

        (iii)   the purpose for which the information is to be used by that person.

812   Court supervision of purpose for which rights may be exercised

(1)   Where a company receives a request under section 811 (register of interests disclosed: right to inspect and require copy), it must—

(a) comply with the request if it is satisfied that it is made for a proper purpose, and

(b) refuse the request if it is not so satisfied.

(2) If the company refuses the request, it must inform the person making the request, stating the reason why it is not satisfied.

(3) A person whose request is refused may apply to the court.

(4) If an application is made to the court—

(a) the person who made the request must notify the company, and

(b) the company must use its best endeavours to notify any persons whose details would be disclosed if the company were required to comply with the request.

(5) If the court is not satisfied that the inspection or copy is sought for a proper purpose, it shall direct the company not to comply with the request.

(6) If the court makes such a direction and it appears to the court that the company is or may be subject to other requests made for a similar purpose (whether made by the same person or different persons), it may direct that the company is not to comply with any such request.

The order must contain such provision as appears to the court appropriate to identify the requests to which it applies.

(7) If the court does not direct the company not to comply with the request, the company must comply with the request immediately upon the court giving its decision or, as the case may be, the proceedings being discontinued.

813   Register of interests disclosed: refusal of inspection or default in providing copy

(1) If an inspection required under section 811 (register of interests disclosed: right to inspect and require copy) is refused or default is made in providing a copy required under that section, otherwise than in accordance with section 812, an offence is committed by—

(a) the company, and

(b) every officer of the company who is in default.

(2) A person guilty of an offence under this section is liable on summary conviction to a fine not exceeding level 3 on the standard scale and, for continued contravention, a daily default fine not exceeding one-tenth of level 3 on the standard scale.

(3) In the case of any such refusal or default the court may by order compel an immediate inspection or, as the case may be, direct that the copy required be sent to the person requesting it.

814   Register of interests disclosed: offences in connection with request for or disclosure of information

(1) It is an offence for a person knowingly or recklessly to make in a request under section 811 (register of interests disclosed: right to inspect or require copy) a statement that is misleading, false or deceptive in a material particular.

(2) It is an offence for a person in possession of information obtained by exercise of either of the rights conferred by that section—

(a) to do anything that results in the information being disclosed to another person, or

(b) to fail to do anything with the result that the information is disclosed to another person,

knowing, or having reason to suspect, that person may use the information for a purpose that is not a proper purpose.

(3) A person guilty of an offence under this section is liable—

(a) on conviction on indictment, to imprisonment for a term not exceeding two years or a fine (or both);

(b) on summary conviction—

(i) in England and Wales, to imprisonment for a term not exceeding twelve months or to a fine not exceeding the statutory maximum (or both);

(ii) in Scotland or Northern Ireland, to imprisonment for a term not exceeding six months, or to a fine not exceeding the statutory maximum (or both).

815   Entries not to be removed from register

(1)   Entries in the register kept under section 808 (register of interests disclosed) must not be deleted except in accordance with—
         section 816 (old entries), or
         section 817 (incorrect entry relating to third party).

(2)   If an entry is deleted in contravention of subsection (1), the company must restore it as soon as reasonably practicable.

(3)   If default is made in complying with subsection (1) or (2), an offence is committed by—
         (a)   the company, and
         (b)   every officer of the company who is in default.

(4)   A person guilty of an offence under this section is liable on summary conviction to a fine not exceeding level 3 on the standard scale and, for continued contravention of subsection (2), a daily default fine not exceeding one-tenth of level 3 on the standard scale.

816   Removal of entries from register: old entries

         A company may remove an entry from the register kept under section 808 (register of interests disclosed) if more than six years have elapsed since the entry was made.

817   Removal of entries from register: incorrect entry relating to third party

(1)   This section applies where in pursuance of an obligation imposed by a notice under section 793 (notice requiring information about interests in company's shares) a person gives to a company the name and address of another person as being interested in shares in the company.

(2)   That other person may apply to the company for the removal of the entry from the register.

(3)   If the company is satisfied that the information in pursuance of which the entry was made is incorrect, it shall remove the entry.

(4)   If an application under subsection (3) is refused, the applicant may apply to the court for an order directing the company to remove the entry in question from the register.
         The court may make such an order if it thinks fit.

818   Adjustment of entry relating to share acquisition agreement

(1)   If a person who is identified in the register kept by a company under section 808 (register of interests disclosed) as being a party to an agreement to which section 824 applies (certain share acquisition agreements) ceases to be a party to the agreement, he may apply to the company for the inclusion of that information in the register.

(2)   If the company is satisfied that he has ceased to be a party to the agreement, it shall record that information (if not already recorded) in every place where his name appears in the register as a party to the agreement.

(3)   If an application under this section is refused (otherwise than on the ground that the information has already been recorded), the applicant may apply to the court for an order directing the company to include the information in question in the register.
         The court may make such an order if it thinks fit.

819   Duty of company ceasing to be public company

(1)   If a company ceases to be a public company, it must continue to keep any register kept under section 808 (register of interests disclosed), and any associated index, until the end of the period of six years after it ceased to be such a company.

(2)   If default is made in complying with this section, an offence is committed by—
         (a)   the company, and
         (b)   every officer of the company who is in default.

(3)   A person guilty of an offence under this section is liable on summary conviction to a fine not exceeding level 3 on the standard scale and, for continued contravention, a daily default fine not exceeding one-tenth of level 3 on the standard scale.

Meaning of interest in shares

820 Interest in shares: general

(1) This section applies to determine for the purposes of this Part whether a person has an interest in shares.

(2) In this Part—
(a) a reference to an interest in shares includes an interest of any kind whatsoever in the shares, and
(b) any restraints or restrictions to which the exercise of any right attached to the interest is or may be subject shall be disregarded.

(3) Where an interest in shares is comprised in property held on trust, every beneficiary of the trust is treated as having an interest in the shares.

(4) A person is treated as having an interest in shares if—
(a) he enters into a contract to acquire them, or
(b) not being the registered holder, he is entitled—
(i) to exercise any right conferred by the holding of the shares, or
(ii) to control the exercise of any such right.

(5) For the purposes of subsection (4)(b) a person is entitled to exercise or control the exercise of a right conferred by the holding of shares if he—
(a) has a right (whether subject to conditions or not) the exercise of which would make him so entitled, or
(b) is under an obligation (whether subject to conditions or not) the fulfilment of which would make him so entitled.

(6) A person is treated as having an interest in shares if—
(a) he has a right to call for delivery of the shares to himself or to his order, or
(b) he has a right to acquire an interest in shares or is under an obligation to take an interest in shares.
This applies whether the right or obligation is conditional or absolute.

(7) Persons having a joint interest are treated as each having that interest.

(8) It is immaterial that shares in which a person has an interest are unidentifiable.

821 Interest in shares: right to subscribe for shares

(1) Section 793 (notice by company requiring information about interests in its shares) applies in relation to a person who has, or previously had, or is or was entitled to acquire, a right to subscribe for shares in the company as it applies in relation to a person who is or was interested in shares in that company.

(2) References in that section to an interest in shares shall be read accordingly.

822 Interest in shares: family interests

(1) For the purposes of this Part a person is taken to be interested in shares in which—
(a) his spouse or civil partner, or
(b) any infant child or step-child of his,
is interested.

(2) In relation to Scotland "infant" means a person under the age of 18 years.

823 Interest in shares: corporate interests

(1) For the purposes of this Part a person is taken to be interested in shares if a body corporate is interested in them and—
(a) the body or its directors are accustomed to act in accordance with his directions or instructions, or
(b) he is entitled to exercise or control the exercise of one-third or more of the voting power at general meetings of the body.

(2) For the purposes of this section a person is treated as entitled to exercise or control the exercise of voting power if—

(a)   another body corporate is entitled to exercise or control the exercise of that voting power, and

(b)   he is entitled to exercise or control the exercise of one-third or more of the voting power at general meetings of that body corporate.

(3)   For the purposes of this section a person is treated as entitled to exercise or control the exercise of voting power if—

(a)   he has a right (whether or not subject to conditions) the exercise of which would make him so entitled, or

(b)   he is under an obligation (whether or not subject to conditions) the fulfilment of which would make him so entitled.

824   Interest in shares: agreement to acquire interests in a particular company

(1)   For the purposes of this Part an interest in shares may arise from an agreement between two or more persons that includes provision for the acquisition by any one or more of them of interests in shares of a particular public company (the "target company" for that agreement).

(2)   This section applies to such an agreement if—

(a)   the agreement includes provision imposing obligations or restrictions on any one or more of the parties to it with respect to their use, retention or disposal of their interests in the shares of the target company acquired in pursuance of the agreement (whether or not together with any other interests of theirs in the company's shares to which the agreement relates), and

(b)   an interest in the target company's shares is in fact acquired by any of the parties in pursuance of the agreement.

(3)   The reference in subsection (2) to the use of interests in shares in the target company is to the exercise of any rights or of any control or influence arising from those interests (including the right to enter into an agreement for the exercise, or for control of the exercise, of any of those rights by another person).

(4)   Once an interest in shares in the target company has been acquired in pursuance of the agreement, this section continues to apply to the agreement so long as the agreement continues to include provisions of any description mentioned in subsection (2).

This applies irrespective of—

(a)   whether or not any further acquisitions of interests in the company's shares take place in pursuance of the agreement;

(b)   any change in the persons who are for the time being parties to it;

(c)   any variation of the agreement.

References in this subsection to the agreement include any agreement having effect (whether directly or indirectly) in substitution for the original agreement.

(5)   In this section—

(a)   "agreement" includes any agreement or arrangement, and

(b)   references to provisions of an agreement include—

(i)   undertakings, expectations or understandings operative under an arrangement, and

(ii)   any provision whether express or implied and whether absolute or not.

References elsewhere in this Part to an agreement to which this section applies have a corresponding meaning.

(6)   This section does not apply—

(a)   to an agreement that is not legally binding unless it involves mutuality in the undertakings, expectations or understandings of the parties to it; or

(b)   to an agreement to underwrite or sub-underwrite an offer of shares in a company, provided the agreement is confined to that purpose and any matters incidental to it.

825   Extent of obligation in case of share acquisition agreement

(1)   For the purposes of this Part each party to an agreement to which section 824 applies is treated as interested in all shares in the target company in which any other party to the agreement is

interested apart from the agreement (whether or not the interest of the other party was acquired, or includes any interest that was acquired, in pursuance of the agreement).

(2) For those purposes an interest of a party to such an agreement in shares in the target company is an interest apart from the agreement if he is interested in those shares otherwise than by virtue of the application of section 824 (and this section) in relation to the agreement.

(3) Accordingly, any such interest of the person (apart from the agreement) includes for those purposes any interest treated as his under section 822 or 823 (family or corporate interests) or by the application of section 824 (and this section) in relation to any other agreement with respect to shares in the target company to which he is a party.

(4) A notification with respect to his interest in shares in the target company made to the company under this Part by a person who is for the time being a party to an agreement to which section 824 applies must—

(a) state that the person making the notification is a party to such an agreement,

(b) include the names and (so far as known to him) the addresses of the other parties to the agreement, identifying them as such, and

(c) state whether or not any of the shares to which the notification relates are shares in which he is interested by virtue of section 824 (and this section) and, if so, the number of those shares.

Other supplementary provisions

826 Information protected from wider disclosure

(1) Information in respect of which a company is for the time being entitled to any exemption conferred by regulations under section 409(3) (information about related undertakings to be given in notes to accounts: exemption where disclosure harmful to company's business)—

(a) must not be included in a report under section 805 (report to members on outcome of investigation), and

(b) must not be made available under section 811 (right to inspect and request copy of entries).

(2) Where any such information is omitted from a report under section 805, that fact must be stated in the report.

827 Reckoning of periods for fulfilling obligations

Where the period allowed by any provision of this Part for fulfilling an obligation is expressed as a number of days, any day that is not a working day shall be disregarded in reckoning that period.

828 Power to make further provision by regulations

(1) The Secretary of State may by regulations amend—

(a) the definition of shares to which this Part applies (section 792),

(b) the provisions as to notice by a company requiring information about interests in its shares (section 793), and

(c) the provisions as to what is taken to be an interest in shares (sections 820 and 821).

(2) The regulations may amend, repeal or replace those provisions and make such other consequential amendments or repeals of provisions of this Part as appear to the Secretary of State to be appropriate.

(3) Regulations under this section are subject to affirmative resolution procedure.

PART 23
DISTRIBUTIONS

CHAPTER 1
RESTRICTIONS ON WHEN DISTRIBUTIONS MAY BE MADE

Introductory

829 Meaning of "distribution"

(1) In this Part "distribution" means every description of distribution of a company's assets to its members, whether in cash or otherwise, subject to the following exceptions.

(2)   The following are not distributions for the purposes of this Part—
        (a)   an issue of shares as fully or partly paid bonus shares;
        (b)   the reduction of share capital—
             (i)   by extinguishing or reducing the liability of any of the members on any of the company's shares in respect of share capital not paid up, or
             (ii)   by repaying paid-up share capital;
        (c)   the redemption or purchase of any of the company's own shares out of capital (including the proceeds of any fresh issue of shares) or out of unrealised profits in accordance with Chapter 3, 4 or 5 of Part 18;
        (d)   a distribution of assets to members of the company on its winding up.

General rules

830   Distributions to be made only out of profits available for the purpose

(1)   A company may only make a distribution out of profits available for the purpose.

(2)   A company's profits available for distribution are its accumulated, realised profits, so far as not previously utilised by distribution or capitalisation, less its accumulated, realised losses, so far as not previously written off in a reduction or reorganisation of capital duly made.

(3)   Subsection (2) has effect subject to sections 832, 833A and 835 (investment companies and Solvency 2 insurance companies).

831   Net asset restriction on distributions by public companies

(1)   A public company may only make a distribution—
        (a)   if the amount of its net assets is not less than the aggregate of its called-up share capital and undistributable reserves, and
        (b)   if, and to the extent that, the distribution does not reduce the amount of those assets to less than that aggregate.

(2)   For this purpose a company's "net assets" means the aggregate of the company's assets less the aggregate of its liabilities.

(3)   "Liabilities" here includes—
        (a)   where the relevant accounts are Companies Act accounts, provisions of a kind specified for the purposes of this subsection by regulations under section 396;
        (b)   where the relevant accounts are IAS accounts, provisions of any kind.

(4)   A company's undistributable reserves are—
        (a)   its share premium account;
        (b)   its capital redemption reserve;
        (c)   the amount by which its accumulated, unrealised profits (so far as not previously utilised by capitalisation) exceed its accumulated, unrealised losses (so far as not previously written off in a reduction or reorganisation of capital duly made);
        (d)   any other reserve that the company is prohibited from distributing—
             (i)   by any enactment (other than one contained in this Part), or
             (ii)   by its articles.
     The reference in paragraph (c) to capitalisation does not include a transfer of profits of the company to its capital redemption reserve.

(5)   A public company must not include any uncalled share capital as an asset in any accounts relevant for purposes of this section.

(6)   Subsection (1) has effect subject to sections 832 and 835 (investment companies etc: distributions out of accumulated revenue profits).

Distributions by investment companies or Solvency 2 insurance companies

832   Distributions by investment companies out of accumulated revenue profits

(1)   An investment company may make a distribution out of its accumulated, realised revenue profits if the following conditions are met.

(2) It may make such a distribution only if, and to the extent that, its accumulated, realised revenue profits, so far as not previously utilised by a distribution or capitalisation, exceed its accumulated revenue losses (whether realised or unrealised), so far as not previously written off in a reduction or reorganisation of capital duly made.

(3) It may make such a distribution only—

    (a) if the amount of its assets is at least equal to one and a half times the aggregate of its liabilities to creditors, and

    (b) if, and to the extent that, the distribution does not reduce that amount to less than one and a half times that aggregate.

(4) For this purpose a company's liabilities to creditors include—

    (a) in the case of Companies Act accounts, provisions of a kind specified for the purposes of this subsection by regulations under section 396;

    (b) in the case of IAS accounts, provisions for liabilities to creditors.

(5) The following conditions must also be met—

    (a) the company's shares must be shares admitted to trading on a UK regulated market;

    (b) during the relevant period it must not have—

        (i) ...

        (ii) applied any unrealised profits ... in paying up debentures or amounts unpaid on its issued shares;

    (c) it must have given notice to the registrar under section 833(1) (notice of intention to carry on business as an investment company)—

        (i) before the beginning of the relevant period, or

        (ii) as soon as reasonably practicable after the date of its incorporation.

(6) For the purposes of this section—

    (a) ...

    (b) the "relevant period" is the period beginning with—

        (i) the first day of the accounting reference period immediately preceding that in which the proposed distribution is to be made, or

        (ii) where the distribution is to be made in the company's first accounting reference period, the first day of that period, and ending with the date of the distribution.

(7) The company must not include any uncalled share capital as an asset in any accounts relevant for purposes of this section.

833 Meaning of "investment company"

(1) In this Part an "investment company" means a public company that—

    (a) has given notice (which has not been revoked) to the registrar of its intention to carry on business as an investment company, and

    (b) since the date of that notice has complied with the following requirement.

(2) The requirement is—

    (a) that the business of the company consists of investing its funds in shares, land or other assets, with the aim of spreading investment risk and giving members of the company the benefit of the results of the management of its funds;

    (b)–(d) ...

(3) ...

(4) Notice to the registrar under this section may be revoked at any time by the company on giving notice to the registrar that it no longer wishes to be an investment company within the meaning of this section.

(5) On giving such a notice, the company ceases to be such a company.

833A Distributions by insurance companies authorised under the Solvency 2 Directive

(1) This section applies in relation to any authorised insurance company carrying on long-term business that is authorised in accordance with Article 14 of the Solvency 2 Directive.

(2)   For the purposes of section 830(2), the realised profit or loss of the company for the period in respect of which its relevant accounts (within the meaning of section 836) are prepared is taken to be the amount given by the formula in subsection (4) (with a positive figure taken to be a realised profit and a negative figure taken to be a realised loss).

(3)   But the company's profits available for distribution are limited to an amount that does not exceed its accumulated profits (whether realised or not), so far as not previously utilised by distribution or capitalisation, less its accumulated losses (whether realised or not), so far as not previously written off in a reduction or reorganisation of capital duly made.

(4)   The formula is A - L - D,
        where—
                "A" is the total value of the company's assets;
                "L" is the total value of the company's liabilities; and
                "D" is the total value of the items within subsection (5) relating to the company;
                and, in each case, the value is to be determined as at the date of the company's balance sheet that forms part of the accounts mentioned in subsection (2).

(5)   The items within this subsection are—
        (a)   if the value of shares held by the company in a qualifying investment subsidiary exceeds the value of the consideration given by it for their acquisition, the amount of that excess;
        (b)   any asset of the company representing a surplus in a defined benefit pension scheme;
        (c)   if the value of the assets held by the company in a ring-fenced fund exceeds the value of the liabilities incurred by the company in respect of that fund, the amount of that excess;
        (d)   the amount of any liability of the company in respect of deferred tax shown in the company's balance sheet that relates to any asset within paragraph (a), (b) or (c);
        (e)   if—
                (i)   the company has permission under regulation 42 of the Solvency 2 Regulations 2015 to apply a matching adjustment to a relevant risk-free interest rate term structure to calculate the best estimate of a portfolio of the company's life insurance or reinsurance obligations, and
                (ii)   the value of the portfolio of the company's assets assigned by the company to cover the best estimate exceeds the value of the portfolio of the company's life insurance or reinsurance obligations, the amount of that excess; and
        (f)   the following capital items of the company—
                (i)   paid-in ordinary share capital together with any related share premium account;
                (ii)   paid-in preference shares which are not liabilities of the company together with any related share premium account;
                (iii)   capital redemption reserve; and
                (iv)   any other reserve that the company is prohibited from distributing (ignoring this Part for this purpose).

(6)   So far as anything falls within more than one of the above paragraphs of subsection (5), its value is to be taken into account only once.

(7)   The company's assets and liabilities must be valued in accordance with—
        (a)   rules made by the Prudential Regulation Authority under Part 9A of the Financial Services and Markets Act 2000 implementing Articles 75 to 85, and 308b to 308e, of the Solvency 2 Directive; and
        (b)   Articles 7 to 61 of Commission Delegated Regulation (EU) 2015/35 supplementing that directive.

(8)   If the company carries on both long-term business and other insurance business—
        (a)   this section is to be applied on the assumption that the company carries on only the long-term business; and
        (b)   the remainder of this Part is to be applied on the assumption that the company carries on only that other insurance business;

and, in applying paragraph (a) or (b), such apportionments of amounts referable to the long-term business or other insurance business are to be made as are just and reasonable.

(9)   In this section—

"best estimate", "paid-in ordinary share capital", "paid-in preference shares", "relevant risk-free interest rate term structure" and "ring-fenced fund" have the same meaning as in the Solvency 2 Directive and any directly applicable regulations made under it;

"defined benefit pension scheme" means a pension scheme (as defined by section 1(5) of the Pension Schemes Act 1993) which is a defined benefits scheme within the meaning given by section 2 of the Pension Schemes Act 2015;

"long-term business" means business that consists of effecting or carrying out contracts of long-term insurance (and this definition must be read with section 22 of the Financial Services and Markets Act 2000, any relevant order under that section and Schedule 2 to that Act);

"qualifying investment subsidiary" means an undertaking in which the company holds a participation within the meaning given by Article 13(20) of the Solvency 2 Directive and which is not held by the company as part of its portfolio of investments;

"Solvency 2 Directive" means Directive 2009/138/EC of the European Parliament and of the Council on the taking-up and pursuit of the business of Insurance and Reinsurance (Solvency II).

834, 835 …

CHAPTER 2
JUSTIFICATION OF DISTRIBUTION BY REFERENCE TO ACCOUNTS

Justification of distribution by reference to accounts

836   Justification of distribution by reference to relevant accounts

(1)   Whether a distribution may be made by a company without contravening this Part is determined by reference to the following items as stated in the relevant accounts—

(a)   profits, losses, assets and liabilities;

(b)   provisions of the following kinds—

(i)   where the relevant accounts are Companies Act accounts, provisions of a kind specified for the purposes of this subsection by regulations under section 396;

(ii)   where the relevant accounts are IAS accounts, provisions of any kind;

(c)   share capital and reserves (including undistributable reserves).

(2)   The relevant accounts are the company's last annual accounts, except that—

(a)   where the distribution would be found to contravene this Part by reference to the company's last annual accounts, it may be justified by reference to interim accounts, and

(b)   where the distribution is proposed to be declared during the company's first accounting reference period, or before any accounts have been circulated in respect of that period, it may be justified by reference to initial accounts.

(3)   The requirements of—

section 837 (as regards the company's last annual accounts), section 838 (as regards interim accounts), and

section 839 (as regards initial accounts),

must be complied with, as and where applicable.

(4)   If any applicable requirement of those sections is not complied with, the accounts may not be relied on for the purposes of this Part and the distribution is accordingly treated as contravening this Part.

Requirements applicable in relation to relevant accounts

837   Requirements where last annual accounts used

(1)   The company's last annual accounts means the company's individual accounts—

(a)   that were last circulated to members in accordance with section 423 (duty to circulate copies of annual accounts and reports), ...

(b)   ...

(2)   The accounts must have been properly prepared in accordance with this Act, or have been so prepared subject only to matters that are not material for determining (by reference to the items mentioned in section 836(1)) whether the distribution would contravene this Part.

(3)   Unless the company is exempt from audit and the directors take advantage of that exemption, the auditor must have made his report on the accounts.

(4)   If that report was qualified—

(a)   the auditor must have stated in writing (either at the time of his report or subsequently) whether in his opinion the matters in respect of which his report is qualified are material for determining whether a distribution would contravene this Part, and

(b)   a copy of that statement must—

(i)   in the case of a private company, have been circulated to members in accordance with section 423, or

(ii)   in the case of a public company, have been laid before the company in general meeting.

(5)   An auditor's statement is sufficient for the purposes of a distribution if it relates to distributions of a description that includes the distribution in question, even if at the time of the statement it had not been proposed.

838   Requirements where interim accounts used

(1)   Interim accounts must be accounts that enable a reasonable judgment to be made as to the amounts of the items mentioned in section 836(1).

(2)   Where interim accounts are prepared for a proposed distribution by a public company, the following requirements apply.

(3)   The accounts must have been properly prepared, or have been so prepared subject to matters that are not material for determining (by reference to the items mentioned in section 836(1)) whether the distribution would contravene this Part.

(4)   "Properly prepared" means prepared in accordance with sections 395 to 397 (requirements for company individual accounts), applying those requirements with such modifications as are necessary because the accounts are prepared otherwise than in respect of an accounting reference period.

(5)   The balance sheet comprised in the accounts must have been signed in accordance with section 414.

(6)   A copy of the accounts must have been delivered to the registrar. Any requirement of Part 35 of this Act as to the delivery of a certified translation into English of any document forming part of the accounts must also have been met.

839   Requirements where initial accounts used

(1)   Initial accounts must be accounts that enable a reasonable judgment to be made as to the amounts of the items mentioned in section 836(1).

(2)   Where initial accounts are prepared for a proposed distribution by a public company, the following requirements apply.

(3)   The accounts must have been properly prepared, or have been so prepared subject to matters that are not material for determining (by reference to the items mentioned in section 836(1)) whether the distribution would contravene this Part.

(4)   "Properly prepared" means prepared in accordance with sections 395 to 397 (requirements for company individual accounts), applying those requirements with such modifications as are necessary because the accounts are prepared otherwise than in respect of an accounting reference period.

(5)   The company's auditor must have made a report stating whether, in his opinion, the accounts have been properly prepared.

(6)   If that report was qualified—

     (a)   the auditor must have stated in writing (either at the time of his report or subsequently) whether in his opinion the matters in respect of which his report is qualified are material for determining whether a distribution would contravene this Part, and

     (b)   a copy of that statement must have been laid before the company in general meeting.

(7)   A copy of the accounts, of the auditor's report and of any auditor's statement must have been delivered to the registrar.

Any requirement of Part 35 of this Act as to the delivery of a certified translation into English of any of those documents must also have been met.

Application of provisions to successive distributions etc

840   Successive distributions etc by reference to the same accounts

(1)   In determining whether a proposed distribution may be made by a company in a case where—

     (a)   one or more previous distributions have been made in pursuance of a determination made by reference to the same relevant accounts, or

     (b)   relevant financial assistance has been given, or other relevant payments have been made, since those accounts were prepared,

the provisions of this Part apply as if the amount of the proposed distribution was increased by the amount of the previous distributions, financial assistance and other payments.

(2)   The financial assistance and other payments that are relevant for this purpose are—

     (a)   financial assistance lawfully given by the company out of its distributable profits;

     (b)   financial assistance given by the company in contravention of section 678 or 679 (prohibited financial assistance) in a case where the giving of that assistance reduces the company's net assets or increases its net liabilities;

     (c)   payments made by the company in respect of the purchase by it of shares in the company, except a payment lawfully made otherwise than out of distributable profits;

     (d)   payments of any description specified in section 705 (payments apart from purchase price of shares to be made out of distributable profits).

(3)   In this section "financial assistance" has the same meaning as in Chapter 2 of Part 18 (see section 677).

(4)   For the purpose of applying subsection (2)(b) in relation to any financial assistance—

     (a)   "net assets" means the amount by which the aggregate amount of the company's assets exceeds the aggregate amount of its liabilities, and

     (b)   "net liabilities" means the amount by which the aggregate amount of the company's liabilities exceeds the aggregate amount of its assets,

taking the amount of the assets and liabilities to be as stated in the company's accounting records immediately before the financial assistance is given.

(5)   For this purpose a company's liabilities include any amount retained as reasonably necessary for the purposes of providing for any liability—

     (a)   the nature of which is clearly defined, and

     (b)   which is either likely to be incurred or certain to be incurred but uncertain as to amount or as to the date on which it will arise.

CHAPTER 3
SUPPLEMENTARY PROVISIONS

Accounting matters

841   Realised losses and profits and revaluation of fixed assets

(1)   The following provisions have effect for the purposes of this Part.

(2)   The following are treated as realised losses—

     (a)   in the case of Companies Act accounts, provisions of a kind specified for the purposes of this paragraph by regulations under section 396 (except revaluation provisions);

       (b)   in the case of IAS accounts, provisions of any kind (except revaluation provisions).

(3)   A "revaluation provision" means a provision in respect of a diminution in value of a fixed asset appearing on a revaluation of all the fixed assets of the company, or of all of its fixed assets other than goodwill.

(4)   For the purpose of subsections (2) and (3) any consideration by the directors of the value at a particular time of a fixed asset is treated as a revaluation provided—

       (a)   the directors are satisfied that the aggregate value at that time of the fixed assets of the company that have not actually been revalued is not less than the aggregate amount at which they are then stated in the company's accounts, and

       (b)   it is stated in a note to the accounts—

          (i)   that the directors have considered the value of some or all of the fixed assets of the company without actually revaluing them,

          (ii)   that they are satisfied that the aggregate value of those assets at the time of their consideration was not less than the aggregate amount at which they were then stated in the company's accounts, and

          (iii)   that accordingly, by virtue of this subsection, amounts are stated in the accounts on the basis that a revaluation of fixed assets of the company is treated as having taken place at that time.

(5)   Where—

       (a)   on the revaluation of a fixed asset, an unrealised profit is shown to have been made, and

       (b)   on or after the revaluation, a sum is written off or retained for depreciation of that asset over a period,

an amount equal to the amount by which that sum exceeds the sum which would have been so written off or retained for the depreciation of that asset over that period, if that profit had not been made, is treated as a realised profit made over that period.

842   Determination of profit or loss in respect of asset where records incomplete

In determining for the purposes of this Part whether a company has made a profit or loss in respect of an asset where—

       (a)   there is no record of the original cost of the asset, or

       (b)   a record cannot be obtained without unreasonable expense or delay, its cost is taken to be the value ascribed to it in the earliest available record of its value made on or after its acquisition by the company.

843   Realised profits and losses of long-term insurance business of certain insurance companies

(1)   The provisions of this section have effect for the purposes of this Part as it applies in relation to an authorised insurance company carrying on long-term business, other than—

       (a)   a person to whom section 833A applies; or

       (b)   an insurance special purpose vehicle.

(2)   An amount included in the relevant part of the company's balance sheet that—

       (a)   represents a surplus in the fund or funds maintained by it in respect of its long-term business, and

       (b)   has not been allocated to policy holders or, as the case may be, carried forward unappropriated in accordance with asset identification rules made under Part 9A of the Financial Services and Markets Act 2000,

is treated as a realised profit.

(3)   For the purposes of subsection (2)—

       (a)   the relevant part of the balance sheet is that part of the balance sheet that represents accumulated profit or loss;

       (b)   a surplus in the fund or funds maintained by the company in respect of its long-term business means an excess of the assets representing that fund or those funds over the liabilities of the company attributable to its long-term business, as shown by an actuarial investigation.

(4)   A deficit in the fund or funds maintained by the company in respect of its long-term business is treated as a realised loss.

For this purpose a deficit in any such fund or funds means an excess of the liabilities of the company attributable to its long-term business over the assets representing that fund or those funds, as shown by an actuarial investigation.

(5)   Subject to subsections (2) and (4), any profit or loss arising in the company's long-term business is to be left out of account.

(6)   For the purposes of this section an "actuarial investigation" means an investigation made into the financial condition of an authorised insurance company in respect of its long-term business—

(a)   carried out once in every period of twelve months in accordance with rules made under Part 9A of the Financial Services and Markets Act 2000, or

(b)   carried out in accordance with a requirement imposed under section 166 of that Act,

by an actuary appointed as actuary to the company.

(7)   In this section "long-term business" means business that consists of effecting or carrying out contracts of long-term insurance.

This definition must be read with section 22 of the Financial Services and Markets Act 2000, any relevant order under that section and Schedule 2 to that Act.

(8)   In this section "insurance special purpose vehicle" means a special purpose vehicle within the meaning of Article 13(26) of Directive 2009/138/EC of the European Parliament and of the Council of 25 November 2009 on the taking-up and pursuit of the business of Insurance and Reinsurance (Solvency II).

844   Treatment of development costs

(1)   Where development costs are shown or included as an asset in a company's accounts, any amount shown or included in respect of those costs is treated—

(a)   for the purposes of section 830 (distributions to be made out of profits available for the purpose) as a realised loss, and

(b)   for the purposes of section 832 (distributions by investment companies out of accumulated revenue profits) as a realised revenue loss. This is subject to the following exceptions.

(2)   Subsection (1) does not apply to any part of that amount representing an unrealised profit made on revaluation of those costs.

(3)   Subsection (1) does not apply if—

(a)   there are special circumstances in the company's case justifying the directors in deciding that the amount there mentioned is not to be treated as required by subsection (1),

(b)   it is stated—

(i)   in the case of Companies Act accounts, in the note required by regulations under section 396 as to the reasons for showing development costs as an asset, or

(ii)   in the case of IAS accounts, in any note to the accounts,

that the amount is not to be so treated, and

(c)   the note explains the circumstances relied upon to justify the decision of the directors to that effect.

Distributions in kind

845   Distributions in kind: determination of amount

(1)   This section applies for determining the amount of a distribution consisting of or including, or treated as arising in consequence of, the sale, transfer or other disposition by a company of a non-cash asset where—

(a)   at the time of the distribution the company has profits available for distribution, and

(b)   if the amount of the distribution were to be determined in accordance with this section, the company could make the distribution without contravening this Part.

(2)   The amount of the distribution (or the relevant part of it) is taken to be—

(a)   in a case where the amount or value of the consideration for the disposition is not less than the book value of the asset, zero;

(b)   in any other case, the amount by which the book value of the asset exceeds the amount or value of any consideration for the disposition.

(3)   For the purposes of subsection (1) (a) the company's profits available for distribution are treated as increased by the amount (if any) by which the amount or value of any consideration for the disposition exceeds the book value of the asset.

(4)   In this section "book value", in relation to an asset, means—

(a)   the amount at which the asset is stated in the relevant accounts, or

(b)   where the asset is not stated in those accounts at any amount, zero.

(5)   The provisions of Chapter 2 (justification of distribution by reference to accounts) have effect subject to this section.

846   Distributions in kind: treatment of unrealised profits

(1)   This section applies where—

(a)   a company makes a distribution consisting of or including, or treated as arising in consequence of, the sale, transfer or other disposition by the company of a non-cash asset, and

(b)   any part of the amount at which that asset is stated in the relevant accounts represents an unrealised profit.

(2)   That profit is treated as a realised profit—

(a)   for the purpose of determining the lawfulness of the distribution in accordance with this Part (whether before or after the distribution takes place), and

(b)   for the purpose of the application, in relation to anything done with a view to or in connection with the making of the distribution, of any provision of regulations under section 396 under which only realised profits are to be included in or transferred to the profit and loss account.

Consequences of unlawful distribution

847   Consequences of unlawful distribution

(1)   This section applies where a distribution, or part of one, made by a company to one of its members is made in contravention of this Part.

(2)   If at the time of the distribution the member knows or has reasonable grounds for believing that it is so made, he is liable—

(a)   to repay it (or that part of it, as the case may be) to the company, or

(b)   in the case of a distribution made otherwise than in cash, to pay the company a sum equal to the value of the distribution (or part) at that time.

(3)   This is without prejudice to any obligation imposed apart from this section on a member of a company to repay a distribution unlawfully made to him.

(4)   This section does not apply in relation to—

(a)   financial assistance given by a company in contravention of section 678 or 679, or

(b)   any payment made by a company in respect of the redemption or purchase by the company of shares in itself.

Other matters

848   Saving for certain older provisions in articles

(1)   Where immediately before the relevant date a company was authorised by a provision of its articles to apply its unrealised profits in paying up in full or in part unissued shares to be allotted to members of the company as fully or partly paid bonus shares, that provision continues (subject to any alteration of the articles) as authority for those profits to be so applied after that date.

(2)   For this purpose the relevant date is—

(a)   for companies registered in Great Britain, 22nd December 1980;

(b)   for companies registered in Northern Ireland, 1st July 1983.

849   Restriction on application of unrealised profits

A company must not apply an unrealised profit in paying up debentures or any amounts unpaid on its issued shares.

850   Treatment of certain older profits or losses

(1)   Where the directors of a company are, after making all reasonable enquiries, unable to determine whether a particular profit made before the relevant date is realised or unrealised, they may treat the profit as realised.

(2)   Where the directors of a company, after making all reasonable enquiries, are unable to determine whether a particular loss made before the relevant date is realised or unrealised, they may treat the loss as unrealised.

(3)   For the purposes of this section the relevant date is—

(a)   for companies registered in Great Britain, 22nd December 1980;

(b)   for companies registered in Northern Ireland, 1st July 1983.

851   Application of rules of law restricting distributions

(1)   Except as provided in this section, the provisions of this Part are without prejudice to any rule of law restricting the sums out of which, or the cases in which, a distribution may be made.

(2)   For the purposes of any rule of law requiring distributions to be paid out of profits or restricting the return of capital to members—

(a)   section 845 (distributions in kind: determination of amount) applies to determine the amount of any distribution or return of capital consisting of or including, or treated as arising in consequence of the sale, transfer or other disposition by a company of a non-cash asset; and

(b)   section 846 (distributions in kind: treatment of unrealised profits) applies as it applies for the purposes of this Part.

(3)   In this section references to distributions are to amounts regarded as distributions for the purposes of any such rule of law as is referred to in subsection (1).

852   Saving for other restrictions on distributions

The provisions of this Part are without prejudice to any enactment, or any provision of a company's articles, restricting the sums out of which, or the cases in which, a distribution may be made.

853   Minor definitions

(1)   The following provisions apply for the purposes of this Part.

(2)   References to profit or losses of any description—

(a)   are to profits or losses of that description made at any time, and

(b)   except where the context otherwise requires, are to profits or losses of a revenue or capital character.

(3)   "Capitalisation", in relation to a company's profits, means any of the following operations (whenever carried out)—

(a)   applying the profits in wholly or partly paying up unissued shares in the company to be allotted to members of the company as fully or partly paid bonus shares, or

(b)   transferring the profits to capital redemption reserve.

(4)   References to "realised profits" and "realised losses", in relation to a company's accounts, are to such profits or losses of the company as fall to be treated as realised in accordance with principles generally accepted at the time when the accounts are prepared, with respect to the determination for accounting purposes of realised profits or losses.

(5)   Subsection (4) is without prejudice to—

(a)   the construction of any other expression (where appropriate) by reference to accepted accounting principles or practice, or

(b)   any specific provision for the treatment of profits or losses of any description as realised.

(6)   "Fixed assets" means assets of a company which are intended for use on a continuing basis in the company's activities.

PART 24

ANNUAL CONFIRMATION OF ACCURACY OF INFORMATION ON REGISTER

853A   Duty to deliver confirmation statements

(1)   Every company must, before the end of the period of 14 days after the end of each review period, deliver to the registrar—

    (a)   such information as is necessary to ensure that the company is able to make the statement referred to in paragraph (b), and

    (b)   a statement (a "confirmation statement") confirming—

       (i)   that the company has delivered to the registrar, or is delivering to the registrar at the same time as the confirmation statement, all of the information that it is required to deliver in relation to the confirmation period concerned under any duty to notify a relevant event (see section 853B),

       (ii)   that the company is delivering to the registrar at the same time as the confirmation statement any information that it is required to deliver by virtue of a duty imposed by any of sections 853BA to 853H, and

       (iii)   in the case of a company's first statement under this paragraph, that the company has delivered to the registrar, or is delivering to the registrar at the same time as the confirmation statement, any information that it is required to deliver under section 167I, 279I or 790LG (pre-incorporation changes).

(2)   ...

(3)   In this Part "confirmation period"—

    (a)   in relation to a company's first confirmation statement, means the period beginning with the day of the company's incorporation and ending with the date specified in the statement ("the confirmation date");

    (b)   in relation to any other confirmation statement of a company, means the period beginning with the day after the confirmation date of the last such statement and ending with the confirmation date of the confirmation statement concerned.

(4)   The confirmation date of a confirmation statement must be no later than the last day of the review period concerned.

(5)   For the purposes of this Part, each of the following is a review period—

    (a)   the period of 12 months beginning with the day of the company's incorporation;

    (b)   each period of 12 months beginning with the day after the end of the previous review period.

(6)   But where a company delivers a confirmation statement with a confirmation date which is earlier than the last day of the review period concerned, the next review period is the period of 12 months beginning with the day after the confirmation date.

(7)   For the purpose of making a confirmation statement a company is entitled to assume that information that has been delivered to the registrar has been properly delivered unless the registrar has notified the company otherwise.

853B   Duties to notify a relevant event

The following duties are duties to notify a relevant event—

    (a)   ...

    (b)   in the case of a company in respect of which an election is in force under section 128B (election to keep membership information on central register), the duty to deliver anything as mentioned in section 128E;

    (c)   the duty to give notice of a change as mentioned in section 167 (change in directors or in particulars required to be included in register of directors or register of directors' residential addresses);

(d)   in the case of a company in respect of which an election is in force under section 167A (election to keep information in register of directors or register of directors' residential addresses on central register), the duty to deliver anything as mentioned in section 167D;

(e)   in the case of a private company with a secretary or a public company, the duty to give notice of a change as mentioned in section 276 (change in secretary or joint secretaries or in particulars required to be included in register of secretaries);

(f)   in the case of a private company with a secretary in respect of which an election is in force under section 279A (election to keep information in register of secretaries on central register), the duty to deliver anything as mentioned in section 279D;

(fa)   in the case of a company to which Part 21A (information about people with significant control) applies, and in respect of which an election is not in force under section 790X (election to keep information in PSC register on central register), the duty to give notice of a change as mentioned in section 790VA (notification to the registrar of changes to the company's PSC register);

(g)   in the case of a company in respect of which an election is in force under section 790X (election to keep information in PSC

(h)   in the case of a company which, in accordance with regulations under section 1136, keeps any company records at a place other than its registered office, any duty under the regulations to give notice of a change in the address of that place.

853BA Duty to confirm lawful purpose

Where a company makes a confirmation statement it must at the same time deliver to the registrar a statement that the intended future activities of the company are lawful.

853C   Duty to notify a change in company's principal business activities

(1)   This section applies where—
       (a)   a company makes a confirmation statement, and
       (b)   there has been a change in the company's principal business activities during the confirmation period concerned.

(1A)   This section also applies where—
       (a)   a company makes its first confirmation statement, and
       (b)   by the time of its incorporation, the company's principal business activities had changed from those specified in the statement under section 9(5)(c).

(2)   The company must give notice to the registrar of the change at the same time as it delivers the confirmation statement.

(3)   The information as to the company's new principal business activities may be given by reference to one or more categories of any prescribed system of classifying business activities.

853CA Duty to notify a change in registered office

(1)   This section applies where—
       (a)   a company makes a confirmation statement,
       (b)   the company's registered office is not at an appropriate address within the meaning given by section 86(2), and
       (c)   the company has not given a notice under section 87 (change of registered office) that is awaiting registration by the registrar.

(2)   The company must deliver a notice under section 87 at the same time as it delivers the confirmation statement.

853CB Duty to notify a change in registered email address

(1)   This section applies where—
       (a)   a company makes a confirmation statement,
       (b)   the company's registered email address is not an appropriate email address within the meaning given by section 88A(2), and

(c)   the company has not given a notice under section 88B (change of registered email address) that is awaiting registration by the registrar.

(2)   The company must deliver a notice under section 88B at the same time as it delivers the confirmation statement.

853D   Duty to deliver statement of capital

(1)   This section applies where a company having a share capital makes a confirmation statement.

(2)   The company must deliver a statement of capital to the registrar at the same time as it delivers the confirmation statement.

(3)   Subsection (2) does not apply if there has been no change in any of the matters required to be dealt with by the statement of capital since the last such statement was delivered to the registrar.

(4)   The statement of capital must state with respect to the company's share capital at the confirmation date—

    (a)   the total number of shares of the company,

    (b)   the aggregate nominal value of those shares,

    (c)   the aggregate amount (if any) unpaid on those shares (whether on account of their nominal value or by way of premium), and

    (d)   for each class of shares—

        (i)   prescribed particulars of the rights attached to the shares,

        (ii)   the total number of shares of that class, and

        (iii)   the aggregate nominal value of shares of that class.

853E   Duty to notify trading status of shares

(1)   This section applies where a company having a share capital makes a confirmation statement.

(2)   The company must deliver to the registrar a statement dealing with the matters mentioned in subsection (4) at the same time as it delivers the confirmation statement.

(3)   Subsection (2) does not apply if and to the extent that the last statement delivered to the registrar under this section applies equally to the confirmation period concerned.

(4)   The matters are—

    (a)   whether any of the company's shares were, at any time during the confirmation period concerned, shares admitted to trading on a relevant market or on any other market which is outside the United Kingdom, and

    (b)   if so, whether both of the conditions mentioned in subsection (5) were satisfied throughout the confirmation period concerned.

(5)   The conditions are that—

    (a)   there were shares of the company which were shares admitted to trading on a relevant market;

    (b)   the company was a DTR5 issuer.

(6)   In this Part—

"DTR5 issuer" means an issuer to which Chapter 5 of the Disclosure Rules and Transparency Rules sourcebook made by the Financial Conduct Authority (as amended or replaced from time to time) applies;

"relevant market" means—

    (a)   a recognised investment exchange, as defined in section 285(1)(a) (exemption for recognised exemption exchanges and clearance houses) of the Financial Services and Markets Act 2000 ("the Act"); and

    (b)   any other market which is a UK regulated market or an EU regulated market,

but not an overseas investment exchange, as defined by section 313 (interpretation of Part 18) of the Act.

853F   Duty to deliver shareholder information: non-traded companies

(1)   This section applies where—

    (a)   a non-traded company makes a confirmation statement, and

    (b)   there is no election in force under section 128B in respect of the company.

(2)   A "non-traded company" is a company none of whose shares were, at any time during the confirmation period concerned, shares admitted to trading on a relevant market or on any other market which is outside the United Kingdom.

(3)   The company must deliver the information falling within subsection (5) to the registrar at the same time as it delivers the confirmation statement.

(4)   Subsection (3) does not apply if and to the extent that the information most recently delivered to the registrar under this section applies equally to the confirmation period concerned.

(5)   The information is—

    (a)   the name (as it appears in the company's register of members) of every person who was at any time during the confirmation period a member of the company,

    (b)   the number of shares of each class held at the end of the confirmation date concerned by each person who was a member of the company at that time,

    (c)   the number of shares of each class transferred during the confirmation period concerned by or to each person who was a member of the company at any time during that period, and

    (d)   the dates of registration of those transfers.

(6)   The registrar may impose requirements about the form in which information of the kind mentioned in subsection (5)(a) is delivered for the purpose of enabling the entries on the register relating to any given person to be easily found.

853G   Duty to deliver shareholder information: certain traded companies

(1)   This section applies where a traded company makes a confirmation statement.

(2)   A "traded company" is a company any of whose shares were, at any time during the confirmation period concerned, shares admitted to trading on a relevant market or on any other market which is outside the United Kingdom.

(3)   But a company is not a traded company if throughout the confirmation period concerned—

    (a)   there were shares of the company which were shares admitted to trading on a relevant market, and

    (b)   the company was a DTR5 issuer.

(4)   The company must deliver the information falling within subsection (6) to the registrar at the same time as it delivers the confirmation statement.

(5)   Subsection (4) does not apply if and to the extent the information most recently delivered to the registrar under this section applies equally to the confirmation period concerned.

(6)   The information is—

    (a)   the name and address (as they appear in the company's register of members) of each person who, at the end of the confirmation date concerned, held at least 5% of the issued shares of any class of the company, and

    (b)   the number of shares of each class held by each such person at that time.

853H   Duty to deliver information about exemption from Part 21A

(1)   This section applies where a company … to which Part 21A does not apply (information about people with significant control, see section 790B), makes a confirmation statement.

(2)   The company must deliver to the registrar a statement of the fact that it is a company to which Part 21A does not apply at the same time as it delivers the confirmation statement.

(3)   Subsection (2) does not apply if the last statement delivered to the registrar under this section applies equally to the confirmation period concerned.

853I   …

853J   Power to amend duties to deliver certain information

(1)   The Secretary of State may by regulations make provision about the duties on a company in relation to the delivery of information falling within section 853E(4), 853F(5), 853G(6) or 853H(2) (referred to in this section as "relevant information").

(2)   The regulations may, in particular, make provision requiring relevant information to be delivered—

(a)   on such occasions as may be prescribed;

(b)   at such intervals as may be prescribed.

(3)   The regulations may amend or repeal the provisions of sections 853A, 853B and 853E to 853H.

(4)   The regulations may provide—

(a)   that where a company fails to comply with any duty to deliver relevant information an offence is committed by—

(i)   the company, and

(ii)   every officer of the company who is in default;

(b)   that a person guilty of such an offence is liable on summary conviction—

(i)   in England and Wales, to a fine and, for continued contravention, a daily default fine not exceeding the greater of £500 and one-tenth of level 4 on the standard scale;

(ii)   in Scotland or Northern Ireland, to a fine not exceeding level 5 on the standard scale and, for continued contravention, a daily default fine not exceeding one- tenth of level 5 on the standard scale;

(c)   that, in the case of continued contravention, an offence is also committed by every officer of the company who did not commit an offence under provision made under paragraph (a) in relation to the initial contravention but who is in default in relation to the continued contravention;

(d)   that a person guilty of such an offence is liable on summary conviction—

(i)   in England and Wales, to a fine not exceeding the greater of £500 and one-tenth of level 4 on the standard scale for each day on which the contravention continues and the person is in default;

(ii)   in Scotland or Northern Ireland, to a fine not exceeding one-tenth of level 5 on the standard scale for each day on which the contravention continues and the person is in default.

(5)   The regulations may provide that, for the purposes of any provision made under subsection (4), a shadow director is to be treated as a director.

(6)   Regulations under this section are subject to affirmative resolution procedure.

853K   Confirmation statements: power to make further provision by regulations

(1)   The Secretary of State may by regulations make further provision as to the duties to deliver information to the registrar to which a confirmation statement is to relate.

(2)   The regulations may—

(a)   amend or repeal the provisions of sections 853A to 853H, and

(b)   provide for exceptions from the requirements of those sections as they have effect from time to time.

(3)   Regulations under this section which provide that a confirmation statement must relate to a duty to deliver information not for the time being mentioned in section 853A(1)(b) are subject to affirmative resolution procedure.

(4)   Any other regulations under this section are subject to negative resolution procedure.

853L   Failure to deliver confirmation statement

(1)   If a company fails to deliver a confirmation statement before the end of the period of 14 days after the end of a review period an offence is committed by—

(a)   the company, and

(b)   every officer of the company who is in default,

For this purpose a shadow director is treated as a director.

(2)   A person guilty of an offence under subsection (1) is liable on summary conviction—

(a)   in England and Wales to a fine, and, for continued contravention, a daily default fine not exceeding the greater of £500 and one-tenth of level 4 on the standard scale;

(b) in Scotland or Northern Ireland, to a fine not exceeding level 5 on the standard scale and, for continued contravention, a daily default fine not exceeding one-tenth of level 5 on the standard scale.

(3) The contravention continues until such time as a confirmation statement specifying a confirmation date no later than the last day of the review period concerned is delivered by the company to the registrar.

(4) ...

(5) In the case of continued contravention, an offence is also committed by every officer of the company who did not commit an offence under subsection (1) in relation to the initial contravention but who is in default in relation to the continued contravention.

(6) A person guilty of an offence under subsection (5) is liable on summary conviction—

(a) in England and Wales, to a fine not exceeding the greater of £500 and one-tenth of level 4 on the standard scale for each day on which the contravention continues and the person is in default;

(b) in Scotland or Northern Ireland, to a fine not exceeding one- tenth of level 5 on the standard scale for each day on which the contravention continues and the person is in default.

PART 25
COMPANY CHARGES

CHAPTER A1
REGISTRATION OF COMPANY CHARGES

Company charges

859A Charges created by a company

(1) Subject to subsection (6), this section applies where a company creates a charge.

(2) The registrar must register the charge if, before the end of the period allowed for delivery, the company or any person interested in the charge delivers to the registrar for registration a section 859D statement of particulars.

(3) Where the charge is created or evidenced by an instrument, the registrar is required to register it only if a certified copy of the instrument is delivered to the registrar with the statement of particulars.

(4) "The period allowed for delivery" is 21 days beginning with the day after the date of creation of the charge (see section 859E), unless an order allowing an extended period is made under section 859F(3).

(5) Where an order is made under section 859F(3) a copy of the order must be delivered to the registrar with the statement of particulars.

(6) This section does not apply to—

(a) a charge in favour of a landlord on a cash deposit given as a security in connection with the lease of land;

(b) a charge created by a member of Lloyd's (within the meaning of the Lloyd's Act 1982) to secure its obligations in connection with its underwriting business at Lloyd's;

(c) a charge excluded from the application of this section by or under any other Act.

(7) In this Part—

"cash" includes foreign currency,

"charge" includes—

(a) a mortgage;

(b) a standard security, assignation in security, and any other right in security constituted under the law of Scotland, including any heritable security, but not including a pledge, and

"company" means a UK-registered company.

859B Charge in series of debentures

(1) This section applies where—

(a)   a company creates a series of debentures containing a charge, or giving a charge by
       reference to another instrument, and

(b)   debenture holders of that series are entitled to the benefit of the charge pari passu.

(2)   The registrar must register the charge if, before the end of the period allowed for delivery, the
       company or any person interested in the charge delivers to the registrar for registration, a
       section 859D statement of particulars which also contains the following—

       (a)   either—

              (i)   the name of each of the trustees for the debenture holders, or

              (ii)   where there are more than four such persons, the names of any four persons listed in
                      the charge instrument as trustees for the debenture holders, and a statement that
                      there are other such persons;

       (b)   the dates of the resolutions authorising the issue of the series;

       (c)   the date of the covering instrument (if any) by which the series is created or defined.

(3)   Where the charge is created or evidenced by an instrument, the registrar is required to register it
       only if a certified copy of the instrument is delivered to the registrar with the statement of
       particulars.

(4)   Where the charge is not created or evidenced by an instrument, the registrar is required to register
       it only if a certified copy of one of the debentures in the series is delivered to the registrar with the
       statement of particulars.

(5)   For the purposes of this section a statement of particulars is taken to be a section 859D statement
       of particulars even if it does not contain the names of the debenture holders.

(6)   "The period allowed for delivery" is—

       (a)   if there is a deed containing the charge, 21 days beginning with the day after the date on
              which the deed is executed;

       (b)   if there is no deed containing the charge, 21 days beginning with the day after the date on
              which the first debenture of the series is executed.

(7)   Where an order is made under section 859F(3) a copy of the order must be delivered to the
       registrar with the statement of particulars.

(8)   In this section "deed" means—

       (a)   a deed governed by the law of England and Wales or Northern Ireland, or

       (b)   an instrument governed by a law other than the law of England and Wales or Northern
              Ireland which requires delivery under that law in order to take effect.

859C   Charges existing on property or undertaking acquired

(1)   This section applies where a company acquires property or undertaking which is subject to a
       charge of a kind which would, if it had been created by the company after the acquisition of the
       property or undertaking, have been capable of being registered under section 859A.

(2)   The registrar must register the charge if the company or any person interested in the charge
       delivers to the registrar for registration a section 859D statement of particulars.

(3)   Where the charge is created or evidenced by an instrument, the registrar is required to register it
       only if a certified copy of the instrument is delivered to the registrar with the statement of
       particulars.

859D   Particulars to be delivered to registrar

(1)   A statement of particulars relating to a charge created by a company is a "section 859D statement
       of particulars" if it contains the following particulars—

       (a)   the registered name and number of the company;

       (b)   the date of creation of the charge and (if the charge is one to which section 859C applies) the
              date of acquisition of the property or undertaking concerned;

       (c)   where the charge is created or evidenced by an instrument, the particulars listed in
              subsection (2);

       (d)   where the charge is not created or evidenced by an instrument, the particulars listed in
              subsection (3).

(2)   The particulars referred to in subsection (1)(c) are—

     (a)   any of the following—

          (i)   the name of each of the persons in whose favour the charge has been created or of the security agents or trustees holding the charge for the benefit of one or more persons; or,

          (ii)   where there are more than four such persons, security agents or trustees, the names of any four such persons, security agents or trustees listed in the charge instrument, and a statement that there are other such persons, security agents or trustees;

     (b)   whether the instrument is expressed to contain a floating charge and, if so, whether it is expressed to cover all the property and undertaking of the company;

     (c)   whether any of the terms of the charge prohibit or restrict the company from creating further security that will rank equally with or ahead of the charge;

     (d)   whether (and if so, a short description of) any land, ship, aircraft or intellectual property that is registered or required to be registered in the United Kingdom, is subject to a charge (which is not a floating charge) or fixed security included in the instrument;

     (e)   whether the instrument includes a charge (which is not a floating charge) or fixed security over—

          (i)   any tangible or corporeal property, or

          (ii)   any intangible or incorporeal property,

     not described in paragraph (d).

(3)   The particulars referred to in subsection (1)(d) are—

     (a)   a statement that there is no instrument creating or evidencing the charge;

     (b)   the names of each of the persons in whose favour the charge has been created or the names of any security agents or trustees holding the charge for the benefit of one or more persons;

     (c)   the nature of the charge;

     (d)   a short description of the property or undertaking charged;

     (e)   the obligations secured by the charge.

(4)   In this section "fixed security" has the meaning given in section 486(1) of the Companies Act 1985.

(5)   In this section "intellectual property" includes—

     (a)   any patent, trade mark, registered design, copyright or design right;

     (b)   any licence under or in respect of any such right.

859E   Date of creation of charge

(1)   For the purposes of this Part, a charge of the type described in column 1 of the Table below is taken to be created on the date given in relation to it in column 2 of that Table.

1 Type of charge	2 When charge created
Standard security	The date of its recording in the Register of Sasines or its registration in the Land Register of Scotland
Charge other than a standard security, where created or evidenced by an instrument	Where the instrument is a deed that has been executed and has immediate effect on execution and delivery, the date of delivery
	Where the instrument is a deed that has been executed and held in escrow, the date of delivery into escrow
	Where the instrument is a deed that has been executed and held as undelivered, the date of delivery

1 Type of charge	2 When charge created
	Where the instrument is not a deed and has immediate effect on execution, the date of execution
	Where the instrument is not a deed and does not have immediate effect on execution, the date on which the instrument takes effect
Charge other than a standard security, where not created or evidenced by an instrument	The date on which the charge comes into effect.

(2)   Where a charge is created or evidenced by an instrument made between two or more parties, references in the Table in subsection (1) to execution are to execution by all the parties to the instrument whose execution is essential for the instrument to take effect as a charge.

(3)   This section applies for the purposes of this Chapter even if further forms, notices, registrations or other actions or proceedings are necessary to make the charge valid or effectual for any other purposes.

(4)   For the purposes of this Chapter, the registrar is entitled without further enquiry to accept a charge as created on the date given as the date of creation of the charge in a section 859D statement of particulars.

(5)   In this section "deed" means—
(a)   a deed governed by the law of England and Wales or Northern Ireland, or
(b)   an instrument governed by a law other than the law of England and Wales or Northern Ireland which requires delivery under that law in order to take effect.

(6)   References in this section to delivery, in relation to a deed, include delivery as a deed where required.

859F   Extension of period allowed for delivery

(1)   Subsection (3) applies if the court is satisfied that—
(a)   neither the company nor any other person interested in the charge has delivered to the registrar the documents required under section 859A or (as the case may be) 859B before the end of the period allowed for delivery under the section concerned, and
(b)   the requirement in subsection (2) is met.

(2)   The requirement is—
(a)   that the failure to deliver those documents—
(i)   was accidental or due to inadvertence or to some other sufficient cause, or
(ii)   is not of a nature to prejudice the position of creditors or shareholders of the company, or
(b)   that on other grounds it is just and equitable to grant relief.

(3)   The court may, on the application of the company or a person interested, and on such terms and conditions as seem to the court just and expedient, order that the period allowed for delivery be extended.

859G   Personal information etc in certified copies

(1)   The following are not required to be included in a certified copy of an instrument or debenture delivered to the registrar for the purposes of any provision of this Chapter—
(a)   personal information relating to an individual (other than the name of an individual);
(b)   the number or other identifier of a bank or securities account of a company or individual;
(c)   a signature.

(2)   The registrar is entitled without further enquiry, to accept the certified copy of an instrument whether or not any of the information in subsection (1) is contained within the instrument.

Consequence of non-delivery

859H Consequence of failure to deliver charges

(1) This section applies if—

    (a) a company creates a charge to which section 859A or 859B applies, and

    (b) the documents required by section 859A or (as the case may be) 859B are not delivered to the registrar by the company or another person interested in the charge before the end of the relevant period allowed for delivery.

(2) "The relevant period allowed for delivery" is—

    (a) the period allowed for delivery under the section in question, or

    (b) if an order under section 859F(3) has been made, the period allowed by the order.

(3) Where this section applies, the charge is void (so far as any security on the company's property or undertaking is conferred by it) against—

    (a) a liquidator of the company,

    (b) an administrator of the company, and

    (c) a creditor of the company.

(4) Subsection (3) is without prejudice to any contract or obligation for repayment of the money secured by the charge; and when a charge becomes void under this section, the money secured by it immediately becomes payable.

The register

859I Entries on the register

(1) This section applies where a charge is registered in accordance with a provision of this Chapter.

(2) The registrar must—

    (a) allocate to the charge a unique reference code and place a note in the register recording that reference code; and

    (b) include in the register any documents delivered under section 859A(3) or (5), 859B(3), (4) or (7), or 859C(3).

(3) The registrar must give a certificate of the registration of the charge to the person who delivered to the registrar a section 859D statement of particulars relating to the charge.

(4) The certificate must state—

    (a) the registered name and number of the company in respect of which the charge was registered; and

    (b) the unique reference code allocated to the charge.

(5) The certificate must be signed by the registrar or authenticated by the registrar's official seal.

(6) In the case of registration under section 859A or 859B, the certificate is conclusive evidence that the documents required by the section concerned were delivered to the registrar before the end of the relevant period allowed for delivery.

(7) "The relevant period allowed for delivery" is—

    (a) the period allowed for delivery under the section in question, or

    (b) if an order under section 859F(3) has been made, the period allowed by the order.

859J Company holding property or undertaking as trustee

(1) Where a company is acting as trustee of property or undertaking which is the subject of a charge delivered for registration under this Chapter, the company or any person interested in the charge may deliver to the registrar a statement to that effect.

(2) A statement delivered after the delivery for registration of the charge must include—

    (a) the registered name and number of the company; and

    (b) the unique reference code allocated to the charge.

859K Registration of enforcement of security

(1) Subsection (2) applies where a person—

    (a)   obtains an order for the appointment of a receiver or manager of a company's property or undertaking, or

    (b)   appoints such a receiver or manager under powers contained in an instrument.

(2)   The person must, within 7 days of the order or of the appointment under those powers—

    (a)   give notice to the registrar of that fact, and

    (b)   if the order was obtained, or the appointment made, by virtue of a registered charge held by the person give the registrar a notice containing—

        (i)   in the case of a charge created before 6th April 2013, the information specified in subsection (4);

        (ii)   in the case of a charge created on or after 6th April 2013, the unique reference code allocated to the charge.

(3)   Where a person appointed receiver or manager of a company's property or undertaking under powers contained in an instrument ceases to act as such a receiver or manager, the person must, on so ceasing—

    (a)   give notice to the registrar of that fact, and

    (b)   give the registrar a notice containing—

        (i)   in the case of a charge created before 6th April 2013, the information specified in subsection (4), or

        (ii)   in the case of a charge created on or after 6th April 2013, the unique reference code allocated to the charge.

(4)   The information referred to in subsections (2)(b)(i) and (3)(b)(i) is—

    (a)   the date of the creation of the charge;

    (b)   a description of the instrument (if any) creating or evidencing the charge;

    (c)   short particulars of the property or undertaking charged.

(5)   The registrar must include in the register—

    (a)   a fact of which notice is given under subsection (2)(a), and

    (b)   a fact of which notice is given under subsection (3)(a).

(6)   A person who makes default in complying with the requirements of subsections (2) or (3) of this section commits an offence.

(7)   A person guilty of an offence under this section is liable on summary conviction to a fine not exceeding level 3 on the standard scale and, for continued contravention, a daily default fine not exceeding one-tenth of level 3 on the standard scale.

(8)   This section applies only to a receiver or manager appointed—

    (a)   by a court in England and Wales or Northern Ireland, or

    (b)   under an instrument governed by the law of England and Wales or Northern Ireland.

(9)   This section does not apply to a receiver appointed under Chapter 2 of Part 3 of the Insolvency Act 1986 (receivers (Scotland)).

859L   Entries of satisfaction and release

(1)   Subsection (5) applies if the statement set out in subsection (2) and the particulars set out in subsection (4) are delivered to the registrar with respect to a registered charge.

(2)   The statement referred to in subsection (1) is a statement to the effect that—

    (a)   the debt for which the charge was given has been paid or satisfied in whole or in part, or

    (b)   all or part of the property or undertaking charged—

        (i)   has been released from the charge, or

        (ii)   has ceased to form part of the company's property or undertaking.

(3)   Where a statement within subsection (2)(b) relates to part only of the property or undertaking charged, the statement must include a short description of that part.

(4)   The particulars referred to in subsection (1) are—

    (a)   the name and address of the person delivering the statement and an indication of their interest in the charge;

    (b)   the registered name and number of the company that—

        (i)   created the charge (in a case within section 859A or 859B), or

        (ii)   acquired the property or undertaking subject to the charge (in a case within section 859C);

(c)   in respect of a charge created before 6th April 2013—

        (i)   the date of creation of the charge;

        (ii)   a description of the instrument (if any) by which the charge is created or evidenced;

        (iii)   short particulars of the property or undertaking charged;

(d)   in respect of a charge created on or after 6th April 2013, the unique reference code allocated to the charge.

(5)   The registrar must include in the register—

(a)   a statement of satisfaction in whole or in part, or

(b)   a statement of the fact that all or part of the property or undertaking has been released from the charge or has ceased to form part of the company's property or undertaking (as the case may be).

859M   Rectification of register

(1)   Subsection (3) applies if the court is satisfied that—

(a)   there has been an omission or mis-statement in any statement or notice delivered to the registrar in accordance with this Chapter, and

(b)   the requirement in subsection (2) is met.

(2)   The requirement is that the court is satisfied—

(a)   that the omission or mis-statement—

        (i)   was accidental or due to inadvertence or to some other sufficient cause, or

        (ii)   is not of a nature to prejudice the position of creditors or shareholders of the company, or

(b)   that on other grounds it is just and equitable to grant relief.

(3)   The court may, on the application of the company or a person interested, and on such terms and conditions as seem to the court just and expedient, order that the omission or mis-statement be rectified.

(4)   A copy of the court's order must be sent by the applicant to the registrar for registration.

859N   Replacement of instrument or debenture

(1)   Subsection (2) applies if the court is satisfied that—

(a)   a copy of an instrument or debenture delivered to the registrar under this Chapter contains material which could have been omitted under section 859G;

(b)   the wrong instrument or debenture was delivered to the registrar; or

(c)   the copy was defective.

(2)   The court may, on the application of the company or a person interested, and on such terms and conditions as seem to the court just and expedient, order that the copy of the instrument or debenture be removed from the register and replaced.

(3)   A copy of the court's order must be sent by the applicant to the registrar for registration.

859O   Notification of addition to or amendment of charge

(1)   This section applies where, after the creation of a charge, the charge is amended by adding or amending a term that—

(a)   prohibits or restricts the creation of any fixed security or any other charge having priority over, or ranking pari passu with, the charge; or

(b)   varies, or otherwise regulates the order of, the ranking of the charge in relation to any fixed security or any other charge.

(2)   Either the company that created the charge or the person taking the benefit of the charge (or another charge referred to in subsection (1)(b)) may deliver to the registrar for registration—

(a)   a certified copy of the instrument effecting the amendment, variation or regulation, and

(b)   a statement of the particulars set out in subsection (3).

(3)   The particulars to be included in the statement are—

(a)   the registered name and number of the company;

(b) in the case of a charge created before 6th April 2013—
    (i) the date of creation of the charge;
    (ii) a description of the instrument (if any) by which the charge was created or evidenced;
    (iii) short particulars of the property or undertaking charged as set out when the charge was registered;
(c) in the case of a charge created on or after 6th April 2013, (where allocated) the unique reference code allocated to the charge.

(4) Subsections (1) to (3) do not affect the continued application of section 466 of the Companies Act 1985.

(5) In this section "fixed security" has the meaning given in section 486(1) of the Companies Act 1985.

Companies' records and registers

859P Companies to keep copies of instruments creating and amending charges

(1) A company must keep available for inspection a copy of every—
    (a) instrument creating a charge capable of registration under this Chapter, and
    (b) instrument effecting any variation or amendment of such a charge.

(2) In the case of a charge contained in a series of uniform debentures, a copy of one of the debentures of the series is sufficient for the purposes of subsection (1)(a).

(3) If the particulars referred to in section 859D(1) or the particulars of the property or undertaking charged are not contained in the instrument creating the charge, but are instead contained in other documents which are referred to in or otherwise incorporated into the instrument, then the company must also keep available for inspection a copy of those other documents.

(4) It is sufficient for the purposes of subsection (1)(a) if the company keeps a copy of the instrument in the form delivered to the registrar under section 859A(3), 859B(3) or (4) or 859C(3).

(5) Where a translation has been delivered to the registrar in accordance with section 1105, the company must keep available for inspection a copy of the translation.

859Q Instruments creating charges to be available for inspection

(1) This section applies to documents required to be kept available for inspection under section 859P (copies of instruments creating and amending charges).

(2) The documents must be kept available for inspection—
    (a) at the company's registered office, or
    (b) at a place specified in regulations under section 1136.

(3) The company must give notice to the registrar—
    (a) of the place at which the documents are kept available for inspection, and
    (b) of any change in that place,
unless they have at all times been kept at the company's registered office.

(4) The documents must be open to the inspection—
    (a) of any creditor or member of the company, without charge, and
    (b) of any other person, on payment of such fee as may be prescribed.

(5) If default is made for 14 days in complying with subsection (3) or an inspection required under subsection (4) is refused, an offence is committed by—
    (a) the company, and
    (b) every officer of the company who is in default.

(6) A person guilty of an offence under this section is liable on summary conviction to a fine not exceeding level 3 on the standard scale and, for continued contravention, a daily default fine not exceeding one-tenth of level 3 on the standard scale.

(7) If an inspection required under subsection (4) is refused the court may by order compel an immediate inspection.

(8) Where the company and a person wishing to carry out an inspection under subsection (4) agree, the inspection may be carried out by electronic means.

CHAPTER 3
POWERS OF THE SECRETARY OF STATE

893   Power to make provision for effect of registration in special register

(1)   In this section a "special register" means a register, other than the register, in which a charge to which Chapter A1 applies is required or authorised to be registered.

(2)   The Secretary of State may by order make provision for facilitating the making of information-sharing arrangements between the person responsible for maintaining a special register ("the responsible person") and the registrar that meet the requirement in subsection (4).
          "Information-sharing arrangements" are arrangements to share and make use of information held by the registrar or by the responsible person.

(3)   If the Secretary of State is satisfied that appropriate information-sharing arrangements have been made, he may by order provide that—
          (a)   the registrar is authorised not to register a charge of a specified description under Chapter A1,
          (b)   a charge of a specified description that is registered in the special register within a specified period is to be treated as if it had been registered (and certified by the registrar as registered) in accordance with the requirements of Chapter A1, and
          (c)   the other provisions of Chapter A1 apply to a charge so treated with specified modifications.

(4)   The information-sharing arrangements must ensure that persons inspecting the register—
          (a)   are made aware, in a manner appropriate to the inspection, of the existence of charges in the special register which are treated in accordance with provision so made, and
          (b)   are able to obtain information from the special register about any such charge.

(5)   An order under this section may—
          (a)   modify any enactment or rule of law which would otherwise restrict or prevent the responsible person from entering into or giving effect to information-sharing arrangements,
          (b)   authorise the responsible person to require information to be provided to him for the purposes of the arrangements,
          (c)   make provision about—
                 (i)   the charging by the responsible person of fees in connection with the arrangements and the destination of such fees (including provision modifying any enactment which would otherwise apply in relation to fees payable to the responsible person), and
                 (ii)   the making of payments under the arrangements by the registrar to the responsible person,
          (d)   require the registrar to make copies of the arrangements available to the public (in hard copy or electronic form).

(6)   In this section "specified" means specified in an order under this section.

(7)   A description of charge may be specified, in particular, by reference to one or more of the following—
          (a)   the type of company by which it is created,
          (b)   the form of charge which it is,
          (c)   the description of assets over which it is granted,
          (d)   the length of the period between the date of its registration in the special register and the date of its creation.

(8)   Provision may be made under this section relating to registers maintained under the law of a country or territory outside the United Kingdom.

(9)   An order under this section is subject to negative resolution procedure.

894   General power to make amendments to this Part

(1)   The Secretary of State may by regulations under this section—

(a)   amend this Part by altering, adding or repealing provisions,

(b)   make consequential amendments or repeals in this Act or any other enactment (whether passed or made before or after this Act).

(2)   Regulations under this section are subject to affirmative resolution procedure.

PART 26
ARRANGEMENTS AND RECONSTRUCTIONS: GENERAL

Application of this Part

895   Application of this Part

(1)   The provisions of this Part apply where a compromise or arrangement is proposed between a company and—

(a)   its creditors, or any class of them, or

(b)   its members, or any class of them.

(2)   In this Part—

"arrangement" includes a reorganisation of the company's share capital by the consolidation of shares of different classes or by the division of shares into shares of different classes, or by both of those methods; and

"company"—

(a)   in section 900 (powers of court to facilitate reconstruction or amalgamation) means a company within the meaning of this Act, and

(b)   elsewhere in this Part means any company liable to be wound up under the Insolvency Act 1986 or the Insolvency (Northern Ireland) Order 1989.

(3)   The provisions of this Part have effect subject to Part 27 (mergers and divisions of public companies) where that Part applies (see sections 902 and 903).

Meeting of creditors or members

896   Court order for holding of meeting

(1)   The court may, on an application under this section, order a meeting of the creditors or class of creditors, or of the members of the company or class of members (as the case may be), to be summoned in such manner as the court directs.

(2)   An application under this section may be made by—

(a)   the company,

(b)   any creditor or member of the company,

(c)   if the company is being wound up, the liquidator, or

(d)   if the company is in administration, the administrator.

(3)   Section 323 (representation of corporations at meetings) applies to a meeting of creditors under this section as to a meeting of the company (references to a member of the company being read as references to a creditor).

(4)   This section is subject to section 899A (moratorium debts, etc).

897   Statement to be circulated or made available

(1)   Where a meeting is summoned under section 896—

(a)   every notice summoning the meeting that is sent to a creditor or member must be accompanied by a statement complying with this section, and

(b)   every notice summoning the meeting that is given by advertisement must either—

(i)   include such a statement, or

(ii)   state where and how creditors or members entitled to attend the meeting may obtain copies of such a statement.

(2)   The statement must—

(a)   explain the effect of the compromise or arrangement, and

(b)   in particular, state—

(i)   any material interests of the directors of the company (whether as directors or as members or as creditors of the company or otherwise), and

(ii)   the effect on those interests of the compromise or arrangement, in so far as it is different from the effect on the like interests of other persons.

(3)   Where the compromise or arrangement affects the rights of debenture holders of the company, the statement must give the like explanation as respects the trustees of any deed for securing the issue of the debentures as it is required to give as respects the company's directors.

(4)   Where a notice given by advertisement states that copies of an explanatory statement can be obtained by creditors or members entitled to attend the meeting, every such creditor or member is entitled, on making application in the manner indicated by the notice, to be provided by the company with a copy of the statement free of charge.

(5)   If a company makes default in complying with any requirement of this section, an offence is committed by—

(a)   the company, and

(b)   every officer of the company who is in default.

This is subject to subsection (7) below.

(6)   For this purpose the following are treated as officers of the company—

(a)   a liquidator or administrator of the company, and

(b)   a trustee of a deed for securing the issue of debentures of the company.

(7)   A person is not guilty of an offence under this section if he shows that the default was due to the refusal of a director or trustee for debenture holders to supply the necessary particulars of his interests.

(8)   A person guilty of an offence under this section is liable—

(a)   on conviction on indictment, to a fine;

(b)   on summary conviction, to a fine not exceeding the statutory maximum.

898   Duty of directors and trustees to provide information

(1)   It is the duty of—

(a)   any director of the company, and

(b)   any trustee for its debenture holders,

to give notice to the company of such matters relating to himself as may be necessary for the purposes of section 897 (explanatory statement to be circulated or made available).

(2)   Any person who makes default in complying with this section commits an offence.

(3)   A person guilty of an offence under this section is liable on summary conviction to a fine not exceeding level 3 on the standard scale.

Court sanction for compromise or arrangement

899   Court sanction for compromise or arrangement

(1)   If a majority in number representing 75% in value of the creditors or class of creditors or members or class of members (as the case may be), present and voting either in person or by proxy at the meeting summoned under section 896, agree a compromise or arrangement, the court may, on an application under this section, sanction the compromise or arrangement.

(1A) Subsection (1) is subject to section 899A (moratorium debts, etc).

(2)   An application under this section may be made by—

(a)   the company,

(b)   any creditor or member of the company,

(c)   if the company is being wound up, the liquidator, or

(d)   if the company is in administration, the administrator.

(3)   A compromise or arrangement sanctioned by the court is binding on—

(a)   all creditors or the class of creditors or on the members or class of members (as the case may be), and

(b)   the company or, in the case of a company in the course of being wound up, the liquidator and contributories of the company.

(4)   The court's order has no effect until a copy of it has been delivered to the registrar.

(5)   ...

Special cases

899A Moratorium debts, etc

(1)   This section applies where—

   (a)   an application under section 896 in respect of a compromise or arrangement is made before the end of the period of 12 weeks beginning with the day after the end of any moratorium for the company under Part A1 of the Insolvency Act 1986 or Part 1A of the Insolvency (Northern Ireland) Order 1989 (S.I. 1989/2405 (NI 19)), and

   (b)   the creditors with whom the compromise or arrangement is proposed include any relevant creditors (see subsection (2)).

(2)   In this section "relevant creditor" means—

   (a)   a creditor in respect of a moratorium debt, or

   (b)   a creditor in respect of a priority pre-moratorium debt.

(3)   The relevant creditors may not participate in the meeting summoned under section 896.

(4)   For the purposes of section 897 (statement to be circulated or made available)—

   (a)   the requirement in section 897(1)(a) is to be read as including a requirement to send each relevant creditor a statement complying with section 897;

   (b)   any reference to creditors entitled to attend the meeting summoned under section 896 includes a reference to relevant creditors.

(5)   The court may not sanction the compromise or arrangement under section 899 if it includes provision in respect of any relevant creditor who has not agreed to it.

(6)   In this section—

"moratorium debt"—

   (a)   in the case of a moratorium under Part A1 of the Insolvency Act 1986, has the same meaning as in section 174A of that Act;

   (b)   in the case of a moratorium under Part 1A of the Insolvency (Northern Ireland) Order 1989, has the same meaning as in Article 148A of that Order;

"priority pre-moratorium debt"—

   (a)   in the case of a moratorium under Part A1 of the Insolvency Act 1986, has the same meaning as in section 174A of that Act;

   (b)   in the case of a moratorium under Part 1A of the Insolvency (Northern Ireland) Order 1989, has the same meaning as in Article 148A of that Order.

Reconstructions and amalgamations

900 Powers of court to facilitate reconstruction or amalgamation

(1)   This section applies where application is made to the court under section 899 to sanction a compromise or arrangement and it is shown that—

   (a)   the compromise or arrangement is proposed for the purposes of, or in connection with, a scheme for the reconstruction of any company or companies, or the amalgamation of any two or more companies, and

   (b)   under the scheme the whole or any part of the undertaking or the property of any company concerned in the scheme ("a transferor company") is to be transferred to another company ("the transferee company").

(2)   The court may, either by the order sanctioning the compromise or arrangement or by a subsequent order, make provision for all or any of the following matters—

   (a)   the transfer to the transferee company of the whole or any part of the undertaking and of the property or liabilities of any transferor company;

   (b)   the allotting or appropriation by the transferee company of any shares, debentures, policies or other like interests in that company which under the compromise or arrangement are to be allotted or appropriated by that company to or for any person;

(c)   the continuation by or against the transferee company of any legal proceedings pending by or against any transferor company;

(d)   the dissolution, without winding up, of any transferor company;

(e)   the provision to be made for any persons who, within such time and in such manner as the court directs, dissent from the compromise or arrangement;

(f)   such incidental, consequential and supplemental matters as are necessary to secure that the reconstruction or amalgamation is fully and effectively carried out.

(3)   If an order under this section provides for the transfer of property or liabilities—

(a)   the property is by virtue of the order transferred to, and vests in, the transferee company, and

(b)   the liabilities are, by virtue of the order, transferred to and become liabilities of that company.

(4)   The property (if the order so directs) vests freed from any charge that is by virtue of the compromise or arrangement to cease to have effect.

(5)   In this section—

"property" includes property, rights and powers of every description; and

"liabilities" includes duties.

(6)   Every company in relation to which an order is made under this section must cause a copy of the order to be delivered to the registrar within seven days after its making.

(7)   If default is made in complying with subsection (6) an offence is committed by—

(a)   the company, and

(b)   every officer of the company who is in default.

(8)   A person guilty of an offence under subsection (7) is liable on summary conviction to a fine not exceeding level 3 on the standard scale and, for continued contravention, a daily default fine not exceeding one-tenth of level 3 on the standard scale.

Obligations of company with respect to articles etc

901   Obligations of company with respect to articles etc

(1)   This section applies—

(a)   to any order under section 899 (order sanctioning compromise or arrangement), and

(b)   to any order under section 900 (order facilitating reconstruction or amalgamation) that alters the company's constitution.

(2)   If the order amends—

(a)   the company's articles, or

(b)   any resolution or agreement to which Chapter 3 of Part 3 applies (resolution or agreement affecting a company's constitution),

the copy of the order delivered to the registrar by the company under section 899(4) or section 900(6) must be accompanied by a copy of the company's articles, or the resolution or agreement in question, as amended.

(3)   Every copy of the company's articles issued by the company after the order is made must be accompanied by a copy of the order, unless the effect of the order has been incorporated into the articles by amendment.

(4)   In this section—

(a)   references to the effect of the order include the effect of the compromise or arrangement to which the order relates; and

(b)   in the case of a company not having articles, references to its articles shall be read as references to the instrument constituting the company or defining its constitution.

(5)   If a company makes default in complying with this section an offence is committed by—

(a)   the company, and

(b)   every officer of the company who is in default.

(6)   A person guilty of an offence under this section is liable on summary conviction to a fine not exceeding level 3 on the standard scale.

PART 26A
ARRANGEMENTS AND RECONSTRUCTIONS: COMPANIES IN FINANCIAL DIFFICULTY

Application of this Part

901A   Application of this Part

(1)   The provisions of this Part apply where conditions A and B are met in relation to a company.

(2)   Condition A is that the company has encountered, or is likely to encounter, financial difficulties that are affecting, or will or may affect, its ability to carry on business as a going concern.

(3)   Condition B is that—

(a)   a compromise or arrangement is proposed between the company and—

(i)   its creditors, or any class of them, or

(ii)   its members, or any class of them, and

(b)   the purpose of the compromise or arrangement is to eliminate, reduce or prevent, or mitigate the effect of, any of the financial difficulties mentioned in subsection (2).

(4)   In this Part—

"arrangement" includes a reorganisation of the company's share capital by the consolidation of shares of different classes or by the division of shares into shares of different classes, or by both of those methods;

"company"—

(a)   in section 901J (powers of court to facilitate reconstruction or amalgamation) means a company within the meaning of this Act, and

(b)   elsewhere in this Part means any company liable to be wound up under the Insolvency Act 1986 or the Insolvency (Northern Ireland) Order 1989 (S.I. 1989/2405 (NI 19)).

(5)   The provisions of this Part have effect subject to Part 27 (mergers and divisions of public companies) where that Part applies (see sections 902 and 903).

901B   Power to exclude companies providing financial services, etc

(1)   The Secretary of State may by regulations provide that this Part does not apply—

(a)   where the company in respect of which a compromise or arrangement is proposed is an authorised person, or an authorised person of a specified description;

(b)   where—

(i)   a compromise or arrangement is proposed between a company, or a company of a specified description, and any creditors of the company, and

(ii)   those creditors consist of or include creditors of a specified description.

(2)   In this section—

"authorised person" has the same meaning as in the Financial Services and Markets Act 2000 (see section 31 of that Act);

"specified" means specified in the regulations.

(3)   Regulations under this section are subject to affirmative resolution procedure.

Meeting of creditors or members

901C   Court order for holding of meeting

(1)   The court may, on an application under this subsection, order a meeting of the creditors or class of creditors, or of the members of the company or class of members (as the case may be), to be summoned in such manner as the court directs.

(2)   An application under subsection (1) may be made by—

(a)   the company,

(b)   any creditor or member of the company,

(c)   if the company is being wound up, the liquidator, or

(d)   if the company is in administration, the administrator.

(3)   Every creditor or member of the company whose rights are affected by the compromise or arrangement must be permitted to participate in a meeting ordered to be summoned under subsection (1).

(4)   But subsection (3) does not apply in relation to a class of creditors or members of the company if, on an application under this subsection, the court is satisfied that none of the members of that class has a genuine economic interest in the company.

(5)   An application under subsection (4) is to be made by the person who made the application under subsection (1) in respect of the compromise or arrangement.

(6)   Section 323 (representation of corporations at meetings) applies to a meeting of creditors under this section as to a meeting of the company (references to a member of the company being read as references to a creditor).

(7)   This section is subject to section 901H (moratorium debts, etc).

901D   Statement to be circulated or made available

(1)   Where a meeting is summoned under section 901C—

(a)   every notice summoning the meeting that is sent to a creditor or member must be accompanied by a statement complying with this section, and

(b)   every notice summoning the meeting that is given by advertisement must either—

(i)   include such a statement, or

(ii)   state where and how creditors or members entitled to attend the meeting may obtain copies of such a statement.

(2)   The statement must—

(a)   explain the effect of the compromise or arrangement, and

(b)   in particular, state—

(i)   any material interests of the directors of the company (whether as directors or as members or as creditors of the company or otherwise), and

(ii)   the effect on those interests of the compromise or arrangement, in so far as it is different from the effect on the like interests of other persons.

(3)   Where the compromise or arrangement affects the rights of debenture holders of the company, the statement must give the like explanation as respects the trustees of any deed for securing the issue of the debentures as it is required to give as respects the company's directors.

(4)   Where a notice given by advertisement states that copies of an explanatory statement can be obtained by creditors or members entitled to attend the meeting, every such creditor or member is entitled, on making application in the manner indicated by the notice, to be provided by the company with a copy of the statement free of charge.

(5)   If a company makes default in complying with any requirement of this section, an offence is committed by—

(a)   the company, and

(b)   every officer of the company who is in default.

This is subject to subsection (7).

(6)   For this purpose the following are treated as officers of the company—

(a)   a liquidator or administrator of the company, and

(b)   a trustee of a deed for securing the issue of debentures of the company.

(7)   A person is not guilty of an offence under this section if the person shows that the default was due to the refusal of a director or trustee for debenture holders to supply the necessary particulars of the director's or (as the case may be) the trustee's interests.

(8)   A person guilty of an offence under this section is liable—

(a)   on conviction on indictment, to a fine;

(b)   on summary conviction in England and Wales, to a fine;

(c)   on summary conviction in Scotland or Northern Ireland, to a fine not exceeding the statutory maximum.

901E Duty of directors and trustees to provide information

(1) It is the duty of—

  (a) any director of the company, and

  (b) any trustee for its debenture holders,

to give notice to the company of such matters relating to that director or trustee as may be necessary for the purposes of section 901D (explanatory statement to be circulated or made available).

(2) Any person who makes default in complying with this section commits an offence.

(3) A person guilty of an offence under this section is liable on summary conviction to a fine not exceeding level 3 on the standard scale.

Court sanction for compromise or arrangement

901F Court sanction for compromise or arrangement

(1) If a number representing 75% in value of the creditors or class of creditors or members or class of members (as the case may be), present and voting either in person or by proxy at the meeting summoned under section 901C, agree a compromise or arrangement, the court may, on an application under this section, sanction the compromise or arrangement.

(2) Subsection (1) is subject to—

  (a) section 901G (sanction for compromise or arrangement where one or more classes dissent), and

  (b) section 901H (moratorium debts, etc).

(3) An application under this section may be made by—

  (a) the company,

  (b) any creditor or member of the company,

  (c) if the company is being wound up, the liquidator, or

  (d) if the company is in administration, the administrator.

(4) Where the court makes an order under this section in relation to a company that is in administration or is being wound up, the court may by the order—

  (a) provide for the appointment of the administrator or liquidator to cease to have effect;

  (b) stay or sist all proceedings in the administration or the winding up;

  (c) impose any requirements with respect to the conduct of the administration or the winding up which the court thinks appropriate for facilitating the compromise or arrangement.

(5) A compromise or arrangement sanctioned by the court is binding—

  (a) on all creditors or the class of creditors or on the members or class of members (as the case may be), and

  (b) on the company or, in the case of a company in the course of being wound up, the liquidator and contributories of the company.

(6) The court's order has no effect until a copy of it has been—

  (a) in the case of an overseas company that is not required to register particulars under section 1046, published in the Gazette, or

  (b) in any other case, delivered to the registrar.

901G Sanction for compromise or arrangement where one or more classes dissent

(1) This section applies if the compromise or arrangement is not agreed by a number representing at least 75% in value of a class of creditors or (as the case may be) of members of the company ("the dissenting class"), present and voting either in person or by proxy at the meeting summoned under section 901C.

(2) If conditions A and B are met, the fact that the dissenting class has not agreed the compromise or arrangement does not prevent the court from sanctioning it under section 901F.

(3) Condition A is that the court is satisfied that, if the compromise or arrangement were to be sanctioned under section 901F, none of the members of the dissenting class would be any worse off than they would be in the event of the relevant alternative (see subsection (4)).

(4)   For the purposes of this section "the relevant alternative" is whatever the court considers would be most likely to occur in relation to the company if the compromise or arrangement were not sanctioned under section 901F.

(5)   Condition B is that the compromise or arrangement has been agreed by a number representing 75% in value of a class of creditors or (as the case may be) of members, present and voting either in person or by proxy at the meeting summoned under section 901C, who would receive a payment, or have a genuine economic interest in the company, in the event of the relevant alternative.

(6)   The Secretary of State may by regulations amend this section for the purpose of—

      (a)   adding to the conditions that must be met for the purposes of this section;

      (b)   removing or varying any of those conditions.

(7)   Regulations under subsection (6) are subject to affirmative resolution procedure.

Special cases

901H   Moratorium debts, etc

(1)   This section applies where—

      (a)   an application under section 901C(1) in respect of a compromise or arrangement is made before the end of the period of 12 weeks beginning with the day after the end of any moratorium for the company under Part A1 of the Insolvency Act 1986 or Part 1A of the Insolvency (Northern Ireland) Order 1989 (S.I. 1989/2405 (NI 19)), and

      (b)   the creditors with whom the compromise or arrangement is proposed include any relevant creditors (see subsection (2)).

(2)   In this section "relevant creditor" means—

      (a)   a creditor in respect of a moratorium debt, or

      (b)   a creditor in respect of a priority pre-moratorium debt.

(3)   The relevant creditors may not participate in the meeting summoned under section 901C.

(4)   For the purposes of section 901D (statement to be circulated or made available)—

      (a)   the requirement in section 901D(1)(a) is to be read as including a requirement to send each relevant creditor a statement complying with section 901D;

      (b)   any reference to creditors entitled to attend the meeting summoned under section 901C includes a reference to relevant creditors.

(5)   The court may not sanction the compromise or arrangement under section 901F if it includes provision in respect of any relevant creditor who has not agreed to it.

(6)   In this section—

      "moratorium debt"—

      (a)   in the case of a moratorium under Part A1 of the Insolvency Act 1986, has the same meaning as in section 174A of that Act;

      (b)   in the case of a moratorium under Part 1A of the Insolvency (Northern Ireland) Order 1989, has the same meaning as in Article 148A of that Order;

      "priority pre-moratorium debt"—

      (a)   in the case of a moratorium under Part A1 of the Insolvency Act 1986, has the same meaning as in section 174A of that Act;

      (b)   in the case of a moratorium under Part 1A of the Insolvency (Northern Ireland) Order 1989, has the same meaning as in Article 148A of that Order.

901I   Pension schemes

(1)   In a case where the company in respect of which a compromise or arrangement is proposed is or has been an employer in respect of an occupational pension scheme that is not a money purchase scheme, any notice or other document required to be sent to a creditor of the company must also be sent to the Pensions Regulator.

(2)   In a case where the company in respect of which a compromise or arrangement is proposed is an employer in respect of an eligible scheme, any notice or other document required to be sent to a

creditor of the company must also be sent to the Board of the Pension Protection Fund ("the Board").

(3)   The Secretary of State may by regulations provide that, in a case where—

(a)   the company in respect of which a compromise or arrangement is proposed is an employer in respect of an eligible scheme, and

(b)   the trustees or managers of the scheme are a creditor of the company,

the Board may exercise any rights, or any rights of a specified description, that are exercisable under this Part by the trustees or managers as a creditor of the company.

(4)   Regulations under this section may provide that the Board may exercise any such rights—

(a)   to the exclusion of the trustees or managers of the scheme, or

(b)   in addition to the exercise of those rights by the trustees or managers of the scheme.

(5)   Regulations under this section—

(a)   may specify conditions that must be met before the Board may exercise any such rights;

(b)   may provide for any such rights to be exercisable by the Board for a specified period;

(c)   may make provision in connection with any such rights ceasing to be so exercisable at the end of such a period.

(6)   Regulations under this section are subject to affirmative resolution procedure (but see subsection (7)).

(7)   During the period of six months beginning with the day on which this section comes into force, regulations under this section are subject to approval after being made (and subsection (6) does not apply).

(8)   For the purposes of subsection (7), section 1291 has effect as if any reference in that section to a period of 28 days were to a period of 40 days.

(9)   In this section—

"eligible scheme" means any pension scheme that is an eligible scheme for the purposes of section 126 of the Pensions Act 2004 or Article 110 of the Pensions (Northern Ireland) Order 2005 (S.I. 2005/255 (NI 1));

"employer"—

(a)   in subsection (1), means an employer within the meaning of section 318(1) of the Pensions Act 2004 or Article 2(2) of the Pensions (Northern Ireland) Order 2005;

(b)   in subsections (2) and (3)—

    (i)   in the case of a pension scheme that is an eligible scheme for the purposes of section 126 of the Pensions Act 2004, has the same meaning as it has for the purposes of Part 2 of that Act (see section 318(1) and (4) of that Act);

    (ii)   in the case of a pension scheme that is an eligible scheme for the purposes of Article 110 of the Pensions (Northern Ireland) Order 2005, has the same meaning as it has for the purposes of Part 3 of that Order (see Article 2(2) and (5) of that Order);

"money purchase scheme" means a pension scheme that is a money purchase scheme for the purposes of the Pension Schemes Act 1993 (see section 181(1) of that Act) or the Pension Schemes (Northern Ireland) Act 1993 (see section 176(1) of that Act);

"occupational pension scheme" and "pension scheme" have the meaning given by section 1 of the Pension Schemes Act 1993;

"specified" means specified in regulations under this section.

Reconstructions and amalgamations

901J   Powers of court to facilitate reconstruction or amalgamation

(1)   This section applies where application is made to the court under section 901F to sanction a compromise or arrangement and it is shown that—

(a)   the compromise or arrangement is proposed in connection with a scheme for the reconstruction of any company or companies, or the amalgamation of any two or more companies, and

(b)   under the scheme the whole or any part of the undertaking or the property of any company concerned in the scheme (a "transferor company") is to be transferred to another company ("the transferee company").

(2)   The court may, either by the order sanctioning the compromise or arrangement or by a subsequent order, make provision for all or any of the following matters—

(a)   the transfer to the transferee company of the whole or any part of the undertaking and of the property or liabilities of any transferor company;

(b)   the allotting or appropriation by the transferee company of any shares, debentures, policies or other like interests in that company which under the compromise or arrangement are to be allotted or appropriated by that company to or for any person;

(c)   the continuation by or against the transferee company of any legal proceedings pending by or against any transferor company;

(d)   the dissolution, without winding up, of any transferor company;

(e)   the provision to be made for any persons who, within such time and in such manner as the court directs, dissent from the compromise or arrangement;

(f)   such incidental, consequential and supplemental matters as are necessary to secure that the reconstruction or amalgamation is fully and effectively carried out.

(3)   If an order under this section provides for the transfer of property or liabilities—

(a)   the property is by virtue of the order transferred to, and vests in, the transferee company, and

(b)   the liabilities are, by virtue of the order, transferred to and become liabilities of that company.

(4)   The property (if the order so directs) vests freed from any charge that is by virtue of the compromise or arrangement to cease to have effect.

(5)   In this section—

"property" includes property, rights and powers of every description; and
"liabilities" includes duties.

(6)   Every company in relation to which an order is made under this section must cause a copy of the order to be delivered to the registrar within seven days after its making.

(7)   If default is made in complying with subsection (6) an offence is committed by—

(a)   the company, and

(b)   every officer of the company who is in default.

(8)   A person guilty of an offence under subsection (7) is liable on summary conviction to a fine not exceeding level 3 on the standard scale and, for continued contravention, a daily default fine not exceeding one-tenth of level 3 on the standard scale.

Obligations of company with respect to articles etc

901K   Obligations of company with respect to articles etc

(1)   This section applies—

(a)   to any order under section 901F (order sanctioning compromise or arrangement), and

(b)   to any order under section 901J (order facilitating reconstruction or amalgamation) that alters the company's constitution.

(2)   If—

(a)   the order amends—

(i)   the company's articles, or

(ii)   any resolution or agreement to which Chapter 3 of Part 3 applies (resolution or agreement affecting a company's constitution), and

(b)   a copy of the order is required to be delivered to the registrar by the company under section 901F(6)(b) or section 901J(6),

the copy of the order delivered to the registrar must be accompanied by a copy of the company's articles, or the resolution or agreement in question, as amended.

(3)   Every copy of the company's articles issued by the company after the order is made must be accompanied by a copy of the order, unless the effect of the order has been incorporated into the articles by amendment.

(4)   In this section—

(a)   references to the effect of the order include the effect of the compromise or arrangement to which the order relates, and

(b)   in the case of a company not having articles, references to its articles are to be read as references to the instrument constituting the company or defining its constitution.

(5)   If a company makes default in complying with this section an offence is committed by—

(a)   the company, and

(b)   every officer of the company who is in default.

(6)   A person guilty of an offence under this section is liable on summary conviction to a fine not exceeding level 3 on the standard scale.

Power to amend Act

901L   Power to amend Act

(1)   The Secretary of State may by regulations make any amendment of this Act which the Secretary of State considers necessary or expedient for the purposes of, in consequence of, or for giving full effect to this Part.

(2)   Regulations under this section are subject to affirmative resolution procedure.

PART 27
MERGERS AND DIVISIONS OF PUBLIC COMPANIES

CHAPTER 1
INTRODUCTORY

902   Application of this Part

(1)   This Part applies where—

(a)   a compromise or arrangement is proposed between a public company and—

(i)   its creditors or any class of them, or

(ii)   its members or any class of them,

for the purposes of, or in connection with, a scheme for the reconstruction of any company or companies or the amalgamation of any two or more companies,

(b)   the scheme involves—

(i)   a merger (as defined in section 904), or

(ii)   a division (as defined in section 919), and

(c)   the consideration for the transfer (or each of the transfers) envisaged is to be shares in the transferee company (or one or more of the transferee companies) receivable by members of the transferor company (or transferor companies), with or without any cash payment to members.

(2)   In this Part—

(a)   a "new company" means a company formed for the purposes of, or in connection with, the scheme, and

(b)   an "existing company" means a company other than one formed for the purposes of, or in connection with, the scheme.

(3)   This Part does not apply where the company in respect of which the compromise or arrangement is proposed is being wound up.

903   Relationship of this Part to Parts 26 and 26A

(1)   The court must not sanction the compromise or arrangement under Part 26 (arrangements and reconstructions: general) or Part 26A (arrangements and reconstructions: companies in financial difficulty) unless the relevant requirements of this Part have been complied with.

(2) The requirements applicable to a merger are specified in sections 905 to 914. Certain of those requirements, and certain general requirements of Parts 26 and 26A, are modified or excluded by the provisions of sections 915 to 918A.

(3) The requirements applicable to a division are specified in sections 920 to 930. Certain of those requirements, and certain general requirements of Parts 26 and 26A, are modified or excluded by the provisions of sections 931 to 934.

CHAPTER 2

MERGER

Introductory

904 Mergers and merging companies

(1) The scheme involves a merger where under the scheme—

    (a) the undertaking, property and liabilities of one or more public companies, including the company in respect of which the compromise or arrangement is proposed, are to be transferred to another existing public company (a "merger by absorption"), or

    (b) the undertaking, property and liabilities of two or more public companies, including the company in respect of which the compromise or arrangement is proposed, are to be transferred to a new company, whether or not a public company, (a "merger by formation of a new company").

(2) References in this Part to "the merging companies" are—

    (a) in relation to a merger by absorption, to the transferor and transferee companies;

    (b) in relation to a merger by formation of a new company, to the transferor companies.

Requirements applicable to merger

905 Draft terms of scheme (merger)

(1) A draft of the proposed terms of the scheme must be drawn up and adopted by the directors of the merging companies.

(2) The draft terms must give particulars of at least the following matters—

    (a) in respect of each transferor company and the transferee company—

        (i) its name,

        (ii) the address of its registered office, and

        (iii) whether it is a company limited by shares or a company limited by guarantee and having a share capital;

    (b) the number of shares in the transferee company to be allotted to members of a transferor company for a given number of their shares (the "share exchange ratio") and the amount of any cash payment;

    (c) the terms relating to the allotment of shares in the transferee company;

    (d) the date from which the holding of shares in the transferee company will entitle the holders to participate in profits, and any special conditions affecting that entitlement;

    (e) the date from which the transactions of a transferor company are to be treated for accounting purposes as being those of the transferee company;

    (f) any rights or restrictions attaching to shares or other securities in the transferee company to be allotted under the scheme to the holders of shares or other securities in a transferor company to which any special rights or restrictions attach, or the measures proposed concerning them;

    (g) any amount of benefit paid or given or intended to be paid or given—

        (i) to any of the experts referred to in section 909 (expert's report), or

        (ii) to any director of a merging company,

    and the consideration for the payment of benefit.

(3) The requirements in subsection (2)(b), (c) and (d) are subject to section 915 (circumstances in which certain particulars not required).

906   Publication of draft terms by registrar (merger)

(1)   The directors of each of the merging companies must deliver a copy of the draft terms to the registrar.

(2)   The registrar must publish in the Gazette notice of receipt by him from that company of a copy of the draft terms.

(3)   That notice must be published at least one month before the date of any meeting of that company summoned for the purpose of approving the scheme.

(4)   The requirements in this section are subject to section 906A (publication of draft terms on company website).

906A   Publication of draft terms on company website (merger)

(1)   Section 906 does not apply in respect of a company if the conditions in subsections (2) to (6) are met.

(2)   The first condition is that the draft terms are made available on a website which—

        (a)   is maintained by or on behalf of the company, and

        (b)   identifies the company.

(3)   The second condition is that neither access to the draft terms on the website nor the supply of a hard copy of them from the website is conditional on payment of a fee or otherwise restricted.

(4)   The third condition is that the directors of the company deliver to the registrar a notice giving details of the website.

(5)   The fourth condition is that the registrar publishes the notice in the Gazette at least one month before the date of any meeting of the company summoned for the purpose of approving the scheme.

(6)   The fifth condition is that the draft terms remain available on the website throughout the period beginning one month before, and ending on, the date of any such meeting.

907   Approval of members of merging companies

(1)   The scheme must be approved by a majority in number, representing 75% in value, of each class of members of each of the merging companies, present and voting either in person or by proxy at a meeting.

(2)   This requirement is subject to sections 916, 917, 917A and 918 (circumstances in which meetings of members not required).

908   Directors' explanatory report (merger)

(1)   The directors of each of the merging companies must draw up and adopt a report.

(2)   The report must consist of—

        (a)   the required statement explaining the effect of the compromise or arrangement, and

        (b)   insofar as that statement does not deal with the following matters, a further statement—

                (i)   setting out the legal and economic grounds for the draft terms, and in particular for the share exchange ratio, and

                (ii)   specifying any special valuation difficulties.

(2A)   In subsection (2) "the required statement explaining the effect of the compromise or arrangement" means—

        (a)   in a case where a meeting is summoned under section 896 in relation to the compromise or arrangement, the statement required by section 897;

        (b)   in a case where a meeting is summoned under section 901C in relation to the compromise or arrangement, the statement required by section 901D.

(3)   The requirement in this section is subject to section 915 (circumstances in which reports not required), section 915A (other circumstances in which reports and inspection not required) and section 918A (agreement to dispense with reports etc).

909   Expert's report (merger)

(1)   An expert's report must be drawn up on behalf of each of the merging companies.

(2)   The report required is a written report on the draft terms to the members of the company.

(3)   The court may on the joint application of all the merging companies approve the appointment of a joint expert to draw up a single report on behalf of all those companies.

If no such appointment is made, there must be a separate expert's report to the members of each merging company drawn up by a separate expert appointed on behalf of that company.

(4)   The expert must be a person who—

(a)   is eligible for appointment as a statutory auditor (see section 1212), and

(b)   meets the independence requirement in section 936.

(5)   The expert's report must—

(a)   indicate the method or methods used to arrive at the share exchange ratio;

(b)   give an opinion as to whether the method or methods used are reasonable in all the circumstances of the case, indicate the values arrived at using each such method and (if there is more than one method) give an opinion on the relative importance attributed to such methods in arriving at the value decided on;

(c)   describe any special valuation difficulties that have arisen;

(d)   state whether in the expert's opinion the share exchange ratio is reasonable; and

(e)   in the case of a valuation made by a person other than himself (see section 935), state that it appeared to him reasonable to arrange for it to be so made or to accept a valuation so made.

(6)   The expert (or each of them) has—

(a)   the right of access to all such documents of all the merging companies, and

(b)   the right to require from the companies' officers all such information, as he thinks necessary for the purposes of making his report.

(7)   The requirement in this section is subject to section 915 (circumstances in which reports not required), section 915A (other circumstances in which reports and inspection not required) and section 918A (agreement to dispense with expert's report).

910   Supplementary accounting statement (merger)

(1)   This section applies if the last annual accounts of any of the merging companies relate to a financial year ending before—

(a)   the date seven months before the first meeting of the company summoned for the purposes of approving the scheme, or

(b)   if no meeting of the company is required (by virtue of any of sections 916 to 918), the date six months before the directors of the company adopt the draft terms of the scheme.

(1A)   If the company has not made public a half-yearly financial report relating to a period ending on or after the date mentioned in subsection (1), the directors of the company must prepare a supplementary accounting statement.

(2)   That statement must consist of—

(a)   a balance sheet dealing with the state of affairs of the company as at a date not more than three months before the draft terms were adopted by the directors, and

(b)   where the company would be required under section 399 to prepare group accounts if that date were the last day of a financial year, a consolidated balance sheet dealing with the state of affairs of the company and the undertakings that would be included in such a consolidation.

(3)   The requirements of this Act ... as to the balance sheet forming part of a company's annual accounts, and the matters to be included in notes to it, apply to the balance sheet required for an accounting statement under this section, with such modifications as are necessary by reason of its being prepared otherwise than as at the last day of a financial year.

(4)   The provisions of section 414 as to the approval and signing of accounts apply to the balance sheet required for an accounting statement under this section.

(5)   In this section "half-yearly financial report" means a report of that description required to be made public by rules under section 89A of the Financial Services and Markets Act 2000 (transparency rules).

(6)   The requirement in this section is subject to section 915A (other circumstances in which reports and inspection not required) and section 918A (agreement to dispense with reports etc).

911   Inspection of documents (merger)

(1)   The members of each of the merging companies must be able, during the period specified below—

     (a)   to inspect at the registered office of that company copies of the documents listed below relating to that company and every other merging company, and

     (b)   to obtain copies of those documents or any part of them on request free of charge.

(2)   The period referred to above is the period—

     (a)   beginning one month before, and

     (b)   ending on the date of,

   the first meeting of the members, or any class of members, of the company for the purposes of approving the scheme.

(3)   The documents referred to above are—

     (a)   the draft terms;

     (b)   the directors' explanatory report;

     (c)   the expert's report;

     (d)   the company's annual accounts and reports for the last three financial years ending on or before the first meeting of the members, or any class of members, of the company summoned for the purposes of approving the scheme; ...

     (e)   any supplementary accounting statement required by section 910; and

     (f)   if no statement is required by section 910 because the company has made public a recent half-yearly financial report (see subsection (1A) of that section), that report.

(3A)   The requirement in subsection (1)(a) is subject to section 911A(1) (publication of documents on company website).

(4)   The requirements of subsection (3)(b) and (c) are subject to section 915 (circumstances in which reports not required) and section 918A (agreement to dispense with reports etc).

(5)   Section 1145 (right to hard copy) does not apply to a document sent or supplied in accordance with subsection (1)(b) to a member who has consented to information being sent or supplied by the company by electronic means and has not revoked that consent.

(6)   Part 4 of Schedule 5 (communications by means of a website) does not apply for the purposes of subsection (1)(b) (but see section 911A(5)).

(7)   The requirements in this section are subject to section 915A (other circumstances in which reports and inspection not required).

911A   Publication of documents on company website (merger)

(1)   Section 911(1)(a) does not apply to a document if the conditions in subsections (2) to (4) are met in relation to that document.

   This is subject to subsection (6).

(2)   The first condition is that the document is made available on a website which—

     (a)   is maintained by or on behalf of the company, and

     (b)   identifies the company.

(3)   The second condition is that access to the document on the website is not conditional on payment of a fee or otherwise restricted.

(4)   The third condition is that the document remains available on the website throughout the period beginning one month before, and ending on, the date of any meeting of the company summoned for the purpose of approving the scheme.

(5)   A person is able to obtain a copy of a document as required by section 911(1)(b) if—

     (a)   the conditions in subsections (2) and (3) are met in relation to that document, and

     (b)   the person is able, throughout the period specified in subsection (4)—

          (i)   to retain a copy of the document as made available on the website, and

          (ii)   to produce a hard copy of it.

(6)   Where members of a company are able to obtain copies of a document only as mentioned in subsection (5), section 911(1)(a) applies to that document even if the conditions in subsections (2) to (4) are met.

911B Report on material changes of assets of merging companies

(1)   The directors of each of the merging companies must report—

(a)   to every meeting of the members, or any class of members, of that company summoned for the purpose of agreeing to the scheme, and

(b)   to the directors of every other merging company,

any material changes in the property and liabilities of that company between the date when the draft terms were adopted and the date of the meeting in question.

(2)   The directors of each of the other merging companies must in turn—

(a)   report those matters to every meeting of the members, or any class of members, of that company summoned for the purpose of agreeing to the scheme, or

(b)   send a report of those matters to every member entitled to receive notice of such a meeting.

(3)   The requirement in this section is subject to section 915A (other circumstances in which reports and inspection not required) and section 918A (agreement to dispense with reports etc).

912 Approval of articles of new transferee company (merger)

(1)   In the case of a merger by formation of a new company, the articles of the transferee company, or a draft of them, must be approved by ordinary resolution of ... each of the transferor companies. This is subject to subsection (2).

(2)   In the case of a compromise or arrangement to be sanctioned under Part 26A, it is not necessary for the articles of the transferee company (or a draft of them) to be approved by ordinary resolution of the company in respect of which the compromise or arrangement is proposed.

913 Protection of holders of securities to which special rights attached (merger)

(1)   The scheme must provide that where any securities of a transferor company (other than shares) to which special rights are attached are held by a person otherwise than as a member or creditor of the company, that person is to receive rights in the transferee company of equivalent value.

(2)   Subsection (1) does not apply if—

(a)   the holder has agreed otherwise, or

(b)   the holder is, or under the scheme is to be, entitled to have the securities purchased by the transferee company on terms that the court considers reasonable.

914 No allotment of shares to transferor company or transferee company (merger)

The scheme must not provide for any shares in the transferee company to be allotted to—

(a)   a transferor company (or its nominee) in respect of shares in the transferor company held by the transferor company itself (or its nominee); or

(b)   the transferee company (or its nominee) in respect of shares in a transferor company held by the transferee company (or its nominee).

Exceptions where shares of transferor company held by transferee company

915 Circumstances in which certain particulars and reports not required (merger)

(1)   This section applies in the case of a merger by absorption where all of the relevant securities of the transferor company (or, if there is more than one transferor company, of each of them) are held by or on behalf of the transferee company.

(2)   The draft terms of the scheme need not give the particulars mentioned in section 905(2)(b), (c) or (d) (particulars relating to allotment of shares to members of transferor company).

(3)   In a case where a meeting has been summoned under section 896 in relation to the compromise or arrangement, section 897 (explanatory statement to be circulated or made available) does not apply.

(3A)   In a case where a meeting has been summoned under section 901C in relation to the compromise or arrangement, section 901D (explanatory statement to be circulated or made available) does not apply.

(4)   The requirements of the following sections do not apply—

section 908 (directors' explanatory report),

section 909 (expert's report).

(5)   The requirements of section 911 (inspection of documents) so far as relating to any document required to be drawn up under the provisions mentioned in subsection (4) above do not apply.

(6)   In this section "relevant securities", in relation to a company, means shares or other securities carrying the right to vote at general meetings of the company.

915A   Other circumstances in which reports and inspection not required (merger)

(1)   This section applies in the case of a merger by absorption where 90% or more (but not all) of the relevant securities of the transferor company (or, if there is more than one transferor company, of each of them) are held by or on behalf of the transferee company.

(2)   If the conditions in subsections (3) and (4) are met, the requirements of the following sections do not apply—

    (a)   section 908 (directors' explanatory report),

    (b)   section 909 (expert's report),

    (c)   section 910 (supplementary accounting statement),

    (d)   section 911 (inspection of documents), and

    (e)   section 911B (report on material changes of assets of merging company).

(3)   The first condition is that the scheme provides that every other holder of relevant securities has the right to require the transferee company to acquire those securities.

(4)   The second condition is that, if a holder of securities exercises that right, the consideration to be given for those securities is fair and reasonable.

(5)   The powers of the court under section 900(2) or, as the case may be, section 901J(2) (power to facilitate reconstruction or amalgamation) include the power to determine, or make provision for the determination of, the consideration to be given for securities acquired under this section.

(6)   In this section—

"other holder" means a person who holds securities of the transferor company otherwise than on behalf of the transferee company (and does not include the transferee company itself);

"relevant securities", in relation to a company, means shares or other securities carrying the right to vote at general meetings of the company.

916   Circumstances in which meeting of members of transferee company not required (merger)

(1)   This section applies in the case of a merger by absorption where 90% or more (but not all) of the relevant securities of the transferor company (or, if there is more than one transferor company, of each of them) are held by or on behalf of the transferee company.

(2)   It is not necessary for the scheme to be approved at a meeting of the members, or any class of members, of the transferee company if the court is satisfied that the following conditions have been complied with.

(3)   The first condition is that either subsection (3A) or subsection (3B) is satisfied.

(3A)   This subsection is satisfied if publication of notice of receipt of the draft terms by the registrar took place in respect of the transferee company at least one month before the date of the first meeting of members, or any class of members, of the transferor company summoned for the purpose of agreeing to the scheme.

(3B)   This subsection is satisfied if—

    (a)   the conditions in section 906A(2) to (4) are met in respect of the transferee company,

    (b)   the registrar published the notice mentioned in subsection (4) of that section in the Gazette at least one month before the date of the first meeting of members, or any class of members, of the transferor company summoned for the purpose of agreeing to the scheme, and

    (c)   the draft terms remained available on the website throughout the period beginning one month before, and ending on, that date.

(4)   The second condition is that subsection (4A) or (4B) is satisfied for each of the documents listed in the applicable paragraphs of section 911(3)(a) to (f) relating to the transferee company and the transferor company (or, if there is more than one transferor company, each of them).

(4A)   This subsection is satisfied for a document if the members of the transferee company were able during the period beginning one month before, and ending on, the date mentioned in subsection (3A) to inspect that document at the registered office of that company.

(4B)   This subsection is satisfied for a document if—

(a)   the document is made available on a website which is maintained by or on behalf of the transferee company and identifies the company,

(b)   access to the document on the website is not conditional on the payment of a fee or otherwise restricted, and

(c)   the document remains available on the website throughout the period beginning one month before, and ending on, the date mentioned in subsection (3A).

(4C)   The third condition is that the members of the transferee company were able to obtain copies of the documents mentioned in subsection (4), or any part of those documents, on request and free of charge, throughout the period beginning one month before, and ending on, the date mentioned in subsection (3A).

(4D)   For the purposes of subsection (4C)—

(a)   section 911A(5) applies as it applies for the purposes of section 911(1)(b), and

(b)   Part 4 of Schedule 5 (communications by means of a website) does not apply.

(5)   The fourth condition is that—

(a)   one or more members of the transferee company, who together held not less than 5% of the paid-up capital of the company which carried the right to vote at general meetings of the company (excluding any shares in the company held as treasury shares) would have been able, during that period, to require a meeting of each class of members to be called for the purpose of deciding whether or not to agree to the scheme, and

(b)   no such requirement was made.

(6)   In this section "relevant securities", in relation to a company, means shares or other securities carrying the right to vote at general meetings of the company.

917   Circumstances in which no meetings required (merger)

(1)   This section applies in the case of a merger by absorption where all of the relevant securities of the transferor company (or, if there is more than one transferor company, of each of them) are held by or on behalf of the transferee company.

(2)   It is not necessary for the scheme to be approved at a meeting of the members, or any class of members, of any of the merging companies if the court is satisfied that the following conditions have been complied with.

(3)   The first condition is that either subsection (3A) or subsection (3B) is satisfied.

(3A)   This subsection is satisfied if publication of notice of receipt of the draft terms by the registrar took place in respect of all the merging companies at least one month before the date of the court's order.

(3B)   This subsection is satisfied if—

(a)   the conditions in section 906A(2) to (4) are met in respect of each of the merging companies,

(b)   in each case, the registrar published the notice mentioned in subsection (4) of that section in the Gazette at least one month before the date of the court's order, and

(c)   the draft terms remained available on the website throughout the period beginning one month before, and ending on, that date.

(4)   The second condition is that subsection (4A) or (4B) is satisfied for each of the documents listed in the applicable paragraphs of section 911(3)(a) to (f) relating to the transferee company and the transferor company (or, if there is more than one transferor company, each of them).

(4A)   This subsection is satisfied for a document if the members of the transferee company were able during the period beginning one month before, and ending on, the date mentioned in subsection (3A) to inspect that document at the registered office of that company.

(4B)   This subsection is satisfied for a document if—

(a)   the document is made available on a website which is maintained by or on behalf of the transferee company and identifies the company,

(b)   access to the document on the website is not conditional on the payment of a fee or otherwise restricted, and

(c)   the document remains available on the website throughout the period beginning one month before, and ending on, the date mentioned in subsection (3A).

(4C)   The third condition is that the members of the transferee company were able to obtain copies of the documents mentioned in subsection (4), or any part of those documents, on request and free of charge, throughout the period beginning one month before, and ending on, the date mentioned in subsection (3A).

(4D)   For the purposes of subsection (4C)—

(a)   section 911A(5) applies as it applies for the purposes of section 911(1)(b), and

(b)   Part 4 of Schedule 5 (communications by means of a website) does not apply.

(5)   The fourth condition is that—

(a)   one or more members of the transferee company, who together held not less than 5% of the paid-up capital of the company which carried the right to vote at general meetings of the company (excluding any shares in the company held as treasury shares) would have been able, during that period, to require a meeting of each class of members to be called for the purpose of deciding whether or not to agree to the scheme, and

(b)   no such requirement was made.

(6)   In this section "relevant securities", in relation to a company, means shares or other securities carrying the right to vote at general meetings of the company.

Other exceptions

917A   **Other circumstances in which meeting of members of transferor company not required (merger)**

In the case of a compromise or arrangement to be sanctioned under Part 26A, it is not necessary for the scheme to be approved by the members of the company in respect of which the compromise or arrangement is proposed.

918   **Other circumstances in which meeting of members of transferee company not required (merger)**

(1)   In the case of any merger by absorption, it is not necessary for the scheme to be approved by the members of the transferee company if the court is satisfied that the following conditions have been complied with.

(2)   The first condition is that either subsection (2A) or subsection (2B) is satisfied.

(2A)   This subsection is satisfied if publication of notice of receipt of the draft terms by the registrar took place in respect of the transferee company at least one month before the date of the first meeting of members, or any class of members, of the transferor company (or, if there is more than one transferor company, any of them) summoned for the purposes of agreeing to the scheme.

(2B)   This subsection is satisfied if—

(a)   the conditions in section 906A(2) to (4) are met in respect of the transferee company,

(b)   the registrar published the notice mentioned in subsection (4) of that section in the Gazette at least one month before the date of the first meeting of members, or any class of members, of the transferor company (or, if there is more than one transferor company, any of them) summoned for the purposes of agreeing to the scheme, and

(c)   the draft terms remained available on the website throughout the period beginning one month before, and ending on, that date.

(3)   The second condition is that subsection (3A) or (3B) is satisfied for each of the documents listed in the applicable paragraphs of section 911(3) relating to the transferee company and the transferor company (or, if there is more than one transferor company, each of them).

(3A)   This subsection is satisfied for a document if the members of the transferee company were able during the period beginning one month before, and ending on, the date of any such meeting as is mentioned in subsection (2A) to inspect that document at the registered office of that company.

(3B)   This subsection is satisfied for a document if—

(a)   the document is made available on a website which is maintained by or on behalf of the transferee company and identifies the company,

(b)   access to the document on the website is not conditional on the payment of a fee or otherwise restricted, and

(c)   the document remains available on the website throughout the period beginning one month before, and ending on, the date of any such meeting as is mentioned in subsection (2A).

(3C)   The third condition is that the members of the transferee company were able to obtain copies of the documents mentioned in subsection (3), or any part of those documents, on request and free of charge, throughout the period beginning one month before, and ending on, the date of any such meeting as is mentioned in subsection (2A).

(3D)   For the purposes of subsection (3C)—

(a)   section 911A(5) applies as it applies for the purposes of section 911(1)(b), and

(b)   Part 4 of Schedule 5 (communications by means of a website) does not apply.

(4)   The fourth condition is that—

(a)   one or more members of that company, who together held not less than 5 % of the paid-up capital of the company which carried the right to vote at general meetings of the company (excluding any shares in the company held as treasury shares) would have been able, during that period, to require a meeting of each class of members to be called for the purpose of deciding whether or not to agree to the scheme, and

(b)   no such requirement was made.

918A   Agreement to dispense with reports etc

(1)   If all members holding shares in, and all persons holding other securities of, the merging companies, being shares or securities that carry a right to vote in general meetings of the company in question, so agree, the following requirements do not apply.

(1A)   The requirements that may be dispensed with under this section are—

(a)   the requirements of—

(i)   section 908 (directors' explanatory report),

(ii)   section 909 (expert's report),

(iii)   section 910 (supplementary accounting statement), and

(iv)   section 911B (report on material changes of assets of merging company); and

(b)   the requirements of section 911 (inspection of documents) so far as relating to any document required to be drawn up under sections 908, 909 or 910.

(2)   For the purposes of this section—

(a)   the members, or holders of other securities, of a company, and

(b)   whether shares or other securities carry a right to vote in general meetings of the company, are determined as at the date of the relevant application.

(3)   In subsection (2) "the relevant application" means—

(a)   in the case of a compromise or arrangement to be sanctioned under Part 26, the application to the court under section 896;

(b)   in the case of a compromise or arrangement to be sanctioned under Part 26A, the application to the court under section 901C(1).

CHAPTER 3
DIVISION

Introductory

919   **Divisions and companies involved in a division**

(1)   The scheme involves a division where under the scheme the undertaking, property and liabilities of the company in respect of which the compromise or arrangement is proposed are to be divided among and transferred to two or more companies each of which is either—

(a)   an existing public company, or

(b)   a new company (whether or not a public company).

(2)   References in this Part to the companies involved in the division are to the transferor company and any existing transferee companies.

Requirements to be complied with in case of division

920   **Draft terms of scheme (division)**

(1)   A draft of the proposed terms of the scheme must be drawn up and adopted by the directors of each of the companies involved in the division.

(2)   The draft terms must give particulars of at least the following matters—

(a)   in respect of the transferor company and each transferee company—

(i)   its name,

(ii)   the address of its registered office, and

(iii)   whether it is a company limited by shares or a company limited by guarantee and having a share capital;

(b)   the number of shares in a transferee company to be allotted to members of the transferor company for a given number of their shares (the "share exchange ratio") and the amount of any cash payment;

(c)   the terms relating to the allotment of shares in a transferee company;

(d)   the date from which the holding of shares in a transferee company will entitle the holders to participate in profits, and any special conditions affecting that entitlement;

(e)   the date from which the transactions of the transferor company are to be treated for accounting purposes as being those of a transferee company;

(f)   any rights or restrictions attaching to shares or other securities in a transferee company to be allotted under the scheme to the holders of shares or other securities in the transferor company to which any special rights or restrictions attach, or the measures proposed concerning them;

(g)   any amount of benefit paid or given or intended to be paid or given—

(i)   to any of the experts referred to in section 924 (expert's report), or

(ii)   to any director of a company involved in the division,

and the consideration for the payment of benefit.

(3)   The draft terms must also—

(a)   give particulars of the property and liabilities to be transferred (to the extent that these are known to the transferor company) and their allocation among the transferee companies;

(b)   make provision for the allocation among and transfer to the transferee companies of any other property and liabilities that the transferor company has acquired or may subsequently acquire; and

(c)   specify the allocation to members of the transferor company of shares in the transferee companies and the criteria upon which that allocation is based.

921   **Publication of draft terms by registrar (division)**

(1)   The directors of each company involved in the division must deliver a copy of the draft terms to the registrar.

(2)   The registrar must publish in the Gazette notice of receipt by him from that company of a copy of the draft terms.

(3)   That notice must be published at least one month before the date of any meeting of that company summoned for the purposes of approving the scheme.

(4)   The requirements in this section are subject to section 921A (publication of draft terms on company website) and section 934 (power of court to exclude certain requirements).

921A   Publication of draft terms on company website (division)

(1)   Section 921 does not apply in respect of a company if the conditions in subsections (2) to (6) are met.

(2)   The first condition is that the draft terms are made available on a website which—
        (a)   is maintained by or on behalf of the company, and
        (b)   identifies the company.

(3)   The second condition is that neither access to the draft terms on the website nor the supply of a hard copy of them from the website is conditional on payment of a fee or otherwise restricted.

(4)   The third condition is that the directors of the company deliver to the registrar a notice giving details of the website.

(5)   The fourth condition is that the registrar publishes the notice in the Gazette at least one month before the date of any meeting of the company summoned for the purpose of approving the scheme.

(6)   The fifth condition is that the draft terms remain available on the website throughout the period beginning one month before, and ending on, the date of any such meeting.

922   Approval of members of companies involved in the division

(1)   The scheme must be approved by a majority in number, representing 75% in value, of each class of members of each of the companies involved in the division, present and voting either in person or by proxy at a meeting.

(2)   This requirement is subject to sections 931, 931A and 932 (circumstances in which meeting of members not required).

923   Directors' explanatory report (division)

(1)   The directors of the transferor and each existing transferee company must draw up and adopt a report.

(2)   The report must consist of—
        (a)   the required statement explaining the effect of the compromise or arrangement, and
        (b)   insofar as that statement does not deal with the following matters, a further statement—
               (i)   setting out the legal and economic grounds for the draft terms, and in particular for the share exchange ratio and for the criteria on which the allocation to the members of the transferor company of shares in the transferee companies was based, and
               (ii)   specifying any special valuation difficulties.

(2A)   In subsection (2) "the required statement explaining the effect of the compromise or arrangement" means—
        (a)   in a case where a meeting is summoned under section 896 in relation to the compromise or arrangement, the statement required by section 897;
        (b)   in a case where a meeting is summoned under section 901C in relation to the compromise or arrangement, the statement required by section 901D.

(3)   The report must also state—
        (a)   whether a report has been made to any transferee company under section 593 (valuation of non-cash consideration for shares), and
        (b)   if so, whether that report has been delivered to the registrar of companies.

(4)   The requirement in this section is subject to section 933 (agreement to dispense with reports etc) and section 933A (certain requirements excluded where shareholders given proportional rights).

924   Expert's report (division)

(1)   An expert's report must be drawn up on behalf of each company involved in the division.

(2)   The report required is a written report on the draft terms to the members of the company.

(3)   The court may on the joint application of the companies involved in the division approve the appointment of a joint expert to draw up a single report on behalf of all those companies.

If no such appointment is made, there must be a separate expert's report to the members of each company involved in the division drawn up by a separate expert appointed on behalf of that company.

(4)   The expert must be a person who—

    (a)   is eligible for appointment as a statutory auditor (see section 1212), and

    (b)   meets the independence requirement in section 936.

(5)   The expert's report must—

    (a)   indicate the method or methods used to arrive at the share exchange ratio;

    (b)   give an opinion as to whether the method or methods used are reasonable in all the circumstances of the case, indicate the values arrived at using each such method and (if there is more than one method) give an opinion on the relative importance attributed to such methods in arriving at the value decided on;

    (c)   describe any special valuation difficulties that have arisen;

    (d)   state whether in the expert's opinion the share exchange ratio is reasonable; and

    (e)   in the case of a valuation made by a person other than himself (see section 935), state that it appeared to him reasonable to arrange for it to be so made or to accept a valuation so made.

(6)   The expert (or each of them) has—

    (a)   the right of access to all such documents of the companies involved in the division, and

    (b)   the right to require from the companies' officers all such information, as he thinks necessary for the purposes of making his report.

(7)   The requirement in this section is subject to section 933 (agreement to dispense with reports etc) and section 933A (certain requirements excluded where shareholders given proportional rights).

925   Supplementary accounting statement (division)

(1)   This section applies if the last annual accounts of a company involved in the division relate to a financial year ending before—

    (a)   the date seven months before the first meeting of the company summoned for the purposes of approving the scheme, or

    (b)   if no meeting of the company is required (by virtue of section 931, 931A or 932), the date six months before the directors of the company adopt the draft terms of the scheme.

(1A)   If the company has not made public a half-yearly financial report relating to a period ending on or after the date mentioned in subsection (1), the directors of the company must prepare a supplementary accounting statement.

(2)   That statement must consist of—

    (a)   a balance sheet dealing with the state of affairs of the company as at a date not more than three months before the draft terms were adopted by the directors, and

    (b)   where the company would be required under section 399 to prepare group accounts if that date were the last day of a financial year, a consolidated balance sheet dealing with the state of affairs of the company and the undertakings that would be included in such a consolidation.

(3)   The requirements of this Act ... as to the balance sheet forming part of a company's annual accounts, and the matters to be included in notes to it, apply to the balance sheet required for an accounting statement under this section, with such modifications as are necessary by reason of its being prepared otherwise than as at the last day of a financial year.

(4)   The provisions of section 414 as to the approval and signing of accounts apply to the balance sheet required for an accounting statement under this section.

(4A)   In this section "half-yearly financial report" means a report of that description required to be made public by rules under section 89A of the Financial Services and Markets Act 2000 (transparency rules).

(5)   The requirement in this section is subject to section 933 (agreement to dispense with reports etc) and section 933A (certain requirements excluded where shareholders given proportional rights).

926   Inspection of documents (division)

(1)   The members of each company involved in the division must be able, during the period specified below—

    (a)   to inspect at the registered office of that company copies of the documents listed below relating to that company and every other company involved in the division, and

    (b)   to obtain copies of those documents or any part of them on request free of charge.

(2)   The period referred to above is the period—

    (a)   beginning one month before, and

    (b)   ending on the date of,

the first meeting of the members, or any class of members, of the company for the purposes of approving the scheme.

(3)   The documents referred to above are—

    (a)   the draft terms;

    (b)   the directors' explanatory report;

    (c)   the expert's report;

    (d)   the company's annual accounts and reports for the last three financial years ending on or before the first meeting of the members, or any class of members, of the company summoned for the purposes of approving the scheme; …

    (e)   any supplementary accounting statement required by section 925; and

    (f)   if no statement is required by section 925 because the company has made public a recent half-yearly financial report (see subsection (1A) of that section), that report.

(3A)   The requirement in subsection (1)(a) is subject to section 926A(1) (publication of documents on company website).

(4)   The requirements in subsection (3)(b), (c) and (e) are subject to section 933 (agreement to dispense with reports etc), section 933A (certain requirements excluded where shareholders given proportional rights) and section 934 (power of court to exclude certain requirements).

(5)   Section 1145 (right to hard copy) does not apply to a document sent or supplied in accordance with subsection (1)(b) to a member who has consented to information being sent or supplied by the company by electronic means and has not revoked that consent.

(6)   Part 4 of Schedule 5 (communications by means of a website) does not apply for the purposes of subsection (1)(b) (but see section 926A(5)).

926A   Publication of documents on company website (division)

(1)   Section 926(1)(a) does not apply to a document if the conditions in subsections (2) to (4) are met in relation to that document.

This is subject to subsection (6).

(2)   The first condition is that the document is made available on a website which—

    (a)   is maintained by or on behalf of the company, and

    (b)   identifies the company.

(3)   The second condition is that access to the document on the website is not conditional on payment of a fee or otherwise restricted.

(4)   The third condition is that the document remains available on the website throughout the period beginning one month before, and ending on, the date of any meeting of the company summoned for the purpose of approving the scheme.

(5)   A person is able to obtain a copy of a document as required by section 926(1)(b) if—

    (a)   the conditions in subsections (2) and (3) are met in relation to that document, and

    (b)   the person is able, throughout the period specified in subsection (4)—

        (i)   to retain a copy of the document as made available on the website, and

        (ii)   to produce a hard copy of it.

(6)   Where members of a company are able to obtain copies of a document only as mentioned in subsection (5), section 926(1)(a) applies to that document even if the conditions in subsections (2) to (4) are met.

927   Report on material changes of assets of transferor company (division)

(1)   The directors of the transferor company must report—

      (a)   to every meeting of the members, or any class of members, of that company summoned for the purpose of agreeing to the scheme, and

      (b)   to the directors of each existing transferee company,

      any material changes in the property and liabilities of the transferor company between the date when the draft terms were adopted and the date of the meeting in question.

(2)   The directors of each existing transferee company must in turn—

      (a)   report those matters to every meeting of the members, or any class of members, of that company summoned for the purpose of agreeing to the scheme, or

      (b)   send a report of those matters to every member entitled to receive notice of such a meeting.

(3)   The requirement in this section is subject to section 933 (agreement to dispense with reports etc) and section 933A (certain requirements excluded where shareholders given proportional rights).

928   Approval of articles of new transferee company (division)

(1)   The articles of every new transferee company, or a draft of them, must be approved by ordinary resolution of the transferor company.

(2)   Subsection (1) does not apply in the case of a compromise or arrangement to be sanctioned under Part 26A.

929   Protection of holders of securities to which special rights attached (division)

(1)   The scheme must provide that where any securities of the transferor company (other than shares) to which special rights are attached are held by a person otherwise than as a member or creditor of the company, that person is to receive rights in a transferee company of equivalent value.

(2)   Subsection (1) does not apply if—

      (a)   the holder has agreed otherwise, or

      (b)   the holder is, or under the scheme is to be, entitled to have the securities purchased by a transferee company on terms that the court considers reasonable.

930   No allotment of shares to transferor company or to transferee company (division)

      The scheme must not provide for any shares in a transferee company to be allotted to—

      (a)   the transferor company (or its nominee) in respect of shares in the transferor company held by the transferor company itself (or its nominee); or

      (b)   a transferee company (or its nominee) in respect of shares in the transferor company held by the transferee company (or its nominee).

Exceptions where shares of transferor company held by transferee company

931   Circumstances in which meeting of members of transferor company not required (division)

(1)   This section applies in the case of a division where all of the shares or other securities of the transferor company carrying the right to vote at general meetings of the company are held by or on behalf of one or more existing transferee companies.

(2)   It is not necessary for the scheme to be approved by a meeting of the members, or any class of members, of the transferor company if the court is satisfied that the following conditions have been complied with.

(3)   The first condition is that either subsection (3A) or subsection (3B) is satisfied.

(3A)   This subsection is satisfied if publication of notice of receipt of the draft terms by the registrar took place in respect of all the companies involved in the division at least one month before the date of the court's order.

(3B)   This subsection is satisfied if—

(a)   the conditions in section 921A(2) to (4) are met in respect of each of the companies involved in the division,

(b)   in each case, the registrar published the notice mentioned in subsection (4) of that section in the Gazette at least one month before the date of the court's order, and

(c)   the draft terms remained available on the website throughout the period beginning one month before, and ending on, that date.

(4)   The second condition is that subsection (4A) or (4B) is satisfied for each of the documents listed in the applicable paragraphs of section 926(3) relating to every company involved in the division.

(4A) This subsection is satisfied for a document if the members of every company involved in the division were able during the period beginning one month before, and ending on, the date of the court's order to inspect that document at the registered office of their company.

(4B) This subsection is satisfied for a document if—

(a)   the document is made available on a website which is maintained by or on behalf of the company to which it relates and identifies the company,

(b)   access to the document on the website is not conditional on payment of a fee or otherwise restricted, and

(c)   the document remains available on the website throughout the period beginning one month before, and ending on, the date of the court's order.

(4C) The third condition is that the members of every company involved in the division were able to obtain copies of the documents mentioned in subsection (4), or any part of those documents, on request and free of charge, throughout the period beginning one month before, and ending on, the date of the court's order.

(4D) For the purposes of subsection (4C)—

(a)   section 926A(5) applies as it applies for the purposes of section 926(1)(b), and

(b)   Part 4 of Schedule 5 (communications by means of a website) does not apply.

(5)   ...

(6)   The fourth condition is that the directors of the transferor company have sent—

(a)   to every member who would have been entitled to receive notice of a meeting to agree to the scheme (had any such meeting been called), and

(b)   to the directors of every existing transferee company,

a report of any material change in the property and liabilities of the transferor company between the date when the terms were adopted by the directors and the date one month before the date of the court's order.

931A   Other circumstances in which meeting of members of transferor company not required (division)

In the case of a compromise or arrangement to be sanctioned under Part 26A, it is not necessary for the scheme to be approved by the members of the transferor company.

Other exceptions

932   Circumstances in which meeting of members of transferee company not required (division)

(1)   In the case of a division, it is not necessary for the scheme to be approved by the members of a transferee company if the court is satisfied that the following conditions have been complied with in relation to that company.

(2)   The first condition is that either subsection (2A) or subsection (2B) is satisfied.

(2A) This subsection is satisfied if publication of notice of receipt of the draft terms by the registrar took place in respect of the transferee company at least one month before the date of the first meeting of members of the transferor company summoned for the purposes of agreeing to the scheme.

(2B) This subsection is satisfied if—

(a)   the conditions in section 921A(2) to (4) are met in respect of the transferee company,

     (b)   the registrar published the notice mentioned in subsection (4) of that section in the Gazette at least one month before the date of the first meeting of members of the transferor company summoned for the purposes of agreeing to the scheme, and

     (c)   the draft terms remained available on the website throughout the period beginning one month before, and ending on, that date.

(3)   The second condition is that subsection (3A) or (3B) is satisfied for each of the documents listed in the applicable paragraphs of section 926(3) relating to the transferee company and every other company involved in the division.

(3A)   This subsection is satisfied for a document if the members of the transferee company were able during the period beginning one month before, and ending on, the date mentioned in subsection (2A) to inspect that document at the registered office of that company.

(3B)   This subsection is satisfied for a document if—

     (a)   the document is made available on a website which is maintained by or on behalf of the transferee company and identifies the company,

     (b)   access to the document on the website is not conditional on payment of a fee or otherwise restricted, and

     (c)   the document remains available on the website throughout the period beginning one month before, and ending on, the date mentioned in subsection (2A).

(3C)   The third condition is that the members of the transferee company were able to obtain copies of the documents mentioned in subsection (3), or any part of those documents, on request and free of charge, throughout the period beginning one month before, and ending on, the date mentioned in subsection (2A).

(3D)   For the purposes of subsection (3C)—

     (a)   section 926A(5) applies as it applies for the purposes of section 926(1)(b), and

     (b)   Part 4 of Schedule 5 (communications by means of a website) does not apply.

(4)   The fourth condition is that—

     (a)   one or more members of that company, who together held not less than 5 % of the paid-up capital of the company which carried the right to vote at general meetings of the company (excluding any shares in the company held as treasury shares) would have been able, during that period, to require a meeting of each class of members to be called for the purpose of deciding whether or not to agree to the scheme, and

     (b)   no such requirement was made.

(5)   The first, second and third conditions above are subject to section 934 (power of court to exclude certain requirements).

933   Agreement to dispense with reports etc (division)

(1)   If all members holding shares in, and all persons holding other securities of, the companies involved in the division, being shares or securities that carry a right to vote in general meetings of the company in question, so agree, the following requirements do not apply.

(2)   The requirements that may be dispensed with under this section are—

     (a)   the requirements of—

         (i)   section 923 (directors' explanatory report),

         (ii)   section 924 (expert's report),

         (iii)   section 925 (supplementary accounting statement), and

         (iv)   section 927 (report on material changes in assets of transferor company); and

     (b)   the requirements of section 926 (inspection of documents) so far as relating to any document required to be drawn up under the provisions mentioned in paragraph (a)(i), (ii) or (iii) above.

(3)   For the purposes of this section—

     (a)   the members, or holders of other securities, of a company, and

     (b)   whether shares or other securities carry a right to vote in general meetings of the company, are determined as at the date of the relevant application.

(4)   In subsection (3) "the relevant application" means—

(a)   in the case of a compromise or arrangement to be sanctioned under Part 26, the application to the court under section 896;

(b)   in the case of a compromise or arrangement to be sanctioned under Part 26A, the application to the court under section 901C(1).

933A   Certain requirements excluded where shareholders given proportional rights (division)

(1)   This section applies in the case of a division where each of the transferee companies is a new company.

(2)   If all the shares in each of the transferee companies are to be allotted to the members of the transferor company in proportion to their rights in the allotted share capital of the transferor company, the following requirements do not apply.

(3)   The requirements which do not apply are—

    (a)   the requirements of—

        (i)   section 923 (directors' explanatory report),

        (ii)   section 924 (expert's report),

        (iii)   section 925 (supplementary accounting statement), and

        (iv)   section 927 (report on material changes in assets of transferor company); and

    (b)   the requirements of section 926 (inspection of documents) so far as relating to any document required to be drawn up under the provisions mentioned in paragraph (a)(i), (ii) or (iii) above.

934   Power of court to exclude certain requirements (division)

(1)   In the case of a division, the court may by order direct that—

    (a)   in relation to any company involved in the division, the requirements of—

        (i)   section 921 (publication of draft terms), and

        (ii)   section 926 (inspection of documents),

    do not apply, and

    (b)   in relation to an existing transferee company, section 932 (circumstances in which meeting of members of transferee company not required) has effect with the omission of the first, second and third conditions specified in that section,

if the court is satisfied that the following conditions will be fulfilled in relation to that company.

(2)   The first condition is that the members of that company will have received, or will have been able to obtain free of charge, copies of the documents listed in section 926—

    (a)   in time to examine them before the date of the first meeting of the members, or any class of members, of that company summoned for the purposes of agreeing to the scheme, or

    (b)   in the case of an existing transferee company where in the circumstances described in section 932 no meeting is held, in time to require a meeting as mentioned in subsection (4) of that section.

(3)   The second condition is that the creditors of that company will have received or will have been able to obtain free of charge copies of the draft terms in time to examine them—

    (a)   before the date of the first meeting of the members, or any class of members, of the company summoned for the purposes of agreeing to the scheme, or

    (b)   in the circumstances mentioned in subsection (2)(b) above, at the same time as the members of the company.

(4)   The third condition is that no prejudice would be caused to the members or creditors of the transferor company or any transferee company by making the order in question.

CHAPTER 4
SUPPLEMENTARY PROVISIONS

Expert's report and related matters

935   Expert's report: valuation by another person

(1)   Where it appears to an expert—

(a) that a valuation is reasonably necessary to enable him to draw up his report, and

(b) that it is reasonable for that valuation, or part of it, to be made by (or for him to accept a valuation made by) another person who—

   (i) appears to him to have the requisite knowledge and experience to make the valuation or that part of it, and

   (ii) meets the independence requirement in section 936,

he may arrange for or accept such a valuation, together with a report which will enable him to make his own report under section 909 or 924.

(2) Where any valuation is made by a person other than the expert himself, the latter's report must state that fact and must also—

(a) state the former's name and what knowledge and experience he has to carry out the valuation, and

(b) describe so much of the undertaking, property and liabilities as was valued by the other person, and the method used to value them, and specify the date of the valuation.

936 Experts and valuers: independence requirement

(1) A person meets the independence requirement for the purposes of section 909 or 924 (expert's report) or section 935 (valuation by another person) only if—

(a) he is not—

   (i) an officer or employee of any of the companies concerned in the scheme, or

   (ii) a partner or employee of such a person, or a partnership of which such a person is a partner;

(b) he is not—

   (i) an officer or employee of an associated undertaking of any of the companies concerned in the scheme, or

   (ii) a partner or employee of such a person, or a partnership of which such a person is a partner; and

(c) there does not exist between—

   (i) the person or an associate of his, and

   (ii) any of the companies concerned in the scheme or an associated undertaking of such a company,

   a connection of any such description as may be specified by regulations made by the Secretary of State.

(2) An auditor of a company is not regarded as an officer or employee of the company for this purpose.

(3) For the purposes of this section—

(a) the "companies concerned in the scheme" means every transferor and existing transferee company;

(b) "associated undertaking", in relation to a company, means—

   (i) a parent undertaking or subsidiary undertaking of the company, or

   (ii) a subsidiary undertaking of a parent undertaking of the company; and

(c) "associate" has the meaning given by section 937.

(4) Regulations under this section are subject to negative resolution procedure.

937 Experts and valuers: meaning of "associate"

(1) This section defines "associate" for the purposes of section 936 (experts and valuers: independence requirement).

(2) In relation to an individual, "associate" means—

(a) that individual's spouse or civil partner or minor child or step-child,

(b) any body corporate of which that individual is a director, and

(c) any employee or partner of that individual.

(3) In relation to a body corporate, "associate" means—

(a) any body corporate of which that body is a director,

(b)　any body corporate in the same group as that body, and

(c)　any employee or partner of that body or of any body corporate in the same group.

(4)　In relation to a partnership that is a legal person under the law by which it is governed, "associate" means—

(a)　any body corporate of which that partnership is a director,

(b)　any employee of or partner in that partnership, and

(c)　any person who is an associate of a partner in that partnership.

(5)　In relation to a partnership that is not a legal person under the law by which it is governed, "associate" means any person who is an associate of any of the partners.

(6)　In this section, in relation to a limited liability partnership, for "director" read "member".

Powers of the court

938　Power of court to summon meeting of members or creditors of existing transferee company

(1)　The court may order a meeting of—

(a)　the members of an existing transferee company, or any class of them, or

(b)　the creditors of an existing transferee company, or any class of them,

to be summoned in such manner as the court directs.

(2)　An application for such an order may be made by—

(a)　the company concerned,

(b)　a member or creditor of the company, or

(c)　if the company is being wound up, the liquidator, or

(d)　if the company is in administration, the administrator.

(3)　Section 323 (representation of corporations at meetings) applies to a meeting of creditors under this section as to a meeting of the company (references to a member being read as references to a creditor).

939　Court to fix date for transfer of undertaking etc of transferor company

(1)　Where the court sanctions the compromise or arrangement, it must—

(a)　in the order sanctioning the compromise or arrangement, or

(b)　in a subsequent order under section 900 or, as the case may be, section 901J (powers of court to facilitate reconstruction or amalgamation),

fix a date on which the transfer (or transfers) to the transferee company (or transferee companies) of the undertaking, property and liabilities of the transferor company is (or are) to take place.

(2)　Any such order that provides for the dissolution of the transferor company must fix the same date for the dissolution.

(3)　If it is necessary for the transferor company to take steps to ensure that the undertaking, property and liabilities are fully transferred, the court must fix a date, not later than six months after the date fixed under subsection (1), by which such steps must be taken.

(4)　In that case, the court may postpone the dissolution of the transferor company until that date.

(5)　The court may postpone or further postpone the date fixed under subsection (3) if it is satisfied that the steps mentioned cannot be completed by the date (or latest date) fixed under that subsection.

Liability of transferee companies

940　Liability of transferee companies for each other's defaults

(1)　In the case of a division, each transferee company is jointly and severally liable for any liability transferred to any other transferee company under the scheme to the extent that the other company has made default in satisfying that liability.

This is subject to the following provisions.

(2)　If, in the case of a compromise or arrangement to be sanctioned under Part 26, a majority in number representing 75% in value of the creditors or any class of creditors of the transferor company, present and voting either in person or by proxy at a meeting summoned for the purposes of agreeing to the scheme, so agree, subsection (1) does not apply in relation to the liabilities owed to the creditors or that class of creditors.

(2A)   If, in the case of a compromise or arrangement to be sanctioned under Part 26A, a number representing 75% in value of the creditors or any class of creditors of the transferor company, present and voting either in person or by proxy at a meeting summoned for the purposes of agreeing to the scheme, so agree, subsection (1) does not apply in relation to the liabilities owed to the creditors or that class of creditors.

(3)   A transferee company is not liable under this section for an amount greater than the net value transferred to it under the scheme.

         The "net value transferred" is the value at the time of the transfer of the property transferred to it under the scheme less the amount at that date of the liabilities so transferred.

Disruption of websites

940A   Disregard of website failures beyond control of company

(1)   A failure to make information or a document available on the website throughout a period specified in any of the provisions mentioned in subsection (2) is to be disregarded if—
         (a)   it is made available on the website for part of that period, and
         (b)   the failure to make it available throughout that period is wholly attributable to circumstances that it would not be reasonable to have expected the company to prevent or avoid.

(2)   The provisions referred to above are—
         (a)   section 906A(6),
         (b)   section 911A(4),
         (c)   section 916(3B) and (4B),
         (d)   section 917(3B) and (4B),
         (e)   section 918(2B) and (3B),
         (f)   section 921A(6),
         (g)   section 926A(4),
         (h)   section 931(3B) and (4B), and
         (i)   section 932(2B) and (3B).

Interpretation

941   Meaning of "liabilities" and "property"

         In this Part—
         "liabilities" includes duties;
         "property" includes property, rights and powers of every description.

PART 28
TAKEOVERS ETC

CHAPTER 1
THE TAKEOVER PANEL

The Panel and its rules

942   The Panel

(1)   The body known as the Panel on Takeovers and Mergers ("the Panel") is to have the functions conferred on it by or under this Chapter.

(2)   The Panel may do anything that it considers necessary or expedient for the purposes of, or in connection with, its functions.

(3)   The Panel may make arrangements for any of its functions to be discharged by—
         (a)   a committee or sub-committee of the Panel, or
         (b)   an officer or member of staff of the Panel, or a person acting as such. This is subject to section 943(4) and (5).

943   Rules

(1)   The Panel must make rules—

(a)   giving effect to the general principles in Part 1 of Schedule 1C, and

(b)   in accordance with Part 2 of that Schedule.

(1A)   Rules must specify the percentage of voting rights that gives a person control of a company for the purposes of this Chapter and how it is to be calculated.

(2)   Rules made by the Panel may also make other provision—

(a)   for or in connection with the regulation of—

(i)   takeover bids,

(ii)   merger transactions, and

(iii)   transactions (not falling within sub-paragraph (i) or (ii)) that have or may have, directly or indirectly, an effect on the ownership or control of companies;

(b)   for or in connection with the regulation of things done in consequence of, or otherwise in relation to, any such bid or transaction;

(c)   about cases where—

(i)   any such bid or transaction is, or has been, contemplated or apprehended, or

(ii)   an announcement is made denying that any such bid or transaction is intended.

(3)   The provision that may be made under subsection (2) includes, in particular, provision for a matter that is, or is similar to, a matter provided for by the Panel in the City Code on Takeovers and Mergers as it had effect immediately before the passing of this Act.

(4)   In relation to rules made by virtue of section 957 (fees and charges), functions under this section may be discharged either by the Panel itself or by a committee of the Panel (but not otherwise).

(5)   In relation to rules of any other description, the Panel must discharge its functions under this section by a committee of the Panel.

(6)   Section 1 (meaning of "company") does not apply for the purposes of this section.

(7)   In this section "takeover bid" includes a takeover bid within the meaning given by paragraph 20(1) of Schedule 1C.

(8)   …

(9)   A reference to rules in the following provisions of this Chapter is to rules under this section.

944   Further provisions about rules

(1)   Rules may—

(a)   make different provision for different purposes;

(b)   make provision subject to exceptions or exemptions;

(c)   contain incidental, supplemental, consequential or transitional provision;

(d)   authorise the Panel to dispense with or modify the application of rules in particular cases and by reference to any circumstances.

Rules made by virtue of paragraph (d) must require the Panel to give reasons for acting as mentioned in that paragraph.

(2)   Rules must be made by an instrument in writing.

(3)   Immediately after an instrument containing rules is made, the text must be made available to the public, with or without payment, in whatever way the Panel thinks appropriate.

(4)   A person is not to be taken to have contravened a rule if he shows that at the time of the alleged contravention the text of the rule had not been made available as required by subsection (3).

(5)   The production of a printed copy of an instrument purporting to be made by the Panel on which is endorsed a certificate signed by an officer of the Panel authorised by it for that purpose and stating—

(a)   that the instrument was made by the Panel,

(b)   that the copy is a true copy of the instrument, and

(c)   that on a specified date the text of the instrument was made available to the public as required by subsection (3),

is evidence (or in Scotland sufficient evidence) of the facts stated in the certificate.

(6)   A certificate purporting to be signed as mentioned in subsection (5) is to be treated as having been properly signed unless the contrary is shown.

(7)   A person who wishes in any legal proceedings to rely on an instrument by which rules are made may require the Panel to endorse a copy of the instrument with a certificate of the kind mentioned in subsection (5).

945   Rulings

(1)   The Panel may give rulings on the interpretation, application or effect of rules.

(2)   To the extent and in the circumstances specified in rules, and subject to any review or appeal, a ruling has binding effect.

946   Directions

Rules may contain provision conferring power on the Panel to give any direction that appears to the Panel to be necessary in order—

(a)   to restrain a person from acting (or continuing to act) in breach of rules;

(b)   to restrain a person from doing (or continuing to do) a particular thing, pending determination of whether that or any other conduct of his is or would be a breach of rules;

(c)   otherwise to secure compliance with rules.

Information

947   Power to require documents and information

(1)   The Panel may by notice in writing require a person—

(a)   to produce any documents that are specified or described in the notice;

(b)   to provide, in the form and manner specified in the notice, such information as may be specified or described in the notice.

(2)   A requirement under subsection (1) must be complied with—

(a)   at a place specified in the notice, and

(b)   before the end of such reasonable period as may be so specified.

(3)   This section applies only to documents and information reasonably required in connection with the exercise by the Panel of its functions.

(4)   The Panel may require—

(a)   any document produced to be authenticated, or

(b)   any information provided (whether in a document or otherwise) to be verified,

in such manner as it may reasonably require.

(5)   The Panel may authorise a person to exercise any of its powers under this section.

(6)   A person exercising a power by virtue of subsection (5) must, if required to do so, produce evidence of his authority to exercise the power.

(7)   The production of a document in pursuance of this section does not affect any lien that a person has on the document.

(8)   The Panel may take copies of or extracts from a document produced in pursuance of this section.

(9)   A reference in this section to the production of a document includes a reference to the production of—

(a)   a hard copy of information recorded otherwise than in hard copy form, or

(b)   information in a form from which a hard copy can be readily obtained.

(10)   A person is not required by this section to disclose documents or information in respect of which a claim to legal professional privilege (in Scotland, to confidentiality of communications) could be maintained in legal proceedings.

948   Restrictions on disclosure

(1)   This section applies to information (in whatever form)—

(a)   relating to the private affairs of an individual, or

(b)   relating to any particular business,

that is provided to the Panel in connection with the exercise of its functions.

(2)   No such information may, during the lifetime of the individual or so long as the business continues to be carried on, be disclosed without the consent of that individual or (as the case may be) the person for the time being carrying on that business.

(3)   Subsection (2) does not apply to any disclosure of information that—

(a)   is made for the purpose of facilitating the carrying out by the Panel of any of its functions,

(b)   is made to a person specified in Part 1 of Schedule 2,

(c)   is of a description specified in Part 2 of that Schedule, or

(d)   is made in accordance with Part 3 of that Schedule.

(4)   The Secretary of State may amend Schedule 2 by order subject to negative resolution procedure.

(5)   An order under subsection (4) must not—

(a)   amend Part 1 of Schedule 2 by specifying a person unless the person exercises functions of a public nature (whether or not he exercises any other function);

(b)   amend Part 2 of Schedule 2 by adding or modifying a description of disclosure unless the purpose for which the disclosure is permitted is likely to facilitate the exercise of a function of a public nature;

(c)   amend Part 3 of Schedule 2 so as to have the effect of permitting disclosures to be made to a body other than one that exercises functions of a public nature in a country or territory outside the United Kingdom.

(6)   Subsection (2) does not apply to—

(a)   the disclosure by an authority within subsection (7) of information disclosed to it by the Panel in reliance on subsection (3);

(b)   the disclosure of such information by anyone who has obtained it directly or indirectly from an authority within subsection (7).

(7)   The authorities within this subsection are—

(a)   the Financial Conduct Authority;

(aa) the Prudential Regulation Authority;

(ab) the Bank of England;

(b), (c)...

(8)   This section does not prohibit the disclosure of information if the information is or has been available to the public from any other source.

(9)   Nothing in this section authorises the making of a disclosure in contravention of the data protection legislation.

949   Offence of disclosure in contravention of section 948

(1)   A person who discloses information in contravention of section 948 is guilty of an offence, unless—

(a)   he did not know, and had no reason to suspect, that the information had been provided as mentioned in section 948(1), or

(b)   he took all reasonable steps and exercised all due diligence to avoid the commission of the offence.

(2)   A person guilty of an offence under this section is liable—

(a)   on conviction on indictment, to imprisonment for a term not exceeding two years or a fine (or both);

(b)   on summary conviction—

(i)   in England and Wales, to imprisonment for a term not exceeding twelve months or to a fine not exceeding the statutory maximum (or both);

(ii)   in Scotland or Northern Ireland, to imprisonment for a term not exceeding six months, or to a fine not exceeding the statutory maximum (or both).

(3)   Where a company or other body corporate commits an offence under this section, an offence is also committed by every officer of the company or other body corporate who is in default.

Co-operation

950   Panel's duty of co-operation

(1)   The Panel must take such steps as it considers appropriate to co-operate with—

     (a)   the Financial Conduct Authority;

     (aa)   the Prudential Regulation Authority;

     (ab)   the Bank of England;

     (b)   ...

     (c)   any other person or body that exercises functions of a public nature, under legislation in any country or territory outside the United Kingdom, that appear to the Panel to be similar to its own functions or those of the Financial Conduct Authority or the Prudential Regulation Authority or similar to the regulatory functions of the Bank of England.

(2)   Co-operation may include the sharing of information that the Panel is not prevented from disclosing.

Hearings and appeals

951   Hearings and appeals

(1)   Rules must provide for a decision of the Panel to be subject to review by a committee of the Panel (the "Hearings Committee") at the instance of such persons affected by the decision as are specified in the rules.

(2)   Rules may also confer other functions on the Hearings Committee.

(3)   Rules must provide for there to be a right of appeal against a decision of the Hearings Committee to an independent tribunal (the "Takeover Appeal Board") in such circumstances and subject to such conditions as are specified in the rules.

(4)   Rules may contain—

     (a)   provision as to matters of procedure in relation to proceedings before the Hearings Committee (including provision imposing time limits);

     (b)   provision about evidence in such proceedings;

     (c)   provision as to the powers of the Hearings Committee dealing with a matter referred to it;

     (d)   provision about enforcement of decisions of the Hearings Committee and the Takeover Appeal Board.

(5)   Rules must contain provision—

     (a)   requiring the Panel, when acting in relation to any proceedings before the Hearings Committee or the Takeover Appeal Board, to do so by an officer or member of staff of the Panel (or a person acting as such);

     (b)   preventing a person who is or has been a member of the committee mentioned in section 943(5) from being a member of the Hearings Committee or the Takeover Appeal Board;

     (c)   preventing a person who is a member of the committee mentioned in section 943(5), of the Hearings Committee or of the Takeover Appeal Board from acting as mentioned in paragraph (a).

Contravention of rules etc

952   Sanctions

(1)   Rules may contain provision conferring power on the Panel to impose sanctions on a person who has—

     (a)   acted in breach of rules, or

     (b)   failed to comply with a direction given by virtue of section 946.

(2)   Subsection (3) applies where rules made by virtue of subsection (1) confer power on the Panel to impose a sanction of a kind not provided for by the City Code on Takeovers and Mergers as it had effect immediately before the passing of this Act.

(3)   The Panel must prepare a statement (a "policy statement") of its policy with respect to—

     (a)   the imposition of the sanction in question, and

(b) where the sanction is in the nature of a financial penalty, the amount of the penalty that may be imposed.

An element of the policy must be that, in making a decision about any such matter, the Panel has regard to the factors mentioned in subsection (4).

(4) The factors are—
   (a) the seriousness of the breach or failure in question in relation to the nature of the rule or direction contravened;
   (b) the extent to which the breach or failure was deliberate or reckless;
   (c) whether the person on whom the sanction is to be imposed is an individual.

(5) The Panel may at any time revise a policy statement.

(6) The Panel must prepare a draft of any proposed policy statement (or revised policy statement) and consult such persons about the draft as the Panel considers appropriate.

(7) The Panel must publish, in whatever way it considers appropriate, any policy statement (or revised policy statement) that it prepares.

(8) In exercising, or deciding whether to exercise, its power to impose a sanction within subsection (2) in the case of any particular breach or failure, the Panel must have regard to any relevant policy statement published and in force at the time when the breach or failure occurred.

953 Failure to comply with rules about bid documentation

(1) This section applies where a takeover bid is made for a company that has securities carrying voting rights admitted to trading on a regulated market in the United Kingdom.

(2) Where an offer document published in respect of the bid does not comply with offer document rules, an offence is committed by—
   (a) the person making the bid, and
   (b) where the person making the bid is a body of persons, any director, officer or member of that body who caused the document to be published.

(3) A person commits an offence under subsection (2) only if—
   (a) he knew that the offer document did not comply, or was reckless as to whether it complied, and
   (b) he failed to take all reasonable steps to secure that it did comply.

(4) Where a response document published in respect of the bid does not comply with response document rules, an offence is committed by any director or other officer of the company referred to in subsection (1) who—
   (a) knew that the response document did not comply, or was reckless as to whether it complied, and
   (b) failed to take all reasonable steps to secure that it did comply.

(5) Where an offence is committed under subsection (2)(b) or (4) by a company or other body corporate ("the relevant body")—
   (a) subsection (2)(b) has effect as if the reference to a director, officer or member of the person making the bid included a reference to a director, officer or member of the relevant body;
   (b) subsection (4) has effect as if the reference to a director or other officer of the company referred to in subsection (1) included a reference to a director, officer or member of the relevant body.

(6) A person guilty of an offence under this section is liable—
   (a) on conviction on indictment, to a fine;
   (b) on summary conviction, to a fine not exceeding the statutory maximum.

(7) Nothing in this section affects any power of the Panel in relation to the enforcement of its rules.

(8) Section 1 (meaning of "company") does not apply for the purposes of this section.

(9) In this section—
"designated" means designated in rules;
"offer document" means a document required to be published by rules made in accordance with paragraph 12(1) to (3) of Schedule 1C;

"offer document rules" means rules under section 943(1) designated as rules made in accordance with paragraph 12(4) of Schedule 1C;

"response document" means a document required to be published by rules made in accordance with paragraph 18 of Schedule 1C

"response document rules" means rules under section 943(1) designated as rules made in accordance with paragraph 18(1) of Schedule 1C;

"securities" means shares or debentures;

"takeover bid" has the meaning given by paragraph 20(1) of Schedule 1C;

"voting rights" means rights to vote at general meetings of the company in question, including rights that arise only in certain circumstances.

954   Compensation

(1)   Rules may confer power on the Panel to order a person to pay such compensation as it thinks just and reasonable if he is in breach of a rule the effect of which is to require the payment of money.

(2)   Rules made by virtue of this section may include provision for the payment of interest (including compound interest).

955   Enforcement by the court

(1)   If, on the application of the Panel, the court is satisfied—

   (a)   that there is a reasonable likelihood that a person will contravene a rule-based requirement, or

   (b)   that a person has contravened a rule-based requirement or a disclosure requirement,

   the court may make any order it thinks fit to secure compliance with the requirement.

(2)   In subsection (1) "the court" means the High Court or, in Scotland, the Court of Session.

(3)   Except as provided by subsection (1), no person—

   (a)   has a right to seek an injunction, or

   (b)   in Scotland, has title or interest to seek an interdict or an order for specific performance,

   to prevent a person from contravening (or continuing to contravene) a rule-based requirement or a disclosure requirement.

(4)   In this section—

   "contravene" includes fail to comply;

   "disclosure requirement" means a requirement imposed under section 947;

   "rule-based requirement" means a requirement imposed by or under rules.

956   No action for breach of statutory duty etc

(1)   Contravention of a rule-based requirement or a disclosure requirement does not give rise to any right of action for breach of statutory duty.

(2)   Contravention of a rule-based requirement does not make any transaction void or unenforceable or (subject to any provision made by rules) affect the validity of any other thing.

(3)   In this section—

   (a)   "contravention" includes failure to comply;

   (b)   "disclosure requirement" and "rule-based requirement" have the same meaning as in section 955.

Funding

957   Fees and charges

(1)   Rules may provide for fees or charges to be payable to the Panel for the purpose of meeting any part of its expenses.

(2)   A reference in this section or section 958 to expenses of the Panel is to any expenses that have been or are to be incurred by the Panel in, or in connection with, the discharge of its functions, including in particular—

   (a)   payments in respect of the expenses of the Takeover Appeal Board;

(b) the cost of repaying the principal of, and of paying any interest on, any money borrowed by the Panel;

(c) the cost of maintaining adequate reserves.

958 Levy

(1) For the purpose of meeting any part of the expenses of the Panel, the Secretary of State may by regulations provide for a levy to be payable to the Panel—

(a) by specified persons or bodies, or persons or bodies of a specified description, or

(b) on transactions, of a specified description, in securities on specified markets.

In this subsection "specified" means specified in the regulations.

(2) The power to specify (or to specify descriptions of) persons or bodies must be exercised in such a way that the levy is payable only by persons or bodies that appear to the Secretary of State—

(a) to be capable of being directly affected by the exercise of any of the functions of the Panel, or

(b) otherwise to have a substantial interest in the exercise of any of those functions.

(3) Regulations under this section may in particular—

(a) specify the rate of the levy and the period in respect of which it is payable at that rate;

(b) make provision as to the times when, and the manner in which, payments are to be made in respect of the levy.

(4) In determining the rate of the levy payable in respect of a particular period, the Secretary of State—

(a) must take into account any other income received or expected by the Panel in respect of that period;

(b) may take into account estimated as well as actual expenses of the Panel in respect of that period.

(5) The Panel must—

(a) keep proper accounts in respect of any amounts of levy received by virtue of this section;

(b) prepare, in relation to each period in respect of which any such amounts are received, a statement of account relating to those amounts in such form and manner as is specified in the regulations.

Those accounts must be audited, and the statement certified, by persons appointed by the Secretary of State.

(6) Regulations under this section—

(a) are subject to affirmative resolution procedure if subsection (7) applies to them;

(b) otherwise, are subject to negative resolution procedure.

(7) This subsection applies to—

(a) the first regulations under this section;

(b) any other regulations under this section that would result in a change in the persons or bodies by whom, or the transactions on which, the levy is payable.

(8) If a draft of an instrument containing regulations under this section would, apart from this subsection, be treated for the purposes of the Standing Orders of either House of Parliament as a hybrid instrument, it is to proceed in that House as if it were not such an instrument.

959 Recovery of fees, charges or levy

An amount payable by any person or body by virtue of section 957 or 958 is a debt due from that person or body to the Panel, and is recoverable accordingly.

Miscellaneous and supplementary

960 Panel as party to proceedings

The Panel is capable (despite being an unincorporated body) of—

(a) bringing proceedings under this Chapter in its own name;

(b) bringing or defending any other proceedings in its own name.

961   Exemption from liability in damages

(1)   Neither the Panel, nor any person within subsection (2), is to be liable in damages for anything done (or omitted to be done) in, or in connection with, the discharge or purported discharge of the Panel's functions.

(2)   A person is within this subsection if—

(a)   he is (or is acting as) a member, officer or member of staff of the Panel, or

(b)   he is a person authorised under section 947(5).

(3)   Subsection (1) does not apply—

(a)   if the act or omission is shown to have been in bad faith, or

(b)   so as to prevent an award of damages in respect of the act or omission on the ground that it was unlawful as a result of section 6(1) of the Human Rights Act 1998 (acts of public authorities incompatible with Convention rights).

962   Privilege against self-incrimination

(1)   A statement made by a person in response to—

(a)   a requirement under section 947(1), or

(b)   an order made by the court under section 955 to secure compliance with such a requirement,

may not be used against him in criminal proceedings in which he is charged with an offence to which this subsection applies.

(2)   Subsection (1) applies to any offence other than an offence under one of the following provisions (which concern false statements made otherwise than on oath)—

(a)   section 5 of the Perjury Act 1911;

(b)   section 44(2) of the Criminal Law (Consolidation) (Scotland) Act 1995;

(c)   Article 10 of the Perjury (Northern Ireland) Order 1979.

963   Annual reports

(1)   After the end of each financial year the Panel must publish a report.

(2)   The report must—

(a)   set out how the Panel's functions were discharged in the year in question;

(b)   include the Panel's accounts for that year;

(c)   mention any matters the Panel considers to be of relevance to the discharge of its functions.

964   Amendments to Financial Services and Markets Act 2000

(1)   The Financial Services and Markets Act 2000 is amended as follows.

(2)   Section 143 (power to make rules endorsing the City Code on Takeovers and Mergers etc) is repealed.

(3)   ...

(4)   In section 349 (exceptions from restrictions on disclosure of confidential information), after subsection (3) insert—

"(3A)   Section 348 does not apply to—

(a)   the disclosure by a recipient to which subsection (3B) applies of confidential information disclosed to it by the Authority in reliance on subsection (1);

(b)   the disclosure of such information by a person obtaining it directly or indirectly from a recipient to which subsection (3B) applies.

(3B)   This subsection applies to—

(a)   the Panel on Takeovers and Mergers;

(b)   an authority designated as a supervisory authority for the purposes of Article 4.1 of the Takeovers Directive;

(c)   any other person or body that exercises public functions, under legislation in an EEA State other than the United Kingdom, that are similar to the Authority's functions or those of the Panel on Takeovers and Mergers.".

(5)   ...

(6)   In section 417(1) (definitions), insert at the appropriate place—

""Takeovers Directive" means Directive 2004/25/EC of the European Parliament and of the Council;".

965 Power to extend to Isle of Man and Channel Islands

Her Majesty may by Order in Council direct that any of the provisions of this Chapter extend, with such modifications as may be specified in the Order, to the Isle of Man or any of the Channel Islands.

CHAPTER 2
IMPEDIMENTS TO TAKEOVERS

Opting in and opting out

966 Opting in and opting out

(1) A company may by special resolution (an "opting-in resolution") opt in for the purposes of this Chapter if the following five conditions are met in relation to the company.

(2) The first condition is that the company has voting shares admitted to trading on a UK regulated market.

(3) The second condition is that the company's articles of association do not contain any restrictions on the transfer of shares or, if they do contain any such restrictions, provide that they are not to apply to—

    (a) transfers to the offeror, or at the offeror's direction to another person, during the offer period, or

    (b) transfers to any person at a time during the offer period when the offeror holds shares amounting to not less than 75% in value of all the voting shares in the company.

(3A) The third condition is that the company's articles of association—

    (a) do not contain any restrictions on rights to vote at a general meeting of the company, or

    (b) if they do contain any such restrictions, provide that they are not to have effect on rights to vote at a general meeting of the company that—

        (i) decides whether to take any action which might result in the frustration of the takeover bid, or

        (ii) is held at a time when the offeror holds shares amounting to not less than 75% in value of all the voting shares in the company,

    unless the restrictions are compensated for by specific pecuniary advantages.

(3B) The fourth condition is that the company's articles of association do not contain any other provision which would be incompatible with the requirements of subsection (3C).

(3C) Those requirements are—

    (a) multiple-vote shares are to carry only one vote each at a general meeting of the company that decides whether to take any action which might result in the frustration of the takeover bid,

    (b) multiple-vote shares are to carry only one vote each at a general meeting of the company which—

        (i) is the first such meeting to be held after the end of the offer period,

        (ii) is held at a time when the offeror holds shares amounting to not less than 75% in value of all the voting shares in the company, and

        (iii) is called at the offeror's request under section 969 in order to amend the company's articles of association or to appoint or remove members of the board of directors, and

    (c) at a time during the offer period when the offeror holds shares amounting to not less than 75% in value of all the voting shares in the company, shareholders are not to have any extraordinary rights to appoint or remove members of the board of directors.

(3D) The references in subsections (3A)(b) and (3C)(a) to voting at a general meeting of the company that decides whether to take any action which might result in the frustration of the takeover bid includes a reference to voting on a written resolution concerned with that question.

(3E)   For the purposes of subsections (3A)(b)(i) and (3C)(a), action which might result in the frustration of the takeover bid is any action of that kind specified in rules under section 943(1) made in accordance with paragraphs 17 or 18 of Schedule 1C.

(3F)   The references in subsections (3), (3A) and (3C) to voting shares in the company do not include—

(a)   debentures, or

(b)   shares that, under the company's articles of association, do not normally carry rights to vote at its general meetings (for example, shares carrying rights to vote that, under those articles, arise only where specified pecuniary advantages are not provided).

(3G)   In subsection (3C), "multiple-vote shares" means shares included in a distinct and separate class and carrying more than one vote each.

(4)   The fifth condition is that—

(a)   no shares conferring special rights in the company are held by—

(i)   a minister,

(ii)   a nominee of, or any other person acting on behalf of, a minister, or

(iii)   a company directly or indirectly controlled by a minister, and

(b)   no such rights are exercisable by or on behalf of a minister under any enactment.

(5)   A company may revoke an opting-in resolution by a further special resolution (an "opting-out resolution").

(6)   ...

(7)   In subsection (4) "minister" means—

(a)   the holder of an office in Her Majesty's Government in the United Kingdom;

(b)   the Scottish Ministers;

(c)   a Minister within the meaning given by section 7(3) of the Northern Ireland Act 1998;

(d)   the Welsh Ministers;

and for the purposes of that subsection "minister" also includes the Treasury, the Board of Trade and, the Defence Council ...

(8)   The Secretary of State may by order subject to negative resolution procedure provide that subsection (4) applies in relation to a specified person or body that exercises functions of a public nature as it applies in relation to a minister. "Specified" means specified in the order.

967   Further provision about opting-in and opting-out resolutions

(1)   An opting-in resolution or an opting-out resolution must specify the date from which it is to have effect (the "effective date").

(2)   The effective date of an opting-in resolution may not be earlier than the date on which the resolution is passed.

(3)   The second, third, fourth and fifth conditions in section 966 must be met at the time when an opting-in resolution is passed, but the first one does not need to be met until the effective date.

(4)   An opting-in resolution passed before the time when voting shares of the company are admitted to trading on a UK regulated market complies with the requirement in subsection (1) if, instead of specifying a particular date, it provides for the resolution to have effect from that time.

(5)   An opting-in resolution passed before the commencement of this section complies with the requirement in subsection (1) if, instead of specifying a particular date, it provides for the resolution to have effect from that commencement.

(6)   The effective date of an opting-out resolution may not be earlier than the first anniversary of the date on which a copy of the opting-in resolution was forwarded to the registrar.

(7)   Where a company has passed an opting-in resolution, any alteration of its articles of association that would prevent the second, third or fourth condition in section 966 from being met is of no effect until the effective date of an opting-out resolution passed by the company.

Consequences of opting in

968   Effect on contractual restrictions

(1)   The following provisions have effect where a takeover bid is made for an opted-in company.

(2)   An agreement to which this section applies is invalid in so far as it places any restriction—

   (a)   on the transfer to the offeror, or at his direction to another person, of shares in the company during the offer period;

   (b)   on the transfer to any person of shares in the company at a time during the offer period when the offeror holds shares amounting to not less than 75% in value of all the voting shares in the company;

   (c)   on rights to vote at a general meeting of the company that decides whether to take any action which might result in the frustration of the bid;

   (d)   on rights to vote at a general meeting of the company that—

      (i)   is the first such meeting to be held after the end of the offer period, and

      (ii)   is held at a time when the offeror holds shares amounting to not less than 75% in value of all the voting shares in the company.

(3)   This section applies to an agreement—

   (a)   entered into between a person holding shares in the company and another such person on or after 21st April 2004, or

   (b)   entered into at any time between such a person and the company, and it applies to such an agreement even if the law applicable to the agreement (apart from this section) is not the law of a part of the United Kingdom.

(4)   The reference in subsection (2)(c) to rights to vote at a general meeting of the company that decides whether to take any action which might result in the frustration of the bid includes a reference to rights to vote on a written resolution concerned with that question.

(5)   For the purposes of subsection (2)(c), action which might result in the frustration of a bid is any action of that kind specified in rules under section 943(1) made in accordance with paragraph 17 or 18 of Schedule 1C.

(6)   If a person suffers loss as a result of any act or omission that would (but for this section) be a breach of an agreement to which this section applies, he is entitled to compensation, of such amount as the court considers just and equitable, from any person who would (but for this section) be liable to him for committing or inducing the breach.

(7)   In subsection (6) "the court" means the High Court or, in Scotland, the Court of Session.

(8)   A reference in this section to voting shares in the company does not include—

   (a)   debentures, or

   (b)   shares that, under the company's articles of association, do not normally carry rights to vote at its general meetings (for example, shares carrying rights to vote that, under those articles, arise only where specified pecuniary advantages are not provided).

969   Power of offeror to require general meeting to be called

(1)   Where a takeover bid is made for an opted-in company, the offeror may by making a request to the directors of the company require them to call a general meeting of the company if, at the date at which the request is made, he holds shares amounting to not less than 75% in value of all the voting shares in the company.

(2)   The reference in subsection (1) to voting shares in the company does not include—

   (a)   debentures, or

   (b)   shares that, under the company's articles of association, do not normally carry rights to vote at its general meetings (for example, shares carrying rights to vote that, under those articles, arise only where specified pecuniary advantages are not provided).

(3)   Sections 303 to 305 (members' power to require general meetings to be called) apply as they would do if subsection (1) above were substituted for subsections (1) to (3) of section 303, and with any other necessary modifications.

Supplementary

970   Communication of decisions

(1)   A company that has passed an opting-in resolution or an opting-out resolution must notify—

   (a)   the Panel, …

(b) ...

(2)   Notification must be given within 15 days after the resolution is passed ...

(3)   If a company fails to comply with this section, an offence is committed by—

        (a)   the company, and

        (b)   every officer of it who is in default.

(4)   A person guilty of an offence under this section is liable on summary conviction to a fine not exceeding level 3 on the standard scale and, for continued contravention, a daily default fine not exceeding one-tenth of level 3 on the standard scale.

971   Interpretation of this Chapter

(1)   In this Chapter—

"offeror", in relation to a takeover bid, means the person making the bid;

"offer period", in relation to a takeover bid, means the time allowed for acceptance of the bid by—

        (a)   rules under section 943(1) made in accordance with paragraph 13 of Schedule 1C;

"opted-in company" means a company in relation to which—

        (a)   an opting-in resolution has effect, and

        (b)   the conditions in section 966(2) and (4) continue to be met;

"opting-in resolution" has the meaning given by section 966(1);

"opting-out resolution" has the meaning given by section 966(5);

"takeover bid" has the meaning given by paragraph 20(1) of Schedule 1C;

...

"voting rights" means rights to vote at general meetings of the company in question, including rights that arise only in certain circumstances;

"voting shares" means shares carrying voting rights.

(2)   For the purposes of this Chapter—

        (a)   securities of a company are treated as shares in the company if they are convertible into or entitle the holder to subscribe for such shares;

        (b)   debentures issued by a company are treated as shares in the company if they carry voting rights.

972   Transitory provision

(1)   Where a takeover bid is made for an opted-in company, section 368 of the Companies Act 1985 (extraordinary general meeting on members' requisition) and section 378 of that Act (extraordinary and special resolutions) have effect as follows until their repeal by this Act.

(2)   Section 368 has effect as if a members' requisition included a requisition of a person who—

        (a)   is the offeror in relation to the takeover bid, and

        (b)   holds at the date of the deposit of the requisition shares amounting to

        not less than 75% in value of all the voting shares in the company.

(3)   In relation to a general meeting of the company that—

        (a)   is the first such meeting to be held after the end of the offer period, and

        (b)   is held at a time when the offeror holds shares amounting to not less than 75% in value of all the voting shares in the company,

section 378(2) (meaning of "special resolution") has effect as if "14 days' notice" were substituted for "21 days' notice".

(4)   A reference in this section to voting shares in the company does not include—

        (a)   debentures, or

        (b)   shares that, under the company's articles of association, do not normally carry rights to vote at its general meetings (for example, shares carrying rights to vote that, under those articles, arise only where specified pecuniary advantages are not provided).

973 Power to extend to Isle of Man and Channel Islands

Her Majesty may by Order in Council direct that any of the provisions of this Chapter extend, with such modifications as may be specified in the Order, to the Isle of Man or any of the Channel Islands.

CHAPTER 3
"SQUEEZE-OUT" AND "SELL-OUT"

Takeover offers

974 Meaning of "takeover offer"

(1) For the purposes of this Chapter an offer to acquire shares in a company is a "takeover offer" if the following two conditions are satisfied in relation to the offer.

(2) The first condition is that it is an offer to acquire—

    (a)   all the shares in a company, or

    (b)   where there is more than one class of shares in a company, all the shares of one or more classes,

other than shares that at the date of the offer are already held by the offeror.

Section 975 contains provision supplementing this subsection.

(3) The second condition is that the terms of the offer are the same—

    (a)   in relation to all the shares to which the offer relates, or

    (b)   where the shares to which the offer relates include shares of different classes, in relation to all the shares of each class.

Section 976 contains provision treating this condition as satisfied in certain circumstances.

(4) In subsections (1) to (3) "shares" means shares, other than relevant treasury shares, that have been allotted on the date of the offer (but see subsection (5)).

(5) A takeover offer may include among the shares to which it relates—

    (a)   all or any shares that are allotted after the date of the offer but before a specified date;

    (b)   all or any relevant treasury shares that cease to be held as treasury shares before a specified date;

    (c)   all or any other relevant treasury shares.

(6) In this section—

"relevant treasury shares" means shares that—

    (a)   are held by the company as treasury shares on the date of the offer, or

    (b)   become shares held by the company as treasury shares after that date but before a specified date;

"specified date" means a date specified in or determined in accordance with the terms of the offer.

(7) Where the terms of an offer make provision for their revision and for acceptances on the previous terms to be treated as acceptances on the revised terms, then, if the terms of the offer are revised in accordance with that provision—

    (a)   the revision is not to be regarded for the purposes of this Chapter as the making of a fresh offer, and

    (b)   references in this Chapter to the date of the offer are accordingly to be read as references to the date of the original offer.

975 Shares already held by the offeror etc

(1) The reference in section 974(2) to shares already held by the offeror includes a reference to shares that he has contracted to acquire, whether unconditionally or subject to conditions being met.

This is subject to subsection (2).

(2) The reference in section 974(2) to shares already held by the offeror does not include a reference to shares that are the subject of a contract—

    (a)   intended to secure that the holder of the shares will accept the offer when it is made, and

    (b)   entered into—

        (i)   by deed and for no consideration,

        (ii)   for consideration of negligible value, or

        (iii)   for consideration consisting of a promise by the offeror to make the offer.

(3)   In relation to Scotland, this section applies as if the words "by deed and" in subsection (2)(b)(i) were omitted.

(4)   The condition in section 974(2) is treated as satisfied where—

      (a)   the offer does not extend to shares that associates of the offeror hold or have contracted to acquire (whether unconditionally or subject to conditions being met), and

      (b)   the condition would be satisfied if the offer did extend to those shares.

      (For further provision about such shares, see section 977(2)).

976   Cases where offer treated as being on same terms

(1)   The condition in section 974(3) (terms of offer to be the same for all shares or all shares of particular classes) is treated as satisfied where subsection (2) or (3) below applies.

(2)   This subsection applies where—

      (a)   shares carry an entitlement to a particular dividend which other shares of the same class, by reason of being allotted later, do not carry,

      (b)   there is a difference in the value of consideration offered for the shares allotted earlier as against that offered for those allotted later,

      (c)   that difference merely reflects the difference in entitlement to the dividend, and

      (d)   the condition in section 974(3) would be satisfied but for that difference.

(3)   This subsection applies where—

      (a)   the law of a country or territory outside the United Kingdom—

          (i)   precludes an offer of consideration in the form, or any of the forms, specified in the terms of the offer ("the specified form"), or

          (ii)   precludes it except after compliance by the offeror with conditions with which he is unable to comply or which he regards as unduly onerous,

      (b)   the persons to whom an offer of consideration in the specified form is precluded are able to receive consideration in another form that is of substantially equivalent value, and

      (c)   the condition in section 974(3) would be satisfied but for the fact that an offer of consideration in the specified form to those persons is precluded.

977   Shares to which an offer relates

(1)   Where a takeover offer is made and, during the period beginning with the date of the offer and ending when the offer can no longer be accepted, the offeror—

      (a)   acquires or unconditionally contracts to acquire any of the shares to which the offer relates, but

      (b)   does not do so by virtue of acceptances of the offer,

      those shares are treated for the purposes of this Chapter as excluded from those to which the offer relates.

(2)   For the purposes of this Chapter shares that an associate of the offeror holds or has contracted to acquire, whether at the date of the offer or subsequently, are not treated as shares to which the offer relates, even if the offer extends to such shares.

      In this subsection "contracted" means contracted unconditionally or subject to conditions being met.

(3)   This section is subject to section 979(8) and (9).

978   Effect of impossibility etc of communicating or accepting offer

(1)   Where there are holders of shares in a company to whom an offer to acquire shares in the company is not communicated, that does not prevent the offer from being a takeover offer for the purposes of this Chapter if—

      (a)   those shareholders have no registered address in the United Kingdom,

      (b)   the offer was not communicated to those shareholders in order not to contravene the law of a country or territory outside the United Kingdom, and

      (c)   either—

(i)   the offer is published in the Gazette, or

(ii)   the offer can be inspected, or a copy of it obtained, at a place in the United Kingdom or on a website, and a notice is published in the Gazette specifying the address of that place or website.

(2)   Where an offer is made to acquire shares in a company and there are persons for whom, by reason of the law of a country or territory outside the United Kingdom, it is impossible to accept the offer, or more difficult to do so, that does not prevent the offer from being a takeover offer for the purposes of this Chapter.

(3)   It is not to be inferred—

(a)   that an offer which is not communicated to every holder of shares in the company cannot be a takeover offer for the purposes of this Chapter unless the requirements of paragraphs (a) to (c) of subsection (1) are met, or

(b)   that an offer which is impossible, or more difficult, for certain persons to accept cannot be a takeover offer for those purposes unless the reason for the impossibility or difficulty is the one mentioned in subsection (2).

"Squeeze-out"

979   Right of offeror to buy out minority shareholder

(1)   Subsection (2) applies in a case where a takeover offer does not relate to shares of different classes.

(2)   If the offeror has, by virtue of acceptances of the offer, acquired or unconditionally contracted to acquire—

(a)   not less than 90% in value of the shares to which the offer relates, and

(b)   in a case where the shares to which the offer relates are voting shares, not less than 90% of the voting rights carried by those shares,

he may give notice to the holder of any shares to which the offer relates which the offeror has not acquired or unconditionally contracted to acquire that he desires to acquire those shares.

(3)   Subsection (4) applies in a case where a takeover offer relates to shares of different classes.

(4)   If the offeror has, by virtue of acceptances of the offer, acquired or unconditionally contracted to acquire—

(a)   not less than 90% in value of the shares of any class to which the offer relates, and

(b)   in a case where the shares of that class are voting shares, not less than 90% of the voting rights carried by those shares,

he may give notice to the holder of any shares of that class to which the offer relates which the offeror has not acquired or unconditionally contracted to acquire that he desires to acquire those shares.

(5)   In the case of a takeover offer which includes among the shares to which it relates—

(a)   shares that are allotted after the date of the offer, or

(b)   relevant treasury shares (within the meaning of section 974) that cease to be held as treasury shares after the date of the offer,

the offeror's entitlement to give a notice under subsection (2) or (4) on any particular date shall be determined as if the shares to which the offer relates did not include any allotted, or ceasing to be held as treasury shares, on or after that date.

(6)   Subsection (7) applies where—

(a)   the requirements for the giving of a notice under subsection (2) or (4) are satisfied, and

(b)   there are shares in the company which the offeror, or an associate of his, has contracted to acquire subject to conditions being met, and in relation to which the contract has not become unconditional.

(7)   The offeror's entitlement to give a notice under subsection (2) or (4) shall be determined as if—

(a)   the shares to which the offer relates included shares falling within paragraph (b) of subsection (6), and

      (b)   in relation to shares falling within that paragraph, the words "by virtue of acceptances of the offer" in subsection (2) or (4) were omitted.

(8)   Where—

      (a)   a takeover offer is made,

      (b)   during the period beginning with the date of the offer and ending when the offer can no longer be accepted, the offeror—

           (i)   acquires or unconditionally contracts to acquire any of the shares to which the offer relates, but

          (ii)   does not do so by virtue of acceptances of the offer, and

      (c)   subsection (10) applies,

then for the purposes of this section those shares are not excluded by section 977(1) from those to which the offer relates, and the offeror is treated as having acquired or contracted to acquire them by virtue of acceptances of the offer.

(9)   Where—

      (a)   a takeover offer is made,

      (b)   during the period beginning with the date of the offer and ending when the offer can no longer be accepted, an associate of the offeror acquires or unconditionally contracts to acquire any of the shares to which the offer relates, and

      (c)   subsection (10) applies,

then for the purposes of this section those shares are not excluded by section 977(2) from those to which the offer relates.

(10)   This subsection applies if—

      (a)   at the time the shares are acquired or contracted to be acquired as mentioned in subsection (8) or (9) (as the case may be), the value of the consideration for which they are acquired or contracted to be acquired ("the acquisition consideration") does not exceed the value of the consideration specified in the terms of the offer, or

      (b)   those terms are subsequently revised so that when the revision is announced the value of the acquisition consideration, at the time mentioned in paragraph (a), no longer exceeds the value of the consideration specified in those terms.

980   Further provision about notices given under section 979

(1)   A notice under section 979 must be given in the prescribed manner.

(2)   No notice may be given under section 979(2) or (4) after the end of—

      (a)   the period of three months beginning with the day after the last day on which the offer can be accepted, or

      (b)   the period of six months beginning with the date of the offer, where that period ends earlier and the offer is one to which subsection (3) below applies.

(3)   This subsection applies to an offer if the time allowed for acceptance of the offer is not governed by rules under section 943(1) made in accordance with paragraph 13 or 14 of Schedule 1C.

(4)   At the time when the offeror first gives a notice under section 979 in relation to an offer, he must send to the company—

      (a)   a copy of the notice, and

      (b)   a statutory declaration by him in the prescribed form, stating that the conditions for the giving of the notice are satisfied.

(5)   Where the offeror is a company (whether or not a company within the meaning of this Act) the statutory declaration must be signed by a director.

(6)   A person commits an offence if—

      (a)   he fails to send a copy of a notice or a statutory declaration as required by subsection (4), or

      (b)   he makes such a declaration for the purposes of that subsection knowing it to be false or without having reasonable grounds for believing it to be true.

(7)   It is a defence for a person charged with an offence for failing to send a copy of a notice as required by subsection (4) to prove that he took reasonable steps for securing compliance with that subsection.

(8) A person guilty of an offence under this section is liable—

    (a) on conviction on indictment, to imprisonment for a term not exceeding two years or a fine (or both);

    (b) on summary conviction—

        (i) in England and Wales, to imprisonment for a term not exceeding twelve months or to a fine not exceeding the statutory maximum (or both) and, for continued contravention, a daily default fine not exceeding one-fiftieth of the greater of £5,000 or the amount corresponding to level 4 on the standard scale for summary offences;

        (ii) in Scotland or Northern Ireland, to imprisonment for a term not exceeding six months, or to a fine not exceeding the statutory maximum (or both) and, for continued contravention, a daily default fine not exceeding one-fiftieth of the statutory maximum.

981 Effect of notice under section 979

(1) Subject to section 986 (applications to the court), this section applies where the offeror gives a shareholder a notice under section 979.

(2) The offeror is entitled and bound to acquire the shares to which the notice relates on the terms of the offer.

(3) Where the terms of an offer are such as to give the shareholder a choice of consideration, the notice must give particulars of the choice and state—

    (a) that the shareholder may, within six weeks from the date of the notice, indicate his choice by a written communication sent to the offeror at an address specified in the notice, and

    (b) which consideration specified in the offer will apply if he does not indicate a choice.

The reference in subsection (2) to the terms of the offer is to be read accordingly.

(4) Subsection (3) applies whether or not any time-limit or other conditions applicable to the choice under the terms of the offer can still be complied with.

(5) If the consideration offered to or (as the case may be) chosen by the shareholder—

    (a) is not cash and the offeror is no longer able to provide it, or

    (b) was to have been provided by a third party who is no longer bound or able to provide it,

the consideration is to be taken to consist of an amount of cash, payable by the offeror, which at the date of the notice is equivalent to the consideration offered or (as the case may be) chosen.

(6) At the end of six weeks from the date of the notice the offeror must immediately—

    (a) send a copy of the notice to the company, and

    (b) pay or transfer to the company the consideration for the shares to which the notice relates.

Where the consideration consists of shares or securities to be allotted by the offeror, the reference in paragraph (b) to the transfer of the consideration is to be read as a reference to the allotment of the shares or securities to the company.

(7) If the shares to which the notice relates are registered, the copy of the notice sent to the company under subsection (6)(a) must be accompanied by an instrument of transfer executed on behalf of the holder of the shares by a person appointed by the offeror.

On receipt of that instrument the company must register the offeror as the holder of those shares.

(8) If the shares to which the notice relates are transferable by the delivery of warrants or other instruments, the copy of the notice sent to the company under subsection (6)(a) must be accompanied by a statement to that effect. On receipt of that statement the company must issue the offeror with warrants or other instruments in respect of the shares, and those already in issue in respect of the shares become void.

(9) The company must hold any money or other consideration received by it under subsection (6)(b) on trust for the person who, before the offeror acquired them, was entitled to the shares in respect of which the money or other consideration was received.

Section 982 contains further provision about how the company should deal with such money or other consideration.

982   **Further provision about consideration held on trust under section 981(9)**

(1)   This section applies where an offeror pays or transfers consideration to the company under section 981(6).

(2)   The company must pay into a separate bank account that complies with subsection (3)—

    (a)   any money it receives under paragraph (b) of section 981(6), and

    (b)   any dividend or other sum accruing from any other consideration it receives under that paragraph.

(3)   A bank account complies with this subsection if the balance on the account—

    (a)   bears interest at an appropriate rate, and

    (b)   can be withdrawn by such notice (if any) as is appropriate.

(4)   If—

    (a)   the person entitled to the consideration held on trust by virtue of section 981(9) cannot be found, and

    (b)   subsection (5) applies,

the consideration (together with any interest, dividend or other benefit that has accrued from it) must be paid into court.

(5)   This subsection applies where—

    (a)   reasonable enquiries have been made at reasonable intervals to find the person, and

    (b)   twelve years have elapsed since the consideration was received, or the company is wound up.

(6)   In relation to a company registered in Scotland, subsections (7) and (8) apply instead of subsection (4).

(7)   If the person entitled to the consideration held on trust by virtue of section 981(9) cannot be found and subsection (5) applies—

    (a)   the trust terminates,

    (b)   the company or (if the company is wound up) the liquidator must sell any consideration other than cash and any benefit other than cash that has accrued from the consideration, and

    (c)   a sum representing—

        (i)   the consideration so far as it is cash,

        (ii)   the proceeds of any sale under paragraph (b), and

        (iii)   any interest, dividend or other benefit that has accrued from the consideration,

        must be deposited in the name of the Accountant of Court in a separate bank account complying with subsection (3) and the receipt for the deposit must be transmitted to the Accountant of Court.

(8)   Section 150 of the Bankruptcy (Scotland) Act 2016 (so far as consistent with this Act) applies (with any necessary modifications) to sums deposited under subsection (7) as it applies to sums deposited under section 148(3) of that Act.

(9)   The expenses of any such enquiries as are mentioned in subsection (5) may be paid out of the money or other property held on trust for the person to whom the enquiry relates.

"Sell-out"

983   **Right of minority shareholder to be bought out by offeror**

(1)   Subsections (2) and (3) apply in a case where a takeover offer relates to all the shares in a company.

For this purpose a takeover offer relates to all the shares in a company if it is an offer to acquire all the shares in the company within the meaning of section 974.

(2)   The holder of any voting shares to which the offer relates who has not accepted the offer may require the offeror to acquire those shares if, at any time before the end of the period within which the offer can be accepted—

    (a)   the offeror has by virtue of acceptances of the offer acquired or unconditionally contracted to acquire some (but not all) of the shares to which the offer relates, and

    (b)   those shares, with or without any other shares in the company which he has acquired or contracted to acquire (whether unconditionally or subject to conditions being met)—

        (i)   amount to not less than 90% in value of all the voting shares in the company (or would do so but for section 990(1)), and

        (ii)   carry not less than 90% of the voting rights in the company (or would do so but for section 990(1)).

(3)   The holder of any non-voting shares to which the offer relates who has not accepted the offer may require the offeror to acquire those shares if, at any time before the end of the period within which the offer can be accepted—

    (a)   the offeror has by virtue of acceptances of the offer acquired or unconditionally contracted to acquire some (but not all) of the shares to which the offer relates, and

    (b)   those shares, with or without any other shares in the company which he has acquired or contracted to acquire (whether unconditionally or subject to conditions being met), amount to not less than 90% in value of all the shares in the company (or would do so but for section 990(1)).

(4)   If a takeover offer relates to shares of one or more classes and at any time before the end of the period within which the offer can be accepted—

    (a)   the offeror has by virtue of acceptances of the offer acquired or unconditionally contracted to acquire some (but not all) of the shares of any class to which the offer relates, and

    (b)   those shares, with or without any other shares of that class which he has acquired or contracted to acquire (whether unconditionally or subject to conditions being met)—

        (i)   amount to not less than 90% in value of all the shares of that class, and

        (ii)   in a case where the shares of that class are voting shares, carry not less than 90% of the voting rights carried by the shares of that class,

the holder of any shares of that class to which the offer relates who has not accepted the offer may require the offeror to acquire those shares.

(5)   For the purposes of subsections (2) to (4), in calculating 90% of the value of any shares, shares held by the company as treasury shares are to be treated as having been acquired by the offeror.

(6)   Subsection (7) applies where—

    (a)   a shareholder exercises rights conferred on him by subsection (2), (3) or (4),

    (b)   at the time when he does so, there are shares in the company which the offeror has contracted to acquire subject to conditions being met, and in relation to which the contract has not become unconditional, and

    (c)   the requirement imposed by subsection (2)(b), (3)(b) or (4)(b) (as the case may be) would not be satisfied if those shares were not taken into account.

(7)   The shareholder is treated for the purposes of section 985 as not having exercised his rights under this section unless the requirement imposed by paragraph (b) of subsection (2), (3) or (4) (as the case may be) would be satisfied if—

    (a)   the reference in that paragraph to other shares in the company which the offeror has contracted to acquire unconditionally or subject to conditions being met were a reference to such shares which he has unconditionally contracted to acquire, and

    (b)   the reference in that subsection to the period within which the offer can be accepted were a reference to the period referred to in section 984(2).

(8)   A reference in subsection (2)(b), (3)(b), (4)(b), (6) or (7) to shares which the offeror has acquired or contracted to acquire includes a reference to shares which an associate of his has acquired or contracted to acquire.

984   Further provision about rights conferred by section 983

(1)   Rights conferred on a shareholder by subsection (2), (3) or (4) of section 983 are exercisable by a written communication addressed to the offeror.

(2)   Rights conferred on a shareholder by subsection (2), (3) or (4) of that section are not exercisable after the end of the period of three months from—

    (a)   the end of the period within which the offer can be accepted, or

(b)   if later, the date of the notice that must be given under subsection (3) below.

(3)   Within one month of the time specified in subsection (2), (3) or (4) (as the case may be) of that section, the offeror must give any shareholder who has not accepted the offer notice in the prescribed manner of—

(a)   the rights that are exercisable by the shareholder under that subsection, and

(b)   the period within which the rights are exercisable.

If the notice is given before the end of the period within which the offer can be accepted, it must state that the offer is still open for acceptance.

(4)   Subsection (3) does not apply if the offeror has given the shareholder a notice in respect of the shares in question under section 979.

(5)   An offeror who fails to comply with subsection (3) commits an offence.

If the offeror is a company, every officer of that company who is in default or to whose neglect the failure is attributable also commits an offence.

(6)   If an offeror other than a company is charged with an offence for failing to comply with subsection (3), it is a defence for him to prove that he took all reasonable steps for securing compliance with that subsection.

(7)   A person guilty of an offence under this section is liable—

(a)   on conviction on indictment, to a fine;

(b)   on summary conviction, to a fine not exceeding the statutory maximum and, for continued contravention, a daily default fine not exceeding one-fiftieth of the greater of £5,000 or the amount corresponding to level 4 on the standard scale for summary offences.

985   Effect of requirement under section 983

(1)   Subject to section 986, this section applies where a shareholder exercises his rights under section 983 in respect of any shares held by him.

(2)   The offeror is entitled and bound to acquire those shares on the terms of the offer or on such other terms as may be agreed.

(3)   Where the terms of an offer are such as to give the shareholder a choice of consideration—

(a)   the shareholder may indicate his choice when requiring the offeror to acquire the shares, and

(b)   the notice given to the shareholder under section 984(3)—

(i)   must give particulars of the choice and of the rights conferred by this subsection, and

(ii)   may state which consideration specified in the offer will apply if he does not indicate a choice.

The reference in subsection (2) to the terms of the offer is to be read accordingly.

(4)   Subsection (3) applies whether or not any time-limit or other conditions applicable to the choice under the terms of the offer can still be complied with.

(5)   If the consideration offered to or (as the case may be) chosen by the shareholder—

(a)   is not cash and the offeror is no longer able to provide it, or

(b)   was to have been provided by a third party who is no longer bound or able to provide it,

the consideration is to be taken to consist of an amount of cash, payable by the offeror, which at the date when the shareholder requires the offeror to acquire the shares is equivalent to the consideration offered or (as the case may be) chosen.

Supplementary

986   Applications to the court

(1)   Where a notice is given under section 979 to a shareholder the court may, on an application made by him, order—

(a)   that the offeror is not entitled and bound to acquire the shares to which the notice relates, or

(b)   that the terms on which the offeror is entitled and bound to acquire the shares shall be such as the court thinks fit.

(2)   An application under subsection (1) must be made within six weeks from the date on which the notice referred to in that subsection was given.

If an application to the court under subsection (1) is pending at the end of that period, section 981(6) does not have effect until the application has been disposed of.

(3) Where a shareholder exercises his rights under section 983 in respect of any shares held by him, the court may, on an application made by him or the offeror, order that the terms on which the offeror is entitled and bound to acquire the shares shall be such as the court thinks fit.

(4) On an application under subsection (1) or (3)—

(a) the court may not require consideration of a higher value than that specified in the terms of the offer ("the offer value") to be given for the shares to which the application relates unless the holder of the shares shows that the offer value would be unfair;

(b) the court may not require consideration of a lower value than the offer value to be given for the shares.

(5) No order for costs or expenses may be made against a shareholder making an application under subsection (1) or (3) unless the court considers that—

(a) the application was unnecessary, improper or vexatious,

(b) there has been unreasonable delay in making the application, or

(c) there has been unreasonable conduct on the shareholder's part in conducting the proceedings on the application.

(6) A shareholder who has made an application under subsection (1) or (3) must give notice of the application to the offeror.

(7) An offeror who is given notice of an application under subsection (1) or (3) must give a copy of the notice to—

(a) any person (other than the applicant) to whom a notice has been given under section 979;

(b) any person who has exercised his rights under section 983.

(8) An offeror who makes an application under subsection (3) must give notice of the application to—

(a) any person to whom a notice has been given under section 979;

(b) any person who has exercised his rights under section 983.

(9) Where a takeover offer has not been accepted to the extent necessary for entitling the offeror to give notices under subsection (2) or (4) of section 979 the court may, on an application made by him, make an order authorising him to give notices under that subsection if it is satisfied that—

(a) the offeror has after reasonable enquiry been unable to trace one or more of the persons holding shares to which the offer relates,

(b) the requirements of that subsection would have been met if the person, or all the persons, mentioned in paragraph (a) above had accepted the offer, and

(c) the consideration offered is fair and reasonable.

This is subject to subsection (10).

(10) The court may not make an order under subsection (9) unless it considers that it is just and equitable to do so having regard, in particular, to the number of shareholders who have been traced but who have not accepted the offer.

987 Joint offers

(1) In the case of a takeover offer made by two or more persons jointly, this Chapter has effect as follows.

(2) The conditions for the exercise of the rights conferred by section 979 are satisfied—

(a) in the case of acquisitions by virtue of acceptances of the offer, by the joint offerors acquiring or unconditionally contracting to acquire the necessary shares jointly;

(b) in other cases, by the joint offerors acquiring or unconditionally contracting to acquire the necessary shares either jointly or separately.

(3) The conditions for the exercise of the rights conferred by section 983 are satisfied—

(a) in the case of acquisitions by virtue of acceptances of the offer, by the joint offerors acquiring or unconditionally contracting to acquire the necessary shares jointly;

(b) in other cases, by the joint offerors acquiring or contracting (whether unconditionally or subject to conditions being met) to acquire the necessary shares either jointly or separately.

(4)   Subject to the following provisions, the rights and obligations of the offeror under sections 979 to 985 are respectively joint rights and joint and several obligations of the joint offerors.

(5)   A provision of sections 979 to 986 that requires or authorises a notice or other document to be given or sent by or to the joint offerors is complied with if the notice or document is given or sent by or to any of them (but see subsection (6)).

(6)   The statutory declaration required by section 980(4) must be made by all of the joint offerors and, where one or more of them is a company, signed by a director of that company.

(7)   In sections 974 to 977, 979(9), 981(6), 983(8) and 988 references to the offeror are to be read as references to the joint offerors or any of them.

(8)   In section 981(7) and (8) references to the offeror are to be read as references to the joint offerors or such of them as they may determine.

(9)   In sections 981(5)(a) and 985(5)(a) references to the offeror being no longer able to provide the relevant consideration are to be read as references to none of the joint offerors being able to do so.

(10)   In section 986 references to the offeror are to be read as references to the joint offerors, except that—

(a)   an application under subsection (3) or (9) may be made by any of them, and

(b)   the reference in subsection (9)(a) to the offeror having been unable to trace one or more of the persons holding shares is to be read as a reference to none of the offerors having been able to do so.

Interpretation

988   Associates

(1)   In this Chapter "associate", in relation to an offeror, means—

(a)   a nominee of the offeror,

(b)   a holding company, subsidiary or fellow subsidiary of the offeror or a nominee of such a holding company, subsidiary or fellow subsidiary,

(c)   a body corporate in which the offeror is substantially interested,

(d)   a person who is, or is a nominee of, a party to a share acquisition agreement with the offeror, or

(e)   (where the offeror is an individual) his spouse or civil partner and any minor child or step-child of his.

(2)   For the purposes of subsection (1)(b) a company is a fellow subsidiary of another body corporate if both are subsidiaries of the same body corporate but neither is a subsidiary of the other.

(3)   For the purposes of subsection (1)(c) an offeror has a substantial interest in a body corporate if—

(a)   the body or its directors are accustomed to act in accordance with his directions or instructions, or

(b)   he is entitled to exercise or control the exercise of one-third or more of the voting power at general meetings of the body.

Subsections (2) and (3) of section 823 (which contain provision about when a person is treated as entitled to exercise or control the exercise of voting power) apply for the purposes of this subsection as they apply for the purposes of that section.

(4)   For the purposes of subsection (1)(d) an agreement is a share acquisition agreement if—

(a)   it is an agreement for the acquisition of, or of an interest in, shares to which the offer relates,

(b)   it includes provisions imposing obligations or restrictions on any one or more of the parties to it with respect to their use, retention or disposal of such shares, or their interests in such shares, acquired in pursuance of the agreement (whether or not together with any other shares to which the offer relates or any other interests of theirs in such shares), and

(c)   it is not an excluded agreement (see subsection (5)).

(5)   An agreement is an "excluded agreement"—

(a)   if it is not legally binding, unless it involves mutuality in the undertakings, expectations or understandings of the parties to it, or

(b) if it is an agreement to underwrite or sub-underwrite an offer of shares in a company, provided the agreement is confined to that purpose and any matters incidental to it.

(6) The reference in subsection (4)(b) to the use of interests in shares is to the exercise of any rights or of any control or influence arising from those interests (including the right to enter into an agreement for the exercise, or for control of the exercise, of any of those rights by another person).

(7) In this section—

(a) "agreement" includes any agreement or arrangement;

(b) references to provisions of an agreement include—

(i) undertakings, expectations or understandings operative under an arrangement, and

(ii) any provision whether express or implied and whether absolute or not.

989 Convertible securities

(1) For the purposes of this Chapter securities of a company are treated as shares in the company if they are convertible into or entitle the holder to subscribe for such shares.
References to the holder of shares or a shareholder are to be read accordingly.

(2) Subsection (1) is not to be read as requiring any securities to be treated—

(a) as shares of the same class as those into which they are convertible or for which the holder is entitled to subscribe, or

(b) as shares of the same class as other securities by reason only that the shares into which they are convertible or for which the holder is entitled to subscribe are of the same class.

990 Debentures carrying voting rights

(1) For the purposes of this Chapter debentures issued by a company to which subsection (2) applies are treated as shares in the company if they carry voting rights.

(2) This subsection applies to a company that has voting shares, or debentures carrying voting rights, which are admitted to trading on a regulated market.

(3) In this Chapter, in relation to debentures treated as shares by virtue of subsection (1)—

(a) references to the holder of shares or a shareholder are to be read accordingly;

(b) references to shares being allotted are to be read as references to debentures being issued.

991 Interpretation

(1) In this Chapter—

"the company" means the company whose shares are the subject of a takeover offer;

"date of the offer" means—

(a) where the offer is published, the date of publication;

(b) where the offer is not published, or where any notices of the offer are given before the date of publication, the date when notices of the offer (or the first such notices) are given;

and references to the date of the offer are to be read in accordance with section 974(7) (revision of offer terms) where that applies;

"non-voting shares" means shares that are not voting shares;

"offeror" means (subject to section 987) the person making a takeover offer;

"voting rights" means rights to vote at general meetings of the company, including rights that arise only in certain circumstances;

"voting shares" means shares carrying voting rights.

(2) For the purposes of this Chapter a person contracts unconditionally to acquire shares if his entitlement under the contract to acquire them is not (or is no longer) subject to conditions or if all conditions to which it was subject have been met.
A reference to a contract becoming unconditional is to be read accordingly.

CHAPTER 4

AMENDMENTS TO PART 7 OF THE COMPANIES ACT 1985

992   Matters to be dealt with in directors' report

(1)   Part 7 of the Companies Act 1985 (accounts and audit) is amended as follows.

(2)   In Schedule 7 (matters to be dealt with in directors' report), after Part 6 insert—

"PART 7

DISCLOSURE REQUIRED BY CERTAIN PUBLICLY-TRADED COMPANIES

13   (1)   This Part of this Schedule applies to the directors' report for a financial year if the company had securities carrying voting rights admitted to trading on a regulated market at the end of that year.

(2)   The report shall contain detailed information, by reference to the end of that year, on the following matters—

(a)   the structure of the company's capital, including in particular—

(i)   the rights and obligations attaching to the shares or, as the case may be, to each class of shares in the company, and

(ii)   where there are two or more such classes, the percentage of the total share capital represented by each class;

(b)   any restrictions on the transfer of securities in the company, including in particular—

(i)   limitations on the holding of securities, and

(ii)   requirements to obtain the approval of the company, or of other holders of securities in the company, for a transfer of securities;

(c)   in the case of each person with a significant direct or indirect holding of securities in the company, such details as are known to the company of—

(i)   the identity of the person,

(ii)   the size of the holding, and

(iii)   the nature of the holding;

(d)   in the case of each person who holds securities carrying special rights with regard to control of the company—

(i)   the identity of the person, and

(ii)   the nature of the rights;

(e)   where—

(i)   the company has an employees' share scheme, and

(ii)   shares to which the scheme relates have rights with regard to control of the company that are not exercisable directly by the employees,

how those rights are exercisable;

(f)   any restrictions on voting rights, including in particular—

(i)   limitations on voting rights of holders of a given percentage or number of votes,

(ii)   deadlines for exercising voting rights, and

(iii)   arrangements by which, with the company's co-operation, financial rights carried by securities are held by a person other than the holder of the securities;

(g)   any agreements between holders of securities that are known to the company and may result in restrictions on the transfer of securities or on voting rights;

(h)   any rules that the company has about—

(i)   appointment and replacement of directors, or

(ii)   amendment of the company's articles of association;

(i)   the powers of the company's directors, including in particular any powers in relation to the issuing or buying back by the company of its shares;

(j)   any significant agreements to which the company is a party that take effect, alter or terminate upon a change of control of the company following a takeover bid, and the effects of any such agreements;

(k)   any agreements between the company and its directors or employees providing for compensation for loss of office or employment (whether through resignation, purported redundancy or otherwise) that occurs because of a takeover bid.

(3)   For the purposes of sub-paragraph (2)(a) a company's capital includes any securities in the company that are not admitted to trading on a regulated market.

(4)   For the purposes of sub-paragraph (2)(c) a person has an indirect holding of securities if—

(a)   they are held on his behalf, or

(b)   he is able to secure that rights carried by the securities are exercised in accordance with his wishes.

(5)   Sub-paragraph (2)(j) does not apply to an agreement if—

(a)   disclosure of the agreement would be seriously prejudicial to the company, and

(b)   the company is not under any other obligation to disclose it.

(6)   In this paragraph—

"securities" means shares or debentures;

"takeover bid" has the same meaning as in the Takeovers Directive;

"the Takeovers Directive" means Directive 2004/25/EC of the European Parliament and of the Council;

"voting rights" means rights to vote at general meetings of the company in question, including rights that arise only in certain circumstances.".

(3)   In section 234ZZA (requirements of directors' reports), at the end of subsection (4) (contents of Schedule 7) insert—

"Part 7 specifies information to be disclosed by certain publicly-traded companies.".

(4)   After that subsection insert—

"(5) A directors' report shall also contain any necessary explanatory material with regard to information that is required to be included in the report by Part 7 of Schedule 7.".

(5)   In section 251 (summary financial statements), after subsection (2ZA) insert—

"(2ZB) A company that sends to an entitled person a summary financial statement instead of a copy of its directors' report shall—

(a)   include in the statement the explanatory material required to be included in the directors' report by section 234ZZA(5), or

(b)   send that material to the entitled person at the same time as it sends the statement.

For the purposes of paragraph (b), subsections (2A) to (2E) apply in relation to the material referred to in that paragraph as they apply in relation to a summary financial statement.".

(6)   The amendments made by this section apply in relation to directors' reports for financial years beginning on or after 20th May 2006.

PART 29
FRAUDULENT TRADING

993   Offence of fraudulent trading

(1)   If any business of a company is carried on with intent to defraud creditors of the company or creditors of any other person, or for any fraudulent purpose, every person who is knowingly a party to the carrying on of the business in that manner commits an offence.

(2)   This applies whether or not the company has been, or is in the course of being, wound up.

(3)   A person guilty of an offence under this section is liable—

(a)   on conviction on indictment, to imprisonment for a term not exceeding ten years or a fine (or both);

(b)   on summary conviction—

(i)   in England and Wales, to imprisonment for a term not exceeding twelve months or a fine not exceeding the statutory maximum (or both);

(ii)   in Scotland or Northern Ireland, to imprisonment for a term not exceeding six months or a fine not exceeding the statutory maximum (or both).

PART 30
PROTECTION OF MEMBERS AGAINST UNFAIR PREJUDICE

Main provisions

994   Petition by company member

(1)   A member of a company may apply to the court by petition for an order under this Part on the ground—

(a)   that the company's affairs are being or have been conducted in a manner that is unfairly prejudicial to the interests of members generally or of some part of its members (including at least himself), or

(b)   that an actual or proposed act or omission of the company (including an act or omission on its behalf) is or would be so prejudicial.

(1A)   For the purposes of subsection (1)(a), a removal of the company's auditor from office—

(a)   on grounds of divergence of opinions on accounting treatments or audit procedures, or

(b)   on any other improper grounds,

shall be treated as being unfairly prejudicial to the interests of some part of the company's members.

(2)   The provisions of this Part apply to a person who is not a member of a company but to whom shares in the company have been transferred or transmitted by operation of law as they apply to a member of a company.

(3)   In this section, and so far as applicable for the purposes of this section in the other provisions of this Part, "company" means—

(a)   a company within the meaning of this Act, ...

(b)   ...

995   Petition by Secretary of State

(1)   This section applies to a company in respect of which—

(a)   the Secretary of State has received a report under section 437 of the Companies Act 1985 (inspector's report);

(b)   the Secretary of State has exercised his powers under section 447 or 448 of that Act (powers to require documents and information or to enter and search premises);

(c)   the Secretary of State, the Financial Conduct Authority, the Prudential Regulation Authority or the Bank of England has exercised his or its powers under Part 11 of the Financial Services and Markets Act 2000 (information gathering and investigations); or

(d)   the Secretary of State has received a report from an investigator appointed by him, the Financial Conduct Authority, the Prudential Regulation Authority or the Bank of England under that Part.

(2)   If it appears to the Secretary of State that in the case of such a company—

(a)   the company's affairs are being or have been conducted in a manner that is unfairly prejudicial to the interests of members generally or of some part of its members, or

(b)   an actual or proposed act or omission of the company (including an act or omission on its behalf) is or would be so prejudicial,

he may apply to the court by petition for an order under this Part.

(3)   The Secretary of State may do this in addition to, or instead of, presenting a petition for the winding up of the company.

(4)   In this section, and so far as applicable for the purposes of this section in the other provisions of this Part, "company" means any body corporate that is liable to be wound up under the Insolvency Act 1986 or the Insolvency (Northern Ireland) Order 1989.

996   Powers of the court under this Part

(1)   If the court is satisfied that a petition under this Part is well founded, it may make such order as it thinks fit for giving relief in respect of the matters complained of.

(2)   Without prejudice to the generality of subsection (1), the court's order may—

    (a)   regulate the conduct of the company's affairs in the future;

    (b)   require the company—

        (i)   to refrain from doing or continuing an act complained of, or

        (ii)   to do an act that the petitioner has complained it has omitted to do;

    (c)   authorise civil proceedings to be brought in the name and on behalf of the company by such person or persons and on such terms as the court may direct;

    (d)   require the company not to make any, or any specified, alterations in its articles without the leave of the court;

    (e)   provide for the purchase of the shares of any members of the company by other members or by the company itself and, in the case of a purchase by the company itself, the reduction of the company's capital accordingly.

Supplementary provisions

997   Application of general rule-making powers

The power to make rules under section 411 of the Insolvency Act 1986 or Article 359 of the Insolvency (Northern Ireland) Order 1989, so far as relating to a winding-up petition, applies for the purposes of a petition under this Part.

998   Copy of order affecting company's constitution to be delivered to registrar

(1)   Where an order of the court under this Part—

    (a)   alters the company's constitution, or

    (b)   gives leave for the company to make any, or any specified, alterations to its constitution,

the company must deliver a copy of the order to the registrar.

(2)   It must do so within 14 days from the making of the order or such longer period as the court may allow.

(3)   If a company makes default in complying with this section, an offence is committed by—

    (a)   the company, and

    (b)   every officer of the company who is in default.

(4)   A person guilty of an offence under this section is liable on summary conviction to a fine not exceeding level 3 on the standard scale and, for continued contravention, a daily default fine not exceeding one-tenth of level 3 on the standard scale.

999   Supplementary provisions where company's constitution altered

(1)   This section applies where an order under this Part alters a company's constitution.

(2)   If the order amends—

    (a)   a company's articles, or

    (b)   any resolution or agreement to which Chapter 3 of Part 3 applies (resolution or agreement affecting a company's constitution),

the copy of the order delivered to the registrar by the company under section 998 must be accompanied by a copy of the company's articles, or the resolution or agreement in question, as amended.

(3)   Every copy of a company's articles issued by the company after the order is made must be accompanied by a copy of the order, unless the effect of the order has been incorporated into the articles by amendment.

(4)   If a company makes default in complying with this section an offence is committed by—

(a)   the company, and

(b)   every officer of the company who is in default.

(5)   A person guilty of an offence under this section is liable on summary conviction to a fine not exceeding level 3 on the standard scale.

PART 31

DISSOLUTION AND RESTORATION TO THE REGISTER

CHAPTER 1

STRIKING OFF

Registrar's power to strike off defunct company

1000   Power to strike off company not carrying on business or in operation

(1)   If the registrar has reasonable cause to believe that a company is not carrying on business or in operation, the registrar may send to the company a communication inquiring whether the company is carrying on business or in operation.

(2)   If the registrar does not within 14 days of sending the communication receive any answer to it, the registrar must within 14 days after the expiration of that period send to the company a second communication referring to the first communication, and stating—

(a)   that no answer to it has been received, and

(b)   that if an answer is not received to the second communication within 14 days from its date, a notice will be published in the Gazette with a view to striking the company's name off the register.

(3)   If the registrar—

(a)   receives an answer to the effect that the company is not carrying on business or in operation, or

(b)   does not within 14 days after sending the second communication receive any answer,

the registrar may publish in the Gazette, and send to the company ..., a notice that at the expiration of 2 months from the date of the notice the name of the company mentioned in it will, unless cause is shown to the contrary, be struck off the register and the company will be dissolved.

(4)   At the expiration of the time mentioned in the notice the registrar may, unless cause to the contrary is previously shown by the company, strike its name off the register.

(5)   The registrar must publish notice in the Gazette of the company's name having been struck off the register.

(6)   On the publication of the notice in the Gazette the company is dissolved.

(7)   However—

(a)   the liability (if any) of every director, managing officer and member of the company continues and may be enforced as if the company had not been dissolved, and

(b)   nothing in this section affects the power of the court to wind up a company the name of which has been struck off the register.

1001   Duty to act in case of company being wound up

(1)   If, in a case where a company is being wound up—

(a)   the registrar has reasonable cause to believe—

(i)   that no liquidator is acting, or

(ii)   that the affairs of the company are fully wound up, and

(b)   the returns required to be made by the liquidator have not been made for a period of six consecutive months,

the registrar must publish in the Gazette and send to the company or the liquidator (if any) a notice that at the expiration of 2 months from the date of the notice the name of the company mentioned in it will, unless cause is shown to the contrary, be struck off the register and the company will be dissolved.

(2) At the expiration of the time mentioned in the notice the registrar may, unless cause to the contrary is previously shown by the company, strike its name off the register.

(3) The registrar must publish notice in the Gazette of the company's name having been struck off the register.

(4) On the publication of the notice in the Gazette the company is dissolved.

(5) However—

 (a) the liability (if any) of every director, managing officer and member of the company continues and may be enforced as if the company had not been dissolved, and

 (b) nothing in this section affects the power of the court to wind up a company the name of which has been struck off the register.

1002 Supplementary provisions as to service of communication or notice

(1) If the registrar is not able to send a communication or notice under section 1000 or 1001 to a company in accordance with Schedule 4, the communication may be sent to an officer of the company at an address for that officer that has been notified to the registrar by the company.

(2) If there is no officer of the company whose name and address are known to the registrar, the communication or notice may be sent to each of the persons who subscribed the memorandum (if their addresses are known to the registrar).

(3) A notice to be sent to a liquidator under section 1001 may be sent to the address of the liquidator's last known place of business or to an address specified by the liquidator to the registrar for the purpose of receiving notices, or notices of that kind.

(4) In this section "address" has the same meaning as in section 1148(1).

Voluntary striking off

1003 Striking off on application by company

(1) On application by a company, the registrar of companies may strike the company's name off the register.

(2) The application—

 (a) must be made on the company's behalf by its directors or by a majority of them, and

 (b) must contain the prescribed information.

(3) The registrar may not strike a company off under this section until after the expiration of 2 months from the publication by the registrar in the Gazette of a notice—

 (a) stating that the registrar may exercise the power under this section in relation to the company, and

 (b) inviting any person to show cause why that should not be done.

(4) The registrar must publish notice in the Gazette of the company's name having been struck off.

(5) On the publication of the notice in the Gazette the company is dissolved.

(6) However—

 (a) the liability (if any) of every director, managing officer and member of the company continues and may be enforced as if the company had not been dissolved, and

 (b) nothing in this section affects the power of the court to wind up a company the name of which has been struck off the register.

1004 Circumstances in which application not to be made: activities of company

(1) An application under section 1003 (application for voluntary striking off) on behalf of a company must not be made if, at any time in the previous three months, the company has—

 (a) changed its name,

 (b) traded or otherwise carried on business,

 (c) made a disposal for value of property or rights that, immediately before ceasing to trade or otherwise carry on business, it held for the purpose of disposal for gain in the normal course of trading or otherwise carrying on business, or

 (d) engaged in any other activity, except one which is—

        (i)   necessary or expedient for the purpose of making an application under that section, or deciding whether to do so,

        (ii)   necessary or expedient for the purpose of concluding the affairs of the company,

        (iii)   necessary or expedient for the purpose of complying with any statutory requirement, or

        (iv)   specified by the Secretary of State by order for the purposes of this sub-paragraph.

(2)   For the purposes of this section, a company is not to be treated as trading or otherwise carrying on business by virtue only of the fact that it makes a payment in respect of a liability incurred in the course of trading or otherwise carrying on business.

(3)   The Secretary of State may by order amend subsection (1) for the purpose of altering the period in relation to which the doing of the things mentioned in paragraphs (a) to (d) of that subsection is relevant.

(4)   An order under this section is subject to negative resolution procedure.

(5)   It is an offence for a person to make an application in contravention of this section.

(6)   In proceedings for such an offence it is a defence for the accused to prove that he did not know, and could not reasonably have known, of the existence of the facts that led to the contravention.

(7)   A person guilty of an offence under this section is liable—

     (a)   on conviction on indictment, to a fine;

     (b)   on summary conviction, to a fine not exceeding the statutory maximum.

1005   Circumstances in which application not to be made: other proceedings not concluded

(1)   An application under section 1003 (application for voluntary striking off) on behalf of a company must not be made at a time when—

     (a)   an application to the court under Part 26 or 26A has been made on behalf of the company for the sanctioning of a compromise or arrangement and the matter has not been finally concluded;

     (b)   a voluntary arrangement in relation to the company has been proposed under Part 1 of the Insolvency Act 1986 or Part 2 of the Insolvency (Northern Ireland) Order 1989 and the matter has not been finally concluded;

     (c)   the company is in administration under Part 2 of that Act or Part 3 of that Order;

     (d)   paragraph 44 of Schedule B1 to that Act or paragraph 45 of Schedule B1 to that Order applies (interim moratorium on proceedings where application to the court for an administration order has been made or notice of intention to appoint administrator has been filed);

     (e)   the company is being wound up under Part 4 of that Act or Part 5 of that Order, whether voluntarily or by the court, or a petition under that Part for winding up of the company by the court has been presented and not finally dealt with or withdrawn;

     (f)   there is a receiver or manager of the company's property;

     (g)   the company's estate is being administered by a judicial factor.

(2)   For the purposes of subsection (1)(a), the matter is finally concluded if—

     (a)   the application has been withdrawn,

     (b)   the application has been finally dealt with without a compromise or arrangement being sanctioned by the court, or

     (c)   a compromise or arrangement has been sanctioned by the court and has, together with anything required to be done under any provision made in relation to the matter by order of the court, been fully carried out.

(3)   For the purposes of subsection (1)(b), the matter is finally concluded if—

     (a)   no meetings are to be summoned under section 3 of the Insolvency Act 1986 or Article 16 of the Insolvency (Northern Ireland) Order 1989,

     (b)   meetings summoned under that section or Article fail to approve the arrangement with no, or the same, modifications,

(c)   an arrangement approved by meetings summoned under that section, or in consequence of a direction under section 6(4)(b) of that Act or Article 19(4)(b) of that Order, has been fully implemented, or

(d)   the court makes an order under section 6(5) of that Act or Article 19(5) of that Order revoking approval given at previous meetings and, if the court gives any directions under section 6(6) of that Act or Article 19(6) of that Order, the company has done whatever it is required to do under those directions.

(4)   It is an offence for a person to make an application in contravention of this section.

(5)   In proceedings for such an offence it is a defence for the accused to prove that he did not know, and could not reasonably have known, of the existence of the facts that led to the contravention.

(6)   A person guilty of an offence under this section is liable—

(a)   on conviction on indictment, to a fine;

(b)   on summary conviction, to a fine not exceeding the statutory maximum.

1006   Copy of application to be given to members, employees, etc

(1)   A person who makes an application under section 1003 (application for voluntary striking off) on behalf of a company must secure that, within seven days from the day on which the application is made, a copy of it is given to every person who at any time on that day is—

(a)   a member of the company,

(b)   an employee of the company,

(c)   a creditor of the company,

(d)   a director of the company,

(e)   a manager or trustee of any pension fund established for the benefit of employees of the company, or

(f)   a person of a description specified for the purposes of this paragraph by regulations made by the Secretary of State.

Regulations under paragraph (f) are subject to negative resolution procedure.

(2)   Subsection (1) does not require a copy of the application to be given to a director who is a party to the application.

(3)   The duty imposed by this section ceases to apply if the application is withdrawn before the end of the period for giving the copy application.

(4)   A person who fails to perform the duty imposed on him by this section commits an offence.

If he does so with the intention of concealing the making of the application from the person concerned, he commits an aggravated offence.

(5)   In proceedings for an offence under this section it is a defence for the accused to prove that he took all reasonable steps to perform the duty.

(6)   A person guilty of an offence under this section (other than an aggravated offence) is liable—

(a)   on conviction on indictment, to a fine;

(b)   on summary conviction, to a fine not exceeding the statutory maximum.

(7)   A person guilty of an aggravated offence under this section is liable—

(a)   on conviction on indictment, to imprisonment for a term not exceeding seven years or a fine (or both);

(b)   on summary conviction—

(i)   in England and Wales, to imprisonment for a term not exceeding twelve months or to a fine not exceeding the statutory maximum (or both);

(ii)   in Scotland or Northern Ireland, to imprisonment for a term not exceeding six months, or to a fine not exceeding the statutory maximum (or both).

1007   Copy of application to be given to new members, employees, etc

(1)   This section applies in relation to any time after the day on which a company makes an application under section 1003 (application for voluntary striking off) and before the day on which the application is finally dealt with or withdrawn.

(2)   A person who is a director of the company at the end of a day on which a person (other than himself) becomes—

    (a)   a member of the company,

    (b)   an employee of the company,

    (c)   a creditor of the company,

    (d)   a director of the company,

    (e)   a manager or trustee of any pension fund established for the benefit of employees of the company, or

    (f)   a person of a description specified for the purposes of this paragraph by regulations made by the Secretary of State,

must secure that a copy of the application is given to that person within seven days from that day. Regulations under paragraph (f) are subject to negative resolution procedure.

(3)   The duty imposed by this section ceases to apply if the application is finally dealt with or withdrawn before the end of the period for giving the copy application.

(4)   A person who fails to perform the duty imposed on him by this section commits an offence.

        If he does so with the intention of concealing the making of the application from the person concerned, he commits an aggravated offence.

(5)   In proceedings for an offence under this section it is a defence for the accused to prove—

    (a)   that at the time of the failure he was not aware of the fact that the company had made an application under section 1003, or

    (b)   that he took all reasonable steps to perform the duty.

(6)   A person guilty of an offence under this section (other than an aggravated offence) is liable—

    (a)   on conviction on indictment, to a fine;

    (b)   on summary conviction, to a fine not exceeding the statutory maximum.

(7)   A person guilty of an aggravated offence under this section is liable—

    (a)   on conviction on indictment, to imprisonment for a term not exceeding seven years or a fine (or both);

    (b)   on summary conviction—

        (i)   in England and Wales, to imprisonment for a term not exceeding twelve months or to a fine not exceeding the statutory maximum (or both);

        (ii)   in Scotland or Northern Ireland, to imprisonment for a term not exceeding six months, or to a fine not exceeding the statutory maximum (or both).

1008   Copy of application: provisions as to service of documents

(1)   The following provisions have effect for the purposes of—

        section 1006 (copy of application to be given to members, employees, etc), and

        section 1007 (copy of application to be given to new members, employees, etc).

(2)   A document is treated as given to a person if it is—

    (a)   delivered to him, or

    (b)   left at his proper address, or

    (c)   sent by post to him at that address.

(3)   For the purposes of subsection (2) and section 7 of the Interpretation Act 1978 (service of documents by post) as it applies in relation to that subsection, the proper address of a person is—

    (a)   in the case of a firm incorporated or formed in the United Kingdom, its registered or principal office;

    (b)   in the case of a firm incorporated or formed outside the United Kingdom—

        (i)   if it has a place of business in the United Kingdom, its principal office in the United Kingdom, or

        (ii)   if it does not have a place of business in the United Kingdom, its registered or principal office;

    (c)   in the case of an individual, his last known address.

(4)   In the case of a creditor of the company a document is treated as given to him if it is left or sent by post to him—

(a)   at the place of business of his with which the company has had dealings by virtue of which he is a creditor of the company, or

(b)   if there is more than one such place of business, at each of them.

1009   Circumstances in which application to be withdrawn

(1)   This section applies where, at any time on or after the day on which a company makes an application under section 1003 (application for voluntary striking off) and before the day on which the application is finally dealt with or withdrawn—

    (a)   the company—

        (i)   changes its name,

        (ii)   trades or otherwise carries on business,

        (iii)   makes a disposal for value of any property or rights other than those which it was necessary or expedient for it to hold for the purpose of making, or proceeding with, an application under that section, or

        (iv)   engages in any activity, except one to which subsection (4) applies;

    (b)   an application is made to the court under Part 26 or 26A on behalf of the company for the sanctioning of a compromise or arrangement;

    (c)   a voluntary arrangement in relation to the company is proposed under Part 1 of the Insolvency Act 1986 or Part 2 of the Insolvency (Northern Ireland) Order 1989;

    (d)   an application to the court for an administration order in respect of the company is made under paragraph 12 of Schedule B1 to that Act or paragraph 13 of Schedule B1 to that Order;

    (e)   an administrator is appointed in respect of the company under paragraph 14 or 22 of Schedule B1 to that Act or paragraph 15 or 23 of Schedule B1 to that Order, or a copy of notice of intention to appoint an administrator of the company under any of those provisions is filed with the court;

    (f)   there arise any of the circumstances in which, under section 84(1) of that Act or Article 70 of that Order, the company may be voluntarily wound up;

    (g)   a petition is presented for the winding up of the company by the court under Part 4 of that Act or Part 5 of that Order;

    (h)   a receiver or manager of the company's property is appointed; or

    (i)   a judicial factor is appointed to administer the company's estate.

(2)   A person who, at the end of a day on which any of the events mentioned in subsection (1) occurs, is a director of the company must secure that the company's application is withdrawn forthwith.

(3)   For the purposes of subsection (1)(a), a company is not treated as trading or otherwise carrying on business by virtue only of the fact that it makes a payment in respect of a liability incurred in the course of trading or otherwise carrying on business.

(4)   The excepted activities referred to in subsection (1)(a)(iv) are—

    (a)   any activity necessary or expedient for the purposes of—

        (i)   making, or proceeding with, an application under section 1003 (application for voluntary striking off),

        (ii)   concluding affairs of the company that are outstanding because of what has been necessary or expedient for the purpose of making, or proceeding with, such an application, or

        (iii)   complying with any statutory requirement;

    (b)   any activity specified by the Secretary of State by order for the purposes of this subsection.

    An order under paragraph (b) is subject to negative resolution procedure.

(5)   A person who fails to perform the duty imposed on him by this section commits an offence.

(6)   In proceedings for an offence under this section it is a defence for the accused to prove—

    (a)   that at the time of the failure he was not aware of the fact that the company had made an application under section 1003, or

    (b)   that he took all reasonable steps to perform the duty.

(7)   A person guilty of an offence under this section is liable—

    (a)   on conviction on indictment, to a fine;

    (b)   on summary conviction, to a fine not exceeding the statutory maximum.

1010   Withdrawal of application

An application under section 1003 is withdrawn by notice to the registrar.

1011   Meaning of "creditor"

In this Chapter "creditor" includes a contingent or prospective creditor.

CHAPTER 2
PROPERTY OF DISSOLVED COMPANY

Property vesting as bona vacantia

1012   Property of dissolved company to be bona vacantia

(1)   When a company is dissolved, all property and rights whatsoever vested in or held on trust for the company immediately before its dissolution (including leasehold property, but not including property held by the company on trust for another person) are deemed to be *bona vacantia* and—

    (a)   accordingly belong to the Crown, or to the Duchy of Lancaster or to the Duke of Cornwall for the time being (as the case may be), and

    (b)   vest and may be dealt with in the same manner as other *bona vacantia* accruing to the Crown, to the Duchy of Lancaster or to the Duke of Cornwall.

(2)   Subsection (1) has effect subject to the possible restoration of the company to the register under Chapter 3 (see section 1034).

1013   Crown disclaimer of property vesting as bona vacantia

(1)   Where property vests in the Crown under section 1012, the Crown's title to it under that section may be disclaimed by a notice signed by the Crown representative, that is to say the Treasury Solicitor, or, in relation to property in Scotland, the Queen's and Lord Treasurer's Remembrancer.

(2)   The right to execute a notice of disclaimer under this section may be waived by or on behalf of the Crown either expressly or by taking possession.

(3)   A notice of disclaimer must be executed within three years after—

    (a)   the date on which the fact that the property may have vested in the Crown under section 1012 first comes to the notice of the Crown representative, or

    (b)   if ownership of the property is not established at that date, the end of the period reasonably necessary for the Crown representative to establish the ownership of the property.

(4)   If an application in writing is made to the Crown representative by a person interested in the property requiring him to decide whether he will or will not disclaim, any notice of disclaimer must be executed within twelve months after the making of the application or such further period as may be allowed by the court.

(5)   A notice of disclaimer under this section is of no effect if it is shown to have been executed after the end of the period specified by subsection (3) or (4).

(6)   A notice of disclaimer under this section must be delivered to the registrar and retained and registered by him.

(7)   Copies of it must be published in the Gazette and sent to any persons who have given the Crown representative notice that they claim to be interested in the property.

(8)   This section applies to property vested in the Duchy of Lancaster or the Duke of Cornwall under section 1012 as if for references to the Crown and the Crown representative there were respectively substituted references to the Duchy of Lancaster and to the Solicitor to that Duchy, or to the Duke of Cornwall and to the Solicitor to the Duchy of Cornwall, as the case may be.

1014   Effect of Crown disclaimer

(1)   Where notice of disclaimer is executed under section 1013 as respects any property, that property is deemed not to have vested in the Crown under section 1012.

(2)   The following sections contain provisions as to the effect of the Crown disclaimer—
        sections 1015 to 1019 apply in relation to property in England and Wales or Northern Ireland;
        sections 1020 to 1022 apply in relation to property in Scotland.

Effect of Crown disclaimer: England and Wales and Northern Ireland

1015   General effect of disclaimer

(1)   The Crown's disclaimer operates so as to terminate, as from the date of the disclaimer, the rights, interests and liabilities of the company in or in respect of the property disclaimed.

(2)   It does not, except so far as is necessary for the purpose of releasing the company from any liability, affect the rights or liabilities of any other person.

1016   Disclaimer of leaseholds

(1)   The disclaimer of any property of a leasehold character does not take effect unless a copy of the disclaimer has been served (so far as the Crown representative is aware of their addresses) on every person claiming under the company as underlessee or mortgagee, and either—
        (a)   no application under section 1017 (power of court to make vesting order) is made with respect to that property before the end of the period of 14 days beginning with the day on which the last notice under this paragraph was served, or
        (b)   where such an application has been made, the court directs that the disclaimer shall take effect.

(2)   Where the court gives a direction under subsection (1)(b) it may also, instead of or in addition to any order it makes under section 1017, make such order as it thinks fit with respect to fixtures, tenant's improvements and other matters arising out of the lease.

(3)   In this section the "Crown representative" means—
        (a)   in relation to property vested in the Duchy of Lancaster, the Solicitor to that Duchy;
        (b)   in relation to property vested in the Duke of Cornwall, the Solicitor to the Duchy of Cornwall;
        (c)   in relation to property in Scotland, the Queen's and Lord Treasurer's Remembrancer;
        (d)   in relation to other property, the Treasury Solicitor.

1017   Power of court to make vesting order

(1)   The court may on application by a person who—
        (a)   claims an interest in the disclaimed property, or
        (b)   is under a liability in respect of the disclaimed property that is not discharged by the disclaimer,
        make an order under this section in respect of the property.

(2)   An order under this section is an order for the vesting of the disclaimed property in, or its delivery to—
        (a)   a person entitled to it (or a trustee for such a person), or
        (b)   a person subject to such a liability as is mentioned in subsection (1)(b) (or a trustee for such a person).

(3)   An order under subsection (2)(b) may only be made where it appears to the court that it would be just to do so for the purpose of compensating the person subject to the liability in respect of the disclaimer.

(4)   An order under this section may be made on such terms as the court thinks fit.

(5)   On a vesting order being made under this section, the property comprised in it vests in the person named in that behalf in the order without conveyance, assignment or transfer.

1018   Protection of persons holding under a lease

(1)   The court must not make an order under section 1017 vesting property of a leasehold nature in a person claiming under the company as underlessee or mortgagee except on terms making that person—

(a)   subject to the same liabilities and obligations as those to which the company was subject under the lease, or

(b)   if the court thinks fit, subject to the same liabilities and obligations as if the lease had been assigned to him.

(2)   Where the order relates to only part of the property comprised in the lease, subsection (1) applies as if the lease had comprised only the property comprised in the vesting order.

(3)   A person claiming under the company as underlessee or mortgagee who declines to accept a vesting order on such terms is excluded from all interest in the property.

(4)   If there is no person claiming under the company who is willing to accept an order on such terms, the court has power to vest the company's estate and interest in the property in any person who is liable (whether personally or in a representative character, and whether alone or jointly with the company) to perform the lessee's covenants in the lease.

(5)   The court may vest that estate and interest in such a person freed and discharged from all estates, incumbrances and interests created by the company.

1019   Land subject to rentcharge

Where in consequence of the disclaimer land that is subject to a rentcharge vests in any person, neither he nor his successors in title are subject to any personal liability in respect of sums becoming due under the rentcharge, except sums becoming due after he, or some person claiming under or through him, has taken possession or control of the land or has entered into occupation of it.

Effect of Crown disclaimer: Scotland

1020   General effect of disclaimer

(1)   The Crown's disclaimer operates to determine, as from the date of the disclaimer, the rights, interests and liabilities of the company, and the property of the company, in or in respect of the property disclaimed.

(2)   It does not (except so far as is necessary for the purpose of releasing the company and its property from liability) affect the rights or liabilities of any other person.

1021   Power of court to make vesting order

(1)   The court may—

(a)   on application by a person who either claims an interest in disclaimed property or is under a liability not discharged by this Act in respect of disclaimed property, and

(b)   on hearing such persons as it thinks fit,

make an order for the vesting of the property in or its delivery to any persons entitled to it, or to whom it may seem just that the property should be delivered by way of compensation for such liability, or a trustee for him.

(2)   The order may be made on such terms as the court thinks fit.

(3)   On a vesting order being made under this section, the property comprised in it vests accordingly in the person named in that behalf in the order, without conveyance or assignation for that purpose.

1022   Protection of persons holding under a lease

(1)   Where the property disclaimed is held under a lease the court must not make a vesting order in favour of a person claiming under the company, whether—

(a)   as sub-lessee, or

(b)   as creditor in a duly registered or (as the case may be) recorded heritable security over a lease,

except on the following terms.

(2)   The person must by the order be made subject—

(a)   to the same liabilities and obligations as those to which the company was subject under the lease in respect of the property, or

(b)   if the court thinks fit, only to the same liabilities and obligations as if the lease had been assigned to him.

In either event (if the case so requires) the liabilities and obligations must be as if the lease had comprised only the property comprised in the vesting order.

(3)   A sub-lessee or creditor declining to accept a vesting order on such terms is excluded from all interest in and security over the property.

(4)   If there is no person claiming under the company who is willing to accept an order on such terms, the court has power to vest the company's estate and interest in the property in any person liable (either personally or in a representative character, and either alone or jointly with the company) to perform the lessee's obligations under the lease.

(5)   The court may vest that estate and interest in such a person freed and discharged from all interests, rights and obligations created by the company in the lease or in relation to the lease.

(6)   For the purposes of this section a heritable security—

(a)   is duly recorded if it is recorded in the Register of Sasines, and

(b)   is duly registered if registered in accordance with the Land Registration etc (Scotland) Act 2012 (asp 5)

Supplementary provisions

1023   Liability for rentcharge on company's land after dissolution

(1)   This section applies where on the dissolution of a company land in England and Wales or Northern Ireland that is subject to a rentcharge vests by operation of law in the Crown or any other person ("the proprietor").

(2)   Neither the proprietor nor his successors in title are subject to any personal liability in respect of sums becoming due under the rentcharge, except sums becoming due after the proprietor, or some person claiming under or through him, has taken possession or control of the land or has entered into occupation of it.

(3)   In this section "company" includes any body corporate.

CHAPTER 3
RESTORATION TO THE REGISTER

Administrative restoration to the register

1024   Application for administrative restoration to the register

(1)   An application may be made to the registrar to restore to the register a company that has been struck off the register under section 1000 or 1001 (power of registrar to strike off defunct company).

(2)   An application under this section may be made whether or not the company has in consequence been dissolved.

(3)   An application under this section may only be made by a former director or former member of the company.

(4)   An application under this section may not be made after the end of the period of six years from the date of the dissolution of the company.

For this purpose an application is made when it is received by the registrar.

1025   Requirements for administrative restoration

(1)   On an application under section 1024 the registrar shall restore the company to the register if, and only if, the following conditions are met.

(2)   The first condition is that the company was carrying on business or in operation at the time of its striking off.

(3)   The second condition is that, if any property or right previously vested in or held on trust for the company has vested as *bona vacantia,* the Crown representative has signified to the registrar in writing consent to the company's restoration to the register.

(4)   It is the applicant's responsibility to obtain that consent and to pay any costs (in Scotland, expenses) of the Crown representative—
         (a)   in dealing with the property during the period of dissolution, or
         (b)   in connection with the proceedings on the application,
         that may be demanded as a condition of giving consent.

(5)   The third condition is that the applicant has delivered to the registrar such documents relating to the company as are necessary to ensure that if the company is restored to the register the records kept by the registrar relating to the company will be up to date.

(5A)   The fourth condition is—
         (a)   that any outstanding penalties under section 453 or corresponding earlier provisions (civil penalty for failure to deliver accounts) in relation to the company have been paid, and
         (b)   that each relevant person has paid any outstanding fines or financial penalties imposed on them in respect of an offence under the Companies Acts relating to the company.

(5B)   In subsection (5A)(b) "relevant person" means—
         (a)   the applicant,
         (b)   any person who—
               (i)   was a director of the company immediately before it was dissolved or struck off, and
               (ii)   if the company is restored to the register, will be a director immediately after its restoration, or
         (c)   any person who is a relevant officer of a firm where the firm is—
               (i)   a person mentioned in paragraph (a) or (b), or
               (ii)   a person falling within this paragraph.

(5C)   In subsection (5B)(c) "relevant officer"—
         (a)   in relation to a company, means a director;
         (b)   in relation to a firm the affairs of which are managed by its members, means one of those members;
         (c)   in relation to any other firm, means an officer of the firm whose functions correspond to that of a director of a company.

(6)   In this section the "Crown representative" means—
         (a)   in relation to property vested in the Duchy of Lancaster, the Solicitor to that Duchy;
         (b)   in relation to property vested in the Duke of Cornwall, the Solicitor to the Duchy of Cornwall;
         (c)   in relation to property in Scotland, the Queen's and Lord Treasurer's Remembrancer;
         (d)   in relation to other property, the Treasury Solicitor.

1026   Application to be accompanied by statement of compliance

(1)   An application under section 1024 (application for administrative restoration to the register) must be accompanied by a statement of compliance.

(2)   The statement of compliance required is a statement—
         (a)   that the person making the application has standing to apply (see subsection (3) of that section), and
         (b)   that the requirements for administrative restoration (see section 1025) are met.

(3)   The registrar may accept the statement of compliance as sufficient evidence of those matters.

1027   Registrar's decision on application for administrative restoration

(1)   The registrar must give notice to the applicant of the decision on an application under section 1024 (application for administrative restoration to the register).

(2)   If the decision is that the company should be restored to the register, the restoration takes effect as from the date that notice is sent.

(3)   In the case of such a decision, the registrar must—
         (a)   enter on the register a note of the date as from which the company's restoration to the register takes effect, and

    (b)   cause notice of the restoration to be published in the Gazette.

(4)   The notice under subsection (3)(b) must state—

    (a)   the name of the company or, if the company is restored to the register under a different name (see section 1033), that name and its former name,

    (b)   the company's registered number, and

    (c)   the date as from which the restoration of the company to the register takes effect.

1028 Effect of administrative restoration

(1)   The general effect of administrative restoration to the register is that the company is deemed to have continued in existence as if it had not been dissolved or struck off the register.

(2)   The company is not liable to a penalty under section 453 or any corresponding earlier provision (civil penalty for failure to deliver accounts) for a financial year in relation to which the period for filing accounts and reports ended—

    (a)   after the date of dissolution or striking off, and

    (b)   before the restoration of the company to the register.

(3)   The court may give such directions and make such provision as seems just for placing the company and all other persons in the same position (as nearly as may be) as if the company had not been dissolved or struck off the register.

(4)   An application to the court for such directions or provision may be made any time within three years after the date of restoration of the company to the register.

Restoration to the register by the court

1028A Administrative restoration of company with share warrants

(1)   This section applies in relation to a company which has been struck off the register under section 1000 or 1001 and which, at the time it was struck off, had any share warrant in issue.

(2)   If the registrar restores the company to the register under section 1025, the share warrant and the shares specified in it are cancelled with effect from the date the restoration takes effect.

(3)   If as a result of subsection (2) the company has no issued share capital, the company must, before the end of the period of one month beginning with the date the restoration takes effect, allot at least one share in the company; and section 549(1) does not apply to such an allotment.

(4)   The company must, before the end of the period of 15 days beginning with the date the restoration takes effect, deliver a statement of capital to the registrar.

(5)   Subsection (4) does not apply in a case where the company is required under subsection (3) to make an allotment (because in such a case section 555 will apply).

(6)   The statement of capital must state with respect to the company's share capital as reduced by the cancellation of the share warrant and the shares specified in it—

    (a)   the total number of shares of the company,

    (b)   the aggregate nominal value of those shares,

    (c)   the aggregate amount (if any) unpaid on those shares (whether on account of their nominal value or by way of premium), and

    (d)   for each class of shares—

        (i)   prescribed particulars of the rights attached to the shares,

        (ii)   the total number of shares of that class, and

        (iii)   the aggregate nominal value of shares of that class.

(7)   Where a share warrant is cancelled in accordance with subsection (2), the company must, as soon as reasonably practicable—

    (a)   enter the date the cancellation takes effect in its register of members, or

    (b)   where an election is in force under section 128B of the Companies Act 2006 (option to keep membership information on central register) in respect of the company, deliver that information to the registrar as if it were information required to be delivered under section 128E of that Act.

(8)   Subsection (9) applies where—

(a)   any property or right previously vested in or held on trust for the company in respect of any share specified in a share warrant has vested as bona vacantia (see section 1012), and

(b)   the warrant and the share are cancelled on the restoration of the company in accordance with this section.

(9)   On restoration of the company, that property or right—

(a)   may not be returned to the company, and

(b)   accordingly, remains vested as bona vacantia.

(10) If default is made in complying with subsection (3) or (4), an offence is committed by—

(a)   the company, and

(b)   every officer of the company who is in default.

For this purpose a shadow director is treated as an officer of the company.

(11) A person guilty of an offence under this section is liable--

(a)   on conviction on indictment, to a fine;

(b)   on summary conviction—

(i)   in England and Wales, to a fine;

(ii)   in Scotland or Northern Ireland, to a fine not exceeding the statutory maximum.

1029   Application to court for restoration to the register

(1)   An application may be made to the court to restore to the register a company—

(a)   that has been dissolved under Chapter 9 of Part 4 of the Insolvency Act 1986 or Chapter 9 of Part 5 of the Insolvency (Northern Ireland) Order 1989 (dissolution of company after winding up),

(b)   that is deemed to have been dissolved under paragraph 84(6) of Schedule B1 to that Act or paragraph 85(6) of Schedule B1 to that Order (dissolution of company following administration), or

(c)   that has been struck off the register—

(i)   under section 1000 or 1001 (power of registrar to strike off defunct company), or

(ii)   under section 1003 (voluntary striking off),

whether or not the company has in consequence been dissolved.

(2)   An application under this section may be made by—

(a)   the Secretary of State,

(b)   any former director of the company,

(c)   any person having an interest in land in which the company had a superior or derivative interest,

(d)   any person having an interest in land or other property—

(i)   that was subject to rights vested in the company, or

(ii)   that was benefited by obligations owed by the company,

(e)   any person who but for the company's dissolution would have been in a contractual relationship with it,

(f)   any person with a potential legal claim against the company,

(g)   any manager or trustee of a pension fund established for the benefit of employees of the company,

(h)   any former member of the company (or the personal representatives of such a person),

(i)   any person who was a creditor of the company at the time of its striking off or dissolution,

(j)   any former liquidator of the company,

(k)   where the company was struck off the register under section 1003 (voluntary striking off), any person of a description specified by regulations under section 1006(1)(f) or 1007(2)(f) (persons entitled to notice of application for voluntary striking off),

or by any other person appearing to the court to have an interest in the matter.

1030   When application to the court may be made

(1)   An application to the court for restoration of a company to the register may be made at any time for the purpose of—

    (a)   bringing proceedings against the company for damages for personal injury;

    (b)   an insurer (within the meaning of the Third Parties (Rights Against Insurers) Act 2010) bringing proceedings against a third party in the name of that company in respect of that company's liability for damages for personal injury.

(2)   No order shall be made on such an application if it appears to the court that the proceedings would fail by virtue of any enactment as to the time within which proceedings must be brought.

(3)   In making that decision the court must have regard to its power under section 1032(3) (power to give consequential directions etc) to direct that the period between the dissolution (or striking off) of the company and the making of the order is not to count for the purposes of any such enactment.

(4)   In any other case an application to the court for restoration of a company to the register may not be made after the end of the period of six years from the date of the dissolution of the company, subject as follows.

(5)   In a case where—

    (a)   the company has been struck off the register under section 1000 or 1001 (power of registrar to strike off defunct company),

    (b)   an application to the registrar has been made under section 1024 (application for administrative restoration to the register) within the time allowed for making such an application, and

    (c)   the registrar has refused the application,

an application to the court under this section may be made within 28 days of notice of the registrar's decision being issued by the registrar, even if the period of six years mentioned in subsection (4) above has expired.

(6)   For the purposes of this section—

    (a)   "personal injury" includes any disease and any impairment of a person's physical or mental condition; and

    (b)   references to damages for personal injury include—

        (i)   any sum claimed by virtue of section 1(2)(c) of the Law Reform (Miscellaneous Provisions) Act 1934 or section 14(2)(c) of the Law Reform (Miscellaneous Provisions) Act (Northern Ireland) 1937 (funeral expenses)), and

        (ii)   damages under the Fatal Accidents Act 1976, the Damages (Scotland) Act 2011 (asp 7) or the Fatal Accidents (Northern Ireland) Order 1977.

1031 Decision on application for restoration by the court

(1)   On an application under section 1029 the court may order the restoration of the company to the register—

    (a)   if the company was struck off the register under section 1000 or 1001 (power of registrar to strike off defunct companies) and the company was, at the time of the striking off, carrying on business or in operation;

    (b)   if the company was struck off the register under section 1003 (voluntary striking off) and any of the requirements of sections 1004 to 1009 was not complied with;

    (c)   if in any other case the court considers it just to do so.

(2)   If the court orders restoration of the company to the register, the restoration takes effect on a copy of the court's order being delivered to the registrar.

(3)   The registrar must cause to be published in the Gazette notice of the restoration of the company to the register.

(4)   The notice must state—

    (a)   the name of the company or, if the company is restored to the register under a different name (see section 1033), that name and its former name,

    (b)   the company's registered number, and

    (c)   the date on which the restoration took effect.

1032   Effect of court order for restoration to the register

(1)   The general effect of an order by the court for restoration to the register is that the company is deemed to have continued in existence as if it had not been dissolved or struck off the register.

(2)   The company is not liable to a penalty under section 453 or any corresponding earlier provision (civil penalty for failure to deliver accounts) for a financial year in relation to which the period for filing accounts and reports ended—

    (a)   after the date of dissolution or striking off, and

    (b)   before the restoration of the company to the register.

(3)   The court may give such directions and make such provision as seems just for placing the company and all other persons in the same position (as nearly as may be) as if the company had not been dissolved or struck off the register.

(4)   The court may also give directions as to—

    (a)   the delivery to the registrar of such documents relating to the company as are necessary to bring up to date the records kept by the registrar,

    (b)   the payment of the costs (in Scotland, expenses) of the registrar in connection with the proceedings for the restoration of the company to the register,

    (c)   where any property or right previously vested in or held on trust for the company has vested as *bona vacantia*, the payment of the costs (in Scotland, expenses) of the Crown representative—

        (i)   in dealing with the property during the period of dissolution, or

        (ii)   in connection with the proceedings on the application.

(5)   In this section the "Crown representative" means—

    (a)   in relation to property vested in the Duchy of Lancaster, the Solicitor to that Duchy;

    (b)   in relation to property vested in the Duke of Cornwall, the Solicitor to the Duchy of Cornwall;

    (c)   in relation to property in Scotland, the Queen's and Lord Treasurer's Remembrancer;

    (d)   in relation to other property, the Treasury Solicitor.

1032A Restoration by court of company with share warrants

(1)   This section applies in relation to a company falling within section 1029(1) if, at the time it was dissolved, deemed to be dissolved or (as the case may be) struck off, it had any share warrant in issue.

(2)   If the court orders the restoration of the company to the register, the order must also cancel the share warrant and the shares specified in it with effect from the date the restoration takes effect.

(3)   If as a result of subsection (2) the company has no issued share capital, the company must, before the end of the period of one month beginning with the date the restoration takes effect, allot at least one share in the company; and section 549(1) does not apply to such an allotment.

(4)   Subsection (6) applies in a case where—

    (a)   the application under section 1029 was made by a person mentioned in subsection (2)(b) or (h) of that section, or

    (b)   the court order specifies that it applies.

(5)   But subsection (6) does not apply in any case where the company is required under subsection (3) to make an allotment (because in such a case section 555 will apply).

(6)   In a case where this subsection applies, the company must, before the end of the period of 15 days beginning with the date the restoration takes effect, deliver a statement of capital to the registrar.

(7)   The statement of capital must state with respect to the company's share capital as reduced by the cancellation of the share warrant and the shares specified in it—

    (a)   the total number of shares of the company,

    (b)   the aggregate nominal value of those shares,

    (c)   the aggregate amount (if any) unpaid on those shares (whether on account of their nominal value or by way of premium), and

    (d)   for each class of shares—

        (i)   prescribed particulars of the rights attached to the shares,

          (ii)   the total number of shares of that class, and

          (iii)   the aggregate nominal value of shares of that class.

(8)   Where a share warrant is cancelled by an order as mentioned in subsection (2), the company must, as soon as reasonably practicable—

     (a)   enter the date the cancellation takes effect in its register of members, or

     (b)   where an election is in force under section 128B of the Companies Act 2006 (option to keep membership information on central register) in respect of the company, deliver that information to the registrar as if it were information required to be delivered under section 128E of that Act.

(9)   Subsection (10) applies where—

     (a)   any property or right previously vested in or held on trust for the company in respect of any share specified in a share warrant has vested as bona vacantia (see section 1012), and

     (b)   the warrant and the share are cancelled on the restoration of the company in accordance with this section.

(10)   On restoration of the company, that property or right—

     (a)   may not be returned to the company, and

     (b)   accordingly, remains vested as bona vacantia.

(11)   If default is made in complying with subsection (3) or (6), an offence is committed by—

     (a)   the company, and

     (b)   every officer of the company who is in default.

     For this purpose a shadow director is treated as an officer of the company.

(12)   A person guilty of an offence under this section is liable—

     (a)   on conviction on indictment, to a fine;

     (b)   on summary conviction—

          (i)   in England and Wales, to a fine;

          (ii)   in Scotland or Northern Ireland, to a fine not exceeding the statutory maximum.

Supplementary provisions

1033   Company's name on restoration

(1)   A company is restored to the register with the name it had before it was dissolved or struck off the register, subject to the following provisions.

(2)   If at the date of restoration the company could not be registered under its former name without contravening section 66 (name not to be the same as another in the registrar's index of company names), it must be restored to the register—

     (a)   under another name specified—

          (i)   in the case of administrative restoration, in the application to the registrar, or

          (ii)   in the case of restoration under a court order, in the court's order, or

     (b)   as if its registered number was also its name.

     References to a company's being registered in a name, and to registration in that context, shall be read as including the company's being restored to the register.

(3)   If a company is restored to the register under a name specified in the application to the registrar, the provisions of—

     section 80 (change of name: registration and issue of new certificate of incorporation), and

     section 81 (change of name: effect),

     apply as if the application to the registrar were notice of a change of name.

(4)   If a company is restored to the register under a name specified in the court's order, the provisions of—

     section 80 (change of name: registration and issue of new certificate of incorporation), and

     section 81 (change of name: effect),

     apply as if the copy of the court order delivered to the registrar were notice of a change a name.

(5)   If the company is restored to the register as if its registered number was also its name—

     (a)   the company must change its name within 14 days after the date of the restoration, (b)　the change may be made by resolution of the directors (without prejudice to any other method of changing the company's name),

(c)　the company must give notice to the registrar of the change, and

(d)　sections 80 and 81 apply as regards the registration and effect of the change.

(6)　If the company fails to comply with subsection (5) (a) or (c) an offence is committed by—

(a)　the company, and

(b)　every officer of the company who is in default.

(7)　A person guilty of an offence under subsection (6) is liable on summary conviction to a fine not exceeding level 5 on the standard scale and, for continued contravention, a daily default fine not exceeding one-tenth of the greater of £5,000 or level 4 on the standard scale.

1034　Effect of restoration to the register where property has vested as bona vacantia

(1)　The person in whom any property or right is vested by section 1012 (property of dissolved company to be *bona vacantia)* may dispose of, or of an interest in, that property or right despite the fact that the company may be restored to the register under this Chapter.

(2)　If the company is restored to the register—

(a)　the restoration does not affect the disposition (but without prejudice to its effect in relation to any other property or right previously vested in or held on trust for the company), and

(b)　the Crown or, as the case may be, the Duke of Cornwall shall pay to the company an amount equal to—

(i)　the amount of any consideration received for the property or right or, as the case may be, the interest in it, or

(ii)　the value of any such consideration at the time of the disposition,

or, if no consideration was received an amount equal to the value of the property, right or interest disposed of, as at the date of the disposition.

(3)　There may be deducted from the amount payable under subsection (2)(b) the reasonable costs of the Crown representative in connection with the disposition (to the extent that they have not been paid as a condition of administrative restoration or pursuant to a court order for restoration).

(4)　Where a liability accrues under subsection (2) in respect of any property or right which before the restoration of the company to the register had accrued as *bona vacantia* to the Duchy of Lancaster, the Attorney General of that Duchy shall represent Her Majesty in any proceedings arising in connection with that liability.

(5)　Where a liability accrues under subsection (2) in respect of any property or right which before the restoration of the company to the register had accrued as *bona vacantia* to the Duchy of Cornwall, such persons as the Duke of Cornwall (or other possessor for the time being of the Duchy) may appoint shall represent the Duke (or other possessor) in any proceedings arising out of that liability.

(6)　In this section the "Crown representative" means—

(a)　in relation to property vested in the Duchy of Lancaster, the Solicitor to that Duchy;

(b)　in relation to property vested in the Duke of Cornwall, the Solicitor to the Duchy of Cornwall;

(c)　in relation to property in Scotland, the Queen's and Lord Treasurer's Remembrancer;

(d)　in relation to other property, the Treasury Solicitor.

...

PART 34
OVERSEAS COMPANIES

Introductory

1044　Overseas companies

In the Companies Acts an "overseas company" means a company incorporated outside the United Kingdom.

1045 Company contracts and execution of documents by companies

(1) The Secretary of State may make provision by regulations applying sections 43 to 52 (formalities of doing business and other matters) to overseas companies, subject to such exceptions, adaptations or modifications as may be specified in the regulations.

(2) Regulations under this section are subject to negative resolution procedure.

Registration of particulars

1046 Duty to register particulars

(1) The Secretary of State may make provision by regulations requiring an overseas company—

    (a) to deliver to the registrar for registration a return containing specified particulars, and

    (b) to deliver to the registrar with the return specified documents.

(2) The regulations—

    (a) must, in the case of a company other than a Gibraltar company, require the company to register particulars if the company opens a branch in the United Kingdom, and

    (b) may, in the case of a Gibraltar company, require the company to register particulars if the company opens a branch in the United Kingdom, and

    (c) may, in any case, require the registration of particulars in such other circumstances as may be specified.

(3) In subsection (2)—

"branch" means a branch within the meaning of the Eleventh Company Law Directive (89/666/ EEC);

"Gibraltar company" means a company incorporated in Gibraltar.

(4) The regulations may provide that where a company has registered particulars under this section and any alteration is made—

    (a) in the specified particulars, or

    (b) in any document delivered with the return,

the company must deliver to the registrar for registration a return containing specified particulars of the alteration.

(5) The regulations may make provision—

    (a) requiring the return under this section to be delivered for registration to the registrar for a specified part of the United Kingdom, and

    (b) requiring it to be so delivered before the end of a specified period.

(6) The regulations may make different provision according to—

    (a) the place where the company is incorporated, and

    (b) the activities carried on (or proposed to be carried on) by it. This is without prejudice to the general power to make different provision for different cases.

(7) In this section "specified" means specified in the regulations.

(8) Regulations under this section are subject to affirmative resolution procedure.

1047 Registered name of overseas company

(1) Regulations under section 1046 (duty to register particulars) must require an overseas company that is required to register particulars to register its name.

(2) This may be—

    (a) the company's corporate name (that is, its name under the law of the country or territory in which it is incorporated) or

    (b) an alternative name specified in accordance with section 1048.

(3) ...

(4) ... the following provisions of Part 5 (a company's name) apply in relation to the registration of the name of an overseas company—

    (a) section 53 (prohibited names);

    (aa) section 53A (names for criminal purposes);

    (b) sections 54 to 56 (sensitive words and expressions);

(bza) section 56A (names suggesting connection with foreign governments etc);

(ba) section 57 (permitted characters etc);

(bb) section 57A (names containing computer code);

(bc) section 57B (restriction on re-registering name following direction);

(bd) section 57C (names that another company has been directed to change);

(c)   section 65 (inappropriate use of indications of company type or legal form);

(d)   sections 66 to 74 (similarity to other names);

(e)   section 75 (provision of misleading information etc);

(f)   section 76 (misleading indication of activities);

(g)   section 76A (power to direct change of name used for criminal purposes);

(h)   section 76B (direction to change name wrongly registered);

(i)   section 76C (registrar's power to change name containing computer code);

(j)   section 76D (registrar's power to change name for failure to comply with direction).

(5)   ...

(6)   Any reference in the provisions mentioned in subsection (4) ... to a change of name shall be read as a reference to registration of a different name under section 1048.

1048 Registration under alternative name

(1)   An overseas company that is required to register particulars under section 1046 may at any time deliver to the registrar for registration a statement specifying a name, other than its corporate name, under which it proposes to carry on business in the United Kingdom.

(2)   An overseas company that has registered an alternative name may at any time deliver to the registrar of companies for registration a statement specifying a different name under which it proposes to carry on business in the United Kingdom (which may be its corporate name or a further alternative) in substitution for the name previously registered.

(3)   The alternative name for the time being registered under this section is treated for all purposes of the law applying in the United Kingdom as the company's corporate name.

(4)   This does not—

(a)   affect the references in this section or section 1047 to the company's corporate name,

(b)   affect any rights or obligation of the company, or

(c)   render defective any legal proceedings by or against the company.

(5)   Any legal proceedings that might have been continued or commenced against the company by its corporate name, or any name previously registered under this section, may be continued or commenced against it by its name for the time being so registered.

Other requirements

1049 Accounts and reports: general

(1)   The Secretary of State may make provision by regulations requiring an overseas company that is required to register particulars under section 1046—

(a)   to prepare the like accounts and strategic report and directors' report, and

(b)   to cause to be prepared such an auditor's report,

as would be required if the company were formed and registered under this Act.

(2)   The regulations may for this purpose apply, with or without modifications, all or any of the provisions of—

Part 15 (accounts and reports), and

Part 16 (audit).

(3)   The Secretary of State may make provision by regulations requiring an overseas company to deliver to the registrar copies of—

(a)   the accounts and reports prepared in accordance with the regulations, or

(b)   the accounts and reports that it is required to prepare and have audited under the law of the country in which it is incorporated.

(4)   Regulations under this section are subject to negative resolution procedure.

1050   Accounts and reports: credit or financial institutions

(1)   This section applies to a credit or financial institution—

   (a)   that is incorporated or otherwise formed outside the United Kingdom and Gibraltar,

   (b)   whose head office is outside the United Kingdom and Gibraltar, and

   (c)   that has a branch in the United Kingdom.

(2)   In subsection (1) "branch" means a place of business that forms a legally dependent part of the institution and conducts directly all or some of the operations inherent in its business.

(3)   The Secretary of State may make provision by regulations requiring an institution to which this section applies—

   (a)   to prepare the like accounts and strategic report and directors' report, and

   (b)   to cause to be prepared such an auditor's report,

   as would be required if the institution were a company formed and registered under this Act.

(4)   The regulations may for this purpose apply, with or without modifications, all or any of the provisions of—

   Part 15 (accounts and reports), and

   Part 16 (audit).

(5)   The Secretary of State may make provision by regulations requiring an institution to which this section applies to deliver to the registrar copies of—

   (a)   accounts and reports prepared in accordance with the regulations, or

   (b)   accounts and reports that it is required to prepare and have audited under the law of the country in which the institution has its head office.

(6)   Regulations under this section are subject to negative resolution procedure.

1051   Trading disclosures

(1)   The Secretary of State may by regulations make provision requiring overseas companies carrying on business in the United Kingdom—

   (a)   to display specified information in specified locations,

   (b)   to state specified information in specified descriptions of document or communication, and

   (c)   to provide specified information on request to those they deal with in the course of their business.

(2)   The regulations—

   (a)   shall in every case require a company that has registered particulars under section 1046 to disclose the name registered by it under section 1047, and

   (b)   may make provision as to the manner in which any specified information is to be displayed, stated or provided.

(3)   The regulations may make provision corresponding to that made by—

   section 83 (civil consequences of failure to make required disclosure), and

   section 84 (criminal consequences of failure to make required disclosure).

(4)   In this section "specified" means specified in the regulations.

(5)   Regulations under this section are subject to affirmative resolution procedure.

1052   Company charges

(1)   The Secretary of State may by regulations make provision about the registration of specified charges over property in the United Kingdom of a registered overseas company.

(2)   The power in subsection (1) includes power to make provision about—

   (a)   a registered overseas company that—

      (i)   has particulars registered in more than one part of the United Kingdom;

      (ii)   has property in more than one part of the United Kingdom;

   (b)   the circumstances in which property is to be regarded, for the purposes of the regulations, as being, or not being, in the United Kingdom or in a particular part of the United Kingdom;

   (c)   the keeping by a registered overseas company of records and registers about specified charges and their inspection;

   (d)   the consequences of a failure to register a charge in accordance with the regulations;

(e)   the circumstances in which a registered overseas company ceases to be subject to the regulations.

(3)   The regulations may for this purpose apply, with or without modifications, any of the provisions of Part 25 (company charges).

(4)   The regulations may modify any reference in an enactment to Part 25, or to a particular provision of that Part, so as to include a reference to the regulations or to a specified provision of the regulations.

(5)   Regulations under this section are subject to negative resolution procedure.

(6)   In this section—

"registered overseas company" means an overseas company that has registered particulars under section 1046(1), and

"specified" means specified in the regulations.

1053   Other returns etc

(1)   This section applies to overseas companies that are required to register particulars under section 1046.

(2)   The Secretary of State may make provision by regulations requiring the delivery to the registrar of returns—

   (a)   by a company to which this section applies that—

     (i)   is being wound up, or

     (ii)   becomes or ceases to be subject to insolvency proceedings, or an arrangement or composition or any analogous proceedings;

   (b)   by the liquidator of a company to which this section applies.

(3)   The regulations may specify—

   (a)   the circumstances in which a return is to be made,

   (b)   the particulars to be given in it, and

   (c)   the period within which it is to be made.

(4)   The Secretary of State may make provision by regulations requiring notice to be given to the registrar of the appointment in relation to a company to which this section applies of a judicial factor (in Scotland).

(5)   The regulations may include provision corresponding to any provision made by section 1154 of this Act (duty to notify registrar of certain appointments).

(6)   Regulations under this section are subject to affirmative resolution procedure.

Supplementary

1054   Offences

(1)   Regulations under this Part may specify the person or persons responsible for complying with any specified requirement of the regulations.

(2)   Regulations under this Part may make provision for offences, including provision as to—

   (a)   the person or persons liable in the case of any specified contravention of the regulations, and

   (b)   circumstances that are, or are not, to be a defence on a charge of such an offence.

(3)   The regulations must not provide—

   (a)   for imprisonment, or

   (b)   for the imposition on summary conviction of a fine exceeding level 5 on the standard scale and, for continued contravention, a daily default fine not exceeding one-tenth of the greater of £5,000 or level 4 on the standard scale.

(4)   In this section "specified" means specified in the regulations.

1055   Disclosure of individual's residential address: protection from disclosure

Where regulations under section 1046 (overseas companies: duty to register particulars) require an overseas company to register particulars of an individual's usual residential address, they must contain provision corresponding to that made by Chapter 8 of Part 10 (directors' residential addresses: protection from disclosure).

1056 Requirement to identify persons authorised to accept service of documents

Regulations under section 1046 (overseas companies: duty to register particulars) must require an overseas company to register—

(a) particulars identifying every person resident in the United Kingdom authorised to accept service of documents on behalf of the company, or

(b) a statement that there is no such person.

1057 Registrar to whom returns, notices etc to be delivered

(1) This section applies to an overseas company that is required to register or has registered particulars under section 1046 in more than one part of the United Kingdom.

(2) The Secretary of State may provide by regulations that, in the case of such a company, anything authorised or required to be delivered to the registrar under this Part is to be delivered—

(a) to the registrar for each part of the United Kingdom in which the company is required to register or has registered particulars, or

(b) to the registrar for such part or parts of the United Kingdom as may be specified in or determined in accordance with the regulations.

(3) Regulations under this section are subject to negative resolution procedure.

1058 Duty to give notice of ceasing to have registrable presence

(1) The Secretary of State may make provision by regulations requiring an overseas company—

(a) if it has registered particulars following the opening of a branch, in accordance with regulations under section 1046(2)(a) or (b), to give notice to the registrar if it closes that branch;

(b) if it has registered particulars in other circumstances, in accordance with regulations under section 1046(2)(c), to give notice to the registrar if the circumstances that gave rise to the obligation to register particulars cease to obtain.

(2) The regulations must provide for the notice to be given to the registrar for the part of the United Kingdom to which the original return of particulars was delivered.

(3) The regulations may specify the period within which notice must be given.

(4) Regulations under this section are subject to negative resolution procedure.

1059 Application of provisions in case of relocation of branch

For the purposes of this Part—

(a) the relocation of a branch from one part of the United Kingdom to another counts as the closing of one branch and the opening of another;

(b) the relocation of a branch within the same part of the United Kingdom does not.

...

PART 36
OFFENCES UNDER THE COMPANIES ACTS AND FINANCIAL PENALTIES

Liability of officer in default

1121 Liability of officer in default

(1) This section has effect for the purposes of any provision of the Companies Acts to the effect that, in the event of contravention of an enactment in relation to a company, an offence is committed by every officer of the company who is in default.

(2) For this purpose "officer" includes—

(a) any director, manager or secretary, and

(b) any person who is to be treated as an officer of the company for the purposes of the provision in question.

(3) An officer is "in default" for the purposes of the provision if he authorises or permits, participates in, or fails to take all reasonable steps to prevent, the contravention.

1122   Liability of company as officer in default

(1)   Where a company is an officer of another company, it does not commit an offence as an officer in default unless one of its officers is in default.

(2)   Where any such offence is committed by a company the officer in question also commits the offence and is liable to be proceeded against and punished accordingly.

(3)   In this section "officer" and "in default" have the meanings given by section 1121.

1123   Application to bodies other than companies

(1)   Section 1121 (liability of officers in default) applies to a body other than a company as it applies to a company.

(2)   As it applies in relation to a body corporate other than a company—

    (a)   the reference to a director of the company shall be read as referring—

        (i)   where the body's affairs are managed by its members, to a member of the body,

        (ii)   in any other case, to any corresponding officer of the body, and

    (b)   the reference to a manager or secretary of the company shall be read as referring to any manager, secretary or similar officer of the body.

(3)   As it applies in relation to a partnership—

    (a)   the reference to a director of the company shall be read as referring to a member of the partnership, and

    (b)   the reference to a manager or secretary of the company shall be read as referring to any manager, secretary or similar officer of the partnership.

(4)   As it applies in relation to an unincorporated body other than a partnership—

    (a)   the reference to a director of the company shall be read as referring—

        (i)   where the body's affairs are managed by its members, to a member of the body,

        (ii)   in any other case, to a member of the governing body, and

    (b)   the reference to a manager or secretary of the company shall be read as referring to any manager, secretary or similar officer of the body.

Offences under the Companies Act 1985

1124   Amendments of the Companies Act 1985

Schedule 3 contains amendments of the Companies Act 1985 relating to offences.

General provisions

1125   Meaning of "daily default fine"

(1)   This section defines what is meant in the Companies Acts where it is provided that a person guilty of an offence is liable on summary conviction to a fine not exceeding a specified amount "and, for continued contravention, a daily default fine" not exceeding a specified amount.

(2)   This means that the person is liable on a second or subsequent summary conviction of the offence to a fine not exceeding the latter amount for each day on which the contravention is continued (instead of being liable to a fine not exceeding the former amount).

1126   Consents required for certain prosecutions

(1)   This section applies to proceedings for an offence under any of the following provisions—

section 458, 460 or 949 of this Act (offences of unauthorised disclosure of information);

section 953 of this Act (failure to comply with rules about takeover bid documents);

section 448, 449, 450, 451 or 453A of the Companies Act 1985 (offences in connection with company investigations);

section 798 of this Act or section 455 of the Companies Act 1985 (offence of attempting to evade restrictions on shares);

section 1112 or 1112A of this Act (false statement offences);

paragraph 5 or 6 of Schedule 1B to this Act (breach of certain restrictions imposed under that Schedule).

(2)   No such proceedings are to be brought in England and Wales except by or with the consent of—

    (a)   in the case of an offence under—

        (i)   section 458, 460 or 949 of, or paragraph 5 or 6 of Schedule 1B to, this Act,

        (ii)   section 953 of this Act, …

        (iii)   section 448, 449, 450, 451 or 453A of the Companies Act 1985, or,

        (iv)   section 1112 or 1112A of this Act,

        the Secretary of State or the Director of Public Prosecutions;

    (b)   in the case of an offence under section 798 of, or paragraph 5 or 6 of Schedule 1B to, this Act or section 455 of the Companies Act 1985, the Secretary of State.

(3)   No such proceedings are to be brought in Northern Ireland except by or with the consent of—

    (a)   in the case of an offence under—

        (i)   section 458, 460 or 949 of this Act,

        (ii)   section 953 of this Act, …

        (iii)   section 448, 449, 450, 451 or 453A of the Companies Act 1985, or

        (iv)   section 1112 or 1112A of this Act,

        the Secretary of State or the Director of Public Prosecutions for Northern Ireland;

    (b)   in the case of an offence under section 798 of, or paragraph 5 or 6 of Schedule 1B to, this Act or section 455 of the Companies Act 1985, the Secretary of State.

1127 Summary proceedings: venue

(1)   Summary proceedings for any offence under the Companies Acts may be taken—

    (a)   against a body corporate, at any place at which the body has a place of business, and

    (b)   against any other person, at any place at which he is for the time being.

(2)   This is without prejudice to any jurisdiction exercisable apart from this section.

1128 Summary proceedings: time limit for proceedings

(1)   An information relating to an offence under the Companies Acts that is triable by a magistrates' court in England and Wales may be so tried if it is laid—

    (a)   at any time within three years after the commission of the offence, and

    (b)   within twelve months after the date on which evidence sufficient in the opinion of the Director of Public Prosecutions or the Secretary of State (as the case may be) to justify the proceedings comes to his knowledge.

(2)   Summary proceedings in Scotland for an offence under the Companies Acts—

    (a)   must not be commenced after the expiration of three years from the commission of the offence;

    (b)   subject to that, may be commenced at any time—

        (i)   within twelve months after the date on which evidence sufficient in the Lord Advocate's opinion to justify the proceedings came to his knowledge, or

        (ii)   where such evidence was reported to him by the Secretary of State, within twelve months after the date on which it came to the knowledge of the latter.

    Section 136(3) of the Criminal Procedure (Scotland) Act 1995 (date when proceedings deemed to be commenced) applies for the purposes of this subsection as for the purposes of that section.

(3)   A magistrates' court in Northern Ireland has jurisdiction to hear and determine a complaint charging the commission of a summary offence under the Companies Acts provided that the complaint is made—

    (a)   within three years from the time when the offence was committed, and

    (b)   within twelve months from the date on which evidence sufficient in the opinion of the Director of Public Prosecutions for Northern Ireland or the Secretary of State (as the case may be) to justify the proceedings comes to his knowledge.

(4)   For the purposes of this section a certificate of the Director of Public Prosecutions, the Lord Advocate, the Director of Public Prosecutions for Northern Ireland or the Secretary of State (as the case may be) as to the date on which such evidence as is referred to above came to his notice is conclusive evidence.

1129   Legal professional privilege

In proceedings against a person for an offence under the Companies Acts, nothing in those Acts is to be taken to require any person to disclose any information that he is entitled to refuse to disclose on grounds of legal professional privilege (in Scotland, confidentiality of communications).

1130   Proceedings against unincorporated bodies

(1)   Proceedings for an offence under the Companies Acts alleged to have been committed by an unincorporated body must be brought in the name of the body (and not in that of any of its members).

(2)   For the purposes of such proceedings—

    (a)   any rules of court relating to the service of documents have effect as if the body were a body corporate, and

    (b)   the following provisions apply as they apply in relation to a body corporate—

        (i)   in England and Wales, section 33 of the Criminal Justice Act 1925 and Schedule 3 to the Magistrates' Courts Act 1980,

        (ii)   in Scotland, sections 70 and 143 of the Criminal Procedure (Scotland) Act 1995,

        (iii)   in Northern Ireland, section 18 of the Criminal Justice Act (Northern Ireland) 1945 and Article 166 of and Schedule 4 to the Magistrates' Courts (Northern Ireland) Order 1981.

(3)   A fine imposed on an unincorporated body on its conviction of an offence under the Companies Acts must be paid out of the funds of the body.

1131   Imprisonment on summary conviction in England and Wales: transitory provision

(1)   This section applies to any provision of the Companies Acts that provides that a person guilty of an offence is liable on summary conviction in England and Wales to imprisonment for a term not exceeding the general limit in a magistrates' court.

(2)   In relation to an offence committed before 2 May 2022, for "the general limit in a magistrates' court" substitute "six months".

Production and inspection of documents

1132   Production and inspection of documents where offence suspected

(1)   An application under this section may be made—

    (a)   in England and Wales, to a judge of the High Court by the Director of Public Prosecutions, the Secretary of State or a chief officer of police;

    (b)   in Scotland, to one of the Lords Commissioners of Justiciary by the Lord Advocate;

    (c)   in Northern Ireland, to the High Court by the Director of Public Prosecutions for Northern Ireland, the Department of Enterprise, Trade and Investment or a chief superintendent of the Police Service of Northern Ireland.

(2)   If on an application under this section there is shown to be reasonable cause to believe—

    (a)   that any person has, while an officer of a company, committed an offence in connection with the management of the company's affairs, and

    (b)   that evidence of the commission of the offence is to be found in any documents in the possession or control of the company,

an order under this section may be made.

(3)   The order may—

    (a)   authorise any person named in it to inspect the documents in question, or any of them, for the purpose of investigating and obtaining evidence of the offence, or

    (b)   require the secretary of the company, or such other officer of it as may be named in the order, to produce the documents (or any of them) to a person named in the order at a place so named.

(4)   This section applies also in relation to documents in the possession or control of a person carrying on the business of banking, so far as they relate to the company's affairs, as it applies to

documents in the possession or control of the company, except that no such order as is referred to in subsection (3) (b) may be made by virtue of this subsection.

(5) The decision under this section of a judge of the High Court, any of the Lords Commissioners of Justiciary or the High Court is not appealable.

(6) In this section "document" includes information recorded in any form.

Financial penalties

1132A Power to make provision for financial penalties

(1) The Secretary of State may by regulations make provision conferring power on the registrar to impose a financial penalty on a person if satisfied, beyond reasonable doubt, that the person has engaged in conduct amounting to a relevant offence under this Act.

(2) "Relevant offence under this Act" means any offence under this Act other than an offence under a provision contained in—
  (a) Part 12 (company secretaries);
  (b) Part 13 (resolutions and meetings);
  (c) Part 16 (audit).

(3) The regulations may include provision—
  (a) about the procedure to be followed in imposing penalties;
  (b) about the amount of penalties;
  (c) for the imposition of interest or additional penalties for late payment;
  (d) conferring rights of appeal against penalties;
  (e) about the enforcement of penalties.

(4) Provision made under subsection (3)(b) must ensure that the maximum financial penalty that may be imposed does not exceed £10,000.

(5) The regulations must provide that—
  (a) no financial penalty may be imposed under the regulations on a person in respect of conduct amounting to an offence if—
    (i) proceedings have been brought against the person for that offence in respect of that conduct and the proceedings are ongoing, or
    (ii) the person has been convicted of that offence in respect of that conduct, and
  (b) no proceedings may be brought against a person in respect of conduct amounting to an offence if the person has been given a financial penalty under the regulations in respect of that conduct.

(6) Amounts recovered by the registrar under the regulations are to be paid into the Consolidated Fund.

(7) Regulations under this section are subject to affirmative resolution procedure.

(8) In this section "conduct" means an act or omission.

Supplementary

1133 Transitional provision

The provisions of this Part except section 1132 do not apply to offences committed before the commencement of the relevant provision.

PART 37
COMPANIES: SUPPLEMENTARY PROVISIONS

Company records

1134 Meaning of "company records"

In this Part "company records" means—
  (a) any register, index, accounting records, agreement, memorandum, minutes or other document required by the Companies Acts to be kept by a company, and
  (b) any register kept by a company of its debenture holders.

1135   Form of company records

(1)   Company records—

(a)   may be kept in hard copy or electronic form, and

(b)   may be arranged in such manner as the directors of the company think fit,

provided the information in question is adequately recorded for future reference.

(2)   Where the records are kept in electronic form, they must be capable of being reproduced in hard copy form.

(3)   If a company fails to comply with this section, an offence is committed by every officer of the company who is in default.

(4)   A person guilty of an offence under this section is liable on summary conviction to a fine not exceeding level 3 on the standard scale and, for continued contravention, a daily default fine not exceeding one-tenth of level 3 on the standard scale.

(5)   Any provision of an instrument made by a company before 12th February 1979 that requires a register of holders of the company's debentures to be kept in hard copy form is to be read as requiring it to be kept in hard copy or electronic form.

1136   Regulations about where certain company records to be kept available for inspection

(1)   The Secretary of State may make provision by regulations specifying places other than a company's registered office at which company records required to be kept available for inspection under a relevant provision may be so kept in compliance with that provision.

(2)   The "relevant provisions" are—

section 114 (register of members);

section 128D (historic register of members);

section 162 (register of directors);

section 228 (directors' service contracts);

section 237 (directors' indemnities);

section 275 (register of secretaries);

section 358 (records of resolutions etc);

section 702 (contracts relating to purchase of own shares);

section 720 (documents relating to redemption or purchase of own shares out of capital by private company);

section 743 (register of debenture holders);

section 790M (register of people with significant control over a company);

section 790Z (historic PSC register);

section 805 (report to members of outcome of investigation by public company into interests in its shares);

section 809 (register of interests in shares disclosed to public company);

section 859Q (instruments creating charges).

(3)   The regulations may specify a place by reference to the company's principal place of business, the part of the United Kingdom in which the company is registered, the place at which the company keeps any other records available for inspection or in any other way.

(4)   The regulations may provide that a company does not comply with a relevant provision by keeping company records available for inspection at a place specified in the regulations unless conditions specified in the regulations are met.

(5)   The regulations—

(a)   need not specify a place in relation to each relevant provision;

(b)   may specify more than one place in relation to a relevant provision.

(6)   A requirement under a relevant provision to keep company records available for inspection is not complied with by keeping them available for inspection at a place specified in the regulations unless all the company's records subject to the requirement are kept there.

(7)   Regulations under this section are subject to negative resolution procedure.

1137   Regulations about inspection of records and provision of copies

(1)   The Secretary of State may make provision by regulations as to the obligations of a company that is required by any provision of the Companies Acts—

(a)   to keep available for inspection any company records, or

(b)   to provide copies of any company records.

(2)   A company that fails to comply with the regulations is treated as having refused inspection or, as the case may be, having failed to provide a copy.

(3)   The regulations may—

(a)   make provision as to the time, duration and manner of inspection, including the circumstances in which and extent to which the copying of information is permitted in the course of inspection, and

(b)   define what may be required of the company as regards the nature, extent and manner of extracting or presenting any information for the purposes of inspection or the provision of copies.

(4)   Where there is power to charge a fee, the regulations may make provision as to the amount of the fee and the basis of its calculation.

(5)   Nothing in any provision of this Act or in the regulations shall be read as preventing a company—

(a)   from affording more extensive facilities than are required by the regulations, or

(b)   where a fee may be charged, from charging a lesser fee than that prescribed or none at all.

(6)   Regulations under this section are subject to negative resolution procedure.

1138   Duty to take precautions against falsification

(1)   Where company records are kept otherwise than in bound books, adequate precautions must be taken—

(a)   to guard against falsification, and

(b)   to facilitate the discovery of falsification.

(2)   If a company fails to comply with this section, an offence is committed by every officer of the company who is in default.

(3)   A person guilty of an offence under this section is liable on summary conviction to a fine not exceeding level 3 on the standard scale and, for continued contravention, a daily default fine not exceeding one-tenth of level 3 on the standard scale.

(4)   This section does not apply to the documents required to be kept under—

(a)   section 228 (copy of director's service contract or memorandum of its terms); or

(b)   section 237 (qualifying indemnity provision).

Service addresses

1139   Service of documents on company

(1)   A document may be served on a company registered under this Act by leaving it at, or sending it by post to, the company's registered office.

(2)   A document may be served on an overseas company whose particulars are registered under section 1046—

(a)   by leaving it at, or sending it by post to, the registered address of any person resident in the United Kingdom who is authorised to accept service of documents on the company's behalf, or

(b)   if there is no such person, or if any such person refuses service or service cannot for any other reason be effected, by leaving it at or sending by post to any place of business of the company in the United Kingdom.

(3)   For the purposes of this section a person's "registered address" means any address for the time being shown as a current address in relation to that person in the part of the register available for public inspection.

(4)   Where a company registered in Scotland or Northern Ireland carries on business in England and Wales, the process of any court in England and Wales may be served on the company by leaving

it at, or sending it by post to, the company's principal place of business in England and Wales, addressed to the manager or other head officer in England and Wales of the company.

Where process is served on a company under this subsection, the person issuing out the process must send a copy of it by post to the company's registered office.

(5) Further provision as to service and other matters is made in the company communications provisions (see section 1143).

1140 Service of documents on directors, secretaries and others

(1) A document may be served on a person to whom this section applies by leaving it at, or sending it by post to, the person's registered address.

(2) This section applies to—

   (a) a director or secretary of a company;

   (aa) a person who is a registrable person or a registrable relevant legal entity in relation to a company (within the meanings given by section 790C);

   (b) in the case of an overseas company whose particulars are registered under section 1046, a person holding any such position as may be specified for the purposes of this section by regulations under that section;

   (c) a person appointed in relation to a company as—

      (i) a judicial factor (in Scotland),

      (ii) an interim manager appointed under section 76 of the Charities Act 2011, or

      (iii) a manager appointed under section 47 of the Companies (Audit, Investigations and Community Enterprise) Act 2004.

(3) This section applies whatever the purpose of the document in question.

It is not restricted to service for purposes arising out of or in connection with the appointment or position mentioned in subsection (2) or in connection with the company concerned.

(4) For the purposes of this section a person's "registered address" means any address for the time being shown as a current address in relation to that person in the part of the register available for public inspection.

(5) If notice of a change of that address is given to the registrar, a person may validly serve a document at the address previously registered until the end of the period of 14 days beginning with the date on which notice of the change is registered.

(6) Service may not be effected by virtue of this section at an address—

   (a) if notice has been registered of the termination of the appointment in relation to which the address was registered and the address is not a registered address of the person concerned in relation to any other appointment;

   (b) in the case of a person holding any such position as is mentioned in subsection (2)(b), if the overseas company has ceased to have any connection with the United Kingdom by virtue of which it is required to register particulars under section 1046.

(7) Further provision as to service and other matters is made in the company communications provisions (see section 1143).

(8) Nothing in this section shall be read as affecting any enactment or rule of law under which permission is required for service out of the jurisdiction.

1141 Service addresses

(1) In the Companies Acts a "service address", in relation to a person, means an address at which documents may be effectively served on that person.

(2) The Secretary of State may by regulations specify conditions with which a service address must comply.

(3) Regulations under this section are subject to negative resolution procedure.

1142 Requirement to give service address

Any obligation under the Companies Acts to give a person's address is, unless otherwise expressly provided, to give a service address for that person.

Sending or supplying documents or information

1143   The company communications provisions

(1)   The provisions of sections 1144 to 1148 and Schedules 4 and 5 ("the company communications provisions") have effect for the purposes of any provision of the Companies Acts that authorises or requires documents or information to be sent or supplied by or to a company.

(2)   The company communications provisions have effect subject to any requirements imposed, or contrary provision made, by or under any enactment.

(3)   In particular, in their application in relation to documents or information to be sent or supplied to the registrar, they have effect subject to the provisions of Part 35.

(4)   For the purposes of subsection (2), provision is not to be regarded as contrary to the company communications provisions by reason only of the fact that it expressly authorises a document or information to be sent or supplied in hard copy form, in electronic form or by means of a website.

1144   Sending or supplying documents or information

(1)   Documents or information to be sent or supplied to a company must be sent or supplied in accordance with the provisions of Schedule 4.

(2)   Documents or information to be sent or supplied by a company must be sent or supplied in accordance with the provisions of Schedule 5.

(3)   The provisions referred to in subsection (2) apply (and those referred to in subsection (1) do not apply) in relation to documents or information that are to be sent or supplied by one company to another.

1145   Right to hard copy version

(1)   Where a member of a company or a holder of a company's debentures has received a document or information from the company otherwise than in hard copy form, he is entitled to require the company to send him a version of the document or information in hard copy form.

(2)   The company must send the document or information in hard copy form within 21 days of receipt of the request from the member or debenture holder.

(3)   The company may not make a charge for providing the document or information in that form.

(4)   If a company fails to comply with this section, an offence is committed by the company and every officer of it who is in default.

(5)   A person guilty of an offence under this section is liable on summary conviction to a fine not exceeding level 3 on the standard scale and, for continued contravention, a daily default fine not exceeding one-tenth of level 3 on the standard scale.

1146   Requirement of authentication

(1)   This section applies in relation to the authentication of a document or information sent or supplied by a person to a company.

(2)   A document or information sent or supplied in hard copy form is sufficiently authenticated if it is signed by the person sending or supplying it.

(3)   A document or information sent or supplied in electronic form is sufficiently authenticated—

    (a)   if the identity of the sender is confirmed in a manner specified by the company, or

    (b)   where no such manner has been specified by the company, if the communication contains or is accompanied by a statement of the identity of the sender and the company has no reason to doubt the truth of that statement.

(4)   Where a document or information is sent or supplied by one person on behalf of another, nothing in this section affects any provision of the company's articles under which the company may require reasonable evidence of the authority of the former to act on behalf of the latter.

1147   Deemed delivery of documents and information

(1)   This section applies in relation to documents and information sent or supplied by a company.

(2)   Where—

(a)   the document or information is sent by post (whether in hard copy or electronic form) to an address in the United Kingdom, and

(b)   the company is able to show that it was properly addressed, prepaid and posted,

it is deemed to have been received by the intended recipient 48 hours after it was posted.

(3)   Where—

(a)   the document or information is sent or supplied by electronic means, and

(b)   the company is able to show that it was properly addressed,

it is deemed to have been received by the intended recipient 48 hours after it was sent.

(4)   Where the document or information is sent or supplied by means of a website, it is deemed to have been received by the intended recipient—

(a)   when the material was first made available on the website, or

(b)   if later, when the recipient received (or is deemed to have received) notice of the fact that the material was available on the website.

(5)   In calculating a period of hours for the purposes of this section, no account shall be taken of any part of a day that is not a working day.

(6)   This section has effect subject to—

(a)   in its application to documents or information sent or supplied by a company to its members, any contrary provision of the company's articles;

(b)   in its application to documents or information sent or supplied by a company to its debentures holders, any contrary provision in the instrument constituting the debentures;

(c)   in its application to documents or information sent or supplied by a company to a person otherwise than in his capacity as a member or debenture holder, any contrary provision in an agreement between the company and that person.

1148   Interpretation of company communications provisions

(1)   In the company communications provisions—

"address" includes a number or address used for the purposes of sending or receiving documents or information by electronic means;

"company" includes any body corporate;

"document" includes summons, notice, order or other legal process and registers.

(2)   References in the company communications provisions to provisions of the Companies Acts authorising or requiring a document or information to be sent or supplied include all such provisions, whatever expression is used, and references to documents or information being sent or supplied shall be construed accordingly.

(3)   References in the company communications provisions to documents or information being sent or supplied by or to a company include references to documents or information being sent or supplied by or to the directors of a company acting on behalf of the company.

Requirements as to independent valuation

1149   Application of valuation requirements

The provisions of sections 1150 to 1153 apply to the valuation and report required by—

section 93 (re-registration as public company: recent allotment of shares for non-cash consideration);

section 593 (allotment of shares of public company in consideration of non-cash asset);

section 599 (transfer of non-cash asset to public company).

1150   Valuation by qualified independent person

(1)   The valuation and report must be made by a person ("the valuer") who—

(a)   is eligible for appointment as a statutory auditor (see section 1212), and

(b)   meets the independence requirement in section 1151.

(2)   However, where it appears to the valuer to be reasonable for the valuation of the consideration, or part of it, to be made by (or for him to accept a valuation made by) another person who—

(a)   appears to him to have the requisite knowledge and experience to value the consideration or that part of it, and

(b)   is not an officer or employee of—

    (i)   the company, or

    (ii)   any other body corporate that is that company's subsidiary or holding company or a subsidiary of that company's holding company,

or a partner of or employed by any such officer or employee,

he may arrange for or accept such a valuation, together with a report which will enable him to make his own report under this section.

(3)   The references in subsection (2) (b) to an officer or employee do not include an auditor.

(4)   Where the consideration or part of it is valued by a person other than the valuer himself, the latter's report must state that fact and shall also—

(a)   state the former's name and what knowledge and experience he has to carry out the valuation, and

(b)   describe so much of the consideration as was valued by the other person, and the method used to value it, and specify the date of that valuation.

1151   The independence requirement

(1)   A person meets the independence requirement for the purposes of section 1150 only if—

(a)   he is not—

    (i)   an officer or employee of the company, or

    (ii)   a partner or employee of such a person, or a partnership of which such a person is a partner;

(b)   he is not—

    (i)   an officer or employee of an associated undertaking of the company, or

    (ii)   a partner or employee of such a person, or a partnership of which such a person is a partner; and

(c)   there does not exist between—

    (i)   the person or an associate of his, and

    (ii)   the company or an associated undertaking of the company, a connection of any such description as may be specified by regulations made by the Secretary of State.

(2)   An auditor of the company is not regarded as an officer or employee of the company for this purpose.

(3)   In this section—

"associated undertaking" means—

(a)   a parent undertaking or subsidiary undertaking of the company, or

(b)   a subsidiary undertaking of a parent undertaking of the company; and

"associate" has the meaning given by section 1152.

(4)   Regulations under this section are subject to negative resolution procedure.

1152   Meaning of "associate"

(1)   This section defines "associate" for the purposes of section 1151 (valuation: independence requirement).

(2)   In relation to an individual, "associate" means—

(a)   that individual's spouse or civil partner or minor child or step-child,

(b)   any body corporate of which that individual is a director, and

(c)   any employee or partner of that individual.

(3)   In relation to a body corporate, "associate" means—

(a)   any body corporate of which that body is a director,

(b)   any body corporate in the same group as that body, and

(c)   any employee or partner of that body or of any body corporate in the same group.

(4)   In relation to a partnership that is a legal person under the law by which it is governed, "associate" means—

(a)   any body corporate of which that partnership is a director,

(b)   any employee of or partner in that partnership, and

(c)   any person who is an associate of a partner in that partnership.

(5)   In relation to a partnership that is not a legal person under the law by which it is governed, "associate" means any person who is an associate of any of the partners.

(6)   In this section, in relation to a limited liability partnership, for "director" read "member".

1153   Valuer entitled to full disclosure

(1)   A person carrying out a valuation or making a report with respect to any consideration proposed to be accepted or given by a company, is entitled to require from the officers of the company such information and explanation as he thinks necessary to enable him to—

(a)   carry out the valuation or make the report, and

(b)   provide any note required by section 596(3) or 600(3) (note required where valuation carried out by another person).

(2)   A person who knowingly or recklessly makes a statement to which this subsection applies that is misleading, false or deceptive in a material particular commits an offence.

(3)   Subsection (2) applies to a statement—

(a)   made (whether orally or in writing) to a person carrying out a valuation or making a report, and

(b)   conveying or purporting to convey any information or explanation which that person requires, or is entitled to require, under subsection (1).

(4)   A person guilty of an offence under subsection (2) is liable—

(a)   on conviction on indictment, to imprisonment for a term not exceeding two years or a fine (or both);

(b)   on summary conviction—

(i)   in England and Wales, to imprisonment for a term not exceeding twelve months or to a fine not exceeding the statutory maximum (or both);

(ii)   in Scotland or Northern Ireland, to imprisonment for a term not exceeding six months, or to a fine not exceeding the statutory maximum (or both).

Notice of appointment of certain officers

1154   Duty to notify registrar of certain appointments etc

(1)   Notice must be given to the registrar of the appointment in relation to a company of—

(a)   a judicial factor (in Scotland),

(b)   an interim manager appointed under section 76 of the Charities Act 2011, or

(c)   a manager appointed under section 47 of the Companies (Audit, Investigations and Community Enterprise) Act 2004.

(2)   The notice must be given—

(a)   in the case of appointment of a judicial factor, by the judicial factor;

(b)   in the case of appointment of an interim manager under section 76 of the Charities Act 2011, by the Charity Commission;

(c)   in the case of appointment of a manager under section 47 of the Companies (Audit, Investigations and Community Enterprise) Act 2004, by the Regulator of Community Interest Companies.

(3)   The notice must specify an address at which service of documents (including legal process) may be effected on the person appointed.

Notice of a change in the address for service may be given to the registrar by the person appointed.

(4)   Where notice has been given under this section of the appointment of a person, notice must also be given to the registrar of the termination of the appointment. This notice must be given by the person specified in subsection (2).

1155   Offence of failure to give notice

(1)   If a judicial factor fails to give notice of his appointment in accordance with section 1154 within the period of 14 days after the appointment he commits an offence.

(2)   A person guilty of an offence under this section is liable on summary conviction to a fine not exceeding level 5 on the standard scale and, for continued contravention, a daily default fine not exceeding one-tenth of level 5 on the standard scale.

Courts and legal proceedings

1156   Meaning of "the court"

(1)   Except as otherwise provided, in the Companies Acts "the court" means—
    (a)   in England and Wales, the High Court or the county court;
    (b)   in Scotland, the Court of Session or the sheriff court;
    (c)   in Northern Ireland, the High Court.

(2)   The provisions of the Companies Acts conferring jurisdiction on "the court" as defined above have effect subject to any enactment or rule of law relating to the allocation of jurisdiction or distribution of business between courts in any part of the United Kingdom.

(3), (4)   ...

1157   Power of court to grant relief in certain cases

(1)   If in proceedings for negligence, default, breach of duty or breach of trust against—
    (a)   an officer of a company, or
    (b)   a person employed by a company as auditor (whether he is or is not an officer of the company),
    it appears to the court hearing the case that the officer or person is or may be liable but that he acted honestly and reasonably, and that having regard to all the circumstances of the case (including those connected with his appointment) he ought fairly to be excused, the court may relieve him, either wholly or in part, from his liability on such terms as it thinks fit.

(2)   If any such officer or person has reason to apprehend that a claim will or might be made against him in respect of negligence, default, breach of duty or breach of trust—
    (a)   he may apply to the court for relief, and
    (b)   the court has the same power to relieve him as it would have had if it had been a court before which proceedings against him for negligence, default, breach of duty or breach of trust had been brought.

(3)   Where a case to which subsection (1) applies is being tried by a judge with a jury, the judge, after hearing the evidence, may, if he is satisfied that the defendant (in Scotland, the defender) ought in pursuance of that subsection to be relieved either in whole or in part from the liability sought to be enforced against him, withdraw the case from the jury and forthwith direct judgment to be entered for the defendant (in Scotland, grant decree of absolvitor) on such terms as to costs (in Scotland, expenses) or otherwise as the judge may think proper.

PART 38
COMPANIES: INTERPRETATION

Meaning of "UK-registered company"

1158   Meaning of "UK-registered company"

In the Companies Acts "UK-registered company" means a company registered under this Act. The expression does not include an overseas company that has registered particulars under section 1046.

Meaning of "subsidiary" and related expressions

1159   Meaning of "subsidiary" etc

(1)   A company is a "subsidiary" of another company, its "holding company", if that other company—

(a)   holds a majority of the voting rights in it, or

(b)   is a member of it and has the right to appoint or remove a majority of its board of directors, or

(c)   is a member of it and controls alone, pursuant to an agreement with other members, a majority of the voting rights in it,

or if it is a subsidiary of a company that is itself a subsidiary of that other company.

(2)   A company is a "wholly-owned subsidiary" of another company if it has no members except that other and that other's wholly-owned subsidiaries or persons acting on behalf of that other or its wholly-owned subsidiaries.

(3)   Schedule 6 contains provisions explaining expressions used in this section and otherwise supplementing this section.

(4)   In this section and that Schedule "company" includes any body corporate.

1160   Meaning of "subsidiary" etc: power to amend

(1)   The Secretary of State may by regulations amend the provisions of section 1159 (meaning of "subsidiary" etc) and Schedule 6 (meaning of "subsidiary" etc: supplementary provisions) so as to alter the meaning of the expressions "subsidiary", "holding company" or "wholly-owned subsidiary".

(2)   Regulations under this section are subject to negative resolution procedure.

(3)   Any amendment made by regulations under this section does not apply for the purposes of enactments outside the Companies Acts unless the regulations so provide.

(4)   So much of section 23(3) of the Interpretation Act 1978 as applies section 17(2)(a) of that Act (effect of repeal and re-enactment) to deeds, instruments and documents other than enactments does not apply in relation to any repeal and re-enactment effected by regulations under this section.

Meaning of "undertaking" and related expressions

1161   Meaning of "undertaking" and related expressions

(1)   In the Companies Acts "undertaking" means—

(a)   a body corporate or partnership, or

(b)   an unincorporated association carrying on a trade or business, with or without a view to profit.

(2)   In the Companies Acts references to shares—

(a)   in relation to an undertaking with capital but no share capital, are to rights to share in the capital of the undertaking; and

(b)   in relation to an undertaking without capital, are to interests—

(i)   conferring any right to share in the profits or liability to contribute to the losses of the undertaking, or

(ii)   giving rise to an obligation to contribute to the debts or expenses of the undertaking in the event of a winding up.

(3)   Other expressions appropriate to companies shall be construed, in relation to an undertaking which is not a company, as references to the corresponding persons, officers, documents or organs, as the case may be, appropriate to undertakings of that description.

This is subject to provision in any specific context providing for the translation of such expressions.

(4)   References in the Companies Acts to "fellow subsidiary undertakings" are to undertakings which are subsidiary undertakings of the same parent undertaking but are not parent undertakings or subsidiary undertakings of each other.

(5)   In the Companies Acts "group undertaking", in relation to an undertaking, means an undertaking which is—

(a)   a parent undertaking or subsidiary undertaking of that undertaking, or

(b)   a subsidiary undertaking of any parent undertaking of that undertaking.

1162 **Parent and subsidiary undertakings**

(1) This section (together with Schedule 7) defines "parent undertaking" and "subsidiary undertaking" for the purposes of the Companies Acts.

(2) An undertaking is a parent undertaking in relation to another undertaking, a subsidiary undertaking, if—

    (a) it holds a majority of the voting rights in the undertaking, or

    (b) it is a member of the undertaking and has the right to appoint or remove a majority of its board of directors, or

    (c) it has the right to exercise a dominant influence over the undertaking—

        (i) by virtue of provisions contained in the undertaking's articles, or

        (ii) by virtue of a control contract, or

    (d) it is a member of the undertaking and controls alone, pursuant to an agreement with other shareholders or members, a majority of the voting rights in the undertaking.

(3) For the purposes of subsection (2) an undertaking shall be treated as a member of another undertaking—

    (a) if any of its subsidiary undertakings is a member of that undertaking, or

    (b) if any shares in that other undertaking are held by a person acting on behalf of the undertaking or any of its subsidiary undertakings.

(4) An undertaking is also a parent undertaking in relation to another undertaking, a subsidiary undertaking, if—

    (a) it has the power to exercise, or actually exercises, dominant influence or control over it, or

    (b) it and the subsidiary undertaking are managed on a unified basis.

(5) A parent undertaking shall be treated as the parent undertaking of undertakings in relation to which any of its subsidiary undertakings are, or are to be treated as, parent undertakings; and references to its subsidiary undertakings shall be construed accordingly.

(6) Schedule 7 contains provisions explaining expressions used in this section and otherwise supplementing this section.

(7) In this section and that Schedule references to shares, in relation to an undertaking, are to allotted shares.

Other definitions

1163 **"Non-cash asset"**

(1) In the Companies Acts "non-cash asset" means any property or interest in property, other than cash.

For this purpose "cash" includes foreign currency.

(2) A reference to the transfer or acquisition of a non-cash asset includes—

    (a) the creation or extinction of an estate or interest in, or a right over, any property, and

    (b) the discharge of a liability of any person, other than a liability for a liquidated sum.

1164 **Meaning of "banking company" and "banking group"**

(1) This section defines "banking company" and "banking group" for the purposes of the Companies Acts.

(2) "Banking company" means a person who has permission under Part 4A of the Financial Services and Markets Act 2000 to accept deposits, other than—

    (a) a person who is not a company, and

    (b) a person who has such permission only for the purpose of carrying on another regulated activity in accordance with permission under that Part.

(3) The definition in subsection (2) must be read with section 22 of that Act, any relevant order under that section and Schedule 2 to that Act.

(4) References to a banking group are to a group where the parent company is a banking company or where—

(a) the parent company's principal subsidiary undertakings are wholly or mainly credit institutions, and

(b) the parent company does not itself carry on any material business apart from the acquisition, management and disposal of interests in subsidiary undertakings.

"Group" here means a parent undertaking and its subsidiary undertakings.

(5) For the purposes of subsection (4)—

(a) a parent company's principal subsidiary undertakings are the subsidiary undertakings of the company whose results or financial position would principally affect the figures shown in the group accounts, and

(b) the management of interests in subsidiary undertakings includes the provision of services to such undertakings.

1165 Meaning of "insurance company" and related expressions

(1) This section defines "insurance company", "authorised insurance company", "insurance group" and "insurance market activity" for the purposes of the Companies Acts.

(2) An "authorised insurance company" means a person (whether incorporated or not) who has permission under Part 4A of the Financial Services and Markets Act 2000 to effect or carry out contracts of insurance.

(3) An "insurance company" means—

(a) an authorised insurance company, or

(b) any other person (whether incorporated or not) who—

    (i) carries on insurance market activity, or

    (ii) may effect or carry out contracts of insurance under which the benefits provided by that person are exclusively or primarily benefits in kind in the event of accident to or breakdown of a vehicle.

(4) Neither expression includes a friendly society within the meaning of the Friendly Societies Act 1992.

(5) References to an insurance group are to a group where the parent company is an insurance company or where—

(a) the parent company's principal subsidiary undertakings are wholly or mainly insurance companies, and

(b) the parent company does not itself carry on any material business apart from the acquisition, management and disposal of interests in subsidiary undertakings.

"Group" here means a parent undertaking and its subsidiary undertakings.

(6) For the purposes of subsection (5)—

(a) a parent company's principal subsidiary undertakings are the subsidiary undertakings of the company whose results or financial position would principally affect the figures shown in the group accounts, and

(b) the management of interests in subsidiary undertakings includes the provision of services to such undertakings.

(7) "Insurance market activity" has the meaning given in section 316(3) of the Financial Services and Markets Act 2000.

(8) References in this section to contracts of insurance and to the effecting or carrying out of such contracts must be read with section 22 of that Act, any relevant order under that section and Schedule 2 to that Act.

1166 "Employees' share scheme"

For the purposes of the Companies Acts an employees' share scheme is a scheme for encouraging or facilitating the holding of shares in or debentures of a company by or for the benefit of—

(a) the bona fide employees or former employees of—

    (i) the company,

    (ii) any subsidiary of the company, or

          (iii)   the company's holding company or any subsidiary of the company's holding company, or

    (b)   the spouses, civil partners, surviving spouses, surviving civil partners, or minor children or step-children of such employees or former employees.

1167   Meaning of "prescribed"

In the Companies Acts "prescribed" means prescribed (by order or by regulations) by the Secretary of State.

1168   Hard copy and electronic form and related expressions

(1)   The following provisions apply for the purposes of the Companies Acts.

(2)   A document or information is sent or supplied in hard copy form if it is sent or supplied in a paper copy or similar form capable of being read.
References to hard copy have a corresponding meaning.

(3)   A document or information is sent or supplied in electronic form if it is sent or supplied—
    (a)   by electronic means (for example, by e-mail or fax), or
    (b)   by any other means while in an electronic form (for example, sending a disk by post).
References to electronic copy have a corresponding meaning.

(4)   A document or information is sent or supplied by electronic means if it is—
    (a)   sent initially and received at its destination by means of electronic equipment for the processing (which expression includes digital compression) or storage of data, and
    (b)   entirely transmitted, conveyed and received by wire, by radio, by optical means or by other electromagnetic means.
References to electronic means have a corresponding meaning.

(5)   A document or information authorised or required to be sent or supplied in electronic form must be sent or supplied in a form, and by a means, that the sender or supplier reasonably considers will enable the recipient—
    (a)   to read it, and
    (b)   to retain a copy of it.

(6)   For the purposes of this section, a document or information can be read only if—
    (a)   it can be read with the naked eye, or
    (b)   to the extent that it consists of images (for example photographs, pictures, maps, plans or drawings), it can be seen with the naked eye.

(7)   The provisions of this section apply whether the provision of the Companies Acts in question uses the words "sent" or "supplied" or uses other words (such as "deliver", "provide", "produce" or, in the case of a notice, "give") to refer to the sending or supplying of a document or information.

1169   Dormant companies

(1)   For the purposes of the Companies Acts a company is "dormant" during any period in which it has no significant accounting transaction.

(2)   A "significant accounting transaction" means a transaction that is required by section 386 to be entered in the company's accounting records.

(3)   In determining whether or when a company is dormant, there shall be disregarded—
    (a)   any transaction arising from the taking of shares in the company by a subscriber to the memorandum as a result of an undertaking of his in connection with the formation of the company;
    (b)   any transaction consisting of the payment of—
        (i)   a fee to the registrar on a change of the company's name,
        (ii)   a fee to the registrar on the re-registration of the company,
        (iii) a penalty under section 453 (penalty for failure to file accounts), or
        (iv) a fee to the registrar for the registration of a confirmation statement.

(4)   Any reference in the Companies Acts to a body corporate other than a company being dormant has a corresponding meaning.

1170   Meaning of "EEA State" and related expressions

In the Companies Acts—

"EEA State" has the meaning given by Schedule 1 to the Interpretation Act 1978;

"EEA company" and "EEA undertaking" mean a company or undertaking governed by the law of an EEA State.

1170A   Receiver or manager and certain related references

(1)   Any reference in the Companies Acts to a receiver or manager of the property of a company, or to a receiver of it, includes a receiver or manager or (as the case may be) a receiver of part only of that property and a receiver only of the income arising from the property or from part of it.

(2)   Any reference in the Companies Acts to the appointment of a receiver or manager under powers contained in an instrument includes an appointment made under powers that by virtue of an enactment are implied in and have effect as if contained in an instrument.

1170B   Meaning of "contributory"

(1)   In the Companies Acts "contributory" means every person liable to contribute to the assets of a company in the event of its being wound up.

(2)   For the purposes of all proceedings for determining, and all proceedings prior to the final determination of, the persons who are to be deemed contributories, the expression includes any person alleged to be a contributory.

(3)   The reference in subsection (1) to persons liable to contribute to the assets does not include a person so liable by virtue of a declaration by the court under—

(a)   section 213 of the Insolvency Act 1986 or Article 177 of the Insolvency (Northern Ireland) Order 1989 (fraudulent trading), or

(b)   section 214 of that Act or Article 178 of that Order (wrongful trading).

1171   The former Companies Acts

In the Companies Acts—

"the former Companies Acts" means—

(a)   the Joint Stock Companies Acts, the Companies Act 1862, the Companies (Consolidation) Act 1908, the Companies Act 1929, the Companies Act (Northern Ireland) 1932, the Companies Acts 1948 to 1983, the Companies Act (Northern Ireland) 1960, the Companies (Northern Ireland) Order 1986 and the Companies Consolidation (Consequential Provisions) (Northern Ireland) Order 1986, and

(b)   the provisions of the Companies Act 1985 and the Companies Consolidation (Consequential Provisions) Act 1985 that are no longer in force;

"the Joint Stock Companies Acts" means the Joint Stock Companies Act 1856, the Joint Stock Companies Acts 1856, 1857, the Joint Stock Banking Companies Act 1857, and the Act to enable Joint Stock Banking Companies to be formed on the principle of limited liability, but does not include the Joint Stock Companies Act 1844.

General

1172   References to requirements of this Act

References in the company law provisions of this Act to the requirements of this Act include the requirements of regulations and orders made under it.

1173   Minor definitions: general

(1)   In the Companies Acts—

"the Audit Regulation" means Regulation 537/2014 of the European Parliament and of the Council on specific requirements regarding statutory audit of public interest entities;

"body corporate" and "corporation" include a body incorporated outside the United Kingdom, but do not include—

(a)   a corporation sole, or

(b)   a partnership that, whether or not a legal person, is not regarded as a body corporate under the law by which it is governed;

"the competent authority" means the Financial Reporting Council Limited;

"credit institution" means a credit institution as defined in Article 4(1)(1) of Regulation (EU) No. 575/2013 of the European Parliament and of the Council;

"the data protection legislation" has the same meaning as in the Data Protection Act 2018 (see section 3 of that Act);

"EU regulated market" has the meaning given in Article 2.1.13B of Regulation (EU) No. 600/2014 of the European Parliament and of the Council of 15 May 2014 and amending Regulation (EU) No. 648/2012;

"financial institution" means a financial institution within the meaning of Article 1.1 of the Council Directive on the obligations of branches established in a Member State of credit and financial institutions having their head offices outside that Member State regarding the publication of annual accounting documents (the Bank Branches Directive, 89/117/ EEC);

"firm" means any entity, whether or not a legal person, that is not an individual and includes a body corporate, a corporation sole and a partnership or other unincorporated association;

"the Gazette" means—

(a)   as respects companies registered in England and Wales, the London Gazette,

(b)   as respects companies registered in Scotland, the Edinburgh Gazette, and

(c)   as respects companies registered in Northern Ireland, the Belfast Gazette;

"hire-purchase agreement" has the same meaning as in the Consumer Credit Act 1974;

"officer", in relation to a body corporate, includes a director, manager or secretary;

"parent company" means a company that is a parent undertaking (see section 1162 and Schedule 7);

"regulated activity" has the meaning given in section 22 of the Financial Services and Markets Act 2000;

"regulated market" has the meaning given in Article 2.1.13 of Regulation (EU) No. 600/2014 of the European Parliament and of the Council of 15 May 2014 and amending Regulation (EU) No. 648/2012;

"transferable securities" has the meaning given by Article 2.1.24 of Regulation (EU) No 600/2014 of the European Parliament and of the Council of 15 May 2014 and amending Regulation (EU) No 648/2012;

"UK regulated market" has the meaning given in Article 2.1.13A of Regulation (EU) No. 600/2014 of the European Parliament and of the Council of 15 May 2014 and amending Regulation (EU) No. 648/2012;

"working day", in relation to a company, means a day that is not a Saturday or Sunday, Christmas Day, Good Friday or any day that is a bank holiday under the Banking and Financial Dealings Act 1971 in the part of the United Kingdom where the company is registered.

(2)   ...

1174   Index of defined expressions

Schedule 8 contains an index of provisions defining or otherwise explaining expressions used in the Companies Acts.

...

PART 41
BUSINESS NAMES

CHAPTER 1
RESTRICTED OR PROHIBITED NAMES

Introductory

1192   Application of this Chapter

(1)   Subject to any express provision to the contrary, this Chapter applies to any person carrying on business in the United Kingdom.

(2)   The provisions of this Chapter do not prevent—

(a)   an individual carrying on business under a name consisting of his surname without any addition other than a permitted addition, or

(b)   individuals carrying on business in partnership under a name consisting of the surnames of all the partners without any addition other than a permitted addition.

(3)   The following are the permitted additions—

(a)   in the case of an individual, his forename or initial;

(b)   in the case of a partnership—

(i)   the forenames of individual partners or the initials of those forenames, or

(ii)   where two or more individual partners have the same surname, the addition of "s" at the end of that surname;

(c)   in either case, an addition merely indicating that the business is carried on in succession to a former owner of the business.

Sensitive words or expressions

1193   Name suggesting connection with government or public authority

(1)   A person must not, without the approval of the Secretary of State, carry on business in the United Kingdom under a name that would be likely to give the impression that the business is connected with—

(a)   Her Majesty's Government, any part of the Scottish administration, the Welsh Assembly Government or Her Majesty's Government in Northern Ireland,

(b)   any local authority, or

(c)   any public authority specified for the purposes of this section by regulations made by the Secretary of State.

(2)   For the purposes of this section—
"local authority" means—

(a)   a local authority within the meaning of the Local Government Act 1972, the Common Council of the City of London or the Council of the Isles of Scilly,

(b)   a council constituted under section 2 of the Local Government etc. (Scotland) Act 1994, or

(c)   a district council in Northern Ireland;
"public authority" includes any person or body having functions of a public nature.

(3)   Regulations under this section are subject to affirmative resolution procedure.

(4)   A person who contravenes this section commits an offence.

(5)   Where an offence under this section is committed by a body corporate, an offence is also committed by every officer of the body who is in default.

(6)   A person guilty of an offence under this section is liable on summary conviction to a fine not exceeding level 3 on the standard scale and, for continued contravention, a daily default fine not exceeding one-tenth of level 3 on the standard scale.

1194   Other sensitive words or expressions

(1)   A person must not, without the approval of the Secretary of State, carry on business in the United Kingdom under a name that includes a word or expression for the time being specified in regulations made by the Secretary of State under this section.

(2)   Regulations under this section are subject to approval after being made.

(3)   A person who contravenes this section commits an offence.

(4)   Where an offence under this section is committed by a body corporate, an offence is also committed by every officer of the body who is in default.

(5)   A person guilty of an offence under this section is liable on summary conviction to a fine not exceeding level 3 on the standard scale and, for continued contravention, a daily default fine not exceeding one-tenth of level 3 on the standard scale.

1195   Requirement to seek comments of government department or other relevant body

(1)   The Secretary of State may by regulations under—
    (a)   section 1193 (name suggesting connection with government or public authority), or
    (b)   section 1194 (other sensitive words or expressions),
    require that, in connection with an application for the approval of the Secretary of State under that section, the applicant must seek the view of a specified Government department or other body.

(2)   Where such a requirement applies, the applicant must request the specified department or other body (in writing) to indicate whether (and if so why) it has any objections to the proposed name.

(3)   He must submit to the Secretary of State a statement that such a request has been made and a copy of any response received from the specified body.

(4)   If these requirements are not complied with, the Secretary of State may refuse to consider the application for approval.

(5)   In this section "specified" means specified in the regulations.

1196   Withdrawal of Secretary of State's approval

(1)   This section applies to approval given for the purposes of—
    section 1193 (name suggesting connection with government or public authority), or
    section 1194 (other sensitive words or expressions).

(2)   If it appears to the Secretary of State that there are overriding considerations of public policy that require such approval to be withdrawn, the approval may be withdrawn by notice in writing given to the person concerned.

(3)   The notice must state the date as from which approval is withdrawn.

1196A   Names suggesting connection with foreign governments etc

(1)   A person must not carry on business in the United Kingdom under a name that would be likely to give the false impression that the business is connected with—
    (a)   a foreign government or an agency or authority of a foreign government, or
    (b)   an international organisation whose members include two or more countries or territories (or their governments).

(2)   A person who contravenes this section commits an offence.

(3)   Where an offence under this section is committed by a body corporate, an offence is also committed by every officer of the body who is in default.

(4)   A person guilty of an offence under this section is liable on summary conviction to a fine not exceeding level 3 on the standard scale and, for continued contravention, a daily default fine not exceeding one-tenth of level 3 on the standard scale.

Misleading names

1197   Name containing inappropriate indication of company type or legal form

(1)   The Secretary of State may make provision by regulations prohibiting a person from carrying on business in the United Kingdom under a name consisting of or containing specified words, expressions or other indications—
    (a)   that are associated with a particular type of company or form of organisation, or
    (b)   that are similar to words, expressions or other indications associated with a particular type of company or form of organisation.

(2)   The regulations may prohibit the use of words, expressions or other indications—

      (a)   in a specified part, or otherwise than in a specified part, of a name;

      (b)   in conjunction with, or otherwise than in conjunction with, such other words, expressions or indications as may be specified.

(3)   In this section "specified" means specified in the regulations.

(4)   Regulations under this section are subject to negative resolution procedure.

(5)   A person who uses a name in contravention of regulations under this section commits an offence.

(6)   Where an offence under this section is committed by a body corporate, an offence is also committed by every officer of the body who is in default.

(7)   A person guilty of an offence under this section is liable on summary conviction to a fine not exceeding level 3 on the standard scale and, for continued contravention, a daily default fine not exceeding one-tenth of level 3 on the standard scale.

1198   Name giving misleading indication of activities

(1)   A person must not carry on business in the United Kingdom under a name that gives so misleading an indication of the nature of the activities of the business as to pose a risk of harm to the public in the United Kingdom or elsewhere.

(2)   A person who uses a name in contravention of this section commits an offence.

(3)   Where an offence under this section is committed by a body corporate, an offence is also committed by every officer of the body who is in default.

(4)   A person guilty of an offence under this section is liable on summary conviction to a fine not exceeding level 3 on the standard scale and, for continued contravention, a daily default fine not exceeding one-tenth of level 3 on the standard scale.

Restrictions where a company has been required to change a name

1198A   Name that a company has been required to change

(1)   Where a relevant direction has been given to a company to change its name, or it has been ordered under section 73 to change its name, the company must not carry on business in the United Kingdom under the name that it was directed or ordered to change, except as mentioned in subsection (2).

(2)   Subsection (1) does not prevent the use by a company of a name if—

      (a)   the period for complying with the direction or order has not yet expired,

      (b)   the company complied with the direction or order and has since become registered with the name again following approval given under section 57B, or

      (c)   the direction was given, or the order was made, before section 25 of the Economic Crime and Corporate Transparency Act 2023 came fully into force.

(3)   If a company uses a name in contravention of this section an offence is committed by—

      (a)   the company, and

      (b)   every officer of the company who is in default.

(4)   A person guilty of an offence under this section is liable on summary conviction to a fine not exceeding level 3 on the standard scale and, for continued contravention, a daily default fine not exceeding one-tenth of level 3 on the standard scale.

(5)   In this section—

      "company" includes an overseas company;

      "relevant direction" means a direction under section 67, 75, 76, 76A or 76B, other than a direction under section 76B(1)(b) given on the basis that, at the time at which a company's name was registered, the Secretary of State had proper grounds for forming the opinion mentioned in section 57A.

1198B   Name that another company has been required to change

(1)   Where a relevant direction has been given to a company to change its name, or it has been ordered under section 73 to change its name, another company must not carry on business in the United Kingdom under the name that the first company was directed or ordered to change if there is a person who has, or has had, a relevant relationship with both companies.

(2)   Subsection (1) does not prevent the use by a company of a name if—
    (a)   it is registered under this Act by that name,
    (b)   the period for complying with the direction or order has not yet expired, or
    (c)   the direction was given, or the order was made, before section 26 of the Economic Crime and Corporate Transparency Act 2023 came fully into force.

(3)   For the purposes of subsection (1) it is irrelevant whether the person has, or has had, a relevant relationship with both companies at the same time.

(4)   For the purposes of this section a person has a "relevant relationship" with a company if the person is—
    (a)   an officer, or
    (b)   a member or former member.

(5)   If a company uses a name in contravention of this section an offence is committed by—
    (a)   the company, and
    (b)   every officer of the company who is in default.

(6)   A person guilty of an offence under this section is liable on summary conviction to a fine not exceeding level 3 on the standard scale and, for continued contravention, a daily default fine not exceeding one-tenth of level 3 on the standard scale.

(7)   In this section—
    "company" includes an overseas company;
    "relevant direction" means a direction under section 67, 75, 76A or 76B, other than a direction under section 76B(1)(b) given on the basis that, at the time at which a company's name was registered, the Secretary of State had proper grounds for forming the opinion mentioned in section 57A.

Supplementary

1199   Savings for existing lawful business names

(1)   This section has effect in relation to—
sections 1192 to 1196 (sensitive words or expressions), and
section 1197 (inappropriate indication of company type or legal form).

(2)   Those sections do not apply to the carrying on of a business by a person who—
    (a)   carried on the business immediately before the date on which this Chapter came into force, and
    (b)   continues to carry it on under the name that immediately before that date was its lawful business name.

(3)   Where—
    (a)   a business is transferred to a person on or after the date on which this Chapter came into force, and
    (b)   that person carries on the business under the name that was its lawful business name immediately before the transfer,
those sections do not apply in relation to the carrying on of the business under that name during the period of twelve months beginning with the date of the transfer.

(4)   In this section "lawful business name", in relation to a business, means a name under which the business was carried on without contravening—
    (a)   section 2(1) of the Business Names Act 1985 or Article 4(1) of the Business Names (Northern Ireland) Order 1986, or
    (b)   after this Chapter has come into force, the provisions of this Chapter.

1199A Exceptions based on national security etc

(1)   The Secretary of State may, by written notice given to a person, provide that a prohibition imposed by this Chapter does not apply in relation to the carrying on of a business by that person under a name specified in the notice, if satisfied that to do so is necessary—
    (a)   in the interests of national security, or
    (b)   for the purposes of preventing or detecting serious crime.

(2)   For the purposes of subsection (1)(b)—
(a)   "crime" means conduct which—
(i)   constitutes a criminal offence, or
(ii)   is, or corresponds to, any conduct which, if it all took place in any one part of the United Kingdom, would constitute a criminal offence, and
(b)   crime is "serious" if—
(i)   the offence which is or would be constituted by the conduct is an offence for which the maximum sentence (in any part of the United Kingdom) is imprisonment for 3 years or more, or
(ii)   the conduct involves the use of violence, results in substantial financial gain or is conduct by a large number of persons in pursuit of a common purpose.

CHAPTER 2
DISCLOSURE REQUIRED IN CASE OF INDIVIDUAL OR PARTNERSHIP

Introductory

1200   Application of this Chapter

(1)   This Chapter applies to an individual or partnership carrying on business in the United Kingdom under a business name.
References in this Chapter to "a person to whom this Chapter applies" are to such an individual or partnership.

(2)   For the purposes of this Chapter a "business name" means a name other than—
(a)   in the case of an individual, his surname without any addition other than a permitted addition;
(b)   in the case of a partnership—
(i)   the surnames of all partners who are individuals, and
(ii)   the corporate names of all partners who are bodies corporate, without any addition other than a permitted addition.

(3)   The following are the permitted additions—
(a)   in the case of an individual, his forename or initial;
(b)   in the case of a partnership—
(i)   the forenames of individual partners or the initials of those forenames, or
(ii)   where two or more individual partners have the same surname, the addition of "s" at the end of that surname;
(c)   in either case, an addition merely indicating that the business is carried on in succession to a former owner of the business.

1201   Information required to be disclosed

(1)   The "information required by this Chapter" is—
(a)   in the case of an individual, the individual's name;
(b)   in the case of a partnership, the name of each member of the partnership;
and, in relation to each person so named, an address at which service of any document relating in any way to the business will be effective.

(2)   If the individual or partnership has a place of business in the United Kingdom, the address must be in the United Kingdom.

(3)   If the individual or partnership does not have a place of business in the United Kingdom, the address must be an address at which service of documents can be effected by physical delivery and the delivery of documents is capable of being recorded by the obtaining of an acknowledgement of delivery.

Disclosure requirements

1202   Disclosure required: business documents etc

(1)   A person to whom this Chapter applies must state the information required by this Chapter, in legible characters, on all—

    (a)   business letters,

    (b)   written orders for goods or services to be supplied to the business,

    (c)   invoices and receipts issued in the course of the business, and

    (d)   written demands for payment of debts arising in the course of the business.

This subsection has effect subject to section 1203 (exemption for large partnerships if certain conditions met).

(2)   A person to whom this Chapter applies must secure that the information required by this Chapter is immediately given, by written notice, to any person with whom anything is done or discussed in the course of the business and who asks for that information.

(3)   The Secretary of State may by regulations require that such notices be given in a specified form.

(4)   Regulations under this section are subject to negative resolution procedure.

1203   Exemption for large partnerships if certain conditions met

(1)   Section 1202(1) (disclosure required in business documents) does not apply in relation to a document issued by a partnership of more than 20 persons if the following conditions are met.

(2)   The conditions are that—

    (a)   the partnership maintains at its principal place of business a list of the names of all the partners,

    (b)   no partner's name appears in the document, except in the text or as a signatory, and

    (c)   the document states in legible characters the address of the partnership's principal place of business and that the list of the partners' names is open to inspection there.

(3)   Where a partnership maintains a list of the partners' names for the purposes of this section, any person may inspect the list during office hours.

(4)   Where an inspection required by a person in accordance with this section is refused, an offence is committed by any member of the partnership concerned who without reasonable excuse refused the inspection or permitted it to be refused.

(5)   A person guilty of an offence under subsection (4) is liable on summary conviction to a fine not exceeding level 3 on the standard scale and, for continued contravention, a daily default fine not exceeding one-tenth of level 3 on the standard scale.

1204   Disclosure required: business premises

(1)   A person to whom this Chapter applies must, in any premises—

    (a)   where the business is carried on, and

    (b)   to which customers of the business or suppliers of goods or services to the business have access,

display in a prominent position, so that it may easily be read by such customers or suppliers, a notice containing the information required by this Chapter.

(2)   The Secretary of State may by regulations require that such notices be displayed in a specified form.

(3)   Regulations under this section are subject to negative resolution procedure.

Consequences of failure to make required disclosure

1205   Criminal consequences of failure to make required disclosure

(1)   A person who without reasonable excuse fails to comply with the requirements of—

section 1202 (disclosure required: business documents etc), or

section 1204 (disclosure required: business premises),

commits an offence.

(2)   Where an offence under this section is committed by a body corporate, an offence is also committed by every officer of the body who is in default.

(3)   A person guilty of an offence under this section is liable on summary conviction to a fine not exceeding level 3 on the standard scale and, for continued contravention, a daily default fine not exceeding one-tenth of level 3 on the standard scale.

(4)   References in this section to the requirements of section 1202 or 1204 include the requirements of regulations under that section.

1206   Civil consequences of failure to make required disclosure

(1)   This section applies to any legal proceedings brought by a person to whom this Chapter applies to enforce a right arising out of a contract made in the course of a business in respect of which he was, at the time the contract was made, in breach of section 1202(1) or (2) (disclosure in business documents etc) or section 1204(1) (disclosure at business premises).

(2)   The proceedings shall be dismissed if the defendant (in Scotland, the defender) to the proceedings shows—

       (a)   that he has a claim against the claimant (pursuer) arising out of the contract that he has been unable to pursue by reason of the latter's breach of the requirements of this Chapter, or

       (b)   that he has suffered some financial loss in connection with the contract by reason of the claimant's (pursuer's) breach of those requirements,

     unless the court before which the proceedings are brought is satisfied that it is just and equitable to permit the proceedings to continue.

(3)   References in this section to the requirements of this Chapter include the requirements of regulations under this Chapter.

(4)   This section does not affect the right of any person to enforce such rights as he may have against another person in any proceedings brought by that person.

CHAPTER 3
SUPPLEMENTARY

1207   Application of general provisions about offences

     The provisions of sections 1121 to 1123 (liability of officer in default) and 1125 to 1131 (general provisions about offences) apply in relation to offences under this Part as in relation to offences under the Companies Acts.

1208   Interpretation

In this Part—

       "business" includes a profession;

       "initial" includes any recognised abbreviation of a name;

       "partnership" means—

       (a)   a partnership within the Partnership Act 1890, or

       (b)   a limited partnership registered under the Limited Partnerships Act 1907,

       or a firm or entity of a similar character formed under the law of a country or territory outside the United Kingdom;

       "surname", in relation to a peer or person usually known by a British title different from his surname, means the title by which he is known.

. . .

PART 45
NORTHERN IRELAND

1284   Extension of Companies Acts to Northern Ireland

(1)   The Companies Acts as defined by this Act (see section 2) extend to Northern Ireland.

(2)   The Companies (Northern Ireland) Order 1986, the Companies Consolidation (Consequential Provisions) (Northern Ireland) Order 1986 and Part 3 of the Companies (Audit, Investigations and Community Enterprise) Order 2005 shall cease to have effect accordingly.

1285   Extension of GB enactments relating to UK Societas

(1)   The enactments in force in Great Britain relating to UK Societas extend to Northern Ireland.

(2)   The following enactments shall cease to have effect accordingly—
   (a)   the European Public Limited-Liability Company Regulations (Northern Ireland) 2004, and
   (b)   the European Public Limited-Liability Company (Fees) Regulations (Northern Ireland) 2004.

(3)   In this section "UK Societas" means a United Kingdom Societas within the meaning of Council Regulation 2157/2001/EC of 8 October 2001 on the Statute for a European Company.

1286   Extension of GB enactments relating to certain other forms of business organisation

(1)   The enactments in force in Great Britain relating to—
   (a)   limited liability partnerships,
   (b)   limited partnerships,
   (c)   open-ended investment companies, ...
   (d)   European Economic Interest Groupings, and
   (e)   UK Economic Interest Groupings,
extend to Northern Ireland.

(2)   The following enactments shall cease to have effect accordingly—
   (a)   the Limited Liability Partnerships Act (Northern Ireland) 2002;
   (b)   the Limited Partnerships Act 1907 as it formerly had effect in Northern Ireland;
   (c)   the Open-Ended Investment Companies Act (Northern Ireland) 2002;
   (d)   the European Economic Interest Groupings Regulations (Northern Ireland) 1989.

1287   Extension of enactments relating to business names

(1)   The provisions of Part 41 of this Act (business names) extend to Northern Ireland.

(2)   The Business Names (Northern Ireland) Order 1986 shall cease to have effect accordingly.

...

PART 47

FINAL PROVISIONS

1298   Short title

The short title of this Act is the Companies Act 2006.

1299   Extent

Except as otherwise provided (or the context otherwise requires), the provisions of this Act extend to the whole of the United Kingdom.

1300   Commencement

(1)   The following provisions come into force on the day this Act is passed—
   (a)   Part 43 (transparency obligations and related matters), except the amendment in paragraph 11(2) of Schedule 15 of the definition of "regulated market" in Part 6 of the Financial Services and Markets Act 2000,
   (b)   in Part 44 (miscellaneous provisions)—
   section 1274 (grants to bodies concerned with actuarial standards etc), and
   section 1276 (application of provisions to Scotland and Northern Ireland),
   (c)   Part 46 (general supplementary provisions), except section 1295 and Schedule 16 (repeals), and
   (d)   this Part.

(2)   The other provisions of this Act come into force on such day as may be appointed by order of the Secretary of State or the Treasury.

SCHEDULES

SCHEDULE 1   Sections 254 and 255
CONNECTED PERSONS: REFERENCES TO AN INTEREST IN SHARES OR DEBENTURES

Introduction

1   (1)   The provisions of this Schedule have effect for the interpretation of references in sections 254 and 255 (directors connected with or controlling a body corporate) to an interest in shares or debentures.

         (2)   The provisions are expressed in relation to shares but apply to debentures as they apply to shares.

General provisions

2   (1)   A reference to an interest in shares includes any interest of any kind whatsoever in shares.

         (2)   Any restraints or restrictions to which the exercise of any right attached to the interest is or may be subject shall be disregarded.

         (3)   It is immaterial that the shares in which a person has an interest are not identifiable.

         (4)   Persons having a joint interest in shares are deemed each of them to have that interest.

Rights to acquire shares

3   (1)   A person is taken to have an interest in shares if he enters into a contract to acquire them.

         (2)   A person is taken to have an interest in shares if—

             (a)   he has a right to call for delivery of the shares to himself or to his order, or

             (b)   he has a right to acquire an interest in shares or is under an obligation to take an interest in shares,

         whether the right or obligation is conditional or absolute.

         (3)   Rights or obligations to subscribe for shares are not to be taken for the purposes of sub-paragraph (2) to be rights to acquire or obligations to take an interest in shares.

         (4)   A person ceases to have an interest in shares by virtue of this paragraph—

             (a)   on the shares being delivered to another person at his order—

                 (i)   in fulfilment of a contract for their acquisition by him, or

                (ii)   in satisfaction of a right of his to call for their delivery;

             (b)   on a failure to deliver the shares in accordance with the terms of such a contract or on which such a right falls to be satisfied;

             (c)   on the lapse of his right to call for the delivery of shares.

Right to exercise or control exercise of rights

4   (1)   A person is taken to have an interest in shares if, not being the registered holder, he is entitled—

             (a)   to exercise any right conferred by the holding of the shares, or

             (b)   to control the exercise of any such right.

         (2)   For this purpose a person is taken to be entitled to exercise or control the exercise of a right conferred by the holding of shares if he—

             (a)   has a right (whether subject to conditions or not) the exercise of which would make him so entitled, or

             (b)   is under an obligation (whether or not so subject) the fulfilment of which would make him so entitled.

         (3)   A person is not by virtue of this paragraph taken to be interested in shares by reason only that—

             (a)   he has been appointed a proxy to exercise any of the rights attached to the shares, or

             (b)   he has been appointed by a body corporate to act as its representative at any meeting of a company or of any class of its members.

Bodies corporate

5   (1)   A person is taken to be interested in shares if a body corporate is interested in them and—

        (a)   the body corporate or its directors are accustomed to act in accordance with his directions or instructions, or

        (b)   he is entitled to exercise or control the exercise of more than one-half of the voting power at general meetings of the body corporate.

    (2)   For the purposes of sub-paragraph (1)(b) where—

        (a)   a person is entitled to exercise or control the exercise of more than one-half of the voting power at general meetings of a body corporate, and

        (b)   that body corporate is entitled to exercise or control the exercise of any of the voting power at general meetings of another body corporate,

    the voting power mentioned in paragraph (b) above is taken to be exercisable by that person.

Trusts

6   (1)   Where an interest in shares is comprised in property held on trust, every beneficiary of the trust is taken to have an interest in shares, subject as follows.

    (2)   So long as a person is entitled to receive, during the lifetime of himself or another, income from trust property comprising shares, an interest in the shares in reversion or remainder or (as regards Scotland) in fee shall be disregarded.

    (3)   A person is treated as not interested in shares if and so long as he holds them—

        (a)   under the law in force in any part of the United Kingdom, as a bare trustee or as a custodian trustee, or

        (b)   under the law in force in Scotland, as a simple trustee.

    (4)   There shall be disregarded any interest of a person subsisting by virtue of—

        (a)   an authorised unit trust scheme (within the meaning of section 237 of the Financial Services and Markets Act 2000;

        (b)   a scheme made under section 22 or 22A of the Charities Act 1960, section 25 of the Charities Act (Northern Ireland) 1964, section 24 or 25 of the Charities Act 1993 or section 96 or 100 of the Charities Act 2011, section 11 of the Trustee Investments Act 1961 or section 42 of the Administration of Justice Act 1982; or

        (c)   the scheme set out in the Schedule to the Church Funds Investment Measure 1958.

    (5)   There shall be disregarded any interest—

        (a)   of the Church of Scotland General Trustees or of the Church of Scotland Trust in shares held by them;

        (b)   of any other person in shares held by those Trustees or that Trust otherwise than as simple trustees.

Note. Paragraph 6(4)(b) is amended by the Charities Act (Northern Ireland) 2008, s. 183, Sch. 8, para. 13(6), as from a day to be appointed.

Section 790C

SCHEDULE 1A
REFERENCES TO PEOPLE WITH SIGNIFICANT CONTROL OVER A COMPANY

PART 1
THE SPECIFIED CONDITIONS

Introduction

1   This Part of this Schedule specifies the conditions at least one of which must be met by an individual ("X") in relation to a company ("company Y") in order for the individual to be a person with "significant control" over the company.

Ownership of shares

2   The first condition is that X holds, directly or indirectly, more than 25% of the shares in company Y.

Ownership of voting rights

3   The second condition is that X holds, directly or indirectly, more than 25% of the voting rights in company Y.

Ownership of right to appoint or remove directors

4   The third condition is that X holds the right, directly or indirectly, to appoint or remove a majority of the board of directors of company Y.

Significant influence or control

5   The fourth condition is that X has the right to exercise, or actually exercises, significant influence or control over company Y.

Trusts, partnerships etc

6   The fifth condition is that—
         (a)   the trustees of a trust or the members of a firm that, under the law by which it is governed, is not a legal person meet any of the other specified conditions (in their capacity as such) in relation to company Y, or would do so if they were individuals, and
         (b)   X has the right to exercise, or actually exercises, significant influence or control over the activities of that trust or firm.

PART 2
HOLDING AN INTEREST IN A COMPANY ETC

Introduction

7   This Part of this Schedule specifies the circumstances in which, for the purposes of section 790C(4) or (8)—
         (a)   a person ("V") is to be regarded as holding an interest in a company ("company W");
         (b)   an interest held by V in company W is to be regarded as held through a legal entity.

Holding an interest

8   (1)   V holds an interest in company W if—
               (a)   V holds shares in company W, directly or indirectly,
               (b)   V holds, directly or indirectly, voting rights in company W,
               (c)   V holds, directly or indirectly, the right to appoint or remove any member of the board of directors of company W,
               (d)   V has the right to exercise, or actually exercises, significant influence or control over company W, or
               (e)   sub-paragraph (2) is satisfied.
         (2)   This sub-paragraph is satisfied where—
               (a)   the trustees of a trust or the members of a firm that, under the law by which it is governed, is not a legal person hold an interest in company W in a way mentioned in sub- paragraph (1)(a) to (d), and
               (b)   V has the right to exercise, or actually exercises, significant influence or control over the activities of that trust or firm.

Interests held through a legal entity

9   (1)   This paragraph applies where V—
               (a)   holds an interest in company W by virtue of indirectly holding shares or a right, and
               (b)   does so by virtue of having a majority stake (see paragraph 18) in—
                      (i)   a legal entity ("L") which holds the shares or right directly, or

           (ii)   a legal entity that is part of a chain of legal entities such as is described in paragraph 18(1)(b) or (2)(b) that includes L.

    (2)   Where this paragraph applies, V holds the interest in company W—

        (a)   through L, and

        (b)   through each other legal entity in the chain mentioned in sub-paragraph (1)(b)(ii).

PART 3
SUPPLEMENTARY PROVISION

Introduction

10   This Part sets out rules for the interpretation of this Schedule.

Joint interests

11   If two or more persons each hold a share or right jointly, each of them is treated for the purposes of this Schedule as holding that share or right.

Joint arrangements

12   (1)   If shares or rights held by a person and shares or rights held by another person are the subject of a joint arrangement between those persons, each of them is treated for the purposes of this Schedule as holding the combined shares or rights of both of them.

    (2)   A "joint arrangement" is an arrangement between the holders of shares (or rights) that they will exercise all or substantially all the rights conferred by their respective shares (or rights) jointly in a way that is pre-determined by the arrangement.

    (3)   "Arrangement" has the meaning given by paragraph 21.

Calculating shareholdings

13   (1)   In relation to a legal entity that has a share capital, a reference to holding "more than 25% of the shares" in that entity is to holding shares comprised in the issued share capital of that entity of a nominal value exceeding (in aggregate) 25% of that share capital.

    (2)   In relation to a legal entity that does not have a share capital—

        (a)   a reference to holding shares in that entity is to holding a right to share in the capital or, as the case may be, profits of that entity;

        (b)   a reference to holding "more than 25% of the shares" in that entity is to holding a right or rights to share in more than 25% of the capital or, as the case may be, profits of that entity.

Voting rights

14   (1)   A reference to the voting rights in a legal entity is to the rights conferred on shareholders in respect of their shares (or, in the case of an entity not having a share capital, on members) to vote at general meetings of the entity on all or substantially all matters.

    (2)   In relation to a legal entity that does not have general meetings at which matters are decided by the exercise of voting rights—

        (a)   a reference to exercising voting rights in the entity is to be read as a reference to exercising rights in relation to the entity that are equivalent to those of a person entitled to exercise voting rights in a company;

        (b)   a reference to exercising more than 25% of the voting rights in the entity is to be read as a reference to exercising the right under the constitution of the entity to block changes to the overall policy of the entity or to the terms of its constitution.

15   In applying this Schedule, the voting rights in a legal entity are to be reduced by any rights held by the entity itself.

Rights to appoint or remove members of the board

16   A reference to the right to appoint or remove a majority of the board of directors of a legal entity is to the right to appoint or remove directors holding a majority of the voting rights at meetings of the board on all or substantially all matters.

17   References to a board of directors, in the case of an entity that does not have such a board, are to be read as references to the equivalent management body of that entity.

Shares or rights held "indirectly"

18   (1)   A person holds a share "indirectly" if the person has a majority stake in a legal entity and that entity—
        (a)   holds the share in question, or
        (b)   is part of a chain of legal entities—
            (i)   each of which (other than the last) has a majority stake in the entity immediately below it in the chain, and
            (ii)   the last of which holds the share.

    (2)   A person holds a right "indirectly" if the person has a majority stake in a legal entity and that entity—
        (a)   holds that right, or
        (b)   is part of a chain of legal entities—
            (i)   each of which (other than the last) has a majority stake in the entity immediately below it in the chain, and
            (ii)   the last of which holds that right.

    (3)   For these purposes, A has a "majority stake" in B if—
        (a)   A holds a majority of the voting rights in B,
        (b)   A is a member of B and has the right to appoint or remove a majority of the board of directors of B,
        (c)   A is a member of B and controls alone, pursuant to an agreement with other shareholders or members, a majority of the voting rights in B, or
        (d)   A has the right to exercise, or actually exercises, dominant influence or control over B.

    (4)   In the application of this paragraph to the right to appoint or remove a majority of the board of directors, a legal entity is to be treated as having the right to appoint a director if—
        (a)   a person's appointment as director follows necessarily from that person's appointment as director of the legal entity, or
        (b)   the directorship is held by the legal entity itself.

Shares held by nominees

19   A share held by a person as nominee for another is to be treated for the purposes of this Schedule as held by the other (and not by the nominee).

Rights treated as held by person who controls their exercise

20   (1)   Where a person controls a right, the right is to be treated for the purposes of this Schedule as held by that person (and not by the person who in fact holds the right, unless that person also controls it).

    (2)   A person "controls" a right if, by virtue of any arrangement between that person and others, the right is exercisable only—
        (a)   by that person,
        (b)   in accordance with that person's directions or instructions, or
        (c)   with that person's consent or concurrence.

21   (1)   "Arrangement" includes—
        (a)   any scheme, agreement or understanding, whether or not it is legally enforceable, and
        (b)   any convention, custom or practice of any kind.

(2) But something does not count as an arrangement unless there is at least some degree of stability about it (whether by its nature or terms, the time it has been in existence or otherwise).

Rights exercisable only in certain circumstances etc

22 (1) Rights that are exercisable only in certain circumstances are to be taken into account only—

    (a) when the circumstances have arisen, and for so long as they continue to obtain, or

    (b) when the circumstances are within the control of the person having the rights.

(2) But rights that are exercisable by an administrator or by creditors while a legal entity is in relevant insolvency proceedings are not to be taken into account even while the entity is in those proceedings.

(3) "Relevant insolvency proceedings" means—

    (a) administration within the meaning of the Insolvency Act 1986,

    (b) administration within the meaning of the Insolvency (Northern Ireland) Order 1989 (S.I. 1989/2405 (N.I. 19)), or

    (c) proceedings under the insolvency law of another country or territory during which an entity's assets and affairs are subject to the control or supervision of a third party or creditor.

(4) Rights that are normally exercisable but are temporarily incapable of exercise are to continue to be taken into account.

Rights attached to shares held by way of security

23 Rights attached to shares held by way of security provided by a person are to be treated for the purposes of this Schedule as held by that person—

    (a) where apart from the right to exercise them for the purpose of preserving the value of the security, or of realising it, the rights are exercisable only in accordance with that person's instructions, and

    (b) where the shares are held in connection with the granting of loans as part of normal business activities and apart from the right to exercise them for the purpose of preserving the value of the security, or of realising it, the rights are exercisable only in that person's interests.

Significant influence or control

24 (1) The Secretary of State must issue guidance about the meaning of "significant influence or control" for the purposes of this Schedule.

(2) Regard must be had to that guidance in interpreting references in this Schedule to "significant influence or control".

(3) Before issuing guidance under this paragraph the Secretary of State must lay a draft of it before Parliament.

(4) If, within the 40-day period, either House of Parliament resolves not to approve the draft guidance, the Secretary of State must take no further steps in relation to it.

(5) If no such resolution is made within that period, the Secretary of State must issue and publish the guidance in the form of the draft.

(6) Sub-paragraph (4) does not prevent a new draft of proposed guidance from being laid before Parliament.

(7) In this section "the 40-day period", in relation to draft guidance, means the period of 40 days beginning with the day on which the draft is laid before Parliament (or, if it is not laid before each House on the same day, the later of the days on which it is laid).

(8) In calculating the 40-day period, no account is to be taken of any period during which—

    (a) Parliament is dissolved or prorogued, or

    (b) both Houses are adjourned for more than 4 days.

(9) The Secretary of State may revise guidance issued under this paragraph, and a reference in this paragraph to guidance includes a reference to revised guidance.

Limited partnerships

25   (1)   An individual does not meet the specified condition in paragraph 2, 3 or 4 in relation to a
               company by virtue only of being a limited partner.

        (2)   An individual does not meet the specified condition in paragraph 2, 3 or 4 in relation to a
               company by virtue only of, directly or indirectly—
               (a)   holding shares, or
               (b)   holding a right,
               in or in relation to a limited partner which (in its capacity as such) would meet the condition
               if it were an individual.

        (3)   Sub-paragraphs (1) and (2) do not apply for the purposes of determining whether the
               requirement set out in paragraph (a) of the specified condition in paragraph 6 is met.

        (4)   In this paragraph "limited partner" means—
               (a)   a limited partner in a limited partnership registered under the Limited Partnerships
                        Act 1907 (other than one who takes part in the management of the partnership
                        business), or
               (b)   a foreign limited partner.

        (5)   In this paragraph "foreign limited partner" means an individual who—
               (a)   participates in arrangements established under the law of a country or territory
                        outside the United Kingdom, and
               (b)   has the characteristics prescribed by regulations made by the Secretary of State.

        (6)   Regulations under this paragraph may, in particular, prescribe characteristics by reference
               to—
               (a)   the nature of arrangements;
               (b)   the nature of an individual's participation in the arrangements.

        (7)   Regulations under this paragraph are subject to affirmative resolution procedure.

PART 4
POWER TO AMEND THRESHOLDS ETC

26   (1)   The Secretary of State may by regulations amend this Schedule for a permitted purpose.
        (2)   The permitted purposes are—
               (a)   to replace any or all references in this Schedule to a percentage figure with
                        references to some other (larger or smaller) percentage figure;
               (b)   to change or supplement the specified conditions in Part 1 of this Schedule so as to
                        include circumstances (for example, circumstances involving more complex
                        structures) that give individuals a level of control over company Y broadly similar
                        to the level of control given by the other specified conditions;
               (c)   in consequence of any provision made by virtue of paragraph (b), to change or
                        supplement Part 2 of this Schedule so that circumstances specified in that Part in
                        which a person is to be regarded as holding an interest in a company correspond to
                        any of the specified conditions, or would do so but for the extent of the interest.

        (3)   Regulations under this paragraph are subject to affirmative resolution procedure.

SCHEDULE 1B   Section 790I
ENFORCEMENT OF DISCLOSURE REQUIREMENTS

Right to issue restrictions notice

1   (1)   This paragraph applies if—
               (a)   a notice under section 790D or 790E is served by a company on a person who has a
                        relevant interest in the company, and
               (b)   the person fails to comply with that notice within the time specified in it.

(2) The company may give the person a notice under this paragraph (a "warning notice") informing the person that it is proposing to issue the person with a notice (a "restrictions notice") with respect to the relevant interest.

(3) The company may issue the restrictions notice if, by the end of the period of one month beginning with the date on which the warning notice was given—

(a) the person has not complied with the notice served under section 790D or 790E, and

(b) the company has not been provided with a valid reason sufficient to justify the person's failure to comply with the notice served under that section.

(4) A restrictions notice is issued on a person by sending the notice to the person.

(5) The effect of a restrictions notice is set out in paragraph 3.

(6) In deciding whether to issue a restrictions notice, the company must have regard to the effect of the notice on the rights of third parties in respect of the relevant interest.

Relevant interests

2   (1) For the purposes of this Schedule, a person has a relevant interest in a company if the person—

(a) holds any shares in the company,

(b) holds any voting rights in the company, or

(c) holds the right to appoint or remove any member of the board of directors of the company.

(2) References to "the relevant interest" are to the shares or right in question.

(3) Part 3 of Schedule 1A applies for the interpretation of sub- paragraph (1) save that, where the relevant interest is by virtue of paragraph 19 or 20 of that Schedule treated for the purposes of that Schedule as held by a person other than the person who in fact holds the interest, both the holder and the other person are to be regarded for the purposes of this Schedule as having the relevant interest.

Effect of restrictions notice

3   (1) The effect of a restrictions notice issued under paragraph 1 with respect to a relevant interest is as follows—

(a) any transfer of the interest is void,

(b) no rights are exercisable in respect of the interest,

(c) no shares may be issued in right of the interest or in pursuance of an offer made to the interest-holder,

(d) except in a liquidation, no payment may be made of sums due from the company in respect of the interest, whether in respect of capital or otherwise.

(2) An agreement to transfer an interest that is subject to the restriction in sub-paragraph (1)(a) is void.

(3) Sub-paragraph (2) does not apply to an agreement to transfer the interest on the making of an order under paragraph 8 made by virtue of sub-paragraph (3)(b) of that paragraph (removal of restrictions in case of court-approved transfer).

(4) An agreement to transfer any associated right (otherwise than in a liquidation) is void.

(5) Sub-paragraph (4) does not apply to an agreement to transfer any such right on the making of an order under paragraph 8 made by virtue of sub-paragraph (3)(b) of that paragraph (removal of restrictions in case of court-approved transfer).

(6) An "associated right", in relation to a relevant interest, is—

(a) a right to be issued with any shares issued in right of the relevant interest, or

(b) a right to receive payment of any sums due from the company in respect of the relevant interest.

(7) The provisions of this section are subject to any directions given under paragraph 4.

Protection of third party rights

4   (1)   The court may give a direction under this paragraph if, on application by any person aggrieved, the court is satisfied that a restrictions notice issued by the company under paragraph 1 unfairly affects the rights of third parties in respect of the relevant interest.

         (2)   The direction is given for the purpose of protecting those third party rights.

         (3)   The direction is a direction that certain acts will not constitute a breach of the restrictions placed on the relevant interest by the restrictions notice.

         (4)   An order containing a direction under this paragraph—
                (a)   must specify the acts that will not constitute a breach of the restrictions, and
                (b)   may confine the direction to cases where those acts are done by persons, or for purposes, described in the order.

         (5)   The direction may be given subject to such terms as the court thinks fit.

Breach of restrictions

5   (1)   A person commits an offence if the person does anything listed in sub-paragraph (2) knowing that the interest is subject to restrictions.

         (2)   The things are—
                (a)   exercising or purporting to exercise any right to dispose of a relevant interest,
                (b)   exercising or purporting to exercise any right to dispose of any right to be issued with a relevant interest, or
                (c)   voting in respect of a relevant interest (whether as holder of the interest or as proxy) or appointing a proxy to vote in respect of a relevant interest.

         (3)   A person who has a relevant interest that the person knows to be subject to restrictions commits an offence if the person—
                (a)   knows a person to be entitled (apart from the restrictions) to vote in respect of the interest, whether as holder or as proxy,
                (b)   does not know the person to be aware of the fact that the interest is subject to restrictions, and
                (c)   fails to notify the person of that fact.

         (4)   A person commits an offence if the person—
                (a)   either has a relevant interest that the person knows to be subject to restrictions or is entitled to an associated right, and
                (b)   enters in that capacity into an agreement that is void by virtue of paragraph 3(2) or (4).

         (5)   References in this Schedule to an interest being "subject to restrictions" are to an interest being subject to restrictions by virtue of a restrictions notice under paragraph 1.

6   If shares in a company are issued in contravention of a restriction imposed by virtue of a restrictions notice under paragraph 1, an offence is committed by—
                (a)   the company, and
                (b)   very officer of the company who is in default.

7   (1)   A person guilty of an offence under paragraph 5 or 6 is liable—
                (a)   on conviction on indictment, to a fine;
                (b)   on summary conviction—
                       (i)   in England and Wales, to a fine,
                       (ii)   in Scotland or Northern Ireland, to a fine not exceeding the statutory maximum.

         (2)   The provisions of those paragraphs are subject to any direction given under paragraph 4 or 8.

Relaxation of restrictions

8   (1)   An application may be made to the court for an order directing that the relevant interest cease to be subject to restrictions.

(2) An application for an order under this paragraph may be made by the company in question or by any person aggrieved.

(3) The court must not make an order under this paragraph unless—

    (a) it is satisfied that the information required by the notice served under section 790D or 790E has been disclosed to the company and no unfair advantage has accrued to any person as a result of the earlier failure to make that disclosure, or

    (b) the relevant interest is to be transferred for valuable consideration and the court approves the transfer.

(4) An order under this paragraph made by virtue of sub-paragraph (3)(b) may continue, in whole or in part, the restrictions mentioned in paragraph 3(1)(c) and (d) so far as they relate to a right acquired or offer made before the transfer.

(5) Where any restrictions continue in force under sub-paragraph (4)—

    (a) an application may be made under this paragraph for an order directing that the relevant interest cease to be subject to those restrictions, and

    (b) sub-paragraph (3) does not apply in relation to the making of such an order.

Orders for sale

9 (1) The court may order that the relevant interest subject to restrictions be sold subject to the court's approval as to the sale.

(2) An application for an order under sub-paragraph (1) may only be made by the company in question.

(3) If the court makes an order under this paragraph, it may make such further order relating to the sale or transfer of the interest as it thinks fit.

(4) An application for an order under sub-paragraph (3) may be made—

    (a) by the company in question,

    (b) by the person appointed by or in pursuance of the order to effect the sale, or

    (c) by any person with an interest in the relevant interest.

(5) On making an order under sub-paragraph (1) or (3), the court may order that the applicant's costs (in Scotland, expenses) be paid out of the proceeds of sale.

10 (1) If a relevant interest is sold in pursuance of an order under paragraph 9, the proceeds of the sale, less the costs of the sale, must be paid into court for the benefit of those who are beneficially interested in the relevant interest.

(2) A person who is beneficially interested in the relevant interest may apply to the court for the whole or part of those proceeds to be paid to that person.

(3) On such an application, the court must order the payment to the applicant of—

    (a) the whole of the proceeds of sale together with any interest on the proceeds, or

    (b) if another person was also beneficially interested in the relevant interest at the time of the sale, such proportion of the proceeds (and any interest) as the value of the applicant's interest bears to the total value of the relevant interest.

(4) If the court has ordered under paragraph 9 that the costs (in Scotland, expenses) of an applicant under that paragraph are to be paid out of the proceeds of sale, the applicant is entitled to payment of those costs (or expenses) out of the proceeds before any person receives any part of the proceeds under this paragraph.

Company's power to withdraw restrictions notice

11 A company that issues a person with a restrictions notice under paragraph 1 must by notice withdraw the restrictions notice if—

    (a) it is satisfied that there is a valid reason sufficient to justify the person's failure to comply with the notice served under section 790D or 790E,

    (b) the notice served under section 790D or 790E is complied with, or

    (c) it discovers that the rights of a third party in respect of the relevant interest are being unfairly affected by the restrictions notice.

Supplementary provision

12   (1)   The Secretary of State may by regulations make provision about the procedure to be
               followed by companies in issuing and withdrawing restrictions notices.

        (2)   The regulations may in particular make provision about—

               (a)   the form and content of warning notices and restrictions notices, and the manner in
                       which they must be given,

               (b)   the factors to be taken into account in deciding what counts as a "valid reason"
                       sufficient to justify a person's failure to comply with a notice under section 790D or
                       790E, and

               (c)   the effect of withdrawing a restrictions notice on matters that are pending with
                       respect to the relevant interest when the notice is withdrawn.

        (3)   Regulations under this paragraph are subject to negative resolution procedure.

Offences for failing to comply with notices

13   (1)   A person to whom a notice under section 790D or 790E is addressed commits an offence if
               the person—

               (a)   fails to comply with the notice, or

               (b)   in purported compliance with the notice—

                       (i)   makes a statement that the person knows to be false in a material particular, or

                       (ii)   recklessly makes a statement that is false in a material particular.

        (2)   Where the person is a legal entity, an offence is also committed by every officer of the entity
               who is in default.

        (3)   A person does not commit an offence under sub-paragraph (1)(a) (or sub-paragraph (2) as it
               applies in relation to that sub- paragraph) if the person proves that the requirement to give
               information was frivolous or vexatious.

        (4)   A person guilty of an offence under this paragraph is liable—

               (a)   on conviction on indictment, to imprisonment for a term not exceeding two years or
                       a fine (or both);

               (b)   on summary conviction—

                       (i)   in England and Wales, to imprisonment for a term not exceeding twelve
                              months or to a fine (or both);

                       (ii)   in Scotland, to imprisonment for a term not exceeding twelve months or to a
                              fine not exceeding the statutory maximum (or both);

                       (iii) in Northern Ireland, to imprisonment for a term not exceeding six months or
                              to a fine not exceeding the statutory maximum (or both).

Offences for failing to provide information

14   (1)   A person commits an offence if the person—

               (a)   fails to comply with a duty under section 790G or 790H, or

               (b)   in purported compliance with such a duty—

                       (i)   makes a statement that the person knows to be false in a material particular, or

                       (ii)   recklessly makes a statement that is false in a material particular.

        (2)   Where the person is a legal entity, an offence is also committed by every officer of the entity
               who is in default.

        (3)   A person guilty of an offence under this paragraph is liable—

               (a)   on conviction on indictment, to imprisonment for a term not exceeding two years or
                       a fine (or both);

               (b)   on summary conviction—

                       (i)   in England and Wales, to imprisonment for a term not exceeding twelve
                              months or to a fine (or both);

                       (ii)   in Scotland, to imprisonment for a term not exceeding twelve months or to a
                              fine not exceeding the statutory maximum (or both);

        (iii) in Northern Ireland, to imprisonment for a term not exceeding six months or to a fine not exceeding the statutory maximum (or both).

...

SCHEDULE 4   Section 1144(1)

DOCUMENTS AND INFORMATION SENT OR SUPPLIED TO A COMPANY

PART 1

INTRODUCTION

Application of Schedule

1   (1) This Schedule applies to documents or information sent or supplied to a company.

        (2) It does not apply to documents or information sent or supplied by another company (see section 1144(3) and Schedule 5).

PART 2

COMMUNICATIONS IN HARD COPY FORM

Introduction

2   A document or information is validly sent or supplied to a company if it is sent or supplied in hard copy form in accordance with this Part of this Schedule.

Method of communication in hard copy form

3   (1) A document or information in hard copy form may be sent or supplied by hand or by post to an address (in accordance with paragraph 4).

        (2) For the purposes of this Schedule, a person sends a document or information by post if he posts a prepaid envelope containing the document or information.

Address for communications in hard copy form

4   A document or information in hard copy form may be sent or supplied—

        (a) to an address specified by the company for the purpose;

        (b) to the company's registered office;

        (c) to an address to which any provision of the Companies Acts authorises the document or information to be sent or supplied.

PART 2A

COMMUNICATIONS IN ELECTRONIC FORM FROM THE REGISTRAR OR THE SECRETARY OF STATE

4A   (1) A document or information is validly sent or supplied to a company by the registrar or the Secretary of State if it is sent or supplied in electronic form in accordance with sub-paragraph (2) or (3).

        (2) Where the document or information is sent or supplied by electronic means it may only be sent—

        (a) in the case of a company registered under this Act, to the company's registered email address;

        (b) in the case of any company, to an address specified by the company for that purpose (generally or specifically).

        (3) Where the document or information is sent or supplied in electronic form by hand or by post, it must be sent or supplied to an address to which it could be validly sent if it were in hard copy form.

PART 3
COMMUNICATIONS IN ELECTRONIC FORM IN OTHER CASES

Introduction

5   A document or information is validly sent or supplied to a company by a person other than the
         registrar or the Secretary of State if it is sent or supplied in electronic form in accordance with this
         Part of this Schedule.

Conditions for use of communications in electronic form

6   A document or information may only be sent or supplied to a company in electronic form if—
         (a)   the company has agreed (generally or specifically) that the document or information may be
               sent or supplied in that form (and has not revoked that agreement), or
         (b)   the company is deemed to have so agreed by a provision in the Companies Acts.

Address for communications in electronic form

7   (1)   Where the document or information is sent or supplied by electronic means, it may only be
               sent or supplied to an address—
               (a)   specified for the purpose by the company (generally or specifically), or
               (b)   deemed by a provision in the Companies Acts to have been so specified.
         (2)   Where the document or information is sent or supplied in electronic form by hand or by
               post, it must be sent or supplied to an address to which it could be validly sent if it were in
               hard copy form.

PART 4
OTHER AGREED FORMS OF COMMUNICATION

8   A document or information that is sent or supplied to a company otherwise than in hard copy
         form or electronic form is validly sent or supplied if it is sent or supplied in a form or manner that
         has been agreed by the company.

SCHEDULE 5   Section 1144(2)
COMMUNICATIONS BY A COMPANY

PART 1
INTRODUCTION

Application of this Schedule

1   This Schedule applies to documents or information sent or supplied by a
         company.

PART 2
COMMUNICATIONS IN HARD COPY FORM

Introduction

2   A document or information is validly sent or supplied by a company if it is sent or supplied in
         hard copy form in accordance with this Part of this Schedule.

Method of communication in hard copy form

3   (1)   A document or information in hard copy form must be—
               (a)   handed to the intended recipient, or
               (b)   sent or supplied by hand or by post to an address (in accordance with paragraph 4).
         (2)   For the purposes of this Schedule, a person sends a document or information by post if he
               posts a prepaid envelope containing the document or information.

Address for communications in hard copy form

4   (1)   A document or information in hard copy form may be sent or supplied by the company—
        (a)   to an address specified for the purpose by the intended recipient;
        (b)   to a company at its registered office;
        (c)   to a person in his capacity as a member of the company at his address as shown in the company's register of members;
        (d)   to a person in his capacity as a director of the company at his address as shown in the company's register of directors;
        (e)   to an address to which any provision of the Companies Acts authorises the document or information to be sent or supplied.
    (1A) Sub-paragraph (1) has effect—
        (a)   where an election under section 128B is in force, as if the reference in paragraph (c) to the company's register of members were a reference to the register kept by the registrar under section 1080, and
        (b)   where an election under section 167A is in force in respect of the company's register of directors, as if the reference in paragraph (d) to the company's register of directors were a reference to the register kept by the registrar under section 1080.
    (2)   Where the company is unable to obtain an address falling within sub-paragraph (1), the document or information may be sent or supplied to the intended recipient's last address known to the company.

PART 3
COMMUNICATIONS IN ELECTRONIC FORM

Introduction

5   A document or information is validly sent or supplied by a company if it is sent in electronic form in accordance with this Part of this Schedule.

Agreement to communications in electronic form

6   A document or information may only be sent or supplied by a company in electronic form—
    (a)   to a person who has agreed (generally or specifically) that the document or information may be sent or supplied in that form (and has not revoked that agreement), or
    (b)   to a company that is deemed to have so agreed by a provision in the Companies Acts.

Address for communications in electronic form

7   (1)   Where the document or information is sent or supplied by electronic means, it may only be sent or supplied to an address—
        (a)   specified for the purpose by the intended recipient (generally or specifically), or
        (b)   where the intended recipient is a company, deemed by a provision of the Companies Acts to have been so specified.
    (2)   Where the document or information is sent or supplied in electronic form by hand or by post, it must be—
        (a)   handed to the intended recipient, or
        (b)   sent or supplied to an address to which it could be validly sent if it were in hard copy form.

PART 4
COMMUNICATIONS BY MEANS OF A WEBSITE

Use of website

8   A document or information is validly sent or supplied by a company if it is made available on a website in accordance with this Part of this Schedule.

Agreement to use of website

9   A document or information may only be sent or supplied by the company to a person by being
       made available on a website if the person—
       (a)   has agreed (generally or specifically) that the document or information may be sent or
              supplied to him in that manner, or
       (b)   is taken to have so agreed under—
              (i)   paragraph 10 (members of the company etc), or
              (ii)   paragraph 11 (debenture holders),
              and has not revoked that agreement.

Deemed agreement of members of company etc to use of website

10   (1)   This paragraph applies to a document or information to be sent or supplied to a person—
              (a)   as a member of the company, or
              (b)   as a person nominated by a member in accordance with the company's articles to
                     enjoy or exercise all or any specified rights of the member in relation to the
                     company, or
              (c)   as a person nominated by a member under section 146 to enjoy information rights.
       (2)   To the extent that—
              (a)   the members of the company have resolved that the company may send or supply
                     documents or information to members by making them available on a website, or
              (b)   the company's articles contain provision to that effect,
              a person in relation to whom the following conditions are met is taken to have agreed that
              the company may send or supply documents or information to him in that manner.
       (3)   The conditions are that—
              (a)   the person has been asked individually by the company to agree that the company
                     may send or supply documents or information generally, or the documents or
                     information in question, to him by means of a website, and
              (b)   the company has not received a response within the period of 28 days beginning
                     with the date on which the company's request was sent.
       (4)   A person is not taken to have so agreed if the company's request—
              (a)   did not state clearly what the effect of a failure to respond would be, or
              (b)   was sent less than twelve months after a previous request made to him for the
                     purposes of this paragraph in respect of the same or a similar class of documents or
                     information.
       (5)   Chapter 3 of Part 3 (resolutions affecting a company's constitution) applies to a resolution
              under this paragraph.

Deemed agreement of debenture holders to use of website

11   (1)   This paragraph applies to a document or information to be sent or supplied to a person as
              holder of a company's debentures.
       (2)   To the extent that—
              (a)   the relevant debenture holders have duly resolved that the company may send or
                     supply documents or information to them by making them available on a website,
                     or
              (b)   the instrument creating the debenture in question contains provision to that effect,
              a debenture holder in relation to whom the following conditions are met is taken to have
              agreed that the company may send or supply documents or information to him in that
              manner.
       (3)   The conditions are that—
              (a)   the debenture holder has been asked individually by the company to agree that the
                     company may send or supply documents or information generally, or the documents
                     or information in question, to him by means of a website, and

    (b)   the company has not received a response within the period of 28 days beginning with the date on which the company's request was sent.

(4) A person is not taken to have so agreed if the company's request—

    (a)   did not state clearly what the effect of a failure to respond would be, or

    (b)   was sent less than twelve months after a previous request made to him for the purposes of this paragraph in respect of the same or a similar class of documents or information.

(5) For the purposes of this paragraph—

    (a)   the relevant debenture holders are the holders of debentures of the company ranking *pari passu* for all purposes with the intended recipient, and

    (b)   a resolution of the relevant debenture holders is duly passed if they agree in accordance with the provisions of the instruments creating the debentures.

Availability of document or information

12 (1) A document or information authorised or required to be sent or supplied by means of a website must be made available in a form, and by a means, that the company reasonably considers will enable the recipient—

    (a)   to read it, and

    (b)   to retain a copy of it.

(2) For this purpose a document or information can be read only if—

    (a)   it can be read with the naked eye, or

    (b)   to the extent that it consists of images (for example photographs, pictures, maps, plans or drawings), it can be seen with the naked eye.

Notification of availability

13 (1) The company must notify the intended recipient of—

    (a)   the presence of the document or information on the website,

    (b)   the address of the website,

    (c)   the place on the website where it may be accessed, and

    (d)   how to access the document or information.

(2) The document or information is taken to be sent—

    (a)   on the date on which the notification required by this paragraph is sent, or

    (b)   if later, the date on which the document or information first appears on the website after that notification is sent.

Period of availability on website

14 (1) The company must make the document or information available on the website throughout—

    (a)   the period specified by any applicable provision of the Companies Acts, or

    (b)   if no such period is specified, the period of 28 days beginning with the date on which the notification required under paragraph 13 is sent to the person in question.

(2) For the purposes of this paragraph, a failure to make a document or information available on a website throughout the period mentioned in sub-paragraph (1) shall be disregarded if—

    (a)   it is made available on the website for part of that period, and

    (b)   the failure to make it available throughout that period is wholly attributable to circumstances that it would not be reasonable to have expected the company to prevent or avoid.

PART 5
OTHER AGREED FORMS OF COMMUNICATION

15 A document or information that is sent or supplied otherwise than in hard copy or electronic form or by means of a website is validly sent or supplied if it is sent or supplied in a form or manner that has been agreed by the intended recipient.

PART 6
SUPPLEMENTARY PROVISIONS

Joint holders of shares or debentures

16   (1)   This paragraph applies in relation to documents or information to be sent or supplied to joint holders of shares or debentures of a company.

(2)   Anything to be agreed or specified by the holder must be agreed or specified by all the joint holders.

(3)   Anything authorised or required to be sent or supplied to the holder may be sent or supplied either—

(a)   to each of the joint holders, or

(b)   to the holder whose name appears first in the register of members or the relevant register of debenture holders.

(3A)   Where an election under section 128B is in force, the reference in sub-paragraph (3)(b) to the register of members is to be read as a reference to the register kept by the registrar under section 1080.

(4)   This paragraph has effect subject to anything in the company's articles.

Death or bankruptcy of holder of shares

17   (1)   This paragraph has effect in the case of the death or bankruptcy of a holder of a company's shares.

(2)   Documents or information required or authorised to be sent or supplied to the member may be sent or supplied to the persons claiming to be entitled to the shares in consequence of the death or bankruptcy—

(a)   by name, or

(b)   by the title of representatives of the deceased, or trustee of the bankrupt, or by any like description,

at the address in the United Kingdom supplied for the purpose by those so claiming.

(3)   Until such an address has been so supplied, a document or information may be sent or supplied in any manner in which it might have been sent or supplied if the death or bankruptcy had not occurred.

(4)   This paragraph has effect subject to anything in the company's articles.

(5)   References in this paragraph to the bankruptcy of a person include—

(a)   the sequestration of the estate of a person;

(b)   a person's estate being the subject of a protected trust deed (within the meaning of the Bankruptcy (Scotland) Act 2016).

In such a case the reference in sub-paragraph (2)(b) to the trustee of the bankrupt is to be read as the trustee or interim trustee (under that Act) on the sequestrated estate or, as the case may be, the trustee under the protected deed.

SCHEDULE 6   Section 1159
MEANING OF "SUBSIDIARY" ETC: SUPPLEMENTARY PROVISIONS

Introduction

1   The provisions of this Part of this Schedule explain expressions used in section 1159 (meaning of "subsidiary" etc) and otherwise supplement that section.

Voting rights in a company

2   In section 1159(1)(a) and (c) the references to the voting rights in a company are to the rights conferred on shareholders in respect of their shares or, in the case of a company not having a share capital, on members, to vote at general meetings of the company on all, or substantially all, matters.

Right to appoint or remove a majority of the directors

3   (1)   In section 1159(1)(b) the reference to the right to appoint or remove a majority of the board of directors is to the right to appoint or remove directors holding a majority of the voting rights at meetings of the board on all, or substantially all, matters.

     (2)   A company shall be treated as having the right to appoint to a directorship if—

            (a)   a person's appointment to it follows necessarily from his appointment as director of the company, or

            (b)   the directorship is held by the company itself.

     (3)   A right to appoint or remove which is exercisable only with the consent or concurrence of another person shall be left out of account unless no other person has a right to appoint or, as the case may be, remove in relation to that directorship.

Rights exercisable only in certain circumstances or temporarily incapable of exercise

4   (1)   Rights which are exercisable only in certain circumstances shall be taken into account only—

            (a)   when the circumstances have arisen, and for so long as they continue to obtain, or

            (b)   when the circumstances are within the control of the person having the rights.

     (2)   Rights which are normally exercisable but are temporarily incapable of exercise shall continue to be taken into account.

Rights held by one person on behalf of another

5   Rights held by a person in a fiduciary capacity shall be treated as not held by him.

6   (1)   Rights held by a person as nominee for another shall be treated as held by the other.

     (2)   Rights shall be regarded as held as nominee for another if they are
            exercisable only on his instructions or with his consent or concurrence.

Rights attached to shares held by way of security

7   Rights attached to shares held by way of security shall be treated as held by the person providing the security—

     (a)   where apart from the right to exercise them for the purpose of preserving the value of the security, or of realising it, the rights are exercisable only in accordance with his instructions, and

     (b)   where the shares are held in connection with the granting of loans as part of normal business activities and apart from the right to exercise them for the purpose of preserving the value of the security, or of realising it, the rights are exercisable only in his interests.

Rights attributed to holding company

8   (1)   Rights shall be treated as held by a holding company if they are held by any of its subsidiary companies.

     (2)   Nothing in paragraph 6 or 7 shall be construed as requiring rights held by a holding company to be treated as held by any of its subsidiaries.

     (3)   For the purposes of paragraph 7 rights shall be treated as being exercisable in accordance with the instructions or in the interests of a company if they are exercisable in accordance with the instructions of or, as the case may be, in the interests of—

            (a)   any subsidiary or holding company of that company, or

            (b)   any subsidiary of a holding company of that company.

Disregard of certain rights

9   The voting rights in a company shall be reduced by any rights held by the company itself.

Supplementary

10   References in any provision of paragraphs 5 to 9 to rights held by a person include rights falling to be treated as held by him by virtue of any other provision of those paragraphs but not rights which by virtue of any such provision are to be treated as not held by him.

SCHEDULE 7   Section 1162

PARENT AND SUBSIDIARY UNDERTAKINGS: SUPPLEMENTARY PROVISIONS

Introduction

1   The provisions of this Schedule explain expressions used in section 1162 (parent and subsidiary undertakings) and otherwise supplement that section.

Voting rights in an undertaking

2   (1)   In section 1162(2)(a) and (d) the references to the voting rights in an undertaking are to the rights conferred on shareholders in respect of their shares or, in the case of an undertaking not having a share capital, on members, to vote at general meetings of the undertaking on all, or substantially all, matters.

     (2)   In relation to an undertaking which does not have general meetings at which matters are decided by the exercise of voting rights the references to holding a majority of the voting rights in the undertaking shall be construed as references to having the right under the constitution of the undertaking to direct the overall policy of the undertaking or to alter the terms of its constitution.

Right to appoint or remove a majority of the directors

3   (1)   In section 1162(2)(b) the reference to the right to appoint or remove a majority of the board of directors is to the right to appoint or remove directors holding a majority of the voting rights at meetings of the board on all, or substantially all, matters.

     (2)   An undertaking shall be treated as having the right to appoint to a directorship if—

            (a)   a person's appointment to it follows necessarily from his appointment as director of the undertaking, or

            (b)   the directorship is held by the undertaking itself.

     (3)   A right to appoint or remove which is exercisable only with the consent or concurrence of another person shall be left out of account unless no other person has a right to appoint or, as the case may be, remove in relation to that directorship.

Right to exercise dominant influence

4   (1)   For the purposes of section 1162(2) (c) an undertaking shall not be regarded as having the right to exercise a dominant influence over another undertaking unless it has a right to give directions with respect to the operating and financial policies of that other undertaking which its directors are obliged to comply with whether or not they are for the benefit of that other undertaking.

     (2)   A "control contract" means a contract in writing conferring such a right which—

            (a)   is of a kind authorised by the articles of the undertaking in relation to which the right is exercisable, and

            (b)   is permitted by the law under which that undertaking is established.

     (3)   This paragraph shall not be read as affecting the construction of section 1162(4)(a).

Rights exercisable only in certain circumstances or temporarily incapable of exercise

5   (1)   Rights which are exercisable only in certain circumstances shall be taken into account only—

            (a)   when the circumstances have arisen, and for so long as they continue to obtain, or

            (b)   when the circumstances are within the control of the person having the rights.

     (2)   Rights which are normally exercisable but are temporarily incapable of exercise shall continue to be taken into account.

Rights held by one person on behalf of another

6   Rights held by a person in a fiduciary capacity shall be treated as not held by him.

7   (1)   Rights held by a person as nominee for another shall be treated as held by the other.

     (2)   Rights shall be regarded as held as nominee for another if they are exercisable only on his instructions or with his consent or concurrence.

Rights attached to shares held by way of security

8   Rights attached to shares held by way of security shall be treated as held by the person providing the security—

     (a)   where apart from the right to exercise them for the purpose of preserving the value of the security, or of realising it, the rights are exercisable only in accordance with his instructions, and

     (b)   where the shares are held in connection with the granting of loans as part of normal business activities and apart from the right to exercise them for the purpose of preserving the value of the security, or of realising it, the rights are exercisable only in his interests.

Rights attributed to parent undertaking

9   (1)   Rights shall be treated as held by a parent undertaking if they are held by any of its subsidiary undertakings.

     (2)   Nothing in paragraph 7 or 8 shall be construed as requiring rights held by a parent undertaking to be treated as held by any of its subsidiary undertakings.

     (3)   For the purposes of paragraph 8 rights shall be treated as being exercisable in accordance with the instructions or in the interests of an undertaking if they are exercisable in accordance with the instructions of or, as the case may be, in the interests of any group undertaking.

Disregard of certain rights

10   The voting rights in an undertaking shall be reduced by any rights held by the undertaking itself.

Supplementary

11   References in any provision of paragraphs 6 to 10 to rights held by a person include rights falling to be treated as held by him by virtue of any other provision of those paragraphs but not rights which by virtue of any such provision are to be treated as not held by him.

SCHEDULE 8   Section 1174

INDEX OF DEFINED EXPRESSIONS

...

annual accounts and reports (in Part 15)	section 471
annual general meeting	section 336
...	
appropriate audit authority (in sections 522, 523 and 524)	section 525(1)
appropriate rate of interest	
— in Chapter 5 of Part 17	section 592
— in Chapter 6 of Part 17	section 609
approval after being made, in relation to regulations and orders	section 1291
arrangement	
— in Chapter 7 of Part 17	section 616(1)
— in Part 26	section 895(2)
— in Part 26A	section 901A(4)
articles	section 18
associate (in Chapter 3 of Part 28)	section 988
associated bodies corporate and associated company (in Part 10)	section 256
the Audit Regulation	section 1173(1)
authenticated, in relation to a document or information sent or supplied to a company	section 1146
authorised group, of members of a company (in Part 14)	section 370(3)
authorised insurance company	section 1165(2)
authorised minimum (in relation to share capital of public company)	section 763
available profits (in Chapter 5 of Part 18)	section 711 and 712
banking company and banking group	section 1164
body corporate	section 1173(1)
called-up share capital	section 547
capital redemption reserve	section 733
capitalisation in relation to a company's profits (in Part 23)	section 853(3)
cash (in relation to paying up or allotting shares)	section 583
cause of action, in relation to derivative proceedings (in Chapter 2 of Part 11)	section 265(7)
the central register	
— in Chapter 2A of Part 8	section 128A(2)
— in Chapter 4 of Part 21A	section 790W(2)
certified translation (in Part 35)	section 1107
charge (in Chapter A1 of Part 25)	section 859A(7)
circulation date, in relation to a written resolution (in Part 13)	section 290
class of shares	section 629
the Companies Acts	section 2
Companies Act accounts	sections 395(1)(a) and 403(2)(a)
Companies Act group accounts	section 403(2)(a)
Companies Act individual accounts	section 395(1)
companies involved in the division (in Part 27)	section 919(2)
company	
— generally in the Companies Acts	section 1

— in Chapter 7 of Part 17	section 616(1)
— in Chapter A1 of Part 25	section 859A(7)
...	...
— in Part 26	section 895(2)
— in Part 26A	section 901A(4)
— in Schedule 1C (see Chapter 1 of Part 28)	paragraph 21 of Schedule 1C
— in Chapter 3 of Part 28	section 991(1)
— in the company communications provisions	section 1148(1)
the company communications provisions	section 1143
the company law provisions of this Act	section 2(2)
company records (in Part 37)	section 1134
the competent authority	section 1173(1)
confirmation date (in Part 24)	section 853A(3)
confirmation period (in Part 24)	section 853A(3)
confirmation statement	section 853A(1)
connected with, in relation to a director (in Part 10)	sections 252 to 254
constitution, of a company	section
— generally in the Companies Acts	section 17
— in Part 10	section 257
contributory	section 1170B
controlling, of a body corporate by a director (in Part 10)	section 255
corporate governance statement and separate corporate governance statement	
— in Part 15	section 472A
— in Part 16	section 538A
corporation	section 1173(1)
the court	section 1156
credit institution	section 1173(1)
credit transaction (in Chapter 4 of Part 10)	section 202
creditor (in Chapter 1 of Part 31)	section 1011
daily default fine	section 1125
the data protection legislation	section 1173(1)
date of the offer (in Chapter 3 of Part 28)	section 991(1)
debenture	section 738
derivative claim (in Chapter 1 of Part 11)	section 260
derivative proceedings (in Chapter 2 of Part 11)	section 265
...	
director	
— generally in the Companies Acts	section 250
— in Chapter 8 of Part 10	section 240(3)
— in Chapter 1 of Part 11	section 260(5)
— in Chapter 2 of Part 11	section 265(7)
— in Part 14	section 379(1)
directors' remuneration report	section 420

directors' remuneration policy (in Chapter 4A of Part 10)	section 226A(1)
directors' report	section 415
disqualified under the directors disqualification legislation	section 159A(2)
distributable profits	
— in Chapter 2 of Part 18	section 683(1)
— elsewhere in Part 18	section 736
distribution	
— in Chapter 2 of Part 18	section 683(1)
— in Part 23	section 829
division (in Part 27)	section 919
document	section 226A(1)
— in Part 35	section 1114(1)
— in the company communications provisions	section 1148(1)
dormant, in relation to a company or other body corporate	section 1169
DTR5 issuer (in Part 24)	section 853E(6)
EEA State and related expressions	section 1170
electronic form, electronic copy, electronic means	
— generally in the Companies Acts	section 1168(3) and (4)
— in relation to communications to a company	Part 3 of Schedule 4
— in relation to communications by a company	Part 3 of Schedule 5
eligible members, in relation to a written resolution	section 289
e-money issuer	
— in Part 15	section 474(1)
— in Part 16	section 539
employees' share scheme	section 1166
employer and employee (in Chapter 1 of Part 18)	section 676
enactment	section 1293
enhanced disclosure documents	section 1078
equity securities (in Chapter 3 of Part 17)	section 560(1)
equity share capital	section 548
equity shares (in Chapter 7 of Part 17)	section 616(1)
establishment of an overseas company (in Part 35)	section 1067(6)
EU regulated market	section 1173(1)
exempt reasons, in relation to a auditor of a company ceasing to hold office (in Chapter 4 of Part 16)	Section 519A
existing company (in Part 27)	section 902(2)
fellow subsidiary undertakings	section 1161(4)
financial assistance (in Chapter 2 of Part 18)	section 677
financial institution	section 1173(1)
financial year, of a company	section 390
firm	section 1173(1)
fixed assets (in Part 23)	section 853
the former Companies Acts	section 1171
the Gazette	section 1173(1)

group (in Part 15)	section 474(1)
group undertaking	section 1161(5)
hard copy form and hard copy	
— generally in the Companies Acts	section 1168(2)
— in relation to communications to a company	Part 2 of Schedule 4
— in relation to communications by a company	Part 2 of Schedule 5
hire-purchase agreement	section 1173(1)
holder of shares (in Chapter 3 of Part 17)	section 574
holding company	section 1159 (and see section 1160 and Schedule 6)
IAS accounts	sections395(1)(b) and 403(1) and (2)(b)
IAS group accounts	section 403(1) and (2)(b)
IAS individual accounts	section 395(1)(b)
…	…
included in the consolidation, in relation to group accounts (in Part 15)	section 474(1)
individual accounts	section 394
information rights (in Part 9)	section 146(3)
insurance company	section 1165(3)
insurance group	section 1165(5)
insurance market activity	section 1165(7)
interest in shares (for the purposes of Part 22)	sections 820 to 825
international accounting standards (in Part 15)	section 474(1)
investment company (in Part 23)	section 833
…	
issued share capital and issued shares	section 546(1)(a) and (2)
the issuing company (in Chapter 7 of Part 17)	section 610(6)
the Joint Stock Companies Acts	section 1171
legal entity (in Part 21A)	section 790C(5)
liabilities (in Part 27)	section 941
liability, references to incurring, reducing or discharging (in Chapter 2 of Part 18)	section 683(2)
limited by guarantee	section 3(3)
limited by shares	section 3(2)
limited company	section 3
the main register (of members) (in Chapter 3 of Part 8)	section 131(1)
…	
market purchase, by a company of its own shares (in Chapter 4 of Part 18)	section 694(4)
member, of a company	
— generally in the Companies Acts	section 112
— in Chapter 1 of Part 11	section 260(5)
— in Chapter 2 of Part 11	section 265(7)
memorandum of association	section 8
merger (in Part 27)	section 904

permissible capital payment (in Chapter 5 of Part 18)	section 710
political donation (in Part 14)	section 364
political expenditure (in Part 14)	section 365
political organisation (in Part 14)	section 363(2)
prescribed	section 1167
private company	section 4
profit and loss account (in Part 15)	section 474(1) and (2)
profits and losses (in Part 23)	section 853(2)
profits available for distribution (for the purposes of Part 23)	section 830(2)
property (in Part 27)	section 941
protected information (in Chapter 8 of Part 10)	section 240
provision for entrenchment, in relation to a company's articles	section 22
PSC register	section 790C(10)
public company	section 4
public interest company (in Chapter 4 of Part 16)	section 519A
publication, in relation to accounts and reports (in sections 433 to 435)	section 436
qualified, in relation to an auditor's report etc	
— in Part 15	section 474(1)
— in Part 16	section 539
qualifying shares (in Chapter 6 of Part 18)	section 724(2)
qualifying third party indemnity provision (in Chapter 7 of Part 10)	section 234
qualifying pension scheme indemnity provision (in Chapter 7 of Part 10)	section 235
quasi-loan (in Chapter 4 of Part 10)	section 199
quoted company	
— in Chapter 4A of Part 10	section 226A(1)
— in Part 13	section 361
— in Part 15	section 385
— in Chapter 5 of Part 16	section 531 (and section 385)
realised profits and losses (in Part 23)	section 853(4)
receiver or manager (and certain related references)	section 1170A
redeemable shares	section 684(1)
redenominate	section 622(1)
redenomination reserve	section 628
the register	section 1080
...	...
register of directors	section 162
register of directors' residential addresses	section 165
register of members	section 113
register of secretaries	section 275
...	...
registered number, of a company (or an overseas company)	section 1066 (and section 1059A(5))
registered number, of a UK establishment of an overseas company	section 1067
registered office, of a company	section 86

registrable person (in Part 21A)	section 790C(4)
registrable relevant legal entity (in Part 21A)	section 790C(8)
registrar and registrar of companies	section 1060
registrar's index of company names	section 1099
registrar's rules	section 1117
registration in a particular part of the United Kingdom	section 1060(4)
regulated activity	
— generally in the Companies Acts	section 1173(1)
— in Part 15	section 474(1)
regulated market	section 1173(1)
relevant accounts (in Part 23)	section 836(2)
relevant legal entity (in Part 21A)	section 790C(6)
relevant market (in Part 24)	section 853E(6)
remuneration payment (in Chapter 4A of Part 10)	section 226A(1)
requirements for proper delivery (in Part 35)	section 1072 (and see section 1073)
requirements of this Act	section 1172
...	...
review period (in Part 24)	section 853A(5) and (6)
section 172(1) statement	section 414CZA(1)
securities (and related expressions)	
— in Chapter 1 of Part 20	section 755(5)
— in Chapter 2 of Part 21	section 783
senior statutory auditor	section 504
sent or supplied, in relation to documents or information (in the company communications provisions)	section 1148(2) and (3)
service address	section 1141
service contract, of a director (in Part 10)	section 227
shadow director	section 251
share	
— generally in the Companies Acts	section 540 (and see section 1161(2))
— in Part 22	section 792
— in section 1162 and Schedule 7	section 1162(7)
share capital, company having a	section 545
share exchange ratio	
— in Chapter 2 of Part 27	section 905(2)
— in Chapter 3 of Part 27	section 920(2)
share premium account	section 610(1)
share warrant	section 779(1)
significant control (in Part 21A)	section 790C(2)
small companies exemption (in relation to directors' report)	section 415A
small companies regime (for accounts)	section 381
solvency statement (in sections 641 to 644)	section 643
special notice, in relation to a resolution	section 312

special resolution	section 283
statutory accounts	section 434(3)
subsidiary	section 1159 (and see section 1160 and Schedule 6)
subsidiary undertaking	section 1162 (and see Schedule 7)
…	…
takeover bid	
— in section 943	section 943(7)
— in Schedule 1C	paragraph 20(1) of Schedule 1C
— in section 953	section 953(9)
— in Chapter 2 of Part 28	section 971(1)
takeover offer (in Chapter 3 of Part 28)	section 974
…	…
traded company	
— in Part 13	section 360C
— in Part 15	section 474(1)
…	
trading certificate	section 761(1)
transfer, in relation to a non-cash asset	section 1163(2)
transferable securities	section 1173(1)
treasury shares	section 724(5)
turnover	
— in Part 15	section 474(1)
— in Part 16	section 539
UCITS management company	
— in Part 15	section 474(1)
— in Part 16	section 539
UK-adopted international accounting standards (in Part 15)	section 474(1)
UK establishment of an overseas company (in Part 35)	section 1067(6)
UK-registered company	section 1158
UK regulated market	section 1173(1)
uncalled share capital	section 547
unconditional, in relation to a contract to acquire shares (in Chapter 3 of Part 28)	section 991(2)
undistributable reserves	section 831(4)
undertaking	section 1161(1)
unique identifier	section 1082
unlimited company	section 3
unquoted company (in Part 15)	section 385
unquoted traded company (in Chapter 4A of Part 10)	section 226A(1)
voting rights	
— in Schedule 1C (see Chapter 1 of Part 28)	paragraph 20(1) of Schedule 1C

— in Chapter 2 of Part 28	section 971(1)
— in Chapter 3 of Part 28	section 991(1)
— in section 1159 and Schedule 6	paragraph 2 of Schedule 6
— in section 1162 and Schedule 7	paragraph 2 of Schedule 7
voting shares	
— in Chapter 2 of Part 28	section 971(1)
— in Chapter 3 of Part 28	section 991(1)
website, communication by a company by means of	section Part 4 of Schedule 5
Welsh company	section 88
wholly-owned subsidiary	section 1159(2) (and see section 1160 and Schedule 6)
working day, in relation to a company	section 1173(1)
written resolution	section 288

...

Company Directors Disqualification Act 1986

1986 c. 46

An Act to consolidate certain enactments relating to the disqualification of persons from being directors of companies, and from being otherwise concerned with a company's affairs

[25th July 1986]

Preliminary

1.   Disqualification orders: general

(1)   In the circumstances specified below in this Act a court may, and under sections 6, 8ZF and 9A shall, make against a person a disqualification order, that is to say an order that for a period specified in the order—

(a)   he shall not be a director of a company, act as receiver of a company's property or in any way, whether directly or indirectly, be concerned or take part in the promotion, formation or management of a company unless (in each case) he has the leave of the court, and

(b)   he shall not act as an insolvency practitioner.

(2)   In each section of this Act which gives to a court power or, as the case may be, imposes on it the duty to make a disqualification order there is specified the maximum (and, in sections 6, 8ZA and 8ZF, the minimum) period of disqualification which may or (as the case may be) must be imposed by means of the order and, unless the court otherwise orders, the period of disqualification so imposed shall begin at the end of the period of 21 days beginning with the date of the order.

(3)   Where a disqualification order is made against a person who is already subject to such an order or to a disqualification undertaking, the periods specified in those orders or, as the case may be, in the order and the undertaking shall run concurrently.

(4)   A disqualification order may be made on grounds which are or include matters other than criminal convictions, notwithstanding that the person in respect of whom it is to be made may be criminally liable in respect of those matters.

1A.   Disqualification undertakings: general

(1)   In the circumstances specified in sections 5A, 7, 8, 8ZC, 8ZE, 8ZF and 8ZG the appropriate authority may accept a disqualification undertaking, that is to say an undertaking by any person that, for a period specified in the undertaking, the person—

(a)   will not be a director of a company, act as receiver of a company's property or in any way, whether directly or indirectly, be concerned or take part in the promotion, formation or management of a company unless (in each case) he has the leave of a court, and

(b)   will not act as an insolvency practitioner.

(2)   The maximum period which may be specified in a disqualification undertaking is 15 years; and the minimum period which may be specified in a disqualification undertaking under section 7, 8ZC or 8ZF is two years.

(3)   Where a disqualification undertaking by a person who is already subject to such an undertaking or to a disqualification order is accepted, the periods specified in those undertakings or (as the case may be) the undertaking and the order shall run concurrently.

(4)   In determining whether to accept a disqualification undertaking by any person, the appropriate authority may take account of matters other than criminal convictions, notwithstanding that the person may be criminally liable in respect of those matters.

(5)   In this section "the appropriate authority" means—

(a)   in relation to an undertaking under section 8ZF or 8ZG, an officer of Revenue and Customs;

(b)   in any other case, the Secretary of State.

Disqualification for general misconduct in connection with companies

2.   Disqualification on conviction of indictable offence

(1)   The court may make a disqualification order against a person where he is convicted of an indictable offence (whether on indictment or summarily) in connection with the promotion, formation, management, liquidation or striking off of a company, with the receivership of a company's property or with his being an administrative receiver of a company.

(1A)   In subsection (1), "company" includes overseas company.

(2)   "The court" for this purpose means—

(a)   any court having jurisdiction to wind up the company in relation to which the offence was committed, or

(aa)   in relation to an overseas company not falling within paragraph (a), the High Court or, in Scotland, the Court of Session, or

(b)   the court by or before which the person is convicted of the offence, or

(c)   in the case of a summary conviction in England and Wales, any other magistrates' court acting in the same local justice area;

and for the purposes of this section the definition of "indictable offence" in Schedule 1 to the Interpretation Act 1978 applies for Scotland as it does for England and Wales.

(3)   The maximum period of disqualification under this section is—

(a)   where the disqualification order is made by a court of summary jurisdiction, 5 years, and

(b)   in any other case, 15 years.

3.   Disqualification for persistent breaches of companies legislation

(1)   The court may make a disqualification order against a person where it appears to it that he has been persistently in default in relation to provisions of the companies legislation requiring any return, account or other document to be filed with, delivered or sent, or notice of any matter to be given, to the registrar of companies.

(2)   On an application to the court for an order to be made under this section, the fact that a person has been persistently in default in relation to such provisions as are mentioned above may (without prejudice to its proof in any other manner) be conclusively proved by showing that in the 5 years ending with the date of the application he has been adjudged guilty (whether or not on the same occasion) of three or more defaults in relation to those provisions.

(3)   A person is to be treated under subsection (2) as being adjudged guilty of a default in relation to any provision of that legislation if—

(a)   he is convicted (whether on indictment or summarily) of an offence consisting in a contravention of or failure to comply with that provision (whether on his own part or on the part of any company), or

(b)   a default order is made against him, that is to say an order under any of the following provisions—

(i)   section 452 of the Companies Act 2006 (order requiring delivery of company accounts),

(ia)   section 456 of that Act (order requiring preparation of revised accounts),

(ii)   section 1113 of that Act (enforcement of company's filing obligations),

(iii)   section 41 of the Insolvency Act 1986 (enforcement of receiver's or manager's duty to make returns), or

(iv)   section 170 of that Act (corresponding provision for liquidator in winding up),

in respect of any such contravention of or failure to comply with that provision (whether on his own part or on the part of any company).

(3A)   In this section "company" includes overseas company.

(4)   In this section "the court" means—

(a)   any court having jurisdiction to wind up any of the companies in relation to which the offence or other default has been or is alleged to have been committed, or

    (b)   in relation to an overseas company not falling within paragraph (a), the High Court or, in Scotland, the Court of Session.

(4A)   In this section "the companies legislation" means the Companies Acts and Parts 1 to 7 of the Insolvency Act 1986 (company insolvency and winding up).

(5)   The maximum period of disqualification under this section is 5 years.

4.   **Disqualification for fraud, etc, in winding up**

(1)   The court may make a disqualification order against a person if, in the course of the winding up of a company, it appears that he—

    (a)   has been guilty of an offence for which he is liable (whether he has been convicted or not) under section 993 of the Companies Act 2006 (fraudulent trading), or

    (b)   has otherwise been guilty, while an officer or liquidator of the company receiver of the company's property or administrative receiver of the company, of any fraud in relation to the company or of any breach of his duty as such officer, liquidator, receiver or administrative receiver.

(2)   In this section "the court" means any court having jurisdiction to wind up any of the companies in relation to which the offence or other default has been or is alleged to have been committed; and "officer" includes a shadow director.

(3)   The maximum period of disqualification under this section is 15 years.

5.   **Disqualification on summary conviction**

(1)   An offence counting for the purposes of this section is one of which a person is convicted (either on indictment or summarily) in consequence of a contravention of, or failure to comply with, any provision of the companies legislation requiring a return, account or other document to be filed with, delivered or sent, or notice of any matter to be given, to the registrar of companies (whether the contravention or failure is on the person's own part or on the part of any company).

(2)   Where a person is convicted of a summary offence counting for those purposes, the court by which he is convicted (or, in England and Wales, any other magistrates' court acting in the same local justice area) may make a disqualification order against him if the circumstances specified in the next subsection are present.

(3)   Those circumstances are that, during the 5 years ending with the date of the conviction, the person has had made against him, or has been convicted of, in total not less than 3 default orders and offences counting for the purposes of this section; and those offences may include that of which he is convicted as mentioned in subsection (2) and any other offence of which he is convicted on the same occasion.

(4)   For the purposes of this section—

    (a)   the definition of "summary offence" in Schedule 1 to the Interpretation Act 1978 applies for Scotland as for England and Wales, and

    (b)   "default order" means the same as in section 3(3)(b).

(4A)   In this section "the companies legislation" means the Companies Acts and Parts 1 to 7 of the Insolvency Act 1986 (company insolvency and winding up).

(4B)   In this section "company" includes overseas company.

(5)   The maximum period of disqualification under this section is 5 years.

5A.   **Disqualification for certain convictions abroad**

(1)   If it appears to the Secretary of State that it is expedient in the public interest that a disqualification order under this section should be made against a person, the Secretary of State may apply to the court for such an order.

(2)   The court may, on an application under subsection (1), make a disqualification order against a person who has been convicted of a relevant foreign offence.

(3)   A "relevant foreign offence" is an offence committed outside Great Britain—

    (a)   in connection with—

        (i)   the promotion, formation, management, liquidation or striking off of a company (or any similar procedure),

        (ii)   the receivership of a company's property (or any similar procedure), or

        (iii) a person being an administrative receiver of a company (or holding a similar position), and

    (b)   which corresponds to an indictable offence under the law of England and Wales or (as the case may be) an indictable offence under the law of Scotland.

(4)   Where it appears to the Secretary of State that, in the case of a person who has offered to give a disqualification undertaking—

    (a)   the person has been convicted of a relevant foreign offence, and

    (b)   it is expedient in the public interest that the Secretary of State should accept the undertaking (instead of applying, or proceeding with an application, for a disqualification order), the Secretary of State may accept the undertaking.

(5)   In this section—

"company" includes an overseas company;

"the court" means the High Court or, in Scotland, the Court of Session.

(6)   The maximum period of disqualification under an order under this section is 15 years.

Disqualification for unfitness

6.   **Duty of court to disqualify unfit directors ...**

(1)   The court shall make a disqualification order against a person in any case where, on an application under this section, ...—

    (a)   the court is satisfied—

        (i)   that the person is or has been a director of a company which has at any time become insolvent (whether while the person was a director or subsequently), or

        (ii) that the person has been a director of a company which has at any time been dissolved without becoming insolvent (whether while the person was a director or subsequently), and

    (b)   the court is satisfied that the person's conduct as a director of that company (either taken alone or taken together with the person's conduct as a director of one or more other companies or overseas companies) makes the person unfit to be concerned in the management of a company.

(1A)   In this section references to a person's conduct as a director of any company or overseas company include, where that company or overseas company has become insolvent, references to that person's conduct in relation to any matter connected with or arising out of the insolvency.

(2)   For the purposes of this section ..., a company becomes insolvent if—

    (a)   the company goes into liquidation at a time when its assets are insufficient for the payment of its debts and other liabilities and the expenses of the winding up,

    (b)   the company enters administration, or

    (c)   an administrative receiver of the company is appointed;

    ...

(2A)   For the purposes of this section, an overseas company becomes insolvent if the company enters into insolvency proceedings of any description (including interim proceedings) in any jurisdiction.

(3)   In this section and section 7(2), "the court" means—

    (a)   where the company in question is being or has been wound up by the court, that court,

    (b)   where the company in question is being or has been wound up voluntarily, any court which has or (as the case may be) had jurisdiction to wind it up,

    (c)   where neither paragraph (a) nor (b) applies but an administrator or administrative receiver has at any time been appointed in respect of the company in question, any court which has jurisdiction to wind it up,

    (d)   where the company in question has been dissolved without becoming insolvent, a court which at the time it was dissolved had jurisdiction to wind it up.

(3A)   Sections 117 and 120 of the Insolvency Act 1986 (jurisdiction) shall apply for the purposes of subsection (3) as if the references in the definitions of "registered office" to the presentation of the petition for winding up were references—

(a)   in a case within paragraph (b) of that subsection, to the passing of the resolution for voluntary winding up,

(b)   in a case within paragraph (c) of that subsection, to the appointment of the administrator or (as the case may be) administrative receiver.

(3B)   Nothing in subsection (3) invalidates any proceedings by reason of their being taken in the wrong court; and proceedings—

(a)   for or in connection with a disqualification order under this section, or

(b)   in connection with a disqualification undertaking accepted under section 7,

may be retained in the court in which the proceedings were commenced, although it may not be the court in which they ought to have been commenced.

(3C)   In this section and section 7, "director" includes a shadow director.

(4)   Under this section the minimum period of disqualification is 2 years, and the maximum period is 15 years.

7.   Disqualification orders under section 6: applications and acceptance of undertakings

(1)   If it appears to the Secretary of State that it is expedient in the public interest that a disqualification order under section 6 should be made against any person, an application for the making of such an order against that person may be made—

(a)   by the Secretary of State, or

(b)   if the Secretary of State so directs in the case of a person who is or has been a director of a company which is being or has been wound up by the court in England and Wales, by the official receiver.

(2)   Except with the leave of the court, an application for the making under that section of a disqualification order against any person shall not be made after the end of the period of 3 years beginning with—

(a)   in a case where the person is or has been a director of a company which has become insolvent, the day on which the company became insolvent, or

(b)   in a case where the person has been a director of a company which has been dissolved without becoming insolvent, the day on which the company was dissolved.

(2A)   If it appears to the Secretary of State that the conditions mentioned in section 6(1) are satisfied as respects any person who has offered to give him a disqualification undertaking, he may accept the undertaking if it appears to him that it is expedient in the public interest that he should do so (instead of applying, or proceeding with an application, for a disqualification order).

(3)   ...

(4)   The Secretary of State or the official receiver may require any person—

(a)   to furnish him with such information with respect to that person's or another person's conduct as a director of a company which has at any time become insolvent or been dissolved without becoming insolvent (whether while the person was a director or subsequently), and

(b)   to produce and permit inspection of such books, papers and other records as are considered by the Secretary of State or (as the case may be) the official receiver to be relevant to that person's or another person's conduct as such a director,

as the Secretary of State or the official receiver may reasonably require for the purpose of determining whether to exercise, or of exercising, any function of his under this section.

(5)   Subsections (1A) and (2) of section 6 apply for the purposes of this section as they apply for the purposes of that section.

7A.   Office-holder's report on conduct of directors

(1)   The office-holder in respect of a company which is insolvent must prepare a report (a "conduct report") about the conduct of each person who was a director of the company—

(a)   on the insolvency date, or

(b)   at any time during the period of 3 years ending with that date.

(2)   For the purposes of this section a company is insolvent if—

(a)   the company is in liquidation and at the time it went into liquidation its assets were insufficient for the payment of its debts and other liabilities and the expenses of the winding up,

(b)   the company has entered administration, or

(c)   an administrative receiver of the company has been appointed;

and subsection (1A) of section 6 applies for the purposes of this section as it applies for the purpose of that section.

(3)   A conduct report must, in relation to each person, describe any conduct of the person which may assist the Secretary of State in deciding whether to exercise the power under section 7(1) or (2A) in relation to the person.

(4)   The office-holder must send the conduct report to the Secretary of State before the end of—

(a)   the period of 3 months beginning with the insolvency date, or

(b)   such other longer period as the Secretary of State considers appropriate in the particular circumstances.

(5)   If new information comes to the attention of an office-holder, the office-holder must send that information to the Secretary of State as soon as reasonably practicable.

(6)   "New information" is information which an office-holder considers should have been included in a conduct report prepared in relation to the company, or would have been so included had it been available before the report was sent.

(7)   If there is more than one office-holder in respect of a company at any particular time (because the company is insolvent by virtue of falling within more than one paragraph of subsection (2) at that time), subsection (1) applies only to the first of the office-holders to be appointed.

(8)   In the case of a company which is at different times insolvent by virtue of falling within one or more different paragraphs of subsection (2)—

(a)   the references in subsection (1) to the insolvency date are to be read as references to the first such date during the period in which the company is insolvent, and

(b)   subsection (1) does not apply to an office-holder if at any time during the period in which the company is insolvent a conduct report has already been prepared and sent to the Secretary of State.

(9)   The "office-holder" in respect of a company which is insolvent is—

(a)   in the case of a company being wound up by the court in England and Wales, the official receiver;

(b)   in the case of a company being wound up otherwise, the liquidator;

(c)   in the case of a company in administration, the administrator;

(d)   in the case of a company of which there is an administrative receiver, the receiver.

(10)   The "insolvency date"—

(a)   in the case of a company being wound up by the court, means the date on which the court makes the winding-up order (see section 125 of the Insolvency Act 1986);

(b)   in the case of a company being wound up by way of a members' voluntary winding up, means the date on which the liquidator forms the opinion that the company will be unable to pay its debts in full (together with interest at the official rate) within the period stated in the directors' declaration of solvency under section 89 of the Insolvency Act 1986;

(c)   in the case of a company being wound up by way of a creditors' voluntary winding up where no such declaration under section 89 of that Act has been made, means the date of the passing of the resolution for voluntary winding up;

(d)   in the case of a company which has entered administration, means the date the company did so;

(e)   in the case of a company in respect of which an administrative receiver has been appointed, means the date of that appointment.

(11) For the purposes of subsection (10)(e), any appointment of an administrative receiver to replace an administrative receiver who has died or vacated office pursuant to section 45 of the Insolvency Act 1986 is to be ignored.

(12) In this section—

"court" has the same meaning as in section 6;

"director" includes a shadow director.

8. Disqualification of director on finding of unfitness

(1) If it appears to the Secretary of State ... that it is expedient in the public interest that a disqualification order should be made against a person who is, or has been, a director or shadow director of a company, he may apply to the court for such an order.

(1A) ...

(2) The court may make a disqualification order against a person where, on an application under this section, it is satisfied that his conduct in relation to the company (either taken alone or taken together with his conduct as a director or shadow director of one or more other companies or overseas companies) makes him unfit to be concerned in the management of a company.

(2A) Where it appears to the Secretary of State ... that, in the case of a person who has offered to give him a disqualification undertaking—

    (a) the conduct of the person in relation to a company of which the person is or has been a director or shadow director (either taken alone or taken together with his conduct as a director or shadow director of one or more other companies or overseas companies) makes him unfit to be concerned in the management of a company, and

    (b) it is expedient in the public interest that he should accept the undertaking (instead of applying, or proceeding with an application, for a disqualification order),

he may accept the undertaking.

(2B) Subsection (1A) of section 6 applies for the purposes of this section as it applies for the purposes of that section.

(3) In this section "the court" means the High Court or, in Scotland, the Court of Session.

(4) The maximum period of disqualification under this section is 15 years.

Persons instructing unfit directors

8ZA. Order disqualifying person instructing unfit director ...

(1) The court may make a disqualification order against a person ("P") if, on an application under section 8ZB, it is satisfied—

    (a) either—

        (i) that a disqualification order under section 6 has been made against a person who is or has been a director (but not a shadow director) of a company, or

        (ii) that the Secretary of State has accepted a disqualification undertaking from such a person under section 7(2A), and

    (b) that P exercised the requisite amount of influence over the person.

That person is referred to in this section as "the main transgressor".

(2) For the purposes of this section, P exercised the requisite amount of influence over the main transgressor if any of the conduct—

    (a) for which the main transgressor is subject to the order made under section 6, or

    (b) in relation to which the undertaking was accepted from the main transgressor under section 7(2A),

was the result of the main transgressor acting in accordance with P's directions or instructions.

(3) But P does not exercise the requisite amount of influence over the main transgressor by reason only that the main transgressor acts on advice given by P in a professional capacity.

(4) Under this section the minimum period of disqualification is 2 years and the maximum period is 15 years.

(5)   In this section and section 8ZB "the court" has the same meaning as in section 6; and subsection (3B) of section 6 applies in relation to proceedings mentioned in subsection (6) below as it applies in relation to proceedings mentioned in section 6(3B)(a) and (b).

(6)   The proceedings are proceedings—

(a)   for or in connection with a disqualification order under this section, or

(b)   in connection with a disqualification undertaking accepted under section 8ZC.

8ZB.   Application for order under section 8ZA

(1)   If it appears to the Secretary of State that it is expedient in the public interest that a disqualification order should be made against a person under section 8ZA, the Secretary of State may—

(a)   make an application to the court for such an order, or

(b)   in a case where an application for an order under section 6 against the main transgressor has been made by the official receiver, direct the official receiver to make such an application.

(2)   Except with the leave of the court, an application for a disqualification order under section 8ZA must not be made after the end of the period of 3 years beginning with the day on which the company in question became insolvent (within the meaning given by section 6(2)) or was dissolved without becoming insolvent.

(3)   Subsection (4) of section 7 applies for the purposes of this section as it applies for the purposes of that section.

8ZC.   Disqualification undertaking instead of an order under section 8ZA

(1)   If it appears to the Secretary of State that it is expedient in the public interest to do so, the Secretary of State may accept a disqualification undertaking from a person ("P") if—

(a)   any of the following is the case—

(i)   a disqualification order under section 6 has been made against a person who is or has been a director (but not a shadow director) of a company,

(ii)   the Secretary of State has accepted a disqualification undertaking from such a person under section 7(2A), or

(iii) it appears to the Secretary of State that such an undertaking could be accepted from such a person (if one were offered), and

(b)   it appears to the Secretary of State that P exercised the requisite amount of influence over the person.

That person is referred to in this section as "the main transgressor".

(2)   For the purposes of this section, P exercised the requisite amount of influence over the main transgressor if any of the conduct—

(a)   for which the main transgressor is subject to the disqualification order made under section 6,

(b)   in relation to which the disqualification undertaking was accepted from the main transgressor under section 7(2A), or

(c)   which led the Secretary of State to the conclusion set out in subsection (1)(a)(iii),

was the result of the main transgressor acting in accordance with P's directions or instructions.

(3)   But P does not exercise the requisite amount of influence over the main transgressor by reason only that the main transgressor acts on advice given by P in a professional capacity.

(4)   Subsection (4) of section 7 applies for the purposes of this section as it applies for the purposes of that section.

8ZD.   Order disqualifying person instructing unfit director: other cases

(1)   The court may make a disqualification order against a person ("P") if, on an application under this section, it is satisfied—

(a)   either—

(i)   that a disqualification order under section 8 has been made against a person who is or has been a director (but not a shadow director) of a company, or

(ii)   that the Secretary of State has accepted a disqualification undertaking from such a person under section 8(2A), and

(b)   that P exercised the requisite amount of influence over the person.

That person is referred to in this section as "the main transgressor".

(2)   The Secretary of State may make an application to the court for a disqualification order against P under this section if it appears to the Secretary of State that it is expedient in the public interest for such an order to be made.

(3)   For the purposes of this section, P exercised the requisite amount of influence over the main transgressor if any of the conduct—

(a)   for which the main transgressor is subject to the order made under section 8, or

(b)   in relation to which the undertaking was accepted from the main transgressor under section 8(2A),

was the result of the main transgressor acting in accordance with P's directions or instructions.

(4)   But P does not exercise the requisite amount of influence over the main transgressor by reason only that the main transgressor acts on advice given by P in a professional capacity.

(5)   Under this section the maximum period of disqualification is 15 years.

(6)   In this section "the court" means the High Court or, in Scotland, the Court of Session.

8ZE.   Disqualification undertaking instead of an order under section 8ZD

(1)   If it appears to the Secretary of State that it is expedient in the public interest to do so, the Secretary of State may accept a disqualification undertaking from a person ("P") if—

(a)   any of the following is the case—

(i)   a disqualification order under section 8 has been made against a person who is or has been a director (but not a shadow director) of a company,

(ii)   the Secretary of State has accepted a disqualification undertaking from such a person under section 8(2A), or

(iii)   it appears to the Secretary of State that such an undertaking could be accepted from such a person (if one were offered), and

(b)   it appears to the Secretary of State that P exercised the requisite amount of influence over the person.

That person is referred to in this section as "the main transgressor".

(2)   For the purposes of this section, P exercised the requisite amount of influence over the main transgressor if any of the conduct—

(a)   for which the main transgressor is subject to the disqualification order made under section 8,

(b)   in relation to which the disqualification undertaking was accepted from the main transgressor under section 8(2A), or

(c)   which led the Secretary of State to the conclusion set out in subsection (1)(a)(iii),

was the result of the main transgressor acting in accordance with P's directions or instructions.

(3)   But P does not exercise the requisite amount of influence over the main transgressor by reason only that the main transgressor acts on advice given by P in a professional capacity.

Disqualification for promoting tax avoidance

8ZF   Disqualification following winding up under section 85 of Finance Act 2022

(1)   The court must make a disqualification order against a person if, on an application under this section, it is satisfied—

(a)   that the person has at any time after the coming into force of this section been a director of a company while the company was a relevant body within the meaning of section 85(4) of the Finance Act 2022 (winding up of promoters of tax avoidance schemes), and

(b)   that a court has made a winding-up order in respect of the company under section 85(3) of that Act (whether while the person was a director or subsequently).

(2)   An officer of Revenue and Customs may make an application to the court for a disqualification order against a person under this section if it appears to the officer that it is expedient in the public interest for such an order to be made.

(3)   Except with the permission of the court, an application under subsection (2) may not be made after the end of the period of 3 years beginning with the day on which the winding-up order in question is made.

(4)   Under this section the minimum period of disqualification is 2 years, and the maximum is 15 years.

(5)   An officer of Revenue and Customs may accept a disqualification undertaking if it appears to the officer—

    (a)   that the conditions mentioned in subsection (1) are satisfied in relation to the person who has offered to give the disqualification undertaking, and

    (b)   that it is expedient in the public interest that the officer should accept the undertaking (instead of applying, or proceeding with an application, for a disqualification order).

(6)   In this section—

    "company" includes overseas company;

    "court" means—

    (a)   the court having jurisdiction for the purposes of the Insolvency Act 1986, or

    (b)   the High Court in Northern Ireland;

    "director" includes a shadow director.

8ZG   Disqualification on finding of unfitness: promoters of tax avoidance

(1)   The court may make a disqualification order against a person if, on an application under this section, it is satisfied—

    (a)   that the person—

        (i)   is a director of a company that carries on business as a promoter within the meaning of Part 5 of the Finance Act 2014 (promoters of tax avoidance schemes), or

        (ii)   after the coming into force of this section, was a director of a company at a time at which it did so, and

    (b)   that the person's conduct in relation to the company (either taken alone or taken together with the person's conduct as a director of one or more other companies) makes the person unfit to be concerned in the management of a company.

(2)   For the purposes of subsection (1)(a)(i), Part 5 of the Finance Act 2014 has effect as if, in section 234 of that Act—

    (a)   references to "tax" included value added tax and other indirect taxes, and

    (b)   the definition of "tax advantage" also included a tax advantage as defined for VAT in paragraph 6, and for other indirect taxes in paragraph 7, of Schedule 17 to the Finance (No. 2) Act 2017 (disclosure of tax avoidance schemes: VAT and other indirect taxes).

(3)   References in subsection (1)(b) to a person's conduct include conduct occurring before, as well as after, the coming into force of this section.

(4)   An officer of Revenue and Customs may make an application to the court for a disqualification order against a person under this section if it appears to the officer that it is expedient in the public interest for such an order to be made.

(5)   The maximum period of disqualification under this section is 15 years.

(6)   An officer of Revenue and Customs may accept a disqualification undertaking if it appears to the officer—

    (a)   that the conditions mentioned in subsection (1) are satisfied in relation to the person who has offered to give the disqualification undertaking, and

    (b)   that it is expedient in the public interest that the officer should accept the undertaking (instead of applying, or proceeding with an application, for a disqualification order).

(7)   In this section—

    "company" includes overseas company;

    "the court" means—

    (a)   in England and Wales, the High Court;

    (b)   in Scotland, the Court of Session;

    (c)   in Northern Ireland, the High Court in Northern Ireland;

"director" includes a shadow director;

"indirect tax" has the same meaning as in Schedule 17 to the Finance (No. 2) Act 2017 (see paragraph 2(1) of that Schedule).

Further provision about disqualification undertakings

8A. Variation etc of disqualification undertaking

(1)   The court may, on the application of a person who is subject to a disqualification undertaking—

(a)   reduce the period for which the undertaking is to be in force, or

(b)   provide for it to cease to be in force.

(2)   On the hearing of an application under subsection (1), the Secretary of State shall appear and call the attention of the court to any matters which seem to him to be relevant, and may himself give evidence or call witnesses.

(2ZA) Subsection (2) does not apply to an application in the case of an undertaking given under section 8ZF or 8ZG, and in such a case on the hearing of the application an officer of Revenue and Customs—

(a)   must appear and call the attention of the court to any matters which appear to the officer to be relevant;

(b)   may give evidence or call witnesses.

(2A)   Subsection (2) does not apply to an application in the case of an undertaking given under section 9B, and in such a case on the hearing of the application whichever of the Competition and Markets Authority or a specified regulator (within the meaning of section 9E) accepted the undertaking—

(a)   must appear and call the attention of the court to any matters which appear to it or him (as the case may be) to be relevant;

(b)   may give evidence or call witnesses.

(3)   In this section "the court"—

(za)   in the case of an undertaking given under section 8ZC has the same meaning as in section 8ZA;

(zb)   in the case of an undertaking given under section 8ZE means the High Court or, in Scotland, the Court of Session;

(a)   in the case of an undertaking given under section 9B means the High Court or (in Scotland) the Court of Session;

(b)   in any other case has the same meaning as in section 5A(5), 7(2), 8, 8ZF or 8ZG (as the case may be).

9.   ...

Disqualification for competition infringements

9A. Competition disqualification order

(1)   The court must make a disqualification order against a person if the following two conditions are satisfied in relation to him.

(2)   The first condition is that an undertaking which is a company of which he is a director commits a breach of competition law.

(3)   The second condition is that the court considers that his conduct as a director makes him unfit to be concerned in the management of a company.

(4)   An undertaking commits a breach of competition law if it engages in conduct which infringes either of the following—

(a)   the Chapter 1 prohibition (within the meaning of the Competition Act 1998) (prohibition on agreements, etc preventing, restricting or distorting competition);

(b)   the Chapter 2 prohibition (within the meaning of that Act) (prohibition on abuse of a dominant position);

(c), (d)   ...

(5)   For the purpose of deciding under subsection (3) whether a person is unfit to be concerned in the management of a company the court—

(a) must have regard to whether subsection (6) applies to him;

(b) may have regard to his conduct as a director of a company in connection with any other breach of competition law;

(c) must not have regard to the matters mentioned in Schedule 1.

(6)   This subsection applies to a person if as a director of the company—

(a) his conduct contributed to the breach of competition law mentioned in subsection (2);

(b) his conduct did not contribute to the breach but he had reasonable grounds to suspect that the conduct of the undertaking constituted the breach and he took no steps to prevent it;

(c) he did not know but ought to have known that the conduct of the undertaking constituted the breach.

(7)   For the purposes of subsection (6)(a) it is immaterial whether the person knew that the conduct of the undertaking constituted the breach.

(8)   For the purposes of subsection (4)(a) ... references to the conduct of an undertaking are references to its conduct taken with the conduct of one or more other undertakings.

(9)   The maximum period of disqualification under this section is 15 years.

(10)   An application under this section for a disqualification order may be made by the Competition and Markets Authority or by a specified regulator.

(11)   Section 60A of the Competition Act 1998 (certain principles etc to be considered or applied from IP completion day) applies in relation to any question arising by virtue of subsection (4)(a) or (b) above as it applies in relation to any question arising under Part 1 of that Act.

9B.   Competition undertakings

(1)   This section applies if—

(a) the Competition and Markets Authority or a specified regulator thinks that in relation to any person an undertaking which is a company of which he is a director has committed or is committing a breach of competition law,

(b) the Competition and Markets Authority or the specified regulator thinks that the conduct of the person as a director makes him unfit to be concerned in the management of a company, and

(c) the person offers to give the Competition and Markets Authority or the specified regulator (as the case may be) a disqualification undertaking.

(2)   The Competition and Markets Authority or the specified regulator (as the case may be) may accept a disqualification undertaking from the person instead of applying for or proceeding with an application for a disqualification order.

(3)   A disqualification undertaking is an undertaking by a person that for the period specified in the undertaking he will not—

(a) be a director of a company;

(b) act as receiver of a company's property;

(c) in any way, whether directly or indirectly, be concerned or take part in the promotion, formation or management of a company;

(d) act as an insolvency practitioner.

(4)   But a disqualification undertaking may provide that a prohibition falling within subsection (3)(a) to (c) does not apply if the person obtains the leave of the court.

(5)   The maximum period which may be specified in a disqualification undertaking is 15 years.

(6)   If a disqualification undertaking is accepted from a person who is already subject to a disqualification undertaking under this Act or to a disqualification order the periods specified in those undertakings or the undertaking and the order (as the case may be) run concurrently.

(7)   Subsections (4) to (8) of section 9A apply for the purposes of this section as they apply for the purposes of that section but in the application of subsection (5) of that section the reference to the court must be construed as a reference to the Competition and Markets Authority or a specified regulator (as the case may be).

9C. **Competition investigations**

(1)   If the Competition and Markets Authority or a specified regulator has reasonable grounds for suspecting that a breach of competition law has occurred it or he (as the case may be) may carry out an investigation for the purpose of deciding whether to make an application under section 9A for a disqualification order.

(2)   For the purposes of such an investigation sections 26 to 30 of the Competition Act 1998 apply to the Competition and Markets Authority and the specified regulators as they apply to the Competition and Markets Authority for the purposes of an investigation under section 25 of that Act.

(3)   Subsection (4) applies if as a result of an investigation under this section the Competition and Markets Authority or a specified regulator proposes to apply under section 9A for a disqualification order.

(4)   Before making the application the Competition and Markets Authority or regulator (as the case may be) must—

(a)   give notice to the person likely to be affected by the application, and

(b)   give that person an opportunity to make representations.

9D. **Co-ordination**

(1)   The Secretary of State may make regulations for the purpose of co-ordinating the performance of functions under sections 9A to 9C (relevant functions) which are exercisable concurrently by two or more persons.

(2)   Section 54(5) to (7) of the Competition Act 1998 (c. 41) applies to regulations made under this section as it applies to regulations made under that section and for that purpose in that section—

(a)   references to Part 1 functions must be read as references to relevant functions;

(b)   references to a regulator must be read as references to a specified regulator;

(ba)   the reference in subsection (6A)(b) to notice under section 31(1) of the Competition Act 1998 that the regulator proposes to make a decision within the meaning given by section 31(2) of that Act is to be read as notice under section 9C(4) that the specified regulator proposes to apply under section 9A for a disqualification order;

(c)   a competent person also includes any of the specified regulators.

(3)   The power to make regulations under this section must be exercised by statutory instrument subject to annulment in pursuance of a resolution of either House of Parliament.

(4)   Such a statutory instrument may—

(a)   contain such incidental, supplemental, consequential and transitional provision as the Secretary of State thinks appropriate;

(b)   make different provision for different cases.

9E. **Interpretation**

(1)   This section applies for the purposes of sections 9A to 9D.

(2)   Each of the following is a specified regulator for the purposes of a breach of competition law in relation to a matter in respect of which he or it has a function—

(a)   the Office of Communications;

(b)   the Gas and Electricity Markets Authority;

(c)   the Water Services Regulation Authority;

(d)   the Office of Rail and Road;

(e)   the Civil Aviation Authority;

(f)   Monitor;

(g)   the Payment Systems Regulator established under section 40 of the Financial Services (Banking Reform) Act 2013;

(h)   the Financial Conduct Authority.

(3)   The court is the High Court or (in Scotland) the Court of Session.

(4)   Conduct includes omission.

(5)   Director includes shadow director.

Other cases of disqualification

10.   Participation in wrongful trading

(1)   Where the court makes a declaration under section 213 or 214 of the Insolvency Act 1986 that a person is liable to make a contribution to a company's assets, then, whether or not an application for such an order is made by any person, the court may, if it thinks fit, also make a disqualification order against the person to whom the declaration relates.

(2)   The maximum period of disqualification under this section is 15 years.

(3)   In this section "company" includes overseas company.

11.   Undischarged bankrupts

(1)   It is an offence for a person to act as director of a company or directly or indirectly to take part in or be concerned in the promotion, formation or management of a company, without the leave of the court, at a time when any of the circumstances mentioned in subsection (2) apply to the person.

(2)   The circumstances are—

    (a)   the person is an undischarged bankrupt—

        (i)   in England and Wales or Scotland, or

        (ii)   in Northern Ireland,

    (b)   a bankruptcy restrictions order or undertaking is in force in respect of the person under—

        (i)   the Bankruptcy (Scotland) Act 1985 or 2016 or the Insolvency Act 1986, or

        (ii)   the Insolvency (Northern Ireland) Order 1989,

    (c)   a debt relief restrictions order or undertaking is in force in respect of the person under—

        (i)   the Insolvency Act 1986, or

        (ii)   the Insolvency (Northern Ireland) Order 1989,

    (d)   a moratorium period under a debt relief order applies in relation to the person under—

        (i)   the Insolvency Act 1986, or

        (ii)   the Insolvency (Northern Ireland) Order 1989.

(2A)   In subsection (1) "the court" means—

    (a)   for the purposes of subsection (2)(a)(i)—

        (i)   the court by which the bankruptcy order was made or (if the order was not made by a court) the court to which a debtor may appeal against a refusal to make a bankruptcy order, or

        (ii)   in Scotland, the court by which sequestration of the person's estate was awarded or, if awarded other than by the court, the court which would have jurisdiction in respect of sequestration of the person's estate,

    (b)   for the purposes of subsection (2)(b)(i)—

        (i)   the court which made the order,

        (ii)   in Scotland, if the order has been made other than by the court, the court to which the person may appeal against the order, or

        (iii)   the court to which the person may make an application for annulment of the undertaking,

    (c)   for the purposes of subsection (2)(c)(i)—

        (i)   the court which made the order, or

        (ii)   the court to which the person may make an application for annulment of the undertaking,

    (d)   for the purposes of subsection (2)(d)(i), the court to which the person would make an application under section 251M(1) of the Insolvency Act 1986 (if the person were dissatisfied as mentioned there),

    (e)   for the purposes of paragraphs (a)(ii), (b)(ii), (c)(ii) and (d)(ii) of subsection (2), the High Court of Northern Ireland.

(3)   In England and Wales, the leave of the court shall not be given unless notice of intention to apply for it has been served on the official receiver; and it is the latter's duty, if he is of opinion that it is

contrary to the public interest that the application should be granted, to attend on the hearing of the application and oppose it.

(4)   In this section "company" includes a company incorporated outside Great Britain that has an established place of business in Great Britain.

11A   Designated persons under sanctions legislation

(1)   It is an offence for a person who is subject to director disqualification sanctions to act as a director of a company or directly or indirectly to take part in or be concerned in the promotion, formation or management of a company (but see subsection (2)).

(2)   Subsection (1) does not apply—

(a)   to the extent that an exception from subsection (1) has been created by virtue of section 15(3A) of the Sanctions and Anti-Money Laundering Act 2018, or

(b)   to anything done under the authority of a licence issued by virtue of section 15(3A) of that Act.

(3)   It is a defence for a person charged with an offence under this section to prove that they did not know and could not reasonably have been expected to know that they were subject to director disqualification sanctions at the time at which they engaged in that conduct.

(4)   In this section "person who is subject to director disqualification sanctions" means a person who under regulations under section 1 of the Sanctions and Anti-Money Laundering Act 2018 is a person subject to director disqualification sanctions for the purposes of this section and Article 15A of the Company Directors Disqualification (Northern Ireland) Order 2002 (see section 3A of the Sanctions and Anti-Money Laundering Act 2018).

12.   *Failure to pay under county court administration order*

(1)   The following has effect where a court under section 429 of the Insolvency Act revokes an administration order under Part VI of the County Courts Act 1984.

(2)   A person to whom *that section applies by virtue of the order under section 429(2)(b)* shall not, except with the leave of the court which made the order, act as director or liquidator of, or directly or indirectly take part or be concerned in the promotion, formation or management of, a company.

Note. This section is amended as follows by the Tribunals, Courts and Enforcement Act 2007, ss. 106(2), 146, Sch. 16, para. 5, Sch. 23, Pt. 5, as from a day to be appointed: the section heading is substituted by the words "Disabilities on revocation of administration order"; subsection (1) is repealed; and in subsection (2) the italicized words are repealed and substituted by the words "section 429 of the Insolvency Act 1986 applies by virtue of an order under subsection (2) of that section".

12A.   Northern Irish disqualification orders

A person subject to a disqualification order under the Company Directors Disqualification (Northern Ireland) Order 2002 or made by the High Court of Northern Ireland under section 8ZF or 8ZG—

(a)   shall not be a director of a company, act as receiver of a company's property or in any way, whether directly or indirectly, be concerned or take part in the promotion, formation or management of a company unless (in each case) he has the leave of the High Court of Northern Ireland, and

(b)   shall not act as an insolvency practitioner.

12B.   Northern Irish disqualification undertakings

A person subject to a disqualification undertaking under section 8ZF or 8ZG so far as they extend to Northern Ireland or under the Company Directors Disqualification (Northern Ireland) Order 2002—

(a)   shall not be a director of a company, act as receiver of a company's property or in any way, whether directly or indirectly, be concerned or take part in the promotion, formation or management of a company unless (in each case) he has the leave of the High Court of Northern Ireland, and

(b)   shall not act as an insolvency practitioner.

12C.   **Determining unfitness etc: matters to be taken into account**

(1)   This section applies where a court must determine—

    (a)   whether a person's conduct as a director of one or more companies or overseas companies makes the person unfit to be concerned in the management of a company;

    (b)   whether to exercise any discretion it has to make a disqualification order under any of sections 2 to 4, 5A, 8, 8ZG or 10;

    (c)   where the court has decided to make a disqualification order under any of those sections or is required to make an order under section 6 or 8ZF, what the period of disqualification should be.

(2)   But this section does not apply where the court in question is one mentioned in section 2(2)(b) or (c).

(3)   This section also applies where the Secretary of State must determine—

    (a)   whether a person's conduct as a director of one or more companies or overseas companies makes the person unfit to be concerned in the management of a company;

    (b)   whether to exercise any discretion the Secretary of State has to accept a disqualification undertaking under section 5A, 7 or 8.

(3A)   This section also applies where an officer of Revenue and Customs must determine—

    (a)   whether a person's conduct as a director of one or more companies or overseas companies makes the person unfit to be concerned in the management of a company;

    (b)   whether to exercise any discretion the officer has to accept a disqualification undertaking under section 8ZF or 8ZG.

(4)   In making any such determination in relation to a person, the court or the Secretary of State or the officer (as the case may be) must—

    (a)   in every case, have regard in particular to the matters set out in paragraphs 1 to 4 of Schedule 1;

    (b)   in a case where the person concerned is or has been a director of a company or overseas company, also have regard in particular to the matters set out in paragraphs 5 to 7 of that Schedule.

(5)   In this section "director" includes a shadow director.

(6)   Subsection (1A) of section 6 applies for the purposes of this section as it applies for the purposes of that section.

(7)   The Secretary of State may by order modify Schedule 1; and such an order may contain such transitional provision as may appear to the Secretary of State to be necessary or expedient.

(8)   The power to make an order under this section is exercisable by statutory instrument.

(9)   An order under this section may not be made unless a draft of the instrument containing it has been laid before, and approved by a resolution of, each House of Parliament.

Consequences of contravention

13.   **Criminal penalties**

(1)   If a person acts in contravention of a disqualification order or disqualification undertaking or in contravention of section 12(2), 12A or 12B, or is guilty of an offence under section 11 or 11A, he is liable—

    (a)   on conviction on indictment, to imprisonment for not more than 2 years or a fine, or both; and

    (b)   on summary conviction, to imprisonment for not more than 6 months or a fine not exceeding the statutory maximum, or both.

14.   **Offences by body corporate**

(1)   Where—

    (a)   a body corporate is—

        (i)   guilty of an offence of acting in contravention of a disqualification order or disqualification undertaking or in contravention of section 12A or 12B, or

        (ii)   guilty of an offence under section 11A, and

(b)   it is proved that the offence occurred with the consent or connivance of, or was attributable to any neglect on the part of any director, manager, secretary or other similar officer of the body corporate, or any person who was purporting to act in any such capacity,

the person, as well as the body corporate, is guilty of the offence and liable to be proceeded against and punished accordingly.

(2)   Where the affairs of a body corporate are managed by its members, subsection (1) applies in relation to the acts and defaults of a member in connection with his functions of management as if he were a director of the body corporate.

15.   Personal liability for company's debts where person acts while disqualified

(1)   A person is personally responsible for all the relevant debts of a company if at any time—

(a)   in contravention of a disqualification order or disqualification undertaking or in contravention of section 11, 11A, 12A or 12B of this Act he is involved in the management of the company, ...

(b)   as a person who is involved in the management of the company, he acts or is willing to act on instructions given without the leave of the court by a person whom he knows at that time—

(i)   to be the subject of a disqualification order made or disqualification undertaking accepted under this Act or under the Company Directors Disqualification (Northern Ireland) Order 2002, or

(ii)   to be an undischarged bankrupt, or

(c)   as a person who is involved in the management of the company, they act or are willing to act on instructions where—

(i)   the instructions are given by a person whom they know at that time to be subject to director disqualification sanctions (within the meaning of section 11A),

(ii)   the giving of the instructions does not fall within any exception from section 11A(1) created by virtue of section 15(3A) of the Sanctions and Anti-Money Laundering Act 2018, and

(iii)   the instructions are not authorised,

(but see subsection (3A)).

(2)   Where a person is personally responsible under this section for the relevant debts of a company, he is jointly and severally liable in respect of those debts with the company and any other person who, whether under this section or otherwise, is so liable.

(3)   For the purposes of this section the relevant debts of a company are—

(a)   in relation to a person who is personally responsible under paragraph (a) of subsection (1), such debts and other liabilities of the company as are incurred at a time when that person was involved in the management of the company, and

(b)   in relation to a person who is personally responsible under paragraph (b) or (c) of that subsection, such debts and other liabilities of the company as are incurred at a time when that person was acting or was willing to act on instructions given as mentioned in that paragraph.

(3A)   But—

(a)   a person who is subject to director disqualification sanctions (within the meaning of section 11A) is not personally responsible under subsection (1)(a) for any relevant debts of the company incurred at a time when the person did not know and could not reasonably have been expected to know that they were subject to director disqualification sanctions;

(b)   a person is not personally responsible under subsection (1)(c) for any relevant debts of the company incurred at a time when the person reasonably believed that the instructions were authorised.

(4)   For the purposes of this section, a person is involved in the management of a company if he is a director of the company or if he is concerned, whether directly or indirectly, or takes part, in the management of the company.

(5) For the purposes of this section a person who, as a person involved in the management of a company, has at any time acted on instructions given without the leave of the court by a person whom he knew at that time—

  (a) to be the subject of a disqualification order made or disqualification undertaking accepted under this Act or under the Company Directors Disqualification (Northern Ireland) Order 2002, or

  (b) to be an undischarged bankrupt,

is presumed, unless the contrary is shown, to have been willing at any time thereafter to act on any instructions given by that person.

(6) Subsection (7) applies where a person ("P") at any time—

  (a) was involved in the management of a company, and

  (b) acted on instructions where—

    (i) the instructions were given by a person ("D") whom P knew at that time to be subject to director disqualification sanctions (within the meaning of section 11A),

    (ii) the giving of the instructions did not fall within any exception from section 11A(1) created by virtue of section 15(3A) of the Sanctions and Anti-Money Laundering Act 2018, and

    (iii) the instructions were not authorised,

unless P reasonably believed at that time that the instructions were authorised.

(7) For the purposes of this section P is presumed, unless the contrary is shown, to have been willing at any time thereafter to act on any instructions given by D.

(8) For the purposes of this section instructions are "authorised" if they are given under the authority of a licence issued by virtue of section 15(3A) of the Sanctions and Anti-Money Laundering Act 2018.

Compensation orders and undertakings

15A. Compensation orders and undertakings

(1) The court may make a compensation order against a person on the application of the Secretary of State if it is satisfied that the conditions mentioned in subsection (3) are met.

(2) If it appears to the Secretary of State that the conditions mentioned in subsection (3) are met in respect of a person who has offered to give the Secretary of State a compensation undertaking, the Secretary of State may accept the undertaking instead of applying, or proceeding with an application, for a compensation order.

(3) The conditions are that—

  (a) the person is subject to a disqualification order or disqualification undertaking under this Act, and

  (b) conduct for which the person is subject to the order or undertaking has caused loss to one or more creditors of an insolvent company, or a company which has been dissolved without becoming insolvent, of which the person has at any time been a director.

(4) An "insolvent company" is a company that is or has been insolvent and a company becomes insolvent if—

  (a) the company goes into liquidation at a time when its assets are insufficient for the payment of its debts and other liabilities and the expenses of the winding up,

  (b) the company enters administration, or

  (c) an administrative receiver of the company is appointed.

(5) The Secretary of State may apply for a compensation order at any time before the end of the period of two years beginning with the date on which the disqualification order referred to in paragraph (a) of subsection (3) was made, or the disqualification undertaking referred to in that paragraph was accepted.

(6) In the case of a person subject to a disqualification order under section 8ZA or 8ZD, or a disqualification undertaking under section 8ZC or 8ZE, the reference in subsection (3)(b) to

conduct is a reference to the conduct of the main transgressor in relation to which the person has exercised the requisite amount of influence.

(7)   In this section and sections 15B and 15C "the court" means—

(a)   in a case where a disqualification order has been made, the court that made the order,

(b)   in any other case, the High Court or, in Scotland, the Court of Session.

15B.   **Amounts payable under compensation orders and undertakings**

(1)   A compensation order is an order requiring the person against whom it is made to pay an amount specified in the order—

(a)   to the Secretary of State for the benefit of—

(i)   a creditor or creditors specified in the order;

(ii)   a class or classes of creditor so specified;

(b)   as a contribution to the assets of a company so specified.

(2)   A compensation undertaking is an undertaking to pay an amount specified in the undertaking—

(a)   to the Secretary of State for the benefit of—

(i)   a creditor or creditors specified in the undertaking;

(ii)   a class or classes of creditor so specified;

(b)   as a contribution to the assets of a company so specified.

(3)   When specifying an amount the court (in the case of an order) and the Secretary of State (in the case of an undertaking) must in particular have regard to—

(a)   the amount of the loss caused;

(b)   the nature of the conduct mentioned in section 15A(3)(b);

(c)   whether the person has made any other financial contribution in recompense for the conduct (whether under a statutory provision or otherwise).

(4)   An amount payable by virtue of subsection (2) under a compensation undertaking is recoverable as if payable under a court order.

(5)   An amount payable under a compensation order or compensation undertaking is provable as a bankruptcy debt.

15C.   **Variation and revocation of compensation undertakings**

(1)   The court may, on the application of a person who is subject to a compensation undertaking—

(a)   reduce the amount payable under the undertaking, or

(b)   provide for the undertaking not to have effect.

(2)   On the hearing of an application under subsection (1), the Secretary of State must appear and call the attention of the court to any matters which the Secretary of State considers relevant, and may give evidence or call witnesses.

Supplementary provisions

16.   **Application for disqualification order**

(1)   A person intending to apply for the making of a disqualification order ... shall give not less than 10 days' notice of his intention to the person against whom the order is sought; and on the hearing of the application the last-mentioned person may appear and himself give evidence or call witnesses.

(2)   An application to a court, other than a court mentioned in section 2(2)(b) or (c), for the making against any person of a disqualification order under any of sections 2 to 4 may be made by the Secretary of State or the official receiver, or by the liquidator or any past or present member or creditor of any company or overseas company in relation to which that person has committed or is alleged to have committed an offence or other default.

(3)   On the hearing of any application under this Act made by a person falling within subsection (4), the applicant shall appear and call the attention of the court to any matters which seem to him to be relevant, and may himself give evidence or call witnesses.

(4)   The following fall within this subsection—

(a)   the Secretary of State;

(b)   the official receiver;
(ba)   an officer of Revenue and Customs;
(c)   the Competition and Markets Authority;
(d)   the liquidator;
(e)   a specified regulator (within the meaning of section 9E).

17.   Application for leave under an order or undertaking

(1)   Where a person is subject to a disqualification order made by a court having jurisdiction to wind up companies, any application for leave for the purposes of section 1(1)(a) shall be made to that court.

(2)   Where—
(a)   a person is subject to a disqualification order made under section 2 by a court other than a court having jurisdiction to wind up companies, or
(b)   a person is subject to a disqualification order made under section 5,
any application for leave for the purposes of section 1(1)(a) shall be made to any court which, when the order was made, had jurisdiction to wind up the company (or, if there is more than one such company, any of the companies) to which the offence (or any of the offences) in question related.

(3)   Where a person is subject to a disqualification undertaking accepted at any time under section 5A, 7 or 8, any application for leave for the purposes of section 1A(1)(a) shall be made to any court to which, if the Secretary of State had applied for a disqualification order under the section in question at that time, his application could have been made.

(3ZA) Where a person is subject to a disqualification undertaking accepted at any time under section 8ZC, any application for leave for the purposes of section 1A(1)(a) must be made to any court to which, if the Secretary of State had applied for a disqualification order under section 8ZA at that time, that application could have been made.

(3ZB) Where a person is subject to a disqualification undertaking accepted at any time under section 8ZE, any application for leave for the purposes of section 1A(1)(a) must be made to the High Court or, in Scotland, the Court of Session.

(3ZC) Where a person is subject to a disqualification undertaking accepted at any time under section 8ZF or 8ZG, any application for leave for the purposes of section 1A(1)(a) must be made to any court to which, if an officer of Revenue and Customs had applied for a disqualification order under the section in question at that time, the application could have been made.

(3A)   Where a person is subject to a disqualification undertaking accepted at any time under section 9B any application for leave for the purposes of section 9B(4) must be made to the High Court or (in Scotland) the Court of Session.

(4)   But where a person is subject to two or more disqualification orders or undertakings (or to one or more disqualification orders and to one or more disqualification undertakings), any application for leave for the purposes of section 1(1)(a), 1A(1)(a) or 9B(4) shall be made to any court to which any such application relating to the latest order to be made, or undertaking to be accepted, could be made.

(5)   On the hearing of an application for leave for the purposes of section 1(1)(a) or 1A(1)(a), the Secretary of State shall appear and call the attention of the court to any matters which seem to him to be relevant, and may himself give evidence or call witnesses.

(5A)   Subsection (5) does not apply to an application for leave—
(a)   for the purposes of section 1(1)(a) if the application for the disqualification order was made by an officer of Revenue and Customs, or
(b)   for the purposes of section 1A(1)(a) if the disqualification undertaking was accepted by an officer of Revenue and Customs.

(5B)   In such a case, on the hearing of the application an officer of Revenue and Customs—
(a)   must appear and call the attention of the court to any matters which appear to the officer to be relevant;
(b)   may give evidence or call witnesses.

(6)   Subsection (5) does not apply to an application for leave for the purposes of section 1(1)(a) if the application for the disqualification order was made under section 9A.

(7)   In such a case and in the case of an application for leave for the purposes of section 9B(4) on the hearing of the application whichever of the Competition and Markets Authority or a specified regulator (within the meaning of section 9E) applied for the order or accepted the undertaking (as the case may be)—

   (a)   must appear and draw the attention of the court to any matters which appear to it or him (as the case may be) to be relevant;

   (b)   may give evidence or call witnesses.

18.   Register of disqualification orders and undertakings

(1)   The Secretary of State may make regulations requiring officers of courts to furnish him with such particulars as the regulations may specify of cases in which—

   (a)   a disqualification order is made, or

   (b)   any action is taken by a court in consequence of which such an order or a disqualification undertaking is varied or ceases to be in force, or

   (c)   leave is granted by a court for a person subject to such an order to do any thing which otherwise the order prohibits him from doing, or

   (d)   leave is granted by a court for a person subject to such an undertaking to do anything which otherwise the undertaking prohibits him from doing;

   and the regulations may specify the time within which, and the form and manner in which, such particulars are to be furnished.

(2)   The Secretary of State shall, from the particulars so furnished, continue to maintain the register of orders, and of cases in which leave has been granted as mentioned in subsection (1)(c), ...

(2A)   The Secretary of State must include in the register such particulars as he considers appropriate of—

   (a)   disqualification undertakings accepted by him under section 5A, 7, 8, 8ZC or 8ZE;

   (aa)   disqualification undertakings accepted by an officer of Revenue and Customs under section 8ZF or 8ZG;

   (b)   disqualification undertakings accepted by the Competition and Markets Authority or a specified regulator under section 9B;

   (c)   cases in which leave has been granted as mentioned in subsection (1)(d);

   (d)   persons who are subject to director disqualification sanctions within the meaning of section 11A;

   (e)   any licences issued by virtue of section 15(3A) of the Sanctions and Anti-Money Laundering Act 2018.

(3)   When an order or undertaking of which entry is made in the register ceases to be in force, the Secretary of State shall delete the entry from the register and all particulars relating to it which have been furnished to him under this section or any previous corresponding provision and, in the case of a disqualification undertaking, any other particulars he has included in the register.

(4)   The register shall be open to inspection on payment of such fee as may be specified by the Secretary of State in regulations.

(4A)   Regulations under this section may extend the preceding provisions of this section, to such extent and with such modifications as may be specified in the regulations, to disqualification orders ... or disqualification undertakings made under the Company Directors Disqualification (Northern Ireland) Order 2002.

(5)   Regulations under this section shall be made by statutory instrument subject to annulment in pursuance of a resolution of either House of Parliament.

19.   Special savings from repealed enactments

Schedule 2 to this Act has effect—

   (a)   in connection with certain transitional cases arising under sections 93 and 94 of the Companies Act 1981, so as to limit the power to make a disqualification order, or to restrict the duration of an order, by reference to events occurring or things done before the sections came into force,

(b)   to preserve orders made under section 28 of the Companies Act 1976 (repealed by the Act of 1981), and

(c)   to preclude any applications for a disqualification order under section 6 or 8, where the relevant company went into liquidation before 28th April 1986.

Miscellaneous and general

20.   Admissibility in evidence of statements

(1)   In any proceedings (whether or not under this Act), any statement made in pursuance of a requirement imposed by or under sections 5A, 6 to 10, 12C, 15 to 15C or 19(c) of, or Schedule 1 to, this Act, or by or under rules made for the purposes of this Act under the Insolvency Act 1986 or under the 1989 Order, may be used in evidence against any person making or concurring in making the statement.

(2)   However, in criminal proceedings in which any such person is charged with an offence to which this subsection applies—

(a)   no evidence relating to the statement may be adduced, and

(b)   no question relating to it may be asked,

by or on behalf of the prosecution, unless evidence relating to it is adduced, or a question relating to it is asked, in the proceedings by or on behalf of that person.

(3)   Subsection (2) applies to any offence other than—

(a)   an offence which is—

(i)   created by rules made for the purposes of this Act under the Insolvency Act 1986, and

(ii)   designated for the purposes of this subsection by such rules or by regulations made by the Secretary of State;

(b)   an offence which is—

(i)   created by regulations made under any such rules, and

(ii)   designated for the purposes of this subsection by such regulations;

(c)   an offence under section 5 of the Perjury Act 1911 (false statements made otherwise than on oath); ...

(d)   an offence under section 44(2) of the Criminal Law (Consolidation) (Scotland) Act 1995 (false statements made otherwise than on oath); or

(e)   an offence under Article 10 of the Perjury (Northern Ireland) Order 1979 (S.I. 1979/1714 (N.I. 19)) (false statements made otherwise than on oath).

(4)   Regulations under subsection (3)(a)(ii) shall be made by statutory instrument and, after being made, shall be laid before each House of Parliament.

(5)   In subsection (1), "the 1989 Order" means the Insolvency (Northern Ireland) Order 1989 (S.I. 1989/2405 (N.I. 19)).

20A.   Legal professional privilege

In proceedings against a person for an offence under this Act nothing in this Act is to be taken to require any person to disclose any information that he is entitled to refuse to disclose on grounds of legal professional privilege (in Scotland, confidentiality of communications).

21.   Interaction with Insolvency Act 1986 etc

(1)   References in this Act to the official receiver, in relation to the winding up of a company or the bankruptcy of an individual, are to any person who, by virtue of section 399 of the Insolvency Act 1986, is authorised to act as the official receiver in relation to that winding up or bankruptcy; and, in accordance with section 401(2) of that Act, references in this Act to an official receiver includes a person appointed as his deputy.

(2)   Sections 1A, 5A, 6 to 10, 12C, 15 to 15C, 19(c) and 20 of, and Schedule 1 to, this Act and sections 1 and 17 of this Act as they apply for the purposes of those provisions are deemed

included in Parts I to VII of the Insolvency Act 1986 for the purposes of the following sections of that Act—

section 411 (power to make insolvency rules);

section 414 (fees orders);

section 420 (orders extending provisions about insolvent companies to insolvent partnerships);

section 422 (modification of such provisions in their application to recognised banks); …

…

(3)   Section 434 of that Act (Crown application) applies to sections 1A, 5A, 6 to 10, 12C, 15 to 15C, 19(c) and 20 of, and Schedule 1 to, this Act and sections 1 and 17 of this Act as they apply for the purposes of those provisions as it does to the provisions of that Act which are there mentioned.

(4)   For the purposes of summary proceedings in Scotland, section 431 of that Act applies to summary proceedings for an offence under section 11, 11A or 13 of this Act as it applies to summary proceedings for an offence under Parts I to VII of that Act.

(5)   Sections 8ZF and 8ZG and the other provisions of this Act so far as relating to applications and orders made, and undertakings accepted, under those provisions in Northern Ireland, are deemed included in Parts 2 to 7 of the Insolvency (Northern Ireland) Order 1989 (S.I. 1989/2405 (N.I. 19)) for the purposes of the following Articles of that Order—

> Article 359 (power to make insolvency rules);
>
> Article 361 (fees orders).

21A.   Bank insolvency

Section 121 of the Banking Act 2009 provides for this Act to apply in relation to bank insolvency as it applies in relation to liquidation.

21B.   Bank administration

Section 155 of the Banking Act 2009 provides for this Act to apply in relation to bank administration as it applies in relation to liquidation.

21C.   Building society insolvency and special administration

Section 90E of the Building Societies Act 1986 provides for this Act to apply in relation to building society insolvency and building society special administration as it applies in relation to liquidation.

22.   Interpretation

(1)   This section has effect with respect to the meaning of expressions used in this Act, and applies unless the context otherwise requires.

(2)   "Company" means—

(a)   a company registered under the Companies Act 2006 in Great Britain, or

(b)   a company that may be wound up under Part 5 of the Insolvency Act 1986 (unregistered companies).

(2A)   An "overseas company" is a company incorporated or formed outside Great Britain.

(2B)   So far as this Act extends to Northern Ireland, subsections (2) and (2A) do not apply and instead—

"company" means—

(a)   a company registered under the Companies Act 2006 in Northern Ireland, or

(b)   a company that may be wound up under Part 6 of the Insolvency (Northern Ireland) Order 1989 (S.I. 1989/2405 (N.I. 19)) (unregistered companies), and

"overseas company" means a company which is incorporated or formed outside Northern Ireland.

(3)   Section 247 in Part VII of the Insolvency Act 1986 (interpretation for the first Group of Parts to that Act) applies as regards references to a company's insolvency and to its going into liquidation; and "administrative receiver" has the meaning given by section 251 of that Act and references to acting as an insolvency practitioner are to be read in accordance with section 388 of that Act.

(4)   "Director" includes any person occupying the position of director, by whatever name called … .

(5)   "Shadow director", in relation to a company, means a person in accordance with whose directions or instructions the directors of the company are accustomed to act, but so that a person is not deemed a shadow director by reason only that the directors act—

      (a)   on advice given by that person in a professional capacity;

      (b)   in accordance with instructions, a direction, guidance or advice given by that person in the exercise of a function conferred by or under an enactment;

      (c)   in accordance with guidance or advice given by that person in that person's capacity as a Minister of the Crown (within the meaning of the Ministers of the Crown Act 1975).

(6)   "Body corporate" and "officer" have the same meaning as in the Companies Acts (see section 1173(1) of the Companies Act 2006).

(7)   "The Companies Acts" has the meaning given by section 2(1) of the Companies Act 2006.

(8)   Any reference to provisions, or a particular provision, of the Companies Acts or the Insolvency Act 1986 includes the corresponding provisions or provision of corresponding earlier legislation.

(9)   Subject to the provisions of this section, expressions that are defined for the purposes of the Companies Acts (see section 1174 of, and Schedule 8 to, the Companies Act 2006) have the same meaning in this Act.

(10)   Any reference to acting as receiver—

      (a)   includes acting as manager or as both receiver and manager, but

      (b)   does not include acting as administrative receiver;

      and "receivership" is to be read accordingly.

22A.   Application of Act to building societies

(1)   This Act applies to building societies as it applies to companies.

(2)   References in this Act to a company, or to a director or an officer of a company include, respectively, references to a building society within the meaning of the Building Societies Act 1986 or to a director or officer, within the meaning of that Act, of a building society.

(3)   In relation to a building society the definition of "shadow director" in section 22(5) applies with the substitution of "building society" for "company".

(3A)   In relation to a building society, this Act applies as if—

      (a)   sections 6(1)(a)(ii) and (3)(d), 7(2)(b) and 11A were omitted;

      (b)   references in sections 7(4)(a), 8ZB(2) and 15A(3)(b) to a company which has been dissolved without becoming insolvent were omitted.

(4)   ...

22B.   Application of Act to incorporated friendly societies

(1)   This Act applies to incorporated friendly societies as it applies to companies.

(2)   References in this Act to a company, or to a director or an officer of a company include, respectively, references to an incorporated friendly society within the meaning of the Friendly Societies Act 1992 or to a member of the committee of management or officer, within the meaning of the Act, of an incorporated friendly society.

(3)   In relation to an incorporated friendly society every reference to a shadow director shall be omitted.

(3A)   In relation to an incorporated friendly society, this Act applies as if—

      (a)   sections 6(1)(a)(ii) and (3)(d), 7(2)(b), 8ZA to 8ZE and 11A were omitted;

      (b)   references in sections 7(4)(a) and 15A(3)(b) to a company which has been dissolved without becoming insolvent were omitted.

(4)   ...

22C.   Application of Act to NHS foundation trusts

(1)   This Act applies to NHS foundation trusts as it applies to companies within the meaning of this Act.

(2)   References in this Act to a company, or to a director or officer of a company, include, respectively, references to an NHS foundation trust or to a director or officer of the trust; but references to shadow directors are omitted.

(2A)   In relation to an NHS foundation trust, this Act applies as if—

(a)   sections 6(1)(a)(ii) and (3)(d), 7(2)(b) and 11A were omitted;

(b)   references in sections 7(4)(a), 8ZB(2) and 15A(3)(b) to a company which has been dissolved without becoming insolvent were omitted.

(3)   ...

22D.   ...

22E.   Application of Act to registered societies

(1)   In this section "registered society" has the same meaning as in the Co-operative and Community Benefit Societies Act 2014 ("the 2014 Act").

(2)   This Act applies to registered societies as it applies to companies.

(3)   Accordingly, in this Act—

(a)   references to a company include a registered society, and

(b)   references to a director or an officer of a company include a member of the committee or an officer of a registered society.

In paragraph (b) "committee" and "officer" have the same meaning as in the 2014 Act: see section 149 of that Act.

(4)   As they apply in relation to registered societies, the provisions of this Act have effect with the following modifications—

(a)   in section 2(1) (disqualification on conviction of indictable offence), the reference to striking off includes cancellation of the registration of a society under the 2014 Act;

(b)   in section 3 (disqualification for persistent breaches) and section 5 (disqualification on summary conviction), references to the companies legislation shall be read as references to the legislation relating to registered societies;

(c)   ...

(d)   references to the registrar shall be read as references to the Financial Conduct Authority;

(e)   references to a shadow director shall be disregarded;

(f)   sections 6(1)(a)(ii) and (3)(d), 7(2)(b), 8ZA to 8ZE and 11A are to be disregarded;

(g)   references in sections 7(4)(a) and 15A(3)(b) to a company which has been dissolved without becoming insolvent are to be disregarded.

(5)   ...

(6)   "The legislation relating to registered societies" means the Credit Unions Act 1979 and the Co-operative and Community Benefit Societies Act 2014.

22F.   Application of Act to charitable incorporated organisations

(1)   This Act applies to charitable incorporated organisations ("CIOs") as it applies to companies.

(2)   Accordingly, in this Act—

(a)   references to a company are to be read as including references to a CIO;

(b)   references to a director or an officer of a company are to be read as including references to a charity trustee of a CIO; and

(c)   any reference to the Insolvency Act 1986 is to be read as including a reference to that Act as it applies to CIOs.

(3)   As they apply in relation to CIOs, the provisions of this Act have effect with the following modifications—

(a)   in section 2(1), the reference to striking off is to be read as including a reference to dissolution;

(b)   in section 4(1)(a), the reference to an offence under section 993 of the Companies Act 2006 is to be read as including a reference to an offence under regulation 60 of the Charitable Incorporated Organisations (General) Regulations 2012 (fraudulent trading);

(ba)   sections 6(1)(a)(ii) and (3)(d) and 7(2)(b) are to be disregarded;

(bb)   references in sections 7(4)(a), 8ZB(2) and 15A(3)(b) to a company which has been dissolved without becoming insolvent are to be disregarded;

(c)   sections 9A to 9E are to be disregarded;

    (d)   references to any of sections 9A to 9E are to be disregarded;

    (da) section 11A is to be disregarded;

    (e)   references to a shadow director are to be disregarded.

(4)   ...

(5)   In this section "charity trustees" has the meaning given by section 177 of the Charities Act 2011.

22G.   **Application of Act to further education bodies**

(1)   This Act applies to further education bodies as it applies to companies.

(2)   Accordingly, in this Act—

    (a)   references to a company are to be read as including references to a further education body;

    (b)   references to a director or an officer of a company are to be read as including references to a member of a further education body;

    (c)   any reference to the Insolvency Act 1986 is to be read as including a reference to that Act as it applies to further education bodies.

(3)   As they apply in relation to further education bodies, the provisions of this Act have effect with the following modifications—

    (a)   in section 2(1), the reference to striking off is to be read as including a reference to dissolution;

    (aa) sections 6(1)(a)(ii) and (3)(d) and 7(2)(b) are to be disregarded;

    (ab) references in sections 7(4)(a), 8ZB(2) and 15A(3)(b) to a company which has been dissolved without becoming insolvent are to be disregarded;

    (b)   sections 9A to 9E are to be disregarded;

    (c)   references to any of sections 9A to 9E are to be disregarded;

    (d)   section 11A is to be disregarded.

(4)   In this section—

"further education body" means—

    (a)   a further education corporation, or

    (b)   a sixth form college corporation;

"further education corporation" means a body corporate that—

    (a)   is established under section 15 or 16 of the Further and Higher Education Act 1992, or

    (b)   has become a further education corporation by virtue of section 33D or 47 of that Act;

"sixth form college corporation" means a body corporate—

    (a)   designated as a sixth form college corporation under section 33A or 33B of the Further and Higher Education Act 1992, or

    (b)   established under section 33C of that Act.

22H.   **Application of Act to protected cell companies**

(1)   In this section—

    (a)   so far as this section extends to England and Wales and Scotland, "protected cell company" means a protected cell company incorporated under Part 4 of the Risk Transformation Regulations 2017 which has its registered office in England and Wales (or Wales) or Scotland; and

    (aa) so far as this section extends to Northern Ireland, "protected cell company" means a protected cell company incorporated under Part 4 of the Risk Transformation Regulations 2017 which has its registered office in Northern Ireland;

    (b)   a reference to a part of a protected cell company is a reference to the core or a cell of the protected cell company (see regulations 42 and 43 of the Risk Transformation Regulations 2017).

(2)   This Act applies to protected cell companies as it applies to companies.

(3)   Accordingly, in this Act, references to a company are to be read as including references to a protected cell company.

(4)   As they apply in relation to protected cell companies, the provisions of this Act have effect with the following modifications—

(za) sections 6(1)(a)(ii) and (3)(d), 7(2)(b) and 11A are to be disregarded;

(zb) references in sections 7(4)(a), 8ZB(2) and 15A(3)(b) to a company which has been dissolved without becoming insolvent are to be disregarded;

(a) references to the administration, insolvency, liquidation or winding up of a company are to be read as references to the administration, insolvency, liquidation or winding up of a part of a protected cell company;

(b) references to striking off are to be read as including references to dissolution;

(c) references to a director of a company which is or has been insolvent are to be read as references to the director of a protected cell company, a part of which is or has been insolvent;

(d) references to a director of a company which is being or has been wound up are to be read as references to the director of a protected cell company, a part of which is being or has been wound up;

(e) references to the court with jurisdiction to wind up a company are to be read as references to the court with jurisdiction to wind up the parts of a protected cell company;

(f) references to the companies legislation are to be read as references to Part 4 of, and Schedules 1 to 3 to, the Risk Transformation Regulations 2017;

(g) references to the Insolvency Act 1986 are to be read as references to that Act as applied by Part 4 of, and Schedules 1 to 3 to, the Risk Transformation Regulations 2017;

(h) references to section 452 and 456 of the Companies Act 2006 are to be read as references to those sections as applied by regulation 163 of the Risk Transformation Regulations 2017;

(i) references to the registrar of companies are to be read as references to the Financial Conduct Authority; and

(j) so far as this section extends to England and Wales and Scotland, references to an overseas company include references to a protected cell company incorporated under the Risk Transformation Regulations 2017 which has its registered office in Northern Ireland;

(k) so far as this section extends to Northern Ireland, references to an overseas company include references to a protected cell company incorporated under the Risk Transformation Regulations 2017 which has its registered office in England and Wales (or Wales) or Scotland.

(5) Where two or more parts of a protected cell company are or have been insolvent, then sections 6 to 7A and 8ZA to 8ZC apply in relation to each part separately.

(6) A contribution to the assets of a protected cell company given in accordance with a compensation order under section 15A(1) or a compensation undertaking under section 15A(2) is to be held by the protected cell company on behalf of the part of the protected cell company specified in the order or undertaking.

23. Transitional provisions, savings, repeals

(1) The transitional provisions and savings in Schedule 3 to this Act have effect, and are without prejudice to anything in the Interpretation Act 1978 with regard to the effect of repeals.

(2) The enactments specified in the second column of Schedule 4 to this Act are repealed to the extent specified in the third column of that Schedule.

24. Extent

(1) This Act extends to England and Wales and to Scotland.

(2) Subsections (1) to (2A) of section 11 also extend to Northern Ireland.

(3) For provision extending this Act (other than sections 13 to 15) to Northern Ireland so far as relating to applications and orders made, and undertakings accepted, under section 8ZF or 8ZG, see paragraph 4 of Schedule 13 to the Finance Act 2024.

25. Commencement

This Act comes into force simultaneously with the Insolvency Act 1986.

26.   Citation

This Act may be cited as the Company Directors Disqualification Act 1986.

SCHEDULE 1 Section 12C

DETERMINING UNFITNESS ETC: MATTERS TO BE TAKEN INTO ACCOUNT

Matters to be taken into account in all cases

1.   The extent to which the person was responsible for the causes of any material contravention by a company or overseas company of any applicable legislative or other requirement.
2.   Where applicable, the extent to which the person was responsible for the causes of a company or overseas company becoming insolvent.
3.   The frequency of conduct of the person which falls within paragraph 1 or 2.
4.   The nature and extent of any loss or harm caused, or any potential loss or harm which could have been caused, by the person's conduct in relation to a company or overseas company.

Additional matters to be taken into account where person is or has been a director

5.   Any misfeasance or breach of any fiduciary duty by the director in relation to a company or overseas company.
6.   Any material breach of any legislative or other obligation of the director which applies as a result of being a director of a company or overseas company.
7.   The frequency of conduct of the director which falls within paragraph 5 or 6.

Interpretation

8.   Subsections (1A) to (2A) of section 6 apply for the purposes of this Schedule as they apply for the purposes of that section.
9.   In this Schedule "director" includes a shadow director.

SCHEDULE 2 Section 19

SAVINGS FROM COMPANIES ACT 1981 SS 93, 94, AND
INSOLVENCY ACT 1985 SCHEDULE 9

1.   Sections 2 and 4(1)(b) do not apply in relation to anything done before 15th June 1982 by a person in his capacity as liquidator of a company or as receiver or manager of a company's property.
2.   Subject to paragraph 1—
    (a)   section 2 applies in a case where a person is convicted on indictment of an offence which he committed (and, in the case of a continuing offence, has ceased to commit) before 15th June 1982; but in such a case a disqualification order under that section shall not be made for a period in excess of 5 years;
    (b)   that section does not apply in a case where a person is convicted summarily—
        (i)   in England and Wales, if he had consented so to be tried before that date, or
        (ii)   in Scotland, if the summary proceedings commenced before that date.
3.   Subject to paragraph 1, section 4 applies in relation to an offence committed or other thing done before 15th June 1982; but a disqualification order made on the grounds of such an offence or other thing done shall not be made for a period in excess of 5 years.
4.   The powers of a court under section 5 are not exercisable in a case where a person is convicted of an offence which he committed (and, in the case of a continuing offence, had ceased to commit) before 15th June 1982.
5.   For purposes of section 3(1) and section 5, no account is to be taken of any offence which was committed, or any default order which was made, before 1st June 1977.
6.   An order made under section 28 of the Companies Act 1976 has effect as if made under section 3 of this Act; and an application made before 15th June 1982 for such an order is to be treated as an application for an order under the section last mentioned.

7.   Where—
        (a)   an application is made for a disqualification order under section 6 of this Act by virtue of
                paragraph (a) of subsection (2) of that section, and
        (b)   the company in question went into liquidation before 28th April 1986 (the coming into force
                of the provision replaced by section 6),
        the court shall not make an order under that section unless it could have made a disqualification
        order under section 300 of the Companies Act 1985 as it had effect immediately before the date
        specified in sub-paragraph (b) above.

8.   An application shall not be made under section 8 of this Act in relation to a report made or
        information or documents obtained before 28th April 1986.

SCHEDULE 3   Section 23(1)

TRANSITIONAL PROVISIONS AND SAVINGS

1.   In this Schedule, "the former enactments" means so much of the Companies Act 1985, and so
        much of the Insolvency Act 1986, as is repealed and replaced by this Act; and "the appointed
        day" means the day on which this Act comes into force.

2.   So far as anything done or treated as done under or for the purposes of any provision of the former
        enactments could have been done under or for the purposes of the corresponding provision of this
        Act, it is not invalidated by the repeal of that provision but has effect as if done under or for the
        purposes of the corresponding provision; and any order, regulation, rule or other instrument made
        or having effect under any provision of the former enactments shall, insofar as its effect is
        preserved by this paragraph, be treated for all purposes as made and having effect under the
        corresponding provision.

3.   Where any period of time specified in a provision of the former enactments is current
        immediately before the appointed day, this Act has effect as if the corresponding provision had
        been in force when the period began to run; and (without prejudice to the foregoing) any period of
        time so specified and current is deemed for the purposes of this Act—
        (a)   to run from the date or event from which it was running immediately before the appointed
                day, and
        (b)   to expire (subject to any provision of this Act for its extension) whenever it would have
                expired if this Act had not been passed;
        and any rights, priorities, liabilities, reliefs, obligations, requirements, powers, duties or exemp-
        tions dependent on the beginning, duration or end of such a period as above mentioned shall be
        under this Act as they were or would have been under the former enactments.

4.   Where in any provision of this Act there is a reference to another such provision, and the first-
        mentioned provision operates, or is capable of operating, in relation to things done or omitted, or
        events occurring or not occurring, in the past (including in particular past acts of compliance with
        any enactment, failures of compliance, contraventions, offences and convictions of offences) the
        reference to the other provision is to be read as including a reference to the corresponding
        provision of the former enactments.

5.   Offences committed before the appointed day under any provision of the former enactments may,
        notwithstanding any repeal by this Act, be prosecuted and punished after that day as if this Act
        had not passed.

6.   A reference in any enactment, instrument or document (whether express or implied, and in
        whatever phraseology) to a provision of the former enactments (including the corresponding
        provision of any yet earlier enactment) is to be read, where necessary to retain for the enactment,
        instrument or document the same force and effect as it would have had but for the passing of this
        Act, as, or as including, a reference to the corresponding provision by which it is replaced in this
        Act.

Companies (Model Articles) Regulations 2008

S.I. 2008/3229

1.   Citation and Commencement

These Regulations may be cited as the Companies (Model Articles) Regulations 2008 and come into force on 1st October 2009.

2.   Model articles for private companies limited by shares

Schedule 1 to these Regulations prescribes the model articles of association for private companies limited by shares.

3.   Model articles for private companies limited by guarantee

Schedule 2 to these Regulations prescribes the model articles of association for private companies limited by guarantee.

4.   Model articles for public companies

Schedule 3 to these Regulations prescribes the model articles of association for public companies.

SCHEDULE 1   Regulation 2

MODEL ARTICLES FOR PRIVATE COMPANIES LIMITED BY SHARES

PART 1

INTERPRETATION AND LIMITATION OF LIABILITY

1.   Defined terms

In the articles, unless the context requires otherwise—

"articles" means the company's articles of association;

"bankruptcy" includes individual insolvency proceedings in a jurisdiction other than England and Wales or Northern Ireland which have an effect similar to that of bankruptcy;

"chairman" has the meaning given in article 12;

"chairman of the meeting" has the meaning given in article 39;

"Companies Acts" means the Companies Acts (as defined in section 2 of the Companies Act 2006), in so far as they apply to the company;

"director" means a director of the company, and includes any person occupying the position of director, by whatever name called;

"distribution recipient" has the meaning given in article 31;

"document" includes, unless otherwise specified, any document sent or supplied in electronic form;

"electronic form" has the meaning given in section 1168 of the Companies Act 2006;

"fully paid" in relation to a share, means that the nominal value and any premium to be paid to the company in respect of that share have been paid to the company;

"hard copy form" has the meaning given in section 1168 of the Companies Act 2006;

"holder" in relation to shares means the person whose name is entered in the register of members as the holder of the shares;

"instrument" means a document in hard copy form;

"ordinary resolution" has the meaning given in section 282 of the Companies Act 2006;

"paid" means paid or credited as paid;

"participate", in relation to a directors' meeting, has the meaning given in article 10;

"proxy notice" has the meaning given in article 45;

"shareholder" means a person who is the holder of a share;

"shares" means shares in the company;

"special resolution" has the meaning given in section 283 of the Companies Act 2006;

"subsidiary" has the meaning given in section 1159 of the Companies Act 2006;

"transmittee" means a person entitled to a share by reason of the death or bankruptcy of a shareholder or otherwise by operation of law; and

"writing" means the representation or reproduction of words, symbols or other information in a visible form by any method or combination of methods, whether sent or supplied in electronic form or otherwise.

Unless the context otherwise requires, other words or expressions contained in these articles bear the same meaning as in the Companies Act 2006 as in force on the date when these articles become binding on the company.

2.   **Liability of members**

The liability of the members is limited to the amount, if any, unpaid on the shares held by them.

PART 2

DIRECTORS

Directors' Powers and Responsibilities

3.   **Directors' general authority**

Subject to the articles, the directors are responsible for the management of the company's business, for which purpose they may exercise all the powers of the company.

4.   **Shareholders' reserve power**

(1)   The shareholders may, by special resolution, direct the directors to take, or refrain from taking, specified action.

(2)   No such special resolution invalidates anything which the directors have done before the passing of the resolution.

5.   **Directors may delegate**

(1)   Subject to the articles, the directors may delegate any of the powers which are conferred on them under the articles—

(a)   to such person or committee;

(b)   by such means (including by power of attorney);

(c)   to such an extent;

(d)   in relation to such matters or territories; and

(e)   on such terms and conditions;

as they think fit.

(2)   If the directors so specify, any such delegation may authorise further delegation of the directors' powers by any person to whom they are delegated.

(3)   The directors may revoke any delegation in whole or part, or alter its terms and conditions.

6.   **Committees**

(1)   Committees to which the directors delegate any of their powers must follow procedures which are based as far as they are applicable on those provisions of the articles which govern the taking of decisions by directors.

(2)   The directors may make rules of procedure for all or any committees, which prevail over rules derived from the articles if they are not consistent with them.

Decision-Making by Directors

7.   **Directors to take decisions collectively**

(1)   The general rule about decision-making by directors is that any decision of the directors must be either a majority decision at a meeting or a decision taken in accordance with article 8.

(2)   If—

(a)   the company only has one director, and

(b)   no provision of the articles requires it to have more than one director,

the general rule does not apply, and the director may take decisions without regard to any of the provisions of the articles relating to directors' decision-making.

8. **Unanimous decisions**

(1)   A decision of the directors is taken in accordance with this article when all eligible directors indicate to each other by any means that they share a common view on a matter.

(2)   Such a decision may take the form of a resolution in writing, copies of which have been signed by each eligible director or to which each eligible director has otherwise indicated agreement in writing.

(3)   References in this article to eligible directors are to directors who would have been entitled to vote on the matter had it been proposed as a resolution at a directors' meeting.

(4)   A decision may not be taken in accordance with this article if the eligible directors would not have formed a quorum at such a meeting.

9. **Calling a directors' meeting**

(1)   Any director may call a directors' meeting by giving notice of the meeting to the directors or by authorising the company secretary (if any) to give such notice.

(2)   Notice of any directors' meeting must indicate—

(a)   its proposed date and time;

(b)   where it is to take place; and

(c)   if it is anticipated that directors participating in the meeting will not be in the same place, how it is proposed that they should communicate with each other during the meeting.

(3)   Notice of a directors' meeting must be given to each director, but need not be in writing.

(4)   Notice of a directors' meeting need not be given to directors who waive their entitlement to notice of that meeting, by giving notice to that effect to the company not more than 7 days after the date on which the meeting is held. Where such notice is given after the meeting has been held, that does not affect the validity of the meeting, or of any business conducted at it.

10. **Participation in directors' meetings**

(1)   Subject to the articles, directors participate in a directors' meeting, or part of a directors' meeting, when—

(a)   the meeting has been called and takes place in accordance with the articles, and

(b)   they can each communicate to the others any information or opinions they have on any particular item of the business of the meeting.

(2)   In determining whether directors are participating in a directors' meeting, it is irrelevant where any director is or how they communicate with each other.

(3)   If all the directors participating in a meeting are not in the same place, they may decide that the meeting is to be treated as taking place wherever any of them is.

11. **Quorum for directors' meetings**

(1)   At a directors' meeting, unless a quorum is participating, no proposal is to be voted on, except a proposal to call another meeting.

(2)   The quorum for directors' meetings may be fixed from time to time by a decision of the directors, but it must never be less than two, and unless otherwise fixed it is two.

(3)   If the total number of directors for the time being is less than the quorum required, the directors must not take any decision other than a decision—

(a)   to appoint further directors, or

(b)   to call a general meeting so as to enable the shareholders to appoint further directors.

12. **Chairing of directors' meetings**

(1)   The directors may appoint a director to chair their meetings.

(2)   The person so appointed for the time being is known as the chairman.

(3)   The directors may terminate the chairman's appointment at any time.

(4)   If the chairman is not participating in a directors' meeting within ten minutes of the time at which it was to start, the participating directors must appoint one of themselves to chair it.

13.   Casting vote

(1)   If the numbers of votes for and against a proposal are equal, the chairman or other director chairing the meeting has a casting vote.

(2)   But this does not apply if, in accordance with the articles, the chairman or other director is not to be counted as participating in the decision-making process for quorum or voting purposes.

14.   Conflicts of interest

(1)   If a proposed decision of the directors is concerned with an actual or proposed transaction or arrangement with the company in which a director is interested, that director is not to be counted as participating in the decision-making process for quorum or voting purposes.

(2)   But if paragraph (3) applies, a director who is interested in an actual or proposed transaction or arrangement with the company is to be counted as participating in the decision-making process for quorum and voting purposes.

(3)   This paragraph applies when—

(a)   the company by ordinary resolution disapplies the provision of the articles which would otherwise prevent a director from being counted as participating in the decision-making process;

(b)   the director's interest cannot reasonably be regarded as likely to give rise to a conflict of interest; or

(c)   the director's conflict of interest arises from a permitted cause.

(4)   For the purposes of this article, the following are permitted causes—

(a)   a guarantee given, or to be given, by or to a director in respect of an obligation incurred by or on behalf of the company or any of its subsidiaries;

(b)   subscription, or an agreement to subscribe, for shares or other securities of the company or any of its subsidiaries, or to underwrite, sub-underwrite, or guarantee subscription for any such shares or securities; and

(c)   arrangements pursuant to which benefits are made available to employees and directors or former employees and directors of the company or any of its subsidiaries which do not provide special benefits for directors or former directors.

(5)   For the purposes of this article, references to proposed decisions and decision-making processes include any directors' meeting or part of a directors' meeting.

(6)   Subject to paragraph (7), if a question arises at a meeting of directors or of a committee of directors as to the right of a director to participate in the meeting (or part of the meeting) for voting or quorum purposes, the question may, before the conclusion of the meeting, be referred to the chairman whose ruling in relation to any director other than the chairman is to be final and conclusive.

(7)   If any question as to the right to participate in the meeting (or part of the meeting) should arise in respect of the chairman, the question is to be decided by a decision of the directors at that meeting, for which purpose the chairman is not to be counted as participating in the meeting (or that part of the meeting) for voting or quorum purposes.

15.   Records of decisions to be kept

The directors must ensure that the company keeps a record, in writing, for at least 10 years from the date of the decision recorded, of every unanimous or majority decision taken by the directors.

16.   Directors' discretion to make further rules

Subject to the articles, the directors may make any rule which they think fit about how they take decisions, and about how such rules are to be recorded or communicated to directors.

Appointment of Directors

17.   Methods of appointing directors

(1)   Any person who is willing to act as a director, and is permitted by law to do so, may be appointed to be a director—

(a)   by ordinary resolution, or

(b)   by a decision of the directors.

(2)   In any case where, as a result of death, the company has no shareholders and no directors, the personal representatives of the last shareholder to have died have the right, by notice in writing, to appoint a person to be a director.

(3)   For the purposes of paragraph (2), where 2 or more shareholders die in circumstances rendering it uncertain who was the last to die, a younger shareholder is deemed to have survived an older shareholder.

18.   Termination of director's appointment

A person ceases to be a director as soon as—

(a)   that person ceases to be a director by virtue of any provision of the Companies Act 2006 or is prohibited from being a director by law;

(b)   a bankruptcy order is made against that person;

(c)   a composition is made with that person's creditors generally in satisfaction of that person's debts;

(d)   a registered medical practitioner who is treating that person gives a written opinion to the company stating that that person has become physically or mentally incapable of acting as a director and may remain so for more than three months;

(e)   ...

(f)   notification is received by the company from the director that the director is resigning from office, and such resignation has taken effect in accordance with its terms.

19.   Directors' remuneration

(1)   Directors may undertake any services for the company that the directors decide.

(2)   Directors are entitled to such remuneration as the directors determine—

(a)   for their services to the company as directors, and

(b)   for any other service which they undertake for the company.

(3)   Subject to the articles, a director's remuneration may—

(a)   take any form, and

(b)   include any arrangements in connection with the payment of a pension, allowance or gratuity, or any death, sickness or disability benefits, to or in respect of that director.

(4)   Unless the directors decide otherwise, directors' remuneration accrues from day to day.

(5)   Unless the directors decide otherwise, directors are not accountable to the company for any remuneration which they receive as directors or other officers or employees of the company's subsidiaries or of any other body corporate in which the company is interested.

20.   Directors' expenses

The company may pay any reasonable expenses which the directors properly incur in connection with their attendance at—

(a)   meetings of directors or committees of directors,

(b)   general meetings, or

(c)   separate meetings of the holders of any class of shares or of debentures of the company,

or otherwise in connection with the exercise of their powers and the discharge of their responsibilities in relation to the company.

PART 3
SHARES AND DISTRIBUTIONS

Shares

21.   All shares to be fully paid up

(1)   No share is to be issued for less than the aggregate of its nominal value and any premium to be paid to the company in consideration for its issue.

(2)   This does not apply to shares taken on the formation of the company by the subscribers to the company's memorandum.

22.   Powers to issue different classes of share

(1)   Subject to the articles, but without prejudice to the rights attached to any existing share, the company may issue shares with such rights or restrictions as may be determined by ordinary resolution.

(2)   The company may issue shares which are to be redeemed, or are liable to be redeemed at the option of the company or the holder, and the directors may determine the terms, conditions and manner of redemption of any such shares.

23.   Company not bound by less than absolute interests

Except as required by law, no person is to be recognised by the company as holding any share upon any trust, and except as otherwise required by law or the articles, the company is not in any way to be bound by or recognise any interest in a share other than the holder's absolute ownership of it and all the rights attaching to it.

24.   Share certificates

(1)   The company must issue each shareholder, free of charge, with one or more certificates in respect of the shares which that shareholder holds.

(2)   Every certificate must specify—

(a)   in respect of how many shares, of what class, it is issued;

(b)   the nominal value of those shares;

(c)   that the shares are fully paid; and

(d)   any distinguishing numbers assigned to them.

(3)   No certificate may be issued in respect of shares of more than one class.

(4)   If more than one person holds a share, only one certificate may be issued in respect of it.

(5)   Certificates must—

(a)   have affixed to them the company's common seal, or

(b)   be otherwise executed in accordance with the Companies Acts.

25.   Replacement share certificates

(1)   If a certificate issued in respect of a shareholder's shares is—

(a)   damaged or defaced, or

(b)   said to be lost, stolen or destroyed,

that shareholder is entitled to be issued with a replacement certificate in respect of the same shares.

(2)   A shareholder exercising the right to be issued with such a replacement certificate—

(a)   may at the same time exercise the right to be issued with a single certificate or separate certificates;

(b)   must return the certificate which is to be replaced to the company if it is damaged or defaced; and

(c)   must comply with such conditions as to evidence, indemnity and the payment of a reasonable fee as the directors decide.

26.   Share transfers

(1)   Shares may be transferred by means of an instrument of transfer in any usual form or any other form approved by the directors, which is executed by or on behalf of the transferor.

(2) No fee may be charged for registering any instrument of transfer or other document relating to or affecting the title to any share.

(3) The company may retain any instrument of transfer which is registered.

(4) The transferor remains the holder of a share until the transferee's name is entered in the register of members as holder of it.

(5) The directors may refuse to register the transfer of a share, and if they do so, the instrument of transfer must be returned to the transferee with the notice of refusal unless they suspect that the proposed transfer may be fraudulent.

27.   Transmission of shares

(1) If title to a share passes to a transmittee, the company may only recognise the transmittee as having any title to that share.

(2) A transmittee who produces such evidence of entitlement to shares as the directors may properly require—

    (a) may, subject to the articles, choose either to become the holder of those shares or to have them transferred to another person, and

    (b) subject to the articles, and pending any transfer of the shares to another person, has the same rights as the holder had.

(3) But transmittees do not have the right to attend or vote at a general meeting, or agree to a proposed written resolution, in respect of shares to which they are entitled, by reason of the holder's death or bankruptcy or otherwise, unless they become the holders of those shares.

28.   Exercise of transmittees' rights

(1) Transmittees who wish to become the holders of shares to which they have become entitled must notify the company in writing of that wish.

(2) If the transmittee wishes to have a share transferred to another person, the transmittee must execute an instrument of transfer in respect of it.

(3) Any transfer made or executed under this article is to be treated as if it were made or executed by the person from whom the transmittee has derived rights in respect of the share, and as if the event which gave rise to the transmission had not occurred.

29.   Transmittees bound by prior notices

If a notice is given to a shareholder in respect of shares and a transmittee is entitled to those shares, the transmittee is bound by the notice if it was given to the shareholder before the transmittee's name has been entered in the register of members.

Dividends and Other Distributions

30.   Procedure for declaring dividends

(1) The company may by ordinary resolution declare dividends, and the directors may decide to pay interim dividends.

(2) A dividend must not be declared unless the directors have made a recommendation as to its amount. Such a dividend must not exceed the amount recommended by the directors.

(3) No dividend may be declared or paid unless it is in accordance with shareholders' respective rights.

(4) Unless the shareholders' resolution to declare or directors' decision to pay a dividend, or the terms on which shares are issued, specify otherwise, it must be paid by reference to each shareholder's holding of shares on the date of the resolution or decision to declare or pay it.

(5) If the company's share capital is divided into different classes, no interim dividend may be paid on shares carrying deferred or non-preferred rights if, at the time of payment, any preferential dividend is in arrear.

(6) The directors may pay at intervals any dividend payable at a fixed rate if it appears to them that the profits available for distribution justify the payment.

(7) If the directors act in good faith, they do not incur any liability to the holders of shares conferring preferred rights for any loss they may suffer by the lawful payment of an interim dividend on shares with deferred or non-preferred rights.

31.   Payment of dividends and other distributions

(1)   Where a dividend or other sum which is a distribution is payable in respect of a share, it must be paid by one or more of the following means—

(a)   transfer to a bank or building society account specified by the distribution recipient either in writing or as the directors may otherwise decide;

(b)   sending a cheque made payable to the distribution recipient by post to the distribution recipient at the distribution recipient's registered address (if the distribution recipient is a holder of the share), or (in any other case) to an address specified by the distribution recipient either in writing or as the directors may otherwise decide;

(c)   sending a cheque made payable to such person by post to such person at such address as the distribution recipient has specified either in writing or as the directors may otherwise decide; or

(d)   any other means of payment as the directors agree with the distribution recipient either in writing or by such other means as the directors decide.

(2)   In the articles, "the distribution recipient" means, in respect of a share in respect of which a dividend or other sum is payable—

(a)   the holder of the share; or

(b)   if the share has two or more joint holders, whichever of them is named first in the register of members; or

(c)   if the holder is no longer entitled to the share by reason of death or bankruptcy, or otherwise by operation of law, the transmittee.

32.   No interest on distributions

The company may not pay interest on any dividend or other sum payable in respect of a share unless otherwise provided by—

(a)   the terms on which the share was issued, or

(b)   the provisions of another agreement between the holder of that share and the company.

33.   Unclaimed distributions

(1)   All dividends or other sums which are—

(a)   payable in respect of shares, and

(b)   unclaimed after having been declared or become payable,

may be invested or otherwise made use of by the directors for the benefit of the company until claimed.

(2)   The payment of any such dividend or other sum into a separate account does not make the company a trustee in respect of it.

(3)   If—

(a)   twelve years have passed from the date on which a dividend or other sum became due for payment, and

(b)   the distribution recipient has not claimed it,

the distribution recipient is no longer entitled to that dividend or other sum and it ceases to remain owing by the company.

34.   Non-cash distributions

(1)   Subject to the terms of issue of the share in question, the company may, by ordinary resolution on the recommendation of the directors, decide to pay all or part of a dividend or other distribution payable in respect of a share by transferring non-cash assets of equivalent value (including, without limitation, shares or other securities in any company).

(2)   For the purposes of paying a non-cash distribution, the directors may make whatever arrangements they think fit, including, where any difficulty arises regarding the distribution—

(a)   fixing the value of any assets;

(b)   paying cash to any distribution recipient on the basis of that value in order to adjust the rights of recipients; and

(c)   vesting any assets in trustees.

35.   Waiver of distributions

Distribution recipients may waive their entitlement to a dividend or other distribution payable in respect of a share by giving the company notice in writing to that effect, but if—

(a)   the share has more than one holder, or

(b)   more than one person is entitled to the share, whether by reason of the death or bankruptcy of one or more joint holders, or otherwise,

the notice is not effective unless it is expressed to be given, and signed, by all the holders or persons otherwise entitled to the share.

Capitalisation of Profits

36.   Authority to capitalise and appropriation of capitalised sums

(1)   Subject to the articles, the directors may, if they are so authorised by an ordinary resolution—

(a)   decide to capitalise any profits of the company (whether or not they are available for distribution) which are not required for paying a preferential dividend, or any sum standing to the credit of the company's share premium account or capital redemption reserve; and

(b)   appropriate any sum which they so decide to capitalise (a "capitalised sum") to the persons who would have been entitled to it if it were distributed by way of dividend (the "persons entitled") and in the same proportions.

(2)   Capitalised sums must be applied—

(a)   on behalf of the persons entitled, and

(b)   in the same proportions as a dividend would have been distributed to them.

(3)   Any capitalised sum may be applied in paying up new shares of a nominal amount equal to the capitalised sum which are then allotted credited as fully paid to the persons entitled or as they may direct.

(4)   A capitalised sum which was appropriated from profits available for distribution may be applied in paying up new debentures of the company which are then allotted credited as fully paid to the persons entitled or as they may direct.

(5)   Subject to the articles the directors may—

(a)   apply capitalised sums in accordance with paragraphs (3) and (4) partly in one way and partly in another;

(b)   make such arrangements as they think fit to deal with shares or debentures becoming distributable in fractions under this article (including the issuing of fractional certificates or the making of cash payments); and

(c)   authorise any person to enter into an agreement with the company on behalf of all the persons entitled which is binding on them in respect of the allotment of shares and debentures to them under this article.

PART 4

DECISION-MAKING BY SHAREHOLDERS

Organisation of General Meetings

37.   Attendance and speaking at general meetings

(1)   A person is able to exercise the right to speak at a general meeting when that person is in a position to communicate to all those attending the meeting, during the meeting, any information or opinions which that person has on the business of the meeting.

(2)   A person is able to exercise the right to vote at a general meeting when—

(a)   that person is able to vote, during the meeting, on resolutions put to the vote at the meeting, and

(b)　that person's vote can be taken into account in determining whether or not such resolutions are passed at the same time as the votes of all the other persons attending the
meeting.

(3)　The directors may make whatever arrangements they consider appropriate to enable those
attending a general meeting to exercise their rights to speak or vote at it.

(4)　In determining attendance at a general meeting, it is immaterial whether any two or more
members attending it are in the same place as each other.

(5)　Two or more persons who are not in the same place as each other attend a general meeting if
their circumstances are such that if they have (or were to have) rights to speak and vote at
that meeting, they are (or would be) able to exercise them.

38.　Quorum for general meetings

No business other than the appointment of the chairman of the meeting is to be transacted at a
general meeting if the persons attending it do not constitute a quorum.

39.　Chairing general meetings

(1)　If the directors have appointed a chairman, the chairman shall chair general meetings if
present and willing to do so.

(2)　If the directors have not appointed a chairman, or if the chairman is unwilling to chair the
meeting or is not present within ten minutes of the time at which a meeting was due to
start—
(a)　the directors present, or
(b)　(if no directors are present), the meeting,
must appoint a director or shareholder to chair the meeting, and the appointment of the
chairman of the meeting must be the first business of the meeting.

(3)　The person chairing a meeting in accordance with this article is referred to as "the chairman
of the meeting".

40.　Attendance and speaking by directors and non-shareholders

(1)　Directors may attend and speak at general meetings, whether or not they are shareholders.

(2)　The chairman of the meeting may permit other persons who are not—
(a)　shareholders of the company, or
(b)　otherwise entitled to exercise the rights of shareholders in relation to general meetings,
to attend and speak at a general meeting.

41.　Adjournment

(1)　If the persons attending a general meeting within half an hour of the time at which the
meeting was due to start do not constitute a quorum, or if during a meeting a quorum ceases
to be present, the chairman of the meeting must adjourn it.

(2)　The chairman of the meeting may adjourn a general meeting at which a quorum is present
if—
(a)　the meeting consents to an adjournment, or
(b)　it appears to the chairman of the meeting that an adjournment is necessary to protect
the safety of any person attending the meeting or ensure that the business of the meeting is conducted in an orderly manner.

(3)　The chairman of the meeting must adjourn a general meeting if directed to do so by the
meeting.

(4)　When adjourning a general meeting, the chairman of the meeting must—
(a)　either specify the time and place to which it is adjourned or state that it is to continue
at a time and place to be fixed by the directors, and
(b)　have regard to any directions as to the time and place of any adjournment which have
been given by the meeting.

(5) If the continuation of an adjourned meeting is to take place more than 14 days after it was adjourned, the company must give at least 7 clear days' notice of it (that is, excluding the day of the adjourned meeting and the day on which the notice is given)—

    (a) to the same persons to whom notice of the company's general meetings is required to be given, and

    (b) containing the same information which such notice is required to contain.

(6) No business may be transacted at an adjourned general meeting which could not properly have been transacted at the meeting if the adjournment had not taken place.

Voting at General Meetings

42. Voting: general

A resolution put to the vote of a general meeting must be decided on a show of hands unless a poll is duly demanded in accordance with the articles.

43. Errors and disputes

(1) No objection may be raised to the qualification of any person voting at a general meeting except at the meeting or adjourned meeting at which the vote objected to is tendered, and every vote not disallowed at the meeting is valid.

(2) Any such objection must be referred to the chairman of the meeting, whose decision is final.

44. Poll votes

(1) A poll on a resolution may be demanded—

    (a) in advance of the general meeting where it is to be put to the vote, or

    (b) at a general meeting, either before a show of hands on that resolution or immediately after the result of a show of hands on that resolution is declared.

(2) A poll may be demanded by—

    (a) the chairman of the meeting;

    (b) the directors;

    (c) two or more persons having the right to vote on the resolution; or

    (d) a person or persons representing not less than one tenth of the total voting rights of all the shareholders having the right to vote on the resolution.

(3) A demand for a poll may be withdrawn if—

    (a) the poll has not yet been taken, and

    (b) the chairman of the meeting consents to the withdrawal.

(4) Polls must be taken immediately and in such manner as the chairman of the meeting directs.

45. Content of proxy notices

(1) Proxies may only validly be appointed by a notice in writing (a "proxy notice") which—

    (a) states the name and address of the shareholder appointing the proxy;

    (b) identifies the person appointed to be that shareholder's proxy and the general meeting in relation to which that person is appointed;

    (c) is signed by or on behalf of the shareholder appointing the proxy, or is authenticated in such manner as the directors may determine; and

    (d) is delivered to the company in accordance with the articles and any instructions contained in the notice of the general meeting to which they relate.

(2) The company may require proxy notices to be delivered in a particular form, and may specify different forms for different purposes.

(3) Proxy notices may specify how the proxy appointed under them is to vote (or that the proxy is to abstain from voting) on one or more resolutions.

(4) Unless a proxy notice indicates otherwise, it must be treated as—

    (a) allowing the person appointed under it as a proxy discretion as to how to vote on any ancillary or procedural resolutions put to the meeting, and

    (b)   appointing that person as a proxy in relation to any adjournment of the general meeting to which it relates as well as the meeting itself.

46.   Delivery of proxy notices

(1)   A person who is entitled to attend, speak or vote (either on a show of hands or on a poll) at a general meeting remains so entitled in respect of that meeting or any adjournment of it, even though a valid proxy notice has been delivered to the company by or on behalf of that person.

(2)   An appointment under a proxy notice may be revoked by delivering to the company a notice in writing given by or on behalf of the person by whom or on whose behalf the proxy notice was given.

(3)   A notice revoking a proxy appointment only takes effect if it is delivered before the start of the meeting or adjourned meeting to which it relates.

(4)   If a proxy notice is not executed by the person appointing the proxy, it must be accompanied by written evidence of the authority of the person who executed it to execute it on the appointor's behalf.

47.   Amendments to resolutions

(1)   An ordinary resolution to be proposed at a general meeting may be amended by ordinary resolution if—

    (a)   notice of the proposed amendment is given to the company in writing by a person entitled to vote at the general meeting at which it is to be proposed not less than 48 hours before the meeting is to take place (or such later time as the chairman of the meeting may determine), and

    (b)   the proposed amendment does not, in the reasonable opinion of the chairman of the meeting, materially alter the scope of the resolution.

(2)   A special resolution to be proposed at a general meeting may be amended by ordinary resolution, if—

    (a)   the chairman of the meeting proposes the amendment at the general meeting at which the resolution is to be proposed, and

    (b)   the amendment does not go beyond what is necessary to correct a grammatical or other non-substantive error in the resolution.

(3)   If the chairman of the meeting, acting in good faith, wrongly decides that an amendment to a resolution is out of order, the chairman's error does not invalidate the vote on that resolution.

PART 5
ADMINISTRATIVE ARRANGEMENTS

48.   Means of communication to be used

(1)   Subject to the articles, anything sent or supplied by or to the company under the articles may be sent or supplied in any way in which the Companies Act 2006 provides for documents or information which are authorised or required by any provision of that Act to be sent or supplied by or to the company.

(2)   Subject to the articles, any notice or document to be sent or supplied to a director in connection with the taking of decisions by directors may also be sent or supplied by the means by which that director has asked to be sent or supplied with such notices or documents for the time being.

(3)   A director may agree with the company that notices or documents sent to that director in a particular way are to be deemed to have been received within a specified time of their being sent, and for the specified time to be less than 48 hours.

49.   Company seals

(1)   Any common seal may only be used by the authority of the directors.

(2)   The directors may decide by what means and in what form any common seal is to be used.

(3)   Unless otherwise decided by the directors, if the company has a common seal and it is affixed to a document, the document must also be signed by at least one authorised person in the presence of a witness who attests the signature.

(4)   For the purposes of this article, an authorised person is—

   (a)   any director of the company;

   (b)   the company secretary (if any); or

   (c)   any person authorised by the directors for the purpose of signing documents to which the common seal is applied.

50.   No right to inspect accounts and other records

Except as provided by law or authorised by the directors or an ordinary resolution of the company, no person is entitled to inspect any of the company's accounting or other records or documents merely by virtue of being a shareholder.

51.   Provision for employees on cessation of business

The directors may decide to make provision for the benefit of persons employed or formerly employed by the company or any of its subsidiaries (other than a director or former director or shadow director) in connection with the cessation or transfer to any person of the whole or part of the undertaking of the company or that subsidiary.

Directors' Indemnity and Insurance

52.   Indemnity

(1)   Subject to paragraph (2), a relevant director of the company or an associated company may be indemnified out of the company's assets against—

   (a)   any liability incurred by that director in connection with any negligence, default, breach of duty or breach of trust in relation to the company or an associated company,

   (b)   any liability incurred by that director in connection with the activities of the company or an associated company in its capacity as a trustee of an occupational pension scheme (as defined in section 235(6) of the Companies Act 2006),

   (c)   any other liability incurred by that director as an officer of the company or an associated company.

(2)   This article does not authorise any indemnity which would be prohibited or rendered void by any provision of the Companies Acts or by any other provision of law.

(3)   In this article—

   (a)   companies are associated if one is a subsidiary of the other or both are subsidiaries of the same body corporate, and

   (b)   a "relevant director" means any director or former director of the company or an associated company.

53.   Insurance

(1)   The directors may decide to purchase and maintain insurance, at the expense of the company, for the benefit of any relevant director in respect of any relevant loss.

(2)   In this article—

   (a)   a "relevant director" means any director or former director of the company or an associated company,

   (b)   a "relevant loss" means any loss or liability which has been or may be incurred by a relevant director in connection with that director's duties or powers in relation to the company, any associated company or any pension fund or employees' share scheme of the company or associated company, and

   (c)   companies are associated if one is a subsidiary of the other or both are subsidiaries of the same body corporate.

SCHEDULE 3   Regulation 4
MODEL ARTICLES FOR PUBLIC COMPANIES

PART 1
INTERPRETATION AND LIMITATION OF LIABILITY

1.   **Defined terms**
In the articles, unless the context requires otherwise—
"alternate" or "alternate director" has the meaning given in article 25;
"appointor" has the meaning given in article 25;
"articles" means the company's articles of association;
"bankruptcy" includes individual insolvency proceedings in a jurisdiction other than England and Wales or Northern Ireland which have an effect similar to that of bankruptcy;
"call" has the meaning given in article 54;
"call notice" has the meaning given in article 54;
"certificate" means a paper certificate (other than a share warrant) evidencing a person's title to specified shares or other securities;
"certificated" in relation to a share, means that it is not an uncertificated share or a share in respect of which a share warrant has been issued and is current;
"chairman" has the meaning given in article 12;
"chairman of the meeting" has the meaning given in article 31;
"Companies Acts" means the Companies Acts (as defined in section 2 of the Companies Act 2006), in so far as they apply to the company;
"company's lien" has the meaning given in article 52;
"director" means a director of the company, and includes any person occupying the position of director, by whatever name called;
"distribution recipient" has the meaning given in article 72;
"document" includes, unless otherwise specified, any document sent or supplied in electronic form;
"electronic form" has the meaning given in section 1168 of the Companies Act 2006;
"fully paid" in relation to a share, means that the nominal value and any premium to be paid to the company in respect of that share have been paid to the company;
"hard copy form" has the meaning given in section 1168 of the Companies Act 2006;
"holder" in relation to shares means the person whose name is entered in the register of members as the holder of the shares, or, in the case of a share in respect of which a share warrant has been issued (and not cancelled), the person in possession of that warrant;
"instrument" means a document in hard copy form;
"lien enforcement notice" has the meaning given in article 53;
"member" has the meaning given in section 112 of the Companies Act 2006;
"ordinary resolution" has the meaning given in section 282 of the Companies Act 2006;
"paid" means paid or credited as paid;
"participate", in relation to a directors' meeting, has the meaning given in article 9;
"partly paid" in relation to a share means that part of that share's nominal value or any premium at which it was issued has not been paid to the company;
"proxy notice" has the meaning given in article 38;
"securities seal" has the meaning given in article 47;
"shares" means shares in the company;
"special resolution" has the meaning given in section 283 of the Companies Act 2006;
"subsidiary" has the meaning given in section 1159 of the Companies Act 2006;
"transmittee" means a person entitled to a share by reason of the death or bankruptcy of a shareholder or otherwise by operation of law;

"uncertificated" in relation to a share means that, by virtue of legislation (other than section 778 of the Companies Act 2006) permitting title to shares to be evidenced and transferred without a certificate, title to that share is evidenced and may be transferred without a certificate; and

"writing" means the representation or reproduction of words, symbols or other information in a visible form by any method or combination of methods, whether sent or supplied in electronic form or otherwise.

Unless the context otherwise requires, other words or expressions contained in these articles bear the same meaning as in the Companies Act 2006 as in force on the date when these articles become binding on the company.

2.   **Liability of members**

The liability of the members is limited to the amount, if any, unpaid on the shares held by them.

PART 2

DIRECTORS

Directors' Powers and Responsibilities

3.   **Directors' general authority**

Subject to the articles, the directors are responsible for the management of the company's business, for which purpose they may exercise all the powers of the company.

4.   **Members' reserve power**

(1)   The members may, by special resolution, direct the directors to take, or refrain from taking, specified action.

(2)   No such special resolution invalidates anything which the directors have done before the passing of the resolution.

5.   **Directors may delegate**

(1)   Subject to the articles, the directors may delegate any of the powers which are conferred on them under the articles—

(a)   to such person or committee;

(b)   by such means (including by power of attorney);

(c)   to such an extent;

(d)   in relation to such matters or territories; and

(e)   on such terms and conditions;

as they think fit.

(2)   If the directors so specify, any such delegation may authorise further delegation of the directors' powers by any person to whom they are delegated.

(3)   The directors may revoke any delegation in whole or part, or alter its terms and conditions.

6.   **Committees**

(1)   Committees to which the directors delegate any of their powers must follow procedures which are based as far as they are applicable on those provisions of the articles which govern the taking of decisions by directors.

(2)   The directors may make rules of procedure for all or any committees, which prevail over rules derived from the articles if they are not consistent with them.

Decision-Making by Directors

7.   **Directors to take decisions collectively**

Decisions of the directors may be taken—

(a)   at a directors' meeting, or

(b)   in the form of a directors' written resolution.

8.   Calling a directors' meeting

(1)   Any director may call a directors' meeting.

(2)   The company secretary must call a directors' meeting if a director so requests.

(3)   A directors' meeting is called by giving notice of the meeting to the directors.

(4)   Notice of any directors' meeting must indicate—

    (a)   its proposed date and time;

    (b)   where it is to take place; and

    (c)   if it is anticipated that directors participating in the meeting will not be in the same place, how it is proposed that they should communicate with each other during the meeting.

(5)   Notice of a directors' meeting must be given to each director, but need not be in writing.

(6)   Notice of a directors' meeting need not be given to directors who waive their entitlement to notice of that meeting, by giving notice to that effect to the company not more than 7 days after the date on which the meeting is held. Where such notice is given after the meeting has been held, that does not affect the validity of the meeting, or of any business conducted at it.

9.   Participation in directors' meetings

(1)   Subject to the articles, directors participate in a directors' meeting, or part of a directors' meeting, when—

    (a)   the meeting has been called and takes place in accordance with the articles, and

    (b)   they can each communicate to the others any information or opinions they have on any particular item of the business of the meeting.

(2)   In determining whether directors are participating in a directors' meeting, it is irrelevant where any director is or how they communicate with each other.

(3)   If all the directors participating in a meeting are not in the same place, they may decide that the meeting is to be treated as taking place wherever any of them is.

10.   Quorum for directors' meetings

(1)   At a directors' meeting, unless a quorum is participating, no proposal is to be voted on, except a proposal to call another meeting.

(2)   The quorum for directors' meetings may be fixed from time to time by a decision of the directors, but it must never be less than two, and unless otherwise fixed it is two.

11.   Meetings where total number of directors less than quorum

(1)   This article applies where the total number of directors for the time being is less than the quorum for directors' meetings.

(2)   If there is only one director, that director may appoint sufficient directors to make up a quorum or call a general meeting to do so.

(3)   If there is more than one director—

    (a)   a directors' meeting may take place, if it is called in accordance with the articles and at least two directors participate in it, with a view to appointing sufficient directors to make up a quorum or calling a general meeting to do so, and

    (b)   if a directors' meeting is called but only one director attends at the appointed date and time to participate in it, that director may appoint sufficient directors to make up a quorum or call a general meeting to do so.

12.   Chairing directors' meetings

(1)   The directors may appoint a director to chair their meetings.

(2)   The person so appointed for the time being is known as the chairman.

(3)   The directors may appoint other directors as deputy or assistant chairmen to chair directors' meetings in the chairman's absence.

(4)   The directors may terminate the appointment of the chairman, deputy or assistant chairman at any time.

(5) If neither the chairman nor any director appointed generally to chair directors' meetings in the chairman's absence is participating in a meeting within ten minutes of the time at which it was to start, the participating directors must appoint one of themselves to chair it.

13. Voting at directors' meetings: general rules

(1) Subject to the articles, a decision is taken at a directors' meeting by a majority of the votes of the participating directors.

(2) Subject to the articles, each director participating in a directors' meeting has one vote.

(3) Subject to the articles, if a director has an interest in an actual or proposed transaction or arrangement with the company—

    (a) that director and that director's alternate may not vote on any proposal relating to it, but

    (b) this does not preclude the alternate from voting in relation to that transaction or arrangement on behalf of another appointor who does not have such an interest.

14. Chairman's casting vote at directors' meetings

(1) If the numbers of votes for and against a proposal are equal, the chairman or other director chairing the meeting has a casting vote.

(2) But this does not apply if, in accordance with the articles, the chairman or other director is not to be counted as participating in the decision-making process for quorum or voting purposes.

15. Alternates voting at directors' meetings

A director who is also an alternate director has an additional vote on behalf of each appointor who is—

(a) not participating in a directors' meeting, and

(b) would have been entitled to vote if they were participating in it.

16. Conflicts of interest

(1) If a directors' meeting, or part of a directors' meeting, is concerned with an actual or proposed transaction or arrangement with the company in which a director is interested, that director is not to be counted as participating in that meeting, or part of a meeting, for quorum or voting purposes.

(2) But if paragraph (3) applies, a director who is interested in an actual or proposed transaction or arrangement with the company is to be counted as participating in a decision at a directors' meeting, or part of a directors' meeting, relating to it for quorum and voting purposes.

(3) This paragraph applies when—

    (a) the company by ordinary resolution disapplies the provision of the articles which would otherwise prevent a director from being counted as participating in, or voting at, a directors' meeting;

    (b) the director's interest cannot reasonably be regarded as likely to give rise to a conflict of interest; or

    (c) the director's conflict of interest arises from a permitted cause.

(4) For the purposes of this article, the following are permitted causes—

    (a) a guarantee given, or to be given, by or to a director in respect of an obligation incurred by or on behalf of the company or any of its subsidiaries;

    (b) subscription, or an agreement to subscribe, for shares or other securities of the company or any of its subsidiaries, or to underwrite, sub-underwrite, or guarantee subscription for any such shares or securities; and

    (c) arrangements pursuant to which benefits are made available to employees and directors or former employees and directors of the company or any of its subsidiaries which do not provide special benefits for directors or former directors.

(5) Subject to paragraph (6), if a question arises at a meeting of directors or of a committee of directors as to the right of a director to participate in the meeting (or part of the meeting) for voting or quorum purposes, the question may, before the conclusion of the meeting, be referred to the chairman whose ruling in relation to any director other than the chairman is to be final and conclusive.

(6) If any question as to the right to participate in the meeting (or part of the meeting) should arise in respect of the chairman, the question is to be decided by a decision of the directors at that meeting, for which purpose the chairman is not to be counted as participating in the meeting (or that part of the meeting) for voting or quorum purposes.

17. Proposing directors' written resolutions

(1) Any director may propose a directors' written resolution.
(2) The company secretary must propose a directors' written resolution if a director so requests.
(3) A directors' written resolution is proposed by giving notice of the proposed resolution to the directors.
(4) Notice of a proposed directors' written resolution must indicate—
   (a) the proposed resolution, and
   (b) the time by which it is proposed that the directors should adopt it.
(5) Notice of a proposed directors' written resolution must be given in writing to each director.
(6) Any decision which a person giving notice of a proposed directors' written resolution takes regarding the process of adopting that resolution must be taken reasonably in good faith.

18. Adoption of directors' written resolutions

(1) A proposed directors' written resolution is adopted when all the directors who would have been entitled to vote on the resolution at a directors' meeting have signed one or more copies of it, provided that those directors would have formed a quorum at such a meeting.
(2) It is immaterial whether any director signs the resolution before or after the time by which the notice proposed that it should be adopted.
(3) Once a directors' written resolution has been adopted, it must be treated as if it had been a decision taken at a directors' meeting in accordance with the articles.
(4) The company secretary must ensure that the company keeps a record, in writing, of all directors' written resolutions for at least ten years from the date of their adoption.

19. Directors' discretion to make further rules

Subject to the articles, the directors may make any rule which they think fit about how they take decisions, and about how such rules are to be recorded or communicated to directors.

Appointment of Directors

20. Methods of appointing directors

Any person who is willing to act as a director, and is permitted by law to do so, may be appointed to be a director—
(a) by ordinary resolution, or
(b) by a decision of the directors.

21. Retirement of directors by rotation

(1) At the first annual general meeting all the directors must retire from office.
(2) At every subsequent annual general meeting any directors—
   (a) who have been appointed by the directors since the last annual general meeting, or
   (b) who were not appointed or reappointed at one of the preceding two annual general meetings,
must retire from office and may offer themselves for reappointment by the members.

22. Termination of director's appointment

A person ceases to be a director as soon as—

(a)   that person ceases to be a director by virtue of any provision of the Companies Act 2006 or is prohibited from being a director by law;

(b)   a bankruptcy order is made against that person;

(c)   a composition is made with that person's creditors generally in satisfaction of that person's debts;

(d)   a registered medical practitioner who is treating that person gives a written opinion to the company stating that that person has become physically or mentally incapable of acting as a director and may remain so for more than three months;

(e)   ...

(f)   notification is received by the company from the director that the director is resigning from office as director, and such resignation has taken effect in accordance with its terms.

23.   Directors' remuneration

(1)   Directors may undertake any services for the company that the directors decide.

(2)   Directors are entitled to such remuneration as the directors determine—

    (a)   for their services to the company as directors, and

    (b)   for any other service which they undertake for the company.

(3)   Subject to the articles, a director's remuneration may—

    (a)   take any form, and

    (b)   include any arrangements in connection with the payment of a pension, allowance or gratuity, or any death, sickness or disability benefits, to or in respect of that director.

(4)   Unless the directors decide otherwise, directors' remuneration accrues from day to day.

(5)   Unless the directors decide otherwise, directors are not accountable to the company for any remuneration which they receive as directors or other officers or employees of the company's subsidiaries or of any other body corporate in which the company is interested.

24.   Directors' expenses

The company may pay any reasonable expenses which the directors properly incur in connection with their attendance at—

(a)   meetings of directors or committees of directors,

(b)   general meetings, or

(c)   separate meetings of the holders of any class of shares or of debentures of the company,

or otherwise in connection with the exercise of their powers and the discharge of their responsibilities in relation to the company.

Alternate Directors

25.   Appointment and removal of alternates

(1)   Any director (the "appointor") may appoint as an alternate any other director, or any other person approved by resolution of the directors, to—

    (a)   exercise that director's powers, and

    (b)   carry out that director's responsibilities,

in relation to the taking of decisions by the directors in the absence of the alternate's appointor.

(2)   Any appointment or removal of an alternate must be effected by notice in writing to the company signed by the appointor, or in any other manner approved by the directors.

(3)   The notice must—

    (a)   identify the proposed alternate, and

    (b)   in the case of a notice of appointment, contain a statement signed by the proposed alternate that the proposed alternate is willing to act as the alternate of the director giving the notice.

26.   **Rights and responsibilities of alternate directors**

(1)   An alternate director has the same rights, in relation to any directors' meeting or directors' written resolution, as the alternate's appointor.

(2)   Except as the articles specify otherwise, alternate directors—

(a)   are deemed for all purposes to be directors;

(b)   are liable for their own acts and omissions;

(c)   are subject to the same restrictions as their appointors; and

(d)   are not deemed to be agents of or for their appointors.

(3)   A person who is an alternate director but not a director—

(a)   may be counted as participating for the purposes of determining whether a quorum is participating (but only if that person's appointor is not participating), and

(b)   may sign a written resolution (but only if it is not signed or to be signed by that person's appointor).

No alternate may be counted as more than one director for such purposes.

(4)   An alternate director is not entitled to receive any remuneration from the company for serving as an alternate director except such part of the alternate's appointor's remuneration as the appointor may direct by notice in writing made to the company.

27.   **Termination of alternate directorship**

An alternate director's appointment as an alternate terminates—

(a)   when the alternate's appointor revokes the appointment by notice to the company in writing specifying when it is to terminate;

(b)   on the occurrence in relation to the alternate of any event which, if it occurred in relation to the alternate's appointor, would result in the termination of the appointor's appointment as a director;

(c)   on the death of the alternate's appointor; or

(d)   when the alternate's appointor's appointment as a director terminates, except that an alternate's appointment as an alternate does not terminate when the appointor retires by rotation at a general meeting and is then re-appointed as a director at the same general meeting.

PART 3
DECISION-MAKING BY MEMBERS

Organisation of General Meetings

28.   **Members can call general meeting if not enough directors**

If—

(a)   the company has fewer than two directors, and

(b)   the director (if any) is unable or unwilling to appoint sufficient directors to make up a quorum or to call a general meeting to do so,

then two or more members may call a general meeting (or instruct the company secretary to do so) for the purpose of appointing one or more directors.

29.   **Attendance and speaking at general meetings**

(1)   A person is able to exercise the right to speak at a general meeting when that person is in a position to communicate to all those attending the meeting, during the meeting, any information or opinions which that person has on the business of the meeting.

(2)   A person is able to exercise the right to vote at a general meeting when—

(a)   that person is able to vote, during the meeting, on resolutions put to the vote at the meeting, and

(b)   that person's vote can be taken into account in determining whether or not such resolutions are passed at the same time as the votes of all the other persons attending the meeting.

(3) The directors may make whatever arrangements they consider appropriate to enable those attending a general meeting to exercise their rights to speak or vote at it.

(4) In determining attendance at a general meeting, it is immaterial whether any two or more members attending it are in the same place as each other.

(5) Two or more persons who are not in the same place as each other attend a general meeting if their circumstances are such that if they have (or were to have) rights to speak and vote at that meeting, they are (or would be) able to exercise them.

30. Quorum for general meetings

No business other than the appointment of the chairman of the meeting is to be transacted at a general meeting if the persons attending it do not constitute a quorum.

31. Chairing general meetings

(1) If the directors have appointed a chairman, the chairman shall chair general meetings if present and willing to do so.

(2) If the directors have not appointed a chairman, or if the chairman is unwilling to chair the meeting or is not present within ten minutes of the time at which a meeting was due to start—

    (a) the directors present, or

    (b) (if no directors are present), the meeting,

must appoint a director or member to chair the meeting, and the appointment of the chairman of the meeting must be the first business of the meeting.

(3) The person chairing a meeting in accordance with this article is referred to as "the chairman of the meeting".

32. Attendance and speaking by directors and non-members

(1) Directors may attend and speak at general meetings, whether or not they are members.

(2) The chairman of the meeting may permit other persons who are not—

    (a) members of the company, or

    (b) otherwise entitled to exercise the rights of members in relation to general meetings,

to attend and speak at a general meeting.

33. Adjournment

(1) If the persons attending a general meeting within half an hour of the time at which the meeting was due to start do not constitute a quorum, or if during a meeting a quorum ceases to be present, the chairman of the meeting must adjourn it.

(2) The chairman of the meeting may adjourn a general meeting at which a quorum is present if—

    (a) the meeting consents to an adjournment, or

    (b) it appears to the chairman of the meeting that an adjournment is necessary to protect the safety of any person attending the meeting or ensure that the business of the meeting is conducted in an orderly manner.

(3) The chairman of the meeting must adjourn a general meeting if directed to do so by the meeting.

(4) When adjourning a general meeting, the chairman of the meeting must—

    (a) either specify the time and place to which it is adjourned or state that it is to continue at a time and place to be fixed by the directors, and

    (b) have regard to any directions as to the time and place of any adjournment which have been given by the meeting.

(5) If the continuation of an adjourned meeting is to take place more than 14 days after it was adjourned, the company must give at least 7 clear days' notice of it (that is, excluding the day of the adjourned meeting and the day on which the notice is given)—

    (a) to the same persons to whom notice of the company's general meetings is required to be given, and

      (b)   containing the same information which such notice is required to contain.

  (6)   No business may be transacted at an adjourned general meeting which could not properly have been transacted at the meeting if the adjournment had not taken place.

Voting at General Meetings

34.   Voting: general

A resolution put to the vote of a general meeting must be decided on a show of hands unless a poll is duly demanded in accordance with the articles.

35.   Errors and disputes

  (1)   No objection may be raised to the qualification of any person voting at a general meeting except at the meeting or adjourned meeting at which the vote objected to is tendered, and every vote not disallowed at the meeting is valid.

  (2)   Any such objection must be referred to the chairman of the meeting whose decision is final.

36.   Demanding a poll

  (1)   A poll on a resolution may be demanded—
      (a)   in advance of the general meeting where it is to be put to the vote, or
      (b)   at a general meeting, either before a show of hands on that resolution or immediately after the result of a show of hands on that resolution is declared.

  (2)   A poll may be demanded by—
      (a)   the chairman of the meeting;
      (b)   the directors;
      (c)   two or more persons having the right to vote on the resolution; or
      (d)   a person or persons representing not less than one tenth of the total voting rights of all the members having the right to vote on the resolution.

  (3)   A demand for a poll may be withdrawn if—
      (a)   the poll has not yet been taken, and
      (b)   the chairman of the meeting consents to the withdrawal.

37.   Procedure on a poll

  (1)   Subject to the articles, polls at general meetings must be taken when, where and in such manner as the chairman of the meeting directs.

  (2)   The chairman of the meeting may appoint scrutineers (who need not be members) and decide how and when the result of the poll is to be declared.

  (3)   The result of a poll shall be the decision of the meeting in respect of the resolution on which the poll was demanded.

  (4)   A poll on—
      (a)   the election of the chairman of the meeting, or
      (b)   a question of adjournment,
     must be taken immediately.

  (5)   Other polls must be taken within 30 days of their being demanded.

  (6)   A demand for a poll does not prevent a general meeting from continuing, except as regards the question on which the poll was demanded.

  (7)   No notice need be given of a poll not taken immediately if the time and place at which it is to be taken are announced at the meeting at which it is demanded.

  (8)   In any other case, at least 7 days' notice must be given specifying the time and place at which the poll is to be taken.

38.   Content of proxy notices

  (1)   Proxies may only validly be appointed by a notice in writing (a "proxy notice") which—
      (a)   states the name and address of the member appointing the proxy;
      (b)   identifies the person appointed to be that member's proxy and the general meeting in relation to which that person is appointed;

    (c)   is signed by or on behalf of the member appointing the proxy, or is authenticated in such manner as the directors may determine; and

    (d)   is delivered to the company in accordance with the articles and any instructions contained in the notice of the general meeting to which they relate.

(2)   The company may require proxy notices to be delivered in a particular form, and may specify different forms for different purposes.

(3)   Proxy notices may specify how the proxy appointed under them is to vote (or that the proxy is to abstain from voting) on one or more resolutions.

(4)   Unless a proxy notice indicates otherwise, it must be treated as—

    (a)   allowing the person appointed under it as a proxy discretion as to how to vote on any ancillary or procedural resolutions put to the meeting, and

    (b)   appointing that person as a proxy in relation to any adjournment of the general meeting to which it relates as well as the meeting itself.

39.   Delivery of proxy notices

(1)   Any notice of a general meeting must specify the address or addresses ("proxy notification address") at which the company or its agents will receive proxy notices relating to that meeting, or any adjournment of it, delivered in hard copy or electronic form.

(2)   A person who is entitled to attend, speak or vote (either on a show of hands or on a poll) at a general meeting remains so entitled in respect of that meeting or any adjournment of it, even though a valid proxy notice has been delivered to the company by or on behalf of that person.

(3)   Subject to paragraphs (4) and (5), a proxy notice must be delivered to a proxy notification address not less than 48 hours before the general meeting or adjourned meeting to which it relates.

(4)   In the case of a poll taken more than 48 hours after it is demanded, the notice must be delivered to a proxy notification address not less than 24 hours before the time appointed for the taking of the poll.

(5)   In the case of a poll not taken during the meeting but taken not more than 48 hours after it was demanded, the proxy notice must be delivered—

    (a)   in accordance with paragraph (3), or

    (b)   at the meeting at which the poll was demanded to the chairman, secretary or any director.

(6)   An appointment under a proxy notice may be revoked by delivering a notice in writing given by or on behalf of the person by whom or on whose behalf the proxy notice was given to a proxy notification address.

(7)   A notice revoking a proxy appointment only takes effect if it is delivered before—

    (a)   the start of the meeting or adjourned meeting to which it relates, or

    (b)   (in the case of a poll not taken on the same day as the meeting or adjourned meeting) the time appointed for taking the poll to which it relates.

(8)   If a proxy notice is not signed by the person appointing the proxy, it must be accompanied by written evidence of the authority of the person who executed it to execute it on the appointor's behalf.

40.   Amendments to resolutions

(1)   An ordinary resolution to be proposed at a general meeting may be amended by ordinary resolution if—

    (a)   notice of the proposed amendment is given to the company secretary in writing by a person entitled to vote at the general meeting at which it is to be proposed not less than 48 hours before the meeting is to take place (or such later time as the chairman of the meeting may determine), and

    (b)   the proposed amendment does not, in the reasonable opinion of the chairman of the meeting, materially alter the scope of the resolution.

(2) A special resolution to be proposed at a general meeting may be amended by ordinary resolution, if—

    (a) the chairman of the meeting proposes the amendment at the general meeting at which the resolution is to be proposed, and

    (b) the amendment does not go beyond what is necessary to correct a grammatical or other non-substantive error in the resolution.

(3) If the chairman of the meeting, acting in good faith, wrongly decides that an amendment to a resolution is out of order, the chairman's error does not invalidate the vote on that resolution.

Restrictions on Members' Rights

41.   No voting of shares on which money owed to company

No voting rights attached to a share may be exercised at any general meeting, at any adjournment of it, or on any poll called at or in relation to it, unless all amounts payable to the company in respect of that share have been paid.

Application of Rules to Class Meetings

42.   Class meetings

The provisions of the articles relating to general meetings apply, with any necessary modifications, to meetings of the holders of any class of shares.

PART 4

SHARES AND DISTRIBUTIONS

Issue of Shares

43.   Powers to issue different classes of share

(1) Subject to the articles, but without prejudice to the rights attached to any existing share, the company may issue shares with such rights or restrictions as may be determined by ordinary resolution.

(2) The company may issue shares which are to be redeemed, or are liable to be redeemed at the option of the company or the holder, and the directors may determine the terms, conditions and manner of redemption of any such shares.

44.   Payment of commissions on subscription for shares

(1) The company may pay any person a commission in consideration for that person—

    (a) subscribing, or agreeing to subscribe, for shares, or

    (b) procuring, or agreeing to procure, subscriptions for shares.

(2) Any such commission may be paid—

    (a) in cash, or in fully paid or partly paid shares or other securities, or partly in one way and partly in the other, and

    (b) in respect of a conditional or an absolute subscription.

Interests in Shares

45.   Company not bound by less than absolute interests

Except as required by law, no person is to be recognised by the company as holding any share upon any trust, and except as otherwise required by law or the articles, the company is not in any way to be bound by or recognise any interest in a share other than the holder's absolute ownership of it and all the rights attaching to it.

Share Certificates

46. Certificates to be issued except in certain cases

(1) The company must issue each member with one or more certificates in respect of the shares which that member holds.

(2) This article does not apply to—

    (a) uncertificated shares;

    (b) shares in respect of which a share warrant has been issued; or

    (c) shares in respect of which the Companies Acts permit the company not to issue a certificate.

(3) Except as otherwise specified in the articles, all certificates must be issued free of charge.

(4) No certificate may be issued in respect of shares of more than one class.

(5) If more than one person holds a share, only one certificate may be issued in respect of it.

47. Contents and execution of share certificates

(1) Every certificate must specify—

    (a) in respect of how many shares, of what class, it is issued;

    (b) the nominal value of those shares;

    (c) the amount paid up on them; and

    (d) any distinguishing numbers assigned to them.

(2) Certificates must—

    (a) have affixed to them the company's common seal or an official seal which is a facsimile of the company's common seal with the addition on its face of the word "Securities" (a "securities seal"), or

    (b) be otherwise executed in accordance with the Companies Acts.

48. Consolidated share certificates

(1) When a member's holding of shares of a particular class increases, the company may issue that member with—

    (a) a single, consolidated certificate in respect of all the shares of a particular class which that member holds, or

    (b) a separate certificate in respect of only those shares by which that member's holding has increased.

(2) When a member's holding of shares of a particular class is reduced, the company must ensure that the member is issued with one or more certificates in respect of the number of shares held by the member after that reduction. But the company need not (in the absence of a request from the member) issue any new certificate if—

    (a) all the shares which the member no longer holds as a result of the reduction, and

    (b) none of the shares which the member retains following the reduction,

    were, immediately before the reduction, represented by the same certificate.

(3) A member may request the company, in writing, to replace—

    (a) the member's separate certificates with a consolidated certificate, or

    (b) the member's consolidated certificate with two or more separate certificates representing such proportion of the shares as the member may specify.

(4) When the company complies with such a request it may charge such reasonable fee as the directors may decide for doing so.

(5) A consolidated certificate must not be issued unless any certificates which it is to replace have first been returned to the company for cancellation.

49. Replacement share certificates

(1) If a certificate issued in respect of a member's shares is—

    (a) damaged or defaced, or

    (b) said to be lost, stolen or destroyed,

that member is entitled to be issued with a replacement certificate in respect of the same shares.

(2) A member exercising the right to be issued with such a replacement certificate—

    (a) may at the same time exercise the right to be issued with a single certificate or separate certificates;

    (b) must return the certificate which is to be replaced to the company if it is damaged or defaced; and

    (c) must comply with such conditions as to evidence, indemnity and the payment of a reasonable fee as the directors decide.

Shares not Held in Certificated Form

50. Uncertificated shares

(1) In this article, "the relevant rules" means—

    (a) any applicable provision of the Companies Acts about the holding, evidencing of title to, or transfer of shares other than in certificated form, and

    (b) any applicable legislation, rules or other arrangements made under or by virtue of such provision.

(2) The provisions of this article have effect subject to the relevant rules.

(3) Any provision of the articles which is inconsistent with the relevant rules must be disregarded, to the extent that it is inconsistent, whenever the relevant rules apply.

(4) Any share or class of shares of the company may be issued or held on such terms, or in such a way, that—

    (a) title to it or them is not, or must not be, evidenced by a certificate, or

    (b) it or they may or must be transferred wholly or partly without a certificate.

(5) The directors have power to take such steps as they think fit in relation to—

    (a) the evidencing of and transfer of title to uncertificated shares (including in connection with the issue of such shares);

    (b) any records relating to the holding of uncertificated shares;

    (c) the conversion of certificated shares into uncertificated shares; or

    (d) the conversion of uncertificated shares into certificated shares.

(6) The company may by notice to the holder of a share require that share—

    (a) if it is uncertificated, to be converted into certificated form, and

    (b) if it is certificated, to be converted into uncertificated form,

to enable it to be dealt with in accordance with the articles.

(7) If—

    (a) the articles give the directors power to take action, or require other persons to take action, in order to sell, transfer or otherwise dispose of shares, and

    (b) uncertificated shares are subject to that power, but the power is expressed in terms which assume the use of a certificate or other written instrument,

the directors may take such action as is necessary or expedient to achieve the same results when exercising that power in relation to uncertificated shares.

(8) In particular, the directors may take such action as they consider appropriate to achieve the sale, transfer, disposal, forfeiture, re-allotment or surrender of an uncertificated share or otherwise to enforce a lien in respect of it.

(9) Unless the directors otherwise determine, shares which a member holds in uncertificated form must be treated as separate holdings from any shares which that member holds in certificated form.

(10) A class of shares must not be treated as two classes simply because some shares of that class are held in certificated form and others are held in uncertificated form.

51. Share warrants

(1) The directors may issue a share warrant in respect of any fully paid share.

(2) Share warrants must be—

      (a)   issued in such form, and

      (b)   executed in such manner,

   as the directors decide.

(3)   A share represented by a share warrant may be transferred by delivery of the warrant representing it.

(4)   The directors may make provision for the payment of dividends in respect of any share represented by a share warrant.

(5)   Subject to the articles, the directors may decide the conditions on which any share warrant is issued. In particular, they may—

      (a)   decide the conditions on which new warrants are to be issued in place of warrants which are damaged or defaced, or said to have been lost, stolen or destroyed;

      (b)   decide the conditions on which bearers of warrants are entitled to attend and vote at general meetings;

      (c)   decide the conditions subject to which bearers of warrants may surrender their warrant so as to hold their shares in certificated or uncertificated form instead; and

      (d)   vary the conditions of issue of any warrant from time to time,

   and the bearer of a warrant is subject to the conditions and procedures in force in relation to it, whether or not they were decided or specified before the warrant was issued.

(6)   Subject to the conditions on which the warrants are issued from time to time, bearers of share warrants have the same rights and privileges as they would if their names had been included in the register as holders of the shares represented by their warrants.

(7)   The company must not in any way be bound by or recognise any interest in a share represented by a share warrant other than the absolute right of the bearer of that warrant to that warrant.

Partly Paid Shares

52.   **Company's lien over partly paid shares**

(1)   The company has a lien ("the company's lien") over every share which is partly paid for any part of—

      (a)   that share's nominal value, and

      (b)   any premium at which it was issued,

   which has not been paid to the company, and which is payable immediately or at some time in the future, whether or not a call notice has been sent in respect of it.

(2)   The company's lien over a share—

      (a)   takes priority over any third party's interest in that share, and

      (b)   extends to any dividend or other money payable by the company in respect of that share and (if the lien is enforced and the share is sold by the company) the proceeds of sale of that share.

(3)   The directors may at any time decide that a share which is or would otherwise be subject to the company's lien shall not be subject to it, either wholly or in part.

53.   **Enforcement of the company's lien**

(1)   Subject to the provisions of this article, if—

      (a)   a lien enforcement notice has been given in respect of a share, and

      (b)   the person to whom the notice was given has failed to comply with it,

   the company may sell that share in such manner as the directors decide.

(2)   A lien enforcement notice—

      (a)   may only be given in respect of a share which is subject to the company's lien, in respect of which a sum is payable and the due date for payment of that sum has passed;

      (b)   must specify the share concerned;

      (c)   must require payment of the sum payable within 14 days of the notice;

      (d)   must be addressed either to the holder of the share or to a person entitled to it by reason of the holder's death, bankruptcy or otherwise; and

(e)   must state the company's intention to sell the share if the notice is not complied with.

(3)   Where shares are sold under this article—
    (a)   the directors may authorise any person to execute an instrument of transfer of the shares to the purchaser or a person nominated by the purchaser, and
    (b)   the transferee is not bound to see to the application of the consideration, and the transferee's title is not affected by any irregularity in or invalidity of the process leading to the sale.

(4)   The net proceeds of any such sale (after payment of the costs of sale and any other costs of enforcing the lien) must be applied—
    (a)   first, in payment of so much of the sum for which the lien exists as was payable at the date of the lien enforcement notice,
    (b)   second, to the person entitled to the shares at the date of the sale, but only after the certificate for the shares sold has been surrendered to the company for cancellation or a suitable indemnity has been given for any lost certificates, and subject to a lien equivalent to the company's lien over the shares before the sale for any money payable in respect of the shares after the date of the lien enforcement notice.

(5)   A statutory declaration by a director or the company secretary that the declarant is a director or the company secretary and that a share has been sold to satisfy the company's lien on a specified date—
    (a)   is conclusive evidence of the facts stated in it as against all persons claiming to be entitled to the share, and
    (b)   subject to compliance with any other formalities of transfer required by the articles or by law, constitutes a good title to the share.

54.   Call notices

(1)   Subject to the articles and the terms on which shares are allotted, the directors may send a notice (a "call notice") to a member requiring the member to pay the company a specified sum of money (a "call") which is payable in respect of shares which that member holds at the date when the directors decide to send the call notice.

(2)   A call notice—
    (a)   may not require a member to pay a call which exceeds the total sum unpaid on that member's shares (whether as to the share's nominal value or any amount payable to the company by way of premium);
    (b)   must state when and how any call to which it relates it is to be paid; and
    (c)   may permit or require the call to be paid by instalments.

(3)   A member must comply with the requirements of a call notice, but no member is obliged to pay any call before 14 days have passed since the notice was sent.

(4)   Before the company has received any call due under a call notice the directors may—
    (a)   revoke it wholly or in part, or
    (b)   specify a later time for payment than is specified in the notice,
    by a further notice in writing to the member in respect of whose shares the call is made.

55.   Liability to pay calls

(1)   Liability to pay a call is not extinguished or transferred by transferring the shares in respect of which it is required to be paid.

(2)   Joint holders of a share are jointly and severally liable to pay all calls in respect of that share.

(3)   Subject to the terms on which shares are allotted, the directors may, when issuing shares, provide that call notices sent to the holders of those shares may require them—
    (a)   to pay calls which are not the same, or
    (b)   to pay calls at different times.

56.   When call notice need not be issued

(1)   A call notice need not be issued in respect of sums which are specified, in the terms on which a share is issued, as being payable to the company in respect of that share (whether in respect of nominal value or premium)—

(a)   on allotment;

(b)   on the occurrence of a particular event; or

(c)   on a date fixed by or in accordance with the terms of issue.

(2)   But if the due date for payment of such a sum has passed and it has not been paid, the holder of the share concerned is treated in all respects as having failed to comply with a call notice in respect of that sum, and is liable to the same consequences as regards the payment of interest and forfeiture.

57.   Failure to comply with call notice: automatic consequences

(1)   If a person is liable to pay a call and fails to do so by the call payment date—

(a)   the directors may issue a notice of intended forfeiture to that person, and

(b)   until the call is paid, that person must pay the company interest on the call from the call payment date at the relevant rate.

(2)   For the purposes of this article—

(a)   the "call payment date" is the time when the call notice states that a call is payable, unless the directors give a notice specifying a later date, in which case the "call payment date" is that later date;

(b)   the "relevant rate" is—

(i)   the rate fixed by the terms on which the share in respect of which the call is due was allotted;

(ii)   such other rate as was fixed in the call notice which required payment of the call, or has otherwise been determined by the directors; or

(iii)   if no rate is fixed in either of these ways, 5 per cent per annum.

(3)   The relevant rate must not exceed by more than 5 percentage points the base lending rate most recently set by the Monetary Policy Committee of the Bank of England in connection with its responsibilities under Part 2 of the Bank of England Act 1998.

(4)   The directors may waive any obligation to pay interest on a call wholly or in part.

58.   Notice of intended forfeiture

A notice of intended forfeiture—

(a)   may be sent in respect of any share in respect of which a call has not been paid as required by a call notice;

(b)   must be sent to the holder of that share or to a person entitled to it by reason of the holder's death, bankruptcy or otherwise;

(c)   must require payment of the call and any accrued interest by a date which is not less than 14 days after the date of the notice;

(d)   must state how the payment is to be made; and

(e)   must state that if the notice is not complied with, the shares in respect of which the call is payable will be liable to be forfeited.

59.   Directors' power to forfeit shares

If a notice of intended forfeiture is not complied with before the date by which payment of the call is required in the notice of intended forfeiture, the directors may decide that any share in respect of which it was given is forfeited, and the forfeiture is to include all dividends or other moneys payable in respect of the forfeited shares and not paid before the forfeiture.

60.   Effect of forfeiture

(1)   Subject to the articles, the forfeiture of a share extinguishes—

(a)   all interests in that share, and all claims and demands against the company in respect of it, and

     (b)   all other rights and liabilities incidental to the share as between the person whose share it was prior to the forfeiture and the company.

(2)   Any share which is forfeited in accordance with the articles—

     (a)   is deemed to have been forfeited when the directors decide that it is forfeited;

     (b)   is deemed to be the property of the company; and

     (c)   may be sold, re-allotted or otherwise disposed of as the directors think fit.

(3)   If a person's shares have been forfeited—

     (a)   the company must send that person notice that forfeiture has occurred and record it in the register of members;

     (b)   that person ceases to be a member in respect of those shares;

     (c)   that person must surrender the certificate for the shares forfeited to the company for cancellation;

     (d)   that person remains liable to the company for all sums payable by that person under the articles at the date of forfeiture in respect of those shares, including any interest (whether accrued before or after the date of forfeiture); and

     (e)   the directors may waive payment of such sums wholly or in part or enforce payment without any allowance for the value of the shares at the time of forfeiture or for any consideration received on their disposal.

(4)   At any time before the company disposes of a forfeited share, the directors may decide to cancel the forfeiture on payment of all calls and interest due in respect of it and on such other terms as they think fit.

61.   Procedure following forfeiture

(1)   If a forfeited share is to be disposed of by being transferred, the company may receive the consideration for the transfer and the directors may authorise any person to execute the instrument of transfer.

(2)   A statutory declaration by a director or the company secretary that the declarant is a director or the company secretary and that a share has been forfeited on a specified date—

     (a)   is conclusive evidence of the facts stated in it as against all persons claiming to be entitled to the share, and

     (b)   subject to compliance with any other formalities of transfer required by the articles or by law, constitutes a good title to the share.

(3)   A person to whom a forfeited share is transferred is not bound to see to the application of the consideration (if any) nor is that person's title to the share affected by any irregularity in or invalidity of the process leading to the forfeiture or transfer of the share.

(4)   If the company sells a forfeited share, the person who held it prior to its forfeiture is entitled to receive from the company the proceeds of such sale, net of any commission, and excluding any amount which—

     (a)   was, or would have become, payable, and

     (b)   had not, when that share was forfeited, been paid by that person in respect of that share,

but no interest is payable to such a person in respect of such proceeds and the company is not required to account for any money earned on them.

62.   Surrender of shares

(1)   A member may surrender any share—

     (a)   in respect of which the directors may issue a notice of intended forfeiture;

     (b)   which the directors may forfeit; or

     (c)   which has been forfeited.

(2)   The directors may accept the surrender of any such share.

(3)   The effect of surrender on a share is the same as the effect of forfeiture on that share.

(4)   A share which has been surrendered may be dealt with in the same way as a share which has been forfeited.

Transfer and Transmission of Shares

63. Transfers of certificated shares

(1) Certificated shares may be transferred by means of an instrument of transfer in any usual form or any other form approved by the directors, which is executed by or on behalf of—

    (a) the transferor, and

    (b) (if any of the shares is partly paid) the transferee.

(2) No fee may be charged for registering any instrument of transfer or other document relating to or affecting the title to any share.

(3) The company may retain any instrument of transfer which is registered.

(4) The transferor remains the holder of a certificated share until the transferee's name is entered in the register of members as holder of it.

(5) The directors may refuse to register the transfer of a certificated share if—

    (a) the share is not fully paid;

    (b) the transfer is not lodged at the company's registered office or such other place as the directors have appointed;

    (c) the transfer is not accompanied by the certificate for the shares to which it relates, or such other evidence as the directors may reasonably require to show the transferor's right to make the transfer, or evidence of the right of someone other than the transferor to make the transfer on the transferor's behalf;

    (d) the transfer is in respect of more than one class of share; or

    (e) the transfer is in favour of more than four transferees.

(6) If the directors refuse to register the transfer of a share, the instrument of transfer must be returned to the transferee with the notice of refusal unless they suspect that the proposed transfer may be fraudulent.

64. Transfer of uncertificated shares

A transfer of an uncertificated share must not be registered if it is in favour of more than four transferees.

65. Transmission of shares

(1) If title to a share passes to a transmittee, the company may only recognise the transmittee as having any title to that share.

(2) Nothing in these articles releases the estate of a deceased member from any liability in respect of a share solely or jointly held by that member.

66. Transmittees' rights

(1) A transmittee who produces such evidence of entitlement to shares as the directors may properly require—

    (a) may, subject to the articles, choose either to become the holder of those shares or to have them transferred to another person, and

    (b) subject to the articles, and pending any transfer of the shares to another person, has the same rights as the holder had.

(2) But transmittees do not have the right to attend or vote at a general meeting in respect of shares to which they are entitled, by reason of the holder's death or bankruptcy or otherwise, unless they become the holders of those shares

67. Exercise of transmittees' rights

(1) Transmittees who wish to become the holders of shares to which they have become entitled must notify the company in writing of that wish.

(2) If the share is a certificated share and a transmittee wishes to have it transferred to another person, the transmittee must execute an instrument of transfer in respect of it.

(3) If the share is an uncertificated share and the transmittee wishes to have it transferred to another person, the transmittee must—

      (a)   procure that all appropriate instructions are given to effect the transfer, or

      (b)   procure that the uncertificated share is changed into certificated form and then execute an instrument of transfer in respect of it.

  (4)   Any transfer made or executed under this article is to be treated as if it were made or executed by the person from whom the transmittee has derived rights in respect of the share, and as if the event which gave rise to the transmission had not occurred.

68.   **Transmittees bound by prior notices**

If a notice is given to a member in respect of shares and a transmittee is entitled to those shares, the transmittee is bound by the notice if it was given to the member before the transmittee's name has been entered in the register of members.

Consolidation of Shares

69.   **Procedure for disposing of fractions of shares**

  (1)   This article applies where—

      (a)   there has been a consolidation or division of shares, and

      (b)   as a result, members are entitled to fractions of shares.

  (2)   The directors may—

      (a)   sell the shares representing the fractions to any person including the company for the best price reasonably obtainable;

      (b)   in the case of a certificated share, authorise any person to execute an instrument of transfer of the shares to the purchaser or a person nominated by the purchaser; and

      (c)   distribute the net proceeds of sale in due proportion among the holders of the shares.

  (3)   Where any holder's entitlement to a portion of the proceeds of sale amounts to less than a minimum figure determined by the directors, that member's portion may be distributed to an organisation which is a charity for the purposes of the law of England and Wales, Scotland or Northern Ireland.

  (4)   The person to whom the shares are transferred is not obliged to ensure that any purchase money is received by the person entitled to the relevant fractions.

  (5)   The transferee's title to the shares is not affected by any irregularity in or invalidity of the process leading to their sale.

Distributions

70.   **Procedure for declaring dividends**

  (1)   The company may by ordinary resolution declare dividends, and the directors may decide to pay interim dividends.

  (2)   A dividend must not be declared unless the directors have made a recommendation as to its amount. Such a dividend must not exceed the amount recommended by the directors.

  (3)   No dividend may be declared or paid unless it is in accordance with members' respective rights.

  (4)   Unless the members' resolution to declare or directors' decision to pay a dividend, or the terms on which shares are issued, specify otherwise, it must be paid by reference to each member's holding of shares on the date of the resolution or decision to declare or pay it.

  (5)   If the company's share capital is divided into different classes, no interim dividend may be paid on shares carrying deferred or non-preferred rights if, at the time of payment, any preferential dividend is in arrear.

  (6)   The directors may pay at intervals any dividend payable at a fixed rate if it appears to them that the profits available for distribution justify the payment.

  (7)   If the directors act in good faith, they do not incur any liability to the holders of shares conferring preferred rights for any loss they may suffer by the lawful payment of an interim dividend on shares with deferred or non-preferred rights.

71.   Calculation of dividends

(1)   Except as otherwise provided by the articles or the rights attached to shares, all dividends must be—

(a)   declared and paid according to the amounts paid up on the shares on which the dividend is paid, and

(b)   apportioned and paid proportionately to the amounts paid up on the shares during any portion or portions of the period in respect of which the dividend is paid.

(2)   If any share is issued on terms providing that it ranks for dividend as from a particular date, that share ranks for dividend accordingly.

(3)   For the purposes of calculating dividends, no account is to be taken of any amount which has been paid up on a share in advance of the due date for payment of that amount.

72.   Payment of dividends and other distributions

(1)   Where a dividend or other sum which is a distribution is payable in respect of a share, it must be paid by one or more of the following means—

(a)   transfer to a bank or building society account specified by the distribution recipient either in writing or as the directors may otherwise decide;

(b)   sending a cheque made payable to the distribution recipient by post to the distribution recipient at the distribution recipient's registered address (if the distribution recipient is a holder of the share), or (in any other case) to an address specified by the distribution recipient either in writing or as the directors may otherwise decide;

(c)   sending a cheque made payable to such person by post to such person at such address as the distribution recipient has specified either in writing or as the directors may otherwise decide; or

(d)   any other means of payment as the directors agree with the distribution recipient either in writing or by such other means as the directors decide.

(2)   In the articles, "the distribution recipient" means, in respect of a share in respect of which a dividend or other sum is payable—

(a)   the holder of the share; or

(b)   if the share has two or more joint holders, whichever of them is named first in the register of members; or

(c)   if the holder is no longer entitled to the share by reason of death or bankruptcy, or otherwise by operation of law, the transmittee.

73.   Deductions from distributions in respect of sums owed to the company

(1)   If—

(a)   a share is subject to the company's lien, and

(b)   the directors are entitled to issue a lien enforcement notice in respect of it,

they may, instead of issuing a lien enforcement notice, deduct from any dividend or other sum payable in respect of the share any sum of money which is payable to the company in respect of that share to the extent that they are entitled to require payment under a lien enforcement notice.

(2)   Money so deducted must be used to pay any of the sums payable in respect of that share.

(3)   The company must notify the distribution recipient in writing of—

(a)   the fact and amount of any such deduction;

(b)   any non-payment of a dividend or other sum payable in respect of a share resulting from any such deduction; and

(c)   how the money deducted has been applied.

74.   No interest on distributions

The company may not pay interest on any dividend or other sum payable in respect of a share unless otherwise provided by—

(a)   the terms on which the share was issued, or

(b)   the provisions of another agreement between the holder of that share and the company.

75.   Unclaimed distributions

(1)   All dividends or other sums which are—

(a)   payable in respect of shares, and

(b)   unclaimed after having been declared or become payable,

may be invested or otherwise made use of by the directors for the benefit of the company until claimed.

(2)   The payment of any such dividend or other sum into a separate account does not make the company a trustee in respect of it.

(3)   If—

(a)   twelve years have passed from the date on which a dividend or other sum became due for payment, and

(b)   the distribution recipient has not claimed it,

the distribution recipient is no longer entitled to that dividend or other sum and it ceases to remain owing by the company.

76.   Non-cash distributions

(1)   Subject to the terms of issue of the share in question, the company may, by ordinary resolution on the recommendation of the directors, decide to pay all or part of a dividend or other distribution payable in respect of a share by transferring non-cash assets of equivalent value (including, without limitation, shares or other securities in any company).

(2)   If the shares in respect of which such a non-cash distribution is paid are uncertificated, any shares in the company which are issued as a non-cash distribution in respect of them must be uncertificated.

(3)   For the purposes of paying a non-cash distribution, the directors may make whatever arrangements they think fit, including, where any difficulty arises regarding the distribution—

(a)   fixing the value of any assets;

(b)   paying cash to any distribution recipient on the basis of that value in order to adjust the rights of recipients; and

(c)   vesting any assets in trustees.

77.   Waiver of distributions

Distribution recipients may waive their entitlement to a dividend or other distribution payable in respect of a share by giving the company notice in writing to that effect, but if—

(a)   the share has more than one holder, or

(b)   more than one person is entitled to the share, whether by reason of the death or bankruptcy of one or more joint holders, or otherwise,

the notice is not effective unless it is expressed to be given, and signed, by all the holders or persons otherwise entitled to the share.

Capitalisation of Profits

78.   Authority to capitalise and appropriation of capitalised sums

(1)   Subject to the articles, the directors may, if they are so authorised by an ordinary resolution—

(a)   decide to capitalise any profits of the company (whether or not they are available for distribution) which are not required for paying a preferential dividend, or any sum standing to the credit of the company's share premium account or capital redemption reserve; and

(b)   appropriate any sum which they so decide to capitalise (a "capitalised sum") to the persons who would have been entitled to it if it were distributed by way of dividend (the "persons entitled") and in the same proportions.

(2) Capitalised sums must be applied—

    (a) on behalf of the persons entitled, and

    (b) in the same proportions as a dividend would have been distributed to them.

(3) Any capitalised sum may be applied in paying up new shares of a nominal amount equal to the capitalised sum which are then allotted credited as fully paid to the persons entitled or as they may direct.

(4) A capitalised sum which was appropriated from profits available for distribution may be applied—

    (a) in or towards paying up any amounts unpaid on existing shares held by the persons entitled, or

    (b) in paying up new debentures of the company which are then allotted credited as fully paid to the persons entitled or as they may direct.

(5) Subject to the articles the directors may—

    (a) apply capitalised sums in accordance with paragraphs (3) and (4) partly in one way and partly in another;

    (b) make such arrangements as they think fit to deal with shares or debentures becoming distributable in fractions under this article (including the issuing of fractional certificates or the making of cash payments); and

    (c) authorise any person to enter into an agreement with the company on behalf of all the persons entitled which is binding on them in respect of the allotment of shares and debentures to them under this article.

PART 5
MISCELLANEOUS PROVISIONS

Communications

79. Means of communication to be used

(1) Subject to the articles, anything sent or supplied by or to the company under the articles may be sent or supplied in any way in which the Companies Act 2006 provides for documents or information which are authorised or required by any provision of that Act to be sent or supplied by or to the company.

(2) Subject to the articles, any notice or document to be sent or supplied to a director in connection with the taking of decisions by directors may also be sent or supplied by the means by which that director has asked to be sent or supplied with such notices or documents for the time being.

(3) A director may agree with the company that notices or documents sent to that director in a particular way are to be deemed to have been received within a specified time of their being sent, and for the specified time to be less than 48 hours.

80. Failure to notify contact details

(1) If—

    (a) the company sends two consecutive documents to a member over a period of at least 12 months, and

    (b) each of those documents is returned undelivered, or the company receives notification that it has not been delivered,

that member ceases to be entitled to receive notices from the company.

(2) A member who has ceased to be entitled to receive notices from the company becomes entitled to receive such notices again by sending the company—

    (a) a new address to be recorded in the register of members, or

    (b) if the member has agreed that the company should use a means of communication other than sending things to such an address, the information that the company needs to use that means of communication effectively.

Administrative Arrangements

81.   Company seals

(1)   Any common seal may only be used by the authority of the directors.

(2)   The directors may decide by what means and in what form any common seal or securities seal is to be used.

(3)   Unless otherwise decided by the directors, if the company has a common seal and it is affixed to a document, the document must also be signed by at least one authorised person in the presence of a witness who attests the signature.

(4)   For the purposes of this article, an authorised person is—

   (a)   any director of the company;

   (b)   the company secretary; or

   (c)   any person authorised by the directors for the purpose of signing documents to which the common seal is applied.

(5)   If the company has an official seal for use abroad, it may only be affixed to a document if its use on that document, or documents of a class to which it belongs, has been authorised by a decision of the directors.

(6)   If the company has a securities seal, it may only be affixed to securities by the company secretary or a person authorised to apply it to securities by the company secretary.

(7)   For the purposes of the articles, references to the securities seal being affixed to any document include the reproduction of the image of that seal on or in a document by any mechanical or electronic means which has been approved by the directors in relation to that document or documents of a class to which it belongs.

82.   Destruction of documents

(1)   The company is entitled to destroy—

   (a)   all instruments of transfer of shares which have been registered, and all other documents on the basis of which any entries are made in the register of members, from six years after the date of registration;

   (b)   all dividend mandates, variations or cancellations of dividend mandates, and notifications of change of address, from two years after they have been recorded;

   (c)   all share certificates which have been cancelled from one year after the date of the cancellation;

   (d)   all paid dividend warrants and cheques from one year after the date of actual payment; and

   (e)   all proxy notices from one year after the end of the meeting to which the proxy notice relates.

(2)   If the company destroys a document in good faith, in accordance with the articles, and without notice of any claim to which that document may be relevant, it is conclusively presumed in favour of the company that—

   (a)   entries in the register purporting to have been made on the basis of an instrument of transfer or other document so destroyed were duly and properly made;

   (b)   any instrument of transfer so destroyed was a valid and effective instrument duly and properly registered;

   (c)   any share certificate so destroyed was a valid and effective certificate duly and properly cancelled; and

   (d)   any other document so destroyed was a valid and effective document in accordance with its recorded particulars in the books or records of the company.

(3)   This article does not impose on the company any liability which it would not otherwise have if it destroys any document before the time at which this article permits it to do so.

(4)   In this article, references to the destruction of any document include a reference to its being disposed of in any manner.

83. No right to inspect accounts and other records

Except as provided by law or authorised by the directors or an ordinary resolution of the company, no person is entitled to inspect any of the company's accounting or other records or documents merely by virtue of being a member.

84. Provision for employees on cessation of business

The directors may decide to make provision for the benefit of persons employed or formerly employed by the company or any of its subsidiaries (other than a director or former director or shadow director) in connection with the cessation or transfer to any person of the whole or part of the undertaking of the company or that subsidiary.

Directors' Indemnity and Insurance

85. Indemnity

(1) Subject to paragraph (2), a relevant director of the company or an associated company may be indemnified out of the company's assets against—

    (a) any liability incurred by that director in connection with any negligence, default, breach of duty or breach of trust in relation to the company or an associated company,

    (b) any liability incurred by that director in connection with the activities of the company or an associated company in its capacity as a trustee of an occupational pension scheme (as defined in section 235(6) of the Companies Act 2006),

    (c) any other liability incurred by that director as an officer of the company or an associated company.

(2) This article does not authorise any indemnity which would be prohibited or rendered void by any provision of the Companies Acts or by any other provision of law.

(3) In this article—

    (a) companies are associated if one is a subsidiary of the other or both are subsidiaries of the same body corporate, and

    (b) a "relevant director" means any director or former director of the company or an associated company.

86. Insurance

(1) The directors may decide to purchase and maintain insurance, at the expense of the company, for the benefit of any relevant director in respect of any relevant loss.

(2) In this article—

    (a) a "relevant director" means any director or former director of the company or an associated company,

    (b) a "relevant loss" means any loss or liability which has been or may be incurred by a relevant director in connection with that director's duties or powers in relation to the company, any associated company or any pension fund or employees' share scheme of the company or associated company, and

    (c) companies are associated if one is a subsidiary of the other or both are subsidiaries of the same body corporate.

Companies (Shares and Share Capital) Order 2009

S.I. 2009/388

1. **Citation, commencement and interpretation**

(1) This Order may be cited as the Companies (Shares and Share Capital) Order 2009 and shall come into force on 1st October 2009.

(2) In this Order, a reference to a section is a reference to a section of the Companies Act 2006.

2. **Statements of capital, and returns of allotment by unlimited companies: prescribed particulars of the rights attached to shares**

(1) The particulars in paragraph (3) are prescribed for the purposes of the provisions in paragraph (2).

(2) The provisions are—

    (a) section 10(2)(c)(i);

    (b) section 32(2)(c)(i);

    (c) section 108(3)(c)(i);

    (d) section 555(4)(c)(i);

    (e) section 556(3);

    (f) section 619(3)(c)(i);

    (g) section 621(3)(c)(i);

    (h) section 625(3)(c)(i);

    (i) section 627(3)(c)(i);

    (j) section 644(2)(c)(i);

    (k) section 649(2)(c)(i);

    (l) section 663(3)(c)(i);

    (m) section 689(3)(c)(i);

    (n) section 708(3)(c)(i); …

    (o) section 730(5)(c)(i); and

    (p) section 853D(4)(d)(i).

(3) The particulars are—

    (a) particulars of any voting rights attached to the shares, including rights that arise only in certain circumstances;

    (b) particulars of any rights attached to the shares, as respects dividends, to participate in a distribution;

    (c) particulars of any rights attached to the shares, as respects capital, to participate in a distribution (including on winding up); and

    (d) whether the shares are to be redeemed or are liable to be redeemed at the option of the company or the shareholder.

3. **Prescribed information for a return of an allotment by a limited company**

(1) The information in paragraph (2) is prescribed for the purposes of section 555(3)(a) (information to be contained in a return of an allotment by a limited company).

(2) The information is—

    (a) the number of shares allotted;

    (b) the amount paid up and the amount (if any) unpaid on each allotted share (whether on account of the nominal value of the share or by way of premium); and

    (c) where the shares are allotted as fully or partly paid up (as to their nominal value or any premium on them) otherwise than in cash, the consideration for the allotment.

4. **Shares deemed paid up in or allotted for cash, and sale of treasury shares for a cash consideration: meaning of cash consideration**

(1) The creation of an obligation on the part of a settlement bank to make a relevant payment in respect of the allotment of a share to a system-member by means of a relevant system is to be regarded as a means of payment falling within section 583(3)(e).

(2) The creation of an obligation on the part of a settlement bank to make a relevant payment in respect of the payment up of a share by a system-member by means of a relevant system is to be regarded as a means of payment falling within section 583(3)(e).

(3) The creation of an obligation on the part of a settlement bank to make a relevant payment in respect of the transfer by a company to a system-member, by means of a relevant system, of a share held by the company as a treasury share is to be regarded as a means of payment falling within section 727(2)(e).

(4) In this article—

    (a) the expressions "Operator", "relevant system", "rules", "settlement bank", "system-member" and "uncertificated" have the meanings given in the Uncertificated Securities Regulations 2001; and

    (b) "relevant payment" means a payment in accordance with the rules and practices of an Operator of a relevant system.

5. **Redemption or purchase of own shares out of capital by a private company: prescribed form of, and information with respect to the nature of the company's business to be contained in, a directors' statement**

(1) The directors' statement required by section 714 (directors' statement to be made where a private company makes a payment out of capital for the redemption or purchase of its own shares) must—

    (a) be in writing;

    (b) indicate that it is a directors' statement made under that section; and

    (c) be signed by each of the company's directors.

(2) The statement must state—

    (a) whether the company's business includes that of a banking company; and

    (b) whether its business includes that of an insurance company.

Companies (Reduction of Share Capital) Order 2008

S.I. 2008/1915

1.   (1)   This Order may be cited as the Companies (Reduction of Share Capital) Order 2008 and comes into force on 1st October 2008.

(2)   In this Order, "the Act" means the Companies Act 2006.

2.   A solvency statement under section 643 of the Act must—

(a)   be in writing,

(b)   indicate that it is a solvency statement for the purposes of section 642 of the Act, and

(c)   be signed by each of the directors.

3.   (1)   If an unlimited company reduces its share capital—

    (a)   the prohibition in section 654(1) of the Act does not apply, and

    (b)   a reserve arising from the reduction is to be treated for the purposes of Part 23 of the Act as a realised profit.

(2)   If a private company limited by shares reduces its share capital and the reduction is supported by a solvency statement but has not been the subject of an application to the court for an order confirming it—

    (a)   the prohibition in section 654(1) of the Act does not apply, and

    (b)   a reserve arising from the reduction is to be treated for the purposes of Part 23 of the Act as a realised profit.

(3)   If a limited company having a share capital reduces its share capital and the reduction is confirmed by order of the court—

    (a)   the prohibition in section 654(1) of the Act does not apply, and

    (b)   a reserve arising from the reduction is to be treated for the purposes of Part 23 of the Act as a realised profit unless the court orders otherwise under section 648(1) of the Act.

(4)   This article is without prejudice to any contrary provision of—

    (a)   an order of, or undertaking given to, the court,

    (b)   the resolution for, or any other resolution relevant to, the reduction of share capital, or

    (c)   the company's memorandum or articles of association.

Companies (Registration) Regulations 2008

S.I. 2008/3014

The prohibition

1. **Citation, commencement and interpretation**
   (1) These Regulations may be cited as the Companies (Registration) Regulations 2008 and come into force on 1st October 2009.
   (2) In these Regulations "the Act" means the Companies Act 2006.

2. **Memorandum of association**
   For the purposes of section 8 of the Act—
   (a) the memorandum of association of a company having a share capital shall be in the form set out in Schedule 1; and
   (b) the memorandum of association of a company not having a share capital shall be in the form set out in Schedule 2.

3. **Statement of capital and initial shareholdings**
   For the purposes of section 10(3) of the Act, the statement of capital and initial shareholdings shall contain the name and address of each subscriber to the memorandum of association.

4. **Statement of guarantee**
   For the purposes of section 11(2) of the Act, the statement of guarantee shall contain the name and address of each subscriber to the memorandum of association.

5. **Form of assent for re-registration of private limited company as unlimited**
   The form set out in Schedule 3 is the form prescribed for the purposes of section 103(2)(a) of the Act.

6. **Form of assent for re-registration of public company as private and unlimited**
   The form set out in Schedule 4 is the form prescribed for the purposes of section 110(2)(a) of the Act.

SCHEDULE 1   Regulation 2(a)

COMPANY HAVING A SHARE CAPITAL

Memorandum of association of [*insert name of company*]

Each subscriber to this memorandum of association wishes to form a company under the Companies Act 2006 and agrees to become a member of the company and to take at least one share.

Name of each subscriber	*Authentication by each subscriber*

Dated

...

Stock Transfer Act 1963

1963 c. 18

An Act to amend the law with respect to the transfer of securities

[10th July 1963]

1.   Simplified transfer of securities

(1)   Registered securities to which this section applies may be transferred by means of an instrument under hand in the form set out in Schedule 1 to this Act (in this Act referred to as a stock transfer), executed by the transferor only and specifying (in addition to the particulars of the consideration, of the description and number or amount of the securities, and of the person by whom the transfer is made) the full name and address of the transferee.

(2)   The execution of a stock transfer need not be attested; and where such a transfer has been executed for the purpose of a stock exchange transaction, the particulars of the consideration and of the transferee may either be inserted in that transfer or, as the case may require, supplied by means of separate instruments in the form set out in Schedule 2 to this Act (in this Act referred to as brokers transfers), identifying the stock transfer and specifying the securities to which each such instrument relates and the consideration paid for those securities.

(3)   Nothing in this section shall be construed as affecting the validity of any instrument which would be effective to transfer securities apart from this section; and any instrument purporting to be made in any form which was common or usual before the commencement of this Act, or in any other form authorised or required for that purpose apart from this section, shall be sufficient, whether or not it is completed in accordance with the form, if it complies with the requirements as to execution and contents which apply to a stock transfer.

(4)   This section applies to fully paid up registered securities of any description, being—

      (a)   securities issued by any company as defined in section 1(1) of the Companies Act 2006 except a company limited by guarantee or an unlimited company;

      (b)   securities issued by any body (other than a company as so defined) incorporated in Great Britain by or under any enactment or by Royal Charter except a building society within the meaning of the Building Societies Act 1986 or registered society within the meaning of the Co-operative and Community Benefit Societies Act 2014;

      (c)   securities issued by the Government of the United Kingdom, except stock or bonds in the National Savings Stock Register ..., and except national savings certificates;

      (d)   securities issued by any local authority;

      (e)   units of an authorised unit trust scheme, an authorised contractual scheme or a recognised scheme within the meaning of Part 17 of the Financial Services and Markets Act 2000;

      (f)   shares issued by an open-ended investment company within the meaning of the Open-Ended Investment Companies Regulations 2001;

      (g)   shares issued by a protected cell company within the meaning of Part 4 of the Risk Transformation Regulations 2017.

2.   Supplementary provisions as to simplified transfer

(1)   Section 1 of this Act shall have effect in relation to the transfer of any securities to which that section applies notwithstanding anything to the contrary in any enactment or instrument relating to the transfer of those securities; but nothing in that section affects—

      (a)   any right to refuse to register a person as the holder of any securities on any ground other than the form in which those securities purport to be transferred to him: or

      (b)   any enactment or rule of law regulating the execution of documents by companies or other bodies corporate, or any articles of association or other instrument regulating the execution of documents by any particular company or body corporate.

(2)   Subject to the provisions of this section, any enactment or instrument relating to the transfer of securities to which section 1 of this Act applies shall, with any necessary modifications, apply in relation to an instrument of transfer authorised by that section as it applies in relation to an instrument of transfer to which it applies apart from this subsection; and without prejudice to the generality of the foregoing provision, the references to an instrument of transfer in section 775 of the Companies Act 2006 (certification of instrument of transfer) shall be construed as including a reference to a brokers transfer.

(3)   In relation to the transfer of securities by means of a stock transfer and a brokers transfer—

     (a)   any reference in any enactment or instrument (including in particular section 770(1)(a) of the Companies Act 2006 (registration of transfer) ...) to the delivery or lodging of an instrument (or proper instrument) of transfer shall be construed as a reference to the delivery or lodging of the stock transfer and the brokers transfer;

     (b)   any such reference to the date on which an instrument of transfer is delivered or lodged shall be construed as a reference to the data by which the later of those transfers to be delivered or lodged has been delivered or lodged; and

     (c)   *subject to the foregoing provisions of this subsection, the brokers transfer (and not the stock transfer) shall be deemed to be the conveyance or transfer for the purposes of the enactments relating to stamp duty.*

(4)   ...

Note. Subsection (3)(c) is repealed by the Finance Act 1990, s. 132, Sch. 19, Pt. VI, as from a day to be appointed.

3.   Additional provisions as to transfer forms

(1)   References in this Act to the forms set out in Schedule 1 and Schedule 2 include references to forms substantially corresponding to those forms respectively.

(2)   The Treasury may by order amend the said Schedules either by altering the forms set out therein or by substituting different forms for those forms or by the addition of forms for use as alternatives to those forms; and references in this Act to the forms set out in those Schedules (including references in this section) shall be construed accordingly.

(3)   Any order under subsection (2) of this section which substitutes a different form for a form set out in Schedule 1 to this Act may direct that subsection (3) of section 1 of this Act shall apply, with any necessary modifications, in relation to the form for which that form is substituted as it applies to any form which was common or usual before the commencement of this Act.

(4)   Any order of the Treasury under this section shall be made by statutory instrument, and may be varied or revoked by a subsequent order; and any statutory instrument made by virtue of this section shall be subject to annulment in pursuance of a resolution of either House of Parliament.

(5)   An order under subsection (2) of this section may—

     (a)   provide for forms on which some of the particulars mentioned in subsection (1) of section 1 of this Act are not required to be specified;

     (b)   provide for that section to have effect, in relation to such forms as are mentioned in the preceding paragraph or other forms specified in the order, subject to such amendments as are so specified (which may include an amendment of the reference in subsection (1) of that section to an instrument under hand);

     (c)   provide for all or any of the provisions of the order to have effect in such cases only as are specified in the order.

4.   Interpretation

(1)   In this Act the following expressions have the meanings hereby respectively assigned to them, that is to say—

     "local authority" means, in relation to England and Wales,

     (a)   a billing authority or a precepting authority, as defined in section 69 of the Local Government Finance Act 1992;

(aa) a fire and rescue authority in Wales constituted by a scheme under section 2 of the Fire and Rescue Services Act 2004 or a scheme to which section 4 of that Act applies;

(b) a levying body within the meaning of section 74 of the Local Government Finance Act 1988; and

(c) a body as regards which section 75 of that Act applies,

and, in relation to Scotland, a county council, a town council and any statutory authority, commissioners or trustees to whom section 270 of the Local Government (Scotland) Act 1947 applies;

"registered securities" means transferable securities the holders of which are entered in a register (whether maintained in Great Britain or not); "securities" means shares, stock, debentures, debenture stock, loan stock, bonds, units of a collective investment scheme within the meaning of the Financial Services and Markets Act 2000, and other securities of any description;

"stock exchange transaction" means a sale and purchase of securities in which each of the parties is a member of a stock exchange acting in the ordinary course of his business as such or is acting through the agency of such a member;

"stock exchange" means the Stock Exchange, London, and any other stock exchange (whether in Great Britain or not) which is declared by order of the Treasury to be a recognised stock exchange for the purposes of this Act.

(2) Any order of the Treasury under this section shall be made by statutory instrument, and may be varied or revoked by a subsequent order.

5.   Application to Northern Ireland

(1) This Act, so far as it applies to things done outside Great Britain, extends to Northern Ireland.

(2) Without prejudice to subsection (1) of this section, the provisions of this Act affecting securities issued by the Government of the United Kingdom shall apply to any such securities entered in a register maintained in Northern Ireland.

(3) ...

(4) Except as provided by this section, this Act shall not extend to Northern Ireland.

6.   Short title and commencement

(1) This Act may be cited as the Stock Transfer Act 1963.

(2) Subsection (3) of section 5 of this Act shall come into force on the passing of this Act, and the remaining provisions of this Act shall come into force on such date as the Treasury may by order made by statutory instrument direct.

SCHEDULES

SCHEDULE 1

	Certificate lodged with the Registrar
STOCK TRANSFER FORM	
Consideration Money £............................	(For completion by the Registrar/ Stock Exchange)

Name of Undertaking.	
Description of Security.	
Number or amount of Shares, Stock or other security and, in figures column only, number and denomination of units, if any.	Words
	Figures
	(units of)
Name(s) of registered holder(s) should be given in full: the address should be given where there is only one holder. If the transfer is not made by the registered holder(s) insert also the name(s) and capacity (eg, Executor(s)), of the person(s) making the transfer.	in the name(s) of

Delete words in italics except for stock exchange transactions.	I/We hereby transfer the above security out of the name(s) aforesaid to the person(s) named below *or to the several persons named in Parts 2 of Brokers Transfer Forms relating to the above security:* Signature(s) of transferor(s)	Stamp of Selling Broker(s) or, for transactions which are not stock exchange transactions, of Agent(s), if any, acting for the Transferor(s).
	1 .... 3	
	2 .... 4	
	A body corporate should execute this transfer under its common seal or otherwise in accordance with applicable statutory requirements.	Date

Full name(s), full postal address(es) (including County or, if applicable, Postal District number) of the person(s) to whom the security is transferred. Please state title, if any, or whether Mr, Mrs or Miss. Please complete in type or in Block Capitals.	

I/We request that such entries be made in the register as are necessary to give effect to this transfer.

Stamp of Buying Broker(s) (if any).	Stamp or name and address of person lodging this form (if other than the Buying Broker(s)).

Reference to the Registrar in this form means the registrar or registration agent of the undertaking, <u>not</u> the Registrar of Companies at Companies House.

(Endorsement for use only in stock exchange transactions)

The security represented by the transfer overleaf has been sold as follows:–

....*Shares/Stock*   ....*Shares/Stock*
....*Shares/Stock*   ....*Shares/Stock*
....*Shares/Stock*   ....*Shares/Stock*
....*Shares/Stock*   ....*Shares/Stock*
....*Shares/Stock*   ....*Shares/Stock*
....*Shares/Stock*   ....*Shares/Stock*

....

Balance (if any) due to Selling Broker(s)

Amount of Certificate(s)

Brokers Transfer Forms for above amount certified

Stamp of certifying Stock Exchange   *Stamp of Selling Broker(s)*

**TALISMAN
SOLD
TRANSFER**

This transfer is
exempt from Transfer
Stamp Duty

Above this line for Registrar's use only

	Bargain Reference No:	Certificate lodged with Registrar

Name of
Undertaking

Description of
Security

(for completion by the Registrars/ Stock Exchange)

Amount of Stock or number of Stock units or shares or other security in words	Figures

In the name(s) of

Account Designation (if any)

Name(s) of registered
holder(s) should be
given in full; the ad-
dress should be given
where there is only
one holder.

If the transfer is not
made by the regis-
tered holder(s) insert
also the name(s) and
capacity (e.g. Execu-
tor(s)) of the per-
son(s) making the
transfer.

PLEASE SIGN HERE ⇨

I/We hereby transfer the above security out of the name(s)
aforesaid into the name of   and request the necessary
entries to be made in the register.

Balance Certificate Required for
(amount or number in figures)

*Bodies corporate should affix their common seal and each signatory should state his/her
representative capacity (e g 'Company Secretary' 'Director') agaist his/her signature*

Stamp of Lodging Agent

1 _____

2 _____

3 _____

4 _____

Date

is lodging this transfer at the direction and on behalf of the Lodging Agent
whose stamp appears herein (''the Original Lodging Agent'') and does not in any manner or
to any extent warrant or represent the validity, genuineness or correctness of the transfer
instructions contained herein or the genuineness of the signature(s) of the transferor(s) The
Original Lodging Agent be delivering this transfer to   authorises
               to lodge this transfer for registration and agrees to be deemed for all
purposes to be the person(s) actually lodging this transfer for registration

INSP Code (if applicable)

Transfer Number

TALISMAN
BOUGHT
TRANSFER

Above this line for Registrar's use only

Name of Undertaking

Rate	Description of Security

Stamp Duty	Bargain Date	Settlement	Price	Transfer Consideration	Figures

Amount of Stock or Number of Stock Units or Shares or Other Security in Words

Hundred Millions	Ten Millions	Millions	Hundred Thousands	Ten Thousands	Thousands	Hundreds	Tens	Units

Transferee Details

Account Designation

Apportionment Date

Registrar	Batch	Company	Security	Bargain Reference	Firm	Transfer Number	Quantity

hereby transfers the above security to the person(s) named under "Transferee Details" and requests the necessary entries to be made in the register. It confirms that the price and transfer consideration have been derived from information supplied by Member Firms

is lodging this transfer at the direction and on behalf of the Member Firm whose code number appears herein ('the Original Lodging Agent') and does not in any manner or to any extent warrant or represent the validity or correctness of the transfer instructions contained herein. The Original Lodging Agent by instructing   to deliver this transfer for registration agrees to be deemed for all purposes to be the person(s) actually lodging this transfer for registration

Dated

It is hereby certified on behalf of The Stock Exchange that the Stamp Duty indicated hereon has been or will be accounted for to the Commissioners of Inland Revenue pursuant to an agreement under Section 33 of the Finance Act 1970 as amended.

Above this line for Registrar's use

TRANSFER

Counter Location Stamp	Barcode or reference

RN

Above this line for completion by the depositing system-user only.

Name of Undertaking.

Consideration Money	Certificate(s) lodged with Registrar (To be completed by Registrar)

Description of Security.

Please complete form in type or in block capitals.

Amount of shares or other security in words	Figures

Name(s) of registered holder(s) should be given in full; the address should be given where there is only one holder.

If the transfer is not made by the registered holder(s) insert also the name(s) and capacity (e.g. executor(s)) of the person(s) making the transfer.

In the name(s) of	Designation (if any)
	Balance certificate(s) required

Please Sign Here →

I/We hereby transfer the above security out of the name(s) aforesaid into the name(s) of the system-member set out below and request that the necessary entries be made in the undertaking's own register of members.

Signature(s) of transferor(s)

1.

2.

3.

4.

A body corporate should execute this transfer under its common seal or otherwise in accordance with applicable statutory requirements.

Stamp of depositing system-user

Date

Full name(s) of the person(s) to whom the security is transferred.

Such person(s) must be a system-member.

Participant ID

Member Account ID

is delivering this transfer at the direction and on behalf of the depositing system-user whose stamp appears herein and does not in any manner or to any extent warrant or represent the validity, genuineness or correctness of the transfer instructions contained herein or the genuineness of the signature(s) of the transferor(s). The depositing system-user by delivering this transfer to   authorises   to deliver this transfer for registration and agrees to be deemed for all purposes to be the person(s) actually so delivering this transfer for registration.

Reference to the Registrar in this form means the registrar or registration agent of the undertaking, not the Registrar of Companies at Companies House.

Theft Act 1968

19. **False statements by company directors, etc**

(1) Where an officer of a body corporate or unincorporated association (or person purporting to act as such), with intent to deceive members or creditors of the body corporate or association about its affairs, publishes or concurs in publishing a written statement or account which to his knowledge is or may be misleading, false or deceptive in a material particular, he shall on conviction on indictment be liable to imprisonment for a term not exceeding seven years.

(2) For purposes of this section a person who has entered into a security for the benefit of a body corporate or association is to be treated as a creditor of it.

(3) Where the affairs of a body corporate or association are managed by its members, this section shall apply to any statement which a member publishes or concurs in publishing in connection with his functions of management as if he were an officer of the body corporate or association.

Register of People with Significant Control Regulations 2016

S.I. 2016/339

PART 1
GENERAL INTRODUCTORY PROVISIONS

1. **Citation and commencement**

    (1) These Regulations may be cited as the Register of People with Significant Control Regulations 2016.

    (2) These Regulations come into force on 6th April 2016 other than paragraph 6 of Schedule 5, which comes into force on 30th June 2016.

2. **Interpretation**

    In these Regulations—

    "the Act" means the Companies Act 2006;

    "the 2009 Regulations" means the Companies (Disclosure of Address) Regulations 2009;

    "the 2016 Regulations" means the Limited Liability Partnerships (Register of People with Significant Control) Regulations 2016;

    "credit institution" has the same meaning as in regulation 10(1) of the Money Laundering, Terrorist Financing and Transfer of Funds (Information on the Payer) Regulations 2017;

    "financial institution" has the same meaning as in regulation 10(2) of the Money Laundering, Terrorist Financing and Transfer of Funds (Information on the Payer) Regulations 2017;

    "former name" means a name by which an individual was formerly known for business purposes;

    "limited liability partnership" means a limited liability partnership incorporated under the Limited Liability Partnerships Act 2000;

    "name" means a person's forename and surname, except that in the case of—

    (a) a peer; or

    (b) an individual usually known by a title,

    the title may be stated instead of that person's forename and surname or in addition to either or both of them;

    "personal representative" means the executor or administrator for the time being of a deceased person;

    "relevant body" means—

    (a) a police force within the meaning of section 101(1) of the Police Act 1996;

    (b) the Police Service of Northern Ireland; and

    (c) the Police Service of Scotland;

    "section 243 decision" means a determination under the 2009 Regulations which is a section 243 decision within the meaning of those Regulations;

    "secured information" means the required particulars (other than the particular required by section 790K(1)(i) of the Act) of a registrable person in relation to a company;

    "specified public authorities" has the meaning given in regulation 22(1);

    "voting rights" means rights to vote at general meetings of the company or legal entity in question, including rights that arise only in certain circumstances, and in relation to a legal entity that does not have general meetings at which matters are decided by the exercise of voting rights, a reference to voting rights is to be read as a reference to rights in relation to the entity that are equivalent to those of a person entitled to exercise voting rights in a company;

"voting shares" means shares carrying voting rights; and

"withdrawal notice" has the meaning given in regulation 21.

PART 2
APPLICATION AND FEES

3.   Companies to which Part 21A of the Act does not apply

A company is specified for the purpose of section 790B(1)(b) of the Act if it has voting shares admitted to trading—

(a)   ...

(b)   on a market listed in Schedule 1.

4.   Legal entities which are subject to their own disclosure requirements

A legal entity (other than one to which section 790C(7)(c) of the Act applies) is specified for the purpose of section 790C(7)(d) of the Act if it has voting shares admitted to trading—

(a)   ...

(b)   on a market listed in Schedule 1.

5.   Modification for persons covered by section 790C(12) of the Act

(1)   The following modification is prescribed for the purpose of section 790C(12) of the Act.

(2)   Sections 790M(2) to (6A) and (10) of the Act are not to be read and do not have effect as if a person within section 790C(12) of the Act were an individual.

6.   Fee for a copy of a company's PSC register

(1)   The fee prescribed for the purpose of section 790O(2) of the Act is £12.

(2)   That fee applies to any single request for a copy of a company's PSC register, or any part of it, regardless of how many parts are required to be copied.

PART 3
NATURE OF CONTROL AND FOREIGN LIMITED PARTNERS

7.   Particulars required as to nature of control

(1)   The particulars required by sections 790K(1)(h), 790K(2)(e) and 790K(3)(f) of the Act (particulars as to nature of control over the company) are—

    (a)   where the person meets the first specified condition, the statement listed in Part 1 of Schedule 2 which is applicable to that person;

    (b)   where the person meets the second specified condition, the statement listed in Part 2 of Schedule 2 which is applicable to that person;

    (c)   where the person meets the third specified condition, the statement listed in Part 3 of Schedule 2;

    (d)   where the person meets the fourth specified condition and does not meet the first, second or third specified condition, the statement listed in Part 4 of Schedule 2;

    (e)   where the person meets the fifth specified condition in connection with a trust, every statement listed in Part 5 of Schedule 2 which is applicable to that person;

    (f)   where the person meets the fifth specified condition in connection with a firm, every statement listed in Part 6 of Schedule 2 which is applicable to that person.

(2)   Part 7 of Schedule 2 sets out a rule for the interpretation of Schedule 2.

8.   Characteristics of a foreign limited partner

(1)   The characteristics prescribed for the purposes of paragraph 25(5)(b) of Schedule 1A to the Act are that the individual—

    (a)   participates in a foreign limited partnership as a limited liability participant; or

    (b)   directly or indirectly, holds shares or a right in or in relation to a legal entity which participates in a foreign limited partnership as a limited liability participant.

(2)   In this regulation—

    (a)   a "foreign limited partnership" is an arrangement which—
        (i)   is established under the law of a country or territory outside the United Kingdom;
        (ii) consists of at least one person who has unlimited liability for the debts and obligations of the arrangement; and
        (iii) consists of at least one person who has no, or limited, liability for the debts and obligations of the arrangement for so long as that person does not take part in the management of the arrangement's business; and
    (b)   a "limited liability participant" is a person who—
        (i)   has no, or limited, liability for the debts and obligations of the foreign limited partnership for so long as that person does not take part in the management of the foreign limited partnership's business; and
        (ii) does not take part in the management of the foreign limited partnership's business.

PART 4
ADDITIONAL MATTERS

9.   **Additional matters to be noted in a PSC register**

(1)   The additional matters required to be noted in a company's PSC register under section 790M(7) of the Act are the matters required to be noted by regulations 10 to 17.

(2)   Where any additional matter noted in a company's PSC register in accordance with regulation 10, 11, 12 or 13 ceases to be true, the company must note in its PSC register—
    (a)   that the additional matter has ceased to be true; and
    (b)   the date on which the additional matter ceased to be true.

10.   **Additional matters where there is no registrable person or registrable relevant legal entity**

(1)   This regulation applies where a company knows or has reasonable cause to believe that there is no registrable person or registrable relevant legal entity in relation to the company.

(2)   The company must note in its PSC register that it knows or has reasonable cause to believe that there is no registrable person or registrable relevant legal entity in relation to the company.

11.   **Additional matters where there is an unidentified registrable person**

(1)   This regulation applies where a company—
    (a)   knows or has reasonable cause to believe that there is a registrable person in relation to the company; and
    (b)   has not been able to identify the registrable person.

(2)   The company must—
    (a)   note in its PSC register that it knows or has reasonable cause to believe that there is a registrable person in relation to the company but it has not identified the registrable person; and
    (b)   make a separate note in its PSC register in respect of each registrable person which the company has been unable to identify.

12.   **Additional matters where an identified registrable person's particulars are not confirmed**

(1)   This regulation applies where—
    (a)   a company has identified a registrable person in relation to the company; and
    (b)   all the required particulars of that person have not been confirmed for the purposes of section 790M of the Act.

(2)   The company must—
    (a)   note in its PSC register that it has identified a registrable person in relation to the company but all the required particulars of that person have not been confirmed; and
    (b)   make a separate note in its PSC register in respect of each registrable person which the company has been unable to identify.

13.   **Additional matters where a company's investigations are ongoing**

(1)   This regulation applies where a company—

    (a)   is not required to place a note in its PSC register by regulation 10, 11 or 12;

    (b)   has not entered, and is not required to enter, the required particulars of any registrable person or registrable relevant legal entity in its PSC register; and

    (c)   has not yet completed taking reasonable steps to find out if there is anyone who is a registrable person or a registrable relevant legal entity in relation to the company under section 790D of the Act.

(2)   The company must note in its PSC register that it has not yet completed taking reasonable steps to find out if there is anyone who is a registrable person or a registrable relevant legal entity in relation to the company.

14.   **Additional matters where there is a failure to comply with a notice given under section 790D of the Act**

(1)   This regulation applies where—

    (a)   a company has given a notice under section 790D of the Act; and

    (b)   the addressee of the notice has failed to comply with the notice within the time specified in it.

(2)   The company must—

    (a)   note in its PSC register that it has given a notice under section 790D of the Act which has not been complied with; and

    (b)   make a separate note in its PSC register in respect of each notice under section 790D which has not been complied with.

15.   **Additional matters where there is a failure to comply with a notice given under section 790E of the Act**

(1)   This regulation applies where—

    (a)   a company has given a notice under section 790E of the Act; and

    (b)   the addressee of the notice has failed to comply with the notice within the time specified in it.

(2)   The company must note in the entry in its PSC register for the addressee that the addressee has failed to comply with a notice given by the company under section 790E of the Act.

16.   **Additional matters where a notice given under section 790D or section 790E of the Act is complied with after the time specified in the notice**

(1)   This regulation applies where—

    (a)   a note has been placed in a company's register under regulation 14 or 15; and

    (b)   the addressee of the notice to which the note relates has complied with the notice after the time specified in the notice.

(2)   The company must note in its PSC register—

    (a)   that the notice has been complied with after the time specified in the notice; and

    (b)   the date on which the notice was complied with.

17.   **Additional matters where a company has issued a restrictions notice**

(1)   This regulation applies where a company has issued a restrictions notice under paragraph 1 of Schedule 1B to the Act.

(2)   The company must—

    (a)   note in its PSC register that it has issued a restrictions notice under paragraph 1 of Schedule 1B to the Act; and

    (b)   make a separate note in its PSC register in respect of each registrable person which the company has been unable to identify.

(3)   Where the company withdraws the restrictions notice under paragraph 11 of Schedule 1B to the Act, the company must note in its PSC register—

    (a)   that it has withdrawn the restrictions notice by giving a withdrawal notice; and

(b)   the date specified in the withdrawal notice as the date on which the withdrawal notice was given.

(4)   Where a court makes an order under paragraph 8 of Schedule 1B to the Act directing that a relevant interest in the company cease to be subject to restrictions, the company must note in its PSC register—

(a)   that the court has made an order under paragraph 8 of Schedule 1B to the Act directing that a relevant interest in the company cease to be subject to restrictions; and

(b)   the date on which that order takes effect.

PART 5
WARNING AND RESTRICTIONS NOTICES

18.   Content of a warning notice

A warning notice given under paragraph 1 of Schedule 1B to the Act must—

(a)   specify the date on which the warning notice is given;

(b)   be accompanied by a copy of the notice given under section 790D or 790E of the Act to which the warning notice relates;

(c)   identify the addressee's relevant interest in the company by reference to the shares or right in question;

(d)   state that the company will consider reasons provided to it as to why the addressee failed to comply with the notice given under section 790D or 790E of the Act;

(e)   explain the effect of a restrictions notice; and

(f)   state that, by virtue of a restrictions notice, certain acts or failures to act may constitute an offence.

19.   Content of a restrictions notice

A restrictions notice issued under paragraph 1 of Schedule 1B to the Act must—

(a)   specify the date on which the restrictions notice is issued;

(b)   be accompanied by a copy of the warning notice which preceded the restrictions notice;

(c)   identify the addressee's relevant interest in the company by reference to the shares or right in question;

(d)   explain the effect of the restrictions notice;

(e)   state that, by virtue of the restrictions notice, certain acts or failures to act may constitute an offence; and

(f)   state that an aggrieved person may apply to the court for an order directing that the relevant interest cease to be subject to restrictions.

20.   Failure to comply with a section 790D or 790E notice: valid reason

A company must take into account any incapacity of the addressee of a notice given under section 790D or 790E of the Act in deciding what counts as a "valid reason" sufficient to justify the addressee's failure to comply with the notice.

21.   Withdrawal of a restrictions notice

Where a company is required to withdraw a restrictions notice under paragraph 11 of Schedule 1B to the Act by notice (a "withdrawal notice"), the withdrawal notice must—

(a)   be given before the end of the period of 14 days beginning with the day on which the company became required to withdraw the restrictions notice under that paragraph;

(b)   specify the date on which the withdrawal notice is given;

(c)   identify the addressee's relevant interest in the company by reference to the shares or right in question; and

(d)   state that the relevant interest is no longer subject to restrictions.

PARTS 6–8 OMITTED

SCHEDULE 1
LIST OF MARKETS

Regulations 3 and 4

In Israel—
 Tel Aviv Stock Exchange
In Japan—
 Fukuoka Stock Exchange
 Nagoya Stock Exchange
 Osaka Securities Exchange
 Sapporo Securities Exchange
 Tokyo Stock Exchange
In Switzerland—
 BX Berne Exchange
 SIX Swiss Exchange
In the United States of America—
 BATS Exchange, Inc
 BATS Y-Exchange, Inc
 BOX Options Exchange LLC
 C2 Options Exchange, Incorporated
 Chicago Board Options Exchange, Incorporated
 Chicago Stock Exchange, Inc
 EDGA Exchange, Inc
 EDGX Exchange, Inc
 International Securities Exchange, LLC
 ISE Gemini LLC
 Miami International Securities Exchange LLC
 NASDAQ OMX BX, Inc
 NASDAQ OMX PHLX LLC
 The NASDAQ Stock Market LLC
 National Stock Exchange, Inc
 New York Stock Exchange LLC
 NYSE Arca, Inc
 NYSE MKT LLC

SCHEDULE 2
PARTICULARS REQUIRED AS TO NATURE OF CONTROL

Regulation 7

PART 1
FIRST CONDITION

1. A statement that the person holds, directly or indirectly, more than 25% but not more than 50% of the shares in the company.
2. A statement that the person holds, directly or indirectly, more than 50% but less than 75% of the shares in the company.
3. A statement that the person holds, directly or indirectly, 75% or more of the shares in the company.

…

PART 2
SECOND CONDITION

4.   A statement that the person holds, directly or indirectly, more than 25% but not more than 50% of the voting rights in the company.

5.   A statement that the person holds, directly or indirectly, more than 50% but less than 75% of the voting rights in the company.

6.   A statement that the person holds, directly or indirectly, 75% or more of the voting rights in the company.

PART 3
THIRD CONDITION

7.   A statement that the person holds the right, directly or indirectly, to appoint or remove a majority of the board of directors of the company.

PART 4
FOURTH CONDITION

8.   A statement that the person has the right to exercise, or actually exercises, significant influence or control over the company.

PART 5
FIFTH CONDITION AND TRUSTS

9.   A statement that—
   (a)   the person has the right to exercise, or actually exercises, significant influence or control over the activities of a trust; and
   (b)   the trustees of that trust (in their capacity as such) hold, directly or indirectly, more than 25% but not more than 50% of the shares in the company.

10.   A statement that—
   (a)   the person has the right to exercise, or actually exercises, significant influence or control over the activities of a trust; and
   (b)   the trustees of that trust (in their capacity as such) hold, directly or indirectly, more than 50% but less than 75% of the shares in the company.

11.   A statement that—
   (a)   the person has the right to exercise, or actually exercises, significant influence or control over the activities of a trust; and
   (b)   the trustees of that trust (in their capacity as such) hold, directly or indirectly, 75% or more of the shares in the company.

12.   A statement that—
   (a)   the person has the right to exercise, or actually exercises, significant influence or control over the activities of a trust; and
   (b)   the trustees of that trust (in their capacity as such) hold, directly or indirectly, more than 25% but not more than 50% of the voting rights in the company.

13.   A statement that—
   (a)   the person has the right to exercise, or actually exercises, significant influence or control over the activities of a trust; and
   (b)   the trustees of that trust (in their capacity as such) hold, directly or indirectly, more than 50% but less than 75% of the voting rights in the company.

14.   A statement that—
   (a)   the person has the right to exercise, or actually exercises, significant influence or control over the activities of a trust; and

    (b)   the trustees of that trust (in their capacity as such) hold, directly or indirectly, 75% or more of the voting rights in the company.

15.   A statement that—
    (a)   the person has the right to exercise, or actually exercises, significant influence or control over the activities of a trust; and
    (b)   the trustees of that trust (in their capacity as such) hold the right, directly or indirectly, to appoint or remove a majority of the board of directors of the company.

16.   A statement that—
    (a)   the person has the right to exercise, or actually exercises, significant influence or control over the activities of a trust; and
    (b)   the trustees of that trust (in their capacity as such) have the right to exercise, or actually exercise, significant influence or control over the company.

PART 6
FIFTH CONDITION AND FIRMS

17.   A statement that—
    (a)   the person has the right to exercise, or actually exercises, significant influence or control over the activities of a firm that, under the law by which it is governed, is not a legal person; and
    (b)   the members of that firm (in their capacity as such) hold, directly or indirectly, more than 25% but not more than 50% of the shares in the company.

18.   A statement that—
    (a)   the person has the right to exercise, or actually exercises, significant influence or control over the activities of a firm that, under the law by which it is governed, is not a legal person; and
    (b)   the members of that firm (in their capacity as such) hold, directly or indirectly, more than 50% but less than 75% of the shares in the company.

19.   A statement that—
    (a)   the person has the right to exercise, or actually exercises, significant influence or control over the activities of a firm that, under the law by which it is governed, is not a legal person; and
    (b)   the members of that firm (in their capacity as such) hold, directly or indirectly, 75% or more of the shares in the company.

20.   A statement that—
    (a)   the person has the right to exercise, or actually exercises, significant influence or control over the activities of a firm that, under the law by which it is governed, is not a legal person; and
    (b)   the members of that firm (in their capacity as such) hold, directly or indirectly, more than 25% but not more than 50% of the voting rights in the company.

21.   A statement that—
    (a)   the person has the right to exercise, or actually exercises, significant influence or control over the activities of a firm that, under the law by which it is governed, is not a legal person; and
    (b)   the members of that firm (in their capacity as such) hold, directly or indirectly, more than 50% but less than 75% of the voting rights in the company.

22.   A statement that—
    (a)   the person has the right to exercise, or actually exercises, significant influence or control over the activities of a firm that, under the law by which it is governed, is not a legal person; and
    (b)   the members of that firm (in their capacity as such) hold, directly or indirectly, 75% or more of the voting rights in the company.

23.   A statement that—

(a)   the person has the right to exercise, or actually exercises, significant influence or control over the activities of a firm that, under the law by which it is governed, is not a legal person; and

(b)   the members of that firm (in their capacity as such) hold the right, directly or indirectly, to appoint or remove a majority of the board of directors of the company.

24.   A statement that—

(a)   the person has the right to exercise, or actually exercises, significant influence or control over the activities of a firm that, under the law by which it is governed, is not a legal person; and

(b)   the members of that firm (in their capacity as such) have the right to exercise, or actually exercise, significant influence or control over the company.

PART 7
INTERPRETATION OF SCHEDULE 2

25.   In relation to a company that does not have a share capital, a reference to holding a particular percentage of shares in a company is to holding a right or rights to share in that percentage of capital or, as the case may be, profits of that company.

SCHEDULES 3–5 OMITTED

Companies (Tables A to F) Regulations 1985

S.I. 1985/805

1. These Regulations may be cited as the Companies (Tables A to F) Regulations 1985 and shall come into operation on 1st July 1985.
2. The regulations in Table A and the forms in Tables B, C, D, E and F in the Schedule to these Regulations shall be the regulations and forms of memorandum and articles of association for the purposes of sections 3 and 8 of the Companies Act 1985.
3. ...

SCHEDULE

Regulation 2

TABLE A

REGULATIONS FOR MANAGEMENT OF A COMPANY LIMITED BY SHARES

INTERPRETATION

1. In these regulations—
    "the Act" means the Companies Act 1985 including any statutory modification or re-enactment thereof for the time being in force.
    "the articles" means the articles of the company.
    "clear days" in relation to the period of a notice means that period excluding the day when the notice is given or deemed to be given and the day for which it is given or on which it is to take effect.
    "communication" means the same as in the Electronic Communications Act 2000.
    "electronic communication" means the same as in the Electronic Communications Act 2000.
    "executed" includes any mode of execution.
    "office" means the registered office of the company.
    "the holder" in relation to shares means the member whose name is entered in the register of members as the holder of the shares.
    "the seal" means the common seal of the company.
    "secretary" means the secretary of the company or any other person appointed to perform the duties of the secretary of the company, including a joint, assistant or deputy secretary.
    "the United Kingdom" means Great Britain and Northern Ireland.
    Unless the context otherwise requires, words or expressions contained in these regulations bear the same meaning as in the Act but excluding any statutory modification thereof not in force when these regulations become binding on the company.

SHARE CAPITAL

2. Subject to the provisions of the Act and without prejudice to any rights attached to any existing shares, any share may be issued with such rights or restrictions as the company may by ordinary resolution determine.
3. Subject to the provisions of the Act, shares may be issued which are to be redeemed or are to be liable to be redeemed at the option of the company or the holder on such terms and in such manner as may be provided by the articles.
4. The company may exercise the powers of paying commissions conferred by the Act. Subject to the provisions of the Act, any such commission may be satisfied by the payment of cash or by the allotment of fully or partly paid shares or partly in one way and partly in the other.
5. Except as required by law, no person shall be recognised by the company as holding any share upon any trust and (except as otherwise provided by the articles or by law) the company shall not

be bound by or recognise any interest in any share except an absolute right to the entirety thereof in the holder.

SHARE CERTIFICATES

6. Every member, upon becoming the holder of any shares, shall be entitled without payment to one certificate for all the shares of each class held by him (and, upon transferring a part of his holding of shares of any class, to a certificate for the balance of such holding) or several certificates each for one or more of his shares of any class, to a certificate for the balance of such holding) or several certificates each for one or more of his shares upon payment for every certificate after the first of such reasonable sum as the directors may determine. Every certificate shall be sealed with the seal and shall specify the number, class and distinguishing numbers (if any) of the shares to which it relates and the amount or respective amounts paid up thereon. The company shall not be bound to issue more than one certificate for shares held jointly by several persons and delivery of a certificate to one joint holder shall be a sufficient delivery to all of them.

7. If a share certificate is defaced, worn-out, lost or destroyed, it may be renewed on such terms (if any) as to evidence and indemnity and payment of the expenses reasonably incurred by the company in investigating evidence as the directors may determine but otherwise free of charge, and (in the case of defacement or wearing-out) on delivery up of the old certificate.

LIEN

8. The company shall have a first and paramount lien on every share (not being a fully paid share) for all moneys (whether presently payable or not) payable at a fixed time or called in respect of that share. The directors may at any time declare any share to be wholly or in part exempt from the provisions of this regulation. The company's lien on a share shall extend to any amount payable in respect of it.

9. The company may sell in such manner as the directors determine any shares on which the company has a lien if a sum in respect of which the lien exists is presently payable and is not paid within fourteen clear days after notice has been given to the holder of the share or to the person entitled to it in consequence of the death or bankruptcy of the holder, demanding payment and stating that if the notice is not complied with the shares may be sold.

10. To give effect to a sale the directors may authorise some person to execute an instrument of transfer of the shares sold to, or in accordance with the directions of, the purchaser. The title of the transferee to the shares shall not be affected by any irregularity in or invalidity of the proceedings in reference to the sale.

11. The net proceeds of the sale, after payment of the costs, shall be applied in payment of so much of the sum for which the lien exists as is presently payable, and any residue shall (upon surrender to the company for cancellation of the certificate for the shares sold and subject to a like lien for any moneys not presently payable as existed upon the shares before the sale) be paid to the person entitled to the shares at the date of the sale.

CALLS ON SHARES AND FORFEITURE

12. Subject to the terms of allotment, the directors may make calls upon the members in respect of any moneys unpaid on their shares (whether in respect of nominal value or premium) and each member shall (subject to receiving at least fourteen clear days' notice specifying when and where payment is to be made) pay to the company as required by the notice the amount called on his shares. A call may be required to be paid by instalments. A call may, before receipt by the company of any sum due thereunder, be revoked in whole or part and payment of a call may be postponed in whole or part. A person upon whom a call is made shall remain liable for calls made upon him notwithstanding the subsequent transfer of the shares in respect whereof the call was made.

13. A call shall be deemed to have been made at the time when the resolution of the directors authorising the call was passed.

14. The joint holders of a share shall be jointly and severally liable to pay all calls in respect thereof.

15. If a call remains unpaid after it has become due and payable the person from whom it is due and payable shall pay interest on the amount unpaid from the day it became due and payable until it is paid at the rate fixed by the terms of allotment of the share or in the notice of the call or, if no rate is fixed, at the appropriate rate (as defined by the Act) but the directors may waive payment of the interest wholly or in part.

16. An amount payable in respect of a share on allotment or at any fixed date, whether in respect of nominal value or premium or as an instalment of a call, shall be deemed to be a call and if it is not paid the provisions of the articles shall apply as if that amount had become due and payable by virtue of a call.

17. Subject to the terms of allotment, the directors may make arrangements on the issue of shares for a difference between the holders in the amounts and times of payment of calls on their shares.

18. If a call remains unpaid after it has become due and payable the directors may give to the person from whom it is due not less than fourteen clear days' notice requiring payment of the amount unpaid together with any interest which may have accrued. The notice shall name the place where payment is to be made and shall state that if the notice is not complied with the shares in respect of which the call was made will be liable to be forfeited.

19. If the notice is not complied with any share in respect of which it was given may, before the payment required by the notice has been made, be forfeited by a resolution of the directors and the forfeiture shall include all dividends or other moneys payable in respect of the forfeited shares and not paid before the forfeiture.

20. Subject to the provisions of the Act, a forfeited share may be sold, re-alloted or otherwise disposed of on such terms and in such manner as the directors determine either to the person who was before the forfeiture the holder or to any other person and at any time before sale, re-allotment or other disposition, the forfeiture may be cancelled on such terms as the directors think fit. Where for the purposes of its disposal a forfeited share is to be transferred to any person the directors may authorise some person to execute an instrument of transfer of the share to that person.

21. A person any of whose shares have been forfeited shall cease to be a member in respect of them and shall surrender to the company for cancellation the certificate for the shares forfeited but shall remain liable to the company for all moneys which at the date of forfeiture were presently payable by him to the company in respect of those shares with interest at the rate at which interest was payable on those moneys before the forfeiture or, if no interest was so payable, at the appropriate rate (as defined in the Act) from the date of forfeiture until payment but the directors may waive payment wholly or in part or enforce payment without any allowance for the value of the shares at the time of forfeiture or for any consideration received on their disposal.

22. A statutory declaration by a director or the secretary that a share has been forfeited on a specified date shall be conclusive evidence of the facts stated in it as against all persons claiming to be entitled to the share and the declaration shall (subject to the execution of an instrument of transfer if necessary) constitute a good title to the share and the person to whom the share is disposed of shall not be bound to see to the application of the consideration, if any, nor shall his title to the share be affected by any irregularity in or invalidity of the proceedings in reference to the forfeiture or disposal of the share.

TRANSFER OF SHARES

23. The instrument of transfer of a share may be in any usual form or in any other form which the directors may approve and shall be executed by or on behalf of the transferor and, unless the share is fully paid, by or on behalf of the transferee.

24.   The directors may refuse to register the transfer of a share which is not fully paid to a person of whom they do not approve and they may refuse to register the transfer of a share on which the company has a lien. They may also refuse to register a transfer unless—

(a)   it is lodged at the office or at such other place as the directors may appoint and is accompanied by the certificate for the shares to which it relates and such other evidence as the directors may reasonably require to show the right of the transferor to make the transfer;

(b)   it is in respect of only one class of shares; and

(c)   it is in favour of not more than four transferees.

25.   If the directors refuse to register a transfer of a share, they shall within two months after the date on which the transfer was lodged with the company send to the transferee notice of the refusal.

26.   The registration of transfers of shares or of transfers of any class of shares may be suspended at such times and for such periods (not exceeding thirty days in any year) as the directors may determine.

27.   No fee shall be charged for the registration of any instrument of transfer or other document relating to or affecting the title to any share.

28.   The company shall be entitled to retain any instrument of transfer which is registered, but any instrument of transfer which the directors refuse to register shall be returned to the person lodging it when notice of the refusal is given.

TRANSMISSION OF SHARES

29.   If a member dies the survivor or survivors where he was a joint holder, and his personal representatives where he was a sole holder or the only survivor of joint holders, shall be the only persons recognised by the company as having any title to his interest; but nothing herein contained shall release the estate of a deceased member from any liability in respect of any share which had been jointly held by him.

30.   A person becoming entitled to a share in consequence of the death or bankruptcy of a member may, upon such evidence being produced as the directors may properly require, elect either to become the holder of the share or to have some person nominated by him registered as the transferee. If he elects to become the holder he shall give notice to the company to that effect. If he elects to have another person registered he shall execute an instrument of transfer of the share to that person. All the articles relating to the transfer of shares shall apply to the notice or instrument of transfer as if it were an instrument of transfer executed by the member and the death or bankruptcy of the member had not occurred.

31.   A person becoming entitled to a share in consequence of the death or bankruptcy of a member shall have the rights to which he would be entitled if he were the holder of the share, except that he shall not, before being registered as the holder of the share, be entitled in respect of it to attend or vote at any meeting of the company or at any separate meeting of the holders of any class of shares in the company.

ALTERATION OF SHARE CAPITAL

32.   The company may by ordinary resolution—

(a)   increase its share capital by new shares of such amount as the resolution prescribes;

(b)   consolidate and divide all or any of its share capital into shares of larger amount than its existing shares;

(c)   subject to the provisions of the Act, sub-divide its shares, or any of them, into shares of smaller amount and the resolution may determine that, as between the shares resulting from the sub-division, any of them may have any preference or advantage as compared with the others; and

(d)   cancel shares which, at the date of the passing of the resolution, have not been taken or agreed to be taken by any person and diminish the amount of its share capital by the amount of the shares so cancelled.

33. Whenever as a result of a consolidation of shares any members would become entitled to fractions of a share, the directors may, on behalf of those members, sell the shares representing the fractions for the best price reasonably obtainable to any person (including, subject to the provisions of the Act, the company) and distribute the net proceeds of sale in due proportion among those members, and the directors may authorise some person to execute an instrument of transfer of the shares to, or in accordance with the directions of, the purchaser. The transferee shall not be bound to see to the application of the purchase money nor shall his title to the shares be affected by any irregularity in or invalidity of the proceedings in reference to the sale.

34. Subject to the provisions of the Act, the company may by special resolution reduce its share capital, any capital redemption reserve and any share premium account in any way.

PURCHASE OF OWN SHARES

35. Subject to the provisions of the Act, the company may purchase its own shares (including any redeemable shares) and, if it is a private company, make a payment in respect of the redemption or purchase of its own shares otherwise than out of distributable profits of the company or the proceeds of a fresh issue of shares.

GENERAL MEETINGS

36. All general meetings other than annual general meetings shall be called extraordinary general meetings.

37. The directors may call general meetings and, on the requisition of members pursuant to the provisions of the Act, shall forthwith proceed to convene an extraordinary general meeting for a date not later than eight weeks after receipt of the requisition. If there are not within the United Kingdom sufficient directors to call a general meeting, any director or any member of the company may call a general meeting.

NOTICE OF GENERAL MEETINGS

38. An annual general meeting and an extraordinary general meeting called for the passing of a special resolution or a resolution appointing a person as a director shall be called by at least twenty-one clear days' notice. All other extraordinary general meetings shall be called by at least fourteen clear days' notice but a general meeting may be called by shorter notice if is so agreed—
    (a) in the case of an annual general meeting, by all the members entitled to attend and vote thereat; and
    (b) in the case of any other meeting by a majority in number of the members having a right to attend and vote being a majority together holding not less than ninety-five per cent in nominal value of the shares giving that right.
    The notice shall specify the time and place of the meeting and the general nature of the business to be transacted and, in the case of an annual general meeting, shall specify the meeting as such.
    Subject to the provisions of the articles and to any restrictions imposed on any shares, the notice shall be given to all the members, to all persons entitled to a share in consequence of the death or bankruptcy of a member and to the directors and auditors.

39. The accidental omission to give notice of a meeting to, or the non-receipt of notice of a meeting by, any person entitled to receive notice shall not invalidate the proceedings at that meeting.

PROCEEDINGS AT GENERAL MEETINGS

40. No business shall be transacted at any meeting unless a quorum is present. Two persons entitled to vote upon the business to be transacted, each being a member or a proxy for a member or a duly authorised representative of a corporation, shall be a quorum.

41. If such a quorum is not present within half an hour from the time appointed for the meeting, or if during a meeting such a quorum ceases to be present, the meeting shall stand adjourned to the

same day in the next week at the same time and place or to such time and place as the directors may determine.

42.   The chairman, if any, of the board of directors or in his absence some other director nominated by the directors shall preside as chairman of the meeting, but if neither the chairman nor such other director (if any) be present within fifteen minutes after the time appointed for holding the meeting and willing to act, the directors present shall elect one of their number to be chairman and, if there is only one director present and willing to act, he shall be chairman.

43.   If no director is willing to act as chairman, or if no director is present within fifteen minutes after the time appointed for holding the meeting, the members present and entitled to vote shall choose one of their number to be chairman.

44.   A director shall, notwithstanding that he is not a member, be entitled to attend and speak at any general meeting and at any separate meeting of the holders of any class of shares in the company.

45.   The chairman may, with the consent of a meeting at which a quorum is present (and shall if so directed by the meeting), adjourn the meeting from time to time and from place to place, but no business shall be transacted at an adjourned meeting other than business which might properly have been transacted at the meeting had the adjournment not taken place. When a meeting is adjourned for fourteen days or more, at least seven clear days' notice shall be given specifying the time and place of the adjourned meeting and the general nature of the business to be transacted. Otherwise it shall not be necessary to give any such notice.

46.   A resolution put to the vote of a meeting shall be decided on a show of hands unless before, or on the declaration of the result of, the show of hands a poll is duly demanded. Subject to the provisions of the Act, a poll may be demanded—

(a)   by the chairman; or

(b)   by at least two members having the right to vote at the meeting; or

(c)   by a member or members representing not less than one-tenth of the total voting rights of all the members having the right to vote at the meeting; or

(d)   by a member or members holding shares conferring a right to vote at the meeting being shares on which an aggregate sum has been paid up equal to not less than one-tenth of the total sum paid up on all the shares conferring that right;

and a demand by a person as proxy for a member shall be the same as a demand by the member.

47.   Unless a poll is duly demanded a declaration by the chairman that a resolution has been carried or carried unanimously, or by a particular majority, or lost, or not carried by a particular majority and an entry to that effect in the minutes of the meeting shall be conclusive evidence of the fact without proof of the number or proportion of the votes recorded in favour of or against the resolution.

48.   The demand for a poll may, before the poll is taken, be withdrawn but only with the consent of the chairman and a demand so withdrawn shall not be taken to have invalidated the result of a show of hands declared before the demand was made.

49.   A poll shall be taken as the chairman directs and he may appoint scrutineers (who need not be members) and fix a time and place for declaring the result of the poll. The result of the poll shall be deemed to be the resolution of the meeting at which the poll was demanded.

50.   In the case of an equality of votes, whether on a show of hands or on a poll, the chairman shall be entitled to a casting vote in addition to any other vote he may have.

51.   A poll demanded on the election of a chairman or on a question of adjournment shall be taken forthwith. A poll demanded on any other question shall be taken either forthwith or at such time and place as the chairman directs not being more than thirty days after the poll is demanded. The demand for a poll shall not prevent the continuance of a meeting for the transaction of any business other than the question on which the poll was demanded. If a poll is demanded before the declaration of the result of a show of hands and the demand is duly withdrawn, the meeting shall continue as if the demand had not been made.

52.   No notice need be given of a poll not taken forthwith if the time and place at which it is to be taken are announced at the meeting at which it is demanded. In any other case at least seven clear days' notice shall be given specifying the time and place at which the poll is to be taken.

53.   A resolution in writing executed by or on behalf of each member who would have been entitled to vote upon it if it had been proposed at a general meeting at which he was present shall be as effectual as if it had been passed at a general meeting duly convened and held and may consist of several instruments in the like form each executed by or on behalf of one or more members.

VOTES OF MEMBERS

54.   Subject to any rights or restrictions attached to any shares, on a show of hands every member who (being an individual) is present in person or (being a corporation) is present by a duly authorised representative, not being himself a member entitled to vote, shall have one vote and on a poll every member shall have one vote for every share of which he is the holder.

55.   In the case of joint holders the vote of the senior who tenders a vote, whether in person or by proxy, shall be accepted to the exclusion of the votes of the other joint holders; and seniority shall be determined by the order in which the names of the holders stand in the register of members.

56.   A member in respect of whom an order has been made by any court having jurisdiction (whether in the United Kingdom or elsewhere) in matters concerning mental disorder may vote, whether on a show of hands or on a poll, by his receiver, curator bonis or other person authorised in that behalf appointed by that court, and any such receiver, curator bonis or other person may, on a poll, vote by proxy. Evidence to the satisfaction of the directors of the authority of the person claiming to exercise the right to vote shall be deposited at the office, or at such other place as is specified in accordance with the articles for the deposit of instruments of proxy, not less than 48 hours before the time appointed for holding the meeting or adjourned meeting at which the right to vote is to be exercised and in default the right to vote shall not be exercisable.

57.   No member shall vote at any general meeting or at any separate meeting of the holders of any class of shares in the company, either in person or by proxy, in respect of any share held by him unless all moneys presently payable by him in respect of that share have been paid.

58.   No objection shall be raised to the qualification of any voter except at the meeting or adjourned meeting at which the vote objected to is tendered, and every vote not disallowed at the meeting shall be valid. Any objection made in due time shall be referred to the chairman whose decision shall be final and conclusive.

59.   On a poll votes may be given either personally or by proxy. A member may appoint more than one proxy to attend on the same occasion.

60.   The appointment of a proxy shall be ..., executed by or on behalf of the appointor and shall be in the following form (or in a form as near thereto as circumstances allow or in any other form which is usual or which the directors may approve)—

" .. .. PLC/Limited .. .. I/We, ..., of .. .., being a member/members of the above-named company, hereby appoint .. .. of .. .., or failing him, ... of .. .., as my/our proxy to vote in my/our names and on my/our behalf at the annual/ extraordinary general meeting of the company to be held on .. .. 19 .. .., and at any adjournment thereof.

Signed on .. .. 19 .. .."

61.   Where it is desired to afford members an opportunity of instructing the proxy how he shall act the appointment of a proxy shall be in the following form (or in a form as near thereto as circumstances allow or in any other form which is usual or which the directors may approve)—

" .. .. PLC/Limited .. .. I/We, ..., of .. .., being a member/members of the above-named company, hereby appoint .. .. of .. .., or failing him .. .. of .. .., as my/our proxy to vote in my/our names and on my/our behalf at the annual/ extraordinary general meeting of the company, to be held on .. .. 19 , ..., and at any adjournment thereof.

This form is to be used in respect of the resolutions mentioned below as follows:

Resolution No. 1 *for *against

Resolution No. 2 *for *against.

*Strike out whichever is not desired.

Unless otherwise instructed, the proxy may vote as he thinks fit or abstain from voting.

Signed this .. .. day of .. .. 19 .. .."

62. The appointment of a proxy and any authority under which it is executed or a copy of such authority certified notarially or in some other way approved by the directors may—

 (a) in the case of an instrument in writing be deposited at the office or at such other place within the United kingdom as is specified in the notice convening the meeting or in any instrument of proxy sent out by the company in relation to the meeting not less than 48 hours before the time for holding the meeting or adjourned meeting at which the person named in the instrument proposes to vote; or

 (aa) in the case of an appointment contained in an electronic communication, where an address has been specified for the purpose of receiving electronic communications—

  (i) in the notice convening the meeting, or

  (ii) in any instrument of proxy sent out by the company in relation to the meeting, or

  (iii) in any invitation contained in an electronic communication to appoint a proxy issued by the company in relation to the meeting,

  be received at such address not less than 48 hours before the time for holding the meeting or adjourned meeting at which the person named in the appointment proposes to vote;

 (b) in the case of a poll taken more than 48 hours after it is demanded, be deposited or received as aforesaid after the poll has been demanded and not less than 24 hours before the time appointed for the taking of the poll; or

 (c) where the poll is not taken forthwith but is taken not more than 48 hours after it was demanded, be delivered at the meeting at which the poll was demanded to the chairman or to the secretary or to any director;

and an appointment of proxy which is not deposited, delivered or received in a manner so permitted shall be invalid.

In this regulation and the next, "address", in relation to electronic communications, includes any number or address used for the purposes of such communications.

63. A vote given or poll demanded by proxy or by the duly authorised representative of a corporation shall be valid notwithstanding the previous determination of the authority of the person voting or demanding a poll unless notice of the determination was received by the company at the office or at such other place at which the instrument of proxy was duly deposited or, where the appointment of the proxy was contained in an electronic communication, at the address at which such appointment was duly received before the commencement of the meeting or adjourned meeting at which the vote is given or the poll demanded or (in the case of a poll taken otherwise than on the same day as the meeting or adjourned meeting) the time appointed for taking the poll.

NUMBER OF DIRECTORS

64. Unless otherwise determined by ordinary resolution, the number of directors (other than alternate directors) shall not be subject to any maximum but shall be not less than two.

ALTERNATE DIRECTORS

65. Any director (other than an alternate director) may appoint any other director, or any other person approved by resolution of the directors and willing to act, to be an alternate director and may remove from office an alternate director so appointed by him.

66. An alternate director shall be entitled to receive notice of all meetings of directors and of all meetings of committees of directors of which his appointor is a member, to attend and vote at any such meeting at which the director appointing him is not personally present and generally to perform all the functions of his appointor as a director in his absence but shall not be entitled to receive any remuneration from the company for his services as an alternate director. But it shall

not be necessary to give notice of such a meeting to an alternate director who is absent from the United Kingdom.

67. An alternate director shall cease to be an alternate director if his appointor ceases to be a director; but, if a director retires by rotation or otherwise but is reappointed or deemed to have been reappointed at the meeting at which he retires, any appointment of an alternate director made by him which was in force immediately prior to his retirement shall continue after his reappointment.

68. Any appointment or removal of an alternate director shall be by notice to the company signed by the director making or revoking the appointment or in any other manner approved by the directors.

69. Save as otherwise provided in the articles, an alternate director shall be deemed for all purposes to be a director and shall alone be responsible for his own acts and defaults and he shall not be deemed to be the agent of the director appointing him.

POWERS OF DIRECTORS

70. Subject to the provisions of the Act, the memorandum and the articles and to any directions given by special resolution, the business of the company shall be managed by the directors who may exercise all the powers of the company. No alteration of the memorandum or articles and no such direction shall invalidate any prior act of the directors which would have been valid if that alteration had not been made or that direction had not been given. The powers given by this regulation shall not be limited by any special power given to the directors by the articles and a meeting of directors at which a quorum is present may exercise all powers exercisable by the directors.

71. The directors may, by power of attorney or otherwise, appoint any person to be the agent of the company for such purposes and on such conditions as they determine, including authority for the agent to delegate all or any of his powers.

DELEGATION OF DIRECTORS' POWERS

72. The directors may delegate any of their powers to any committee consisting of one or more directors. They may also delegate to any managing director or any director holding any other executive office such of their powers as they consider desirable to be exercised by him. Any such delegation may be made subject to any conditions the directors may impose, and either collaterally with or to the exclusion of their own powers and may be revoked or altered. Subject to any such conditions, the proceedings of a committee with two or more members shall be governed by the articles regulating the proceedings of directors so far as they are capable of applying.

APPOINTMENT AND RETIREMENT OF DIRECTORS

73. At the first annual general meeting all the directors shall retire from office, and at every subsequent annual general meeting one-third of the directors who are subject to retirement by rotation or, if their number is not three or a multiple of three, the number nearest to one-third shall retire from office; but, if there is only one director who is subject to retirement by rotation, he shall retire.

74. Subject to the provisions of the Act, the directors to retire by rotation shall be those who have been longest in office since their last appointment or reappointment, but as between persons who became or were last reappointed directors on the same day those to retire shall (unless they otherwise agree among themselves) be determined by lot.

75. If the company, at the meeting at which a director retires by rotation, does not fill the vacancy the retiring director shall, if willing to act, be deemed to have been reappointed unless at the meeting it is resolved not to fill the vacancy or unless a resolution for the reappointment of the director is put to the meeting and lost.

76.   No person other than a director retiring by rotation shall be appointed or reappointed a director at any general meeting unless—

    (a)   he is recommended by the directors; or

    (b)   not less than fourteen nor more than thirty-five clear days before the date appointed for the meeting, notice executed by a member qualified to vote at the meeting has been given to the company of the intention to propose that person for appointment or reappointment stating the particulars which would, if he were so appointed or reappointed, be required to be included in the company's register of directors together with notice executed by that person of his willingness to be appointed or reappointed.

77.   Not less than seven nor more than twenty-eight clear days before the date appointed for holding a general meeting notice shall be given to all who are entitled to receive notice of the meeting of any person (other than a director retiring by rotation at the meeting) who is recommended by the directors for appointment or reappointment as a director at the meeting or in respect of whom notice has been duly given to the company of the intention to propose him at the meeting for appointment or reappointment as a director. The notice shall give the particulars of that person which would, if he were so appointed or reappointed, be required to be included in the company's register of directors.

78.   Subject as aforesaid, the company may by ordinary resolution appoint a person who is willing to act to be a director either to fill a vacancy or as an additional director and may also determine the rotation in which any additional directors are to retire.

79.   The directors may appoint a person who is willing to act to be a director, either to fill a vacancy or as an additional director, provided that the appointment does not cause the number of directors to exceed any number fixed by or in accordance with the articles as the maximum number of directors. A director so appointed shall hold office only until the next following annual general meeting and shall not be taken into account in determining the directors who are to retire by rotation at the meeting. If not reappointed at such annual general meeting, he shall vacate office at the conclusion thereof.

80.   Subject as aforesaid, a director who retires at an annual general meeting may, if willing to act, be reappointed. If he is not reappointed, he shall retain office until the meeting appoints someone in his place, or if it does not do so, until the end of the meeting.

DISQUALIFICATION AND REMOVAL OF DIRECTORS

81.   The office of a director shall be vacated if—

    (a)   he ceases to be a director by virtue of any provision of the Act or he becomes prohibited by law from being a director; or

    (b)   he becomes bankrupt or makes any arrangement or composition with his creditors generally; or

    (c)   he is, or may be, suffering from mental disorder and either—

        (i)   he is admitted to hospital in pursuance of an application for admission for treatment under the Mental Health Act 1983 or, in Scotland, an application for admission under the Mental Health (Scotland) Act 1960, or

        (ii)   an order is made by a court having jurisdiction (whether in the United Kingdom or elsewhere) in matters concerning mental disorder for his detention or for the appointment of a receiver, curator bonis or other person to exercise powers with respect to his property or affairs; or

    (d)   he resigns his office by notice to the company; or

    (e)   he shall for more than six consecutive months have been absent without permission of the directors from meetings of directors held during that period and the directors resolve that his office be vacated.

REMUNERATION OF DIRECTORS

82.   The directors shall be entitled to such remuneration as the company may by ordinary resolution determine and, unless the resolution provides otherwise, the remuneration shall be deemed to accrue from day to day.

DIRECTORS' EXPENSES

83.   The directors may be paid all travelling, hotel, and other expenses properly incurred by them in connection with their attendance at meetings of directors or committees of directors or general meetings or separate meetings of the holders of any class of shares or of debentures of the company or otherwise in connection with the discharge of their duties.

DIRECTORS' APPOINTMENTS AND INTERESTS

84.   Subject to the provisions of the Act, the directors may appoint one or more of their number to the office of managing director or to any other executive office under the company and may enter into an agreement or arrangement with any director for his employment by the company or for the provision by him of any services outside the scope of the ordinary duties of a director. Any such appointment, agreement or arrangement may be made upon such terms as the directors determine and they may remunerate any such director for his services as they think fit. Any appointment of a director to an executive office shall terminate if he ceases to be a director but without prejudice to any claim to damages for breach of the contract of service between the director and the company. A managing director and a director holding any other executive office shall not be subject to retirement by rotation.

85.   Subject to the provisions of the Act, and provided that he has disclosed to the directors the nature and extent of any material interest of his, a director notwithstanding his office—
  (a)   may be a party to, or otherwise interested in, any transaction or arrangement with the company or in which the company is otherwise interested;
  (b)   may be a director or other officer of, or employed by, or a party to any transaction or arrangement with, or otherwise interested in, any body corporate promoted by the company or in which the company is otherwise interested; and
  (c)   shall not, by reason of his office, be accountable to the company for any benefit which he derives from any such office or employment or from any such transaction or arrangement or from any interest in any such body corporate and no such transaction or arrangement shall be liable to be avoided on the ground of any such interest or benefit.

86.   For the purposes of regulation 85—
  (a)   a general notice given to the directors that a director is to be regarded as having an interest of the nature and extent specified in the notice in any transaction or arrangement in which a specified person or class of persons is interested shall be deemed to be a disclosure that the director has an interest in any such transaction of the nature and extent so specified; and
  (b)   an interest of which a director has no knowledge and of which it is unreasonable to expect him to have knowledge shall not be treated as an interest of his.

DIRECTORS' GRATUITIES AND PENSIONS

87.   The directors may provide benefits, whether by the payment of gratuities or pensions or by insurance or otherwise, for any director who has held but no longer holds any executive office or employment with the company or with any body corporate which is or has been a subsidiary of the company or a predecessor in business of the company or of any such subsidiary, and for any member of his family (including a spouse and a former spouse) or any person who is or was dependent on him, and may (as well before as after he ceases to hold such office or employment) contribute to any fund and pay premiums for the purchase or provision of any such benefit.

PROCEEDINGS OF DIRECTORS

88. Subject to the provisions of the articles, the directors may regulate their proceedings as they think fit. A director may, and the secretary at the request of a director shall, call a meeting of the directors. It shall not be necessary to give notice of a meeting to a director who is absent from the United Kingdom. Questions arising at a meeting shall be decided by a majority of votes. In the case of an equality of votes, the chairman shall have a second or casting vote. A director who is also an alternate director shall be entitled in the absence of his appointor to a separate vote on behalf of his appointor in addition to his own vote.

89. The quorum for the transaction of the business of the directors may be fixed by the directors and unless so fixed at any other number shall be two. A person who holds office only as an alternate director shall, if his appointor is not present, be counted in the quorum.

90. The continuing directors or a sole continuing director may act notwithstanding any vacancies in their number, but, if the number of directors is less than the number fixed as the quorum, the continuing directors or director may act only for the purpose of filling vacancies or of calling a general meeting.

91. The directors may appoint one of their number to be the chairman of the board of directors and may at any time remove him from that office. Unless he is unwilling to do so, the director so appointed shall preside at every meeting of directors at which he is present. But if there is no director holding that office, or if the director holding it is unwilling to preside or is not present within five minutes after the time appointed for the meeting, the directors present may appoint one of their number to be chairman of the meeting.

92. All acts done by a meeting of directors, or of a committee of directors, or by a person acting as a director shall, notwithstanding that it be afterwards discovered that there was a defect in the appointment of any director or that any of them were disqualified from holding office, or had vacated office, or were not entitled to vote, be as valid as if every such person had been duly appointed and was qualified and had continued to be a director and had been entitled to vote.

93. A resolution in writing signed by all the directors entitled to receive notice of a meeting of directors or of a committee of directors shall be as valid and effectual as it if had been passed at a meeting of directors or (as the case may be) a committee of directors duly convened and held and may consist of several documents in the like form each signed by one or more directors; but a resolution signed by an alternate director need not also be signed by his appointor and, if it is signed by a director who has appointed an alternate director, it need not be signed by the alternate director in that capacity.

94. Save as otherwise provided by the articles, a director shall not vote at a meeting of directors or of a committee of directors on any resolution concerning a matter in which he has, directly or indirectly, an interest or duty which is material and which conflicts or may conflict with the interests of the company unless his interest or duty arises only because the case falls within one or more of the following paragraphs—

    (a) the resolution relates to the giving to him of a guarantee, security, or indemnity in respect of money lent to, or an obligation incurred by him for the benefit of, the company or any of its subsidiaries;

    (b) the resolution relates to the giving to a third party of a guarantee, security, or indemnity in respect of an obligation of the company or any of its subsidiaries for which the director has assumed responsibility in whole or part and whether alone or jointly with others under a guarantee or indemnity or by the giving of security;

    (c) his interest arises by virtue of his subscribing or agreeing to subscribe for any shares, debentures, or other securities of the company or any of its subsidiaries, or by virtue of his being, or intending to become, a participant in the underwriting or sub-underwriting of an offer of any such shares, debentures, or other securities by the company or any of its subsidiaries for subscription, purchase or exchange;

    (d) the resolution relates in any way to a retirement benefits scheme which has been approved, or is conditional upon approval, by the Board of Inland Revenue for taxation purposes.

For the purposes of this regulation, an interest of a person who is, for any purpose of the Act (excluding any statutory modification thereof not in force when this regulation becomes binding on the company), connected with a director shall be treated as an interest of the director and, in relation to an alternate director, an interest of his appointor shall be treated as an interest of the alternate director without prejudice to any interest which the alternate director has otherwise.

95.   A director shall not be counted in the quorum present at a meeting in relation to a resolution on which he is not entitled to vote.

96.   The company may by ordinary resolution suspend or relax to any extent, either generally or in respect of any particular matter, any provision of the articles prohibiting a director from voting at a meeting of directors or of a committee of directors.

97.   Where proposals are under consideration concerning the appointment of two or more directors to offices or employments with the company or any body corporate in which the company is interested the proposals may be divided and considered in relation to each director separately and (provided he is not for another reason precluded from voting) each of the directors concerned shall be entitled to vote and be counted in the quorum in respect of each resolution except that concerning his own appointment.

98.   If a question arises at a meeting of directors or of a committee of directors as to the right of a director to vote, the question may, before the conclusion of the meeting, be referred to the chairman of the meeting and his ruling in relation to any director other than himself shall be final and conclusive.

SECRETARY

99.   Subject to the provisions of the Act, the secretary shall be appointed by the directors for such term, at such remuneration and upon such conditions as they may think fit; and any secretary so appointed may be removed by them.

MINUTES

100.   The directors shall cause minutes to be made in books kept for the purpose—
(a)   of all appointments of officers made by the directors; and
(b)   of all proceedings at meetings of the company, of the holders of any class of shares in the company, and of the directors, and of committees of directors, including the names of the directors present at each such meeting.

THE SEAL

101.   The seal shall only be used by the authority of the directors or of a committee of directors authorised by the directors. The directors may determine who shall sign any instrument to which the seal is affixed and unless otherwise so determined it shall be signed by a director and by the secretary or by a second director.

DIVIDENDS

102.   Subject to the provisions of the Act, the company may by ordinary resolution declare dividends in accordance with the respective rights of the members, but no dividend shall exceed the amount recommended by the directors.

103.   Subject to the provisions of the Act, the directors may pay interim dividends if it appears to them that they are justified by the profits of the company available for distribution. If the share capital is divided into different classes, the directors may pay interim dividends on shares which confer deferred or non-preferred rights with regard to dividend as well as on shares which confer preferential rights with regard to dividend, but no interim dividend shall be paid on shares carrying deferred or non-preferred rights if, at the time of payment, any preferential dividend is in arrear. The directors may also pay at intervals settled by them any dividend payable at a fixed rate if it appears to them that the profits available for distribution justify the payment. Provided the

directors act in good faith they shall not incur any liability to the holders of shares conferring preferred rights for any loss they may suffer by the lawful payment of an interim dividend on any shares having deferred or non-preferred rights.

104.   Except as otherwise provided by the rights attached to shares, all dividends shall be declared and paid according to the amounts paid up on the shares on which the dividend is paid. All dividends shall be apportioned and paid proportionately to the amounts paid up on the shares during any portion or portions of the period in respect of which the dividend is paid; but, if any share is issued on terms providing that it shall rank for dividend as from a particular date, that share shall rank for dividend accordingly.

105.   A general meeting declaring a dividend may, upon the recommendation of the directors, direct that it shall be satisfied wholly or partly by the distribution of assets and, where any difficulty arises in regard to the distribution, the directors may settle the same and in particular may issue fractional certificates and fix the value for distribution of any assets and may determine that cash shall be paid to any member upon the footing of the value so fixed in order to adjust the rights of members and may vest any assets in trustees.

106.   Any dividend or other moneys payable in respect of a share may be paid by cheque sent by post to the registered address of the person entitled or, if two or more persons are the holders of the share or are jointly entitled to it by reason of the death or bankruptcy of the holder, to the registered address of that one of those persons who is first named in the register of members or to such person and to such address as the person or persons entitled may in writing direct. Every cheque shall be made payable to the order of the person or persons entitled or to such other person as the person or persons entitled may in writing direct and payment of the cheque shall be a good discharge to the company. Any joint holder or other person jointly entitled to a share as aforesaid may give receipts for any dividend or other moneys payable in respect of the share.

107.   No dividend or other moneys payable in respect of a share shall bear interest against the company unless otherwise provided by the rights attached to the share.

108.   Any dividend which has remained unclaimed for twelve years from the date when it became due for payment shall, if the directors so resolve, be forfeited and cease to remain owing by the company.

ACCOUNTS

109.   No member shall (as such) have any right of inspecting any accounting records or other book or document of the company except as conferred by statute or authorised by the directors or by ordinary resolution of the company.

CAPITALISATION OF PROFITS

110.   The directors may with the authority of an ordinary resolution of the company—

(a)   subject as hereinafter provided, resolve to capitalise any undivided profits of the company not required for paying any preferential dividend (whether or not they are available for distribution) or any sum standing to the credit of the company's share premium account or capital redemption reserve;

(b)   appropriate the sum resolved to be capitalised to the members who would have been entitled to it if it were distributed by way of dividend and in the same proportions and apply such sum on their behalf either in or towards paying up the amounts, if any, for the time being unpaid on any shares held by them respectively, or in paying up in full unissued shares or debentures of the company of a nominal amount equal to that sum, and allot the shares or debentures credited as fully paid to those members, or as they may direct, in those proportions, or partly in one way and partly in the other: but the share premium account, the capital redemption reserve, and any profits which are not available for distribution may, for the purposes of this regulation, only be applied in paying up unissued shares to be allotted to members credited as fully paid;

(c)   make such provision by the issue of fractional certificates or by payment in cash or otherwise as they determine in the case of shares or debentures becoming distributable under this regulation in fractions; and

(d)   authorise any person to enter on behalf of all the members concerned into an agreement with the company providing for the allotment to them respectively, credited as fully paid, of any shares or debentures to which they are entitled upon such capitalisation, any agreement made under such authority being binding on all such members.

NOTICES

111.   Any notice to be given to or by any person pursuant to the articles (other than a notice calling a meeting of the directors) shall be in writing or shall be given using electronic communications to an address for the time being notified for that purpose to the person giving the notice.

In this regulation, "address", in relation to electronic communications, includes any number or address used for the purposes of such communications.

112.   The company may give any notice to a member either personally or by sending it by post in a prepaid envelope addressed to the member at his registered address or by leaving it at that address or by giving it using electronic communications to an address for the time being notified to the company by the member. In the case of joint holders of a share, all notices shall be given to the joint holder whose name stands first in the register of members in respect of the joint holding and notice so given shall be sufficient notice to all the joint holders. A member whose registered address is not within the United Kingdom and who gives to the company an address within the United Kingdom at which notices may be given to him, or an address to which notices may be sent using electronic communications, shall be entitled to have notices given to him at that address, but otherwise no such member shall be entitled to receive any notice from the company.

In this regulation and the next, "address", in relation to electronic communications, includes any number or address used for the purposes of such communications.

113.   A member present, either in person or by proxy, at any meeting of the company or of the holders of any class of shares in the company shall be deemed to have received notice of the meeting and, where requisite, of the purposes for which it was called.

114.   Every person who becomes entitled to a share shall be bound by any notice in respect of that share which, before his name is entered in the register of members, has been duly given to a person from whom he derives his title.

115.   Proof that an envelope containing a notice was properly addressed, prepaid and posted shall be conclusive evidence that that the notice was given. Proof that a notice contained in an electronic communication was sent in accordance with guidance issued by the Institute of Chartered Secretaries and Administrators shall be conclusive evidence that the notice was given. A notice shall, ... be deemed to be given at the expiration of 48 hours after the envelope containing it was posted or, in the case of a notice contained in an electronic communication, at the expiration of 48 hours after the time it was sent.

116.   A notice may be given by the company to the persons entitled to a share in consequence of the death or bankruptcy of a member by sending or delivering it, in any manner authorised by the articles for the giving of notice to a member, addressed to them by name, or by the title of representatives of the deceased, or trustee of the bankrupt or by any like description at the address, if any, within the United Kingdom supplied for that purpose by the persons claiming to be so entitled. Until such an address has been supplied, a notice may be given in any manner in which it might have been given if the death or bankruptcy had not occurred.

WINDING UP

117.   If the company is wound up, the liquidator may, with the sanction of an extraordinary resolution of the company and any other sanction required by the Act, divide among the members in specie the whole or any part of the assets of the company and may, for that purpose, value any assets and determine how the division shall be carried out as between the members or different classes of

members. The liquidator may, with the like sanction, vest the whole or any part of the assets in trustees upon such trusts for the benefit of the members as he with the like sanction determines, but no member shall be compelled to accept any assets upon which there is a liability.

INDEMNITY

118. Subject to the provisions of the Act but without prejudice to any indemnity to which a director may otherwise be entitled, every director or other officer or auditor of the company shall be indemnified out of the assets of the company against any liability incurred by him in defending any proceedings, whether civil or criminal, in which judgment is given in his favour or in which he is acquitted or in connection with any application in which relief is granted to him by the court from liability for negligence, default, breach of duty or breach of trust in relation to the affairs of the company.

TABLE B
A PRIVATE COMPANY LIMITED BY SHARES

MEMORANDUM OF ASSOCIATION

1. The company's name is "The South Wales Motor Transport Company cyfyngedig".
2. The company's registered office is to be situated in Wales.
3. The company's objects are the carriage of passengers and goods in motor vehicles between such places as the company may from time to time determine and the doing of all such other things as are incidental or conducive to the attainment of that object.
4. The liability of the members is limited.
5. The company's share capital is £50,000 divided into 50,000 shares of £1 each.

We, the subscribers to this memorandum of association, wish to be formed into a company pursuant to this memorandum; and we agree to take the number of shares shown opposite our respective names.

Names and Addresses of Subscribers	Number of shares taken by each Subscriber
1. Thomas Jones, 138 Mountfield Street,Tredegar.	1
2. Mary Evans, 19 Merthyr Road, Aberystwyth.	1
	Total shares taken 2

Dated .. .. 19 .. ..
Witness to the above signatures,
Anne Brown, "Woodlands", Fieldside Road, Bryn Mawr.

...

Partnership Act 1890

1890 c. 39

An Act to declare and amend the Law of Partnership

[14th August 1890]

Nature of Partnership

1. Definition of Partnership

(1)   Partnership is the relation which subsists between persons carrying on a business in common with a view of profit.

(2)   But the relation between members of any company or association which is—

(a)   registered under the Companies Act 2006, or

(b)   Formed or incorporated by or in pursuance of any other Act of Parliament or letters patent, or Royal Charter …

(c)   …

is not a partnership within the meaning of this Act.

2. Rules for determining existence of partnership

In determining whether a partnership does or does not exist, regard shall be had to the following rules:

(1)   Joint tenancy, tenancy in common, joint property, common property, or part ownership does not of itself create a partnership as to anything so held or owned, whether the tenants or owners do or do not share any profits made by the use thereof.

(2)   The sharing of gross returns does not of itself create a partnership, whether the persons sharing such returns have or have not a joint or common right or interest in any property from which or from the use of which the returns are derived.

(3)   The receipt by a person of a share of the profits of a business is *prima facie* evidence that he is a partner in the business, but receipt of such a share, or of a payment contingent on or varying with the profits of a business, does not of itself make him a partner in the business; and in particular—

(a)   The receipt by a person of a debt or other liquidated amount by instalments or otherwise out of the accruing profits of a business does not of itself make him a partner in the business or liable as such:

(b)   A contract for the remuneration of a servant or agent of a person engaged in a business by a share of the profits of the business does not of itself make the servant or agent a partner in the business or liable as such:

(c)   A person being the widow, widower, surviving civil partner or child of a deceased partner, and receiving by way of annuity a portion of the profits made in the business in which the deceased person was a partner, is not by reason only of such receipt a partner in the business or liable as such:

(d)   The advance of money by way of loan to a person engaged or about to engage in any business on a contract with that person that the lender shall receive a rate of interest varying with the profits, or shall receive a share of the profits arising from carrying on the business, does not of itself make the lender a partner with the person or persons carrying on the business or liable as such. Provided that the contract is in writing, and signed by or on behalf of all the parties thereto:

(e)   A person receiving by way of annuity or otherwise a portion of the profits of a business in consideration of the sale by him of the goodwill of the business is not by reason only of such receipt a partner in the business or liable as such.

3.   Postponement of rights of person lending or selling in consideration of share of profits in case of insolvency

In the event of any person to whom money has been advanced by way of loan upon such a contract as is mentioned in the last foregoing section, or of any buyer of a goodwill in consideration of a share of the profits of the business, being adjudged a bankrupt, entering into an arrangement to pay his creditors less than 100p in the pound, or dying in insolvent circumstances, the lender of the loan shall not be entitled to recover anything in respect of his loan, and the seller of the goodwill shall not be entitled to recover anything in respect of the share of profits contracted for, until the claims of the other creditors of the borrower or buyer for valuable consideration in money or money's worth have been satisfied.

4.   Meaning of firm

(1)   Persons who have entered into partnership with one another are for the purposes of this Act called collectively a firm, and the name under which their business is carried on is called the firm-name.

(2)   In Scotland a firm is a legal person distinct from the partners of whom it is composed, but an individual partner may be charged on a decree or diligence directed against the firm, and on payment of the debts is entitled to relief pro rata from the firm and its other members.

Relations of Partners to persons dealing with them

5.   Power of partner to bind the firm

Every partner is an agent of the firm and his other partners for the purpose of the business of the partnership; and the acts of every partner who does any act for carrying on in the usual way business of the kind carried on by the firm of which he is a member bind the firm and his partners, unless the partner so acting has in fact no authority to act for the firm in the particular matter, and the person with whom he is dealing either knows that he has no authority, or does not know or believe him to be a partner.

6.   Partners bound by acts on behalf of firm

An act or instrument relating to the business of the firm done or executed in the firm-name, or in any other manner showing an intention to bind the firm, by any person thereto authorised, whether a partner or not, is binding on the firm and all the partners.

Provided that this section shall not affect any general rule of law relating to the execution of deeds or negotiable instruments.

7.   Partner using credit of firm for private purposes

Where one partner pledges the credit of the firm for a purpose apparently not connected with the firm's ordinary course of business, the firm is not bound, unless he is in fact specially authorised by the other partners; but this section does not affect any personal liability incurred by an individual partner.

8.   Effect of notice that firm will not be bound by acts of partner

If it has been agreed between the partners that any restriction shall be placed on the power of any one or more of them to bind the firm, no act done in contravention of the agreement is binding on the firm with respect to persons having notice of the agreement.

9.   Liability of partners

Every partner in a firm is liable jointly with the other partners, and in Scotland severally also, for all debts and obligations of the firm incurred while he is a partner; and after his death his estate is also severally liable in a due course of administration for such debts and obligations, so far as they remain unsatisfied, but subject in England or Ireland to the prior payment of his separate debts.

10. Liability of the firm for wrongs

Where, by any wrongful act or omission of any partner acting in the ordinary course of the business of the firm, or with the authority of his co-partners, loss or injury is caused to any person not being a partner in the firm, or any penalty is incurred, the firm is liable therefor to the same extent as the partner so acting or omitting to act.

11. Misapplication of money or property received for or in custody of the firm

In the following cases; namely—

(a) Where one partner acting within the scope of his apparent authority receives the money or property of a third person and misapplies it; and

(b) Where a firm in the course of its business receives money or property of a third person, and the money or property so received is misapplied by one or more of the partners while it is in the custody of the firm;

the firm is liable to make good the loss.

12. Liability for wrongs joint and several

Every partner is liable jointly with his co-partners and also severally for everything for which the firm while he is a partner therein becomes liable under either of the two last preceding sections.

13. Improper employment of trust-property for partnership purposes

If a partner, being a trustee, improperly employs trust-property in the business or on the account of the partnership, no other partner is liable for the trust property to the persons beneficially interested therein:

Provided as follows:—

(1) This section shall not affect any liability incurred by any partner by reason of his having notice of a breach of trust; and

(2) Nothing in this section shall prevent trust money from being followed and recovered from the firm if still in its possession or under its control.

14. Persons liable by "holding out"

(1) Every one who by words spoken or written or by conduct represents himself, or who knowingly suffers himself to be represented, as a partner in a particular firm, is liable as a partner to any one who has on the faith of any such representation given credit to the firm, whether the representation has or has not been made or communicated to the person so giving credit by or with the knowledge of the apparent partner making the representation or suffering it to be made.

(2) Provided that where after a partner's death the partnership business is continued in the old firm's name, the continued use of that name or of the deceased partner's name as part thereof shall not of itself make his executors or administrators estate or effects liable for any partnership debts contracted after his death.

15. Admissions and representation of partners

An admission or representation made by any partner concerning the partnership affairs, and in the ordinary course of its business, is evidence against the firm.

16. Notice to acting partner to be notice to the firm

Notice to any partner who habitually acts in the partnership business of any matter relating to partnership affairs operates as notice to the firm, except in the case of a fraud on the firm committed by or with the consent of that partner.

17. Liabilities of incoming and outgoing partners

(1) A person who is admitted as a partner into an existing firm does not thereby become liable to the creditors of the firm for anything done before he became a partner.

(2) A partner who retires from a firm does not thereby cease to be liable for partnership debts or obligations incurred before his retirement.

(3)   A retiring partner may be discharged from any existing liabilities, by an agreement to that effect between himself and the members of the firm as newly constituted and the creditors, and this agreement may be either expressed or inferred as a fact from the course of dealing between the creditors and the firm as newly constituted.

18.   **Revocation of continuing guaranty by change in firm**

A continuing guaranty or cautionary obligation given either to a firm or to a third person in respect of the transactions of a firm is, in the absence of agreement to the contrary, revoked as to future transactions by any change in the constitution of the firm to which, or of the firm in respect of the transactions of which, the guaranty or obligation was given.

Relations of Partners to one another

19.   **Variation by consent of terms of partnership**

The mutual rights and duties of partners, whether ascertained by agreement or defined by this Act, may be varied by the consent of all the partners, and such consent may be either express or inferred from a course of dealing.

20.   **Partnership property**

(1)   All property and rights and interests in property originally brought into the partnership stock or acquired, whether by purchase or otherwise, on account of the firm, or for the purposes and in the course of the partnership business, are called in this Act partnership property, and must be held and applied by the partners exclusively for the purposes of the partnership and in accordance with the partnership agreement.

(2)   Provided that the legal estate or interest in any land, or in Scotland the title to and interest in any heritable estate, which belongs to the partnership shall devolve according to the nature and tenure thereof, and the general rules of law thereto applicable, but in trust, so far as necessary, for the persons beneficially interested in the land under this section.

(3)   Where co-owners of an estate or interest in any land, or in Scotland of any heritable estate, not being itself partnership property, are partners as to profits made by the use of that land or estate, and purchase other land or estate out of the profits to be used in like manner, the land or estate so purchased belongs to them, in the absence of an agreement to the contrary, not as partners, but as co-owners for the same respective estates and interests as are held by them in the land or estate first mentioned at the date of the purchase.

21.   **Property bought with partnership money**

Unless the contrary intention appears, property bought with money belonging to the firm is deemed to have been bought on account of the firm.

22.   ...

23.   **Procedure against partnership property for a partner's separate judgement debt**

(1)   ... A writ of execution shall not issue against any partnership property except on a judgment against the firm.

(2)   The High Court, or a judge thereof, ..., or the county court in England and Wales or a county court in Northern Ireland, may, on the application by summons of any judgment creditor of a partner, make an order charging that partner's interest in the partnership property and profits with payment of the amount of the judgment debt and interest thereon, and may by the same or a subsequent order appoint a receiver of that partner's share of profits (whether already declared or accruing), and of any other money which may be coming to him in respect of the partnership, and direct all accounts and inquiries, and give all other orders and directions which might have been directed or given if the charge had been made in favour of the judgment creditor by the partner, or which the circumstances of the case may require.

(3)   The other partner or partners shall be at liberty at any time to redeem the interest charged, or in case of a sale being directed, to purchase the same.

(4)   ...

(5)   This section shall not apply to Scotland.

24.   Rules as to interests and duties of partners subject to special agreement

The interests of partners in the partnership property and their rights and duties in relation to the partnership shall be determined, subject to any agreement express or implied between the partners, by the following rules:

(1)   All the partners are entitled to share equally in the capital and profits of the business, and must contribute equally towards the losses whether of capital or otherwise sustained by the firm.

(2)   The firm must indemnify every partner in respect of payments made and personal liabilities incurred by him—

(a)   In the ordinary and proper conduct of the business of the firm; or,

(b)   In or about anything necessarily done for the preservation of the business or property of the firm.

(3)   A partner making, for the purpose of the partnership, any actual payment or advance beyond the amount of capital which he has agreed to subscribe, is entitled to interest at the rate of five per cent. per annum from the date of the payment or advance.

(4)   A partner is not entitled, before the ascertainment of profits, to interest on the capital subscribed by him.

(5)   Every partner may take part in the management of the partnership business.

(6)   No partner shall be entitled to remuneration for acting in the partnership business.

(7)   No person may be introduced as a partner without the consent of all existing partners.

(8)   Any difference arising as to ordinary matters connected with the partnership business may be decided by a majority of the partners, but no change may be made in the nature of the partnership business without the consent of all existing partners.

(9)   The partnership books are to be kept at the place of business of the partnership (or the principal place, if there is more than one), and every partner may, when he thinks fit, have access to and inspect and copy any of them.

25.   Expulsion of partner

No majority of the partners can expel any partner unless a power to do so has been conferred by express agreement between the partners.

26.   Retirement from partnership at will

(1)   Where no fixed term has been agreed upon for the duration of the partnership, any partner may determine the partnership at any time on giving notice of his intention so to do to all the other partners.

(2)   Where the partnership has originally been constituted by deed, a notice in writing, signed by the partner giving it, shall be sufficient for this purpose.

27.   Where partnership for term is continued over, continuance on old terms presumed

(1)   Where a partnership entered into for a fixed term is continued after the term has expired, and without any express new agreement, the rights and duties of the partners remain the same as they were at the expiration of the term, so far as is consistent with the incidents of a partnership at will.

(2)   A continuance of the business by the partners or such of them as habitually acted therein during the term, without any settlement or liquidation of the partnership affairs, is presumed to be a continuance of the partnership.

28.   Duty of partners to render accounts, etc

Partners are bound to render true accounts and full information of all things affecting the partnership to any partner or his legal representatives.

29.   Accountability of partners for private profits

(1)   Every partner must account to the firm for any benefit derived by him without the consent of the other partners from any transaction concerning the partnership, or from any use by him of the partnership property name or business connexion.

(2)   This section applies also to transactions undertaken after a partnership has been dissolved by the death of a partner, and before the affairs thereof have been completely wound up, either by any surviving partner or by the representatives of the deceased partner.

30.   Duty of partner not to compete with firm

If a partner, without the consent of the other partners, carries on any business of the same nature as and competing with that of the firm, he must account for and pay over to the firm all profits made by him in that business.

31.   Rights of assignee of share in partnership

(1)   An assignment by any partner of his share in the partnership, either absolute or by way of mortgage or redeemable charge, does not, as against the other partners, entitle the assignee, during the continuance of the partnership, to interfere in the management or administration of the partnership business or affairs, or to require any accounts of the partnership transactions, or to inspect the partnership books, but entitles the assignee only to receive the share of profits to which the assigning partner would otherwise be entitled, and the assignee must accept the account of profits agreed to by the partners.

(2)   In case of a dissolution of the partnership, whether as respects all the partners or as respects the assigning partner, the assignee is entitled to receive the share of the partnership assets to which the assigning partner is entitled as between himself and the other partners, and, for the purpose of ascertaining that share, to an account as from the date of the dissolution.

Dissolution of Partnership, and its consequences

32.   Dissolution by expiration or notice

Subject to any agreement between the partners, a partnership is dissolved—
(a)   If entered into for a fixed term, by the expiration of that term:
(b)   If entered into for a single adventure or undertaking, by the termination of that adventure or undertaking:
(c)   If entered into for an undefined time, by any partner giving notice to the other or others of his intention to dissolve the partnership.

In the last-mentioned case the partnership is dissolved as from the date mentioned in the notice as the date of dissolution, or, if no date is so mentioned, as from the date of the communication of the notice.

33.   Dissolution by bankruptcy, death or charge

(1)   Subject to any agreement between the partners, every partnership is dissolved as regards all the partners by the death or bankruptcy of any partner.

(2)   A partnership may, at the option of the other partners, be dissolved if any partner suffers his share of the partnership property to be charged under this Act for his separate debt.

34.   Dissolution by illegality of partnership

A partnership is in every case dissolved by the happening of any event which makes it unlawful for the business of the firm to be carried on or for the members of the firm to carry it on in partnership.

35.   Dissolution by the Court

On application by a partner the Court may decree a dissolution of the partnership in any of the following cases:
(a)   ...

(b) When a partner, other than the partner suing, becomes in any other way permanently incapable of performing his part of the partnership contract:

(c) When a partner, other than the partner suing, has been guilty of such conduct as, in the opinion of the Court, regard being had to the nature of the business, is calculated to prejudicially affect the carrying on of the business:

(d) When a partner, other than the partner suing, wilfully or persistently commits a breach of the partnership agreement, or otherwise so conducts himself in matters relating to the partnership business that it is not reasonably practicable for the other partner or partners to carry on the business in partnership with him:

(e) When the business of the partnership can only be carried on at a loss:

(f) Whenever in any case circumstances have arisen which, in the opinion of the Court, render it just and equitable that the partnership be dissolved.

36. Rights of persons dealing with firm against apparent members of firm

(1) Where a person deals with a firm after a change in its constitution he is entitled to treat all apparent members of the old firm as still being members of the firm until he has notice of the change.

(2) An advertisement in the London Gazette as to a firm whose principal place of business is in England or Wales, in the Edinburgh Gazette as to a firm whose principal place of business is in Scotland, and in the Belfast Gazette as to a firm whose principal place of business is in Ireland, shall be notice as to persons who had not dealings with the firm before the date of the dissolution or change so advertised.

(3) The estate of a partner who dies, or who becomes bankrupt, or of a partner who, not having been known to the person dealing with the firm to be a partner, retires from the firm, is not liable for partnership debts contracted after the date of the death, bankruptcy, or retirement respectively.

37. Right of partners to notify dissolution

On the dissolution of a partnership or retirement of a partner any partner may publicly notify the same, and may require the other partner or partners to concur for that purpose in all necessary or proper acts, if any, which cannot be done without his or their concurrence.

38. Continuing authority of partners for purposes of winding up

After the dissolution of a partnership the authority of each partner to bind the firm, and the other rights and obligations of the partners, continue notwithstanding the dissolution so far as may be necessary to wind up the affairs of the partnership, and to complete transactions begun but unfinished at the time of the dissolution, and in relation to any prosecution of the partnership by virtue of section 1 of the Partnerships (Prosecution) (Scotland) Act 2013, but not otherwise.

Provided that the firm is in no case bound by the acts of a partner who has become bankrupt; but this proviso does not affect the liability of any person who has after the bankruptcy represented himself or knowingly suffered himself to be represented as a partner of the bankrupt.

39. Rights of partners as to application of partnership property

On the dissolution of a partnership every partner is entitled, as against the other partners in the firm, and all persons claiming through them in respect of their interests as partners, to have the property of the partnership applied in payment of the debts and liabilities of the firm, and to have the surplus assets after such payment applied in payment of what may be due to the partners respectively after deducting what may be due from them as partners to the firm; and for that purpose any partner or his representatives may on the termination of the partnership apply to the Court to wind up the business and affairs of the firm.

40. Apportionment of premium where partnership prematurely dissolved

Where one partner has paid a premium to another on entering into a partnership for a fixed term, and the partnership is dissolved before the expiration of that term otherwise than by the death of a partner, the Court may order the repayment of the premium, or of such part thereof as it thinks just, having regard to the terms of the partnership contract and to the length of time during which the partnership has continued; unless

(a) the dissolution is, in the judgment of the Court, wholly or chiefly due to the misconduct of the partner who paid the premium; or

(b) the partnership has been dissolved by an agreement containing no provision for a return of any part of the premium.

41.   Rights where partnership dissolved for fraud or misrepresentation

Where a partnership contract is rescinded on the ground of the fraud or misrepresentation of one of the parties thereto, the party entitled to rescind is, without prejudice to any other right, entitled—

(a) to a lien on, or right of retention of, the surplus of the partnership assets, after satisfying the partnership liabilities, for any sum of money paid by him for the purchase of a share in the partnership and for any capital contributed by him, and is

(b) to stand in the place of the creditors of the firm for any payments made by him in respect of the partnership liabilities, and

(c) to be indemnified by the person guilty of the fraud or making the representation against all the debts and liabilities of the firm.

42.   Right of outgoing partner in certain cases to share profits made after dissolution

(1) Where any member of a firm has died or otherwise ceased to be a partner, and the surviving or continuing partners carry on the business of the firm with its capital or assets without any final settlement of accounts as between the firm and the outgoing partner or his estate, then, in the absence of any agreement to the contrary, the outgoing partner or his estate is entitled at the option of himself or his representatives to such share of the profits made since the dissolution as the Court may find to be attributable to the use of his share of the partnership assets, or to interest at the rate of five per cent. per annum on the amount of his share of the partnership assets.

(2) Provided that where by the partnership contract an option is given to surviving or continuing partners to purchase the interest of a deceased or outgoing partner, and that option is duly exercised, the estate of the deceased partner, or the outgoing partner or his estate, as the case may be, is not entitled to any further or other share of profits; but if any partner assuming to act in exercise of the option does not in all material respects comply with the terms thereof, he is liable to account under the foregoing provisions of this section.

43.   Retiring or deceased partner's share to be a debt

Subject to any agreement between the partners, the amount due from surviving or continuing partners to an outgoing partner or the representatives of a deceased partner in respect of the outgoing or deceased partner's share is a debt accruing at the date of the dissolution or death.

44.   Rule for distribution of assets on final settlement of accounts

In settling accounts between the partners after a dissolution of partnership, the following rules shall, subject to any agreement, be observed:

(a) Losses, including losses and deficiencies of capital, shall be paid first out of profits, next out of capital, and lastly, if necessary, by the partners individually in the proportion in which they were entitled to share profits:

(b) The assets of the firm including the sums, if any, contributed by the partners to make up losses or deficiencies of capital, shall be applied in the following manner and order:

1. In paying the debts and liabilities of the firm to persons who are not partners therein:

2. In paying to each partner rateably what is due from the firm to him for advances as distinguished from capital:

3. In paying to each partner rateably what is due from the firm to him in respect of capital:

4. The ultimate residue, if any, shall be divided among the partners in the proportion in which profits are divisible.

Supplemental

45.   Definitions of "court" and "business"

In this Act, unless the contrary intention appears,—

The expression "court" includes every court and judge having jurisdiction in the case:

The expression "business" includes every trade, occupation, or profession.

46.   Saving for rules of equity and common law

The rules of equity and of common law applicable to partnership shall continue in force except so far as they are inconsistent with the express provisions of this Act.

47.   Provision as to bankruptcy in Scotland

(1)   In the application of this Act to Scotland the bankruptcy of a firm or of an individual shall mean sequestration under the Bankruptcy (Scotland) Acts, and also in the case of an individual the issue against him of a decree of cessio bonorum.

(2)   Nothing in this Act shall alter the rules of the law of Scotland relating to the bankruptcy of a firm or of the individual partners thereof.

48, 49. ...

50.   Short title

This Act may be cited as the Partnership Act 1890.

SCHEDULE

...

Limited Liability Partnerships Act 2000

2000 c. 12

An Act to make provision for limited liability partnerships

[20th July 2000]

Introductory

1. Limited liability partnerships

(1) There shall be a new form of legal entity to be known as a limited liability partnership.

(2) A limited liability partnership is a body corporate (with legal personality separate from that of its members) which is formed by being incorporated under this Act; and—

(a) in the following provisions of this Act (except in the phrase "oversea limited liability partnership"), and

(b) in any other enactment (except where provision is made to the contrary or the context otherwise requires),

references to a limited liability partnership are to such a body corporate.

(3) A limited liability partnership has unlimited capacity.

(4) The members of a limited liability partnership have such liability to contribute to its assets in the event of its being wound up as is provided for by virtue of this Act.

(5) Accordingly, except as far as otherwise provided by this Act or any other enactment, the law relating to partnerships does not apply to a limited liability partnership.

(6) The Schedule (which makes provision about the names and registered offices of limited liability partnerships) has effect.

Incorporation

2. Incorporation document etc

(1) For a limited liability partnership to be incorporated—

(a) two or more persons associated for carrying on a lawful business with a view to profit must have subscribed their names to an incorporation document,

(b) the incorporation document or a copy of it must have been delivered to the registrar, and

(c) there must have been so delivered a statement … made by either a solicitor engaged in the formation of the limited liability partnership or anyone who subscribed his name to the incorporation document, that the requirement imposed by paragraph (a) has been complied with.

(2) The incorporation document must—

(a) …

(b) state the name of the limited liability partnership,

(c) state whether the registered office of the limited liability partnership is to be situated in England and Wales, in Wales, in Scotland or in Northern Ireland,

(d) state the address of that registered office, which must be an appropriate address,

(da) state the intended registered email address of the limited liability partnership, which must be an appropriate email address,

(e) give the required particulars of each of the persons who are to be members of the limited liability partnership on incorporation, …

(f) either specify which of those persons are to be designated members or state that every person who from time to time is a member of the limited liability partnership is a designated member, and

(g) include a statement of initial significant control.

(2ZA) The required particulars mentioned in subsection (2)(e) are the particulars required to be stated in the LLP's register of members and register of members' residential addresses.

(2A), (2B)   ...

(3)   If a person makes a false statement under subsection (1)(c) which he—

    (a)   knows to be false, or

    (b)   does not believe to be true,

he commits an offence.

(4)   A person guilty of an offence under subsection (3) is liable—

    (a)   on summary conviction, to imprisonment for a period not exceeding six months or a fine not exceeding the statutory maximum, or to both, or

    (b)   on conviction on indictment, to imprisonment for a period not exceeding two years or a fine, or to both.

(5)   In this section—

"appropriate address" means an address at which, in the ordinary course of events—

    (a)   a document addressed to the limited liability partnership, and delivered there by hand or by post, would be expected to come to the attention of a person acting on behalf of the limited liability partnership, and

    (b)   the delivery of documents there is capable of being recorded by the obtaining of an acknowledgement of delivery;

"appropriate email address" means an email address to which, in the ordinary course of events, emails sent by the registrar would be expected to come to the attention of a person acting on behalf of the limited liability partnership.

3.   Incorporation by registration

(1)   The registrar, if satisfied that the requirements of section 2 are complied with, shall—

    (a)   register the documents delivered under that section, and

    (b)   give a certificate that the limited liability partnership is incorporated.

(1A)   The certificate must state—

    (a)   the name and registered number of the limited liability partnership,

    (b)   the date of its incorporation, and

    (c)   whether the limited liability partnership's registered office is situated in England and Wales (or in Wales), in Scotland or in Northern Ireland.

(2)   The registrar may accept the statement delivered under paragraph (c) of subsection (1) of section 2 as sufficient evidence that the requirement imposed by paragraph (a) of that subsection has been complied with.

(3)   The certificate shall either be signed by the registrar or be authenticated by his official seal.

(4)   The certificate is conclusive evidence that the requirements of section 2 are complied with and that the limited liability partnership is incorporated by the name specified in the incorporation document.

Membership

4.   Members

(1)   On the incorporation of a limited liability partnership its members are the persons who subscribed their names to the incorporation document (other than any who have died or been dissolved).

(2)   Any other person may become a member of a limited liability partnership by and in accordance with an agreement with the existing members.

(3)   A person may cease to be a member of a limited liability partnership (as well as by death or dissolution) in accordance with an agreement with the other members or, in the absence of agreement with the other members as to cessation of membership, by giving reasonable notice to the other members.

(4)   A member of a limited liability partnership shall not be regarded for any purpose as employed by the limited liability partnership unless, if he and the other members were partners in a partnership, he would be regarded for that purpose as employed by the partnership.

4A.   Minimum membership for carrying on business

(1)   This section applies where a limited liability partnership carries on business without having at least two members, and does so for more than 6 months.

(2)   A person who, for the whole or any part of the period that it so carries on business after those 6 months—

(a)   is a member of the limited liability partnership, and

(b)   knows that it is carrying on business with only one member,

is liable (jointly and severally with the limited liability partnership) for the payment of the limited liability partnership's debts contracted during the period or, as the case may be, that part of it.

5.   Relationship of members etc

(1)   Except as far as otherwise provided by this Act or any other enactment, the mutual rights and duties of the members of a limited liability partnership, and the mutual rights and duties of a limited liability partnership and its members, shall be governed—

(a)   by agreement between the members, or between the limited liability partnership and its members, or

(b)   in the absence of agreement as to any matter, by any provision made in relation to that matter by regulations under section 15(c).

(2)   An agreement made before the incorporation of a limited liability partnership between the persons who subscribe their names to the incorporation document may impose obligations on the limited liability partnership (to take effect at any time after its incorporation).

6.   Members as agents

(1)   Every member of a limited liability partnership is the agent of the limited liability partnership.

(2)   But a limited liability partnership is not bound by anything done by a member in dealing with a person if—

(a)   the member in fact has no authority to act for the limited liability partnership by doing that thing, and

(b)   the person knows that he has no authority or does not know or believe him to be a member of the limited liability partnership.

(3)   Where a person has ceased to be a member of a limited liability partnership, the former member is to be regarded (in relation to any person dealing with the limited liability partnership) as still being a member of the limited liability partnership unless—

(a)   the person has notice that the former member has ceased to be a member of the limited liability partnership, or

(b)   notice that the former member has ceased to be a member of the limited liability partnership has been delivered to the registrar.

(4)   Where a member of a limited liability partnership is liable to any person (other than another member of the limited liability partnership) as a result of a wrongful act or omission of his in the course of the business of the limited liability partnership or with its authority, the limited liability partnership is liable to the same extent as the member.

7.   Ex-members

(1)   This section applies where a member of a limited liability partnership has either ceased to be a member or—

(a)   has died,

(b)   has become bankrupt or had his estate sequestrated or has been wound up,

(c)   has granted a trust deed for the benefit of his creditors, or

(d)   has assigned the whole or any part of his share in the limited liability partnership (absolutely or by way of charge or security).

(2)   In such an event the former member or—

(a)   his personal representative,

(b) his trustee in bankruptcy, the trustee or interim trustee in the sequestration, under the Bankruptcy (Scotland) Act 2016, of the former member's estate or the former member's liquidator,

(c) his trustee under the trust deed for the benefit of his creditors, or

(d) his assignee,

may not interfere in the management or administration of any business or affairs of the limited liability partnership.

(3) But subsection (2) does not affect any right to receive an amount from the limited liability partnership in that event.

8. Designated members

(1) If the incorporation document specifies who are to be designated members—

(a) they are designated members on incorporation, and

(b) any member may become a designated member by and in accordance with an agreement with the other members,

and a member may cease to be a designated member in accordance with an agreement with the other members.

(2) But if there would otherwise be no designated members, or only one, every member is a designated member.

(3) If the incorporation document states that every person who from time to time is a member of the limited liability partnership is a designated member, every member is a designated member.

(4) A limited liability partnership may at any time deliver to the registrar—

(a) notice that specified members are to be designated members, or

(b) notice that every person who from time to time is a member of the limited liability partnership is a designated member,

and, once it is delivered, subsection (1) (apart from paragraph (a)) and subsection (2), or subsection (3), shall have effect as if that were stated in the incorporation document.

(5) ...

(6) A person ceases to be a designated member if he ceases to be a member.

9. Registration of membership changes

(1) A limited liability partnership must ensure that—

(a) where a person becomes or ceases to be a member or designated member, notice is delivered to the registrar within fourteen days, and

(b) where there is any change in the particulars contained in its register of members or its register of members' residential addresses, notice is delivered to the registrar within 14 days.

(2) Where all the members from time to time of a limited liability partnership are designated members, subsection (1)(a) does not require notice that a person has become or ceased to be a designated member as well as a member.

(3) A notice delivered under subsection (1) that relates to a person becoming a member or designated member must contain—

(a) a statement that the member or designated member consents to acting in that capacity, and

(b) in the case of a person becoming a member, a statement of the particulars of the new member that are required to be included in the limited liability partnership's register of members and its register of residential addresses.

(3ZA) Where—

(a) a limited liability partnership gives notice of a change of a member's service address as stated in its register of members, and

(b) the notice is not accompanied by notice of any resulting change in the particulars contained in its register of members' residential addresses,

the notice must be accompanied by a statement that no such change is required.

(3A), (3B) ...

(4)   If a limited liability partnership fails to comply with this section, the partnership and every designated member commits an offence.

(5)   But it is a defence for a designated member charged with an offence under subsection (4) to prove that he took all reasonable steps for securing that this section was complied with.

(6)   A person guilty of an offence under subsection (4) is liable on summary conviction to a fine not exceeding level 5 on the standard scale.

Taxation

10, 11. ...

12.   Stamp duty

(1)   Stamp duty shall not be chargeable on an instrument by which property is conveyed or transferred by a person to a limited liability partnership in connection with its incorporation within the period of one year beginning with the date of incorporation if the following two conditions are satisfied.

(2)   The first condition is that at the relevant time the person—

    (a)   is a partner in a partnership comprised of all the persons who are or are to be members of the limited liability partnership (and no-one else), or

    (b)   holds the property conveyed or transferred as nominee or bare trustee for one or more of the partners in such a partnership.

(3)   The second condition is that—

    (a)   the proportions of the property conveyed or transferred to which the persons mentioned in subsection (2)(a) are entitled immediately after the conveyance or transfer are the same as those to which they were entitled at the relevant time, or

    (b)   none of the differences in those proportions has arisen as part of a scheme or arrangement of which the main purpose, or one of the main purposes, is avoidance of liability to any duty or tax.

(4)   For the purposes of subsection (2) a person holds property as bare trustee for a partner if the partner has the exclusive right (subject only to satisfying any outstanding charge, lien or other right of the trustee to resort to the property for payment of duty, taxes, costs or other outgoings) to direct how the property shall be dealt with.

(5)   In this section "the relevant time" means—

    (a)   if the person who conveyed or transferred the property to the limited liability partnership acquired the property after its incorporation, immediately after he acquired the property, and

    (b)   in any other case, immediately before its incorporation.

(6)   An instrument in respect of which stamp duty is not chargeable by virtue of subsection (1) shall not be taken to be duly stamped unless—

    (a)   it has, in accordance with section 12 of the Stamp Act 1891, been stamped with a particular stamp denoting that it is not chargeable with any duty or that it is duly stamped, or

    (b)   it is stamped with the duty to which it would be liable apart from that subsection.

**13.   ** ...

Regulations

14.   Insolvency and winding up

(1)   Regulations shall make provision about the insolvency and winding up of limited liability partnerships by applying or incorporating, with such modifications—

    (a)   in relation to a limited liability partnership registered in Great Britain, Parts A1 to 4, 6 and 7 of the Insolvency Act 1986;

    (b)   in relation to a limited liability partnership registered in Northern Ireland, Parts 1A to 5 and 7 of the Insolvency (Northern Ireland) Order 1989, and so much of Part 1 of that Order as applies for the purposes of those Parts.

(2) Regulations may make other provision about the insolvency and winding up of limited liability partnerships, and provision about the insolvency and winding up of oversea limited liability partnerships, by—

    (a) applying or incorporating, with such modifications as appear appropriate, any law relating to the insolvency or winding up of companies or other corporations which would not otherwise have effect in relation to them, or

    (b) providing for any law relating to the insolvency or winding up of companies or other corporations which would otherwise have effect in relation to them not to apply to them or to apply to them with such modifications as appear appropriate.

(3) In this Act "oversea limited liability partnership" means a body incorporated or otherwise established outside the United Kingdom and having such connection with the United Kingdom, and such other features, as regulations may prescribe.

15. Application of company law etc

Regulations may make provision about limited liability partnerships and oversea limited liability partnerships (not being provision about insolvency or winding up) by—

    (a) applying or incorporating, with such modifications as appear appropriate, any law relating to companies or other corporations which would not otherwise have effect in relation to them,

    (b) providing for any law relating to companies or other corporations which would otherwise have effect in relation to them not to apply to them or to apply to them with such modifications as appear appropriate, or

    (c) applying or incorporating, with such modifications as appear appropriate, any law relating to partnerships.

16. Consequential amendments

(1) Regulations may make in any enactment such amendments or repeals as appear appropriate in consequence of this Act or regulations made under it.

(2) The regulations may, in particular, make amendments and repeals affecting companies or other corporations or partnerships

17. General

(1) In this Act "regulations" means regulations made by the Secretary of State by statutory instrument.

(2) Regulations under this Act may in particular—

    (a) make provisions for dealing with non-compliance with any of the regulations (including the creation of criminal offences),

    (b) impose fees (which shall be paid into the Consolidated Fund), and

    (c) provide for the exercise of functions by persons prescribed by the regulations.

(3) Regulations under this Act may—

    (a) contain any appropriate consequential, incidental, supplementary or transitional provisions or savings, and

    (b) make different provision for different purposes.

(4) No regulations to which this subsection applies shall be made unless a draft of the statutory instrument containing the regulations (whether or not together with other provisions) has been laid before, and approved by a resolution of, each House of Parliament.

(5) Subsection (4) applies to—

    (a) regulations under section 14(2) not consisting entirely of the application or incorporation (with or without modifications) of provisions contained in or made under the Insolvency Act 1986 or the Insolvency (Northern Ireland) Order 1989,

    (b) regulations under section 15 not consisting entirely of the application or incorporation (with or without modifications) of provisions contained in or made under the following provisions of the Companies Act 2006 (c 46)—

        Part 4 (a company's capacity and related matters);

Part 5 (a company's name);
Part 6 (a company's registered office);
Chapters 1 and 8 of Part 10 (register of directors);
Part 15 (accounts and reports);
Part 16 (audit);
Part 19 (debentures);
Part 21 (certification and transfer of securities);
Part 24 (a company's annual return);
Part 25 (company charges);
Part 26 (arrangements and reconstructions: general);
Part 26A (arrangements and reconstructions: companies in financial difficulty);
Part 29 (fraudulent trading);
Part 30 (protection of members against unfair prejudice);
Part 31 (dissolution and restoration to the register);
Part 35 (the registrar of companies);
Part 36 (offences under the Companies Acts);
Part 37 (supplementary provisions);
Part 38 (interpretation),

(c) regulations under section 14 or 15 making provision about oversea limited liability partnerships, and

(d) regulations under section 16.

(6) A statutory instrument containing regulations under this Act shall (unless a draft of it has been approved by a resolution of each House of Parliament) be subject to annulment in pursuance of a resolution of either House of Parliament.

Supplementary

18. Interpretation

In this Act—

...

"business" includes every trade, profession and occupation,

"designated member" shall be construed in accordance with section 8,

"enactment" includes subordinate legislation (within the meaning of the Interpretation Act 1978),

"incorporation document" shall be construed in accordance with section 2,

"limited liability partnership" has the meaning given by section 1(2),

"member" shall be construed in accordance with section 4,

"modifications" includes additions and omissions,

"name", in relation to a member of a limited liability partnership, means—

(a) if an individual, his forename and surname (or, in the case of a peer or other person usually known by a title, his title instead of or in addition to either or both his forename and surname), and

(b) if a corporation or Scottish firm, its corporate or firm name,

"oversea limited liability partnership" has the meaning given by section 14(3),

"the registrar" means—

(a) if the registered office of the limited liability partnership is, or is to be, in England and Wales (or Wales), the registrar of companies for England and Wales,

(b) if the registered office of the limited liability partnership is, or is to be, in Scotland, the registrar of companies for Scotland, and

(c) if the registered office of the limited liability partnership is, or is to be, in Northern Ireland, the registrar of companies for Northern Ireland;

"regulations" has the meaning given by section 17(1).

19. Commencement, extent and short title

(1)　The preceding provisions of this Act shall come into force on such day as the Secretary of State may by order made by statutory instrument appoint; and different days may be appointed for different purposes.

(2)　The Secretary of State may by order made by statutory instrument make any transitional provisions and savings which appear appropriate in connection with the coming into force of any provision of this Act.

(3)　For the purposes of the Scotland Act 1998 this Act shall be taken to be a pre-commencement enactment within the meaning of that Act.

(4)　This Act extends to the whole of the United Kingdom.

(5)　This Act may be cited as the Limited Liability Partnerships Act 2000.

SCHEDULE

NAMES ...

Section 1

PART I

NAMES

1.　　...

Name to indicate status

2.—　(1)　The name of a limited liability partnership must end with—
　　　　(a)　the expression "limited liability partnership", or
　　　　(b)　the abbreviation "llp" or "LLP".

　　　(2)　But if the incorporation document for a limited liability partnership states that the registered office is to be situated in Wales, its name must end with—
　　　　(a)　one of the expressions "limited liability partnership" and "partneriaeth atebolrwydd cyfyngedig", or
　　　　(b)　one of the abbreviations "llp", "LLP", "pac" and "PAC".

Registration of names

3.　　...

Change of name

4.—　(1)　A limited liability partnership may change its name at any time.

　　　(2)　The name of a limited liability partnership may also be changed—
　　　　(a)　on the determination of a new name by a company names adjudicator under section 73 of the Companies Act 2006 (C 46) as applied to limited liability partnerships (powers of adjudicator on upholding objection to name);
　　　　(b)　on the determination of a new name by the court under section 74 of the Companies Act 2006 as so applied (appeal against decision of company names adjudicator);
　　　　(ba)　on the determination of a new name by the registrar under section 76C or 76D of the Companies Act 2006 as so applied (names containing computer code or failure to comply with direction);
　　　　(c)　under section 1033 as so applied (name on restoration to the register).

Notification of change of name

5.—　(1)　Where a limited liability partnership changes its name it shall deliver notice of the change to the registrar.

　　　(2)–(4) ...

Registration of a change of name

5A.— (1) This paragraph applies where—

    (a) the registrar receives notice of a change of name of a limited liability partnership and the new name is one by which a limited liability partnership may be registered, or

    (b) the registrar determines a new name for a limited liability partnership under a provision mentioned in paragraph 4(2)(ba).

  (2) The registrar shall—

    (a) enter the new name on the register in place of the former name, and

    (b) issue a certificate of the change of name.

  (3) The change of name has effect from the date on which the certificate is issued.

Effect of change of name

6. A change of name by a limited liability partnership does not—

  (a) affect any of its rights or duties,

  (b) render defective any legal proceedings by or against it,

and any legal proceedings that might have been commenced or continued against it by its former name may be commenced or continued against it by its new name.

Improper use of "limited liability partnership" etc

7.— (1) If any person carries on a business under a name or title which includes as the last words—

    (a) the expression "limited liability partnership" or "partneriaeth atebolrwydd cyfyngedig", or

    (b) any contraction or imitation of either of those expressions,

that person, unless a limited liability partnership or oversea limited liability partnership, commits an offence.

  (2) A person guilty of an offence under sub-paragraph (1) is liable on summary conviction to a fine not exceeding level 3 on the standard scale.

8. ...

PART II

...

Limited Liability Partnerships Regulations 2001

S.I. 2001/1090

PART I

CITATION, COMMENCEMENT AND INTERPRETATION

1.   Citation and commencement

These Regulations may be cited as the Limited Liability Partnerships Regulations 2001 and shall come into force on 6th April 2001.

2.   Interpretation

In these Regulations—

"the 1985 Act" means the Companies Act 1985;

"the 1986 Act" means the Insolvency Act 1986;

"the 2000 Act" means the Financial Services and Markets Act 2000;

"devolved", in relation to the provisions of the 1986 Act, means the provisions of the 1986 Act which are listed in Schedule 4 and, in their application to Scotland, concern wholly or partly, matters which are set out in Section C 2 of Schedule 5 to the Scotland Act 1998 as being exceptions to the reservations made in that Act in the field of insolvency;

"limited liability partnership agreement", in relation to a limited liability partnership, means any agreement express or implied between the members of the limited liability partnership or between the limited liability partnership and the members of the limited liability partnership which determines the mutual rights and duties of the members, and their rights and duties in relation to the limited liability partnership;

"the principal Act" means the Limited Liability Partnerships Act 2000; and

"shadow member", in relation to limited liability partnerships, means a person in accordance with whose directions or instructions the members of the limited liability partnership are accustomed to act (but so that a person is not deemed a shadow member by reason only that the members of the limited partnership act on advice given by him in a professional capacity).

2A.   Application of provisions

(1)   The provisions of these Regulations applying—

(a)   the Company Directors Disqualification Act 1986, or

(b)   provisions of the Insolvency Act 1986,

have effect only in relation to limited liability partnerships registered in Great Britain.

(2)   The other provisions of these Regulations have effect in relation to limited liability partnerships registered in any part of the United Kingdom.

...

PART III

COMPANIES ACT 1985 AND COMPANY DIRECTORS DISQUALIFICATION ACT 1986

4.   Application of certain provisions of the 1985 Act and of the provisions of the Company Directors Disqualification Act 1986 to limited liability partnerships

(1)   The provisions of the 1985 Act specified in the first column of Part I of Schedule 2 to these Regulations shall apply to limited liability partnerships, except where the context otherwise requires, with the following modifications—

(a) references to a company shall include references to a limited liability partnership;

(b) ...

(c) references to the Insolvency Act 1986 shall include references to that Act as it applies to limited liability partnerships by virtue of Part IV of these Regulations;

(d) references in a provision of the 1985 Act to—

    (i) other provisions of that Act, or

    (ii) provisions of the Companies Act 2006,

shall include references to those provisions as they apply to limited liability partnerships;

(e), (f) ...

(g) references to a director of a company or to an officer of a company shall include references to a member of a limited liability partnership;

(h) the modifications, if any, specified in the second column of Part I of Schedule 2 opposite the provision specified in the first column; and

(i) such further modifications as the context requires for the purpose of giving effect to that legislation as applied by these Regulations.

(2) The provisions of the Company Director Disqualification Act 1986 shall apply to limited liability partnerships, except where the context otherwise requires, with the following modifications—

(a) references to a company shall include references to a limited liability partnership;

(b) references to the Companies Acts shall include references to the principal Act and regulations made thereunder;

(c) references to the Insolvency Act 1986 shall include references to that Act as it applies to limited liability partnerships by virtue of Part IV of these Regulations;

(d) references in a provision of the 1985 Act to other provisions of that Act shall include references to those other provisions as they apply to limited liability partnerships by virtue of these Regulations;

(e) ...

(f) references to a shadow director shall include references to a shadow member;

(g) references to a director of a company or to an officer of a company shall include references to a member of a limited liability partnership;

(h) the modifications, if any, specified in the second column of Part II of Schedule 2 opposite the provision specified in the first column; and

(i) such further modifications as the context requires for the purpose of giving effect to that legislation as applied by these Regulations.

PART IV

WINDING UP AND INSOLVENCY

5. **Application of the 1986 Act to limited liability partnerships**

(1) Subject to paragraphs (2) and (3), the following provisions of the 1986 Act, shall apply to limited liability partnerships—

(a) Parts A1, I, II, III, IV, VI and VII of the First Group of Parts (company insolvency; companies winding up),

(b) the Third Group of Parts (miscellaneous matters bearing on both company and individual insolvency; general interpretation; final provisions).

(2) The provisions of the 1986 Act referred to in paragraph (1) shall apply to limited liability partnerships, except where the context otherwise requires, with the following modifications—

(a) references to a company shall include references to a limited liability partnership;

(b) references to a director or to an officer of a company shall include references to a member of a limited liability partnership;

(c) references to a shadow director shall include references to a shadow member;

(d) references to the Companies Acts, the Company Directors Disqualification Act 1986, the Companies Act 1989 or to any provisions of those Acts or to any provisions of the 1986 Act shall include references to those Acts or provisions as they apply to limited liability partnerships by virtue of the principal Act;

(e) references ... to the articles of association of a company shall include references to the limited liability partnership agreement of a limited liability partnership;

(f) the modifications set out in Schedule 3 to these Regulations; and

(g) such further modifications as the context requires for the purpose of giving effect to that legislation as applied by these Regulations.

(3) In the application of this regulation to Scotland, the provisions of the 1986 Act referred to in paragraph (1) shall not include the provisions listed in Schedule 4 to the extent specified in that Schedule.

PART V

FINANCIAL SERVICES AND MARKETS

6. Application of provisions contained in Parts XV and XXIV of the 2000 Act to limited liability partnerships

(1) Subject to paragraph (2), sections 215(3),(4) and (6), 356, 359(1) to (4), 361 to 365, 367, 370 and 371 of the 2000 Act shall apply to limited liability partnerships.

(2) The provisions of the 2000 Act referred to in paragraph (1) shall apply to limited liability partnerships, except where the context otherwise requires, with the following modifications—

(a) references to a company shall include references to a limited liability partnership;

(b) references to body shall include references to a limited liability partnership; and

(c) references to the 1985 Act, the 1986 Act or to any of the provisions of those Acts shall include references to those Acts or provisions as they apply to limited liability partnerships by virtue of the principal Act.

PART VI

DEFAULT PROVISION

7. Default provision for limited liability partnerships

The mutual rights and duties of the members and the mutual rights and duties of the limited liability partnership and the members shall be determined, subject to the provisions of the general law and to the terms of any limited liability partnership agreement, by the following rules:

(1) All the members of a limited liability partnership are entitled to share equally in the capital and profits of the limited liability partnership.

(2) The limited liability partnership must indemnify each member in respect of payments made and personal liabilities incurred by him—

(a) in the ordinary and proper conduct of the business of the limited liability partnership; or

(b) in or about anything necessarily done for the preservation of the business or property of the limited liability partnership.

(3) Every member may take part in the management of the limited liability partnership.

(4) No member shall be entitled to remuneration for acting in the business or management of the limited liability partnership.

(5) No person may be introduced as a member or voluntarily assign an interest in a limited liability partnership without the consent of all existing members.

(6) Any difference arising as to ordinary matters connected with the business of the limited liability partnership may be decided by a majority of the members, but no change may be made in the nature of the business of the limited liability partnership without the consent of all the members.

(7)   The books and records of the limited liability partnership are to be made available for inspection at the registered office of the limited liability partnership or at such other place as the members think fit and every member of the limited liability partnership may when he thinks fit have access to and inspect and copy any of them.

(8)   Each member shall render true accounts and full information of all things affecting the limited liability partnership to any member or his legal representatives.

(9)   If a member, without the consent of the limited liability partnership, carries on any business of the same nature as and competing with the limited liability partnership, he must account for and pay over to the limited liability partnership all profits made by him in that business.

(10)   Every member must account to the limited liability partnership for any benefit derived by him without the consent of the limited liability partnership from any transaction concerning the limited liability partnership, or from any use by him of the property of the limited liability partnership, name or business connection.

8.   Expulsion

No majority of the members can expel any member unless a power to do so has been conferred by express agreement between the members.

PART VII

MISCELLANEOUS

9.   General and consequential amendments

(1)   Subject to paragraph (2), the enactments mentioned in Schedule 5 shall have effect subject to the amendments specified in that Schedule.

(2)   In the application of this regulation to Scotland—

    (a)   paragraph 15 of Schedule 5 which amends section 110 of the 1986 Act shall not extend to Scotland; and

    (b)   paragraph 22 of Schedule 5 which applies to limited liability partnerships the culpable officer provisions in existing primary legislation shall not extend to Scotland insofar as it relates to matters which have not been reserved by Schedule 5 to the Scotland Act 1998.

10.   Application of subordinate legislation

(1)   The subordinate legislation specified in Schedule 6 shall apply as from time to time in force to limited liability partnerships and—

    (a)   in the case of the subordinate legislation listed in Part I of that Schedule with such modifications as the context requires for the purpose of giving effect to the provisions of the Companies Act 1985 which are applied by these Regulations;

    (b)   in the case of the subordinate legislation listed in Part II of that Schedule with such modifications as the context requires for the purpose of giving effect to the provisions of the Insolvency Act 1986 which are applied by these Regulations; and

    (c)   in the case of the subordinate legislation listed in Part III of that Schedule with such modifications as the context requires for the purpose of giving effect to the provisions of … the Company Directors Disqualification Act 1986 which are applied by these Regulations.

(2)   In the case of any conflict between any provision of the subordinate legislation applied by paragraph (1) and any provision of these Regulations, the latter shall prevail.

...

SCHEDULE 6

APPLICATION OF SUBORDINATE LEGISLATION

Regulation 10

PART I

REGULATIONS MADE UNDER THE 1985 ACT

...

7. The Companies Act 1985 (Power to Enter and Remain on Premises: Procedural) Regulations 2005

PART II

REGULATIONS MADE UNDER THE 1986 ACT

1. Insolvency Practitioners Regulations 1990
2. The Insolvency Practitioners (Recognised Professional Bodies) Order 1986
3. The Insolvency (England and Wales) Rules 2016 and the Insolvency (Scotland) Rules 1986 (except in so far as they relate to the exceptions to the reserved matters specified in section C 2 of Part II of Schedule 5 to the Scotland Act 1998)
4. The Insolvency Fees Order 1986
5. The Co-operation of Insolvency Courts (Designation of Relevant Countries and Territories) Order 1986
6. The Co-operation of Insolvency Courts (Designation of Relevant Countries and Territories) Order 1996
7. The Co-operation of Insolvency Courts (Designation of Relevant Country) Order 1998
8. Insolvency Proceedings (Monetary Limits) Order 1986
9. ...
10. Insolvency Regulations 1994
11. Insolvency (Amendment) Regulations 2000

PART III

REGULATIONS MADE UNDER OTHER LEGISLATION

1. ...
2. The Companies (Disqualification Orders) Regulations 1986
3. The Insolvent Companies (Disqualification of Unfit Directors) Proceedings Rules 1987
4. The Contracting Out (Functions of the Official Receiver) Order 1995
5. The Uncertificated Securities Regulations 1995
6. The Insolvent Companies (Reports on Conduct of Directors) (England and Wales) Rules 2016
7. The Insolvent Companies (Reports on Conduct of Directors) (Scotland) Rules 2016

...

Company, Limited Liability Partnership and Business Names (Sensitive Words and Expressions) Regulations 2014

S.I. 2014/3140

1.   Citation and commencement

These Regulations may be cited as the Company, Limited Liability Partnership and Business Names (Sensitive Words and Expressions) Regulations 2014 and come into force on 31st January 2015.

2.   Interpretation

(1)   In these Regulations "the 2006 Act" means the Companies Act 2006.

(2)   Any reference in these Regulations to section 55 or 88 of the 2006 Act includes a reference to that section as applied by regulation 8 or 17 of the Limited Liability Partnerships (Application of Companies Act 2006) Regulations 2009.

3.   Specified words and expressions to which sections 55 and 1194 of the 2006 Act apply

The following words and expressions are specified for the purposes of sections 55(1) and 1194(1) of the 2006 Act—

(a)   the words and expressions set out in Part 1 of Schedule 1;

(b)   the plural and possessive forms of those words and expressions, and, where relevant, the feminine form; and

(c)   in the case of the words and expressions set out in Part 1 of Schedule 1 which are marked with an asterisk, the grammatically mutated forms of those words and expressions.

4.   Specified words and expressions to which section 55 of the 2006 Act applies

The following words and expressions are specified for the purposes of section 55(1) of the 2006 Act—

(a)   the words and expressions set out in Part 2 of Schedule 1;

(b)   the plural and possessive forms of those words and expressions, and, where relevant, the feminine form; and

(c)   in the case of the words and expressions set out in Part 2 of Schedule 1 which are marked with an asterisk, the grammatically mutated forms of those words and expressions.

5.   Applications where situation of registered office or principal place of business is irrelevant

In connection with an application for the approval of the Secretary of State under section 55 or 1194 of the 2006 Act in relation to a name that includes a word or expression specified in column (1) of Part 1 of Schedule 2, the applicant must seek the view of the Government department or other body set out opposite that word or expression in column (2) of Part 1 of Schedule 2.

6.   Applications where situation of registered office or principal place of business is relevant

In connection with an application for the approval of the Secretary of State under section 55 or 1194 of the 2006 Act in relation to a name that includes a word or expression specified in column (1) of Part 2 of Schedule 2, the applicant must seek the view of a Government department or other body as follows—

(a)   in the case of—

    (i)   a company or limited liability partnership that has already been registered, whose registered office is situated in England and Wales;

    (ii)   a proposed company or limited liability partnership that has not yet been registered under the 2006 Act, whose registered office is to be situated in England and Wales;

       (iii) a business, whose principal place of business is or is to be situated in England; and

       (iv) an overseas company (see section 1044 of the 2006 Act),

      the Government department or other body set out in column (2) of Part 2 of Schedule 2 opposite that word or expression;

  (b) in the case of—

       (i) a company or limited liability partnership that has already been registered, that is a Welsh company or Welsh LLP (see section 88 of the 2006 Act);

       (ii) a proposed company or limited liability partnership that has not yet been registered, that is to be a Welsh company or Welsh LLP; and

       (iii) a business, whose principal place of business is or is to be situated in Wales,

      the Government department or other body set out in column (3) of Part 2 of Schedule 2 opposite that word or expression;

  (c) in the case of—

       (i) a company or limited liability partnership that has already been registered, whose registered office is situated in Scotland;

       (ii) a proposed company or limited liability partnership that has not yet been registered, whose registered office is to be situated in Scotland; and

       (iii) a business, whose principal place of business is or is to be situated in Scotland,

      the Government department or other body set out in column (4) of Part 2 of Schedule 2 opposite that word or expression; and

  (d) in the case of—

       (i) a company or limited liability partnership that has already been registered, whose registered office is situated in Northern Ireland;

       (ii) a proposed company or limited liability partnership that has not yet been registered, whose registered office is to be situated in Northern Ireland; and

       (iii) a business, whose principal place of business is or is to be situated in Northern Ireland, the Government department or other body set out in column (5) of Part 2 of Schedule 2 opposite that word or expression.

7.   **Revocation**

The Company, Limited Liability Partnership and Business Names (Sensitive Words and Expressions) Regulations 2009 are revoked.

SCHEDULE 1   Regulations 3 and 4

SPECIFIED WORDS AND EXPRESSIONS

PART 1

WORDS AND EXPRESSIONS SPECIFIED FOR THE PURPOSES OF SECTIONS 55(1) AND 1194(1) OF THE 2006 ACT

Accredit	Benevolent	Child maintenance
Accreditation	*Breatannach	Child support
Accredited	*Breatainn	*Coimisean
Accrediting	*Brenhinol	*Comhairle
Adjudicator	*Brenin	*Comisiwn
Association	*Brenhiniaeth	Commission
Assurance	Britain	Co-operative
Assurer	British	Council
Audit office	Chamber of commerce	*Cyngor
Auditor General	Charitable	Dental
*Banc	Charity	Dentistry
Bank	Charter	*Diùc
Banking	Chartered	*Dug

Duke	NHS	*Riaghaltas
Ei Fawrhydi	Northern Ireland	*Rìgh
England	Northern Irish	Rìoghachd Aonaichte
English	Nurse	Rìoghail
Federation	Nursing	Rìoghalachd
Friendly Society	Oifis sgrùdaidh	Royal
Foundation	*Oilthigh	Royalty
Fund	Ombudsman	Scotland
Government	*Ombwdsmon	Scottish
*Gwasanaeth iechyd	*Parlamaid	Senedd
Health centre	Parliament	Sheffield
Health service	Parliamentarian	Siambr fasnach
Health visitor	Parliamentary	Social service
His Majesty	Patent	Society
HPSS	Patentee	Special school
HSC	Police	Standards
Inspectorate	Polytechnic	Stock exchange
Institute	Post office	Swyddfa archwilio
Institution	*Prifysgol	*Teyrnas Gyfunol
Insurance	Prince	*Teyrnas Unedig
Insurer	*Prionnsa	Trade union
Judicial appointment	*Prydain	Tribunal
King	*Prydeinig	Trust
Licensing	Queen	*Tywysog
*Llywodraeth	Reassurance	Underwrite
Medical centre	Reassurer	Underwriting
Midwife	Registrar	University
Midwifery	Regulator	Wales
*Mòrachd	Reinsurance	Welsh
Mutual	Reinsurer	Windsor

PART 2
WORDS AND EXPRESSIONS SPECIFIED FOR THE PURPOSES OF SECTION 55(1) OF THE 2006 ACT

Alba	Na h-Alba	*Cymraeg
Albannach	*Cymru	*Cymreig

SCHEDULE 2 — Regulations 5 and 6
LIST OF GOVERNMENT DEPARTMENTS AND OTHER BODIES WHOSE VIEWS MUST BE SOUGHT

PART 1
APPLICATIONS WHERE SITUATION OF REGISTERED OFFICE OR PRINCIPAL PLACE OF BUSINESS IS IRRELEVANT

Column (1)	Column (2)
Word or expression specified under regulation 3	Specified Government department or other body whose view must be sought
Accredit	Department for Business and Trade
Accreditation	Department for Business and Trade
Accredited	Department for Business and Trade

Column (1)	Column (2)
Word or expression specified under regulation 3	Specified Government department or other body whose view must be sought
Accrediting	Department for Business and Trade
Assurance	Financial Conduct Authority
Assurer	Financial Conduct Authority
Banc	Financial Conduct Authority
Bank	Financial Conduct Authority
Banking	Financial Conduct Authority
Brenhinol	The Welsh Assembly Government
Brenin	The Welsh Assembly Government
Brenhiniaeth	The Welsh Assembly Government
Child maintenance	Department for Work and Pensions
Child support	Department for Work and Pensions
Dental	General Dental Council
Dentistry	General Dental Council
Diùc	The Scottish Government
Dug	The Welsh Assembly Government
Ei Fawrhydi	The Welsh Assembly Government
Friendly Society	Financial Conduct Authority
Fund	Financial Conduct Authority
Gwasanaeth iechyd	The Welsh Assembly Government
Health visitor	Nursing & Midwifery Council
HPSS	Department of Health, Social Services and Public Safety
HSC	Department of Health, Social Services and Public Safety
Insurance	Financial Conduct Authority
Insurer	Financial Conduct Authority
Judicial appointment	Ministry of Justice
Llywodraeth	The Welsh Assembly Government
Medical centre	Department of Health, Social Services and Public Safety
Midwife	Nursing & Midwifery Council
Midwifery	Nursing & Midwifery Council
Mòrachd	The Scottish Government
Mutual	Financial Conduct Authority
NHS	Department of Health and Social Care
Nurse	Nursing & Midwifery Council
Nursing	Nursing & Midwifery Council
Oifis sgrùdaidh	Audit Scotland
Oilthigh	The Scottish Government
Parlamaid	The Scottish Parliamentary Corporate Body
Parliament	The Corporate Officer of the House of Lords and The Corporate Officer of the House of Commons

Column (1)	Column (2)
Word or expression specified under regulation 3	Specified Government department or other body whose view must be sought
Parliamentarian	The Corporate Officer of the House of Lords and The Corporate Officer of the House of Commons
Parliamentary	The Corporate Officer of the House of Lords and The Corporate Officer of the House of Commons
Patent	The Patent Office
Patentee	The Patent Office
Polytechnic	Department for Education
Prifysgol	The Welsh Assembly Government
Prionnsa	The Scottish Government
Reassurance	Financial Conduct Authority
Reassurer	Financial Conduct Authority
Reinsurance	Financial Conduct Authority
Reinsurer	Financial Conduct Authority
Riaghaltas	The Scottish Government
Rìgh	The Scottish Government
Rìoghail	The Scottish Government
Rìoghalachd	The Scottish Government
Senedd	The National Assembly for Wales
Sheffield	The Company of Cutlers in Hallamshire
Swyddfa archwilio	Auditor General for Wales
Tywysog	The Welsh Assembly Government
Underwrite	Financial Conduct Authority
Underwriting	Financial Conduct Authority

PART 2

APPLICATIONS WHERE SITUATION OF REGISTERED OFFICE OR PRINCIPAL PLACE OF BUSINESS IS RELEVANT

Column (1)	Column (2)	Column (3)	Column (4)	Column (5)
Word or expression specified under regulation 3	Specified Government department or other body whose view must be sought			
	under regulation 6(a)	under regulation 6(b)	under regulation 6(c)	under regulation 6(d)
Audit office	Comptroller & Auditor General	Auditor General for Wales	Audit Scotland	Northern Ireland Audit Office
Charitable Charity	The Charity Commission	The Charity Commission	Office of the Scottish Charity Regulator	The Charity Commission

Column (1)	Column (2)	Column (3)	Column (4)	Column (5)
Word or expression specified under regulation 3	Specified Government department or other body whose view must be sought			
	under regulation 6(a)	under regulation 6(b)	under regulation 6(c)	under regulation 6(d)
Duke	Ministry of Justice	The Welsh Assembly Government	The Scottish Government	Ministry of Justice
His Majesty				
King				
Prince				
Queen				
Royal				
Royalty				
Windsor				
Health centre	Department of Health and Social Care	The Welsh Assembly Government	The Scottish Government	Department of Health, Social Services and Public Safety
Health service				
Police	The Home Office	The Home Office	The Scottish Government	Department of Justice in Northern Ireland
Special school	Department for Education	The Welsh Assembly Government	The Scottish Government	Department of Education
University	Department for Education	The Welsh Assembly Government	The Scottish Government	Department for Employment and Learning

Company, Limited Liability Partnership and Business (Names and Trading Disclosures) Regulations 2015

S.I. 2015/17

PART 1
INTRODUCTORY

1. **Citation, commencement and interpretation**

(1) These Regulations may be cited as the Company, Limited Liability Partnership and Business (Names and Trading Disclosures) Regulations 2015 and come into force on 31st January 2015.

(2) In these Regulations, "the Act" means the Companies Act 2006.

PART 2
COMPANY NAMES

2. **Permitted characters**

(1) This regulation sets out the characters, signs, symbols (including accents and other diacritical marks) and punctuation that may be used in the name of a company registered under the Act ("the permitted characters").

(2) The following permitted characters may be used in any part of the name—

    (a) any character, character with an accent or other diacritical mark, sign or symbol set out in table 1 in Schedule 1;

    (b) 0, 1, 2, 3, 4, 5, 6, 7, 8 or 9;

    (c) full stop, comma, colon, semi-colon or hyphen; and

    (d) any other punctuation referred to in column 1 of table 2 in Schedule 1 but only in one of the forms set out opposite that punctuation in column 2 of that table.

(3) The signs and symbols set out in table 3 in Schedule 1 are permitted characters that may be used but not as one of the first three permitted characters of the name.

(4) The name must not consist of more than 160 permitted characters.

(5) For the purposes of computing the number of permitted characters in paragraph (4) of this regulation (but not in paragraph (3) of this regulation), any blank space between one permitted character and another in the name shall be counted as though it was a permitted character.

3. **Exemption from requirement as to use of "limited"**

(1) A private company limited by guarantee is exempt from section 59 of the Act (requirement to have name ending with "limited" or permitted alternative) so long as it meets the following two conditions.

(2) The first condition is that the objects of that company are the promotion or regulation of commerce, art, science, education, religion, charity or any profession, and anything incidental or conducive to any of those objects.

(3) The second condition is that the company's articles—

    (a) require its income to be applied in promoting its objects;

    (b) prohibit the payment of dividends, or any return of capital, to its members; and

    (c) require all the assets that would otherwise be available to its members generally to be transferred on its winding up either—

        (i) to another body with objects similar to its own; or

        (ii) to another body the objects of which are the promotion of charity and anything incidental or conducive thereto,

(whether or not the body is a member of the company).

4.   **Inappropriate indication of company type or legal form: generally applicable provisions**

(1)   A company must not be registered under the Act by a name that includes, otherwise than at the end of the name, an expression or abbreviation specified in inverted commas in paragraph 3(a) to (f) of Schedule 2 (or any expression or abbreviation specified as similar).

(2)   A company must not be registered under the Act by a name that includes in any part of the name an expression or abbreviation specified in inverted commas in paragraph 3(g) or (h) of Schedule 2 (or any expression or abbreviation specified as similar) unless that company is a RTE company within the meaning of section 4A of the Leasehold Reform, Housing and Urban Development Act 1993.

(3)   A company must not be registered under the Act by a name that includes in any part of the name an expression or abbreviation specified in inverted commas in paragraph 3(i) or (j) of Schedule 2 (or any expression or abbreviation specified as similar) unless that company is a RTM company within the meaning of section 73 of the Commonhold and Leasehold Reform Act 2002.

(4)   A company must not be registered under the Act by a name that includes in any part of the name an expression or abbreviation specified in inverted commas in paragraph 3(k) to (x) of Schedule 2 (or any expression or abbreviation specified as similar).

(5)   A company must not be registered under the Act by a name that includes immediately before an expression or abbreviation specified in inverted commas in paragraph 3(a) to (j) of Schedule 2 an abbreviation specified in inverted commas in paragraph 3(y) of that Schedule (or any abbreviation specified as similar).

(6)   Paragraph (1) is subject to regulations 5(b) and 6(b).

5.   **Inappropriate indication of company type or legal form: company exempt from requirement to have name ending in "limited"**

A company which is exempt from section 59 of the Act (requirement to have name ending with "limited" or permitted alternative) under section 60 of the Act must not be registered under the Act by a name that concludes with—

(a)   a word specified in inverted commas in paragraph 1(c) or (d) of Schedule 2 (or any word specified as similar); or

(b)   an expression or abbreviation specified in inverted commas in paragraph 3(a) to (f) or (y) of Schedule 2 (or any expression or abbreviation specified as similar).

6.   **Inappropriate indication of company type or legal form: unlimited company**

An unlimited company must not be registered under the Act by a name that concludes with—

(a)   a word or abbreviation specified in inverted commas in paragraph 1(a) or (b) of Schedule 2 (or any word or abbreviation specified as similar); or

(b)   an expression or abbreviation specified in inverted commas in paragraph 3(a) to (f) or (y) of Schedule 2 (or any expression or abbreviation specified as similar).

7.   **Name not to be the same as another in the registrar's index of company names**

For the purposes of section 66 of the Act (determining whether a name to be registered under the Act is the same as another name appearing in the registrar's index of company names) Schedule 3 has effect for setting out—

(a)   the matters that are to be disregarded; and

(b)   the words, expressions, signs and symbols that are to be regarded as the same.

8.   **Consent to registration of a name which is the same as another in the registrar's index of company names**

(1)   A company may be registered under the Act by a proposed same name if the conditions in paragraph (2) are met.

(2)   The conditions are—

    (a)   the company or other body whose name already appears in the registrar's index of company names ("Body X") consents to the proposed same name being the name of a company ("Company Y");

    (b)   Company Y forms, or is to form, part of the same group as Body X; and

    (c)   Company Y provides to the registrar a copy of a statement made by Body X indicating—

        (i)   the consent of Body X as referred to in sub-paragraph (a); and

        (ii)   that Company Y forms, or is to form, part of the same group as Body X.

(3)   If the proposed same name is to be taken by a company which has not yet been incorporated, the copy of such statement must be provided to the registrar instead by the person who delivers to the registrar the application for registration of the company (and the reference in paragraph (1) to the conditions in paragraph (2) shall be read accordingly).

(4)   The registrar may accept the statement referred to in paragraph (2)(c) as sufficient evidence that the conditions referred to in paragraph (2)(a) and (b) have been met.

(5)   If the consent referred to in paragraph (2)(a) is given by Body X, a subsequent withdrawal of that consent does not affect the registration of Company Y by that proposed same name.

(6)   In this regulation—

    (a)   "group" has the meaning given in section 474(1) of the Act; and

    (b)   "proposed same name" means a name which is, due to the application of regulation 8 and Schedule 3, considered the same as a name appearing in the registrar's index of company names and differs from that name appearing in the index by any of the matters set out in inverted commas in paragraph 5 of Schedule 3.

9.   **Names with connection to Public Authorities**

(1)   Each of the persons and bodies set out in column (1) of Schedule 4 is specified for the purposes of section 54 of the Act.

(2)   In connection with an application for the approval of the Secretary of State under section 54 of the Act in relation to a name that would be likely to give the impression of a connection with a public authority set out in column (1) of Schedule 4 the applicant must seek the view of the Government department or other body set out opposite that public authority in column (2) of Schedule 4.

10.   **Interpretation**

In this Part—

    (a)   "expression or abbreviation specified as similar" has the meaning given in paragraph 4 of Schedule 2 and "abbreviation specified as similar" has the meaning that would be given to it in that paragraph if that paragraph made no reference to "expressions";

    (b)   "permitted characters" has the meaning given in regulation 2(1);

    (c)   "word or abbreviation specified as similar" has the meaning given in paragraph 2 of Schedule 2; and

    (d)   "word specified as similar" has the meaning given in paragraph 2 of Schedule 2.

PART 3

LIMITED LIABILITY PARTNERSHIP NAMES

11.   **Application to Limited Liability Partnerships**

(1)   In regulation 9 of these Regulations, any reference to section 54 of the Act includes a reference to that section as applied by regulation 8 of the Limited Liability Partnerships (Application of Companies Act 2006) Regulations 2009.

(2)   The Limited Liability Partnerships (Application of Companies Act 2006) Regulations 2009 are amended by Schedule 5.

PART 4
OVERSEAS COMPANY NAMES

12.   **Interpretation and permitted characters**

Regulations 2 and 10 apply to the name of an overseas company which is registered by that company under Part 34 of the Act (overseas companies) as they apply to the name of a company formed and registered under the Act.

13.   **Inappropriate indication of company type or legal form**

(1)   An overseas company must not be registered under the Act by a name that concludes with a word or abbreviation specified in inverted commas in paragraph 1(a) or (b) of Schedule 2 (or any word or abbreviation specified as similar) unless the liability of the members of the company is limited by its constitution.

(2)   An overseas company must not be registered under the Act by a name that concludes with a word specified in inverted commas in paragraph 1(c) or (d) of Schedule 2 (or any word specified as similar) unless the liability of the members of the company is not limited by its constitution.

(3)   An overseas company must not be registered under the Act by a name that includes in any part of the name an expression or abbreviation specified in inverted commas in paragraph 3 of Schedule 2 (or any expression or abbreviation specified as similar).

14.   **Name not to be the same as another in the registrar's index of company names**

Regulation 7 applies to the name of an overseas company which is registered by that company under Part 34 of the Act as it applies to the name of a company formed and registered under the Act.

15.   **Consent to registration of a name which is the same as another in the registrar's index of company names**

(1)   Regulation 8 applies to the proposed same name of an overseas company as it applies to the proposed same name of a company formed and registered under the Act.

(2)   In this regulation "proposed same name" has the same meaning as in regulation 8.

PART 5
BUSINESS NAMES

16.   **"Limited" and permitted alternatives**

(1)   A person must not carry on business in the United Kingdom under a name that concludes with any word or abbreviation set out in inverted commas in paragraph 1(a) or (b) of Schedule 2 unless that person is—

(a)   a company or an overseas company registered in the United Kingdom by that name;

(b)   an overseas company incorporated with that name;

(c)   a society registered under the Co-operative and Community Benefit Societies Act 2014 or the Industrial and Provident Societies Act (Northern Ireland) 1969 by that name;

(d)   an incorporated friendly society (as defined in section 116 of the Friendly Societies Act 1992) which has that name; ...

(e)   a company to which section 1040 of the Act (companies authorised to register under the Companies Act 2006) applies which has that name; or

(f)   a company registered under Part 4 of the Risk Transformation Regulations 2017 with that name.

(2)   A person must not carry on business in the United Kingdom under a name that concludes with any word or abbreviation specified as similar to any word or abbreviation set out in inverted commas in paragraph 1(a) or (b) of Schedule 2.

17. **Other indications of legal form**

(1) A person must not carry on business in the United Kingdom under a name that includes any expression or abbreviation set out in inverted commas in paragraph 3 of Schedule 2 unless that person is such a company, partnership, grouping or organisation as is indicated in that expression or abbreviation.

(2) A person must not carry on business in the United Kingdom under a name that includes any expression or abbreviation specified as similar to any expression or abbreviation set out in inverted commas in paragraph 3 of Schedule 2.

18. **Names with connection to Public Authorities**

(1) Each of the persons and bodies set out in column (1) of Schedule 4 is specified for the purposes of section 1193 of the Act.

(2) In connection with an application for the approval of the Secretary of State under section 1193 of the Act in relation to a name that would be likely to give the impression of a connection with a public authority set out in column (1) of Schedule 4 the applicant must seek the view of the Government department or other body set out opposite that public authority in column (2) of Schedule 4.

19. **Savings and Transitional provisions**

(1) Regulation 17 does not apply to the carrying on of a business under a name by a person who—

   (a) carried on that business under that name immediately before these Regulations came into force; and

   (b) continues to carry it on under that name,

if it was lawful for the business to be carried on under that name immediately before these Regulations came into force.

(2) Regulation 17 does not apply to the carrying on of a business under a name by a person to whom the business is transferred on or after the date on which these Regulations came into force—

   (a) where that person continues to carry on the business under that name; and

   (b) where it was lawful for the business to be carried on under that name immediately before the transfer, during the period of 12 months beginning with the date of the transfer.

(3) Regulation 18 does not apply to the carrying on of a business by a person who—

   (a) carried on the business immediately before the date on which these Regulations came into force, and

   (b) continues to carry it on under the name that immediately before that date was its lawful business name.

(4) Regulation 18 does not apply in relation to the carrying on of the business under that name during the period of twelve months beginning with the date of the transfer where—

   (a) a business is transferred to a person on or after the date on which these Regulations came into force, and

   (b) that person carries on the business under the name that was its lawful business name immediately before the transfer,

(5) In this regulation "lawful business name", in relation to a business, means a name under which the business was carried on without contravening the provisions of Chapter 1 of Part 41 of the Act.

PART 6
TRADING DISCLOSURES

20. Legibility of displays and disclosures

Any display or disclosure of information required by this Part must be in characters that can be read with the naked eye.

21. Requirement to display registered name at registered office and inspection place

(1) A company shall display its registered name at—
  (a) its registered office; and
  (b) any inspection place.

(2) But paragraph (1) does not apply to any company which has at all times since its incorporation been dormant.

(3) Paragraph (1) shall also not apply to the registered office or an inspection place of a company where—
  (a) in respect of that company, a liquidator, administrator or administrative receiver has been appointed; and
  (b) the registered office or inspection place is also a place of business of that liquidator, administrator or administrative receiver.

22. Requirement to display registered name at other business locations

(1) This regulation applies to a location other than a company's registered office or any inspection place.

(2) A company shall display its registered name at any such location at which it carries on business.

(3) But paragraph (2) shall not apply to a location which is primarily used for living accommodation.

(4) Paragraph (2) shall also not apply to any location at which business is carried on by a company where—
  (a) in respect of that company, a liquidator, administrator or administrative receiver has been appointed; and
  (b) the location is also a place of business of that liquidator, administrator or administrative receiver.

(5) Paragraph (2) shall also not apply to any location at which business is carried on by a company of which every director who is an individual is a relevant director.

(6) In this regulation—
  (a) "administrative receiver" has the meaning given—
    (i) in England and Wales or Scotland, by section 251 of the Insolvency Act 1986, and
    (ii) in Northern Ireland, by Article 5 of the Insolvency (Northern Ireland) Order 1989;
  (b) "credit reference agency" has the meaning given in section 243(7) of the Act;
  (c) "protected information" has the meaning given in section 240 of the Act; and
  (d) "relevant director" means an individual in respect of whom the registrar is required by regulations made pursuant to section 243(4) of the Act to refrain from disclosing protected information to a credit reference agency.

23. Manner of display of registered name

(1) This regulation applies where a company is required to display its registered name at any office, place or location.

(2) Where that office, place or location is shared by no more than five companies, the registered name—
  (a) shall be so positioned that it may be easily seen by any visitor to that office, place or location; and

    (b)   shall be displayed continuously.

(3)   Where any such office, place or location is shared by six or more companies, each such company must ensure that either—

    (a)   its registered name is displayed for at least fifteen continuous seconds at least once every three minutes; or

    (b)   its registered name is available for inspection on a register by any visitor to that office, place or location.

24.   **Registered name to appear in communications**

(1)   Every company shall disclose its registered name on—

    (a)   its business letters, notices and other official publications;

    (b)   its bills of exchange, promissory notes, endorsements and order forms;

    (c)   cheques purporting to be signed by or on behalf of the company;

    (d)   orders for money, goods or services purporting to be signed by or on behalf of the company;

    (e)   its bills of parcels, invoices and other demands for payment, receipts and letters of credit;

    (f)   its applications for licences to carry on a trade or activity; and

    (g)   all other forms of its business correspondence and documentation.

(2)   Every company shall disclose its registered name on its websites.

25.   **Further particulars to appear in business letters, order forms and websites**

(1)   Every company shall disclose the particulars set out in paragraph (2) on—

    (a)   its business letters;

    (b)   its order forms; and

    (c)   its websites.

(2)   The particulars are—

    (a)   the part of the United Kingdom in which the company is registered;

    (b)   the company's registered number;

    (c)   the address of the company's registered office;

    (d)   in the case of a limited company exempt from the obligation to use the word "limited" as part of its registered name under section 60 of the Act, the fact that it is a limited company;

    (e)   in the case of a community interest company which is not a public company, the fact that it is a limited company; and

    (f)   in the case of an investment company within the meaning of section 833 of the Act, the fact that it is such a company.

(3)   If, in the case of a company having a share capital, there is a disclosure as to the amount of share capital on—

    (a)   its business letters;

    (b)   its order forms; or

    (c)   its websites,

that disclosure must be as to paid up share capital.

26.   **Disclosure of names of directors**

(1)   Where a company's business letter includes the name of any director of that company, other than in the text or as a signatory, the letter must disclose the name of every director of that company.

(2)   In paragraph (1), "name" has the following meanings—

    (a)   in the case of a director who is an individual, "name" has the meaning given in section 163(2) of the Act; and

    (b)   in the case of a director who is a body corporate or a firm that is a legal person under the law by which it is governed, "name" means corporate name or firm name.

27. Disclosures relating to registered office and inspection place

    (1)   A company shall disclose—

        (a)   the address of its registered office;

        (b)   any inspection place; and

        (c)   the type of company records which are kept at that office or place,

    to any person it deals with in the course of business who makes a written request to the company for that information.

    (2)   The company shall send a written response to that person within five working days of the receipt of that request.

28. Offence

    (1)   Where a company fails, without reasonable excuse, to comply with any requirement in regulations 20 to 27, an offence is committed by—

        (a)   the company; and

        (b)   every officer of the company who is in default.

    (2)   A person guilty of an offence under paragraph (1) is liable on summary conviction to—

        (a)   a fine not exceeding level 3 on the standard scale; and

        (b)   for continued contravention, a daily default fine not exceeding one-tenth of level 3 on the standard scale.

    (3)   For the purposes of this regulation a shadow director is to be treated as an officer of the company.

29. Interpretation

In this Part—

    (a)   "company record" means—

        (i)   any register, index, accounting records, agreement, memorandum, minutes or other document required by the Companies Acts to be kept by a company; and

        (ii)   any register kept by a company of its debenture holders;

    (b)   "inspection place" means any location, other than a company's registered office, at which a company keeps available for inspection any company record which it is required under the Companies Acts to keep available for inspection;

    (c)   a reference to any type of document is a reference to a document of that type in hard copy, electronic or any other form; and

    (d)   in relation to a company, a reference to "its websites" includes a reference to any part of a website relating to that company which that company has caused or authorised to appear.

PART 7

MISCELLANEOUS

30. Revocations and Consequential Amendments

Schedule 6 (which contains revocations and consequential amendments) has effect.

SCHEDULE 1
Regulation 2
Characters, Signs, Symbols (including Accents and other Diacritical Marks) and Punctuation

Table 1

Characters, signs and symbols				
A	À	Á	Â	Ã
Ä	Å	Ā	Ă	Ą
Å	Æ	Æ	B	C
Ç	Ć	Ĉ	Ċ	Č
D	Þ	Ď	Đ	E
È	É	Ê	Ë	Ē

Characters, signs and symbols				
Ĕ	Ė	Ę	Ě	F
G	Ĝ	Ğ	Ġ	Ģ
H	Ĥ	Ħ	I	Ì
Í	Î	Ï	Ĩ	Ī
Ĭ	Į	İ	J	Ĵ
K	Ķ	L	Ĺ	Ļ
Ľ	Ŀ	Ł	M	N
Ñ	Ń	Ņ	Ň	Ŋ
O	Ò	Ó	Ô	Õ
Ö	Ø	Ō	Ŏ	Ő
Ǿ	Œ	P	Q	R
Ŕ	Ŗ	Ř	S	Ś
Ŝ	Ş	Š	T	Ţ
Ť	Ŧ	U	Ù	Ú
Û	Ü	Ũ	Ū	Ŭ
Ů	Ű	Ų	V	W
Ŵ	Ẇ	Ẃ	Ẅ	X
Y	Ỳ	Ý	Ŷ	Ÿ
Z	Ź	Ż	Ž	&
@	£	$	€	¥

Table 2

Column 1 (type of punctuation)	Column 2 (punctuation mark)
Apostrophe	'
	,
	'
Bracket	(
	)
	[
	]
	{
	}
	<
	>
Exclamation mark	!
Guillemet	«
	»
Inverted comma	"
	"
	"
Question mark	?
Solidus	\
	∕

Table 3

Signs and symbols
*
=
#
%
+

SCHEDULE 2   Regulations 4 to 6, 10, 13, 16 and 17

SPECIFIED WORDS, EXPRESSIONS AND ABBREVIATIONS

1.   The words and abbreviations specified are—
   - (a)   "LIMITED" or (with or without full stops) the abbreviation "LTD";
   - (b)   "CYFYNGEDIG" or (with or without full stops) the abbreviation "CYF";
   - (c)   "UNLIMITED"; and
   - (d)   "ANGHYFYNGEDIG".

2.   The words and abbreviations specified as similar to the words and abbreviations set out in inverted commas in paragraph 1(a) and (b) and the words specified as similar to the words set out in inverted commas in paragraph 1(c) and (d) are any in which—
   - (a)   one or more permitted characters has been omitted;
   - (b)   one or more permitted characters has been added; or
   - (c)   each of one or more permitted characters has been substituted by one or more other permitted characters,

   in such a way as to be likely to mislead the public as to the legal form of a company or business if included in the registered name of the company or in a business name.

3.   The expressions and abbreviations specified are—
   - (a)   "PUBLIC LIMITED COMPANY" or (with or without full stops) the abbreviation "PLC";
   - (b)   "CWMNI CYFYNGEDIG CYHOEDDUS" or (with or without full stops) the abbreviation "CCC";
   - (c)   "COMMUNITY INTEREST COMPANY" or (with or without full stops) the abbreviation "CIC";
   - (d)   "CWMNI BUDDIANT CYMUNEDOL" or (with or without full stops) the abbreviation "CBC";
   - (e)   "COMMUNITY INTEREST PUBLIC LIMITED COMPANY" or (with or without full stops) the abbreviation "COMMUNITY INTEREST PLC";
   - (f)   "CWMNI BUDDIANT CYMUNEDOL CYHOEDDUS CYFYNGEDIG" or (with or without full stops) the abbreviation "CWMNI BUDDIANT CYMUNEDOL CCC";
   - (g)   "RIGHT TO ENFRANCHISEMENT" or (with or without full stops) the abbreviation "RTE";
   - (h)   "HAWL I RYDDFREINIAD";
   - (i)   "RIGHT TO MANAGE" or (with or without full stops) the abbreviation "RTM";
   - (j)   "CWMNI RTM CYFYNGEDIG";
   - (k)   "UK ECONOMIC INTEREST GROUPING" or the abbreviation (with or without full stops) "UKEIG";
   - (l)   "INVESTMENT COMPANY WITH VARIABLE CAPITAL";
   - (m)   "CWMNI BUDDSODDI Â CHYFALAF NEWIDIOL";
   - (n)   "LIMITED PARTNERSHIP";
   - (o)   "PARTNERIAETH CYFYNGEDIG";
   - (p)   "LIMITED LIABILITY PARTNERSHIP";
   - (q)   "PARTNERIAETH ATEBOLRWYDD CYFYNGEDIG";
   - (r)   "OPEN-ENDED INVESTMENT COMPANY";

(s)   "CWMNI BUDDSODDIAD PENAGORED";

(t)   "CHARITABLE INCORPORATED ORGANISATION";

(u)   "SEFYDLIAD ELUSENNOL CORFFOREDIG";

(v)   "INDUSTRIAL AND PROVIDENT SOCIETY";

(w)   "CO-OPERATIVE SOCIETY"

(wa) "PROTECTED CELL COMPANY" or (with or without full stops) the abbreviations "PCC LIMITED" and "PCC LTD";

(wb) "CWMNI UNEDAU GWARCHODEDIG" or (with or without full stops) the abbreviations "CUG CYFYNGEDIG" and "CUG CYF";

(x)   "COMMUNITY BENEFIT SOCIETY"; and

(y)   the following abbreviations (with or without full stops) of the expressions specified in sub-paragraphs (n), (o), (p), (q), (t) and (u) respectively, namely "LP", "PC", "LLP", "PAC", "CIO" and "SEC".

4.   The expressions and abbreviations specified as similar to the expressions and abbreviations set out in inverted commas in paragraph 3 are any in which—

(a)   one or more permitted characters has been omitted;

(b)   one or more permitted characters has been added; or

(c)   each of one or more permitted characters has been substituted by one or more other permitted characters,

in such a way as to be likely to mislead the public as to the legal form of a company or business if included in the registered name of the company or in a business name.

SCHEDULE 3   Regulations 7 and 8

NAME SAME AS ANOTHER IN THE REGISTRAR'S INDEX OF COMPANY NAMES

1.   In determining whether a name is the same as another name appearing in the registrar's index of company names the provisions in this Schedule are to be applied in the order set out in the Schedule.

2.   Regard each permitted character set out in column 1 of the table to this paragraph as the same as a corresponding permitted character, or combination of permitted characters, in column 2.

Column 1 (permitted characters)	Column 2 (to be treated the same as)
À Á Â Ã Ä Å Ā Ă Ą Å	A
Æ Ǽ	AE
Ç Ć Ĉ Č	C
Þ Ď Đ	D
È É Ê Ë Ē Ĕ Ė Ę Ě	E
Ĝ Ğ Ġ Ģ	G
Ĥ Ħ	H
Ì Í Î Ï Ĩ Ī Ĭ Į İ	I
Ĵ	J
Ķ	K
Ĺ Ļ Ľ Ŀ Ł	L
Ñ Ń Ņ Ň Ŋ	N
Ò Ó Ô Õ Ö Ø Ō Ŏ Ő	O
Œ	OECE
Ŕ Ŗ Ř	R
Ś Ŝ Ş Š	S
Ţ Ť Ŧ	T

Column 1 (permitted characters)	Column 2 (to be treated the same as)
Ù Ú Û Ü Ũ Ū Ŭ Ů Ű Ų	U
Ŵ Ẁ Ẃ Ẅ	W
Ŷ Ý Ỳ Ÿ	Y
Ź Ż Ž	Z

3.   Taking the name remaining after the application of paragraph 2, disregard any word, expression or abbreviation set out in inverted commas in Schedule 2 where it appears at the end of the name.

4.—   (1)   Taking the name remaining after the application of paragraphs 2 and 3, regard each of the words, expressions, signs and symbols set out in inverted commas in any of the paragraphs of sub-paragraph (2) ("relevant matters") as the same as the other relevant matters set out in that paragraph where each relevant matter—

         (a)   is preceded by and followed by a blank space; or

         (b)   where the relevant matter is at the beginning of the name, where it is followed by a blank space.

      (2)   The words, expressions, signs and symbols are—

         (a)   "AND" and "&";

         (b)   "PLUS" and "+";

         (c)   "0", "ZERO" and "O";

         (d)   "1" and "ONE";

         (e)   "2", "TWO", "TO" and "TOO";

         (f)   "3" and "THREE";

         (g)   "4", "FOUR" and "FOR";

         (h)   "5" and "FIVE";

         (i)   "6" and "SIX";

         (j)   "7" and "SEVEN";

         (k)   "8" and "EIGHT";

         (l)   "9" and "NINE";

         (m)   "£" and "POUND";

         (n)   " EUR " and "EURO";

         (o)   "$" and "DOLLAR";

         (p)   "¥" and "YEN";

         (q)   "%", "PER CENT", "PERCENT", "PER CENTUM" and "PERCENTUM"; and

         (r)   "@" and "AT".

5.—   (1)   Taking the name remaining after the application of paragraphs 2 to 4, disregard at the end of the name the matters set out in inverted commas in sub-paragraph (2) (or any combination of such matters) where the matter (or combination) is preceded by a blank space or by the following punctuation or symbol in inverted commas—

         (a)   a full stop; or

         (b)   "@".

      (2)   The matters are—

         (a)   "& CO";

         (b)   "& COMPANY";

         (c)   "AND CO";

         (d)   "AND COMPANY";

         (e)   "BIZ";

         (f)   "CO";

         (g)   "CO UK";

         (h)   "CO.UK";

         (i)   "COM";

         (j)   "COMPANY";

         (k)   "EU";

       (l)   "GB";

      (m) "GREAT BRITAIN";

      (n)   "NET";

      (o)   "NI";

      (p)   "NORTHERN IRELAND";

      (q)   "ORG";

      (r)   "ORG UK";

      (s)   "ORG.UK";

      (t)   "UK";

      (u)   "UNITED KINGDOM";

      (v)   "WALES";

      (w) "& CWMNI";

      (x)   "A'R CWMNI";

      (y)   "CWMNI";

      (z)   "CYM";

     (aa) "CYMRU";

     (bb) "DU";

     (cc) "PF";

     (dd) "PRYDAIN FAWR"; and

     (ee) "Y DEYRNAS UNEDIG".

(3)   The matters in sub-paragraph (2) include any matter in inverted commas that is preceded by and followed by brackets set out in column 2 of table 2 in Schedule 1.

6.   Taking the name remaining after the application of paragraphs 2 to 5, disregard the following matters in any part of the name—

    (a)   any punctuation set out in regulation 2(2)(c) or in column 2 of table 2 in Schedule 1; and

    (b)   the following words and symbols set out in inverted commas—

        (i)   "*";

       (ii)   "="; and

      (iii)   "#".

7.   Taking the name remaining after the application of paragraphs 2 to 6, disregard the letter "S" at the end of the name.

8.—   (1)   Taking the name remaining after the application of paragraphs 2 to 7, disregard any permitted character after the first 60 permitted characters of the name.

    (2)   For the purposes of computing the number of permitted characters in this paragraph, any blank space between one permitted character and another in the name shall be counted as though it was a permitted character.

9.   Taking the name remaining after the application of paragraphs 2 to 8, disregard the following matters or any combination of the following matters set out in inverted commas where they appear at the beginning of the name—

    (a)   "@";

    (b)   "THE" (but only where followed by a blank space); and

    (c)   "WWW".

10.   Taking the name remaining after the application of paragraphs 2 to 9, disregard blank spaces between permitted characters.

SCHEDULE 4   Regulations 9 and 18

SPECIFIED "PUBLIC AUTHORITIES" AND LIST OF GOVERNMENT DEPARTMENTS AND OTHER BODIES WHOSE VIEWS MUST BE SOUGHT

Column (1)	*Column (2)*
Public authority	*Government department or other body whose view must be sought*
Accounts Commission for Scotland	Accounts Commission for Scotland
Audit Commission for Local Authorities and the National Health Service in England	Audit Commission for Local Authorities and the National Health Service in England
Audit Scotland	Audit Scotland
Auditor General for Scotland	Auditor General For Scotland
Auditor General for Wales (known in Welsh as "Archwilydd Cyffredinol Cymru")	Auditor General for Wales (known in Welsh as "Archwilydd Cyffredinol Cymru")
Comptroller and Auditor General	Comptroller and Auditor General
Comptroller and Auditor General for Northern Ireland	Comptroller and Auditor General for Northern Ireland
Financial Reporting Council	Financial Reporting Council
Financial Conduct Authority	Financial Conduct Authority
Health and Safety Executive	Health and Safety Executive
House of Commons	The Corporate Officer of the House of Commons
House of Lords	The Corporate Officer of the House of Lords
Law Commission	Ministry of Justice
Money and Pensions Service	Department for Work and Pensions
National Assembly for Wales (known in Welsh as "Cynulliad Cenedlaethol Cymru")	National Assembly for Wales Commission (known in Welsh as "Comisiwn Cynulliad Cenedlaethol Cymru")
National Assembly for Wales Commission (known in Welsh as "Comisiwn Cynulliad Cenedlaethol Cymru")	National Assembly for Wales Commission (known in Welsh as "Comisiwn Cynulliad Cenedlaethol Cymru")
Northern Ireland Assembly	Northern Ireland Assembly Commission
Northern Ireland Assembly Commission	Northern Ireland Assembly Commission
Northern Ireland Audit Office	Northern Ireland Audit Office
Office for Nuclear Regulation	Office for Nuclear Regulation
Prudential Regulation Authority	the Governor and Company of the Bank of England
Regional Agency for Public Health and Social Wellbeing	Regional Agency for Public Health and Social Wellbeing
Regional Health and Social Care Board	Regional Health and Social Care Board
Scottish Law Commission	Scottish Law Commission
The Governor and Company of the Bank of England	The Governor and Company of the Bank of England
The Pensions Advisory Service	Department for Work and Pensions
The Scottish Parliament	The Scottish Parliamentary Corporate Body
The Scottish Parliamentary Corporate Body	The Scottish Parliamentary Corporate Body

Column (1)	Column (2)
Public authority	*Government department or other body whose view must be sought*
Wales Audit Office (known in Welsh as "Swyddfa Archwilio Cymru")	Wales Audit Office (known in Welsh as "Swyddfa Archwilio Cymru")

SCHEDULE 5   Regulation 11

AMENDMENT TO THE LIMITED LIABILITY PARTNERSHIPS
(APPLICATION OF COMPANIES ACT 2006) REGULATIONS 2009

1.   The Limited Liability Partnerships (Application of Companies Act 2006) Regulations 2009 are amended as follows.

2.   In regulation 9, for section 57 of the Act, as applied with modifications by that regulation, substitute—

"57. Permitted characters etc

(1)   The provisions of the Company, Limited Liability Partnership and Business (Names and Trading Disclosures) Regulations 2015 relating to the characters, signs or symbols and punctuation that may be used in a registered name apply to LLPs.

(2)   Those provisions are—

    (a)   regulation 2 and Schedule 1, and

    (b)   any other provisions of those Regulations having effect for the purpose of those provisions.

(3)   In those provisions as they apply to LLPs—

    (a)   for "company" substitute "LLP", and

    (b)   for "the Act" substitute "the Limited Liability Partnerships Act 2000".

(4)   An LLP may not be registered under the Limited Liability Partnerships Act 2000 by a name that consists of or includes anything that is not permitted in accordance with the provisions applied by this section."

3.   In regulation 10, for section 65 of the Act, as applied with modifications by that regulation, substitute—

"65. Inappropriate use of indications of company type or legal form

(1)   The provisions of the Company, Limited Liability Partnership and Business (Names and Trading Disclosures) Regulations 2015 relating to inappropriate use of indications of company type or legal form apply to LLPs.

(2)   Those provisions are—

    (a)   regulation 4 and Schedule 2, and

    (b)   any other provisions of those Regulations having effect for the purpose of those provisions.

(3)   As applied to LLPs regulation 4 is modified so as to read as follows—

"4.   Inappropriate indication of legal form: generally applicable provisions

(1)   An LLP must not be registered under the Limited Liability Partnerships Act 2000 by a name that includes in any part of the name—

    (a)   an expression or abbreviation specified in inverted commas in paragraph 3(a) to (o) or (r) to (y) in Schedule 2 (other than the abbreviation "LLP" or "PAC" (with or without full stops) at the end of its name), or

    (b)   an expression or abbreviation specified as similar.

(2)   An LLP must not be registered under the Limited Liability Partnerships Act 2000 by a name that includes, immediately before the expression "LIMITED LIABILITY PARTNERSHIP" OR "PARTNERIAETH ATE-BOLRWYDD CYFYNGEDIG" or the abbreviations "LLP" or "PAC", an abbreviation specified in inverted commas in paragraph 3(y) of that Schedule (or any abbreviation specified as similar)".

4.   In regulation 11, for section 66 of the Act, as applied with modifications by that regulation, substitute—

"66. Name not to be the same as another in the index

(1)   An LLP must not be registered under the Limited Liability Partnerships Act 2000 by a name that is the same as another name appearing in the registrar's index of company names.

(2)   The provisions of the Company, Limited Liability Partnership and Business (Names and Trading Disclosures) Regulations 2015 supplementing this section apply to LLPs.

(3)   Those provisions are—

(a)   regulation 7 and Schedule 3 (matters that are to be disregarded and words, expressions, signs and symbols that are to be regarded as the same),

(b)   regulation 8 (consent to registration of a name which is LLP is the same as another in the registrar's index of company names), and

(c)   any other provisions of those Regulations having effect for the purpose of those provisions.

(4)   In regulation 8 as applied to LLPs—

(a)   for "a company" or "the company" substitute "an LLP" or "the LLP",

(b)   for "Company Y" substitute "LLP Y", and

(c)   in paragraph (1), for "the Act" substitute "the Limited Liability Partnerships Act 2000"."

5.   In regulation 14, for sections 82 and 83 of the Act, as applied with modifications by that regulation, substitute—

"82. Requirements to disclose LLP name etc

(1)   The provisions of the Company, Limited Liability Partnership and Business (Names and Trading Disclosures) Regulations 2015 relating to Trading Disclosures apply to LLPs.

(2)   As they apply to LLPs—

(a)   read references to a company as references to an LLP;

(b)   read references to a director as references to a member of an LLP;

(c)   read references to an officer of a company as references to a designated member of an LLP;

(d)   in regulation 25 (further particulars to appear in business letters, order forms and websites), for paragraphs (2)(d) to (f) and (3) substitute—

"(d) in the case of an LLP whose name ends with the abbreviation "llp", "LLP", "pac" or "PAC", the fact that it is an LLP or a partneriaeth atebolrwydd cyfyngedig.";

(e)   in regulation 26 (disclosure of names of members)—

(i)   at the beginning of paragraph (1) insert "Subject to paragraph (3)," and

(ii)   after paragraph (2) insert—

"(3) Paragraph (1) does not apply in relation to any document issued by an LLP with more than 20 members which maintains at its principal place of business a list of the names of all the members if the document states in legible characters the address of the principal place of business of the LLP and that the list of the members' names is open to inspection at that place.

(4)   Where an LLP maintains a list of the members' names for the purposes of paragraph (3), any person may inspect the list during office hours.";

(f)   omit regulation 28(3) (offences: shadow directors).

83.   Civil consequences of failure to make required disclosure

(1)   This section applies to any legal proceedings brought by an LLP to which section 82 applies (requirement to disclose LLP name etc) to enforce a right arising out of a con-

tract made in the course of a business in respect of which the LLP was, at the time the contract was made, in breach of the Company, Limited Liability Partnership and Business (Names and Trading Disclosures) Regulations 2015.

(2) The proceedings shall be dismissed if the defendant (in Scotland, the defender) to the proceedings shows—

(a) that he has a claim against the claimant (pursuer) arising out of the contract that he has been unable to pursue by reason of the latter's breach of the regulations, or

(b) that he has suffered some financial loss in connection with the contract by reason of the claimant's (pursuer's) breach of the regulations, unless the court before which the proceedings are brought is satisfied that it is just and equitable to permit the proceedings to continue.

(3) This section does not affect the right of any person to enforce such rights as he may have against another person in any proceedings brought by that person.".

6. In regulation 15, for section 85 of the Act, as applied with modifications by that regulation, substitute—

"85. Minor variation in form of name to be left out of account

(1) For the purposes of this Chapter, in considering an LLP's name no account is to be taken of—

(a) whether upper or lower case characters (or a combination of the two) are used,

(b) whether diacritical marks or punctuation are present or absent,

provided there is no real likelihood of names differing only in those respects being taken to be different names.

(2) This does not affect the operation of provisions of the Company, Limited Liability Partnership and Business (Names and Trading Disclosures) Regulations 2015 permitting only specified characters or punctuation.".

SCHEDULE 6   Regulation 30

REVOCATIONS AND CONSEQUENTIAL AMENDMENTS

1. The following Regulations are revoked—

(a) The Company and Business Names (Miscellaneous Provisions) Regulations 2009;

(b) The Company, Limited Liability Partnership and Business Names (Miscellaneous Provisions) (Amendment) Regulations 2009;

(c) The Company, Limited Liability Partnership and Business Names (Public Authorities) Regulations 2009;

(d) The Companies (Trading Disclosures) Regulations 2008;

(e) The Companies (Trading Disclosures) (Amendment) Regulations 2009.

2. In the European Economic Interest Grouping Regulations 1989—

(a) in regulation 10(1)(a), for "Company and Business Names (Miscellaneous Provisions) Regulations 2009" substitute "Company, Limited Liability Partnership and Business (Names and Trading Disclosures) Regulations 2015"; and

(b) in regulation 10(1)(c), for "(v)" substitute "(y)".

3. In the Transport Act 2000, for section 56(5)(e) substitute—

"(e) regulation 28(3) of the Companies, Limited Liability Partnership and Business (Names and Trading Disclosures) Regulations 2015 (liability for offence), as it applies in relation to an offence under regulation 26 (disclosure of names of directors)."

4. In Schedule 1 to the Enterprise Act 2002 (Part 8 Domestic Infringements) Order 2003 for the entry for the Company (Trading Disclosure) Regulations 2008, substitute the following entry—

"Company, Limited Liability Partnership and Business (Names and Trading Disclosures) Regulations 2015	Part 6 of the Company, Limited Liability Partnership and Business (Names and Trading Disclosures) Regulations 2015 and any other provision of those Regulations having effect for the purpose of Part 6"

5.   In the Registrar of Companies and Application for Striking Off Regulations 2009, for the table in the Schedule substitute—

Characters and symbols referred to in regulation 8(3)(a)									
A	À	Á	Â	Ã	Ä	Å	Ā	Ă	Ą
Å	a	à	á	â	ã	ä	å	ā	ă
ą	å	Æ	Æ	æ	æ	B	b	C	Ç
Ć	Ĉ	Ċ	Č	c	ç	ć	ĉ	ċ	č
D	Þ	Ď	Đ	d	þ	đ	đ	E	È
É	Ê	Ë	Ē	Ĕ	Ė	Ę	Ě	e	è
é	ê	ë	ē	ĕ	ė	ę	ě	F	f
G	Ĝ	Ğ	Ġ	Ģ	g	ĝ	ğ	ġ	ģ
H	Ĥ	Ħ	h	ĥ	ħ	I	Ì	Í	Î
Ï	Ĩ	Ī	Ĭ	Į	İ	i	ì	í	î
Ï	ĩ	ī	ĭ	į	J	Ĵ	j	ĵ	K
Ķ	k	ķ	L	Ĺ	Ļ	Ľ	Ŀ	Ł	l
Í	ļ	ľ	ŀ	ł	M	m	N	Ñ	Ń
Ņ	Ň	Ŋ	n	ñ	ń	ņ	ň	ŋ	O
Ò	Ó	Ô	Õ	Ö	Ø	Ō	Ŏ	Ő	Ø
o	ò	ó	ô	õ	ö	ø	ō	ŏ	ő
ø	Œ	œ	P	p	Q	q	R	Ŕ	Ŗ
Ř	r	ŕ	ŗ	ř	S	Ś	Ŝ	Ş	Š
s	ś	ŝ	ş	š	T	Ţ	Ť	Ŧ	t
ţ	ť	ŧ	U	Ù	Ú	Û	Ü	Ũ	Ū
Ů	Ủ	Ű	Ų	u	ù	ú	û	ü	ũ
ū	ŭ	ů	ű	ų	V	v	W	Ŵ	Ẁ
Ẃ	Ẅ	w	ŵ	ẁ	ẃ	ẅ	X	x	Y
Ỳ	Ý	Ŷ	Ÿ	y	ỳ	ý	ŷ	ÿ	Z
Ź	Ż	Ž	z	ź	ż	ž	&	@	£
$	€	¥	*	=	#	%	+	'	'
'	(	)	[	]	{	}	<	>	!
«	»	?	"	"	"	\	/		

6.   In paragraph 1 of Schedule 6 to the Investment Bank Special Administration Regulations 2011, in the list of secondary legislation, for "Companies (Trading Disclosures) Regulations 2008" substitute "Company, Limited Liability Partnership and Business (Names and Trading Disclosures) Regulations 2015".

Insolvency Act 1986

1986 c. 45

An Act to consolidate the enactments relating to company insolvency and winding up (including the winding up of companies that are not insolvent, and of unregistered companies); enactments relating to the insolvency and bankruptcy of individuals; and other enactments bearing on those two subject matters, including the functions and qualification of insolvency practitioners, the public administration of insolvency, the penalisation and redress of malpractice and wrongdoing, and the avoidance of certain transactions at an undervalue

[25th July 1986]

THE FIRST GROUP OF PARTS
COMPANY INSOLVENCY; COMPANIES WINDING UP

PART A1
MORATORIUM

CHAPTER 1
INTRODUCTORY

A1 **Overview**

(1) This Part contains provision that enables an eligible company, in certain circumstances, to obtain a moratorium, giving it various protections from creditors set out in this Part.

(2) In this Chapter section A2 introduces Schedule ZA1 (which defines what is meant by an "eligible" company).

(3) Chapter 2 sets out how an eligible company may obtain a moratorium.

(4) Chapter 3 sets out for how long a moratorium has effect.

(5) Chapter 4 sets out the effects of a moratorium on the company and its creditors.

(6) Chapter 5 contains provision about the monitor.

(7) Chapter 6 contains provision about challenges.

(8) Chapter 7 contains provision about certain offences.

(9) Chapter 8 contains miscellaneous and general provision, including—

    (a) special provision for certain kinds of company;

    (b) definitions for the purposes of this Part;

    (c) provision about regulations under this Part.

A2 **Eligible companies**

Schedule ZA1 contains provision for determining whether a company is an eligible company for the purposes of this Part.

CHAPTER 2
OBTAINING A MORATORIUM

A3 **Obtaining a moratorium by filing or lodging documents at court**

(1) This section applies to an eligible company that—

    (a) is not subject to an outstanding winding-up petition, and

    (b) is not an overseas company.

(2) The directors of the company may obtain a moratorium for the company by filing the relevant documents with the court (for the relevant documents, see section A6).

(3) For the purposes of this Chapter a company is "subject to an outstanding winding-up petition" if—

    (a) a petition for the winding up of the company has been presented, and

(b)   the petition has not been withdrawn or determined.

A4   Obtaining a moratorium for company subject to winding-up petition

(1)   This section applies to an eligible company that is subject to an outstanding winding-up petition.

(2)   The directors of the company may apply to the court for a moratorium for the company.

(3)   The application must be accompanied by the relevant documents (for the relevant documents, see section A6).

(4)   On hearing the application the court may—

(a)   make an order that the company should be subject to a moratorium, or

(b)   make any other order which the court thinks appropriate.

(5)   The court may make an order under subsection (4)(a) only if it is satisfied that a moratorium for the company would achieve a better result for the company's creditors as a whole than would be likely if the company were wound up (without first being subject to a moratorium)

A5   Obtaining a moratorium for other overseas companies

(1)   This section applies to an eligible company that—

(a)   is not subject to an outstanding winding-up petition, and

(b)   is an overseas company.

(2)   The directors of the company may apply to the court for a moratorium for the company.

(3)   The application must be accompanied by the relevant documents (for the relevant documents, see section A6).

(4)   On hearing the application the court may—

(a)   make an order that the company should be subject to a moratorium, or

(b)   make any other order which the court thinks appropriate.

A6   The relevant documents

(1)   For the purposes of this Chapter, "the relevant documents" are—

(a)   a notice that the directors wish to obtain a moratorium,

(b)   a statement from a qualified person ("the proposed monitor") that the person—

(i)   is a qualified person, and

(ii)   consents to act as the monitor in relation to the proposed moratorium,

(c)   a statement from the proposed monitor that the company is an eligible company,

(d)   a statement from the directors that, in their view, the company is, or is likely to become, unable to pay its debts, and

(e)   a statement from the proposed monitor that, in the proposed monitor's view, it is likely that a moratorium for the company would result in the rescue of the company as a going concern.

(2)   Where it is proposed that more than one person should act as the monitor in relation to the proposed moratorium—

(a)   each of them must make a statement under subsection (1)(b), (c) and (e), and

(b)   the statement under subsection (1)(b) must specify—

(i)   which functions (if any) are to be exercised by the persons acting jointly, and

(ii)   which functions (if any) are to be exercised by any or all of the persons.

(3)   The rules may make provision about the date on which a statement comprised in the relevant documents must be made.

(4)   The Secretary of State may by regulations amend this section for the purposes of adding to the list of documents in subsection (1).

(5)   Regulations under subsection (4) are subject to the affirmative resolution procedure.

A7   Beginning of moratorium and appointment of monitor

(1)   A moratorium for a company comes into force at the time at which—

(a)   in the case of a company to which section A3 applies, the relevant documents are filed with the court under subsection (2) of that section;

(b) in the case of a company to which section A4 applies, an order is made under section A4(4)(a);

(c) in the case of a company to which section A5 applies, an order is made under section A5(4)(a).

(2) On the coming into force of a moratorium, the person or persons who made the statement mentioned in section A6(1)(b) become the monitor in relation to the moratorium.

A8   Obligations to notify where moratorium comes into force

(1) As soon as reasonably practicable after a moratorium for a company comes into force, the directors must notify the monitor of that fact.

(2) As soon as reasonably practicable after receiving a notice under subsection (1), the monitor must notify the following that a moratorium for the company has come into force—

(a) the registrar of companies,

(b) every creditor of the company of whose claim the monitor is aware,

(c) in a case where the company is or has been an employer in respect of an occupational pension scheme that is not a money purchase scheme, the Pensions Regulator, and

(d) in a case where the company is an employer in respect of such a pension scheme that is an eligible scheme within the meaning given by section 126 of the Pensions Act 2004, the Board of the Pension Protection Fund.

(3) A notice under subsection (2) must specify—

(a) when the moratorium came into force, and

(b) when, subject to any alteration under or by virtue of any of the provisions mentioned in section A9(3) or (4), the moratorium will come to an end.

(4) If the directors fail to comply with subsection (1), any director who did not have a reasonable excuse for the failure commits an offence.

(5) If the monitor without reasonable excuse fails to comply with subsection (2), the monitor commits an offence.

CHAPTER 3
LENGTH OF MORATORIUM

Initial period

A9   End of the moratorium

(1) A moratorium ends at the end of the initial period unless it is extended, or comes to an end sooner, under or by virtue of a provision mentioned in subsection (3) or (4).

(2) In this Chapter "the initial period", in relation to a moratorium, means the period of 20 business days beginning with the business day after the day on which the moratorium comes into force.

(3) For provision under or by virtue of which a moratorium is or may be extended, see—
section A10 (extension by directors without creditor consent);
section A11 (extension by directors with creditor consent);
section A13 (extension by court on application of directors);
section A14 (extension while proposal for CVA pending);
section A15 (extension by court in course of other proceedings)

(4) For provision under or by virtue of which the moratorium is or may be terminated, see—
section A16 (termination on entry into insolvency procedure etc);
section A38 (termination by monitor);
section A42 or A44 (termination by court).

(5) A moratorium may not be extended under a provision mentioned in subsection (3) once it has come to an end.

(6) Where the application of two or more of the provisions mentioned in subsections (3) and (4) would produce a different length of moratorium, the provision that applies last is to prevail (irrespective of whether that results in a shorter or longer moratorium).

Extension of moratorium

A10   Extension by directors without creditor consent

(1)   During the initial period, but after the first 15 business days of that period, the directors may extend the moratorium by filing with the court—

(a)   a notice that the directors wish to extend the moratorium,

(b)   a statement from the directors that all of the following that have fallen due have been paid or otherwise discharged—

(i)   moratorium debts, and

(ii)   pre-moratorium debts for which the company does not have a payment holiday during the moratorium (see section A18),

(c)   a statement from the directors that, in their view, the company is, or is likely to become, unable to pay its pre-moratorium debts, and

(d)   a statement from the monitor that, in the monitor's view, it is likely that the moratorium will result in the rescue of the company as a going concern.

(2)   The rules may make provision about the date on which a statement mentioned in subsection (1) must be made.

(3)   On the filing with the court of the documents mentioned in subsection (1), the moratorium is extended so that it ends at the end of the period—

(a)   beginning immediately after the initial period ends, and

(b)   ending with the 20th business day after the initial period ends.

A11   Extension by directors with creditor consent

(1)   At any time after the first 15 business days of the initial period the directors may, if they have obtained creditor consent, extend the moratorium by filing with the court—

(a)   a notice that the directors wish to extend the moratorium,

(b)   a statement from the directors that all of the following that have fallen due have been paid or otherwise discharged—

(i)   moratorium debts, and

(ii)   pre-moratorium debts for which the company does not have a payment holiday during the moratorium (see section A18),

(c)   a statement from the directors that, in their view, the company is, or is likely to become, unable to pay its pre-moratorium debts,

(d)   a statement from the monitor that, in the monitor's view, it is likely that the moratorium will result in the rescue of the company as a going concern, and

(e)   a statement from the directors that creditor consent has been obtained, and of the revised end date for which that consent was obtained.

(2)   The rules may make provision about the date on which a statement mentioned in subsection (1) must be made.

(3)   On the filing with the court of the documents mentioned in subsection (1), the moratorium is extended so that it ends with the revised end date mentioned in the statement under subsection (1)(e).

(4)   A moratorium may be extended under this section more than once.

A12   Creditor consent for the purposes of section A11

(1)   References in section A11 to creditor consent are to the consent of pre-moratorium creditors to a revised end date for the moratorium.

(2)   The decision as to consent is to be made using a qualifying decision procedure.

(3)   The revised end date must be a date before the end of the period of one year beginning with the first day of the initial period.

(4)   In this section "pre-moratorium creditor" means a creditor in respect of a pre-moratorium debt—

(a)   for which the company has a payment holiday during the moratorium (see section A18), and

(b)   which has not been paid or otherwise discharged.

(5)   In determining for the purposes of subsection (4) what counts as a pre-moratorium debt for which the company has a payment holiday during the moratorium, sections A18(3) and A53(1)(b) apply as if the references to the moratorium were to the moratorium as proposed to be extended.

(6)   The Secretary of State may by regulations amend this section for the purposes of changing the definition of "pre-moratorium creditor".

(7)   Regulations under subsection (6) are subject to the affirmative resolution procedure.

A13   Extension by court on application of directors

(1)   At any time after the first 15 business days of the initial period, the directors may apply to the court for an order that the moratorium be extended.

(2)   The application must be accompanied by—
(a)   a statement from the directors that all of the following that have fallen due have been paid or otherwise discharged—
(i)   moratorium debts, and
(ii)   pre-moratorium debts for which the company does not have a payment holiday during the moratorium (see section A18),
(b)   a statement from the directors that, in their view, the company is, or is likely to become, unable to pay its pre-moratorium debts,
(c)   a statement from the directors as to whether pre-moratorium creditors (as defined by section A12(4) and (5)) have been consulted about the application and if not why not, and
(d)   a statement from the monitor that, in the monitor's view, it is likely that the moratorium will result in the rescue of the company as a going concern.

(3)   The rules may make provision about the date on which a statement mentioned in subsection (2) must be made.

(4)   On hearing the application the court may—
(a)   make an order that the moratorium be extended to such date as is specified in the order, or
(b)   make any other order which the court thinks appropriate.

(5)   In deciding whether to make an order under subsection (4)(a) the court must, in particular, consider the following—
(a)   the interests of pre-moratorium creditors, as defined by section A12(4) and (5), and
(b)   the likelihood that the extension of the moratorium will result in the rescue of the company as a going concern.

(6)   Subsection (7) applies where—
(a)   an application under this section is made, and
(b)   apart from that subsection, the moratorium would end at a time before the application has been disposed of.

(7)   The moratorium—
(a)   does not end at the time mentioned in subsection (6)(b), and
(b)   instead, ends—
(i)   in a case in which the court makes an order under subsection (4)(a), in accordance with the order;
(ii)   otherwise, when the application is withdrawn or disposed of.

(8)   A moratorium may be extended under this section more than once.

A14   Extension while proposal for CVA pending

(1)   Subsection (2) applies where—
(a)   at any time, the directors make a proposal under Part 1 (company voluntary arrangements), and
(b)   apart from that subsection, the moratorium would end at a time before the proposal is disposed of.

(2)   The moratorium—
(a)   does not end at the time mentioned in subsection (1)(b), and
(b)   instead, ends when the proposal is disposed of.

(3)   For the purposes of this section a proposal under Part 1 is "disposed of" when any of the following takes place—

    (a)   the company and its creditors both decide under section 4 not to approve the voluntary arrangement contained in the proposal;

    (b)   the decisions taken by the company and its creditors under section 4 differ, and—

        (i)   the period for making an application under section 4A(3) expires and either no application has been made within that period or any application made within that period has been withdrawn, or

        (ii)   an application is made under section 4A(3) and that application is disposed of, or it is withdrawn after the expiry of the period for making an application under section 4A(3);

    (c)   the voluntary arrangement contained in the proposal takes effect under section 5;

    (d)   the proposal is withdrawn.

A15   Extension by court in the course of other proceedings

(1)   Subsection (2) applies where—

    (a)   an application is made under section 896 or 901C(1) of the Companies Act 2006 (arrangements and reconstructions: court order for holding of meeting) in respect of a company, and

    (b)   during proceedings before a court in connection with the application, a moratorium for the company is in force.

(2)   The court may make an order that the moratorium be extended to such date as is specified in the order.

Early termination on certain grounds

A16   Company enters into insolvency procedure etc

(1)   A moratorium comes to an end at any time at which the company—

    (a)   enters into a compromise or arrangement (see subsection (2)), or

    (b)   enters into a relevant insolvency procedure (see subsection (3))

(2)   For the purposes of this section a company enters into a compromise or arrangement if an order under section 899 or 901F of the Companies Act 2006 (court sanction for compromise or arrangement) comes into effect in relation to the company.

(3)   For the purposes of this section a company enters into a relevant insolvency procedure if—

    (a)   a voluntary arrangement takes effect under section 5 in relation to the company,

    (b)   the company enters administration (within the meaning of Schedule B1 (see paragraph 1(2)(b) of that Schedule)),

    (c)   paragraph 44 of Schedule B1 (administration: interim moratorium) begins to apply in relation to the company, or

    (d)   the company goes into liquidation (see section 247)

Obligations to notify change in end of moratorium

A17   Obligations to notify change in end of moratorium

(1)   The table imposes obligations on the directors of a company to notify the monitor where a moratorium for the company is extended or comes to an end.

	Where a moratorium is extended or comes to an end under or by virtue of the following provision	*the directors must*
1	Section A10	Notify the monitor of the extension.
2	Section A11	Notify the monitor of the extension and of the revised end date.

	Where a moratorium is extended or comes to an end under or by virtue of the following provision	the directors must
3	Section A13(4)	Notify the monitor of the extension and provide the monitor with the court order under section A13(4).
4	Section A13(7)(a)	Notify the monitor of the extension.
5	Section A13(7)(b)(ii)	Notify the monitor that the moratorium has come to an end and of the date that it ended.
6	Section A14(2)(a)	Notify the monitor of the extension.
7	Section A14(2)(b)	Notify the monitor that the moratorium has come to an end and of the date that it ended.
8	Section A15	Notify the monitor of the extension and provide the monitor with any court order under section A15.
9	Section A16	Notify the monitor that the moratorium has come to an end.
10	Section A42	Notify the monitor that the moratorium has come to an end and provide the monitor with the court order under section A42.
11	Section A44	Notify the monitor that the moratorium has come to an end and provide the monitor with the court order under section A44.

(2) After receiving a notice under subsection (1), other than a notice under entry 4 or 6 of the table, the monitor must notify the relevant persons of when the moratorium ended or, subject to any alteration under or by virtue of any of the provisions mentioned in section A9(3) or (4), the moratorium will come to an end.

(3) After receiving a notice under entry 4 or 6 of the table, the monitor must notify the relevant persons.

(4) If a moratorium comes to an end under section A38 (termination by monitor), the monitor must notify the company and the relevant persons of when the moratorium ended.

(5) The rules may—
    (a) make further provision about the timing of a notice required to be given under this section;
    (b) require a notice to be accompanied by other documents.

(6) If the directors fail to comply with subsection (1), any director who did not have a reasonable excuse for the failure commits an offence.

(7) If the monitor without reasonable excuse fails to comply with any of subsections (2) to (4), the monitor commits an offence.

(8) In this section "the relevant persons" means—
    (a) the registrar of companies,
    (b) every creditor of the company of whose claim the monitor is aware,
    (c) in a case where the company is or has been an employer in respect of an occupational pension scheme that is not a money purchase scheme, the Pensions Regulator, and
    (d) in a case where the company is an employer in respect of such a pension scheme that is an eligible scheme within the meaning given by section 126 of the Pensions Act 2004, the Board of the Pension Protection Fund.

CHAPTER 4
EFFECTS OF MORATORIUM

Introductory

A18   Overview and construction of references to payment holidays

(1)   This Chapter makes provision about the main effects of a moratorium for a company.

(2)   The provision made by this Chapter includes restrictions on the enforcement or payment of the debts that are defined by subsection (3) as pre-moratorium debts for which a company has a payment holiday during a moratorium.

(3)   In this Part a reference to pre-moratorium debts for which a company has a payment holiday during a moratorium is to its pre-moratorium debts that have fallen due before the moratorium, or that fall due during the moratorium, except in so far as they consist of amounts payable in respect of—

    (a)   the monitor's remuneration or expenses,

    (b)   goods or services supplied during the moratorium,

    (c)   rent in respect of a period during the moratorium,

    (d)   wages or salary arising under a contract of employment,

    (e)   redundancy payments, or

    (f)   debts or other liabilities arising under a contract or other instrument involving financial services.

(4)   The rules may make provision as to what is, or is not, to count as the supply of goods or services for the purposes of subsection (3)(b).

(5)   The Secretary of State may by regulations amend this section for the purposes of changing the list in subsection (3).

(6)   Regulations under subsection (5) are subject to the affirmative resolution procedure.

(7)   In this section—

"contract or other instrument involving financial services" has the meaning given by Schedule ZA2;

"monitor's remuneration or expenses" does not include remuneration in respect of anything done by a proposed monitor before the moratorium begins;

"redundancy payment" means—

    (a)   a redundancy payment under Part 11 of the Employment Rights Act 1996 or Part 12 of the Employment Rights (Northern Ireland) Order 1996, or

    (b)   a payment made to a person who agrees to the termination of their employment in circumstances where they would have been entitled to a redundancy payment under that Part if dismissed;

"wages or salary" includes—

    (a)   a sum payable in respect of a period of holiday (for which purpose the sum is to be treated as relating to the period by reference to which the entitlement to holiday accrued),

    (b)   a sum payable in respect of a period of absence through illness or other good cause,

    (c)   a sum payable in lieu of holiday, and

    (d)   a contribution to an occupational pension scheme.

Publicity about moratorium

A19   Publicity about moratorium

(1)   During a moratorium, the company must, in any premises—

    (a)   where business of the company is carried on, and

    (b)   to which customers of the company or suppliers of goods or services to the company have access,

display, in a prominent position so that it may easily be read by such customers or suppliers, a notice containing the required information.

(2)   During a moratorium, any websites of the company must state the required information.

(3) During a moratorium, every business document issued by or on behalf of the company must state the required information.

(4) For the purposes of subsections (1), (2) and (3), "the required information" is—

    (a) that a moratorium is in force in relation to the company, and

    (b) the name of the monitor.

(5) If subsection (1), (2) or (3) is contravened—

    (a) the company commits an offence, and

    (b) any officer of the company who without reasonable excuse authorised or permitted the contravention commits an offence.

(6) In this section "business document" means—

    (a) an invoice,

    (b) an order for goods or services,

    (c) a business letter, and

    (d) an order form,

whether in hard copy, electronic or any other form.

Effect on creditors etc

A20 Restrictions on insolvency proceedings etc

(1) During a moratorium—

    (a) no petition may be presented for the winding up of the company, except by the directors,

    (b) no resolution may be passed for the voluntary winding up of the company under section 84(1)(a),

    (c) a resolution for the voluntary winding up of the company under section 84(1)(b) may be passed only if the resolution is recommended by the directors,

    (d) no order may be made for the winding up of the company, except on a petition by the directors,

    (e) no administration application may be made in respect of the company, except by the directors,

    (f) no notice of intention to appoint an administrator of the company under paragraph 14 or 22(1) of Schedule B1 may be filed with the court,

    (g) no administrator of the company may be appointed under paragraph 14 or 22(1) of Schedule B1, and

    (h) no administrative receiver of the company may be appointed.

(2) Subsection (1)(a) does not apply to an excepted petition; and subsection (1)(d) does not apply to an order on an excepted petition.

(3) For these purposes, "excepted petition" means a petition under—

    (a) section 124A, 124B or 124C, or

    (b) section 367 of the Financial Services and Markets Act 2000 on the ground mentioned in subsection (3)(b) of that section.

A21 Restrictions on enforcement and legal proceedings

(1) During a moratorium—

    (a) a landlord or other person to whom rent is payable may not exercise a right of forfeiture by peaceable re-entry in relation to premises let to the company, except with the permission of the court,

    (b) in Scotland, a landlord or other person to whom rent is payable may not exercise a right of irritancy in relation to premises let to the company, except with the permission of the court,

    (c) no steps may be taken to enforce any security over the company's property except—

        (i) steps to enforce a collateral security charge (within the meaning of the Financial Markets and Insolvency (Settlement Finality) Regulations 1999 (S.I. 1999/2979)),

        (ii) steps to enforce security created or otherwise arising under a financial collateral arrangement (within the meaning of regulation 3 of the Financial Collateral Arrangements (No. 2) Regulations 2003 (S.I. 2003/3226)), or

            (iii) steps taken with the permission of the court,

    (d)   no steps may be taken to repossess goods in the company's possession under any hire-purchase agreement, except with the permission of the court, and

    (e)   no legal process (including legal proceedings, execution, distress or diligence) may be instituted, carried out or continued against the company or its property except—

            (i)   employment tribunal proceedings or any legal process arising out of such proceedings,

            (ii)   proceedings, not within sub-paragraph (i), involving a claim between an employer and a worker, or

            (iii) a legal process instituted, carried out or continued with the permission of the court.

(2)   An application may not be made for permission under subsection (1) for the purposes of enforcing a pre-moratorium debt for which the company has a payment holiday during the moratorium.

(3)   An application may not be made for permission under subsection (1)(c), (d) or (e) with a view to obtaining—

    (a)   the crystallisation of a floating charge, or

    (b)   the imposition, by virtue of provision in an instrument creating a floating charge, of any restriction on the disposal of any property of the company.

(4)   Permission of the court under subsection (1) may be given subject to conditions.

(5)   Subsection (1)(c)(iii) is subject to section A23(1).

(6)   In this section—

"agency worker" has the meaning given by section 13(2) of the Employment Relations Act 1999;

"employer"—

    (a)   in relation to an agency worker, has the meaning given by section 13(2) of the Employment Relations Act 1999;

    (b)   otherwise, has the meaning given by section 230(4) of the Employment Rights Act 1996;

"worker" means an individual who is—

    (a)   a worker within the meaning of section 230(3) of the Employment Rights Act 1996, or

    (b)   an agency worker.

A22   Floating charges

(1)   This section applies where there is an uncrystallised floating charge on the property of a company for which a moratorium is in force.

(2)   During the moratorium, the holder of the floating charge may not give any notice which would have the effect of—

    (a)   causing the floating charge to crystallise, or

    (b)   causing the imposition, by virtue of provision in the instrument creating the charge, of any restriction on the disposal of property of the company.

(3)   No other event occurring during the moratorium is to have the effect mentioned in subsection (2)(a) or (b).

(4)   Subsection (5) applies where—

    (a)   the holder of a floating charge ("the chargee") is prevented by subsection (2) from giving a notice mentioned there during the moratorium, and

    (b)   under the terms of the floating charge, the time for giving such a notice ends during the moratorium or before the chargee is given notice of the end of the moratorium under section A17.

(5)   The chargee may give notice later than is required under the terms of the floating charge, but only if the chargee does so as soon as is practicable after—

    (a)   the end of the moratorium, or

    (b)   if later, the day on which the chargee is notified of the end of the moratorium.

(6)   Where—

    (a)   subsection (3) prevents an event which occurs during the moratorium from having the effect mentioned there, and

(b) the holder of the floating charge gives notice of the event to the company as soon as is practicable after—

    (i) the end of the moratorium, or

    (ii) if later, the day on which the chargee is notified of the end of the moratorium,

the event is to be treated as if it had occurred when the notice was given.

(7) This section does not apply in relation to a floating charge that is—

    (a) a collateral security (as defined by section A27);

    (b) a market charge (as defined by section A27);

    (c) a security financial collateral arrangement (within the meaning of regulation 3 of the Financial Collateral Arrangements (No. 2) Regulations 2003 (S.I. 2003/3226));

    (d) a system-charge (as defined by section A27).

A23 Enforcement of security granted during moratorium

(1) Security granted by a company during a moratorium in relation to the company may be enforced only if the monitor consented to the grant of security under section A26.

(2) See also section A21(1)(c), which restricts enforcement during a moratorium.

Notification of insolvency proceedings

A24 Duty of directors to notify monitor of insolvency proceedings etc

(1) The directors of a company must notify the monitor before taking any of the following steps during a moratorium—

    (a) presenting a petition for the winding up of the company;

    (b) making an administration application in respect of the company;

    (c) appointing an administrator under paragraph 22(2) of Schedule B1.

(2) The directors of a company must notify the monitor if, during a moratorium for the company, they recommend that the company passes a resolution for voluntary winding up under section 84(1)(b)

(3) The rules may make provision about the timing of a notice required to be given under subsection (1) or (2).

(4) If the directors fail to comply with subsection (1) or (2), any director who did not have a reasonable excuse for the failure commits an offence.

Restrictions on transactions

A25 Restrictions on obtaining credit

(1) During a moratorium, the company may not obtain credit to the extent of £500 or more from a person unless the person has been informed that a moratorium is in force in relation to the company.

(2) The reference to the company obtaining credit includes—

    (a) the company entering into a conditional sale agreement in accordance with which goods are to be sold to the company,

    (b) the company entering into any other form of hire-purchase agreement under which goods are to be bailed (in Scotland, hired) to the company, and

    (c) the company being paid in advance (whether in money or otherwise) for the supply of goods or services.

(3) If a company contravenes subsection (1)—

    (a) the company commits an offence, and

    (b) any officer of the company who without reasonable excuse authorised or permitted the obtaining of the credit commits an offence.

A26 Restrictions on grant of security etc

(1) During a moratorium, the company may grant security over its property only if the monitor consents.

(2) The monitor may give consent under subsection (1) only if the monitor thinks that the grant of security will support the rescue of the company as a going concern.

(3)   In deciding whether to give consent under subsection (1), the monitor is entitled to rely on information provided by the company unless the monitor has reason to doubt its accuracy.

(4)   If the company grants security over its property during the moratorium otherwise than as authorised by subsection (1)—
        (a)   the company commits an offence, and
        (b)   any officer of the company who without reasonable excuse authorised or permitted the grant of the security commits an offence.

(5)   For the consequences of a company granting security over its property in contravention of subsection (1), see also section A23.

(6)   The monitor may not give consent under this section if the granting of security is an offence under section A27.

A27   Prohibition on entering into market contracts etc

(1)   If a company enters into a transaction to which this section applies during a moratorium for the company—
        (a)   the company commits an offence, and
        (b)   any officer of the company who without reasonable excuse authorised or permitted the company to enter into the transaction commits an offence.

(2)   A company enters into a transaction to which this section applies if it—
        (a)   enters into a market contract,
        (b)   enters into a financial collateral arrangement,
        (c)   gives a transfer order,
        (d)   grants a market charge or a system-charge, or
        (e)   provides any collateral security.

(3)   Where during the moratorium a company enters into a transaction to which this section applies, nothing done by or in pursuance of the transaction is to be treated as done in contravention of any of sections A19, A21, A25, A26 and A28 to A32.

(4)   In this section—
        "collateral security" has the same meaning as in the Financial Markets and Insolvency (Settlement Finality) Regulations 1999 (S.I. 1999/2979);
        "financial collateral arrangement" has the same meaning as in the Financial Collateral Arrangements (No. 2) Regulations 2003 (S.I. 2003/3226);
        "market charge" has the same meaning as in Part 7 of the Companies Act 1989;
        "market contract" has the same meaning as in Part 7 of the Companies Act 1989;
        "system-charge" has the meaning given by the Financial Markets and Insolvency Regulations 1996 (S.I. 1996/1469);
        "transfer order" has the same meaning as in the Financial Markets and Insolvency (Settlement Finality) Regulations 1999.

Restrictions on payments and disposal of property

A28   Restrictions on payment of certain pre-moratorium debts

(1)   During a moratorium, the company may make one or more relevant payments to a person that (in total) exceed the specified maximum amount only if—
        (a)   the monitor consents,
        (b)   the payment is in pursuance of a court order, or
        (c)   the payment is required by section A31(3) or A32(3).

(2)   In subsection (1)—
        "relevant payments" means payments in respect of pre-moratorium debts for which the company has a payment holiday during the moratorium (see section A18);
        "specified maximum amount" means an amount equal to the greater of—
        (a)   £5000, and

(b) 1% of the value of the debts and other liabilities owed by the company to its unsecured creditors when the moratorium began, to the extent that the amount of such debts and liabilities can be ascertained at that time.

(3) The monitor may give consent under subsection (1)(a) only if the monitor thinks that it will support the rescue of the company as a going concern.

(4) In deciding whether to give consent under subsection (1)(a), the monitor is entitled to rely on information provided by the company unless the monitor has reason to doubt its accuracy.

(5) If the company makes a payment to which subsection (1) applies otherwise than as authorised by that subsection—

(a) the company commits an offence, and

(b) any officer of the company who without reasonable excuse authorised or permitted the payment commits an offence.

A29 Restrictions on disposal of property

(1) During a moratorium, the company may dispose of its property only if authorised by subsection (2) or (5).

(2) In the case of property that is not subject to a security interest, the company may dispose of the property if—

(a) the disposal is made in the ordinary way of the company's business,

(b) the monitor consents, or

(c) the disposal is in pursuance of a court order.

(3) The monitor may give consent under subsection (2)(b) only if the monitor thinks that it will support the rescue of the company as a going concern.

(4) In deciding whether to give consent under subsection (2)(b), the monitor is entitled to rely on information provided by the company unless the monitor has reason to doubt its accuracy.

(5) In the case of property that is subject to a security interest, the company may dispose of the property if the disposal is in accordance with—

(a) section A31(1), or

(b) the terms of the security.

(6) If the company disposes of its property during the moratorium otherwise than as authorised by this section—

(a) the company commits an offence, and

(b) any officer of the company who without reasonable excuse authorised or permitted the disposal commits an offence.

A30 Restrictions on disposal of hire-purchase property

(1) During a moratorium, the company may dispose of any goods in the possession of the company under a hire-purchase agreement only if the disposal is in accordance with —

(a) section A32(1), or

(b) the terms of the agreement.

(2) If the company disposes of goods in the possession of the company under a hire-purchase agreement otherwise than as authorised by subsection (1)—

(a) the company commits an offence, and

(b) any officer of the company who without reasonable excuse authorised or permitted the disposal commits an offence.

Disposals of property free from charges etc

A31 Disposal of charged property free from charge

(1) During a moratorium, the company may, with the permission of the court, dispose of property which is subject to a security interest as if it were not subject to the security interest.

(2) The court may give permission under subsection (1) only if the court thinks that it will support the rescue of the company as a going concern.

(3)   Where the court gives permission under subsection (1) other than in relation to a floating charge, the company must apply the following towards discharging the sums secured—
    (a) the net proceeds of disposal of the property, and
    (b) any money required to be added to the net proceeds so as to produce the amount determined by the court as the net amount which would be realised on a sale of the property in the open market by a willing vendor.

(4)   Where the permission relates to two or more security interests, the condition in subsection (3) requires the application of money in the order of the priorities of the security interests.

(5)   Where property subject to a floating charge is disposed of under subsection (1), the holder of the floating charge has the same priority in respect of acquired property as they had in respect of the property disposed of.

(6)   In subsection (5) "acquired property" means property of the company which directly or indirectly represents the property disposed of.

(7)   Where the court makes an order giving permission under subsection (1), the directors must, within the period of 14 days beginning with the date of the order, send a copy of it to the registrar of companies.

(8)   If the directors fail to comply with subsection (7), any director who did not have a reasonable excuse for the failure commits an offence.

(9)   Where property in Scotland is disposed of under subsection (1), the company must grant to the disponee an appropriate document of transfer or conveyance of the property, and—
    (a) that document, or
    (b) recording, intimation or registration of that document (where recording, intimation or registration of the document is a legal requirement for completion of title to the property),
has the effect of disencumbering the property of or, as the case may be, freeing the property from, the security interest.

(10)   If a company fails to comply with subsection (3) or (9)—
    (a) the company commits an offence, and
    (b) any officer of the company who without reasonable excuse authorised or permitted the failure commits an offence.

(11)   Subsection (1) does not apply in relation to any property which is subject to a financial collateral arrangement, a market charge, a system-charge or a collateral security (as defined by section A27).

A32   Disposal of hire-purchase property

(1)   During a moratorium, the company may, with the permission of the court, dispose of goods which are in the possession of the company under a hire-purchase agreement as if all of the rights of the owner under the agreement were vested in the company.

(2)   The court may give permission under subsection (1) only if the court thinks that it will support the rescue of the company as a going concern.

(3)   Where the court gives permission under subsection (1), the company must apply the following towards discharging the sums payable under the hire-purchase agreement—
    (a) the net proceeds of disposal of the goods, and
    (b) any additional money required to be added to the net proceeds so as to produce the amount determined by the court as the net amount which would be realised on a sale of the goods in the open market by a willing vendor.

(4)   If a company fails to comply with subsection (3)—
    (a) the company commits an offence, and
    (b) any officer of the company who without reasonable excuse authorised or permitted the failure commits an offence.

(5)   Where the court makes an order giving permission under subsection (1), the directors must, within the period of 14 days beginning with the date of the order, send a copy of it to the registrar of companies.

(6)   If the directors fail to comply with subsection (5), any director who did not have a reasonable excuse for the failure commits an offence.

(7)   In Scotland, where goods in the possession of the company under a hire-purchase agreement are disposed of under subsection (1), the disposal has the effect of extinguishing, as against the disponee, all rights of the owner of the goods under the agreement.

Effect of contravention of certain provisions of Chapter

A33   Contravention of certain requirements imposed under this Chapter

The fact that a company contravenes section A19 or any of sections A25 to A32 does not—

(a)   make any transaction void or unenforceable, or

(b)   affect the validity of any other thing.

CHAPTER 5
THE MONITOR

A34   Status of monitor

The monitor in relation to a moratorium is an officer of the court.

A35   Monitoring

(1)   During a moratorium, the monitor must monitor the company's affairs for the purpose of forming a view as to whether it remains likely that the moratorium will result in the rescue of the company as a going concern.

(2)   In forming the view mentioned in subsection (1), the monitor is entitled to rely on information provided by the company, unless the monitor has reason to doubt its accuracy.

A36   Provision of information to monitor

(1)   The monitor may require the directors of the company to provide any information required by the monitor for the purpose of carrying out the monitor's functions.

(2)   The directors must comply with a requirement to provide information as soon as practicable.

(3)   For the potential consequences of failing to comply with a requirement to provide information, see section A38.

A37   Application by monitor for directions

The monitor in relation to a moratorium may apply to the court for directions about the carrying out of the monitor's functions.

A38   Termination of moratorium by monitor

(1)   The monitor must bring a moratorium to an end by filing a notice with the court if—

    (a)   the monitor thinks that the moratorium is no longer likely to result in the rescue of the company as a going concern,

    (b)   the monitor thinks that the objective of rescuing the company as a going concern has been achieved,

    (c)   the monitor thinks that, by reason of a failure by the directors to comply with a requirement under section A36, the monitor is unable properly to carry out the monitor's functions, or

    (d)   the monitor thinks that the company is unable to pay any of the following that have fallen due—

        (i)   moratorium debts;

        (ii)   pre-moratorium debts for which the company does not have a payment holiday during the moratorium (see section A18).

(2)   The rules may provide for debts that are to be disregarded for the purposes of subsection (1)(d).

(3)   On the filing with the court of a notice under subsection (1), the moratorium comes to an end.

(4)   The rules may make provision about the timing of a notice required to be given under subsection (1).

(5)   The Secretary of State may by regulations amend this section for the purposes of changing the circumstances in which the monitor must bring a moratorium to an end under subsection (1).

(6)   Regulations under subsection (5) are subject to the affirmative resolution procedure.

(7)   See also section A17 (obligations to notify change in end of moratorium).

A39   Replacement of monitor or appointment of additional monitor

(1)   The court may make an order authorising the appointment of a qualified person to act as the monitor in relation to a moratorium instead of, or in addition to, a person who already acts as the monitor.

(2)   The court may make an order providing that a person ceases to act as the monitor in relation to a moratorium.

(3)   An order under subsection (1) or (2) may be made only on an application by the directors or the monitor.

(4)   The court may make an order authorising the appointment of a monitor under subsection (1) only if the person has provided the court with a statement that the person—

    (a)   is a qualified person, and

    (b)   consents to act as the monitor in relation to the moratorium.

(5)   Where it is proposed that more than one person should act as the monitor in relation to the moratorium, the statement under subsection (4) must specify—

    (a)   which functions (if any) are to be exercised by the persons acting jointly, and

    (b)   which functions (if any) are to be exercised by any or all of the persons.

(6)   The rules may make provision about the date on which the statement under subsection (4) must be made.

(7)   Where the court makes an order under subsection (1) or (2) the person begins to act as the monitor, or ceases to act as the monitor, in relation to the moratorium at the time specified in, or determined in accordance with, the order ("the relevant time")

(8)   As soon as reasonably practicable after the relevant time, the monitor must notify the following of the effect of the order—

    (a)   the registrar of companies,

    (b)   every creditor of the company of whose claim the monitor is aware,

    (c)   in a case where the company is or has been an employer in respect of an occupational pension scheme that is not a money purchase scheme, the Pensions Regulator, and

    (d)   in a case where the company is an employer in respect of such a pension scheme that is an eligible scheme within the meaning given by section 126 of the Pensions Act 2004, the Board of the Pension Protection Fund.

(9)   If the monitor without reasonable excuse fails to comply with subsection (8), the monitor commits an offence.

A40   Application of Part where two or more persons act as monitor

(1)   Where two or more persons act jointly as the monitor—

    (a)   a reference in this Act to the monitor is a reference to those persons acting jointly;

    (b)   where an offence of omission is committed by the monitor, each of the persons appointed to act jointly—

        (i)   commits the offence, and

        (ii)   may be proceeded against and punished individually.

(2)   Where persons act jointly in respect of only some of the functions of the monitor, subsection (1) applies only in relation to those functions.

(3)   Where two or more persons act concurrently as the monitor a reference in this Act to the monitor is a reference to any of the persons appointed (or any combination of them).

A41   Presumption of validity

    An act of the monitor is valid in spite of a defect in the monitor's appointment or qualification.

CHAPTER 6

CHALLENGES

A42 Challenge to monitor's actions

(1) Any of the persons specified below may apply to the court on the ground that an act, omission or decision of the monitor during a moratorium has unfairly harmed the interests of the applicant.

(2) The persons who may apply are—

    (a) a creditor, director or member of the company, or

    (b) any other person affected by the moratorium.

(3) An application under subsection (1) may be made during the moratorium or after it has ended.

(4) On an application under subsection (1) the court may—

    (a) confirm, reverse or modify any act or decision of the monitor,

    (b) give the monitor directions, or

    (c) make such other order as it thinks fit (but may not, under this paragraph, order the monitor to pay any compensation).

(5) Where an application under subsection (1) relates to a failure by the monitor to bring the moratorium to an end under section A38(1), an order under subsection (4) may, in particular, bring the moratorium to an end and make such consequential provision as the court thinks fit.

(6) Where an application under subsection (1) relates to the monitor bringing a moratorium to an end under section A38(1), an order under subsection (4) may, in particular, provide that the moratorium is not to be taken into account for the purposes of paragraph 2(1)(b) of Schedule ZA1 (company not eligible for moratorium if moratorium in force within previous 12 months).

(7) In making an order under subsection (4) the court must have regard to the need to safeguard the interests of persons who have dealt with the company in good faith and for value.

(8) See also section A17 (obligations to notify change in end of moratorium).

A43 Challenges to monitor remuneration in insolvency proceedings

(1) The rules may confer on an administrator or liquidator of a company the right to apply to the court on the ground that remuneration charged by the monitor in relation to a prior moratorium for the company was excessive.

(2) Rules under subsection (1) may (among other things) make provision as to—

    (a) time limits;

    (b) disposals available to the court;

    (c) the treatment of costs (or, in Scotland, the expenses) of the application in the administration or winding up.

A44 Challenge to directors' actions

(1) A creditor or member of a company may apply to the court for an order under this section on the ground that—

    (a) during a moratorium, the company's affairs, business and property are being or have been managed by the directors in a manner which has unfairly harmed the interests of its creditors or members generally or of some part of its creditors or members (including at least the applicant), or

    (b) any actual or proposed act or omission of the directors during a moratorium causes or would cause such harm.

(2) An application under subsection (1) may be made during the moratorium or after it has ended.

(3) On an application under subsection (1) the court may make such order as it thinks fit.

(4) An order under subsection (3) may in particular—

    (a) regulate the management by the directors of the company's affairs, business and property during the remainder of the moratorium,

    (b) require the directors to refrain from doing or continuing an act complained of by the applicant or to do an act which the applicant has complained they have omitted to do,

(c)   require a decision of the company's creditors to be sought (using a qualifying decision procedure) on such matters as the court may direct, or

(d)   bring the moratorium to an end and make such consequential provision as the court thinks fit.

(5)   In making an order under subsection (3) the court must have regard to the need to safeguard the interests of persons who have dealt with the company in good faith and for value.

(6)   See also section A17 (obligations to notify change in end of moratorium).

A45   Challenge brought by Board of the Pension Protection Fund

(1)   This section applies where—

(a)   a moratorium—

(i)   is in force in relation to a company that is an employer in respect of an eligible scheme, or

(ii)   is or has been in force in relation to a company that has been an employer in respect of an eligible scheme at any time during the moratorium, and

(b)   the trustees or managers of the scheme are a creditor of the company.

(2)   The Board of the Pension Protection Fund may make any application under section A42(1) or A44(1) that could be made by the trustees or managers as a creditor.

(3)   For the purposes of such an application, any reference in section A42(1) or A44(1) to the interests of the applicant is to be read as a reference to the interests of the trustees or managers as a creditor.

(4)   In this section "eligible scheme" has the meaning given by section 126 of the Pensions Act 2004.

CHAPTER 7
OFFENCES: GENERAL

A46   Offence of fraud etc during or in anticipation of moratorium

(1)   An officer of a company commits an offence if, during a moratorium for the company or at any time within the period of 12 months ending with the day on which a moratorium for the company comes into force, the officer—

(a)   does any of the things mentioned in subsection (2), or

(b)   was privy to the doing by others of any of the things mentioned in subsection (2)(c), (d) and (e).

(2)   Those things are—

(a)   concealing any part of the company's property to the value of £500 or more, or concealing any debt due to or from the company,

(b)   fraudulently removing any part of the company's property to the value of £500 or more,

(c)   concealing, destroying, mutilating or falsifying any document affecting or relating to the company's property or affairs,

(d)   making any false entry in any document affecting or relating to the company's property or affairs,

(e)   fraudulently parting with, altering or making any omission in any document affecting or relating to the company's property or affairs, or

(f)   pawning, pledging or disposing of any property of the company which has been obtained on credit and has not been paid for (unless the pawning, pledging or disposal was in the ordinary way of the company's business).

(3)   It is a defence—

(a)   for a person charged with an offence under subsection (1) in respect of any of the things mentioned in subsection (2)(a) or (f) to prove that the person had no intent to defraud, and

(b)   for a person charged with an offence under subsection (1) in respect of any of the things mentioned in subsection (2)(c) or (d) to prove that the person had no intent to conceal the state of affairs of the company or to defeat the law.

(4)   Where a person pawns, pledges or disposes of any property of a company in circumstances which amount to an offence under subsection (1), every person who takes in pawn or pledge, or otherwise receives, the property commits an offence if the person knows it to be pawned, pledged or disposed of in circumstances which—

(a)   amount to an offence under subsection (1), or

(b)   would, if a moratorium were obtained for the company within the period of 12 months beginning with the day on which the pawning, pledging or disposal took place, amount to an offence under subsection (1).

(5)   In this section, "officer" includes a shadow director.

A47   Offence of false representation etc to obtain a moratorium

(1)   An officer of a company commits an offence if, for the purpose of obtaining a moratorium for the company or an extension of a moratorium for the company, the officer—

(a)   makes any false representation, or

(b)   fraudulently does, or omits to do, anything.

(2)   Subsection (1) applies even if no moratorium or extension is obtained.

(3)   In this section, "officer" includes a shadow director.

A48   Prosecution of delinquent officers of company

(1)   This section applies where a moratorium has been obtained for a company.

(2)   If it appears to the monitor that any past or present officer of the company has committed an offence in connection with the moratorium, the monitor must forthwith—

(a)   report the matter to the appropriate authority, and

(b)   provide the appropriate authority with such information and give the authority such access to and facilities for inspecting and taking copies of documents (being information or documents in the possession or under the control of the monitor and relating to the matter in question) as the authority requires.

(3)   In subsection (2), "the appropriate authority"—

(a)   in the case of a company registered in England and Wales, means the Secretary of State,

(b)   in the case of a company registered in Scotland, means the Lord Advocate, and

(c)   in the case of an unregistered company means—

(i)   if it has a principal place of business in England and Wales but not Scotland, the Secretary of State,

(ii)   if it has a principal place of business in Scotland but not England and Wales, the Lord Advocate,

(iii)   if it has a principal place of business in both England and Wales and Scotland, the Secretary of State and the Lord Advocate, and

(iv)   if it does not have a principal place of business in England and Wales or Scotland, the Secretary of State.

(4)   Where a matter is reported to the Secretary of State under subsection (2), the Secretary of State may, for the purpose of investigating the matter and such other matters relating to the affairs of the company as appear to the Secretary of State to require investigation, exercise any of the powers which are exercisable by inspectors appointed under section 431 or 432 of the Companies Act 1985.

(5)   For the purpose of such an investigation any obligation imposed on a person by any provision of the Companies Acts to produce documents or give information to, or otherwise to assist, inspectors so appointed is to be regarded as an obligation similarly to assist the Secretary of State in the Secretary of State's investigation.

(6)   Where a question is put to a person in exercise of the powers conferred by subsection (4), the person's answer may be used in evidence against them.

(7)   However, in criminal proceedings in which the person is charged with an offence other than a false statement offence—

(a)   no evidence relating to the answer may be adduced, and

(b)   no question relating to it may be asked,

by or on behalf of the prosecution, unless evidence relating to it is adduced, or a question relating to it is asked, in the proceedings by or on behalf of the person.

(8)   In subsection (7) "false statement offence" means—

    (a)   an offence under section 2 or 5 of the Perjury Act 1911 (false statements made on oath otherwise than in judicial proceedings or made otherwise than on oath), or

    (b)   an offence under section 44(1) or (2) of the Criminal Law (Consolidation) (Scotland) Act 1995 (false statements made on oath or otherwise than on oath)

(9)   Where a prosecuting authority institutes criminal proceedings following any report under subsection (2), the monitor, and every officer and agent of the company past and present (other than the defendant or defender), must give the authority all assistance in connection with the prosecution which they are reasonably able to give.

(10)   For this purpose—

"agent" includes any banker or solicitor of the company and any person employed by the company as auditor, whether that person is or is not an officer of the company;

"prosecuting authority" means the Director of Public Prosecutions, the Lord Advocate or the Secretary of State.

(11)   The court may, on the application of the prosecuting authority, direct a person who has failed to comply with subsection (9) to comply with it.

CHAPTER 8
MISCELLANEOUS AND GENERAL

Special rules for certain kinds of company etc

A49   Regulated companies: modifications to this Part

(1)   For the purposes of sections A3 and A4 as they apply in relation to a regulated company, section A6(1) has effect as if the documents listed there included a reference to the written consent of the appropriate regulator to the appointment of the proposed monitor.

(2)   The remaining provisions of this section apply in relation to a moratorium for a regulated company.

(3)   Any notice under section A8(2), A17(2) to (4) or A39(8) must also be sent by the monitor to the appropriate regulator.

(4)   The directors must give the appropriate regulator notice of any qualifying decision procedure by which a decision of the company's creditors is sought for the purposes of section A12(2) or A44(4)(c).

(5)   If the directors fail to comply with subsection (4), any director who did not have a reasonable excuse for the failure commits an offence.

(6)   The appropriate regulator, or a person appointed by the appropriate regulator, may in the way provided for by the rules, participate (but not vote) in any qualifying decision procedure by which a decision of the company's creditors is sought for the purposes of this Part.

(7)   The appropriate regulator is entitled to be heard on any application to the court for permission under section A31(1) or A32(1) (disposal of charged property, etc).

(8)   The court may make an order under section A39(1) only if the appropriate regulator has given its written consent to the appointment of the proposed monitor.

(9)   The persons who may apply to the court under section A39(3), A42(1) or A44(1) include the appropriate regulator.

(10)   If a person other than a regulator applies to the court under section A39(3), A42(1) or A44(1) the appropriate regulator is entitled to be heard on the application.

(11)   If either regulator makes an application to the court under section A39(3), A42(1) or A44(1) in relation to a PRA-regulated company, the other regulator is entitled to be heard on the application.

(12)   This section does not affect any right that the appropriate regulator has (apart from this section) as a creditor of a regulated company.

(13) In this section—

"the appropriate regulator" means—

    (a) where the regulated company is a PRA-regulated company, each of the Financial Conduct Authority and the Prudential Regulation Authority, and

    (b) where the regulated company is not a PRA-regulated company, the Financial Conduct Authority;

"PRA-authorised person" has the meaning given by section 2B(5) of the Financial Services and Markets Act 2000;

"PRA-regulated company" means a regulated company which—

    (a) is, or has been, a PRA-authorised person,

    (b) is, or has been, an appointed representative within the meaning given by section 39 of the Financial Services and Markets Act 2000, whose principal (or one of whose principals) is, or was, a PRA-authorised person, or

    (c) is carrying on, or has carried on, a PRA-regulated activity (within the meaning of section 22A of that Act) in contravention of the general prohibition;

"regulated activity" has the meaning given by section 22 of the Financial Services and Markets Act 2000, taken with Schedule 2 to that Act and any order under that section;

"regulated company" means a company which—

    (a) is, or has been, an authorised person within the meaning given by section 31 of the Financial Services and Markets Act 2000,

    (b) is, or has been, an appointed representative within the meaning given by section 39 of that Act, or

    (c) is carrying on, or has carried on, a regulated activity in contravention of the general prohibition within the meaning given by section 19 of that Act;

"regulator" means the Financial Conduct Authority or the Prudential Regulation Authority.

(14) The Secretary of State may by regulations amend this section for the purposes of changing the definition of "regulated company" in subsection (13).

(15) Regulations under subsection (14) are subject to the affirmative resolution procedure.

A50 Power to modify this Part etc in relation to certain companies

(1) The Secretary of State may by regulations make provision under the law of England and Wales or Scotland—

    (a) to modify this Part as it applies in relation to a company for which there is a special administration regime, or

    (b) in connection with the interaction between this Part and any other insolvency procedure in relation to such a company.

(2) The Welsh Ministers may by regulations make provision under the law of England and Wales—

    (a) to modify this Part as it applies in relation to a company that is a social landlord registered under Part 1 of the Housing Act 1996, or

    (b) make provision in connection with the interaction between this Part and any other insolvency procedure in relation to such a company.

(3) The Scottish Ministers may by regulations make provision under the law of Scotland—

    (a) to modify this Part as it applies in relation to a company that is a social landlord registered under Part 2 of the Housing (Scotland) Act 2010 (asp 17), or

    (b) make provision in connection with the interaction between this Part and any other insolvency procedure in relation to such a company.

(4) The Secretary of State may, by regulations, make any provision under the law of England and Wales, Scotland or Northern Ireland that appears to the Secretary of State to be appropriate in view of provision made under subsection (1), (2) or (3).

(5) The power in subsection (1), (2), (3) or (4) may, in particular, be used to amend, repeal, revoke or otherwise modify any provision made by an enactment.

(6) Regulations under subsection (1) or (4) are subject to the affirmative resolution procedure.

(7)   A statutory instrument containing regulations under subsection (2) may not be made unless a draft of the statutory instrument containing them has been laid before and approved by a resolution of Senedd Cymru.

(8)   Regulations made by the Scottish Ministers under subsection (3) are subject to the affirmative procedure (see section 29 of the Interpretation and Legislative Reform (Scotland) Act 2010 (asp 10)).

(9)   In this section—

"insolvency procedure" includes—

    (a)   in relation to subsection (1)(b), the provision made by sections 143A to 159 of the Housing and Regeneration Act 2008;

    (b)   in relation to subsection (2)(b), the provision made by sections 39 to 50 of the Housing Act 1996;

    (c)   in relation to subsection (3)(b), the provision made by Part 7 of the Housing (Scotland) Act 2010;

"ordinary administration" means the insolvency procedure provided for by Schedule B1;

"special administration regime" means provision made by an enactment for an insolvency procedure that—

    (a)   is similar or corresponds to ordinary administration, and

    (b)   provides for the administrator to have one or more special objectives instead of or in addition to the objectives of ordinary administration.

A51   Power to make provision in connection with pension schemes

(1)   The Secretary of State may by regulations provide that, in a case where—

    (a)   a moratorium—

        (i)   is in force in relation to a company that is an employer in respect of an eligible scheme, or

        (ii)   is or has been in force in relation to a company that has been an employer in respect of an eligible scheme at any time during the moratorium, and

    (b)   the trustees or managers of the scheme are a creditor of the company,

the Board of the Pension Protection Fund may exercise any of the following rights.

(2)   The rights are those which are exercisable by the trustees or managers as a creditor of the company under or by virtue of—

    (a)   section A12, or

    (b)   a court order under section A44(4)(c).

(3)   Regulations under subsection (1) may provide that the Board may exercise any such rights—

    (a)   to the exclusion of the trustees or managers of the scheme, or

    (b)   in addition to the exercise of those rights by the trustees or managers of the scheme.

(4)   Regulations under subsection (1)—

    (a)   may specify conditions that must be met before the Board may exercise any such rights;

    (b)   may provide for any such rights to be exercisable by the Board for a specified period;

    (c)   may make provision in connection with any such rights ceasing to be so exercisable at the end of such a period.

(5)   Regulations under subsection (1) are subject to the affirmative resolution procedure.

(6)   In this section "eligible scheme" has the meaning given by section 126 of the Pensions Act 2004.

Floating charges

A52   Void provisions in floating charge documents

(1)   A provision in an instrument creating a floating charge is void if it provides for the obtaining of a moratorium, or anything done with a view to obtaining a moratorium, to be—

    (a)   an event causing the floating charge to crystallise,

    (b)   an event causing restrictions which would not otherwise apply to be imposed on the disposal of property by the company, or

    (c)   a ground for the appointment of a receiver.

(2)   The reference in subsection (1) to anything done with a view to obtaining a moratorium includes any preliminary decision or investigation.

(3)   In subsection (1) "receiver" includes a manager and a person who is appointed both receiver and manager.

(4)   Subsection (1) does not apply to a provision in an instrument creating a floating charge that is—

(a)   a collateral security (as defined by section A27);

(b)   a market charge (as defined by section A27);

(c)   a security financial collateral arrangement (within the meaning of regulation 3 of the Financial Collateral Arrangements (No. 2) Regulations 2003 (S.I. 2003/3226));

(d)   a system-charge (as defined by section A27).

Interpretation of this Part

A53   Meaning of "pre-moratorium debt" and "moratorium debt"

(1)   In this Part "pre-moratorium debt", in relation to a company for which a moratorium is or has been in force, means—

(a)   any debt or other liability to which the company becomes subject before the moratorium comes into force, or

(b)   any debt or other liability to which the company has become or may become subject during the moratorium by reason of any obligation incurred before the moratorium comes into force,

but this is subject to subsection (3).

(2)   In this Part "moratorium debt", in relation to a company for which a moratorium is or has been in force, means—

(a)   any debt or other liability to which the company becomes subject during the moratorium, other than by reason of an obligation incurred before the moratorium came into force, or

(b)   any debt or other liability to which the company has become or may become subject after the end of the moratorium by reason of an obligation incurred during the moratorium,

but this is subject to subsection (3).

(3)   For the purposes of this Part—

(a)   a liability in tort or delict is a "pre-moratorium debt" if either—

(i)   the cause of action has accrued before the moratorium comes into force, or

(ii)   all the elements necessary to establish the cause of action exist before the moratorium comes into force except for actionable damage;

(b)   a liability in tort or delict is a "moratorium debt" if it does not fall within paragraph (a) and either—

(i)   the cause of action has accrued during the moratorium, or

(ii)   all the elements necessary to establish the cause of action exist before the moratorium comes to an end except for actionable damage.

(4)   The Secretary of State may by regulations amend this section for the purposes of changing the definition of "pre-moratorium debt" or "moratorium debt" in this Part.

(5)   Regulations under subsection (4) are subject to the affirmative resolution procedure.

A54   Interpretation of this Part: general

(1)   In this Part—

"company" means—

(a)   a company registered under the Companies Act 2006 in England and Wales or Scotland, or

(b)   an unregistered company that may be wound up under Part 5 of this Act;

"the court" means such court as is prescribed;

"eligible", in relation to a company, has the meaning given by Schedule ZA1;

"employer", in relation to a pension scheme—

(a)   in sections A8(2)(c), A17(8)(c) and A39(8)(c), means an employer within the meaning of section 318(1) of the Pensions Act 2004;

(b)   elsewhere in this Part, has the same meaning that it has for the purposes of Part 2 of the Pensions Act 2004 (see section 318(1) and (4) of that Act);

"enactment" includes an Act of the Scottish Parliament and an instrument made under such an Act;

"hire-purchase agreement" includes a conditional sale agreement, a chattel leasing agreement and a retention of title agreement;

"liability" means (subject to subsection (2)) a liability to pay money or money's worth, including any liability under an enactment, a liability for breach of trust, any liability in contract, tort, delict or bailment, and any liability arising out of an obligation to make restitution;

"money purchase scheme" has the meaning given by section 181(1) of the Pension Schemes Act 1993;

"the monitor", in relation to a moratorium, means the person who has the functions of the monitor in relation to the moratorium (see also section A40 for cases where two or more persons act as the monitor);

"moratorium" means a moratorium under this Part;

"moratorium debt" has the meaning given by section A53;

"occupational pension scheme" has the meaning given by section 1 of the Pension Schemes Act 1993;

"pension scheme" has the meaning given by section 1 of the Pension Schemes Act 1993;

"pre-moratorium debt" has the meaning given by section A53;

"qualified person" means a person qualified to act as an insolvency practitioner;

"unable to pay its debts"—

(a)   in relation to a registered company, has the same meaning as in Part 4 (see section 123);

(b)   in relation to an unregistered company, has the same meaning as in Part 5 (see sections 222 to 224).

(2)   For the purposes of references in any provision of this Part to a debt or liability it is immaterial whether the debt or liability is present or future, whether it is certain or contingent, or whether its amount is fixed or liquidated, or is capable of being ascertained by fixed rules or as a matter of opinion.

(3)   In this Part references to filing a document with the court are, in relation to a court in Scotland, references to lodging it in court.

(4)   The Secretary of State may by regulations amend this section for the purposes of changing the definition of "qualified person" in subsection (1).

(5)   Regulations under subsection (4) are subject to the affirmative resolution procedure.

Regulations

A55   **Regulations**

(1)   Regulations under this Part may make—

(a)   different provision for different purposes;

(b)   consequential, supplementary, incidental or transitional provision or savings.

(2)   Regulations under this Part are to be made by statutory instrument, unless they are made by the Scottish Ministers.

(3)   Where regulations of the Secretary of State under this Part are subject to "the affirmative resolution procedure", they may not be made unless a draft of the statutory instrument containing them has been laid before Parliament and approved by a resolution of each House of Parliament.

PART I

COMPANY VOLUNTARY ARRANGEMENTS

The proposal

1. **Those who may propose an arrangement**

(1) The directors of a company (other than one which is in administration or being wound up) may make a proposal under this Part to the company and to its creditors for a composition in satisfaction of its debts or a scheme of arrangement of its affairs (from here on referred to, in either case, as a "voluntary arrangement").

(2) A proposal under this Part is one which provides for some person ("the nominee") to act in relation to the voluntary arrangement either as trustee or otherwise for the purpose of supervising its implementation; and the nominee must be a person who is qualified to act as an insolvency practitioner ... in relation to the voluntary arrangement.

(3) Such a proposal may also be made—

(a) where the company is in administration, by the administrator, and

(b) where the company is being wound up, by the liquidator.

(4) In this Part "company" means—

(a) a company registered under the Companies Act 2006 in England and Wales or Scotland;

(b) a company incorporated in an EEA ...; or

(c) a company not incorporated in an EEA State but having its centre of main interests in a member State (other than Denmark) or in the United Kingdom.

(5) In subsection (4), in relation to a company, "centre of main interests" has the same meaning as in Article 3 of the EU Regulation.

(6) If a company incorporated outside the United Kingdom has a principal place of business in Northern Ireland, no proposal under this Part shall be made in relation to it unless it also has a principal place of business in England and Wales or Scotland (or both in England and Wales or Scotland).

1A. ...

2. **Procedure where nominee is not the liquidator or administrator**

(1) This section applies where the nominee under section 1 is not the liquidator or administrator of the company ...

(2) The nominee shall, within 28 days (or such longer period as the court may allow) after he is given notice of the proposal for a voluntary arrangement, submit a report to the court stating—

(a) whether, in his opinion, the proposed voluntary arrangement has a reasonable prospect of being approved and implemented,

(b) whether, in his opinion, the proposal should be considered by a meeting of the company and by the company's creditors, and

(c) if in his opinion it should, the date on which, and time and place at which, he proposes a meeting of the company should be held.

(3) For the purposes of enabling the nominee to prepare his report, the person intending to make the proposal shall submit to the nominee—

(a) a document setting out the terms of the proposed voluntary arrangement, and

(b) a statement of the company's affairs containing—

(i) such particulars of its creditors and of its debts and other liabilities and of its assets as may be prescribed, and

(ii) such other information as may be prescribed.

(4) The court may—

(a) on an application made by the person intending to make the proposal, in a case where the nominee has failed to submit the report required by this section or has died, or

(b) on an application made by that person or the nominee, in a case where it is impracticable or inappropriate for the nominee to continue to act as such, direct that the nominee be replaced as such by another person qualified to act as an insolvency practitioner … in relation to the voluntary arrangement.

3.   Consideration of proposal

(1)   Where the nominee under section 1 is not the liquidator or administrator, and it has been reported to the court under section 2(2) that the proposal should be considered by a meeting of the company and by the company's creditors, the person making the report shall (unless the court otherwise directs)—

     (a)   summon a meeting of the company to consider the proposal for the time, date and place proposed in the report, and

     (b)   seek a decision from the company's creditors as to whether they approve the proposal.

(2)   Where the nominee is the liquidator or administrator, he shall—

     (a)   summon a meeting of the company to consider the proposal for such time, date and place as he thinks fit, and

     (b)   seek a decision from the company's creditors as to whether they approve the proposal.

(3)   A decision of the company's creditors as to whether they approve the proposal is to be made by a qualifying decision procedure.

(4)   Notice of the qualifying decision procedure must be given to every creditor of the company of whose claim and address the person seeking the decision is aware.

Consideration and implementation of proposal

4.   Decisions of the company and its creditors

(1)   This section applies where, under section 3—

     (a)   a meeting of the company is summoned to consider the proposed voluntary arrangement, and

     (b)   the company's creditors are asked to decide whether to approve the proposed voluntary arrangement.

(1A)   The company and its creditors may approve the proposed voluntary arrangement with or without modifications.

(2)   The modifications may include one conferring the functions proposed to be conferred on the nominee on another person qualified to act as an insolvency practitioner … in relation to the voluntary arrangement.

But they shall not include any modification by virtue of which the proposal ceases to be a proposal such as is mentioned in section 1.

(3)   Neither the company nor its creditors may approve any proposal or modification which affects the right of a secured creditor of the company to enforce his security, except with the concurrence of the creditor concerned.

(4)   Subject as follows, neither the company nor its creditors may approve any proposal or modification under which—

     (a)   any preferential debt of the company is to be paid otherwise than in priority to such of its debts as are not preferential debts, …

     (aa)   any ordinary preferential debt of the company is to be paid otherwise than in priority to any secondary preferential debts that it may have,

     (b)   a preferential creditor of the company is to be paid an amount in respect of an ordinary preferential debt that bears to that debt a smaller proportion than is borne to another ordinary preferential debt by the amount that is to be paid in respect of that other debt, …

     (c)   a preferential creditor of the company is to be paid an amount in respect of a secondary preferential debt that bears to that debt a smaller proportion than is borne to another secondary preferential debt by the amount that is to be paid in respect of that other debt, or

     (d)   in the case of a company which is a relevant financial institution (see section 387A), any non-preferential debt is to be paid otherwise than in accordance with the rules in section 176AZA(2) or (3).

However, … such a proposal or modification may be approved with the concurrence of the … creditor concerned.

(4A) Subject to subsection (4B), where the nominee's report under section 2(2) is submitted to the court before the end of the period of 12 weeks beginning with the day after the end of any moratorium for the company under Part A1, neither the company nor its creditors may approve any proposal or modification under which the following are to be paid otherwise than in full—

    (a) moratorium debts (within the meaning given by section 174A);

    (b) priority pre-moratorium debts (within the meaning given by section 174A).

(4B) Subsection (4A) does not prevent the approval of such a proposal or modification with the concurrence of the creditor concerned.

(5) Subject as above, the meeting of the company and the qualifying decision procedure shall be conducted in accordance with the rules.

(6) After the conclusion of the company meeting in accordance with the rules, the chairman of the meeting shall report the result of the meeting to the court, and, immediately after reporting to the court, shall give notice of the result of the meeting to such persons as may be prescribed.

(6A) After the company's creditors have decided whether to approve the proposed voluntary arrangement the person who sought the decision must—

    (a) report the creditors' decision to the court, and

    (b) immediately after reporting to the court, give notice of the creditors' decision to such persons as may be prescribed.

(7) References in this section to preferential debts, ordinary preferential debts, secondary preferential debts and preferential creditors are to be read in accordance with section 386 in Part XII of this Act.

4A.   Approval of arrangement

(1) This section applies to a decision, under section 4, with respect to the approval of a proposed voluntary arrangement.

(2) The decision has effect if, in accordance with the rules—

    (a) it has been taken by the meeting of the company summoned under section 3 and by the company's creditors pursuant to that section, or

    (b) (subject to any order made under subsection (6)) it has been taken by the company's creditors pursuant to that section.

(3) If the decision taken by the company's creditors differs from that taken by the company meeting, a member of the company may apply to the court.

(4) An application under subsection (3) shall not be made after the end of the period of 28 days beginning with—

    (a) the day on which the decision was taken by the company's creditors, or

    (b) where the decision of the company meeting was taken on a later day, that day.

(5) Where a member of a regulated company, as defined by section A49(13), applies to the court under subsection (3), the appropriate regulator is entitled to be heard on the application.

(5A) The "appropriate regulator" means—

    (a) where the regulated company is a PRA-regulated company as defined by section A49(13), the Financial Conduct Authority and the Prudential Regulation Authority, and

    (b) in any other case, the Financial Conduct Authority.

(6) On an application under subsection (3), the court may—

    (a) order the decision of the company meeting to have effect instead of the decision of the company's creditors, or

    (b) make such other order as it thinks fit.

5.   Effect of approval

(1) This section applies where a decision approving a voluntary arrangement has effect under section 4A.

(2) The … voluntary arrangement—

(a) takes effect as if made by the company at the time the creditors decided to approve the voluntary arrangement, and

(b) binds every person who in accordance with the rules—

    (i) was entitled to vote in the qualifying decision procedure by which the creditors' decision to approve the voluntary arrangement was made, or

    (ii) would have been so entitled if he had had notice of it,

as if he were a party to the voluntary arrangement.

(2A) If—

(a) when the arrangement ceases to have effect any amount payable under the arrangement to a person bound by virtue of subsection (2)(b)(ii) has not been paid, and

(b) the arrangement did not come to an end prematurely,

the company shall at that time become liable to pay to that person the amount payable under the arrangement.

(3) Subject as follows, if the company is being wound up or is in administration, the court may do one or both of the following, namely—

(a) by order stay or sist all proceedings in the winding up or provide for the appointment of the administrator to cease to have effect;

(b) give such directions with respect to the conduct of the winding up or the administration as it thinks appropriate for facilitating the implementation of the … voluntary arrangement.

(3A) Where immediately before the voluntary arrangement took effect a moratorium for the company was in force under Part A1 and a petition for the winding up of the company, other than an excepted petition within the meaning of section A20, was presented before the beginning of the moratorium, the court must dismiss the petition.

(4) The court shall not make an order under subsection (3)(a) or dismiss a petition under subsection (3A)—

(a) at any time before the end of the period of 28 days beginning with the first day on which each of the reports required by section 4(6) and (6A) has been made to the court, or

(b) at any time when an application under the next section or an appeal in respect of such an application is pending, or at any time in the period within which such an appeal may be brought.

(5) Where the company is in energy administration, the court shall not make an order or give a direction under subsection (3) unless—·

(a) the court has given the Secretary of State or the Gas and Electricity Markets Authority a reasonable opportunity of making representations to it about the proposed order or direction; and

(b) the order or direction is consistent with the objective of the energy administration.

(6) In subsection (5) "in energy administration" and "objective of the energy administration" are to be construed in accordance with Schedule B1 to this Act, as applied by Part 1 of Schedule 20 to the Energy Act 2004.

6.   Challenge of decisions

(1) Subject to this section, an application to the court may be made, by any of the persons specified below, on one or both of the following grounds, namely—

(a) that a voluntary arrangement which has effect under section 4A unfairly prejudices the interests of a creditor, member or contributory of the company;

(b) that there has been some material irregularity at or in relation to the meeting of the company, or in relation to the relevant qualifying decision procedure.

(1A) In this section—

(a) the "relevant qualifying decision procedure" means the qualifying decision procedure in which the company's creditors decide whether to approve a voluntary arrangement;

(b) references to a decision made in the relevant qualifying decision procedure include any other decision made in that qualifying decision procedure.

(2) The persons who may apply under subsection (1) are—

(a) a person entitled, in accordance with the rules, to vote at the meeting of the company or in the relevant qualifying decision procedure;

(aa) a person who would have been entitled, in accordance with the rules, to vote in the relevant qualifying decision procedure if he had had notice of it;

(b) the nominee or any person who has replaced him under section 2(4) or 4(2); and

(c) if the company is being wound up or is in administration, the liquidator or administrator.

(2A) Subject to this section, where a voluntary arrangement in relation to a company in energy administration is approved at the meetings summoned under section 3, an application to the court may be made—

(a) by the Secretary of State, or

(b) with the consent of the Secretary of State, by the Gas and Electricity Markets Authority,

on the ground that the voluntary arrangement is not consistent with the achievement of the objective of the energy administration.

(3) An application under this section shall not be made—

(a) after the end of the period of 28 days beginning with the first day on which each of the reports required by section 4(6) and (6A) has been made to the court, or

(b) in the case of a person who was not given notice of the relevant qualifying decision procedure, after the end of the period of 28 days beginning with the day on which he became aware that the relevant qualifying decision procedure had taken place,

but (subject to that) an application made by a person within subsection (2)(aa) on the ground that the voluntary arrangement prejudices his interests may be made after the arrangement has ceased to have effect, unless it came to an end prematurely.

(4) Where on such an application the court is satisfied as to either of the grounds mentioned in subsection (1) or, in the case of an application under subsection (2A), as to the ground mentioned in that subsection, it may do any of the following, namely—

(a) revoke or suspend any decision approving the voluntary arrangement which has effect under section 4A or, in a case falling within subsection (1)(b), any decision taken by the meeting of the company, or in the relevant qualifying decision procedure, which has effect under that section;

(b) give a direction to any person for the summoning of a further company meeting to consider any revised proposal the person who made the original proposal may make or, in a case falling within subsection (1)(b) and relating to the company meeting, a further company meeting to reconsider the original proposal;

(c) direct any person—

(i) to seek a decision from the company's creditors (using a qualifying decision procedure) as to whether they approve any revised proposal the person who made the original proposal may make, or

(ii) in a case falling within subsection (1)(b) and relating to the relevant qualifying decision procedure, to seek a decision from the company's creditors (using a qualifying decision procedure) as to whether they approve the original proposal.

(5) Where at any time after giving a direction under subsection (4)(b) or (c) in relation to a revised proposal the court is satisfied that the person who made the original proposal does not intend to submit a revised proposal, the court shall revoke the direction and revoke or suspend any decision approving the voluntary arrangement which has effect under section 4A.

(6) In a case where the court, on an application under this section with respect to any meeting or relevant qualifying decision procedure—

(a) gives a direction under subsection (4)(b) or (c), or

(b) revokes or suspends an approval under subsection (4)(a) or (5),

the court may give such supplemental directions as it thinks fit and, in particular, directions with respect to things done under the voluntary arrangement since it took effect.

(7) Except in pursuance of the preceding provisions of this section,

(a)   a decision taken at a company meeting summoned under section 3 is not invalidated by any irregularity at or in relation to the meeting, and

(b)   a decision of the company's creditors made in the relevant qualifying decision procedure is not invalidated by any irregularity in relation to the relevant qualifying decision procedure.

(8)   In this section "in energy administration" and "objective of the energy administration" are to be construed in accordance with Schedule B1 to this Act, as applied by Part 1 of Schedule 20 to the Energy Act 2004.

6A.   False representations, etc

(1)   If, for the purpose of obtaining the approval of the members or creditors of a company to a proposal for a voluntary arrangement, a person who is an officer of the company—

(a)   makes any false representation, or

(b)   fraudulently does, or omits to do, anything,

he commits an offence.

(2)   Subsection (1) applies even if the proposal is not approved.

(3)   For purposes of this section "officer" includes a shadow director.

(4)   A person guilty of an offence under this section is liable to imprisonment or a fine, or both.

7.   Implementation of proposal

(1)   This section applies where a voluntary arrangement has effect under section 4A.

(2)   The person who is for the time being carrying out in relation to the voluntary arrangement the functions conferred—

(a)   on the nominee by virtue of the approval of the voluntary arrangement by the company or its creditors (or both) pursuant to section 3,

(b)   by virtue of section 2(4) or 4(2) on a person other than the nominee,

shall be known as the supervisor of the voluntary arrangement.

(3)   If any of the company's creditors or any other person is dissatisfied by any act, omission or decision of the supervisor, he may apply to the court; and on the application the court may—

(a)   confirm, reverse or modify any act or decision of the supervisor,

(b)   give him directions, or

(c)   make such other order as it thinks fit.

(4)   The supervisor—

(a)   may apply to the court for directions in relation to any particular matter arising under the voluntary arrangement, and

(b)   is included among the persons who may apply to the court for the winding up of the company or for an administration order to be made in relation to it.

(5)   The court may, whenever—

(a)   it is expedient to appoint a person to carry out the functions of the supervisor, and

(b)   it is inexpedient, difficult or impracticable for an appointment to be made without the assistance of the court,

make an order appointing a person who is qualified to act as an insolvency practitioner ... in relation to the voluntary arrangement, either in substitution for the existing supervisor or to fill a vacancy.

(6)   The power conferred by subsection (5) is exercisable so as to increase the number of persons exercising the functions of supervisor or, where there is more than one person exercising those functions, so as to replace one or more of those persons.

7A.   Prosecution of delinquent officers of company

(1)   This section applies where the approval of a voluntary arrangement in relation to a company has taken effect under section 4A.

(2)   If it appears to the supervisor that any past or present officer of the company has committed an offence in connection with the voluntary arrangement, the supervisor must forthwith—

(a)   report the matter to the appropriate authority, and

(b) provide the appropriate authority with such information and give the authority such access to and facilities for inspecting and taking copies of documents (being information or documents in the possession or under the control of the ... supervisor and relating to the matter in question) as the authority requires.

In this subsection, "the appropriate authority" means—

(i) in the case of a company registered in England and Wales, the Secretary of State, and

(ii) in the case of a company registered in Scotland, the Lord Advocate.

(3) Where a report is made to the Secretary of State under subsection (2), he may, for the purpose of investigating the matter reported to him and such other matters relating to the affairs of the company as appear to him to require investigation, exercise any of the powers which are exercisable by inspectors appointed under section 431 or 432 of the Companies Act 1985 to investigate a company's affairs.

(4) For the purpose of such an investigation any obligation imposed on a person by any provision of the Companies Acts to produce documents or give information to, or otherwise to assist, inspectors so appointed is to be regarded as an obligation similarly to assist the Secretary of State in his investigation.

(5) An answer given by a person to a question put to him in exercise of the powers conferred by subsection (3) may be used in evidence against him.

(6) However, in criminal proceedings in which that person is charged with an offence to which this subsection applies—

(a) no evidence relating to the answer may be adduced, and

(b) no question relating to it may be asked,

by or on behalf of the prosecution, unless evidence relating to it is adduced, or a question relating to it is asked, in the proceedings by or on behalf of that person.

(7) Subsection (6) applies to any offence other than—

(a) an offence under section 2 or 5 of the Perjury Act 1911 (false statements made on oath otherwise than in judicial proceedings or made otherwise than on oath), or

(b) an offence under section 44(1) or (2) of the Criminal Law (Consolidation) (Scotland) Act 1995 (false statements made on oath or otherwise than on oath).

(8) Where a prosecuting authority institutes criminal proceedings following any report under subsection (2), the ... supervisor, and every officer and agent of the company past and present (other than the defendant or defender), shall give the authority all assistance in connection with the prosecution which he is reasonably able to give.

For this purpose—

"agent" includes any banker or solicitor of the company and any person employed by the company as auditor, whether that person is or is not an officer of the company,

"prosecuting authority" means the Director of Public Prosecutions, the Lord Advocate or the Secretary of State.

(9) The court may, on the application of the prosecuting authority, direct any person referred to in subsection (8) to comply with that subsection if he has failed to do so.

7B. Arrangements coming to an end prematurely

For the purposes of this Part, a voluntary arrangement the approval of which has taken effect under section 4A ... comes to an end prematurely if, when it ceases to have effect, it has not been fully implemented in respect of all persons bound by the arrangement by virtue of section 5(2)(b)(i) ...

PART II

ADMINISTRATION

8. Administration

Schedule B1 to this Act (which makes provision about the administration of companies) shall have effect.

9–27. ...

PART III
RECEIVERSHIP

CHAPTER I
RECEIVERS AND MANAGERS (ENGLAND AND WALES)

Preliminary and general provisions

28.   Extent of this Chapter

(1)   In this Chapter "company" means a company registered under the Companies Act 2006 in England and Wales or Scotland.

(2)   This Chapter does not apply to receivers appointed under Chapter 2 of this Part (Scotland).

29.   Definitions

(1)   It is hereby declared that, except where the context otherwise requires—

(a)   any reference in ... this Act to a receiver or manager of the property of a company, or to a receiver of it, includes a receiver or manager, or (as the case may be) a receiver of part only of that property and a receiver only of the income arising from the property or from part of it; and

(b)   any reference in ... this Act to the appointment of a receiver or manager under powers contained in an instrument includes an appointment made under powers which, by virtue of any enactment, are implied in and have effect as if contained in an instrument.

(2)   In this Chapter "administrative receiver" means—

(a)   a receiver or manager of the whole (or substantially the whole) of a company's property appointed by or on behalf of the holders of any debentures of the company secured by a charge which, as created, was a floating charge, or by such a charge and one or more other securities; or

(b)   a person who would be such a receiver or manager but for the appointment of some other person as the receiver of part of the company's property.

30.   Disqualification of body corporate from acting as receiver

A body corporate is not qualified for appointment as receiver of the property of a company, and any body corporate which acts as such a receiver is liable to a fine.

31.   Disqualification of bankrupt or person in respect of whom a debt relief order is made

(1)   A person commits an offence if he acts as receiver or manager of the property of a company on behalf of debenture holders while—

(a)   he is an undischarged bankrupt,

(aa)   a moratorium period under a debt relief order applies in relation to him,

(b)   a bankruptcy restrictions order or a debt relief restrictions order is in force in respect of him.

(2)   A person guilty of an offence under subsection (1) shall be liable to imprisonment, a fine or both.

(3)   This section does not apply to a receiver or manager acting under an appointment made by the court.

32.   Power for court to appoint official receiver

Where application is made to the court to appoint a receiver on behalf of the debenture holders or other creditors of a company which is being wound up by the court, the official receiver may be appointed.

Receivers and managers appointed out of court

33. Time for which appointment is effective

(1) The appointment of a person as a receiver or manager of a company's property under powers contained in an instrument—

    (a) is of no effect unless it is accepted by that person before the end of the business day next following that on which the instrument of appointment is received by him or on his behalf, and

    (b) subject to this, is deemed to be made at the time at which the instrument of appointment is so received.

(2) This section applies to the appointment of two or more persons as joint receivers or managers of a company's property under powers contained in an instrument, subject to such modifications as may be prescribed by the rules.

34. Liability for invalid appointment

Where the appointment of a person as the receiver or manager of a company's property under powers contained in an instrument is discovered to be invalid (whether by virtue of the invalidity of the instrument or otherwise), the court may order the person by whom or on whose behalf the appointment was made to indemnify the person appointed against any liability which arises solely by reason of the invalidity of the appointment.

35. Application to court for directions

(1) A receiver or manager of the property of a company appointed under powers contained in an instrument, or the persons by whom or on whose behalf a receiver or manager has been so appointed, may apply to the court for directions in relation to any particular matter arising in connection with the performance of the functions of the receiver or manager.

(2) On such an application, the court may give such directions, or may make such order declaring the rights of persons before the court or otherwise, as it thinks just.

36. Court's power to fix remuneration

(1) The court may, on an application made by the liquidator of a company, by order fix the amount to be paid by way of remuneration to a person who, under powers contained in an instrument, has been appointed receiver or manager of the company's property.

(2) The court's power under subsection (1), where no previous order has been made with respect thereto under the subsection—

    (a) extends to fixing the remuneration for any period before the making of the order or the application for it,

    (b) is exercisable notwithstanding that the receiver or manager has died or ceased to act before the making of the order or the application, and

    (c) where the receiver or manager has been paid or has retained for his remuneration for any period before the making of the order any amount in excess of that so fixed for that period, extends to requiring him or his personal representatives to account for the excess or such part of it as may be specified in the order.

But the power conferred by paragraph (c) shall not be exercised as respects any period before the making of the application for the order under this section, unless in the court's opinion there are special circumstances making it proper for the power to be exercised.

(3) The court may from time to time on an application made either by the liquidator or by the receiver or manager, vary or amend an order made under subsection (1).

37. Liability for contracts, etc

(1) A receiver or manager appointed under powers conferred in an instrument (other than an administrative receiver) is, to the same extent as if he had been appointed by order of the court—

(a)   personally liable on any contract entered into by him in the performance of his functions (except in so far as the contract otherwise provides) and on any contract of employment adopted by him in the performance of those functions, and

(b)   entitled in respect of that liability to indemnity out of the assets.

(2)   For the purposes of subsection (1)(a), the receiver or manager is not to be taken to have adopted a contract of employment by reason of anything done or omitted to be done within 14 days after his appointment.

(3)   Subsection (1) does not limit any right to indemnity which the receiver or manager would have apart from it, nor limit his liability on contracts entered into without authority, nor confer any right to indemnity in respect of that liability.

(4)   Where at any time the receiver or manager so appointed vacates office—

(a)   his remuneration and any expenses properly incurred by him, and

(b)   any indemnity to which he is entitled out of the assets of the company,

shall be charged on and paid out of any property of the company which is in his custody or under his control at that time in priority to any charge or other security held by the person by or on whose behalf he was appointed.

38.   Receivership accounts to be delivered to registrar

(1)   Except in the case of an administrative receiver, every receiver or manager of a company's property who has been appointed under powers contained in an instrument shall deliver to the registrar of companies for registration the requisite accounts of his receipts and payments.

(2)   The accounts shall be delivered within one month (or such longer period as the registrar may allow) after the expiration of 12 months from the date of his appointment and of every subsequent period of 6 months, and also within one month after he ceases to act as receiver or manager.

(3)   The requisite accounts shall be an abstract in the prescribed form showing—

(a)   receipts and payments during the relevant period of 12 or 6 months, or

(b)   where the receiver or manager ceases to act, receipts and payments during the period from the end of the period of 12 or 6 months to which the last preceding abstract related (or, if no preceding abstract has been delivered under this section, from the date of his appointment) up to the date of his so ceasing, and the aggregate amount of receipts and payments during all preceding periods since his appointment.

(4)   In this section "prescribed" means prescribed by regulations made by statutory instrument by the Secretary of State.

(5)   A receiver or manager who makes default in complying with this section is liable to a fine and, for continued contravention, to a daily default fine.

Provisions applicable to every receivership

39.   Notification that receiver or manager appointed

(1)   Where a receiver or manager of the property of a company has been appointed—

(a)   every invoice, order for goods or services, business letter or order form (whether in hard copy, electronic or any other form) issued by or on behalf of the company or the receiver or manager or the liquidator of the company; and

(b)   all the company's websites,

must contain a statement that a receiver or manager has been appointed.

(2)   If default is made in complying with this section, the company and any of the following persons, who knowingly and wilfully authorises or permits the default, namely, any officer of the company, any liquidator of the company and any receiver or manager, is liable to a fine.

40.   Payment of debts out of assets subject to floating charge

(1)   The following applies, in the case of a company, where a receiver is appointed on behalf of the holders of any debentures of the company secured by a charge which, as created, was a floating charge.

(2) If the company is not at the time in course of being wound up, its preferential debts (within the meaning given to that expression by section 386 in Part XII) shall be paid out of the assets coming to the hands of the receiver in priority to any claims for principal or interest in respect of the debentures.

(3) Payments made under this section shall be recouped, as far as may be, out of the assets of the company available for payment of general creditors.

41.   Enforcement of duty to make returns

(1) If a receiver or manager of a company's property—

(a) having made default in filing, delivering or making any return, account or other document, or in giving any notice, which a receiver or manager is by law required to file, deliver, make or give, fails to make good the default within 14 days after the service on him of a notice requiring him to do so, or

(b) having been appointed under powers contained in an instrument, has, after being required at any time by the liquidator of the company to do so, failed to render proper accounts of his receipts and payments and to vouch them and pay over to the liquidator the amount properly payable to him,

the court may, on an application made for the purpose, make an order directing the receiver or manager (as the case may be) to make good the default within such time as may be specified in the order.

(2) In the case of the default mentioned in subsection (1)(a), application to the court may be made by any member or creditor of the company or by the registrar of companies; and in the case of the default mentioned in subsection (1)(b), the application shall be made by the liquidator.

In either case the court's order may provide that all costs of and incidental to the application shall be borne by the receiver or manager, as the case may be.

(3) Nothing in this section prejudices the operation of any enactment imposing penalties on receivers in respect of any such default as is mentioned in subsection (1).

Administrative receivers: general

42.   General powers

(1) The powers conferred on the administrative receiver of a company by the debentures by virtue of which he was appointed are deemed to include (except in so far as they are inconsistent with any of the provisions of those debentures) the powers specified in Schedule 1 to this Act.

(2) In the application of Schedule 1 to the administrative receiver of a company—

(a) the words "he" and "him" refer to the administrative receiver, and

(b) references to the property of the company are to the property of which he is or, but for the appointment of some other person as the receiver of part of the company's property, would be the receiver or manager.

(3) A person dealing with the administrative receiver in good faith and for value is not concerned to inquire whether the receiver is acting within his powers.

43.   Power to dispose of charged property, etc

(1) Where, on an application by the administrative receiver, the court is satisfied that the disposal (with or without other assets) of any relevant property which is subject to a security would be likely to promote a more advantageous realisation of the company's assets than would otherwise be effected, the court may by order authorise the administrative receiver to dispose of the property as if it were not subject to the security.

(2) Subsection (1) does not apply in the case of any security held by the person by or on whose behalf the administrative receiver was appointed, or of any security to which a security so held has priority.

(3) It shall be a condition of an order under this section that—

(a) the net proceeds of the disposal, and

(b)   where those proceeds are less than such amount as may be determined by the court to be the net amount which would be realised on a sale of the property in the open market by a willing vendor, such sums as may be required to make good the deficiency,

shall be applied towards discharging the sums secured by the security.

(4)   Where a condition imposed in pursuance of subsection (3) relates to two or more securities, that condition shall require the net proceeds of the disposal and, where paragraph (b) of that subsection applies, the sums mentioned in that paragraph to be applied towards discharging the sums secured by those securities in the order of their priorities.

(5)   A copy of an order under this section shall, within 14 days of the making of the order, be sent by the administrative receiver to the registrar of companies.

(6)   If the administrative receiver without reasonable excuse fails to comply with subsection (5), he is liable to a fine and, for continued contravention, to a daily default fine.

(7)   In this section "relevant property", in relation to the administrative receiver, means the property of which he is or, but for the appointment of some other person as the receiver of part of the company's property, would be the receiver or manager.

44.   Agency and liability for contracts

(1)   The administrative receiver of a company—
   (a)   is deemed to be the company's agent, unless and until the company goes into liquidation;
   (b)   is personally liable on any contract entered into by him in the carrying out of his functions (except in so far as the contract otherwise provides) and, to the extent of any qualifying liability, on any contract of employment adopted by him in the carrying out of those functions; and
   (c)   is entitled in respect of that liability to an indemnity out of the assets of the company.

(2)   For the purposes of subsection (1)(b) the administrative receiver is not to be taken to have adopted a contract of employment by reason of anything done or omitted to be done within 14 days after his appointment.

(2A)   For the purposes of subsection (1)(b), a liability under a contract of employment is a qualifying liability if—
   (a)   it is a liability to pay a sum by way of wages or salary or contribution to an occupational pension scheme,
   (b)   it is incurred while the administrative receiver is in office, and
   (c)   it is in respect of services rendered wholly or partly after the adoption of the contract.

(2B)   Where a sum payable in respect of a liability which is a qualifying liability for the purposes of subsection (1)(b) is payable in respect of services rendered partly before and partly after the adoption of the contract, liability under subsection (1)(b) shall only extend to so much of the sum as is payable in respect of services rendered after the adoption of the contract.

(2C)   For the purposes of subsections (2A) and (2B)—
   (a)   wages or salary payable in respect of a period of holiday or absence from work through sickness or other good cause are deemed to be wages or (as the case may be) salary in respect of services rendered in that period, and
   (b)   a sum payable in lieu of holiday is deemed to be wages or (as the case may be) salary in respect of services rendered in the period by reference to which the holiday entitlement arose.

(2D)   …

(3)   This section does not limit any right to indemnity which the administrative receiver would have apart from it, nor limit his liability on contracts entered into or adopted without authority, nor confer any right to indemnity in respect of that liability.

45.   Vacation of office

(1)   An administrative receiver of a company may at any time be removed from office by order of the court (but not otherwise) and may resign his office by giving notice of his resignation in the prescribed manner to such persons as may be prescribed.

(2) An administrative receiver shall vacate office if he ceases to be qualified to act as an insolvency practitioner in relation to the company.

(3) Where at any time an administrative receiver vacates office—

(a) his remuneration and any expenses properly incurred by him, and

(b) any indemnity to which he is entitled out of the assets of the company,

shall be charged on and paid out of any property of the company which is in his custody or under his control at that time in priority to any security held by the person by or on whose behalf he was appointed.

(4) Where an administrative receiver vacates office otherwise than by death, he shall, within 14 days after his vacation of office, send a notice to that effect to the registrar of companies.

(5) If an administrative receiver without reasonable excuse fails to comply with subsection (4), he is liable to a fine *and, for continued contravention, to a daily default fine.*

Note. The italicized words in subsection (5) are repealed by the Companies Act 1989, s. 212, Sch. 24, as from a day to be appointed.

Administrative receivers:
ascertainment and investigation of company's affairs

46. Information to be given by administrative receiver

(1) Where an administrative receiver is appointed, he shall—

(a) forthwith send to the company and publish in the prescribed manner a notice of his appointment, and

(b) within 28 days after his appointment, unless the court otherwise directs, send such a notice to all the creditors of the company (so far as he is aware of their addresses).

(2) This section and the next do not apply in relation to the appointment of an administrative receiver to act—

(a) with an existing administrative receiver, or

(b) in place of an administrative receiver dying or ceasing to act,

except that, where they apply to an administrative receiver who dies or ceases to act before they have been fully complied with, the references in this section and the next to the administrative receiver include (subject to the next subsection) his successor and any continuing administrative receiver.

(3) If the company is being wound up, this section and the next apply notwithstanding that the administrative receiver and the liquidator are the same person, but with any necessary modifications arising from that fact.

(4) If the administrative receiver without reasonable excuse fails to comply with this section, he is liable to a fine and, for continued contravention, to a daily default fine.

47. Statement of affairs to be submitted

(1) Where an administrative receiver is appointed, he shall forthwith require some or all of the persons mentioned below to make out and submit to him a statement in the prescribed form as to the affairs of the company.

(2) A statement submitted under this section shall be verified by a statement of truth by the persons required to submit it and shall show—

(a) particulars of the company's assets, debts and liabilities;

(b) the names and addresses of its creditors;

(c) the securities held by them respectively;

(d) the dates when the securities were respectively given; and

(e) such further or other information as may be prescribed.

(3) The persons referred to in subsection (1) are—

(a) those who are or have been officers of the company;

(b) those who have taken part in the company's formation at any time within one year before the date of the appointment of the administrative receiver;

      (c)   those who are in the company's employment, or have been in its employment within that year, and are in the administrative receiver's opinion capable of giving the information required;

      (d)   those who are or have been within that year officers of or in the employment of a company which is, or within that year was, an officer of the company.

In this subsection "employment" includes employment under a contract for services.

(4)   Where any persons are required under this section to submit a statement of affairs to the administrative receiver, they shall do so (subject to the next subsection) before the end of the period of 21 days beginning with the day after that on which the prescribed notice of the requirement is given to them by the administrative receiver.

(5)   The administrative receiver, if he thinks fit, may—

      (a)   at any time release a person from an obligation imposed on him under subsection (1) or (2), or

      (b)   either when giving notice under subsection (4) or subsequently, extend the period so mentioned;

and where the administrative receiver has refused to exercise a power conferred by this subsection, the court, if it thinks fit, may exercise it.

(6)   If a person without reasonable excuse fails to comply with any obligation imposed under this section, he is liable to a fine and, for continued contravention, to a daily default fine.

48.   **Report by administrative receiver**

(1)   Where an administrative receiver is appointed, he shall, within 3 months (or such longer period as the court may allow) after his appointment, send to the registrar of companies, to any trustees for secured creditors of the company and (so far as he is aware of their addresses) to all such creditors, other than opted-out creditors, a report as to the following matters, namely—

      (a)   the events leading up to his appointment, so far as he is aware of them;

      (b)   the disposal or proposed disposal by him of any property of the company and the carrying on or proposed carrying on by him of any business of the company;

      (c)   the amounts of principal and interest payable to the debenture holders by whom or on whose behalf he was appointed and the amounts payable to preferential creditors; and

      (d)   the amount (if any) likely to be available for the payment of other creditors.

(2)   The administrative receiver shall also, within 3 months (or such longer period as the court may allow) after his appointment, either—

      (a)   send a copy of the report (so far as he is aware of their addresses) to all unsecured creditors of the company, other than opted-out creditors, or

      (b)   publish in the prescribed manner a notice stating an address to which unsecured creditors of the company should write for copies of the report to be sent to them free of charge,

      ...

(3)   ...

(4)   Where the company has gone or goes into liquidation, the administrative receiver—

      (a)   shall, within 7 days after his compliance with subsection (1) or, if later, the nomination or appointment of the liquidator, send a copy of the report to the liquidator, and

      (b)   where he does so within the time limited for compliance with subsection (2), is not required to comply with that subsection.

(5)   A report under this section shall include a summary of the statement of affairs made out and submitted to the administrative receiver under section 47 and of his comments (if any) upon it.

(6)   Nothing in this section is to be taken as requiring any such report to include any information the disclosure of which would seriously prejudice the carrying out by the administrative receiver of his functions.

(7)   Section 46(2) applies for the purposes of this section also.

(8)   If the administrative receiver without reasonable excuse fails to comply with this section, he is liable to a fine and, for continued contravention, to a default fine.

49.   Committee of creditors

(1)   Where an administrative receiver has sent or published a report as mentioned in section 48(2) the company's unsecured creditors may, in accordance with the rules, establish a committee ("the creditors' committee") to exercise the functions conferred on it by or under this Act.

(2)   If such a committee is established, the committee may, on giving not less than 7 days' notice, require the administrative receiver to attend before it at any reasonable time and furnish it with such information relating to the carrying out by him of his functions as it may reasonably require.

CHAPTER II
RECEIVERS (SCOTLAND)

50.   Extent of this Chapter

This Chapter extends to Scotland only.

51.   Power to appoint receiver

(1)   It is competent under the law of Scotland for the holder of a floating charge over all or any part of the property (including uncalled capital), which may from time to time be comprised in the property and undertaking of an incorporated company (whether a company registered under the Companies Act 2006 or not)—

    (a)   which the Court of Session has jurisdiction to wind up; or

    (b)   where paragraph (a) does not apply, in respect of which a court of a member state ... has under the EU Regulation jurisdiction to open insolvency proceedings,

to appoint a receiver of such part of the property of the company as is subject to the charge.

(2)   It is competent under the law of Scotland for the court, on the application of the holder of such a floating charge, to appoint a receiver of such part of the property of the company as is subject to the charge.

(2ZA)   ...

(2A)   Subsections (1) and (2) are subject to section 72A.

(3)   The following are disqualified from being appointed as receiver—

    (a)   a body corporate;

    (b)   an undischarged bankrupt; and

    (ba)   a person subject to a bankruptcy restrictions order;

    (c)   a firm according to the law of Scotland.

(4)   A body corporate or a firm according to the law of Scotland which acts as a receiver is liable to a fine.

(5)   An undischarged bankrupt or a person subject to a bankruptcy restrictions order who so acts is liable to imprisonment or a fine, or both.

(6)   In this section, "receiver" includes joint receivers; and

"bankruptcy restrictions order" means—

    (a)   a bankruptcy restrictions order made under section 155 of the Bankruptcy (Scotland) Act 2016;

    (b)   ...

    (c)   a bankruptcy restrictions order made under paragraph 1 of Schedule 4A to this Act; or

    (d)   a bankruptcy restrictions undertaking entered into under paragraph 7 of that Schedule.

"the EU Regulation" is Regulation (EU) 2015/848 of the European Parliament and of the Council on insolvency proceedings as that Regulation has effect in the law of the European Union;

"court" is to be construed in accordance with Article 2(6) of the EU Regulation;

"insolvency proceedings" is to be construed in accordance with Article 2(4) of the EU Regulation.

52.   Circumstances justifying appointment

(1)   A receiver may be appointed under section 51(1) by the holder of the floating charge on the occurrence of any event which, by the provisions of the instrument creating the charge, entitles

the holder of the charge to make that appointment and, in so far as not otherwise provided for by the instrument, on the occurrence of any of the following events, namely—

(a)   the expiry of a period of 21 days after the making of a demand for payment of the whole or any part of the principal sum secured by the charge, without payment having been made;

(b)   the expiry of a period of 2 months during the whole of which interest due and payable under the charge has been in arrears;

(c)   the making of an order or the passing of a resolution to wind up the company;

(d)   the appointment of a receiver by virtue of any other floating charge created by the company.

(2)   A receiver may be appointed by the court under section 51(2) on the occurrence of any event which, by the provisions of the instrument creating the floating charge, entitles the holder of the charge to make that appointment and, in so far as not otherwise provided for by the instrument, on the occurrence of any of the following events, namely—

(a)   where the court, on the application of the holder of the charge, pronounces itself satisfied that the position of the holder of the charge is likely to be prejudiced if no such appointment is made;

(b)   any of the events referred to in paragraphs (a) to (c) of subsection (1).

53.   Mode of appointment by holder of charge

(1)   The appointment of a receiver by the holder of the floating charge under section 51(1) shall be by means of an instrument subscribed in accordance with the Requirements of Writing (Scotland) Act 1995 ("the instrument of appointment"), a copy (certified in the prescribed manner to be a correct copy) whereof shall be delivered by or on behalf of the person making the appointment to the registrar of companies for registration within 7 days of its execution and shall be accompanied by a notice in the prescribed form.

(2)   If any person without reasonable excuse makes default in complying with the requirements of subsection (1), he is liable to a fine *and, for continued contravention, to a daily default fine.*

(3)   ...

(4)   If the receiver is to be appointed by the holders of a series of secured debentures, the instrument of appointment may be executed on behalf of the holders of the floating charge by any person authorised by resolution of the debenture-holders to execute the instrument.

(5)   On receipt of the certified copy of the instrument of appointment in accordance with subsection (1), the registrar shall, on payment of the prescribed fee, enter the particulars of the appointment in the register.

(6)   The appointment of a person as a receiver by an instrument of appointment in accordance with subsection (1)—

(a)   is of no effect unless it is accepted by that person before the end of the business day next following that on which the instrument of appointment is received by him or on his behalf, and

(b)   subject to paragraph (a), is deemed to be made on the day on and at the time at which the instrument of appointment is so received, as evidenced by a written docquet by that person or on his behalf;

and this subsection applies to the appointment of joint receivers subject to such modifications as may be prescribed.

(7)   On the appointment of a receiver under this section, the floating charge by virtue of which he was appointed attaches to the property then subject to the charge; and such attachment has effect as if the charge was a fixed security over the property to which it has attached.

Note. The italicized words in subsection (2) are repealed by the Companies Act 1989, s. 212, Sch. 24, as from a day to be appointed.

54.   Appointment by court

(1)   Application for the appointment of a receiver by the court under section 51(2) shall be by petition to the court, which shall be served on the company.

(2)   On such an application, the court shall, if it thinks fit, issue an interlocutor making the appointment of the receiver.

(3)   A copy (certified by the clerk of the court to be a correct copy) of the court's interlocutor making the appointment shall be delivered by or on behalf of the petitioner to the registrar of companies for registration, accompanied by a notice in the prescribed form, within 7 days of the date of the interlocutor or such longer period as the court may allow.

If any person without reasonable excuse makes default in complying with the requirements of this subsection, he is liable to a fine *and, for continued contravention, to a daily default fine.*

(4)   On receipt of the certified copy interlocutor in accordance with subsection (3), the registrar shall, on payment of the prescribed fee, enter the particulars of the appointment in the register.

(5)   The receiver is to be regarded as having been appointed on the date of his being appointed by the court.

(6)   On the appointment of a receiver under this section, the floating charge by virtue of which he was appointed attaches to the property then subject to the charge; and such attachment has effect as if the charge were a fixed security over the property to which it has attached.

(7)   In making rules of court for the purposes of this section, the Court of Session shall have regard to the need for special provision for cases which appear to the court to require to be dealt with as a matter of urgency.

Note. The italicized words in subsection (3) are repealed by the Companies Act 1989, s. 212, Sch. 24, as from a day to be appointed.

55.   Powers of receiver

(1)   Subject to the next subsection, a receiver has in relation to such part of the property of the company as is attached by the floating charge by virtue of which he was appointed, the powers, if any, given to him by the instrument creating that charge.

(2)   In addition, the receiver has under this Chapter the powers as respects that property (in so far as these are not inconsistent with any provision contained in that instrument) which are specified in Schedule 2 to this Act.

(3)   Subsections (1) and (2) apply—

    (a)   subject to the rights of any person who has effectually executed diligence on all or any part of the property of the company prior to the appointment of the receiver, and

    (b)   subject to the rights of any person who holds over all or any part of the property of the company a fixed security or floating charge having priority over, or ranking pari passu with, the floating charge by virtue of which the receiver was appointed.

(4)   A person dealing with a receiver in good faith and for value is not concerned to enquire whether the receiver is acting within his powers.

56.   Precedence among receivers

(1)   Where there are two or more floating charges subsisting over all or any part of the property of the company, a receiver may be appointed under this Chapter by virtue of each such charge; but a receiver appointed by, or on the application of, the holder of a floating charge having priority of ranking over any other floating charge by virtue of which a receiver has been appointed has the powers given to a receiver by section 55 and Schedule 2 to the exclusion of any other receiver.

(2)   Where two or more floating charges rank with one another equally, and two or more receivers have been appointed by virtue of such charges, the receivers so appointed are deemed to have been appointed as joint receivers.

(3)   Receivers appointed, or deemed to have been appointed, as joint receivers shall act jointly unless the instrument of appointment or respective instruments of appointment otherwise provide.

(4)   Subject to subsection (5) below, the powers of a receiver appointed by, or on the application of, the holder of a floating charge are suspended by, and as from the date of, the appointment of a receiver by, or on the application of, the holder of a floating charge having priority of ranking over that charge to such extent as may be necessary to enable the receiver second mentioned to exercise his powers under section 55 and Schedule 2; and any powers so suspended take effect

again when the floating charge having priority of ranking ceases to attach to the property then subject to the charge, whether such cessation is by virtue of section 62(6) or otherwise.

(5)   The suspension of the powers of a receiver under subsection (4) does not have the effect of requiring him to release any part of the property (including any letters or documents) of the company from his control until he receives from the receiver superseding him a valid indemnity (subject to the limit of the value of such part of the property of the company as is subject to the charge by virtue of which he was appointed) in respect of any expenses, charges and liabilities he may have incurred in the performance of his functions as receiver.

(6)   The suspension of the powers of a receiver under subsection (4) does not cause the floating charge by virtue of which he was appointed to cease to attach to the property to which it attached by virtue of section 53(7) or 54(6).

(7)   Nothing in this section prevents the same receiver being appointed by virtue of two or more floating charges.

57.   **Agency and liability of receiver for contracts**

(1)   A receiver is deemed to be the agent of the company in relation to such property of the company as is attached by the floating charge by virtue of which he was appointed.

(1A)   Without prejudice to subsection (1), a receiver is deemed to be the agent of the company in relation to any contract of employment adopted by him in the carrying out of his functions.

(2)   A receiver (including a receiver whose powers are subsequently suspended under section 56) is personally liable on any contract entered into by him in the performance of his functions, except in so far as the contract otherwise provides, and, to the extent of any qualifying liability, on any contract of employment adopted by him in the carrying out of those functions.

(2A)   For the purposes of subsection (2), a liability under a contract of employment is a qualifying liability if—

         (a)   it is a liability to pay a sum by way of wages or salary or contribution to an occupational pension scheme,

         (b)   it is incurred while the receiver is in office, and

         (c)   it is in respect of services rendered wholly or partly after the adoption of the contract.

(2B)   Where a sum payable in respect of a liability which is a qualifying liability for the purposes of subsection (2) is payable in respect of services rendered partly before and partly after the adoption of the contract, liability under that subsection shall only extend to so much of the sum as is payable in respect of services rendered after the adoption of the contract.

(2C)   For the purposes of subsections (2A) and (2B)—

         (a)   wages or salary payable in respect of a period of holiday or absence from work through sickness or other good cause are deemed to be wages or (as the case may be) salary in respect of services rendered in that period, and

         (b)   a sum payable in lieu of holiday is deemed to be wages or (as the case may be) salary in respect of services rendered in the period by reference to which the holiday entitlement arose.

(2D)   ...

(3)   A receiver who is personally liable by virtue of subsection (2) is entitled to be indemnified out of the property in respect of which he was appointed.

(4)   Any contract entered into by or on behalf of the company prior to the appointment of a receiver continues in force (subject to its terms) notwithstanding that appointment, but the receiver does not by virtue only of his appointment incur any personal liability on any such contract.

(5)   For the purposes of subsection (2), a receiver is not to be taken to have adopted a contract of employment by reason of anything done or omitted to be done within 14 days after his appointment.

(6)   This section does not limit any right to indemnity which the receiver would have apart from it, nor limit his liability on contracts entered into or adopted without authority, nor confer any right to indemnity in respect of that liability.

(7) Any contract entered into by a receiver in the performance of his functions continues in force (subject to its terms) although the powers of the receiver are subsequently suspended under section 56.

58. Remuneration of receiver

(1) The remuneration to be paid to a receiver is to be determined by agreement between the receiver and the holder of the floating charge by virtue of which he was appointed.

(2) Where the remuneration to be paid to the receiver has not been determined under subsection (1), or where it has been so determined but is disputed by any of the persons mentioned in paragraphs (a) to (d) below, it may be fixed instead by the Auditor of the Court of Session on application made to him by—
   (a) the receiver;
   (b) the holder of any floating charge or fixed security over all or any part of the property of the company;
   (c) the company; or
   (d) the liquidator of the company.

(3) Where the receiver has been paid or has retained for his remuneration for any period before the remuneration has been fixed by the Auditor of the Court of Session under subsection (2) any amount in excess of the remuneration so fixed for that period, the receiver or his personal representatives shall account for the excess.

59. Priority of debts

(1) Where a receiver is appointed and the company is not at the time of the appointment in course of being wound up, the debts which fall under subsection (2) of this section shall be paid out of any assets coming to the hands of the receiver in priority to any claim for principal or interest by the holder of the floating charge by virtue of which the receiver was appointed.

(2) Debts falling under this subsection are preferential debts (within the meaning given by section 386 in Part XII) which, by the end of a period of 6 months after advertisement by the receiver for claims in the Edinburgh Gazette and in a newspaper circulating in the district where the company carries on business either—
   (i) have been intimated to him, or
   (ii) have become known to him.

(3) Any payments made under this section shall be recouped as far as may be out of the assets of the company available for payment of ordinary creditors.

60. Distribution of moneys

(1) Subject to the next section, and to the rights of any of the following categories of persons (which rights shall, except to the extent otherwise provided in any instrument, have the following order of priority), namely—
   (a) the holder of any fixed security which is over property subject to the floating charge and which ranks prior to, or pari passu with, the floating charge;
   (b) all persons who have effectually executed diligence on any part of the property of the company which is subject to the charge by virtue of which the receiver was appointed;
   (c) creditors in respect of all liabilities, charges and expenses incurred by or on behalf of the receiver;
   (d) the receiver in respect of his liabilities, expenses and remuneration, and any indemnity to which he is entitled out of the property of the company; and
   (e) the preferential creditors entitled to payment under section 59,
the receiver shall pay moneys received by him to the holder of the floating charge by virtue of which the receiver was appointed in or towards satisfaction of the debt secured by the floating charge.

(2) Any balance of moneys remaining after the provisions of subsection (1) and section 61 below have been satisfied shall be paid in accordance with their respective rights and interests to the following persons, as the case may require—

        (a)   any other receiver;

        (b)   the holder of a fixed security which is over property subject to the floating charge;

        (c)   the company or its liquidator, as the case may be.

(3)   Where any question arises as to the person entitled to a payment under this section, or where a receipt or a discharge of a security cannot be obtained in respect of any such payment, the receiver shall consign the amount of such payment in any joint stock bank of issue in Scotland in name of the Accountant of Court for behoof of the person or persons entitled thereto.

61.   Disposal of interest in property

(1)   Where the receiver sells or disposes, or is desirous of selling or disposing, of any property or interest in property of the company which is subject to the floating charge by virtue of which the receiver was appointed and which is—

        (a)   subject to any security or interest of, or burden or encumbrance in favour of, a creditor the ranking of which is prior to, or pari passu with, or postponed to the floating charge, or

        (b)   property or an interest in property affected or attached by effectual diligence executed by any person,

      and the receiver is unable to obtain the consent of such creditor or, as the case may be, such person to such a sale or disposal, the receiver may apply to the court for authority to sell or dispose of the property or interest in property free of such security, interest, burden, encumbrance or diligence.

(1A)   For the purposes of subsection (1) above, an inhibition which takes effect after the creation of the floating charge by virtue of which the receiver was appointed is not an effectual diligence.

(1B)   For the purposes of subsection (1) above, an arrestment is an effectual diligence only where it is executed before the floating charge, by virtue of which the receiver was appointed, attaches to the property comprised in the company's property and undertaking.

(2)   Subject to the next subsection, on such an application the court may, if it thinks fit, authorise the sale or disposal of the property or interest in question free of such security, interest, burden, encumbrance or diligence, and such authorisation may be on such terms or conditions as the court thinks fit.

(3)   In the case of an application where a fixed security over the property or interest in question which ranks prior to the floating charge has not been met or provided for in full, the court shall not authorise the sale or disposal of the property or interest in question unless it is satisfied that the sale or disposal would be likely to provide a more advantageous realisation of the company's assets than would otherwise be effected.

(4)   It shall be a condition of an authorisation to which subsection (3) applies that—

        (a)   the net proceeds of the disposal, and

        (b)   where those proceeds are less than such amount as may be determined by the court to be the net amount which would be realised on a sale of the property or interest in the open market by a willing seller, such sums as may be required to make good the deficiency,

      shall be applied towards discharging the sums secured by the fixed security.

(5)   Where a condition imposed in pursuance of subsection (4) relates to two or more such fixed securities, that condition shall require the net proceeds of the disposal and, where paragraph (b) of that subsection applies, the sums mentioned in that paragraph to be applied towards discharging the sums secured by those fixed securities in the order of their priorities.

(6)   A copy of an authorisation under subsection (2) ... shall, within 14 days of the granting of the authorisation, be sent by the receiver to the registrar of companies.

(7)   If the receiver without reasonable excuse fails to comply with subsection (6), he is liable to a fine and, for continued contravention, to a daily default fine.

(8)   Where any sale or disposal is effected in accordance with the authorisation of the court under subsection (2), the receiver shall grant to the purchaser or disponee an appropriate document of transfer or conveyance of the property or interest in question, and that document has the effect, or, where recording, intimation or registration of that document is a legal requirement for completion

of title to the property or interest, then that recording, intimation or registration (as the case may be) has the effect, of—

(a) disencumbering the property or interest of the security, interest, burden or encumbrance affecting it, and

(b) freeing the property or interest from the diligence executed upon it.

(9) Nothing in this section prejudices the right of any creditor of the company to rank for his debt in the winding up of the company.

Note. Subsection (1B) is inserted by the Bankruptcy and Diligence etc. (Scotland) Act 2007, s. 226(1), Sch. 5, para. 14, as from a day to be appointed.

62. Cessation of appointment of receiver

(1) A receiver may be removed from office by the court under subsection (3) below and may resign his office by giving notice of his resignation in the prescribed manner to such persons as may be prescribed.

(2) A receiver shall vacate office if he ceases to be qualified to act as an insolvency practitioner in relation to the company.

(3) Subject to the next subsection, a receiver may, on application to the court by the holder of the floating charge by virtue of which he was appointed, be removed by the court on cause shown.

(4) Where at any time a receiver vacates office—

(a) his remuneration and any expenses properly incurred by him, and

(b) any indemnity to which he is entitled out of the property of the company,

shall be paid out of the property of the company which is subject to the floating charge and shall have priority as provided for in section 60(1).

(5) When a receiver ceases to act as such otherwise than by death he shall, and, when a receiver is removed by the court, the holder of the floating charge by virtue of which he was appointed shall, within 14 days of the cessation or removal (as the case may be) give the registrar of companies notice to that effect, and the registrar shall enter the notice in the register.

If the receiver or the holder of the floating charge (as the case may require) makes default in complying with the requirements of this subsection, he is liable to a fine *and, for continued contravention, to a daily default fine.*

(6) If by the expiry of a period of one month following upon the removal of the receiver or his ceasing to act as such no other receiver has been appointed, the floating charge by virtue of which the receiver was appointed—

(a) thereupon ceases to attach to the property then subject to the charge, and

(b) again subsists as a floating charge;

and for the purposes of calculating the period of one month under this subsection no account shall be taken of any period during which the company is in administration, under Part II of this Act …

Note. The italicized words in subsection (5) are repealed by the Companies Act 1989, s. 212, Sch. 24, as from a day to be appointed.

63. Powers of court

(1) The court on the application of—

(a) the holder of a floating charge by virtue of which a receiver was appointed, or

(b) a receiver appointed under section 51,

may give directions to the receiver in respect of any matter arising in connection with the performance by him of his functions.

(2) Where the appointment of a person as a receiver by the holder of a floating charge is discovered to be invalid (whether by virtue of the invalidity of the instrument or otherwise), the court may order the holder of the floating charge to indemnify the person appointed against any liability which arises solely by reason of the invalidity of the appointment.

64. Notification that receiver appointed

(1) Where a receiver has been appointed—

(a)   every invoice, order for goods or services, business letter or order form (whether in hard copy, electronic or any other form) issued by or on behalf of the company or the receiver or the liquidator of the company; and

(b)   all the company's websites,

must contain a statement that a receiver has been appointed.

(2)   If default is made in complying with the requirements of this section, the company and any of the following persons who knowingly and wilfully authorises or permits the default, namely any officer of the company, any liquidator of the company and any receiver, is liable to a fine.

65.   Information to be given by receiver

(1)   Where a receiver is appointed, he shall—

(a)   forthwith send to the company and publish notice of his appointment, and

(b)   within 28 days after his appointment, unless the court otherwise directs, send such notice to all the creditors of the company (so far as he is aware of their addresses).

(2)   This section and the next do not apply in relation to the appointment of a receiver to act—

(a)   with an existing receiver, or

(b)   in place of a receiver who has died or ceased to act,

except that, where they apply to a receiver who dies or ceases to act before they have been fully complied with, the references in this section and the next to the receiver include (subject to subsection (3) of this section) his successor and any continuing receiver.

(3)   If the company is being wound up, this section and the next apply notwithstanding that the receiver and the liquidator are the same person, but with any necessary modifications arising from that fact.

(4)   If a person without reasonable excuse fails to comply with this section, he is liable to a fine and, for continued contravention, to a daily default fine.

66.   Company's statement of affairs

(1)   Where a receiver of a company is appointed, the receiver shall forthwith require some or all of the persons mentioned in subsection (3) below to make out and submit to him a statement in the prescribed form as to the affairs of the company.

(2)   A statement submitted under this section contain a statutory declaration by the persons required to submit it and shall show—

(a)   particulars of the company's assets, debts and liabilities;

(b)   the names and addresses of its creditors;

(c)   the securities held by them respectively;

(d)   the dates when the securities were respectively given; and

(e)   such further or other information as may be prescribed.

(3)   The persons referred to in subsection (1) are—

(a)   those who are or have been officers of the company;

(b)   those who have taken part in the company's formation at any time within one year before the date of the appointment of the receiver;

(c)   those who are in the company's employment or have been in its employment within that year, and are in the receiver's opinion capable of giving the information required;

(d)   those who are or have been within that year officers of or in the employment of a company which is, or within that year was, an officer of the company.

In this subsection "employment" includes employment under a contract for services.

(4)   Where any persons are required under this section to submit a statement of affairs to the receiver they shall do so (subject to the next subsection) before the end of the period of 21 days beginning with the day after that on which the prescribed notice of the requirement is given to them by the receiver.

(5)   The receiver, if he thinks fit, may—

(a)   at any time release a person from an obligation imposed on him under subsection (1) or (2), or (b)　either when giving the notice mentioned in subsection (4) or subsequently extend the period so mentioned,

and where the receiver has refused to exercise a power conferred by this subsection, the court, if it thinks fit, may exercise it.

(6)　If a person without reasonable excuse fails to comply with any obligation imposed under this section, he is liable to a fine and, for continued contravention, to a daily default fine.

67.　Report by receiver

(1)　Where a receiver is appointed under section 51, he shall within 3 months (or such longer period as the court may allow) after his appointment, send to the registrar of companies, to the holder of the floating charge by virtue of which he was appointed and to any trustees for secured creditors of the company and (so far as he is aware of their addresses) to all such creditors, other than opted-out creditors, a report as to the following matters, namely—

(a)　the events leading up to his appointment, so far as he is aware of them;

(b)　the disposal or proposed disposal by him of any property of the company and the carrying on or proposed carrying on by him of any business of the company;

(c)　the amounts of principal and interest payable to the holder of the floating charge by virtue of which he was appointed and the amounts payable to preferential creditors; and

(d)　the amount (if any) likely to be available for the payment of other creditors.

(2)　The receiver shall also, within 3 months (or such longer period as the court may allow) after his appointment, either—

(a)　send a copy of the report (so far as he is aware of their addresses) to all unsecured creditors of the company, other than opted-out creditors, or

(b)　publish in the prescribed manner a notice stating an address to which unsecured creditors of the company should write for copies of the report to be sent to them free of charge,

...

(3)　...

(4)　Where the company has gone or goes into liquidation, the receiver—

(a)　shall, within 7 days after his compliance with subsection (1) or, if later, the nomination or appointment of the liquidator, send a copy of the report to the liquidator, and

(b)　where he does so within the time limited for compliance with subsection (2), is not required to comply with that subsection.

(5)　A report under this section shall include a summary of the statement of affairs made out and submitted under section 66 and of his comments (if any) on it.

(6)　Nothing in this section shall be taken as requiring any such report to include any information the disclosure of which would seriously prejudice the carrying out by the receiver of his functions.

(7)　Section 65(2) applies for the purposes of this section also.

(8)　If a person without reasonable excuse fails to comply with this section, he is liable to a fine and, for continued contravention, to a daily default fine.

(9)　In this section "secured creditor", in relation to a company, means a creditor of the company who holds in respect of his debt a security over property of the company, and "unsecured creditor" shall be construed accordingly.

68.　Committee of creditors

(1)　Where a receiver has sent or published a report as mentioned in section 67(2) the company's unsecured creditors may, in accordance with the rules, establish a committee ("the creditors' committee") to exercise the functions conferred on it by or under this Act.

(2)　If such a committee is established, the committee may on giving not less than 7 days' notice require the receiver to attend before it at any reasonable time and furnish it with such information relating to the carrying out by him of his functions as it may reasonably require.

69.　Enforcement of receiver's duty to make returns, etc

(1)　If any receiver—

(a)   having made default in filing, delivering or making any return, account or other document, or in giving any notice, which a receiver is by law required to file, deliver, make or give, fails to make good the default within 14 days after the service on him of a notice requiring him to do so; or

(b)   has, after being required at any time by the liquidator of the company so to do, failed to render proper accounts of his receipts and payments and to vouch the same and to pay over to the liquidator the amount properly payable to him,

the court may, on an application made for the purpose, make an order directing the receiver to make good the default within such time as may be specified in the order.

(2)   In the case of any such default as is mentioned in subsection (1)(a), an application for the purposes of this section may be made by any member or creditor of the company or by the registrar of companies; and, in the case of any such default as is mentioned in subsection (1)(b), the application shall be made by the liquidator; and, in either case, the order may provide that all expenses of and incidental to the application shall be borne by the receiver.

(3)   Nothing in this section prejudices the operation of any enactments imposing penalties on receivers in respect of any such default as is mentioned in subsection (1).

70.   Interpretation for Chapter II

(1)   In this Chapter, unless the contrary intention appears, the following expressions have the following meanings respectively assigned to them—

"company" means an incorporated company (whether or not a company registered under the Companies Act 2006) which the Court of Session has jurisdiction to wind up;

"fixed security", in relation to any property of a company, means any security, other than a floating charge or a charge having the nature of a floating charge, which on the winding up of the company in Scotland would be treated as an effective security over that property, and (without prejudice to that generality) includes a security over that property, being a heritable security within the meaning of the Conveyancing and Feudal Reform (Scotland) Act 1970;

"instrument of appointment" has the meaning given by section 53(1);

. . .

"prescribed fee" means the fee prescribed by regulations made under this Chapter by the Secretary of State;

"receiver" means a receiver of such part of the property of the company as is subject to the floating charge by virtue of which he has been appointed under section 51;

"the register" has the meaning given by section 1080 of the Companies Act 2006;

"secured debenture" means a bond, debenture, debenture stock or other security which, either itself or by reference to any other instrument, creates a floating charge over all or any part of the property of the company, but does not include a security which creates no charge other than a fixed security; and

"series of secured debentures" means two or more secured debentures created as a series by the company in such a manner that the holders thereof are entitled pari passu to the benefit of the floating charge.

(2)   Where a floating charge, secured debenture or series of secured debentures has been created by the company, then, except where the context otherwise requires, any reference in this Chapter to the holder of the floating charge shall—

(a)   where the floating charge, secured debenture or series of secured debentures provides for a receiver to be appointed by any person or body, be construed as a reference to that person or body;

(b)   where, in the case of a series of secured debentures, no such provision has been made therein but—

(i)   there are trustees acting for the debenture-holders under and in accordance with a trust deed, be construed as a reference to those trustees, and

(ii)   where no such trustees are acting, be construed as a reference to—

       (aa) a majority in nominal value of those present or represented by proxy and voting at a meeting of debenture-holders at which the holders of at least one-third in nominal value of the outstanding debentures of the series are present or so represented, or

       (bb) where no such meeting is held, the holders of at least one-half in nominal value of the outstanding debentures of the series.

(3)   Any reference in this Chapter to a floating charge, secured debenture, series of secured debentures or instrument creating a charge includes, except where the context otherwise requires, a reference to that floating charge, debenture, series of debentures or instrument as varied by any instrument.

(4)   References in this Chapter to the instrument by which a floating charge was created are, in the case of a floating charge created by words in a bond or other written acknowledgement, references to the bond or, as the case may be, the other written acknowledgement.

Note. This section is amended by the Moveable Transactions (Scotland) Act 2023, s. 61, as from a day to be appointed.

71.   Prescription of forms etc; regulations

(1)   The notice referred to in section 62(5), and the notice referred to in section 65(1)(a) shall be in such form as may be prescribed.

(2)   Any power conferred by this Chapter on the Secretary of State to make regulations is exercisable by statutory instrument; and a statutory instrument made in the exercise of the power so conferred to prescribe a fee is subject to annulment in pursuance of a resolution of either House of Parliament.

CHAPTER III

RECEIVERS' POWERS IN GREAT BRITAIN AS A WHOLE

72.   Cross-border operation of receivership provisions

(1)   A receiver appointed under the law of either part of Great Britain in respect of the whole or any part of any property or undertaking of a company and in consequence of the company having created a charge which, as created, was a floating charge may exercise his powers in the other part of Great Britain so far as their exercise is not inconsistent with the law applicable there.

(2)   In subsection (1) "receiver" includes a manager and a person who is appointed both receiver and manager.

CHAPTER IV

PROHIBITION OF APPOINTMENT OF

ADMINISTRATIVE RECEIVER

72A.   Floating charge holder not to appoint administrative receiver

(1)   The holder of a qualifying floating charge in respect of a company's property may not appoint an administrative receiver of the company.

(2)   In Scotland, the holder of a qualifying floating charge in respect of a company's property may not appoint or apply to the court for the appointment of a receiver who on appointment would be an administrative receiver of property of the company.

(3)   In subsections (1) and (2)—

       "holder of a qualifying floating charge in respect of a company's property" has the same meaning as in paragraph 14 of Schedule B1 to this Act, and

       "administrative receiver" has the meaning given by section 251.

(4)   This section applies—

       (a) to a floating charge created on or after a date appointed by the Secretary of State by order made by statutory instrument, and

       (b) in spite of any provision of an agreement or instrument which purports to empower a person to appoint an administrative receiver (by whatever name).

(5)   An order under subsection (4)(a) may—

(a)   make provision which applies generally or only for a specified purpose;

(b)   make different provision for different purposes;

(c)   make transitional provision.

(6)   This section is subject to the exceptions specified in sections 72B to 72GA.

72B.   First exception: capital market

(1)   Section 72A does not prevent the appointment of an administrative receiver in pursuance of an agreement which is or forms part of a capital market arrangement if—

(a)   a party incurs or, when the agreement was entered into was expected to incur, a debt of at least £50 million under the arrangement, and

(b)   the arrangement involves the issue of a capital market investment.

(2)   In subsection (1)—

"capital market arrangement" means an arrangement of a kind described in paragraph 1 of Schedule 2A, and

"capital market investment" means an investment of a kind described in paragraph 2 or 3 of that Schedule.

72C.   Second exception: public-private partnership

(1)   Section 72A does not prevent the appointment of an administrative receiver of a project company of a project which—

(a)   is a public-private partnership project, and

(b)   includes step-in rights.

(2)   In this section "public-private partnership project" means a project—

(a)   the resources for which are provided partly by one or more public bodies and partly by one or more private persons, or

(b)   which is designed wholly or mainly for the purpose of assisting a public body to discharge a function.

(3)   In this section—

"step-in rights" has the meaning given by paragraph 6 of Schedule 2A, and

"project company" has the meaning given by paragraph 7 of that Schedule.

72D.   Third exception: utilities

(1)   Section 72A does not prevent the appointment of an administrative receiver of a project company of a project which—

(a)   is a utility project, and

(b)   includes step-in rights.

(2)   In this section—

(a)   "utility project" means a project designed wholly or mainly for the purpose of a regulated business,

(b)   "regulated business" means a business of a kind listed in paragraph 10 of Schedule 2A,

(c)   "step-in rights" has the meaning given by paragraph 6 of that Schedule, and

(d)   "project company" has the meaning given by paragraph 7 of that Schedule.

72DA.   Exception in respect of urban regeneration projects

(1)   Section 72A does not prevent the appointment of an administrative receiver of a project company of a project which—

(a)   is designed wholly or mainly to develop land which at the commencement of the project is wholly or partly in a designated disadvantaged area outside Northern Ireland, and

(b)   includes step-in rights.

(2)   In subsection (1) "develop" means to carry out—

(a)   building operations,

(b)   any operation for the removal of substances or waste from land and the levelling of the surface of the land, or

(c)   engineering operations in connection with the activities mentioned in paragraph (a) or (b).

(3)   In this section—

"building" includes any structure or erection, and any part of a building as so defined, but does not include plant and machinery comprised in a building,

"building operations" includes—

(a) demolition of buildings,

(b) filling in of trenches,

(c) rebuilding,

(d) structural alterations of, or additions to, buildings, and

(e) other operations normally undertaken by a person carrying on business as a builder,

"designated disadvantaged area" means an area designated as a disadvantaged area under section 92 of the Finance Act 2001,

"engineering operations" includes the formation and laying out of means of access to highways,

"project company" has the meaning given by paragraph 7 of Schedule 2A,

"step-in rights" has the meaning given by paragraph 6 of that Schedule,

"substance" means any natural or artificial substance whether in solid or liquid form or in the form of a gas or vapour, and

"waste" includes any waste materials, spoil, refuse or other matter deposited on land.

72E. Fourth exception: project finance

(1) Section 72A does not prevent the appointment of an administrative receiver of a project company of a project which—

(a) is a financed project, and

(b) includes step-in rights.

(2) In this section—

(a) a project is "financed" if under an agreement relating to the project a project company incurs, or when the agreement is entered into is expected to incur, a debt of at least £50 million for the purposes of carrying out the project,

(b) "project company" has the meaning given by paragraph 7 of Schedule 2A, and

(c) "step-in rights" has the meaning given by paragraph 6 of that Schedule.

72F. Fifth exception: financial market

Section 72A does not prevent the appointment of an administrative receiver of a company by virtue of—

(a) a market charge within the meaning of section 173 of the Companies Act 1989,

(b) a system-charge within the meaning of the Financial Markets and Insolvency Regulations 1996,

(c) a collateral security charge within the meaning of the Financial Markets and Insolvency (Settlement Finality) Regulations 1999.

72G. Sixth exception: social landlords

Section 72A does not prevent the appointment of an administrative receiver of a company which is—

(a) a private registered provider of social housing, or

(b) registered as a social landlord under Part I of the Housing Act 1996 (c 52) or under Part 2 of the Housing (Scotland) Act 2010 (asp 17).

72GA. Exception in relation to protected railway companies etc

Section 72A does not prevent the appointment of an administrative receiver of—

(a) a company holding an appointment under Chapter I of Part II of the Water Industry Act 1991,

(b) a protected railway company within the meaning of section 59 of the Railways Act 1993 (including that section as it has effect by virtue of section 19 of the Channel Tunnel Rail Link Act 1996), or

(c) a licence company within the meaning of section 26 of the Transport Act 2000.

72H.   Sections 72A to 72G: supplementary

(1)   Schedule 2A (which supplements sections 72B to 72G) shall have effect.

(2)   The Secretary of State may by order—

        (a)   insert into this Act provision creating an additional exception to section 72A(1) or (2);

        (b)   provide for a provision of this Act which creates an exception to section 72A(1) or (2) to cease to have effect;

        (c)   amend section 72A in consequence of provision made under paragraph (a) or (b);

        (d)   amend any of sections 72B to 72G;

        (e)   amend Schedule 2A.

(3)   An order under subsection (2) must be made by statutory instrument.

(4)   An order under subsection (2) may make—

        (a)   provision which applies generally or only for a specified purpose;

        (b)   different provision for different purposes;

        (c)   consequential or supplementary provision;

        (d)   transitional provision.

(5)   An order under subsection (2)—

        (a)   in the case of an order under subsection (2)(e), shall be subject to annulment in pursuance of a resolution of either House of Parliament,

        (b)   in the case of an order under subsection (2)(d) varying the sum specified in section 72B(1)(a) or 72E(2)(a) (whether or not the order also makes consequential or transitional provision), shall be subject to annulment in pursuance of a resolution of either House of Parliament, and

        (c)   in the case of any other order under subsection (2)(a) to (d), may not be made unless a draft has been laid before and approved by resolution of each House of Parliament.

PART IV
WINDING UP OF COMPANIES REGISTERED
UNDER THE COMPANIES ACTS

CHAPTER I
PRELIMINARY

Introductory

73.   Scheme of this Part

(1)   This Part applies to the winding up of a company registered under the Companies Act 2006 in England and Wales or Scotland.

(2)   The winding up may be either—

        (a)   voluntary (see Chapters 2 to 5), or

        (b)   by the court (see Chapter 6).

(3)   This Chapter and Chapters 7 to 10 relate to winding up generally, except where otherwise stated.

Contributories

74.   Liability as contributories of present and past members

(1)   When a company is wound up, every present and past member is liable to contribute to its assets to any amount sufficient for payment of its debts and liabilities, and the expenses of the winding up, and for the adjustment of the rights of the contributories among themselves.

(2)   This is subject as follows—

        (a)   a past member is not liable to contribute if he has ceased to be a member for one year or more before the commencement of the winding up;

        (b)   a past member is not liable to contribute in respect of any debt or liability of the company contracted after he ceased to be a member;

(c) a past member is not liable to contribute, unless it appears to the court that the existing members are unable to satisfy the contributions required to be made by them ...;

(d) in the case of a company limited by shares, no contribution is required from any member exceeding the amount (if any) unpaid on the shares in respect of which he is liable as a present or past member;

(e) nothing in the Companies Acts or this Act invalidates any provision contained in a policy of insurance or other contract whereby the liability of individual members on the policy or contract is restricted, or whereby the funds of the company are alone made liable in respect of the policy or contract;

(f) a sum due to any member of the company (in his character of a member) by way of dividends, profits or otherwise is not deemed to be a debt of the company, payable to that member in a case of competition between himself and any other creditor not a member of the company, but any such sum may be taken into account for the purpose of the final adjustment of the rights of the contributories among themselves.

(3) In the case of a company limited by guarantee, no contribution is required from any member exceeding the amount undertaken to be contributed by him to the company's assets in the event of its being wound up; but if it is a company with a share capital, every member of it is liable (in addition to the amount so undertaken to be contributed to the assets), to contribute to the extent of any sums unpaid on shares held by him.

75. ...

76. Liability of past directors and shareholders

(1) This section applies where a company is being wound up and—

(a) it has under Chapter 5 of Part 18 of the Companies Act 2006 (acquisition by limited company of its own shares: redemption or purchase by private company out of capital) made a payment out of capital in respect of the redemption or purchase of any of its own shares (the payment being referred to below as "the relevant payment"), and

(b) the aggregate amount of the company's assets and the amounts paid by way of contribution to its assets (apart from this section) is not sufficient for payment of its debts and liabilities, and the expenses of the winding up.

(2) If the winding up commenced within one year of the date on which the relevant payment was made, then—

(a) the person from whom the shares were redeemed or purchased, and

(b) the directors who signed the statement made in accordance with section 714(1) to (3) of the Companies Act 2006 for purposes of the redemption or purchase (except a director who shows that he had reasonable grounds for forming the opinion set out in the statement),

are, so as to enable that insufficiency to be met, liable to contribute to the following extent to the company's assets.

(3) A person from whom any of the shares were redeemed or purchased is liable to contribute an amount not exceeding so much of the relevant payment as was made by the company in respect of his shares; and the directors are jointly and severally liable with that person to contribute that amount.

(4) A person who has contributed any amount to the assets in pursuance of this section may apply to the court for an order directing any other person jointly and severally liable in respect of that amount to pay him such amount as the court thinks just and equitable.

(5) Section 74 does not apply in relation to liability accruing by virtue of this section.

(6) ...

77. Limited company formerly unlimited

(1) This section applies in the case of a company being wound up which was at some former time registered as unlimited but has re-registered as a limited company.

(2) Notwithstanding section 74(2)(a) above, a past member of the company who was a member of it at the time of re-registration, if the winding up commences within the period of 3 years beginning

with the day on which the company was re-registered, is liable to contribute to the assets of the company in respect of debts and liabilities contracted before that time.

(3) If no persons who were members of the company at that time are existing members of it, a person who at that time was a present or past member is liable to contribute as above notwithstanding that the existing members have satisfied the contributions required to be made by them ...

This applies subject to section 74(2)(a) above and to subsection (2) of this section, but notwithstanding section 74(2)(c).

(4) Notwithstanding section 74(2)(d) and (3), there is no limit on the amount which a person who, at that time, was a past or present member of the company is liable to contribute as above.

78. Unlimited company formerly limited

(1) This section applies in the case of a company being wound up which was at some former time registered as limited but has been re-registered as unlimited ...

(2) A person who, at the time when the application for the company to be re-registered was lodged, was a past member of the company and did not after that again become a member of it is not liable to contribute to the assets of the company more than he would have been liable to contribute had the company not been re-registered.

79. Meaning of "contributory"

(1) In this Act ... the expression "contributory" means every person liable to contribute to the assets of a company in the event of its being wound up, and for the purposes of all proceedings for determining, and all proceedings prior to the final determination of, the persons who are to be deemed contributories, includes any person alleged to be a contributory.

(2) The reference in subsection (1) to persons liable to contribute to the assets does not include a person so liable by virtue of a declaration by the court under section 213 (imputed responsibility for company's fraudulent trading) or section 214 (wrongful trading) in Chapter X of this Part.

(3) A reference in a company's articles to a contributory does not (unless the context requires) include a person who is a contributory only by virtue of section 76.

...

80. Nature of contributory's liability

The liability of a contributory creates a debt (in England and Wales in the nature of an ordinary contract debt) accruing due from him at the time when his liability commenced, but payable at the times when calls are made for enforcing the liability.

81. Contributories in case of death of a member

(1) If a contributory dies either before or after he has been placed on the list of contributories, his personal representatives, and the heirs and legatees of heritage of his heritable estate in Scotland, are liable in a due course of administration to contribute to the assets of the company in discharge of his liability and are contributories accordingly.

(2) Where the personal representatives are placed on the list of contributories, the heirs or legatees of heritage need not be added, but they may be added as and when the court thinks fit.

(3) If in England and Wales the personal representatives make default in paying any money ordered to be paid by them, proceedings may be taken for administering the estate of the deceased contributory and for compelling payment out of it of the money due.

82. Effect of contributory's bankruptcy

(1) The following applies if a contributory becomes bankrupt, either before or after he has been placed on the list of contributories.

(2) His trustee in bankruptcy represents him for all purposes of the winding up, and is a contributory accordingly.

(3) The trustee may be called on to admit to proof against the bankrupt's estate, or otherwise allow to be paid out of the bankrupt's assets in due course of law, any money due from the bankrupt in respect of his liability to contribute to the company's assets.

(4)　There may be proved against the bankrupt's estate the estimated value of his liability to future calls as well as calls already made.

83.　Companies registered but not formed under the Companies Act 2006

(1)　The following applies in the event of a company being wound up which is registered but not formed under the Companies Act 2006.

(2)　Every person is a contributory, in respect of the company's debts and liabilities contracted before registration, who is liable—

(a)　to pay, or contribute to the payment of, any debt or liability so contracted, or

(b)　to pay, or contribute to the payment of, any sum for the adjustment of the rights of the members among themselves in respect of any such debt or liability, or

(c)　to pay, or contribute to the amount of, the expenses of winding up the company, so far as relates to the debts or liabilities above-mentioned.

(3)　Every contributory is liable to contribute to the assets of the company, in the course of the winding up, all sums due from him in respect of any such liability.

(4)　In the event of the death, bankruptcy or insolvency of any contributory, provisions of this Act, with respect to the personal representatives, to the heirs and legatees of heritage of the heritable estate in Scotland of deceased contributories and to the trustees of bankrupt or insolvent contributories respectively, apply.

CHAPTER II
VOLUNTARY WINDING UP
(INTRODUCTORY AND GENERAL)

Resolutions for, and commencement of, voluntary winding up

84.　Circumstances in which company may be wound up voluntarily

(1)　A company may be wound up voluntarily—

(a)　when the period (if any) fixed for the duration of the company by the articles expires, or the event (if any) occurs, on the occurrence of which the articles provide that the company is to be dissolved, and the company in general meeting has passed a resolution requiring it to be wound up voluntarily;

(b)　if the company resolves by special resolution that it be wound up voluntarily;

(c)　...

(2)　In this Act the expression "a resolution for voluntary winding up" means a resolution passed under either of the paragraphs of subsection (1).

(2A)　Before a company passes a resolution for voluntary winding up it must give written notice of the resolution to the holder of any qualifying floating charge to which section 72A applies.

(2B)　Where notice is given under subsection (2A) a resolution for voluntary winding up may be passed only—

(a)　after the end of the period of five business days beginning with the day on which the notice was given, or

(b)　if the person to whom the notice was given has consented in writing to the passing of the resolution.

(3)　Chapter 3 of Part 3 of the Companies Act 2006 (resolutions affecting a company's constitution) applies to a resolution under paragraph (a) of subsection (1) as well as a special resolution under paragraph (b).

(4)　This section has effect subject to section 43 of the Commonhold and Leasehold Reform Act 2002.

85.　Notice of resolution to wind up

(1)　When a company has passed a resolution for voluntary winding up, it shall, within 14 days after the passing of the resolution, give notice of the resolution by advertisement in the Gazette.

(2)　If default is made in complying with this section, the company and every officer of it who is in default is liable to a fine and, for continued contravention, to a daily default fine.

For the purposes of this subsection the liquidator is deemed an officer of the company.

86.   Commencement of winding up

A voluntary winding up is deemed to commence at the time of the passing of the resolution for voluntary winding up.

Consequences of resolution to wind up

87.   Effect on business and status of company

(1)   In case of a voluntary winding up, the company shall from the commencement of the winding up cease to carry on its business, except so far as may be required for its beneficial winding up.

(2)   However, the corporate state and corporate powers of the company, notwithstanding anything to the contrary in its articles, continue until the company is dissolved.

88.   Avoidance of share transfers, etc after winding-up resolution

Any transfer of shares, not being a transfer made to or with the sanction of the liquidator, and any alteration in the status of the company's members, made after the commencement of a voluntary winding up, is void.

Declaration of solvency

89.   Statutory declaration of solvency

(1)   Where it is proposed to wind up a company voluntarily, the directors (or, in the case of a company having more than two directors, the majority of them) may at a directors' meeting make a statutory declaration to the effect that they have made a full inquiry into the company's affairs and that, having done so, they have formed the opinion that the company will be able to pay its debts in full, together with interest at the official rate (as defined in section 251), within such period, not exceeding 12 months from the commencement of the winding up, as may be specified in the declaration.

(2)   Such a declaration by the directors has no effect for purposes of this Act unless—

(a)   it is made within the 5 weeks immediately preceding the date of the passing of the resolution for winding up, or on that date but before the passing of the resolution, and

(b)   it embodies a statement of the company's assets and liabilities as at the latest practicable date before the making of the declaration.

(3)   A copy of the declaration shall be delivered to the registrar of companies before the expiration of 15 days immediately following the date on which the resolution for winding up is passed.

(4)   A director making a declaration under this section without having reasonable grounds for the opinion that the company will be able to pay its debts in full, together with interest at the official rate, within the period specified is liable to imprisonment or a fine, or both.

(5)   If the company is wound up in pursuance of a resolution passed within 5 weeks after the making of the declaration, and its debts (together with interest at the official rate) are not paid or provided for in full within the period specified, it is to be presumed (unless the contrary is shown) that the director did not have reasonable grounds for his opinion.

(6)   If a copy of a declaration required by subsection (3) to be delivered to the registrar is not so delivered within the time prescribed by that subsection, the company and every officer in default is liable to a fine and, for continued contravention, to a daily default fine.

90.   Distinction between "members'" and "creditors'" voluntary winding up

A winding up in the case of which a directors' statutory declaration under section 89 has been made is a "members' voluntary winding up"; and a winding up in the case of which such a declaration has not been made is a "creditors' voluntary winding up".

CHAPTER III
MEMBERS' VOLUNTARY WINDING UP

91. Appointment of liquidator

(1) In a members' voluntary winding up, the company in general meeting shall appoint one or more liquidators for the purpose of winding up the company's affairs and distributing its assets.

(2) On the appointment of a liquidator all the powers of the directors cease, except so far as the company in general meeting or the liquidator sanctions their continuance.

92. Power to fill vacancy in office of liquidator

(1) If a vacancy occurs by death, resignation or otherwise in the office of liquidator appointed by the company, the company in general meeting may, subject to any arrangement with its creditors, fill the vacancy.

(2) For that purpose a general meeting may be convened by any contributory or, if there were more liquidators than one, by the continuing liquidators.

(3) The meeting shall be held in manner provided by this Act or by the articles, or in such manner as may, on application by any contributory or by the continuing liquidators, be determined by the court.

92A. Progress report to company ...

(1) Subject to section 96, ... the liquidator must—
    (a) for each prescribed period produce a progress report relating to the prescribed matters; and
    (b) within such period commencing with the end of the period referred to in paragraph (a) as may be prescribed send a copy of the progress report to—
        (i) the members of the company; and
        (ii) such other persons as may be prescribed.

(2) A liquidator who fails to comply with this section is liable to a fine.

93. ...

94. Final account prior to dissolution

(1) As soon as the company's affairs are fully wound up the liquidator must make up an account of the winding up, showing how it has been conducted and the company's property has been disposed of.

(2) The liquidator must send a copy of the account to the members of the company before the end of the period of 14 days beginning with the day on which the account is made up.

(3) The liquidator must send a copy of the account to the registrar of companies before the end of that period (but not before sending it to the members of the company).

(4) If the liquidator does not comply with subsection (2) the liquidator is liable to a fine.

(5) If the liquidator does not comply with subsection (3) the liquidator is liable to a fine and, for continued contravention, a daily default fine.

95. Effect of company's insolvency

(1) This section applies where the liquidator is of the opinion that the company will be unable to pay its debts in full (together with interest at the official rate) within the period stated in the directors' declaration under section 89.

(1A) The liquidator must before the end of the period of 7 days beginning with the day after the day on which the liquidator formed that opinion—
    (a) make out a statement in the prescribed form as to the affairs of the company, and
    (b) send it to the company's creditors.

(2), (2A), (3) ...

(4) The statement as to the affairs of the company ... shall show—
    (a) particulars of the company's assets, debts and liabilities;
    (b) the names and addresses of the company's creditors;

(c)   the securities held by them respectively;
(d)   the dates when the securities were respectively given; and
(e)   such further or other information as may be prescribed.

(4A)   The statement as to the affairs of the company ... —
(a) in the case of a winding up of a company registered in England and Wales, be verified by the liquidator by a statement of truth; and
(b)   in the case of a winding up of a company registered in Scotland, contain a statutory declaration by the liquidator.

(4B)   The company's creditors may in accordance with the rules nominate a person to be liquidator.

(4C)   The liquidator must in accordance with the rules seek such a nomination from the company's creditors.

(5)–(7) ...

(8)   If the liquidator without reasonable excuse fails to comply with subsections (1) to (4A), he is liable to a fine.

96.   Conversion to creditors' voluntary winding up

(1)   The winding up becomes a creditors' voluntary winding up as from the day on which—
(a)   the company's creditors under section 95 nominate a person to be liquidator, or
(b)   the procedure by which the company's creditors were to have made such a nomination concludes without a nomination having been made.

(2)   As from that day this Act has effect as if the directors' declaration under section 89 had not been made.

(3)   The liquidator in the creditors' voluntary winding up is to be the person nominated by the company's creditors under section 95 or, where no person has been so nominated, the existing liquidator.

(4)   In the case of the creditors nominating a person other than the existing liquidator any director, member or creditor of the company may, within 7 days after the date on which the nomination was made by the creditors, apply to the court for an order either—
(a)   directing that the existing liquidator is to be liquidator instead of or jointly with the person nominated by the creditors, or
(b)   appointing some other person to be liquidator instead of the person nominated by the creditors.

(4A)   The court shall grant an application under subsection (4) made by the holder of a qualifying floating charge in respect of the company's property (within the meaning of paragraph 14 of Schedule B1) unless the court thinks it right to refuse the application because of the particular circumstances of the case.

(5)   The "existing liquidator" is the person who is liquidator immediately before the winding up becomes a creditors' voluntary winding up.

CHAPTER IV
CREDITORS' VOLUNTARY WINDING UP

97.   Application of this Chapter

(1)   Subject as follows, this Chapter applies in relation to a creditors' voluntary winding up.

(2)   Sections 99 and 100 do not apply where, under section 96 in Chapter III, a members' voluntary winding up has become a creditors' voluntary winding up.

98.   ...

99.   Directors to lay statement of affairs before creditors

(1)   The directors of the company must, before the end of the period of 7 days beginning with the day after the day on which the company passes a resolution for voluntary winding up—
(a)   make out a statement in the prescribed form as to the affairs of the company, and
(b)   send the statement to the company's creditors.

(2)   The statement as to the affairs of the company ... shall show—
    (a)   particulars of the company's assets, debts and liabilities;
    (b)   the names and addresses of the company's creditors;
    (c)   the securities held by them respectively;
    (d)   the dates when the securities were respectively given; and
    (e)   such further or other information as may be prescribed.

(2A) The statement as to the affairs of the company shall ... —
    (a)   in the case of a winding up of a company registered in England and Wales, be verified by some or all of the directors by a statement of truth; and
    (b)   in the case of a winding up of a company registered in Scotland, contain a statutory declaration by some or all of the directors.

(3)   If the directors without reasonable excuse fail to comply with subsection (1), (2) or (2A), they are guilty of an offence and liable to a fine.

100.   Appointment of liquidator

(1)   The company may nominate a person to be liquidator at the company meeting at which the resolution for voluntary winding up is passed.

(1A) The company's creditors may in accordance with the rules nominate a person to be liquidator.

(1B) The directors of the company must in accordance with the rules seek such a nomination from the company's creditors.

(2)   The liquidator shall be the person nominated by the creditors or, where no person has been so nominated, the person (if any) nominated by the company.

(3)   In the case of different persons being nominated, any director, member or creditor of the company may, within 7 days after the date on which the nomination was made by the creditors, apply to the court for an order either—
    (a)   directing that the person nominated as liquidator by the company shall be liquidator instead of or jointly with the person nominated by the creditors, or
    (b)   appointing some other person to be liquidator instead of the person nominated by the creditors.

(4)   The court shall grant an application under subsection (3) made by the holder of a qualifying floating charge in respect of the company's property (within the meaning of paragraph 14 of Schedule B1) unless the court thinks it right to refuse the application because of the particular circumstances of the case.

Note. Subsection (4) is inserted by the Enterprise Act 2002, s. 248(3), Sch. 17, paras. 9, 14, as from a day to be appointed.

101.   Appointment of liquidation committee

(1)   The creditors may in accordance with the rules appoint a committee ("the liquidation committee") of not more than 5 persons to exercise the functions conferred on it by or under this Act.

(2)   If such a committee is appointed, the company may, either at the meeting at which the resolution for voluntary winding up is passed or at any time subsequently in general meeting, appoint such number of persons as they think fit to act as members of the committee, not exceeding 5.

(3)   However, the creditors may, if they think fit, decide that all or any of the persons so appointed by the company ought not to be members of the liquidation committee; and if the creditors so decide—
    (a)   those persons are not then, unless the court otherwise directs, qualified to act as members of the committee; and
    (b)   on any application to the court under this provision the court may, if it thinks fit, appoint other persons to act as such members in place of those persons.

(4)   In Scotland, the liquidation committee has, in addition to the powers and duties conferred and imposed on it by this Act, such of the powers and duties of commissioners on a bankrupt estate as may be conferred and imposed on liquidation committees by the rules.

Note. Subsection (4) is repealed, in relation to Scotland, by S.S.I. 2017/209, art. 3, as from a day to be appointed (save for certain purposes).

102.   ...

103.   Cesser of directors' powers

On the appointment of a liquidator, all the powers of the directors cease, except so far as the liquidation committee (or, if there is no such committee, the creditors) sanction their continuance.

104.   Vacancy in office of liquidator

If a vacancy occurs, by death, resignation or otherwise, in the office of a liquidator (other than a liquidator appointed by, or by the direction of, the court) the creditors may fill the vacancy.

104A.   Progress report to company and creditors ...

(1)   The liquidator must—
(a)   for each prescribed period produce a progress report relating to the prescribed matters; and
(b)   within such period commencing with the end of the period referred to in paragraph (a) as may be prescribed send a copy of the progress report to—
(i)   the members and creditors, other than opted-out creditors of the company; and
(ii)   such other persons as may be prescribed.

(2)   A liquidator who fails to comply with this section is liable to a fine.

105.   ...

106.   Final account prior to dissolution

(1)   As soon as the company's affairs are fully wound up the liquidator must make up an account of the winding up, showing how it has been conducted and the company's property has been disposed of.

(2)   The liquidator must, before the end of the period of 14 days beginning with the day on which the account is made up—
(a)   send a copy of the account to the company's members,
(b)   send a copy of the account to the company's creditors (other than opted-out creditors), and
(c)   give the company's creditors (other than opted-out creditors) a notice explaining the effect of section 173(2)(e) and how they may object to the liquidator's release.

(3)   The liquidator must during the relevant period send to the registrar of companies--
(a)   a copy of the account, and
(b)   a statement of whether any of the company's creditors objected to the liquidator's release.

(4)   The relevant period is the period of 7 days beginning with the day after the last day of the period prescribed by the rules as the period within which the creditors may object to the liquidator's release.

(4A), (4B)   ...

(5)   If the liquidator does not comply with subsection (2) the liquidator is liable to a fine.

(6)   If the liquidator does not comply with subsection (3) the liquidator is liable to a fine and, for continued contravention, a daily default fine.

(7), (8)   ...

CHAPTER V
PROVISIONS APPLYING TO BOTH KINDS OF VOLUNTARY WINDING UP

107.   Distribution of company's property

Subject to the provisions of this Act as to preferential payments, the company's property in a voluntary winding up shall on the winding up be applied in satisfaction of the company's liabilities pari passu and, subject to that application, shall (unless the articles otherwise provide) be distributed among the members according to their rights and interests in the company.

108. Appointment or removal of liquidator by the court

(1) If from any cause whatever there is no liquidator acting, the court may appoint a liquidator.

(2) The court may, on cause shown, remove a liquidator and appoint another.

109. Notice by liquidator of his appointment

(1) The liquidator shall, within 14 days after his appointment, publish in the Gazette and deliver to the registrar of companies for registration a notice of his appointment in the form prescribed by statutory instrument made by the Secretary of State.

(2) If the liquidator fails to comply with this section, he is liable to a fine and, for continued contravention, to a daily default fine.

110. Acceptance of shares, etc, as consideration for sale of company property

(1) This section applies, in the case of a company proposed to be, or being, wound up voluntarily, where the whole or part of the company's business or property is proposed to be transferred or sold—

    (a) to another company ("the transferee company"), whether or not the latter is a company registered under the Companies Act 2006, or

    (b) to a limited liability partnership (the "transferee limited liability partnership").

(2) With the requisite sanction, the liquidator of the company being, or proposed to be, wound up ("the transferor company") may receive, in compensation or part compensation for the transfer or sale—

    (a) in the case of the transferee company, shares, policies or other like interests in the transferee company for distribution among the members of the transferor company, or

    (b) in the case of the transferee limited liability partnership, membership in the transferee limited liability partnership for distribution among the members of the transferor company.

(3) The sanction requisite under subsection (2) is—

    (a) in the case of a members' voluntary winding up, that of a special resolution of the company, conferring either a general authority on the liquidator or an authority in respect of any particular arrangement, and

    (b) in the case of a creditors' voluntary winding up, that of either the court or the liquidation committee.

(4) Alternatively to subsection (2), the liquidator may (with that sanction) enter into any other arrangement whereby the members of the transferor company may—

    (a) in the case of the transferee company, in lieu of receiving cash, shares, policies or other like interests (or in addition thereto) participate in the profits of, or receive any other benefit from, the transferee company, or

    (b) in the case of the transferee limited liability partnership, in lieu of receiving cash or membership (or in addition thereto), participate in some other way in the profits of, or receive any other benefit from, the transferee limited liability partnership.

(5) A sale or arrangement in pursuance of this section is binding on members of the transferor company.

(6) A special resolution is not invalid for purposes of this section by reason that it is passed before or concurrently with a resolution for voluntary winding up or for appointing liquidators; but, if an order is made within a year for winding up the company by the court, the special resolution is not valid unless sanctioned by the court.

111. Dissent from arrangement under s 110

(1) This section applies in the case of a voluntary winding up where, for the purposes of section 110(2) or (4), there has been passed a special resolution of the transferor company providing the sanction requisite for the liquidator under that section.

(2) If a member of the transferor company who did not vote in favour of the special resolution expresses his dissent from it in writing, addressed to the liquidator and left at the company's registered office within 7 days after the passing of the resolution, he may require the liquidator

either to abstain from carrying the resolution into effect or to purchase his interest at a price to be determined by agreement or by arbitration under this section.

(3) If the liquidator elects to purchase the member's interest, the purchase money must be paid before the company is dissolved and be raised by the liquidator in such manner as may be determined by special resolution.

(4) For purposes of an arbitration under this section, the provisions of the Companies Clauses Consolidation Act 1845 or, in the case of a winding up in Scotland, the Companies Clauses Consolidation (Scotland) Act 1845 with respect to the settlement of disputes by arbitration are incorporated with this Act, and—

 (a) in the construction of those provisions this Act is deemed the special Act and "the company" means the transferor company, and

 (b) any appointment by the incorporated provisions directed to be made under the hand of the secretary or any two of the directors may be made in writing by the liquidator (or, if there is more than one liquidator, then any two or more of them).

112. Reference of questions to court

(1) The liquidator or any contributory or creditor may apply to the court to determine any question arising in the winding up of a company, or to exercise, as respects the enforcing of calls or any other matter, all or any of the powers which the court might exercise if the company were being wound up by the court.

(2) The court, if satisfied that the determination of the question or the required exercise of power will be just and beneficial, may accede wholly or partially to the application on such terms and conditions as it thinks fit, or may make such other order on the application as it thinks just.

(3) A copy of an order made by virtue of this section staying the proceedings in the winding up shall forthwith be forwarded by the company, or otherwise as may be prescribed, to the registrar of companies, who shall enter it in his records relating to the company.

113. Court's power to control proceedings (Scotland)

If the court, on the application of the liquidator in the winding up of a company registered in Scotland, so directs, no action or proceeding shall be proceeded with or commenced against the company except by leave of the court and subject to such terms as the court may impose.

114. No liquidator appointed or nominated by company

(1) This section applies where, in the case of a voluntary winding up, no liquidator has been appointed or nominated by the company.

(2) The powers of the directors shall not be exercised, except with the sanction of the court or (in the case of a creditors' voluntary winding up) so far as may be necessary to secure compliance with sections … 99 (statement of affairs) and 100(1B) (nomination of liquidator by creditors), during the period before the appointment or nomination of a liquidator of the company.

(3) Subsection (2) does not apply in relation to the powers of the directors—

 (a) to dispose of perishable goods and other goods the value of which is likely to diminish if they are not immediately disposed of, and

 (b) to do all such other things as may be necessary for the protection of the company's assets.

(4) If the directors of the company without reasonable excuse fail to comply with this section, they are liable to a fine.

115. Expenses of voluntary winding up

After the payment of any liabilities to which section 174A applies, all expenses properly incurred in the winding up, including the remuneration of the liquidator, are payable out of the company's assets in priority to all other claims.

116. Saving for certain rights

The voluntary winding up of a company does not bar the right of any creditor or contributory to have it wound up by the court; but in the case of an application by a contributory the court must be satisfied that the rights of the contributories will be prejudiced by a voluntary winding up.

CHAPTER VI
WINDING UP BY THE COURT

Jurisdiction (England and Wales)

117. High Court and county court jurisdiction

(1) The High Court has jurisdiction to wind up any company registered in England and Wales.

(2) Where in the case of a company registered in England and Wales the amount of its share capital paid up or credited as paid up does not exceed £120,000, then (subject to this section) the county court ... has concurrent jurisdiction with the High Court to wind up the company.

(2A) Despite subsection (2), proceedings for the exercise of the jurisdiction to wind up a company registered in England and Wales may be commenced only in the High Court if the place which has longest been the company's registered office during the 6 months immediately preceding the presentation of the petition for winding up is in the district that is the London insolvency district for the purposes of the second Group of Parts of the Act.

(3) The money sum for the time being specified in subsection (2) is subject to increase or reduction by order under section 416 in Part XV.

(4) ...

(5) Every court in England and Wales having winding-up jurisdiction has for the purposes of that jurisdiction all the powers of the High Court; and every prescribed officer of the court shall perform any duties which an officer of the High Court may discharge by order of a judge of that court or otherwise in relation to winding up.

(6) ...

(7) ...

(8) The Lord Chief Justice may nominate a judicial office holder (as defined in section 109(4) of the Constitutional Reform Act 2005) to exercise his functions under this section.

118. Proceedings taken in wrong court

(1) Nothing in section 117 invalidates a proceeding by reason of its being taken in the wrong court.

(2) The winding up of a company by the court in England and Wales, or any proceedings in the winding up, may be retained in the court in which the proceedings were commenced, although it may not be the court in which they ought to have been commenced.

119. Proceedings in county court; case stated for High Court

(1) If any question arises in any winding-up proceedings in a county court which all the parties to the proceedings, or which one of them and the judge of the court, desire to have determined in the first instance in the High Court, the judge shall state the facts in the form of a special case for the opinion of the High Court.

(2) Thereupon the special case and the proceedings (or such of them as may be required) shall be transmitted to the High Court for the purposes of the determination.

Jurisdiction (Scotland)

120. Court of Session and sheriff court jurisdiction

(1) The Court of Session has jurisdiction to wind up any company registered in Scotland.

(2) When the Court of Session is in vacation, the jurisdiction conferred on that court by this section may (subject to the provisions of this Part) be exercised by the judge acting as vacation judge ...

(3)   Where the amount of a company's share capital paid up or credited as paid up does not exceed £120,000, the sheriff court of the sheriffdom in which the company's registered office is situated has concurrent jurisdiction with the Court of Session to wind up the company; but—

(a)   the Court of Session may, if it thinks expedient having regard to the amount of the company's assets to do so—

(i)   remit to sheriff court any petition presented to the Court of Session for winding up such a company, or

(ii)   require such a petition presented to a sheriff court to be remitted to the Court of Session; and

(b)   the Court of Session may require any such petition as above-mentioned presented to one sheriff court to be remitted to another sheriff court; and

(c)   in a winding up in the sheriff court the sheriff may submit a stated case for the opinion of the Court of Session on any question of law arising in that winding up.

(4)   For purposes of this section, the expression "registered office" means the place which has longest been the company's registered office during the 6 months immediately preceding the presentation of the petition for winding up.

(5)   The money sum for the time being specified in subsection (3) is subject to increase or reduction by order under section 416 in Part XV.

(6)   ...

121.   Power to remit winding up to Lord Ordinary

(1)   The Court of Session may, by Act of Sederunt, make provision for the taking of proceedings in a winding up before one of the Lords Ordinary; and, where provision is so made, the Lord Ordinary has, for the purposes of the winding up, all the powers and jurisdiction of the court.

(2)   However, the Lord Ordinary may report to the Inner House any matter which may arise in the course of a winding up.

Grounds and effect of winding-up petition

122.   Circumstances in which company may be wound up by the court

(1)   A company may be wound up by the court if—

(a)   the company has by special resolution resolved that the company be wound up by the court,

(b)   being a public company which was registered as such on its original incorporation, the company has not been issued with a trading certificate under section 761 of the Companies Act 2006 (requirement as to minimum share capital) and more than a year has expired since it was so registered,

(c)   it is an old public company, within the meaning of Schedule 3 to the Companies Act 2006 (Consequential Amendments, Transitional Provisions and Savings) Order 2009,

(d)   the company does not commence its business within a year from its incorporation or suspends its business for a whole year,

(e)   ...

(f)   the company is unable to pay its debts,

(fa)   ...

(g)   the court is of the opinion that it is just and equitable that the company should be wound up.

(2)   In Scotland, a company which the Court of Session has jurisdiction to wind up may be wound up by the Court if there is subsisting a floating charge over property comprised in the company's property and undertaking, and the court is satisfied that the security of the creditor entitled to the benefit of the floating charge is in jeopardy.

For this purpose a creditor's security is deemed to be in jeopardy if the Court is satisfied that events have occurred or are about to occur which render it unreasonable in the creditor's interests that the company should retain power to dispose of the property which is subject to the floating charge.

123. **Definition of inability to pay debts**

(1) A company is deemed unable to pay its debts—

    (a) if a creditor (by assignment or otherwise) to whom the company is indebted in a sum exceeding £750 then due has served on the company, by leaving it at the company's registered office, a written demand (in the prescribed form) requiring the company to pay the sum so due and the company has for 3 weeks thereafter neglected to pay the sum or to secure or compound for it to the reasonable satisfaction of the creditor, or

    (b) if, in England and Wales, execution or other process issued on a judgment, decree or order of any court in favour of a creditor of the company is returned unsatisfied in whole or in part, or

    (c) if, in Scotland, the induciae of a charge for payment on an extract decree, or an extract registered bond, or an extract registered protest, have expired without payment being made, or

    (d) if, in Northern Ireland, a certificate of unenforceability has been granted in respect of a judgment against the company, or

    (e) if it is proved to the satisfaction of the court that the company is unable to pay its debts as they fall due.

(2) A company is also deemed unable to pay its debts if it is proved to the satisfaction of the court that the value of the company's assets is less than the amount of its liabilities, taking into account its contingent and prospective liabilities.

(3) The money sum for the time being specified in subsection (1)(a) is subject to increase or reduction by order under section 416 in Part XV.

124. **Application for winding up**

(1) Subject to the provisions of this section, an application to the court for the winding up of a company shall be by petition presented either by the company, or the directors, or by any creditor or creditors (including any contingent or prospective creditor or creditors), contributory or contributories, ... or by the designated officer for a magistrates' court in the exercise of the power conferred by section 87A of the Magistrates' Courts Act 1980 (enforcement of fines imposed on companies), or by all or any of those parties, together or separately.

(2) Except as mentioned below, a contributory is not entitled to present a winding-up petition unless either—

    (a) the number of members is reduced below 2, or

    (b) the shares in respect of which he is a contributory, or some of them, either were originally allotted to him, or have been held by him, and registered in his name, for at least 6 months during the 18 months before the commencement of the winding up, or have devolved on him through the death of a former holder.

(3) A person who is liable under section 76 to contribute to a company's assets in the event of its being wound up may petition on either of the grounds set out in section 122(1)(f) and (g), and subsection (2) above does not then apply; but unless the person is a contributory otherwise than under section 76, he may not in his character as contributory petition on any other ground.

    ...

(3A) ...

(4) A winding-up petition may be presented by the Secretary of State—

    (a) if the ground of the petition is that in section 122(1)(b) or (c), or

    (b) in a case falling within section 124A or 124B below.

(4AA) A winding up petition may be presented by the Financial Conduct Authority in a case falling within section 124C(1) or (2).

(4A) A winding-up petition may be presented by the Regulator of Community Interest Companies in a case falling within section 50 of the Companies (Audit, Investigations and Community Enterprise) Act 2004.

(5) Where a company is being wound up voluntarily in England and Wales, a winding-up petition may be presented by the official receiver attached to the court as well as by any other person

authorised in that behalf under the other provisions of this section; but the court shall not make a winding-up order on the petition unless it is satisfied that the voluntary winding up cannot be continued with due regard to the interests of the creditors or contributories.

124A.   Petition for winding up on grounds of public interest

(1)   Where it appears to the Secretary of State from—

    (a)   any report made or information obtained under Part XIV (except section 448A) of the Companies Act 1985 (company investigations, &c.),

    (b)   any report made by inspectors under—

        (i)   section 167, 168, 169 or 284 of the Financial Services and Markets Act 2000, or

        (ii)   where the company is an open-ended investment company (within the meaning of that Act), regulations made as a result of section 262(2)(k) of that Act,

    (bb)   any information or documents obtained under section 165, 171, 172, 173 or 175 of that Act,

    (c)   any information obtained under section 2 of the Criminal Justice Act 1987 or section 52 of the Criminal Justice (Scotland) Act 1987 (fraud investigations), or

    (d)   any information obtained under section 83 of the Companies Act 1989 (powers exercisable for purpose of assisting overseas regulatory authorities),

that it is expedient in the public interest that a company should be wound up, he may present a petition for it to be wound up if the court thinks it just and equitable for it to be so.

(2)   This section does not apply if the company is already being wound up by the court.

124B.   ...

124C.   ...

125.   Powers of court on hearing of petition

(1)   On hearing a winding-up petition the court may dismiss it, or adjourn the hearing conditionally or unconditionally, or make an interim order, or any other order that it thinks fit; but the court shall not refuse to make a winding-up order on the ground only that the company's assets have been mortgaged to an amount equal to or in excess of those assets, or that the company has no assets.

(2)   If the petition is presented by members of the company as contributories on the ground that it is just and equitable that the company should be wound up, the court, if it is of opinion—

    (a)   that the petitioners are entitled to relief either by winding up the company or by some other means, and

    (b)   that in the absence of any other remedy it would be just and equitable that the company should be wound up,

shall make a winding-up order; but this does not apply if the court is also of the opinion both that some other remedy is available to the petitioners and that they are acting unreasonably in seeking to have the company wound up instead of pursuing that other remedy.

126.   Power to stay or restrain proceedings against company

(1)   At any time after the presentation of a winding-up petition, and before a winding-up order has been made, the company, or any creditor or contributory, may—

    (a)   where any action or proceeding against the company is pending in the High Court or Court of Appeal in England and Wales or Northern Ireland, apply to the court in which the action or proceeding is pending for a stay of proceedings therein, and

    (b)   where any other action or proceeding is pending against the company, apply to the court having jurisdiction to wind up the company to restrain further proceedings in the action or proceeding;

and the court to which application is so made may (as the case may be) stay, sist or restrain the proceedings accordingly on such terms as it thinks fit.

(2)   In the case of a company registered but not formed under the Companies Act 2006, where the application to stay, sist or restrain is by a creditor, this section extends to actions and proceedings against any contributory of the company.

(3)   Subsection (1) applies in relation to any action being taken in respect of the company under Part 1 of Schedule 8 to the Finance (No 2) Act 2015 (enforcement by deduction from accounts) as it applies in relation to any action or proceeding mentioned in paragraph (b) of that subsection.

127. **Avoidance of property dispositions, etc**

(1)   In a winding up by the court, any disposition of the company's property, and any transfer of shares, or alteration in the status of the company's members, made after the commencement of the winding up is, unless the court otherwise orders, void.

(2)   This section has no effect in respect of anything done by an administrator of a company while a winding-up petition is suspended under paragraph 40 of Schedule B1.

(3)   This section has no effect in respect of anything done during a moratorium under Part A1, or during a period mentioned in section 5(4)(a) following the end of a moratorium, where the winding-up order was made on a petition presented before the moratorium begins, unless the petition was presented under section 367 of the Financial Services and Markets Act 2000 on the ground mentioned in section 367(3)(b) of that Act.

128. **Avoidance of attachments, etc**

(1)   Where a company registered in England and Wales is being wound up by the court, any attachment, sequestration, distress or execution put in force against the estate or effects of the company after the commencement of the winding up is void.

(2)   This section, so far as relates to any estate or effects of the company situated in England and Wales, applies in the case of a company registered in Scotland as it applies in the case of a company registered in England and Wales.

(3)   In subsection (1) "attachment" includes a hold notice or a deduction notice under Part 1 of Schedule 8 to the Finance (No 2) Act 2015 (enforcement by deduction from accounts) and, if subsection (1) has effect in relation to a deduction notice, it also has effect in relation to the hold notice to which the deduction notice relates (whenever the hold notice was given).

Commencement of winding up

129. **Commencement of winding up by the court**

(1)   If, before the presentation of a petition for the winding up of a company by the court, a resolution has been passed by the company for voluntary winding up, the winding up of the company is deemed to have commenced at the time of the passing of the resolution; and unless the court, on proof of fraud or mistake, directs otherwise, all proceedings taken in the voluntary winding up are deemed to have been validly taken.

(1A)   Where the court makes a winding-up order by virtue of paragraph 13(1)(e) of Schedule B1, the winding up is deemed to commence on the making of the order.

(2)   In any other case, the winding up of a company by the court is deemed to commence at the time of the presentation of the petition for winding up.

130. **Consequences of winding-up order**

(1)   On the making of a winding-up order, a copy of the order must forthwith be forwarded by the company (or otherwise as may be prescribed) to the registrar of companies, who shall enter it in his records relating to the company.

(2)   When a winding-up order has been made or a provisional liquidator has been appointed, no action or proceeding shall be proceeded with or commenced against the company or its property, except by leave of the court and subject to such terms as the court may impose.

(3)   When an order has been made for winding up a company registered but not formed under the Companies Act 2006, no action or proceeding shall be commenced or proceeded with against the company or its property or any contributory of the company, in respect of any debt of the company, except by leave of the court, and subject to such terms as the court may impose.

(3A)   In subsections (2) and (3), the reference to an action or proceeding includes action in respect of the company under Part 1 of Schedule 8 to the Finance (No 2) Act 2015 (enforcement by deduction from accounts).

(4)   An order for winding up a company operates in favour of all the creditors and of all contributories of the company as if made on the joint petition of a creditor and of a contributory.

Investigation procedures

131.   Company's statement of affairs

(1)   Where the court has made a winding-up order or appointed a provisional liquidator, the official receiver may require some or all of the persons mentioned in subsection (3) below to make out and submit to him a statement in the prescribed form as to the affairs of the company.

(2)   The statement ... shall show—
    (a)   particulars of the company's assets, debts and liabilities;
    (b)   the names and addresses of the company's creditors;
    (c)   the securities held by them respectively;
    (d)   the dates when the securities were respectively given; and
    (e)   such further or other information as may be prescribed or as the official receiver may require.

(2A)   The statement shall ...—
    (a)   in the case of an appointment of a provisional liquidator or a winding up by the court in England and Wales, be verified by the persons required to submit it by a statement of truth; and
    (b)   in the case of an appointment of a provisional liquidator or a winding up by the court in Scotland, contain a statutory declaration by the persons required to submit it.

(3)   The persons referred to in subsection (1) are—
    (a)   those who are or have been officers of the company;
    (b)   those who have taken part in the formation of the company at any time within one year before the relevant date;
    (c)   those who are in the company's employment, or have been in its employment within that year, and are in the official receiver's opinion capable of giving the information required;
    (d)   those who are or have been within that year officers of, or in the employment of, a company which is, or within that year was, an officer of the company.

(4)   Where any persons are required under this section to submit a statement of affairs to the official receiver, they shall do so (subject to the next subsection) before the end of the period of 21 days beginning with the day after that on which the prescribed notice of the requirement is given to them by the official receiver.

(5)   The official receiver, if he thinks fit, may—
    (a)   at any time release a person from an obligation imposed on him under subsection (1) or (2) above; or
    (b)   either when giving the notice mentioned in subsection (4) or subsequently, extend the period so mentioned;
    and where the official receiver has refused to exercise a power conferred by this subsection, the court, if it thinks fit, may exercise it.

(6)   In this section—
    "employment" includes employment under a contract for services; and
    "the relevant date" means—
    (a)   in a case where a provisional liquidator is appointed, the date of his appointment; and
    (b)   in a case where no such appointment is made, the date of the winding-up order.

(7)   If a person without reasonable excuse fails to comply with any obligation imposed under this section, he is liable to a fine and, for continued contravention, to a daily default fine.

(8)   In the application of this section to Scotland references to the official receiver are to the liquidator or, in a case where a provisional liquidator is appointed, the provisional liquidator.

132. Investigation by official receiver

(1) Where a winding-up order is made by the court in England and Wales, it is the duty of the official receiver to investigate—

(a) if the company has failed, the causes of the failure; and

(b) generally, the promotion, formation, business, dealings and affairs of the company,

and to make such report (if any) to the court as he thinks fit.

(2) The report is, in any proceedings, prima facie evidence of the facts stated in it.

133. Public examination of officers

(1) Where a company is being wound up by the court, the official receiver or, in Scotland, the liquidator may at any time before the dissolution of the company apply to the court for the public examination of any person who—

(a) is or has been an officer of the company; or

(b) has acted as liquidator or administrator of the company or as receiver or manager or, in Scotland, receiver of its property; or

(c) not being a person falling within paragraph (a) or (b), is or has been concerned, or has taken part, in the promotion, formation or management of the company.

(2) Unless the court otherwise orders, the official receiver or, in Scotland, the liquidator shall make an application under subsection (1) if he is requested in accordance with the rules to do so by—

(a) one-half, in value, of the company's creditors; or

(b) three-quarters, in value, of the company's contributories.

(3) On an application under subsection (1), the court shall direct that a public examination of the person to whom the application relates shall be held on a day appointed by the court; and that person shall attend on that day and be publicly examined as to the promotion, formation or management of the company or as to the conduct of its business and affairs, or his conduct or dealings in relation to the company.

(4) The following may take part in the public examination of a person under this section and may question that person concerning the matters mentioned in subsection (3), namely—

(a) the official receiver;

(b) the liquidator of the company;

(c) any person who has been appointed as special manager of the company's property or business;

(d) any creditor of the company who has tendered a proof or, in Scotland, submitted a claim in the winding up;

(e) any contributory of the company.

134. Enforcement of s 133

(1) If a person without reasonable excuse fails at any time to attend his public examination under section 133, he is guilty of a contempt of court and liable to be punished accordingly.

(2) In a case where a person without reasonable excuse fails at any time to attend his examination under section 133 or there are reasonable grounds for believing that a person has absconded, or is about to abscond, with a view to avoiding or delaying his examination under that section, the court may cause a warrant to be issued to a constable or prescribed officer of the court—

(a) for the arrest of that person; and

(b) for the seizure of any books, papers, records, money or goods in that person's possession.

(3) In such a case the court may authorise the person arrested under the warrant to be kept in custody, and anything seized under such a warrant to be held, in accordance with the rules, until such time as the court may order.

Appointment of liquidator

135. Appointment and powers of provisional liquidator

(1) Subject to the provisions of this section, the court may, at any time after the presentation of a winding-up petition, appoint a liquidator provisionally.

(2)   In England and Wales, the appointment of a provisional liquidator may be made at any time before the making of a winding-up order; and either the official receiver or any other fit person may be appointed.

(3)   In Scotland, such an appointment may be made at any time before the first appointment of liquidators.

(4)   The provisional liquidator shall carry out such functions as the court may confer on him.

(5)   When a liquidator is provisionally appointed by the court, his powers may be limited by the order appointing him.

136.   Functions of official receiver in relation to office of liquidator

(1)   The following provisions of this section have effect, subject to section 140 below, on a winding-up order being made by the court in England and Wales.

(2)   The official receiver, by virtue of his office, becomes the liquidator of the company and continues in office until another person becomes liquidator under the provisions of this Part.

(3)   The official receiver is, by virtue of his office, the liquidator during any vacancy.

(4)   At any time when he is the liquidator of the company, the official receiver may in accordance with the rules seek nominations from the company's creditors and contributories for the purpose of choosing a person to be liquidator of the company in place of the official receiver.

(5)   It is the duty of the official receiver—

     (a)   as soon as practicable in the period of 12 weeks beginning with the day on which the winding-up order was made, to decide whether to exercise his power under subsection (4) …, and

     (b)   if in pursuance of paragraph (a) he decides not to exercise that power, to give notice of his decision, before the end of that period, to the court and to the company's creditors and contributories, and

     (c)   (whether or not he has decided to exercise that power) to exercise his power … under subsection (4) if he is at any time requested, in accordance with the rules, to do so by one-quarter, in value, of the company's creditors;

     and accordingly, where the duty imposed by paragraph (c) arises before the official receiver has performed a duty imposed by paragraph (a) or (b), he is not required to perform the latter duty.

(6)   A notice given under subsection (5)(b) to the company's creditors shall contain an explanation of the creditors' power under subsection (5)(c) to require the official receiver to seek nominations from the company's creditors and contributories.

137.   Appointment by Secretary of State

(1)   In a winding up by the court in England and Wales the official receiver may, at any time when he is the liquidator of the company, apply to the Secretary of State for the appointment of a person as liquidator in his place.

(2)   If nominations are sought from the company's creditors and contributories in pursuance of a decision under section 136(5)(a), but no person is chosen to be liquidator as a result …, it is the duty of the official receiver to decide whether to refer the need for an appointment to the Secretary of State.

(3)   On an application under subsection (1), or a reference made in pursuance of a decision under subsection (2), the Secretary of State shall either make an appointment or decline to make one.

(4)   Where a liquidator has been appointed by the Secretary of State under subsection (3), the liquidator shall give notice of his appointment to the company's creditors or, if the court so allows, shall advertise his appointment in accordance with the directions of the court.

(5)   In that notice or advertisement the liquidator must explain the procedure for establishing a liquidation committee under section 141.

138.   Appointment of liquidator in Scotland

(1)   Where a winding-up order is made by the court in Scotland, a liquidator shall be appointed by the court at the time when the order is made.

(2)   The liquidator so appointed (here referred to as "the interim liquidator") continues in office until another person becomes liquidator in his place under this section or the next.

(3)   The interim liquidator shall (subject to the next subsection) as soon as practicable in the period of 28 days beginning with the day on which the winding-up order was made or such longer period as the court may allow, in accordance with the rules seek nominations from the company's creditors and contributories for the purpose of choosing a person (who may be the person who is the interim liquidator) to be liquidator of the company in place of the interim liquidator.

(4)   If it appears to the interim liquidator, in any case where a company is being wound up on grounds including its inability to pay its debts, that it would be inappropriate to seek a nomination from the company's contributories under subsection (3), he may seek a nomination only from the company's creditors for the purpose mentioned in that subsection.

(5)   If a nomination is sought from the company's creditors, or nominations are sought from the company's creditors and contributories, in pursuance of this section but no person is appointed or nominated as a result, the interim liquidator shall make a report to the court which shall appoint either the interim liquidator or some other person to be liquidator of the company.

(6)   A person who becomes liquidator of the company in place of the interim liquidator shall, unless he is appointed by the court, forthwith notify the court of that fact.

139.   Choice of liquidator by creditors and contributories

(1)   This section applies where a company is being wound up by the court and nominations are sought from the company's creditors and contributories for the purpose of choosing a person to be liquidator of the company.

(2)   The creditors and the contributories may in accordance with the rules nominate a person to be liquidator.

(3)   The liquidator shall be the person nominated by the creditors or, where no person has been so nominated, the person (if any) nominated by the contributories.

(4)   In the case of different persons being nominated, any contributory or creditor may, within 7 days after the date on which the nomination was made by the creditors, apply to the court for an order either—

(a)   appointing the person nominated as liquidator by the contributories to be a liquidator instead of, or jointly with, the person nominated by the creditors; or

(b)   appointing some other person to be liquidator instead of the person nominated by the creditors.

140.   Appointment by the court following administration or voluntary arrangement

(1)   Where a winding-up order is made immediately upon the appointment of an administrator ceasing to have effect, the court may appoint as liquidator of the company the person whose appointment as administrator has ceased to have effect.

(2)   Where a winding-up order is made at a time when there is a supervisor of a voluntary arrangement approved in relation to the company under Part I, the court may appoint as liquidator of the company the person who is the supervisor at the time when the winding-up order is made.

(3)   Where the court makes an appointment under this section, the official receiver does not become the liquidator as otherwise provided by section 136(2), and section 136(5)(a) and (b) does not apply.

Liquidation committees

141.   Liquidation committee (England and Wales)

(1)   This section applies where a winding up order has been made by the court in England and Wales.

(2)   If both the company's creditors and the company's contributories decide that a liquidation committee should be established, a liquidation committee is to be established in accordance with the rules.

(3)   If only the company's creditors, or only the company's contributories, decide that a liquidation committee should be established, a liquidation committee is to be established in accordance with the rules unless the court orders otherwise.

(3A)   A "liquidation committee" is a committee having such functions as are conferred on it by or under this Act.

(3B)   The liquidator must seek a decision from the company's creditors and contributories as to whether a liquidation committee should be established if requested, in accordance with the rules, to do so by one-tenth in value of the company's creditors.

(3C)   Subsection (3B) does not apply where the liquidator is the official receiver.

(4)   The liquidation committee is not to be able or required to carry out its functions at any time when the official receiver is liquidator; but at any such time its functions are vested in the Secretary of State except to the extent that the rules otherwise provide.

(5)   Where there is for the time being no liquidation committee, and the liquidator is a person other than the official receiver, the functions of such a committee are vested in the Secretary of State except to the extent that the rules otherwise provide.

142.   Liquidation committee (Scotland)

(1)   This section applies where a winding up order has been made by the court in Scotland.

(2)   If both the company's creditors and the company's contributories decide that a liquidation committee should be established, a liquidation committee is to be established in accordance with the rules.

(3)   If only the company's creditors, or only the company's contributories, decide that a liquidation committee should be established, a liquidation committee is to be established in accordance with the rules unless the court orders otherwise.

(4)   A liquidator appointed by the court other than under section 139(4)(a) must seek a decision from the company's creditors and contributories as to whether a liquidation committee should be established if requested, in accordance with the rules, to do so by one-tenth in value of the company's creditors.

(5)   Where in the case of any winding up there is for the time being no liquidation committee, the functions of such a committee are vested in the court except to the extent that the rules otherwise provide.

(6)   A "liquidation committee" is a committee having the powers and duties conferred and imposed on it by this Act, and such of the powers and duties of commissioners in a sequestration as may be conferred and imposed on such committees by the rules.

Note. This section is amended, in relation to Scotland, by S.S.I. 2017/209, art. 4, as from a day to be appointed (save for certain purposes).

The liquidator's functions

143.   General functions in winding up by the court

(1)   The functions of the liquidator of a company which is being wound up by the court are to secure that the assets of the company are got in, realised and distributed to the company's creditors and, if there is a surplus, to the persons entitled to it.

(2)   It is the duty of the liquidator of a company which is being wound up by the court in England and Wales, if he is not the official receiver—

(a)   to furnish the official receiver with such information,

(b)   to produce to the official receiver, and permit inspection by the official receiver of, such books, papers and other records, and

(c)   to give the official receiver such other assistance,

as the official receiver may reasonably require for the purposes of carrying out his functions in relation to the winding up.

144. Custody of company's property

(1) When a winding-up order has been made, or where a provisional liquidator has been appointed, the liquidator or the provisional liquidator (as the case may be) shall take into his custody or under his control all the property and things in action to which the company is or appears to be entitled.

(2) In a winding up by the court in Scotland, if and so long as there is no liquidator, all the property of the company is deemed to be in the custody of the court.

145. Vesting of company property in liquidator

(1) When a company is being wound up by the court, the court may on the application of the liquidator by order direct that all or any part of the property of whatsoever description belonging to the company or held by trustees on its behalf shall vest in the liquidator by his official name; and thereupon the property to which the order relates vests accordingly.

(2) The liquidator may, after giving such indemnity (if any) as the court may direct, bring or defend in his official name any action or other legal proceeding which relates to that property or which it is necessary to bring or defend for the purpose of effectually winding up the company and recovering its property.

146. Final account

(1) This section applies where a company is being wound up by the court and the liquidator is not the official receiver.

(2) If it appears to the liquidator that the winding up of the company is for practical purposes complete the liquidator must make up an account of the winding up, showing how it has been conducted and the company's property has been disposed of.

(3) The liquidator must—
    (a) send a copy of the account to the company's creditors (other than opted-out creditors), and
    (b) give the company's creditors (other than opted-out creditors) a notice explaining the effect of section 174(4)(d) and how they may object to the liquidator's release.

(4) The liquidator must during the relevant period send to the court and the registrar of companies—
    (a) a copy of the account, and
    (b) a statement of whether any of the company's creditors objected to the liquidator's release.

(5) The relevant period is the period of 7 days beginning with the day after the last day of the period prescribed by the rules as the period within which the creditors may object to the liquidator's release.

(6), (7) ...

146A. ...

General powers of court

147. Power to stay or sist winding up

(1) The court may at any time after an order for winding up, on the application either of the liquidator or the official receiver or any creditor or contributory, and on proof to the satisfaction of the court that all proceedings in the winding up ought to be stayed or sisted, make an order staying or sisting the proceedings, either altogether or for a limited time, on such terms and conditions as the court thinks fit.

(2) The court may, before making an order, require the official receiver to furnish to it a report with respect to any facts or matters which are in his opinion relevant to the application.

(3) A copy of every order made under this section shall forthwith be forwarded by the company, or otherwise as may be prescribed, to the registrar of companies, who shall enter it in his records relating to the company.

148.   Settlement of list of contributories and application of assets

(1)   As soon as may be after making a winding-up order, the court shall settle a list of contributories, with power to rectify the register of members in all cases where rectification is required ..., and shall cause the company's assets to be collected, and applied in discharge of its liabilities.

(2)   If it appears to the court that it will not be necessary to make calls on or adjust the rights of contributories, the court may dispense with the settlement of a list of contributories.

(3)   In settling the list, the court shall distinguish between persons who are contributories in their own right and persons who are contributories as being representatives of or liable for the debts of others.

149.   Debts due from contributory to company

(1)   The court may, at any time after making a winding-up order, make an order on any contributory for the time being on the list of contributories to pay, in manner directed by the order, any money due from him (or from the estate of the person who he represents) to the company, exclusive of any money payable by him or the estate by virtue of any call ...

(2)   The court in making such an order may—

(a)   in the case of an unlimited company, allow to the contributory by way of set-off any money due to him or the estate which he represents from the company on any independent dealing or contract with the company, but not any money due to him as a member of the company in respect of any dividend or profit, and

(b)   in the case of a limited company, make to any director or manager whose liability is unlimited or to his estate the like allowance.

(3)   In the case of any company, whether limited or unlimited, when all the creditors are paid in full (together with interest at the official rate), any money due on any account whatever to a contributory from the company may be allowed to him by way of set-off against any subsequent call.

150.   Power to make calls

(1)   The court may, at any time after making a winding-up order, and either before or after it has ascertained the sufficiency of the company's assets, make calls on all or any of the contributories for the time being settled on the list of the contributories to the extent of their liability, for payment of any money which the court considers necessary to satisfy the company's debts and liabilities, and the expenses of winding up, and for the adjustment of the rights of the contributories among themselves, and make an order for payment of any calls so made.

(2)   In making a call the court may take into consideration the probability that some of the contributories may partly or wholly fail to pay it.

151.   ...

152.   Order on contributory to be conclusive evidence

(1)   An order made by the court on a contributory is conclusive evidence that the money (if any) thereby appearing to be due or ordered to be paid is due, but subject to any right of appeal.

(2)   All other pertinent matters stated in the order are to be taken as truly stated as against all persons and in all proceedings except proceedings in Scotland against the heritable estate of a deceased contributory; and in that case the order is only prima facie evidence for the purpose of charging his heritable estate, unless his heirs or legatees of heritage were on the list of contributories at the time of the order being made.

153.   Power to exclude creditors not proving in time

The court may fix a time or times within which creditors are to prove their debts or claims or to be excluded from the benefit of any distribution made before those debts are proved.

154.   Adjustment of rights of contributories

The court shall adjust the rights of the contributories among themselves and distribute any surplus among the persons entitled to it.

155. Inspection of books by creditors, etc

(1) The court may, at any time after making a winding-up order, make such order for inspection of the company's books and papers by creditors and contributories as the court thinks just; and any books and papers in the company's possession may be inspected by creditors and contributories accordingly, but not further or otherwise.

(2) Nothing in this section excludes or restricts any statutory rights of a government department or person acting under the authority of a government department.

(3) For the purposes of subsection (2) above, references to a government department shall be construed as including references to any part of the Scottish Administration.

156. Payment of expenses of winding up

The court may, in the event of the assets being insufficient to satisfy the liabilities, make an order as to the payment out of the assets of the expenses incurred in the winding up in such order of priority as the court thinks just.

157. Attendance at company meetings (Scotland)

In the winding up by the court of a company registered in Scotland, the court has power to require the attendance of any officer of the company at any meeting of creditors or of contributories, or of a liquidation committee, for the purpose of giving information as to the trade, dealings, affairs or property of the company.

158. Power to arrest absconding contributory

The court, at any time either before or after making a winding-up order, on proof of probable cause for believing that a contributory is about to quit the United Kingdom or otherwise to abscond or to remove or conceal any of his property for the purpose of evading payment of calls, may cause the contributory to be arrested and his books and papers and movable personal property to be seized and him and them to be kept safely until such time as the court may order.

159. Powers of court to be cumulative

Powers conferred on the court by this Act are in addition to, and not in restriction of, any existing powers of instituting proceedings against a contributory or debtor of the company, or the estate of any contributory or debtor, for the recovery of any call or other sums.

160. Delegation of powers to liquidator (England and Wales)

(1) Provision may be made by rules for enabling or requiring all or any of the powers and duties conferred and imposed on the court in England and Wales ... in respect of the following matters—

(a) the seeking of decisions on any matter from creditors and contributories,

(b) the settling of lists of contributories and the rectifying of the register of members where required, and the collection and application of the assets,

(c) the payment, delivery, conveyance, surrender or transfer of money, property, books or papers to the liquidator,

(d) the making of calls,

(e) the fixing of a time within which debts and claims must be proved,

to be exercised or performed by the liquidator as an officer of the court, and subject to the court's control.

(2) But the liquidator shall not, without the special leave of the court, rectify the register of members, and shall not make any call without either that special leave or the sanction of the liquidation committee.

Enforcement of, and appeal from, orders

161. Orders for calls on contributories (Scotland)

(1) In Scotland, where an order, interlocutor or decree has been made for winding up a company by the court, it is competent to the court, on production by the liquidators of a list certified by them

of the names of the contributories liable in payment of any calls, and of the amount due by each contributory, and of the date when that amount became due, to pronounce forthwith a decree against those contributories for payment of the sums so certified to be due, with interest from that date until payment (at 5 per cent. per annum) in the same way and to the same effect as if they had severally consented to registration for execution, on a charge of 6 days, of a legal obligation to pay those calls and interest.

(2) The decree may be extracted immediately, and no suspension of it is competent, except on caution or consignation, unless with special leave of the court.

162. Appeals from orders in Scotland

(1) Subject to the provisions of this section and to rules of court, an appeal from any order or decision made or given in the winding up of a company by the court in Scotland under this Act lies in the same manner and subject to the same conditions as an appeal from an order or decision of the court in cases within its ordinary jurisdiction.

(2) In regard to orders or judgments pronounced by the judge acting as vacation judge ... —

    (a) none of the orders specified in Part I of Schedule 3 to this Act are subject to review, reduction, suspension or stay of execution, and

    (b) every other order or judgment (except as mentioned below) may be submitted to review by the Inner House by reclaiming motion enrolled within 14 days from the date of the order or judgment.

(3) However, an order being one of those specified in Part II of that Schedule shall, from the date of the order and notwithstanding that it has been submitted to review as above, be carried out and receive effect until the Inner House have disposed of the matter.

(4) In regard to orders or judgments pronounced in Scotland by a Lord Ordinary before whom proceedings in a winding up are being taken, any such order or judgment may be submitted to review by the Inner House by reclaiming motion enrolled within 14 days from its date; but should it not be so submitted to review during session, the provisions of this section in regard to orders or judgments pronounced by the judge acting as vacation judge apply.

(5) Nothing in this section affects provisions of the Companies Acts or this Act in reference to decrees in Scotland for payment of calls in the winding up of companies, whether voluntary or by the court.

CHAPTER VII
LIQUIDATORS

Preliminary

163. Style and title of liquidators

The liquidator of a company shall be described—

    (a) where a person other than the official receiver is liquidator, by the style of "the liquidator" of the particular company, or

    (b) where the official receiver is liquidator, by the style of "the official receiver and liquidator" of the particular company;

and in neither case shall he be described by an individual name.

164. Corrupt inducement affecting appointment

A person who gives, or agrees or offers to give, to any member or creditor of a company any valuable consideration with a view to securing his own appointment or nomination, or to securing or preventing the appointment or nomination of some person other than himself, as the company's liquidator is liable to a fine.

Liquidator's powers and duties

165.   Voluntary winding up

(1)   This section has effect where a company is being wound up voluntarily, but subject to section 166 below in the case of a creditors' voluntary winding up.

(2)   The liquidator may exercise any of the powers specified in Parts 1 to 3 of Schedule 4.

(3)   ...

(4)   The liquidator may—

   (a)   exercise the court's power of settling a list of contributories (which list is prima facie evidence of the liability of the persons named in it to be contributories),

   (b)   exercise the court's power of making calls,

   (c)   summon general meetings of the company for the purpose of obtaining its sanction by special resolution or for any other purpose he may think fit.

(5)   The liquidator shall pay the company's debts and adjust the rights of the contributories among themselves.

(6)   Where the liquidator in exercise of the powers conferred on him by this Act disposes of any property of the company to a person who is connected with the company (within the meaning of section 249 in Part VII), he shall, if there is for the time being a liquidation committee, give notice to the committee of that exercise of his powers.

166.   Creditors' voluntary winding up

(1)   This section applies where, in the case of a creditors' voluntary winding up, a liquidator has been nominated by the company.

(1A)   The exercise by the liquidator of the power specified in paragraph 6 of Schedule 4 to this Act (power to sell any of the company's property) shall not be challengeable on the ground of any prior inhibition.

(2)   The powers conferred on the liquidator by section 165 shall not be exercised, except with the sanction of the court, before—

   (a)   the company's creditors under section 100 nominate a person to be liquidator, or

   (b)   the procedure by which the company's creditors were to have made such a nomination concludes without a nomination having been made.

(3)   Subsection (2) does not apply in relation to the power of the liquidator—

   (a)   to take into his custody or under his control all the property to which the company is or appears to be entitled;

   (b)   to dispose of perishable goods and other goods the value of which is likely to diminish if they are not immediately disposed of; and

   (c)   to do all such other things as may be necessary for the protection of the company's assets.

(4)   ...

(5)   If the directors fail to comply with—

   (a)   section 99(1), (2) or (2A), or

   (b)   section 100(1B),

   the liquidator shall, within 7 days of the relevant day, apply to the court for directions as to the manner in which that default is to be remedied.

(6)   "The relevant day" means the day on which the liquidator was nominated by the company or the day on which he first became aware of the default, whichever is the later.

(7)   If the liquidator without reasonable excuse fails to comply with this section, he is liable to a fine.

167.   Winding up by the court

(1)   Where a company is being wound up by the court, the liquidator may exercise any of the powers specified in Parts 1 to 3 of Schedule 4.

(2)   Where the liquidator (not being the official receiver), in exercise of the powers conferred on him by this Act—

   (a)   disposes of any property of the company to a person who is connected with the company (within the meaning of section 249 in Part VII), or

(b)   employs a solicitor to assist him in the carrying out of his functions,

he shall, if there is for the time being a liquidation committee, give notice to the committee of that exercise of his powers.

(3)   The exercise by the liquidator in a winding up by the court of the powers conferred by this section is subject to the control of the court, and any creditor or contributory may apply to the court with respect to any exercise or proposed exercise of any of those powers.

168.   Supplementary powers (England and Wales)

(1)   This section applies in the case of a company which is being wound up by the court in England and Wales.

(2)   The liquidator may seek a decision on any matter from the company's creditors or contributories; and must seek a decision on a matter—

(a)   from the company's creditors, if requested to do so by one-tenth in value of the creditors;

(b)   from the company's contributories, if requested to do so by one-tenth in value of the contributories.

(3)   The liquidator may apply to the court (in the prescribed manner) for directions in relation to any particular matter arising in the winding up.

(4)   Subject to the provisions of this Act, the liquidator shall use his own discretion in the management of the assets and their distribution among the creditors.

(5)   If any person is aggrieved by an act or decision of the liquidator, that person may apply to the court; and the court may confirm, reverse or modify the act or decision complained of, and make such order in the case as it thinks just.

(5A)   Where at any time after a winding-up petition has been presented to the court against any person (including an insolvent partnership or other body which may be wound up under Part V of the Act as an unregistered company), whether by virtue of the provisions of the Insolvent Partnerships Order 1994 or not, the attention of the court is drawn to the fact that the person in question is a member of an insolvent partnership, the court may make an order as to the future conduct of the insolvency proceedings and any such order may apply any provisions of that Order with any necessary modifications.

(5B)   Any order or directions under subsection (5A) may be made or given on the application of the official receiver, any responsible insolvency practitioner, the trustee of the partnership or any other interested person and may include provisions as to the administration of the joint estate of the partnership, and in particular how it and the separate estate of any member are to be administered.

(5C)   Where the court makes an order for the winding up of an insolvent partnership under—

(a)   section 72(1)(a) of the Financial Services Act 1986;

(b)   section 92(1)(a) of the Banking Act 1987; or

(c)   section 367(3)(a) of the Financial Services and Markets Act 2000,

the court may make an order as to the future conduct of the winding up proceedings, and any such order may apply any provisions of the Insolvent Partnerships Order 1994 with any necessary modifications.

169.   Supplementary powers (Scotland)

(1)   ...

(2)   In a winding up by the court in Scotland, the liquidator has (subject to the rules) the same powers as a trustee on a bankrupt estate.

170.   Enforcement of liquidator's duty to make returns, etc

(1)   If a liquidator who has made any default—

(a)   in filing, delivering or making any return, account or other document, or

(b)   in giving any notice which he is by law required to file, deliver, make or give,

fails to make good the default within 14 days after the service on him of a notice requiring him to do so, the court has the following powers.

(2)   On an application made by any creditor or contributory of the company, or by the registrar of companies, the court may make an order directing the liquidator to make good the default within such time as may be specified in the order.

(3)   The court's order may provide that all costs of and incidental to the application shall be borne by the liquidator.

(4)   Nothing in this section prejudices the operation of any enactment imposing penalties on a liquidator in respect of any such default as is mentioned above.

Removal; vacation of office

171.   Removal, etc (voluntary winding up)

(1)   This section applies with respect to the removal from office and vacation of office of the liquidator of a company which is being wound up voluntarily.

(2)   Subject to the next subsection, the liquidator may be removed from office only by an order of the court or—

(a)   in the case of a members' voluntary winding up, by a general meeting of the company summoned specially for that purpose, or

(b)   in the case of a creditors' voluntary winding up, by a decision of the company's creditors made by a qualifying decision procedure instigated specially for that purpose in accordance with the rules.

(3)   Where the liquidator in a members' voluntary winding up was appointed by the court under section 108, a meeting such as is mentioned in subsection (2)(a) shall be summoned only if—

(a)   the liquidator thinks fit,

(b)   the court so directs, or

(c)   the meeting is requested in accordance with the rules by members representing not less than one-half of the total voting rights of all the members having at the date of the request a right to vote at the meeting.

(3A)   Where the liquidator in a creditors' voluntary winding up was appointed by the court under section 108, a qualifying decision procedure such as is mentioned in subsection (2)(b) is to be instigated only if—

(a)   the liquidator thinks fit,

(b)   the court so directs, or

(c)   it is requested in accordance with the rules by not less than one-half in value of the company's creditors.

(4)   A liquidator shall vacate office if he ceases to be a person who is qualified to act as an insolvency practitioner in relation to the company.

(5)   A liquidator may, in the prescribed circumstances, resign his office by giving notice of his resignation to the registrar of companies.

(6)   In the case of a members' voluntary winding up where the liquidator has produced an account of the winding up under section 94 (final account), the liquidator vacates office as soon as the liquidator has complied with section 94(3) (requirement to send final account to registrar).

(7)   In the case of a creditors' voluntary winding up where the liquidator has produced an account of the winding up under section 106 (final account), the liquidator vacates office as soon as the liquidator has complied with section 106(3) (requirement to send final account etc to registrar).

172.   Removal, etc (winding up by the court)

(1)   This section applies with respect to the removal from office and vacation of office of the liquidator of a company which is being wound up by the court, or of a provisional liquidator.

(2)   Subject as follows, the liquidator may be removed from office only by an order of the court or by a decision of the company's creditors made by a qualifying decision procedure instigated specially for that purpose in accordance with the rules; and a provisional liquidator may be removed from office only by an order of the court.

(3)   Where—

(a)   the official receiver is liquidator otherwise than in succession under section 136(3) to a person who held office as a result of a nomination by ... the company's creditors or contributories, or

(b)   the liquidator was appointed by the court otherwise than under section 139(4)(a) or 140(1), or was appointed by the Secretary of State,

a qualifying decision procedure such as is mentioned in subsection (2) shall be instigated only if the liquidator thinks fit, the court so directs, or it is requested, in accordance with the rules, by not less that one-quarter, in value, of the creditors.

(4)   If appointed by the Secretary of State, the liquidator may be removed from office by a direction of the Secretary of State.

(5)   A liquidator or provisional liquidator, not being the official receiver, shall vacate office if he ceases to be a person who is qualified to act as an insolvency practitioner in relation to the company.

(6)   A liquidator may, in the prescribed circumstances, resign his office by giving notice of his resignation to the court.

(7)   Where an order is made under section 204 (early dissolution in Scotland) for the dissolution of the company, the liquidator shall vacate office when the dissolution of the company takes effect in accordance with that section.

(8)   Where the liquidator has produced an account of the winding up under section 146 (final account), the liquidator vacates office as soon as the liquidator has complied with section 146(4) (requirement to send account etc to registrar and to court).

(9)   Subsection (10) applies where, immediately before a liquidator gives notice to the court and the registrar under subsection (8) (or, where the liquidator gives notice to the court and the registrar on different days, immediately before the liquidator gives the first of those notices), there are EU insolvency proceedings open in respect of the company in one or more other member States.

(10)   The liquidator must send to the court and the registrar, with the notice, a statement—

(a)   identifying those proceedings,

(b)   identifying the member State liquidator appointed in each of those proceedings, and

(c)   indicating, in relation to each of those member State liquidators, whether that member State liquidator consents to the company being dissolved.

Release of liquidator

173.   Release (voluntary winding up)

(1)   This section applies with respect to the release of the liquidator of a company which is being wound up voluntarily.

(2)   A person who has ceased to be a liquidator shall have his release with effect from the following time, that is to say—

(a)   in the following cases, the time at which notice is given to the registrar of companies in accordance with the rules that the person has ceased to hold office—

(i)   the person has been removed from office by a general meeting of the company,

(ii)   the person has been removed from office by a decision of the company's creditors and the company's creditors have not decided against his release,

(iii) the person has died;

(b)   in the following cases, such time as the Secretary of State may, on the application of the person, determine—

(i)   the person has been removed from office by a decision of the company's creditors and the company's creditors have decided against his release,

(ii)   the person has been removed from office by the court,

(iii) the person has vacated office under section 171(4);

(c)   in the case of a person who has resigned, such time as may be prescribed;

(d)   in the case of a person who has vacated office under subsection (6) of section 171, the time at which he vacated office;

(e)   in the case of a person who has vacated office under section 171(7)—

      (i)   if any of the company's creditors objected to the person's release before the end of the period for so objecting prescribed by the rules, such time as the Secretary of State may, on an application by that person, determine, and

      (ii)   otherwise, the time at which the person vacated office.

(2A)   Where the person is removed from office by a decision of the company's creditors, any decision of the company's creditors as to whether the person should have his release must be made by a qualifying decision procedure.

(3)   In the application of subsection (2) to the winding up of a company registered in Scotland, the references to a determination by the Secretary of State as to the time from which a person who has ceased to be liquidator shall have his release are to be read as references to such a determination by the Accountant of Court.

(4)   Where a liquidator has his release under subsection (2), he is, with effect from the time specified in that subsection, discharged from all liability both in respect of acts or omissions of his in the winding up and otherwise in relation to his conduct as liquidator.

But nothing in this section prevents the exercise, in relation to a person who has had his release under subsection (2), of the court's powers under section 212 of this Act (summary remedy against delinquent directors, liquidators, etc).

174.   **Release (winding up by the court)**

(1)   This section applies with respect to the release of the liquidator of a company which is being wound up by the court, or of a provisional liquidator.

(2)   Where the official receiver has ceased to be liquidator and a person becomes liquidator in his stead, the official receiver has his release with effect from the following time, that is to say—

    (a)   in a case where that person was nominated by the company's creditors or contributories, or was appointed by the Secretary of State, the time at which the official receiver gives notice to the court that he has been replaced;

    (b)   in a case where that person is appointed by the court, such time as the court may determine.

(3)   If the official receiver while he is a liquidator gives notice to the Secretary of State that the winding up is for practical purposes complete, he has his release with effect from such time as the Secretary of State may determine.

(4)   A person other than the official receiver who has ceased to be a liquidator has his release with effect from the following time, that is to say—

    (a)   in the following cases, the time at which notice is given to the court in accordance with the rules that the person has ceased to hold office—

      (i)   the person has been removed from office by a decision of the company's creditors and the company's creditors have not decided against his release,

      (ii)   the person has died;

    (b)   in the following cases, such time as the Secretary of State may, on the application of the person, determine—

      (i)   the person has been removed from office by a decision of the company's creditors and the company's creditors have decided against his release;

      (ii)   the person has been removed from office by the court or the Secretary of State;

      (iii) the person has vacated office under section 172(5) or (7);

    (c)   in the case of a person who has resigned, such time as may be prescribed;

    (d)   in the case of a person who has vacated office under section 172(8)—

      (i)   if any of the company's creditors objected to the person's release before the end of the period for so objecting prescribed by the rules, such time as the Secretary of State may, on an application by that person, determine, and

      (ii)   otherwise, the time at which the person vacated office.

(4A)   Where a winding-up order made by the court in England and Wales is rescinded, the person (whether the official receiver or another person) who is the liquidator of the company at the time the order is rescinded has his release with effect from such time as the court may determine.

(4ZA)   Where the person is removed from office by a decision of the company's creditors, any decision of the company's creditors as to whether the person should have his release must be made by a qualifying decision procedure.

(5)   A person who has ceased to hold office as a provisional liquidator has his release with effect from such time as the court may, on an application by him, determine.

(6)   Where the official receiver or a liquidator or provisional liquidator has his release under this section, he is, with effect from the time specified in the preceding provisions of this section, discharged from all liability both in respect of acts or omissions of his in the winding up and otherwise in relation to his conduct as liquidator or provisional liquidator.

        But nothing in this section prevents the exercise, in relation to a person who has had his release under this section, of the court's powers under section 212 (summary remedy against delinquent directors, liquidators, etc).

(7)   In the application of this section to a case where the order for winding up has been made by the court in Scotland, the references to a determination by the Secretary of State as to the time from which a person who has ceased to be liquidator has his release are to such a determination by the Accountant of Court.

CHAPTER VIII
PROVISIONS OF GENERAL APPLICATION IN WINDING UP

Moratorium: order of priority of payment of debts

174A.   Moratorium debts etc: priority

(1)   This section applies where proceedings for the winding up of a company are begun before the end of the period of 12 weeks beginning with the day after the end of any moratorium for the company under Part A1.

(2)   In the winding up, the following are payable out of the company's assets (in the order of priority shown) in preference to all other claims—
        (a)   any prescribed fees or expenses of the official receiver acting in any capacity in relation to the company;
        (b)   moratorium debts and priority pre-moratorium debts.

(3)   In subsection (2)(b) "priority pre-moratorium debt" means—
        (a)   any pre-moratorium debt that is payable in respect of—
              (i)   the monitor's remuneration or expenses,
              (ii)   goods or services supplied during the moratorium,
              (iii) rent in respect of a period during the moratorium, or
              (iv)   wages or salary arising under a contract of employment, so far as relating to a period of employment before or during the moratorium,
        (b)   any pre-moratorium debt that—
              (i)   consists of a liability to make a redundancy payment, and
              (ii)   fell due before or during the moratorium, and
        (c)   any pre-moratorium debt that—
              (i)   arises under a contract or other instrument involving financial services,
              (ii)   fell due before or during the moratorium, and
              (iii) is not relevant accelerated debt (see subsection (4)).

(4)   For the purposes of subsection (3)(c)—
        "relevant accelerated debt" means any pre-moratorium debt that fell due during the relevant period by reason of the operation of, or the exercise of rights under, an acceleration or early termination clause in a contract or other instrument involving financial services;
        "the relevant period" means the period—
        (a)   beginning with the day on which the statement under section A6(1)(e) is made, and
        (b)   ending with the last day of the moratorium.

(5) The rules may make provision as to the order in which the debts mentioned in subsection (2)(b) rank among themselves in a case where the assets of the company are insufficient to meet them in full.

(6) The Secretary of State may by regulations made by statutory instrument amend this section for the purposes of changing the definition of "moratorium debt" or "priority pre-moratorium debt" in this section.

(7) Regulations under subsection (6) may make consequential, supplementary, incidental or transitional provision or savings.

(8) A statutory instrument containing regulations under subsection (6) may not be made unless a draft of the instrument has been laid before and approved by a resolution of each House of Parliament.

(9) For the purposes of this section proceedings for the winding up of a company are begun when—
   (a)   a winding-up petition is presented, or
   (b)   a resolution for voluntary winding up is passed.

(10) Any rules made under section A18(4) (meaning of supply of goods or services) apply also for the purposes of subsection (3)(a)(ii) of this section.

(11) In this section—
"acceleration or early termination clause", in relation to a contract or other instrument involving financial services, means a provision of the contract or other instrument—
   (a)   under which, on the happening of an event—
      (i)   a debt or other liability falls due earlier than it otherwise would, or
      (ii)   a debt or other liability is terminated and replaced by another debt or liability, or
   (b)   which confers on a party a right which, if exercised, will result in—
      (i)   a debt or other liability falling due earlier than it otherwise would, or
      (ii)   a debt or other liability being terminated and replaced by another debt or liability;
"contract or other instrument involving financial services" has the same meaning as it has for the purposes of section A18 (see Schedule ZA2);
"monitor's remuneration or expenses" has the meaning given by section A18;
"moratorium debt" has the meaning given by section A53;
"pre-moratorium debt" has the meaning given by section A53;
"redundancy payment" has the meaning given by section A18;
"wages or salary" has the meaning given by section A18.

Preferential debts

175. Preferential debts (general provision)

(1) In a winding up the company's preferential debts ... shall be paid in priority to all other debts after the payment of—
   (a)   any liabilities to which section 174A applies, and
   (b)   expenses of the winding up.

(1A) Ordinary preferential debts rank equally among themselves ... and shall be paid in full, unless the assets are insufficient to meet them, in which case they abate in equal proportions.

(1B) Secondary preferential debts rank equally among themselves after the ordinary preferential debts and shall be paid in full, unless the assets are insufficient to meet them, in which case they abate in equal proportions.

(2) Preferential debts—
   (a)   ...
   (b)   so far as the assets of the company available for payment of general creditors are insufficient to meet them, have priority over the claims of holders of debentures secured by, or holders of, any floating charge created by the company, and shall be paid accordingly out of any property comprised in or subject to that charge.

(3) In this section "preferential debts", "ordinary preferential debts" and "secondary preferential debts" each has the meaning given in section 386 in Part 12.

176. **Preferential charge on goods distrained, etc**

(1)   This section applies where a company is being wound up by the court in England and Wales, and is without prejudice to section 128 (avoidance of attachments, etc).

(2)   (2)   Subsection (2A) applies where—

    (a)   any person (whether or not a landlord or person entitled to rent) has distrained upon the goods or effects of the company, or

    (b)   Her Majesty's Revenue and Customs has been paid any amount from an account of the company under Part 1 of Schedule 8 to the Finance (No 2) Act 2015 (enforcement by deduction from accounts),

in the period of 3 months ending with the date of the winding-up order.

(2A)   Where this subsection applies—

    (a)   in a case within subsection (2)(a), the goods or effects, or the proceeds of their sale, and

    (b)   in a case within subsection (2)(b), the amount in question,

is charged for the benefit of the company with the preferential debts of the company to the extent that the company's property is for the time being insufficient for meeting those debts.

(3)   Where by virtue of a charge under subsection (2A) any person surrenders any goods or effects to a company or makes a payment to a company, that person ranks, in respect of the amount of the proceeds of sale of those goods or effects by the liquidator or (as the case may be) the amount of the payment, as a preferential creditor of the company, except as against so much of the company's property as is available for the payment of preferential creditors by virtue of the surrender or payment.

Non-preferential debts

176AZA.Non-preferential debts of financial institutions

(1)   This section applies in the winding up of a company which is a relevant financial institution.

(2)   The company's ordinary non-preferential debts shall be paid in priority to its secondary non-preferential debts.

(3)   The company's secondary non-preferential debts—

    (a)   shall be paid in priority to its tertiary non-preferential debts, and

    (b)   rank equally among themselves after the ordinary non-preferential debts and shall be paid in full, unless the assets are insufficient to meet them, in which case they abate in equal proportions.

(4)   See section 387A for definitions relevant to this section.

Property subject to floating charge

176ZA. Payment of expenses of winding up (England and Wales)

(1)   The expenses of winding up in England and Wales, so far as the assets of the company available for payment of general creditors are insufficient to meet them, have priority over any claims to property comprised in or subject to any floating charge created by the company and shall be paid out of any such property accordingly.

(2)   In subsection (1)—

    (a)   the reference to assets of the company available for payment of general creditors does not include any amount made available under section 176A(2)(a);

    (b)   the reference to claims to property comprised in or subject to a floating charge is to the claims of—

        (i)   the holders of debentures secured by, or holders of, the floating charge, and

        (ii)   any preferential creditors entitled to be paid out of that property in priority to them.

(3)   Provision may be made by rules restricting the application of subsection (1), in such circumstances as may be prescribed, to expenses authorised or approved—

    (a)   by the holders of debentures secured by, or holders of, the floating charge and by any preferential creditors entitled to be paid in priority to them, or

    (b)   by the court.

(4) References in this section to the expenses of the winding up are to all expenses properly incurred in the winding up, including the remuneration of the liquidator.

176ZB. Application of proceeds of office-holder claims

(1) This section applies where—
    (a) there is a floating charge (whether created before or after the coming into force of this section) which relates to property of a company which—
        (i) is in administration, or
        (ii) has gone into liquidation; and
    (b) the administrator or the liquidator (referred to in this section as "the office-holder") has—
        (i) brought a claim under any provision mentioned in subsection (3), or
        (ii) made an assignment (or, in Scotland, assignation) in relation to a right of action under any such provision under section 246ZD.

(2) The proceeds of the claim or assignment (or, in Scotland, assignation) are not to be treated as part of the company's net property, that is to say the amount of its property which would be available for satisfaction of claims of holders of debentures secured by, or holders of, any floating charge created by the company.

(3) The provisions are—
    (a) section 213 or 246ZA (fraudulent trading);
    (b) section 214 or 246ZB (wrongful trading);
    (c) section 238 (transactions at an undervalue (England and Wales));
    (d) section 239 (preferences (England and Wales));
    (e) section 242 (gratuitous alienations (Scotland));
    (f) section 243 (unfair preferences (Scotland));
    (g) section 244 (extortionate credit transactions).

(4) Subsection (2) does not apply to a company if or in so far as it is disapplied by—
    (a) a voluntary arrangement in respect of the company, or
    (b) a compromise or arrangement agreed under Part 26 or 26A of the Companies Act 2006 (arrangements and reconstructions).

176A. Share of assets for unsecured creditors

(1) This section applies where a floating charge relates to property of a company—
    (a) which has gone into liquidation,
    (b) which is in administration,
    (c) of which there is a provisional liquidator, or
    (d) of which there is a receiver.

(2) The liquidator, administrator or receiver—
    (a) shall make a prescribed part of the company's net property available for the satisfaction of unsecured debts, and
    (b) shall not distribute that part to the proprietor of a floating charge except in so far as it exceeds the amount required for the satisfaction of unsecured debts.

(3) Subsection (2) shall not apply to a company if—
    (a) the company's net property is less than the prescribed minimum, and
    (b) the liquidator, administrator or receiver thinks that the cost of making a distribution to unsecured creditors would be disproportionate to the benefits.

(4) Subsection (2) shall also not apply to a company if or in so far as it is disapplied by—
    (a) a voluntary arrangement in respect of the company, or
    (b) a compromise or arrangement agreed under Part 26 or 26A of the Companies Act 2006 (arrangements and reconstructions).

(5) Subsection (2) shall also not apply to a company if—
    (a) the liquidator, administrator or receiver applies to the court for an order under this subsection on the ground that the cost of making a distribution to unsecured creditors would be disproportionate to the benefits, and

(b)   the court orders that subsection (2) shall not apply.

(6)   In subsections (2) and (3) a company's net property is the amount of its property which would, but for this section, be available for satisfaction of claims of holders of debentures secured by, or holders of, any floating charge created by the company.

(7)   An order under subsection (2) prescribing part of a company's net property may, in particular, provide for its calculation—

(a)   as a percentage of the company's net property, or

(b)   as an aggregate of different percentages of different parts of the company's net property.

(8)   An order under this section—

(a)   must be made by statutory instrument, and

(b)   shall be subject to annulment pursuant to a resolution of either House of Parliament.

(9)   In this section—

"floating charge" means a charge which is a floating charge on its creation and which is created after the first order under subsection (2)(a) comes into force, and

"prescribed" means prescribed by order by the Secretary of State.

(10)   An order under this section may include transitional or incidental provision.

Special managers

177.   Power to appoint special manager

(1)   Where a company has gone into liquidation or a provisional liquidator has been appointed, the court may, on an application under this section, appoint any person to be the special manager of the business or property of the company.

(2)   The application may be made by the liquidator or provisional liquidator in any case where it appears to him that the nature of the business or property of the company, or the interests of the company's creditors or contributories or members generally, require the appointment of another person to manage the company's business or property.

(3)   The special manager has such powers as may be entrusted to him by the court.

(4)   The court's power to entrust powers to the special manager includes power to direct that any provision of this Act that has effect in relation to the provisional liquidator or liquidator of a company shall have the like effect in relation to the special manager for the purposes of the carrying out by him of any of the functions of the provisional liquidator or liquidator.

(5)   The special manager shall—

(a)   give such security or, in Scotland, caution as may be prescribed;

(b)   prepare and keep such accounts as may be prescribed; and

(c)   produce those accounts in accordance with the rules to the Secretary of State or to such other persons as may be prescribed.

Disclaimer (England and Wales only)

178.   Power to disclaim onerous property

(1)   This and the next two sections apply to a company that is being wound up in England and Wales.

(2)   Subject as follows, the liquidator may, by the giving of the prescribed notice, disclaim any onerous property and may do so notwithstanding that he has taken possession of it, endeavoured to sell it, or otherwise exercised rights of ownership in relation to it.

(3)   The following is onerous property for the purposes of this section—

(a)   any unprofitable contract, and

(b)   any other property of the company which is unsaleable or not readily saleable or is such that it may give rise to a liability to pay money or perform any other onerous act.

(4)   A disclaimer under this section—

(a)   operates so as to determine, as from the date of the disclaimer, the rights, interests and liabilities of the company in or in respect of the property disclaimed; but

(b)   does not, except so far as is necessary for the purpose of releasing the company from any liability, affect the rights or liabilities of any other person.

(5) A notice of disclaimer shall not be given under this section in respect of any property if—

    (a) a person interested in the property has applied in writing to the liquidator or one of his predecessors as liquidator requiring the liquidator or that predecessor to decide whether he will disclaim or not, and

    (b) the period of 28 days beginning with the day on which that application was made, or such longer period as the court may allow, has expired without a notice of disclaimer having been given under this section in respect of that property.

(6) Any person sustaining loss or damage in consequence of the operation of a disclaimer under this section is deemed a creditor of the company to the extent of the loss or damage and accordingly may prove for the loss or damage in the winding up.

179. Disclaimer of leaseholds

(1) The disclaimer under section 178 of any property of a leasehold nature does not take effect unless a copy of the disclaimer has been served (so far as the liquidator is aware of their addresses) on every person claiming under the company as underlessee or mortgagee and either—

    (a) no application under section 181 below is made with respect to that property before the end of the period of 14 days beginning with the day on which the last notice served under this subsection was served; or

    (b) where such an application has been made, the court directs that the disclaimer shall take effect.

(2) Where the court gives a direction under subsection (1)(b) it may also, instead of or in addition to any order it makes under section 181, make such orders with respect to fixtures, tenant's improvements and other matters arising out of the lease as it thinks fit.

180. Land subject to rentcharge

(1) The following applies where, in consequence of the disclaimer under section 178 of any land subject to a rentcharge, that land vests by operation of law in the Crown or any other person (referred to in the next subsection as "the proprietor").

(2) The proprietor and the successors in title of the proprietor are not subject to any personal liability in respect of any sums becoming due under the rentcharge except sums becoming due after the proprietor, or some person claiming under or through the proprietor, has taken possession or control of the land or has entered into occupation of it.

181. Powers of court (general)

(1) This section and the next apply where the liquidator has disclaimed property under section 178.

(2) An application under this section may be made to the court by—

    (a) any person who claims an interest in the disclaimed property, or

    (b) any person who is under any liability in respect of the disclaimed property, not being a liability discharged by the disclaimer.

(3) Subject as follows, the court may on the application make an order, on such terms as it thinks fit, for the vesting of the disclaimed property in, or for its delivery to—

    (a) a person entitled to it or a trustee for such a person, or

    (b) a person subject to such a liability as is mentioned in subsection (2)(b) or a trustee for such a person.

(4) The court shall not make an order under subsection (3)(b) except where it appears to the court that it would be just to do so for the purpose of compensating the person subject to the liability in respect of the disclaimer.

(5) The effect of any order under this section shall be taken into account in assessing for the purpose of section 178(6) the extent of any loss or damage sustained by any person in consequence of the disclaimer.

(6) An order under this section vesting property in any person need not be completed by conveyance, assignment or transfer.

182.   Powers of court (leaseholds)

(1)   The court shall not make an order under section 181 vesting property of a leasehold nature in any person claiming under the company as underlessee or mortgagee except on terms making that person—

    (a)   subject to the same liabilities and obligations as the company was subject to under the lease at the commencement of the winding up, or

    (b)   if the court thinks fit, subject to the same liabilities and obligations as that person would be subject to if the lease had been assigned to him at the commencement of the winding up.

(2)   For the purposes of an order under section 181 relating to only part of any property comprised in a lease, the requirements of subsection (1) apply as if the lease comprised only the property to which the order relates.

(3)   Where subsection (1) applies and no person claiming under the company as underlessee or mortgagee is willing to accept an order under section 181 on the terms required by virtue of that subsection, the court may, by order under that section, vest the company's estate or interest in the property in any person who is liable (whether personally or in a representative capacity, and whether alone or jointly with the company) to perform the lessee's covenants in the lease.
The court may vest that estate and interest in such a person freed and discharged from all estates, incumbrances and interests created by the company.

(4)   Where subsection (1) applies and a person claiming under the company as underlessee or mortgagee declines to accept an order under section 181, that person is excluded from all interest in the property.

Execution, attachment and the Scottish equivalents

183.   Effect of execution or attachment (England and Wales)

(1)   Where a creditor has issued execution against the goods or land of a company or has attached any debt due to it, and the company is subsequently wound up, he is not entitled to retain the benefit of the execution or attachment against the liquidator unless he has completed the execution or attachment before the commencement of the winding up.

(2)   However—

    (a)   if a creditor has had notice of a meeting having been called at which a resolution for voluntary winding up is to be proposed, the date on which he had notice is substituted, for the purpose of subsection (1), for the date of commencement of the winding up;

    (b)   a person who purchases in good faith under a sale by the enforcement officer or other officer charged with the execution of the writ any goods of a company on which execution has been levied in all cases acquires a good title to them against the liquidator; and

    (c)   the rights conferred by subsection (1) on the liquidator may be set aside by the court in favour of the creditor to such extent and subject to such terms as the court thinks fit.

(3)   For the purposes of this Act—

    (a)   an execution against goods is completed by seizure and sale, or by the making of a charging order under section 1 of the Charging Orders Act 1979;

    (b)   an attachment of a debt is completed by receipt of the debt; and

    (c)   an execution against land is completed by seizure, by the appointment of a receiver, or by the making of a charging order under section 1 of the Act above-mentioned.

(4)   In this section "goods" includes all chattels personal; and "enforcement officer" means an individual who is authorised to act as an enforcement officer under the Courts Act 2003.

(4A)   For the purposes of this section, Her Majesty's Revenue and Customs is to be regarded as having attached a debt due to a company if it has taken action under Part 1 of Schedule 8 to the Finance (No 2) Act 2015 (enforcement by deduction for accounts) as a result of which an amount standing to the credit of an account held by the company is—

    (a)   subject to arrangements made under paragraph 6(3) of that Schedule, or

    (b)   the subject of a deduction notice under paragraph 13 of that Schedule.

(5)   This section does not apply in the case of a winding up in Scotland.

184. **Duties of officers charged with execution of writs and other processes (England and Wales)**

(1) The following applies where a company's goods are taken in execution and, before their sale or the completion of the execution (by the receipt or recovery of the full amount of the levy), notice is served on the enforcement officer, or other officer, charged with execution of the writ or other process, that a provisional liquidator has been appointed or that a winding-up order has been made, or that a resolution for voluntary winding up has been passed.

(2) The enforcement officer or other officer shall, on being so required, deliver the goods and any money seized or received in part satisfaction of the execution to the liquidator; but the costs of execution are a first charge on the goods or money so delivered, and the liquidator may sell the goods, or a sufficient part of them, for the purpose of satisfying the charge.

(3) If under an execution in respect of a judgment for a sum exceeding £500 a company's goods are sold or money is paid in order to avoid sale, the enforcement officer or other officer shall deduct the costs of the execution from the proceeds of sale or the money paid and retain the balance for 14 days.

(4) If within that time notice is served on the enforcement officer or other officer of a petition for the winding up of the company having been presented, or of a meeting having been called at which there is to be proposed a resolution for voluntary winding up, and an order is made or a resolution passed (as the case may be), the enforcement officer or other officer shall pay the balance to the liquidator, who is entitled to retain it as against the execution creditor.

(5) The rights conferred by this section on the liquidator may be set aside by the court in favour of the creditor to such extent and subject to such terms as the court thinks fit.

(6) In this section, "goods" includes all chattels personal; and "enforcement officer" means an individual who is authorised to act as an enforcement officer under the Courts Act 2003.

(7) The money sum for the time being specified in subsection (3) is subject to increase or reduction by order under section 416 in Part XV.

(8) This section does not apply in the case of a winding up in Scotland.

185. **Effect of diligence (Scotland)**

(1) In the winding up of a company registered in Scotland, the following provisions of the Bankruptcy (Scotland) Act 2016—

(a) subsections (3) to (10) of section 23A (effect of sequestration on land attachment) and section 24 (effect of sequestration on diligence generally); and

(b) subsections (6), (7), (10) and (11) of section 109 (management and realisation of estate),

apply, so far as consistent with this Act, in like manner as they apply in the sequestration of a debtor's estate, with the substitutions specified below and with any other necessary modifications.

(2) The substitutions to be made in those sections of the Act of 2016 are as follows—

(a) for references to the debtor, substitute references to the company;

(b) for references to the sequestration, substitute references to the winding up;

(c) for references to the date of sequestration, substitute references to the commencement of the winding up of the company; and

(d) for references to the ... trustee, substitute references to the liquidator.

(3) In this section, "the commencement of the winding up of the company" means, where it is being wound up by the court, the day on which the winding-up order is made.

(4) This section, so far as relating to any estate or effects of the company situated in Scotland, applies in the case of a company registered in England and Wales as in the case of one registered in Scotland.

Miscellaneous matters

186. **Rescission of contracts by the court**

(1) The court may, on the application of a person who is, as against the liquidator, entitled to the benefit or subject to the burden of a contract made with the company, make an order rescinding the contract on such terms as to payment by or to either party of damages for the non-performance of the contract, or otherwise as the court thinks just.

(2)   Any damages payable under the order to such a person may be proved by him as a debt in the winding up.

187.   Power to make over assets to employees

(1)   On the winding up of a company (whether by the court or voluntarily), the liquidator may, subject to the following provisions of this section, make any payment which the company has, before the commencement of the winding up, decided to make under section 247 of the Companies Act 2006 (power to provide for employees or former employees on cessation or transfer of business).

(2)   The liquidator may, after the winding up has commenced, make any such provision as is mentioned in section 247(1) if—

      (a)   the company's liabilities have been fully satisfied and provision has been made for the expenses of the winding up,

      (b)   the exercise of the power has been sanctioned by a resolution of the company, and

      (c)   any requirements of the company's articles as to the exercise of the power conferred by section 247(1) are complied with.

(3)   Any payment which may be made by a company under this section (that is, a payment after the commencement of its winding up) may be made out of the company's assets which are available to the members on the winding up.

(4)   On a winding up by the court, the exercise by the liquidator of his powers under this section is subject to the court's control, and any creditor or contributory may apply to the court with respect to any exercise or proposed exercise of the power.

(5)   Subsections (1) and (2) above have effect notwithstanding anything in any rule of law or in section 107 of this Act (property of company after satisfaction of liabilities to be distributed among members).

188.   Notification that company is in liquidation

(1)   When a company is being wound up, whether by the court or voluntarily—

      (a)   every invoice, order for goods or services, business letter or order form (whether in hard copy, electronic or any other form) issued by or on behalf of the company, or a liquidator of the company or a receiver or manager of the company's property…, and

      (b)   all the company's websites,

    must contain a statement that the company is being wound up.

(2)   If default is made in complying with this section, the company and any of the following persons who knowingly and wilfully authorises or permits the default, namely, any officer of the company, any liquidator of the company and any receiver or manager, is liable to a fine.

189.   Interest on debts

(1)   In a winding up interest is payable in accordance with this section on any debt proved in the winding up, including so much of any such debt as represents interest on the remainder.

(2)   Any surplus remaining after the payment of the debts proved in a winding up shall, before being applied for any other purpose, be applied in paying interest on those debts in respect of the periods during which they have been outstanding since the company went into liquidation.

(3)   All interest under this section ranks equally, whether or not the debts on which it is payable rank equally.

(4)   The rate of interest payable under this section in respect of any debt ("the official rate" for the purposes of any provision of this Act in which that expression is used) is whichever is the greater of—

      (a)   the rate specified in section 17 of the Judgments Act 1838 on the day on which the company went into liquidation, and

      (b)   the rate applicable to that debt apart from the winding up.

(5)   In the application of this section to Scotland—

      (a)   references to a debt proved in a winding up have effect as references to a claim accepted in a winding up, and

      (b)   the reference to section 17 of the Judgments Act 1838 has effect as a reference to the rules.

190. Documents exempt from stamp duty

(1) In the case of a winding up by the court, or of a creditors' voluntary winding up, the following has effect as regards exemption from duties chargeable under the enactments relating to stamp duties.

(2) If the company is registered in England and Wales, the following documents are exempt from stamp duty—

    (a) every assurance relating solely to freehold or leasehold property, or to any estate, right or interest in, any real or personal property, which forms part of the company's assets and which, after the execution of the assurance, either at law or in equity, is or remains part of those assets, and

    (b) every writ, order, certificate, or other instrument or writing relating solely to the property of any company which is being wound up as mentioned in subsection (1), or to any proceeding under such a winding up.

"Assurance" here includes deed, conveyance, assignment and surrender.

(3) If the company is registered in Scotland, the following documents are exempt from stamp duty—

    (a) every conveyance relating solely to property which forms part of the company's assets and which, after the execution of the conveyance, is or remains the company's property for the benefit of its creditors,

    (b) any articles of roup or sale, submission and every other instrument and writing whatsoever relating solely to the company's property, and

    (c) every deed or writing forming part of the proceedings in the winding up.

"Conveyance" here includes assignation, instrument, discharge, writing and deed.

191. Company's books to be evidence

Where a company is being wound up, all books and papers of the company and of the liquidators are, as between the contributories of the company, prima facie evidence of the truth of all matters purporting to be recorded in them.

192. Information as to pending liquidations

(1) If the winding up of a company is not concluded within one year after its commencement, the liquidator shall, at such intervals as may be prescribed, until the winding up is concluded, send to the registrar of companies a statement in the prescribed form and containing the prescribed particulars with respect to the proceedings in, and position of, the liquidation.

(2) If a liquidator fails to comply with this section, he is liable to a fine and, for continued contravention, to a daily default fine.

193. Unclaimed dividends (Scotland)

(1) The following applies where a company registered in Scotland has been wound up, and is about to be dissolved.

(2) The liquidator shall lodge in an appropriate bank or institution as defined in section 228(1) of the Bankruptcy (Scotland) Act 2016 (not being a bank or institution in or of which the liquidator is acting partner, manager, agent or cashier) in the name of the Accountant of Court the whole unclaimed dividends and unapplied or undistributable balances, and the deposit receipts shall be transmitted to the Accountant of Court.

(3) The provisions of section 150 of the Bankruptcy (Scotland) Act 2016 (so far as consistent with this Act and the Companies Acts) apply with any necessary modifications to sums lodged in a bank or institution under this section as they apply to sums deposited under section 148 of the Act first mentioned.

194. ...

195. Court's powers to ascertain wishes of creditors or contributories

(1) The court may—

    (a) as to all matters relating to the winding up of a company, have regard to the wishes of the creditors or contributories (as proved to it by any sufficient evidence), and

(b)   if it thinks fit, for the purpose of ascertaining those wishes, direct qualifying decision procedures to be instigated or the deemed consent procedure to be used in accordance with any directions given by the court, and appoint a person to report the result to the court.

(2)   In the case of creditors, regard shall be had to the value of each creditor's debt.

(3)   In the case of contributories, regard shall be had to the number of votes conferred on each contributory ...

196.   Judicial notice of court documents

In all proceedings under this Part, all courts, judges and persons judicially acting, and all officers, judicial or ministerial, of any court, or employed in enforcing the process of any court shall take judicial notice—

(a)   of the signature of any officer of the High Court or of the county court in England and Wales, or of the Court of Session or a sheriff court in Scotland, or of the High Court in Northern Ireland, and also

(b)   of the official seal or stamp of the several offices of the High Court in England and Wales or Northern Ireland, or of the Court of Session, appended to or impressed on any document made, issued or signed under the provisions of this Act or the Companies Acts, or any official copy of such a document.

197.   Commission for receiving evidence

(1)   When a company is wound up in England and Wales or in Scotland, the court may refer the whole or any part of the examination of witnesses—

(a)   to the county court in England and Wales, or

(b)   to the sheriff principal for a special sheriffdom in Scotland, or

(c)   to the High Court in Northern Ireland or a specified Northern Ireland County Court,

("specified" meaning specified in the order of the winding-up court).

(2)   Any person exercising jurisdiction as a judge of the court to which the reference is made (or, in Scotland, the sheriff principal to whom it is made) shall then, by virtue of this section, be a commissioner for the purpose of taking the evidence of those witnesses.

(3)   The judge or sheriff principal has in the matter referred the same power of summoning and examining witnesses, of requiring the production and delivery of documents, of punishing defaults by witnesses, and of allowing costs and expenses to witnesses, as the court which made the winding-up order.

These powers are in addition to any which the judge or sheriff principal might lawfully exercise apart from this section.

(4)   The examination so taken shall be returned or reported to the court which made the order in such manner as that court requests.

(5)   This section extends to Northern Ireland.

198.   Court order for examination of persons in Scotland

(1)   The court may direct the examination in Scotland of any person for the time being in Scotland (whether a contributory of the company or not), in regard to the trade, dealings, affairs or property of any company in course of being wound up, or of any person being a contributory of the company, so far as the company may be interested by reason of his being a contributory.

(2)   The order or commission to take the examination shall be directed to the sheriff principal of the sheriffdom in which the person to be examined is residing or happens to be for the time; and the sheriff principal shall summon the person to appear before him at a time and place to be specified in the summons for examination on oath as a witness or as a haver, and to produce any books or papers called for which are in his possession or power.

(3)   The sheriff principal may take the examination either orally or on written interrogatories, and shall report the same in writing in the usual form to the court, and shall transmit with the report the books and papers produced, if the originals are required and specified by the order or commission, or otherwise copies or extracts authenticated by the sheriff.

(4)   If a person so summoned fails to appear at the time and place specified, or refuses to be examined or to make the production required, the sheriff principal shall proceed against him as a witness or haver duly cited; and failing to appear or refusing to give evidence or make production may be proceeded against by the law of Scotland.

(5)   The sheriff principal is entitled to such fees, and the witness is entitled to such allowances, as sheriffs principal when acting as commissioners under appointment from the Court or Session and as witnesses and havers are entitled to in the like cases according to the law and practice of Scotland.

(6)   If any objection is stated to the sheriff principal by the witness, either on the ground of his incompetency as a witness, or as to the production required, or on any other ground, the sheriff principal may, if he thinks fit, report the objection to the court, and suspend the examination of the witness until it has been disposed of by the court.

199.   Costs of application for leave to proceed (Scottish companies)

Where a petition or application for leave to proceed with an action or proceeding against a company which is being wound up in Scotland is unopposed and is granted by the court, the costs of the petition or application shall, unless the court otherwise directs, be added to the amount of the petitioner's or applicant's claim against the company.

200.   Affidavits etc in United Kingdom and overseas

(1)   An affidavit required to be sworn under or for the purposes of this Part may be sworn in the United Kingdom, or elsewhere in Her Majesty's dominions, before any court, judge or person lawfully authorised to take and receive affidavits, or before any of Her Majesty's consuls or vice-consuls in any place outside Her dominions.

(2)   All courts, judges, justices, commissioners and persons acting judicially shall take judicial notice of the seal or stamp or signature (as the case may be) of any such court, judge, person, consul or vice-consul attached, appended or subscribed to any such affidavit, or to any other document to be used for the purposes of this Part.

CHAPTER IX
DISSOLUTION OF COMPANIES AFTER WINDING UP

201.   Dissolution (voluntary winding up)

(1)   This section applies, in the case of a company wound up voluntarily, where the liquidator has sent to the registrar of companies his final account ... under section 94 (members' voluntary) or his final account and statement under section 106 (creditors' voluntary).

(2)   The registrar on receiving the account ..., or the account and statement, ... shall forthwith register it or them; and on the expiration of 3 months from the registration of the account the company is deemed to be dissolved ....

(2A), (2B) ...

(3)   However, the court may, on the application of the liquidator or any other person who appears to the court to be interested, make an order deferring the date at which the dissolution of the company is to take effect for such time as the court thinks fit.

(4)   It is the duty of the person on whose application an order of the court under this section is made within 7 days after the making of the order to deliver to the registrar a copy of the order for registration; and if that person fails to do so he is liable to a fine and, for continued contravention, to a daily default fine.

202.   Early dissolution (England and Wales)

(1)   This section applies where an order for the winding up of a company has been made by the court in England and Wales.

(2)   The official receiver, if—

(a)   he is the liquidator of the company, and

(b)   it appears to him—

      (i)   that the realisable assets of the company are insufficient to cover the expenses of the winding up, and

      (ii)   that the affairs of the company do not require any further investigation,

may at any time apply to the registrar of companies for the early dissolution of the company.

(2A), (2B) ...

(3)   Before making an application under subsection (2), the official receiver shall give not less than 28 days' notice of his intention to do so to the company's creditors, other than opted-out creditors, and contributories and, if there is an administrative receiver of the company, to that receiver.

(4)   With the giving of that notice the official receiver ceases (subject to any directions under the next section) to be required to perform any duties imposed on him in relation to the company, its creditors or contributories by virtue of any provision of this Act, apart from a duty to make an application under subsection (2) ....

(5)   On the receipt of the official receiver's application under subsection (2) ... the registrar shall forthwith register it ... and, at the end of the period of 3 months beginning with the day of the registration of the application, the company shall be dissolved ....

(6), (7) ...

(8)   However, the Secretary of State may, on the application of the official receiver or any other person who appears to the Secretary of State to be interested, give directions under section 203 at any time before the end of the period in subsection (5) ....

203.   Consequence of notice under s 202

(1)   Where a notice has been given under section 202(3), the official receiver or any creditor or contributory of the company, or the administrative receiver of the company (if there is one) may apply to the Secretary of State for directions under this section.

(2)   The grounds on which that application may be made are—

     (a)   that the realisable assets of the company are sufficient to cover the expenses of the winding up;

     (b)   that the affairs of the company do require further investigation; or

     (c)   that for any other reason the early dissolution of the company is inappropriate.

(3)   Directions under this section—

     (a)   are directions making such provision as the Secretary of State thinks fit for enabling the winding up of the company to proceed as if no notice had been given under section 202(3), and

     (b)   may, in the case of an application under section 202(8), include a direction deferring the date at which the dissolution of the company is to take effect for such period as the Secretary of State thinks fit.

(4)   An appeal to the court lies from any decision of the Secretary of State on an application for directions under this section.

(5)   It is the duty of the person on whose application any directions are given under this section, or in whose favour an appeal with respect to an application for such directions is determined, within 7 days after the giving of the directions or the determination of the appeal, to deliver to the registrar of companies for registration such a copy of the directions or determination as is prescribed.

(6)   If a person without reasonable excuse fails to deliver a copy as required by subsection (5), he is liable to a fine and, for continued contravention, to a daily default fine.

204.   Early dissolution (Scotland)

(1)   This section applies where a winding-up order has been made by the court in Scotland.

(2)   If after a liquidator has been appointed under section 138 (appointment of liquidator in Scotland) it appears to the liquidator that the realisable assets of the company are insufficient to cover the expenses of the winding up, the liquidator may at any time apply to the court for an order that the company be dissolved.

(3)   Where the liquidator makes that application, if the court is satisfied that the realisable assets of the company are insufficient to cover the expenses of the winding up and it appears to the court

appropriate to do so, the court shall make an order that the company be dissolved in accordance with this section.

(4) A copy of the order shall within 14 days from its date be forwarded by the liquidator to the registrar of companies, who shall forthwith register it; and, at the end of the period of 3 months beginning with the day of the registration of the order, the company shall be dissolved.

(4A)–(4E) ...

(5) The court may, on an application by any person who appears to the court to have an interest, order that the date at which the dissolution of the company is to take effect shall be deferred for such period as the court thinks fit.

(6) It is the duty of the person on whose application an order is made under subsection (5), within 7 days after the making of the order, to deliver to the registrar of companies such a copy of the order as is prescribed.

(7) If the liquidator without reasonable excuse fails to comply with the requirements of subsection (4), he is liable to a fine and, for continued contravention, to a daily default fine.

(8) If a person without reasonable excuse fails to deliver a copy as required by subsection (6), he is liable to a fine and, for continued contravention, to a daily default fine.

205. Dissolution otherwise than under ss 202–204

(1) This section applies where the registrar of companies receives—
   (a) a final account and statement sent under section 146(4) (final account), or
   (b) a notice from the official receiver that the winding up of a company by the court is complete.

(2) The registrar shall, on receipt of the final account and statement or the notice ..., forthwith register them or it; and, subject as follows, at the end of the period of 3 months beginning with the day of the registration of the final account or notice ..., the company shall be dissolved.

(2A), (2B) ...

(3) The Secretary of State may, on the application of the official receiver or any other person who appears to the Secretary of State to be interested, give a direction deferring the date at which the dissolution of the company is to take effect for such period as the Secretary of State thinks fit.

(4) An appeal to the court lies from any decision of the Secretary of State on an application for a direction under subsection (3).

(5) Subsection (3) does not apply in a case where the winding-up order was made by the court in Scotland, but in such a case the court may, on an application by any person appearing to the court to have an interest, order that the date at which the dissolution of the company is to take effect shall be deferred for such period as the court thinks fit.

(6) It is the duty of the person—
   (a) on whose application a direction is given under subsection (3);
   (b) in whose favour an appeal with respect to an application for such a direction is determined; or
   (c) on whose application an order is made under subsection (5),
within 7 days after the giving of the direction, the determination of the appeal or the making of the order, to deliver to the registrar for registration such a copy of the direction, determination or order as is prescribed.

(7) If a person without reasonable excuse fails to deliver a copy as required by subsection (6), he is liable to a fine and, for continued contravention to a daily default fine.

CHAPTER X
MALPRACTICE BEFORE AND DURING LIQUIDATION; PENALISATION OF COMPANIES AND COMPANY OFFICERS; INVESTIGATIONS AND PROSECUTIONS

Offences of fraud, deception, etc

206. Fraud, etc in anticipation of winding up

(1) When a company is ordered to be wound up by the court, or passes a resolution for voluntary winding up, any person, being a past or present officer of the company, is deemed to have

committed an offence if, within the 12 months immediately preceding the commencement of the
winding up, he has—

   (a) concealed any part of the company's property to the value of £500 or more, or concealed
        any debt due to or from the company, or
   (b) fraudulently removed any part of the company's property to the value of £500 or more, or
   (c) concealed, destroyed, mutilated or falsified any book or paper affecting or relating to the
        company's property or affairs, or
   (d) made any false entry in any book or paper affecting or relating to the company's property or
        affairs, or
   (e) fraudulently parted with, altered or made any omission in any document affecting or relating
        to the company's property or affairs, or
   (f) pawned, pledged or disposed of any property of the company which has been obtained on
        credit and has not been paid for (unless the pawning, pledging or disposal was in the
        ordinary way of the company's business).

(2)   Such a person is deemed to have committed an offence if within the period above mentioned he
      has been privy to the doing by others of any of the things mentioned in paragraphs (c), (d) and (e)
      of subsection (1); and he commits an offence if, at any time after the commencement of the
      winding up, he does any of the things mentioned in paragraphs (a) to (f) of that subsection, or is
      privy to the doing by others of any of the things mentioned in paragraphs (c) to (e) of it.

(3)   For purposes of this section, "officer" includes a shadow director.

(4)   It is a defence—

   (a) for a person charged under paragraph (a) or (f) of subsection (1) (or under subsection (2) in
        respect of the things mentioned in either of those two paragraphs) to prove that he had no
        intent to defraud, and
   (b) for a person charged under paragraph (c) or (d) of subsection (1) (or under subsection (2) in
        respect of the things mentioned in either of those two paragraphs) to prove that he had no
        intent to conceal the state of affairs of the company or to defeat the law.

(5)   Where a person pawns, pledges or disposes of any property in circumstances which amount to an
      offence under subsection (1)(f), every person who takes in pawn or pledge, or otherwise receives,
      the property knowing it to be pawned, pledged or disposed of in such circumstances, is guilty of
      an offence.

(6)   A person guilty of an offence under this section is liable to imprisonment or a fine, or both.

(7)   The money sums specified in paragraphs (a) and (b) of subsection (1) are subject to increase or
      reduction by order under section 416 in Part XV.

207.   Transactions in fraud of creditors

(1)   When a company is ordered to be wound up by the court or passes a resolution for voluntary
      winding up, a person is deemed to have committed an offence if he, being at the time an officer of
      the company—

   (a) has made or caused to be made any gift or transfer of, or charge on, or has caused or
        connived at the levying of any execution against, the company's property, or
   (b) has concealed or removed any part of the company's property since, or within 2 months
        before, the date of any unsatisfied judgment or order for the payment of money obtained
        against the company.

(2)   A person is not guilty of an offence under this section—

   (a) by reason of conduct constituting an offence under subsection (1)(a) which occurred more
        than 5 years before the commencement of the winding up, or
   (b) if he proves that, at the time of the conduct constituting the offence, he had no intent to
        defraud the company's creditors.

(3)   A person guilty of an offence under this section is liable to imprisonment or a fine, or both.

208. Misconduct in course of winding up

(1) When a company is being wound up, whether by the court or voluntarily, any person, being a past or present officer of the company, commits an offence if he—

    (a) does not to the best of his knowledge and belief fully and truly discover to the liquidator all the company's property, and how and to whom and for what consideration and when the company disposed of any part of that property (except such part as has been disposed of in the ordinary way of the company's business), or

    (b) does not deliver up to the liquidator (or as he directs) all such part of the company's property as is in his custody or under his control, and which he is required by law to deliver up, or

    (c) does not deliver up to the liquidator (or as he directs) all books and papers in his custody or under his control belonging to the company and which he is required by law to deliver up, or

    (d) knowing or believing that a false debt has been proved by any person in the winding up, fails to inform the liquidator as soon as practicable, or

    (e) after the commencement of the winding up, prevents the production of any book or paper affecting or relating to the company's property or affairs.

(2) Such a person commits an offence if after the commencement of the winding up he attempts to account for any part of the company's property by fictitious losses or expenses; and he is deemed to have committed that offence if he has so attempted in connection with any qualifying decision procedure or deemed consent procedure of the company's creditors within the 12 months immediately preceding the commencement of the winding up.

(3) For purposes of this section, "officer" includes a shadow director.

(4) It is a defence—

    (a) for a person charged under paragraph (a), (b) or (c) of subsection (1) to prove that he had no intent to defraud, and

    (b) for a person charged under paragraph (e) of that subsection to prove that he had no intent to conceal the state of affairs of the company or to defeat the law.

(5) A person guilty of an offence under this section is liable to imprisonment or a fine, or both.

209. Falsification of company's books

(1) When a company is being wound up, an officer or contributory of the company commits an offence if he destroys, mutilates, alters or falsifies any books, papers or securities, or makes or is privy to the making of any false or fraudulent entry in any register, book of account or document belonging to the company with intent to defraud or deceive any person.

(2) A person guilty of an offence under this section is liable to imprisonment or a fine, or both.

210. Material omissions from statement relating to company's affairs

(1) When a company is being wound up, whether by the court or voluntarily, any person, being a past or present officer of the company, commits an offence if he makes any material omission in any statement relating to the company's affairs.

(2) When a company has been ordered to be wound up by the court, or has passed a resolution for voluntary winding up, any such person is deemed to have committed that offence if, prior to the winding up, he has made any material omission in any such statement.

(3) For purposes of this section, "officer" includes a shadow director.

(4) It is a defence for a person charged under this section to prove that he had no intent to defraud.

(5) A person guilty of an offence under this section is liable to imprisonment or a fine, or both.

211. False representations to creditors

(1) When a company is being wound up, whether by the court or voluntarily, any person, being a past or present officer of the company—

    (a) commits an offence if he makes any false representation or commits any other fraud for the purpose of obtaining the consent of the company's creditors or any of them to an agreement with reference to the company's affairs or to the winding up, and

(b)   is deemed to have committed that offence if, prior to the winding up, he has made any false representation, or committed any other fraud, for that purpose.

(2)   For purposes of this section, "officer" includes a shadow director.

(3)   A person guilty of an offence under this section is liable to imprisonment or a fine, or both.

Penalisation of directors and officers

212.   Summary remedy against delinquent directors, liquidators, etc

(1)   This section applies if in the course of the winding up of a company it appears that a person who—

(a)   is or has been an officer of the company,

(b)   has acted as liquidator… or administrative receiver of the company, or

(c)   not being a person falling within paragraph (a) or (b), is or has been concerned, or has taken part, in the promotion, formation or management of the company,

has misapplied or retained, or become accountable for, any money or other property of the company, or been guilty of any misfeasance or breach of any fiduciary or other duty in relation to the company.

(2)   The reference in subsection (1) to any misfeasance or breach of any fiduciary or other duty in relation to the company includes, in the case of a person who has acted as liquidator … of the company, any misfeasance or breach of any fiduciary or other duty in connection with the carrying out of his functions as liquidator … of the company.

(3)   The court may, on the application of the official receiver or the liquidator, or of any creditor or contributory, examine into the conduct of the person falling within subsection (1) and compel him—

(a)   to repay, restore or account for the money or property or any part of it, with interest at such rate as the court thinks just, or

(b)   to contribute such sum to the company's assets by way of compensation in respect of the misfeasance or breach of fiduciary or other duty as the court thinks just.

(4)   The power to make an application under subsection (3) in relation to a person who has acted as liquidator … of the company is not exercisable, except with the leave of the court, after he has had his release.

(5)   The power of a contributory to make an application under subsection (3) is not exercisable except with the leave of the court, but is exercisable notwithstanding that he will not benefit from any order the court may make on the application.

213.   Fraudulent trading

(1)   If in the course of the winding up of a company it appears that any business of the company has been carried on with intent to defraud creditors of the company or creditors of any other person, or for any fraudulent purpose, the following has effect.

(2)   The court, on the application of the liquidator may declare that any persons who were knowingly parties to the carrying on of the business in the manner above-mentioned are to be liable to make such contributions (if any) to the company's assets as the court thinks proper.

214.   Wrongful trading

(1)   Subject to subsection (3) below, if in the course of the winding up of a company it appears that subsection (2) of this section applies in relation to a person who is or has been a director of the company, the court, on the application of the liquidator, may declare that that person is to be liable to make such contribution (if any) to the company's assets as the court thinks proper.

(2)   This subsection applies in relation to a person if—

(a)   the company has gone into insolvent liquidation,

(b)   at some time before the commencement of the winding up of the company, that person knew or ought to have concluded that there was no reasonable prospect that the company would avoid going into insolvent liquidation or entering insolvent administration, and

(c)   that person was a director of the company at that time;

but the court shall not make a declaration under this section in any case where the time mentioned in paragraph (b) above was before 28th April 1986.

(3)   The court shall not make a declaration under this section with respect to any person if it is satisfied that after the condition specified in subsection (2)(b) was first satisfied in relation to him that person took every step with a view to minimising the potential loss to the company's creditors as (on the assumption that he had knowledge of the matter mentioned in subsection (2)(b)) he ought to have taken.

(4)   For the purposes of subsections (2) and (3), the facts which a director of a company ought to know or ascertain, the conclusions which he ought to reach and the steps which he ought to take are those which would be known or ascertained, or reached or taken, by a reasonably diligent person having both—

(a)   the general knowledge, skill and experience that may reasonably be expected of a person carrying out the same functions as are carried out by that director in relation to the company, and

(b)   the general knowledge, skill and experience that that director has.

(5)   The reference in subsection (4) to the functions carried out in relation to a company by a director of the company includes any functions which he does not carry out but which have been entrusted to him.

(6)   For the purposes of this section a company goes into insolvent liquidation if it goes into liquidation at a time when its assets are insufficient for the payment of its debts and other liabilities and the expenses of the winding up.

(6A)   For the purposes of this section a company enters insolvent administration if it enters administration at a time when its assets are insufficient for the payment of its debts and other liabilities and the expenses of the administration.

(7)   In this section "director" includes a shadow director.

(8)   This section is without prejudice to section 213.

215.   Proceedings under ss 213, 214

(1)   On the hearing of an application under section 213 or 214, the liquidator may himself give evidence or call witnesses.

(2)   Where under either section the court makes a declaration, it may give such further directions as it thinks proper for giving effect to the declaration; and in particular, the court may—

(a)   provide for the liability of any person under the declaration to be a charge on any debt or obligation due from the company to him, or on any mortgage or charge or any interest in a mortgage or charge on assets of the company held by or vested in him, or any person on his behalf, or any person claiming as assignee from or through the person liable or any person acting on his behalf, and

(b)   from time to time make such further order as may be necessary for enforcing any charge imposed under this subsection.

(3)   For the purposes of subsection (2), "assignee"—

(a)   includes a person to whom or in whose favour, by the directions of the person made liable, the debt, obligation, mortgage or charge was created, issued or transferred or the interest created, but

(b)   does not include an assignee for valuable consideration (not including consideration by way of marriage or the formation of a civil partnership) given in good faith and without notice of any of the matters on the ground of which the declaration is made.

(4)   Where the court makes a declaration under either section in relation to a person who is a creditor of the company, it may direct that the whole or any part of any debt owed by the company to that person and any interest thereon shall rank in priority after all other debts owed by the company and after any interest on those debts.

(5)   Sections 213 and 214 have effect notwithstanding that the person concerned may be criminally liable in respect of matters on the ground of which the declaration under the section is to be made.

216. **Restriction on re-use of company names**

(1)   This section applies to a person where a company ("the liquidating company") has gone into insolvent liquidation on or after the appointed day and he was a director or shadow director of the company at any time in the period of 12 months ending with the day before it went into liquidation.

(2)   For the purposes of this section, a name is a prohibited name in relation to such a person if—

    (a)   it is a name by which the liquidating company was known at any time in that period of 12 months, or

    (b)   it is a name which is so similar to a name falling within paragraph (a) as to suggest an association with that company.

(3)   Except with leave of the court or in such circumstances as may be prescribed, a person to whom this section applies shall not at any time in the period of 5 years beginning with the day on which the liquidating company went into liquidation—

    (a)   be a director of any other company that is known by a prohibited name, or

    (b)   in any way, whether directly or indirectly, be concerned or take part in the promotion, formation or management of any such company, or

    (c)   in any way, whether directly or indirectly, be concerned or take part in the carrying on of a business carried on (otherwise than by a company) under a prohibited name.

(4)   If a person acts in contravention of this section, he is liable to imprisonment or a fine, or both.

(5)   In subsection (3) "the court" means any court having jurisdiction to wind up companies; and on an application for leave under that subsection, the Secretary of State or the official receiver may appear and call the attention of the court to any matters which seem to him to be relevant.

(6)   References in this section, in relation to any time, to a name by which a company is known are to the name of the company at that time or to any name under which the company carries on business at that time.

(7)   For the purposes of this section a company goes into insolvent liquidation if it goes into liquidation at a time when its assets are insufficient for the payment of its debts and other liabilities and the expenses of the winding up.

(8)   In this section "company" includes a company which may be wound up under Part V of this Act.

217. **Personal liability for debts, following contravention of s 216**

(1)   A person is personally responsible for all the relevant debts of a company if at any time—

    (a)   in contravention of section 216, he is involved in the management of the company, or

    (b)   as a person who is involved in the management of the company, he acts or is willing to act on instructions given (without the leave of the court) by a person whom he knows at that time to be in contravention in relation to the company of section 216.

(2)   Where a person is personally responsible under this section for the relevant debts of a company, he is jointly and severally liable in respect of those debts with the company and any other person who, whether under this section or otherwise, is so liable.

(3)   For the purposes of this section the relevant debts of a company are—

    (a)   in relation to a person who is personally responsible under paragraph (a) of subsection (1), such debts and other liabilities of the company as are incurred at a time when that person was involved in the management of the company, and

    (b)   in relation to a person who is personally responsible under paragraph (b) of that subsection, such debts and other liabilities of the company as are incurred at a time when that person was acting or was willing to act on instructions given as mentioned in that paragraph.

(4)   For the purposes of this section, a person is involved in the management of a company if he is a director of the company or if he is concerned, whether directly or indirectly, or takes part, in the management of the company.

(5)   For the purposes of this section a person who, as a person involved in the management of a company, has at any time acted on instructions given (without the leave of the court) by a person whom he knew at that time to be in contravention in relation to the company of section 216 is

presumed, unless the contrary is shown, to have been willing at any time thereafter to act on any instructions given by that person.

(6)   In this section "company" includes a company which may be wound up under Part V.

Investigation and prosecution of malpractice

218.   Prosecution of delinquent officers and members of company

(1)   If it appears to the court in the course of a winding up by the court that any past or present officer, or any member, of the company has been guilty of any offence in relation to the company for which he is criminally liable, the court may (either on the application of a person interested in the winding up or of its own motion) direct the liquidator to refer the matter

　　　　(a)   in the case of a winding up in England and Wales, to the Secretary of State, and

　　　　(b)   in the case of a winding up in Scotland, to the Lord Advocate.

(2)   ...

(3)   If in the case of a winding up by the court in England and Wales it appears to the liquidator, not being the official receiver, that any past or present officer of the company, or any member of it, has been guilty of an offence in relation to the company for which he is criminally liable, the liquidator shall report the matter to the official receiver.

(4)   If it appears to the liquidator in the course of a voluntary winding up that any past or present officer of the company, or any member of it, has been guilty of an offence in relation to the company for which he is criminally liable, he shall forthwith report the matter—

　　　　(a)   in the case of a winding up in England and Wales, to the Secretary of State, and

　　　　(b)   in the case of a winding up in Scotland, to the Lord Advocate,

and shall furnish to the Secretary of State or (as the case may be) the Lord Advocate such information and give to him such access to and facilities for inspecting and taking copies of documents (being information or documents in the possession or under the control of the liquidator and relating to the matter in question) as the Secretary of State or (as the case may be) the Lord Advocate requires.

(5)   Where a report is made to the Secretary of State under subsection (4) he may, for the purpose of investigating the matter reported to him and such other matters relating to the affairs of the company as appear to him to require investigation, exercise any of the powers which are exercisable by inspectors appointed under section 431 or 432 of the Companies Act 1985 to investigate a company's affairs.

(6)   If it appears to the court in the course of a voluntary winding up that—

　　　　(a)   any past or present officer of the company, or any member of it, has been guilty as above-mentioned, and

　　　　(b)   no report with respect to the matter has been made by the liquidator ... under subsection (4),

the court may (on the application of any person interested in the winding up or of its own motion) direct the liquidator to make such a report.

On a report being made accordingly, this section has effect as though the report had been made in pursuance of subsection (4).

219.   Obligations arising under s 218

(1)   For the purpose of an investigation by the Secretary of State in consequence of a report made to him under section 218(4), any obligation imposed on a person by any provision of the Companies Act 1985 to produce documents or give information to, or otherwise to assist, inspectors appointed as mentioned in section 218(5) is to be regarded as an obligation similarly to assist the Secretary of State in his investigation.

(2)   An answer given by a person to a question put to him in exercise of the powers conferred by section 218(5) may be used in evidence against him.

(2A)   However, in criminal proceedings in which that person is charged with an offence to which this subsection applies—

　　　　(a)   no evidence relating to the answer may be adduced, and

　　　　(b)   no question relating to it may be asked,

by or on behalf of the prosecution, unless evidence relating to it is adduced, or a question relating to it is asked, in the proceedings by or on behalf of that person.

(2B)   Subsection (2A) applies to any offence other than—

    (a)   an offence under section 2 or 5 of the Perjury Act 1911 (false statements made on oath otherwise than in judicial proceedings or made otherwise than on oath), or

    (b)   an offence under section 44(1) or (2) of the Criminal Law (Consolidation) (Scotland) Act 1995 (false statements made on oath or otherwise than on oath).

(3)   Where criminal proceedings are instituted by the Director of Public Prosecutions, the Lord Advocate or the Secretary of State following any report or reference under section 218, it is the duty of the liquidator and every officer and agent of the company past and present (other than the defendant or defender) to give to the Director of Public Prosecutions, the Lord Advocate or the Secretary of State (as the case may be) all assistance in connection with the prosecution which he is reasonably able to give.

For this purpose "agent" includes any banker or solicitor of the company and any person employed by the company as auditor, whether that person is or is not an officer of the company.

(4)   If a person fails or neglects to give assistance in the manner required by subsection (3), the court may, on the application of the Director of Public Prosecutions, the Lord Advocate or the Secretary of State (as the case may be) direct the person to comply with that subsection; and if the application is made with respect to a liquidator, the court may (unless it appears that the failure or neglect to comply was due to the liquidator not having in his hands sufficient assets of the company to enable him to do so) direct that the costs shall be borne by the liquidator personally.

PART V
WINDING UP OF UNREGISTERED COMPANIES

220.   Meaning of "unregistered company"

For the purposes of this Part "unregistered company" includes any association and any company, with the exception of a company registered under the Companies Act 2006 in any part of the United Kingdom.

221.   Winding up of unregistered companies

(1)   Subject to the provisions of this Part, any unregistered company may be wound up under this Act; and all the provisions of this Act ... about winding up apply to an unregistered company with the exceptions and additions mentioned in the following subsections.

(2)   If an unregistered company has a principal place of business situated in Northern Ireland, it shall not be wound up under this Part unless it has a principal place of business situated in England and Wales or Scotland, or in both England and Wales and Scotland.

(3)   For the purpose of determining a court's winding-up jurisdiction, an unregistered company is deemed—

    (a)   to be registered in England and Wales or Scotland, according as its principal place of business is situated in England and Wales or Scotland, or

    (b)   if it has a principal place of business situated in both countries, to be registered in both countries;

and the principal place of business situated in that part of Great Britain in which proceedings are being instituted is, for all purposes of the winding up, deemed to be the registered office of the company.

(4)   No unregistered company shall be wound up under this Act voluntarily, except in accordance with the EU Regulation.

(5)   The circumstances in which an unregistered company may be wound up are as follows—

    (a)   if the company is dissolved, or has ceased to carry on business, or is carrying on business only for the purpose of winding up its affairs;

    (b)   if the company is unable to pay its debts;

    (c)   if the court is of opinion that it is just and equitable that the company should be wound up.

(6)   ...

(7)   In Scotland, an unregistered company which the Court of Session has jurisdiction to wind up may be wound up by the court if there is subsisting a floating charge over property comprised in the company's property and undertaking, and the court is satisfied that the security of the creditor entitled to the benefit of the floating charge is in jeopardy.

For this purpose a creditor's security is deemed to be in jeopardy if the court is satisfied that events have occurred or are about to occur which render it unreasonable in the creditor's interests that the company should retain power to dispose of the property which is subject to the floating charge.

222.   Inability to pay debts: unpaid creditor for £750 or more

(1)   An unregistered company is deemed (for the purposes of section 221) unable to pay its debts if there is a creditor, by assignment or otherwise, to whom the company is indebted in a sum exceeding £750 then due and—

(a)   the creditor has served on the company, by leaving at its principal place of business, or by delivering to the secretary or some director, manager or principal officer of the company, or by otherwise serving in such manner as the court may approve or direct, a written demand in the prescribed form requiring the company to pay the sum due, and

(b)   the company has for 3 weeks after the service of the demand neglected to pay the sum or to secure or compound for it to the creditor's satisfaction.

(2)   The money sum for the time being specified in subsection (1) is subject to increase or reduction by regulations under section 417 in Part XV; but no increase in the sum so specified affects any case in which the winding-up petition was presented before the coming into force of the increase.

223.   Inability to pay debts: debt remaining unsatisfied after action brought

An unregistered company is deemed (for the purposes of section 221) unable to pay its debts if an action or other proceeding has been instituted against any member for any debt or demand due, or claimed to be due, from the company, or from him in his character of member, and—

(a)   notice in writing of the institution of the action or proceeding has been served on the company by leaving it at the company's principal place of business (or by delivering it to the secretary, or some director, manager or principal officer of the company, or by otherwise serving it in such manner as the court may approve or direct), and

(b)   the company has not within 3 weeks after service of the notice paid, secured or compounded for the debt or demand, or procured the action or proceeding to be stayed or sisted, or indemnified the defendant or defender to his reasonable satisfaction against the action or proceeding, and against all costs, damages and expenses to be incurred by him because of it.

224.   Inability to pay debts: other cases

(1)   An unregistered company is deemed (for purposes of section 221) unable to pay its debts—

(a)   if in England and Wales execution or other process issued on a judgment, decree or order obtained in any court in favour of a creditor against the company, or any member of it as such, or any person authorised to be sued as nominal defendant on behalf of the company, is returned unsatisfied;

(b)   if in Scotland the induciae of a charge for payment on an extract decree, or an extract registered bond, or an extract registered protest, have expired without payment being made;

(c)   if in Northern Ireland a certificate of unenforceability has been granted in respect of any judgment, decree or order obtained as mentioned in paragraph (a);

(d)   if it is otherwise proved to the satisfaction of the court that the company is unable to pay its debts as they fall due.

(2)   An unregistered company is also deemed unable to pay its debts if it is proved to the satisfaction of the court that the value of the company's assets is less than the amount of its liabilities, taking into account its contingent and prospective liabilities.

225. Company incorporated outside Great Britain may be wound up though dissolved

(1) Where a company incorporated outside Great Britain which has been carrying on business in Great Britain ceases to carry on business in Great Britain, it may be wound up as an unregistered company under this Act, notwithstanding that it has been dissolved or otherwise ceased to exist as a company under or by virtue of the laws of the country under which it was incorporated.

(2) ...

226. Contributories in winding up of unregistered company

(1) In the event of an unregistered company being wound up, every person is deemed a contributory who is liable to pay or contribute to the payment of any debt or liability of the company, or to pay or contribute to the payment of any sum for the adjustment of the rights of members among themselves, or to pay or contribute to the payment of the expenses of winding up the company.

(2) Every contributory is liable to contribute to the company's assets all sums due from him in respect of any such liability as is mentioned above.

(3) In the case of an unregistered company engaged in or formed for working mines within the stannaries, a past member is not liable to contribute to the assets if he has ceased to be a member for 2 years or more either before the mine ceased to be worked or before the date of the winding-up order.

(4) ...

227. Power of court to stay, sist or restrain proceedings

The provisions of this Part with respect to staying, sisting or restraining actions and proceedings against a company at any time after the presentation of a petition for winding up and before the making of a winding-up order extend, in the case of an unregistered company, where the application to stay, sist or restrain is presented by a creditor, to actions and proceedings against any contributory of the company.

228. Actions stayed on winding-up order

Where an order has been made for winding up an unregistered company, no action or proceeding shall be proceeded with or commenced against any contributory of the company in respect of any debt of the company, except by leave of the court, and subject to such terms as the court may impose.

229. Provisions of this Part to be cumulative

(1) The provisions of this Part with respect to unregistered companies are in addition to and not in restriction of any provisions in Part IV with respect to winding up companies by the court; and the court or liquidator may exercise any powers or do any act in the case of unregistered companies which might be exercised or done by it or him in winding up companies registered under the Companies Act 2006 in England and Wales or Scotland.

(2) ...

PART VI
MISCELLANEOUS PROVISIONS APPLYING TO COMPANIES
WHICH ARE INSOLVENT OR IN LIQUIDATION

Office-holders

230. Holders of office to be qualified insolvency practitioners

(1) ...

(2) Where an administrative receiver of a company is appointed, he must be a person who is so qualified.

(3) Where a company goes into liquidation, the liquidator must be a person who is so qualified.

(4) Where a provisional liquidator is appointed, he must be a person who is so qualified.

(5) Subsections (3) and (4) are without prejudice to any enactment under which the official receiver is to be, or may be, liquidator or provisional liquidator.

231. Appointment to office of two or more persons

(1)   This section applies if an appointment or nomination of any person to the office of ... administrative receiver, liquidator or provisional liquidator—

(a)   relates to more than one person, or

(b)   has the effect that the office is to be held by more than one person.

(2)   The appointment or nomination shall declare whether any act required or authorised under any enactment to be done by the ... administrative receiver, liquidator or provisional liquidator is to be done by all or any one or more of the persons for the time being holding the office in question.

232. Validity of office-holder's acts

The acts of an individual as ... administrative receiver, liquidator or provisional liquidator of a company are valid notwithstanding any defect in his appointment, nomination or qualifications.

Management by administrators, liquidators, etc

233. Supplies of gas, water, electricity, etc

(1)   This section applies in the case of a company where—

(a)   the company enters administration, or

(b)   an administrative receiver is appointed, or

(ba)   ...

(c)   a voluntary arrangement approved under Part I, has taken effect, or

(d)   the company goes into liquidation, or

(e)   a provisional liquidator is appointed;

and "the office-holder" means the administrator, the administrative receiver, ... the supervisor of the voluntary arrangement, the liquidator or the provisional liquidator, as the case may be.

(2)   If a request is made by or with the concurrence of the office-holder for the giving, after the effective date, of any of the supplies mentioned in the next subsection, the supplier—

(a)   may make it a condition of the giving of the supply that the office-holder personally guarantees the payment of any charges in respect of the supply, but

(b)   shall not make it a condition of the giving of the supply, or do anything which has the effect of making it a condition of the giving of the supply, that any outstanding charges in respect of a supply given to the company before the effective date are paid.

(3)   The supplies referred to in subsection (2) are—

(a)   a supply of gas by a gas supplier within the meaning of Part I of the Gas Act 1986;

(aa)   a supply of gas by a person within paragraph 1 of Schedule 2A to the Gas Act 1986 (supply by landlords etc);

(b)   a supply of electricity by an electricity supplier within the meaning of Part I of the Electricity Act 1989;

(ba)   a supply of electricity by a class of person within Class A (small suppliers) or Class B (resale) of Schedule 4 to the Electricity (Class Exemptions from the Requirement for a Licence) Order 2001 (S.I. 2001/3270);

(c)   a supply of water by a water undertaker or, in Scotland, Scottish Water,

(ca)   a supply of water by a water supply licensee within the meaning of the Water Industry Act 1991;

(cb)   a supply of water by a water services provider within the meaning of the Water Services etc (Scotland) Act 2005;

(cc)   a supply of water by a person who has an interest in the premises to which the supply is given;

(d)   a supply of communications services by a provider of a public electronic communications service;

(e)   a supply of communications services by a person who carries on a business which includes giving such supplies;

(f)   a supply of goods or services mentioned in subsection (3A) by a person who carries on a business which includes giving such supplies, where the supply is for the purpose of enabling or facilitating anything to be done by electronic means.

(3A)   The goods and services referred to in subsection (3)(f) are—

(a)   point of sale terminals;

(b)   computer hardware and software;

(c)   information, advice and technical assistance in connection with the use of information technology;

(d)   data storage and processing;

(e)   website hosting.

(4)   "The effective date" for the purposes of this section is whichever is applicable of the following dates—

(a)   the date on which the company entered administration,

(b)   the date on which the administrative receiver was appointed (or, if he was appointed in succession to another administrative receiver, the date on which the first of his predecessors was appointed),

(ba)   ...

(c)   the date on which the voluntary arrangement took effect,

(d)   the date on which the company went into liquidation,

(e)   the date on which the provisional liquidator was appointed.

(5)   The following applies to expressions used in subsection (3)—

(a)–(c)...

(d)   "communications services" do not include electronic communications services to the extent that they are used to broadcast or otherwise transmit programme services (within the meaning of the Communications Act 2003).

233A.   Further protection of essential supplies

(1)   An insolvency-related term of a contract for the supply of essential goods or services to a company ceases to have effect if—

(a)   the company enters administration, or

(b)   a voluntary arrangement approved under Part 1 takes effect in relation to the company.

(2)   An insolvency-related term of a contract does not cease to have effect by virtue of subsection (1) to the extent that—

(a)   it provides for the contract or the supply to terminate, or any other thing to take place, because the company becomes subject to an insolvency procedure other than administration or a voluntary arrangement;

(b)   it entitles a supplier to terminate the contract or the supply, or do any other thing, because the company becomes subject to an insolvency procedure other than administration or a voluntary arrangement; or

(c)   it entitles a supplier to terminate the contract or the supply because of an event that occurs, or may occur, after the company enters administration or the voluntary arrangement takes effect.

(3)   Where an insolvency-related term of a contract ceases to have effect under this section the supplier may—

(a)   terminate the contract, if the condition in subsection (4) is met;

(b)   terminate the supply, if the condition in subsection (5) is met.

(4)   The condition in this subsection is that—

(a)   the insolvency office-holder consents to the termination of the contract,

(b)   the court grants permission for the termination of the contract, or

(c)   any charges in respect of the supply that are incurred after the company entered administration or the voluntary arrangement took effect are not paid within the period of 28 days beginning with the day on which payment is due.

The court may grant permission under paragraph (b) only if satisfied that the continuation of the contract would cause the supplier hardship.

(5) The condition in this subsection is that—

    (a) the supplier gives written notice to the insolvency office-holder that the supply will be terminated unless the office-holder personally guarantees the payment of any charges in respect of the continuation of the supply after the company entered administration or the voluntary arrangement took effect, and

    (b) the insolvency office-holder does not give that guarantee within the period of 14 days beginning with the day the notice is received.

(6) For the purposes of securing that the interests of suppliers are protected, where—

    (a) an insolvency-related term of a contract (the "original term") ceases to have effect by virtue of subsection (1), and

    (b) the company subsequently enters administration, or a voluntary arrangement subsequently has effect in relation to it,

the contract is treated for the purposes of subsections (1) to (5) as if, immediately before the subsequent administration is entered into or the subsequent voluntary arrangement takes effect, it included an insolvency-related term identical to the original term.

(7) A contract for the supply of essential goods or services is a contract for a supply mentioned in section 233(3).

(8) An insolvency-related term of a contract for the supply of essential goods or services to a company is a provision of the contract under which—

    (a) the contract or the supply would terminate, or any other thing would take place, because the company enters administration or the voluntary arrangement takes effect,

    (b) the supplier would be entitled to terminate the contract or the supply, or to do any other thing, because the company enters administration or the voluntary arrangement takes effect, or

    (c) the supplier would be entitled to terminate the contract or the supply because of an event that occurred before the company enters administration or the voluntary arrangement takes effect.

(9) In this section "insolvency office-holder" means—

    (a) in a case where a company enters administration, the administrator;

    (b) in a case where a voluntary arrangement under Part 1 takes effect in relation to a company, the supervisor of the voluntary arrangement.

(10) Subsection (1) does not have effect in relation to a contract entered into before 1st October 2015.

233B. Protection of supplies of goods and services

(1) This section applies where a company becomes subject to a relevant insolvency procedure.

(2) A company becomes subject to a relevant insolvency procedure for the purposes of this section where—

    (a) a moratorium under Part A1 comes into force for the company,

    (b) the company enters administration,

    (c) an administrative receiver of the company is appointed (otherwise than in succession to another administrative receiver),

    (d) a voluntary arrangement approved under Part 1 takes effect in relation to the company,

    (e) the company goes into liquidation,

    (f) a provisional liquidator of the company is appointed (otherwise than in succession to another provisional liquidator), or

    (g) a court order is made under section 901C(1) of the Companies Act 2006 in relation to the company (order summoning meeting relating to compromise or arrangement).

(3) A provision of a contract for the supply of goods or services to the company ceases to have effect when the company becomes subject to the relevant insolvency procedure if and to the extent that, under the provision—

(a) the contract or the supply would terminate, or any other thing would take place, because the company becomes subject to the relevant insolvency procedure, or

(b) the supplier would be entitled to terminate the contract or the supply, or to do any other thing, because the company becomes subject to the relevant insolvency procedure.

(4) Where—

(a) under a provision of a contract for the supply of goods or services to the company the supplier is entitled to terminate the contract or the supply because of an event occurring before the start of the insolvency period, and

(b) the entitlement arises before the start of that period,

the entitlement may not be exercised during that period.

(5) Where a provision of a contract ceases to have effect under subsection (3) or an entitlement under a provision of a contract is not exercisable under subsection (4), the supplier may terminate the contract if—

(a) in a case where the company has become subject to a relevant insolvency procedure as specified in subsection (2)(b), (c), (e) or (f), the office-holder consents to the termination of the contract,

(b) in any other case, the company consents to the termination of the contract, or

(c) the court is satisfied that the continuation of the contract would cause the supplier hardship and grants permission for the termination of the contract.

(6) Where a provision of a contract ceases to have effect under subsection (3) and the company becomes subject to a further relevant insolvency procedure, the supplier may terminate the contract in accordance with subsection (5)(a) to (c).

(7) The supplier shall not make it a condition of any supply of goods and services after the time when the company becomes subject to the relevant insolvency procedure, or do anything which has the effect of making it a condition of such a supply, that any outstanding charges in respect of a supply made to the company before that time are paid.

(8) In this section "the insolvency period", in relation to a relevant insolvency procedure, means the period beginning when the company becomes subject to the relevant insolvency procedure and ending—

(a) in the case of a moratorium under Part A1, when the moratorium comes to an end,

(b) in the case of the company entering administration, when the appointment of the administrator ceases to have effect under—

(i) paragraphs 76 to 84 of Schedule B1, or

(ii) an order under section 901F of the Companies Act 2006,

(c) in the case of the appointment of an administrative receiver of the company, when the receiver or any successor to the receiver ceases to hold office without a successor being appointed,

(d) in the case of a voluntary arrangement approved under Part 1 taking effect in relation to the company, when the arrangement ceases to have effect,

(e) in the case of the company going into liquidation, when—

(i) the liquidator complies with section 94(2), 106(2) or 146(3) (duties relating to final account), or

(ii) the appointment of the liquidator ceases to have effect under an order under section 901F of the Companies Act 2006,

(f) in the case of the appointment of a provisional liquidator for the company, when the provisional liquidator or any successor to the provisional liquidator ceases to hold office without a successor being appointed, and

(g) in the case of the making of a court order under section 901C(1) of the Companies Act 2006 in relation to the company, when—

(i) an order made by the court under section 901F of that Act takes effect, or

(ii) the court decides not to make such an order.

(9) In this section "office-holder", in relation to a company which has entered into an insolvency procedure as specified in subsection (2)(b), (c), (e) or (f), means the administrator, administrative receiver, liquidator or provisional liquidator respectively.

(10) Schedule 4ZZA provides for exclusions from the operation of this section.

233C. Powers to amend section 233B and Schedule 4ZZA

(1) The Secretary of State may by regulations omit any of paragraphs (a) to (g) of section 233B(2) (relevant insolvency procedures).

(2) The Secretary of State may by regulations amend Schedule 4ZZA so as to—

    (a) remove or amend any exclusion from section 233B for the time being specified there, or

    (b) add further exclusions from section 233B.

(3) In subsection (2), references to exclusions from section 233B are to circumstances in which section 233B, or any provision of that section, does not apply.

(4) The circumstances referred to in subsection (3) may be framed by reference to kinds of company, supplier, contract, goods or services or in any other way.

(5) Regulations under this section may make—

    (a) different provision for different purposes;

    (b) consequential provision;

    (c) transitional and supplementary provision.

(6) Regulations under this section made by virtue of subsection (5) may in particular make provision amending this Act or any other enactment whenever passed or made (including, if paragraph 1(1) or (2) of Schedule 4ZZA is omitted, provision omitting section 233A or 233 respectively).

(7) Regulations under subsection (1) may not omit section 233B(2)(c) unless the Secretary of State has first consulted the Scottish Ministers.

(8) In this section "enactment" includes an Act of the Scottish Parliament and an instrument made under such an Act.

(9) Regulations under this section are to be made by statutory instrument.

(10) A statutory instrument containing regulations under this section may not be made unless a draft of the instrument has been laid before and approved by a resolution of each House of Parliament.

234. Getting in the company's property

(1) This section applies in the case of a company where—

    (a) the company enters administration, or

    (b) an administrative receiver is appointed, or

    (c) the company goes into liquidation, or

    (d) a provisional liquidator is appointed;

and "the office-holder" means the administrator, the administrative receiver, the liquidator or the provisional liquidator, as the case may be.

(2) Where any person has in his possession or control any property, books, papers or records to which the company appears to be entitled, the court may require that person forthwith (or within such period as the court may direct) to pay, deliver, convey, surrender or transfer the property, books, papers or records to the office-holder.

(3) Where the office-holder—

    (a) seizes or disposes of any property which is not property of the company, and

    (b) at the time of seizure or disposal believes, and has reasonable grounds for believing, that he is entitled (whether in pursuance of an order of the court or otherwise) to seize or dispose of that property,

the next subsection has effect.

(4) In that case the office-holder—

    (a) is not liable to any person in respect of any loss or damage resulting from the seizure or disposal except in so far as that loss or damage is caused by the office-holder's own negligence, and

(b)   has a lien on the property, or the proceeds of its sale, for such expenses as were incurred in connection with the seizure or disposal.

235.   Duty to co-operate with office-holder

(1)   This section applies as does section 234; and it also applies, in the case of a company in respect of which a winding-up order has been made by the court in England and Wales, as if references to the office-holder included the official receiver, whether or not he is the liquidator.

(2)   Each of the persons mentioned in the next subsection shall—

    (a)   give to the office-holder such information concerning the company and its promotion, formation, business, dealings, affairs or property as the office-holder may at any time after the effective date reasonably require, and

    (b)   attend on the office-holder at such times as the latter may reasonably require.

(3)   The persons referred to above are—

    (a)   those who are or have at any time been officers of the company,

    (b)   those who have taken part in the formation of the company at any time within one year before the effective date,

    (c)   those who are in the employment of the company, or have been in its employment (including employment under a contract for services) within that year, and are in the office-holder's opinion capable of giving information which he requires,

    (d)   those who are, or have within that year been, officers of, or in the employment (including employment under a contract for services) of, another company which is, or within that year was, an officer of the company in question, and

    (e)   in the case of a company being wound up by the court, any person who has acted as administrator, administrative receiver or liquidator of the company.

(4)   For the purposes of subsections (2) and (3), "the effective date" is whichever is applicable of the following dates—

    (a)   the date on which the company entered administration,

    (b)   the date on which the administrative receiver was appointed or, if he was appointed in succession to another administrative receiver, the date on which the first of his predecessors was appointed,

    (c)   the date on which the provisional liquidator was appointed, and

    (d)   the date on which the company went into liquidation.

(5)   If a person without reasonable excuse fails to comply with any obligation imposed by this section, he is liable to a fine and, for contravention, to a daily default fine.

236.   Inquiry into company's dealings, etc

(1)   This section applies as does section 234; and it also applies in the case of a company in respect of which a winding-up order has been made by the court in England and Wales as if references to the office-holder included the official receiver, whether or not he is the liquidator.

(2)   The court may, on the application of the office-holder, summon to appear before it—

    (a)   any officer of the company,

    (b)   any person known or suspected to have in his possession any property of the company or supposed to be indebted to the company, or

    (c)   any person whom the court thinks capable of giving information concerning the promotion, formation, business, dealings, affairs or property of the company.

(3)   The court may require any such person as is mentioned in subsection (2)(a) to (c) to submit to the court an account of his dealings with the company or to produce any books, papers or other records in his possession or under his control relating to the company or the matters mentioned in paragraph (c) of the subsection.

(3A)   An account submitted to the court under subsection (3) must be contained in—

    (a)   a witness statement verified by a statement of truth (in England and Wales), and

    (b)   an affidavit (in Scotland).

(4)   The following applies in a case where—

(a) a person without reasonable excuse fails to appear before the court when he is summoned to do so under this section, or

(b) there are reasonable grounds for believing that a person has absconded, or is about to abscond, with a view to avoiding his appearance before the court under this section.

(5) The court may, for the purpose of bringing that person and anything in his possession before the court, cause a warrant to be issued to a constable or prescribed officer of the court—

(a) for the arrest of that person, and

(b) for the seizure of any books, papers, records, money or goods in that person's possession.

(6) The court may authorise a person arrested under such a warrant to be kept in custody, and anything seized under such a warrant to be held, in accordance with the rules, until that person is brought before the court under the warrant or until such other time as the court may order.

237. Court's enforcement powers under s 236

(1) If it appears to the court, on consideration of any evidence obtained under section 236 or this section, that any person has in his possession any property of the company, the court may, on the application of the office-holder, order that person to deliver the whole or any part of the property to the office-holder at such time, in such manner and on such terms as the court thinks fit.

(2) If it appears to the court, on consideration of any evidence so obtained, that any person is indebted to the company, the court may, on the application of the office-holder, order that person to pay to the office-holder, at such time and in such manner as the court may direct, the whole or any part of the amount due, whether in full discharge of the debt or otherwise, as the court thinks fit.

(3) The court may, if it thinks fit, order that any person who if within the jurisdiction of the court would be liable to be summoned to appear before it under section 236 or this section shall be examined in any part of the United Kingdom where he may for the time being be, or in a place outside the United Kingdom.

(4) Any person who appears or is brought before the court under section 236 or this section may be examined on oath, either orally or (except in Scotland) by interrogatories, concerning the company or the matters mentioned in section 236(2)(c).

Adjustment of prior transactions (administration and liquidation)

238. Transactions at an undervalue (England and Wales)

(1) This section applies in the case of a company where—

(a) the company enters administration, or

(b) the company goes into liquidation;

and "the office-holder" means the administrator or the liquidator, as the case may be.

(2) Where the company has at a relevant time (defined in section 240) entered into a transaction with any person at an undervalue, the office-holder may apply to the court for an order under this section.

(3) Subject as follows, the court shall, on such an application, make such order as it thinks fit for restoring the position to what it would have been if the company had not entered into that transaction.

(4) For the purposes of this section and section 241, a company enters into a transaction with a person at an undervalue if—

(a) the company makes a gift to that person or otherwise enters into a transaction with that person on terms that provide for the company to receive no consideration, or

(b) the company enters into a transaction with that person for a consideration the value of which, in money or money's worth, is significantly less than the value, in money or money's worth, of the consideration provided by the company.

(5) The court shall not make an order under this section in respect of a transaction at an undervalue if it is satisfied—

(a) that the company which entered into the transaction did so in good faith and for the purpose of carrying on its business, and

(b)   that at the time it did so there were reasonable grounds for believing that the transaction would benefit the company.

239.   Preferences (England and Wales)

(1)   This section applies as does section 238.

(2)   Where the company has at a relevant time (defined in the next section) given a preference to any person, the office-holder may apply to the court for an order under this section.

(3)   Subject as follows, the court shall, on such an application, make such order as it thinks fit for restoring the position to what it would have been if the company had not given that preference.

(4)   For the purposes of this section and section 241, a company gives a preference to a person if—

(a)   that person is one of the company's creditors or a surety or guarantor for any of the company's debts or other liabilities, and

(b)   the company does anything or suffers anything to be done which (in either case) has the effect of putting that person into a position which, in the event of the company going into insolvent liquidation, will be better than the position he would have been in if that thing had not been done.

(5)   The court shall not make an order under this section in respect of a preference given to any person unless the company which gave the preference was influenced in deciding to give it by a desire to produce in relation to that person the effect mentioned in subsection (4)(b).

(6)   A company which has given a preference to a person connected with the company (otherwise than by reason only of being its employee) at the time the preference was given is presumed, unless the contrary is shown, to have been influenced in deciding to give it by such a desire as is mentioned in subsection (5).

(7)   The fact that something has been done in pursuance of the order of a court does not, without more, prevent the doing or suffering of that thing from constituting the giving of a preference.

240.   "Relevant time" under ss 238, 239

(1)   Subject to the next subsection, the time at which a company enters into a transaction at an undervalue or gives a preference is a relevant time if the transaction is entered into, or the preference given—

(a)   in the case of a transaction at an undervalue or of a preference which is given to a person who is connected with the company (otherwise than by reason only of being its employee), at a time in the period of 2 years ending with the onset of insolvency (which expression is defined below),

(b)   in the case of a preference which is not such a transaction and is not so given, at a time in the period of 6 months ending with the onset of insolvency, ...

(c)   in either case, at a time between the making of an administration application in respect of the company and the making of an administration order on that application, and

(d)   in either case, at a time between the filing with the court of a copy of notice of intention to appoint an administrator under paragraph 14 or 22 of Schedule B1 and the making of an appointment under that paragraph.

(2)   Where a company enters into a transaction at an undervalue or gives a preference at a time mentioned in subsection (1)(a) or (b), that time is not a relevant time for the purposes of section 238 or 239 unless the company—

(a)   is at that time unable to pay its debts within the meaning of section 123 in Chapter VI of Part IV, or

(b)   becomes unable to pay its debts within the meaning of that section in consequence of the transaction or preference;

but the requirements of this subsection are presumed to be satisfied, unless the contrary is shown, in relation to any transaction at an undervalue which is entered into by a company with a person who is connected with the company.

(3)   For the purposes of subsection (1), the onset of insolvency is—

    (a)   in a case where section 238 or 239 applies by reason of an administrator of a company being appointed by administration order, the date on which the administration application is made,

    (b)   in a case where section 238 or 239 applies by reason of an administrator of a company being appointed under paragraph 14 or 22 of Schedule B1 following filing with the court of a copy of a notice of intention to appoint under that paragraph, the date on which the copy of the notice is filed,

    (c)   in a case where section 238 or 239 applies by reason of an administrator of a company being appointed otherwise than as mentioned in paragraph (a) or (b), the date on which the appointment takes effect,

    (d)   in a case where section 238 or 239 applies by reason of a company going into liquidation ... at the time when the appointment of an administrator ceases to have effect, the date on which the company entered administration (or, if relevant, the date on which the application for the administration order was made or a copy of the notice of intention to appoint was filed), and

    (e)   in a case where section 238 or 239 applies by reason of a company going into liquidation at any other time, the date of the commencement of the winding up.

241.   **Orders under ss 238, 239**

(1)   Without prejudice to the generality of sections 238(3) and 239(3), an order under either of those sections with respect to a transaction or preference entered into or given by a company may (subject to the next subsection)—

    (a)   require any property transferred as part of the transaction, or in connection with the giving of the preference, to be vested in the company,

    (b)   require any property to be so vested if it represents in any person's hands the application either of the proceeds of sale of property so transferred or of money so transferred,

    (c)   release or discharge (in whole or in part) any security given by the company,

    (d)   require any person to pay, in respect of benefits received by him from the company, such sums to the office-holder as the court may direct,

    (e)   provide for any surety or guarantor whose obligations to any person were released or discharged (in whole or in part) under the transaction, or by the giving of the preference, to be under such new or revived obligations to that person as the court thinks appropriate,

    (f)   provide for security to be provided for the discharge of any obligation imposed by or arising under the order, for such an obligation to be charged on any property and for the security or charge to have the same priority as a security or charge released or discharged (in whole or in part) under the transaction or by the giving of the preference, and

    (g)   provide for the extent to which any person whose property is vested by the order in the company, or on whom obligations are imposed by the order, is to be able to prove in the winding up of the company for debts or other liabilities which arose from, or were released or discharged (in whole or in part) under or by, the transaction or the giving of the preference.

(2)   An order under section 238 or 239 may affect the property of, or impose any obligation on, any person whether or not he is the person with whom the company in question entered into the transaction or (as the case may be) the person to whom the preference was given; but such an order—

    (a)   shall not prejudice any interest in property which was acquired from a person other than the company and was acquired in good faith and for value, or prejudice any interest deriving from such an interest, and

    (b)   shall not require a person who received a benefit from the transaction or preference in good faith and for value to pay a sum to the office-holder, except where that person was a party to the transaction or the payment is to be in respect of a preference given to that person at a time when he was a creditor of the company.

(2A)   Where a person has acquired an interest in property from a person other than the company in question, or has received a benefit from the transaction or preference, and at the time of that acquisition or receipt—

(a)   he had notice of the relevant surrounding circumstances and of the relevant proceedings, or

(b)   he was connected with, or was an associate of, either the company in question or the person with whom that company entered into the transaction or to whom that company gave the preference,

then, unless the contrary is shown, it shall be presumed for the purposes of paragraph (a) or (as the case may be) paragraph (b) of subsection (2) that the interest was acquired or the benefit was received otherwise than in good faith.

(3)   For the purposes of subsection (2A)(a), the relevant surrounding circumstances are (as the case may require)—

(a)   the fact that the company in question entered into the transaction at an undervalue; or

(b)   the circumstances which amounted to the giving of the preference by the company in question;

and subsections (3A) to (3C) have effect to determine whether, for those purposes, a person has notice of the relevant proceedings.

(3A)   Where section 238 or 239 applies by reason of a company's entering administration, a person has notice of the relevant proceedings if he has notice that—

(a)   an administration application has been made,

(b)   an administration order has been made,

(c)   a copy of a notice of intention to appoint an administrator under paragraph 14 or 22 of Schedule B1 has been filed, or

(d)   notice of the appointment of an administrator has been filed under paragraph 18 or 29 of that Schedule.

(3B)   Where section 238 or 239 applies by reason of a company's going into liquidation at the time when the appointment of an administrator of the company ceases to have effect, a person has notice of the relevant proceedings if he has notice that—

(a)   an administration application has been made,

(b)   an administration order has been made,

(c)   a copy of a notice of intention to appoint an administrator under paragraph 14 or 22 of Schedule B1 has been filed,

(d)   notice of the appointment of an administrator has been filed under paragraph 18 or 29 of that Schedule, or

(e)   the company has gone into liquidation.

(3C)   In a case where section 238 or 239 applies by reason of the company in question going into liquidation at any other time, a person has notice of the relevant proceedings if he has notice—

(a)   where the company goes into liquidation on the making of a winding-up order, of the fact that the petition on which the winding-up order is made has been presented or of the fact that the company has gone into liquidation;

(b)   in any other case, of the fact that the company has gone into liquidation.

(4)   The provisions of sections 238 to 241 apply without prejudice to the availability of any other remedy, even in relation to a transaction or preference which the company had no power to enter into or give.

242.   Gratuitous alienations (Scotland)

(1)   Where this subsection applies and—

(a)   the winding up of a company has commenced, an alienation by the company is challengeable by—

(i)   any creditor who is a creditor by virtue of a debt incurred on or before the date of such commencement, or

(ii)   the liquidator;

(b)   a company enters administration, an alienation by the company is challengeable by the administrator.

(2)   Subsection (1) applies where—

    (a)   by the alienation, whether before or after 1st April 1986 (the coming into force of section 75 of the Bankruptcy (Scotland) Act 1985), any part of the company's property is transferred or any claim or right of the company is discharged or renounced, and

    (b)   the alienation takes place on a relevant day.

(3)   For the purposes of subsection (2)(b), the day on which an alienation takes place is the day on which it becomes completely effectual; and in that subsection "relevant day" means, if the alienation has the effect of favouring—

    (a)   a person who is an associate (within the meaning of the Bankruptcy (Scotland) Act 2016) of the company, a day not earlier than 5 years before the date on which—

        (i)   the winding up of the company commences, or

        (ii)   as the case may be, the company enters administration; or

    (b)   any other person, a day not earlier than 2 years before that date.

(4)   On a challenge being brought under subsection (1), the court shall grant decree of reduction or for such restoration of property to the company's assets or other redress as may be appropriate; but the court shall not grant such a decree if the person seeking to uphold the alienation establishes—

    (a)   that immediately, or at any other time, after the alienation the company's assets were greater than its liabilities, or

    (b)   that the alienation was made for adequate consideration, or

    (c)   that the alienation—

        (i)   was a birthday, Christmas or other conventional gift, or

        (ii)   was a gift made, for a charitable purpose, to a person who is not an associate of the company,

which, having regard to all the circumstances, it was reasonable for the company to make.

Provided that this subsection is without prejudice to any right or interest acquired in good faith and for value from or through the transferee in the alienation.

(5)   In subsection (4) above, "charitable purpose" means any charitable, benevolent or philanthropic purpose, whether or not it is charitable within the meaning of any rule of law.

(6)   For the purposes of the foregoing provisions of this section, an alienation in implementation of a prior obligation is deemed to be one for which there was no consideration or no adequate consideration to the extent that the prior obligation was undertaken for no consideration or no adequate consideration.

(7)   A liquidator and an administrator have the same right as a creditor has under any rule of law to challenge an alienation of a company made for no consideration or no adequate consideration.

(8)   This section applies to Scotland only.

243.   **Unfair preferences (Scotland)**

(1)   Subject to subsection (2) below, subsection (4) below applies to a transaction entered into by a company, whether before or after 1st April 1986, which has the effect of creating a preference in favour of a creditor to the prejudice of the general body of creditors, being a preference created not earlier than 6 months before the commencement of the winding up of the company or the company enters administration.

(2)   Subsection (4) below does not apply to any of the following transactions—

    (a)   a transaction in the ordinary course of trade or business;

    (b)   a payment in cash for a debt which when it was paid had become payable, unless the transaction was collusive with the purpose of prejudicing the general body of creditors;

    (c)   a transaction whereby the parties to it undertake reciprocal obligations (whether the performance by the parties of their respective obligations occurs at the same time or at different times) unless the transaction was collusive as aforesaid;

    (d)   the granting of a mandate by a company authorising an arrestee to pay over the arrested funds or part thereof to the arrester where—

(i)   there has been a decree for payment or a warrant for summary diligence, and

(ii)   the decree or warrant has been preceded by an arrestment on the dependence of the action or followed by an arrestment in execution.

(3)   For the purposes of subsection (1) above, the day on which a preference was created is the day on which the preference became completely effectual.

(4)   A transaction to which this subsection applies is challengeable by—

(a)   in the case of a winding up—

(i)   any creditor who is a creditor by virtue of a debt incurred on or before the date of commencement of the winding up, or

(ii)   the liquidator; and

(b)   where the company has entered administration, the administrator.

(5)   On a challenge being brought under subsection (4) above, the court, if satisfied that the transaction challenged is a transaction to which this section applies, shall grant decree of reduction or for such restoration of property to the company's assets or other redress as may be appropriate:

Provided that this subsection is without prejudice to any right or interest acquired in good faith and for value from or through the creditor in whose favour the preference was created.

(6)   A liquidator and an administrator have the same right as a creditor has under any rule of law to challenge a preference created by a debtor.

(7)   This section applies to Scotland only.

244.   Extortionate credit transactions

(1)   This section applies as does section 238, and where the company is, or has been, a party to a transaction for, or involving, the provision of credit to the company.

(2)   The court may, on the application of the office-holder, make an order with respect to the transaction if the transaction is or was extortionate and was entered into in the period of 3 years ending with the day on which the company entered administration or went into liquidation.

(3)   For the purposes of this section a transaction is extortionate if, having regard to the risk accepted by the person providing the credit—

(a)   the terms of it are or were such as to require grossly exorbitant payments to be made (whether unconditionally or in certain contingencies) in respect of the provision of the credit, or

(b)   it otherwise grossly contravened ordinary principles of fair dealing;

and it shall be presumed, unless the contrary is proved, that a transaction with respect to which an application is made under this section is or, as the case may be, was extortionate.

(4)   An order under this section with respect to any transaction may contain such one or more of the following as the court thinks fit, that is to say—

(a)   provision setting aside the whole or part of any obligation created by the transaction,

(b)   provision otherwise varying the terms of the transaction or varying the terms on which any security for the purposes of the transaction is held,

(c)   provision requiring any person who is or was a party to the transaction to pay to the office-holder any sums paid to that person, by virtue of the transaction, by the company,

(d)   provision requiring any person to surrender to the office-holder any property held by him as security for the purposes of the transaction,

(e)   provision directing accounts to be taken between any persons.

(5)   The powers conferred by this section are exercisable in relation to any transaction concurrently with any powers exercisable in relation to that transaction as a transaction at an undervalue or under section 242 (gratuitous alienations in Scotland).

245.   Avoidance of certain floating charges

(1)   This section applies as does section 238, but applies to Scotland as well as to England and Wales.

(2)   Subject as follows, a floating charge on the company's undertaking or property created at a relevant time is invalid except to the extent of the aggregate of—

(a) the value of so much of the consideration for the creation of the charge as consists of money paid, or goods or services supplied, to the company at the same time as, or after, the creation of the charge,

(b) the value of so much of that consideration as consists of the discharge or reduction, at the same time as, or after the creation of the charge, of any debt of the company, and

(c) the amount of such interest (if any) as is payable on the amount falling within paragraph (a) or (b) in pursuance of any agreement under which the money was so paid, the goods or services were so supplied or the debt was so discharged or reduced.

(3) Subject to the next subsection, the time at which a floating charge is created by a company is a relevant time for the purposes of this section if the charge is created—

(a) in the case of a charge which is created in favour of a person who is connected with the company, at a time in the period of 2 years ending with the onset of insolvency,

(b) in the case of a charge which is created in favour of any other person, at a time in the period of 12 months ending with the onset of insolvency, ...

(c) in either case, at a time between the making of an administration application in respect of the company and the making of an administration order on that application, or

(d) in either case, at a time between the filing with the court of a copy of notice of intention to appoint an administrator under paragraph 14 or 22 of Schedule B1 and the making of an appointment under that paragraph.

(4) Where a company creates a floating charge at a time mentioned in subsection (3)(b) and the person in favour of whom the charge is created is not connected with the company, that time is not a relevant time for the purposes of this section unless the company—

(a) is at that time unable to pay its debts within the meaning of section 123 in Chapter VI of Part IV, or

(b) becomes unable to pay its debts within the meaning of that section in consequence of the transaction under which the charge is created.

(5) For the purposes of subsection (3), the onset of insolvency is—

(a) in a case where this section applies by reason of an administrator of a company being appointed by administration order, the date on which the administration application is made,

(b) in a case where this section applies by reason of an administrator of a company being appointed under paragraph 14 or 22 of Schedule B1 following filing with the court of a copy of notice of intention to appoint under that paragraph, the date on which the copy of the notice is filed,

(c) in a case where this section applies by reason of an administrator of a company being appointed otherwise than as mentioned in paragraph (a) or (b), the date on which the appointment takes effect, and

(d) in a case where this section applies by reason of a company going into liquidation, the date of the commencement of the winding up.

(6) For the purposes of subsection (2)(a) the value of any goods or services supplied by way of consideration for a floating charge is the amount in money which at the time they were supplied could reasonably have been expected to be obtained for supplying the goods or services in the ordinary course of business and on the same terms (apart from the consideration) as those on which they were supplied to the company.

246. Unenforceability of liens on books, etc

(1) This section applies in the case of a company where—

(a) the company enters administration, or

(b) the company goes into liquidation, or

(c) a provisional liquidator is appointed;

and "the office-holder" means the administrator, the liquidator or the provisional liquidator, as the case may be.

(2)   Subject as follows, a lien or other right to retain possession of any of the books, papers or other records of the company is unenforceable to the extent that its enforcement would deny possession of any books, papers or other records to the office-holder.

(3)   This does not apply to a lien on documents which give a title to property and are held as such.

Administration: penalisation of directors etc

246ZA. Fraudulent trading: administration

(1)   If while a company is in administration it appears that any business of the company has been carried on with intent to defraud creditors of the company or creditors of any other person, or for any fraudulent purpose, the following has effect.

(2)   The court, on the application of the administrator, may declare that any persons who were knowingly parties to the carrying on of the business in the manner mentioned in subsection (1) are to be liable to make such contributions (if any) to the company's assets as the court thinks proper.

246ZB. Wrongful trading: administration

(1)   Subject to subsection (3), if while a company is in administration it appears that subsection (2) applies in relation to a person who is or has been a director of the company, the court, on the application of the administrator, may declare that that person is to be liable to make such contribution (if any) to the company's assets as the court thinks proper.

(2)   This subsection applies in relation to a person if—

(a)   the company has entered insolvent administration,

(b)   at some time before the company entered administration, that person knew or ought to have concluded that there was no reasonable prospect that the company would avoid entering insolvent administration or going into insolvent liquidation, and

(c)   the person was a director of the company at that time.

(3)   The court must not make a declaration under this section with respect to any person if it is satisfied that, after the condition specified in subsection (2)(b) was first satisfied in relation to the person, the person took every step with a view to minimising the potential loss to the company's creditors as (on the assumption that the person had knowledge of the matter mentioned in subsection (2)(b)) the person ought to have taken.

(4)   For the purposes of subsections (2) and (3), the facts which a director of a company ought to know or ascertain, the conclusions which the director ought to reach and the steps which the director ought to take are those which would be known or ascertained, or reached or taken, by a reasonably diligent person having both—

(a)   the general knowledge, skill and experience that may reasonably be expected of a person carrying out the same functions as are carried out by that director in relation to the company, and

(b)   the general knowledge, skill and experience that that director has.

(5)   The reference in subsection (4) to the functions carried out in relation to a company by a director of the company includes any functions which the director does not carry out but which have been entrusted to the director.

(6)   For the purposes of this section—

(a)   a company enters insolvent administration if it enters administration at a time when its assets are insufficient for the payment of its debts and other liabilities and the expenses of the administration;

(b)   a company goes into insolvent liquidation if it goes into liquidation at a time when its assets are insufficient for the payment of its debts and other liabilities and the expenses of the winding up.

(7)   In this section "director" includes shadow director.

(8)   This section is without prejudice to section 246ZA.

246ZC. Proceedings under section 246ZA or 246ZB

Section 215 applies for the purposes of an application under section 246ZA or 246ZB as it applies for the purposes of an application under section 213 but as if the reference in subsection (1) of section 215 to the liquidator was a reference to the administrator.

Power to assign certain causes of action

246ZD. Power to assign

(1) This section applies in the case of a company where—
  (a) the company enters administration, or
  (b) the company goes into liquidation;
  and "the office-holder" means the administrator or the liquidator, as the case may be.

(2) The office-holder may assign a right of action (including the proceeds of an action) arising under or by virtue of any of the following—
  (za) section A43 (challenges to monitor remuneration in subsequent insolvency proceedings);
  (a) section 213 or 246ZA (fraudulent trading);
  (b) section 214 or 246ZB (wrongful trading);
  (c) section 238 (transactions at an undervalue (England and Wales));
  (d) section 239 (preferences (England and Wales));
  (e) section 242 (gratuitous alienations (Scotland));
  (f) section 243 (unfair preferences (Scotland));
  (g) section 244 (extortionate credit transactions).

Decisions by creditors and contributories

246ZE. Decisions by creditors and contributories: general

(1) This section applies where, for the purposes of this Group of Parts, a person ("P") seeks a decision about any matter from a company's creditors or contributories.

(2) The decision may be made by any qualifying decision procedure P thinks fit, except that it may not be made by a creditors' meeting or (as the case may be) a contributories' meeting unless subsection (3) applies.

(3) This subsection applies if at least the minimum number of creditors or (as the case may be) contributories make a request to P in writing that the decision be made by a creditors' meeting or (as the case may be) a contributories' meeting.

(4) If subsection (3) applies P must summon a creditors' meeting or (as the case may be) a contributories' meeting.

(5) Subsection (2) is subject to any provision of this Act, the rules or any other legislation, or any order of the court—
  (a) requiring a decision to be made, or prohibiting a decision from being made, by a particular qualifying decision procedure (other than a creditors' meeting or a contributories' meeting);
  (b) permitting or requiring a decision to be made by a creditors' meeting or a contributories' meeting.

(6) Section 246ZF provides that in certain cases the deemed consent procedure may be used instead of a qualifying decision procedure.

(7) For the purposes of subsection (3) the "minimum number" of creditors or contributories is any of the following—
  (a) 10% in value of the creditors or contributories;
  (b) 10% in number of the creditors or contributories;
  (c) 10 creditors or contributories.

(8) The references in subsection (7) to creditors are to creditors of any class, even where a decision is sought only from creditors of a particular class.

(9) In this section references to a meeting are to a meeting where the creditors or (as the case may be) contributories are invited to be present together at the same place (whether or not it is possible to attend the meeting without being present at that place).

(10)   Except as provided by subsection (8), references in this section to creditors include creditors of a
        particular class.

(11)   In this Group of Parts "qualifying decision procedure" means a procedure prescribed or
        authorised under paragraph 8A of Schedule 8.

246ZF. Deemed consent procedure

(1)   The deemed consent procedure may be used instead of a qualifying decision procedure where a
        company's creditors or contributories are to make a decision about any matter, unless—
        (a)   a decision about the matter is required by virtue of this Act, the rules, or any other
               legislation to be made by a qualifying decision procedure, or
        (b)   the court orders that a decision about the matter is to be made by a qualifying decision
               procedure.

(2)   If the rules provide for a company's creditors or contributories to make a decision about the
        remuneration of any person, they must provide that the decision is to be made by a qualifying
        decision procedure.

(3)   The deemed consent procedure is that the relevant creditors (other than opted-out creditors) or (as
        the case may be) the relevant contributories are given notice of—
        (a)   the matter about which they are to make a decision,
        (b)   the decision that the person giving the notice proposes should be made (the "proposed
               decision"),
        (c)   the effect of subsections (4) and (5), and
        (d)   the procedure for objecting to the proposed decision.

(4)   If less than the appropriate number of relevant creditors or (as the case may be) relevant
        contributories object to the proposed decision in accordance with the procedure set out in the
        notice, the creditors or (as the case may be) the contributories are to be treated as having made the
        proposed decision.

(5)   Otherwise—
        (a)   the creditors or (as the case may be) the contributories are to be treated as not having made a
               decision about the matter in question, and
        (b)   if a decision about that matter is again sought from the creditors or (as the case may be) the
               contributories, it must be sought using a qualifying decision procedure.

(6)   For the purposes of subsection (4) the "appropriate number" of relevant creditors or relevant
        contributories is 10% in value of those creditors or contributories.

(7)   "Relevant creditors" means the creditors who, if the decision were to be made by a qualifying
        decision procedure, would be entitled to vote in the procedure.

(8)   "Relevant contributories" means the contributories who, if the decision were to be made by a
        qualifying decision procedure, would be entitled to vote in the procedure.

(9)   In this section references to creditors include creditors of a particular class.

(10)   The rules may make further provision about the deemed consent procedure.

246ZG. Power to amend sections 246ZE and 246ZF

(1)   The Secretary of State may by regulations amend section 246ZE so as to change the definition
        of—
        (a)   the minimum number of creditors;
        (b)   the minimum number of contributories.

(2)   The Secretary of State may by regulations amend section 246ZF so as to change the definition
        of—
        (a)   the appropriate number of relevant creditors;
        (b)   the appropriate number of relevant contributories.

(3)   Regulations under this section may define the minimum number or the appropriate number by
        reference to any one or more of—
        (a)   a proportion in value,
        (b)   a proportion in number,

(c)   an absolute number,

and the definition may include alternative, cumulative or relative requirements.

(4)   Regulations under subsection (1) may define the minimum number of creditors or contributories by reference to all creditors or contributories, or by reference to creditors or contributories of a particular description.

(5)   Regulations under this section may make provision that will result in section 246ZE or 246ZF having different definitions for different cases, including—

(a)   for creditors and for contributories,

(b)   for different kinds of decisions.

(6)   Regulations under this section may make transitional provision.

(7)   The power of the Secretary of State to make regulations under this section is exercisable by statutory instrument.

(8)   A statutory instrument containing regulations under this section may not be made unless a draft of the instrument has been laid before, and approved by a resolution of, each House of Parliament.

Remote attendance at meetings

246A.   Remote attendance at meetings

(1)   Subject to subsection (2), this section applies to any meeting of the members of a company summoned by the office-holder under this Act or the rules, other than a meeting of the members of the company in a members' voluntary winding up.

(2)   This section does not apply where—

(a)   a company is being wound up in Scotland, or

(b)   a receiver is appointed under section 51 in Chapter 2 of Part 3.

(3)   Where the person summoning a meeting ("the convener") considers it appropriate, the meeting may be conducted and held in such a way that persons who are not present together at the same place may attend it.

(4)   Where a meeting is conducted and held in the manner referred to in subsection (3), a person attends the meeting if that person is able to exercise any rights which that person may have to speak and vote at the meeting.

(5)   For the purposes of this section—

(a)   a person is able to exercise the right to speak at a meeting when that person is in a position to communicate to all those attending the meeting, during the meeting, any information or opinions which that person has on the business of the meeting; and

(b)   a person is able to exercise the right to vote at a meeting when—

(i)   that person is able to vote, during the meeting, on resolutions put to the vote at the meeting, and

(ii)   that person's vote can be taken into account in determining whether or not such resolutions are passed at the same time as the votes of all the other persons attending the meeting.

(6)   The convener of a meeting which is to be conducted and held in the manner referred to in subsection (3) shall make whatever arrangements the convener considers appropriate to—

(a)   enable those attending the meeting to exercise their rights to speak or vote, and

(b)   ensure the identification of those attending the meeting and the security of any electronic means used to enable attendance.

(7)   Where in the reasonable opinion of the convener—

(a)   a meeting will be attended by persons who will not be present together at the same place, and

(b)   it is unnecessary or inexpedient to specify a place for the meeting,

any requirement under this Act or the rules to specify a place for the meeting may be satisfied by specifying the arrangements the convener proposes to enable persons to exercise their rights to speak or vote.

(8)   In making the arrangements referred to in subsection (6) and in forming the opinion referred to in subsection (7)(b), the convener must have regard to the legitimate interests of the members and others attending the meeting in the efficient despatch of the business of the meeting.

(9)   If—

      (a)   the notice of a meeting does not specify a place for the meeting,

      (b)   the convener is requested in accordance with the rules to specify a place for the meeting, and

      (c)   that request is made by members representing not less than ten percent of the total voting rights of all the members having at the date of the request a right to vote at the meeting,

      it shall be the duty of the convener to specify a place for the meeting.

(10)   In this section, "the office-holder", in relation to a company, means—

      (za) the monitor in relation to a moratorium under Part A1,

      (a)   its liquidator, provisional liquidator, administrator, or administrative receiver, or

      (b)   where a voluntary arrangement in relation to the company is proposed or has taken effect under Part 1, the nominee or the supervisor of the voluntary arrangement.

Note. This section is amended, in relation to Scotland, by S.S.I. 2017/209, art. 5, as from a day to be appointed (save for certain purposes).

Giving of notices etc by office-holders

246B.   Use of websites

(1)   Subject to subsection (2), where any provision of this Act or the rules requires the office-holder to give, deliver, furnish or send a notice or other document or information to any person, that requirement is satisfied by making the notice, document or information available on a website—

      (a)   in accordance with the rules, and

      (b)   in such circumstances as may be prescribed.

(2)   ...

(3)   In this section, "the office-holder" means—

      (za) the monitor in relation to a moratorium under Part A1,

      (a)   the liquidator, provisional liquidator, administrator, receiver (appointed under section 51), or administrative receiver of a company, or

      (b)   where a voluntary arrangement in relation to a company is proposed or has taken effect under Part 1, the nominee or the supervisor of the voluntary arrangement.

246C.   Creditors' ability to opt out of receiving certain notices

(1)   Any provision of the rules which requires an office-holder of a company to give a notice to creditors of the company does not apply, in circumstances prescribed by the rules, in relation to opted-out creditors.

(2)   Subsection (1)—

      (a)   does not apply in relation to a notice of a distribution or proposed distribution to creditors;

      (b)   is subject to any order of the court requiring a notice to be given to all creditors (or all creditors of a particular category).

(3)   Except as provided by the rules, a creditor may participate and vote in a qualifying decision procedure or a deemed consent procedure even though, by virtue of being an opted-out creditor, the creditor does not receive notice of it.

(4)   In this section—

      "give" includes deliver, furnish or send;

      "notice" includes any document or information in any other form;

      "office-holder", in relation to a company, means—

      (a)   a liquidator, provisional liquidator, administrator or administrative receiver of the company,

      (b)   a receiver appointed under section 51 in relation to any property of the company, or

      (c)   the supervisor of a voluntary arrangement which has taken effect under Part 1 in relation to the company.

PART VII
INTERPRETATION FOR FIRST GROUP OF PARTS

247. **"Insolvency" and "go into liquidation"**

(1) In this Group of Parts, except in so far as the context otherwise requires, "insolvency", in relation to a company, includes the coming into force of a moratorium for the company under Part A1, the approval of a voluntary arrangement under Part I, or the appointment of an administrator or administrative receiver.

(2) For the purposes of any provision in this Group of Parts, a company goes into liquidation if it passes a resolution for voluntary winding up or an order for its winding up is made by the court at a time when it has not already gone into liquidation by passing such a resolution.

(3) The reference to a resolution for voluntary winding up in subsection (2) includes a reference to a resolution which is deemed to occur by virtue of—

   (a) paragraph 83(6)(b) of Schedule B1, ...

   (b) ...

248. **"Secured creditor", etc**

In this Group of Parts, except in so far as the context otherwise requires—

   (a) "secured creditor", in relation to a company, means a creditor of the company who holds in respect of his debt a security over property of the company, and "unsecured creditor" is to be read accordingly; and

   (b) "security" means—

      (i) in relation to England and Wales, any mortgage, charge, lien or other security, and

      (ii) in relation to Scotland, any security (whether heritable or moveable), any floating charge and any right of lien or preference and any right of retention (other than a right of compensation or set off).

248A. **"Opted-out creditor"**

(1) For the purposes of this Group of Parts "opted-out creditor", in relation to an office-holder of a company, means a person who—

   (a) is a creditor of the company, and

   (b) in accordance with the rules has elected (or is deemed to have elected) to be (and not to cease to be) an opted-out creditor in relation to the office-holder.

(2) In this section, "office-holder", in relation to a company, means—

   (a) a liquidator, provisional liquidator, administrator or administrative receiver of the company,

   (b) a receiver appointed under section 51 in relation to any property of the company, or

   (c) the supervisor of a voluntary arrangement which has taken effect under Part 1 in relation to the company.

249. **"Connected" with a company**

For the purposes of any provision in this Group of Parts, a person is connected with a company if—

   (a) he is a director or shadow director of the company or an associate of such a director or shadow director, or

   (b) he is an associate of the company;

and "associate" has the meaning given by section 435 in Part XVIII of this Act.

250. **"Member" of a company**

For the purposes of any provision in this Group of Parts, a person who is not a member of a company but to whom shares in the company have been transferred, or transmitted by operation of law, is to be regarded as a member of the company, and references to a member or members are to be read accordingly.

251. **Expressions used generally**

In this Group of Parts, except in so far as the context otherwise requires—

"administrative receiver" means—

(a) an administrative receiver as defined by section 29(2) in Chapter I of Part III, or

(b) a receiver appointed under section 51 in Chapter II of that Part in a case where the whole (or substantially the whole) of the company's property is attached by the floating charge;

"agent" does not include a person's counsel acting as such;

"books and papers" and "books or papers" includes accounts, deeds, writing and documents;

"business day" means any day other than a Saturday, a Sunday, Christmas Day, Good Friday or a day which is a bank holiday in any part of Great Britain;

"chattel leasing agreement" means an agreement for the bailment or, in Scotland, the hiring of goods which is capable of subsisting for more than 3 months;

"contributory" has the meaning given by section 79;

"the court", in relation to a company, means a court having jurisdiction to wind up the company;

"deemed consent procedure" means the deemed consent procedure provided for by section 246ZF;

"director" includes any person occupying the position of director, by whatever name called;

"document" includes summons, notice, order and other legal process, and registers;

...

"floating charge" means a charge which, as created, was a floating charge and includes a floating charge within section 462 of the Companies Act (Scottish floating charges);

"the Gazette" means—

(a) as respects companies registered in England and Wales, the London Gazette;

(b) as respects companies registered in Scotland, the Edinburgh Gazette;

...

...

"officer", in relation to a body corporate, includes a director, manager or secretary;

"the official rate", in relation to interest, means the rate payable under section 189(4);

"prescribed" means prescribed by the rules;

"qualifying decision procedure" has the meaning given by section 246ZE(11);

"receiver", in the expression "receiver or manager", does not include a receiver appointed under section 51 in Chapter II of Part III;

"retention of title agreement" means an agreement for the sale of goods to a company, being an agreement—

(a) which does not constitute a charge on the goods, but

(b) under which, if the seller is not paid and the company is wound up, the seller will have priority over all other creditors of the company as respects the goods or any property representing the goods;

"the rules" means rules under section 411 in Part XV; and

"shadow director", in relation to a company, means a person in accordance with whose directions or instructions the directors of the company are accustomed to act, but so that a person is not deemed a shadow director by reason only that the directors act—

(a) on advice given by that person in a professional capacity;

(b) in accordance with instructions, a direction, guidance or advice given by that person in the exercise of a function conferred by or under an enactment (within the meaning given by section 1293 of the Companies Act 2006);

(c) in accordance with guidance or advice given by that person in that person's capacity as a Minister of the Crown (within the meaning of the Ministers of the Crown Act 1975).

THE SECOND GROUP OF PARTS
INSOLVENCY OF INDIVIDUALS; BANKRUPTCY

PART VIIA
DEBT RELIEF ORDERS

Preliminary

251A. Debt relief orders

(1) An individual who is unable to pay his debts may apply for an order under this Part ("a debt relief order") to be made in respect of his qualifying debts.

(2) In this Part "qualifying debt" means (subject to subsection (3)) a debt which—

(a) is for a liquidated sum payable either immediately or at some certain future time; and

(b) is not an excluded debt.

(3) A debt is not a qualifying debt to the extent that it is secured.

(4) In this Part "excluded debt" means a debt of any description prescribed for the purposes of this subsection.

Applications for a debt relief order

251B. Making of application

(1) An application for a debt relief order must be made to the official receiver through an approved intermediary.

(2) The application must include—

(a) a list of the debts to which the debtor is subject at the date of the application, specifying the amount of each debt (including any interest, penalty or other sum that has become payable in relation to that debt on or before that date) and the creditor to whom it is owed;

(b) details of any security held in respect of any of those debts; and

(c) such other information about the debtor's affairs (including his creditors, debts and liabilities and his income and assets) as may be prescribed.

(3) The rules may make further provision as to—

(a) the form of an application for a debt relief order;

(b) the manner in which an application is to be made; and

(c) information and documents to be supplied in support of an application.

(4) For the purposes of this Part an application is not to be regarded as having been made until—

(a) the application has been submitted to the official receiver; and

(b) any fee required in connection with the application by an order under section 415 has been paid to such person as the order may specify.

251C. Duty of official receiver to consider and determine application

(1) This section applies where an application for a debt relief order is made.

(2) The official receiver may stay consideration of the application until he has received answers to any queries raised with the debtor in relation to anything connected with the application.

(3) The official receiver must determine the application by—

(a) deciding whether to refuse the application;

(b) if he does not refuse it, by making a debt relief order in relation to the specified debts he is satisfied were qualifying debts of the debtor at the application date;

but he may only refuse the application if he is authorised or required to do so by any of the following provisions of this section.

(4) The official receiver may refuse the application if he considers that—

(a) the application does not meet all the requirements imposed by or under section 251B;

(b) any queries raised with the debtor have not been answered to the satisfaction of the official receiver within such time as he may specify when they are raised;

(c) the debtor has made any false representation or omission in making the application or on supplying any information or documents in support of it.

(5)   The official receiver must refuse the application if he is not satisfied that—
         (a)   the debtor is an individual who is unable to pay his debts;
         (b)   at least one of the specified debts was a qualifying debt of the debtor at the application date;
         (c)   each of the conditions set out in Part 1 of Schedule 4ZA is met.

(6)   The official receiver may refuse the application if he is not satisfied that each condition specified in Part 2 of Schedule 4ZA is met.

(7)   If the official receiver refuses an application he must give reasons for his refusal to the debtor in the prescribed manner.

(8)   In this section "specified debt" means a debt specified in the application.

251D.   Presumptions applicable to the determination of an application

(1)   The following presumptions are to apply to the determination of an application for a debt relief order.

(2)   The official receiver must presume that the debtor is an individual who is unable to pay his debts at the determination date if—
         (a)   that appears to the official receiver to be the case at the application date from the information supplied in the application and he has no reason to believe that the information supplied is incomplete or inaccurate; and
         (b)   he has no reason to believe that, by virtue of a change in the debtor's financial circumstances since the application date, the debtor may be able to pay his debts.

(3)   The official receiver must presume that a specified debt (of the amount specified in the application and owed to the creditor so specified) is a qualifying debt at the application date if—
         (a)   that appears to him to be the case from the information supplied in the application; and
         (b)   he has no reason to believe that the information supplied is incomplete or inaccurate.

(4)   The official receiver must presume that the condition specified in paragraph 1 of Schedule 4ZA is met if—
         (a)   that appears to him to be the case from the information supplied in the application;
         (b)   any prescribed verification checks relating to the condition have been made; and
         (c)   he has no reason to believe that the information supplied is incomplete or inaccurate.

(5)   The official receiver must presume that any other condition specified in Part 1 or 2 of Schedule 4ZA is met if—
         (a)   that appears to him to have been the case as at the application date from the information supplied in the application and he has no reason to believe that the information supplied is incomplete or inaccurate;
         (b)   any prescribed verification checks relating to the condition have been made; and
         (c)   he has no reason to believe that, by virtue of a change in circumstances since the application date, the condition may no longer be met.

(6)   References in this section to information supplied in the application include information supplied to the official receiver in support of the application.

(7)   In this section "specified debt" means a debt specified in the application.

Making and effect of debt relief order

251E.   Making of debt relief orders

(1)   This section applies where the official receiver makes a debt relief order on determining an application under section 251C

(2)   The order must be made in the prescribed form.

(3)   The order must include a list of the debts which the official receiver is satisfied were qualifying debts of the debtor at the application date, specifying the amount of the debt at that time and the creditor to whom it was then owed.

(4)   The official receiver must—
         (a)   give a copy of the order to the debtor; and
         (b)   make an entry for the order in the register containing the prescribed information about the order or the debtor.

(5) The rules may make provision as to other steps to be taken by the official receiver or the debtor on the making of the order.

(6) Those steps may include in particular notifying each creditor to whom a qualifying debt specified in the order is owed of—

    (a) the making of the order and its effect,

    (b) the grounds on which a creditor may object under section 251K, and

    (c) any other prescribed information.

(7) In this Part the date on which an entry relating to the making of a debt relief order is first made in the register is referred to as "the effective date".

251F. Effect of debt relief order on other debt management arrangements

(1) This section applies if—

    (a) a debt relief order is made, and

    (b) immediately before the order is made, other debt management arrangements are in force in respect of the debtor.

(2) The other debt management arrangements cease to be in force when the debt relief order is made.

(3) In this section "other debt management arrangements" means—

    (a) an administration order under Part 6 of the County Courts Act 1984;

    (b) an enforcement restriction order under Part 6A of that Act;

    (c) a debt repayment plan arranged in accordance with a debt management scheme that is approved under Chapter 4 of Part 5 of the Tribunals, Courts and Enforcement Act 2007.

251G. Moratorium from qualifying debts

(1) A moratorium commences on the effective date for a debt relief order in relation to each qualifying debt specified in the order ("a specified qualifying debt").

(2) During the moratorium, the creditor to whom a specified qualifying debt is owed—

    (a) has no remedy in respect of the debt, and

    (b) may not—

        (i) commence a creditor's petition in respect of the debt, or

        (ii) otherwise commence any action or other legal proceedings against the debtor for the debt,

    except with the permission of the court and on such terms as the court may impose.

(3) If on the effective date a creditor to whom a specified qualifying debt is owed has any such petition, action or other proceeding as mentioned in subsection (2)(b) pending in any court, the court may—

    (a) stay the proceedings on the petition, action or other proceedings (as the case may be), or

    (b) allow them to continue on such terms as the court thinks fit.

(4) In subsection (2)(a) and (b) references to the debt include a reference to any interest, penalty or other sum that becomes payable in relation to that debt after the application date.

(5) Nothing in this section affects the right of a secured creditor of the debtor to enforce his security.

251H. The moratorium period

(1) The moratorium relating to the qualifying debts specified in a debt relief order continues for the period of one year beginning with the effective date for the order, unless—

    (a) the moratorium terminates early; or

    (b) the moratorium period is extended by the official receiver under this section or by the court under section 251M.

(2) The official receiver may only extend the moratorium period for the purpose of—

    (a) carrying out or completing an investigation under section 251K;

    (b) taking any action he considers necessary (whether as a result of an investigation or otherwise) in relation to the order; or

    (c) in a case where he has decided to revoke the order, providing the debtor with the opportunity to make arrangements for making payments towards his debts.

(3)   The official receiver may not extend the moratorium period for the purpose mentioned in subsection (2)(a) without the permission of the court.

(4)   The official receiver may not extend the moratorium period beyond the end of the period of three months beginning after the end of the initial period of one year mentioned in subsection (1).

(5)   The moratorium period may be extended more than once, but any extension (whether by the official receiver or by the court) must be made before the moratorium would otherwise end.

(6)   References in this Part to a moratorium terminating early are to its terminating before the end of what would otherwise be the moratorium period, whether on the revocation of the order or by virtue of any other enactment.

251I.   Discharge from qualifying debts

(1)   Subject as follows, at the end of the moratorium applicable to a debt relief order the debtor is discharged from all the qualifying debts specified in the order (including all interest, penalties and other sums which may have become payable in relation to those debts since the application date).

(2)   Subsection (1) does not apply if the moratorium terminates early.

(3)   Subsection (1) does not apply in relation to any qualifying debt which the debtor incurred in respect of any fraud or fraudulent breach of trust to which the debtor was a party.

(4)   The discharge of the debtor under subsection (1) does not release any other person from—

     (a)   any liability (whether as partner or co-trustee of the debtor or otherwise) from which the debtor is released by the discharge; or

     (b)   any liability as surety for the debtor or as a person in the nature of such a surety.

(5)   If the order is revoked by the court under section 251M after the end of the moratorium period, the qualifying debts specified in the order shall (so far as practicable) be treated as though subsection (1) had never applied to them.

Duties of debtor

251J.   Providing assistance to official receiver etc

(1)   The duties in this section apply to a debtor at any time after the making of an application by him for a debt relief order.

(2)   The debtor must—

     (a)   give to the official receiver such information as to his affairs,

     (b)   attend on the official receiver at such times, and

     (c)   do all such other things,

as the official receiver may reasonably require for the purpose of carrying out his functions in relation to the application or, as the case may be, the debt relief order made as a result of the application.

(3)   The debtor must notify the official receiver as soon as reasonably practicable if he becomes aware of—

     (a)   any error in, or omission from, the information supplied to the official receiver in, or in support of, the application;

     (b)   any change in his circumstances between the application date and the determination date that would affect (or would have affected) the determination of the application.

(4)   The duties under subsections (2) and (3) apply after (as well as before) the determination of the application, for as long as the official receiver is able to exercise functions of the kind mentioned in subsection (2).

(5)   If a debt relief order is made as a result of the application, the debtor must notify the official receiver as soon as reasonably practicable if—

     (a)   there is an increase in his income during the moratorium period applicable to the order;

     (b)   he acquires any property or any property is devolved upon him during that period;

     (c)   he becomes aware of any error in or omission from any information supplied by him to the official receiver after the determination date.

(6)   A notification under subsection (3) or (5) must give the prescribed particulars (if any) of the matter being notified.

Objections, investigations and revocation

251K. Objections and investigations

(1)   Any person specified in a debt relief order as a creditor to whom a specified qualifying debt is owed may object to—

    (a)   the making of the order;

    (b)   the inclusion of the debt in the list of the debtor's qualifying debts; or

    (c)   the details of the debt specified in the order.

(2)   An objection under subsection (1) must be—

    (a)   made during the moratorium period relating to the order and within the prescribed period for objections;

    (b)   made to the official receiver in the prescribed manner;

    (c)   based on a prescribed ground;

    (d)   supported by any information and documents as may be prescribed;

    and the prescribed period mentioned in paragraph (a) must not be less than 28 days after the creditor in question has been notified of the making of the order.

(3)   The official receiver must consider every objection made to him under this section.

(4)   The official receiver may—

    (a)   as part of his consideration of an objection, or

    (b)   on his own initiative,

    carry out an investigation of any matter that appears to the official receiver to be relevant to the making of any decision mentioned in subsection (5) in relation to a debt relief order or the debtor.

(5)   The decisions to which an investigation may be directed are—

    (a)   whether the order should be revoked or amended under section 251L;

    (b)   whether an application should be made to the court under section 251M; or

    (c)   whether any other steps should be taken in relation to the debtor.

(6)   The power to carry out an investigation under this section is exercisable after (as well as during) the moratorium relating to the order.

(7)   The official receiver may require any person to give him such information and assistance as he may reasonably require in connection with an investigation under this section.

(8)   Subject to anything prescribed in the rules as to the procedure to be followed in carrying out an investigation under this section, an investigation may be carried out by the official receiver in such manner as he thinks fit.

251L. Power of official receiver to revoke or amend a debt relief order

(1)   The official receiver may revoke or amend a debt relief order during the applicable moratorium period in the circumstances provided for by this section.

(2)   The official receiver may revoke the order on the ground that—

    (a)   any information supplied to him by the debtor—

        (i)   in, or in support of, the application, or

        (ii) after the determination date,

        was incomplete, incorrect or otherwise misleading;

    (b)   the debtor has failed to comply with a duty under section 251J;

    (c)   a bankruptcy order has been made in relation to the debtor; or

    (d)   the debtor has made a proposal under Part 8 (or has notified the official receiver of his intention to do so).

(3)   The official receiver may revoke the order on the ground that he should not have been satisfied—

    (a)   that the debts specified in the order were qualifying debts of the debtor as at the application date;

    (b)   that the conditions specified in Part 1 of Schedule 4ZA were met;

    (c)   that the conditions specified in Part 2 of that Schedule were met or that any failure to meet such a condition did not prevent his making the order.

(4)   The official receiver may revoke the order on the ground that either or both of the conditions in paragraphs 7 and 8 of Schedule 4ZA (monthly surplus income and property) are not met at any time after the order was made.
        For this purpose those paragraphs are to be read as if references to the determination date were references to the time in question.

(5)   Where the official receiver decides to revoke the order, he may revoke it either—
        (a)   with immediate effect, or
        (b)   with effect from such date (not more than three months after the date of the decision) as he may specify.

(6)   In considering when the revocation should take effect the official receiver must consider (in the light of the grounds on which the decision to revoke was made and all the other circumstances of the case) whether the debtor ought to be given the opportunity to make arrangements for making payments towards his debts.

(7)   If the order has been revoked with effect from a specified date the official receiver may, if he thinks it appropriate to do so at any time before that date, revoke the order with immediate effect.

(8)   The official receiver may amend a debt relief order for the purpose of correcting an error in or omission from anything specified in the order.

(9)   But subsection (8) does not permit the official receiver to add any debts that were not specified in the application for the debt relief order to the list of qualifying debts.

(10)   The rules may make further provision as to the procedure to be followed by the official receiver in the exercise of his powers under this section.

Role of the court

251M. Powers of court in relation to debt relief orders

(1)   Any person may make an application to the court if he is dissatisfied by any act, omission or decision of the official receiver in connection with a debt relief order or an application for such an order.

(2)   The official receiver may make an application to the court for directions or an order in relation to any matter arising in connection with a debt relief order or an application for such an order.

(3)   The matters referred to in subsection (2) include, among other things, matters relating to the debtor's compliance with any duty arising under section 251J.

(4)   An application under this section may, subject to anything in the rules, be made at any time.

(5)   The court may extend the moratorium period applicable to a debt relief order for the purposes of determining an application under this section.

(6)   On an application under this section the court may dismiss the application or do one or more of the following—
        (a)   quash the whole or part of any act or decision of the official receiver;
        (b)   give the official receiver directions (including a direction that he reconsider any matter in relation to which his act or decision has been quashed under paragraph (a));
        (c)   make an order for the enforcement of any obligation on the debtor arising by virtue of a duty under section 251J;
        (d)   extend the moratorium period applicable to the debt relief order;
        (e)   make an order revoking or amending the debt relief order;
        (f)   make an order under section 251N; or
        (g)   make such other order as the court thinks fit.

(7)   An order under subsection (6)(e) for the revocation of a debt relief order—
        (a)   may be made during the moratorium period applicable to the debt relief order or at any time after that period has ended;
        (b)   may be made on the court's own motion if the court has made a bankruptcy order in relation to the debtor during that period;
        (c)   may provide for the revocation of the order to take effect on such terms and at such a time as the court may specify.

(8)   An order under subsection (6)(e) for the amendment of a debt relief order may not add any debts that were not specified in the application for the debt relief order to the list of qualifying debts.

251N. Inquiry into debtor's dealings and property

(1)   An order under this section may be made by the court on the application of the official receiver.

(2)   An order under this section is an order summoning any of the following persons to appear before the court—

(a)   the debtor;

(b)   the debtor's spouse or former spouse or the debtor's civil partner or former civil partner;

(c)   any person appearing to the court to be able to give information or assistance concerning the debtor or his dealings, affairs and property.

(3)   The court may require a person falling within subsection (2)(c)—

(a)   to provide a written account of his dealings with the debtor; or

(b)   to produce any documents in his possession or under his control relating to the debtor or to the debtor's dealings, affairs or property.

(4)   Subsection (5) applies where a person fails without reasonable excuse to appear before the court when he is summoned to do so by an order under this section.

(5)   The court may cause a warrant to be issued to a constable or prescribed officer of the court—

(a)   for the arrest of that person, and

(b)   for the seizure of any records or other documents in that person's possession.

(6)   The court may authorise a person arrested under such a warrant to be kept in custody, and anything seized under such a warrant to be held, in accordance with the rules, until that person is brought before the court under the warrant or until such other time as the court may order.

Offences

251O. False representations and omissions

(1)   A person who makes an application for a debt relief order is guilty of an offence if he knowingly or recklessly makes any false representation or omission in making the application or providing any information or documents to the official receiver in support of the application.

(2)   A person who makes an application for a debt relief order is guilty of an offence if—

(a)   he intentionally fails to comply with a duty under section 251J(3) in connection with the application; or

(b)   he knowingly or recklessly makes any false representation or omission in providing any information to the official receiver in connection with such a duty or otherwise in connection with the application.

(3)   It is immaterial for the purposes of an offence under subsection (1) or (2) whether or not a debt relief order is made as a result of the application.

(4)   A person in respect of whom a debt relief order is made is guilty of an offence if—

(a)   he intentionally fails to comply with a duty under section 251J(5) in connection with the order; or

(b)   he knowingly or recklessly makes any false representation or omission in providing information to the official receiver in connection with such a duty or otherwise in connection with the performance by the official receiver of functions in relation to the order.

(5)   It is immaterial for the purposes of an offence under subsection (4)—

(a)   whether the offence is committed during or after the moratorium period; and

(b)   whether or not the order is revoked after the conduct constituting the offence takes place.

251P. Concealment or falsification of documents

(1)   A person in respect of whom a debt relief order is made is guilty of an offence if, during the moratorium period in relation to that order—

(a)   he does not provide, at the request of the official receiver, all his books, papers and other records of which he has possession or control and which relate to his affairs;

(b)   he prevents the production to the official receiver of any books, papers or other records relating to his affairs;

(c)   he conceals, destroys, mutilates or falsifies, or causes or permits the concealment, destruction, mutilation or falsification of, any books, papers or other records relating his affairs;

(d)   he makes, or causes or permits the making of, any false entries in any book, document or record relating to his affairs; or

(e)   he disposes of, or alters or makes any omission in, or causes or permits the disposal, altering or making of any omission in, any book, document or record relating to his affairs.

(2)   A person in respect of whom a debt relief order is made is guilty of an offence if—

(a)   he did anything falling within paragraphs (c) to (e) of subsection (1) during the period of 12 months ending with the application date; or

(b)   he did anything falling within paragraphs (b) to (e) of subsection (1) after that date but before the effective date.

(3)   A person is not guilty of an offence under this section if he proves that, in respect of the conduct constituting the offence, he had no intent to defraud or to conceal the state of his affairs.

(4)   In its application to a trading record subsection (2)(a) has effect as if the reference to 12 months were a reference to two years.

(5)   In subsection (4) "trading record" means a book, document or record which shows or explains the transactions or financial position of a person's business, including—

(a)   a periodic record of cash paid and received,

(b)   a statement of periodic stock-taking, and

(c)   except in the case of goods sold by way of retail trade, a record of goods sold and purchased which identifies the buyer and seller or enables them to be identified.

(6)   It is immaterial for the purposes of an offence under this section whether or not the debt relief order in question is revoked after the conduct constituting the offence takes place (but no offence is committed under this section by virtue of conduct occurring after the order is revoked).

251Q.   Fraudulent disposal of property

(1)   A person in respect of whom a debt relief order is made is guilty of an offence if he made or caused to be made any gift or transfer of his property during the period between—

(a)   the start of the period of two years ending with the application date; and

(b)   the end of the moratorium period.

(2)   The reference in subsection (1) to making a transfer of any property includes causing or conniving at the levying of any execution against that property.

(3)   A person is not guilty of an offence under this section if he proves that, in respect of the conduct constituting the offence, he had no intent to defraud or to conceal the state of his affairs.

(4)   For the purposes of subsection (3) a person is to be taken to have proved that he had no such intent if—

(a)   sufficient evidence is adduced to raise an issue as to whether he had such intent; and

(b)   the contrary is not proved beyond reasonable doubt.

(5)   It is immaterial for the purposes of this section whether or not the debt relief order in question is revoked after the conduct constituting an offence takes place (but no offence is committed by virtue of conduct occurring after the order is revoked).

251R.   Fraudulent dealing with property obtained on credit

(1)   A person in respect of whom a debt relief order is made is guilty of an offence if during the relevant period he disposed of any property which he had obtained on credit and, at the time he disposed of it, had not paid for it.

(2)   Any other person is guilty of an offence if during the relevant period he acquired or received property from a person in respect of whom a debt relief order was made (the "debtor") knowing or believing—

(a)   that the debtor owed money in respect of the property, and

(b)   that the debtor did not intend, or was unlikely to be able, to pay the money he so owed.

(3)   In subsections (1) and (2) "relevant period" means the period between—

(a)   the start of the period of two years ending with the application date; and

(b)   the determination date.

(4)   A person is not guilty of an offence under subsection (1) or (2) if the disposal, acquisition or receipt of the property was in the ordinary course of a business carried on by the debtor at the time of the disposal, acquisition or receipt.

(5)   In determining for the purposes of subsection (4) whether any property is disposed of, acquired or received in the ordinary course of a business carried on by the debtor, regard may be had, in particular, to the price paid for the property.

(6)   A person is not guilty of an offence under subsection (1) if he proves that, in respect of the conduct constituting the offence, he had no intent to defraud or to conceal the state of his affairs.

(7)   In this section references to disposing of property include pawning or pledging it; and references to acquiring or receiving property shall be read accordingly.

(8)   It is immaterial for the purposes of this section whether or not the debt relief order in question is revoked after the conduct constituting an offence takes place (but no offence is committed by virtue of conduct occurring after the order is revoked).

251S. Obtaining credit or engaging in business

(1)   A person in respect of whom a debt relief order is made is guilty of an offence if, during the relevant period—

(a)   he obtains credit (either alone or jointly with any other person) without giving the person from whom he obtains the credit the relevant information about his status; or

(b)   he engages directly or indirectly in any business under a name other than that in which the order was made without disclosing to all persons with whom he enters into any business transaction the name in which the order was made.

(2)   For the purposes of subsection (1)(a) the relevant information about a person's status is the information that—

(a)   a moratorium is in force in relation to the debt relief order,

(b)   a debt relief restrictions order is in force in respect of him, or

(c)   both a moratorium and a debt relief restrictions order is in force,

as the case may be.

(3)   In subsection (1) "relevant period" means—

(a)   the moratorium period relating to the debt relief order, or

(b)   the period for which a debt relief restrictions order is in force in respect of the person in respect of whom the debt relief order is made, as the case may be.

(4)   Subsection (1)(a) does not apply if the amount of the credit is less than the prescribed amount (if any).

(5)   The reference in subsection (1)(a) to a person obtaining credit includes the following cases—

(a)   where goods are bailed to him under a hire-purchase agreement, or agreed to be sold to him under a conditional sale agreement;

(b)   where he is paid in advance (in money or otherwise) for the supply of goods or services.

251T. Offences: supplementary

(1)   Proceedings for an offence under this Part may only be instituted by the Secretary of State or by or with the consent of the Director of Public Prosecutions.

(2)   It is not a defence in proceedings for an offence under this Part that anything relied on, in whole or in part, as constituting the offence was done outside England and Wales.

(3)   A person guilty of an offence under this Part is liable to imprisonment or a fine, or both (but see section 430).

Supplementary

251U. Approved intermediaries

(1) In this Part "approved intermediary" means an individual for the time being approved by a competent authority to act as an intermediary between a person wishing to make an application for a debt relief order and the official receiver.

(2) In this section "competent authority" means a person or body for the time being designated by the Secretary of State for the purposes of granting approvals under this section.

(3) Designation as a competent authority may be limited so as to permit the authority only to approve persons of a particular description.

(4) The Secretary of State may by regulations make provision as to—
   (a)   the procedure for designating persons or bodies as competent authorities;
   (b)   descriptions of individuals who are ineligible to be approved under this section;
   (c)   the procedure for granting approvals under this section;
   (d)   the withdrawal of designations or approvals under this section;
   and provision made under paragraph (a) or (c) may include provision requiring the payment of fees.

(5) The rules may make provision about the activities to be carried out by an approved intermediary in connection with an application for a debt relief order, which may in particular include—
   (a)   assisting the debtor in making the application;
   (b)   checking that the application has been properly completed;
   (c)   sending the application to the official receiver.

(6) The rules may also make provision about other activities to be carried out by approved intermediaries.

(7) An approved intermediary may not charge a debtor any fee in connection with an application for a debt relief order.

(8) An approved intermediary is not liable to any person in damages for anything done or omitted to be done when acting (or purporting to act) as an approved intermediary in connection with a particular application by a debtor for a debt relief order.

(9) Subsection (8) does not apply if the act or omission was in bad faith.

(10) Regulations under subsection (4) shall be made by statutory instrument subject to annulment in pursuance of a resolution of either House of Parliament.

251V. Debt relief restrictions orders and undertakings

Schedule 4ZB (which makes provision about debt relief restrictions orders and debt relief restrictions undertakings) has effect.

251W. Register of debt relief orders etc

The Secretary of State must maintain a register of matters relating to—
   (a)   debt relief orders;
   (b)   debt relief restrictions orders; and
   (c)   debt relief restrictions undertakings.

251X. Interpretation

(1) In this Part—
   "the application date", in relation to a debt relief order or an application for a debt relief order, means the date on which the application for the order is made to the official receiver;
   "approved intermediary" has the meaning given in section 251U(1);
   "debt relief order" means an order made by the official receiver under this Part;
   "debtor" means—
   (a)   in relation to an application for a debt relief order, the applicant; and
   (b)   in relation to a debt relief order, the person in relation to whom the order is made;
   "debt relief restrictions order" and "debt relief restrictions undertaking" means an order made, or an undertaking accepted, under Schedule 4ZB;

"the determination date", in relation to a debt relief order or an application for a debt relief order, means the date on which the application for the order is determined by the official receiver;

"the effective date" has the meaning given in section 251E(7);

"excluded debt" is to be construed in accordance with section 251A;

"moratorium" and "moratorium period" are to be construed in accordance with sections 251G and 251H;

"qualifying debt", in relation to a debtor, has the meaning given in section 251A(2);

"the register" means the register maintained under section 251W;

"specified qualifying debt" has the meaning given in section 251G(1).

(2) In this Part references to a creditor specified in a debt relief order as the person to whom a qualifying debt is owed by the debtor include a reference to any person to whom the right to claim the whole or any part of the debt has passed, by assignment or operation of law, after the date of the application for the order.

PART VIII
INDIVIDUAL VOLUNTARY ARRANGEMENTS

Moratorium for insolvent debtor

252. Interim order of court

(1) In the circumstances specified below, the court may in the case of a debtor (being an individual) make an interim order under this section.

(2) An interim order has the effect that, during the period for which it is in force—

    (a) no bankruptcy petition relating to the debtor may be presented or proceeded with,

    (aa) no landlord or other person to whom rent is payable may exercise any right of forfeiture by peaceable re-entry in relation to premises let to the debtor in respect of a failure by the debtor to comply with any term or condition of his tenancy of such premises, except with the leave of the court, and

    (b) no other proceedings, and no execution or other legal process, may be commenced or continued and no distress may be levied against the debtor or his property except with the leave of the court.

253. Application for interim order

(1) Application to the court for an interim order may be made where the debtor intends to make a proposal under this Part, that is, a proposal to his creditors for a composition in satisfaction of his debts or a scheme of arrangement of his affairs (from here on referred to, in either case, as a "voluntary arrangement").

(2) The proposal must provide for some person ("the nominee") to act in relation to the voluntary arrangement either as trustee or otherwise for the purpose of supervising its implementation and the nominee must be a person who is qualified to act as an insolvency practitioner, or authorised to act as nominee, in relation to the voluntary arrangement.

(3) Subject as follows, the application may be made—

    (a) if the debtor is an undischarged bankrupt, by the debtor, the trustee of his estate, or the official receiver, and

    (b) in any other case, by the debtor.

(4) An application shall not be made under subsection (3)(a) unless the debtor has given notice of the proposal to the official receiver and, if there is one, the trustee of his estate.

(5) …

254. Effect of application

(1) At any time when an application under section 253 for an interim order is pending,

    (a) no landlord or other person to whom rent is payable may exercise any right of forfeiture by peaceable re-entry in relation to premises let to the debtor in respect of a failure by the debtor to comply with any term or condition of his tenancy of such premises, except with the leave of the court, and

(b)   the court may forbid the levying of any distress on the debtor's property or its subsequent sale, or both, and stay any action, execution or other legal process against the property or person of the debtor.

(2)   Any court in which proceedings are pending against an individual may, on proof that an application under that section has been made in respect of that individual, either stay the proceedings or allow them to continue on such terms as it thinks fit.

255.   Cases in which interim order can be made

(1)   The court shall not make an interim order on an application under section 253 unless it is satisfied—

(a)   that the debtor intends to make a proposal under this Part;

(b)   that on the day of the making of the application the debtor was an undischarged bankrupt or was able to make a bankruptcy application;

(c)   that no previous application has been made by the debtor for an interim order in the period of 12 months ending with that day; and

(d)   that the nominee under the debtor's proposal … is willing to act in relation to the proposal.

(2)   The court may make an order if it thinks that it would be appropriate to do so for the purpose of facilitating the consideration and implementation of the debtor's proposal.

(3)   Where the debtor is an undischarged bankrupt, the interim order may contain provision as to the conduct of the bankruptcy, and the administration of the bankrupt's estate, during the period for which the order is in force.

(4)   Subject as follows, the provision contained in an interim order by virtue of subsection (3) may include provision staying proceedings in the bankruptcy or modifying any provision in this Group of Parts, and any provision of the rules in their application to the debtor's bankruptcy.

(5)   An interim order shall not, in relation to a bankrupt, make provision relaxing or removing any of the requirements of provisions in this Group of Parts, or of the rules, unless the court is satisfied that that provision is unlikely to result in any significant diminution in, or in the value of, the debtor's estate for the purposes of the bankruptcy.

(6)   Subject to the following provisions of this Part, and interim order made on an application under section 253 ceases to have effect at the end of the period of 14 days beginning with the day after the making of the order.

256.   Nominee's report on debtor's proposal

(1)   Where an interim order has been made on an application under section 253, the nominee shall, before the order ceases to have effect, submit a report to the court stating—

(a)   whether, in his opinion, the voluntary arrangement which the debtor is proposing has a reasonable prospect of being approved and implemented, and

(aa) whether, in his opinion, the debtor's creditors should consider the debtor's proposal, …

(b)   …

(2)   For the purpose of enabling the nominee to prepare his report the debtor shall submit to the nominee—

(a)   a document setting out the terms of the voluntary arrangement which the debtor is proposing, and

(b)   a statement of his affairs containing—

(i)   such particulars of his creditors and of his debts and other liabilities and of his assets as may be prescribed, and

(ii) such other information as may be prescribed.

(3)   The court may—

(a)   on an application made by the debtor in a case where the nominee has failed to submit the report required by this section or has died, or

(b)   on an application made by the debtor or the nominee in a case where it is impracticable or inappropriate for the nominee to continue to act as such,

direct that the nominee shall be replaced as such by another person qualified to act as an insolvency practitioner, or authorised to act as nominee, in relation to the voluntary arrangement.

(3A)   The court may, on an application made by the debtor in a case where the nominee has failed to submit the report required by this section, direct that the interim order shall continue, or (if it has ceased to have effect) be renewed, for such further period as the court may specify in the direction.

(4)   The court may, on the application of the nominee, extend the period for which the interim order has effect so as to enable the nominee to have more time to prepare his report.

(5)   If the court is satisfied on receiving the nominee's report that the debtor's creditors should consider the debtor's proposal, the court shall direct that the period for which the interim order has effect shall be extended, for such further period as it may specify in the direction, for the purpose of enabling the debtor's proposal to be considered by his creditors in accordance with the following provisions of this Part.

(6)   The court may discharge the interim order if it is satisfied, on the application of the nominee—

(a)   that the debtor has failed to comply with his obligations under subsection (2), or

(b)   that for any other reason it would be inappropriate for the debtor's creditors to consider the debtor's proposal.

Procedure where no interim order made

256A. Debtor's proposal and nominee's report

(1)   This section applies where a debtor (being an individual)—

(a)   intends to make a proposal under this Part (but an interim order has not been made in relation to the proposal and no application for such an order is pending), and

(b)   if he is an undischarged bankrupt, has given notice of the proposal to the official receiver and, if there is one, the trustee of his estate,

...

(2)   For the purpose of enabling the nominee to prepare a report under subsection (3), the debtor shall submit to the nominee—

(a)   a document setting out the terms of the voluntary arrangement which the debtor is proposing, and

(b)   a statement of his affairs containing—

(i)   such particulars of his creditors and of his debts and other liabilities and of his assets as may be prescribed, and

(ii)   such other information as may be prescribed.

(3)   If the nominee is of the opinion that the debtor is an undischarged bankrupt, or is able to make a bankruptcy application, the nominee shall, within 14 days (or such longer period as the court may allow) after receiving the document and statement mentioned in subsection (2), submit a report to the debtor's creditors stating—

(a)   whether, in his opinion, the voluntary arrangement which the debtor is proposing has a reasonable prospect of being approved and implemented, and

(b)   whether, in his opinion, the debtor's creditors should consider the debtor's proposal, ...

(c)   ...

(4)   The court may—

(a)   on an application made by the debtor in a case where the nominee has failed to submit the report required by this section or has died, or

(b)   on an application made by the debtor or the nominee in a case where it is impracticable or inappropriate for the nominee to continue to act as such,

direct that the nominee shall be replaced as such by another person qualified to act as an insolvency practitioner, or authorised to act as nominee, in relation to the voluntary arrangement.

(5)   The court may, on an application made by the nominee, extend the period within which the nominee is to submit his report.

Creditors' decisions

257.   Consideration of debtor's proposal by creditors

(1)   This section applies where it has been reported to the court under section 256 or to the debtor's creditors under section 256A that the debtor's creditors should consider the debtor's proposal.

(2)   The nominee (or the nominee's replacement under section 256(3) or 256A(4)) must seek a decision from the debtor's creditors as to whether they approve the proposed voluntary arrangement (unless, in the case of a report to which section 256 applies, the court otherwise directs).

(2A)   The decision is to be made by a creditors' decision procedure.

(2B)   Notice of the creditors' decision procedure must be given to every creditor of the debtor of whose claim and address the nominee (or the nominee's replacement) is aware.

(3)   For this purpose the creditors of a debtor who is an undischarged bankrupt include—

    (a)   every person who is a creditor of the bankrupt in respect of a bankruptcy debt, and

    (b)   every person who would be such a creditor if the bankruptcy had commenced on the day on which notice of the creditors' decision procedure is given.

Consideration and implementation of debtor's proposal

258.   Approval of debtor's proposal

(1)   This section applies where under section 257 the debtor's creditors are asked to decide whether to approve the proposed voluntary arrangement.

(2)   The creditors may approve the proposed voluntary arrangement with or without modifications, but shall not approve it with modifications unless the debtor consents to each modification.

(3)   The modifications subject to which the proposed voluntary arrangement may be approved may include one conferring the functions proposed to be conferred on the nominee on another person qualified to act as an insolvency practitioner or authorised to act as nominee, in relation to the voluntary arrangement.

         But they shall not include any modification by virtue of which the proposal ceases to be a proposal under this Part.

(4)   The creditors shall not approve any proposal or modification which affects the right of a secured creditor of the debtor to enforce his security, except with the concurrence of the creditor concerned.

(5)   Subject as follows, the creditors shall not approve any proposal or modification under which—

    (a)   any preferential debt of the debtor is to be paid otherwise than in priority to such of his debts as are not preferential debts, ...

    (aa)   any ordinary preferential debt of the debtor is to be paid otherwise than in priority to any secondary preferential debts that the debtor may have,

    (b)   a preferential creditor of the debtor is to be paid an amount in respect of an ordinary preferential debt that bears to that debt a smaller proportion than is borne to another ordinary preferential debt by the amount that is to be paid in respect of that other debt, ...

    (c)   a preferential creditor of the debtor is to be paid an amount in respect of a secondary preferential debt that bears to that debt a smaller proportion than is borne to another secondary preferential debt by the amount that is to be paid in respect of that other debt, or

    (d)   if the debtor is a relevant financial institution (see section 387A), any non-preferential debt is to be paid otherwise than in accordance with the rules in section 328(3A) (reading references to the bankrupt as references to the debtor).

         However, the creditors may approve such a proposal or modification with the concurrence of the ... creditor concerned.

(6)   ...

(7)   In this section "preferential debt", "ordinary preferential debt" and "secondary preferential debt" each has the meaning given by section 386 in Part XII; and "preferential creditor" is to be construed accordingly.

259.   Report of decisions to court

(1)   When pursuant to section 257 the debtor's creditors have decided whether to approve the debtor's proposal (with or without modifications), the nominee (or the nominee's replacement under section 256(3) or 256A(4)) must—
   (a)   give notice of the creditors' decision to such persons as may be prescribed, and
   (b)   where the creditors considered the debtor's proposal pursuant to a report to the court under section 256(1)(aa), report the creditors' decision to the court.

(2)   If the report is that the creditors have declined (with or without modifications) to approve the voluntary arrangement proposed under section 256, the court may discharge any interim order which is in force in relation to the debtor.

260.   Effect of approval

(1)   This section has effect where pursuant to section 257 the debtor's creditors decide to approve the proposed voluntary arrangement (with or without modifications).

(2)   The approved arrangement—
   (a)   takes effect as if made by the debtor at the time the creditors decided to approve the proposal, and
   (b)   binds every person who in accordance with the rules—
      (i)   was entitled to vote at at the time the creditors decided to approve the proposal, or
      (ii)   would have been so entitled if he had had notice of it,
   as if he were a party to the arrangement.

(2A)   If—
   (a)   when the arrangement ceases to have effect any amount payable under the arrangement to a person bound by virtue of subsection (2)(b)(ii) has not been paid, and
   (b)   the arrangement did not come to an end prematurely,
   the debtor shall at that time become liable to pay to that person the amount payable under the arrangement.

(3)   ...

(4)   Any interim order in force in relation to the debtor immediately before the end of the period of 28 days beginning with the day on which the report with respect to the creditors' decision was made to the court under section 259 ceases to have effect at the end of that period.
   This subsection applies except to such extent as the court may direct for the purposes of any application under section 262 below.

(5)   Where proceedings on a bankruptcy petition have been stayed by an interim order which ceases to have effect under subsection (4), the petition is deemed, unless the court otherwise orders, to have been dismissed.

261.   Additional effect on undischarged bankrupt

(1)   This section applies where—
   (a)   pursuant to section 257 the debtor's creditors decide to approve the proposed voluntary arrangement (with or without modifications), and
   (b)   the debtor is an undischarged bankrupt.

(2)   Where this section applies the court shall annul the bankruptcy order on an application made—
   (a)   by the bankrupt, or
   (b)   where the bankrupt has not made an application within the prescribed period, by the official receiver.

(3)   An application under subsection (2) may not be made—
   (a)   during the period specified in section 262(3)(a) during which the creditors' decision can be challenged by application under section 262,
   (b)   while an application under that section is pending, or

(c)   while an appeal in respect of an application under that section is pending or may be brought.

(4)   Where this section applies the court may give such directions about the conduct of the bankruptcy and the administration of the bankrupt's estate as it thinks appropriate for facilitating the implementation of the approved voluntary arrangement.

262.   Challenge of creditors' decision

(1)   Subject to this section, an application to the court may be made, by any of the persons specified below, on one or both of the following grounds, namely—

    (a)   that a voluntary arrangement approved by a decision of the debtor's creditors pursuant to section 257 unfairly prejudices the interests of a creditor of the debtor;

    (b)   that there has been some material irregularity in relation to a creditors' decision procedure instigated under that section.

(2)   The persons who may apply under this section are—

    (a)   the debtor;

    (b)   a person who—

        (i)   was entitled, in accordance with the rules, to vote in the creditors' decision procedure, or

        (ii)   would have been so entitled if he had had notice of it;

    (c)   the nominee (or his replacement under section 256(3), 256A(4) or 258(3)); and

    (d)   if the debtor is an undischarged bankrupt, the trustee of his estate or the official receiver.

(3)   An application under this section shall not be made—

    (a)   after the end of the period of 28 days beginning with the day on which the creditors decided whether to approve the proposed voluntary arrangement or, where a report was required to be made to the court under section 259(1)(b), the day on which the report was made, or

    (b)   in the case of a person who was not given notice of the creditors' decision procedure, after the end of the period of 28 days beginning with the day on which he became aware that a decision as to whether to approve the proposed voluntary arrangement had been made,

but (subject to that) an application made by a person within subsection (2)(b)(ii) on the ground that the arrangement prejudices his interests may be made after the arrangement has ceased to have effect, unless it has come to an end prematurely.

(4)   Where on an application under this section the court is satisfied as to either of the grounds mentioned in subsection (1), it may do one or both of the following, namely—

    (a)   revoke or suspend any approval given by a decision of the debtor's creditors;

    (b)   direct any person to seek a decision from the debtor's creditors (using a creditors' decision procedure) as to whether they approve—

        (i)   any revised proposal the debtor may make, or

        (ii)   in a case falling within subsection (1)(b), the debtor's original proposal.

(5)   Where at any time after giving a direction under subsection (4)(b) in relation to a revised proposal the court is satisfied that the debtor does not intend to submit such a proposal, the court shall revoke the direction and revoke or suspend any approval previously given by the debtor's creditors.

(6)   Where the court gives a direction under subsection (4)(b), it may also give a direction continuing or, as the case may require, renewing, for such period as may be specified in the direction, the effect in relation to the debtor of any interim order.

(7)   In any case where the court, on an application made under this section with respect to a creditors' decision, gives a direction under subsection (4)(b) or revokes or suspends an approval under subsection (4)(a) or (5), the court may give such supplemental directions as it thinks fit and, in particular, directions with respect to—

    (a)   things done since the decision under any voluntary arrangement approved by the decision, and

    (b)   such things done since the decision as could not have been done if an interim order had been in force in relation to the debtor when they were done.

(8) Except in pursuance of the preceding provisions of this section, the approval of a voluntary arrangement by a decision of the debtor's creditors pursuant to section 257 is not invalidated by any irregularity in relation to the creditors' decision procedure by which the decision was made.

262A. False representations etc

(1) If for the purpose of obtaining the approval of his creditors to a proposal for a voluntary arrangement, the debtor—

(a) makes any false representation, or

(b) fraudulently does, or omits to do, anything,

he commits an offence.

(2) Subsection (1) applies even if the proposal is not approved.

(3) A person guilty of an offence under this section is liable to imprisonment or a fine, or both.

262B. Prosecution of delinquent debtors

(1) This section applies where a voluntary arrangement approved by a decision of the debtor's creditors pursuant to section 257 has taken effect.

(2) If it appears to the nominee or supervisor that the debtor has been guilty of any offence in connection with the arrangement for which he is criminally liable, he shall forthwith—

(a) report the matter to the Secretary of State, and

(b) provide the Secretary of State with such information and give the Secretary of State such access to and facilities for inspecting and taking copies of documents (being information or documents in his possession or under his control and relating to the matter in question) as the Secretary of State requires.

(3) Where a prosecuting authority institutes criminal proceedings following any report under subsection (2), the nominee or, as the case may be, supervisor shall give the authority all assistance in connection with the prosecution which he is reasonably able to give.

For this purpose, "prosecuting authority" means the Director of Public Prosecutions or the Secretary of State.

(4) The court may, on the application of the prosecuting authority, direct a nominee or supervisor to comply with subsection (3) if he has failed to do so.

262C. Arrangements coming to an end prematurely

For the purposes of this Part, a voluntary arrangement approved by a decision of the debtor's creditors pursuant to section 257 comes to an end prematurely if, when it ceases to have effect, it has not been fully implemented in respect of all persons bound by the arrangement by virtue of section 260(2)(b)(i).

263. Implementation and supervision of approved voluntary arrangement

(1) This section applies where a voluntary arrangement approved by a decision of the debtor's creditors pursuant to section 257 has taken effect.

(2) The person who is for the time being carrying out, in relation to the voluntary arrangement, the functions conferred by virtue of the approval on the nominee (or his replacement under section 256(3), 256A(4) or 258(3)) shall be known as the supervisor of the voluntary arrangement.

(3) If the debtor, any of his creditors or any other person is dissatisfied by any act, omission or decision of the supervisor, he may apply to the court; and on such an application the court may—

(a) confirm, reverse or modify any act or decision of the supervisor,

(b) give him directions, or

(c) make such other order as it thinks fit.

(4) The supervisor may apply to the court for directions in relation to any particular matter arising under the voluntary arrangement.

(5) The court may, whenever—

(a) it is expedient to appoint a person to carry out the functions of the supervisor, and

(b) it is inexpedient, difficult or impracticable for an appointment to be made without the assistance of the court,

make an order appointing a person who is qualified to act as an insolvency practitioner or authorised to act as supervisor, in relation to the voluntary arrangement, either in substitution for the
existing supervisor or to fill a vacancy.

...

(6)   The power conferred by subsection (5) is exercisable so as to increase the number of persons
exercising the functions of the supervisor or, where there is more than one person exercising those
functions, so as to replace one or more of those persons.

263A.–263G.   ...

PART IX
BANKRUPTCY

CHAPTER A1
ADJUDICATORS: BANKRUPTCY APPLICATIONS BY DEBTORS AND BANKRUPTCY
ORDERS

263H.   Bankruptcy applications to an adjudicator

(1)   An individual may make an application to an adjudicator in accordance with this Chapter for a
bankruptcy order to be made against him or her.

(2)   An individual may make a bankruptcy application only on the ground that the individual is unable
to pay his or her debts.

263I.   Debtors against whom an adjudicator may make a bankruptcy order

(1)   An adjudicator has jurisdiction to determine a bankruptcy application only if—

   (a)   the centre of the debtor's main interests is in England and Wales, or

   (ab) the centre of the debtor's main interests is in a member State (other than Denmark) and the
debtor has an establishment in England and Wales, or

   (b)   ... the test in subsection (2) is met.

(2)   The test is that—

   (a)   the debtor is domiciled in England and Wales, or

   (b)   at any time in the period of three years ending with the day on which the application is made
to the adjudicator, the debtor—

     (i)   has been ordinarily resident, or has had a place of residence, in England and Wales, or

     (ii) has carried on business in England and Wales.

(3)   The reference in subsection (2) to the debtor carrying on business includes—

   (a)   the carrying on of business by a firm or partnership of which the debtor is a member, and

   (b)   the carrying on of business by an agent or manager for the debtor or for such a firm or
partnership.

(4)   In this section, references to the centre of the debtor's main interests have the same meaning as in
Article 3 of the EC Regulation.

(5)   In this section "establishment" has the same meaning as in Article 2(10) of the EU Regulation.

263J.   Conditions applying to bankruptcy application

(1)   A bankruptcy application must include—

   (a)   such particulars of the debtor's creditors, debts and other liabilities, and assets, as may be
prescribed, and

   (b)   such other information as may be prescribed.

(2)   A bankruptcy application is not to be regarded as having been made unless any fee or deposit
required in connection with the application by an order under section 415 has been paid to such
person, and within such period, as may be prescribed.

(3)   A bankruptcy application may not be withdrawn.

(4)   A debtor must notify the adjudicator if, at any time before a bankruptcy order is made against the
debtor or the adjudicator refuses to make such an order—

(a)   the debtor becomes able to pay his or her debts, or

(b)   a bankruptcy petition has been presented to the court in relation to the debtor.

263K. Determination of bankruptcy application

(1)   After receiving a bankruptcy application, an adjudicator must determine whether the following requirements are met—

(a)   the adjudicator had jurisdiction under section 263I to determine the application on the date the application was made,

(b)   the debtor is unable to pay his or her debts at the date of the determination,

(c)   no bankruptcy petition is pending in relation to the debtor at the date of the determination, and

(d)   no bankruptcy order has been made in respect of any of the debts which are the subject of the application at the date of the determination.

(2)   If the adjudicator is satisfied that each of the requirements in subsection (1) are met, the adjudicator must make a bankruptcy order against the debtor.

(3)   If the adjudicator is not so satisfied, the adjudicator must refuse to make a bankruptcy order against the debtor.

(4)   The adjudicator must make a bankruptcy order against the debtor or refuse to make such an order before the end of the prescribed period ("the determination period").

263L. Adjudicator's requests for further information

(1)   An adjudicator may at any time during the determination period request from the debtor information that the adjudicator considers necessary for the purpose of determining whether a bankruptcy order must be made.

(2)   The adjudicator may specify a date before which information requested under subsection (1) must be provided; but that date must not be after the end of the determination period.

(3)   If the rules so prescribe, a request under subsection (1) may include a request for information to be given orally.

(4)   The rules may make provision enabling or requiring an adjudicator to request information from persons of a prescribed description in prescribed circumstances.

263M. Making of bankruptcy order

(1)   This section applies where an adjudicator makes a bankruptcy order as a result of a bankruptcy application.

(2)   The order must be made in the prescribed form.

(3)   The adjudicator must—

(a)   give a copy of the order to the debtor, and

(b)   give notice of the order to persons of such description as may be prescribed.

263N. Refusal to make a bankruptcy order: review and appeal etc

(1)   Where an adjudicator refuses to make a bankruptcy order on a bankruptcy application, the adjudicator must give notice to the debtor—

(a)   giving the reasons for the refusal, and

(b)   explaining the effect of subsections (2) to (5).

(2)   If requested by the debtor before the end of the prescribed period, the adjudicator must review the information which was available to the adjudicator when the determination that resulted in the refusal was made.

(3)   Following a review under subsection (2) the adjudicator must—

(a)   confirm the refusal to make a bankruptcy order, or

(b)   make a bankruptcy order against the debtor.

(4)   Where the adjudicator confirms a refusal under subsection (3), the adjudicator must give notice to the debtor—

(a)   giving the reasons for the confirmation, and

(b)   explaining the effect of subsection (5).

(5)   If the refusal is confirmed under subsection (3), the debtor may appeal against the refusal to the
        court before the end of the prescribed period.

263O.   False representations and omissions

(1)   It is an offence knowingly or recklessly to make any false representation or omission in—
        (a)   making a bankruptcy application to an adjudicator, or
        (b)   providing any information to an adjudicator in connection with a bankruptcy application.

(2)   It is an offence knowingly or recklessly to fail to notify an adjudicator of a matter in accordance
        with a requirement imposed by or under this Part.

(3)   It is immaterial for the purposes of an offence under this section whether or not a bankruptcy
        order is made as a result of the application.

(4)   It is not a defence in proceedings for an offence under this section that anything relied on, in
        whole or in part, as constituting the offence was done outside England and Wales.

(5)   Proceedings for an offence under this section may only be instituted—
        (a)   by the Secretary of State, or
        (b)   by or with the consent of the Director of Public Prosecutions.

CHAPTER I
THE COURT: BANKRUPTCY PETITIONS AND BANKRUPTCY ORDERS

Preliminary

264.   Who may present a bankruptcy petition

(1)   A petition for a bankruptcy order to be made against an individual may be presented to the court
        in accordance with the following provisions of this Part—
        (a)   by one of the individual's creditors or jointly by more than one of them,
        (b)   ...
        (ba), (bb) ...
        (c)   by the supervisor of, or any person (other than the individual) who is for the time being
              bound by, a voluntary arrangement proposed by the individual and approved under Part
              VIII, *or*
        (d)   *where a criminal bankruptcy order has been made against the individual, by the Official
              Petitioner or by any person specified in the order in pursuance of section 39(3)(b) of the
              Powers of Criminal Courts Act 1973.*

(2)   Subject to those provisions, the court may make a bankruptcy order on any such petition.

        Note. Subsection (1)(d) and the italicized word preceding it are repealed by the Criminal Justice Act 1988,
        s. 170(2), Sch. 16, as from a day to be appointed.

265.   Creditor's petition: debtors against whom the court may make a bankruptcy order

(1)   A bankruptcy petition may be presented to the court under section 264(1)(a) only if—
        (a)   the centre of the debtor's main interests is in England and Wales, or
        (ab)   the centre of the debtor's main interests is in a member State (other than Denmark)
               and the debtor has an establishment in England and Wales, or
        (b)   ... the test in subsection (2) is met.

(2)   The test is that—
        (a)   the debtor is domiciled in England and Wales, or
        (b)   at any time in the period of three years ending with the day on which the petition is
               presented, the debtor—
               (i)   has been ordinarily resident, or has had a place of residence, in England and
                      Wales, or
               (ii)   has carried on business in England and Wales.

(3)   The reference in subsection (2) to the debtor carrying on business includes—
        (a)   the carrying on of business by a firm or partnership of which the debtor is a member,
               and

(b)   the carrying on of business by an agent or manager for the debtor or for such a firm or partnership.

(4)   In this section, references to the centre of the debtor's main interests have the same meaning as in Article 3 of the EU Regulation.

(5)   In this section "establishment" has the same meaning as in Article 2(10) of the EU Regulation.

266.   Other preliminary conditions

(1)   Where a bankruptcy petition relating to an individual is presented by a person who is entitled to present a petition under two or more paragraphs of section 264(1), the petition is to be treated for the purposes of this Part as a petition under such one of those paragraphs as may be specified in the petition.

(2)   A bankruptcy petition shall not be withdrawn without the leave of the court.

(3)   The court has a general power, if it appears to it appropriate to do so on the grounds that there has been a contravention of the rules or for any other reason, to dismiss a bankruptcy petition or to stay proceedings on such a petition; and, where it stays proceedings on a petition, it may do so on such terms and conditions as it thinks fit.

(4)   *Without prejudice to subsection (3), where a petition under section 264(1)(a) ... or (c) in respect of an individual is pending at a time when a criminal bankruptcy order is made against him, or is presented after such an order has been so made, the court may on the application of the Official Petitioner dismiss the petition if it appears to it appropriate to do so.*

Note. Subsection (4) is repealed by the Criminal Justice Act 1988, s. 170(2), Sch. 16, as from a day to be appointed.

Creditor's petition

267.   Grounds of creditor's petition

(1)   A creditor's petition must be in respect of one or more debts owed by the debtor, and the petitioning creditor or each of the petitioning creditors must be a person to whom the debt or (as the case may be) at least one of the debts is owed.

(2)   Subject to the next three sections, a creditor's petition may be presented to the court in respect of a debt or debts only if, at the time the petition is presented—

(a)   the amount of the debt, or the aggregate amount of the debts, is equal to or exceeds the bankruptcy level,

(b)   the debt, or each of the debts, is for a liquidated sum payable to the petitioning creditor, or one or more of the petitioning creditors, either immediately or at some certain, future time, and is unsecured,

(c)   the debt, or each of the debts, is a debt which the debtor appears either to be unable to pay or to have no reasonable prospect of being able to pay, and

(d)   there is no outstanding application to set aside a statutory demand served (under section 268 below) in respect of the debt or any of the debts.

(3)   *A debt is not to be regarded for the purposes of subsection (2) as a debt for a liquidated sum by reason only that the amount of the debt is specified in a criminal bankruptcy order.*

(4)   "The bankruptcy level" is £5,000; but the Secretary of State may by order in a statutory instrument substitute any amount specified in the order for that amount or (as the case may be) for the amount which by virtue of such an order is for the time being the amount of the bankruptcy level.

(5)   An order shall not be made under subsection (4) unless a draft of it has been laid before, and approved by a resolution of, each House of Parliament.

Note. Subsection (3) is repealed by the Criminal Justice Act 1988, s. 170(2), Sch. 16, as from a day to be appointed.

268.   Definition of "inability to pay", etc; the statutory demand

(1)   For the purposes of section 267(2)(c), the debtor appears to be unable to pay a debt if, but only if, the debt is payable immediately and either—

   (a)   the petitioning creditor to whom the debt is owed has served on the debtor a demand (known as "the statutory demand") in the prescribed form requiring him to pay the debt or to secure or compound for it to the satisfaction of the creditor, at least 3 weeks have elapsed since the demand was served and the demand has been neither complied with nor set aside in accordance with the rules, or

   (b)   execution or other process issued in respect of the debt on a judgment or order of any court in favour of the petitioning creditor, or one or more of the petitioning creditors to whom the debt is owed, has been returned unsatisfied in whole or in part.

(2)   For the purposes of section 267(2)(c) the debtor appears to have no reasonable prospect of being able to pay a debt if, but only if, the debt is not immediately payable and—

   (a)   the petitioning creditor to whom it is owed has served on the debtor a demand (also known as "the statutory demand") in the prescribed form requiring him to establish to the satisfaction of the creditor that there is a reasonable prospect that the debtor will be able to pay the debt when it falls due,

   (b)   at least 3 weeks have elapsed since the demand was served, and

   (c)   the demand has been neither complied with nor set aside in accordance with the rules.

269.   Creditor with security

(1)   A debt which is the debt, or one of the debts, in respect of which a creditor's petition is presented need not be unsecured if either—

   (a)   the petition contains a statement by the person having the right to enforce the security that he is willing, in the event of a bankruptcy order being made, to give up his security for the benefit of all the bankrupt's creditors, or

   (b)   the petition is expressed not to be made in respect of the secured part of the debt and contains a statement by that person of the estimated value at the date of the petition of the security for the secured part of the debt.

(2)   In a case falling within subsection (1)(b) the secured and unsecured parts of the debt are to be treated for the purposes of sections 267 and 270 as separate debts.

270.   Expedited petition

In the case of a creditor's petition presented wholly or partly in respect of a debt which is the subject of a statutory demand under section 268, the petition may be presented before the end of the 3-week period there mentioned if there is a serious possibility that the debtor's property or the value of any of his property will be significantly diminished during that period and the petition contains a statement to that effect.

271.   Proceedings on creditor's petition

(1)   The court shall not make a bankruptcy order on a creditor's petition unless it is satisfied that the debt, or one of the debts, in respect of which the petition was presented is either—

   (a)   a debt which, having been payable at the date of the petition or having since become payable, has been neither paid nor secured or compounded for, or

   (b)   a debt which the debtor has no reasonable prospect of being able to pay when it falls due.

(2)   In a case in which the petition contains such a statement as is required by section 270, the court shall not make a bankruptcy order until at least 3 weeks have elapsed since the service of any statutory demand under section 268.

(3)   The court may dismiss the petition if it is satisfied that the debtor is able to pay all his debts or is satisfied—

   (a)   that the debtor has made an offer to secure or compound for a debt in respect of which the petition is presented,

   (b)   that the acceptance of that offer would have required the dismissal of the petition, and

(c)   that the offer has been unreasonably refused;

and, in determining for the purposes of this subsection whether the debtor is able to pay all his debts, the court shall take into account his contingent and prospective liabilities.

(4)   In determining for the purposes of this section what constitutes a reasonable prospect that a debtor will be able to pay a debt when it falls due, it is to be assumed that the prospect given by the facts and other matters known to the creditor at the time he entered into the transaction resulting in the debt was a reasonable prospect.

(5)   Nothing in sections 267 to 271 prejudices the power of the court, in accordance with the rules, to authorise a creditor's petition to be amended by the omission of any creditor or debt and to be proceeded with as if things done for the purposes of those sections had been done only by or in relation to the remaining creditors or debts.

272.–275.   ...

Other cases for special consideration

276.   Default in connection with voluntary arrangement

(1)   The court shall not make a bankruptcy order on a petition under section 264(1)(c) (supervisor of, or person bound by, voluntary arrangement proposed and approved) unless it is satisfied—

(a)   that the debtor has failed to comply with his obligations under the voluntary arrangement, or

(b)   that information which was false or misleading in any material particular or which contained material omissions—

(i)   was contained in any statement of affairs or other document supplied by the debtor under Part VIII to any person, or

(ii)   was otherwise made available by the debtor to his creditors in connection with a creditors' decision procedure instigated under that Part, or

(c)   that the debtor has failed to do all such things as may for the purposes of the voluntary arrangement have been reasonably required of him by the supervisor of the arrangement.

(2)   Where a bankruptcy order is made on a petition under section 264(1)(c), any expenses properly incurred as expenses of the administration of the voluntary arrangement in question shall be a first charge on the bankrupt's estate.

277.   *Petition based on criminal bankruptcy order*

(1)   Subject to section 266(3), the court shall make a bankruptcy order on a petition under section 264(1)(d) on production of a copy of the criminal bankruptcy order on which the petition is based. This does not apply if it appears to the court that the criminal bankruptcy order has been rescinded on appeal.

(2)   Subject to the provisions of this Part, the fact that an appeal is pending against any conviction by virtue of which a criminal bankruptcy order was made does not affect any proceedings on a petition under section 264(1)(d) based on that order.

(3)   For the purposes of this section, an appeal against a conviction is pending—

(a)   in any case, until the expiration of the period of 28 days beginning with the date of conviction;

(b)   if notice of appeal to the Court of Appeal is given during that period and during that period the appellant notifies the official receiver of it, until the determination of the appeal and thereafter for so long as an appeal to the Supreme Court is pending within the meaning of subsection (4).

(4)   For the purposes of subsection (3)(b) an appeal to the Supreme Court shall be treated as pending until any application for leave to appeal is disposed of and, if leave to appeal is granted, until the appeal is disposed of; and for the purposes of this subsection an application for leave to appeal shall be treated as disposed of at the expiration of the time within which it may be made, if it is not made within that time.

Note. This section is repealed by the Criminal Justice Act 1988, s. 170(2), Sch. 16, as from a day to be appointed.

CHAPTER 1A
COMMENCEMENT AND DURATION OF BANKRUPTCY

278.   Commencement and continuance

The bankruptcy of an individual against whom a bankruptcy order has been made—

(a)   commences with the day on which the order is made, and

(b)   continues until the individual is discharged under ... this Chapter.

279.   Duration

(1)   A bankrupt is discharged from bankruptcy at the end of the period of one year beginning with the date on which the bankruptcy commences.

(2)   ...

(3)   On the application of the official receiver or the trustee of a bankrupt's estate, the court may order that the period specified in subsection (1) shall cease to run until—

(a)   the end of a specified period, or

(b)   the fulfilment of a specified condition.

(4)   The court may make an order under subsection (3) only if satisfied that the bankrupt has failed or is failing to comply with an obligation under this Part.

(5)   In subsection (3)(b) "condition" includes a condition requiring that the court be satisfied of something.

(6)   In the case of an individual who is made bankrupt on a petition under section 264(1)(d)—

(a)   subsections (1) to (5) shall not apply, and

(b)   the bankrupt is discharged from bankruptcy by an order of the court under section 280.

(7)   This section is without prejudice to any power of the court to annul a bankruptcy order.

280.   Discharge by order of the court

(1)   An application for an order of the court discharging an individual from bankruptcy in a case falling within section 279(6) may be made by the bankrupt at any time after the end of the period of 5 years beginning with the date on which the bankruptcy commences.

(2)   On an application under this section the court may—

(a)   refuse to discharge the bankrupt from bankruptcy,

(b)   make an order discharging him absolutely, or

(c)   make an order discharging him subject to such conditions with respect to any income which may subsequently become due to him, or with respect to property devolving upon him, or acquired by him, after his discharge, as may be specified in the order.

(3)   The court may provide for an order falling within subsection (2)(b) or (c) to have immediate effect or to have its effect suspended for such period, or until the fulfilment of such conditions (including a condition requiring the court to be satisfied as to any matter), as may be specified in the order.

281.   Effect of discharge

(1)   Subject as follows, where a bankrupt is discharged, the discharge releases him from all the bankruptcy debts, but has no effect—

(a)   on the functions (so far as they remain to be carried out) of the trustee of his estate, or

(b)   on the operation, for the purposes of the carrying out of those functions, of the provisions of this Part;

and, in particular, discharge does not affect the right of any creditor of the bankrupt to prove in the bankruptcy for any debt from which the bankrupt is released.

(2)   Discharge does not affect the right of any secured creditor of the bankrupt to enforce his security for the payment of a debt from which the bankrupt is released.

(3)   Discharge does not release the bankrupt from any bankruptcy debt which he incurred in respect of, or forbearance in respect of which was secured by means of, any fraud or fraudulent breach of trust to which he was a party.

(4)   Discharge does not release the bankrupt from any liability in respect of a fine imposed for an offence or from any liability under a recognisance except, in the case of a penalty imposed for an offence under an enactment relating to the public revenue or of a recognisance, with the consent of the Treasury.

(4A)   In subsection (4) the reference to a fine imposed for an offence includes a reference to—

    (a)   a charge ordered to be paid under section 46 of the Sentencing Code (criminal courts charge), whether on conviction or otherwise;

    (b)   a confiscation order under Part 2, 3 or 4 of the Proceeds of Crime Act 2002.

(5)   Discharge does not, except to such extent and on such conditions as the court may direct, release the bankrupt from any bankruptcy debt which—

    (a)   consists in a liability to pay damages for negligence, nuisance or breach of a statutory, contractual or other duty, or to pay damages by virtue of Part I of the Consumer Protection Act 1987, being in either case damages in respect of personal injuries to any person, or

    (b)   arises under any order made in family proceedings or under a *maintenance assessment [maintenance calculation]* made under the Child Support Act 1991 ... .

(6)   Discharge does not release the bankrupt from such other bankruptcy debts, not being debts provable in his bankruptcy, as are prescribed.

(7)   Discharge does not release any person other than the bankrupt from any liability (whether as partner or co-trustee of the bankrupt or otherwise) from which the bankrupt is released by the discharge, or from any liability as surety for the bankrupt or as a person in the nature of such a surety.

(8)   In this section—

    "family proceedings" means—

    (a)   proceedings in the family court; and

    (b)   family proceedings within the meaning of Part V of the Matrimonial and Family Proceedings Act 1984;

    "fine" means the same as in the Magistrates' Courts Act 1980; and

    "personal injuries" includes death and any disease or other impairment of a person's physical or mental condition.

Note. The words "maintenance assessment" in subsection (5)(b) are repealed and the subsequent italicized words in square brackets are substituted by the Child Support, Pensions and Social Security Act 2000, s. 26, Sch. 3, para. 6, from 3 March 2003 in relation to certain cases (see S.I. 2003/192) and as from a day to be appointed otherwise.

281A.   Post-discharge restrictions

Schedule 4A to this Act (bankruptcy restrictions order and bankruptcy restrictions undertaking) shall have effect.

282.   Court's power to annul bankruptcy order

(1)   The court may annul a bankruptcy order if it at any time appears to the court—

    (a)   that, on the grounds existing at the time the order was made, the order ought not to have been made, or

    (b)   that, to the extent required by the rules, the bankruptcy debts and the expenses of the bankruptcy have all, since the making of the order, been either paid or secured for to the satisfaction of the court.

(2)   *The court may annual a bankruptcy order made against an individual on a petition under paragraph (a) ... or (c) of section 264(1) or on a bankruptcy application if it at any time appears to the court, on an application by the Official Petitioner—*

    (a)   *that the petition was pending or the application was ongoing at a time when a criminal bankruptcy order was made against the individual or was presented after such an order was so made, and*

    (b)   *no appeal is pending (within the meaning of section 277) against the individual's conviction of any offence by virtue of which the criminal bankruptcy order was made;*

and the court shall annul a bankruptcy order made on a petition under section 264(1)(d) if it at
any time appears to the court that the criminal bankruptcy order on which the petition was based
has been rescinded in consequence of an appeal.

(3)   The court may annul a bankruptcy order whether or not the bankrupt has been discharged from
the bankruptcy.

(4)   Where the court annuls a bankruptcy order (whether under this section or under section 261 … in
Part VIII)—

    (a)   any sale or other disposition of property, payment made or other thing duly done, under any
provision in this Group of Parts, by or under the authority of the official receiver or a trustee
of the bankrupt's estate or by the court is valid, but

    (b)   if any of the bankrupt's estate is then vested, under any such provision, in such a trustee, it
shall vest in such person as the court may appoint or, in default of any such appointment,
revert to the bankrupt on such terms (if any) as the court may direct;

and the court may include in its order such supplemental provisions as may be authorised by the
rules.

(5)   …

Note. Subsection (2) is repealed by the Criminal Justice Act 1988, s. 170(2), Sch. 16, as from a day to be
appointed.

CHAPTER II
PROTECTION OF BANKRUPT'S ESTATE AND
INVESTIGATION OF HIS AFFAIRS

283.   Definition of bankrupt's estate

(1)   Subject as follows, a bankrupt's estate for the purposes of any of this Group of Parts comprises—

    (a)   all property belonging to or vested in the bankrupt at the commencement of the bankruptcy,
and

    (b)   any property which by virtue of any of the following provisions of this Part is comprised in
that estate or is treated as falling within the preceding paragraph.

(2)   Subsection (1) does not apply to—

    (a)   such tools, books, vehicles and other items of equipment as are necessary to the bankrupt for
use personally by him in his employment, business or vocation;

    (b)   such clothing, bedding, furniture, household equipment and provisions as are necessary for
satisfying the basic domestic needs of the bankrupt and his family.

This subsection is subject to section 308 in Chapter IV (certain excluded property reclaimable by
trustee).

(3)   Subsection (1) does not apply to—

    (a)   property held by the bankrupt on trust for any other person, or

    (b)   the right of nomination to a vacant ecclesiastical benefice.

(3A)   Subject to section 308A in Chapter IV, subsection (1) does not apply to—

    (a)   a tenancy which is an assured tenancy or an assured agricultural occupancy, within the
meaning of Part I of the Housing Act 1988, and the terms of which inhibit an assignment as
mentioned in section 127(5) of the Rent Act 1977, or

    (aa)   a standard contract within the meaning of section 8 of the Renting Homes (Wales) Act 2016
(anaw 1) and the terms of which inhibit an assignment as mentioned in section 127(5) of the
Rent Act 1977 (c 42), or

    (b)   a protected tenancy, within the meaning of the Rent Act 1977, in respect of which, by virtue
of any provision of Part IX of that Act, no premium can lawfully be required as a condition
of assignment, or

    (c)   a tenancy of a dwelling-house by virtue of which the bankrupt is, within the meaning of the
Rent (Agriculture) Act 1976, a protected occupier of the dwelling-house, and the terms of
which inhibit an assignment as mentioned in section 127(5) of the Rent Act 1977, or

(d)   a secure tenancy, within the meaning of Part IV of the Housing Act 1985, which is not capable of being assigned, except in the cases mentioned in section 91(3) of that Act, or

(e)   a secure contract within the meaning of section 8 of the Renting Homes (Wales) Act 2016 (anaw 1) which is not capable of being assigned, except—

    (i)   in the cases mentioned in section 251 (family property order) of that Act,

    (ii)   in accordance with section 92 (assignment by way of exchange) of the Housing Act 1985 (c 68), or

    (iii)   to a person who would be qualified to succeed the contract-holder if the contract-holder died immediately before the assignment.

(4)   References in any of this Group of Parts to property, in relation to a bankrupt, include references to any power exercisable by him over or in respect of property except in so far as the power is exercisable over or in respect of property not for the time being comprised in the bankrupt's estate and—

(a)   is so exercisable at a time after either the official receiver has had his release in respect of that estate under section 299(2) in Chapter III or the trustee of that estate has vacated office under section 298(8), or

(b)   cannot be so exercised for the benefit of the bankrupt;

and a power exercisable over or in respect of property is deemed for the purposes of any of this Group of Parts to vest in the person entitled to exercise it at the time of the transaction or event by virtue of which it is exercisable by that person (whether or not it becomes so exercisable at that time).

(5)   For the purposes of any such provision in this Group of Parts, property comprised in a bankrupt's estate is so comprised subject to the rights of any person other than the bankrupt (whether as a secured creditor of the bankrupt or otherwise) in relation thereto, but disregarding—

(a)   any rights in relation to which a statement such as is required by section 269(1)(a) was made in the petition on which the bankrupt was made bankrupt, and

(b)   any rights which have been otherwise given up in accordance with the rules.

(6)   This section has effect subject to the provisions of any enactment not contained in this Act under which any property is to be excluded from a bankrupt's estate.

283A. Bankrupt's home ceasing to form part of estate

(1)   This section applies where property comprised in the bankrupt's estate consists of an interest in a dwelling-house which at the date of the bankruptcy was the sole or principal residence of—

(a)   the bankrupt,

(b)   the bankrupt's spouse or civil partner, or

(c)   a former spouse or former civil partner of the bankrupt.

(2)   At the end of the period of three years beginning with the date of the bankruptcy the interest mentioned in subsection (1) shall—

(a)   cease to be comprised in the bankrupt's estate, and

(b)   vest in the bankrupt (without conveyance, assignment or transfer).

(3)   Subsection (2) shall not apply if during the period mentioned in that subsection—

(a)   the trustee realises the interest mentioned in subsection (1),

(b)   the trustee applies for an order for sale in respect of the dwelling-house,

(c)   the trustee applies for an order for possession of the dwelling-house,

(d)   the trustee applies for an order under section 313 in Chapter IV in respect of that interest, or

(e)   the trustee and the bankrupt agree that the bankrupt shall incur a specified liability to his estate (with or without the addition of interest from the date of the agreement) in consideration of which the interest mentioned in subsection (1) shall cease to form part of the estate.

(4)   Where an application of a kind described in subsection (3)(b) to (d) is made during the period mentioned in subsection (2) and is dismissed, unless the court orders otherwise the interest to which the application relates shall on the dismissal of the application—

(a)   cease to be comprised in the bankrupt's estate, and

(b)   vest in the bankrupt (without conveyance, assignment or transfer).

(5)   If the bankrupt does not inform the trustee or the official receiver of his interest in a property before the end of the period of three months beginning with the date of the bankruptcy, the period of three years mentioned in subsection (2)—

(a)   shall not begin with the date of the bankruptcy, but

(b)   shall begin with the date on which the trustee or official receiver becomes aware of the bankrupt's interest.

(6)   The court may substitute for the period of three years mentioned in subsection (2) a longer period—

(a)   in prescribed circumstances, and

(b)   in such other circumstances as the court thinks appropriate.

(7)   The rules may make provision for this section to have effect with the substitution of a shorter period for the period of three years mentioned in subsection (2) in specified circumstances (which may be described by reference to action to be taken by a trustee in bankruptcy).

(8)   The rules may also, in particular, make provision—

(a)   requiring or enabling the trustee of a bankrupt's estate to give notice that this section applies or does not apply;

(b)   about the effect of a notice under paragraph (a);

(c)   requiring the trustee of a bankrupt's estate to make an application to the Chief Land Registrar.

(9)   Rules under subsection (8)(b) may, in particular—

(a)   disapply this section;

(b)   enable a court to disapply this section;

(c)   make provision in consequence of a disapplication of this section;

(d)   enable a court to make provision in consequence of a disapplication of this section;

(e)   make provision (which may include provision conferring jurisdiction on a court or tribunal) about compensation.

284.   Restrictions on dispositions of property

(1)   Where a person is made bankrupt, any disposition of property made by that person in the period to which this section applies is void except to the extent that it is or was made with the consent of the court, or is or was subsequently ratified by the court.

(2)   Subsection (1) applies to a payment (whether in cash or otherwise) as it applies to a disposition of property and, accordingly, where any payment is void by virtue of that subsection, the person paid shall hold the sum paid for the bankrupt as part of his estate.

(3)   This section applies to the period beginning with the day of the making of the bankruptcy application or (as the case may be) the presentation of the bankruptcy petition and ending with the vesting, under Chapter IV of this Part, of the bankrupt's estate in a trustee.

(4)   The preceding provisions of this section do not give a remedy against any person—

(a)   in respect of any property or payment which he received before the commencement of the bankruptcy in good faith, for value and without notice that the bankruptcy application had been made or (as the case may be) that the bankruptcy petition had been presented, or

(b)   in respect of any interest in property which derives from an interest in respect of which there is, by virtue of this subsection, no remedy.

(5)   Where after the commencement of his bankruptcy the bankrupt has incurred a debt to a banker or other person by reason of the making of a payment which is void under this section, that debt is deemed for the purposes of any of this Group of Parts to have been incurred before the commencement of the bankruptcy unless—

(a)   that banker or person had notice of the bankruptcy before the debt was incurred, or

(b)   it is not reasonably practicable for the amount of the payment to be recovered from the person to whom it was made.

(6) A disposition of property is void under this section notwithstanding that the property is not or, as the case may be, would not be comprised in the bankrupt's estate; but nothing in this section affects any disposition made by a person of property held by him on trust for any other person.

285. **Restriction on proceedings and remedies**

(1) At any time when proceedings on a bankruptcy application are ongoing or proceedings on a bankruptcy petition are pending or an individual has been made bankrupt the court may stay any action, execution or other legal process against the property or person of the debtor or, as the case may be, of the bankrupt.

(2) Any court in which proceedings are pending against any individual may, on proof that a bankruptcy application has been made or a bankruptcy petition has been presented in respect of that individual or that he is an undischarged bankrupt, either stay the proceedings or allow them to continue on such terms as it thinks fit.

(3) After the making of a bankruptcy order no person who is a creditor of the bankrupt in respect of a debt provable in the bankruptcy shall—

(a) have any remedy against the property or person of the bankrupt in respect of that debt, or

(b) before the discharge of the bankrupt, commence any action or other legal proceedings against the bankrupt except with the leave of the court and on such terms as the court may impose.

This is subject to sections 346 (enforcement procedures) and 347 (limited right to distress).

(4) Subject as follows, subsection (3) does not affect the right of a secured creditor of the bankrupt to enforce his security.

(5) Where any goods of an undischarged bankrupt are held by any person by way of pledge, pawn or other security, the official receiver may, after giving notice in writing of his intention to do so, inspect the goods.

Where such a notice has been given to any person, that person is not entitled, without leave of the court, to realise his security unless he has given the trustee of the bankrupt's estate a reasonable opportunity of inspecting the goods and of exercising the bankrupt's right of redemption.

(6) References in this section to the property or goods of the bankrupt are to any of his property or goods, whether or not comprised in his estate.

286. **Power to appoint interim receiver**

(1) The court may, if it is shown to be necessary for the protection of the debtor's property, at any time after the presentation of a bankruptcy petition and before making a bankruptcy order, appoint the official receiver or an insolvency practitioner to be interim receiver of the debtor's property.

(2) ...

(3) The court may by an order appointing any person to be an interim receiver direct that his powers shall be limited or restricted in any respect; but, save as so directed, an interim receiver has, in relation to the debtor's property, all the rights, powers, duties and immunities given by the next section.

(4) An order of the court appointing any person to be an interim receiver shall require that person to take immediate possession of the debtor's property or, as the case may be, the part of it to which his powers as interim receiver are limited.

(5) Where an interim receiver has been appointed, the debtor shall give him such inventory of his property and such other information, and shall attend on the interim receiver at such times, as the latter may for the purpose of carrying out his functions under this section reasonably require.

(6) Where an interim receiver is appointed, section 285(3) applies for the period between the appointment and the making of a bankruptcy order on the petition, or the dismissal of the petition, as if the appointment were the making of such an order.

(7) A person ceases to be interim receiver of a debtor's property if the bankruptcy petition relating to the debtor is dismissed, if a bankruptcy order is made on the petition or if the court by order otherwise terminates the appointment.

(8)   References in this section to the debtor's property are to all his property, whether or not it would
         be comprised in his estate if he were made bankrupt.

287.   Powers of interim receiver

(1)   An interim receiver appointed under section 286 is the receiver and (subject to section 370
         (special manager)) the manager of the debtor's property and is under a duty to act as such.

(2)   The function of an interim receiver while acting as receiver or manager of the debtor's property
         under this section is to protect the property; and for this purpose—
         (a)   he has the same powers as if he were a receiver or manager appointed by the High Court,
               and
         (b)   he is entitled to sell or otherwise dispose of any perishable goods comprised in the property
               and any other goods so comprised the value of which is likely to diminish if they are not
               disposed of.

(3)   An interim receiver while acting as receiver or manager of the debtor's property under this
         section—
         (a)   shall take all such steps as he thinks fit for protecting the debtor's property,
         (b)   is not required to do anything that involves his incurring expenditure, except in pursuance of
               directions given by—
               (i)   the Secretary of State, where the official receiver is the interim receiver, or
               (ii)   the court, in any other case,
         (c)   may, if he thinks fit (and shall, if so directed by the court) at any time seek a decision on a
               matter from the debtor's creditors.

(4)   Where—
         (a)   an interim receiver acting as receiver or manager of the debtor's property under this section
               seizes or disposes of any property which is not the debtor's property, and
         (b)   at the time of the seizure or disposal the interim receiver believes, and has reasonable
               grounds for believing, that he is entitled (whether in pursuance of an order of the court or
               otherwise) to seize or dispose of that property,
         the interim receiver is not to be liable to any person in respect of any loss or damage resulting
         from the seizure or disposal except in so far as that loss or damage is caused by his negligence;
         and he has a lien on the property, or the proceeds of its sale, for such of the expenses of the
         interim receivership as were incurred in connection with the seizure or disposal.

(5)   …

288.   Statement of affairs

(1)   Where a bankruptcy order has been made otherwise than on a bankruptcy application, the official
         receiver may at any time before the discharge of the bankrupt require the bankrupt to submit to
         the official receiver a statement of affairs.

(2)   The statement of affairs shall contain—
         (a)   such particulars of the bankrupt's creditors and of his debts and other liabilities and of his
               assets as may be prescribed, and
         (b)   such other information as may be prescribed.

(2A)   Where a bankrupt is required under subsection (1) to submit a statement of affairs to the official
         receiver, the bankrupt shall do so (subject to subsection (3)) before the end of the period of 21
         days beginning with the day after that on which the prescribed notice of the requirement is given
         to the bankrupt by the official receiver.

(3)   The official receiver may, if he thinks fit—
         (a)   release a bankrupt from an obligation imposed on the bankrupt under subsection (1), or
         (b)   either when giving the notice mentioned in subsection (2A) or subsequently, extend the
               period mentioned in that subsection,
         and where the official receiver has refused to exercise a power conferred by this section, the
         court, if it thinks fit, may exercise it.

(4)   A bankrupt who—

      (a)   without reasonable excuse fails to comply with an obligation imposed under this section, or

      (b)   without reasonable excuse submits a statement of affairs that does not comply with the prescribed requirements,

is guilty of a contempt of court and liable to be punished accordingly (in addition to any other punishment to which he may be subject).

289.   Investigatory duties of official receiver

(1)   The official receiver shall—

      (a)   investigate the conduct and affairs of each bankrupt (including his conduct and affairs before the making of the bankruptcy order), and

      (b)   make such report (if any) to the court as the official receiver thinks fit.

(2)   Subsection (1) shall not apply to a case in which the official receiver thinks an investigation under that subsection unnecessary.

(3)   Where a bankrupt makes an application for discharge under section 280—

      (a)   the official receiver shall make a report to the court about such matters as may be prescribed, and

      (b)   the court shall consider the report before determining the application.

(4)   A report by the official receiver under this section shall in any proceedings be prima facie evidence of the facts stated in it.

290.   Public examination of bankrupt

(1)   Where a bankruptcy order has been made, the official receiver may at any time before the discharge of the bankrupt apply to the court for the public examination of the bankrupt.

(2)   Unless the court otherwise orders, the official receiver shall make an application under subsection (1) if notice requiring him to do so is given to him, in accordance with the rules, by one of the bankrupt's creditors with the concurrence of not less than one-half, in value, of those creditors (including the creditor giving notice).

(3)   On an application under subsection (1), the court shall direct that a public examination of the bankrupt shall be held on a day appointed by the court; and the bankrupt shall attend on that day and be publicly examined as to his affairs, dealings and property.

(4)   The following may take part in the public examination of the bankrupt and may question him concerning his affairs, dealings and property and the causes of his failure, namely—

      (a)   the official receiver and, in the case of an individual made bankrupt on a petition under section 264(1)(d), the Official Petitioner,

      (b)   the trustee of the bankrupt's estate, if his appointment has taken effect,

      (c)   any person who has been appointed as special manager of the bankrupt's estate or business,

      (d)   any creditor of the bankrupt who has tendered a proof in the bankruptcy.

(5)   If a bankrupt without reasonable excuse fails at any time to attend his public examination under this section he is guilty of a contempt of court and liable to be punished accordingly (in addition to any other punishment to which he may be subject).

291.   Duties of bankrupt in relation to official receiver

(1)–(3) ...

(4)   The bankrupt shall give the official receiver such inventory of his estate and such other information, and shall attend on the official receiver at such times, as the official receiver may reasonably require—

      (a)   for a purpose of this Chapter, or

      (b)   in connection with the making of a bankruptcy restrictions order.

(5)   Subsection (4) applies to a bankrupt after his discharge.

(6)   If the bankrupt without reasonable excuse fails to comply with any obligation imposed by this section, he is guilty of a contempt of court and liable to be punished accordingly (in addition to any other punishment to which he may be subject).

CHAPTER III
TRUSTEES IN BANKRUPTCY

Tenure of office as trustee

291A.   **First trustee in bankruptcy**

(1)   On the making of a bankruptcy order the official receiver becomes trustee of the bankrupt's estate, unless the court appoints another person under subsection (2).

(2)   If when the order is made there is a supervisor of a voluntary arrangement approved in relation to the bankrupt under Part 8, the court may on making the order appoint the supervisor of the arrangement as the trustee.

(3)   Where a person becomes trustee of a bankrupt's estate under this section, the person must give notice of that fact to the bankrupt's creditors (or, if the court so allows, advertise it in accordance with the court's directions).

(4)   A notice or advertisement given by a trustee appointed under subsection (2) must explain the procedure for establishing a creditors' committee under section 301.

292.   **Appointment of trustees: general provision**

(1)   This section applies to any appointment of a person (other than the official receiver) as trustee of a bankrupt's estate.

(2)   No person may be appointed as trustee of a bankrupt's estate unless he is, at the time of the appointment, qualified to act as an insolvency practitioner in relation to the bankrupt.

(3)   Any power to appoint a person as trustee of a bankrupt's estate includes power to appoint two or more persons as joint trustees; but such an appointment must make provision as to the circumstances in which the trustees must act together and the circumstances in which one or more of them may act for the others.

(4)   The appointment of any person as trustee takes effect only if that person accepts the appointment in accordance with the rules. Subject to this, the appointment of any person as trustee takes effect at the time specified in his certificate of appointment.

(5)   ...

293–5.   ...

296.   **Appointment of trustee by Secretary of State**

(1)   At any time when the official receiver is the trustee of a bankrupt's estate by virtue of any provision of this Chapter ... he may apply to the Secretary of State for the appointment of a person as trustee instead of the official receiver.

(2)   On an application under subsection (1) the Secretary of State shall either make an appointment or decline to make one.

(3)   Such an application may be made notwithstanding that the Secretary of State has declined to make an appointment either on a previous application under subsection (1) ... or under section 300(4) below.

(4)   Where the trustee of a bankrupt's estate has been appointed by the Secretary of State (whether under this section or otherwise), the trustee shall give notice to the bankrupt's creditors of his appointment or, if the court so allows, shall advertise his appointment in accordance with the court's directions.

(5)   In that notice or advertisement the trustee shall explain the procedure for establishing a creditors' committee under section 301.

297.   ...

298.   **Removal of trustee; vacation of office**

(1)   Subject as follows, the trustee of a bankrupt's estate may be removed from office only by an order of the court or by a decision of the bankrupt's creditors made by a creditors' decision procedure instigated specially for that purpose in accordance with the rules.

(2), (3) ...

(4) Where the official receiver is trustee by virtue of section 291A(1) or a trustee is appointed by the Secretary of State or (otherwise than under section 291A(2)) by the court, a creditors' decision procedure may be instigated for the purpose of removing the trustee only if—

    (a) the trustee thinks fit, or

    (b) the court so directs, or

    (c) ... one of the bankrupt's creditors so requests, with the concurrence of not less than one-quarter, in value, of the creditors (including the creditor making the request).

(4A) Where the bankrupt's creditors decide to remove a trustee, they may in accordance with the rules appoint another person as trustee in his place.

(4B) Where the decision to remove a trustee is made under subsection (4), the decision does not take effect until the bankrupt's creditors appoint another person as trustee in his place.

(5) If the trustee was appointed by the Secretary of State, he may be removed by a direction of the Secretary of State.

(6) The trustee (not being the official receiver) shall vacate office if he ceases to be a person who is for the time being qualified to act as an insolvency practitioner in relation to the bankrupt.

(7) The trustee may, in the prescribed circumstances, resign his office by giving notice of his resignation to the prescribed person.

(8) The trustee shall vacate office on giving notice to the prescribed person that the trustee has given notice under section 331(2).

(8A) A notice under subsection (8)—

    (a) must not be given before the end of the period prescribed by the rules as the period within which the bankrupt's creditors may object to the trustee's release, and

    (b) must state whether any of the bankrupt's creditors objected to the trustee's release.

(9) The trustee shall vacate office if the bankruptcy order is annulled.

299. Release of trustee

(1) Where the official receiver has ceased to be the trustee of a bankrupt's estate and a person is appointed in his stead, the official receiver shall have his release with effect from the following time, that is to say—

    (a) where that person is appointed by ... the bankrupt's creditors or by the Secretary of State, the time at which the official receiver gives notice under this paragraph to the prescribed person that he has been replaced, and

    (b) where that person is appointed by the court, such time as the court may determine.

(2) If the official receiver while he is the trustee gives notice to the Secretary of State that the administration of the bankrupt's estate in accordance with Chapter IV of this Part is for practical purposes complete, he shall have his release with effect from such time as the Secretary of State may determine.

(3) A person other than the official receiver who has ceased to be the trustee shall have his release with effect from the following time, that is to say—

    (a) in the following cases, the time at which notice is given to the prescribed person in accordance with the rules that that person has ceased to hold office—

        (i) the person has been removed from office by a decision of the bankrupt's creditors and the creditors have not decided against his release,

        (ii) the person has died;

    (b) in the following cases, such time as the Secretary of State may, on an application by the person, determine—

        (i) the person has been removed from office by a decision of the bankrupt's creditors and the creditors have decided against his release,

        (ii) the person has been removed from office by the court or by the Secretary of State,

        (iii) the person has vacated office under section 298(6);

    (c) in the case of a person who has resigned, such time as may be prescribed;

    (d) in the case of a person who has vacated office under section 298(8)—

(i)   if any of the bankrupt's creditors objected to the person's release before the end of the period for so objecting prescribed by the rules, such time as the Secretary of State may, on an application by that person, determine, and

(ii)   otherwise, the time at which the person vacated office.

(3A)   Where the person is removed from office by a decision of the bankrupt's creditors, any decision of the bankrupt's creditors as to whether the person should have his release must be made by a creditors' decision procedure.

(4)   Where a bankruptcy order is annulled, the trustee at the time of the annulment has his release with effect from such time as the court may determine.

(5)   Where the official receiver or the trustee has his release under this section, he shall, with effect from the time specified in the preceding provisions of this section, be discharged from all liability both in respect of acts or omissions of his in the administration of the estate and otherwise in relation to his conduct as trustee.

But nothing in this section prevents the exercise, in relation to a person who has had his release under this section, of the court's powers under section 304.

300.   Vacancy in office of trustee

(1)   This section applies where the appointment of any person as trustee of a bankrupt's estate fails to take effect or, such an appointment having taken effect, there is otherwise a vacancy in the office of trustee.

(2)   The official receiver shall be trustee until the vacancy is filled.

(3)   The official receiver may ask the bankrupt's creditors to appoint a person as trustee, and must do so if so requested by not less than one tenth in value of the bankrupt's creditors.

(3A)   If the official receiver makes such a request the bankrupt's creditors may in accordance with the rules appoint a person as trustee.

(4)   If at the end of the period of 28 days beginning with the day on which the vacancy first came to the official receiver's attention he has not asked, and is not proposing to ask, the bankrupt's creditors to appoint a person as trustee, he shall refer the need for an appointment to the Secretary of State.

(5)   ...

(6)   On a reference to the Secretary of State under subsection (4) ... the Secretary of State shall either make an appointment or decline to make one.

(7)   If on a reference under subsection (4) ... no appointment is made, the official receiver shall continue to be trustee of the bankrupt's estate, but without prejudice to his power to make a further reference.

(8)   References in this section to a vacancy include a case where it is necessary, in relation to any property which is or may be comprised in a bankrupt's estate, to revive the trusteeship of that estate after the vacation of office by the trustee under section 298(8) or the giving by the official receiver of notice under section 299(2).

Control of trustee

301.   Creditors' committee

(1)   Subject as follows, a bankrupt's creditors may, in accordance with the rules, establish a committee (known as "the creditors' committee") to exercise the functions conferred on it by or under this Act.

(2)   The bankrupt's creditors shall not establish such a committee, or confer any functions on such a committee, at any time when the official receiver is the trustee of the bankrupt's estate, except in connection with the appointment of a person to be trustee instead of the official receiver.

302.   Exercise by Secretary of State of functions of creditors' committee

(1)   The creditors' committee is not to be able or required to carry out its functions at any time when the official receiver is trustee of the bankrupt's estate; but at any such time the functions of the

committee under this Act shall be vested in the Secretary of State, except to the extent that the rules otherwise provide.

(2)   Where in the case of any bankruptcy there is for the time being no creditors' committee and the trustee of the bankrupt's estate is a person other than the official receiver, the functions of such a committee shall be vested in the Secretary of State, except to the extent that the rules otherwise provide.

303.   General control of trustee by the court

(1)   If a bankrupt or any of his creditors or any other person is dissatisfied by any act, omission or decision of a trustee of the bankrupt's estate, he may apply to the court; and on such an application the court may confirm, reverse or modify any act or decision of the trustee, may give him directions or may make such other order as it thinks fit.

(2)   The trustee of a bankrupt's estate may apply to the court for directions in relation to any particular matter arising under the bankruptcy.

(2A)   Where at any time after a bankruptcy petition has been presented to the court against any person, whether under the provisions of the Insolvent Partnerships Order 1994 or not, the attention of the court is drawn to the fact that the person in question is a member of an insolvent partnership, the court may make an order as to the future conduct of the insolvency proceedings and any such order may apply any provisions of that Order with any necessary modifications.

(2B)   Where a bankruptcy petition has been presented against more than one individual in the circumstances mentioned in subsection (2A) above, the court may give such directions for consolidating the proceedings, or any of them, as it thinks just.

(2C)   Any order or directions under subsection (2A) or (2B) may be made or given on the application of the official receiver, any responsible insolvency practitioner, the trustee of the partnership or any other interested person and may include provisions as to the administration of the joint estate of the partnership, and in particular how it and the separate estate of any member are to be administered.

304.   Liability of trustee

(1)   Where on an application under this section the court is satisfied—

(a)   that the trustee of a bankrupt's estate has misapplied or retained, or become accountable for, any money or other property comprised in the bankrupt's estate, or

(b)   that a bankrupt's estate has suffered any loss in consequence of any misfeasance or breach of fiduciary or other duty by a trustee of the estate in the carrying out of his functions,

the court may order the trustee, for the benefit of the estate, to repay, restore or account for money or other property (together with interest at such rate as the court thinks just) or, as the case may require, to pay such sum by way of compensation in respect of the misfeasance or breach of fiduciary or other duty as the court thinks just.

This is without prejudice to any liability arising apart from this section.

(2)   An application under this section may be made by the official receiver, the Secretary of State, a creditor of the bankrupt or (whether or not there is, or is likely to be, a surplus for the purposes of section 330(5) (final distribution)) the bankrupt himself.

But the leave of the court is required for the making of an application if it is to be made by the bankrupt or if it is to be made after the trustee has had his release under section 299.

(3)   Where—

(a)   the trustee seizes or disposes of any property which is not comprised in the bankrupt's estate, and

(b)   at the time of the seizure or disposal the trustee believes, and has reasonable grounds for believing, that he is entitled (whether in pursuance of an order of the court or otherwise) to seize or dispose of that property,

the trustee is not liable to any person (whether under this section or otherwise) in respect of any loss or damage resulting from the seizure or disposal except in so far as that loss or damage is caused by the negligence of the trustee; and he has a lien on the property, or the proceeds of its sale, for such of the expenses of the bankruptcy as were incurred in connection with the seizure or disposal.

CHAPTER IV
ADMINISTRATION BY TRUSTEE

Preliminary

305.   General functions of trustee

(1)   This Chapter applies in relation to any bankruptcy where either—
   (a)   the appointment of a person as trustee of a bankrupt's estate takes effect, or
   (b)   the official receiver becomes trustee of a bankrupt's estate.

(2)   The function of the trustee is to get in, realise and distribute the bankrupt's estate in accordance with the following provisions of this Chapter; and in the carrying out of that function and in the management of the bankrupt's estate the trustee is entitled, subject to those provisions, to use his own discretion.

(3)   It is the duty of the trustee, if he is not the official receiver—
   (a)   to furnish the official receiver with such information,
   (b)   to produce to the official receiver, and permit inspection by the official receiver of, such books, papers and other records, and
   (c)   to give the official receiver such other assistance,
   as the official receiver may reasonably require for the purpose of enabling him to carry out his functions in relation to the bankruptcy.

(4)   The official name of the trustee shall be "the trustee of the estate of .. .., a bankrupt" (inserting the name of the bankrupt); be he may be referred to as "the trustee in bankruptcy" of the particular bankrupt.

Acquisition, control and realisation of bankrupt's estate

306.   Vesting of bankrupt's estate in trustee

(1)   The bankrupt's estate shall vest in the trustee immediately on his appointment taking effect or, in the case of the official receiver, on his becoming trustee.

(2)   Where any property which is, or is to be, comprised in the bankrupt's estate vests in the trustee (whether under this section or under any other provision of this Part), it shall so vest without any conveyance, assignment or transfer.

306A.   Property subject to restraint order

(1)   This section applies where—
   (a)   property is excluded from the bankrupt's estate by virtue of section 417(2)(a) of the Proceeds of Crime Act 2002 (property subject to a restraint order),
   (b)   an order under section section 50, 67A, 128, 131A, 198 or 215A of that Act has not been made in respect of the property, ...
   (c)   the restraint order is discharged, and
   (d)   immediately after the discharge of the restraint order the property is not detained under or by virtue of section 44A, 47J, 122A, 127J, 193A or 195J of that Act.

(2)   The property vests in the trustee as part of the bankrupt's estate.

(3)   But subsection (2) does not apply to the proceeds of property realised by a management receiver under section 49(2)(d) or 197(2)(d) of that Act (realisation of property to meet receiver's remuneration and expenses).

306AA. Property released from detention

(1)   This section applies where—
   (a)   property is excluded from the bankrupt's estate by virtue of section 417(2)(b) of the Proceeds of Crime Act 2002 (property detained under certain provisions),

(b)   no order is in force in respect of the property under section 41, 50, 120, 128, 190 or 198 of that Act, and

(c)   the property is released.

(2)   The property vests in the trustee as part of the bankrupt's estate.

306B.   Property in respect of which receivership or administration order made

(1)   This section applies where—

(a)   property is excluded from the bankrupt's estate by virtue of section section 417(2)(c) of the Proceeds of Crime Act 2002 (property in respect of which an order for the appointment of a receiver or administrator under certain provisions of that Act is in force),

(b)   a confiscation order is made under section 6, 92 or 156 of that Act,

(c)   the amount payable under the confiscation order is fully paid, and

(d)   any of the property remains in the hands of the receiver or administrator (as the case may be).

(2)   The property vests in the trustee as part of the bankrupt's estate.

306BA. Property in respect of which realisation order made

(1)   This section applies where—

(a)   property is excluded from the bankrupt's estate by virtue of section 417(2)(d) of the Proceeds of Crime Act 2002 (property in respect of which an order has been made authorising realisation of the property by an appropriate officer),

(b)   a confiscation order is made under section 6, 92 or 156 of that Act,

(c)   the amount payable under the confiscation order is fully paid, and

(d)   any of the property remains in the hands of the appropriate officer.

(2)   The property vests in the trustee as part of the bankrupt's estate.

306C.   Property subject to certain orders where confiscation order discharged or quashed

(1)   This section applies where—

(a)   property is excluded from the bankrupt's estate by virtue of section 417(2)(a), (b), (c) or (d) of the Proceeds of Crime Act 2002 (property excluded from bankrupt's estate),

(b)   a confiscation order is made under section 6, 92 or 156 of that Act, and

(c)   the confiscation order is discharged under section 30, 114 or 180 of that Act (as the case may be) or quashed under that Act or in pursuance of any enactment relating to appeals against conviction or sentence.

(2)   Any such property vests in the trustee as part of the bankrupt's estate if it is in the hands of—

(a)   a receiver appointed under Part 2 or 4 of that Act,

(b)   an administrator appointed under Part 3 of that Act,

(c)   an appropriate officer (within the meaning of section 41A, 120A or 190A of that Act).

(3)   But subsection (2) does not apply to the proceeds of property realised by a management receiver under section 49(2)(d) or 197(2)(d) of that Act (realisation of property to meet receiver's remuneration and expenses).

307.   After-acquired property

(1)   Subject to this section and section 309, the trustee may by notice in writing claim for the bankrupt's estate any property which has been acquired by, or has devolved upon, the bankrupt since the commencement of the bankruptcy.

(2)   A notice under this section shall not served in respect of—

(a)   any property falling within subsection (2) or (3) of section 283 in Chapter II,

(aa) any property vesting in the bankrupt by virtue of section 283A in Chapter II,

(b)   any property which by virtue of any other enactment is excluded from the bankrupt's estate, or

(c)   without prejudice to section 280(2)(c) (order of court on application for discharge), any property which is acquired by or, devolves upon, the bankrupt after his discharge.

(3)   Subject to subsections (4) and (4A), upon the service on the bankrupt of a notice under this section the property to which the notice relates shall vest in the trustee as part of the bankrupt's estate; and the trustee's title to that property has relation back to the time at which the property was acquired by, or devolved upon, the bankrupt.

(4)   Where, whether before or after service on the bankrupt of a notice under this section—

     (a)   a person acquires property in good faith, for value and without notice of the bankruptcy, ...

     (b)   ...

     the trustee is not in respect of that property ... entitled by virtue of this section to any remedy against that person ..., or any person whose title to any property derives from that person ... .

(4A)   Where a banker enters into a transaction before service on the banker of a notice under this section (and whether before or after service on the bankrupt of a notice under this section) the trustee is not in respect of that transaction entitled by virtue of this section to any remedy against the banker.

     This subsection applies whether or not the banker has notice of the bankruptcy.

(5)   References in this section to property do not include any property which, as part of the bankrupt's income, may be the subject of an income payments order under section 310.

308.   Vesting in trustee of certain items of excess value

(1)   Subject to section 309, where—

     (a)   property is excluded by virtue of section 283(2) (tools of trade, household effects, etc) from the bankrupt's estate, and

     (b)   it appears to the trustee that the realisable value of the whole or any part of that property exceeds the cost of a reasonable replacement for that property or that part of it,

     the trustee may by notice in writing claim that property or, as the case may be, that part of it for the bankrupt's estate.

(2)   Upon the service on the bankrupt of a notice under this section, the property to which the notice relates vests in the trustee as part of the bankrupt's estate; and, except against a purchaser in good faith, for value and without notice of the bankruptcy, the trustee's title to that property has relation back to the commencement of the bankruptcy.

(3)   The trustee shall apply funds comprised in the estate to the purchase by or on behalf of the bankrupt of a reasonable replacement for any property vested in the trustee under this section; and the duty imposed by this subsection has priority over the obligation of the trustee to distribute the estate.

(4)   For the purposes of this section property is a reasonable replacement for other property if it is reasonably adequate for meeting the needs met by the other property.

308A.   Vesting in trustee of certain tenancies

     Upon the service on the bankrupt by the trustee of a notice in writing under this section, any tenancy—

     (a)   which is excluded by virtue of section 283(3A) from the bankrupt's estate, and

     (b)   to which the notice relates,

     vests in the trustee as part of the bankrupt's estate; and, except against a purchaser in good faith, for value and without notice of the bankruptcy, the trustee's title to that tenancy has relation back to the commencement of the bankruptcy.

309.   Time-limit for notice under s 307 or 308

(1)   Except with the leave of the court, a notice shall not be served—

     (a)   under section 307, after the end of the period of 42 days beginning with the day on which it first came to the knowledge of the trustee that the property in question had been acquired by, or had devolved upon, the bankrupt;

     (b)   under section 308 or section 308A, after the end of the period of 42 days beginning with the day on which the property or tenancy in question first came to the knowledge of the trustee.

(2)   For the purposes of this section—

(a) anything which comes to the knowledge of the trustee is deemed in relation to any successor of his as trustee to have come to the knowledge of the successor at the same time; and

(b) anything which comes (otherwise than under paragraph (a)) to the knowledge of a person before he is the trustee is deemed to come to his knowledge on his appointment taking effect or, in the case of the official receiver, on his becoming trustee.

310. Income payments orders

(1) The court may, ... make an order ("an income payments order") claiming for the bankrupt's estate so much of the income of the bankrupt during the period for which the order is in force as may be specified in the order.

(1A) An income payments order may be made only on an application instituted—

(a) by the trustee, and

(b) before the discharge of the bankrupt.

(2) The court shall not make an income payments order the effect of which would be to reduce the income of the bankrupt when taken together with any payments to which subsection (8) applies below what appears to the court to be necessary for meeting the reasonable domestic needs of the bankrupt and his family.

(3) An income payments order shall, in respect of any payment of income to which it is to apply, either—

(a) require the bankrupt to pay the trustee an amount equal to so much of that payment as is claimed by the order, or

(b) require the person making the payment to pay so much of it as is so claimed to the trustee, instead of to the bankrupt.

(4) Where the court makes an income payments order it may, if it thinks fit, discharge or vary any attachment of earnings order that is for the time being in force to secure payments by the bankrupt.

(5) Sums received by the trustee under an income payments order form part of the bankrupt's estate.

(6) An income payments order must specify the period during which it is to have effect; and that period—

(a) may end after the discharge of the bankrupt, but

(b) may not end after the period of three years beginning with the date on which the order is made.

(6A) An income payments order may (subject to subsection (6)(b)) be varied on the application of the trustee or the bankrupt (whether before or after discharge).

(7) For the purposes of this section the income of the bankrupt comprises every payment in the nature of income which is from time to time made to him or to which he from time to time becomes entitled, including any payment in respect of the carrying on of any business or in respect of any office or employment and (despite anything in section 11 or 12 of the Welfare Reform and Pensions Act 1999) any payment under a pension scheme but excluding any payment to which subsection (8) applies.

(8) This subsection applies to—

(a) payments by way of guaranteed minimum pension; ...

(b) ...

(9) In this section, "guaranteed minimum pension" has the same meaning as in the Pension Schemes Act 1993.

310A. Income payments agreement

(1) In this section "income payments agreement" means a written agreement between a bankrupt and his trustee or between a bankrupt and the official receiver which provides—

(a) that the bankrupt is to pay to the trustee or the official receiver an amount equal to a specified part or proportion of the bankrupt's income for a specified period, or

(b) that a third person is to pay to the trustee or the official receiver a specified proportion of money due to the bankrupt by way of income for a specified period.

(2)   A provision of an income payments agreement of a kind specified in subsection (1)(a) or (b) may be enforced as if it were a provision of an income payments order.

(3)   While an income payments agreement is in force the court may, on the application of the bankrupt, his trustee or the official receiver, discharge or vary an attachment of earnings order that is for the time being in force to secure payments by the bankrupt.

(4)   The following provisions of section 310 shall apply to an income payments agreement as they apply to an income payments order—

    (a)   subsection (5) (receipts to form part of estate), and

    (b)   subsections (7) to (9) (meaning of income).

(5)   An income payments agreement must specify the period during which it is to have effect; and that period—

    (a)   may end after the discharge of the bankrupt, but

    (b)   may not end after the period of three years beginning with the date on which the agreement is made.

(6)   An income payments agreement may (subject to subsection (5)(b)) be varied—

    (a)   by written agreement between the parties, or

    (b)   by the court on an application made by the bankrupt, the trustee or the official receiver.

(7)   The court—

    (a)   may not vary an income payments agreement so as to include provision of a kind which could not be included in an income payments order, and

    (b)   shall grant an application to vary an income payments agreement if and to the extent that the court thinks variation necessary to avoid the effect mentioned in section 310(2).

311.   Acquisition by trustee of control

(1)   The trustee shall take possession of all books, papers and other records which relate to the bankrupt's estate or affairs and which belong to him or are in his possession or under his control (including any which would be privileged from disclosure in any proceedings).

(2)   In relation to, and for the purpose of acquiring or retaining possession of, the bankrupt's estate, the trustee is in the same position as if he were a receiver of property appointed by the High Court; and the court may, on his application, enforce such acquisition or retention accordingly.

(3)   Where any part of the bankrupt's estate consists of stock or shares in a company, shares in a ship or any other property transferable in the books of a company, office or person, the trustee may exercise the right to transfer the property to the same extent as the bankrupt might have exercised it if he had not become bankrupt.

(4)   Where any part of the estate consists of things in action, they are deemed to have been assigned to the trustee; but notice of the deemed assignment need not be given except in so far as it is necessary, in a case where the deemed assignment is from the bankrupt himself, for protecting the priority of the trustee.

(5)   Where any goods comprised in the estate are held by any person by way of pledge, pawn or other security and no notice has been served in respect of those goods by the official receiver under subsection (5) of section 285 (restriction on realising security), the trustee may serve such a notice in respect of the goods; and whether or not a notice has been served under this subsection or that subsection, the trustee may, if he thinks fit, exercise the bankrupt's right of redemption in respect of any such goods.

(6)   A notice served by the trustee under subsection (5) has the same effect as a notice served by the official receiver under section 285(5).

312.   Obligation to surrender control to trustee

(1)   The bankrupt shall deliver up to the trustee possession of any property, books, papers or other records of which he has possession or control and of which the trustee is required to take possession.

This is without prejudice to the general duties of the bankrupt under section 333 in this Chapter.

(2) If any of the following is in possession of any property, books, papers or other records of which the trustee is required to take possession, namely—

(a) the official receiver,

(b) a person who has ceased to be trustee of the bankrupt's estate, or

(c) a person who has been the supervisor of a voluntary arrangement approved in relation to the bankrupt under Part VIII,

the official receiver or, as the case may be, that person shall deliver up possession of the property, books, papers or records to the trustee.

(3) Any banker or agent of the bankrupt or any other person who holds any property to the account of, or for, the bankrupt shall pay or deliver to the trustee all property in his possession or under his control which forms part of the bankrupt's estate and which he is not by law entitled to retain as against the bankrupt or trustee.

(4) If any person without reasonable excuse fails to comply with any obligation imposed by this section, he is guilty of a contempt of court and liable to be punished accordingly (in addition to any other punishment to which he may be subject).

313. Charge on bankrupt's home

(1) Where any property consisting of an interest in a dwelling house which is occupied by the bankrupt or by his spouse or former spouse or by his civil partner or former civil partner is comprised in the bankrupt's estate and the trustee is, for any reason, unable for the time being to realise that property, the trustee may apply to the court for an order imposing a charge on the property for the benefit of the bankrupt's estate.

(2) If on an application under this section the court imposes a charge on any property, the benefit of that charge shall be comprised in the bankrupt's estate and is enforceable, up to the charged value from time to time, for the payment of any amount which is payable otherwise than to the bankrupt out of the estate and of interest on that amount at the prescribed rate.

(2A) In subsection (2) the charged value means—

(a) the amount specified in the charging order as the value of the bankrupt's interest in the property at the date of the order, plus

(b) interest on that amount from the date of the charging order at the prescribed rate.

(2B) In determining the value of an interest for the purposes of this section the court shall disregard any matter which it is required to disregard by the rules.

(3) An order under this section made in respect of property vested in the trustee shall provide, in accordance with the rules, for the property to cease to be comprised in the bankrupt's estate and, subject to the charge (and any prior charge), to vest in the bankrupt.

(4) Subsection (1), (2), (4), (5) and (6) of section 3 of the Charging Orders Act 1979 (supplemental provisions with respect to charging orders) have effect in relation to orders under this section as in relation to charging orders under that Act.

(5) But an order under section 3(5) of that Act may not vary a charged value.

313A. Low value home: application for sale, possession or charge

(1) This section applies where—

(a) property comprised in the bankrupt's estate consists of an interest in a dwelling-house which at the date of the bankruptcy was the sole or principal residence of—

(i) the bankrupt,

(ii) the bankrupt's spouse or civil partner, or

(iii) a former spouse or former civil partner of the bankrupt, and

(b) the trustee applies for an order for the sale of the property, for an order for possession of the property or for an order under section 313 in respect of the property.

(2) The court shall dismiss the application if the value of the interest is below the amount prescribed for the purposes of this subsection.

(3)   In determining the value of an interest for the purposes of this section the court shall disregard any matter which it is required to disregard by the order which prescribes the amount for the purposes of subsection (2).

314.   Powers of trustee

(1)   The trustee may exercise any of the powers specified in Parts 1 and 2 of Schedule 5.

(2)   ... the trustee may appoint the bankrupt—

(a)   to superintend the management of his estate or any part of it,

(b)   to carry on his business (if any) for the benefit of his creditors, or

(c)   in any other respect to assist in administering the estate in such manner and on such terms as the trustee may direct.

(3), (4) ...

(5)   Part III of Schedule 5 to this Act has effect with respect to the things which the trustee is able to do for the purposes of, or in connection with, the exercise of any of his powers under any of this Group of Parts.

(6)   Where the trustee (not being the official receiver) in exercise of the powers conferred on him by any provision in this Group of Parts—

(a)   disposes of any property comprised in the bankrupt's estate to an associate of the bankrupt, or

(b)   employs a solicitor,

he shall, if there is for the time being a creditors' committee, give notice to the committee of that exercise of his powers.

(7)   Without prejudice to the generality of subsection (5) and Part III of Schedule 5, the trustee may, if he thinks fit, at any time seek a decision on a matter from the bankrupt's creditors.

Subject to the preceding provisions in this Group of Parts, he shall seek a decision on a matter if he is requested to do so by a creditor of the bankrupt and the request is made with the concurrence of not less than one-tenth, in value, of the bankrupt's creditors (including the creditor making the request).

(8)   Nothing in this Act is to be construed as restricting the capacity of the trustee to exercise any of his powers outside England and Wales.

Disclaimer of onerous property

315.   Disclaimer (general power)

(1)   Subject as follows, the trustee may, by the giving of the prescribed notice, disclaim any onerous property and may do so notwithstanding that he has taken possession of it, endeavoured to sell it or otherwise exercised rights of ownership in relation to it.

(2)   The following is onerous property for the purposes of this section, that is to say—

(a)   any unprofitable contract, and

(b)   any other property comprised in the bankrupt's estate which is unsaleable or not readily saleable, or is such that it may give rise to a liability to pay money or perform any other onerous act.

(3)   A disclaimer under this section—

(a)   operates so as to determine, as from the date of the disclaimer, the rights, interests and liabilities of the bankrupt and his estate in or in respect of the property disclaimed, and

(b)   discharges the trustee from all personal liability in respect of that property as from the commencement of his trusteeship,

but does not, except so far as is necessary for the purpose of releasing the bankrupt, the bankrupt's estate and the trustee from any liability, affect the rights or liabilities of any other person.

(4)   A notice of disclaimer shall not be given under this section in respect of any property that has been claimed for the estate under section 307 (after-acquired property) or 308 (personal property of bankrupt exceeding reasonable replacement value) or 308A, except with the leave of the court.

(5)   Any person sustaining loss or damage in consequence of the operation of a disclaimer under this section is deemed to be a creditor of the bankrupt to the extent of the loss or damage and accordingly may prove for the loss or damage as a bankruptcy debt.

316.   Notice requiring trustee's decision

(1)   Notice of disclaimer shall not be given under section 315 in respect of any property if—

   (a)   a person interested in the property has applied in writing to the trustee or one of his predecessors as trustee requiring the trustee or that predecessor to decide whether he will disclaim or not, and

   (b)   the period of 28 days beginning with the day on which that application was made has expired without a notice of disclaimer having been given under section 315 in respect of that property.

(2)   The trustee is deemed to have adopted any contract which by virtue of this section he is not entitled to disclaim.

317.   Disclaimer of leaseholds

(1)   The disclaimer of any property of a leasehold nature does not take effect unless a copy of the disclaimer has been served (so far as the trustee is aware of their addresses) on every person claiming under the bankrupt as underlessee or mortgagee and either—

   (a)   no application under section 320 below is made with respect to the property before the end of the period of 14 days beginning with the day on which the last notice served under this subsection was served, or

   (b)   where such an application has been made, the court directs that the disclaimer is to take effect.

(2)   Where the court gives a direction under subsection (1)(b) it may also, instead of or in addition to any order it makes under section 320, make such orders with respect to fixtures, tenant's improvements and other matters arising out of the lease as it thinks fit.

318.   Disclaimer of dwelling house

Without prejudice to section 317, the disclaimer of any property in a dwelling house does not take effect unless a copy of the disclaimer has been served (so far as the trustee is aware of their addresses) on every person in occupation of or claiming a right to occupy the dwelling house and either—

   (a)   no application under section 320 is made with respect to the property before the end of the period of 14 days beginning with the day on which the last notice served under this section was served, or

   (b)   where such an application has been made, the court directs that the disclaimer is to take effect.

319.   Disclaimer of land subject to rentcharge

(1)   The following applies where, in consequence of the disclaimer under section 315 of any land subject to a rentcharge, that land vests by operation of law in the Crown or any other person (referred to in the next subsection as "the proprietor").

(2)   The proprietor, and the successors in title of the proprietor, are not subject to any personal liability in respect of any sums becoming due under the rentcharge, except sums becoming due after the proprietor, or some person claiming under or through the proprietor, has taken possession or control of the land or has entered into occupation of it.

320.   Court order vesting disclaimed property

(1)   This section and the next apply where the trustee has disclaimed property under section 315.

(2)   An application may be made to the court under this section by—

   (a)   any person who claims an interest in the disclaimed property,

   (b)   any person who is under any liability in respect of the disclaimed property, not being a liability discharged by the disclaimer, or

(c)   where the disclaimed property is property in a dwelling-house, any person who at the time when the bankruptcy application was made or (as the case may be) the bankruptcy petition was presented was in occupation of or entitled to occupy the dwelling house.

(3)   Subject as follows in this section and the next, the court may, on an application under this section, make an order on such terms as it thinks fit for the vesting of the disclaimed property in, or for its delivery to—

(a)   a person entitled to it or a trustee for such a person,

(b)   a person subject to such a liability as is mentioned in subsection (2)(b) or a trustee for such a person, or

(c)   where the disclaimed property is property in a dwelling-house, any person who at the time when the bankruptcy application was made or (as the case may be) the bankruptcy petition was presented was in occupation of or entitled to occupy the dwelling house.

(4)   The court shall not make an order by virtue of subsection (3)(b) except where it appears to the court that it would be just to do so for the purpose of compensating the person subject to the liability in respect of the disclaimer.

(5)   The effect of any order under this section shall be taken into account in assessing for the purposes of section 315(5) the extent of any loss or damage sustained by any person in consequence of the disclaimer.

(6)   An order under this section vesting property in any person need not be completed by any conveyance, assignment or transfer.

321.   Order under s 320 in respect of leaseholds

(1)   The court shall not make an order under section 320 vesting property of a leasehold nature in any person, except on terms making that person—

(a)   subject to the same liabilities and obligations as the bankrupt was subject to under the lease on the day the bankruptcy application was made or (as the case may be) the bankruptcy petition was presented, or

(b)   if the court thinks fit, subject to the same liabilities and obligations as that person would be subject to if the lease had been assigned to him on that day.

(2)   For the purposes of an order under section 320 relating to only part of any property comprised in a lease, the requirements of subsection (1) apply as if the lease comprised only the property to which the order relates.

(3)   Where subsection (1) applies and no person is willing to accept an order under section 320 on the terms required by that subsection, the court may (by order under section 320) vest the estate or interest of the bankrupt in the property in any person who is liable (whether personally or in a representative capacity and whether alone or jointly with the bankrupt) to perform the lessee's covenants in the lease.

The court may by virtue of this subsection vest that estate and interest in such a person freed and discharged from all estates, incumbrances and interests created by the bankrupt.

(4)   Where subsection (1) applies and a person declines to accept any order under section 320, that person shall be excluded from all interest in the property.

Distribution of bankrupt's estate

322.   Proof of debts

(1)   Subject to this section and the next, the proof of any bankruptcy debt by a secured or unsecured creditor of the bankrupt and the admission or rejection of any proof shall take place in accordance with the rules.

(2)   Where a bankruptcy debt bears interest, that interest is provable as part of the debt except in so far as it is payable in respect of any period after the commencement of the bankruptcy.

(3)   The trustee shall estimate the value of any bankruptcy debt which, by reason of its being subject to any contingency or contingencies or for any other reason, does not bear a certain value.

(4)   Where the value of a bankruptcy debt is estimated by the trustee under subsection (3) or, by virtue of section 303 in Chapter III, by the court, the amount provable in the bankruptcy in respect of the debt is the amount of the estimate.

323.   Mutual credit and set-off

(1)   This section applies where before the commencement of the bankruptcy there have been mutual credits, mutual debts or other mutual dealings between the bankrupt and any creditor of the bankrupt proving or claiming to prove for a bankruptcy debt.

(2)   An account shall be taken of what is due from each party to the other in respect of the mutual dealings and the sums due from one party shall be set off against the sums due from the other.

(3)   Sums due from the bankrupt to another party shall not be included in the account taken under subsection (2) if that other party had notice at the time they became due that proceedings on a bankruptcy application relating to the bankrupt were ongoing or that a bankruptcy petition relating to the bankrupt was pending.

(4)   Only the balance (if any) of the account taken under subsection (2) is provable as a bankruptcy debt or, as the case may be, to be paid to the trustee as part of the bankrupt's estate.

324.   Distribution by means of dividend

(1)   Whenever the trustee has sufficient funds in hand for the purpose he shall, subject to the retention of such sums as may be necessary for the expenses of the bankruptcy, declare and distribute dividends among the creditors in respect of the bankruptcy debts which they have respectively proved.

(2)   The trustee shall give notice of his intention to declare and distribute a dividend.

(3)   Where the trustee has declared a dividend, he shall give notice of the dividend and of how it is proposed to distribute it; and a notice given under this subsection shall contain the prescribed particulars of the bankrupt's estate.

(4)   In the calculation and distribution of a dividend the trustee shall make provision—

(a)   for any bankruptcy debts which appear to him to be due to persons who, by reason of the distance of their place of residence, may not have had sufficient time to tender and establish their proofs,

(b)   for any bankruptcy debts which are the subject of claims which have not yet been determined, and

(c)   for disputed proofs and claims.

325.   Claims by unsatisfied creditors

(1)   A creditor who has not proved his debt before the declaration of any dividend is not entitled to disturb, by reason that he has not participated in it, the distribution of that dividend or any other dividend declared before his debt was proved, but—

(a)   when he has proved that debt he is entitled to be paid, out of any money for the time being available for the payment of any further dividend, any dividend or dividends which he has failed to receive; and

(b)   any dividend or dividends payable under paragraph (a) shall be paid before that money is applied to the payment of any such further dividend.

(2)   No action lies against the trustee for a dividend, but if the trustee refuses to pay a dividend the court may, if it thinks fit, order him to pay it and also to pay, out of his own money—

(a)   interest on the dividend, at the rate for the time being specified in section 17 of the Judgments Act 1838, from the time it was withheld, and

(b)   the costs of the proceedings in which the order to pay is made.

326.   Distribution of property in specie

(1)   Without prejudice to sections 315 to 319 (disclaimer), the trustee may, with the permission of the creditors' committee, divide in its existing form amongst the bankrupt's creditors, according to its estimated value, any property which from its peculiar nature or other special circumstances cannot be readily or advantageously sold.

(2)   A permission given for the purposes of subsection (1) shall not be a general permission but shall relate to a particular proposed exercise of the power in question; and a person dealing with the trustee in good faith and for value is not to be concerned to enquire whether any permission required by subsection (1) has been given.

(3)   Where the trustee has done anything without the permission required by subsection (1), the court or the creditors' committee may, for the purpose of enabling him to meet his expenses out of the bankrupt's estate, ratify what the trustee has done.

But the committee shall not do so unless it is satisfied that the trustee acted in a case of urgency and has sought its ratification without undue delay.

327.   *Distribution in criminal bankruptcy*

Where the bankruptcy order was made on a petition under section 264(1)(d) (criminal bankruptcy), no distribution shall be made under sections 324 to 326 so long as an appeal is pending (within the meaning of section 277) against the bankrupt's conviction of any offence by virtue of which the criminal bankruptcy order on which the petition was based was made.

Note. This section is repealed by the Criminal Justice Act 1988, s. 170(2), Sch. 16, as from a day to be appointed.

328.   **Priority of debts**

(1)   In the distribution of the bankrupt's estate, his preferential debts ... shall be paid in priority to other debts.

(1A)   Ordinary preferential debts rank equally among themselves after the expenses of the bankruptcy and shall be paid in full, unless the bankrupt's estate is insufficient to meet them, in which case they abate in equal proportions between themselves.

(1B)   Secondary preferential debts rank equally among themselves after the ordinary preferential debts and shall be paid in full, unless the bankrupt's estate is insufficient to meet them, in which case they abate in equal proportions between themselves.

(2)   ...

(3)   Debts which are neither preferential debts nor debts to which the next section applies also rank equally between themselves and, after the preferential debts, shall be paid in full unless the bankrupt's estate is insufficient for meeting them, in which case they abate in equal proportions between themselves.

(3A)   If the bankrupt is a relevant financial institution, subsection (3) does not apply but—

    (a)   the bankrupt's ordinary non-preferential debts shall be paid in priority to the bankrupt's secondary non-preferential debts,

    (b)   the bankrupt's ordinary non-preferential debts rank equally among themselves after the secondary preferential debts and shall be paid in full, unless the bankrupt's estate is insufficient to meet them, in which case they abate in equal proportions,

    (c)   the bankrupt's secondary non-preferential debts shall be paid in priority to the bankrupt's tertiary non-preferential debts, and

    (d)   the bankrupt's secondary non-preferential debts rank equally among themselves after the ordinary non-preferential debts and shall be paid in full, unless the bankrupt's estate is insufficient to meet them, in which case they abate in equal proportions.

See section 387A for definitions relevant to this subsection.

(4)   Any surplus remaining after the payment of the debts—

    (a)   where subsection (3) applies, that are preferential or rank equally under that subsection, or

    (b)   where subsection (3A) applies, that are preferential or are referred to in that subsection,

shall be applied in paying interest on those debts in respect of the periods during which they have been outstanding since the commencement of the bankruptcy; and interest on preferential debts ranks equally with interest on debts other than preferential debts.

(5)   The rate of interest payable under subsection (4) in respect of any debt is whichever is the greater of the following—

(a) the rate specified in section 17 of the Judgments Act 1838 at the commencement of the bankruptcy, and

(b) the rate applicable to that debt apart from the bankruptcy.

(6) This section and the next are without prejudice to any provision of this Act or any other Act under which the payment of any debt or the making of any other payment is, in the event of bankruptcy, to have a particular priority or to be postponed.

(7) In this section "preferential debts", "ordinary preferential debts" and "secondary preferential debts" each has the meaning given in section 386 in Part 12.

329. Debts to spouse or civil partner

(1) This section applies to bankruptcy debts owed in respect of credit provided by a person who (whether or not the bankrupt's spouse or civil partner at the time the credit was provided) was the bankrupt's spouse or civil partner at the commencement of the bankruptcy.

(2) Such debts—

(a) rank in priority after the … interest required to be paid in pursuance of section 328(4), and

(b) are payable with interest at the rate specified in section 328(5) in respect of the period during which they have been outstanding since the commencement of the bankruptcy;

and the interest payable under paragraph (b) has the same priority as the debts on which it is payable.

330. Final distribution

(1) When the trustee has realised all the bankrupt's estate or so much of it as can, in the trustee's opinion, be realised without needlessly protracting the trusteeship, he shall give notice in the prescribed manner either—

(a) of his intention to declare a final dividend, or

(b) that no dividend, or further dividend, will be declared.

(1A) A notice under subsection (1)(b) need not be given to opted-out creditors.

(2) The notice under subsection (1) shall contain the prescribed particulars and shall require claims against the bankrupt's estate to be established by a date ("the final date") specified in the notice.

(3) The court may, on the application of any person, postpone the final date.

(4) After the final date, the trustee shall—

(a) defray any outstanding expenses of the bankruptcy out of the bankrupt's estate, and

(b) if he intends to declare a final dividend, declare and distribute that dividend without regard to the claim of any person in respect of a debt not already proved in the bankruptcy.

(5) If a surplus remains after payment in full and with interest of all the bankrupt's creditors and the payment of the expenses of the bankruptcy, the bankrupt is entitled to the surplus.

(6) …

331. Final report

(1) Subject as follows in this section and the next, this section applies where—

(a) it appears to the trustee that the administration of the bankrupt's estate in accordance with this Chapter is for practical purposes complete, and

(b) the trustee is not the official receiver.

(2) The trustee must give the bankrupt's creditors (other than opted-out creditors) notice that it appears to the trustee that the administration of the bankrupt's estate is for practical purposes complete.

(2A) The notice must—

(a) be accompanied by a report of the trustee's administration of the bankrupt's estate;

(b) explain the effect of section 299(3)(d) and how the creditors may object to the trustee's release.

(3), (4) …

332. Saving for bankrupt's home

(1) This section applies where—

(a) there is comprised in the bankrupt's estate property consisting of an interest in a dwelling house which is occupied by the bankrupt or by his spouse or former spouse or by his civil partner or former civil partner, and

(b) the trustee has been unable for any reason to realise that property.

(2) The trustee shall not give notice under section 331(2) unless either—

(a) the court has made an order under section 313 imposing a charge on that property for the benefit of the bankrupt's estate, or

(b) the court has declined, on an application under that section, to make such an order, or

(c) the Secretary of State has issued a certificate to the trustee stating that it would be inappropriate or inexpedient for such an application to be made in the case in question.

Supplemental

333. Duties of bankrupt in relation to trustee

(1) The bankrupt shall—

(a) give to the trustee such information as to his affairs,

(b) attend on the trustee at such times, and

(c) do all such other things,

as the trustee may for the purposes of carrying out his functions under any of this Group of Parts reasonably require.

(2) Where at any time after the commencement of the bankruptcy any property is acquired by, or devolves upon, the bankrupt or there is an increase of the bankrupt's income, the bankrupt shall, within the prescribed period, give the trustee notice of the property or, as the case may be, of the increase.

(3) Subsection (1) applies to a bankrupt after his discharge.

(4) If the bankrupt without reasonable excuse fails to comply with any obligation imposed by this section, he is guilty of a contempt of court and liable to be punished accordingly (in addition to any other punishment to which he may be subject).

334. Stay of distribution in case of second bankruptcy

(1) This section and the next apply where a bankruptcy order is made against an undischarged bankrupt; and in both sections—

(a) "the later bankruptcy" means the bankruptcy arising from that order,

(b) "the earlier bankruptcy" means the bankruptcy (or, as the case may be, most recent bankruptcy) from which the bankrupt has not been discharged at the commencement of the later bankruptcy, and

(c) "the existing trustee" means the trustee (if any) of the bankrupt's estate for the purposes of the earlier bankruptcy.

(2) Where the existing trustee has been given the prescribed notice of the making of the application or (as the case may be) the presentation of the petition for the later bankruptcy, any distribution or other disposition by him of anything to which the next subsection applies, if made after the giving of the notice, is void except to the extent that it was made with the consent of the court or is or was subsequently ratified by the court.

This is without prejudice to section 284 (restrictions on dispositions of property following bankruptcy order).

(3) This subsection applies to—

(a) any property which is vested in the existing trustee under section 307(3) (after-acquired property);

(b) any money paid to the existing trustee in pursuance of an income payments order under section 310; and

(c) any property or money which is, or in the hands of the existing trustee represents, the proceeds of sale or application of property or money falling within paragraph (a) or (b) of this subsection.

335. Adjustment between earlier and later bankruptcy estates

(1) With effect from the commencement of the later bankruptcy anything to which section 334(3) applies which, immediately before the commencement of that bankruptcy, is comprised in the bankrupt's estate for the purposes of the earlier bankruptcy is to be treated as comprised in the bankrupt's estate for the purposes of the later bankruptcy and, until there is a trustee of that estate, is to be dealt with by the existing trustee in accordance with the rules.

(2) Any sums which in pursuance of an income payments order under section 310 are payable after the commencement of the later bankruptcy to the existing trustee shall form part of the bankrupt's estate for the purposes of the later bankruptcy; and the court may give such consequential directions for the modification of the order as it thinks fit.

(3) Anything comprised in a bankrupt's estate by virtue of subsection (1) or (2) is so comprised subject to a first charge in favour of the existing trustee for any bankruptcy expenses incurred by him in relation thereto.

(4) Except as provided above and in section 334, property which is, or by virtue of section 308 (personal property of bankrupt exceeding reasonable replacement value) or section 308A (vesting in trustee of certain tenancies) is capable of being, comprised in the bankrupt's estate for the purposes of the earlier bankruptcy, or of any bankruptcy prior to it, shall not be comprised in his estate for the purposes of the later bankruptcy.

(5) The creditors of the bankrupt in the earlier bankruptcy and the creditors of the bankrupt in any bankruptcy prior to the earlier one, are not to be creditors of his in the later bankruptcy in respect of the same debts; but the existing trustee may prove in the later bankruptcy for—

(a) the unsatisfied balance of the debts (including any debt under this subsection) provable against the bankrupt's estate in the earlier bankruptcy;

(b) any interest payable on that balance; and

(c) any unpaid expenses of the earlier bankruptcy.

(6) Any amount provable under subsection (5) ranks in priority after all the other debts provable in the later bankruptcy and after interest on those debts and, accordingly, shall not be paid unless those debts and that interest have first been paid in full.

CHAPTER V
EFFECT OF BANKRUPTCY ON CERTAIN RIGHTS, TRANSACTIONS, ETC

Rights under trusts of land

335A. Rights under trusts of land

(1) Any application by a trustee of a bankrupt's estate under section 14 of the Trusts of Land and Appointment of Trustees Act 1996 (powers of court in relation to trusts of land) for an order under that section for the sale of land shall be made to the court having jurisdiction in relation to the bankruptcy.

(2) On such an application the court shall make such order as it thinks just and reasonable having regard to—

(a) the interests of the bankrupt's creditors;

(b) where the application is made in respect of land which includes a dwelling house which is or has been the home of the bankrupt or the bankrupt's spouse or civil partner or former spouse or former civil partner—

(i) the conduct of the spouse, civil partner, former spouse or former civil partner, so far as contributing to the bankruptcy,

(ii) the needs and financial resources of the spouse, civil partner, former spouse or former civil partner, and

(iii) the needs of any children; and

(c) all the circumstances of the case other than the needs of the bankrupt.

(3) Where such an application is made after the end of the period of one year beginning with the first vesting under Chapter IV of this Part of the bankrupt's estate in a trustee, the court shall assume,

unless the circumstances of the case are exceptional, that the interests of the bankrupt's creditors outweigh all other considerations.

(4)   The powers conferred on the court by this section are exercisable on an application whether it is made before or after the commencement of this section.

Rights of occupation

336.   Rights of occupation etc of bankrupt's spouse or civil partner

(1)   Nothing occurring in the initial period of the bankruptcy (that is to say, the period beginning with the day of the making of the bankruptcy application or (as the case may be) the presentation of the bankruptcy petition and ending with the vesting of the bankrupt's estate in a trustee) is to be taken as having given rise to any home rights under Part IV of the Family Law Act 1996 in relation to a dwelling house comprised in the bankrupt's estate.

(2)   Where a spouse's or civil partner's home rights under the Act of 1996 are a charge on the estate or interest of the other spouse or civil partner, or of trustees for the other spouse or civil partner, and the other spouse or civil partner is made bankrupt—

    (a)   the charge continues to subsist notwithstanding the bankruptcy and, subject to the provisions of that Act, binds the trustee of the bankrupt's estate and persons deriving title under that trustee, and

    (b)   any application for an order under section 33 of that Act shall be made to the court having jurisdiction in relation to the bankruptcy.

(3)   ...

(4)   On such an application as is mentioned in subsection (2) ... the court shall make such order under section 33 of the Act of 1996 ... as it thinks just and reasonable having regard to—

    (a)   the interests of the bankrupt's creditors,

    (b)   the conduct of the spouse or former spouse or civil partner or former civil partner, so far as contributing to the bankruptcy,

    (c)   the needs and financial resources of the spouse or former spouse or civil partner or former civil partner,

    (d)   the needs of any children, and

    (e)   all the circumstances of the case other than the needs of the bankrupt.

(5)   Where such an application is made after the end of the period of one year beginning with the first vesting under Chapter IV of this Part of the bankrupt's estate in a trustee, the court shall assume, unless the circumstances of the case are exceptional, that the interests of the bankrupt's creditors outweigh all other considerations.

337.   Rights of occupation of bankrupt

(1)   This section applies where—

    (a)   a person who is entitled to occupy a dwelling house by virtue of a beneficial estate or interest is made bankrupt, and

    (b)   any persons under the age of 18 with whom that person had at some time occupied that dwelling house had their home with that person at the time when the bankruptcy application was made or (as the case may be) the bankruptcy petition was presented and at the commencement of the bankruptcy.

(2)   Whether or not the bankrupt's spouse or civil partner (if any) has home rights under Part IV of the Family Law Act 1996—

    (a)   the bankrupt has the following rights as against the trustee of his estate—

        (i)   if in occupation, a right not to be evicted or excluded from the dwelling house or any part of it, except with the leave of the court,

        (ii)   if not in occupation, a right with the leave of the court to enter into and occupy the dwelling house, and

    (b)   the bankrupt's rights are a charge, having the like priority as an equitable interest created immediately before the commencement of the bankruptcy, on so much of his estate or interest in the dwelling house as vests in the trustee.

(3)   The Act of 1996 has effect, with the necessary modifications, as if—
  (a)   the rights conferred by paragraph (a) of subsection (2) were home rights under that Act,
  (b)   any application for such leave as is mentioned in that paragraph were an application for an order under section 33 of that Act, and
  (c)   any charge under paragraph (b) of that subsection on the estate or interest of the trustee were a charge under that Act on the estate or interest of a spouse or civil partner.

(4)   Any application for leave such as is mentioned in subsection (2)(a) or otherwise by virtue of this section for an order under section 33 of the Act of 1996 shall be made to the court having jurisdiction in relation to the bankruptcy.

(5)   On such an application the court shall make such order under section 33 of the Act of 1996 as it thinks just and reasonable having regard to the interests of the creditors, to the bankrupt's financial resources, to the needs of the children and to all the circumstances of the case other than the needs of the bankrupt.

(6)   Where such an application is made after the end of the period of one year beginning with the vesting (under Chapter IV of this Part) of the bankrupt's estate in a trustee, the court shall assume, unless the circumstances of the case are exceptional, that the interests of the bankrupt's creditors outweigh all other considerations.

338.   Payments in respect of premises occupied by bankrupt

Where any premises comprised in a bankrupt's estate are occupied by him (whether by virtue of the preceding section or otherwise) on condition that he makes payments towards satisfying any liability arising under a mortgage of the premises or otherwise towards the outgoings of the premises, the bankrupt does not, by virtue of those payments, acquire any interest in the premises.

Adjustment of prior transactions, etc

339.   Transactions at an undervalue

(1)   Subject as follows in this section and sections 341 and 342, where an individual is made bankrupt and he has at a relevant time (defined in section 341) entered into a transaction with any person at an undervalue, the trustee of the bankrupt's estate may apply to the court for an order under this section.

(2)   The court shall, on such an application, make such order as it thinks fit for restoring the position to what it would have been if that individual had not entered into that transaction.

(3)   For the purposes of this section and sections 341 and 342, an individual enters into a transaction with a person at an undervalue if—
  (a)   he makes a gift to that person or he otherwise enters into a transaction with that person on terms that provide for him to receive no consideration,
  (b)   he enters into a transaction with that person in consideration of marriage or the formation of a civil partnership, or
  (c)   he enters into a transaction with that person for a consideration the value of which, in money or money's worth, is significantly less than the value, in money or money's worth, of the consideration provided by the individual.

340.   Preferences

(1)   Subject as follows in this and the next two sections, where an individual is made bankrupt and he has at a relevant time (defined in section 341) given a preference to any person, the trustee of the bankrupt's estate may apply to the court for an order under this section.

(2)   The court shall, on such an application, make such order as it thinks fit for restoring the position to what it would have been if that individual had not given that preference.

(3)   For the purposes of this and the next two sections, an individual gives a preference to a person if—
  (a)   that person is one of the individual's creditors or a surety or guarantor for any of his debts or other liabilities, and

(b)   the individual does anything or suffers anything to be done which (in either case) has the effect of putting that person into a position which, in the event of the individual's bankruptcy, will be better than the position he would have been in if that thing had not been done.

(4)   The court shall not make an order under this section in respect of a preference given to any person unless the individual who gave the preference was influenced in deciding to give it by a desire to produce in relation to that person the effect mentioned in subsection (3)(b) above.

(5)   An individual who has given a preference to a person who, at the time the preference was given, was an associate of his (otherwise than by reason only of being his employee) is presumed, unless the contrary is shown, to have been influenced in deciding to give it by such a desire as is mentioned in subsection (4).

(6)   The fact that something has been done in pursuance of the order of a court does not, without more, prevent the doing or suffering of that thing from constituting the giving of a preference.

341.   "Relevant time" under ss 339, 340

(1)   Subject as follows, the time at which an individual enters into a transaction at an undervalue or gives a preference is a relevant time if the transaction is entered into or the preference given—

(a)   in the case of a transaction at an undervalue, at a time in the period of 5 years ending with the day of the making of the bankruptcy application as a result of which, or (as the case may be) the presentation of the bankruptcy petition on which, the individual is made bankrupt,

(b)   in the case of a preference which is not a transaction at an undervalue and is given to a person who is an associate of the individual (otherwise than by reason only of being his employee), at a time in the period of 2 years ending with that day, and

(c)   in any other case of a preference which is not a transaction at an undervalue, at a time in the period of 6 months ending with that day.

(2)   Where an individual enters into a transaction at an undervalue or gives a preference at a time mentioned in paragraph (a), (b) or (c) of subsection (1) (not being, in the case of a transaction at an undervalue, a time less than 2 years before the end of the period mentioned in paragraph (a)), that time is not a relevant time for the purposes of sections 339 and 340 unless the individual—

(a)   is insolvent at that time, or

(b)   becomes insolvent in consequence of the transaction or preference;

but the requirements of this subsection are presumed to be satisfied, unless the contrary is shown, in relation to any transaction at an undervalue which is entered into by an individual with a person who is an associate of his (otherwise than by reason only of being his employee).

(3)   For the purposes of subsection (2), an individual is insolvent if—

(a)   he is unable to pay his debts as they fall due, or

(b)   the value of his assets is less than the amount of his liabilities, taking into account his contingent and prospective liabilities.

(4)   *A transaction entered into or preference given by a person who is subsequently adjudged bankrupt on a petition under section 264(1)(d) (criminal bankruptcy) is to be treated as having been entered into or given at a relevant time for the purposes of sections 339 and 340 if it was entered into or given at any time on or after the date specified for the purposes of this subsection in the criminal bankruptcy order on which the petition was based.*

(5)   *No order shall be made under section 339 or 340 by virtue of subsection (4) of this section where an appeal is pending (within the meaning of section 277) against the individual's conviction of any offence by virtue of which the criminal bankruptcy order was made.*

Note. Subsections (4) and (5) are repealed by the Criminal Justice Act 1988, s. 170(2), Sch. 16, as from a day to be appointed.

342.   Orders under ss 339, 340

(1)   Without prejudice to the generality of section 339(2) or 340(2), an order under either of those sections with respect to a transaction or preference entered into or given by an individual who is subsequently made bankrupt may (subject as follows)—

   (a)   require any property transferred as part of the transaction, or in connection with the giving of the preference, to be vested in the trustee of the bankrupt's estate as part of that estate;

   (b)   require any property to be so vested if it represents in any person's hands the application either of the proceeds of sale of property so transferred or of money so transferred;

   (c)   release or discharge (in whole or in part) any security given by the individual;

   (d)   require any person to pay, in respect of benefits received by him from the individual, such sums to the trustee of his estate as the court may direct;

   (e)   provide for any surety or guarantor whose obligations to any person were released or discharged (in whole or in part) under the transaction or by the giving of the preference to be under such new or revived obligations to that person as the court thinks appropriate;

   (f)   provide for security to be provided for the discharge of any obligation imposed by or arising under the order, for such an obligation to be charged on any property and for the security or charge to have the same priority as a security or charge released or discharged (in whole or in part) under the transaction or by the giving of the preference; and

   (g)   provide for the extent to which any person whose property is vested by the order in the trustee of the bankrupt's estate, or on whom obligations are imposed by the order, is to be able to prove in the bankruptcy for debts or other liabilities which arose from, or were released or discharged (in whole or in part) under or by, the transaction or the giving of the preference.

(2)   An order under section 339 or 340 may affect the property of, or impose any obligation on, any person whether or not he is the person with whom the individual in question entered into the transaction or, as the case may be, the person to whom the preference was given; but such an order—

   (a)   shall not prejudice any interest in property which was acquired from a person other than that individual and was acquired in good faith and for value, or prejudice any interest deriving from such an interest, and

   (b)   shall not require a person who received a benefit from the transaction or preference in good faith and for value to pay a sum to the trustee of the bankrupt's estate, except where he was a party to the transaction or the payment is to be in respect of a preference given to that person at a time when he was a creditor of that individual.

(2A)   Where a person has acquired an interest in property from a person other than the individual in question, or has received a benefit from the transaction or preference, and at the time of that acquisition or receipt—

   (a)   he had notice of the relevant surrounding circumstances and of the relevant proceedings, or

   (b)   he was an associate of, or was connected with, either the individual in question or the person with whom that individual entered into the transaction or to whom that individual gave the preference,

then, unless the contrary is shown, it shall be presumed for the purposes of paragraph (a) or (as the case may be) paragraph (b) of subsection (2) that the interest was acquired or the benefit was received otherwise than in good faith.

(3)   Any sums required to be paid to the trustee in accordance with an order under section 339 or 340 shall be comprised in the bankrupt's estate.

(4)   For the purposes of subsection (2A)(a), the relevant surrounding circumstances are (as the case may require)—

   (a)   the fact that the individual in question entered into the transaction at an undervalue; or

   (b)   the circumstances which amounted to the giving of the preference by the individual in question.

(5)   For the purposes of subsection (2A)(a), a person has notice of the relevant proceedings if he has notice—

   (a)   of the fact that the bankruptcy application as a result of which, or (as the case may be) the bankruptcy petition on which, the individual in question is made bankrupt has been made or presented; or

(b)   of the fact that the individual in question has been made bankrupt.

(6)   Section 249 in Part VII of this Act shall apply for the purposes of subsection (2A)(b) as it applies for the purposes of the first Group of Parts.

342A.   Recovery of excessive pension contributions

(1)   Where an individual who is made bankrupt—

        (a)   has rights under an approved pension arrangement, or

        (b)   has excluded rights under an unapproved pension arrangement,

     the trustee of the bankrupt's estate may apply to the court for an order under this section.

(2)   If the court is satisfied—

        (a)   that the rights under the arrangement are to any extent, and whether directly or indirectly, the fruits of relevant contributions, and

        (b)   that the making of any of the relevant contributions ("the excessive contributions") has unfairly prejudiced the individual's creditors,

     the court may make such order as it thinks fit for restoring the position to what it would have been had the excessive contributions not been made.

(3)   Subsection (4) applies where the court is satisfied that the value of the rights under the arrangement is, as a result of rights of the individual under the arrangement or any other pension arrangement having at any time become subject to a debit under section 29(1)(a) of the Welfare Reform and Pensions Act 1999 (debits giving effect to pension-sharing), less than it would otherwise have been.

(4)   Where this subsection applies—

        (a)   any relevant contributions which were represented by the rights which became subject to the debit shall, for the purposes of subsection (2), be taken to be contributions of which the rights under the arrangement are the fruits, and

        (b)   where the relevant contributions represented by the rights under the arrangement (including those so represented by virtue of paragraph (a)) are not all excessive contributions, relevant contributions which are represented by the rights under the arrangement otherwise than by virtue of paragraph (a) shall be treated as excessive contributions before any which are so represented by virtue of that paragraph.

(5)   In subsections (2) to (4) "relevant contributions" means contributions to the arrangement or any other pension arrangement—

        (a)   which the individual has at any time made on his own behalf, or

        (b)   which have at any time been made on his behalf.

(6)   The court shall, in determining whether it is satisfied under subsection (2)(b), consider in particular—

        (a)   whether any of the contributions were made for the purpose of putting assets beyond the reach of the individual's creditors or any of them, and

        (b)   whether the total amount of any contributions—

             (i)   made by or on behalf of the individual to pension arrangements, and

             (ii)   represented (whether directly or indirectly) by rights under approved pension arrangements or excluded rights under unapproved pension arrangements,

     is an amount which is excessive in view of the individual's circumstances when those contributions were made.

(7)   For the purposes of this section and sections 342B and 342C ("the recovery provisions"), rights of an individual under an unapproved pension arrangement are excluded rights if they are rights which are excluded from his estate by virtue of regulations under section 12 of the Welfare Reform and Pensions Act 1999.

(8)   In the recovery provisions—

        "approved pension arrangement" has the same meaning as in section 11 of the Welfare Reform and Pensions Act 1999;

        "unapproved pension arrangement" has the same meaning as in section 12 of that Act.

342B. **Orders under section 342A**

(1)   Without prejudice to the generality of section 342A(2), an order under section 342A may include provision—

(a)   requiring the person responsible for the arrangement to pay an amount to the individual's trustee in bankruptcy,

(b)   adjusting the liabilities of the arrangement in respect of the individual,

(c)   adjusting any liabilities of the arrangement in respect of any other person that derive, directly or indirectly, from rights of the individual under the arrangement,

(d)   for the recovery by the person responsible for the arrangement (whether by deduction from any amount which that person is ordered to pay or otherwise) of costs incurred by that person in complying in the bankrupt's case with any requirement under section 342C(1) or in giving effect to the order.

(2)   In subsection (1), references to adjusting the liabilities of the arrangement in respect of a person include (in particular) reducing the amount of any benefit or future benefit to which that person is entitled under the arrangement.

(3)   In subsection (1)(c), the reference to liabilities of the arrangement does not include liabilities in respect of a person which result from giving effect to an order or provision falling within section 28(1) of the Welfare Reform and Pensions Act 1999 (pension sharing orders and agreements).

(4)   The maximum amount which the person responsible for an arrangement may be required to pay by an order under section 342A is the lesser of—

(a)   the amount of the excessive contributions, and

(b)   the value of the individual's rights under the arrangement (if the arrangement is an approved pension arrangement) or of his excluded rights under the arrangement (if the arrangement is an unapproved pension arrangement).

(5)   An order under section 342A which requires the person responsible for an arrangement to pay an amount ("the restoration amount") to the individual's trustee in bankruptcy must provide for the liabilities of the arrangement to be correspondingly reduced.

(6)   For the purposes of subsection (5), liabilities are correspondingly reduced if the difference between—

(a)   the amount of the liabilities immediately before the reduction, and

(b)   the amount of the liabilities immediately after the reduction,

is equal to the restoration amount.

(7)   An order under section 342A in respect of an arrangement—

(a)   shall be binding on the person responsible for the arrangement, and

(b)   overrides provisions of the arrangement to the extent that they conflict with the provisions of the order.

342C. **Orders under section 342A: supplementary**

(1)   The person responsible for—

(a)   an approved pension arrangement under which a bankrupt has rights,

(b)   an unapproved pension arrangement under which a bankrupt has excluded rights, or

(c)   a pension arrangement under which a bankrupt has at any time had rights,

shall, on the bankrupt's trustee in bankruptcy making a written request, provide the trustee with such information about the arrangement and rights as the trustee may reasonably require for, or in connection with, the making of applications under section 342A.

(2)   Nothing in—

(a)   any provision of section 159 of the Pension Schemes Act 1993 or section 91 of the Pensions Act 1995 (which prevent assignment and the making of orders that restrain a person from receiving anything which he is prevented from assigning),

(b)   any provision of any enactment (whether passed or made before or after the passing of the Welfare Reform and Pensions Act 1999) corresponding to any of the provisions mentioned in paragraph (a), or

(c)   any provision of the arrangement in question corresponding to any of those provisions, applies to a court exercising its powers under section 342A.

(3)   Where any sum is required by an order under section 342A to be paid to the trustee in bankruptcy, that sum shall be comprised in the bankrupt's estate.

(4)   Regulations may, for the purposes of the recovery provisions, make provision about the calculation and verification of—

(a)   any such value as is mentioned in section 342B(4)(b);

(b)   any such amounts as are mentioned in section 342B(6)(a) and (b).

(5)   The power conferred by subsection (4) includes power to provide for calculation or verification—

(a)   in such manner as may, in the particular case, be approved by a prescribed person; or

(b)   in accordance with guidance from time to time prepared by a prescribed person.

(6)   References in the recovery provisions to the person responsible for a pension arrangement are to—

(a)   the trustees, managers or provider of the arrangement, or

(b)   the person having functions in relation to the arrangement corresponding to those of a trustee, manager or provider.

(7)   In this section and sections 342A and 342B—

"prescribed" means prescribed by regulations;

"the recovery provisions" means this section and sections 342A and 342B;

"regulations" means regulations made by the Secretary of State.

(8)   Regulations under the recovery provisions may—

(a)   make different provision for different cases;

(b)   contain such incidental, supplemental and transitional provisions as appear to the Secretary of State necessary or expedient.

(9)   Regulations under the recovery provisions shall be made by statutory instrument subject to annulment in pursuance of a resolution of either House of Parliament.

342D. Recovery of excessive contributions in pension-sharing cases

(1)   For the purposes of sections 339, 341 and 342, a pension-sharing transaction shall be taken—

(a)   to be a transaction, entered into by the transferor with the transferee, by which the appropriate amount is transferred by the transferor to the transferee; and

(b)   to be capable of being a transaction entered into at an undervalue only so far as it is a transfer of so much of the appropriate amount as is recoverable.

(2)   For the purposes of sections 340 to 342, a pension-sharing transaction shall be taken—

(a)   to be something (namely a transfer of the appropriate amount to the transferee) done by the transferor; and

(b)   to be capable of being a preference given to the transferee only so far as it is a transfer of so much of the appropriate amount as is recoverable.

(3)   If on an application under section 339 or 340 any question arises as to whether, or the extent to which, the appropriate amount in the case of a pension-sharing transaction is recoverable, the question shall be determined in accordance with subsections (4) to (8).

(4)   The court shall first determine the extent (if any) to which the transferor's rights under the shared arrangement at the time of the transaction appear to have been (whether directly or indirectly) the fruits of contributions ("personal contributions")—

(a)   which the transferor has at any time made on his own behalf, or

(b)   which have at any time been made on the transferor's behalf,

to the shared arrangement or any other pension arrangement.

(5)   Where it appears that those rights were to any extent the fruits of personal contributions, the court shall then determine the extent (if any) to which those rights appear to have been the fruits of personal contributions whose making has unfairly prejudiced the transferor's creditors ("the unfair contributions").

(6)   If it appears to the court that the extent to which those rights were the fruits of the unfair contributions is such that the transfer of the appropriate amount could have been made out of

rights under the shared arrangement which were not the fruits of the unfair contributions, then the appropriate amount is not recoverable.

(7) If it appears to the court that the transfer could not have been wholly so made, then the appropriate amount is recoverable to the extent to which it appears to the court that the transfer could not have been so made.

(8) In making the determination mentioned in subsection (5) the court shall consider in particular—

    (a) whether any of the personal contributions were made for the purpose of putting assets beyond the reach of the transferor's creditors or any of them, and

    (b) whether the total amount of any personal contributions represented, at the time the pension-sharing transaction was made, by rights under pension arrangements is an amount which is excessive in view of the transferor's circumstances when those contributions were made.

(9) In this section and sections 342E and 342F—

    "appropriate amount", in relation to a pension-sharing transaction, means the appropriate amount in relation to that transaction for the purposes of section 29(1) of the Welfare Reform and Pensions Act 1999 (creation of pension credits and debits);

    "pension-sharing transaction" means an order or provision falling within section 28(1) of the Welfare Reform and Pensions Act 1999 (orders and agreements which activate pension-sharing);

    "shared arrangement", in relation to a pension-sharing transaction, means the pension arrangement to which the transaction relates;

    "transferee", in relation to a pension-sharing transaction, means the person for whose benefit the transaction is made;

    "transferor", in relation to a pension-sharing transaction, means the person to whose rights the transaction relates.

342E. Orders under section 339 or 340 in respect of pension-sharing transactions

(1) This section and section 342F apply if the court is making an order under section 339 or 340 in a case where—

    (a) the transaction or preference is, or is any part of, a pension-sharing transaction, and

    (b) the transferee has rights under a pension arrangement ("the destination arrangement", which may be the shared arrangement or any other pension arrangement) that are derived, directly or indirectly, from the pension-sharing transaction.

(2) Without prejudice to the generality of section 339(2) or 340(2), or of section 342, the order may include provision—

    (a) requiring the person responsible for the destination arrangement to pay an amount to the transferor's trustee in bankruptcy,

    (b) adjusting the liabilities of the destination arrangement in respect of the transferee,

    (c) adjusting any liabilities of the destination arrangement in respect of any other person that derive, directly or indirectly, from rights of the transferee under the destination arrangement,

    (d) for the recovery by the person responsible for the destination arrangement (whether by deduction from any amount which that person is ordered to pay or otherwise) of costs incurred by that person in complying in the transferor's case with any requirement under section 342F(1) or in giving effect to the order,

    (e) for the recovery, from the transferor's trustee in bankruptcy, by the person responsible for a pension arrangement, of costs incurred by that person in complying in the transferor's case with any requirement under section 342F(2) or (3).

(3) In subsection (2), references to adjusting the liabilities of the destination arrangement in respect of a person include (in particular) reducing the amount of any benefit or future benefit to which that person is entitled under the arrangement.

(4) The maximum amount which the person responsible for the destination arrangement may be required to pay by the order is the smallest of—

    (a) so much of the appropriate amount as, in accordance with section 342D, is recoverable,

      (b)   so much (if any) of the amount of the unfair contributions (within the meaning given by section 342D(5)) as is not recoverable by way of an order under section 342A containing provision such as is mentioned in section 342B(1)(a), and

      (c)   the value of the transferee's rights under the destination arrangement so far as they are derived, directly or indirectly, from the pension-sharing transaction.

(5)   If the order requires the person responsible for the destination arrangement to pay an amount ("the restoration amount") to the transferor's trustee in bankruptcy it must provide for the liabilities of the arrangement to be correspondingly reduced.

(6)   For the purposes of subsection (5), liabilities are correspondingly reduced if the difference between—

      (a)   the amount of the liabilities immediately before the reduction, and

      (b)   the amount of the liabilities immediately after the reduction,

is equal to the restoration amount.

(7)   The order—

      (a)   shall be binding on the person responsible for the destination arrangement, and

      (b)   overrides provisions of the destination arrangement to the extent that they conflict with the provisions of the order.

342F.   **Orders under section 339 or 340 in pension-sharing cases: supplementary**

(1)   On the transferor's trustee in bankruptcy making a written request to the person responsible for the destination arrangement, that person shall provide the trustee with such information about—

      (a)   the arrangement,

      (b)   the transferee's rights under it, and

      (c)   where the destination arrangement is the shared arrangement, the transferor's rights under it,

as the trustee may reasonably require for, or in connection with, the making of applications under sections 339 and 340.

(2)   Where the shared arrangement is not the destination arrangement, the person responsible for the shared arrangement shall, on the transferor's trustee in bankruptcy making a written request to that person, provide the trustee with such information about—

      (a)   the arrangement, and

      (b)   the transferor's rights under it,

as the trustee may reasonably require for, or in connection with, the making of applications under sections 339 and 340.

(3)   On the transferor's trustee in bankruptcy making a written request to the person responsible for any intermediate arrangement, that person shall provide the trustee with such information about—

      (a)   the arrangement, and

      (b)   the transferee's rights under it,

as the trustee may reasonably require for, or in connection with, the making of applications under sections 339 and 340.

(4)   In subsection (3) "intermediate arrangement" means a pension arrangement, other than the shared arrangement or the destination arrangement, in relation to which the following conditions are fulfilled—

      (a)   there was a time when the transferee had rights under the arrangement that were derived (directly or indirectly) from the pension-sharing transaction, and

      (b)   the transferee's rights under the destination arrangement (so far as derived from the pension-sharing transaction) are to any extent derived (directly or indirectly) from the rights mentioned in paragraph (a).

(5)   Nothing in—

      (a)   any provision of section 159 of the Pension Schemes Act 1993 or section 91 of the Pensions Act 1995 (which prevent assignment and the making of orders which restrain a person from receiving anything which he is prevented from assigning),

(b)   any provision of any enactment (whether passed or made before or after the passing of the Welfare Reform and Pensions Act 1999) corresponding to any of the provisions mentioned in paragraph (a), or

(c)   any provision of the destination arrangement corresponding to any of those provisions,

applies to a court exercising its powers under section 339 or 340.

(6)   Regulations may, for the purposes of sections 339 to 342, sections 342D and 342E and this section, make provision about the calculation and verification of—

(a)   any such value as is mentioned in section 342E(4)(c);

(b)   any such amounts as are mentioned in section 342E(6)(a) and (b).

(7)   The power conferred by subsection (6) includes power to provide for calculation or verification—

(a)   in such manner as may, in the particular case, be approved by a prescribed person; or

(b)   in accordance with guidance from time to time prepared by a prescribed person.

(8)   In section 342E and this section, references to the person responsible for a pension arrangement are to—

(a)   the trustees, managers or provider of the arrangement, or

(b)   the person having functions in relation to the arrangement corresponding to those of a trustee, manager or provider.

(9)   In this section—

"prescribed" means prescribed by regulations;

"regulations" means regulations made by the Secretary of State.

(10)   Regulations under this section may—

(a)   make different provision for different cases;

(b)   contain such incidental, supplemental and transitional provisions as appear to the Secretary of State necessary or expedient.

(11)   Regulations under this section shall be made by statutory instrument subject to annulment in pursuance of a resolution of either House of Parliament.

343.   Extortionate credit transactions

(1)   This section applies where a person is made bankrupt who is or has been a party to a transaction for, or involving, the provision to him of credit.

(2)   The court may, on the application of the trustee of the bankrupt's estate, make an order with respect to the transaction if the transaction is or was extortionate and was not entered into more than 3 years before the commencement of the bankruptcy.

(3)   For the purposes of this section a transaction is extortionate if, having regard to the risk accepted by the person providing the credit—

(a)   the terms of it are or were such as to require grossly exorbitant payments to be made (whether unconditionally or in certain contingencies) in respect of the provision of the credit, or

(b)   it otherwise grossly contravened ordinary principles of fair dealing;

and it shall be presumed, unless the contrary is proved, that a transaction with respect to which an application is made under this section is or, as the case may be, was extortionate.

(4)   An order under this section with respect to any transaction may contain such one or more of the following as the court thinks fit, that is to say—

(a)   provision setting aside the whole or part of any obligation created by the transaction;

(b)   provision otherwise varying the terms of the transaction or varying the terms on which any security for the purposes of the transaction is held;

(c)   provision requiring any person who is or was party to the transaction to pay to the trustee any sums paid to that person, by virtue of the transaction, by the bankrupt;

(d)   provision requiring any person to surrender to the trustee any property held by him as security for the purposes of the transaction;

(e)   provision directing accounts to be taken between any persons.

(5)   Any sums or property required to be paid or surrendered to the trustee in accordance with an order under this section shall be comprised in the bankrupt's estate.

(6)   ...

The powers conferred by this section are exercisable in relation to any transaction concurrently with any powers exercisable under this Act in relation to that transaction as a transaction at an undervalue.

344.   Avoidance of general assignment of book debts

(1)   The following applies where a person engaged in any business makes a general assignment to another person of his existing or future book debts, or any class of them, and is subsequently made bankrupt.

(2)   The assignment is void against the trustee of the bankrupt's estate as regards book debts which were not paid before the making of the bankruptcy application or (as the case may be) the presentation of the bankruptcy petition, unless the assignment has been registered under the Bills of Sale Act 1878.

(3)   For the purposes of subsections (1) and (2)—

    (a)   "assignment" includes an assignment by way of security or charge on book debts, and

    (b)   "general assignment" does not include—

        (i)   an assignment of book debts due at the date of the assignment from specified debtors or of debts becoming due under specified contracts, or

        (ii)   an assignment of book debts included either in a transfer of a business made in good faith and for value or in an assignment of assets for the benefit of creditors generally.

(4)   For the purposes of registration under the Act of 1878 an assignment of book debts is to be treated as if it were a bill of sale given otherwise than by way of security for the payment of a sum of money; and the provisions of that Act with respect to the registration of bills of sale apply accordingly with such necessary modifications as may be made by rules under that Act.

345.   Contracts to which bankrupt is a party

(1)   The following applies where a contract has been made with a person who is subsequently made bankrupt.

(2)   The court may, on the application of any other party to the contract, make an order discharging obligations under the contract on such terms as to payment by the applicant or the bankrupt of damages for non-performance or otherwise as appear to the court to be equitable.

(3)   Any damages payable by the bankrupt by virtue of an order of the court under this section are provable as a bankruptcy debt.

(4)   Where an undischarged bankrupt is a contractor in respect of any contract jointly with any person, that person may sue or be sued in respect of the contract without the joinder of the bankrupt.

346.   Enforcement procedures

(1)   Subject to section 285 in Chapter II (restrictions on proceedings and remedies) and to the following provisions of this section, where the creditor of any person who is made bankrupt has, before the commencement of the bankruptcy—

    (a)   issued execution against the goods or land of that person, or

    (b)   attached a debt due to that person from another person,

that creditor is not entitled, as against the official receiver or trustee of the bankrupt's estate, to retain the benefit of the execution or attachment, or any sums paid to avoid it, unless the execution or attachment was completed, or the sums were paid, before the commencement of the bankruptcy.

(1A)   For the purposes of this section, Her Majesty's Revenue and Customs is to be regarded as having attached a debt due to a person if it has taken action under Part 1 of Schedule 8 to the Finance (No 2) Act 2015 (enforcement by deduction from accounts) as a result of which an amount standing to the credit of an account held by that person is—

    (a)   subject to arrangements made under paragraph 6(3) of that Schedule, or

    (b)   the subject of a deduction notice under paragraph 13 of that Schedule.

(2) Subject as follows, where any goods of a person have been taken in execution, then, if before the completion of the execution notice is given to the enforcement officer or other officer charged with the execution that that person has been made bankrupt—

(a) the enforcement officer or other officer shall on request deliver to the official receiver or trustee of the bankrupt's estate the goods and any money seized or recovered in part satisfaction of the execution, but

(b) the costs of the execution are a first charge on the goods or money so delivered and the official receiver or trustee may sell the goods or a sufficient part of them for the purpose of satisfying the charge.

(3) Subject to subsection (6) below, where—

(a) under an execution in respect of a judgment for a sum exceeding such sum as may be prescribed for the purposes of this subsection, the goods of any person are sold or money is paid in order to avoid a sale, and

(b) before the end of the period of 14 days beginning with the day of the sale or payment the enforcement officer or other officer charged with the execution is given notice that a bankruptcy application has been made or a bankruptcy petition has been presented in relation to that person, and

(c) a bankruptcy order is or has been made as a result of that application or on that petition,

the balance of the proceeds of sale or money paid, after deducting the costs of execution, shall (in priority to the claim of the execution creditor) be comprised in the bankrupt's estate.

(4) Accordingly, in the case of an execution in respect of a judgment for a sum exceeding the sum prescribed for the purposes of subsection (3), the enforcement officer or other officer charged with the execution—

(a) shall not dispose of the balance mentioned in subsection (3) at any time within the period of 14 days so mentioned or while proceedings on a bankruptcy application are ongoing or (as the case may be) there is pending a bankruptcy petition of which he has been given notice under that subsection, and

(b) shall pay that balance, where by virtue of that subsection it is comprised in the bankrupt's estate, to the official receiver or (if there is one) to the trustee of that estate.

(5) For the purposes of this section—

(a) an execution against goods is completed by seizure and sale or by the making of a charging order under section 1 of the Charging Orders Act 1979;

(b) an execution against land is completed by seizure, by the appointment of a receiver or by the making of a charging order under that section;

(c) an attachment of a debt is completed by the receipt of the debt.

(6) The rights conferred by subsections (1) to (3) on the official receiver or the trustee may, to such extent and on such terms as it thinks fit, be set aside by the court in favour of the creditor who has issued the execution or attached the debt.

(7) Nothing in this section entitles the trustee of a bankrupt's estate to claim goods from a person who has acquired them in good faith under a sale by an enforcement officer or other officer charged with an execution.

(8) Neither subsection (2) nor subsection (3) applies in relation to any execution against property which has been acquired by or has devolved upon the bankrupt since the commencement of the bankruptcy, unless, at the time the execution is issued or before it is completed—

(a) the property has been or is claimed for the bankrupt's estate under section 307 (after-acquired property), and

(b) a copy of the notice given under that section has been or is served on the enforcement officer or other officer charged with the execution.

(9) In this section "enforcement officer" means an individual who is authorised to act as an enforcement officer under the Courts Act 2003.

347.   **Distress, etc**

(1)   CRAR (the power of commercial rent arrears recovery under section 72(1) of the Tribunals, Courts and Enforcement Act 2007) is exercisable where the tenant is an undischarged bankrupt (subject to sections 252(2)(b) and 254(1) above and subsection (5) below) against goods and effects comprised in the bankrupt's estate, but only for 6 months' rent accrued due before the commencement of the bankruptcy.

(2)   Where CRAR has been exercised to recover rent from an individual to whom a bankruptcy application or a bankruptcy petition relates and a bankruptcy order is subsequently made as a result of that application or on that petition, any amount recovered by way of CRAR which—

    (a)   is in excess of the amount which by virtue of subsection (1) would have been recoverable after the commencement of the bankruptcy, or

    (b)   is in respect of rent for a period or part of a period after goods were taken control of under CRAR,

shall be held for the bankrupt as part of his estate.

(3)   Subsection (3A) applies where—

    (a)   any person (whether or not a landlord or person entitled to rent) has distrained upon the goods or effects of an individual who is adjudged bankrupt before the end of the period of 3 months beginning with the distraint, or

    (b)   Her Majesty's Revenue and Customs has been paid any amount from an account of an individual under Part 1 of Schedule 8 to the Finance (No 2) Act 2015 (enforcement by deduction from accounts) and the individual is adjudged bankrupt before the end of the period of 3 months beginning with the payment.

(3A)   Where this subsection applies—

    (a)   in a case within subsection (3)(a), the goods or effects, or the proceeds of their sale, and

    (b)   in a case within subsection (3)(b), the amount in question,

is charged for the benefit of the bankrupt's estate with the preferential debts of the bankrupt to the extent that the bankrupt's estate is for the time being insufficient for meeting them.

(4)   Where by virtue of any charge under subsection (3A) any person surrenders any goods or effects to the trustee of a bankrupt's estate or makes a payment to such a trustee, that person ranks, in respect of the amount of the proceeds of the sale of those goods or effects by the trustee or, as the case may be, the amount of the payment, as a preferential creditor of the bankrupt, except as against so much of the bankrupt's estate as is available for the payment of preferential creditors by virtue of the surrender or payment.

(5)   CRAR is not exercisable at any time after the discharge of a bankrupt against any goods or effects comprised in the bankrupt's estate.

(6), (7)   …

(8)   Subject to sections 252(2)(b) and 254(1) above nothing in this Group of Parts affects any right to distrain otherwise than for rent; and any such right is at any time exercisable without restriction against property comprised in a bankrupt's estate, even if that right is expressed by any enactment to be exercisable in like manner as a right to distrain for rent.

(9)   Any right to distrain against property comprised in a bankrupt's estate is exercisable notwithstanding that the property has vested in the trustee.

(10)   The provisions of this section are without prejudice to a landlord's right in a bankruptcy to prove for any bankruptcy debt in respect of rent.

(11)   …

348.   **Apprenticeships, etc**

(1)   This section applies where—

    (a)   a bankruptcy order is made in respect of an individual to whom another individual was an apprentice or articled clerk at the time when the application for the order was made or (as the case may be) the petition for the order was presented, and

    (b)   the bankrupt or the apprentice or clerk gives notice to the trustee terminating the apprenticeship or articles.

(2)   Subject to subsection (6) below, the indenture of apprenticeship or, as the case may be, the articles of agreement shall be discharged with effect from the commencement of the bankruptcy.

(3)   If any money has been paid by or on behalf of the apprentice or clerk to the bankrupt as a fee, the trustee may, on an application made by or on behalf of the apprentice or clerk, pay such sum to the apprentice or clerk as the trustee thinks reasonable, having regard to—

(a)   the amount of the fee,

(b)   the proportion of the period in respect of which the fee was paid that has been served by the apprentice or clerk before the commencement of the bankruptcy, and

(c)   the other circumstances of the case.

(4)   The power of the trustee to make a payment under subsection (3) has priority over his obligation to distribute the bankrupt's estate.

(5)   Instead of making a payment under subsection (3), the trustee may, if it appears to him expedient to do so on an application made by or on behalf of the apprentice or clerk, transfer the indenture or articles to a person other than the bankrupt.

(6)   Where a transfer is made under subsection (5), subsection (2) has effect only as between the apprentice or clerk and the bankrupt.

349.   Unenforceability of liens on books, etc

(1)   Subject as follows, a lien or other right to retain possession of any of the books, papers or other records of a bankrupt is unenforceable to the extent that its enforcement would deny possession of any books, papers or other records to the official receiver or the trustee of the bankrupt's estate.

(2)   Subsection (1) does not apply to a lien on documents which give a title to property and are held as such.

349A.   Arbitration agreements to which bankrupt is party

(1)   This section applies where a bankrupt had become party to a contract containing an arbitration agreement before the commencement of his bankruptcy.

(2)   If the trustee in bankruptcy adopts the contract, the arbitration agreement is enforceable by or against the trustee in relation to matters arising from or connected with the contract.

(3)   If the trustee in bankruptcy does not adopt the contract and a matter to which the arbitration agreement applies requires to be determined in connection with or for the purposes of the bankruptcy proceedings—

(a)   the trustee with the consent of the creditors' committee, or

(b)   any other party to the agreement,

may apply to the court which may, if it thinks fit in all the circumstances of the case, order that the matter be referred to arbitration in accordance with the arbitration agreement.

(4)   In this section—

"arbitration agreement" has the same meaning as in Part I of the Arbitration Act 1996; and

"the court" means the court which has jurisdiction in the bankruptcy proceedings.

CHAPTER VI

BANKRUPTCY OFFENCES

Preliminary

350.   Scheme of this Chapter

(1)   Subject to section 360(3) below, this Chapter applies—

(a)   where an adjudicator has made a bankruptcy order as a result of a bankruptcy application, or

(b)   where the court has made a bankruptcy order on a bankruptcy petition.

(2)   This Chapter applies whether or not the bankruptcy order is annulled, but proceedings for an offence under this Chapter shall not be instituted after the annulment.

(3)   Without prejudice to his liability in respect of a subsequent bankruptcy, the bankrupt is not guilty of an offence under this Chapter in respect of anything done after his discharge; but nothing in this Group of Parts prevents the institution of proceedings against a discharged bankrupt for an offence committed before his discharge.

(3A)   Subsection (3) is without prejudice to any provision of this Chapter which applies to a person in respect of whom a bankruptcy restrictions order is in force.

(4)   It is not a defence in proceedings for an offence under this Chapter that anything relied on, in whole or in part, as constituting that offence was done outside England and Wales.

(5)   Proceedings for an offence under this Chapter or under the rules shall not be instituted except by the Secretary of State or by or with the consent of the Director of Public Prosecutions.

(6)   A person guilty of an offence under this Chapter is liable to imprisonment or a fine, or both.

351.   Definitions

In the following provisions of this Chapter—

(a)   references to property comprised in the bankrupt's estate or to property possession of which is required to be delivered up to the official receiver or the trustee of the bankrupt's estate include any property which would be such property if a notice in respect of it were given under section 307 (after-acquired property), section 308 (personal property and effects of bankrupt having more than replacement value) or section 308A (vesting in trustee of certain tenancies);

(b)   "the initial period" means the period between the making of the bankruptcy application or (as the case may be) the presentation of the bankruptcy petition and the commencement of the bankruptcy; ...

(c)   ...

352.   Defence of innocent intention

Where in the case of an offence under any provision of this Chapter it is stated that this section applies, a person is not guilty of the offence if he proves that, at the time of the conduct constituting the offence, he had no intent to defraud or to conceal the state of his affairs.

Wrongdoing by the bankrupt before and after bankruptcy

353.   Non-disclosure

(1)   The bankrupt is guilty of an offence if—

(a)   he does not to the best of his knowledge and belief disclose all the property comprised in his estate to the official receiver or the trustee, or

(b)   he does not inform the official receiver or the trustee of any disposal of any property which but for the disposal would be so comprised, stating how, when, to whom and for what consideration the property was disposed of.

(2)   Subsection (1)(b) does not apply to any disposal in the ordinary course of a business carried on by the bankrupt or to any payment of the ordinary expenses of the bankrupt or his family.

(3)   Section 352 applies to this offence.

354.   Concealment of property

(1)   The bankrupt is guilty of an offence if—

(a)   he does not deliver up possession to the official receiver or trustee, or as the official receiver or trustee may direct, of such part of the property comprised in his estate as is in his possession or under his control and possession of which he is required by law so to deliver up,

(b)   he conceals any debt due to or from him or conceals any property the value of which is not less than the prescribed amount and possession of which he is required to deliver up to the official receiver or trustee, or

(c)   in the 12 months before the making of the bankruptcy application or (as the case may be) the presentation of the bankruptcy petition, or in the initial period, he did anything which would have been an offence under paragraph (b) above if the bankruptcy order had been made immediately before he did it.

Section 352 applies to this offence.

(2)   The bankrupt is guilty of an offence if he removes, or in the initial period removed, any property the value of which was not less than the prescribed amount and possession of which he has or would have been required to deliver up to the official receiver or the trustee.

       Section 352 applies to this offence.

(3)   The bankrupt is guilty of an offence if he without reasonable excuse fails, on being required to do so by the official receiver, the trustee or the court—

       (a)   to account for the loss of any substantial part of his property incurred in the 12 months before the making of the bankruptcy application or (as the case may be) the presentation of the bankruptcy petition or in the initial period, or

       (b)   to give a satisfactory explanation of the manner in which such a loss was incurred.

355.   Concealment of books and papers; falsification

(1)   The bankrupt is guilty of an offence if he does not deliver up possession to the official receiver or the trustee, or as the official receiver or trustee may direct, of all books, papers and other records of which he has possession or control and which relate to his estate or his affairs.

       Section 352 applies to this offence.

(2)   The bankrupt is guilty of an offence if—

       (a)   he prevents, or in the initial period prevented, the production of any books, papers or records relating to his estate or affairs;

       (b)   he conceals, destroys, mutilates or falsifies, or causes or permits the concealment, destruction, mutilation or falsification of, any books, papers or other records relating to his estate or affairs;

       (c)   he makes, or causes or permits the making of, any false entries in any book, document or record relating to his estate or affairs; or

       (d)   in the 12 months before the making of the bankruptcy application or (as the case may be) the presentation of the bankruptcy petition, or in the initial period, he did anything which would have been an offence under paragraph (b) or (c) above if the bankruptcy order had been made before he did it.

       Section 352 applies to this offence.

(3)   The bankrupt is guilty of an offence if—

       (a)   he disposes of, or alters or makes any omission in, or causes or permits the disposal, altering or making of any omission in, any book, document or record relating to his estate or affairs, or

       (b)   in the 12 months before the making of the bankruptcy application or (as the case may be) the presentation of the bankruptcy petition, or in the initial period, he did anything which would have been an offence under paragraph (a) if the bankruptcy order had been made before he did it.

       Section 352 applies to this offence.

(4)   In their application to a trading record subsections (2)(d) and (3)(b) shall have effect as if the reference to 12 months were a reference to two years.

(5)   In subsection (4) "trading record" means a book, document or record which shows or explains the transactions or financial position of a person's business, including—

       (a)   a periodic record of cash paid and received,

       (b)   a statement of periodic stock-taking, and

       (c)   except in the case of goods sold by way of retail trade, a record of goods sold and purchased which identifies the buyer and seller or enables them to be identified.

356.   False statements

(1)   The bankrupt is guilty of an offence if he makes or has made any material omission in any statement made under any provision in this Group of Parts and relating to his affairs.

       Section 352 applies to this offence.

(2)   The bankrupt is guilty of an offence if—

       (a)   knowing or believing that a false debt has been proved by any person under the bankruptcy, he fails to inform the trustee as soon as practicable; or

(b)   he attempts to account for any part of his property by fictitious losses or expenses; or

(c)   in connection with any creditors' decision procedure or deemed consent procedure in the 12 months before the making of the bankruptcy application or (as the case may be) the presentation of the bankruptcy petition or (whether or not in connection with such a procedure) at any time in the initial period, he did anything which would have been an offence under paragraph (b) if the bankruptcy order had been made before he did it; or

(d)   he is, or at any time has been, guilty of any false representation or other fraud for the purpose of obtaining the consent of his creditors, or any of them, to an agreement with reference to his affairs or to his bankruptcy.

357.   Fraudulent disposal of property

(1)   The bankrupt is guilty of an offence if he makes or causes to be made, or has in the period of 5 years ending with the commencement of the bankruptcy made or caused to be made, any gift or transfer of, or any charge on, his property.

Section 352 applies to this offence.

(2)   The reference to making a transfer of or charge on any property includes causing or conniving at the levying of any execution against that property.

(3)   The bankrupt is guilty of an offence if he conceals or removes, or has at any time before the commencement of the bankruptcy concealed or removed, any part of his property after, or within 2 months before, the date on which a judgment or order for the payment of money has been obtained against him, being a judgment or order which was not satisfied before the commencement of the bankruptcy.

Section 352 applies to this offence.

358.   Absconding

The bankrupt is guilty of an offence if—

(a)   he leaves, or attempts or makes preparations to leave, England and Wales with any property the value of which is not less than the prescribed amount and possession of which he is required to deliver up to the official receiver or the trustee, or

(b)   in the 6 months before the making of the bankruptcy application or (as the case may be) the presentation of the bankruptcy petition, or in the initial period, he did anything which would have been an offence under paragraph (a) if the bankruptcy order had been made immediately before he did it.

Section 352 applies to this offence.

359.   Fraudulent dealing with property obtained on credit

(1)   The bankrupt is guilty of an offence if, in the 12 months before the making of the bankruptcy application or (as the case may be) the presentation of the bankruptcy petition, or in the initial period, he disposed of any property which he had obtained on credit and, at the time he disposed of it, had not paid for.

Section 352 applies to this offence.

(2)   A person is guilty of an offence if, in the 12 months before the making of the bankruptcy application or (as the case may be) the presentation of the bankruptcy petition or in the initial period, he acquired or received property from the bankrupt knowing or believing—

(a)   that the bankrupt owed money in respect of the property, and

(b)   that the bankrupt did not intend, or was unlikely to be able, to pay the money he so owed.

(3)   A person is not guilty of an offence under subsection (1) or (2) if the disposal, acquisition or receipt of the property was in the ordinary course of a business carried on by the bankrupt at the time of the disposal, acquisition or receipt.

(4)   In determining for the purposes of this section whether any property is disposed of, acquired or received in the ordinary course of a business carried on by the bankrupt, regard may be had, in particular, to the price paid for the property.

(5)   In this section references to disposing of property include pawning or pledging it; and references to acquiring or receiving property shall be read accordingly.

360.   Obtaining credit; engaging in business

(1)   The bankrupt is guilty of an offence if—

(a)   either alone or jointly with any other person, he obtains credit to the extent of the prescribed amount or more without giving the person from whom he obtains it the relevant information about his status; or

(b)   he engages (whether directly or indirectly) in any business under a name other than that in which he was made bankrupt without disclosing to all persons with whom he enters into any business transaction the name in which he was so made.

(2)   The reference to the bankrupt obtaining credit includes the following cases—

(a)   where goods are bailed to him under a hire-purchase agreement, or agreed to be sold to him under a conditional sale agreement, and

(b)   where he is paid in advance (whether in money or otherwise) for the supply of goods or services.

(3)   A person whose estate has been sequestrated in Scotland, or who has been adjudged bankrupt in Northern Ireland, is guilty of an offence if, before his discharge, he does anything in England and Wales which would be an offence under subsection (1) if he were an undischarged bankrupt and the sequestration of his estate or the adjudication in Northern Ireland were an adjudication under this Part.

(4)   For the purposes of subsection (1)(a), the relevant information about the status of the person in question is the information that he is an undischarged bankrupt or, as the case may be, that his estate has been sequestrated in Scotland and that he has not been discharged.

(5)   This section applies to the bankrupt after discharge while a bankruptcy restrictions order is in force in respect of him.

(6)   For the purposes of subsection (1)(a) as it applies by virtue of subsection (5), the relevant information about the status of the person in question is the information that a bankruptcy restrictions order is in force in respect of him.

361, 362....

CHAPTER VII

POWERS OF COURT IN BANKRUPTCY

363.   General control of court

(1)   Every bankruptcy is under the general control of the court and, subject to the provisions in this Group of Parts, the court has full power to decide all questions of priorities and all other questions, whether of law or fact, arising in any bankruptcy.

(2)   Without prejudice to any other provision in this Group of Parts, an undischarged bankrupt or a discharged bankrupt whose estate is still being administered under Chapter IV of this Part shall do all such things as he may be directed to do by the court for the purposes of his bankruptcy or, as the case may be, the administration of that estate.

(3)   The official receiver or the trustee of a bankrupt's estate may at any time apply to the court for a direction under subsection (2).

(4)   If any person without reasonable excuse fails to comply with any obligation imposed on him by subsection (2), he is guilty of a contempt of court and liable to be punished accordingly (in addition to any other punishment to which he may be subject).

364.   Power of arrest

(1)   In the cases specified in the next subsection the court may cause a warrant to be issued to a constable or prescribed officer of the court—

(a)   for the arrest of a debtor to whom a bankruptcy application or a bankruptcy petition relates or of an undischarged bankrupt, or of a discharged bankrupt whose estate is still being administered under Chapter IV of this Part, and

(b)   for the seizure of any books, papers, records, money or goods in the possession of a person arrested under the warrant, and may authorise a person arrested under such a warrant to be kept in custody, and anything seized under such a warrant to be held, in accordance with the rules, until such time as the court may order.

(2)   The powers conferred by subsection (1) are exercisable in relation to a debtor or undischarged or discharged bankrupt if, at any time after the making of the bankruptcy application or the presentation of the bankruptcy petition relating to him or the making of the bankruptcy order against him, it appears to the court—

      (a)   that there are reasonable grounds for believing that he has absconded, or is about to abscond, with a view to avoiding or delaying the payment of any of his debts or his appearance to a bankruptcy petition or to avoiding, delaying or disrupting any proceedings in bankruptcy against him or any examination of his affairs, or

      (b)   that he is about to remove his goods with a view to preventing or delaying possession being taken of them by the official receiver or the trustee of his estate, or

      (c)   that there are reasonable grounds for believing that he has concealed or destroyed, or is about to conceal or destroy, any of his goods or any books, papers or records which might be of use to his creditors in the course of his bankruptcy or in connection with the administration of his estate, or

      (d)   that he has, without the leave of the official receiver or the trustee of his estate, removed any goods in his possession which exceed in value such sum as may be prescribed for the purposes of this paragraph, or

      (e)   that he has failed, without reasonable excuse, to attend any examination ordered by the court.

365.   Seizure of bankrupt's property

(1)   At any time after a bankruptcy order has been made, the court may, on the application of the official receiver or the trustee of the bankrupt's estate, issue a warrant authorising the person to whom it is directed to seize any property comprised in the bankrupt's estate which is, or any books, papers or records relating to the bankrupt's estate or affairs which are, in the possession or under the control of the bankrupt or any other person who is required to deliver the property, books, papers or records to the official receiver or trustee.

(2)   Any person executing a warrant under this section may, for the purpose of seizing any property comprised in the bankrupt's estate or any books, papers or records relating to the bankrupt's estate or affairs, break open any premises where the bankrupt or anything that may be seized under the warrant is or is believed to be and any receptacle of the bankrupt which contains or is believed to contain anything that may be so seized.

(3)   If, after a bankruptcy order has been made, the court is satisfied that any property comprised in the bankrupt's estate is, or any books, papers or records relating to the bankrupt's estate or affairs are, concealed in any premises not belonging to him, it may issue a warrant authorising any constable or prescribed officer of the court to search those premises for the property, books, papers or records.

(4)   A warrant under subsection (3) shall not be executed except in the prescribed manner and in accordance with its terms.

366.   Inquiry into bankrupt's dealings and property

(1)   At any time after a bankruptcy order has been made the court may, on the application of the official receiver or the trustee of the bankrupt's estate, summon to appear before it—

      (a)   the bankrupt or the bankrupt's spouse or former spouse or civil partner or former civil partner,

      (b)   any person known or believed to have any property comprised in the bankrupt's estate in his possession or to be indebted to the bankrupt,

      (c)   any person appearing to the court to be able to give information concerning the bankrupt or the bankrupt's dealings, affairs or property.

The court may require any such person as is mentioned in paragraph (b) or (c) to submit a witness statement verified by a statement of truth to the court containing an account of his dealings with the bankrupt or to produce any documents in his possession or under his control relating to the bankrupt or the bankrupt's dealings, affairs or property.

(2) Without prejudice to section 364, the following applies in a case where—

    (a) a person without reasonable excuse fails to appear before the court when he is summoned to do so under this section, or

    (b) there are reasonable grounds for believing that a person has absconded, or is about to abscond, with a view to avoiding his appearance before the court under this section.

(3) The court may, for the purpose of bringing that person and anything in his possession before the court, cause a warrant to be issued to a constable or prescribed officer of the court—

    (a) for the arrest of that person, and

    (b) for the seizure of any books, papers, records, money or goods in that person's possession.

(4) The court may authorise a person arrested under such a warrant to be kept in custody, and anything seized under such a warrant to be held, in accordance with the rules, until that person is brought before the court under the warrant or until such other time as the court may order.

367. Court's enforcement powers under s 366

(1) If it appears to the court, on consideration of any evidence obtained under section 366 or this section, that any person has in his possession any property comprised in the bankrupt's estate, the court may, on the application of the official receiver or the trustee of the bankrupt's estate, order that person to deliver the whole or any part of the property to the official receiver or the trustee at such time, in such manner and on such terms as the court thinks fit.

(2) If it appears to the court, on consideration of any evidence obtained under section 366 or this section, that any person is indebted to the bankrupt, the court may, on the application of the official receiver or the trustee of the bankrupt's estate, order that person to pay to the official receiver or trustee, at such time and in such manner as the court may direct, the whole or part of the amount due, whether in full discharge of the debt or otherwise as the court thinks fit.

(3) The court may, if it thinks fit, order that any person who if within the jurisdiction of the court would be liable to be summoned to appear before it under section 366 shall be examined in any part of the United Kingdom where he may be for the time being, or in any place outside the United Kingdom.

(4) Any person who appears or is brought before the court under section 366 or this section may be examined on oath, either orally or by interrogatories, concerning the bankrupt or the bankrupt's dealings, affairs and property.

368. Provision corresponding to s 366, where interim receiver appointed

Sections 366 and 367 apply where an interim receiver has been appointed under section 286 as they apply where a bankruptcy order has been made, as if—

    (a) references to the official receiver or the trustee were to the interim receiver, and

    (b) references to the bankrupt and to his estate were (respectively) to the debtor and his property.

369. Order for production of documents by inland revenue

(1) For the purposes of an examination under section 290 (public examination of bankrupt) or proceedings under sections 366 to 368, the court may, on the application of the official receiver or the trustee of the bankrupt's estate, order an inland revenue official to produce to the court—

    (a) any return, account or accounts submitted (whether before or after the commencement of the bankruptcy) by the bankrupt to any inland revenue official,

    (b) any assessment or determination made (whether before or after the commencement of the bankruptcy) in relation to the bankrupt by any inland revenue official, or

    (c) any correspondence (whether before or after the commencement of the bankruptcy) between the bankrupt and any inland revenue official.

(2)   Where the court has made an order under subsection (1) for the purposes of any examination or proceedings, the court may, at any time after the document to which the order relates is produced to it, by order authorise the disclosure of the document, or of any part of its contents, to the official receiver, the trustee of the bankrupt's estate or the bankrupt's creditors.

(3)   The court shall not address an order under subsection (1) to an inland revenue official unless it is satisfied that that official is dealing, or has dealt, with the affairs of the bankrupt.

(4)   Where any document to which an order under subsection (1) relates is not in the possession of the official to whom the order is addressed, it is the duty of that official to take all reasonable steps to secure possession of it and, if he fails to do so, to report the reasons for his failure to the court.

(5)   Where any document to which an order under subsection (1) relates is in the possession of an inland revenue official other than the one to whom the order is addressed, it is the duty of the official in possession of the document, at the request of the official to whom the order is addressed, to deliver it to the official making the request.

(6)   In this section "inland revenue official" means any inspector or collector of taxes appointed by the Commissioners of Inland Revenue or any person appointed by the Commissioners to serve in any other capacity.

(7)   This section does not apply for the purposes of an examination under sections 366 and 367 which takes place by virtue of section 368 (interim receiver).

370.   Power to appoint special manager

(1)   The court may, on an application under this section, appoint any person to be the special manager—
    (a)   of a bankrupt's estate, or
    (b)   of the business of an undischarged bankrupt, or
    (c)   of the property or business of a debtor in whose case an interim receiver has been appointed under section 286.

(2)   An application under this section may be made by the interim receiver or the trustee of the bankrupt's estate in any case where it appears to the interim receiver or trustee that the nature of the estate, property or business, or the interests of the creditors generally, require the appointment of another person to manage the estate, property or business.

(3)   A special manager appointed under this section has such powers as may be entrusted to him by the court.

(4)   The power of the court under subsection (3) to entrust powers to a special manager includes power to direct that any provision in this Group of Parts that has effect in relation to the official receiver, interim receiver or trustee shall have the like effect in relation to the special manager for the purposes of the carrying out by the special manager of any of the functions of the official receiver, interim receiver or trustee.

(5)   A special manager appointed under this section shall—
    (a)   give such security as may be prescribed,
    (b)   prepare and keep such accounts as may be prescribed, and
    (c)   produce those accounts in accordance with the rules to the Secretary of State or to such other persons as may be prescribed.

371.   Re-direction of bankrupt's letters, etc

(1)   Where a bankruptcy order has been made, the court may from time to time, on the application of the official receiver or the trustee of the bankrupt's estate, order a postal operator (within the meaning of Part 3 of the Postal Services Act 2011) to re-direct and send or deliver to the official receiver or trustee or otherwise any postal packet (within the meaning of that Act) which would otherwise be sent or delivered by the operator concerned to the bankrupt at such place or places as may be specified in the order.

(2)   An order under this section has effect for such period, not exceeding 3 months, as may be specified in the order.

PART X
INDIVIDUAL INSOLVENCY: GENERAL PROVISIONS

372. Supplies of gas, water, electricity, etc

(1) This section applies where on any day ("the relevant day")—

    (a) a bankruptcy order is made against an individual or an interim receiver of an individual's property is appointed, or

    (b) a voluntary arrangement proposed by an individual is approved under Part VIII, ...

    (c) ...

and in this section "the office-holder" means the official receiver, the trustee in bankruptcy, the interim receiver, or the supervisor of the voluntary arrangement, as the case may be.

(2) If a request falling within the next subsection is made for the giving after the relevant day of any of the supplies mentioned in subsection (4), the supplier—

    (a) may make it a condition of the giving of the supply that the office-holder personally guarantees the payment of any charges in respect of the supply, but

    (b) shall not make it a condition of the giving of the supply, or do anything which has the effect of making it a condition of the giving of the supply, that any outstanding charges in respect of a supply given to the individual before the relevant day are paid.

(3) A request falls within this subsection if it is made—

    (a) by or with the concurrence of the office-holder, and

    (b) for the purposes of any business which is or has been carried on by the individual, by a firm or partnership of which the individual is or was a member, or by an agent or manager for the individual or for such a firm or partnership.

(4) The supplies referred to in subsection (2) are—

    (a) a supply of gas by a gas supplier within the meaning of Part I of the Gas Act 1986;

    (aa) a supply of gas by a person within paragraph 1 of Schedule 2A to the Gas Act 1986 (supply by landlords etc);

    (b) a supply of electricity by an electricity supplier within the meaning of Part I of the Electricity Act 1989;

    (ba) a supply of electricity by a class of person within Class A (small suppliers) or Class B (resale) of Schedule 4 to the Electricity (Class Exemptions from the Requirement for a Licence) Order 2001 (S.I. 2001/3270);

    (c) a supply of water by a water undertaker,

    (ca) a supply of water by a water supply licensee within the meaning of the Water Industry Act 1991;

    (cb) a supply of water by a person who has an interest in the premises to which the supply is given;

    (d) a supply of communications services by a provider of a public electronic communications service;

    (e) a supply of communications services by a person who carries on a business which includes giving such supplies;

    (f) a supply of goods or services mentioned in subsection (4A) by a person who carries on a business which includes giving such supplies, where the supply is for the purpose of enabling or facilitating anything to be done by electronic means.

(4A) The goods and services referred to in subsection (4)(f) are—

    (a) point of sale terminals;

    (b) computer hardware and software;

    (c) information, advice and technical assistance in connection with the use of information technology;

    (d) data storage and processing;

    (e) website hosting.

(5) The following applies to expressions used in subsection (4)—

    (a) ...

(b)   … and

(c)   "communications services" do not include electronic communications services to the extent that they are used to broadcast or otherwise transmit programme services (within the meaning of the Communications Act 2003).

372A.   Further protection of essential supplies

(1)   An insolvency-related term of a contract for the supply of essential goods or services to an individual ceases to have effect if—

(a)   a voluntary arrangement proposed by the individual is approved under Part 8, and

(b)   the supply is for the purpose of a business which is or has been carried on by the individual, by a firm or partnership of which the individual is or was a member, or by an agent or manager for the individual or for such a firm or partnership.

(2)   An insolvency-related term of a contract does not cease to have effect by virtue of subsection (1) to the extent that—

(a)   it provides for the contract or the supply to terminate, or any other thing to take place, because the individual becomes subject to an insolvency procedure other than a voluntary arrangement;

(b)   it entitles a supplier to terminate the contract or the supply, or do any other thing, because the individual becomes subject to an insolvency procedure other than a voluntary arrangement; or

(c)   it entitles a supplier to terminate the contract or the supply because of an event that occurs, or may occur, after the voluntary arrangement proposed by the individual is approved.

(3)   Where an insolvency-related term of a contract ceases to have effect under this section the supplier may—

(a)   terminate the contract, if the condition in subsection (4) is met;

(b)   terminate the supply, if the condition in subsection (5) is met.

(4)   The condition in this subsection is that—

(a)   the supervisor of the voluntary arrangement consents to the termination of the contract,

(b)   the court grants permission for the termination of the contract, or

(c)   any charges in respect of the supply that are incurred after the voluntary arrangement is approved are not paid within the period of 28 days beginning with the day on which payment is due.

The court may grant permission under paragraph (b) only if satisfied that the continuation of the contract would cause the supplier hardship.

(5)   The condition in this subsection is that—

(a)   the supplier gives written notice to the supervisor of the voluntary arrangement that the supply will be terminated unless the supervisor personally guarantees the payment of any charges in respect of the continuation of the supply after the arrangement was approved, and

(b)   the supervisor does not give that guarantee within the period of 14 days beginning with the day the notice is received.

(6)   For the purposes of securing that the interests of suppliers are protected, where—

(a)   an insolvency-related term of a contract (the "original term") ceases to have effect by virtue of subsection (1), and

(b)   a subsequent voluntary arrangement proposed by the individual is approved,

the contract is treated for the purposes of subsections (1) to (5) as if, immediately before the subsequent voluntary arrangement proposed by the individual is approved, it included an insolvency-related term identical to the original term.

(7)   A contract for the supply of essential goods or services is a contract for a supply mentioned in section 372(4).

(8)   An insolvency-related term of a contract for the supply of essential goods or services to an individual is a provision of the contract under which—

(a)   the contract or the supply would terminate, or any other thing would take place, because the voluntary arrangement proposed by the individual is approved,

(b)   the supplier would be entitled to terminate the contract or the supply, or to do any other thing, because the voluntary arrangement proposed by the individual is approved, or

(c)   the supplier would be entitled to terminate the contract or the supply because of an event that occurred before the voluntary arrangement proposed by the individual is approved.

(9)   Subsection (1) does not have effect in relation to a contract entered into before 1st October 2015.

373.   Jurisdiction in relation to insolvent individuals

(1)   The High Court and the county court have jurisdiction throughout England and Wales for the purposes of the Parts in this Group.

(2)   For the purposes of those Parts, the county court has, in addition to its ordinary jurisdiction, all the powers and jurisdiction of the High Court; and the orders of the court may be enforced accordingly in the prescribed manner.

(3)   Jurisdiction for the purposes of those Parts is exercised—

(a)   by the High Court or the county court in relation to the proceedings which, in accordance with the rules, are allocated to the London insolvency district, and

(b)   by the county court in relation to the proceedings which are so allocated to any other insolvency district.

(4)   Subsection (3) is without prejudice to the transfer of proceedings from one court to another in the manner prescribed by the rules; and nothing in that subsection invalidates any proceedings on the grounds that they were initiated or continued in the wrong court.

374.   Insolvency districts

(1)   The Lord Chancellor may, with the concurrence of the Lord Chief Justice, by order designate the areas which are for the time being to be comprised, for the purposes of the Parts in this Group, in the London Insolvency district and the insolvency district, or districts, of the county court.

(2)   An order under this section may contain such incidental, supplemental and transitional provisions as may appear to the Lord Chancellor and the Lord Chief Justice necessary or expedient.

(3)   An order under this section shall be made by statutory instrument and, after being made, shall be laid before each House of Parliament.

(4)   Subject to any order under this section—

(a)   the district which, immediately before the appointed day, is the London bankruptcy district becomes, on that day, the London insolvency district;

(b)   any district which immediately before that day is the bankruptcy district of a county court becomes, on that day, the insolvency district of that court, and

(c)   any county court which immediately before that day is excluded from having jurisdiction in bankruptcy is excluded, on and after that day, from having jurisdiction for the purposes of the Parts in this Group.

(5)   The Lord Chief Justice may nominate a judicial office holder (as defined in section 109(4) of the Constitutional Reform Act 2005) to exercise his functions under this section.

375.   Appeals etc from courts exercising insolvency jurisdiction

(1)   Every court having jurisdiction for the purposes of the Parts in this Group may review, rescind or vary any order made by it in the exercise of that jurisdiction.

(2)   An appeal from a decision made in the exercise of jurisdiction for the purposes of those Parts by the county court or by an insolvency and companies court judge lies to a single judge of the High Court; and an appeal from a decision of that judge on such an appeal lies… to the Court of Appeal.

(3)   The county court is not, in the exercise of its jurisdiction for the purposes of those Parts, to be subject to be restrained by the order of any other court, and no appeal lies from its decision in the exercise of that jurisdiction except as provided by this section.

376.   Time-limits

Where by any provision in this Group of Parts or by the rules the time for doing anything (including anything in relation to a bankruptcy application) is limited, the court may extend the time, either before or after it has expired, on such terms, if any, as it thinks fit.

377.   Formal defects

The acts of a person as the trustee of a bankrupt's estate or as a special manager, and the acts of the creditors' committee established for any bankruptcy, are valid notwithstanding any defect in the appointment, election or qualifications of the trustee or manager or, as the case may be, of any member of the committee.

378.   Exemption from stamp duty

Stamp duty shall not be charged on—

(a)   any document, being a deed, conveyance, assignment, surrender, admission or other assurance relating solely to property which is comprised in a bankrupt's estate and which, after the execution of that document, is or remains at law or in equity the property of the bankrupt or of the trustee of that estate,

(b)   any writ, order, certificate or other instrument relating solely to the property of a bankrupt or to any bankruptcy proceedings.

379.   Annual report

As soon as practicable after the end of 1986 and each subsequent calendar year, the Secretary of State shall prepare and lay before each House of Parliament a report about the operation during that year of so much of this Act as is comprised in this Group of Parts ...

Creditors' decisions

379ZA. Creditors' decisions: general

(1)   This section applies where, for the purposes of this Group of Parts, a person ("P") seeks a decision from an individual's creditors about any matter.

(2)   The decision may be made by any creditors' decision procedure P thinks fit, except that it may not be made by a creditors' meeting unless subsection (3) applies.

(3)   This subsection applies if at least the minimum number of creditors request in writing that the decision be made by a creditors' meeting.

(4)   If subsection (3) applies, P must summon a creditors' meeting.

(5)   Subsection (2) is subject to any provision of this Act, the rules or any other legislation, or any order of the court—

(a)   requiring a decision to be made, or prohibiting a decision from being made, by a particular creditors' decision procedure (other than a creditors' meeting);

(b)   permitting or requiring a decision to be made by a creditors' meeting.

(6)   Section 379ZB provides that in certain cases the deemed consent procedure may be used instead of a creditors' decision procedure.

(7)   For the purposes of subsection (3) the "minimum number" of creditors is any of the following—

(a)   10% in value of the creditors;

(b)   10% in number of the creditors;

(c)   10 creditors.

(8)   The references in subsection (7) to creditors are to creditors of any class, even where a decision is sought only from creditors of a particular class.

(9)   In this section references to a meeting are to a meeting where the creditors are invited to be present together at the same place (whether or not it is possible to attend the meeting without being present at that place).

(10)   Except as provided by subsection (8), references in this section to creditors include creditors of a particular class.

(11)   In this Group of Parts "creditors' decision procedure" means a procedure prescribed or authorised under paragraph 11A of Schedule 9.

379ZB. Deemed consent procedure

(1)   The deemed consent procedure may be used instead of a creditors' decision procedure where an individual's creditors are to make a decision about any matter, unless—

(a) a decision about the matter is required by virtue of this Act, the rules or any other legislation to be made by a creditors' decision procedure, or

(b) the court orders that a decision about the matter is to be made by a creditors' decision procedure.

(2) If the rules provide for an individual's creditors to make a decision about the remuneration of any person, they must provide that the decision is to be made by a creditors' decision procedure.

(3) The deemed consent procedure is that the relevant creditors (other than opted-out creditors) are given notice of—

(a) the matter about which the creditors are to make a decision,

(b) the decision the person giving the notice proposes should be made (the "proposed decision"),

(c) the effect of subsections (4) and (5), and

(d) the procedure for objecting to the proposed decision.

(4) If less than the appropriate number of relevant creditors object to the proposed decision in accordance with the procedure set out in the notice, the creditors are to be treated as having made the proposed decision.

(5) Otherwise—

(a) the creditors are to be treated as not having made a decision about the matter in question, and

(b) if a decision about that matter is again sought from the creditors, it must be sought using a creditors' decision procedure.

(6) For the purposes of subsection (4) the "appropriate number" of relevant creditors is 10% in value of those creditors.

(7) "Relevant creditors" means the creditors who, if the decision were to be made by a creditors' decision procedure, would be entitled to vote in the procedure.

(8) In this section references to creditors include creditors of a particular class.

(9) The rules may make further provision about the deemed consent procedure.

379ZC. Power to amend sections 379ZA and 379ZB

(1) The Secretary of State may by regulations amend section 379ZA so as to change the definition of the minimum number of creditors.

(2) The Secretary of State may by regulations amend section 379ZB so as to change the definition of the appropriate number of relevant creditors.

(3) Regulations under this section may define the minimum number or the appropriate number by reference to any one or more of—

(a) a proportion in value,

(b) a proportion in number,

(c) an absolute number,

and the definition may include alternative, cumulative or relative requirements.

(4) Regulations under subsection (1) may define the minimum number of creditors by reference to all creditors, or by reference to creditors of a particular description.

(5) Regulations under this section may make provision that will result in section 379ZA or 379ZB having different definitions for different cases, including for different kinds of decisions.

(6) Regulations under this section may make transitional provision.

(7) The power of the Secretary of State to make regulations under this section is exercisable by statutory instrument.

(8) A statutory instrument containing regulations under this section may not be made unless a draft of the instrument has been laid before, and approved by a resolution of, each House of Parliament.

379A. ...

Giving of notices etc by office-holders

379B. Use of websites

(1)   This section applies where—

    (a)   a bankruptcy order is made against an individual or an interim receiver of an individual's property is appointed, or

    (b)   a voluntary arrangement in relation to an individual is proposed or is approved under Part 8, and "the office-holder" means the official receiver, the trustee in bankruptcy, the interim receiver, the nominee or the supervisor of the voluntary arrangement, as the case may be.

(2)   Where any provision of this Act or the rules requires the office-holder to give, deliver, furnish or send a notice or other document or information to any person, that requirement is satisfied by making the notice, document or information available on a website—

    (a)   in accordance with the rules, and

    (b)   in such circumstances as may be prescribed.

379C. Creditors' ability to opt out of receiving certain notices

(1)   Any provision of the rules which requires an office-holder to give a notice to creditors of an individual does not apply, in circumstances prescribed by the rules, in relation to opted-out creditors.

(2)   Subsection (1)—

    (a)   does not apply in relation to a notice of a distribution or proposed distribution to creditors;

    (b)   is subject to any order of the court requiring a notice to be given to all creditors (or all creditors of a particular category).

(3)   Except as provided by the rules, a creditor may participate and vote in a creditors' decision procedure or a deemed consent procedure even though, by virtue of being an opted-out creditor, the creditor does not receive notice of it.

(4)   In this section—

"give" includes deliver, furnish or send;

"notice" includes any document or information in any other form;

"office-holder", in relation to an individual, means—

    (a)   where a bankruptcy order is made against the individual, the official receiver or the trustee in bankruptcy;

    (b)   where an interim receiver of the individual's property is appointed, the interim receiver;

    (c)   the supervisor of a voluntary arrangement approved under Part 8 in relation to the individual.

PART XI
INTERPRETATION FOR SECOND GROUP OF PARTS

380. Introductory

The next five sections have effect for the interpretation of the provisions of this Act which are comprised in this Group of Parts; and where a definition is provided for a particular expression, it applies except so far as the context otherwise requires.

381. "Bankrupt" and associated terminology

(1)   "Bankrupt" means an individual who has been made bankrupt and, in relation to a bankruptcy order, it means the individual made bankrupt by that order.

(1A)   "Bankruptcy application" means an application to an adjudicator for a bankruptcy order.

(2)   "Bankruptcy order" means an order making an individual bankrupt.

(3)   "Bankruptcy petition" means a petition to the court for a bankruptcy order.

382. "Bankruptcy debt", "liability"

(1)   "Bankruptcy debt", in relation to a bankrupt, means (subject to the next subsection) any of the following—

(a) any debt or liability to which he is subject at the commencement of the bankruptcy,

(b) any debt or liability to which he may become subject after the commencement of the bankruptcy (including after his discharge from bankruptcy) by reason of any obligation incurred before the commencement of the bankruptcy,

(c) *any amount specified in pursuance of section 39(3)(c) of the Powers of Criminal Courts Act 1973 in any criminal bankruptcy order made against him before the commencement of the bankruptcy, and*

(d) any interest provable as mentioned in section 322(2) in Chapter IV of Part IX.

(2) In determining for the purposes of any provision in this Group of Parts whether any liability in tort is a bankruptcy debt, the bankrupt is deemed to become subject to that liability by reason of an obligation incurred at the time when the cause of action accrued.

(3) For the purposes of references in this Group of Parts to a debt or liability, it is immaterial whether the debt or liability is present or future, whether it is certain or contingent or whether its amount is fixed or liquidated, or is capable of being ascertained by fixed rules or as a matter of opinion; and references in this Group of Parts to owing a debt are to be read accordingly.

(4) In this Group of Parts, except in so far as the context otherwise requires, "liability" means (subject to subsection (3) above) a liability to pay money or money's worth, including any liability under an enactment, any liability for breach of trust, any liability in contract, tort or bailment and any liability arising out of an obligation to make restitution.

(5) Liability under the Child Support Act 1991 to pay child support maintenance to any person is not a debt or liability for the purposes of Part 8.

Note. Subsection (1)(c) is repealed by the Criminal Justice Act 1988, s. 170(2), Sch. 16, as from a day to be appointed.

383. **"Creditor", "security", etc**

(1) "Creditor"—

(a) in relation to a bankrupt, means a person to whom any of the bankruptcy debts is owed *(being, in the case of an amount falling within paragraph (c) of the definition in section 382(1) of "bankruptcy debt", the person in respect of whom that amount is specified in the criminal bankruptcy order in question)*, and

(b) in relation to an individual to whom a bankruptcy application or bankruptcy petition relates, means a person who would be a creditor in the bankruptcy if a bankruptcy order were made on that application or petition.

(2) Subject to the next two subsections and any provision of the rules requiring a creditor to give up his security for the purposes of proving a debt, a debt is secured for the purposes of this Group of Parts to the extent that the person to whom the debt is owed holds any security for the debt (whether a mortgage, charge, lien or other security) over any property of the person by whom the debt is owed.

(3) Where a statement such as is mentioned in section 269(1)(a) in Chapter I of Part IX has been made by a secured creditor for the purposes of any bankruptcy petition and a bankruptcy order is subsequently made on that petition, the creditor is deemed for the purposes of the Parts in this Group to have given up the security specified in the statement.

(4) In subsection (2) the reference to a security does not include a lien on books, papers or other records, except to the extent that they consist of documents which give a title to property and are held as such.

Note. The italicized words in subsection (1)(a) are repealed by the Criminal Justice Act 1988, s. 170(2), Sch. 16, as from a day to be appointed.

383A. **"Opted-out creditor"**

(1) For the purposes of this Group of Parts "opted-out creditor" in relation to an office-holder for an individual means a person who—

(a) is a creditor of the individual, and

(b)   in accordance with the rules has elected (or is deemed to have elected) to be (and not to cease to be) an opted-out creditor in relation to the office-holder.

(2)   In this section, "office-holder", in relation to an individual, means—

(a)   where a bankruptcy order is made against the individual, the official receiver or the trustee in bankruptcy;

(b)   where an interim receiver of the individual's property is appointed, the interim receiver;

(c)   the supervisor of a voluntary arrangement approved under Part 8 in relation to the individual.

384.   "Prescribed" and "the rules"

(1)   Subject to the next subsection and sections 342C(7) and 342F(9) in Chapter V of Part IX, "prescribed" means prescribed by the rules; and "the rules" means rules made under section 412 in Part XV.

(2)   References in this Group of Parts to the amount prescribed for the purposes of any of the following provisions—

section 251S(4);

...

section 313A;

section 346(3);

section 354(1) and (2);

section 358;

section 360(1);

section 361(2); ...

section 364(2)(d),

paragraphs 6 to 8 of Schedule 4ZA.

and references in those provisions to the prescribed amount are to be read in accordance with section 418 in Part XV and orders made under that section.

385.   Miscellaneous definitions

(1)   The following definitions have effect—

"adjudicator" means a person appointed by the Secretary of State under section 398A;

"the court", in relation to any matter, means the court to which, in accordance with section 373 in Part X and the rules, proceedings with respect to that matter are allocated or transferred;

"creditors' decision procedure" has the meaning given by section 379ZA(11);

"creditor's petition" means a bankruptcy petition under section 264(1)(a);

"criminal bankruptcy order" means an order under section 39(1) of the Powers of Criminal Courts Act 1973;

"debt" is to be construed in accordance with section 382(3);

"the debtor"—

(za)   in relation to a debt relief order or an application for such an order, has the same meaning as in Part 7A,

(a)   in relation to a proposal for the purposes of Part VIII, means the individual making or intending to make that proposal, and

(b)   in relation to a bankruptcy application or a bankruptcy petition, means the individual to whom the application or petition relates;

...

"debt relief order" means an order made by the official receiver under Part 7A;

"deemed consent procedure" means the deemed consent procedure provided for by section 379ZB;

"determination period" has the meaning given in section 263K(4);

"dwelling house" includes any building or part of a building which is occupied as a dwelling and any yard, garden, garage or outhouse belonging to the dwelling house and occupied with it;

"estate", in relation to a bankrupt is to be construed in accordance with section 283 in Chapter II of Part IX;

"family", in relation to a bankrupt, means the persons (if any) who are living with him and are dependent on him;

"insolvency administration order" means an order for the administration in bankruptcy of the insolvent estate of a deceased debtor (being an individual at the date of his death);

"insolvency administration petition" means a petition for an insolvency administration order;

"the Rules" means the Insolvency (England and Wales) Rules 2016;

"secured" and related expressions are to be construed in accordance with section 383; and

"the trustee", in relation to a bankruptcy and the bankrupt, means the trustee of the bankrupt's estate.

(2)   References in this Group of Parts to a person's affairs include his business, if any.

Note. The italicized definition of "criminal bankruptcy order" in subsection (1) is repealed by the Criminal Justice Act 1988, s. 170(2), Sch. 16, as from a day to be appointed.

THE THIRD GROUP OF PARTS
MISCELLANEOUS MATTERS BEARING ON BOTH COMPANY AND INDIVIDUAL INSOLVENCY; GENERAL INTERPRETATION; FINAL PROVISIONS

PART XII
PREFERENTIAL AND NON-PREFERENTIAL DEBTS IN COMPANY AND INDIVIDUAL INSOLVENCY

386.   Categories of preferential debts

(1)   A reference in this Act to the preferential debts of a company or an individual is to the debts listed in Schedule 6 to this Act (contributions to occupational pension schemes; remuneration, &c of employees; levies on coal and steel production; debts owed to the Financial Services Compensation Scheme; deposits covered by Financial Services Compensation Scheme; other deposits; certain HMRC debts); and references to preferential creditors are to be read accordingly.

(1A)   A reference in this Act to the "ordinary preferential debts" of a company or an individual is to the preferential debts listed in any of paragraphs 8 to 15B of Schedule 6 to this Act.

(1B)   A reference in this Act to the "secondary preferential debts" of a company or an individual is to the preferential debts listed in paragraph 15BA, 15BB or 15D of Schedule 6 to this Act.

(2)   In Schedule 6 "the debtor" means the company or the individual concerned.

(3)   Schedule 6 is to be read with Schedule 4 to the Pension Schemes Act 1993 (occupational pension scheme contributions).

387.   "The relevant date"

(1)   This section explains references in Schedule 6 to the relevant date (being the date which determines the existence and amount of a preferential debt).

(2)   For the purposes of section 4 in Part I (consideration of company voluntary arrangement), the relevant date in relation to a company which is not being wound up is—

(a)   if the company is in administration, the date on which it entered administration, and

(b)   if the company is not in administration, the date on which the voluntary arrangement takes effect.

(2A)   ...

(3)   In relation to a company which is being wound up, the following applies—

(a) if the winding up is by the court, and the winding-up order was made immediately upon the discharge of an administration order, the relevant date is the date on which the company entered administration;

(aa), (ab) ...

(b) if the case does not fall within paragraph (a) ... and the company—

    (i) is being wound up by the court, and

    (ii) had not commenced to be wound up voluntarily before the date of the making of the winding-up order,

the relevant date is the date of the appointment (or first appointment) of a provisional liquidator or, if no such appointment has been made, the date of the winding-up order;

(ba) if the case does not fall within paragraph (a) ... or (b) and the company is being wound up following administration pursuant to paragraph 83 of Schedule B1, the relevant date is the date on which the company entered administration;

(c) if the case does not fall within paragraph (a), ... (b) or (ba), the relevant date is the date of the passing of the resolution for the winding up of the company.

(3A) In relation to a company which is in administration (and to which no other provision of this section applies) the relevant date is the date on which the company enters administration.

(4) In relation to a company in receivership (where section 40 or, as the case may be, section 59 applies), the relevant date is—

(a) in England and Wales, the date of the appointment of the receiver by debenture-holders, and

(b) in Scotland, the date of the appointment of the receiver under section 53(6) or (as the case may be) 54(5).

(5) For the purposes of section 258 in Part VIII (individual voluntary arrangements), the relevant date is, in relation to a debtor who is not an undischarged bankrupt—

(a) where an interim order has been made under section 252 with respect to his proposal, the date of that order, and

(b) in any other case, the date on which the voluntary arrangement takes effect.

(6) In relation to a bankrupt, the following applies—

(a) where at the time the bankruptcy order was made there was an interim receiver appointed under section 286, the relevant date is the date on which the interim receiver was first appointed after the making of the bankruptcy application or (as the case may be) the presentation of the bankruptcy petition;

(b) otherwise, the relevant date is the date of the making of the bankruptcy order.

387A. Financial institutions and their non-preferential debts

(1) In this Act "relevant financial institution" means any of the following—

(a) a credit institution,

(b) an investment firm,

(c) a financial holding company,

(d) a mixed financial holding company,

(da) an investment holding company,

(e) a financial institution which is—

    (i) a subsidiary of an entity referred to in paragraphs (a) to (da), and

    (ii) covered by the supervision of that entity on a consolidated basis by the Financial Conduct Authority in accordance with Part 9C rules or by the Prudential Regulation Authority in accordance with Regulation (EU) No 575/2013 of the European Parliament and of the Council of 26 June 2013 on prudential requirements for credit institutions and investment firms or CRR rules, or,

(f) a mixed-activity holding company.

(2) The definitions in Article 4 of Regulation (EU) No 575/2013 apply for the purposes of subsection (1), except for the definitions of "consolidated basis" and "consolidated situation".

(2A) For the purposes of subsection (1)—

"on a consolidated basis" means on the basis of the consolidated situation;

"consolidated situation" means the situation that results from an entity being treated, for the purposes of Part 9C rules, Regulation (EU) 575/2013 or CRR rules (as appropriate), as if that entity and one or more other entities formed a single entity;

"CRR rules" has the meaning given in section 144A of the Financial Services and Markets Act 2000;

"Part 9C rules" has the meaning given in section 143F of the Financial Services and Markets Act 2000.

(3) In this Act, in relation to a relevant financial institution—

(a) "ordinary non-preferential debts" means non-preferential debts which are neither secondary non-preferential debts nor tertiary non-preferential debts;

(b) "secondary non-preferential debts" means non-preferential debts issued under an instrument where—

(i) the original contractual maturity of the instrument is of at least one year,

(ii) the instrument is not a derivative and contains no embedded derivative, and

(iii) the relevant contractual documentation and where applicable the prospectus related to the issue of the debts explain the priority of the debts under this Act, and

(c) "tertiary non-preferential debts" means all subordinated debts, including (but not limited to) debts under Common Equity Tier 1 instruments, Additional Tier 1 instruments and Tier 2 instruments (all within the meaning of Part 1 of the Banking Act 2009).

(4) In subsection (3)(b), "derivative" has the same meaning as in Article 2(5) of Regulation (EU) No 648/2012.

(5) For the purposes of subsection (3)(b)(ii) an instrument does not contain an embedded derivative merely because—

(a) it provides for a variable interest rate derived from a broadly used reference rate, or

(b) it is not denominated in the domestic currency of the person issuing the debt (provided that the principal, repayment and interest are denominated in the same currency).

...

PART XVI
PROVISIONS AGAINST DEBT AVOIDANCE
(ENGLAND AND WALES ONLY)

423. Transactions defrauding creditors

(1) This section relates to transactions entered into at an undervalue; and a person enters into such a transaction with another person if—

(a) he makes a gift to the other person or he otherwise enters into a transaction with the other on terms that provide for him to receive no consideration;

(b) he enters into a transaction with the other in consideration of marriage or the formation of a civil partnership; or

(c) he enters into a transaction with the other for a consideration the value of which, in money or money's worth, is significantly less than the value, in money or money's worth, of the consideration provided by himself.

(2) Where a person has entered into such a transaction, the court may, if satisfied under the next subsection, make such order as it thinks fit for—

(a) restoring the position to what it would have been if the transaction had not been entered into, and

(b) protecting the interests of persons who are victims of the transaction.

(3) In the case of a person entering into such a transaction, an order shall only be made if the court is satisfied that it was entered into by him for the purpose—

(a) of putting assets beyond the reach of a person who is making, or may at some time make, a claim against him, or

(b)   of otherwise prejudicing the interests of such a person in relation to the claim which he is making or may make.

(4)   In this section "the court" means the High Court or—

    (a)   if the person entering into the transaction is an individual, any other court which would have jurisdiction in relation to a bankruptcy petition relating to him;

    (b)   if that person is a body capable of being wound up under Part IV or V of this Act, any other court having jurisdiction to wind it up.

(5)   In relation to a transaction at an undervalue, references here and below to a victim of the transaction are to a person who is, or is capable of being, prejudiced by it; and in the following two sections the person entering into the transaction is referred to as "the debtor".

424.   Those who may apply for an order under s 423

(1)   An application for an order under section 423 shall not be made in relation to a transaction except—

    (a)   in a case where the debtor has been made bankrupt or is a body corporate which is being wound up or is in administration, by the official receiver, by the trustee of the bankrupt's estate or the liquidator or administrator of the body corporate or (with the leave of the court) by a victim of the transaction;

    (b)   in a case where a victim of the transaction is bound by a voluntary arrangement approved under Part I or Part VIII of this Act, by the supervisor of the voluntary arrangement or by any person who (whether or not so bound) is such a victim; or

    (c)   in any other case, by a victim of the transaction.

(2)   An application made under any of the paragraphs of subsection (1) is to be treated as made on behalf of every victim of the transaction.

425.   Provision which may be made by order under s 423

(1)   Without prejudice to the generality of section 423, an order made under that section with respect to a transaction may (subject as follows)—

    (a)   require any property transferred as part of the transaction to be vested in any person, either absolutely or for the benefit of all the persons on whose behalf the application for the order is treated as made;

    (b)   require any property to be so vested if it represents, in any person's hands, the application either of the proceeds of sale of property so transferred or of money so transferred;

    (c)   release or discharge (in whole or in part) any security given by the debtor;

    (d)   require any person to pay to any other person in respect of benefits received from the debtor such sums as the court may direct;

    (e)   provide for any surety or guarantor whose obligations to any person were released or discharged (in whole or in part) under the transaction to be under such new or revived obligations as the court thinks appropriate;

    (f)   provide for security to be provided for the discharge of any obligation imposed by or arising under the order, for such an obligation to be charged on any property and for such security or charge to have the same priority as a security or charge released or discharged (in whole or in part) under the transaction.

(2)   An order under section 423 may affect the property of, or impose any obligation on, any person whether or not he is the person with whom the debtor entered into the transaction; but such an order—

    (a)   shall not prejudice any interest in property which was acquired from a person other than the debtor and was acquired in good faith, for value and without notice of the relevant circumstances, or prejudice any interest deriving from such an interest, and

    (b)   shall not require a person who received a benefit from the transaction in good faith, for value and without notice of the relevant circumstances to pay any sum unless he was a party to the transaction.

(3)   For the purposes of this section the relevant circumstances in relation to a transaction are the circumstances by virtue of which an order under section 423 may be made in respect of the transaction.

(4)   In this section "security" means any mortgage, charge, lien or other security.

PART XVII
MISCELLANEOUS AND GENERAL

426.   Co-operation between courts exercising jurisdiction in relation to insolvency

(1)   An order made by a court in any part of the United Kingdom in the exercise of jurisdiction in relation to insolvency law shall be enforced in any other part of the United Kingdom as if it were made by a court exercising the corresponding jurisdiction in that other part.

(2)   However, without prejudice to the following provisions of this section, nothing in subsection (1) requires a court in any part of the United Kingdom to enforce, in relation to property situated in that part, any order made by a court in any other part of the United Kingdom.

(3)   The Secretary of State, with the concurrence in relation to property situated in England and Wales of the Lord Chancellor, may by order make provision for securing that a trustee or assignee under the insolvency law of any part of the United Kingdom has, with such modifications as may be specified in the order, the same rights in relation to any property situated in another part of the United Kingdom as he would have in the corresponding circumstances if he were a trustee or assignee under the insolvency law of that other part.

(4)   The courts having jurisdiction in relation to insolvency law in any part of the United Kingdom shall assist the courts having the corresponding jurisdiction in any other part of the United Kingdom or any relevant country or territory.

(5)   For the purposes of subsection (4) a request made to a court in any part of the United Kingdom by a court in any other part of the United Kingdom or in a relevant country or territory is authority for the court to which the request is made to apply, in relation to any matters specified in the request, the insolvency law which is applicable by either court in relation to comparable matters falling within its jurisdiction.

        In exercising its discretion under this subsection, a court shall have regard in particular to the rules of private international law.

(6)   Where a person who is a trustee or assignee under the insolvency law of any part of the United Kingdom claims property situated in any other part of the United Kingdom (whether by virtue of an order under subsection (3) or otherwise), the submission of that claim to the court exercising jurisdiction in relation to insolvency law in that other part shall be treated in the same manner as a request made by a court for the purpose of subsection (4).

(7)   Section 38 of the Criminal Law Act 1977 (execution of warrant of arrest throughout the United Kingdom) applies to a warrant which, in exercise of any jurisdiction in relation to insolvency law, is issued in any part of the United Kingdom for the arrest of a person as it applies to a warrant issued in that part of the United Kingdom for the arrest of a person charged with an offence.

(8)   Without prejudice to any power to make rules of court, any power to make provision by subordinate legislation for the purpose of giving effect in relation to companies or individuals to the insolvency law of any part of the United Kingdom includes power to make provision for the purpose of giving effect in that part to any provision made by or under the preceding provisions of this section.

(9)   An order under subsection (3) shall be made by statutory instrument subject to annulment in pursuance of a resolution of either House of Parliament.

(10)   In this section "insolvency law" means—

        (a)   in relation to England and Wales, provision extending to England and Wales and made by or under this Act or sections 1A, 6 to 10, 12 to 15, 19(c) and 20 (with Schedule 1) of the Company Directors Disqualification Act 1986 and sections 1 to 17 of that Act as they apply for the purposes of those provisions of that Act;

(b)   in relation to Scotland, provision extending to Scotland and made by or under this Act, sections 1A, 6 to 10, 12 to 15, 19(c) and 20 (with Schedule 1) of the Company Directors Disqualification Act 1986 and sections 1 to 17 of that Act as they apply for the purposes of those provisions of that Act, Part XVIII of the Companies Act or the Bankruptcy (Scotland) Act 2016;

(c)   in relation to Northern Ireland, provision made by or under the Insolvency (Northern Ireland) Order 1989 *or Part II of the Companies (Northern Ireland) Order 1989* [*or the Company Directors Disqualification (Northern Ireland) Order 2002*];

(d)   in relation to any relevant country or territory, so much of the law of that country or territory as corresponds to provisions falling within any of the foregoing paragraphs;

and references in this subsection to any enactment include, in relation to any time before the coming into force of that enactment the corresponding enactment in force at that time.

(11)   In this section "relevant country or territory" means—

(a)   any of the Channel Islands or the Isle of Man, or

(b)   any country or territory designated for the purposes of this section by the Secretary of State by order made by statutory instrument.

(12)   In the application of this section to Northern Ireland—

(a)   for any reference to the Secretary of State there is substituted a reference to the Department of Economic Development in Northern Ireland;

(b)   in subsection (3) for the words "another part of the United Kingdom" and the words "that other part" there are substituted the words "Northern Ireland";

(c)   for subsection (9) there is substituted the following subsection—

"(9) An order made under subsection (3) by the Department of Economic Development in Northern Ireland shall be a statutory rule for the purposes of the Statutory Rules (Northern Ireland) Order 1979 and shall be subject to negative resolution within the meaning of section 41(6) of the Interpretation Act (Northern Ireland) 1954.".

(13)   Section 129 of the Banking Act 2009 provides for provisions of that Act about bank insolvency to be "insolvency law" for the purposes of this section.

(14)   Section 165 of the Banking Act 2009 provides for provisions of that Act about bank administration to be "insolvency law" for the purposes of this section.

Note. The italicized words "or Part II of the Companies (Northern Ireland) Order 1989" in subsection (10)(c) are repealed and the subsequent italicized words in square brackets are substituted by S.I. 2002/3150, art. 26(2), Sch. 3, para. 2, as from a day to be appointed.

426A.   Disqualification from Parliament (England and Wales and Northern Ireland)

(1)   A person in respect of whom a bankruptcy restrictions order or a debt relief restrictions order has effect shall be disqualified—

(a)   from membership of the House of Commons,

(b)   from sitting or voting in the House of Lords, and

(c)   from sitting or voting in a committee of the House of Lords or a joint committee of both Houses.

(2)   If a member of the House of Commons becomes disqualified under this section, his seat shall be vacated.

(3)   If a person who is disqualified under this section is returned as a member of the House of Commons, his return shall be void.

(4)   No writ of summons shall be issued to a member of the House of Lords who is disqualified under this section.

(5)   If a court makes a bankruptcy restrictions order or interim order, or a debt relief restrictions order or an interim debt relief restrictions order, in respect of a member of the House of Commons or the House of Lords the court shall notify the Speaker of that House.

(6)   If the Secretary of State accepts a bankruptcy restrictions undertaking or a debt relief restrictions undertaking made by a member of the House of Commons or the House of Lords, the Secretary of State shall notify the Speaker of that House.

(7)   If the Department of Enterprise, Trade and Investment for Northern Ireland accepts a bankruptcy restrictions undertaking made by a member of the House of Commons or the House of Lords under Schedule 2A to the Insolvency (Northern Ireland) Order 1989, the Department shall notify the Speaker of that House.

(8)   In this section a reference to a bankruptcy restrictions order or an interim order includes a reference to a bankruptcy restrictions order or an interim order made under Schedule 2A to the Insolvency (Northern Ireland) Order 1989.

426B. Devolution

(1)   If a court in England and Wales makes a bankruptcy restrictions order or interim order in respect of a member of the Scottish Parliament, the Northern Ireland Assembly or the National Assembly for Wales, or makes a debt relief restrictions order or interim debt relief restrictions order in respect of such a member, the court shall notify the presiding officer of that body.

(1A)   If the High Court in Northern Ireland makes a bankruptcy restrictions order or interim order under Schedule 2A to the Insolvency (Northern Ireland) Order 1989 in respect of a member of the Scottish Parliament or the National Assembly for Wales, the Court shall notify the presiding officer of that body.

(2)   If the Secretary of State accepts a bankruptcy restrictions undertaking or a debt relief restrictions undertaking made by a member of the Scottish Parliament, the Northern Ireland Assembly or the National Assembly for Wales, the Secretary of State shall notify the presiding officer of that body.

(3)   If the Department of Enterprise, Trade and Investment for Northern Ireland accepts a bankruptcy restrictions undertaking made by a member of the Scottish Parliament or the National Assembly for Wales under Schedule 2A to the Insolvency (Northern Ireland) Order 1989, the Department shall notify the presiding officer of that body.

426C. Irrelevance of privilege

(1)   An enactment about insolvency applies in relation to a member of the House of Commons or the House of Lords irrespective of any Parliamentary privilege.

(2)   In this section "enactment" includes a provision made by or under—
        (a)   an Act of the Scottish Parliament, or
        (b)   Northern Ireland legislation.

427.   Disqualification from Parliament (Scotland ...)

(1)   Where a ... court in Scotland awards sequestration of an individual's estate, the individual is disqualified—
        (a)   for sitting or voting in the House of Lords,
        (b)   for being elected to, or sitting or voting in, the House of Commons, and
        (c)   for sitting or voting in a committee of either House.

(2)   Where an individual is disqualified under this section, the disqualification ceases—
        (a)   except where the award is recalled or reduced without the individual having been first discharged, on the discharge of the individual, and
        (b)   in the excepted case, on the ..., recall or reduction, as the case may be.

(3)   No writ of summons shall be issued to any lord of Parliament who is for the time being disqualified under this section for sitting and voting in the House of Lords.

(4)   Where a member of the House of Commons who is disqualified under this section continues to be so disqualified until the end of the period of 6 months beginning with the day of the ... award, his seat shall be vacated at the end of that period.

(5)   A court which makes an ... award such as is mentioned in subsection (1) in relation to any lord of Parliament or member of the House of Commons shall forthwith certify the ... award to the Speaker of the House of Lords or, as the case may be, to the Speaker of the House of Commons.

(6)   Where a court has certified an ... award to the Speaker of the House of Commons under subsection (5), then immediately after it becomes apparent which of the following certificates is applicable, the court shall certify to the Speaker of the House of Commons—

(a)   that the period of 6 months beginning with the day of the ... award has expired without the ... award having been ... recalled or reduced, or

(b)   that the ... award has been ... recalled or reduced before the end of that period.

(6A) Subsections (4) to (6) have effect in relation to a member of the Scottish Parliament but as if—

(a)   references to the House of Commons were to the Parliament and references to the Speaker were to the Presiding Officer, and

(b)   in subsection (4), for "under this section" there were substituted "under section 15(1)(b) of the Scotland Act 1998 by virtue of this section".

(6B) Subsections (4) to (6) have effect in relation to a member of the National Assembly for Wales but as if—

(a)   references to the House of Commons were to the Assembly and references to the Speaker were to the presiding officer, and

(b)   in subsection (4), for "under this section" there were substituted "under section 16(A1)(a) of the Government of Wales Act 2006 and paragraph 4 of Schedule 1A to that Act".

(6C) Subsections (4) to (6) have effect in relation to a member of the Northern Ireland Assembly but as if—

(a)   references to the House of Commons were to the Assembly and references to the Speaker were to the Presiding Officer; and

(b)   in subsection (4), for "under this section" there were substituted "under section 36(4) of the Northern Ireland Act 1998 by virtue of this section".

(7)   ...

428.   Exemptions from Restrictive Trade Practices Act

(1), (2) ...

(3)   In this section "insolvency services" means the services of persons acting as insolvency practitioners or carrying out under the law of Northern Ireland functions corresponding to those mentioned in section 388(1) or (2) in Part XIII, in their capacity as such....

429.   Disabilities on revocation of administration order against an individual

(1)   The following applies where a person fails to make any payment which he is required to make by virtue of an administration order under Part VI of the County Courts Act 1984.

(2)   The court which is administering that person's estate under the order may, if it thinks fit—

(a)   revoke the administration order, and

(b)   make an order directing that this section and section 12 of the Company Directors Disqualification Act 1986 shall apply to the person for such period, not exceeding one year, as may be specified in the order.

(1)   This section applies if the county court revokes an administration order made in respect of an individual ("the debtor") on one of the relevant grounds.

(2)   The court may, at the time it revokes the administration order, make an order directing that this section and section 12 of the Company Directors Disqualification Act 1986 shall apply to the debtor for such period, not exceeding one year, as may be specified in the order.

(2A) Each of the following is a relevant ground—

(a) the debtor had failed to make two payments (whether consecutive or not) required by the order;

(b)   at the time the order was made—

(i)   the total amount of the debtor's qualifying debts was more than the prescribed maximum for the purposes of Part 6 of the 1984 Act, but

(ii)   because of information provided, or not provided, by the debtor, that amount was thought to be less than, or the same as, the prescribed maximum.

(3)   A person to whom this section so applies shall not—

(a)   either alone or jointly with another person, obtain credit to the extent of the amount prescribed for the purposes of section 360(1)(a) or more, or

(b) enter into any transaction in the course of or for the purposes of any business in which he is directly or indirectly engaged,

without disclosing to the person from whom he obtains the credit, or (as the case may be) with whom the transaction is entered into, the fact that this section applies to him.

(4) The reference in subsection (3) to *a person* obtaining credit includes—

(a) a case where goods are bailed or hired to him under a hire-purchase agreement or agreed to be sold to him under a conditional sale agreement, and

(b) a case where he is paid in advance (whether in money or otherwise) for the supply of goods or services.

(5) *A person* who contravenes this section is guilty of an offence and liable to imprisonment or a fine, or both.

Note. Subsections (1), (2) are substituted by the italicized subsections (1), (2), (2A), and the italicized words "a person" in subsections (3)–(5) are substituted by the words "an individual", by the Tribunals, Courts and Enforcement Act 2007, s. 106, Sch. 16, para. 3, as from a day to be appointed.

430. Provision introducing Schedule of punishments

(1) Schedule 10 to this Act has effect with respect to the way in which offences under this Act are punishable on conviction.

(2) In relation to an offence under a provision of this Act specified in the first column of the Schedule (the general nature of the offence being described in the second column), the third column shows whether the offence is punishable on conviction on indictment, or on summary conviction, or either in the one way or the other.

(3) The fourth column of the Schedule shows, in relation to an offence, the maximum punishment by way of fine or imprisonment under this Act which may be imposed on a person convicted of the offence in the way specified in relation to it in the third column (that is to say, on indictment or summarily) a reference to a period of years or months being to a term of imprisonment of that duration.

(4) The fifth column shows, (in relation to an offence for which there is an entry in that column) that a person convicted of the offence after continued contravention is liable to a daily default fine; that is to say, he is liable on a second or subsequent conviction of the offence to the fine specified in that column for each day on which the contravention is continued (instead of the penalty specified for the offence in the fourth column of the Schedule).

(4A) In relation to an offence committed before 2 May 2022, a reference in Schedule 10 to 12 months on summary conviction in England and Wales is to be read as a reference to 6 months.

(5) For the purpose of any enactment in this Act whereby an officer of a company who is in default is liable to a fine or penalty, the expression "officer who is in default" means any officer of the company who knowingly and wilfully authorises or permits the default, refusal or contravention mentioned in the enactment.

431. Summary proceedings

(1) Summary proceedings for any offence under any of Parts A1 to VII of this Act may (without prejudice to any jurisdiction exercisable apart from this subsection) be taken against a body corporate at any place at which the body has a place of business, and against any other person at any place at which he is for the time being.

(2) Notwithstanding anything in section 127(1) of the Magistrates' Courts Act 1980, an information relating to such an offence which is triable by a magistrates' court in England and Wales may be so tried if it is laid at any time within 3 years after the commission of the offence and within 12 months after the date on which evidence sufficient in the opinion of the Director of Public Prosecutions or the Secretary of State (as the case may be) to justify the proceedings comes to his knowledge.

(3) Summary proceedings in Scotland for such an offence shall not be commenced after the expiration of 3 years from the commission of the offence.

Subject to this (and notwithstanding anything in section 136 of the Criminal Procedure (Scotland) Act 1995), such proceedings may (in Scotland) be commenced at any time within 12 months after the date on which evidence sufficient in the Lord Advocate's opinion to justify the proceedings came to his knowledge or, where such evidence was reported to him by the Secretary of State, within 12 months after the date on which it came to the knowledge of the latter; and subsection (3) of that section applies for the purpose of this subsection as it applies for the purpose of that section.

(4)   For purposes of this section, a certificate of the Director of Public Prosecutions, the Lord Advocate or the Secretary of State (as the case may be) as to the date on which such evidence as is referred to above came to his knowledge is conclusive evidence.

432.   Offences by bodies corporate

(1)   This section applies to offences under this Act other than those excepted by subsection (4).

(2)   Where a body corporate is guilty of an offence to which this section applies and the offence is proved to have been committed with the consent or connivance of, or to be attributable to any neglect on the part of, any director, manager, secretary or other similar officer of the body corporate or any person who was purporting to act in any such capacity he, as well as the body corporate, is guilty of the offence and liable to be proceeded against and punished accordingly.

(3)   Where the affairs of a body corporate are managed by its members, subsection (2) applies in relation to the acts and defaults of a member in connection with his functions of management as if he were a director of the body corporate.

(4)   The offences excepted from this section are those under sections A19(5), A25(3), A26(4), A27(1), A28(5), A29(6), A30(2), A31(10), A32(4), 30, 39, 51, 53, 54, 62, 64, 66, 85, 89, 164, 188, 201, 206, 207, 208, 209, 210 and 211 ....

433.   Admissibility in evidence of statements of affairs, etc

(1)   In any proceedings (whether or not under this Act)—

    (a)   a statement of affairs prepared for the purposes of any provision of this Act which is derived from the Insolvency Act 1985,

    (aa)   a statement made in pursuance of a requirement imposed by or under Part 2 of the Banking Act 2009 (bank insolvency),

    (ab)   a statement made in pursuance of a requirement imposed by or under Part 3 of that Act (bank administration), and

    (b)   any other statement made in pursuance of a requirement imposed by or under any such provision or by or under rules made under this Act,

may be used in evidence against any person making or concurring in making the statement.

(2)   However, in criminal proceedings in which any such person is charged with an offence to which this subsection applies—

    (a)   no evidence relating to the statement may be adduced, and

    (b)   no question relating to it may be asked,

by or on behalf of the prosecution, unless evidence relating to it is adduced, or a question relating to it is asked, in the proceedings by or on behalf of that person.

(3)   Subsection (2) applies to any offence other than—

    (a)   an offence under section 22(6), 47(6), 48(8), 66(6), 67(8), 95(8), ... 99(3), 131(7), 192(2), 208(1)(a) or (d) or (2), 210, 235(5), 353(1), 354(1)(b) or (3) or 356(1) or (2)(a) or (b) or paragraph 4(3)(a) of Schedule 7;

    (b)   an offence which is—

        (i)   created by rules made under this Act, and

        (ii)   designated for the purposes of this subsection by such rules or by regulations made by the Secretary of State;

    (c)   an offence which is—

        (i)   created by regulations made under any such rules, and

        (ii)   designated for the purposes of this subsection by such regulations;

    (d)   an offence under section 1, 2 or 5 of the Perjury Act 1911 (false statements made on oath or made otherwise than on oath); or

(e)   an offence under section 44(1) or (2) of the Criminal Law (Consolidation) (Scotland) Act
       1995 (false statements made on oath or otherwise than on oath).

(4)   Regulations under subsection (3)(b)(ii) shall be made by statutory instrument and, after being
       made, shall be laid before each House of Parliament.

434.   Crown application

For the avoidance of doubt it is hereby declared that provisions of this Act which derive from the
Insolvency Act 1985 and Part A1 and sections 233A and 233B and Schedule 4ZZA bind the Crown
so far as affecting or relating to the following matters, namely—

(a)   remedies against, or against the property of, companies or individuals;

(b)   priorities of debts;

(c)   transactions at an undervalue or preferences;

(d)   voluntary arrangements approved under Part I or Part VIII, and

(e)   discharge from bankruptcy.

PART 17A
SUPPLEMENTARY PROVISIONS

434A.   Introductory

The provisions of this Part have effect for the purposes of—

(a)   the First Group of Parts, and

(b)   sections 411, 413, 414, 416 and 417 in Part 15.

434B.   Representation of corporations in decision procedures and at meetings

(1)   If a corporation is a creditor or debenture-holder, it may by resolution of its directors or other
       governing body authorise a person or persons to act as its representative or representatives—

(a)   in a qualifying decision procedure, held in pursuance of this Act or of rules made under it,
       by which a decision is sought from the creditors of a company, or

(b)   at any meeting of a company held in pursuance of the provisions contained in a debenture or
       trust deed.

(2)   Where the corporation authorises only one person, that person is entitled to exercise the same
       powers on behalf of the corporation as the corporation could exercise if it were an individual
       creditor or debenture-holder.

(3)   Where the corporation authorises more than one person, any one of them is entitled to exercise
       the same powers on behalf of the corporation as the corporation could exercise if it were an
       individual creditor or debenture-holder.

(4)   Where the corporation authorises more than one person and more than one of them purport to
       exercise a power under subsection (3)—

(a)   if they purport to exercise the power in the same way, the power is treated as exercised in
       that way;

(b)   if they do not purport to exercise the power in the same way, the power is treated as not
       exercised.

434C.   Legal professional privilege

In proceedings against a person for an offence under this Act nothing in this Act is to be taken to
require any person to disclose any information that he is entitled to refuse to disclose on grounds
of legal professional privilege (in Scotland, confidentiality of communications).

434D.   Enforcement of company's filing obligations

(1)   This section applies where a company has made default in complying with any obligation under
       this Act—

(a)   to deliver a document to the registrar, or

(b)   to give notice to the registrar of any matter.

(2)   The registrar, or any member or creditor of the company, may give notice to the company requiring it to comply with the obligation.

(3)   If the company fails to make good the default within 14 days after service of the notice, the registrar, or any member or creditor of the company, may apply to the court for an order directing the company, and any specified officer of it, to make good the default within a specified time.

(4)   The court's order may provide that all costs (in Scotland, expenses) of or incidental to the application are to be borne by the company or by any officers of it responsible for the default.

(5)   This section does not affect the operation of any enactment imposing penalties on a company or its officers in respect of any such default.

434E.   Application of filing obligations to overseas companies

The provisions of this Act requiring documents to be forwarded or delivered to, or filed with, the registrar of companies apply in relation to an overseas company that is required to register particulars under section 1046 of the Companies Act 2006 as they apply in relation to a company registered under that Act in England and Wales or Scotland.

PART XVIII
INTERPRETATION

435.   Meaning of "associate"

(1)   For the purposes of this Act any question whether a person is an associate of another person is to be determined in accordance with the following provisions of this section (any provision that a person is an associate of another person being taken to mean that they are associates of each other).

(2)   A person is an associate of an individual if that person is—
        (a)   the individual's husband or wife or civil partner,
        (b)   a relative of—
                (i)   the individual, or
                (ii)   the individual's husband or wife or civil partner, or
        (c)   the husband or wife or civil partner of a relative of—
                (i)   the individual, or
                (ii)   the individual's husband or wife or civil partner.

(3)   A person is an associate of any person with whom he is in partnership, and of the husband or wife or civil partner or a relative of any individual with whom he is in partnership; and a Scottish firm is an associate of any person who is a member of the firm.

(4)   A person is an associate of any person whom he employs or by whom he is employed.

(5)   A person in his capacity as trustee of a trust other than—
        (a)   a trust arising under any of the second Group of Parts or the Bankruptcy (Scotland) Act 2016, or
        (b)   a pension scheme or an employees' share scheme …,
        is an associate of another person if the beneficiaries of the trust include, or the terms of the trust confer a power that may be exercised for the benefit of, that other person or an associate of that other person.

(6)   A company is an associate of another company—
        (a)   if the same person has control of both, or a person has control of one and persons who are his associates, or he and persons who are his associates, have control of the other, or
        (b)   if a group of two or more persons has control of each company, and the groups either consist of the same persons or could be regarded as consisting of the same persons by treating (in one or more cases) a member of either group as replaced by a person of whom he is an associate.

(7)   A company is an associate of another person if that person has control of it or if that person and persons who are his associates together have control of it.

(8) For the purposes of this section a person is a relative of an individual if he is that individual's brother, sister, uncle, aunt, nephew, niece, lineal ancestor or lineal descendant, treating—

(a) any relationship of the half blood as a relationship of the whole blood and the stepchild or adopted child of any person as his child, and

(b) an illegitimate child as the legitimate child of his mother and reputed father;

and references in this section to a husband or wife include a former husband or wife and a reputed husband or wife and references to a civil partner include a former civil partner and a reputed civil partner.

(9) For the purposes of this section any director or other officer of a company is to be treated as employed by that company.

(10) For the purposes of this section a person is to be taken as having control of a company if—

(a) the directors of the company or of another company which has control of it (or any of them) are accustomed to act in accordance with his directions or instructions, or

(b) he is entitled to exercise, or control the exercise of, one third or more of the voting power at any general meeting of the company or of another company which has control of it;

and where two or more persons together satisfy either of the above conditions, they are to be taken as having control of the company.

(11) In this section "company" includes any body corporate (whether incorporated in Great Britain or elsewhere); and references to directors and other officers of a company and to voting power at any general meeting of a company have effect with any necessary modifications.

436. Expressions used generally

(1) In this Act, except in so far as the context otherwise requires (and subject to Parts VII and XI)—

...

"the appointed day" means the day on which this Act comes into force under section 443;

"associate" has the meaning given by section 435;

"body corporate" includes a body incorporated outside Great Britain, but does not include—

(a) a corporation sole, or

(b) a partnership that, whether or not a legal person, is not regarded as a body corporate under the law by which it is governed;

"business" includes a trade or profession;

...

"the Companies Acts" means the Companies Acts (as defined in section 2 of the Companies Act 2006) as they have effect in Great Britain;

"conditional sale agreement" and "hire-purchase agreement" have the same meanings as in the Consumer Credit Act 1974;

"distress" includes use of the procedure in Schedule 12 to the Tribunals, Courts and Enforcement Act 2007, and references to levying distress, seizing goods and related expressions shall be construed accordingly;

...

"EEA State" means a state that is a Contracting Party to the Agreement on the European Economic Area signed at Oporto on 2nd May 1992 as adjusted by the Protocol signed at Brussels on 17th March 1993;

"employees' share scheme" means a scheme for encouraging or facilitating the holding of shares in or debentures of a company by or for the benefit of—

(a) the bona fide employees or former employees of—

(i) the company,

(ii) any subsidiary of the company, or

(iii) the company's holding company or any subsidiary of the company's holding company, or

(b) the spouses, civil partners, surviving spouses, surviving civil partners, or minor children or step-children of such employees or former employees;

"the EU Regulation" means Regulation (EU) 2015/848 of the European Parliament and of the Council of 20 May 2015 on insolvency proceedings as it forms part of domestic law on and after IP completion day;

"modifications" includes additions, alterations and omissions and cognate expressions shall be construed accordingly;

...

"property" includes money, goods, things in action, land and every description of property wherever situated and also obligations and every description of interest, whether present or future or vested or contingent, arising out of, or incidental to, property;

"records" includes computer records and other non-documentary records;

...

"subordinate legislation" has the same meaning as in the Interpretation Act 1978; and

"transaction" includes a gift, agreement or arrangement, and references to entering into a transaction shall be construed accordingly.

...

(2)   The following expressions have the same meaning in this Act as in the Companies Acts—

"articles", in relation to a company (see section 18 of the Companies Act 2006);

"debenture" (see section 738 of that Act);

"holding company" (see sections 1159 and 1160 of, and Schedule 6 to, that Act);

"the Joint Stock Companies Acts" (see section 1171 of that Act);

"overseas company" (see section 1044 of that Act);

"paid up" (see section 583 of that Act);

"private company" and "public company" (see section 4 of that Act);

"registrar of companies" (see section 1060 of that Act);

"share" (see section 540 of that Act);

"subsidiary" (see sections 1159 and 1160 of, and Schedule 6 to, that Act).

436A.   ...

436B.   **References to things in writing**

(1)   A reference in this Act to a thing in writing includes that thing in electronic form.

(2)   Subsection (1) does not apply to the following provisions—

     (a)   section 53 (mode of appointment by holder of charge),

     (b)   ...

     (c)   section 70(4) (reference to instrument creating a charge),

     (d)   section 111(2) (dissent from arrangement under s 110),

     (e)   ...

     (f)   section 123(1) (definition of inability to pay debts),

     (g)   section 198(3) (duties of sheriff principal as regards examination),

     (h)   section 222(1) (inability to pay debts: unpaid creditor for £750 or more), and

     (i)   section 223 (inability to pay debts: debt remaining unsatisfied after action brought).

PART XIX
FINAL PROVISIONS

437.   **Transitional provisions, and savings**

The transitional provisions and savings set out in Schedule 11 to this Act shall have effect, the Schedule comprising the following Parts—

     Part I: company insolvency and winding up (matters arising before appointed day, and continuance of proceedings in certain cases as before that day);

     Part II: individual insolvency (matters so arising, and continuance of bankruptcy proceedings in certain cases as before that day);

     Part III: transactions entered into before the appointed day and capable of being affected by orders of the court under Part XVI of this Act;

Part IV: insolvency practitioners acting as such before the appointed day; and

Part V: general transitional provisions and savings required consequentially on, and in connection with, the repeal and replacement by this Act and the Company Directors Disqualification Act 1986 of provisions of the Companies Act 1985, the greater part of the Insolvency Act 1985 and other enactments.

438. Repeals

The enactments specified in the second column of Schedule 12 to this Act are repealed to the extent specified in the third column of that Schedule.

439. Amendment of enactments

(1) The Companies Act is amended as shown in Parts I and II of Schedule 13 to this Act, being amendments consequential on this Act and the Company Directors Disqualification Act 1986.

(2) The enactments specified in the first column of Schedule 14 to this Act (being enactments which refer, or otherwise relate, to those which are repealed and replaced by this Act or the Company Directors Disqualification Act 1986) are amended as shown in the second column of that Schedule.

(3) The Lord Chancellor may by order make such consequential modifications of any provision contained in any subordinate legislation made before the appointed day and such transitional provisions in connection with those modifications as appear to him necessary or expedient in respect of—

(a) any reference in that subordinate legislation to the Bankruptcy Act 1914;

(b) any reference in that subordinate legislation to any enactment repealed by Part III or IV of Schedule 10 to the Insolvency Act 1985; or

(c) any reference in that subordinate legislation to any matter provided for under the Act of 1914 or under any enactment so repealed.

(4) An order under this section shall be made by statutory instrument subject to annulment in pursuance of a resolution of either House of Parliament.

440. Extent (Scotland)

(1) Subject to the next subsection, provisions of this Act contained in the first Group of Parts extend to Scotland except where otherwise stated.

(2) The following provisions of this Act do not extend to Scotland—

(a) in the first Group of Parts—

section 43;

sections 238 to 241; and

section 246;

(b) the second Group of Parts;

(c) in the third Group of Parts—

sections 399 to 402,

sections 412, 413, 415, 415A(3), 418, 420 and 421,

sections 423 to 425, and

section 429(1) and (2); and

(d) in the Schedules—

Parts II and III of Schedule 11; and

Schedules 12 and 14 so far as they repeal or amend enactments which extend to England and Wales only.

Note. In subsection (2)(c), the italicized words "section 429(1) and (2)" are repealed and substituted by the words "section 429(1) to (2A)" by the Tribunals, Courts and Enforcement Act 2007, s. 106, Sch. 16, para. 4, as from a day to be appointed.

441. Extent (Northern Ireland)

(1) The following provisions of this Act extend to Northern Ireland—

(a) sections 197, 426, 426A, 426B, 427 and 428; and

(b) so much of section 439 and Schedule 14 as relates to enactments which extend to Northern Ireland.

(2) Subject as above, and to any provision expressly relating to companies incorporated elsewhere than in Great Britain, nothing in this Act extends to Northern Ireland or applies to or in relation to companies registered or incorporated in Northern Ireland.

442. Extent (other territories)

Her Majesty may, by Order in Council, direct that such of the provisions of this Act as are specified in the Order, being provisions formerly contained in the Insolvency Act 1985, shall extend to any of the Channel Islands or any colony with such modifications as may be so specified.

443. Commencement

This Act comes into force on the day appointed under section 236(2) of the Insolvency Act 1985 for the coming into force of Part III of that Act (individual insolvency and bankruptcy), immediately after that Part of that Act comes into force for England and Wales.

444. Citation

This Act may be cited as the Insolvency Act 1986.

SCHEDULE ZA1
MORATORIUM: ELIGIBLE COMPANIES

Eligible companies

1   A company is "eligible" for the purposes of this Part unless it is excluded from being eligible by any of the following—
       paragraph 2 (current or recent insolvency procedure);
       paragraph 2A (private registered providers of social housing);
       paragraph 2B (a registered social landlord under Part 2 of the Housing (Scotland) Act 2010);
       paragraph 3 (insurance companies);
       paragraph 4 (banks);
       paragraph 5 (electronic money institutions);
       paragraph 6 (investment banks and investment firms);
       paragraph 7 (market contracts, market charges, etc);
       paragraph 8 (participants in designated systems);
       paragraph 9 (payment institutions);
       paragraph 10 (operators of payment systems, infrastructure providers etc);
       paragraph 11 (recognised investment exchanges, clearing houses and CSDs);
       paragraph 12 (securitisation companies);
       paragraph 13 (parties to capital market arrangements);
       paragraph 15 (public-private partnership project companies);
       paragraph 18 (certain overseas companies).

Companies subject to, or recently subject to, moratorium or an insolvency procedure

2   (1) A company is excluded from being eligible if—
            (a) on the filing date, a moratorium for the company is in force, or
            (b) at any time during the period of 12 months ending with the filing date, a moratorium for the company was in force (but see section A42(6) for power of the court to modify the effect of this paragraph).
       (2) A company is excluded from being eligible if—
            (a) on the filing date, the company is subject to an insolvency procedure, or
            (b) at any time during the period of 12 months ending with the filing date, the company was subject to an insolvency procedure within sub-paragraph (3)(a) or (b).
       (3) For the purposes of sub-paragraph (2), a company is subject to an insolvency procedure at any time if at that time—

      (a)   a voluntary arrangement has effect in relation to the company,

      (b)   the company is in administration,

      (c)   paragraph 44 of Schedule B1 applies in relation to the company (administration: interim moratorium),

      (d)   there is an administrative receiver of the company,

      (e)   there is a provisional liquidator of the company,

      (f)   the company is being wound up, or

      (g)   a relevant petition for the winding up of the company has been presented and has not been withdrawn or determined.

  (4)   In sub-paragraph (3)(g) "relevant petition" means a petition under—

      (a)   section 124A (winding up on grounds of public interest),

      (b)   section 124B (winding up of SE), or

      (c)   section 124C (winding up of SCE).

Private registered providers of social housing

2A   A company is excluded from being eligible if it is a private registered provider of social housing.

Registered social landlord under Part 2 of the Housing (Scotland) Act 2010

2B   A company is excluded from being eligible if it is a registered social landlord under Part 2 of the Housing (Scotland) Act 2010.

Insurance companies

3   (1)   A company is excluded from being eligible if—

      (a)   it carries on the regulated activity of effecting or carrying out contracts of insurance, and

      (b)   it is not an exempt person in relation to that activity.

    (2)   In this paragraph—

      "exempt person", in relation to a regulated activity, has the meaning given by section 417 of the Financial Services and Markets Act 2000;

      "regulated activity" has the meaning given by section 22 of that Act, taken with Schedule 2 to that Act and any order under that section.

Banks

4   (1)   A company is excluded from being eligible if—

      (a)   it has permission under Part 4A of the Financial Services and Markets Act 2000 to carry on the regulated activity of accepting deposits,

      (b)   it is a banking group company within the meaning of Part 1 of the Banking Act 2009 (see section 81D of that Act), or

      (c)   it has a liability in respect of a deposit which it accepted in accordance with the Banking Act 1979 or the Banking Act 1987.

    (2)   In sub-paragraph (1)(a) "regulated activity" has the meaning given by section 22 of the Financial Services and Markets Act 2000, taken with Schedule 2 to that Act and any order under that section.

Electronic money institutions

5   A company is excluded from being eligible if it is an electronic money institution within the meaning of the Electronic Money Regulations 2011 (S.I. 2011/99) (see regulation 2 of those Regulations)

Investment banks and investment firms

6   (1)   A company is excluded from being eligible if it is an investment bank or an investment firm.

    (2)   In this paragraph—

      "investment bank" means a company that has permission under Part 4A of the Financial Services and Markets Act 2000 to carry on the regulated activity of—

(a)   safeguarding and administering investments,

(b)   managing an AIF or a UCITS,

(c)   acting as trustee or depositary of an AIF or a UCITS,

(d)   dealing in investments as principal, or

(e)   dealing in investments as agent,

but does not include a company that has permission to arrange for one or more others to carry on the activity mentioned in paragraph (a) if it does not otherwise have permission to carry on any of the activities mentioned in paragraphs (a) to (e);

"investment firm" has the same meaning as in the Banking Act 2009 (see section 258A of that Act), disregarding any order made under section 258A(2)(b) of that Act;

"regulated activity" has the meaning given by section 22 of the Financial Services and Markets Act 2000, taken with Schedule 2 to that Act and any order under that section.

Companies that are party to market contracts or subject to market charges, etc

7   (1)   A company is excluded from being eligible if it is a party to a market contract for the purposes of Part 7 of the Companies Act 1989 (see section 155 of that Act).

(2)   A company is excluded from being eligible if any of its property is subject to a market charge for the purposes of Part 7 of the Companies Act 1989 (see section 173 of that Act)

(3)   A company is excluded from being eligible if any of its property is subject to a charge that is a system-charge, within the meaning of the Financial Markets and Insolvency Regulations 1996 (S.I. 1996/1469) (see regulation 2 of those Regulations).

Participants in designated systems

8   A company is excluded from being eligible if—

(a)   it is a participant in a designated system, within the meaning of the Financial Markets and Insolvency (Settlement Finality) Regulations 1999 (S.I. 1999/2979) (see regulation 2 of those Regulations), or

(b)   any of its property is subject to a collateral security charge within the meaning of those Regulations (see regulation 2 of those Regulations).

Payment institutions

9   A company is excluded from being eligible if it is an authorised payment institution, a small payment institution or a registered account information service provider within the meaning of the Payment Services Regulations 2017 (S.I. 2017/752) (see regulation 2 of those Regulations).

Operators of payment systems, infrastructure providers etc

10   A company is excluded from being eligible if—

(a)   it is the operator of a payment system or an infrastructure provider within the meaning of Part 5 of the Financial Services (Banking Reform) Act 2013 (see section 42 of that Act), or

(b)   it is an infrastructure company, within the meaning of Part 6 of that Act (see section 112 of that Act).

Recognised investment exchanges, clearing houses and CSDs

11   A company is excluded from being eligible if it is a recognised investment exchange, a recognised clearing house or a recognised CSD within the meaning of the Financial Services and Markets Act 2000 (see section 285 of that Act).

Securitisation companies

12   A company is excluded from being eligible if it is a securitisation company within the meaning of the Taxation of Securitisation Companies Regulations 2006 (S.I. 2006/3296) (see regulation 4 of those Regulations).

Parties to capital market arrangements

13   (1)   A company is excluded from being eligible if, on the filing date—

       (a)   it is a party to an agreement which is or forms part of a capital market arrangement (see sub-paragraph (2)),

       (b)   a party has incurred, or when the agreement was entered into was expected to incur, a debt of at least £10 million under the arrangement (at any time during the life of the capital market arrangement), and

       (c)   the arrangement involves the issue of a capital market investment (see paragraph 14).

  (2)   For the purposes of this paragraph, an arrangement is a "capital market arrangement" if any of the following applies—

       (a)   it involves a grant of security to a person holding it as trustee for a person who holds a capital market investment issued by a party to the arrangement;

       (b)   at least one party guarantees the performance of obligations of another party;

       (c)   at least one party provides security in respect of the performance of obligations of another party;

       (d)   the arrangement involves an investment of a kind described in articles 83 to 85 of the Financial Services and Markets Act 2000 (Regulated Activities) Order 2001 (S.I. 2001/544) (options, futures and contracts for differences).

  (3)   For the purposes of sub-paragraph (2)—

       (a)   a reference to holding a security as trustee includes a reference to holding it as nominee or agent,

       (b)   a reference to holding for a person who holds a capital market investment includes a reference to holding for a number of persons at least one of whom holds a capital market investment, and

       (c)   a reference to holding a capital market investment is to holding a legal or beneficial interest in it.

  (4)   For the purposes of sub-paragraph (1)(b), where a debt is denominated wholly or partly in a foreign currency, the sterling equivalent is to be calculated as at the time when the arrangement is entered into.

14 (1)   For the purposes of paragraph 13 an investment is a "capital market investment" if condition A or B is met.

  (2)   Condition A is that the investment—

       (a)   is within article 77 or 77A of the Financial Services and Markets Act 2000 (Regulated Activities) Order 2001 (S.I. 2001/544) (debt instruments), and

       (b)   is rated, listed or traded or designed to be rated, listed or traded.

  (3)   In sub-paragraph (2)—

"listed" means admitted to the official list within the meaning given by section 103(1) of the Financial Services and Markets Act 2000 (interpretation);

"rated" means rated for the purposes of investment by an internationally recognised rating agency;

"traded" means admitted to trading on a market established under the rules of a recognised investment exchange or on a foreign market.

  (4)   In sub-paragraph (3)—

"foreign market" has the same meaning as "relevant market" in article 67(2) of the Financial Services and Markets Act 2000 (Financial Promotion) Order 2005 (S.I. 2005/1529) (foreign markets);

"recognised investment exchange" has the meaning given by section 285 of the Financial Services and Markets Act 2000 (recognised investment exchange).

  (5)   Condition B is that the investment consists of a bond or commercial paper issued to one or more of the following—

       (a)   an investment professional within the meaning of article 19(5) of the Financial Services and Markets Act 2000 (Financial Promotion) Order 2005 (S.I. 2005/1529);

(b)   a person who, when the agreement mentioned in paragraph 13(1) is entered into, is a ... high net worth individual in relation to a communication within the meaning of article 48(2) of that Order;

(c)   a person to whom article 49(2) of that Order applies (high net worth company, etc);

(d)   a person who, when the agreement mentioned in paragraph 13(1) is entered into, is a certified sophisticated investor in relation to a communication within the meaning of article 50(1) of that Order;

(e)   a person in a State other than the United Kingdom who under the law of that State is not prohibited from investing in bonds or commercial paper.

(6)   For the purposes of sub-paragraph (5)—

(a)   in applying article 19(5) of the Financial Services and Markets Act 2000 (Financial Promotion) Order 2005—

(i)   in article 19(5)(b), ignore the words after "exempt person",

(ii)   in article 19(5)(c)(i), for the words from "the controlled activity" to the end substitute "a controlled activity", and

(iii)   in article 19(5)(e), ignore the words from "where the communication" to the end;

(b)   in applying article 49(2) of that Order, ignore article 49(2)(e);

(c)   "bond" means—

(i)   a bond that is within article 77(1) of the Financial Services and Markets Act 2000 (Regulated Activities) Order 2001, or

(ii)   an alternative finance investment bond within the meaning of article 77A of that Order;

(d)   "commercial paper" has the meaning given by article 9(3) of that Order.

Public-private partnership project companies

15   (1)   A company is excluded from being eligible if, on the filing date, it is a project company of a project which—

(a)   is a public-private partnership project (see paragraph 16), and

(b)   includes step-in rights (see paragraph 17).

(2)   For the purposes of this paragraph a company is a "project company" of a project if any of the following applies—

(a)   it holds property for the purpose of the project;

(b)   it has sole or principal responsibility under an agreement for carrying out all or part of the project;

(c)   it is one of a number of companies which together carry out the project;

(d)   it has the purpose of supplying finance to enable the project to be carried out;

(e)   it is the holding company of a company within any of paragraphs (a) to (d)

(3)   But a company is not a "project company" of a project if—

(a)   it performs a function within sub-paragraph (2)(a) to (d) or is within sub-paragraph (2)(e), but

(b)   it also performs a function which is not—

(i)   within sub-paragraph (2)(a) to (d),

(ii)   related to a function within sub-paragraph (2)(a) to (d), or

(iii)   related to the project.

(4)   For the purposes of this paragraph a company carries out all or part of a project whether or not it acts wholly or partly through agents.

16   (1)   For the purposes of paragraph 15 "public-private partnership project" means a project—

(a)   the resources for which are provided partly by one or more public bodies and partly by one or more private persons, or

(b)   which is designed wholly or mainly for the purpose of assisting a public body to discharge a function.

(2)   In sub-paragraph (1) "public body" means—

(a)   a body which exercises public functions,

    (b)   a body specified for the purposes of this paragraph by the Secretary of State, or

    (c)   a body within a class specified for the purposes of this paragraph by the Secretary of State.

(3)   In sub-paragraph (1)(a) "resources" includes—

    (a)   funds (including payment for the provision of services or facilities);

    (b)   assets;

    (c)   professional skill;

    (d)   the grant of a concession or franchise;

    (e)   any other commercial resource.

(4)   A specification under sub-paragraph (2) may be—

    (a)   general, or

    (b)   for the purpose of the application of paragraph 15 to a specified case.

17   (1)   For the purposes of paragraph 15 a project has "step-in rights" if a person who provides finance in connection with the project has a conditional entitlement under an agreement to—

    (a)   assume sole or principal responsibility under an agreement for carrying out all or part of the project, or

    (b)   make arrangements for carrying out all or part of the project.

(2)   In sub-paragraph (1) a reference to the provision of finance includes a reference to the provision of an indemnity.

Overseas companies with corresponding functions

18   A company is excluded from being eligible if its registered office or head office is outside the United Kingdom and—

    (a)   its functions correspond to those of a company mentioned in any of the previous paragraphs of this Schedule apart from paragraphs 2 and 2A and, if it were a company registered under the Companies Act 2006 in England and Wales or Scotland, it would be excluded from being eligible by that paragraph, or

    (b)   it has entered into a transaction or done anything else that, if done in England and Wales or Scotland by a company registered under the Companies Act 2006 in England and Wales or Scotland, would result in the company being excluded by any of the previous paragraphs of this Schedule apart from paragraphs 2 and 2A.

Interpretation of Schedule

19   (1)   This paragraph applies for the purposes of this Schedule.

(2)   "Agreement" includes any agreement or undertaking effected by—

    (a)   contract,

    (b)   deed, or

    (c)   any other instrument intended to have effect in accordance with the law of England and Wales, Scotland or another jurisdiction.

(3)   "The filing date" means the date on which documents are filed with the court under section A3, A4 or A5.

(4)   "Party" to an arrangement includes a party to an agreement which—

    (a)   forms part of the arrangement,

    (b)   provides for the raising of finance as part of the arrangement, or

    (c)   is necessary for the purposes of implementing the arrangement.

Powers to amend Schedule

20   (1)   The Secretary of State may by regulations amend this Schedule, apart from paragraph 2, so as to alter the circumstances in which a company is "eligible" for the purposes of this Part.

(2)   Regulations under this paragraph are subject to the affirmative resolution procedure.

21   (1)   The Welsh Ministers may by regulations amend this Schedule—

(a)   so as to provide that a social landlord registered under Part 1 of the Housing Act 1996 is excluded from being "eligible" for the purposes of this Part;

(b)   so as to reverse the effect of any provision made under paragraph (a).

(2)   Regulations under this paragraph extend to England and Wales only.

(3)   A statutory instrument containing regulations under this paragraph may not be made unless a draft of the statutory instrument containing them has been laid before and approved by a resolution of Senedd Cymru.

22   (1)   The Scottish Ministers may by regulations amend this Schedule—

(a)   so as to provide that a social landlord registered under Part 2 of the Housing (Scotland) Act 2010 (asp 17) is excluded from being "eligible" for the purposes of this Part;

(b)   so as to reverse the effect of any provision made under paragraph (a).

(2)   Regulations under this paragraph extend to Scotland only.

(3)   Regulations under this paragraph are subject to the affirmative procedure (see section 29 of the Interpretation and Legislative Reform (Scotland) Act 2010 (asp 10)).

SCHEDULE ZA2
MORATORIUM: CONTRACT OR OTHER INSTRUMENT INVOLVING FINANCIAL SERVICES

Introductory

1   For the purposes of section A18 "contract or other instrument involving financial services" means a contract or other instrument to which any of the following paragraphs applies.

Financial contracts

2   (1)   This paragraph applies to a financial contract.

(2)   "Financial contract" means—

(a)   a contract for the provision of financial services consisting of—

(i)   lending (including the factoring and financing of commercial transactions),

(ii)   financial leasing, or

(iii)   providing guarantees or commitments;

(b)   a securities contract, including—

(i)   a contract for the purchase, sale or loan of a security, group or index of securities;

(ii)   an option on a security or group or index of securities;

(iii)   a repurchase or reverse repurchase transaction on any such security, group or index;

(c)   a commodities contract, including—

(i)   a contract for the purchase, sale or loan of a commodity or group or index of commodities for future delivery;

(ii)   an option on a commodity or group or index of commodities;

(iii)   a repurchase or reverse repurchase transaction on any such commodity, group or index;

(d)   a futures or forwards contract, including a contract (other than a commodities contract) for the purchase, sale or transfer of a commodity or property of any other description, service, right or interest for a specified price at a future date;

(e)   a swap agreement, including—

(i)   a swap or option relating to interest rates, spot or other foreign exchange agreements, currency, an equity index or equity, a debt index or debt, commodity indexes or commodities, weather, emissions or inflation;

(ii)   a total return, credit spread or credit swap;

(iii)   any agreement or transaction that is similar to an agreement that is referred to in sub-paragraph (i) or (ii) and is the subject of recurrent dealing in the swaps or derivatives markets;

(f) an inter-bank borrowing agreement where the term of the borrowing is three months or less;

(g) a master agreement for any of the contracts or agreements referred to in paragraphs (a) to (f)

(3) For the purposes of this paragraph "commodities" includes—

(a) units recognised for compliance with the requirements of EU Directive 2003/87/EC establishing a scheme for greenhouse gas emission allowance trading,

(b) allowances under paragraph 5 of Schedule 2 to the Climate Change Act 2008 relating to a trading scheme dealt with under Part 1 of that Schedule (schemes limiting activities relating to emissions of greenhouse gas), and

(c) renewables obligation certificates issued—

(i) by the Gas and Electricity Markets Authority under an order made under section 32B of the Electricity Act 1989, or

(ii) by the Northern Ireland Authority for Utility Regulation under the Energy (Northern Ireland) Order 2003 (S.I. 2003/419 (N.I. 6)) and pursuant to an order made under Articles 52 to 55F of that Order.

Securities financing transactions

3 (1) This paragraph applies to—

(a) a securities financing transaction, and

(b) a master agreement for securities financing transactions.

(2) "Securities financing transaction" has the meaning given by Article 3(11) of Regulation (EU) 2015/2365 on the transparency of securities financing transactions.

(3) But for the purposes of that Article as it applies for the purposes of this paragraph, references to "commodities" in that Regulation are to be taken as including the units, allowances and certificates referred to in paragraph 2(3)(a), (b) and (c).

Derivatives

4 (1) This paragraph applies to—

(a) a derivative, and

(b) a master agreement for derivatives.

(2) "Derivative" has the meaning given by Article 2(5) of Regulation (EU) No. 648/2012.

Spot contracts

5 (1) This paragraph applies to—

(a) a spot contract, and

(b) a master agreement for spot contracts.

(2) "Spot contract" has the meaning given by Article 7(2) or 10(2) of Commission Delegated Regulation of 25.4.2016 supplementing Directive 2014/65/EU of the European Parliament and of the Council as regards organisational requirements and operating conditions for investment firms and defined terms for the purposes of that Directive.

Capital market investments

6 (1) This paragraph applies to an agreement which is, or forms part of, an arrangement involving the issue of a capital market investment.

(2) "Capital market investment" has the meaning given by paragraph 14 of Schedule ZA1.

Contracts forming part of a public-private partnership

7 This paragraph applies to a contract forming part of a public-private partnership project within the meaning given by paragraph 16 of Schedule ZA1.

Market contracts

8 This paragraph applies to a market contract within the meaning of Part 7 of the Companies Act 1989 (see section 155 of that Act).

Qualifying collateral arrangements and qualifying property transfers

9   This paragraph applies to qualifying collateral arrangements and qualifying property transfers within the meaning of Part 7 of the Companies Act 1989 (see section 155A of that Act).

Contracts secured by certain charges or arrangements

10   This paragraph applies to a contract where any obligation under the contract is—
        (a)   secured by a market charge within the meaning of Part 7 of the Companies Act 1989 (see section 173 of that Act),
        (b)   secured by a system-charge within the meaning of the Financial Markets and Insolvency Regulations 1996 (S.I. 1996/1469) (see regulation 2 of those Regulations), or
        (c)   secured or otherwise covered by a financial collateral arrangement within the meaning of the Financial Collateral Arrangements (No. 2) Regulations 2003 (S.I. 2003/3226) (see regulation 3 of those Regulations).

Default arrangements and transfer orders

11   This paragraph applies to a contract which is included in default arrangements, or a transfer order, within the meaning of the Financial Markets and Insolvency (Settlement Finality) Regulations 1999 (S.I. 1999/2979) (see regulation 2 of those Regulations).

Card-based payment transactions

12   This paragraph applies to a contract to accept and process card-based payment transactions within the meaning given by Regulation (EU) 2015/751 of the European Parliament and of the Council of 29th April 2015 on interchange fees for card-based payment transactions.

Power to amend Schedule

13   (1)   The Secretary of State may by regulations amend this Schedule so as to change the meaning of "contract or other instrument involving financial services" for the purposes of section A18.
        (2)   Regulations under this paragraph are subject to the affirmative resolution procedure.

. . .

SCHEDULE B1

ADMINISTRATION

Section 8

ARRANGEMENT OF SCHEDULE

NATURE OF ADMINISTRATION

Administration

1.— (1) For the purposes of this Act "administrator" of a company means a person appointed under this Schedule to manage the company's affairs, business and property.

   (2) For the purposes of this Act—

    (a) a company is "in administration" while the appointment of an administrator of the company has effect,

    (b) a company "enters administration" when the appointment of an administrator takes effect,

    (c) a company ceases to be in administration when the appointment of an administrator of the company ceases to have effect in accordance with this Schedule, and

    (d) a company does not cease to be in administration merely because an administrator vacates office (by reason of resignation, death or otherwise) or is removed from office.

2. A person may be appointed as administrator of a company—

    (a) by administration order of the court under paragraph 10,

    (b) by the holder of a floating charge under paragraph 14, or

    (c) by the company or its directors under paragraph 22.

Purpose of administration

3.— (1) The administrator of a company must perform his functions with the objective of—

    (a) rescuing the company as a going concern, or

    (b) achieving a better result for the company's creditors as a whole than would be likely if the company were wound up (without first being in administration), or

    (c) realising property in order to make a distribution to one or more secured or preferential creditors.

   (2) Subject to sub-paragraph (4), the administrator of a company must perform his functions in the interests of the company's creditors as a whole.

   (3) The administrator must perform his functions with the objective specified in sub-paragraph (1)(a) unless he thinks either—

    (a) that it is not reasonably practicable to achieve that objective, or

    (b) that the objective specified in sub-paragraph (1)(b) would achieve a better result for the company's creditors as a whole.

   (4) The administrator may perform his functions with the objective specified in sub-paragraph (1)(c) only if—

    (a) he thinks that it is not reasonably practicable to achieve either of the objectives specified in sub-paragraph (1)(a) and (b), and

    (b) he does not unnecessarily harm the interests of the creditors of the company as a whole.

4. The administrator of a company must perform his functions as quickly and efficiently as is reasonably practicable.

Status of administrator

5. An administrator is an officer of the court (whether or not he is appointed by the court).

General restrictions

6. A person may be appointed as administrator of a company only if he is qualified to act as an insolvency practitioner in relation to the company.

7. A person may not be appointed as administrator of a company which is in administration (subject to the provisions of paragraphs 90 to 97 and 100 to 103 about replacement and additional administrators).

8.— (1) A person may not be appointed as administrator of a company which is in liquidation by virtue of—

          (a)   a resolution for voluntary winding up, or

          (b)   a winding-up order.

  (2)   Sub-paragraph (1)(a) is subject to paragraph 38.

  (3)   Sub-paragraph (1)(b) is subject to paragraphs 37 and 38.

9.— (1)   A person may not be appointed as administrator of a company which—

          (a)   has a liability in respect of a deposit which it accepted in accordance with the Banking Act 1979 or 1987, but

          (b)   is not an authorised deposit taker.

  (2)   A person may not be appointed as administrator of a company which effects or carries out contracts of insurance.

  (3)   But sub-paragraph (2) does not apply to a company which—

          (a)   is exempt from the general prohibition in relation to effecting or carrying out contracts of insurance, or

          (b)   is an authorised deposit taker effecting or carrying out contracts of insurance in the course of a banking business.

  (4)   In this paragraph—

         "authorised deposit taker" means a person with permission under Part IV of the Financial Services and Markets Act 2000 to accept deposits, and

         "the general prohibition" has the meaning given by section 19 of that Act.

  (5)   This paragraph shall be construed in accordance with—

          (a)   section 22 of the Financial Services and Markets Act 2000 (classes of regulated activity and categories of investment),

          (b)   any relevant order under that section, and

          (c)   Schedule 2 to that Act (regulated activities).

APPOINTMENT OF ADMINISTRATOR BY COURT

Administration order

10.   An administration order is an order appointing a person as the administrator of a company.

Conditions for making order

11.   The court may make an administration order in relation to a company only if satisfied—

  (a)   that the company is or is likely to become unable to pay its debts, and

  (b)   that the administration order is reasonably likely to achieve the purpose of administration.

Administration application

12.— (1)   An application to the court for an administration order in respect of a company (an "administration application") may be made only by—

          (a)   the company,

          (b)   the directors of the company,

          (c)   one or more creditors of the company,

          (d)   designated officer for a magistrates' court in the exercise of the power conferred by section 87A of the Magistrates' Courts Act 1980 (fine imposed on company), or

          (e)   a combination of persons listed in paragraphs (a) to (d).

  (2)   As soon as is reasonably practicable after the making of an administration application the applicant shall notify—

          (a)   any person who has appointed an administrative receiver of the company,

          (b)   any person who is or may be entitled to appoint an administrative receiver of the company,

          (c)   any person who is or may be entitled to appoint an administrator of the company under paragraph 14, and

          (d)   such other persons as may be prescribed.

  (3)   An administration application may not be withdrawn without the permission of the court.

(4) In sub-paragraph (1) "creditor" includes a contingent creditor and a prospective creditor.

(5) Sub-paragraph (1) is without prejudice to section 7(4)(b).

Powers of court

13.— (1) On hearing an administration application the court may—

 (a) make the administration order sought;

 (b) dismiss the application;

 (c) adjourn the hearing conditionally or unconditionally;

 (d) make an interim order;

 (e) treat the application as a winding-up petition and make any order which the court could make under section 125;

 (f) make any other order which the court thinks appropriate.

(2) An appointment of an administrator by administration order takes effect—

 (a) at a time appointed by the order, or

 (b) where no time is appointed by the order, when the order is made.

(3) An interim order under sub-paragraph (1)(d) may, in particular—

 (a) restrict the exercise of a power of the directors or the company;

 (b) make provision conferring a discretion on the court or on a person qualified to act as an insolvency practitioner in relation to the company.

(4) This paragraph is subject to paragraph 39.

APPOINTMENT OF ADMINISTRATOR BY HOLDER OF FLOATING CHARGE

Power to appoint

14.— (1) The holder of a qualifying floating charge in respect of a company's property may appoint an administrator of the company.

(2) For the purposes of sub-paragraph (1) a floating charge qualifies if created by an instrument which—

 (a) states that this paragraph applies to the floating charge,

 (b) purports to empower the holder of the floating charge to appoint an administrator of the company,

 (c) purports to empower the holder of the floating charge to make an appointment which would be the appointment of an administrative receiver within the meaning given by section 29(2), or

 (d) purports to empower the holder of a floating charge in Scotland to appoint a receiver who on appointment would be an administrative receiver.

(3) For the purposes of sub-paragraph (1) a person is the holder of a qualifying floating charge in respect of a company's property if he holds one or more debentures of the company secured—

 (a) by a qualifying floating charge which relates to the whole or substantially the whole of the company's property,

 (b) by a number of qualifying floating charges which together relate to the whole or substantially the whole of the company's property, or

 (c) by charges and other forms of security which together relate to the whole or substantially the whole of the company's property and at least one of which is a qualifying floating charge.

Restrictions on power to appoint

15.— (1) A person may not appoint an administrator under paragraph 14 unless—

 (a) he has given at least two business days' written notice to the holder of any prior floating charge which satisfies paragraph 14(2), or

 (b) the holder of any prior floating charge which satisfies paragraph 14(2) has consented in writing to the making of the appointment.

(2)   One floating charge is prior to another for the purposes of this paragraph if—
    (a)   it was created first, or
    (b)   it is to be treated as having priority in accordance with an agreement to which the holder of each floating charge was party.

(3)   Sub-paragraph (2) shall have effect in relation to Scotland as if the following were substituted for paragraph (a)—
    "(a)   it has priority of ranking in accordance with section 464(4)(b) of the Companies Act 1985,".

16.   An administrator may not be appointed under paragraph 14 while a floating charge on which the appointment relies is not enforceable.

17.   An administrator of a company may not be appointed under paragraph 14 if—
    (a)   a provisional liquidator of the company has been appointed under section 135, or
    (b)   an administrative receiver of the company is in office.

Notice of appointment

18.— (1)   A person who appoints an administrator of a company under paragraph 14 shall file with the court—
    (a)   a notice of appointment, and
    (b)   such other documents as may be prescribed.

(2)   The notice of appointment must include a statutory declaration by or on behalf of the person who makes the appointment—
    (a)   that the person is the holder of a qualifying floating charge in respect of the company's property,
    (b)   that each floating charge relied on in making the appointment is (or was) enforceable on the date of the appointment, and
    (c)   that the appointment is in accordance with this Schedule.

(3)   The notice of appointment must identify the administrator and must be accompanied by a statement by the administrator—
    (a)   that he consents to the appointment,
    (b)   that in his opinion the purpose of administration is reasonably likely to be achieved, and
    (c)   giving such other information and opinions as may be prescribed.

(4)   For the purpose of a statement under sub-paragraph (3) an administrator may rely on information supplied by directors of the company (unless he has reason to doubt its accuracy).

(5)   The notice of appointment and any document accompanying it must be in the prescribed form.

(6)   A statutory declaration under sub-paragraph (2) must be made during the prescribed period.

(7)   A person commits an offence if in a statutory declaration under sub-paragraph (2) he makes a statement—
    (a)   which is false, and
    (b)   which he does not reasonably believe to be true.

Commencement of appointment

19.   The appointment of an administrator under paragraph 14 takes effect when the requirements of paragraph 18 are satisfied.

20.   A person who appoints an administrator under paragraph 14—
    (a)   shall notify the administrator and such other persons as may be prescribed as soon as is reasonably practicable after the requirements of paragraph 18 are satisfied, and
    (b)   commits an offence if he fails without reasonable excuse to comply with paragraph (a).

Invalid appointment: indemnity

21.— (1)   This paragraph applies where—

(a)   a person purports to appoint an administrator under paragraph 14, and

(b)   the appointment is discovered to be invalid.

(2)   The court may order the person who purported to make the appointment to indemnify the person appointed against liability which arises solely by reason of the appointment's invalidity.

APPOINTMENT OF ADMINISTRATOR BY COMPANY OR DIRECTORS

Power to appoint

22.— (1)   A company may appoint an administrator.

(2)   The directors of a company may appoint an administrator.

Restrictions on power to appoint

23.— (1)   This paragraph applies where an administrator of a company is appointed—

(a)   under paragraph 22, or

(b)   on an administration application made by the company or its directors.

(2)   An administrator of the company may not be appointed under paragraph 22 during the period of 12 months beginning with the date on which the appointment referred to in sub-paragraph (1) ceases to have effect.

24.   ...

25.   An administrator of a company may not be appointed under paragraph 22 if—

(a)   a petition for the winding up of the company has been presented and is not yet disposed of,

(b)   an administration application has been made and is not yet disposed of, or

(c)   an administrative receiver of the company is in office.

25A.— (1)   Paragraph 25(a) does not prevent the appointment of an administrator of a company if the petition for the winding up of the company was presented after the person proposing to make the appointment filed the notice of intention to appoint with the court under paragraph 27.

(2)   But sub-paragraph (1) does not apply if the petition was presented under a provision mentioned in paragraph 42(4).

Notice of intention to appoint

26.— (1)   A person who proposes to make an appointment under paragraph 22 shall give at least five business days' written notice to—

(a)   any person who is or may be entitled to appoint an administrative receiver of the company, and

(b)   any person who is or may be entitled to appoint an administrator of the company under paragraph 14.

(2)   A person who gives notice of intention to appoint under sub-paragraph (1) shall also give such notice as may be prescribed to such other persons as may be prescribed.

(3)   A notice under this paragraph must—

(a)   identify the proposed administrator, and

(b)   be in the prescribed form.

27.— (1)   A person who gives notice of intention to appoint under paragraph 26 shall file with the court as soon as is reasonably practicable a copy of—

(a)   the notice, and

(b)   any document accompanying it.

(2)   The copy filed under sub-paragraph (1) must be accompanied by a statutory declaration made by or on behalf of the person who proposes to make the appointment—

(a)   that the company is or is likely to become unable to pay its debts,

(b)   that the company is not in liquidation, and

(c)   that, so far as the person making the statement is able to ascertain, the appointment is not prevented by paragraphs 23 to 25, and

      (d)   to such additional effect, and giving such information, as may be prescribed.

    (3)   A statutory declaration under sub-paragraph (2) must—

      (a)   be in the prescribed form, and

      (b)   be made during the prescribed period.

    (4)   A person commits an offence if in a statutory declaration under sub-paragraph (2) he makes a statement—

      (a)   which is false, and

      (b)   which he does not reasonably believe to be true.

28.— (1)   An appointment may not be made under paragraph 22 unless the person who makes the appointment has complied with any requirement of paragraphs 26 and 27 and—

      (a)   the period of notice specified in paragraph 26(1) has expired, or

      (b)   each person to whom notice has been given under paragraph 26(1) has consented in writing to the making of the appointment.

    (2)   An appointment may not be made under paragraph 22 after the period of ten business days beginning with the date on which the notice of intention to appoint is filed under paragraph 27(1).

Notice of appointment

29.— (1)   A person who appoints an administrator of a company under paragraph 22 shall file with the court—

      (a)   a notice of appointment, and

      (b)   such other documents as may be prescribed.

    (2)   The notice of appointment must include a statutory declaration by or on behalf of the person who makes the appointment—

      (a)   that the person is entitled to make an appointment under paragraph 22,

      (b)   that the appointment is in accordance with this Schedule, and

      (c)   that, so far as the person making the statement is able to ascertain, the statements made and information given in the statutory declaration filed with the notice of intention to appoint remain accurate.

    (3)   The notice of appointment must identify the administrator and must be accompanied by a statement by the administrator—

      (a)   that he consents to the appointment,

      (b)   that in his opinion the purpose of administration is reasonably likely to be achieved, and

      (c)   giving such other information and opinions as may be prescribed.

    (4)   For the purpose of a statement under sub-paragraph (3) an administrator may rely on information supplied by directors of the company (unless he has reason to doubt its accuracy).

    (5)   The notice of appointment and any document accompanying it must be in the prescribed form.

    (6)   A statutory declaration under sub-paragraph (2) must be made during the prescribed period.

    (7)   A person commits an offence if in a statutory declaration under sub-paragraph (2) he makes a statement—

      (a)   which is false, and

      (b)   which he does not reasonably believe to be true.

30.   In a case in which no person is entitled to notice of intention to appoint under paragraph 26(1) (and paragraph 28 therefore does not apply)—

      (a)   the statutory declaration accompanying the notice of appointment must include the statements and information required under paragraph 27(2), and

      (b)   paragraph 29(2)(c) shall not apply.

Commencement of appointment

31. The appointment of an administrator under paragraph 22 takes effect when the requirements of paragraph 29 are satisfied.

32. A person who appoints an administrator under paragraph 22—
   (a) shall notify the administrator and such other persons as may be prescribed as soon as is reasonably practicable after the requirements of paragraph 29 are satisfied, and
   (b) commits an offence if he fails without reasonable excuse to comply with paragraph (a).

33. If before the requirements of paragraph 29 are satisfied the company enters administration by virtue of an administration order or an appointment under paragraph 14—
   (a) the appointment under paragraph 22 shall not take effect, and
   (b) paragraph 32 shall not apply.

Invalid appointment: indemnity

34.— (1) This paragraph applies where—
   (a) a person purports to appoint an administrator under paragraph 22, and
   (b) the appointment is discovered to be invalid.
   (2) The court may order the person who purported to make the appointment to indemnify the person appointed against liability which arises solely by reason of the appointment's invalidity.

ADMINISTRATION APPLICATION—SPECIAL CASES

Application by holder of floating charge

35.— (1) This paragraph applies where an administration application in respect of a company—
   (a) is made by the holder of a qualifying floating charge in respect of the company's property, and
   (b) includes a statement that the application is made in reliance on this paragraph.
   (2) The court may make an administration order—
   (a) whether or not satisfied that the company is or is likely to become unable to pay its debts, but
   (b) only if satisfied that the applicant could appoint an administrator under paragraph 14.

Intervention by holder of floating charge

36.— (1) This paragraph applies where—
   (a) an administration application in respect of a company is made by a person who is not the holder of a qualifying floating charge in respect of the company's property, and
   (b) the holder of a qualifying floating charge in respect of the company's property applies to the court to have a specified person appointed as administrator (and not the person specified by the administration applicant).
   (2) The court shall grant an application under sub-paragraph (1)(b) unless the court thinks it right to refuse the application because of the particular circumstances of the case.

Application where company in liquidation

37.— (1) This paragraph applies where the holder of a qualifying floating charge in respect of a company's property could appoint an administrator under paragraph 14 but for paragraph 8(1)(b).
   (2) The holder of the qualifying floating charge may make an administration application.
   (3) If the court makes an administration order on hearing an application made by virtue of sub-paragraph (2)—
   (a) the court shall discharge the winding-up order,
   (b) the court shall make provision for such matters as may be prescribed,
   (c) the court may make other consequential provision,

    (d)   the court shall specify which of the powers under this Schedule are to be exercisable by the administrator, and

    (e)   this Schedule shall have effect with such modifications as the court may specify.

38.— (1)   The liquidator of a company may make an administration application.

    (2)   If the court makes an administration order on hearing an application made by virtue of sub-paragraph (1)—

    (a)   the court shall discharge any winding-up order in respect of the company,

    (b)   the court shall make provision for such matters as may be prescribed,

    (c)   the court may make other consequential provision,

    (d)   the court shall specify which of the powers under this Schedule are to be exercisable by the administrator, and

    (e)   this Schedule shall have effect with such modifications as the court may specify.

Effect of administrative receivership

39.— (1)   Where there is an administrative receiver of a company the court must dismiss an administration application in respect of the company unless—

    (a)   the person by or on behalf of whom the receiver was appointed consents to the making of the administration order,

    (b)   the court thinks that the security by virtue of which the receiver was appointed would be liable to be released or discharged under sections 238 to 240 (transaction at under-value and preference) if an administration order were made,

    (c)   the court thinks that the security by virtue of which the receiver was appointed would be avoided under section 245 (avoidance of floating charge) if an administration order were made, or

    (d)   the court thinks that the security by virtue of which the receiver was appointed would be challengeable under section 242 (gratuitous alienations) or 243 (unfair preferences) or under any rule of law in Scotland.

    (2)   Sub-paragraph (1) applies whether the administrative receiver is appointed before or after the making of the administration application.

EFFECT OF ADMINISTRATION

Dismissal of pending winding-up petition

40.— (1)   A petition for the winding up of a company—

    (a)   shall be dismissed on the making of an administration order in respect of the company, and

    (b)   shall be suspended while the company is in administration following an appointment under paragraph 14.

    (2)   Sub-paragraph (1)(b) does not apply to a petition presented under—

    (a)   section 124A (public interest), or

   (aa)   section 124B (SEs),

    (b)   section 367 of the Financial Services and Markets Act 2000 (petition by Financial Conduct Authority or Prudential Regulation Authority).

    (3)   Where an administrator becomes aware that a petition was presented under a provision referred to in sub-paragraph (2) before his appointment, he shall apply to the court for directions under paragraph 63.

Dismissal of administrative or other receiver

41.— (1)   When an administration order takes effect in respect of a company any administrative receiver of the company shall vacate office.

    (2)   Where a company is in administration, any receiver of part of the company's property shall vacate office if the administrator requires him to.

(3) Where an administrative receiver or receiver vacates office under sub-paragraph (1) or (2)—

    (a) his remuneration shall be charged on and paid out of any property of the company which was in his custody or under his control immediately before he vacated office, and

    (b) he need not take any further steps under section 40 or 59.

(4) In the application of sub-paragraph (3)(a)—

    (a) "remuneration" includes expenses properly incurred and any indemnity to which the administrative receiver or receiver is entitled out of the assets of the company,

    (b) the charge imposed takes priority over security held by the person by whom or on whose behalf the administrative receiver or receiver was appointed, and

    (c) the provision for payment is subject to paragraph 43.

Moratorium on insolvency proceedings

42.— (1) This paragraph applies to a company in administration.

    (2) No resolution may be passed for the winding up of the company.

    (3) No order may be made for the winding up of the company.

    (4) Sub-paragraph (3) does not apply to an order made on a petition presented under—

        (a) section 124A (public interest), or

        (aa) section 124B (SEs),

        (b) section 367 of the Financial Services and Markets Act 2000 (petition by Financial Conduct Authority or Prudential Regulation Authority).

    (5) If a petition presented under a provision referred to in sub-paragraph (4) comes to the attention of the administrator, he shall apply to the court for directions under paragraph 63.

Moratorium on other legal process

43.— (1) This paragraph applies to a company in administration.

    (2) No step may be taken to enforce security over the company's property except—

        (a) with the consent of the administrator, or

        (b) with the permission of the court.

    (3) No step may be taken to repossess goods in the company's possession under a hire-purchase agreement except—

        (a) with the consent of the administrator, or

        (b) with the permission of the court.

    (4) A landlord may not exercise a right of forfeiture by peaceable re-entry in relation to premises let to the company except—

        (a) with the consent of the administrator, or

        (b) with the permission of the court.

    (5) In Scotland, a landlord may not exercise a right of irritancy in relation to premises let to the company except—

        (a) with the consent of the administrator, or

        (b) with the permission of the court.

    (6) No legal process (including legal proceedings, execution, distress and diligence) may be instituted or continued against the company or property of the company except—

        (a) with the consent of the administrator, or

        (b) with the permission of the court.

    (6A) An administrative receiver of the company may not be appointed.

    (7) Where the court gives permission for a transaction under this paragraph it may impose a condition on or a requirement in connection with the transaction.

    (8) In this paragraph "landlord" includes a person to whom rent is payable.

Interim moratorium

44.— (1) This paragraph applies where an administration application in respect of a company has been made and—

    (a) the application has not yet been granted or dismissed, or

    (b) the application has been granted but the administration order has not yet taken effect.

  (2) This paragraph also applies from the time when a copy of notice of intention to appoint an administrator under paragraph 14 is filed with the court until—

    (a) the appointment of the administrator takes effect, or

    (b) the period of five business days beginning with the date of filing expires without an administrator having been appointed.

  (3) Sub-paragraph (2) has effect in relation to a notice of intention to appoint only if it is in the prescribed form.

  (4) This paragraph also applies from the time when a copy of notice of intention to appoint an administrator is filed with the court under paragraph 27(1) until—

    (a) the appointment of the administrator takes effect, or

    (b) the period specified in paragraph 28(2) expires without an administrator having been appointed.

  (5) The provisions of paragraphs 42 and 43 shall apply (ignoring any reference to the consent of the administrator).

  (6) If there is an administrative receiver of the company when the administration application is made, the provisions of paragraphs 42 and 43 shall not begin to apply by virtue of this paragraph until the person by or on behalf of whom the receiver was appointed consents to the making of the administration order.

  (7) This paragraph does not prevent or require the permission of the court for—

    (a) the presentation of a petition for the winding up of the company under a provision mentioned in paragraph 42(4),

    (b) the appointment of an administrator under paragraph 14,

    (c) the appointment of an administrative receiver of the company, or

    (d) the carrying out by an administrative receiver (whenever appointed) of his functions.

Publicity

45.— (1) While a company is in administration, every business document issued by or on behalf of the company or the administrator, and all the company's websites, must state—

    (a) the name of the administrator, and

    (b) that the affairs, business and property of the company are being managed by the administrator.

  (2) Any of the following persons commits an offence if without reasonable excuse the person authorises or permits a contravention of sub-paragraph (1)—

    (a) the administrator,

    (b) an officer of the company, and

    (c) the company.

  (3) In sub-paragraph (1) "business document" means—

    (a) an invoice,

    (b) an order for goods or services,

    (c) a business letter, and

    (d) an order form,

whether in hard copy, electronic or any other form.

PROCESS OF ADMINISTRATION

Announcement of administrator's appointment

46.— (1) This paragraph applies where a person becomes the administrator of a company.

    (2)   As soon as is reasonably practicable the administrator shall—

        (a)   send a notice of his appointment to the company, and

        (b)   publish a notice of his appointment in the prescribed manner.

    (3)   As soon as is reasonably practicable the administrator shall—

        (a)   obtain a list of the company's creditors, and

        (b)   send a notice of his appointment to each creditor of whose claim and address he is aware.

    (4)   The administrator shall send a notice of his appointment to the registrar of companies before the end of the period of 7 days beginning with the date specified in sub-paragraph (6).

    (5)   The administrator shall send a notice of his appointment to such persons as may be prescribed before the end of the prescribed period beginning with the date specified in sub-paragraph (6).

    (6)   The date for the purpose of sub-paragraphs (4) and (5) is—

        (a)   in the case of an administrator appointed by administration order, the date of the order,

        (b)   in the case of an administrator appointed under paragraph 14, the date on which he receives notice under paragraph 20, and

        (c)   in the case of an administrator appointed under paragraph 22, the date on which he receives notice under paragraph 32.

    (7)   The court may direct that sub-paragraph (3)(b) or (5)—

        (a)   shall not apply, or

        (b)   shall apply with the substitution of a different period.

    (8)   A notice under this paragraph must—

        (a)   contain the prescribed information, and

        (b)   be in the prescribed form.

    (9)   An administrator commits an offence if he fails without reasonable excuse to comply with a requirement of this paragraph.

Statement of company's affairs

47.— (1)   As soon as is reasonably practicable after appointment the administrator of a company shall by notice in the prescribed form require one or more relevant persons to provide the administrator with a statement of the affairs of the company.

    (2)   The statement must—

        (a)   be verified by a statement of truth in accordance with Civil Procedure Rules,

        (b)   be in the prescribed form,

        (c)   give particulars of the company's property, debts and liabilities,

        (d)   give the names and addresses of the company's creditors,

        (e)   specify the security held by each creditor,

        (f)   give the date on which each security was granted, and

        (g)   contain such other information as may be prescribed.

    (3)   In sub-paragraph (1) "relevant person" means—

        (a)   a person who is or has been an officer of the company,

        (b)   a person who took part in the formation of the company during the period of one year ending with the date on which the company enters administration,

        (c)   a person employed by the company during that period, and

        (d)   a person who is or has been during that period an officer or employee of a company which is or has been during that year an officer of the company.

    (4)   For the purpose of sub-paragraph (3) a reference to employment is a reference to employment through a contract of employment or a contract for services.

    (5)   In Scotland, a statement of affairs under sub-paragraph (1) must be a statutory declaration made in accordance with the Statutory Declarations Act 1835 (and sub-paragraph (2)(a) shall not apply).

48.— (1)   A person required to submit a statement of affairs must do so before the end of the period of 11 days beginning with the day on which he receives notice of the requirement.

(2) The administrator may—
   (a) revoke a requirement under paragraph 47(1), or
   (b) extend the period specified in sub-paragraph (1) (whether before or after expiry).
(3) If the administrator refuses a request to act under sub-paragraph (2)—
   (a) the person whose request is refused may apply to the court, and
   (b) the court may take action of a kind specified in sub-paragraph (2).
(4) A person commits an offence if he fails without reasonable excuse to comply with a requirement under paragraph 47(1).

Administrator's proposals

49.— (1) The administrator of a company shall make a statement setting out proposals for achieving the purpose of administration.
(2) A statement under sub-paragraph (1) must, in particular—
   (a) deal with such matters as may be prescribed, and
   (b) where applicable, explain why the administrator thinks that the objective mentioned in paragraph 3(1)(a) or (b) cannot be achieved.
(3) Proposals under this paragraph may include—
   (a) a proposal for a voluntary arrangement under Part I of this Act (although this paragraph is without prejudice to section 4(3));
   (b) a proposal for a compromise or arrangement to be sanctioned under Part 26 or 26A of the Companies Act 2006 (arrangements and reconstructions).
(4) The administrator shall send a copy of the statement of his proposals—
   (a) to the registrar of companies,
   (b) to every creditor of the company, other than an opted-out creditor, of whose claim and address he is aware, and
   (c) to every member of the company of whose address he is aware.
(5) The administrator shall comply with sub-paragraph (4)—
   (a) as soon as is reasonably practicable after the company enters administration, and
   (b) in any event, before the end of the period of eight weeks beginning with the day on which the company enters administration.
(6) The administrator shall be taken to comply with sub-paragraph (4)(c) if he publishes in the prescribed manner a notice undertaking to provide a copy of the statement of proposals free of charge to any member of the company who applies in writing to a specified address.
(7) An administrator commits an offence if he fails without reasonable excuse to comply with sub-paragraph (5).
(8) A period specified in this paragraph may be varied in accordance with paragraph 107.

50. ...

Consideration of administrator's proposals by creditors

51.— (1) The administrator must seek a decision from the company's creditors as to whether they approve the proposals set out in the statement made under paragraph 49(1).
(2) The initial decision date for that decision must be within the period of 10 weeks beginning with the day on which the company enters administration.
(3) The "initial decision date" for that decision—
   (a) if the decision is initially sought using the deemed consent procedure, is the date on which a decision will be made if the creditors by that procedure approve the proposals, and
   (b) if the decision is initially sought using a qualifying decision procedure, is the date on or before which a decision will be made if it is made by that qualifying decision procedure (assuming that date does not change after the procedure is instigated).
(4) A period specified in this paragraph may be varied in accordance with paragraph 107.
(5) An administrator commits an offence if he fails without reasonable excuse to comply with a requirement of this paragraph.

52.— (1) Paragraph 51(1) shall not apply where the statement of proposals states that the administrator thinks—

    (a) that the company has sufficient property to enable each creditor of the company to be paid in full,

    (b) that the company has insufficient property to enable a distribution to be made to unsecured creditors other than by virtue of section 176A(2)(a), or

    (c) that neither of the objectives specified in paragraph 3(1)(a) and (b) can be achieved.

  (2) But the administrator shall seek a decision from the company's creditors as to whether they approve the proposals set out in the statement made under paragraph 49(1) if requested to do so—

    (a) by creditors of the company whose debts amount to at least 10% of the total debts of the company,

    (b) in the prescribed manner, and

    (c) in the prescribed period.

  (3) Where a decision is sought by virtue of sub-paragraph (2) the initial decision date (as defined in paragraph 51(3)) must be within the prescribed period.

  (4) The period prescribed under sub-paragraph (3) may be varied in accordance with paragraph 107.

Creditors' decision

53.— (1) The company's creditors may approve the administrator's proposals—

    (a) without modification, or

    (b) with modification to which the administrator consents.

  (2) The administrator shall as soon as is reasonably practicable report any decision taken by the company's creditors to—

    (a) the court,

    (b) the registrar of companies, and

    (c) such other persons as may be prescribed.

  (3) An administrator commits an offence if he fails without reasonable excuse to comply with sub-paragraph (2).

Revision of administrator's proposals

54.— (1) This paragraph applies where—

    (a) an administrator's proposals have been approved (with or without modification) by the company's creditors,

    (b) the administrator proposes a revision to the proposals, and

    (c) the administrator thinks that the proposed revision is substantial.

  (2) The administrator shall—

    (a) …

    (b) send a statement in the prescribed form of the proposed revision … to each creditor who is not an opted-out creditor,

    (c) send a copy of the statement, within the prescribed period, to each member of the company of whose address he is aware, and

    (d) seek a decision from the company's creditors as to whether they approve the proposed revision.

  (3) The administrator shall be taken to have complied with sub-paragraph (2)(c) if he publishes a notice undertaking to provide a copy of the statement free of charge to any member of the company who applies in writing to a specified address.

  (4) A notice under sub-paragraph (3) must be published—

    (a) in the prescribed manner, and

    (b) within the prescribed period.

  (5) The company's creditors may approve the proposed revision—

    (a) without modification, or

      (b)   with modification to which the administrator consents.

    (6)   The administrator shall as soon as is reasonably practicable report any decision taken by the company's creditors to—

      (a)   the court,

      (b)   the registrar of companies, and

      (c)   such other persons as may be prescribed.

    (7)   An administrator commits an offence if he fails without reasonable excuse to comply with sub-paragraph (6).

Failure to obtain approval of administrator's proposals

55.— (1)   This paragraph applies where an administrator—

      (a)   reports to the court under paragraph 53 that a company's creditors have failed to approve the administrator's proposals, or

      (b)   reports to the court under paragraph 54 that a company's creditors have failed to approve a revision of the administrator's proposals.

(2)   The court may—

      (a)   provide that the appointment of an administrator shall cease to have effect from a specified time;

      (b)   adjourn the hearing conditionally or unconditionally;

      (c)   make an interim order;

      (d)   make an order on a petition for winding up suspended by virtue of paragraph 40(1)(b);

      (e)   make any other order (including an order making consequential provision) that the court thinks appropriate.

Further creditors' decisions

56.— (1)   The administrator of a company shall seek a decision from the company's creditors on a matter if—

      (a)   it is requested in the prescribed manner by creditors of the company whose debts amount to at least 10% of the total debts of the company, or

      (b)   he is directed by the court to do so.

    (2)   An administrator commits an offence if he fails without reasonable excuse to seek a decision from the company's creditors on a matter as required by this paragraph.

Creditors' committee

57.— (1)   The company's creditors may, in accordance with the rules, establish a creditors' committee.

    (2)   A creditors' committee shall carry out functions conferred on it by or under this Act.

    (3)   A creditors' committee may require the administrator—

      (a)   to attend on the committee at any reasonable time of which he is given at least seven days' notice, and

      (b)   to provide the committee with information about the exercise of his functions.

58.   ...

FUNCTIONS OF ADMINISTRATOR

General powers

59.— (1)   The administrator of a company may do anything necessary or expedient for the management of the affairs, business and property of the company.

    (2)   A provision of this Schedule which expressly permits the administrator to do a specified thing is without prejudice to the generality of sub-paragraph (1).

    (3)   A person who deals with the administrator of a company in good faith and for value need not inquire whether the administrator is acting within his powers.

60.— (1)   The administrator of a company has the powers specified in Schedule 1 to this Act.

(2) But the power to sell, hire out or otherwise dispose of property is subject to any regulations that may be made under paragraph 60A.

60A.— (1) The Secretary of State may by regulations make provision for—

   (a) prohibiting, or

   (b) imposing requirements or conditions in relation to,

the disposal, hiring out or sale of property of a company by the administrator to a connected person in circumstances specified in the regulations.

(2) Regulations under this paragraph may in particular require the approval of, or provide for the imposition of requirements or conditions by—

   (a) creditors of the company,

   (b) the court, or

   (c) a person of a description specified in the regulations.

(3) In sub-paragraph (1), "connected person", in relation to a company, means—

   (a) a relevant person in relation to the company, or

   (b) a company connected with the company.

(4) For the purposes of sub-paragraph (3)—

   (a) "relevant person", in relation to a company, means—

      (i) a director or other officer, or shadow director, of the company;

      (ii) a non-employee associate of such a person;

      (iii) a non-employee associate of the company;

   (b) a company is connected with another if any relevant person of one is or has been a relevant person of the other.

(5) In sub-paragraph (4), "non-employee associate" of a person means a person who is an associate of that person otherwise than by virtue of employing or being employed by that person.

(6) Subsection (10) of section 435 (extended definition of company) applies for the purposes of sub-paragraphs (3) to (5) as it applies for the purposes of that section.

(7) Regulations under this paragraph may—

   (a) make different provision for different purposes;

   (b) make incidental, consequential, supplemental and transitional provision.

(8) Regulations under this paragraph are to be made by statutory instrument.

(9) Regulations under this paragraph may not be made unless a draft of the statutory instrument containing the regulations has been laid before Parliament and approved by a resolution of each House of Parliament.

(10) This paragraph expires at the end of June 2021 unless the power conferred by it is exercised before then.

61. The administrator of a company—

   (a) may remove a director of the company, and

   (b) may appoint a director of the company (whether or not to fill a vacancy).

62. The administrator of a company may—

   (a) call a meeting of members of the company;

   (b) seek a decision on any matter from the company's creditors.

63. The administrator of a company may apply to the court for directions in connection with his functions.

64.— (1) A company in administration or an officer of a company in administration may not exercise a management power without the consent of the administrator.

(2) For the purpose of sub-paragraph (1)—

   (a) "management power" means a power which could be exercised so as to interfere with the exercise of the administrator's powers,

   (b) it is immaterial whether the power is conferred by an enactment or an instrument, and

   (c) consent may be general or specific.

Distribution

64A.— (1) This paragraph applies where a company enters administration before the end of the period of 12 weeks beginning with the day after the end of any moratorium for the company under Part A1.

(2) The administrator must make a distribution to the creditors of the company in respect of—
   (a) moratorium debts (within the meaning given by section 174A), and
   (b) priority pre-moratorium debts (within the meaning given by section 174A).

(3) A sum payable under sub-paragraph (2) is to be paid in priority to—
   (a) any security to which paragraph 70 applies or paragraph 115(1) applies;
   (b) any sums payable under paragraph 99.

(4) The administrator must realise any property necessary to comply with sub-paragraph (2).

(5) The rules may make provision as to the order in which the moratorium and priority pre-moratorium debts rank among themselves for the purposes of this paragraph in a case where the assets of the company are insufficient to meet them in full.

65.— (1) If the assets of a company are sufficient to meet any debts or other liabilities payable under paragraph 64A in full, the administrator of the company may make a distribution to any other creditor of the company.

(2) Sections 175 and 176AZA shall apply in relation to a distribution under this paragraph as they apply in relation to a winding up.

(3) A payment may not be made by way of distribution under this paragraph to a creditor of the company who is neither secured nor preferential unless—
   (a) the distribution is made by virtue of section 176A(2)(a), or
   (b) the court gives permission.

66.   If the debts and other liabilities payable under paragraph 64A have been met, the administrator of a company may make a payment otherwise than in accordance with paragraph 65 or paragraph 13 of Schedule 1 if he thinks it likely to assist achievement of the purpose of administration.

General duties

67.   The administrator of a company shall on his appointment take custody or control of all the property to which he thinks the company is entitled.

68.— (1) Subject to sub-paragraph (2), the administrator of a company shall manage its affairs, business and property in accordance with—
   (a) any proposals approved under paragraph 53,
   (b) any revision of those proposals which is made by him and which he does not consider substantial, and
   (c) any revision of those proposals approved under paragraph 54.

(2) If the court gives directions to the administrator of a company in connection with any aspect of his management of the company's affairs, business or property, the administrator shall comply with the directions.

(3) The court may give directions under sub-paragraph (2) only if—
   (a) no proposals have been approved under paragraph 53,
   (b) the directions are consistent with any proposals or revision approved under paragraph 53 or 54,
   (c) the court thinks the directions are required in order to reflect a change in circumstances since the approval of proposals or a revision under paragraph 53 or 54, or
   (d) the court thinks the directions are desirable because of a misunderstanding about proposals or a revision approved under paragraph 53 or 54.

Administrator as agent of company

69.   In exercising his functions under this Schedule the administrator of a company acts as its agent.

Charged property: floating charge

70.— (1) The administrator of a company may dispose of or take action relating to property which is subject to a floating charge as if it were not subject to the charge.

(2) Where property is disposed of in reliance on sub-paragraph (1) the holder of the floating charge shall have the same priority in respect of acquired property as he had in respect of the property disposed of.

(3) In sub-paragraph (2) "acquired property" means property of the company which directly or indirectly represents the property disposed of.

Charged property: non-floating charge

71.— (1) The court may by order enable the administrator of a company to dispose of property which is subject to a security (other than a floating charge) as if it were not subject to the security.

(2) An order under sub-paragraph (1) may be made only—

    (a) on the application of the administrator, and

    (b) where the court thinks that disposal of the property would be likely to promote the purpose of administration in respect of the company.

(3) An order under this paragraph is subject to the condition that there be applied towards discharging the sums secured by the security—

    (a) the net proceeds of disposal of the property, and

    (b) any additional money required to be added to the net proceeds so as to produce the amount determined by the court as the net amount which would be realised on a sale of the property at market value.

(4) If an order under this paragraph relates to more than one security, application of money under sub-paragraph (3) shall be in the order of the priorities of the securities.

(5) An administrator who makes a successful application for an order under this paragraph shall send a copy of the order to the registrar of companies before the end of the period of 14 days starting with the date of the order.

(6) An administrator commits an offence if he fails to comply with sub-paragraph (5) without reasonable excuse.

Hire-purchase property

72.— (1) The court may by order enable the administrator of a company to dispose of goods which are in the possession of the company under a hire-purchase agreement as if all the rights of the owner under the agreement were vested in the company.

(2) An order under sub-paragraph (1) may be made only—

    (a) on the application of the administrator, and

    (b) where the court thinks that disposal of the goods would be likely to promote the purpose of administration in respect of the company.

(3) An order under this paragraph is subject to the condition that there be applied towards discharging the sums payable under the hire-purchase agreement—

    (a) the net proceeds of disposal of the goods, and

    (b) any additional money required to be added to the net proceeds so as to produce the amount determined by the court as the net amount which would be realised on a sale of the goods at market value.

(4) An administrator who makes a successful application for an order under this paragraph shall send a copy of the order to the registrar of companies before the end of the period of 14 days starting with the date of the order.

(5) An administrator commits an offence if he fails without reasonable excuse to comply with sub-paragraph (4).

Protection for priority creditor

73.— (1) An administrator's statement of proposals under paragraph 49 may not include any action which—

     (a)   affects the right of a secured creditor of the company to enforce his security,

     (b)   would result in a preferential debt of the company being paid otherwise than in priority to its non-preferential debts, ...

     (bb) would result in an ordinary preferential debt of the company being paid otherwise than in priority to any secondary preferential debts that it may have,

     (c)   would result in one preferential creditor of the company being paid a smaller proportion of an ordinary preferential debt than another, ...

     (d)   would result in one preferential creditor of the company being paid a smaller proportion of a secondary preferential debt than another, or

     (e)   if the company is a relevant financial institution (see section 387A), would result in any non-preferential debt being paid otherwise than in accordance with the rules in section 176AZA(2) or (3).

  (2) Sub-paragraph (1) does not apply to—

     (a)   action to which the relevant creditor consents,

     (b)   a proposal for a voluntary arrangement under Part I of this Act (although this sub-paragraph is without prejudice to section 4(3)), ...

     (c)   a proposal for a compromise or arrangement to be sanctioned under Part 26 or 26A of the Companies Act 2006 (arrangements and reconstructions), ...

     (d)   ...

  (3) The reference to a statement of proposals in sub-paragraph (1) includes a reference to a statement as revised or modified.

Challenge to administrator's conduct of company

74.— (1) A creditor or member of a company in administration may apply to the court claiming that—

     (a)   the administrator is acting or has acted so as unfairly to harm the interests of the applicant (whether alone or in common with some or all other members or creditors), or

     (b)   the administrator proposes to act in a way which would unfairly harm the interests of the applicant (whether alone or in common with some or all other members or creditors).

  (2) A creditor or member of a company in administration may apply to the court claiming that the administrator is not performing his functions as quickly or as efficiently as is reasonably practicable.

  (3) The court may—

     (a)   grant relief;

     (b)   dismiss the application;

     (c)   adjourn the hearing conditionally or unconditionally;

     (d)   make an interim order;

     (e)   make any other order it thinks appropriate.

  (4) In particular, an order under this paragraph may—

     (a)   regulate the administrator's exercise of his functions;

     (b)   require the administrator to do or not do a specified thing;

     (c)   require a decision of the company's creditors to be sought on a matter;

     (d)   provide for the appointment of an administrator to cease to have effect;

     (e)   make consequential provision.

  (5) An order may be made on a claim under sub-paragraph (1) whether or not the action complained of—

     (a)   is within the administrator's powers under this Schedule;

     (b)   was taken in reliance on an order under paragraph 71 or 72.

  (6) An order may not be made under this paragraph if it would impede or prevent the implementation of—

     (a)   a voluntary arrangement approved under Part I,

(b)   a compromise or arrangement sanctioned under Part 26 or 26A of the Companies Act 2006 (arrangements and reconstructions), ...

(ba) ...

(c)   proposals or a revision approved under paragraph 53 or 54 more than 28 days before the day on which the application for the order under this paragraph is made.

Misfeasance

75.— (1) The court may examine the conduct of a person who—

      (a)   is or purports to be the administrator of a company, or

      (b)   has been or has purported to be the administrator of a company.

(2) An examination under this paragraph may be held only on the application of—

      (a)   the official receiver,

      (b)   the administrator of the company,

      (c)   the liquidator of the company,

      (d)   a creditor of the company, or

      (e)   a contributory of the company.

(3) An application under sub-paragraph (2) must allege that the administrator—

      (a)   has misapplied or retained money or other property of the company,

      (b)   has become accountable for money or other property of the company,

      (c)   has breached a fiduciary or other duty in relation to the company, or

      (d)   has been guilty of misfeasance.

(4) On an examination under this paragraph into a person's conduct the court may order him—

      (a)   to repay, restore or account for money or property;

      (b)   to pay interest;

      (c)   to contribute a sum to the company's property by way of compensation for breach of duty or misfeasance.

(5) In sub-paragraph (3) "administrator" includes a person who purports or has purported to be a company's administrator.

(6) An application under sub-paragraph (2) may be made in respect of an administrator who has been discharged under paragraph 98 only with the permission of the court.

ENDING ADMINISTRATION

Automatic end of administration

76.— (1) The appointment of an administrator shall cease to have effect at the end of the period of one year beginning with the date on which it takes effect.

(2) But—

      (a)   on the application of an administrator the court may by order extend his term of office for a specified period, and

      (b)   an administrator's term of office may be extended for a specified period not exceeding one year by consent.

77.— (1) An order of the court under paragraph 76—

      (a)   may be made in respect of an administrator whose term of office has already been extended by order or by consent, but

      (b)   may not be made after the expiry of the administrator's term of office.

(2) Where an order is made under paragraph 76 the administrator shall as soon as is reasonably practicable notify the registrar of companies.

(3) An administrator who fails without reasonable excuse to comply with sub-paragraph (2) commits an offence.

78.— (1) In paragraph 76(2)(b) "consent" means consent of—

      (a)   each secured creditor of the company, and

      (b)   if the company has unsecured debts, the unsecured creditors of the company.

(2) But where the administrator has made a statement under paragraph 52(1)(b) "consent" means—

    (a) consent of each secured creditor of the company, or

    (b) if the administrator thinks that a distribution may be made to preferential creditors, consent of—

        (i) each secured creditor of the company, and

        (ii) the preferential creditors of the company.

(2A) Whether the company's unsecured creditors or preferential creditors consent is to be determined by the administrator seeking a decision from those creditors as to whether they consent.

(3) ...

(4) An administrator's term of office—

    (a) may be extended by consent only once,

    (b) may not be extended by consent after extension by order of the court, and

    (c) may not be extended by consent after expiry.

(5) Where an administrator's term of office is extended by consent he shall as soon as is reasonably practicable—

    (a) file notice of the extension with the court, and

    (b) notify the registrar of companies.

(6) An administrator who fails without reasonable excuse to comply with sub-paragraph (5) commits an offence.

Court ending administration on application of administrator

79.— (1) On the application of the administrator of a company the court may provide for the appointment of an administrator of the company to cease to have effect from a specified time.

(2) The administrator of a company shall make an application under this paragraph if—

    (a) he thinks the purpose of administration cannot be achieved in relation to the company,

    (b) he thinks the company should not have entered administration, or

    (c) the company's creditors decide that he must make an application under this paragraph.

(3) The administrator of a company shall make an application under this paragraph if—

    (a) the administration is pursuant to an administration order, and

    (b) the administrator thinks that the purpose of administration has been sufficiently achieved in relation to the company.

(4) On an application under this paragraph the court may—

    (a) adjourn the hearing conditionally or unconditionally;

    (b) dismiss the application;

    (c) make an interim order;

    (d) make any order it thinks appropriate (whether in addition to, in consequence of or instead of the order applied for).

Termination of administration where objective achieved

80.— (1) This paragraph applies where an administrator of a company is appointed under paragraph 14 or 22.

(2) If the administrator thinks that the purpose of administration has been sufficiently achieved in relation to the company he may file a notice in the prescribed form—

    (a) with the court, and

    (b) with the registrar of companies.

(3) The administrator's appointment shall cease to have effect when the requirements of sub-paragraph (2) are satisfied.

(4) Where the administrator files a notice he shall within the prescribed period send a copy to every creditor of the company, other than an opted-out creditor, of whose claim and address he is aware.

(5) The rules may provide that the administrator is taken to have complied with sub-paragraph (4) if before the end of the prescribed period he publishes in the prescribed manner a notice undertaking to provide a copy of the notice under sub-paragraph (2) to any creditor of the company who applies in writing to a specified address.

(6) An administrator who fails without reasonable excuse to comply with sub-paragraph (4) commits an offence.

Court ending administration on application of creditor

81.— (1) On the application of a creditor of a company the court may provide for the appointment of an administrator of the company to cease to have effect at a specified time.

(2) An application under this paragraph must allege an improper motive—
  (a) in the case of an administrator appointed by administration order, on the part of the applicant for the order, or
  (b) in any other case, on the part of the person who appointed the administrator.

(3) On an application under this paragraph the court may—
  (a) adjourn the hearing conditionally or unconditionally;
  (b) dismiss the application;
  (c) make an interim order;
  (d) make any order it thinks appropriate (whether in addition to, in consequence of or instead of the order applied for).

Public interest winding-up

82.— (1) This paragraph applies where a winding-up order is made for the winding up of a company in administration on a petition presented under—
  (a) section 124A (public interest), or
  (aa) section 124B (SEs),
  (b) section 367 of the Financial Services and Markets Act 2000 (petition by Financial Conduct Authority or Prudential Regulation Authority).

(2) This paragraph also applies where a provisional liquidator of a company in administration is appointed following the presentation of a petition under any of the provisions listed in sub-paragraph (1).

(3) The court shall order—
  (a) that the appointment of the administrator shall cease to have effect, or
  (b) that the appointment of the administrator shall continue to have effect.

(4) If the court makes an order under sub-paragraph (3)(b) it may also—
  (a) specify which of the powers under this Schedule are to be exercisable by the administrator, and
  (b) order that this Schedule shall have effect in relation to the administrator with specified modifications.

Moving from administration to creditors' voluntary liquidation

83.— (1) This paragraph applies in England and Wales where the administrator of a company thinks—
  (a) that the total amount which each secured creditor of the company is likely to receive has been paid to him or set aside for him, and
  (b) that a distribution will be made to unsecured creditors of the company (if there are any) which is not a distribution by virtue of section 176A(2)(a).

(2) This paragraph applies in Scotland where the administrator of a company thinks—
  (a) that each secured creditor of the company will receive payment in respect of his debt, and
  (b) that a distribution will be made to unsecured creditors (if there are any) which is not a distribution by virtue of section 176A(2)(a).

(3) The administrator may send to the registrar of companies a notice that this paragraph applies.

(4) On receipt of a notice under sub-paragraph (3) the registrar shall register it.

(5) If an administrator sends a notice under sub-paragraph (3) he shall as soon as is reasonably practicable—

    (a) file a copy of the notice with the court, and

    (b) send a copy of the notice to each creditor, other than an opted-out creditor, of whose claim and address he is aware.

(6) On the registration of a notice under sub-paragraph (3)—

    (a) the appointment of an administrator in respect of the company shall cease to have effect, and

    (b) the company shall be wound up as if a resolution for voluntary winding up under section 84 were passed on the day on which the notice is registered.

(7) The liquidator for the purposes of the winding up shall be—

    (a) a person nominated by the creditors of the company in the prescribed manner and within the prescribed period, or

    (b) if no person is nominated under paragraph (a), the administrator.

(8) In the application of Part IV to a winding up by virtue of this paragraph—

    (a) section 85 shall not apply,

    (b) section 86 shall apply as if the reference to the time of the passing of the resolution for voluntary winding up were a reference to the beginning of the date of registration of the notice under sub-paragraph (3),

    (c) section 89 does not apply,

    (d) sections ... 99 and 100 shall not apply,

    (e) section 129 shall apply as if the reference to the time of the passing of the resolution for voluntary winding up were a reference to the beginning of the date of registration of the notice under sub-paragraph (3), and

    (f) any creditors' committee which is in existence immediately before the company ceases to be in administration shall continue in existence after that time as if appointed as a liquidation committee under section 101.

Moving from administration to dissolution

84.— (1) If the administrator of a company thinks that the company has no property which might permit a distribution to its creditors, he shall send a notice to that effect to the registrar of companies.

(1A), (1B) ...

(2) The court may on the application of the administrator of a company disapply sub-paragraph (1) in respect of the company.

(3) On receipt of a notice under sub-paragraph (1) ... the registrar shall register it ...

(4) On the registration of a notice in respect of a company under sub-paragraph (1) the appointment of an administrator of the company shall cease to have effect.

(5) If an administrator sends a notice under sub-paragraph (1) he shall as soon as is reasonably practicable—

    (a) file a copy of the notice with the court, and

    (b) send a copy of the notice to each creditor, other than an opted-out creditor, of whose claim and address he is aware.

(6) At the end of the period of three months beginning with the date of registration of a notice in respect of a company under sub-paragraph (1) the company is deemed to be dissolved ...

(6A), (6B) ...

(7) On an application in respect of a company by the administrator or another interested person the court may—

    (a) extend the period specified in sub-paragraph (6) ...

    (b) suspend that period, or

(c)   disapply sub-paragraph (6) …

(8)   Where an order is made under sub-paragraph (7) in respect of a company the administrator shall as soon as is reasonably practicable notify the registrar of companies.

(9)   An administrator commits an offence if he fails without reasonable excuse to comply with sub-paragraph (5).

Discharge of administration order where administration ends

85.— (1)   This paragraph applies where—

(a)   the court makes an order under this Schedule providing for the appointment of an administrator of a company to cease to have effect, and

(b)   the administrator was appointed by administration order.

(2)   The court shall discharge the administration order.

Notice to Companies Registrar where administration ends

86.— (1)   This paragraph applies where the court makes an order under this Schedule providing for the appointment of an administrator to cease to have effect.

(2)   The administrator shall send a copy of the order to the registrar of companies within the period of 14 days beginning with the date of the order.

(3)   An administrator who fails without reasonable excuse to comply with sub-paragraph (2) commits an offence.

REPLACING ADMINISTRATOR

Resignation of administrator

87.— (1)   An administrator may resign only in prescribed circumstances.

(2)   Where an administrator may resign he may do so only—

(a)   in the case of an administrator appointed by administration order, by notice in writing to the court,

(b)   in the case of an administrator appointed under paragraph 14, by notice in writing to the holder of the floating charge by virtue of which the appointment was made,

(c)   in the case of an administrator appointed under paragraph 22(1), by notice in writing to the company, or

(d)   in the case of an administrator appointed under paragraph 22(2), by notice in writing to the directors of the company.

Removal of administrator from office

88.   The court may by order remove an administrator from office.

Administrator ceasing to be qualified

89.— (1)   The administrator of a company shall vacate office if he ceases to be qualified to act as an insolvency practitioner in relation to the company.

(2)   Where an administrator vacates office by virtue of sub-paragraph (1) he shall give notice in writing—

(a)   in the case of an administrator appointed by administration order, to the court,

(b)   in the case of an administrator appointed under paragraph 14, to the holder of the floating charge by virtue of which the appointment was made,

(c)   in the case of an administrator appointed under paragraph 22(1), to the company, or

(d)   in the case of an administrator appointed under paragraph 22(2), to the directors of the company.

(3)   An administrator who fails without reasonable excuse to comply with sub-paragraph (2) commits an offence.

Supplying vacancy in office of administrator

90.   Paragraphs 91 to 95 apply where an administrator—
         (a)   dies,
         (b)   resigns,
         (c)   is removed from office under paragraph 88, or
         (d)   vacates office under paragraph 89.

91.—   (1)   Where the administrator was appointed by administration order, the court may replace the
               administrator on an application under this sub-paragraph made by—
               (a)   a creditors' committee of the company,
               (b)   the company,
               (c)   the directors of the company,
               (d)   one or more creditors of the company, or
               (e)   where more than one person was appointed to act jointly or concurrently as the admin-
                     istrator, any of those persons who remains in office.
         (2)   But an application may be made in reliance on sub-paragraph (1)(b) to (d) only where—
               (a)   there is no creditors' committee of the company,
               (b)   the court is satisfied that the creditors' committee or a remaining administrator is not
                     taking reasonable steps to make a replacement, or
               (c)   the court is satisfied that for another reason it is right for the application to be made.

92.   Where the administrator was appointed under paragraph 14 the holder of the floating charge by
         virtue of which the appointment was made may replace the administrator.

93.—   (1)   Where the administrator was appointed under paragraph 22(1) by the company it may
               replace the administrator.
         (2)   A replacement under this paragraph may be made only—
               (a)   with the consent of each person who is the holder of a qualifying floating charge in
                     respect of the company's property, or
               (b)   where consent is withheld, with the permission of the court.

94.—   (1)   Where the administrator was appointed under paragraph 22(2) the directors of the company
               may replace the administrator.
         (2)   A replacement under this paragraph may be made only—
               (a)   with the consent of each person who is the holder of a qualifying floating charge in
                     respect of the company's property, or
               (b)   where consent is withheld, with the permission of the court.

95.   The court may replace an administrator on the application of a person listed in paragraph 91(1) if
         the court—
         (a)   is satisfied that a person who is entitled to replace the administrator under any of paragraphs
               92 to 94 is not taking reasonable steps to make a replacement, or
         (b)   that for another reason it is right for the court to make the replacement.

Substitution of administrator: competing floating charge-holder

96.—   (1)   This paragraph applies where an administrator of a company is appointed under paragraph
               14 by the holder of a qualifying floating charge in respect of the company's property.
         (2)   The holder of a prior qualifying floating charge in respect of the company's property may
               apply to the court for the administrator to be replaced by an administrator nominated by the
               holder of the prior floating charge.
         (3)   One floating charge is prior to another for the purposes of this paragraph if—
               (a)   it was created first, or
               (b)   it is to be treated as having priority in accordance with an agreement to which the
                     holder of each floating charge was party.
         (4)   Sub-paragraph (3) shall have effect in relation to Scotland as if the following were
               substituted for paragraph (a)—

"(a) it has priority of ranking in accordance with section 464(4)(b) of the Companies Act 1985,".

Substitution of administrator appointed by company or directors: creditors' decision

97.— (1) This paragraph applies where—
    (a) an administrator of a company is appointed by a company or directors under paragraph 22, and
    (b) there is no holder of a qualifying floating charge in respect of the company's property.
  (2) The administrator may be replaced by a decision of the creditors made by a qualifying decision procedure.
  (3) The decision has effect only if, before the decision is made, the new administrator has consented to act in writing.

Vacation of office: discharge from liability

98.— (1) Where a person ceases to be the administrator of a company (whether because he vacates office by reason of resignation, death or otherwise, because he is removed from office or because his appointment ceases to have effect) he is discharged from liability in respect of any action of his as administrator.
  (2) The discharge provided by sub-paragraph (1) takes effect—
    (a) in the case of an administrator who dies, on the filing with the court of notice of his death,
    (b) in the case of an administrator appointed under paragraph 14 or 22 who has not made a statement under paragraph 52(1)(b), at a time appointed by resolution of the creditors' committee or, if there is no committee, by decision of the creditors,
    (ba) in the case of an administrator appointed under paragraph 14 or 22 who has made a statement under paragraph 52(1)(b), at a time decided by the relevant creditors, or
    (c) in any case, at a time specified by the court.
  (3) For the purposes of sub-paragraph (2)(ba), the "relevant creditors" of a company are—
    (a) each secured creditor of the company, or
    (b) if the administrator has made a distribution to preferential creditors or thinks that a distribution may be made to preferential creditors—
      (i) each secured creditor of the company, and
      (ii) the preferential creditors of the company.
  (3A) In a case where the administrator is removed from office, a decision of the creditors for the purposes of sub-paragraph (2)(b), or of the preferential creditors for the purposes of sub-paragraph (2)(ba), must be made by a qualifying decision procedure.
  (4) Discharge—
    (a) applies to liability accrued before the discharge takes effect, and
    (b) does not prevent the exercise of the court's powers under paragraph 75.

Vacation of office: charges and liabilities

99.— (1) This paragraph applies where a person ceases to be the administrator of a company (whether because he vacates office by reason of resignation, death or otherwise, because he is removed from office or because his appointment ceases to have effect).
  (2) In this paragraph—
    "the former administrator" means the person referred to in sub-paragraph (1), and
    "cessation" means the time when he ceases to be the company's administrator.
  (3) The former administrator's remuneration and expenses shall be—
    (a) charged on and payable out of property of which he had custody or control immediately before cessation, and
    (b) payable in priority to any security to which paragraph 70 applies.
  (4) A sum payable in respect of a debt or liability arising out of a contract entered into by the former administrator or a predecessor before cessation shall be—

       (a)   charged on and payable out of property of which the former administrator had custody or control immediately before cessation, and

       (b)   payable in priority to any charge arising under sub-paragraph (3).

(5)   Sub-paragraph (4) shall apply to a liability arising under a contract of employment which was adopted by the former administrator or a predecessor before cessation; and for that purpose—

       (a)   action taken within the period of 14 days after an administrator's appointment shall not be taken to amount or contribute to the adoption of a contract,

       (b)   no account shall be taken of a liability which arises, or in so far as it arises, by reference to anything which is done or which occurs before the adoption of the contract of employment, and

       (c)   no account shall be taken of a liability to make a payment other than wages or salary.

(6)   In sub-paragraph (5)(c) "wages or salary" includes—

       (a)   a sum payable in respect of a period of holiday (for which purpose the sum shall be treated as relating to the period by reference to which the entitlement to holiday accrued),

       (b)   a sum payable in respect of a period of absence through illness or other good cause,

       (c)   a sum payable in lieu of holiday,

       (d)   ...

       (e)   a contribution to an occupational pension scheme.

GENERAL

Joint and concurrent administrators

100.— (1)   In this Schedule—

       (a)   a reference to the appointment of an administrator of a company includes a reference to the appointment of a number of persons to act jointly or concurrently as the administrator of a company, and

       (b)   a reference to the appointment of a person as administrator of a company includes a reference to the appointment of a person as one of a number of persons to act jointly or concurrently as the administrator of a company.

(2)   The appointment of a number of persons to act as administrator of a company must specify—

       (a)   which functions (if any) are to be exercised by the persons appointed acting jointly, and

       (b)   which functions (if any) are to be exercised by any or all of the persons appointed.

101.— (1)   This paragraph applies where two or more persons are appointed to act jointly as the administrator of a company.

(2)   A reference to the administrator of the company is a reference to those persons acting jointly.

(3)   But a reference to the administrator of a company in paragraphs 87 to 99 of this Schedule is a reference to any or all of the persons appointed to act jointly.

(4)   Where an offence of omission is committed by the administrator, each of the persons appointed to act jointly—

       (a)   commits the offence, and

       (b)   may be proceeded against and punished individually.

(5)   The reference in paragraph 45(1)(a) to the name of the administrator is a reference to the name of each of the persons appointed to act jointly.

(6)   Where persons are appointed to act jointly in respect of only some of the functions of the administrator of a company, this paragraph applies only in relation to those functions.

102.— (1)   This paragraph applies where two or more persons are appointed to act concurrently as the administrator of a company.

(2) A reference to the administrator of a company in this Schedule is a reference to any of the persons appointed (or any combination of them).

103.— (1) Where a company is in administration, a person may be appointed to act as administrator jointly or concurrently with the person or persons acting as the administrator of the company.

(2) Where a company entered administration by administration order, an appointment under sub-paragraph (1) must be made by the court on the application of—

(a) a person or group listed in paragraph 12(1)(a) to (e), or

(b) the person or persons acting as the administrator of the company.

(3) Where a company entered administration by virtue of an appointment under paragraph 14, an appointment under sub-paragraph (1) must be made by—

(a) the holder of the floating charge by virtue of which the appointment was made, or

(b) the court on the application of the person or persons acting as the administrator of the company.

(4) Where a company entered administration by virtue of an appointment under paragraph 22(1), an appointment under sub-paragraph (1) above must be made either by the court on the application of the person or persons acting as the administrator of the company or—

(a) by the company, and

(b) with the consent of each person who is the holder of a qualifying floating charge in respect of the company's property or, where consent is withheld, with the permission of the court.

(5) Where a company entered administration by virtue of an appointment under paragraph 22(2), an appointment under sub-paragraph (1) must be made either by the court on the application of the person or persons acting as the administrator of the company or—

(a) by the directors of the company, and

(b) with the consent of each person who is the holder of a qualifying floating charge in respect of the company's property or, where consent is withheld, with the permission of the court.

(6) An appointment under sub-paragraph (1) may be made only with the consent of the person or persons acting as the administrator of the company.

Presumption of validity

104. An act of the administrator of a company is valid in spite of a defect in his appointment or qualification.

Majority decision of directors

105. A reference in this Schedule to something done by the directors of a company includes a reference to the same thing done by a majority of the directors of a company.

Penalties

106.— (1) A person who is guilty of an offence under this Schedule is liable to a fine (in accordance with section 430 and Schedule 10).

(2) A person who is guilty of an offence under any of the following paragraphs of this Schedule is liable to a daily default fine (in accordance with section 430 and Schedule 10)—

(a) paragraph 20,

(b) paragraph 32,

(c) paragraph 46,

(d) paragraph 48,

(e) paragraph 49,

(f) paragraph 51,

(g) paragraph 53,

(h) paragraph 54,

(i) paragraph 56,

(j)   paragraph 71,

(k)   paragraph 72,

(l)   paragraph 77,

(m)   paragraph 78,

(n)   paragraph 80,

(o)   paragraph 84,

(p)   paragraph 86, and

(q)   paragraph 89.

Extension of time limit

107.— (1)   Where a provision of this Schedule provides that a period may be varied in accordance with this paragraph, the period may be varied in respect of a company—

       (a)   by the court, and

       (b)   on the application of the administrator.

     (2)   A time period may be extended in respect of a company under this paragraph—

       (a)   more than once, and

       (b)   after expiry.

108.— (1)   A period specified in paragraph 49(5) ... or 51(2) may be varied in respect of a company by the administrator with consent.

     (2)   In sub-paragraph (1) "consent" means consent of—

       (a)   each secured creditor of the company, and

       (b)   if the company has unsecured debts, the unsecured creditors of the company.

     (3)   But where the administrator has made a statement under paragraph 52(1)(b) "consent" means—

       (a)   consent of each secured creditor of the company, or

       (b)   if the administrator thinks that a distribution may be made to preferential creditors, consent of—

          (i)   each secured creditor of the company, and

          (ii)   the preferential creditors of the company.

   (3A)   Whether the company's unsecured creditors or preferential creditors consent is to be determined by the administrator seeking a decision from those creditors as to whether they consent.

     (4)   ...

     (5)   The power to extend under sub-paragraph (1)—

       (a)   may be exercised in respect of a period only once,

       (b)   may not be used to extend a period by more than 28 days,

       (c)   may not be used to extend a period which has been extended by the court, and

       (d)   may not be used to extend a period after expiry.

109.   Where a period is extended under paragraph 107 or 108, a reference to the period shall be taken as a reference to the period as extended.

Amendment of provision about time

110.— (1)   The Secretary of State may by order amend a provision of this Schedule which—

       (a)   requires anything to be done within a specified period of time,

       (b)   prevents anything from being done after a specified time, or

       (c)   requires a specified minimum period of notice to be given.

     (2)   An order under this paragraph—

       (a)   must be made by statutory instrument, and

       (b)   shall be subject to annulment in pursuance of a resolution of either House of Parliament.

Interpretation

111.— (1)   In this Schedule—

"administrative receiver" has the meaning given by section 251,

"administrator" has the meaning given by paragraph 1 and, where the context requires, includes a reference to a former administrator,

...

"enters administration" has the meaning given by paragraph 1,

"floating charge" means a charge which is a floating charge on its creation,

"in administration" has the meaning given by paragraph 1,

"hire-purchase agreement" includes a conditional sale agreement, a chattel leasing agreement and a retention of title agreement,

"holder of a qualifying floating charge" in respect of a company's property has the meaning given by paragraph 14,

"market value" means the amount which would be realised on a sale of property in the open market by a willing vendor,

"the purpose of administration" means an objective specified in paragraph 3, and

"unable to pay its debts" has the meaning given by section 123.

(1A) In this Schedule, "company" means—

    (a)   a company registered under the Companies Act 2006 in England and Wales or Scotland,

    (b)   a company incorporated in an EEA State ..., or

    (c)   a company not incorporated in an EEA State but having its centre of main interests in a member State (other than Denmark) or in the United Kingdom.

(1B) In sub-paragraph (1A), in relation to a company, "centre of main interests" has the same meaning as in Article 3 of the EU Regulation.

(2)   ...

(3)   In this Schedule a reference to action includes a reference to inaction.

Non-UK companies

111A.   A company incorporated outside the United Kingdom that has a principal place of business in Northern Ireland may not enter administration under this Schedule unless it also has a principal place of business in England and Wales or Scotland (or both in England and Wales and in Scotland).

Scotland

112.   In the application of this Schedule to Scotland—

    (a)   a reference to filing with the court is a reference to lodging in court, and

    (b)   a reference to a charge is a reference to a right in security.

113.   Where property in Scotland is disposed of under paragraph 70 or 71, the administrator shall grant to the disponee an appropriate document of transfer or conveyance of the property, and—

    (a)   that document, or

    (b)   recording, intimation or registration of that document (where recording, intimation or registration of the document is a legal requirement for completion of title to the property),

has the effect of disencumbering the property of or, as the case may be, freeing the property from, the security.

114.   In Scotland, where goods in the possession of a company under a hire-purchase agreement are disposed of under paragraph 72, the disposal has the effect of extinguishing as against the disponee all rights of the owner of the goods under the agreement.

115.— (1)   In Scotland, the administrator of a company may make, in or towards the satisfaction of the debt secured by the floating charge, a payment to the holder of a floating charge which has attached to the property subject to the charge.

(1A) In Scotland, sub-paragraph (1B) applies in connection with the giving by the court of permission as provided for in paragraph 65(3)(b).

(1B) On the giving by the court of such permission, any floating charge granted by the company shall, unless it has already so attached, attach to the property which is subject to the charge.

(2)   In Scotland, where the administrator thinks that the company has insufficient property to enable a distribution to be made to unsecured creditors other than by virtue of section 176A(2)(a), he may file a notice to that effect with the registrar of companies.

(3)   On delivery of the notice to the registrar of companies, any floating charge granted by the company shall, unless it has already so attached, attach to the property which is subject to the charge ...

(4)   Attachment of a floating charge under sub-paragraph (1B) or (3) has effect as if the charge is a fixed security over the property to which it has attached.

116.   In Scotland, the administrator in making any payment in accordance with paragraph 115 shall make such payment subject to the rights of any of the following categories of persons (which rights shall, except to the extent provided in any instrument, have the following order of priority)—

(a)   the holder of any fixed security which is over property subject to the floating charge and which ranks prior to, or pari passu with, the floating charge,

(b)   creditors in respect of all liabilities and expenses incurred by or on behalf of the administrator,

(c)   the administrator in respect of his liabilities, expenses and remuneration and any indemnity to which he is entitled out of the property of the company,

(d)   the preferential creditors entitled to payment in accordance with paragraph 65,

(e)   the holder of the floating charge in accordance with the priority of that charge in relation to any other floating charge which has attached, and

(f)   the holder of a fixed security, other than one referred to in paragraph (a), which is over property subject to the floating charge.

SCHEDULE 1

POWERS OF ADMINISTRATOR OR ADMINISTRATIVE RECEIVER

Sections 14, 42

1.   Power to take possession of, collect and get in the property of the company and, for that purpose, to take such proceedings as may seem to him expedient.

2.   Power to sell or otherwise dispose of the property of the company by public auction or private contract or, in Scotland, to sell, ... hire out or otherwise dispose of the property of the company by public roup or private bargain.

3.   Power to raise or borrow money and grant security therefor over the property of the company.

4.   Power to appoint a solicitor or accountant or other professionally qualified person to assist him in the performance of his functions.

5.   Power to bring or defend any action or other legal proceedings in the name and on behalf of the company.

6.   Power to refer to arbitration any question affecting the company.

7.   Power to effect and maintain insurances in respect of the business and property of the company.

8.   Power to use the company's seal.

9.   Power to do all acts and to execute in the name and on behalf of the company any deed, receipt or other document.

10.   Power to draw, accept, make and endorse any bill of exchange or promissory note in the name and on behalf of the company.

11.   Power to appoint any agent to do any business which he is unable to do himself or which can more conveniently be done by an agent and power to employ and dismiss employees.

12.   Power to do all such things (including the carrying out of works) as may be necessary for the realisation of the property of the company.

13.   Power to make any payment which is necessary or incidental to the performance of his functions.

14.   Power to carry on the business of the company.

15.   Power to establish subsidiaries of the company.

16. Power to transfer to subsidiaries of the company the whole or any part of the business and property of the company.

17. Power to grant or accept a surrender of a lease or tenancy of any of the property of the company, and to take a lease or tenancy of any property required or convenient for the business of the company.

18. Power to make any arrangement or compromise on behalf of the company.

19. Power to call up any uncalled capital of the company.

20. Power to rank and claim in the bankruptcy, insolvency, sequestration or liquidation of any person indebted to the company and to receive dividends, and to accede to trust deeds for the creditors of any such person.

21. Power to present or defend a petition for the winding up of the company.

22. Power to change the situation of the company's registered office.

23. Power to do all other things incidental to the exercise of the foregoing powers.

SCHEDULE 2

POWERS OF A SCOTTISH RECEIVER (ADDITIONAL TO THOSE CONFERRED ON HIM BY THE INSTRUMENT OF CHARGE)

Section 55

1. Power to take possession of, collect and get in the property from the company or a liquidator thereof or any other person, and for that purpose, to take such proceedings as may seem to him expedient.

2. Power to sell, ... hire out or otherwise dispose of the property by public roup or private bargain and with or without advertisement.

3. Power to raise or borrow money and grant security therefor over the property.

4. Power to appoint a solicitor or accountant or other professionally qualified person to assist him in the performance of his functions.

5. Power to bring or defend any action or other legal proceedings in the name and on behalf of the company.

6. Power to refer to arbitration all questions affecting the company.

7. Power to effect and maintain insurances in respect of the business and property of the company.

8. Power to use the company's seal.

9. Power to do all acts and to execute in the name and on behalf of the company any deed, receipt or other document.

10. Power to draw, accept, make and endorse any bill of exchange or promissory note in the name and on behalf of the company.

11. Power to appoint any agent to do any business which he is unable to do himself or which can more conveniently be done by an agent, and power to employ and dismiss employees.

12. Power to do all such things (including the carrying out of works), as may be necessary for the realisation of the property.

13. Power to make any payment which is necessary or incidental to the performance of his functions.

14. Power to carry on the business of the company or any part of it.

15. Power to grant or accept a surrender of a lease or tenancy of any of the property, and to take a lease or tenancy of any property required or convenient for the business of the company.

16. Power to make any arrangement or compromise on behalf of the company.

17. Power to call up any uncalled capital of the company.

18. Power to establish subsidiaries of the company.

19. Power to transfer to subsidiaries of the company the business of the company or any part of it and any of the property.

20. Power to rank and claim in the bankruptcy, insolvency, sequestration or liquidation of any person or company indebted to the company and to receive dividends, and to accede to trust deeds for creditors of any such person.

21.   Power to present or defend a petition for the winding up of the company.

22.   Power to change the situation of the company's registered office.

23.   Power to do all other things incidental to the exercise of the powers mentioned in section 55(1) of this Act or above in this Schedule.

SCHEDULE 2A

EXCEPTIONS TO PROHIBITION ON APPOINTMENT OF ADMINISTRATIVE RECEIVER: SUPPLEMENTARY PROVISIONS

Section 72H(1)

Capital market arrangement

1.—   (1)   For the purposes of section 72B an arrangement is a capital market arrangement if—

(a)   it involves a grant of security to a person holding it as trustee for a person who holds a capital market investment issued by a party to the arrangement, or

(aa) it involves a grant of security to—

(i)   a party to the arrangement who issues a capital market investment, or

(ii) a person who holds the security as trustee for a party to the arrangement in connection with the issue of a capital market investment, or

(ab) it involves a grant of security to a person who holds the security as trustee for a party to the arrangement who agrees to provide finance to another party, or

(b)   at least one party guarantees the performance of obligations of another party, or

(c)   at least one party provides security in respect of the performance of obligations of another party, or

(d)   the arrangement involves an investment of a kind described in articles 83 to 85 of the Financial Services and Markets Act 2000 (Regulated Activities) Order 2001 (options, futures and contracts for differences).

(2)   For the purposes of sub-paragraph (1)—

(a)   a reference to holding as trustee includes a reference to holding as nominee or agent,

(b)   a reference to holding for a person who holds a capital market investment includes a reference to holding for a number of persons at least one of whom holds a capital market investment, and

(c)   a person holds a capital market investment if he has a legal or beneficial interest in it, and

(d)   the reference to the provision of finance includes the provision of an indemnity.

(3)   In section 72B(1) and this paragraph "party" to an arrangement includes a party to an agreement which—

(a)   forms part of the arrangement,

(b)   provides for the raising of finance as part of the arrangement, or

(c)   is necessary for the purposes of implementing the arrangement.

Capital market investment

2.—   (1)   For the purposes of section 72B an investment is a capital market investment if it—

(a)   is within article 77 or 77A of the Financial Services and Markets Act 2000 (Regulated Activities) Order 2001 (debt instruments), and

(b)   is rated, listed or traded or designed to be rated, listed or traded.

(2)   In sub-paragraph (1)—

"rated" means rated for the purposes of investment by an internationally recognised rating agency,

"listed" means admitted to the official list within the meaning given by section 103(1) of the Financial Services and Markets Act 2000 (interpretation), and "traded" means admitted to trading on a market established under the rules of a recognised investment exchange or on a foreign market.

(3)   In sub-paragraph (2)—

        "recognised investment exchange" has the meaning given by section 285 of the Financial Services and Markets Act 2000 (recognised investment exchange), and

        "foreign market" has the same meaning as "relevant market" in article 67(2) of the Financial Services and Markets Act 2000 (Financial Promotion) Order 2001 (foreign markets).

3.—   (1)   An investment is also a capital market investment for the purposes of section 72B if it consists of a bond or commercial paper issued to one or more of the following—

      (a)   an investment professional within the meaning of article 19(5) of the Financial Services and Markets Act 2000 (Financial Promotion) Order 2005 (S.I. 2005/1529),

      (b)   a person who is, when the agreement mentioned in section 72B(1) is entered into, a … high net worth individual in relation to a communication within the meaning of article 48(2) of that order,

      (c)   a person to whom article 49(2) of that order applies (high net worth company, &c),

      (d)   a person who is, when the agreement mentioned in section 72B(1) is entered into, a certified sophisticated investor in relation to a communication within the meaning of article 50(1) of that order, and

      (e)   a person in a State other than the United Kingdom who under the law of that State is not prohibited from investing in bonds or commercial paper.

(2)   In sub-paragraph (1)—

        "bond" shall be construed in accordance with article 77 of the Financial Services and Markets Act 2000 (Regulated Activities) Order 2001, and includes any instrument falling within article 77A of that Order, and

        "commercial paper" has the meaning given by article 9(3) of that order.

(3)   For the purposes of sub-paragraph (1)—

      (a)   in applying article 19(5) of the Financial Promotion Order for the purposes of sub-paragraph (1)(a)—

          (i)   in article 19(5)(b), ignore the words after "exempt person",

         (ii)   in article 19(5)(c)(i), for the words from "the controlled activity" to the end substitute "a controlled activity", and

       (iii)   in article 19(5)(e) ignore the words from "where the communication" to the end, and

      (b)   in applying article 49(2) of that order for the purposes of sub-paragraph (1)(c), ignore article 49(2)(e).

"Agreement"

4.   For the purposes of sections 72B and 72E and this Schedule "agreement" includes an agreement or undertaking effected by—

    (a)   contract,

    (b)   deed, or

    (c)   any other instrument intended to have effect in accordance with the law of England and Wales, Scotland or another jurisdiction.

Debt

5.   The debt of at least £50 million referred to in section 72B(1)(a) or 72E(2)(a)—

    (a)   may be incurred at any time during the life of the capital market arrangement or financed project, and

    (b)   may be expressed wholly or partly in foreign currency (in which case the sterling equivalent shall be calculated as at the time when the arrangement is entered into or the project begins).

Step-in rights

6.— (1) For the purposes of sections 72C to 72E a project has "step-in rights" if a person who provides finance in connection with the project has a conditional entitlement under an agreement to—

    (a) assume sole or principal responsibility under an agreement for carrying out all or part of the project, or

    (b) make arrangements for carrying out all or part of the project.

(2) In sub-paragraph (1) a reference to the provision of finance includes a reference to the provision of an indemnity.

Project company

7.— (1) For the purposes of sections 72C to 72E a company is a "project company" of a project if—

    (a) it holds property for the purpose of the project,

    (b) it has sole or principal responsibility under an agreement for carrying out all or part of the project,

    (c) it is one of a number of companies which together carry out the project,

    (d) it has the purpose of supplying finance to enable the project to be carried out, or

    (e) it is the holding company of a company within any of paragraphs (a) to (d).

(2) But a company is not a "project company" of a project if—

    (a) it performs a function within sub-paragraph (1)(a) to (d) or is within sub-paragraph (1)(e), but

    (b) it also performs a function which is not—

        (i) within sub-paragraph (1)(a) to (d),

        (ii) related to a function within sub-paragraph (1)(a) to (d), or

        (iii) related to the project.

(3) For the purposes of this paragraph a company carries out all or part of a project whether or not it acts wholly or partly through agents.

"Resources"

8. In section 72C "resources" includes—

    (a) funds (including payment for the provision of services or facilities),

    (b) assets,

    (c) professional skill,

    (d) the grant of a concession or franchise, and

    (e) any other commercial resource.

"Public body"

9.— (1) In section 72C "public body" means—

    (a) a body which exercises public functions,

    (b) a body specified for the purposes of this paragraph by the Secretary of State, and

    (c) a body within a class specified for the purposes of this paragraph by the Secretary of State.

(2) A specification under sub-paragraph (1) may be—

    (a) general, or

    (b) for the purpose of the application of section 72C to a specified case.

Regulated business

10.— (1) For the purposes of section 72D a business is regulated if it is carried on—

    (a) ...

    (b) in reliance on a licence under section 7, 7A or 7B of the Gas Act 1986 (transport and supply of gas),

    (c) in reliance on a licence granted by virtue of section 41C of that Act (power to prescribe additional licensable activity),

(d) in reliance on a licence under section 6 of the Electricity Act 1989 (supply of electricity),

(e) by a water undertaker,

(f) by a sewerage undertaker,

(g) by a universal service provider within the meaning of Part 3 of the Postal Services Act 2011,

(h) by a Post Office company within the meaning of Part 1 of that Act,

(i) ...

(j) in reliance on a licence under section 8 of the Railways Act 1993 (railway services),

(k) in reliance on a licence exemption under section 7 of that Act (subject to sub-paragraph (2) below),

(l) by the operator of a system of transport which is deemed to be a railway for a purpose of Part I of that Act by virtue of section 81(2) of that Act (tramways, &c), ...

(m) by the operator of a vehicle carried on flanged wheels along a system within paragraph (l), or

(n) in reliance on a railway undertaking licence granted pursuant to the Railway (Licensing of Railway Undertakings) Regulations 2005 or a relevant European licence.

(2) Sub-paragraph (1)(k) does not apply to the operator of a railway asset on a railway unless on some part of the railway there is a permitted line speed exceeding 40 kilometres per hour.

(2A) For the purposes of section 72D a business is also regulated to the extent that it consists in the provision of a public electronic communications network or a public electronic communications service.

(2B) ...

(3) In sub-paragraph (1)(n) "relevant European licence" has the meaning given by section 6(2) of the Railways Act 1993.

"Person"

11. A reference to a person in this Schedule includes a reference to a partnership or another unincorporated group of persons.

SCHEDULE 3

ORDERS IN COURSE OF WINDING UP PRONOUNCED IN VACATION (SCOTLAND)

Section 162

PART I
ORDERS WHICH ARE TO BE FINAL

Orders under section 153, as to the time for proving debts and claims.

Orders under section 195 as to meetings for ascertaining wishes of creditors or contributories.

Orders under section 198, as to the examination of witnesses in regard to the property or affairs of a company.

PART II
ORDERS WHICH ARE TO TAKE EFFECT UNTIL MATTER
DISPOSED OF BY INNER HOUSE

Orders under section 126(1), 130(2) or (3), 147, 227 or 228, restraining or permitting the commencement or the continuance of legal proceedings.

Orders under section 135(5), limiting the powers of provisional liquidators.

Orders under section 108, appointing a liquidator to fill a vacancy.

...

Orders under section 158, as to the arrest and detention of an absconding contributory and his property.

SCHEDULE 4

POWERS OF LIQUIDATOR IN A WINDING UP

Sections 165, 167

PART I

...

1.   Power to pay any class of creditors in full.
2.   Power to make any compromise or arrangement with creditors or persons claiming to be creditors, or having or alleging themselves to have any claim (present or future, certain or contingent, ascertained or sounding only in damages) against the company, or whereby the company may be rendered liable.
3.   ... power to compromise, on such terms as may be agreed—
    (a)   all calls and liabilities to calls, all debts and liabilities capable of resulting in debts, and all claims (present or future, certain or contingent, ascertained or sounding only in damages) subsisting or supposed to subsist between the company and a contributory or alleged contributory or other debtor or person apprehending liability to the company, and
    (b)   all questions in any way relating to or affecting the assets or the winding up of the company, and take any security for the discharge of any such call, debt, liability or claim and give a complete discharge in respect of it.
3A.   Power to bring legal proceedings under section 213, 214, 238, 239, 242, 243 or 423.

PART II

...

4.   Power to bring or defend any action or other legal proceeding in the name and on behalf of the company.
5.   Power to carry on the business of the company so far as may be necessary for its beneficial winding up.

PART III

...

6.   Power to sell any of the company's property by public auction or private contract with power to transfer the whole of it to any person or to sell the same in parcels.
6A.   ...
7.   Power to do all acts and execute, in the name and on behalf of the company, all deeds, receipts and other documents and for that purpose to use, when necessary, the company's seal.
8.   Power to prove, rank and claim in the bankruptcy, insolvency or sequestration of any contributory for any balance against his estate, and to receive dividends in the bankruptcy, insolvency or sequestration in respect of that balance, as a separate debt due from the bankrupt or insolvent, and rateably with the other separate creditors.
9.   Power to draw, accept, make and indorse any bill of exchange or promissory note in the name and on behalf of the company, with the same effect with respect to the company's liability as if the bill or note had been drawn, accepted, made or indorsed by or on behalf of the company in the course of its business.
10.   Power to raise on the security of the assets of the company any money requisite.
11.   Power to take out in his official name letters of administration to any deceased contributory, and to do in his official name any other act necessary for obtaining payment of any money due from a contributory or his estate which cannot conveniently be done in the name of the company.
        In all such cases the money due is deemed, for the purpose of enabling the liquidator to take out the letters of administration or recover the money, to be due to the liquidator himself.

12.   Power to appoint an agent to do any business which the liquidator is unable to do himself.

13.   Power to do all such other things as may be necessary for winding up the company's affairs and distributing its assets.

SCHEDULE 4ZZA

PROTECTION OF SUPPLIES UNDER SECTION 233B: EXCLUSIONS

Section 233B

PART 1
ESSENTIAL SUPPLIES

Essential supplies

1.—   (1)   Section 233B(3) and (4) do not apply in relation to provision of a contract if—

(a)   the company becomes subject to a relevant insolvency procedure as specified in section 233B(2)(b) or (d), and

(b)   the provision of the contract ceases to have effect under section 233A(1).

(2)   Section 233B(7) does not apply in relation to a supply to the company if—

(a)   the company becomes subject to a relevant insolvency procedure as specified in section 233B(2)(b) to (f), and

(b)   the supply is a supply mentioned in section 233(3).

PART 2
PERSONS INVOLVED IN FINANCIAL SERVICES

Introductory

2.   Section 233B does not apply in relation to a contract for the supply of goods or services to a company ("the company") where any of paragraphs 3 to 11 applies.

Insurers

3.—   (1)   This paragraph applies where either the company or the supplier—

(a)   carries on the regulated activity of effecting or carrying out contracts of insurance, and

(b)   is not an exempt person in relation to that activity.

(2)   In this paragraph—

"exempt person", in relation to a regulated activity, has the meaning given by section 417 of the Financial Services and Markets Act 2000;

"regulated activity" has the meaning given by section 22 of that Act, taken with Schedule 2 to that Act and any order under that section.

Banks

4.—   (1)   This paragraph applies where either the company or the supplier—

(a)   has permission under Part 4A of the Financial Services and Markets Act 2000 to carry on the regulated activity of accepting deposits,

(b)   is a banking group company within the meaning of Part 1 of the Banking Act 2009 (see section 81D of that Act), or

(c)   has a liability in respect of a deposit which it accepted in accordance with the Banking Act 1979 or the Banking Act 1987.

(2)   In sub-paragraph (1)(a) "regulated activity" has the meaning given by section 22 of the Financial Services and Markets Act 2000 2000, taken with Schedule 2 to that Act and any order under that section.

Electronic money institutions

5.   This paragraph applies where either the company or the supplier is an electronic money institution within the meaning of the Electronic Money Regulations 2011 (S.I. 2011/99) (see regulation 2 of those Regulations).

Investment banks and investment firms

6.—   (1)   This paragraph applies where either the company or the supplier is an investment bank or an investment firm.

        (2)   In this paragraph—

                "investment bank" means a company or other entity that has permission under Part 4A of the Financial Services and Markets Act 2000 to carry on the regulated activity of—

                (a)   safeguarding and administering investments,
                (b)   managing an AIF or a UCITS,
                (c)   acting as trustee or depositary of an AIF or a UCITS,
                (d)   dealing in investments as principal, or
                (e)   dealing in investments as agent;

                        "investment firm" has the same meaning as in the Banking Act 2009 (see section 258A of that Act), disregarding any order made under section 258A(2)(b) of that Act;

                        "regulated activity" has the meaning given by section 22 of the Financial Services and Markets Act 2000, taken with Schedule 2 to that Act and any order under that section.

Payment institutions

7.   This paragraph applies where either the company or the supplier is an authorised payment institution, a small payment institution or a registered account information service provider within the meaning of the Payment Services Regulations 2017 (S.I. 2017/752) (see regulation 2 of those Regulations).

Operators of payment systems, infrastructure providers etc

8.   This paragraph applies where either the company or the supplier is—

        (a)   the operator of a payment system or an infrastructure provider within the meaning of Part 5 of the Financial Services (Banking Reform) Act 2013 (see section 42 of that Act), or

        (b)   an infrastructure company within the meaning of Part 6 of that Act (see section 112 of that Act).

Recognised investment exchanges etc

9.   This paragraph applies where either the company or the supplier is a recognised investment exchange, a recognised clearing house or a recognised CSD within the meaning of the Financial Services and Markets Act 2000 (see section 285 of that Act).

Securitisation companies

10.   This paragraph applies where either the company or the supplier is a securitisation company within the meaning of the Taxation of Securitisation Companies Regulations 2006 (S.I. 2006/3296) (see regulation 4 of those Regulations).

Overseas activities

11.   This paragraph applies where either the company or the supplier does or has done anything outside the United Kingdom which, if done in the United Kingdom, would cause any of the preceding paragraphs of this Part of this Schedule to apply.

PART 3
CONTRACTS INVOLVING FINANCIAL SERVICES

Introductory

12.   To the extent that anything to which any of paragraphs 13 to 18 applies is a contract for the supply of goods or services, section 233B does not apply in relation to it.

Financial contracts

13.— (1)   This paragraph applies to a financial contract.

(2)   "Financial contract" means—

(a)   a contract for the provision of financial services consisting of—

(i)   lending (including the factoring and financing of commercial transactions),

(ii)   financial leasing, or

(iii)   providing guarantees or commitments;

(b)   a securities contract, including—

(i)   a contract for the purchase, sale or loan of a security or group or index of securities;

(ii)   an option on a security or group or index of securities;

(iii)   a repurchase or reverse repurchase transaction on any such security, group or index;

(c)   a commodities contract, including—

(i)   a contract for the purchase, sale or loan of a commodity or group or index of commodities for future delivery;

(ii)   an option on a commodity or group or index of commodities;

(iii)   a repurchase or reverse repurchase transaction on any such commodity, group or index;

(d)   a futures or forwards contract, including a contract (other than a commodities contract) for the purchase, sale or transfer of a commodity or property of any other description, service, right or interest for a specified price at a future date;

(e)   a swap agreement, including—

(i)   a swap or option relating to interest rates, spot or other foreign exchange agreements, currency, an equity index or equity, a debt index or debt, commodity indexes or commodities, weather, emissions or inflation;

(ii)   a total return, credit spread or credit swap;

(iii)   any agreement or transaction similar to an agreement that is referred to in sub-paragraph (i) or (ii) and is the subject of recurrent dealing in the swaps or derivatives markets;

(f)   an inter-bank borrowing agreement where the term of the borrowing is three months or less;

(g)   a master agreement for any of the contracts or agreements referred to in paragraphs (a) to (f).

(3)   For the purposes of this paragraph "commodities" includes—

(a)   units recognised for compliance with the requirements of EU Directive 2003/87/EC establishing a scheme for greenhouse gas emission allowance trading,

(b)   allowances under paragraph 5 of Schedule 2 to the Climate Change Act 2008 relating to a trading scheme dealt with under Part 1 of that Schedule (schemes limiting activities relating to emissions of greenhouse gas), and

(c)   renewables obligation certificates issued—

(i)   by the Gas and Electricity Markets Authority under an order made under section 32B of the Electricity Act 1989, or

(ii)   by the Northern Ireland Authority for Utility Regulation under the Energy (Northern Ireland) Order 2003 (S.I. 2003/419 (NI 6)) and pursuant to an order made under Articles 52 to 55F of that Order.

Securities financing transactions

14.— (1) This paragraph applies to—

     (a) a securities financing transaction, and

     (b) a master agreement for securities financing transactions.

    (2) "Securities financing transaction" has the meaning given by Article 3(11) of Regulation (EU) 2015/2365 on the transparency of securities financing transactions.

    (3) But for the purposes of that Article as it applies for the purposes of this paragraph, references to "commodities" in that Regulation are to be taken as including the units, allowances and certificates referred to in paragraph 13(3)(a) to (c).

Derivatives

15.— (1) This paragraph applies to—

     (a) a derivative, and

     (b) a master agreement for derivatives.

    (2) "Derivative" has the meaning given by Article 2(5) of Regulation (EU) No 648/2012.

Spot contracts

16.— (1) This paragraph applies to—

     (a) a spot contract, and

     (b) a master agreement for spot contracts.

    (2) "Spot contract" has the meaning given by Article 7(2) or 10(2) of Commission Delegated Regulation of 25.4.2016 supplementing Directive 2014/65/EU of the European Parliament and of the Council as regards organisational requirements and operating conditions for investment firms and defined terms for the purposes of that Directive.

Capital market investments

17.— (1) This paragraph applies to an agreement which is, or forms part of, an arrangement involving the issue of a capital market investment.

    (2) "Capital market investment" has the meaning given by paragraph 14 of Schedule ZA1.

Contracts forming part of a public-private partnership

18. This paragraph applies to a contract forming part of a public-private partnership project within the meaning given by paragraph 16 of Schedule ZA1.

PART 4
OTHER EXCLUSIONS

Financial markets and insolvency

19. Nothing in section 233B affects the operation of—

    (a) Part 7 of the Companies Act 1989 (financial markets and insolvency),

    (b) the Financial Markets and Insolvency Regulations 1996 (S.I. 1996/1469),

    (c) the Financial Markets and Insolvency (Settlement Finality) Regulations 1999 (S.I. 1999/2979), or

    (d) the Financial Collateral Arrangements (No 2) Regulations 2003 (S.I. 2003/3226).

Set-off and netting

20. Nothing in section 233B affects any set-off or netting arrangements (within the meanings given by section 48(1)(c) and (d) of the Banking Act 2009).

Aircraft equipment

21. Nothing in section 233B affects the International Interests in Aircraft Equipment (Cape Town Convention) Regulations 2015 (S.I. 2015/912).

SCHEDULE 4ZA

CONDITIONS FOR MAKING A DEBT RELIEF ORDER

PART 1
CONDITIONS WHICH MUST BE MET

Connection with England and Wales

1.— (1) The debtor—
    (a) is domiciled in England and Wales on the application date; or
    (b) at any time during the period of three years ending with that date—
        (i) was ordinarily resident, or had a place of residence, in England and Wales; or
        (ii) carried on business in England and Wales.
  (2) The reference in sub-paragraph (1)(b)(ii) to the debtor carrying on business includes—
    (a) the carrying on of business by a firm or partnership of which he is a member;
    (b) the carrying on of business by an agent or manager for him or for such a firm or partnership.

Debtor's previous insolvency history

2. The debtor is not, on the determination date—
  (a) an undischarged bankrupt;
  (b) subject to an interim order or voluntary arrangement under Part 8; or
  (c) subject to a bankruptcy restrictions order or a debt relief restrictions order.

3. A bankruptcy application under Part 9—
  (a) has not been made before the determination date; or
  (b) has been so made, but proceedings on the application have been finally disposed of before that date.

4. A creditor's petition for the debtor's bankruptcy under Part 9—
  (a) has not been presented against the debtor at any time before the determination date;
  (b) has been so presented, but proceedings on the petition have been finally disposed of before that date; or
  (c) has been so presented and proceedings in relation to the petition remain before the court at that date, but the person who presented the petition has consented to the making of an application for a debt relief order.

5. A debt relief order has not been made in relation to the debtor in the period of six years ending with the determination date.

Limit on debtor's overall indebtedness

6.— (1) The total amount of the debtor's debts on the determination date, other than unliquidated debts and excluded debts, does not exceed the prescribed amount.
  (2) For this purpose an unliquidated debt is a debt that is not for a liquidated sum payable to a creditor either immediately or at some future certain time.

Limit on debtor's monthly surplus income

7.— (1) The debtor's monthly surplus income (if any) on the determination date does not exceed the prescribed amount.
  (2) For this purpose "monthly surplus income" is the amount by which a person's monthly income exceeds the amount necessary for the reasonable domestic needs of himself and his family.
  (3) The rules may—
    (a) make provision as to how the debtor's monthly surplus income is to be determined;
    (b) provide that particular descriptions of income are to be excluded for the purposes of this paragraph.

Limit on value of debtor's property

8.— (1) The total value of the debtor's property on the determination date does not exceed the prescribed amount.

    (2) The rules may—

        (a) make provision as to how the value of a person's property is to be determined;

        (b) provide that particular descriptions of property are to be excluded for the purposes of this paragraph.

PART 2
OTHER CONDITIONS

9.— (1) The debtor has not entered into a transaction with any person at an undervalue during the period between—

        (a) the start of the period of two years ending with the application date; and

        (b) the determination date.

    (2) For this purpose a debtor enters into a transaction with a person at an undervalue if—

        (a) he makes a gift to that person or he otherwise enters into a transaction with that person on terms that provide for him to receive no consideration;

        (b) he enters into a transaction with that person in consideration of marriage or the formation of a civil partnership; or

        (c) he enters into a transaction with that person for a consideration the value of which, in money or money's worth, is significantly less than the value, in money or money's worth, of the consideration provided by the individual.

10.— (1) The debtor has not given a preference to any person during the period between—

        (a) the start of the period of two years ending with the application date; and

        (b) the determination date.

    (2) For this purpose a debtor gives a preference to a person if—

        (a) that person is one of the debtor's creditors to whom a qualifying debt is owed or is a surety or guarantor for any such debt, and

        (b) the debtor does anything or suffers anything to be done which (in either case) has the effect of putting that person into a position which, in the event that a debt relief order is made in relation to the debtor, will be better than the position he would have been in if that thing had not been done.

SCHEDULE 4ZB

DEBT RELIEF RESTRICTIONS ORDERS AND UNDERTAKINGS

Debt relief restrictions order

1.— (1) A debt relief restrictions order may be made by the court in relation to a person in respect of whom a debt relief order has been made.

    (2) An order may be made only on the application of—

        (a) the Secretary of State, or

        (b) the official receiver acting on a direction of the Secretary of State.

Grounds for making order

2.— (1) The court shall grant an application for a debt relief restrictions order if it thinks it appropriate to do so having regard to the conduct of the debtor (whether before or after the making of the debt relief order).

    (2) The court shall, in particular, take into account any of the following kinds of behaviour on the part of the debtor—

        (a) failing to keep records which account for a loss of property by the debtor, or by a business carried on by him, where the loss occurred in the period beginning two years before the application date for the debt relief order and ending with the date of the application for the debt relief restrictions order;

(b)   failing to produce records of that kind on demand by the official receiver;

(c)   entering into a transaction at an undervalue in the period beginning two years before the application date for the debt relief order and ending with the date of the determination of that application;

(d)   giving a preference in the period beginning two years before the application date for the debt relief order and ending with the date of the determination of that application;

(e)   making an excessive pension contribution;

(f)   a failure to supply goods or services that were wholly or partly paid for;

(g)   trading at a time, before the date of the determination of the application for the debt relief order, when the debtor knew or ought to have known that he was himself to be unable to pay his debts;

(h)   incurring, before the date of the determination of the application for the debt relief order, a debt which the debtor had no reasonable expectation of being able to pay;

(i)   failing to account satisfactorily to the court or the official receiver for a loss of property or for an insufficiency of property to meet his debts;

(j)   carrying on any gambling, rash and hazardous speculation or unreasonable extravagance which may have materially contributed to or increased the extent of his inability to pay his debts before the application date for the debt relief order or which took place between that date and the date of the determination of the application for the debt relief order;

(k)   neglect of business affairs of a kind which may have materially contributed to or increased the extent of his inability to pay his debts;

(l)   fraud or fraudulent breach of trust;

(m)   failing to co-operate with the official receiver.

(3)   The court shall also, in particular, consider whether the debtor was an undischarged bankrupt at some time during the period of six years ending with the date of the application for the debt relief order.

(4)   For the purposes of sub-paragraph (2)—

"excessive pension contribution" shall be construed in accordance with section 342A;

"preference" shall be construed in accordance with paragraph 10(2) of Schedule 4ZA;

"undervalue" shall be construed in accordance with paragraph 9(2) of that Schedule.

Timing of application for order

3.   An application for a debt relief restrictions order in respect of a debtor may be made—

(a)   at any time during the moratorium period relating to the debt relief order in question, or

(b)   after the end of that period, but only with the permission of the court.

Duration of order

4.—   (1)   A debt relief restrictions order—

(a)   comes into force when it is made, and

(b)   ceases to have effect at the end of a date specified in the order.

(2)   The date specified in a debt relief restrictions order under sub-paragraph (1)(b) must not be—

(a)   before the end of the period of two years beginning with the date on which the order is made, or

(b)   after the end of the period of 15 years beginning with that date.

Interim debt relief restrictions order

5.—   (1)   This paragraph applies at any time between—

(a)   the institution of an application for a debt relief restrictions order, and

(b)   the determination of the application.

(2) The court may make an interim debt relief restrictions order if the court thinks that—

    (a) there are prima facie grounds to suggest that the application for the debt relief restrictions order will be successful, and

    (b) it is in the public interest to make an interim debt relief restrictions order.

(3) An interim debt relief restrictions order may only be made on the application of—

    (a) the Secretary of State, or

    (b) the official receiver acting on a direction of the Secretary of State.

(4) An interim debt relief restrictions order—

    (a) has the same effect as a debt relief restrictions order, and

    (b) comes into force when it is made.

(5) An interim debt relief restrictions order ceases to have effect—

    (a) on the determination of the application for the debt relief restrictions order,

    (b) on the acceptance of a debt relief restrictions undertaking made by the debtor, or

    (c) if the court discharges the interim debt relief restrictions order on the application of the person who applied for it or of the debtor.

6.— (1) This paragraph applies to a case in which both an interim debt relief restrictions order and a debt relief restrictions order are made.

    (2) Paragraph 4(2) has effect in relation to the debt relief restrictions order as if a reference to the date of that order were a reference to the date of the interim debt relief restrictions order.

Debt relief restrictions undertaking

7.— (1) A debtor may offer a debt relief restrictions undertaking to the Secretary of State.

    (2) In determining whether to accept a debt relief restrictions undertaking the Secretary of State shall have regard to the matters specified in paragraph 2(2) and (3).

8. A reference in an enactment to a person in respect of whom a debt relief restrictions order has effect (or who is "the subject of" a debt relief restrictions order) includes a reference to a person in respect of whom a debt relief restrictions undertaking has effect.

9.— (1) A debt relief restrictions undertaking—

    (a) comes into force on being accepted by the Secretary of State, and

    (b) ceases to have effect at the end of a date specified in the undertaking.

    (2) The date specified under sub-paragraph (1)(b) must not be—

    (a) before the end of the period of two years beginning with the date on which the undertaking is accepted, or

    (b) after the end of the period of 15 years beginning with that date.

    (3) On an application by the debtor the court may—

    (a) annul a debt relief restrictions undertaking;

    (b) provide for a debt relief restrictions undertaking to cease to have effect before the date specified under sub-paragraph (1)(b).

Effect of revocation of debt relief order

10. Unless the court directs otherwise, the revocation at any time of a debt relief order does not—

    (a) affect the validity of any debt relief restrictions order, interim debt relief restrictions order or debt relief restrictions undertaking which is in force in respect of the debtor;

    (b) prevent the determination of any application for a debt relief restrictions order, or an interim debt relief restrictions order, in relation to the debtor that was instituted before that time;

    (c) prevent the acceptance of a debt relief restrictions undertaking that was offered before that time; or

    (d) prevent the institution of an application for a debt relief restrictions order or interim debt relief restrictions order in respect of the debtor, or the offer or acceptance of a debt relief restrictions undertaking by the debtor, after that time.

SCHEDULE 4A

BANKRUPTCY RESTRICTIONS ORDER AND UNDERTAKING

Section 281A

Bankruptcy restrictions order

1.— (1) A bankruptcy restrictions order may be made by the court.

(2) An order may be made only on the application of—

    (a) the Secretary of State, or

    (b) the official receiver acting on a direction of the Secretary of State.

Grounds for making order

2.— (1) The court shall grant an application for a bankruptcy restrictions order if it thinks it appropriate having regard to the conduct of the bankrupt (whether before or after the making of the bankruptcy order).

(2) The court shall, in particular, take into account any of the following kinds of behaviour on the part of the bankrupt—

    (a) failing to keep records which account for a loss of property by the bankrupt, or by a business carried on by him, where the loss occurred in the period beginning 2 years before the making of the bankruptcy application or (as the case may be) the presentation of the bankruptcy petition and ending with the date of the application for the bankruptcy restrictions order;

    (b) failing to produce records of that kind on demand by the official receiver or the trustee;

    (c) entering into a transaction at an undervalue;

    (d) giving a preference;

    (e) making an excessive pension contribution;

    (f) a failure to supply goods or services which were wholly or partly paid for which gave rise to a claim provable in the bankruptcy;

    (g) trading at a time before commencement of the bankruptcy when the bankrupt knew or ought to have known that he was himself to be unable to pay his debts;

    (h) incurring, before commencement of the bankruptcy, a debt which the bankrupt had no reasonable expectation of being able to pay;

    (i) failing to account satisfactorily to the court, the official receiver or the trustee for a loss of property or for an insufficiency of property to meet bankruptcy debts;

    (j) carrying on any gambling, rash and hazardous speculation or unreasonable extravagance which may have materially contributed to or increased the extent of the bankruptcy or which took place between the making of the bankruptcy application or (as the case may be) the presentation of the bankruptcy petition and commencement of the bankruptcy;

    (k) neglect of business affairs of a kind which may have materially contributed to or increased the extent of the bankruptcy;

    (l) fraud or fraudulent breach of trust;

    (m) failing to cooperate with the official receiver or the trustee.

(3) The court shall also, in particular, consider whether the bankrupt was an undischarged bankrupt at some time during the period of six years ending with the date of the bankruptcy to which the application relates.

(4) For the purpose of sub-paragraph (2)—

    ...

    "excessive pension contribution" shall be construed in accordance with section 342A, "preference" shall be construed in accordance with section 340, and "undervalue" shall be construed in accordance with section 339.

Timing of application for order

3.—   (1)   An application for a bankruptcy restrictions order in respect of a bankrupt must be made—
       (a)   before the end of the period of one year beginning with the date on which the bankruptcy commences, or
       (b)   with the permission of the court.
       (2)   The period specified in sub-paragraph (1)(a) shall cease to run in respect of a bankrupt while the period set for his discharge is suspended under section 279(3).

Duration of order

4.—   (1)   A bankruptcy restrictions order—
       (a)   shall come into force when it is made, and
       (b)   shall cease to have effect at the end of a date specified in the order.
       (2)   The date specified in a bankruptcy restrictions order under sub-paragraph (1)(b) must not be—
       (a)   before the end of the period of two years beginning with the date on which the order is made, or
       (b)   after the end of the period of 15 years beginning with that date.

Interim bankruptcy restrictions order

5.—   (1)   This paragraph applies at any time between—
       (a)   the institution of an application for a bankruptcy restrictions order, and
       (b)   the determination of the application.
       (2)   The court may make an interim bankruptcy restrictions order if the court thinks that—
       (a)   there are prima facie grounds to suggest that the application for the bankruptcy restrictions order will be successful, and
       (b)   it is in the public interest to make an interim order.
       (3)   An interim order may be made only on the application of—
       (a)   the Secretary of State, or
       (b)   the official receiver acting on a direction of the Secretary of State.
       (4)   An interim order—
       (a)   shall have the same effect as a bankruptcy restrictions order, and
       (b)   shall come into force when it is made.
       (5)   An interim order shall cease to have effect—
       (a)   on the determination of the application for the bankruptcy restrictions order,
       (b)   on the acceptance of a bankruptcy restrictions undertaking made by the bankrupt, or
       (c)   if the court discharges the interim order on the application of the person who applied for it or of the bankrupt.

6.—   (1)   This paragraph applies to a case in which both an interim bankruptcy restrictions order and a bankruptcy restrictions order are made.
       (2)   Paragraph 4(2) shall have effect in relation to the bankruptcy restrictions order as if a reference to the date of that order were a reference to the date of the interim order.

Bankruptcy restrictions undertaking

7.—   (1)   A bankrupt may offer a bankruptcy restrictions undertaking to the Secretary of State.
       (2)   In determining whether to accept a bankruptcy restrictions undertaking the Secretary of State shall have regard to the matters specified in paragraph 2(2) and (3).

8.   A reference in an enactment to a person in respect of whom a bankruptcy restrictions order has effect (or who is "the subject of" a bankruptcy restrictions order) includes a reference to a person in respect of whom a bankruptcy restrictions undertaking has effect.

9.—   (1)   A bankruptcy restrictions undertaking—
       (a)   shall come into force on being accepted by the Secretary of State, and
       (b)   shall cease to have effect at the end of a date specified in the undertaking.
       (2)   The date specified under sub-paragraph (1)(b) must not be—

      (a)   before the end of the period of two years beginning with the date on which the under-taking is accepted, or

      (b)   after the end of the period of 15 years beginning with that date.

    (3)   On an application by the bankrupt the court may—

      (a)   annul a bankruptcy restrictions undertaking;

      (b)   provide for a bankruptcy restrictions undertaking to cease to have effect before the date specified under sub-paragraph (1)(b).

Effect of annulment of bankruptcy order

10.   Where a bankruptcy order is annulled under section 282(1)(a) or (2)—

    (a)   any bankruptcy restrictions order, interim order or undertaking which is in force in respect of the bankrupt shall be annulled,

    (b)   no new bankruptcy restrictions order or interim order may be made in respect of the bankrupt, and

    (c)   no new bankruptcy restrictions undertaking by the bankrupt may be accepted.

11.   Where a bankruptcy order is annulled under section 261 … or 282(1)(b)—

    (a)   the annulment shall not affect any bankruptcy restrictions order, interim order or undertaking in respect of the bankrupt,

    (b)   the court may make a bankruptcy restrictions order in relation to the bankrupt on an application instituted before the annulment,

    (c)   the Secretary of State may accept a bankruptcy restrictions undertaking offered before the annulment, and

    (d)   an application for a bankruptcy restrictions order or interim order in respect of the bankrupt may not be instituted after the annulment.

Registration

12.   The Secretary of State shall maintain a register of—

    (a)   bankruptcy restrictions orders,

    (b)   interim bankruptcy restrictions orders, and

    (c)   bankruptcy restrictions undertakings.

SCHEDULE 5

POWERS OF TRUSTEE IN BANKRUPTCY

Section 314

PART I

…

1.   Power to carry on any business of the bankrupt so far as may be necessary for winding it up beneficially and so far as the trustee is able to do so without contravening any requirement imposed by or under any enactment.

2.   Power to bring, institute or defend any action or legal proceedings relating to the property comprised in the bankrupt's estate.

2A.   Power to bring legal proceedings under section 339, 340 or 423.

3.   Power to accept as the consideration for the sale of any property comprised in the bankrupt's estate a sum of money payable at a future time subject to such stipulations as to security or otherwise as the creditors' committee or the court thinks fit.

4.   Power to mortgage or pledge any part of the property comprised in the bankrupt's estate for the purpose of raising money for the payment of his debts.

5.   Power, where any right, option or other power forms part of the bankrupt's estate, to make payments or incur liabilities with a view to obtaining, for the benefit of the creditors, any property which is the subject of the right, option or power.

6.   …

7.   Power to make such compromise or other arrangement as may be thought expedient with creditors, or persons claiming to be creditors, in respect of bankruptcy debts.

8.   Power to make such compromise or other arrangement as may be thought expedient with respect to any claim arising out of or incidental to the bankrupt's estate made or capable of being made on the trustee by any person ...

PART II

...

9.   Power to sell any part of the property for the time being comprised in the bankrupt's estate, including the goodwill and book debts of any business.

9A.   Power to refer to arbitration, or compromise on such terms as may be agreed, any debts, claims or liabilities subsisting or supposed to subsist between the bankrupt and any person who may have incurred any liability to the bankrupt.

9B.   Power to make such compromise or other arrangement as may be thought expedient with respect to any claim arising out of or incidental to the bankrupt's estate made or capable of being made by the trustee on any person.

10.   Power to give receipts for any money received by him, being receipts which effectually discharge the person paying the money from all responsibility in respect of its application.

11.   Power to prove, rank, claim and draw a dividend in respect of such debts due to the bankrupt as are comprised in his estate.

12.   Power to exercise in relation to any property comprised in the bankrupt's estate any powers the capacity to exercise which is vested in him under Parts VIII to XI of this Act.

13.   Power to deal with any property comprised in the estate to which the bankrupt is beneficially entitled as tenant in tail in the same manner as the bankrupt might have dealt with it.

PART III

...

14.   For the purposes of, or in connection with, the exercise of any of his powers under Parts VIII to XI of this Act, the trustee may, by his official name—

(a)   hold property of every description,

(b)   make contracts,

(c)   sue and be sued,

(d)   enter into engagements binding on himself and, in respect of the bankrupt's estate, on his successors in office,

(e)   employ an agent,

(f)   execute any power of attorney, deed or other instrument;

and he may do any other act which is necessary or expedient for the purposes of or in connection with the exercise of those powers.

SCHEDULE 6

THE CATEGORIES OF PREFERENTIAL DEBTS

Section 386

1–7. ...

Category 4:
Contributions to occupational pension schemes, etc

8.   Any sum which is owed by the debtor and is a sum to which Schedule 4 to the Pension Schemes Act 1993 applies (contributions to occupational pension schemes and state scheme premiums).

Category 5:
Remuneration, etc, of employees

9.   So much of any amount which—

(a)   is owed by the debtor to a person who is or has been an employee of the debtor, and

(b)   is payable by way of remuneration in respect of the whole or any part of the period of 4 months next before the relevant date,

as does not exceed so much as may be prescribed by order made by the Secretary of State.

10.   An amount owed by way of accrued holiday remuneration, in respect of any period of employment before the relevant date, to a person whose employment by the debtor has been terminated, whether before, on or after that date.

11.   So much of any sum owed in respect of money advanced for the purpose as has been applied for the payment of a debt which, if it had not been paid, would have been a debt falling within paragraph 9 or 10.

12.   So much of any amount which—

(a)   is ordered (whether before or after the relevant date) to be paid by the debtor under the Reserve Forces (Safeguard of Employment) Act 1985, and

(b)   is so ordered in respect of a default made by the debtor before that date in the discharge of his obligations under that Act,

as does no exceed such amount as may be prescribed by order made by the Secretary of State.

Interpretation for Category 5

13.—   (1)   For the purposes of paragraphs 9 to 12, a sum is payable by the debtor to a person by way of remuneration in respect of any period if—

(a)   it is paid as wages or salary (whether payable for time or for piece work or earned wholly or partly by way of commission) in respect of services rendered to the debtor in that period, or

(b)   it is an amount falling within the following sub-paragraph and is payable by the debtor in respect of that period.

(2)   An amount falls within this sub-paragraph if it is—

(a)   a guarantee payment under Part III of the Employment Rights Act 1996 (employee without work to do);

(b)   any payment for time off under section 53 (time off to look for work or arrange training) or section 56 (time off for ante-natal care) of that Act or under section 169 of the Trade Union and Labour Relations (Consolidation) Act 1992 (time off for carrying out trade union duties etc);

(c)   remuneration on suspension on medical grounds, or on maternity grounds, under Part VII of the Employment Rights Act 1996; or

(d)   remuneration under a protective award under section 189 of the Trade Union and Labour Relations (Consolidation) Act 1992 (redundancy dismissal with compensation).

14.—   (1)   This paragraph relates to a case in which a person's employment has been terminated by or in consequence of his employer going into liquidation or being made bankrupt or (his employer being a company not in liquidation) by or in consequence of—

(a)   a receiver being appointed as mentioned in section 40 of this Act (debenture-holders secured by floating charge), or

(b)   the appointment of a receiver under section 53(6) or 54(5) of this Act (Scottish company with property subject to floating charge), or

(c)   the taking of possession by debenture-holders (so secured), as mentioned in section 754 of the Companies Act 2006.

(2)   For the purposes of paragraphs 9 to 12, holiday remuneration is deemed to have accrued to that person in respect of any period of employment if, by virtue of his contract of

employment or of any enactment that remuneration would have accrued in respect of that period if his employment had continued until he became entitled to be allowed the holiday.

(3)   The reference in sub-paragraph (2) to any enactment includes an order or direction made under an enactment.

15.   Without prejudice to paragraphs 13 and 14—

(a)   any remuneration payable by the debtor to a person in respect of a period of holiday or of absence from work through sickness or other good cause is deemed to be wages or (as the case may be) salary in respect of services rendered to the debtor in that period, ...

(b)   ...

Category 6:
Levies on coal and steel production

15A.   Any sums due at the relevant date from the debtor in respect of—

(a)   the levies on the production of coal and steel referred to in Articles 49 and 50 of the E.C.S.C. Treaty, or

(b)   any surcharge for delay provided for in Article 50(3) of that Treaty and Article 6 of Decision 3/52 of the High Authority of the Coal and Steel Community.

Category 6A: Debts owed to the Financial Services Compensation Scheme

15AA.   Any debt owed by the debtor to the scheme manager of the Financial Services Compensation Scheme under section 215(2A) of the Financial Services and Markets Act 2000.

Category 7: Deposits covered by Financial Services Compensation Scheme

15B.   So much of any amount owed at the relevant date by the debtor in respect of an eligible deposit as does not exceed the compensation that would be payable in respect of the deposit under the Financial Services Compensation Scheme to the person or persons to whom the amount is owed.

Category 8: Other deposits

15BA.   So much of any amount owed at the relevant date by the debtor to one or more eligible persons in respect of an eligible deposit as exceeds any compensation that would be payable in respect of the deposit under the Financial Services Compensation Scheme to that person or those persons.

15BB.   An amount owed at the relevant date by the debtor to one or more eligible persons in respect of a deposit that—

(a)   was made through a non-UK branch of a credit institution authorised by the competent authority of the United Kingdom, and

(b)   would have been an eligible deposit if it had been made through a UK branch of that credit institution.

Interpretation for Categories 6A, 7 and 8

15C.—   (A1)   In paragraph 15AA "the scheme manager" has the meaning given in section 212(1) of the Financial Services and Markets Act 2000.

(1)   In paragraphs 15B to 15BB "eligible deposit" means a deposit in respect of which the person, or any of the persons, to whom it is owed would be eligible for compensation under the Financial Services Compensation Scheme.

(2)   For the purposes of those paragraphs and this paragraph a "deposit" means rights of the kind described in—

(a)   paragraph 22 of Schedule 2 to the Financial Services and Markets Act 2000 (deposits), or

(b)   section 1(2)(b) of the Dormant Bank and Building Society Accounts Act 2008 (balances transferred under that Act to authorised reclaim fund).

(3)   In paragraphs 15BA and 15BB, "eligible person" means—

(a)   an individual, or

   (b)   any micro, small and medium-sized enterprise, as defined with regard to the annual
         turn-over criterion referred to in Article 2(1) of the Annex to Commission recommen-
         dation 2003/361/EC.
(4)   In paragraph 15BB—
   (a)   "credit institution" has the meaning given in Article 4.1(1) of the capital requirements
         regulation;
   (b)   "non-UK branch" means a branch, as defined in Article 4.1(17) of the capital require-
         ments regulation, which is established outside the United Kingdom;
   (c)   "UK branch" means a branch, as so defined, which is established in the United
         Kingdom,
   and for this purpose "the capital requirements regulation" means Regulation (EU) No 575/
   2013 of the European Parliament and of the Council of 26th June 2013 on prudential
   requirements for credit institutions and investment firms and amending Regulation (EU) No
   648/2012, as it forms part of retained EU law.

Category 9: Certain HMRC debts

15D.— (1)   Any amount owed at the relevant date by the debtor to the Commissioners in respect of—
   (a)   value added tax, or
   (b)   a relevant deduction.
(2)   In sub-paragraph (1), the reference to "any amount" is subject to any regulations under
      section 99(1) of the Finance Act 2020.
(3)   For the purposes of sub-paragraph (1)(b) a deduction is "relevant" if—
   (a)   the debtor is required, by virtue of an enactment, to make the deduction from a pay-
         ment made to another person and to pay an amount to the Commissioners on account
         of the deduction,
   (b)   the payment to the Commissioners is credited against any liabilities of the other per-
         son, and
   (c)   the deduction is of a kind specified in regulations under section 99(3) of the Finance
         Act 2020.
(4)   In this paragraph "the Commissioners" means the Commissioners for Her Majesty's
      Revenue and Customs.

Orders

16.   An order under paragraph 9 or 12—
   (a)   may contain such transitional provisions as may appear to the Secretary of State necessary
         or expedient;
   (b)   shall be made by statutory instrument subject to annulment in pursuance of a resolution of
         either House of Parliament.

SCHEDULES 7–14

...

Insolvency Act 1986 (Prescribed Part) Order 2003

S.I. 2003/2097

1.   Citation, Commencement and Interpretation

(1)   This Order may be cited as the Insolvency Act 1986 (Prescribed Part) Order 2003 and shall come into force on 15th September 2003.

(2)   In this order "the 1986 Act" means the Insolvency Act 1986.

2.   Minimum value of the company's net property

For the purposes of section 176A(3)(a) of the 1986 Act the minimum value of the company's net property is £10,000.

3.   Calculation of prescribed part

(1)   The prescribed part of the company's net property to be made available for the satisfaction of unsecured debts of the company pursuant to section 176A of the 1986 Act shall be calculated as follows—

(a)   where the company's net property does not exceed £10,000 in value, 50% of that property;

(b)   subject to paragraph (2), where the company's net property exceeds £10,000 in value the sum of—

(i)   50% of the first £10,000 in value; and

(ii)   20% of that part of the company's net property which exceeds £10,000 in value.

(2)   The value of the prescribed part of the company's net property to be made available for the satisfaction of unsecured debts of the company pursuant to section 176A shall not exceed £800,000.

Administration (Restrictions on Disposal etc to Connected Persons) Regulations 2021

S.I. 2021/427

PART 1
INTRODUCTORY PROVISIONS

1. Citation, commencement and application

(1) These Regulations may be cited as the Administration (Restrictions on Disposal etc to Connected Persons) Regulations 2021 and come into force on 30th April 2021.

(2) These Regulations apply only to administrations that commence on or after the day on which these Regulations come into force.

(3) For the purposes of this regulation an administration commences on—

(a) the appointment of an administrator under paragraph 14 or paragraph 22 of Schedule B1, or

(b) the making of an administration order.

2. Interpretation

In these Regulations—

"the Act" means the Insolvency Act 1986;

"the company" means the company whose business or assets are the subject of the substantial disposal;

"qualifying report" has the meaning given to it in regulation 5;

"previous report" has the meaning given to it in regulation 8;

"relevant property" means the property being disposed of, hired out or sold by the substantial disposal;

"Schedule B1" means Schedule B1 to the Act; and

"substantial disposal" has the meaning given to it in regulation 3.

PART 2
RESTRICTIONS ON DISPOSAL OF PROPERTY BY ADMINISTRATORS

CHAPTER 1
GENERAL

3. Conditions and requirements that apply in respect of a substantial disposal by the administrator

(1) An administrator must not make a substantial disposal unless either one of the following two conditions is met—

(a) the approval of the company's creditors for the making of that disposal has been obtained in accordance with regulation 4, or

(b) a qualifying report in respect of the making of that disposal has been obtained.

(2) Where the condition in paragraph (1)(b) is met and an administrator makes a substantial disposal the notification requirements in regulation 9 must be met.

(3) For the purposes of these Regulations a "substantial disposal"—

(a) means a disposal, hiring out or sale to one or more connected persons, during the period of 8 weeks beginning with the day on which the company enters administration, of what is, in the administrator's opinion, all or a substantial part of the company's business or assets, and

(b) includes a disposal which is effected by a series of transactions.

CHAPTER 2
CONDITION AS TO CREDITOR APPROVAL

4. Creditor approval

(1) The approval of the company's creditors is obtained in accordance with this regulation if the requirements specified in paragraph (2) are met.

(2) The requirements specified in this paragraph are as follows—

    (a) the administrator has—

        (i) included proposals for making the disposal (referred to for the purposes of this paragraph as "the proposal") in the statement of administrator's proposals referred to in paragraph 49 of Schedule B1, and

        (ii) subsequently sought a decision from the company's creditors as to whether they approve the proposal; and

    (b) the company's creditors approve the proposal—

        (i) without modification, or

        (ii) with modifications to which the administrator consents.

CHAPTER 3
CONDITION AS TO THE OBTAINING OF A QUALIFYING REPORT

5. Qualifying report: meaning of qualifying report

A qualifying report means a report—

    (a) whose contents the administrator has considered, and

    (b) which the administrator is satisfied—

        (i) meets the requirements specified in regulation 6, and

        (ii) includes the content specified in regulation 7.

6. Qualifying report: requirements to be met in connection with obtaining and considering the report

(1) The requirements specified in this regulation are as follows—

    (a) the report is—

        (i) obtained by a connected person,

        (ii) made by an individual who is an evaluator within the meaning given by Part 3 and in respect of whom the requirements specified in paragraph (2) are met, and

        (iii) given to the administrator;

    (b) the report—

        (i) is in writing,

        (ii) states the date on which it was made, and

        (iii) is authenticated by the evaluator; and

    (c) there have been no material changes since the date on which the report was made to—

        (i) the relevant property,

        (ii) the terms of the substantial disposal, or

        (iii) any circumstances relating to the substantial disposal.

(2) The requirements specified in this paragraph are that the administrator, having regard to the date on which the report was made, is satisfied that the individual making that report had sufficient relevant knowledge and experience to make a qualifying report.

(3) For the purposes of paragraph (1)(a)(ii), the individual making the report is to be taken to have met the requirements for being an evaluator in regulation 10(b) and (c) if the administrator has no reason to believe that the individual did not meet those requirements.

(4) For the purposes of this regulation—

    (a) the requirement that the report must be given to the administrator may be met by giving the administrator a copy of the report, and

      (b)   "authenticate" means to authenticate in accordance with rule 1.5 of the Insolvency (England and Wales) Rules 2016 or rule 1.6 of the Insolvency (Scotland) (Company Voluntary Arrangements and Administration) Rules 2018, as applicable.

7.   Qualifying report: required content

The report must contain the following—

      (a)   a statement that the person making the report is an evaluator within the meaning given by Part 3;

      (b)   a statement as to what relevant knowledge and experience the evaluator has to make the report;

      (c)   the following information concerning the professional indemnity insurance, within the meaning given by regulation 11, taken out by, or on behalf of, the evaluator—

            (i)   the name of the insurer;

            (ii)   the policy number;

            (iii)   the risks covered;

            (iv)   the amount covered; and

            (v)   exclusions from the cover;

      (d)   identification of the relevant property;

      (e)   either—

            (i)   the information specified in regulation 8(3) or, as the case may be,

            (ii)   a statement that the evaluator is satisfied that regulation 8 does not apply;

      (f)   a statement as to the nature of the consideration that is to be provided for the relevant property and the value of that consideration expressed in sterling;

      (g)   identification of the connected person and a statement as to their connection to the company;

      (h)   a statement that either—

            (i)   the evaluator is satisfied that the consideration to be provided for the relevant property and the grounds for the substantial disposal are reasonable in the circumstances or, as the case may be,

            (ii)   the evaluator is not satisfied that the consideration to be provided for the relevant property and the grounds for the substantial disposal are reasonable in the circumstances (a "case not made opinion"); and

      (i)   the evaluator's principal reasons for making the statement in sub-paragraph (h)(i) or (ii) and a summary of the evidence relied upon.

8.   Qualifying report: additional requirements where previous report obtained

    (1)   This regulation applies if, at any time before the date on which a report is made for the purpose of satisfying the condition in regulation 3(1)(b), the individual making that report—

      (a)   becomes aware that the connected person has obtained a previous report, or

      (b)   believes the connected person may have obtained a previous report (but this is subject to paragraph (2)).

    (2)   Where—

      (a)   the connected person makes a statement to the individual making the report as to whether they have obtained a previous report, or a specified number of previous reports, and

      (b)   the individual making the report has no reason to believe that statement is incorrect

the report must be made on the basis that the statement is correct.

    (3)   If this regulation applies, the report must contain the following—

      (a)   if the previous report has been given to the individual making the report, that previous report, a copy of that previous report, or details of the contents of that previous report which relate to the matters referred to in paragraph (6)(c), or

      (b)   if the previous report has not been given to the individual making the report—

            (i)   a statement that the previous report has not been obtained;

        (ii) the reasons why the previous report has not been obtained;

        (iii) details of any steps taken by the individual making the report to obtain the previous report; and

        (iv) if this regulation applies by virtue of the individual making the report having formed the belief referred to in paragraph (1)(b), the reasons why the individual making the report formed that belief.

(4) The requirement in paragraph (3)(b)(ii) may be met by including, if applicable, in the report a statement that the connected person claims that no previous report exists.

(5) Where this regulation applies in respect of two or more previous reports, the report must contain the matters specified in paragraph (3) in relation to each of the previous reports.

(6) For the purposes of this regulation, a "previous report" means an opinion obtained by the connected person which—

    (a) was obtained before the date on which the report is made,

    (b) is concerned with a disposal of property that is the same, or substantially the same, as the relevant property identified in the report, and

    (c) makes reference to whether the person making the previous report is satisfied that—

        (i) the grounds for the disposal are reasonable or, as the case may be, unreasonable, in the circumstances, or

        (ii) the consideration to be provided for the property is reasonable or, as the case may be, unreasonable, in the circumstances.

CHAPTER 4
NOTIFICATION OF QUALIFYING REPORT TO REGISTRAR OF COMPANIES AND TO CREDITORS

9.   **Notification requirements where a qualifying report is obtained**

(1) Where regulation 3(2) applies (administrator makes a substantial disposal following receipt of a qualifying report) the administrator must comply with the requirements specified in paragraphs (2) to (5).

(2) The administrator must send the following to the persons specified in paragraph (5)—

    (a) a copy of the report (excluding any information that, in the administrator's opinion, is confidential or commercially sensitive); and

    (b) where paragraph (3) applies, the information specified in paragraph (4).

(3) This paragraph applies where the qualifying report contains—

    (a) a case not made opinion within the meaning given by regulation 7(h)(ii), or

    (b) details of any previous report where the person making it was satisfied that—

        (i) the grounds for the disposal were not reasonable in the circumstances, or

        (ii) the consideration to be provided for the disposal was not reasonable in the circumstances.

(4) Where paragraph (3) applies the administrator must send together with each copy of the qualifying report a statement setting out their reasons for proceeding with the substantial disposal.

(5) A copy of the report and, where applicable, the additional information specified in paragraph (4) must be sent to—

    (a) the registrar of companies, and

    (b) every creditor of the company, other than an opted-out creditor, of whose claim and address the administrator is aware at the same time as the administrator complies with the requirement in paragraph 49(4)(a) and (b) of Schedule B1 to send a copy of the statement of their proposals to the registrar of companies and to creditors.

PART 3
THE EVALUATOR

10. Requirements for acting as evaluator

For the purposes of these Regulations an evaluator is an individual who—

(a) is satisfied that their relevant knowledge and experience is sufficient for the purposes of making a qualifying report,

(b) meets the—

(i) requirement as to insurance specified in regulation 11, and

(ii) requirement as to independence specified in regulation 12, and

(c) is not excluded from acting as an evaluator by virtue of regulation 13.

11. The requirement as to insurance

(1) An individual meets the requirement as to insurance if there is in force professional indemnity insurance in respect of that individual.

(2) For the purposes of this regulation "professional indemnity insurance" means insurance taken out by, or on behalf of, an individual in respect of potential liabilities to the administrator, the connected person, creditors or any other person, as a result of, or arising from, any matter stated by the individual in a report made by them for the purpose of satisfying the condition in regulation 3(1)(b).

12. Requirement as to independence

(1) An individual meets the requirement as to independence unless they—

(a) are connected with the company,

(b) are an associate of the connected person or connected with the connected person,

(c) know or have reason to believe that they have a conflict of interest with respect to the substantial disposal, or

(d) have, at any time during the period of 12 months ending with the date on which a report is made by that individual for the purpose of satisfying the condition in regulation 3(1)(b) provided advice to, and in respect of, the company or a connected person in relation to the company—

(i) in connection with, or in anticipation of, the commencement of an insolvency procedure under Parts A1 to 5 of the Act, or

(ii) in relation to corporate rescue or restructuring.

(2) In this regulation "conflict of interest" means a financial or other interest which is likely to affect prejudicially the independence of the individual in providing a report made for the purpose of satisfying the condition in regulation 3(1)(b).

(3) Nothing in this regulation limits the scope of an individual's obligation to comply with any professional or regulatory requirements to which that individual is subject.

13. Exclusion from providing the report

An individual is excluded from acting as an evaluator if—

(a) the individual is—

(i) the administrator,

(ii) an associate of the administrator, or

(iii) connected with a company with which the administrator is connected,

(b) the individual has at any time been convicted of an offence involving dishonesty or deception in the United Kingdom or any other jurisdiction and the conviction is not a spent conviction,

(c) the individual has at any time made a composition or arrangement with, or granted a trust deed for, the individual's creditors unless the individual has been discharged in respect of it,

(d) the individual has at any time been made bankrupt under the Act, the Bankruptcy (Scotland) Act 1985, the Bankruptcy (Scotland) Act 2016 or the Insolvency (Northern

Ireland) Order 1989, or sequestration of the individual's estate has been awarded and in either case—

    (i)   the individual has not been discharged, or

    (ii)   the individual has been made the subject of a bankruptcy restrictions order or an interim bankruptcy restrictions order under the Act, the Bankruptcy (Scotland) Act 1985, the Bankruptcy (Scotland) Act 2016 or the Insolvency (Northern Ireland) Order 1989, unless that order has ceased to have effect or has been annulled,

(e)   a moratorium period under a debt relief order under the Act or the Insolvency (Northern Ireland) Order 1989 applies in relation to the individual,

(f)   a debt relief restrictions order under the Act or the Insolvency (Northern Ireland) Order 1989 is in force in respect of the individual,

(g)   the individual is subject to—

    (i)   a disqualification order under section 1 of the Company Directors Disqualification Act 1986,

    (ii)   a disqualification undertaking under section 1A of that Act,

    (iii) a disqualification order under article 3 of the Company Directors Disqualification (Northern Ireland) Order 2002,

    (iv) a disqualification undertaking under article 4 of that Order, or

    (v)   an order made under section 429(2)(b) of the Act (failure to pay under county court administration order),

(h)   the individual has at any time been—

    (i)   removed from the office of charity trustee or trustee for a charity by an order made by the Charity Commission for England and Wales or the High Court on the grounds of any misconduct or mismanagement in the administration of the charity for which the individual was responsible or to which the individual was privy, or which the individual by the individual's conduct contributed to or facilitated, or

    (ii)   removed under section 34 of the Charities and Trustee Investment (Scotland) Act 2005 (powers of the Court of Session) from being concerned in the management or control of any charity or body,

(i)   the individual is a patient within the meaning of section 329(1) of the Mental Health (Care and Treatment) (Scotland) Act 2003 or has had a guardian appointed under the Adults with Incapacity (Scotland) Act 2000,

(j)   the individual lacks capacity, within the meaning of the Mental Capacity Act 2005, to provide the report, or

(k)   the individual has at any time been subject to any measures in another jurisdiction equivalent to those set out in sub-paragraphs (d) to (h) above.

Financial Services and Markets Act 2000

2000 c. 8

An Act to make provision about the regulation of financial services and markets; to provide for the transfer of certain statutory functions relating to building societies, friendly societies, industrial and provident societies and certain other mutual societies; and for connected purposes

[14th June 2000]

PART 1A
THE REGULATORS

CHAPTER 1
THE FINANCIAL CONDUCT AUTHORITY

The Financial Conduct Authority

1A.   The Financial Conduct Authority

(1)   The body corporate previously known as the Financial Services Authority is renamed as the Financial Conduct Authority.

(2)   The Financial Conduct Authority is in this Act referred to as "the FCA".

(3)   The FCA is to have the functions conferred on it by or under this Act.

(4)   The FCA must comply with the requirements as to its constitution set out in Schedule 1ZA.

(5)   Schedule 1ZA also makes provision about the status of the FCA and the exercise of certain of its functions.

(6)   References in this Act or any other enactment to functions conferred on the FCA by or under this Act include references to functions conferred on the FCA by or under—

(a)   the Insolvency Act 1986,

(b)   the Banking Act 2009,

(c)   the Financial Services Act 2012, ...

(cza) the Financial Guidance and Claims Act 2018,

(czb) the Civil Liability Act 2018,

(czc) the Financial Services and Markets Act 2023,

(ca)   the Alternative Investment Fund Managers Regulations 2013, ...

(d)   a qualifying provision that is specified, or of a description specified, for the purposes of this subsection by the Treasury by order, or

(e)   regulations made by the Treasury under section 8 of the European Union (Withdrawal) Act 2018.

The FCA's general duties

1B.   The FCA's general duties

(1)   In discharging its general functions the FCA must, so far as is reasonably possible, act in a way which—

(a)   is compatible with its strategic objective, and

(b)   advances one or more of its operational objectives.

(2)   The FCA's strategic objective is: ensuring that the relevant markets (see section 1F) function well.

(3)   The FCA's operational objectives are—

(a)   the consumer protection objective (see section 1C);

(b)   the integrity objective (see section 1D);

(c)   the competition objective (see section 1E).

(4)   The FCA must, so far as is compatible with acting in a way which advances the consumer protection objective or the integrity objective, discharge its general functions in a way which promotes effective competition in the interests of consumers.

(4A)   When discharging its general functions in the way mentioned in subsection (1) the FCA must, so far as reasonably possible, act in a way which, as a secondary objective, advances the competitiveness and growth objective (see section 1EB).

(5)   In discharging its general functions the FCA must have regard to—
        (a) the regulatory principles in section 3B, and
        (b) the importance of taking action intended to minimise the extent to which it is possible for a business carried on—
             (i)   by an authorised person or a recognised investment exchange, or
             (ii)   in contravention of the general prohibition,
             to be used for a purpose connected with financial crime.

(6)   For the purposes of this Chapter, the FCA's general functions are—
        (a) its function of making rules under this Act (considered as a whole),
        (aa) its function of making technical standards in accordance with Chapter 2A of Part 9A;
        (b) its function of preparing and issuing codes under this Act (considered as a whole),
        (c) its functions in relation to the giving of general guidance under this Act (considered as a whole), and
        (d) its function of determining the general policy and principles by reference to which it performs particular functions under this Act.

(7)   Except to the extent that an order under section 50 of the Financial Services Act 2012 (orders relating to mutual societies functions) so provides, the FCA's general functions do not include functions that are transferred functions within the meaning of section 52 of that Act.

(7A)   ...

(8)   "General guidance" has the meaning given in section 139B(5).

1C.   The consumer protection objective

(1)   The consumer protection objective is: securing an appropriate degree of protection for consumers.

(2)   In considering what degree of protection for consumers may be appropriate, the FCA must have regard to—
        (a) the differing degrees of risk involved in different kinds of investment or other transaction;
        (b) the differing degrees of experience and expertise that different consumers may have;
        (c) the needs that consumers may have for the timely provision of information and advice that is accurate and fit for purpose;
        (d) the general principle that consumers should take responsibility for their decisions;
        (e) the general principle that those providing regulated financial services should be expected to provide consumers with a level of care that is appropriate having regard to the degree of risk involved in relation to the investment or other transaction and the capabilities of the consumers in question;
        (f) the differing expectations that consumers may have in relation to different kinds of investment or other transaction;
        (g) ...
        (h) any information which the scheme operator of the ombudsman scheme has provided to the FCA pursuant to section 232A.

1D.   The integrity objective

(1)   The integrity objective is: protecting and enhancing the integrity of the UK financial system.

(2)   The "integrity" of the UK financial system includes—
        (a) its soundness, stability and resilience,
        (b) its not being used for a purpose connected with financial crime,

    (c)   its not being affected by contraventions by persons of Article 14 (prohibition of insider dealing and of unlawful disclosure of inside information) or Article 15 (prohibition of market manipulation) of the market abuse regulation,

    (d)   the orderly operation of the financial markets, and

    (e)   the transparency of the price formation process in those markets.

1E. **The competition objective**

(1) The competition objective is: promoting effective competition in the interests of consumers in the markets for—

    (a)   regulated financial services, or

    (b)   services provided by a recognised investment exchange in carrying on regulated activities in respect of which it is by virtue of section 285(2) exempt from the general prohibition.

(2) The matters to which the FCA may have regard in considering the effectiveness of competition in the market for any services mentioned in subsection (1) include—

    (a)   the needs of different consumers who use or may use those services, including their need for information that enables them to make informed choices,

    (b)   the ease with which consumers who may wish to use those services, including consumers in areas affected by social or economic deprivation, can access them,

    (c)   the ease with which consumers who obtain those services can change the person from whom they obtain them,

    (d)   the ease with which new entrants can enter the market, and

    (e)   how far competition is encouraging innovation.

1EB. **Competitiveness and growth objective**

The competitiveness and growth objective is: facilitating, subject to aligning with relevant international standards—

    (a)   the international competitiveness of the economy of the United Kingdom (including in particular the financial services sector), and

    (b)   its growth in the medium to long term.

Interpretation of terms used in relation to FCA's general duties

1F. **Meaning of "relevant markets" in strategic objective**

In section 1B(2) "the relevant markets" means—

    (a)   the financial markets,

    (b)   the markets for regulated financial services (see section 1H(2)), and

    (c)   the markets for services that are provided by persons other than authorised persons in carrying on regulated activities but are provided without contravening the general prohibition.

1G. **Meaning of "consumer"**

(1) In sections 1B to 1E "consumers" means persons …—

    (a)   who use, have used or may use—

        (i)   regulated financial services, or

        (ii)   services that are provided by persons other than authorised persons but are provided in carrying on regulated activities,

    (b)   who have relevant rights or interests in relation to any of those services,

    (c)   who have invested, or may invest, in financial instruments, …

    (d)   who have relevant rights or interests in relation to financial instruments, …

    (e)   who have rights, interests or obligations that are affected by the level of a regulated benchmark, or

    (f)   in respect of whom a person carries on an activity which is specified in article 89G of the Financial Services and Markets Act 2000 (Regulated Activities) Order 2001 (seeking out etc claims) whether that activity, as carried on by that person, is a regulated activity, or is, by reason of an exclusion provided for under the 2001 Order or the 2000 Act, not a regulated activity.

(2)   A person ("P") has a "relevant right or interest" in relation to any services within subsection (1)(a) if P has a right or interest—

    (a)   which is derived from, or is otherwise attributable to, the use of the services by others, or

    (b)   which may be adversely affected by the use of the services by persons acting on P's behalf or in a fiduciary capacity in relation to P.

(3)   If a person is providing a service within subsection (1)(a) as trustee, the persons who are, have been or may be beneficiaries of the trust are to be treated as persons who use, have used or may use the service.

(4)   A person who deals with another person ("B") in the course of B providing a service within subsection (1)(a) is to be treated as using the service.

(5)   A person ("P") has a "relevant right or interest" in relation to any financial instrument if P has—

    (a)   a right or interest which is derived from, or is otherwise attributable to, investment in the instrument by others, or

    (b)   a right or interest which may be adversely affected by the investment in the instrument by persons acting on P's behalf or in a fiduciary capacity in relation to P.

1H.   **Further interpretative provisions for sections 1B to 1G**

(1)   The following provisions have effect for the interpretation of sections 1B to 1G.

(2)   "Regulated financial services" means services provided—

    (a)   by authorised persons in carrying on regulated activities;

    (b)   ...

    (c)   by authorised persons in communicating, or approving the communication by others of, invitations or inducements to engage in investment activity or to engage in claims management activity;

    (d)   by authorised persons who are investment firms, or qualifying credit institutions, in providing relevant ancillary services;

    (e)   by persons acting as appointed representatives;

    (f)   by payment service providers in providing payment services;

    (g)   by electronic money issuers in issuing electronic money;

    (h)   by sponsors to issuers of securities;

    (i)   by primary information providers to persons who issue financial instruments.

(3)   "Financial crime" includes any offence involving—

    (a)   fraud or dishonesty,

    (b)   misconduct in, or misuse of information relating to, a financial market,

    (c)   handling the proceeds of crime, or

    (d)   the financing of terrorism.

(4)   "Offence" includes an act or omission which would be an offence if it had taken place in the United Kingdom.

(5)   "Issuer", except in the expression "electronic money issuer", has the meaning given in section 102A(6).

(6)   "Financial instrument" has the meaning given in section 102A(4).

(7)   "Securities" has the meaning given in section 102A(2).

(7A)   "Regulated benchmark" means a benchmark, as defined in section 22 ... (6A), in relation to which any provision made under section 22(1A) ... (c) has effect.

(8)   In this section—

    ...

    "electronic money" has the same meaning as in the Electronic Money Regulations 2011;

    "electronic money issuer" means a person who is an electronic money issuer as defined in regulation 2(1) of the Electronic Money Regulations 2011 other than a person falling within paragraph (f), (g) or (j) of the definition;

    "engage in claims management activity" has the meaning given in section 21;

"engage in investment activity" has the meaning given in section 21;

"financial instrument" has the meaning given in section 102A(4);

"payment services" has the same meaning as in the Payment Services Regulations 2017;

"payment service provider" means a person who is a payment service provider as defined in regulation 2(1) of the Payment Services Regulations 2017 other than a person falling within paragraph (i) or (j) of the definition;

"primary information provider" has the meaning given in section 89P(2);

"relevant ancillary service" means any service of a kind mentioned in Part 3A of Schedule 2 to the Financial Services and Markets Act 2000 (Regulated Activities) Order 2001 the provision of which does not involve the carrying on of a regulated activity;

"sponsor" has the meaning given in section 88(2).

1I. Meaning of "the UK financial system"

In this Act "the UK financial system" means the financial system operating in the United Kingdom and includes—

(a) financial markets and exchanges,

(b) regulated activities (including regulated claims management activities), and

(c) other activities connected with financial markets and exchanges.

Modifications applying if core activity not regulated by PRA

1IA. Modifications applying if core activity not regulated by PRA

(1) If and so long as any regulated activity is a core activity (see section 142B) without also being a PRA-regulated activity (see section 22A), the provisions of this Chapter are to have effect subject to the following modifications.

(2) Section 1B is to have effect as if—

(a) in subsection (3), after paragraph (c) there were inserted—

"(d) in relation to the matters mentioned in section 1EA(2), the continuity objective (see section 1EA).", and

(b) in subsection (4), for "or the integrity objective," there were substituted ", the integrity objective or (in relation to the matters mentioned in section 1EA(2)) the continuity objective,".

(3) After section 1E there is to be taken to be inserted—

"1EA. Continuity objective

(1) In relation to the matters mentioned in subsection (2), the continuity objective is: protecting the continuity of the provision in the United Kingdom of core services (see section 142C).

(2) Those matters are—

(a) Part 9B (ring-fencing);

(b) ring-fenced bodies (see section 142A);

(c) any body corporate incorporated in the United Kingdom that has a ring-fenced body as a member of its group;

(d) applications under Part 4A which, if granted, would result, or would be capable of resulting, in a person becoming a ring-fenced body.

(3) The FCA's continuity objective is to be advanced primarily by—

(a) seeking to ensure that the business of ring-fenced bodies is carried on in a way that avoids any adverse effect on the continuity of the provision in the United Kingdom of core services,

(b) seeking to ensure that the business of ring-fenced bodies is protected from risks (arising in the United Kingdom or elsewhere) that could adversely affect the continuity of the provision in the United Kingdom of core services, and

(c) seeking to minimise the risk that the failure of a ring-fenced body or of a member of a ring-fenced body's group could adversely affect the continuity of the provision in the United Kingdom of core services.

(4)   In subsection (3)(c), "failure" is to be read in accordance with section 2J(3) to (4)."

Power to amend objectives

1J.   Power to amend objectives

The Treasury may by order amend any of the following provisions—
(a)   in section 1E(1), paragraphs (a) and (b),
(b)   section 1G, and
(c)   section 1H(2) and (5) to (8).

Recommendations

1JA.   Recommendations by Treasury in connection with general duties

(1)   The Treasury may at any time by notice in writing to the FCA make recommendations to the FCA about aspects of the economic policy of Her Majesty's Government to which the FCA should have regard when considering—
(a)   how to act in a way which is compatible with its strategic objective,
(b)   how to advance one or more of its operational objectives,
(c)   how to discharge the duty in section 1B(4) (duty to promote effective competition in the interests of consumers),
(ca) how to discharge the duty in section 1B(4A) (duty to advance competitiveness and growth objective),
(d)   the application of the regulatory principles in section 3B, and
(e)   the matter mentioned in section 1B(5)(b) (importance of taking action to minimise the extent to which it is possible for a business to be used for a purpose connected with financial crime).

(2)   The Treasury must make recommendations under subsection (1) at least once in each Parliament.

(2A)   The FCA must respond to each recommendation made to it under subsection (1) by notifying the Treasury in writing of—
(a)   action that the FCA has taken or intends to take in accordance with the recommendation, or
(b)   the reasons why the FCA has not acted or does not intend to act in accordance with the recommendation.

(2B)   The notice under subsection (2A) must be given before the end of 12 months beginning with the date the notice containing the recommendation was given under subsection (1).

(2C)   Where the FCA has given notice under subsection (2A) in relation to a recommendation, the FCA must by notice in writing update the Treasury on the matters mentioned in subsection (2A)(a) and (b) before the end of each subsequent period of 12 months.

(2D)   Subsection (2C) does not apply if the Treasury have notified the FCA in writing that no update (or further update) is required.

(2E)   The FCA is not required under subsection (2A) or (2C) to provide any information whose publication would in the opinion of the FCA be against the public interest.

(3)   The Treasury must—
(a)   publish in such manner as they think fit any notice given under subsection (1), (2A) or (2C), and
(b)   lay a copy of it before Parliament.

Guidance about objectives

1K.   Guidance about objectives

(1)   The general guidance given by the FCA under section 139A must include guidance about how it intends to advance its operational objectives in discharging its general functions in relation to different categories of authorised person or regulated activity.

(1A)   The reference in subsection (1) to the FCA's operational objectives includes, in its application as a secondary objective, the competitiveness and growth objective (see section 1EB).

(2)   Before giving or altering any guidance complying with subsection (1), the FCA must consult the PRA.

Supervision, monitoring and enforcement

1L.   Supervision, monitoring and enforcement

(1)   The FCA must maintain arrangements for supervising authorised persons.

(2)   The FCA must maintain arrangements designed to enable it to determine whether persons other than authorised persons are complying—

    (a)   with requirements imposed on them by or under this Act, in cases where the FCA is the appropriate regulator for the purposes of Part 14 (disciplinary measures), ...

    (aa) with requirements imposed on them by the Alternative Investment Fund Managers Regulations 2013, or

    (b)   with requirements imposed on them by any qualifying provision that is specified, or of a description specified, for the purposes of this subsection by the Treasury by order.

(3)   The FCA must also maintain arrangements for enforcing compliance by persons other than authorised persons with relevant requirements, within the meaning of Part 14, in cases where the FCA is the appropriate regulator for the purposes of any provision of that Part.

...

PART II

REGULATED AND PROHIBITED ACTIVITIES

The general prohibition

19.   The general prohibition

(1)   No person may carry on a regulated activity in the United Kingdom, or purport to do so, unless he is—

    (a)   an authorised person; or

    (b)   an exempt person.

(2)   The prohibition is referred to in this Act as the general prohibition.

Requirement for permission

20.   Authorised persons acting without permission

(1)   If an authorised person other than a PRA-authorised person carries on a regulated activity in the United Kingdom, or purports to do so, otherwise than in accordance with permission—

    (a)   given to that person under Part 4A, or

    (b)   resulting from any other provision of this Act,

he is to be taken to have contravened a requirement imposed on him by the FCA under this Act.

(1A)   If a PRA-authorised person carries on a regulated activity in the United Kingdom, or purports to do so, otherwise than in accordance with permission given to the person under Part 4A or resulting from any other provision of this Act, the person is to be taken to have contravened—

    (a)   a requirement imposed by the FCA, and

    (b)   a requirement imposed by the PRA.

(2)   A contravention within subsection (1) or (1A)—

    (a)   does not, except as provided by section 23(1A), make a person guilty of an offence,

    (b)   does not, except as provided by section 26A, make any transaction void or unenforceable, and

    (c)   does not, except as provided by subsection (3), give rise to any right of action for breach of statutory duty.

(3)   In prescribed cases a contravention within subsection (1) or (1A) is actionable at the suit of a person who suffers loss as a result of the contravention, subject to the defences and other incidents applying to actions for breach of statutory duty.

(4)   Subsections (1) and (1A) are subject to section 39(1D).

(5)   References in this Act to an authorised person acting in contravention of this section are references to the person acting in a way that results in a contravention within subsection (1) or (1A).

Financial promotion

21.   Restrictions on financial promotion

(1)   A person ("A") must not, in the course of business, communicate an invitation or inducement—
     (a)   to engage in investment activity, or
     (b)   to engage in claims management activity.

(2)   But subsection (1) does not apply if—
     (a)   A is an authorised person; or
     (b)   the content of the communication is approved for the purposes of this section by an authorised person.

(2A)   The content of a communication may be approved for the purposes of this section by an authorised person only if the giving of the approval—
     (a)   is permitted under section 55NA (which enables approval to be given with FCA permission), or
     (b)   falls within an exemption conferred by regulations under section 55NB.

(3)   In the case of a communication originating outside the United Kingdom, subsection (1) applies only if the communication is capable of having an effect in the United Kingdom.

(4)   The Treasury may by order specify circumstances in which a person is to be regarded for the purposes of subsection (1) as—
     (a)   acting in the course of business;
     (b)   not acting in the course of business.

(5)   The Treasury may by order specify circumstances (which may include compliance with financial promotion rules) in which subsection (1) does not apply.

(6)   An order under subsection (5) may, in particular, provide that subsection (1) does not apply in relation to communications—
     (a)   of a specified description;
     (b)   originating in a specified country or territory outside the United Kingdom;
     (c)   originating in a country or territory which falls within a specified description of country or territory outside the United Kingdom; or
     (d)   originating outside the United Kingdom.

(7)   The Treasury may by order repeal subsection (3).

(8)   "Engaging in investment activity" means—
     (a)   entering or offering to enter into an agreement the making or performance of which by either party constitutes a controlled activity; or
     (b)   exercising any rights conferred by a controlled investment to acquire, dispose of, underwrite or convert a controlled investment.

(9)   An activity is a controlled activity if—
     (a)   it is an activity of a specified kind or one which falls within a specified class of activity; and
     (b)   it relates to an investment of a specified kind, or to one which falls within a specified class of investment.

(10)   An investment is a controlled investment if it is an investment of a specified kind or one which falls within a specified class of investment.

(10A)   "Engaging in claims management activity" means entering into or offering to enter into an agreement the making or performance of which by either party constitutes a controlled claims management activity.

(10B)   An activity is a "controlled claims management activity" if—
     (a)   it is an activity of a specified kind,
     (b)   it is, or relates to, claims management services, and
     (c)   it is carried on in Great Britain.

(11)   Schedule 2 (except paragraph 26) applies for the purposes of subsections (9) and (10) with references to section 22 being read as references to each of those subsections.

(12)   Nothing in Schedule 2, as applied by subsection (11), limits the powers conferred by subsection (9) or (10).

(12A)   Paragraph 25 of Schedule 2 applies for the purposes of subsection (10B) with the references to section 22 in sub-paragraph (3) of that paragraph being read as references to subsection (10B).

(13)   "Communicate" includes causing a communication to be made.

(14)   "Investment" includes any asset, right or interest (including where an asset, right or interest is, or comprises or represents, a cryptoasset).

(15)   "Specified" means specified in an order made by the Treasury.

Regulated activities

22.   Regulated activities

(1)   An activity is a regulated activity for the purposes of this Act if it is an activity of a specified kind which is carried on by way of business and—
   (a)   relates to an investment of a specified kind; or
   (b)   in the case of an activity of a kind which is also specified for the purposes of this paragraph, is carried on in relation to property of any kind.

(1A)   An activity is also a regulated activity for the purposes of this Act if it is an activity of a specified kind which is carried on by way of business and relates to—
   (a)   information about a person's financial standing, ... or
   (b)   ...
   (c)   administering a benchmark.

(1B)   An activity is also a regulated activity for the purposes of this Act if it is an activity of a specified kind which—
   (a)   is carried on by way of business in Great Britain, and
   (b)   is, or relates to, claims management services.

(2)   Schedule 2 makes provision supplementing this section.

(3)   Nothing in Schedule 2 limits the powers conferred by subsections (1) to (1B).

(4)   "Investment" includes any asset, right or interest (including where an asset, right or interest is, or comprises or represents, a cryptoasset).

(5)   "Specified" means specified in an order made by the Treasury.

(6)   ...

(6A)   For the purposes of subsection (1A)(c), "benchmark" has the meaning given by Article 3 of the EU Benchmarks Regulation 2016, and "administering" a benchmark means acting as an administrator of that benchmark within the meaning of that Article.

22A.   Designation of activities requiring prudential regulation by PRA

(1)   The Treasury may by order specify the regulated activities that are "PRA-regulated activities" for the purposes of this Act.

(2)   An order under subsection (1) may—
   (a)   provide for exceptions;
   (b)   confer powers on the Treasury or either regulator;
   (c)   authorise the making of rules or other instruments by either regulator for purposes of, or connected with, any relevant provision;
   (d)   make provision in respect of any information or document which in the opinion of the Treasury or either regulator is relevant for purposes of, or connected with, any relevant provision;
   (e)   make such consequential, transitional, or supplemental provision as the Treasury consider appropriate for purposes of, or connected with, any relevant provision.

(3)   Provision made as a result of subsection (2)(e) may amend any primary or subordinate legislation, including any provision of, or made under, this Act.

(4)   "Relevant provision" means this section or any provision made under this section.

22B.   Parliamentary control in relation to certain orders under section 22A

(1)   This section applies to the first order made under section 22A(1).

(2)   This section also applies to any subsequent order made under section 22A(1) which—

    (a)   contains a statement by the Treasury that, in their opinion, the effect (or one of the effects) of the proposed order would be—

        (i)   that an activity would become a PRA-regulated activity, or

        (ii)   that a PRA-regulated activity would become a regulated activity that is not a PRA-regulated activity, or

    (b)   amends primary legislation.

(3)   No order to which this section applies may be made unless—

    (a)   a draft of the order has been laid before Parliament and approved by a resolution of each House, or

    (b)   subsection (5) applies.

(4)   Subsection (5) applies if an order to which this section applies contains a statement that the Treasury are of the opinion that, by reason of urgency, it is necessary to make the order without a draft being so laid and approved.

(5)   Where this subsection applies the order—

    (a)   must be laid before Parliament after being made, and

    (b)   ceases to have effect at the end of the relevant period unless before the end of that period the order is approved by a resolution of each House of Parliament (but without that affecting anything done under the order or the power to make a new order).

(6)   The "relevant period" is a period of 28 days beginning with the day on which the order is made.

(7)   In calculating the relevant period no account is to be taken of any time during which Parliament is dissolved or prorogued or during which both Houses are adjourned for more than 4 days.

Offences

23.   Contravention of the general prohibition or section 20(1) or (1A)

(1)   A person who contravenes the general prohibition is guilty of an offence and liable—

    (a)   on summary conviction, to imprisonment for a term not exceeding six months or a fine not exceeding the statutory maximum, or both;

    (b)   on conviction on indictment, to imprisonment for a term not exceeding two years or a fine, or both.

(1A)   An authorised person ("A") is guilty of an offence if A carries on a credit-related regulated activity in the United Kingdom, or purports to do so, otherwise than in accordance with permission—

    (a)   given to that person under Part 4A, or

    (b)   resulting from any other provision of this Act.

(1B)   In this Act "credit-related regulated activity" means a regulated activity of a kind designated by the Treasury by order.

(1C)   The Treasury may designate a regulated activity under subsection (1B) only if the activity involves a person—

    (a)   entering into or administering an agreement under which the person provides another person with credit,

    (b)   exercising or being able to exercise the rights of the lender under an agreement under which another person provides a third party with credit, or

    (c)   taking steps to procure payment of debts due under an agreement under which another person is provided with credit.

(1D)   But a regulated activity may not be designated under subsection (1B) if the agreement in question is one under which the obligation of the borrower is secured on land.

(1E)   "Credit" includes any cash loan or other financial accommodation.

(1F)   A person guilty of an offence under subsection (1A) is liable—

    (a)   on summary conviction, to imprisonment for a term not exceeding the applicable maximum term or a fine not exceeding the statutory maximum, or both;

    (b)   on conviction on indictment, to imprisonment for a term not exceeding two years, or a fine, or both.

(1G)   The "applicable maximum term" is—

    (a)   in England and Wales, the general limit in a magistrates' court (or 6 months, if the offence was committed before 2 May 2022);

    (b)   in Scotland, 12 months;

    (c)   in Northern Ireland, 6 months.

(2)   In this Act "an authorisation offence" means an offence under this section.

(3)   In proceedings for an authorisation offence it is a defence for the accused to show that he took all reasonable precautions and exercised all due diligence to avoid committing the offence.

(4)   Subsection (1A) is subject to section 39(1D).

(5)   No proceedings may be brought against a person in respect of an offence under subsection (1A) in a case where either regulator has taken action under section 205, 206 or 206A in relation to the alleged contravention within section 20(1) or (1A).

23A.   Parliamentary control in relation to certain orders under section 23

(1)   This section applies to the first order made under section 23(1B).

(2)   This section also applies to any subsequent order made under section 23(1B) which contains a statement by the Treasury that, in their opinion, the effect (or one of the effects) of the proposed order would be that an activity would become a credit-related regulated activity.

(3)   An order to which this section applies may not be made unless a draft of the order has been laid before Parliament and approved by a resolution of each House.

24.   False claims to be authorised or exempt

(1)   A person who is neither an authorised person nor, in relation to the regulated activity in question, an exempt person is guilty of an offence if he—

    (a)   describes himself (in whatever terms) as an authorised person;

    (b)   describes himself (in whatever terms) as an exempt person in relation to the regulated activity; or

    (c)   behaves, or otherwise holds himself out, in a manner which indicates (or which is reasonably likely to be understood as indicating) that he is—

        (i)   an authorised person; or

        (ii) an exempt person in relation to the regulated activity.

(2)   In proceedings for an offence under this section it is a defence for the accused to show that he took all reasonable precautions and exercised all due diligence to avoid committing the offence.

(3)   A person guilty of an offence under this section is liable on summary conviction to imprisonment for a term not exceeding six months or a fine not exceeding level 5 on the standard scale, or both.

(4)   ...

25.   Contravention of section 21

(1)   A person who contravenes section 21(1) is guilty of an offence and liable—

    (a)   on summary conviction, to imprisonment for a term not exceeding six months or a fine not exceeding the statutory maximum, or both;

    (b)   on conviction on indictment, to imprisonment for a term not exceeding two years or a fine, or both.

(2)   In proceedings for an offence under this section it is a defence for the accused to show—

    (a)   that he believed on reasonable grounds that the content of the communication was prepared, or approved for the purposes of section 21 in accordance with subsection (2A) of that section, by an authorised person; or

    (b)   that he took all reasonable precautions and exercised all due diligence to avoid committing the offence.

Enforceability of agreements

26. Agreements made by unauthorised persons

(1) An agreement made by a person in the course of carrying on a regulated activity in contravention of the general prohibition is unenforceable against the other party.

(2) The other party is entitled to recover—

(a) any money or other property paid or transferred by him under the agreement; and

(b) compensation for any loss sustained by him as a result of having parted with it.

(3) "Agreement" means an agreement—

(a) made after this section comes into force; and

(b) the making or performance of which constitutes, or is part of, the regulated activity in question.

(4) This section does not apply if the regulated activity is accepting deposits.

26A. Agreements relating to credit

(1) An agreement that is made by an authorised person in contravention of section 20 is unenforceable against the other party if the agreement is entered into in the course of carrying on a credit-related regulated activity involving matters falling within section 23(1C)(a).

(2) The other party is entitled to recover—

(a) any money or other property paid or transferred by that party under the agreement, and

(b) compensation for any loss sustained by that party as a result of having parted with it.

(3) In subsections (1) and (2) "agreement" means an agreement—

(a) which is made after this section comes into force, and

(b) the making or performance of which constitutes, or is part of, the credit-related regulated activity.

(4) If the administration of an agreement involves the carrying on of a credit-related regulated activity, the agreement may not be enforced by a person for the time being exercising the rights of the lender under the agreement unless that person—

(a) has permission, given under Part 4A or resulting from any other provision of this Act, in relation to that activity,

(b) is an appointed representative in relation to that activity,

(c) is an exempt person in relation to that activity, or

(d) is a person to whom, as a result of Part 20, the general prohibition does not apply in relation to that activity.

(5) If the taking of steps to procure payment of debts due under an agreement involves the carrying on of a credit-related regulated activity, the agreement may not be enforced by a person for the time being exercising the rights of the lender under the agreement unless—

(a) the agreement is enforced in accordance with permission—

(i) given under Part 4A to the person enforcing the agreement, or

(ii) resulting from any other provision of this Act,

(b) that person is an appointed representative in relation to that activity,

(c) that person is an exempt person in relation to that activity, or

(d) that person is a person to whom, as a result of Part 20, the general prohibition does not apply in relation to that activity.

27. Agreements made through unauthorised persons

(1) This section applies to an agreement that—

(a) is made by an authorised person ("the provider") in the course of carrying on a regulated activity,

(b) is not made in contravention of the general prohibition,

(c) if it relates to a credit-related regulated activity, is not made in contravention of section 20, and

(d) is made in consequence of something said or done by another person ("the third party") in the course of—

(i) a regulated activity carried on by the third party in contravention of the general prohibition, or

(ii) a credit-related regulated activity carried on by the third party in contravention of section 20.

(1ZA) But this section does not apply to a regulated credit agreement or a regulated consumer hire agreement unless the provider knows before the agreement is made that the third party had some involvement in the making of the agreement or matters preparatory to its making.

(1A) An agreement to which this section applies is unenforceable against the other party.

(2) The other party is entitled to recover—

(a) any money or other property paid or transferred by him under the agreement; and

(b) compensation for any loss sustained by him as a result of having parted with it.

(3) "Agreement" means an agreement—

(a) made after this section comes into force; and

(b) the making or performance of which constitutes, or is part of, the regulated activity in question carried on by the provider.

(4) This section does not apply if the regulated activity is accepting deposits.

(5) For the purposes of subsection (1ZA)—

"regulated consumer hire agreement" has the meaning given by article 60N of the Financial Services and Markets Act 2000 (Regulated Activities) Order 2001 (SI 2001/544);

"regulated credit agreement" has the meaning given by article 60B of that Order.

28. Agreements made unenforceable by section 26 or 27: general cases

(1) This section applies to an agreement which is unenforceable because of section 26 or 27, other than an agreement entered into in the course of carrying on a credit-related regulated activity.

(2) The amount of compensation recoverable as a result of that section is—

(a) the amount agreed by the parties; or

(b) on the application of either party, the amount determined by the court.

(3) If the court is satisfied that it is just and equitable in the circumstances of the case, it may allow—

(a) the agreement to be enforced; or

(b) money and property paid or transferred under the agreement to be retained.

(4) In considering whether to allow the agreement to be enforced or (as the case may be) the money or property paid or transferred under the agreement to be retained the court must—

(a) if the case arises as a result of section 26, have regard to the issue mentioned in subsection (5); or

(b) if the case arises as a result of section 27, have regard to the issue mentioned in subsection (6).

(5) The issue is whether the person carrying on the regulated activity concerned reasonably believed that he was not contravening the general prohibition by making the agreement.

(6) The issue is whether the provider knew that the third party was (in carrying on the regulated activity) contravening the general prohibition.

(7) If the person against whom the agreement is unenforceable—

(a) elects not to perform the agreement, or

(b) as a result of this section, recovers money paid or other property transferred by him under the agreement,

he must repay any money and return any other property received by him under the agreement.

(8) If property transferred under the agreement has passed to a third party, a reference in section 26 or 27 or this section to that property is to be read as a reference to its value at the time of its transfer under the agreement.

(9) The commission of an authorisation offence does not make the agreement concerned illegal or invalid to any greater extent than is provided by section 26 or 27.

28A. Credit-related agreements made unenforceable by section 26, 26A or 27

(1) This section applies to an agreement that—

        (a)   is entered into in the course of carrying on a credit-related regulated activity, and

        (b)   is unenforceable because of section 26, 26A or 27.

(2)   The amount of compensation recoverable as a result of that section is—

        (a)   the amount agreed by the parties, or

        (b)   on the application of either party, the amount specified in a written notice given by the FCA to the applicant.

(3)   If on application by the relevant firm the FCA is satisfied that it is just and equitable in the circumstances of the case, it may by written notice to the applicant allow—

        (a)   the agreement to be enforced, or

        (b)   money paid or property transferred under the agreement to be retained.

(4)   In considering whether to allow the agreement to be enforced or (as the case may be) the money or property paid or transferred under the agreement to be retained the FCA must—

        (a)   if the case arises as a result of section 26 or 26A, have regard to the issue mentioned in subsection (5), or

        (b)   if the case arises as a result of section 27, have regard to the issue mentioned in subsection (6).

(5)   The issue is whether the relevant firm reasonably believed that by making the agreement the relevant firm was neither contravening the general prohibition nor contravening section 20.

(6)   The issue is whether the provider knew that the third party was (in carrying on the credit-related regulated activity) either contravening the general prohibition or contravening section 20.

(7)   An application to the FCA under this section by the relevant firm may relate to specified agreements or to agreements of a specified description or made at a specified time.

(8)   "The relevant firm" means—

        (a)   in a case falling within section 26, the person in breach of the general prohibition;

        (b)   in a case falling within section 26A or 27, the authorised person concerned.

(9)   If the FCA thinks fit, it may when acting under subsection (2)(b) or (3)—

        (a)   limit the determination in its notice to specified agreements, or agreements of a specified description or made at a specified time;

        (b)   make the determination in its notice conditional on the doing of specified acts by the applicant.

28B.   **Decisions under section 28A: procedure**

(1)   A notice under section 28A(2)(b) or (3) must—

        (a)   give the FCA's reasons for its determination, and

        (b)   give an indication of—

            (i)   the right to have the matter referred to the Tribunal that is conferred by subsection (3), and

            (ii)   the procedure on such a reference.

(2)   The FCA must, so far as it is reasonably practicable to do so, give a copy of the notice to any other person who appears to it to be affected by the determination to which the notice relates.

(3)   A person who is aggrieved by the determination of an application under section 28A(2)(b) or (3) may refer the matter to the Tribunal.

29.   **Accepting deposits in breach of general prohibition**

(1)   This section applies to an agreement between a person ("the depositor") and another person ("the deposit-taker") made in the course of the carrying on by the deposit-taker of accepting deposits in contravention of the general prohibition.

(2)   If the depositor is not entitled under the agreement to recover without delay any money deposited by him, he may apply to the court for an order directing the deposit-taker to return the money to him.

(3)   The court need not make such an order if it is satisfied that it would not be just and equitable for the money deposited to be returned, having regard to the issue mentioned in subsection (4).

(4)   The issue is whether the deposit-taker reasonably believed that he was not contravening the general prohibition by making the agreement.

(5)   "Agreement" means an agreement—

    (a)   made after this section comes into force; and

    (b)   the making or performance of which constitutes, or is part of, accepting deposits.

30.   Enforceability of agreements resulting from unlawful communications

(1)   In this section—

        "unlawful communication" means a communication in relation to which there has been a contravention of section 21(1);

        "controlled agreement" means an agreement the making or performance of which by either party constitutes a controlled activity for the purposes of that section; and

        "controlled investment" has the same meaning as in section 21.

(2)   If in consequence of an unlawful communication a person enters as a customer into a controlled agreement, it is unenforceable against him and he is entitled to recover—

    (a)   any money or other property paid or transferred by him under the agreement; and

    (b)   compensation for any loss sustained by him as a result of having parted with it.

(3)   If in consequence of an unlawful communication a person exercises any rights conferred by a controlled investment, no obligation to which he is subject as a result of exercising them is enforceable against him and he is entitled to recover—

    (a)   any money or other property paid or transferred by him under the obligation; and

    (b)   compensation for any loss sustained by him as a result of having parted with it.

(4)   But the court may allow—

    (a)   the agreement or obligation to be enforced, or

    (b)   money or property paid or transferred under the agreement or obligation to be retained,

    if it is satisfied that it is just and equitable in the circumstances of the case.

(5)   In considering whether to allow the agreement or obligation to be enforced or (as the case may be) the money or property paid or transferred under the agreement to be retained the court must have regard to the issues mentioned in subsections (6) and (7).

(6)   If the applicant made the unlawful communication, the issue is whether he reasonably believed that he was not making such a communication.

(7)   If the applicant did not make the unlawful communication, the issue is whether he knew that the agreement was entered into in consequence of such a communication.

(8)   "Applicant" means the person seeking to enforce the agreement or obligation or retain the money or property paid or transferred.

(9)   Any reference to making a communication includes causing a communication to be made.

(10)   The amount of compensation recoverable as a result of subsection (2) or (3) is—

    (a)   the amount agreed between the parties; or

    (b)   on the application of either party, the amount determined by the court.

(11)   If a person elects not to perform an agreement or an obligation which (by virtue of subsection (2) or (3)) is unenforceable against him, he must repay any money and return any other property received by him under the agreement.

(12)   If (by virtue of subsection (2) or (3)) a person recovers money paid or property transferred by him under an agreement or obligation, he must repay any money and return any other property received by him as a result of exercising the rights in question.

(13)   If any property required to be returned under this section has passed to a third party, references to that property are to be read as references to its value at the time of its receipt by the person required to return it.

PART III
AUTHORISATION AND EXEMPTION

Authorisation

31.   Authorised persons

(1)   The following persons are authorised for the purposes of this Act—

(a)   a person who has a Part 4A permission to carry on one or more regulated activities;

(b), (c)...

(d)   a person who is otherwise authorised by a provision of, or made under, this Act.

(2)   In this Act "authorised person" means a person who is authorised for the purposes of this Act.

Note. This section is amended by the Financial Services Act 2021, s. 22(1), (2), as from a day to be appointed.

...

PART VI
OFFICIAL LISTING

...

72, 73. ...

Rules

73A.   Part 6 Rules

(1)   The FCA may make rules ("Part 6 rules") for the purposes of this Part.

(2)   Provisions of Part 6 rules expressed to relate to the official list are referred to in this Part as "listing rules".

(3)   ...

(4)   Provisions of Part 6 rules expressed to relate to transferable securities are referred to in this Part as "prospectus rules".

(5)   In relation to prospectus rules, the purposes of this Part include the purposes of the prospectus regulation.

(6)   Transparency rules and corporate governance rules are not listing rules ... or prospectus rules, but are Part 6 rules.

Note. This section is amended by S.I. 2024/105, reg. 47(a), Sch. 3, Pt. 1, paras. 1, 2, as from a day to be appointed (save for certain purposes).

The official list

74.   The official list

(1)   The FCA must maintain the official list.

(2)   The FCA may admit to the official list such securities and other things as it considers appropriate.

(3)   But—

(a)   nothing may be admitted to the official list except in accordance with this Part; and

(b)   the Treasury may by order provide that anything which falls within a description or category specified in the order may not be admitted to the official list.

(4)   ...

(5)   In the following provisions of this Part—

...

"listing" means being included in the official list in accordance with this Part.

Listing

75.   Applications for listing

(1)   Admission to the official list may be granted only on an application made to the FCA in such manner as may be required by listing rules.

(2)   No application for listing may be entertained by the FCA unless it is made by, or with the consent of, the issuer of the securities concerned.

(3)   No application for listing may be entertained by the FCA in respect of securities which are to be issued by a body of a prescribed kind.

(4)   The FCA may not grant an application for listing unless it is satisfied that—
     (a)   the requirements of listing rules (so far as they apply to the application), and
     (b)   any other requirements imposed by the FCA in relation to the application,
     are complied with.

(5)   An application for listing may be refused if, for a reason relating to the issuer, the FCA considers that granting it would be detrimental to the interests of investors.

(6)   An application for listing securities which are already listed in a country or territory outside the United Kingdom may be refused if the issuer has failed to comply with any obligations to which he is subject as a result of that listing.

76.   Decision on application

(1)   The FCA must notify the applicant of its decision on an application for listing—
     (a)   before the end of the period of six months beginning with the date on which the application is received; or
     (b)   if within that period the FCA has required the applicant to provide further information in connection with the application, before the end of the period of six months beginning with the date on which that information is provided.

(2)   If the FCA fails to comply with subsection (1), it is to be taken to have decided to refuse the application.

(3)   If the FCA decides to grant an application for listing, it must give the applicant written notice.

(4)   If the FCA proposes to refuse an application for listing, it must give the applicant a warning notice.

(5)   If the FCA decides to refuse an application for listing, it must give the applicant a decision notice.

(6)   If the FCA decides to refuse an application for listing, the applicant may refer the matter to the Tribunal.

(7)   If securities are admitted to the official list, their admission may not be called in question on the ground that any requirement or condition for their admission has not been complied with.

77.   Discontinuance and suspension of listing

(1)   The FCA may, in accordance with listing rules, discontinue the listing of any securities if satisfied that there are special circumstances which preclude normal regular dealings in them.

(2)   The FCA may, in accordance with listing rules, suspend the listing of any securities.

(2A)   The FCA may discontinue under subsection (1) or suspend under subsection (2) the listing of any securities on its own initiative or on the application of the issuer of those securities.

(3)   If securities are suspended under subsection (2) they are to be treated, for the purposes of section 96 and paragraph 23(6) of Schedule 1ZA, as still being listed.

(3A)   If securities have been suspended by the Bank of England under section 19, 39B or 48L of the Banking Act 2009 or paragraph 44 or 65 of Schedule 11 to the Financial Services and Markets Act 2023, the FCA may, following consultation with the Bank of England, cancel the suspension.

(4)   This section applies to securities whenever they were admitted to the official list.

(5)   If the FCA discontinues or suspends the listing of any securities, on its own initiative, the issuer may refer the matter to the Tribunal.

78.   Discontinuance or suspension: procedure

(1)   A discontinuance or suspension by the FCA on its own initiative takes effect—
     (a)   immediately, if the notice under subsection (2) states that that is the case;
     (b)   in any other case, on such date as may be specified in that notice.

(2)   If on its own initiative the FCA—
     (a)   proposes to discontinue or suspend the listing of securities, or
     (b)   discontinues or suspends the listing of securities with immediate effect,
     it must give the issuer of the securities written notice.

(3)   The notice must—

(a)   give details of the discontinuance or suspension;

(b)   state the FCA's reasons for the discontinuance or suspension and for choosing the date on which it took effect or takes effect;

(c)   inform the issuer of the securities that he may make representations to the FCA within such period as may be specified in the notice (whether or not he has referred the matter to the Tribunal);

(d)   inform him of the date on which the discontinuance or suspension took effect or will take effect; and

(e)   inform him of his right to refer the matter to the Tribunal.

(4)   The FCA may extend the period within which representations may be made to it.

(5)   If, having considered any representations made by the issuer of the securities, the FCA decides—

(a)   to discontinue or suspend the listing of the securities, or

(b)   if the discontinuance or suspension has taken effect, not to cancel it,

the FCA must give the issuer of the securities written notice.

(6)   A notice given under subsection (5) must inform the issuer of the securities of his right to refer the matter to the Tribunal.

(7)   If a notice informs a person of his right to refer a matter to the Tribunal, it must give an indication of the procedure on such a reference.

(8)   If the FCA decides—

(a)   not to discontinue or suspend the listing of the securities, or

(b)   if the discontinuance or suspension has taken effect, to cancel it,

the FCA must give the issuer of the securities written notice.

(9)   The effect of cancelling a discontinuance is that the securities concerned are to be readmitted, without more, to the official list.

(10)   If—

(a)   the FCA has suspended the listing of securities on its own initiative, or securities have been suspended by the Bank of England under section 19, 39B or 48L of the Banking Act 2009 or paragraph 44 or 65 of Schedule 11 to the Financial Services and Markets Act 2023, and

(b)   the FCA proposes to refuse an application by the issuer of the securities for the cancellation of the suspension,

the FCA must give the issuer a warning notice.

(11)   The FCA must, having considered any representations made in response to the warning notice—

(a)   if it decides to refuse the application, give the issuer of the securities a decision notice;

(b)   if it grants the application, give him written notice of its decision.

(12)   If the FCA decides to refuse an application for the cancellation of the suspension of listed securities, the applicant may refer the matter to the Tribunal.

(13)   "Discontinuance" means a discontinuance of listing under section 77(1).

(14)   "Suspension" means a suspension of listing under section 77(2) and in subsections (10) and (12), includes a suspension of listing under section 19, 39B or 48L of the Banking Act 2009 or paragraph 44 or 65 of Schedule 11 to the Financial Services and Markets Act 2023.

78A.   Discontinuance or suspension at the request of the issuer: procedure

(1)   A discontinuance or suspension by the FCA on the application of the issuer of the securities takes effect—

(a)   immediately, if the notification under subsection (2) so provides;

(b)   in any other case, on such date as may be provided for in that notification.

(2)   If the FCA discontinues or suspends the listing of securities on the application of the issuer of the securities it must notify the issuer (whether in writing or otherwise).

(3)   The notification must—

(a)   notify the issuer of the date on which the discontinuance or suspension took effect or will take effect, and

(b)   notify the issuer of such other matters (if any) as are specified in listing rules.

(4)   If the FCA proposes to refuse an application by the issuer of the securities for the discontinuance or suspension of the listing of the securities, it must give him a warning notice.

(5)   The FCA must, having considered any representations made in response to the warning notice, if it decides to refuse the application, give the issuer of the securities a decision notice.

(6)   If the FCA decides to refuse an application by the issuer of the securities for the discontinuance or suspension of the listing of the securities, the issuer may refer the matter to the Tribunal.

(7)   If the FCA has suspended the listing of securities on the application of the issuer of the securities and proposes to refuse an application by the issuer for the cancellation of the suspension, it must give him a warning notice.

(8)   The FCA must, having considered any representations made in response to the warning notice—
    (a)   if it decides to refuse the application for the cancellation of the suspension, give the issuer of the securities a decision notice;
    (b)   if it grants the application, give him written notice of its decision.

(9)   If the FCA decides to refuse an application for the cancellation of the suspension of listed securities, the applicant may refer the matter to the Tribunal.

(10)   "Discontinuance" means a discontinuance of listing under section 77(1).

(11)   "Suspension" means a suspension of listing under section 77(2).

Listing particulars

79.   Listing particulars and other documents

(1)   Listing rules may provide that securities … of a kind specified in the rules may not be admitted to the official list unless—
    (a)   listing particulars have been submitted to, and approved by, the FCA and published; or
    (b)   in such cases as may be specified by listing rules, such document (other than listing particulars or a prospectus of a kind required by listing rules) as may be so specified has been published.

(2)   "Listing particulars" means a document in such form and containing such information as may be specified in listing rules.

(3)   For the purposes of this Part, the persons responsible for listing particulars are to be determined in accordance with regulations made by the Treasury.

(3A)   Listing rules made under subsection (1) may not specify securities of a kind for which an approved prospectus is required as a result of section 85.

(4)   Nothing in this section affects the FCA's general power to make listing rules.

    Note. This section is amended by S.I. 2024/105, reg. 47(a), Sch. 3, Pt. 1, paras. 1, 3, as from a day to be appointed (save for certain purposes).

80.   General duty of disclosure in listing particulars

(1)   Listing particulars submitted to the FCA under section 79 must contain all such information as investors and their professional advisers would reasonably require, and reasonably expect to find there, for the purpose of making an informed assessment of—
    (a)   the assets and liabilities, financial position, profits and losses, and prospects of the issuer of the securities; and
    (b)   the rights attaching to the securities.

(2)   That information is required in addition to any information required by—
    (a)   listing rules, or
    (b)   the FCA,
    as a condition of the admission of the securities to the official list.

(3)   Subsection (1) applies only to information—
    (a)   within the knowledge of any person responsible for the listing particulars; or
    (b)   which it would be reasonable for him to obtain by making enquiries.

(4)   In determining what information subsection (1) requires to be included in listing particulars, regard must be had (in particular) to—
    (a)   the nature of the securities and their issuer;

    (b)   the nature of the persons likely to consider acquiring them;

    (c)   the fact that certain matters may reasonably be expected to be within the knowledge of professional advisers of a kind which persons likely to acquire the securities may reasonably be expected to consult; and

    (d)   any information available to investors or their professional advisers as a result of requirements imposed on the issuer of the securities by a recognised investment exchange, by listing rules or by or under any other enactment.

81.   Supplementary listing particulars

(1)   If at any time after the preparation of listing particulars which have been submitted to the FCA under section 79 and before the commencement of dealings in the securities concerned following their admission to the official list—

    (a)   there is a significant change affecting any matter contained in those particulars the inclusion of which was required by—

        (i)   section 80,

        (ii) listing rules, or

        (iii) the FCA, or

    (b)   a significant new matter arises, the inclusion of information in respect of which would have been so required if it had arisen when the particulars were prepared,

the issuer must, in accordance with listing rules, submit supplementary listing particulars of the change or new matter to the FCA, for its approval and, if they are approved, publish them.

(2)   "Significant" means significant for the purpose of making an informed assessment of the kind mentioned in section 80(1).

(3)   If the issuer of the securities is not aware of the change or new matter in question, he is not under a duty to comply with subsection (1) unless he is notified of the change or new matter by a person responsible for the listing particulars.

(4)   But it is the duty of any person responsible for those particulars who is aware of such a change or new matter to give notice of it to the issuer.

(5)   Subsection (1) applies also as respects matters contained in any supplementary listing particulars previously published under this section in respect of the securities in question.

82.   Exemptions from disclosure

(1)   The FCA may authorise the omission from listing particulars of any information, the inclusion of which would otherwise be required by section 80 or 81, on the ground—

    (a)   that its disclosure would be contrary to the public interest;

    (b)   that its disclosure would be seriously detrimental to the issuer; or

    (c)   in the case of securities of a kind specified in listing rules, that its disclosure is unnecessary for persons of the kind who may be expected normally to buy or deal in securities of that kind.

(2)   But—

    (a)   no authority may be granted under subsection (1)(b) in respect of essential information; and

    (b)   no authority granted under subsection (1)(b) extends to any such information.

(3)   The Secretary of State or the Treasury may issue a certificate to the effect that the disclosure of any information (including information that would otherwise have to be included in listing particulars for which they are themselves responsible) would be contrary to the public interest.

(4)   The FCA is entitled to act on any such certificate in exercising its powers under subsection (1)(a).

(5)   This section does not affect any powers of the FCA under listing rules made as a result of section 101(2).

(6)   "Essential information" means information which a person considering acquiring securities of the kind in question would be likely to need in order not to be misled about any facts which it is essential for him to know in order to make an informed assessment.

(7)   "Listing particulars" includes supplementary listing particulars.

83.   ...

Transferable securities: public offers and admission to trading

84.   Matters which may be dealt with by prospectus rules

(1)   Prospectus rules may make provision as to—

(a)   the required form and content of a prospectus ...;

(b)   the cases in which a summary need not be included in a prospectus;

(c)   the languages which may be used in a prospectus ...;

(d)   the determination of the persons responsible for a prospectus;

(e)   the manner in which applications to the FCA for the approval of a prospectus are to be made.

(1A)   In subsection (1) "prospectus" includes any part of a prospectus, and in particular includes a summary and a supplement.

(2)   Prospectus rules may also make provision as to—

(a)   the period of validity of a prospectus;

(b)   the disclosure of the maximum price or of the criteria or conditions according to which the final offer price is to be determined, if that information is not contained in a prospectus;

(c)   the disclosure of the amount of the transferable securities which are to be offered to the public or of the criteria or conditions according to which that amount is to be determined, if that information is not contained in a prospectus;

(d)   the required form and content of other summary documents (including the languages which may be used in such a document);

(e)   the ways in which a prospectus that has been approved by the FCA may be made available to the public;

(f)   the disclosure, publication or other communication of such information as the FCA may reasonably stipulate;

(g)   the principles to be observed in relation to advertisements in connection with an offer of transferable securities to the public or admission of transferable securities to trading on a regulated market and the enforcement of those principles;

(h)   the suspension of trading in transferable securities where continued trading would be detrimental to the interests of investors;

(i)   the exercise of entitlements under Article 4 of the prospectus regulation ...

(3)   ...

(4)   Prospectus rules may make provision for the purpose of dealing with matters arising out of or related to any provision of the prospectus regulation.

(5), (6)   ...

(7)   Nothing in this section affects the FCA's general power to make prospectus rules.

Note. This section is repealed, and the preceding cross-heading is amended, by S.I. 2024/105, reg. 47(a), Sch. 3, Pt. 1, paras. 1, 4, 5, as from a day to be appointed (save for certain purposes).

85.   Prohibition of dealing etc in transferable securities without approved prospectus

(1)   It is unlawful for transferable securities to which this subsection applies to be offered to the public in the United Kingdom unless an approved prospectus has been made available to the public before the offer is made.

(2)   It is unlawful to request the admission of transferable securities to which this subsection applies to trading on a regulated market situated or operating in the United Kingdom unless an approved prospectus has been made available to the public before the request is made.

(3)   A person who contravenes subsection (1) or (2) is guilty of an offence and liable—

(a)   on summary conviction, to imprisonment for a term not exceeding 3 months or a fine not exceeding the statutory maximum or both;

(b)   on conviction on indictment, to imprisonment for a term not exceeding 2 years or a fine or both.

(4)   A contravention of subsection (1) or (2) is actionable, at the suit of a person who suffers loss as a result of the contravention, subject to the defences and other incidents applying to actions for breach of statutory duty.

(5)   Subsection (1) applies to all transferable securities other than—

(a)   those listed in Article 1(2) of the prospectus regulation;

(b)   any offered in an offer falling within Article 1(3) of the prospectus regulation.

(6)   Subsection (2) applies to all transferable securities other than those listed in Article 1(2) of the prospectus regulation.

(6A)   Schedule 11A makes provision that applies for the purposes of Article 1(2)(e) of the prospectus regulation.

(7)   "Approved prospectus" means, in relation to transferable securities to which this section applies, a prospectus approved by the FCA.

(8)   ...

Note. This section is amended by S.I. 2024/105, reg. 47(a), Sch. 3, Pt. 1, paras. 1, 6, as from a day to be appointed (save for certain purposes).

86.   *Exempt offers to the public and admissions to trading*

(1)   A person does not contravene section 85(1) if—

(aa)   the offer falls within Article 1(4) of the prospectus regulation; or

(e)   the total consideration for the transferable securities being offered in the United Kingdom cannot exceed 8,000,000 euros (or an equivalent amount); ...

(f)   ...

(1A), (1B) ...

(2)   Where—

(a)   a person ("the client") who is not a qualified investor (as defined in ... Article 2(e) of the prospectus regulation) has engaged a qualified investor falling within paragraph 3(a) of Schedule 1 to the markets in financial instruments regulation to act as his agent, and

(b)   the terms on which the qualified investor is engaged enable him to make decisions concerning the acceptance of offers of transferable securities on the client's behalf without reference to the client,

an offer made to or directed at the qualified investor is not to be regarded for the purposes of subsection (1) as also having been made to or directed at the client.

(3)   For the purposes of subsection (1), the making of an offer of transferable securities to—

(a)   trustees of a trust,

(b)   members of a partnership in their capacity as such, or

(c)   two or more persons jointly,

is to be treated as the making of an offer to a single person.

(4)   In determining whether subsection (1)(e) is satisfied in relation to an offer ("offer A"), offer A is to be taken together with any other offer of transferable securities of the same class made by the same person which—

(a)   was open at any time within the period of 12 months ending with the date on which offer A is first made; and

(b)   had previously satisfied subsection (1)(e).

(4A)   A person does not contravene section 85(2) if the admission to trading falls within Article 1(5) of the prospectus regulation.

(5)   For the purposes of this section, an amount (in relation to an amount denominated in euros) is an "equivalent amount" if it is an amount of equal value denominated wholly or partly in another currency or unit of account.

(6)   The equivalent is to be calculated at the latest practicable date before (but in any event not more than 3 working days before) the date on which the offer is first made.

(7)–(10) ...

Note. This section is repealed by S.I. 2024/105, reg. 47(a), Sch. 3, Pt. 1, paras. 1, 7, as from a day to be appointed (save for certain purposes).

87. ***Election to have prospectus***

(1), (2) ...

(3)   *Listing rules made under section 79 do not apply to securities for which a prospectus is drawn up voluntarily in exercise of entitlement to do so under Article 4 of the prospectus regulation.*

(4)   ...

> **Note.** This section is repealed by S.I. 2024/105, reg. 47(a), Sch. 3, Pt. 1, paras. 1, 7, as from a day to be appointed (save for certain purposes).

Approval of prospectus

87A. ***Criteria for approval of prospectus by FCA***

(1)   *The FCA may not approve a prospectus unless it is satisfied that—*

     (a)   ...

     (b)   *the prospectus contains the information required by Article 6(1) or 14(2) of the prospectus regulation, and*

     (c)   *all of the other requirements imposed by or in accordance with this Part, the prospectus regulation or prospectus rules have been complied with (so far as those requirements apply to a prospectus for the transferable securities in question).*

(2)   *The necessary information is—*

     (a)   *the information required by Article 6(1) of the prospectus regulation, or*

     (b)   *in a case within Article 14(1) of that regulation, the information required by Article 14(2) of that regulation.*

(2A)   *If, in the case of transferable securities to which section 87 applies, the prospectus states that the guarantor is a specified ... State, the prospectus is not required to include other information about the guarantor.*

(3)–(7A) ...

(8)   *"Prospectus" ... includes a supplementary prospectus.*

(9), (10) ...

> **Note.** This section and the preceding cross-heading are repealed by S.I. 2024/105, reg. 47(a), Sch. 3, Pt. 1, paras. 1, 7, as from a day to be appointed (save for certain purposes).

87B. ***Exemptions from disclosure***

(1)   ...

(2)   *The Secretary of State or the Treasury may issue a certificate to the effect that the disclosure of any information would be contrary to the public interest.*

(3)   *The FCA is entitled to act on any such certificate in exercising its powers under Article 18(1)(a) of the prospectus regulation.*

(4)   *This section does not affect any powers of the FCA under prospectus rules.*

(5)   ...

> **Note.** This section is repealed by S.I. 2024/105, reg. 47(a), Sch. 3, Pt. 1, paras. 1, 7, as from a day to be appointed (save for certain purposes).

87C. ***Consideration of application for approval***

(1)–(3) ...

(4)   *The FCA may by notice in writing require a person who has applied for approval of a prospectus to provide—*

     (a)   *specified documents or documents of a specified description, or*

     (b)   *specified information or information of a specified description.*

(5)   ...

(6)   *Subsection (4) applies only to information and documents reasonably required in connection with the exercise by the FCA of its functions in relation to the application.*

(7)   *The FCA may require any information provided under this section to be provided in such form as it may reasonably require.*

(8)   *The FCA may require—*

    (a)   *any information provided, whether in a document or otherwise, to be verified in such manner, or*

    (b)   *any document produced to be authenticated in such manner,*

    as it may reasonably require.

(9)   *... subsections (4) and (6) to (8) apply to an application for approval of a supplementary prospectus as they apply to an application for approval of a prospectus.*

(10), (11) ...

    Note. This section is repealed by S.I. 2024/105, reg. 47(a), Sch. 3, Pt. 1, paras. 1, 7, as from a day to be appointed (save for certain purposes).

87D.   *Procedure for decision to refuse an application for approval*

(1), (1A) ...

(2)   *If the FCA proposes to refuse to approve a prospectus, it must give the applicant written notice.*

(3)   *The notice must state the FCA's reasons for the proposed refusal.*

(4)   *If the FCA decides to refuse to approve a prospectus, it must give the applicant written notice.*

(5)   *The notice must—*

    (a)   *give the FCA's reasons for refusing the application; and*

    (b)   *inform the applicant of his right to refer the matter to the Tribunal.*

(6)   *If the FCA refuses to approve a prospectus, the applicant may refer the matter to the Tribunal.*

(7)   *In this section "prospectus" includes a supplementary prospectus.*

    Note. This section is repealed by S.I. 2024/105, reg. 47(a), Sch. 3, Pt. 1, paras. 1, 7, as from a day to be appointed (save for certain purposes).

87E–87FB. ...

Supplementary prospectus

87G.   *Supplementary prospectus*

(1)–(4) ...

(5)   *Any person who is responsible for a prospectus approved by the FCA and who is aware of any new factor, material mistake or material inaccuracy which may require the submission of a supplementary prospectus in accordance with Article 23 of the prospectus regulation must give notice of it to—*

    (a)   *the issuer of the transferable securities to which the prospectus relates, and*

    (b)   *the person on whose application the prospectus was approved.*

(6), (7) ...

    Note. This section and the preceding cross-heading are repealed by S.I. 2024/105, reg. 47(a), Sch. 3, Pt. 1, paras. 1, 7, as from a day to be appointed (save for certain purposes).

87H, 87I. ...

Transferable securities: powers of FCA

87J.   *Requirements imposed as condition of approval*

(1)   *As a condition of approving a prospectus, the FCA may by notice in writing—*

    (a)   *require the inclusion in the prospectus of such supplementary information necessary for investor protection as the FCA may specify;*

    (b)   *require a person controlling, or controlled by, the applicant to provide specified information or documents;*

    (c)   *require an auditor or manager of the applicant to provide specified information or documents;*

    (d)   *require a financial intermediary commissioned to assist either in carrying out the offer to the public of the transferable securities to which the prospectus relates or in requesting their admission to trading on a regulated market, to provide specified information or documents.*

(2)   *"Specified" means specified in the notice.*

(3)   *"Prospectus" includes a supplementary prospectus.*

Note. This section and the preceding cross-heading are repealed by S.I. 2024/105, reg. 47(a), Sch. 3, Pt. 1, paras. 1, 7, as from a day to be appointed (save for certain purposes).

87JA. *Power to suspend scrutiny of prospectus*

(1) *Where the FCA has received an application for approval of a prospectus, it may suspend its scrutiny of the prospectus on the ground that—*

    (a) *before receiving the application, it had imposed a prohibition or restriction under Article 42 of the markets in financial instruments regulation in relation to any financial activity or practice of the applicant;*

    (b) *in considering the application, it has decided to impose a prohibition or restriction under that Article in relation to the transferable securities to which the prospectus relates or any financial activity or practice of the applicant;*

    (c) *before receiving the application, it had found that a financial activity or practice of the applicant had contravened product intervention rules; or*

    (d) *in considering the application, it has decided that the approval of the prospectus would be likely to result in a contravention of product intervention rules.*

(2) *The FCA must resume its consideration of the application for approval of the prospectus—*

    (a) *where it suspended scrutiny of the prospectus on the ground specified in subsection (1)(a) or (b)—*

        (i) *upon revoking the prohibition or restriction under Article 42(6) of the markets in financial instruments regulation; or*

        (ii) *when it is satisfied that the prohibition or restriction does not have, or no longer has, any bearing on the approval of the prospectus;*

    (b) *where it suspended scrutiny of the prospectus on the ground specified in subsection (1)(c), when it is satisfied that the contravention of product intervention rules does not have, or no longer has, any bearing on the approval of the prospectus;*

    (c) *where it suspended scrutiny of the prospectus on the ground specified in subsection (1)(d), when it is satisfied that its approval of the prospectus would not result in a contravention of product intervention rules;*

    (d) *upon giving notice under section 87O(5) revoking its decision to suspend scrutiny of the prospectus;*

    (e) *where its decision to suspend scrutiny of the prospectus is quashed on a reference to the Tribunal or in other legal proceedings, on the date of the judgment of the Tribunal or of the court concerned.*

(3) *"Product intervention rules" has the same meaning as in section 137D.*

Note. This section is repealed by S.I. 2024/105, reg. 47(a), Sch. 3, Pt. 1, paras. 1, 7, as from a day to be appointed (save for certain purposes).

87JB. *Power to refuse approval of a prospectus*

(1) *Where the FCA is satisfied that a person has repeatedly and seriously infringed provision within subsection (2) (whether or not each infringement is of the same provision), the FCA may decide that, for a period not exceeding 5 years, the FCA will not accept from the person any application for approval of a prospectus.*

(2) *The provisions referred to in subsection (1) are—*

    (a) *any provision of this Part so far as relating to prospectuses;*

    (b) *any provision of prospectus rules;*

    (c) *any provision of the prospectus regulation;*

    (d) *any provision made in accordance with the prospectus regulation.*

(3) *If the FCA proposes that for a period it will not accept any application from a person for approval of a prospectus, the FCA must give the person a warning notice specifying the length of the proposed period.*

(4) *If the FCA decides for a period that it will not accept any application from a person for approval of a prospectus—*

(a)   the FCA must give the person a decision notice;

(b)   the period starts with the date of the notice;

(c)   the person may refer that matter to the Tribunal; and

(d)   the notice must—

     (i)   be dated;

     (ii)   specify the length of the period;

     (iii) state that the period begins with the date of the notice; and

     (iv)   state that the person may refer the matter to the Tribunal.

(5)   If the FCA decides not to accept any application from a person for the approval of a prospectus for a specified period, the person may refer the matter to the Tribunal.

Note. This section is repealed by S.I. 2024/105, reg. 47(a), Sch. 3, Pt. 1, paras. 1, 7, as from a day to be appointed (save for certain purposes).

87K.   Power to suspend, restrict or prohibit offer to the public

(1)   This section applies where a person ("the offeror") has made an offer of transferable securities to the public ... ("the offer").

(2)   If the FCA has reasonable grounds for suspecting that an applicable provision has been infringed, it may—

(a)   require the offeror to suspend the offer for a period not exceeding 10 working days;

(b)   require a person not to advertise the offer, or to take such steps as the FCA may specify to suspend any existing advertisement of the offer, for a period not exceeding 10 working days.

(3)   If the FCA has reasonable grounds for suspecting that it is likely that an applicable provision will be infringed, it may require the offeror to withdraw the offer.

(4)   If the FCA finds that an applicable provision has been infringed, it may require the offeror to withdraw the offer.

(5)   "An applicable provision" means—

(a)   a provision of this Part,

(b)   a provision contained in prospectus rules,

(c)   any provision of, or made in accordance with, the prospectus regulation,

applicable in relation to the offer.

(6)   The FCA may require the offeror to suspend or restrict the offer on the ground that—

(a)   before the offer was made, the FCA had imposed a prohibition or restriction under Article 42 of the markets in financial instruments regulation in relation to any financial activity or practice of the offeror;

(b)   the FCA has decided to impose a prohibition or restriction under that Article in relation to the transferable securities to which the offer relates or any financial activity or practice of the offeror;

(c)   before the offer was made, the FCA had found that a financial activity or practice of the offeror had contravened product intervention rules; or

(d)   the FCA has decided that the offer, if not suspended or restricted, would be likely to result in a contravention of product intervention rules.

(7)   A requirement imposed under subsection (6) ceases to have effect—

(a)   where it was imposed on the ground specified in subsection (6)(a) or (b)—

     (i)   upon revocation of the prohibition or restriction under Article 42(6) of the markets in financial instruments regulation; or

     (ii)   when the FCA notifies the offeror that it is satisfied that the prohibition or restriction does not have, or no longer has, any bearing on the transferable securities to which the offer relates;

(b)   where it was imposed on the ground specified in subsection (6)(c), when the FCA notifies the offeror that it is satisfied that the contravention of product intervention rules does not have, or no longer has, any bearing on the transferable securities to which the offer relates;

      (c)   *where it was imposed on the ground specified in subsection (6)(d), when the FCA notifies the offeror that it is satisfied that the offer, if no longer suspended or restricted, would not result in a contravention of product intervention rules;*

      (d)   *upon the FCA giving notice under section 87O(5) revoking its decision to impose the requirement;*

      (e)   *where the FCA's decision to impose the requirement is quashed on a reference to the Tribunal or in other legal proceedings, on the date of the judgment of the Tribunal or of the court concerned.*

(8)   *"Product intervention rules" has the same meaning as in section 137D.*

Note. This section is repealed by S.I. 2024/105, reg. 47(a), Sch. 3, Pt. 1, paras. 1, 7, as from a day to be appointed (save for certain purposes).

87L.   ***Power to suspend, restrict or prohibit admission to trading on a regulated market***

(1)   *This section applies where a person has requested the admission of transferable securities to trading on a regulated market ...*

(2)   *If the FCA has reasonable grounds for suspecting that an applicable provision has been infringed and the securities have not yet been admitted to trading on the regulated market in question, it may—*

      (a)   *require the person requesting admission to suspend the request for a period not exceeding 10 working days;*

      (b)   *require a person not to advertise the securities to which it relates, or to take such steps as the FCA may specify to suspend any existing advertisement in connection with those securities, for a period not exceeding 10 working days.*

(3)   *If the FCA has reasonable grounds for suspecting that an applicable provision has been infringed and the securities have been admitted to trading on the regulated market in question, it may—*

      (a)   *require the market operator to suspend trading in the securities for a period not exceeding 10 working days;*

      (b)   *require a person not to advertise the securities, or to take such steps as the FCA may specify to suspend any existing advertisement in connection with those securities, for a period not exceeding 10 working days.*

(4)   *If the FCA finds that an applicable provision has been infringed, it may require the market operator to prohibit trading in the securities on the regulated market in question.*

(5)   *"An applicable provision" means—*

      (a)   *a provision of this Part,*

      (b)   *a provision contained in prospectus rules,*

      (c)   *any provision of, or made in accordance with, the prospectus regulation,*

    applicable in relation to the admission of the transferable securities to trading on the regulated market in question.

(6)   *Subsections (7) and (8) apply where—*

      (a)   *before the request was made for the admission of the securities to trading on the regulated market in question ("the request"), the FCA had imposed a prohibition or restriction under Article 42 of the markets in financial instruments regulation in relation to any financial activity or practice of the person who made the request;*

      (b)   *the FCA has decided to impose a prohibition or restriction under that Article in relation to the securities or any financial activity or practice of the person who made the request;*

      (c)   *before the request was made, the FCA had found that a financial activity or practice of the person who made the request had contravened product intervention rules; or*

      (d)   *the FCA has decided that the admission of the securities to trading on the regulated market in question, if not suspended or restricted, would be likely to result in a contravention of product intervention rules.*

(7)   *Where the securities have not yet been admitted to trading on the regulated market in question, the FCA may—*

      (a)   *require the person who made the request to suspend or restrict the request;*

(b) *require a person not to advertise the securities, or to take such steps as the FCA may specify to suspend any existing advertising in connection with the securities.*

(8) *Where the securities have been admitted to trading on the regulated market in question, the FCA may—*

(a) *require the market operator to suspend or restrict trading in the securities;*

(b) *require a person not to advertise the securities, or to take such steps as the FCA may specify to suspend any existing advertising in connection with the securities.*

(9) *A requirement imposed under subsection (7) or (8) ceases to have effect—*

(a) *where it was imposed on the ground mentioned in subsection (6)(a) or (b)—*

   (i) *upon revocation of the prohibition or restriction under Article 42(6) of the markets in financial instruments regulation; or*

   (ii) *when the FCA notifies the person who made the request that it is satisfied that the prohibition or restriction does not have, or no longer has, any bearing on the securities;*

(b) *where it was imposed on the ground mentioned in subsection (6)(c), when the FCA notifies the person who made the request that it is satisfied that the contravention of product intervention rules does not have, or no longer has, any bearing on the securities;*

(c) *where it was imposed on the ground mentioned in subsection (6)(d), when the FCA notifies the person who made the request that it is satisfied that the admission of the securities to trading on the regulated market in question, if no longer suspended or restricted, would not result in a contravention of product intervention rules;*

(d) *upon the FCA giving notice under section 87O(5) revoking its decision to impose the requirement;*

(e) *where the FCA's decision to impose the requirement is quashed on a reference to the Tribunal or in other legal proceedings, on the date of the judgment of the Tribunal or of the court concerned.*

(10) *"Product intervention rules" has the same meaning as in section 137D.*

(11) *Where the FCA considers that the financial or other situation of a person at whose request transferable securities have been admitted to trading on a regulated market is such that trading would be detrimental to the interests of investors, it may require the market operator to suspend trading in the securities.*

Note. This section is repealed by S.I. 2024/105, reg. 47(a), Sch. 3, Pt. 1, paras. 1, 7, as from a day to be appointed (save for certain purposes).

87LA. ***Power of FCA to suspend or prohibit trading on a trading facility***

(1) *This section applies in relation to the trading of transferable securities on a trading facility.*

(2) *If—*

(a) *the FCA has reasonable grounds for suspecting that an applicable provision has been infringed, and*

(b) *the securities have not yet been traded on the trading facility in question,*

the FCA may require the person who proposes to trade the securities to suspend taking any action to implement the proposal for a period not exceeding 10 working days.

(3) *If—*

(a) *the FCA has reasonable grounds for suspecting that an applicable provision has been infringed, and*

(b) *the securities have been traded on the trading facility in question,*

the FCA may require the operator of the facility to suspend trading in the securities for a period not exceeding 10 working days.

(4) *If the FCA finds that an applicable provision has been infringed, it may require the operator of the trading facility in question to prohibit trading in the securities on that facility.*

(5) *In this section—*

"applicable provision" means—

(a) *a provision of this Part,*

(b)   a provision contained in prospectus rules, or

(c)   any provision of, or made in accordance with, the prospectus regulation;

"trading facility" means a UK multilateral trading facility or a UK organised trading facility;

"UK multilateral trading facility" has the meaning given in Article 2(1)(14A) of the markets in financial instruments regulation;

"UK organised trading facility" has the meaning given in Article 2(1)(15A) of the markets in financial instruments regulation.

Note. This section is repealed by S.I. 2024/105, reg. 47(a), Sch. 3, Pt. 1, paras. 1, 7, as from a day to be appointed (save for certain purposes).

87M.   Public censure of issuer

(1)   If the FCA finds that—

(a)   an issuer of transferable securities,

(b)   a person offering transferable securities to the public, or

(c)   a person requesting the admission of transferable securities to trading on a regulated market,

is failing or has failed to comply with his obligations under an applicable provision, it may publish a statement to that effect.

(2)   If the FCA proposes to publish a statement, it must give the person a warning notice setting out the terms of the proposed statement.

(3)   If, after considering any representations made in response to the warning notice, the FCA decides to make the proposed statement, it must give the person a decision notice setting out the terms of the statement.

(4)   "An applicable provision" means—

(a)   a provision of this Part,

(b)   a provision contained in prospectus rules,

(c)   any provision of, or made in accordance with, the prospectus regulation,

applicable to a prospectus in relation to the transferable securities in question.

(5)   "Prospectus" includes a supplementary prospectus and also includes, where final terms (see Article 8 of the prospectus regulation) are contained in a separate document that is neither a prospectus nor a supplementary prospectus, that separate document.

Note. This section is repealed by S.I. 2024/105, reg. 47(a), Sch. 3, Pt. 1, paras. 1, 7, as from a day to be appointed (save for certain purposes).

87N.   Right to refer matters to the Tribunal

(1)   A person to whom a decision notice is given under section 87M may refer the matter to the Tribunal.

(2)   A person to whom a notice is given under section 87O may refer the matter to the Tribunal.

Note. This section is repealed by S.I. 2024/105, reg. 47(a), Sch. 3, Pt. 1, paras. 1, 7, as from a day to be appointed (save for certain purposes).

87O.   Procedure under sections 87JA, 87K, 87L and 87LA

(1)   A requirement under section 87K, 87L or 87LA, or a suspension under section 87JA(1), takes effect—

(a)   immediately, if the notice under subsection (2) states that that is the case;

(b)   in any other case, on such date as may be specified in that notice.

(2)   If the FCA—

(a)   proposes to exercise the powers in section 87JA, 87K, 87L or 87LA in relation to a person, or

(b)   exercises any of those powers in relation to a person with immediate effect,

it must give that person written notice.

(3)   The notice must—

(a)   give details of the FCA's action or proposed action;

(b)   state the FCA's reasons for taking the action in question and choosing the date on which it took effect or takes effect;

(c)   *inform the recipient that he may make representations to the FCA within such period as may be specified by the notice (whether or not he has referred the matter to the Tribunal);*

(d)   *inform him of the date on which the action took effect or takes effect; and*

(e)   *inform him of his right to refer the matter to the Tribunal.*

(4)   *The FCA may extend the period within which representations may be made to it.*

(5)   *If, having considered any representations made to it, the FCA decides to maintain, vary or revoke its earlier decision, it must give written notice to that effect to the person mentioned in subsection (2).*

(6)   *A notice given under subsection (5) must inform that person, where relevant, of his right to refer the matter to the Tribunal.*

(7)   *If a notice informs a person of his right to refer a matter to the Tribunal, it must give an indication of the procedure on such a reference.*

(8)   *If a notice under this section relates to the exercise of the power conferred by section 87L(3), the notice must also be given to the person at whose request the transferable securities were admitted to trading on the regulated market.*

Note. This section is repealed by S.I. 2024/105, reg. 47(a), Sch. 3, Pt. 1, paras. 1, 7, as from a day to be appointed (save for certain purposes).

87P. ...

87Q, 87R. ...

Sponsors

88.   Sponsors

(1)   Listing rules may require a person to make arrangements with a sponsor for the performance by the sponsor of such services in relation to him as may be specified in the rules.

(2)   "Sponsor" means a person approved by the FCA for the purposes of the rules.

(3)   Listing rules made by virtue of subsection (1) may—

(a)   provide for the FCA to maintain a list of sponsors;

(b)   specify services which must be performed by a sponsor;

(c)   impose requirements on a sponsor in relation to the provision of services or specified services;

(d)   specify the circumstances in which a person is qualified for being approved as a sponsor;

(e)   provide for limitations or other restrictions to be imposed on the services to which an approval relates (whether or not the approval has already been granted);

(f)   provide for the approval of a sponsor to be suspended on the application of the sponsor.

(4)   If the FCA proposes—

(a)   to refuse a person's application under sponsor rules,

(aa) to impose limitations or other restrictions on the services to which a person's approval relates, or

(b)   to cancel a person's approval as a sponsor otherwise than at his request,

it must give him a warning notice.

(5)   If, after considering any representations made in response to the warning notice, the FCA decides—

(a)   to grant the application under sponsor rules,

(aa) not to impose limitations or other restrictions on the services to which a person's approval relates, or

(b)   not to cancel the approval,

it must give the person concerned, and any person to whom a copy of the warning notice was given, written notice of its decision.

(6)   If, after considering any representations made in response to the warning notice, the FCA decides—

(a)   to refuse to grant the application under sponsor rules,

(aa) to impose limitations or other restrictions on the services to which a person's approval relates, or

(b)   to cancel the approval,

it must give the person concerned a decision notice.

(7)   A person to whom a decision notice is given under this section may refer the matter to the Tribunal.

(8)   In this section any reference to an application under sponsor rules means—

(a)   an application for approval as a sponsor,

(b)   an application for the suspension of an approval as a sponsor,

(c)   an application for the withdrawal of the suspension of an approval as a sponsor, or

(d)   an application for the withdrawal or variation of a limitation or other restriction on the services to which a sponsor's approval relates.

...

89.   ...

Transparency obligations

89A.   Transparency rules

(1)   The FCA may make rules—

(a)   imposing requirements in relation to the disclosure of periodic or ongoing information about issuers whose securities are admitted to trading on a regulated market, and

(b)   dealing with matters arising out of or relating to such requirements.

(2)   The rules may include provision for dealing with any matters dealt with in the transparency obligations directive or with any matters that, when the United Kingdom was a member State, would have been matters arising out of or related to any provision of the transparency obligations directive.

(3)   The FCA may also make rules—

(a)   for the purpose of ensuring that voteholder information in respect of voting shares traded on a UK market other than a regulated market is made public or notified to the FCA;

(b)   ...

(4)   Rules under this section may, in particular, make provision—

(a)   specifying how the proportion of—

(i)   the total voting rights in respect of shares in an issuer, or

(ii)   the total voting rights in respect of a particular class of shares in an issuer,

held by a person is to be determined;

(b)   specifying the circumstances in which, for the purposes of any determination of the voting rights held by a person ("P") in respect of voting shares in an issuer, any voting rights held, or treated by virtue of subsection (3)(b) as held, by another person in respect of voting shares in the issuer are to be regarded as held by P;

(c)   specifying the nature of the information which must be included in any notification;

(d)   about the form of any notification;

(e)   requiring any notification to be given within a specified period;

(f)   specifying the manner in which any information is to be made public and the period within which it must be made public;

(g)   specifying circumstances in which any of the requirements imposed by rules under this section does not apply.

(4A)   The provision that may be made by virtue of subsection (4)(g) includes (but is not limited to) provision, in the case of an issuer whose registered office is situated in a country or territory outside the United Kingdom, allowing exemption from specified provisions of rules under this section if—

(a)   the law of that country or territory is considered by the FCA to lay down equivalent requirements, or

(b)   the issuer complies with the requirements of the law of a country or territory that the FCA considers as equivalent.

(5) Rules under this section are referred to in this Part as "transparency rules".

(6) Nothing in sections 89B to 89G affects the generality of the power to make rules under this section.

89B. Provision of voteholder information

(1) Transparency rules may make provision for voteholder information in respect of voting shares to be notified, in circumstances specified in the rules—

   (a) to the issuer, or

   (b) to the public,

or to both.

(2) Transparency rules may make provision for voteholder information notified to the issuer to be notified at the same time to the FCA.

(3) In this Part "voteholder information" in respect of voting shares means information relating to the proportion of voting rights held by a person in respect of the shares.

(4) Transparency rules may require notification of voteholder information relating to a person in accordance with the following provisions.

(5) Transparency rules ... may require notification of voteholder information relating to a person only where there is a notifiable change in the proportion of—

   (a) the total voting rights in respect of shares in the issuer, or

   (b) the total voting rights in respect of a particular class of share in the issuer,

held by the person.

(6) For this purpose there is a "notifiable change" in the proportion of voting rights held by a person when the proportion changes—

   (a) from being a proportion less than a designated proportion to a proportion equal to or greater than that designated proportion,

   (b) from being a proportion equal to a designated proportion to a proportion greater or less than that designated proportion, or

   (c) from being a proportion greater than a designated proportion to a proportion equal to or less than that designated proportion.

(7) In subsection (6) "designated" means designated by the rules.

89C. Provision of information by issuers of transferable securities

(1) Transparency rules may make provision requiring the issuer of transferable securities, in circumstances specified in the rules—

   (a) to make public information to which this section applies, or

   (b) to notify to the FCA information to which this section applies,

or to do both.

(2) In the case of every issuer, this section applies to—

   (a) an annual financial report which complies with subsection (5) and with such other requirements as may be specified;

   (aa) in the case of an issuer which is—

     (i) a mining or quarrying undertaking, or

     (ii) a logging undertaking,

    reports complying with specified requirements on payments to governments; and

   (b) information relating to the rights attached to the transferable securities, including information about the terms and conditions of those securities which could indirectly affect those rights; ...

   (c) ...

(3) In the case of an issuer of debt securities, this section also applies to a half-yearly financial report which covers the first 6 months of the financial year and complies with subsection (6) and with such other requirements as may be specified.

(4) In the case of an issuer of shares, this section also applies to—

    (a)   a half-yearly financial report which covers the first 6 months of the financial year and complies with subsection (6) and with such other requirements as may be specified;

    (b)   ...

    (c)   voteholder information—

        (i)   notified to the issuer, or

        (ii)   relating to the proportion of voting rights held by the issuer in respect of shares in the issuer;

    (d)   information relating to the issuer's capital; and

    (e)   information relating to the total number of voting rights in respect of shares or shares of a particular class.

(5)   An issuer's annual financial report must include—

    (a)   audited financial statements complying with specified requirements,

    (b)   a management report complying with specified requirements, and

    (c)   statements which—

        (i)   relate to the financial statements and the management report,

        (ii)   are made by the persons responsible within the issuer, and

        (iii)   comply with specified requirements.

(6)   An issuer's half-yearly financial report must include—

    (a)   a condensed set of financial statements complying with specified requirements,

    (b)   an interim management report complying with specified requirements, and

    (c)   statements which—

        (i)   relate to the condensed set of financial statements and the interim management report,

        (ii)   are made by the persons responsible within the issuer, and

        (iii)   comply with specified requirements.

(7)   In subsection (2)(aa), "mining or quarrying undertaking", "logging undertaking", "payment" and "government" have the same meanings as in the Reports on Payments to Governments Regulations 2014.

(8)   In this section "specified" means specified in, or referred to in, transparency rules.

89D.   **Notification of voting rights held by issuer**

(1)   Transparency rules may require notification of voteholder information relating to the proportion of voting rights held by an issuer in respect of voting shares in the issuer in accordance with the following provisions.

(2)   Transparency rules ... may require notification of voteholder information relating to the proportion of voting rights held by an issuer in respect of voting shares in the issuer only where there is a notifiable change in the proportion of—

    (a)   the total voting rights in respect of shares in the issuer, or

    (b)   the total voting rights in respect of a particular class of share in the issuer,

    held by the issuer.

(3)   For this purpose there is a "notifiable change" in the proportion of voting rights held by a person when the proportion changes—

    (a)   from being a proportion less than a designated proportion to a proportion equal to or greater than that designated proportion,

    (b)   from being a proportion equal to a designated proportion to a proportion greater or less than that designated proportion, or

    (c)   from being a proportion greater than a designated proportion to a proportion equal to or less than that designated proportion.

(4)   In subsection (3) "designated" means designated by the rules.

89E.   ...

89F.   **Transparency rules: interpretation etc**

(1)   For the purposes of sections 89A to 89G—

(a)   the voting rights in respect of any voting shares are the voting rights attached to those shares, and

(b)   a person is to be regarded as holding the voting rights in respect of the shares—

     (i)   if, by virtue of those shares, he is a shareholder within the meaning of Article 2.1(e) of the transparency obligations directive;

     (ii)   if, and to the extent that, he is entitled to acquire, dispose of or exercise those voting rights in one or more of the cases mentioned in Article 10(a) to (h) of the transparency obligations directive;

     (iii)   if he holds, directly or indirectly, a financial instrument which satisfies the conditions set out in Article 13(1)(a) or (b) of the transparency obligations directive; ...

(c)   ...

(1A)   The FCA must establish, publish and periodically update an indicative list of financial instruments that are subject to notification requirements by virtue of subsection (1)(b)(iii), taking into account developments on financial markets.

(1B)   Publication of the indicative list is to be in such manner as the FCA considers appropriate.

(2)   ...

(3)   For the purposes of sections 89A to 89G two or more persons may, at the same time, each be regarded as holding the same voting rights.

(4)   In those sections—

     ...

     ...

"UK market" means a market that is situated or operating in the United Kingdom;

"voting shares" means shares of an issuer to which voting rights are attached.

     ...

Powers exercisable in case of infringement of transparency obligation

89K.   Public censure of issuer

(1)   If the FCA finds that an issuer of securities admitted to trading on a regulated market is failing or has failed to comply with an applicable transparency obligation, it may publish a statement to that effect.

(2)   If the FCA proposes to publish a statement, it must give the issuer a warning notice setting out the terms of the proposed statement.

(3)   If, after considering any representations made in response to the warning notice, the FCA decides to make the proposed statement, it must give the issuer a decision notice setting out the terms of the statement.

(4)   A notice under this section must inform the issuer of his right to refer the matter to the Tribunal (see section 89N) and give an indication of the procedure on such a reference.

(5)   In this section "transparency obligation" means an obligation under qualifying transparency legislation.

(5A)   In this Part "qualifying transparency legislation" means—

(a)   transparency rules,

(b)   any EU regulation, originally made under the transparency obligations directive, that is assimilated direct legislation,

(c)   regulations made by the Treasury under regulation 71 of the Official Listing of Securities, Prospectus and Transparency (Amendment etc) (EU Exit) Regulations 2019 for a purpose specified in paragraphs 10 to 20 of Schedule 2 to those Regulations, or

(d)   technical standards made by the FCA under regulation 72 of those Regulations for a purpose specified in paragraphs 31 to 35 of that Schedule.

(6)   ...

89L.   Power to suspend or prohibit trading of securities

(1)   This section applies to securities admitted to trading on a regulated market.

(2)   If the FCA has reasonable grounds for suspecting that an applicable transparency obligation has been infringed by an issuer, it may—
     (a)   suspend trading in the securities for a period not exceeding 10 days,
     (b)   prohibit trading in the securities, or
     (c)   make a request to the operator of the market on which the issuer's securities are traded—
          (i)   to suspend trading in the securities for a period not exceeding 10 days, or
          (ii)   to prohibit trading in the securities.

(3)   If the FCA has reasonable grounds for suspecting that an applicable transparency obligation has been infringed by a voteholder of an issuer, it may—
     (a)   prohibit trading in the securities, or
     (b)   make a request to the operator of the market on which the issuer's securities are traded to prohibit trading in the securities.

(4)   If the FCA finds that an applicable transparency obligation has been infringed, it may require the market operator to prohibit trading in the securities.

(5)   In this section "transparency obligation" means an obligation under qualifying transparency legislation.

(6)   ...

89M.   Procedure under section 89L

(1)   A requirement under section 89L takes effect—
     (a)   immediately, if the notice under subsection (2) states that that is the case;
     (b)   in any other case, on such date as may be specified in the notice.

(2)   If the FCA—
     (a)   proposes to exercise the powers in section 89L in relation to a person, or
     (b)   exercises any of those powers in relation to a person with immediate effect,
     it must give that person written notice.

(3)   The notice must—
     (a)   give details of the FCA's action or proposed action;
     (b)   state the FCA's reasons for taking the action in question and choosing the date on which it took effect or takes effect;
     (c)   inform the recipient that he may make representations to the FCA within such period as may be specified by the notice (whether or not he had referred the matter to the Tribunal);
     (d)   inform him of the date on which the action took effect or takes effect;
     (e)   inform him of his right to refer the matter to the Tribunal (see section 89N) and give an indication of the procedure on such a reference.

(4)   The FCA may extend the period within which representations may be made to it.

(5)   If, having considered any representations made to it, the FCA decides to maintain, vary or revoke its earlier decision, it must give written notice to that effect to the person mentioned in subsection (2).

89N.   Right to refer matters to the Tribunal

     A person—
     (a)   to whom a decision notice is given under section 89K (public censure), or
     (b)   to whom a notice is given under section 89M (procedure in connection with suspension or prohibition of trading),
     may refer the matter to the Tribunal.

89NA. Voting rights suspension orders

(1)   The court may, on the application of the FCA and in accordance with this section, make a voting rights suspension order in respect of a person who is a voteholder in relation to shares in a particular company which are admitted to trading on a regulated market and identified in the application.

(2)   A voting rights suspension order is an order which suspends the person's exercise of voting rights attaching to the shares to which the order relates.

(3)   The court may make a voting rights suspension order in respect of a person only if it is satisfied—
         (a)   that the person has contravened one or more relevant transparency provisions in respect of any of the shares identified in the application or any other shares in the same company which are admitted to trading on a regulated market, and
         (b)   that the contravention is serious enough to make it appropriate to make the order.

(4)   For the purposes of subsection (3)(b), the court may, in particular, have regard to—
         (a)   whether the contravention was deliberate or repeated;
         (b)   the time taken for the contravention to be remedied;
         (c)   whether the voteholder ignored warnings or requests for compliance from the FCA;
         (d)   the size of the holding of shares to which the contravention relates;
         (e)   any impact of the contravention on the integrity of the UK financial system;
         (f)   the effect of the contravention on any company merger or takeover.

(5)   A voting rights suspension order may be made in relation to some or all of the shares to which the application relates.

(6)   A voting rights suspension order may be made for a specified period or an indefinite period.

(7)   A voting rights suspension order takes effect—
         (a)   on the date specified in the order, or
         (b)   if no date is specified, at the time it is made.

(8)   Where a voting rights suspension order has been made, the FCA, the person to whom it applies or the company which issued the shares to which it relates, may apply to the court for—
         (a)   a variation of the order so as to alter the period for which it has effect or the shares in relation to which it has effect, or
         (b)   the discharge of the order.

(9)   The FCA must consult the PRA before making an application to the court under this section in relation to—
         (a)   a person who is a PRA-authorised person, or
         (b)   shares issued by a PRA-authorised person.

(10)   The jurisdiction conferred by this section is exercisable—
         (a)   in England and Wales and Northern Ireland, by the High Court, and
         (b)   in Scotland, by the Court of Session.

(11)   In this section—
         "relevant transparency provision" means—
         (a)   a provision of the transparency rules which implemented Article 9, 10, 12, 13 or 13a of the transparency obligations directive, ...
         (b)   a provision, originally made under any of those Articles, that is assimilated direct legislation,
         (c)   a provision of regulations made by the Treasury under regulation 71 of the Official Listing of Securities, Prospectus and Transparency (Amendment etc.) (EU Exit) Regulations 2019 for a purpose specified in paragraphs 13 to 16 of Schedule 2 to those Regulations, or
         (d)   a provision of technical standards made by the FCA under regulation 72 of those Regulations for a purpose specified in paragraphs 32 to 35 of that Schedule;
         "voteholder" has the meaning given by section 89J(3).

Corporate governance

89O.   Corporate governance rules

(1)   The FCA may make rules ("corporate governance rules") relating to the corporate governance of issuers who have requested or approved admission of their securities to trading on a regulated market.

(2)   "Corporate governance", in relation to an issuer, includes—
         (a)   the nature, constitution or functions of the organs of the issuer;
         (b)   the manner in which organs of the issuer conduct themselves;
         (c)   the requirements imposed on organs of the issuer;

(d)   the relationship between the different organs of the issuer;

(e)   the relationship between the organs of the issuer and the members of the issuer or holders of the issuer's securities.

(3), (4)   ...

(5)   This section is without prejudice to any other power conferred by this Part to make Part 6 rules.

Primary information providers

89P.   Primary information providers

(1)   Part 6 rules may require issuers of financial instruments to use primary information providers for the purpose of giving information of a specified description to a market of a specified description.

(2)   "Primary information provider" means a person approved by the FCA for the purposes of this section.

(3)   "Specified" means specified in the Part 6 rules.

(4)   Part 6 rules made by virtue of subsection (1) may—

(a)   provide for the FCA to maintain a list of providers;

(b)   impose requirements on a provider in relation to the giving of information or of information of a specified description;

(c)   specify the circumstances in which a person is qualified for being approved as a provider;

(d)   provide for limitations or other restrictions to be imposed on the giving of information to which an approval relates (whether or not the approval has already been granted);

(e)   provide for the approval of a provider to be suspended on the application of the provider.

(5)   If the FCA proposes—

(a)   to refuse a person's application under information provider rules,

(b)   to impose limitations or other restrictions on the giving of information to which a person's approval relates, or

(c)   to cancel a person's approval as a provider otherwise than at the person's request,

it must give the person a warning notice.

(6)   If the FCA decides—

(a)   to grant the application under information provider rules,

(b)   not to impose limitations or other restrictions on the giving of information to which a person's approval relates, or

(c)   not to cancel the approval,

it must give the person concerned written notice of its decision.

(7)   If the FCA decides—

(a)   to refuse to grant the application under information provider rules,

(b)   to impose limitations or other restrictions on the giving of information to which a person's approval relates, or

(c)   to cancel the approval,

it must give the person concerned a decision notice.

(8)   A person to whom a decision notice is given under this section may refer the matter to the Tribunal.

(9)   In this section any reference to an application under information provider rules means—

(a)   an application for approval as a provider,

(b)   an application for the suspension of an approval as a provider,

(c)   an application for the withdrawal of the suspension of an approval as a provider, or

(d)   an application for the withdrawal or variation of a limitation or other restriction on the giving of information to which a provider's approval relates.

89Q.   Disciplinary powers: contravention of s 89P(4)(b) or (d)

(1)   The FCA may take action against a provider under this section if it considers that the provider has contravened a requirement or restriction imposed on the provider by rules made as a result of section 89P(4)(b) or (d).

(2)   If the FCA is entitled to take action under this section against a provider, it may do one or more of
        the following—
        (a)   impose a penalty on the provider of such amount as it considers appropriate;
        (b)   suspend, for such period as it considers appropriate, the provider's approval;
        (c)   impose, for such period as it considers appropriate, such limitations or other restrictions in
              relation to the giving by the provider of information as it considers appropriate;
        (d)   publish a statement to the effect that the provider has contravened a requirement or
              restriction imposed on the provider by rules made as a result of section 89P(4)(b) or (d).
(3)   The period for which a suspension or restriction is to have effect may not exceed 12 months.
(4)   A suspension may relate only to the giving of information in specified circumstances.
(5)   A restriction may, in particular, be imposed so as to require the provider to take, or refrain from
        taking, specified action.
(6)   The FCA may—
        (a)   withdraw a suspension or restriction, or
        (b)   vary a suspension or restriction so as to reduce the period for which it has effect or
              otherwise to limit its effect.
(7)   The FCA may not take action against a provider under this section after the end of the limitation
        period unless, before the end of that period, it has given a warning notice to the provider under
        section 89R(1).
(8)   "The limitation period" means the period of 3 years beginning with the first day on which the
        FCA knew that the provider had contravened the requirement or restriction.
(9)   For this purpose the FCA is to be treated as knowing that a provider has contravened a
        requirement or restriction if it has information from which that can reasonably be inferred.

89R.   Action under s 89Q: procedure and right to refer to Tribunal

(1)   If the FCA proposes to take action against a provider under section 89Q, it must give the provider
        a warning notice.
(2)   A warning notice about a proposal to impose a penalty must state the amount of the penalty.
(3)   A warning notice about a proposal—
        (a)   to suspend an approval, or
        (b)   to impose a restriction in relation to the giving of information,
        must state the period for which the suspension or restriction is to have effect.
(4)   A warning notice about a proposal to publish a statement must set out the terms of the statement.
(5)   If the FCA decides to take action against a provider under section 89Q, it must give the provider a
        decision notice.
(6)   A decision notice about the imposition of a penalty must state the amount of the penalty.
(7)   A decision notice about—
        (a)   the suspension of an approval, or
        (b)   the imposition of a restriction in relation to the giving of information,
        must state the period for which the suspension or restriction is to have effect.
(8)   A decision notice about the publication of a statement must set out the terms of the statement.
(9)   If the FCA decides to take action against a provider under section 89Q, the provider may refer the
        matter to the Tribunal.

89S.   Action under s 89Q: statement of policy

(1)   The FCA must prepare and issue a statement of its policy with respect to—
        (a)   the imposition of penalties, suspensions or restrictions under section 89Q,
        (b)   the amount of penalties under that section,
        (c)   the period for which suspensions or restrictions under that section are to have effect, and
        (d)   the matters in relation to which suspensions or restrictions under that section are to have
              effect.
(2)   The FCA's policy in determining what the amount of a penalty should be, or what the period for
        which a suspension or restriction is to have effect should be, must include having regard to—

(a) the seriousness of the contravention in question in relation to the nature of the requirement concerned,

(b) the extent to which that contravention was deliberate or reckless, and

(c) whether the provider concerned is an individual.

(3) The FCA may at any time alter or replace a statement issued under this section.

(4) If a statement issued under this section is altered or replaced, the FCA must issue the altered or replacement statement.

(5) In exercising, or deciding whether to exercise, its power under section 89Q in the case of any particular contravention, the FCA must have regard to any statement of policy published under this section and in force at a time when the contravention in question occurred.

(6) A statement issued under this section must be published by the FCA in the way appearing to the FCA to be best calculated to bring it to the attention of the public.

(7) The FCA may charge a reasonable fee for providing a person with a copy of the statement.

(8) The FCA must, without delay, give the Treasury a copy of any statement which it publishes under this section.

89T. Statement of policy under s 89S: procedure

(1) Before issuing a statement under section 89S, the FCA must publish a draft of the proposed statement in the way appearing to the FCA to be best calculated to bring it to the attention of the public.

(2) The draft must be accompanied by notice that representations about the proposal may be made to the FCA within a specified time.

(3) Before issuing the proposed statement, the FCA must have regard to any representations made to it in accordance with subsection (2).

(4) If the FCA issues the proposed statement it must publish an account, in general terms, of—

(a) the representations made to it in accordance with subsection (2); and

(b) its response to them.

(5) If the statement differs from the draft published under subsection (1) in a way which is, in the opinion of the FCA, significant, the FCA must (in addition to complying with subsection (4)) publish details of the difference.

(6) The FCA may charge a reasonable fee for providing a person with a copy of a draft published under subsection (1).

(7) This section also applies to a proposal to alter or replace a statement.

89U. Powers exercisable to advance operational objectives

(1) The FCA may take action against a provider under this section if it considers that it is desirable to do so in order to advance one or more of its operational objectives.

(2) If the FCA is entitled to take action under this section against a provider, it may—

(a) suspend, for such period as it considers appropriate, the provider's approval, or

(b) impose, for such period as it considers appropriate, such limitations or other restrictions in relation to the giving by the provider of information as it considers appropriate.

(3) A suspension may relate only to the giving of information in specified circumstances.

(4) A restriction may, in particular, be imposed so as to require the provider to take, or refrain from taking, specified action.

(5) The FCA may—

(a) withdraw a suspension or restriction, or

(b) vary a suspension or restriction so as to reduce the period for which it has effect or otherwise to limit its effect.

(6) A person against whom the FCA takes action under this section may refer the matter to the Tribunal.

89V. Action under s 89U: procedure

(1) Action against a provider under section 89U takes effect—

(a) immediately, if the notice given under subsection (2) so provides, or

      (b)   on such later date as may be specified in the notice.

(2)   If the FCA—

      (a)   proposes to take action against a provider under that section, or

      (b)   takes action against a provider under that section with immediate effect,

     it must give the provider written notice.

(3)   The notice must—

      (a)   give details of the action,

      (b)   state the FCA's reasons for taking the action and for its determination as to when the action takes effect,

      (c)   inform the provider that the provider may make representations to the FCA within such period as may be specified in the notice (whether or not the matter has been referred to the Tribunal),

      (d)   inform the provider of when the action takes effect,

      (e)   inform the provider of the right to refer the matter to the Tribunal, and

      (f)   give an indication of the procedure on such a reference.

(4)   The FCA may extend the period allowed under the notice for making representations.

(5)   If the FCA decides—

      (a)   to take the action in the way proposed, or

      (b)   if the action has taken effect, not to rescind it,

     the FCA must give the provider written notice.

(6)   If the FCA decides—

      (a)   not to take the action in the way proposed,

      (b)   to take action under section 89U that differs from the action originally proposed, or

      (c)   to rescind action which has taken effect,

     the FCA must give the provider written notice.

(7)   A notice under subsection (5) must—

      (a)   inform the provider of the right to refer the matter to the Tribunal, and

      (b)   give an indication of the procedure on such a reference.

(8)   A notice under subsection (6)(b) must comply with subsection (3).

89W.   Storage of regulated information

(1)   The FCA must ensure that there is at least one mechanism for the central storage of regulated information …

(1A)   The mechanism must comply with minimum quality standards of security, certainty as to the information source, time recording and easy access by end users (see provision made under regulation 71 of the Official Listing of Securities, Prospectus and Transparency (Amendment etc.) (EU Exit) Regulations 2019 for the purpose specified in paragraph 19(b) of Schedule 2 to those Regulations).

(1B)   The mechanism must be aligned with the procedure for filing the regulated information with the FCA.

(2)   In this section "regulated information" means information which an issuer, or a person who has applied for the admission of securities to trading on a regulated market without the issuer's consent, is required to disclose under—

      (a)   listing rules,

      (b)   qualifying transparency legislation, or

      (c)   Articles 17 to 19 of the market abuse regulation.

Compensation for false or misleading statements etc

90.   Compensation for statements in listing particulars or prospectus

(1)   Any person responsible for listing particulars is liable to pay compensation to a person who has—

      (a)   acquired securities to which the particulars apply; and

      (b)   suffered loss in respect of them as a result of—

         (i)   any untrue or misleading statement in the particulars; or

        (ii)   the omission from the particulars of any matter required to be included by section 80 or 81.

(2)   Subsection (1) is subject to exemptions provided by Schedule 10.

(3)   If listing particulars are required to include information about the absence of a particular matter, the omission from the particulars of that information is to be treated as a statement in the listing particulars that there is no such matter.

(4)   Any person who fails to comply with section 81 is liable to pay compensation to any person who has—

    (a)   acquired securities of the kind in question; and

    (b)   suffered loss in respect of them as a result of the failure.

(5)   Subsection (4) is subject to exemptions provided by Schedule 10.

(6)   This section does not affect any liability which may be incurred apart from this section.

(7)   References in this section to the acquisition by a person of securities include references to his contracting to acquire them or any interest in them.

(8)   No person shall, by reason of being a promoter of a company or otherwise, incur any liability for failing to disclose information which he would not be required to disclose in listing particulars in respect of a company's securities—

    (a)   if he were responsible for those particulars; or

    (b)   if he is responsible for them, which he is entitled to omit by virtue of section 82.

(9)   The reference in subsection (8) to a person incurring liability includes a reference to any other person being entitled as against that person to be granted any civil remedy or to rescind or repudiate an agreement.

(10)   "Listing particulars", in subsection (1) and Schedule 10, includes supplementary listing particulars.

(11)   This section applies in relation to a prospectus as it applies to listing particulars, with the following modifications—

    (a)   references in this section or in Schedule 10 to listing particulars, supplementary listing particulars or sections 80, 81 or 82 are to be read, respectively, as references to a prospectus, supplementary prospectus and Articles 6 and 14(2), Article 23 and Article 18 of the prospectus regulation;

    (b)   references in Schedule 10 to admission to the official list are to be read as references to admission to trading on a regulated market;

    (c)   in relation to a prospectus, "securities" means "transferable securities".

(11A)   In subsection (11)(a) "supplementary prospectus" includes, where final terms (see Article 8 of the prospectus regulation) are contained in a separate document that is neither a prospectus nor a supplementary prospectus, that separate document.

(12)   A person is not to be subject to civil liability solely on the basis of a summary in a prospectus unless the summary, when read with the rest of the prospectus—

    (a)   is misleading, inaccurate or inconsistent; or

    (b)   does not provide key information specified by Article 7 of the prospectus regulation,

    and in this subsection a summary includes any translation of it.

Note. This section is amended by S.I. 2024/105, reg. 47(a), Sch. 3, Pt. 1, paras. 1, 8, as from a day to be appointed (save for certain purposes).

90ZA. Liability for key investor information

(1)   A person is not to be subject to civil liability solely on the basis of the key investor information produced in relation to a collective investment scheme or a sub-fund of such a scheme in accordance with rules or other provisions originally made in implementation of Chapter IX of the UCITS directive, or of any translation of that information, unless the key investor information is misleading, inaccurate or inconsistent with the relevant parts of the prospectus published for that collective investment scheme or sub-fund in accordance with rules made by the FCA under section 248 or 261J of this Act.

(2)   In this section, a reference to a sub-fund of a collective investment scheme is a reference to a part of the property of the collective investment scheme which forms a separate pool where—

    (a)   the collective investment scheme provides arrangements for separate pooling of the contributions of the participants and the profits and income out of which payments are made to them; and

    (b)   the participants are entitled to exchange rights in one pool for rights in another.

90A.   Liability of issuers in connection with published information

Schedule 10A makes provision about the liability of issuers of securities to pay compensation to persons who have suffered loss as a result of—

    (a)   a misleading statement or dishonest omission in certain published information relating to the securities, or

    (b)   a dishonest delay in publishing such information.

90B.   Power to make further provision about liability for published information

(1)   The Treasury may by regulations make provision about the liability of issuers of securities traded on a regulated market, and other persons, in respect of information published to holders of securities, to the market or to the public generally.

(2)   Regulations under this section may amend any primary or subordinate legislation, including any provision of, or made under, this Act.

Penalties

91.   Penalties for breach of Part 6 rules

(1)   If the FCA considers that—

    (a)   an issuer of listed securities, or

    (b)   an applicant for listing,

has contravened any provision of listing rules, it may impose on him a penalty of such amount as it considers appropriate.

(1ZA)   ...

(1A)   If the FCA considers that—

    (a)   an issuer of transferable securities,

    (b)   a person offering transferable securities to the public or requesting their admission to trading on a regulated market,

    (c)   an applicant for the approval of a prospectus in relation to transferable securities,

    (d)   a person on whom a requirement has been imposed under section 87K or 87L, or

    (e)   any other person to whom any provision of, or made in accordance with, the prospectus regulation applies,

has contravened a provision of this Part or of prospectus rules, or a provision of or made in accordance with the prospectus regulation, or a requirement imposed on him under such a provision, it may impose on him a penalty of such amount as it considers appropriate.

(1B)   If the FCA considers—

    (a)   that a person has contravened—

        (i)   a provision of qualifying transparency legislation, or

        (ii)   a provision of corporate governance rules, or

    (b)   that a person on whom a requirement has been imposed under section 89L (power to suspend or prohibit trading of securities in case of infringement of applicable transparency obligation), has contravened that requirement,

it may impose on the person a penalty of such amount as it considers appropriate.

(2)   If, in the case of a contravention by a person referred to in subsection (1), ... (1A) or (1B)(a)(ii) or (b) ("P"), the FCA considers that another person who was at the material time a director of P was knowingly concerned in the contravention, it may impose upon him a penalty of such amount as it considers appropriate.

(2A)   If—

(a)   a person has contravened a provision mentioned in subsection (1B)(a)(i), and

(b)   the FCA considers that another person ("A"), who was at the material time a relevant officer of the person, was knowingly concerned in the contravention,

the FCA may impose upon A a penalty of such amount as it considers appropriate.

(2B)   In subsection (2A) "relevant officer" of a person means—

(a)   a director or other similar officer of the person, or

(b)   if the affairs of the person are managed by its members, a member of the person.

(3)   If the FCA is entitled to impose a penalty on a person under this section in respect of a particular matter it may, instead of imposing a penalty on him in respect of that matter, publish a statement censuring him.

(4)   Nothing in this section prevents the FCA from taking any other steps which it has power to take under this Part.

(5)   A penalty under this section is payable to the FCA.

(6)   The FCA may not take action against a person under this section after the end of the period of 3 years beginning with the first day on which it knew of the contravention unless proceedings against that person, in respect of the contravention, were begun before the end of that period.

(7)   For the purposes of subsection (6)—

(a)   the FCA is to be treated as knowing of a contravention if it has information from which the contravention can reasonably be inferred; and

(b)   proceedings against a person in respect of a contravention are to be treated as begun when a warning notice is given to him under section 92.

Note. This section is amended by S.I. 2024/105, reg. 47(a), Sch. 3, Pt. 1, paras. 1, 9, as from a day to be appointed (save for certain purposes).

92.   Warning notices

(1)   If the FCA proposes to take action against a person under section 91, it must give him a warning notice.

(2)   A warning notice about a proposal to impose a penalty must state the amount of the proposed penalty.

(3)   A warning notice about a proposal to publish a statement must set out the terms of the proposed statement.

(4)   If the FCA decides to take action against a person under section 91, it must give him a decision notice.

(5)   A decision notice about the imposition of a penalty must state the amount of the penalty.

(6)   A decision notice about the publication of a statement must set out the terms of the statement.

(7)   If the FCA decides to take action against a person under section 91, he may refer the matter to the Tribunal.

93.   Statement of policy

(1)   The FCA must prepare and issue a statement ("its policy statement") of its policy with respect to—

(a)   the imposition of penalties under section 91; and

(b)   the amount of penalties under that section.

(2)   The FCA's policy in determining what the amount of a penalty should be must include having regard to—

(a)   the seriousness of the contravention in question in relation to the nature of the requirement contravened;

(b)   the extent to which that contravention was deliberate or reckless; and

(c)   whether the person on whom the penalty is to be imposed is an individual.

(3)   The FCA may at any time alter or replace its policy statement.

(4)   If its policy statement is altered or replaced, the FCA must issue the altered or replacement statement.

(5)   In exercising, or deciding whether to exercise, its power under section 91 in the case of any particular contravention, the FCA must have regard to any policy statement published under this section and in force at the time when the contravention in question occurred.

(6)   The FCA must publish a statement issued under this section in the way appearing to the FCA to be best calculated to bring it to the attention of the public.

(7)   The FCA may charge a reasonable fee for providing a person with a copy of the statement.

(8)   The FCA must, without delay, give the Treasury a copy of any policy statement which it publishes under this section.

94. Statements of policy: procedure

(1)   Before issuing a statement under section 93, the FCA must publish a draft of the proposed statement in the way appearing to the FCA to be best calculated to bring it to the attention of the public.

(2)   The draft must be accompanied by notice that representations about the proposal may be made to the FCA within a specified time.

(3)   Before issuing the proposed statement, the FCA must have regard to any representations made to it in accordance with subsection (2).

(4)   If the FCA issues the proposed statement it must publish an account, in general terms, of—
(a)   the representations made to it in accordance with subsection (2); and
(b)   its response to them.

(5)   If the statement differs from the draft published under subsection (1) in a way which is, in the opinion of the FCA, significant, the competent authority must (in addition to complying with subsection (4)) publish details of the difference.

(6)   The FCA may charge a reasonable fee for providing a person with a copy of a draft published under subsection (1).

(7)   This section also applies to a proposal to alter or replace a statement.

...

95. ...

Miscellaneous

96. Obligations of issuers of listed securities

(1)   Listing rules may—
(a)   specify requirements to be complied with by issuers of listed securities; and
(b)   make provision with respect to the action that may be taken by the FCA in the event of non-compliance.

(2)   If the rules require an issuer to publish information, they may include provision authorising the FCA to publish it in the event of his failure to do so.

(3)   This section applies whenever the listed securities were admitted to the official list.

96A–97...

97A. *Reporting of infringements*

(1)   This section applies to a person—
(a)   who is the employer of any employees, and
(b)   who—
    (i)   provides regulated financial services,
    (ii)   carries on regulated activities in reliance on the exemption in section 327, or
    (iii)   is a recognised investment exchange, a recognised clearing house, a recognised CSD ... or a third country central counterparty.

(2)   The person must have in place appropriate internal procedures for the person's employees to report, through an independent channel, contraventions and potential contraventions of—
(a)   the prospectus regulation, ...

(b) *any EU regulation, originally made under the prospectus regulation, which is assimilated law, or*

(c) *any subordinate legislation (within the meaning of the Interpretation Act 1978) made under the prospectus regulation on or after IP completion day.*

(3) *In this section—*

"employer" and "employee" have the same meaning given in section 230(1) to (5) of the Employment Rights Act 1996;

"regulated financial services" has the meaning given by section 1H.

Note. This section is repealed by S.I. 2024/105, reg. 47(a), Sch. 3, Pt. 1, paras. 1, 11, as from a day to be appointed (save for certain purposes).

98–100. ...

100A. ...

101. Part 6 rules: general provisions

(1) ...

(2) Part 6 rules may authorise the FCA to dispense with or modify the application of the rules in particular cases and by reference to any circumstances.

(3)–(8) ...

102. ...

Interpretative provisions

102A. Meaning of "securities" etc.

(1) This section applies for the purposes of this Part.

(2) "Securities" means (except in section 74(2) and the expression "transferable securities") anything which has been, or may be, admitted to the official list.

(3) "Transferable securities" means anything which is a transferable security for the purposes of the markets in financial instruments regulation, other than money-market instruments for the purposes of that regulation which have a maturity of less than 12 months.

(3A) "Debt securities" means bonds or other forms of transferable securitised debts, with the exception of—

(a) transferable securities which are equivalent to shares, and

(b) transferable securities which, if converted or if the rights conferred by them are exercised, give rise to a right to acquire—

(i) shares, or

(ii) transferable securities equivalent to shares.

(4) "Financial instrument" means those instruments specified in Part 1 of Schedule 2 to the Financial Services and Markets Act 2000 (Regulated Activities) Order 2001.

(5) "Non-equity transferable securities" means all transferable securities that are not equity securities; and for this purpose the following are "equity securities"—

(a) shares,

(b) other transferable securities which are equivalent to shares, and

(c) transferable securities which—

(i) are within neither of paragraphs (a) and (b),

(ii) give the right to acquire securities within paragraph (a) or (b) if converted or if the rights conferred by them are exercised, and

(iii) are issued by the issuer of the underlying shares or by an entity belonging to the group of that issuer.

(6) "Issuer"—

(a) in relation to an offer of transferable securities to the public or admission of transferable securities to trading on a regulated market for which an approved prospectus is required under the prospectus regulation, means a legal person who issues or proposes to issue the transferable securities in question, (aa) in relation to transparency rules, means a … person whose securities are admitted to trading on a regulated market or whose voting shares are admitted to trading on a UK market other than a regulated market, and in the case of depository receipts admitted to trading on a regulated market, the issuer is the issuer of the securities represented by the depository receipt, whether or not those securities are admitted to trading on a regulated market;

(b) in relation to anything else which is or may be admitted to the official list, has such meaning as may be prescribed by the Treasury, and

(c) in any other case, means a person who issues financial instruments.

Note. This section is amended by S.I. 2024/105, reg. 47(a), Sch. 3, Pt. 1, paras. 1, 12, as from a day to be appointed (save for certain purposes).

102B.   *Meaning of "offer of transferable securities to the public" etc.*

(1)   For the purposes of this Part there is an offer of transferable securities to the public if there is a communication to any person which presents sufficient information on—

(a)   the transferable securities to be offered, and

(b)   the terms on which they are offered,

to enable an investor to decide to buy or subscribe for the securities in question.

(2)   For the purposes of this Part, to the extent that an offer of transferable securities is made to a person in the United Kingdom it is an offer of transferable securities to the public in the United Kingdom.

(3)   The communication may be made—

(a)   in any form;

(b)   by any means.

(4)   Subsection (1) includes the placing of securities through a financial intermediary.

(5)   Subsection (1) does not include a communication in connection with trading on—

(a)   a regulated market, as defined in Article 2(1)(13) of the markets in financial instruments regulation;

(b)   a multilateral trading facility; or

(c)   a prescribed market.

(5A)   The Treasury may make regulations to specify (whether by name or description) the markets which are prescribed markets for the purposes of subsection (5)(c).

(6)   "Multilateral trading facility" has the same meaning as in the markets in financial instruments regulation (see Article 2(1)(14) of that Regulation).

Note. This section is repealed by S.I. 2024/105, reg. 47(a), Sch. 3, Pt. 1, paras. 1, 13, as from a day to be appointed (save for certain purposes).

102C.   …

103.   Interpretation of this Part

(1)   In this Part, save where the context otherwise requires—

…

"listed securities" means anything which has been admitted to the official list;

"listing" has the meaning given in section 74(5);

"listing particulars" has the meaning given in section 79(2);

"listing rules" has the meaning given in section 73A;

"market operator" means a person who manages or operates the business of a regulated market;

"offer of transferable securities to the public" has the meaning given in section 102B;

"the official list" means the list maintained by the FCA as that list has effect for the time being;

"Part 6 rules" has the meaning given in section 73A;

…

"the prospectus regulation" means Regulation (EU) No. 2017/1129 of the European Parliament and of the Council of 14 June 2017 on the prospectus to be published when securities are offered to the public or admitted to trading on a regulated market, and repealing Directive 2003/71/EC;

"prospectus rules" has the meaning given in section 73A;

"qualifying transparency legislation" has the meaning given in section 89K(5A);

"regulated market" (except in section 102B and Schedule 10A) means a UK regulated market, as defined in Article 2(1)(13A) of the markets in financial instruments regulation;

"supplementary prospectus" means a supplement to a prospectus (and here "supplement" has the same meaning as in Article 23 of the prospectus regulation);

"the transparency obligations directive" means Directive 2004/ 109/EC of the European Parliament and of the Council relating to the harmonisation of transparency requirements in relation to information about issuers whose securities are admitted to trading on a regulated market as amended by Directive 2010/73/EU of the European Parliament and of the Council of 24 November 2010 and by Directive 2010/78/EU of the European Parliament and of the Council of 24 November 2010 and by Directive 2013/50/EU of the European Parliament and of the Council of 22 October 2013;

"transparency rules" has the meaning given by section 89A(5);

"voteholder information" has the meaning given by section 89B(3);

"working day" means any day other that a Saturday, a Sunday, Christmas Day, Good Friday or a day which is a bank holiday under the Banking and Financial Dealings Act 1971 in any part of the United Kingdom.

(1A)   ...

(2), (3) ...

Note. This section is amended by S.I. 2024/105, reg. 47(a), Sch. 3, Pt. 1, paras. 1, 14, as from a day to be appointed (save for certain purposes).

...

PART VIII
PROVISIONS RELATING TO MARKET ABUSE

118–122F ...

Other administrative powers

122G. Publication of information and corrective statements by issuers

(1)   If condition A or B is met, the FCA may require an issuer or emission allowance market participant to publish—

   (a)   specified information; or

   (b)   a specified statement.

(2)   Condition A is met if the FCA considers that the publication of the information or statement is necessary for the purpose of protecting—

   (a)   the interests of users of financial markets and exchanges in the United Kingdom; or

   (b)   the orderly operation of financial markets and exchanges in the United Kingdom.

(3)   Condition B is met if—

   (a)   the information or statement corrects false or misleading information made public, or a false or misleading impression given to the public, by that person; and

   (b)   the FCA considers that the publication of the information is necessary for the purpose of the exercise by it of functions under the market abuse regulation or under supplementary market abuse legislation.

(4)   Information or statements required to be published under this section must be published—

   (a)   before the end of such reasonable period as may be specified; and

   (b)   by any method as may be specified.

(5)   If a person fails to comply with a requirement to publish information or a statement under this section, the FCA may publish the information or statement.

(6)   But before doing so, the FCA must give that person an opportunity to make representations to it regarding its decision to publish the information or statement under subsection (5).

(7)   In this section—

"emission allowance market participant" has the same meaning as in Article 3.1.20 (definitions) of the market abuse regulation; and

"specified" means specified by the FCA.

(8)   For the meaning of "issuer", see section 131AB.

122H. Publication of corrective statements generally

(1)   If condition A or B is met, the FCA may, by notice in writing, require a person to publish—

         (a)   specified information; or

         (b)   a specified statement

     correcting false or misleading information made public, or a false or misleading impression given to the public, by that person.

(2)   Condition A is met if the FCA considers that the publication of the information or statement is necessary for the purpose of protecting—

         (a)   the interests of users of financial markets and exchanges in the United Kingdom; or

         (b)   the orderly operation of financial markets and exchanges in the United Kingdom.

(3)   Condition B is met if the FCA considers that the publication of the information or statement is necessary for the purpose of the exercise by it of functions under the market abuse regulation or under supplementary market abuse legislation.

(4)   Information or statements required to be published under this section must be published—

         (a)   before the end of such reasonable period as may be specified; and

         (b)   by any method as may be specified.

(5)   If a person fails to comply with a requirement to publish information or a statement under this section the FCA may publish the information or statement.

(6)   But before doing so, the FCA must give that person an opportunity to make representations to it regarding its decision to publish the information or statement under subsection (5).

(7)   In this section "specified" means specified in the notice.

122HA. ...

122I. Power to suspend trading in financial instruments

(1)   The FCA may suspend trading of a financial instrument where it considers it necessary for the purpose of the exercise by it of functions under the market abuse regulation or under supplementary market abuse legislation.

(2)   If the FCA does so the issuer of the financial instrument may refer the matter to the Tribunal.

(2A)   But subsection (2) does not apply if the financial instrument is an emission allowance.

(3)   The FCA may—

         (a)   cancel a suspension under subsection (1); and

         (b)   impose such conditions for the cancellation to take effect as it considers appropriate.

(4)   The provisions relating to suspension of listing of securities in section 78 (discontinuance or suspension: procedure) apply to a suspension of trading in a financial instrument other than an emission allowance under subsection (1) and for the purposes of this section—

         (a)   the references in section 78 to listing are to be read as references to trading; and

         (b)   the references in section 78 to securities are to be read as references to financial instruments.

(4A)   A suspension of trading in a financial instrument that is an emission allowance takes effect—

         (a)   immediately, if the FCA states that is the case; or

         (b)   on such later date as the FCA specify.

(5)   For the meaning of "issuer" in this Part, see section 131AB.

...

Administrative sanctions

123. Power to impose penalties or issue censure

(1)   The FCA may exercise its power under subsection (2) if it is satisfied that—

    (a)   a person has contravened Article 14 (prohibition of insider dealing and of unlawful disclosure of inside information) or Article 15 (prohibition of market manipulation) of the market abuse regulation;

    (b)   a person has contravened, or been knowingly concerned in the contravention of—

        (i)   a provision of the market abuse regulation other than Article 14 or 15 of that regulation; or

        (ii)   a provision of any supplementary market abuse legislation; or

    (c)   a person other than an authorised person has contravened any requirement—

        (i)   imposed on that person under section 122A, 122B, 122C, 122G, 122H, 122HA, 122I, 122IA, 123A or 123B; or

        (ii)   relating to the market abuse regulation or any supplementary market abuse legislation imposed on that person under Part 11.

(2)   The FCA's power under this subsection is a power to impose a penalty of such amount as it considers appropriate on the person.

(3)   The FCA may, instead of imposing a penalty on a person, publish a statement censuring the person.

123A. Power to prohibit individuals from managing or dealing

(1)   The FCA may exercise its power under subsection (2) if it is satisfied that an individual—

    (a)   has contravened Article 14 (prohibition of insider dealing and of unlawful disclosure of inside information) or Article 15 (prohibition of market manipulation) of the market abuse regulation;

    (b)   has contravened, or been knowingly concerned in the contravention of—

        (i)   a provision of the market abuse regulation other than Article 14 or 15 of that regulation; or

        (ii)   a provision of any supplementary market abuse legislation; or

    (c)   has contravened a requirement imposed on that individual under this section or section 122A, 122B, 122C, 122G, 122H, 122HA, 122I, 122IA or 123B.

(2)   The FCA's power under this subsection is a power to impose one or more of the following—

    (a)   a temporary prohibition on the individual holding an office or position involving responsibility for taking decisions about the management of an investment firm;

    (b)   a temporary prohibition on the individual acquiring or disposing of financial instruments, whether on his or her own account or the account of a third party and whether directly or indirectly;

    (c)   a temporary prohibition on the individual making a bid, on his or her own account or the account of a third party, directly or indirectly, at an auction conducted by a recognised auction platform.

(3)   If the FCA is satisfied that an individual has contravened Article 14 or 15 of the market abuse regulation the FCA may impose a permanent prohibition on the individual holding an office or position involving responsibility for taking decisions about the management of an investment firm.

(4)   A prohibition imposed under subsection (2) may be expressed to expire at the end of such period as the FCA may specify, but the imposition of a prohibition that expires at the end of a specified period does not affect the FCA's power to impose a new prohibition under subsection (2).

(5)   A prohibition imposed under subsection (2)(a) or (3) may be expressed to prohibit an individual holding an office or position involving responsibility for taking decisions about the management of—

    (a)   a named investment firm;

    (b)   an investment firm of a specified description; or

    (c)   any investment firm.

(6)   An investment firm must take reasonable care to ensure that no individual who is subject to a prohibition under subsection (2)(a) or (3) on the holding of an office or position involving

responsibility for taking decisions about the management of the firm holds such an office or position.

(7)   The FCA may vary or revoke a prohibition imposed under this section.

(8)   For the meaning of "recognised auction platform" in this Part, see section 131AB.

123B.   Suspending permission to carry on regulated activities etc

(1)   The FCA may exercise its power under subsection (2) if it is satisfied that an authorised person—

     (a)   has contravened Article 14 (prohibition of insider dealing and of unlawful disclosure of inside information) or Article 15 (prohibition of market manipulation) of the market abuse regulation;

     (b)   has contravened, or been knowingly concerned in the contravention of—

         (i)   a provision of the market abuse regulation other than Article 14 and 15 of that regulation;

         (ii)   a provision of any supplementary market abuse legislation; or

     (c)   has contravened a requirement imposed on that person under this section or section 122A, 122B, 122C, 122G, 122H, 122HA, 122I, 122IA or 123A.

(2)   The FCA's power under this subsection is a power to do either or both of the following—

     (a)   to suspend, for such period as it considers appropriate, any permission which the person has to carry on a regulated activity;

     (b)   to impose, for such period as it considers appropriate, such limitations or other restrictions in relation to the carrying on of a regulated activity by the person as it considers appropriate.

(3)   In subsection (2) "permission" means any permission that the authorised person has, whether given (or treated as given) by the FCA or the PRA or conferred by any provision of this Act.

(4)   The period for which a suspension or restriction is to have effect may not exceed 12 months.

(5)   A suspension may relate only to the carrying on of an activity in specified circumstances.

(6)   A restriction may, in particular, be imposed so as to require the person concerned to take, or refrain from taking, specified action.

(7)   The FCA may—

     (a)   withdraw a suspension or restriction; or

     (b)   vary a suspension or restriction so as to reduce the period for which it has effect or otherwise to limit its effect.

(8)   The power under this section may (but need not) be exercised so as to have effect in relation to all the regulated activities that the person concerned carries on.

123C.   Exercise of administrative sanctions

Any one or more of the powers under sections 123, 123A and 123B may be exercised in relation to the same contravention.

124–125. ...

Procedure

126.   Warning notices

(1)   If the FCA proposes—

     (a)   to impose a penalty on a person under section 123(2);

     (b)   to publish a statement censuring a person under section 123(3);

     (c)   to impose a temporary prohibition on an individual under section 123A(2)(a);

     (d)   to impose a temporary prohibition on an individual under section 123A(2)(b);

     (e)   to impose a permanent prohibition on an individual under section 123A(3); or

     (f)   to impose a suspension or restriction in relation to a person under section 123B;

     it must give the person a warning notice.

(2)   A warning notice about a proposal to impose a penalty under section 123 must state the amount of the proposed penalty.

(3)   A warning notice about a proposal to publish a statement under section 123 must set out the terms of the proposed statement.

(4) A warning notice about a proposal to impose a prohibition under section 123A must set out the terms of the proposed prohibition.

(5) A warning notice about a proposal to impose a suspension or restriction under section 123B must state the period for which the suspension or restriction is to have effect.

127. Decision notices and right to refer to Tribunal

(1) If the FCA decides—
    (a) to impose a penalty on a person under section 123(2);
    (b) to publish a statement censuring a person under section 123(3);
    (c) to impose a temporary prohibition on an individual under section 123A(2)(a);
    (d) to impose a temporary prohibition on an individual under section 123A(2)(b);
    (e) to impose a permanent prohibition on an individual under section 123A(3);
    (f) to impose a suspension or restriction in relation to a person under section 123B;
    it must give the person a decision notice.

(2) A decision notice about the imposition of a penalty under section 123 must state the amount of the penalty.

(3) A decision notice about the publication of a statement under section 123 must set out the terms of the statement.

(3A) A decision notice about the imposition of a prohibition under section 123A must set out the terms of the prohibition.

(3B) A decision notice about the imposition of a suspension or restriction under section 123B must state the period for which the suspension or restriction is to have effect.

(4) If the FCA decides—
    (a) to impose a penalty on a person under section 123(2);
    (b) to publish a statement censuring a person under section 123(3);
    (c) to impose a prohibition on an individual under section 123A; or
    (d) to impose a suspension or restriction in relation to a person under section 123B;
    that person may refer the matter to the Tribunal.

127A. ...

Miscellaneous

128. ...

129. Power of court to impose administrative sanctions in cases of market abuse

(1) The FCA may, on an application to the court under Part 25 which relates to the market abuse regulation, request the court to consider whether it is appropriate to impose one or more of the following on the person to whom the application relates—
    (a) a penalty;
    (b) if the person concerned is an individual, a temporary prohibition or a permanent prohibition; or
    (c) a suspension or restriction.

(2) The court may, if it considers it appropriate, make an order which does one or more of the following—
    (a) requires the person concerned to pay to the FCA a penalty of such amount as the court considers appropriate;
    (b) if the person concerned is an individual, imposes a temporary prohibition or a permanent prohibition on that individual; or
    (c) imposes a suspension or restriction on the person concerned.

(3) But the court may impose a permanent prohibition only where it is satisfied the person concerned has contravened Article 14 (prohibition of insider dealing and of unlawful disclosure of inside information) or Article 15 (prohibition of market manipulation) of the market abuse regulation.

(4) Section 123A(4) to (6) apply to a prohibition imposed by an order made under subsection (2) as they do to a prohibition under section 123A, but with—

    (a)   references to a prohibition under section 123A having effect as references to a prohibition under this section; and

    (b)   references to the FCA having effect as references to the court which makes the order under this section.

(5)   Section 123B(4) to (6) and (8) apply to a suspension or restriction imposed by an order under subsection (2) as they do to a suspension or restriction imposed under section 123B.

(6)   The court may—

    (a)   vary or revoke a prohibition imposed under this section;

    (b)   withdraw a suspension or restriction imposed under this section; or

    (c)   vary a suspension or a restriction imposed under this section so as to reduce the period for which it has effect or otherwise to limit its effect.

(7)   In this section—

    ...

    "permanent prohibition" means a permanent prohibition on an individual holding an office or position involving responsibility for taking decisions about the management of an investment firm;

    "suspension or restriction" means—

    (a)   a suspension of any permission which a person has to carry on a regulated activity for such period as the court considers appropriate; or

    (b)   such limitations or other restrictions as the court considers appropriate in relation to the carrying on of a regulated activity by a person for such period as the court considers appropriate;

    "temporary prohibition" means a temporary prohibition on an individual—

    (a)   holding an office or position involving responsibility for taking decisions about the management of an investment firm; ...

    (b)   acquiring or disposing of financial instruments, whether on his or her own account or the account of a third party and whether directly or indirectly; or

    (c)   making a bid, on his or her own account or the account of a third party, directly or indirectly, at an auction conducted by a recognised auction platform.

(8)   For the meaning of "recognised auction platform" in this Part, see section 131AB.

(9)   An application under Part 25 relates to the market abuse regulation if—

    (a)   it is made under section 380 or 382 and the relevant requirement for the purposes of that section is a requirement imposed by the market abuse regulation or by supplementary market abuse legislation; or

    (b)   it is made under section 381 or 383.

130.   ...

130A.   ...

131.   **Effect on transactions**

The imposition of a penalty under this Part does not make any transaction void or unenforceable.

131A.   **Protected Disclosures**

(1)   A disclosure which satisfies the following three conditions is not to be taken to breach any restriction on the disclosure of information (however imposed).

(2)   The first condition is that the information or other matter—

    (a)   causes the person making the disclosure (the discloser) to know or suspect, or

    (b)   gives him reasonable grounds for knowing or suspecting that another person has engaged in market abuse,

    that another person has contravened Article 14 (prohibition of insider dealing and of unlawful disclosure of inside information) or Article 15 (prohibition of market manipulation) of the market abuse regulation.

(3)   The second condition is that the information or other matter disclosed came to the discloser in the course of his trade, profession, business or employment.

(4)   The third condition is that the disclosure is made ... to a nominated officer as soon as is practicable after the information or other matter comes to the discloser.

(5)   A disclosure to a nominated officer is a disclosure which is made to a person nominated by the discloser's employer to receive disclosures under this section, and is made in the course of the discloser's employment and in accordance with the procedure established by the employer for the purpose.

(6)   For the purposes of this section, references to a person's employer include any body, association or organisation (including a voluntary organisation) in connection with whose activities the person exercises a function (whether or not for gain or reward) and references to employment must be construed accordingly.

131AA. Reporting of infringements

(1)   This section applies to employers who—
   (a)   provide regulated financial services;
   (b)   carry on regulated activities in reliance on the exemption in section 327; or
   (c)   are recognised bodies ... or third country central counterparties.

(2)   Employers must have in place appropriate internal procedures for their employees to report contraventions of the market abuse regulation or any supplementary market abuse legislation.

(3)   In this section—
   "employee" and "employer" have the meaning given in section 230 of the Employment Rights Act 1996;
   "recognised body" has the meaning given in section 313;
   "regulated financial services" has the meaning given in section 1H.

131AB. Interpretation

(1)   In this Part—
   ...
   "emission allowance" means emission allowance as described in paragraph 11 of Part 1 of Schedule 2 to the Financial Services and Markets Act 2000 (Regulated Activities) Order 2001;
   "financial instrument" means any instrument specified in Part 1 of Schedule 2 to the Financial Services and Markets Act 2000 (Regulated Activities) Order, read with Part 2 of that Schedule;
   "issuer" has the meaning given in Article 3.1(21) of the market abuse regulation; and
   "recognised auction platform" has the meaning given in regulation 1(3) of the Recognised Auction Platform Regulations 2011 (S.I. 2011/2699);
   ...

(2)   The following are supplementary market abuse legislation for the purposes of this Part—
   (a)   an EU regulation, originally made under the market abuse regulation, which is assimilated direct legislation; and
   (b)   subordinate legislation (within the meaning of the Interpretation Act 1978) made under the market abuse regulation on or after IP completion day.

131AC. Meaning of "persons closely associated" in the market abuse regulation

(1)   In Article 3.1(26)(a) (definitions) of the market abuse regulation "partner considered to be equivalent to a spouse" includes a civil partner.

(2)   In Article 3.1(26)(b) of the market abuse regulation "dependent child" means a child who—
   (a)   is under the age of 18 years;
   (b)   is unmarried; and
   (c)   does not have a civil partner.

(3)   In this section "child" includes a stepchild.

131AD. Individual liability in respect of legal persons under Articles 8 and 12 of the market abuse regulation

(1)   An individual participates in a decision by a body corporate for the purposes of Article 8.5 (insider dealing) or Article 12.4 (market manipulation) of the market abuse regulation where—
        (a)   the individual was an officer of the body corporate when the decision was made; and
        (b)   the FCA are satisfied that the individual was knowingly concerned in the decision.

(2)   In this section "officer", in relation to a body corporate, means—
        (a)   a director, member of the committee of management, chief executive, manager, secretary or other similar officer of the body, or a person purporting to act in any such capacity; or
        (b)   an individual who is a controller of the body.

131AE. Liability for contraventions of Article 14 or 15 of the market abuse regulation

For the purposes of any enactment a person contravenes Article 14 (prohibition of insider dealing and of unlawful disclosure of inside information) or Article 15 (prohibition of market manipulation) whether the contravention is by that person alone or by that person and one or more other persons jointly or in concert.

...

PART XVIII
RECOGNISED INVESTMENT EXCHANGES AND CLEARING HOUSES

...

PART XX
PROVISION OF FINANCIAL SERVICES BY MEMBERS OF THE PROFESSIONS

325.   FCA's general duty

(1)   The FCA must keep itself informed about—
        (a)   the way in which designated professional bodies supervise and regulate the carrying on of exempt regulated activities by members of the professions in relation to which they are established;
        (b)   the way in which such members are carrying on exempt regulated activities.

(2)   In this Part—
        "exempt regulated activities" means regulated activities which may, as a result of this Part, be carried on by members of a profession which is supervised and regulated by a designated professional body without breaching the general prohibition; and
        "members", in relation to a profession, means persons who are entitled to practise the profession in question and, in practising it, are subject to the rules of the body designated in relation to that profession, whether or not they are members of that body.

(3)   The FCA must keep under review the desirability of exercising any of its powers under this Part.
(4)   Each designated professional body must co-operate with the FCA, by the sharing of information and in other ways, in order to enable the FCA to perform its functions under this Part.

326.   Designation of professional bodies

(1)   The Treasury may by order designate bodies for the purposes of this Part.
(2)   A body designated under subsection (1) is referred to in this Part as a designated professional body.
(3)   The Treasury may designate a body under subsection (1) only if they are satisfied that—
        (a)   the basic condition, and
        (b)   one or more of the additional conditions,
        are met in relation to it.

(4)   The basic condition is that the body has rules applicable to the carrying on by members of the profession in relation to which it is established of regulated activities which, if the body were to be designated, would be exempt regulated activities.

(5)   The additional conditions are that—

    (a)   the body has power under any enactment to regulate the practice of the profession;

    (b)   being a member of the profession is a requirement under any enactment for the exercise of particular functions or the holding of a particular office;

    (c)   the body has been recognised for the purpose of any enactment other than this Act and the recognition has not been withdrawn;

    (d)   ...

(6)   "Enactment" includes an Act of the Scottish Parliament, Northern Ireland legislation and subordinate legislation (whether made under an Act, an Act of the Scottish Parliament or Northern Ireland legislation).

(7)   "Recognised" means recognised by—

    (a)   a Minister of the Crown;

    (b)   the Scottish Ministers;

    (c)   a Northern Ireland Minister;

    (d)   a Northern Ireland department or its head.

327.   Exemption from the general prohibition

(1)   The general prohibition does not apply to the carrying on of a regulated activity by a person ("P") if—

    (a)   the conditions set out in subsections (2) to (7) are satisfied; ...

    (aa)   where the activity is the provision of a service listed in Part 3 of Schedule 2 to the Financial Services and Markets Act 2000 (Regulated Activities) Order 2001 relating to a financial instrument, the condition set out in subsection (7A) is also satisfied; and

    (b)   there is not in force—

        (i)   a direction under section 328, or

        (ii)   an order under section 329,

which prevents this subsection from applying to the carrying on of that activity by him.

(2)   P must be—

    (a)   a member of a profession; or

    (b)   controlled or managed by one or more such members.

(3)   P must not receive from a person other than his client any pecuniary reward or other advantage, for which he does not account to his client, arising out of his carrying on of any of the activities.

(4)   The manner of the provision by P of any service in the course of carrying on the activities must be incidental to the provision by him of professional services.

(5)   P must not carry on, or hold himself out as carrying on, a regulated activity other than—

    (a)   one which rules made as a result of section 332(3) allow him to carry on; or

    (b)   one in relation to which he is an exempt person.

(6)   The activities must not be of a description, or relate to an investment of a description, specified in an order made by the Treasury for the purposes of this subsection.

(7)   The activities must be the only regulated activities carried on by P (other than regulated activities in relation to which he is an exempt person).

(7A)   The condition mentioned in subsection (1)(aa) is that—

    (a)   the service is provided in an incidental manner in the course of a professional activity ...; and

    (b)   the professional activity concerned is the provision of professional services.

(7B)   In subsection (7A) a service is provided in an incidental manner in the course of a professional activity ... if the applicable conditions are satisfied.

(7C)   The applicable conditions for the purposes of subsection (7B) are those set out in paragraph 6(a) to (c) of Schedule 3 to the Financial Services and Markets Act 2000 (Regulated Activities) Order 2001.

(8)   "Professional services" means services—

     (a)   which do not constitute carrying on a regulated activity, and

     (b)   the provision of which is supervised and regulated by a designated professional body.

(9)   The exemption in this section does not apply to the carrying on of a regulated claims management activity in Great Britain.

328.   Directions in relation to the general prohibition

(1)   The FCA may direct that section 327(1) is not to apply to the extent specified in the direction.

(2)   A direction under subsection (1)—

     (a)   must be in writing;

     (b)   may be given in relation to different classes of person or different descriptions of regulated activity.

(3)   A direction under subsection (1) must be published in the way appearing to the FCA to be best calculated to bring it to the attention of the public.

(4)   The FCA may charge a reasonable fee for providing a person with a copy of the direction.

(5)   The FCA must, without delay, give the Treasury a copy of any direction which it gives under this section.

(6)   The FCA may exercise the power conferred by subsection (1) only if it is satisfied ...—

     (a)   that it is desirable to do so in order to protect the interests of clients; ...

     (b)   ...

(7)   In considering whether it is satisfied of the matter specified in subsection (6)(a), the FCA must have regard amongst other things to the effectiveness of any arrangements made by any designated professional body—

     (a)   for securing compliance with rules made under section 332(1);

     (b)   for dealing with complaints against its members in relation to the carrying on by them of exempt regulated activities;

     (c)   in order to offer redress to clients who suffer, or claim to have suffered, loss as a result of misconduct by its members in their carrying on of exempt regulated activities;

     (d)   for co-operating with the FCA under section 325(4).

(8)   In this Part "clients" means—

     (a)   persons who use, have used or are or may be contemplating using, any of the services provided by a member of a profession in the course of carrying on exempt regulated activities;

     (b)   persons who have rights or interests which are derived from, or otherwise attributable to, the use of any such services by other persons; or

     (c)   persons who have rights or interests which may be adversely affected by the use of any such services by persons acting on their behalf or in a fiduciary capacity in relation to them.

(9)   If a member of a profession is carrying on an exempt regulated activity in his capacity as a trustee, the persons who are, have been or may be beneficiaries of the trust are to be treated as persons who use, have used or are or may be contemplating using services provided by that person in his carrying on of that activity.

329.   Orders in relation to the general prohibition

(1)   Subsection (2) applies if it appears to the FCA that a person to whom, as a result of section 327(1), the general prohibition does not apply is not a fit and proper person to carry on regulated activities in accordance with that section.

(2)   The FCA may make an order disapplying section 327(1) in relation to that person to the extent specified in the order.

(3)   The FCA may, on the application of the person named in an order under subsection (1), vary or revoke it.

(4)   "Specified" means specified in the order.

(5)   If a partnership is named in an order under this section, the order is not affected by any change in its membership.

(6) If a partnership named in an order under this section is dissolved, the order continues to have effect in relation to any partnership which succeeds to the business of the dissolved partnership.

(7) For the purposes of subsection (6), a partnership is to be regarded as succeeding to the business of another partnership only if—

(a) the members of the resulting partnership are substantially the same as those of the former partnership; and

(b) succession is to the whole or substantially the whole of the business of the former partnership.

330. Consultation

(1) Before giving a direction under section 328(1), the FCA must publish a draft of the proposed direction.

(2) The draft must be accompanied by—

(a) a cost benefit analysis; and

(b) notice that representations about the proposed direction may be made to the FCA within a specified time.

(3) Before giving the proposed direction, the FCA must have regard to any representations made to it in accordance with subsection (2)(b).

(4) If the FCA gives the proposed direction it must publish an account, in general terms, of—

(a) the representations made to it in accordance with subsection (2)(b); and

(b) its response to them.

(5) If the direction differs from the draft published under subsection (1) in a way which is, in the opinion of the FCA, significant—

(a) the FCA must (in addition to complying with subsection (4)) publish details of the difference; and

(b) those details must be accompanied by a cost benefit analysis.

(6) Subsections (1) to (5) do not apply if the FCA considers that the delay involved in complying with them would prejudice the interests of consumers.

(7) Neither subsection (2)(a) nor subsection (5)(b) applies if the FCA considers—

(a) that, making the appropriate comparison, there will be no increase in costs; or

(b) that, making that comparison, there will be an increase in costs but the increase will be of minimal significance.

(8) The FCA may charge a reasonable fee for providing a person with a copy of a draft published under subsection (1).

(9) When the FCA is required to publish a document under this section it must do so in the way appearing to it to be best calculated to bring it to the attention of the public.

(10) "Cost benefit analysis" means—

(a) an analysis of the costs together with an analysis of the benefits that will arise—

(i) if the proposed direction is given, or

(ii) if subsection (5)(b) applies, from the direction that has been given, and

(b) subject to subsection (10A), an estimate of those costs and of those benefits.

(10A) If, in the opinion of the FCA—

(a) the costs or benefits referred to in subsection (10) cannot reasonably be estimated, or

(b) it is not reasonably practicable to produce an estimate,

the cost benefit analysis need not estimate them, but must include a statement of the FCA's opinion and an explanation of it.

(11) "The appropriate comparison" means—

(a) in relation to subsection (2)(a), a comparison between the overall position if the direction is given and the overall position if it is not given;

(b) in relation to subsection (5)(b), a comparison between the overall position after the giving of the direction and the overall position before it was given.

331.   Procedure on making or varying orders under section 329

(1)   If the FCA proposes to make an order under section 329, it must give the person concerned a warning notice.

(2)   The warning notice must set out the terms of the proposed order.

(3)   If the FCA decides to make an order under section 329, it must give the person concerned a decision notice.

(4)   The decision notice must—

    (a)   name the person to whom the order applies;

    (b)   set out the terms of the order; and

    (c)   be given to the person named in the order.

(5)   Subsections (6) to (8) apply to an application for the variation or revocation of an order under section 329.

(6)   If the FCA decides to grant the application, it must give the applicant written notice of its decision.

(7)   If the FCA proposes to refuse the application, it must give the applicant a warning notice.

(8)   If the FCA decides to refuse the application, it must give the applicant a decision notice.

(9)   A person—

    (a)   against whom the FCA have decided to make an order under section 329, or

    (b)   whose application for the variation or revocation of such an order the FCA had decided to refuse,

may refer the matter to the Tribunal.

(10)   The FCA may not make an order under section 329 unless—

    (a)   the period within which the decision to make to the order may be referred to the Tribunal has expired and no such reference has been made; or

    (b)   if such a reference has been made, the reference has been determined.

332.   Rules in relation to persons to whom the general prohibition does not apply

(1)   The FCA may make rules applicable to persons to whom, as a result of section 327(1), the general prohibition does not apply.

(2)   The power conferred by subsection (1) is to be exercised for the purpose of ensuring that clients are aware that such persons are not authorised persons.

(3)   A designated professional body must make rules—

    (a)   applicable to members of the profession in relation to which it is established who are not authorised persons; and

    (b)   governing the carrying on by those members of regulated activities (other than regulated activities in relation to which they are exempt persons).

(4)   Rules made in compliance with subsection (3) must be designed to secure that, in providing a particular professional service to a particular client, the member carries on only regulated activities which arise out of, or are complementary to, the provision by him of that service to that client.

(5)   Rules made by a designated professional body under subsection (3) require the approval of the FCA.

333.   False claims to be a person to whom the general prohibition does not apply

(1)   A person who—

    (a)   describes himself (in whatever terms) as a person to whom the general prohibition does not apply, in relation to a particular regulated activity, as a result of this Part, or

    (b)   behaves, or otherwise holds himself out, in a manner which indicates (or which is reasonably likely to be understood as indicating) that he is such a person,

is guilty of an offence if he is not such a person.

(2)   In proceedings for an offence under this section it is a defence for the accused to show that he took all reasonable precautions and exercised all due diligence to avoid committing the offence.

(3)   A person guilty of an offence under this section is liable on summary conviction to imprisonment for a term not exceeding six months or a fine not exceeding level 5 on the standard scale, or both.

(4)   But where the conduct constituting the offence involved or included the public display of any material, the maximum fine for the offence is level 5 on the standard scale multiplied by the number of days for which the display continued.

...

PART XXVII
OFFENCES

Miscellaneous offences

397–399. ...

Bodies corporate and partnerships

400.   Offences by bodies corporate etc

(1)   If an offence under this Act committed by a body corporate is shown—
  (a)   to have been committed with the consent or connivance of an officer, or
  (b)   to be attributable to any neglect on his part,
  the officer as well as the body corporate is guilty of the offence and liable to be proceeded against and punished accordingly.

(2)   If the affairs of a body corporate are managed by its members, subsection (1) applies in relation to the acts and defaults of a member in connection with his functions of management as if he were a director of the body.

(3)   If an offence under this Act committed by a partnership is shown—
  (a)   to have been committed with the consent or connivance of a partner, or
  (b)   to be attributable to any neglect on his part,
  the partner as well as the partnership is guilty of the offence and liable to be proceeded against and punished accordingly.

(4)   In subsection (3) "partner" includes a person purporting to act as a partner.

(5)   "Officer", in relation to a body corporate, means—
  (a)   a director, member of the committee of management, chief executive, manager, secretary or other similar officer of the body, or a person purporting to act in any such capacity; and
  (b)   an individual who is a controller of the body.

(6)   If an offence under this Act committed by an unincorporated association (other than a partnership) is shown—
  (a)   to have been committed with the consent or connivance of an officer of the association or a member of its governing body, or
  (b)   to be attributable to any neglect on the part of such an officer or member,
  that officer or member as well as the association is guilty of the offence and liable to be proceeded against and punished accordingly.

(6A)   References in this section to an offence under this Act include a reference to an offence under Part 7 of the Financial Services Act 2012 (offences relating to financial services).

(7)   Regulations may provide for the application of any provision of this section, with such modifications as the Treasury consider appropriate, to a body corporate or unincorporated association formed or recognised under the law of a territory outside the United Kingdom.

...

PART XXX
SUPPLEMENTAL

...

433.   **Short title**

This Act may be cited as the Financial Services and Markets Act 2000.

SCHEDULE 1

...

SCHEDULE 2

REGULATED ACTIVITIES

Section 22(2)

PART I
REGULATED ACTIVITIES: GENERAL

General

1.   The matters with respect to which provision may be made under section 22(1) in respect of activities include, in particular, those described in general terms in this Part of this Schedule.

Dealing in investments

2.— (1) Buying, selling, subscribing for or underwriting investments or offering or agreeing to do so, either as a principal or as an agent.

     (2) In the case of an investment which is a contract of insurance, that includes carrying out the contract.

Arranging deals in investments

3.   Making, or offering or agreeing to make—

     (a) arrangements with a view to another person buying, selling, subscribing for or underwriting a particular investment;

     (b) arrangements with a view to a person who participates in the arrangements buying, selling, subscribing for or underwriting investments.

Deposit taking

4.   Accepting deposits.

Safekeeping and administration of assets

5.— (1) Safeguarding and administering assets belonging to another which consist of or include investments or offering or agreeing to do so.

     (2) Arranging for the safeguarding and administration of assets belonging to another, or offering or agreeing to do so.

Managing investments

6.   Managing, or offering or agreeing to manage, assets belonging to another person where—

     (a) the assets consist of or include investments; or

     (b) the arrangements for their management are such that the assets may consist of or include investments at the discretion of the person managing or offering or agreeing to manage them.

Investment advice

7.   Giving or offering or agreeing to give advice to persons on—

(a)   buying, selling, subscribing for or underwriting an investment; or

(b)   exercising any right conferred by an investment to acquire, dispose of, underwrite or convert an investment.

Establishing collective investment schemes

8.   Establishing, operating or winding up a collective investment scheme, including acting as—

(a)   trustee of a unit trust scheme;

(b)   depositary of a collective investment scheme other than a unit trust scheme; or

(c)   sole director of a body incorporated by virtue of regulations under section 262.

Using computer-based systems for giving investment instructions

9.—   (1)   Sending on behalf of another person instructions relating to an investment by means of a computer-based system which enables investments to be transferred without a written instrument.

(2)   Offering or agreeing to send such instructions by such means on behalf of another person.

(3)   Causing such instructions to be sent by such means on behalf of another person.

(4)   Offering or agreeing to cause such instructions to be sent by such means on behalf of another person.

...

PART II
INVESTMENTS

General

10.   The matters with respect to which provision may be made under section 22(1) in respect of investments include, in particular, those described in general terms in this Part of this Schedule.

Securities

11.—   (1)   Shares or stock in the share capital of a company.

(2)   "Company" includes—

(a)   any body corporate (wherever incorporated), and

(b)   any unincorporated body constituted under the law of a country or territory outside the United Kingdom,

other than an open-ended investment company.

Instruments creating or acknowledging indebtedness

12.   Any of the following—

(a)   debentures;

(b)   debenture stock;

(c)   loan stock;

(d)   bonds;

(e)   certificates of deposit;

(f)   any other instruments creating or acknowledging a present or future indebtedness.

Government and public securities

13.—   (1)   Loan stock, bonds and other instruments—

(a)   creating or acknowledging indebtedness; and

(b)   issued by or on behalf of a government, local authority or public authority.

(2)   "Government, local authority or public authority" means—

(a)   the government of the United Kingdom, of Northern Ireland, or of any country or territory outside the United Kingdom;

(b)   a local authority in the United Kingdom or elsewhere;

(c)   any international organisation the members of which include the United Kingdom ....

Instruments giving entitlement to investments

14.—   (1)   Warrants or other instruments entitling the holder to subscribe for any investment.

        (2)   It is immaterial whether the investment is in existence or identifiable.

Certificates representing securities

15.   Certificates or other instruments which confer contractual or property rights—

        (a)   in respect of any investment held by someone other than the person on whom the rights are conferred by the certificate or other instrument; and

        (b)   the transfer of which may be effected without requiring the consent of that person.

Units in collective investment schemes

16.—   (1)   Shares in or securities of an open-ended investment company.

        (2)   Any right to participate in a collective investment scheme.

Options

17.   Options to acquire or dispose of property.

Futures

18.   Rights under a contract for the sale of a commodity or property of any other description under which delivery is to be made at a future date.

Contracts for differences

19.   Rights under—

        (a)   a contract for differences; or

        (b)   any other contract the purpose or pretended purpose of which is to secure a profit or avoid a loss by reference to fluctuations in—

           (i)   the value or price of property of any description; or

           (ii)   an index or other factor designated for that purpose in the contract.

Contracts of insurance

20.   Rights under a contract of insurance, including rights under contracts falling within head C of Schedule 2 to the Friendly Societies Act 1992.

Participation in Lloyd's syndicates

21.—   (1)   The underwriting capacity of a Lloyd's syndicate.

        (2)   A person's membership (or prospective membership) of a Lloyd's syndicate.

Deposits

22.   Rights under any contract under which a sum of money (whether or not denominated in a currency) is paid on terms under which it will be repaid, with or without interest or a premium, and either on demand or at a time or in circumstances agreed by or on behalf of the person making the payment and the person receiving it.

Loans and other forms of credit

23.—   (1)   Rights under any contract under which one person provides another with credit.

        (2)   "Credit" includes any cash loan or other financial accommodation.

        (3)   "Cash" includes money in any form.

        (4)   It is immaterial for the purposes of sub-paragraph (1) whether or not the obligation of the borrower is secured on property of any kind.

Other finance arrangements involving land

23A.—   (1)   Rights under any arrangement for the provision of finance under which the person providing the finance either—

        (a)   acquires a major interest in land from the person to whom the finance is provided, or

(b)   disposes of a major interest in land to that person,

as part of the arrangement.

(2)   References in sub-paragraph (1) to a "major interest" in land are to—

(a)   in relation to land in England or Wales—

(i)   an estate in fee simple absolute, or

(ii)   a term of years absolute,

whether subsisting at law or in equity;

(b)   in relation to land in Scotland—

(i)   the interest of an owner of land, or

(ii)   the tenant's right over or interest in a property subject to a lease;

(c)   in relation to land in Northern Ireland—

(i)   any freehold estate, or

(ii)   any leasehold estate,

whether subsisting at law or in equity.

(3)   It is immaterial for the purposes of sub-paragraph (1) whether either party acquires or (as the case may be) disposes of the interest in land—

(a)   directly, or

(b)   indirectly.

Contracts for hire of goods

23B.— (1)   Rights under a contract for the bailment or (in Scotland) hiring of goods to a person other than a body corporate.

(2)   "Goods" has the meaning given in section 61(1) of the Sale of Goods Act 1979.

(3)   It is immaterial for the purposes of sub-paragraph (1) whether the rights of the person to whom the goods are bailed or hired have been assigned to a body corporate.

Rights in investments

24.   Any right or interest in anything which is an investment as a result of any other provision made under section 22(1).

...

SCHEDULES 7–9

...

SCHEDULE 10

COMPENSATION: EXEMPTIONS

Section 90(2) and (5)

Statements believed to be true

1.—   (1)   In this paragraph "statement" means—

(a)   any untrue or misleading statement in listing particulars; or

(b)   the omission from listing particulars of any matter required to be included by section 80 or 81.

(2)   A person does not incur any liability under section 90(1) for loss caused by a statement if he satisfies the court that, at the time when the listing particulars were submitted to the FCA, he reasonably believed (having made such enquiries, if any, as were reasonable) that—

(a)   the statement was true and not misleading, or

(b)   the matter whose omission caused the loss was properly omitted,

and that one or more of the conditions set out in sub-paragraph (3) are satisfied.

(3)   The conditions are that—

(a)   he continued in his belief until the time when the securities in question were acquired;

    (b)   they were acquired before it was reasonably practicable to bring a correction to the attention of persons likely to acquire them;

    (c)   before the securities were acquired, he had taken all such steps as it was reasonable for him to have taken to secure that a correction was brought to the attention of those persons;

    (d)   he continued in his belief until after the commencement of dealings in the securities following their admission to the official list and they were acquired after such a lapse of time that he ought in the circumstances to be reasonably excused.

Statements by experts

2.—   (1)   In this paragraph "statement" means a statement included in listing particulars which—

    (a)   purports to be made by, or on the authority of, another person as an expert; and

    (b)   is stated to be included in the listing particulars with that other person's consent.

   (2)   A person does not incur any liability under section 90(1) for loss in respect of any securities caused by a statement if he satisfies the court that, at the time when the listing particulars were submitted to the FCA, he reasonably believed that the other person—

    (a)   was competent to make or authorise the statement, and

    (b)   had consented to its inclusion in the form and context in which it was included,

    and that one or more of the conditions set out in sub-paragraph (3) are satisfied.

   (3)   The conditions are that—

    (a)   he continued in his belief until the time when the securities were acquired;

    (b)   they were acquired before it was reasonably practicable to bring the fact that the expert was not competent, or had not consented, to the attention of persons likely to acquire the securities in question;

    (c)   before the securities were acquired he had taken all such steps as it was reasonable for him to have taken to secure that that fact was brought to the attention of those persons;

    (d)   he continued in his belief until after the commencement of dealings in the securities following their admission to the official list and they were acquired after such a lapse of time that he ought in the circumstances to be reasonably excused.

Corrections of statements

3.—   (1)   In this paragraph "statement" has the same meaning as in paragraph 1.

   (2)   A person does not incur liability under section 90(1) for loss caused by a statement if he satisfies the court—

    (a)   that before the securities in question were acquired, a correction had been published in a manner calculated to bring it to the attention of persons likely to acquire the securities; or

    (b)   that he took all such steps as it was reasonable for him to take to secure such publication and reasonably believed that it had taken place before the securities were acquired.

   (3)   Nothing in this paragraph is to be taken as affecting paragraph 1.

Corrections of statements by experts

4.—   (1)   In this paragraph "statement" has the same meaning as in paragraph 2.

   (2)   A person does not incur liability under section 90(1) for loss caused by a statement if he satisfies the court—

    (a)   that before the securities in question were acquired, the fact that the expert was not competent or had not consented had been published in a manner calculated to bring it to the attention of persons likely to acquire the securities; or

    (b)   that he took all such steps as it was reasonable for him to take to secure such publication and reasonably believed that it had taken place before the securities were acquired.

   (3)   Nothing in this paragraph is to be taken as affecting paragraph 2.

Official statements

5.   A person does not incur any liability under section 90(1) for loss resulting from—

    (a)   a statement made by an official person which is included in the listing particulars, or

    (b)   a statement contained in a public official document which is included in the listing particulars,

if he satisfies the court that the statement is accurately and fairly reproduced.

False or misleading information known about

6.   A person does not incur any liability under section 90(1) or (4) if he satisfies the court that the person suffering the loss acquired the securities in question with knowledge—

    (a)   that the statement was false or misleading,

    (b)   of the omitted matter, or

    (c)   of the change or new matter,

as the case may be.

Belief that supplementary listing particulars not called for

7.   A person does not incur any liability under section 90(4) if he satisfies the court that he reasonably believed that the change or new matter in question was not such as to call for supplementary listing particulars.

Meaning of "expert"

8.   "Expert" includes any engineer, valuer, accountant or other person whose profession, qualifications or experience give authority to a statement made by him.

SCHEDULE 10A

LIABILITY OF ISSUERS IN CONNECTION WITH PUBLISHED INFORMATION

Section 90A

PART 1
SCOPE OF THIS SCHEDULE

Securities to which this Schedule applies

1.—   (1)   This Schedule applies to securities that are, with the consent of the issuer, admitted to trading on a securities market, where—

    (a)   the market is situated or operating in the United Kingdom, or

    (b)   the United Kingdom is the issuer's home State.

   (2)   For the purposes of this Schedule—

    (a)   an issuer of securities is not taken to have consented to the securities being admitted to trading on a securities market by reason only of having consented to their admission to trading on another market as a result of which they are admitted to trading on the first-mentioned market;

    (b)   an issuer who has accepted responsibility (to any extent) for any document prepared for the purposes of the admission of the securities to trading on a securities market (such as a prospectus or listing particulars) is taken to have consented to their admission to trading on that market.

   (3)   For the purposes of this Schedule the United Kingdom is the home State of an issuer if—

    (a)   the transparency rules impose requirements on the issuer in relation to the securities, or

    (b)   the issuer has its registered office (or, if it does not have a registered office, its head office) in the United Kingdom.

Published information to which this Schedule applies

2.—   (1) This Schedule applies to information published by the issuer of securities to which this
             Schedule applies—
             (a)   by recognised means, or
             (b)   by other means where the availability of the information has been announced by the
                   issuer by recognised means.
        (2) It is immaterial whether the information is required to be published (by recognised means or
             otherwise).
        (3) The following are "recognised means"—
             (a)   a recognised information service;
             (b)   other means required or authorised to be used to communicate information to the mar-
                   ket in question, or to the public, when a recognised information service is unavailable.
        (4) A "recognised information service" means—
             (a)   in relation to a securities market situated or operating in the United Kingdom, a ser-
                   vice used for the dissemination of information in accordance with transparency rules;
             (b)   in relation to a securities market situated or operating outside the EEA, a service used
                   for the dissemination of information corresponding to that required to be disclosed
                   under that directive; or
             (c)   in relation to any securities market, any other service used by issuers of securities for
                   the dissemination of information required to be disclosed by the rules of the market.

PART 2
LIABILITY IN CONNECTION WITH PUBLISHED INFORMATION

Liability of issuer for misleading statement or dishonest omission

3.—   (1) An issuer of securities to which this Schedule applies is liable to pay compensation to a
             person who—
             (a)   acquires, continues to hold or disposes of the securities in reliance on published infor-
                   mation to which this Schedule applies, and
             (b)   suffers loss in respect of the securities as a result of—
                   (i)   any untrue or misleading statement in that published information, or
                   (ii)   the omission from that published information of any matter required to be
                          included in it.
        (2) The issuer is liable in respect of an untrue or misleading statement only if a person
             discharging managerial responsibilities within the issuer knew the statement to be untrue or
             misleading or was reckless as to whether it was untrue or misleading.
        (3) The issuer is liable in respect of the omission of any matter required to be included in
             published information only if a person discharging managerial responsibilities within the
             issuer knew the omission to be a dishonest concealment of a material fact.
        (4) A loss is not regarded as suffered as a result of the statement or omission unless the person
             suffering it acquired, continued to hold or disposed of the relevant securities—
             (a)   in reliance on the information in question, and
             (b)   at a time when, and in circumstances in which, it was reasonable for him to rely on it.

4.—   An issuer of securities to which this Schedule applies is not liable under paragraph 3 to pay
       compensation to a person for loss suffered as a result of an untrue or misleading statement in, or
       omission from, published information to which this Schedule applies if—
       (a)   the published information is contained in listing particulars or a prospectus (or
             supplementary listing particulars or a supplementary prospectus), and
       (b)   the issuer is liable under section 90 (compensation for statements in listing particulars or
             prospectus) to pay compensation to the person in respect of the statement or omission.

Liability of issuer for dishonest delay in publishing information

5.— (1) An issuer of securities to which this Schedule applies is liable to pay compensation to a person who—

    (a) acquires, continues to hold or disposes of the securities, and

    (b) suffers loss in respect of the securities as a result of delay by the issuer in publishing information to which this Schedule applies.

  (2) The issuer is liable only if a person discharging managerial responsibilities within the issuer acted dishonestly in delaying the publication of the information.

Meaning of dishonesty

6.— For the purposes of paragraphs 3(3) and 5(2) a person's conduct is regarded as dishonest if (and only if)—

    (a) it is regarded as dishonest by persons who regularly trade on the securities market in question, and

    (b) the person was aware (or must be taken to have been aware) that it was so regarded.

Exclusion of certain other liabilities

7.— (1) The issuer is not subject—

    (a) to any liability other than that provided for by paragraph 3 in respect of loss suffered as a result of reliance by any person on—

        (i) an untrue or misleading statement in published information to which this Schedule applies, or

        (ii) the omission from any such published information of any matter required to be included in it;

    (b) to any liability other than that provided for by paragraph 5 in respect of loss suffered as a result of delay in the publication of information to which this Schedule applies.

  (2) A person other than the issuer is not subject to any liability, other than to the issuer, in respect of any such loss.

  (3) This paragraph does not affect—

    (a) civil liability—

        (i) under section 90 (compensation for statements in listing particulars or prospectus),

        (ii) under rules made by virtue of section 954 of the Companies Act 2006 (compensation),

        (iii) for breach of contract,

        (iv) under the Misrepresentation Act 1967, or

        (v) arising from a person's having assumed responsibility, to a particular person for a particular purpose, for the accuracy or completeness of the information concerned;

    (b) liability to a civil penalty; or

    (c) criminal liability.

  (4) This paragraph does not affect the powers conferred by sections 382 and 384 (powers of the court to make a restitution order and of the Authority to require restitution).

  (5) References in this paragraph to liability, in relation to a person, include a reference to another person being entitled as against that person to be granted any civil remedy or to rescind or repudiate an agreement.

PART 3
SUPPLEMENTARY PROVISIONS

Interpretation

8.— (1) In this Schedule—

    (a) "securities" means transferable securities as defined in Article 2(1)(24) of the markets in financial instruments regulation, other than money market instruments as defined in

Article 2(1)(25A) of that regulation that have a maturity of less than 12 months (and includes instruments outside the United Kingdom);

(b)   "securities market" means—

  (i)   a regulated market as defined in Article 2(1)(13) of the markets in financial instruments regulation, or

  (ii)   a multilateral trading facility as defined in Article 2(1)(14) of that regulation.

(2)   References in this Schedule to the issuer of securities are—

(a)   in relation to a depositary receipt, derivative instrument or other financial instrument representing securities where the issuer of the securities represented has consented to the admission of the instrument to trading as mentioned in paragraph 1(1), to the issuer of the securities represented;

(b)   in any other case, to the person who issued the securities.

(3)   References in this Schedule to the acquisition or disposal of securities include—

(a)   acquisition or disposal of any interest in securities, or

(b)   contracting to acquire or dispose of securities or of any interest in securities,

except where what is acquired or disposed of (or contracted to be acquired or disposed of) is a depositary receipt, derivative instrument or other financial instrument representing securities.

(4)   References to continuing to hold securities have a corresponding meaning.

(5)   For the purposes of this Schedule the following are persons "discharging managerial responsibilities" within an issuer—

(a)   any director of the issuer (or person occupying the position of director, by whatever name called);

(b)   in the case of an issuer whose affairs are managed by its members, any member of the issuer;

(c)   in the case of an issuer that has no persons within paragraph (a) or (b), any senior executive of the issuer having responsibilities in relation to the information in question or its publication.

(6)   The following definitions (which apply generally for the purposes of Part 6 of this Act) do not apply for the purposes of this Schedule:

(a)   section 102A(1), (2) and (6) (meaning of "securities" and "issuer");

(b)   ....

Note. This Schedule is amended by S.I. 2024/105, reg. 47(a), Sch. 3, Pt. 1, paras. 1, 22, as from a day to be appointed (save for certain purposes).

...

Financial Services and Markets Act 2000 (Regulated Activities) Order 2001

S.I. 2001/544

PART I

GENERAL

1. **Citation**

This Order may be cited as the Financial Services and Markets Act 2000 (Regulated Activities) Order 2001.

2. **Commencement**

(1) Except as provided by paragraph (2), this Order comes into force on the day on which section 19 of the Act comes into force.

(2) This Order comes into force—

(a) for the purposes of articles 59, 60 and 87 (funeral plan contracts) on 1st January 2002; and

(b) for the purposes of articles 61 to 63, 88, 90 and 91 (regulated mortgage contracts) on such a day as the Treasury may specify.

(3) Any day specified under paragraph (2)(b) must be caused to be notified in the London, Edinburgh and Belfast Gazettes published not later than one week before that day.

3. **Interpretation**

(1) In this Order—

"the Act" means the Financial Services and Markets Act 2000;

"acting as an insolvency practitioner" is to be read with section 388 of the Insolvency Act 1986 or, as the case may be, article 3 of the Insolvency (Northern Ireland) Order 1989 and, in any provision of this Order which provides for activities to be excluded from a specified activity, references to things done by a person acting—

(a) as an insolvency practitioner, or

(b) in reasonable contemplation of that person's appointment as an insolvency practitioner, include anything done by the person's firm in connection with that person so acting;

"agreement provider" has the meaning given by article 63J(3);

"agreement seller" has the meaning given by article 63J(3);

"AIFM" has the meaning given by regulation 4 of the Alternative Investment Fund Managers Regulations 2013;

"aircraft operator" has the meaning given in article 6 of the trading scheme order;

"alternative investment fund managers directive" means Directive 2011/61/EU of the European Parliament and of the Council of 8 June 2011 on Alternative Investment Fund Managers;

"annuities on human life" does not include superannuation allowances and annuities payable out of any fund applicable solely to the relief and maintenance of persons engaged, or who have been engaged, in any particular profession, trade or employment, or of the dependants of such persons;

"assignment", in relation to a credit agreement, has the meaning given by article 60L;

"auction platform" means a platform on which auctions of greenhouse gas emissions allowances are held in accordance with the emission allowance auctioning regulation or the UK auctioning regulations;

"borrower"—

(a)   in relation to a credit agreement other than a regulated mortgage contract, an article 36H agreement (within the meaning given by article 36H) or an agreement that is a green deal plan, has the meaning given by article 60L;

(b)   in relation to an article 36H agreement (within the meaning given by that article) other than a regulated mortgage contract, has the meaning given by article 36H;

(c)   in relation to a credit agreement that is a green deal plan, has the meaning given by article 60LB;

"buying" includes acquiring for valuable consideration;

"close relative" in relation to a person means—

(a)   his spouse or civil partner;

(b)   his children and step children, his parents and step-parents, his brothers and sisters and his step-brothers and step-sisters; and

(c)   the spouse or civil partner of any person within sub-paragraph (b);

"the Commission Regulation" means Commission Delegated Regulation of 25.4.2016 supplementing Directive 2014/65/EU of the European Parliament and of the Council as regards organisational requirements and operating conditions for investment firms and defined terms for the purposes of that Directive;

"consumer hire agreement" has the meaning given by article 60N;

"contract of general insurance" means any contract falling within Part I of Schedule 1;

"contract of insurance" means any contract of insurance which is a contract of long-term insurance or a contract of general insurance, and includes—

(a)   fidelity bonds, performance bonds, administration bonds, bail bonds, customs bonds or similar contracts of guarantee, where these are—

   (i)   effected or carried out by a person not carrying on a banking business;

   (ii) not effected merely incidentally to some other business carried on by the person effecting them; and

   (iii) effected in return for the payment of one or more premiums;

(b)   tontines;

(c)   capital redemption contracts or pension fund management contracts, where these are effected or carried out by a person who—

   (i)   does not carry on a banking business; and

   (ii) otherwise carries on a regulated activity of the kind specified by article 10(1) or (2);

(d)   contracts to pay annuities on human life;

(e)   contracts of a kind referred to in Article 2(3)(b)(v) of the Solvency 2 Directive; and

(f)   contracts relating to the length of human life that are regulated by or under any enactment relating to social security, in so far as they are effected or carried out at their own risk by undertakings with permission to effect or carry out contracts of long-term insurance as principals;

but does not include a funeral plan contract …;

"contract of long-term insurance" means any contract falling within Part II of Schedule 1;

"contractually based investment" means—

(a)   rights under a qualifying contract of insurance;

(b)   any investment of the kind specified by any of articles 83, 84, 85 and 87; or

(c)   any investment of the kind specified by article 89 so far as relevant to an investment falling within (a) or (b);

"credit agreement"—

(a)   in relation to an agreement other than a green deal plan, has the meaning given by article 60B;

(b)   in relation to a green deal plan, has the meaning given by article 60LB;

…

"deposit" has the meaning given by article 5 except where the definition given in article 60L applies;

...

"electronic money" has the meaning given by regulation 2(1) of the Electronic Money Regulations 2011;

"emission allowance auctioning regulation" means Commission Regulation (EU) No 1031/2010 of 12 November 2010 on the timing, administration and other aspects of auctioning of greenhouse gas emission allowances pursuant to the emission allowance trading directive;

"emission allowance trading directive" means Directive 2003/87/EC of the European Parliament and of the Council of 13 October 2003 establishing a scheme for greenhouse gas emission allowances trading within the Community;

"EU Securitisation Regulation 2017" means Regulation (EU) 2017/2402 of the European Parliament and of the Council of 12 December 2017 laying down a general framework for securitisation and creating a specific framework for simple, transparent and standardised securitisation, and amending Directives 2009/65/EC, 2009/138/EC and 2011/61/EU and Regulations (EC) No 1060/2009 and (EU) No 648/2012 as it forms part of retained EU law;

"financial instrument" means any instrument listed in Part 1 of Schedule 2 read with Articles 5 to 8, 10 and 11 of the Commission Regulation (the text of which is set out in Part 2 of Schedule 2);

"full-scope UK AIFM" has the meaning given by regulation 2(1) of the Alternative Investment Fund Managers Regulations 2013;

"green deal plan" has the meaning given by section 1 of the Energy Act 2011;

"funeral plan contract" has the meaning given by article 59;

"greenhouse gas emissions allowances" mean "allowances" as defined in Article 3(a) of the emission allowance trading directive or in article 4(1) of the trading scheme order;

"hire-purchase agreement" has the meaning given by article 60L;

"hirer" is to be read with the definition of "consumer hire agreement" in article 60N;

...

"home purchase provider" has the meaning given by article 63F(3);

"home purchaser" has the meaning given by article 63F(3);

"home State"—

(a)   in relation to a qualifying credit institution, means the State in which the institution has been granted authorisation;

(b)   in relation to a legal person (other than a qualifying credit institution) that has a registered office under the person's national law, means the State in which that office is located;

(c)   in relation to any other person, means the State in which the person's head office is located;

"instrument" includes any record whether or not in the form of a document;

"investment firm" means a person whose regular occupation or business is the provision or performance of investment services and activities on a professional basis, other than—

(a)   a person excluded by Schedule 3, read with the Commission Regulation and with Commission Delegated Regulation (EU) 2017/592 of 1 December 2016 supplementing Directive 2014/65/EU of the European Parliament and of the Council with regard to regulatory technical standards for the criteria to establish when an activity is considered to be ancillary to the main business;

(b)   a person whose home State is not the United Kingdom and who would be excluded by Schedule 3, read with the Commission Regulation and with Commission Delegated Regulation (EU) 2017/592, if the person's registered office (or head office, in the case of a person that is not a body corporate or a person that is a body corporate but has no registered office) was in the United Kingdom;

...

"joint enterprise" means an enterprise into which two or more persons ("the participators") enter for commercial purposes related to a business or businesses (other than the business of engaging in a regulated activity) carried on by them; and, where a participator is a member of a group, each other member of the group is also to be regarded as a participator in the enterprise;

"lender"—

(c)   in relation to a credit agreement other than a regulated mortgage contract, an article 36H agreement (within the meaning given by article 36H) or an agreement that is a green deal plan, has the meaning given by article 60L;

(d)   in relation to an article 36H agreement (within the meaning given by that article) other than a regulated mortgage contract, has the meaning given by article 36H;

(e)   in relation to a credit agreement that is a green deal plan, has the meaning given by article 60LB;

"local authority" means—

(a)   in England and Wales, a local authority within the meaning of the Local Government Act 1972, the Greater London Authority, the Common Council of the City of London or the Council of the Isles of Scilly;

(b)   in Scotland, a local authority within the meaning of the Local Government (Scotland) Act 1973;

(c)   in Northern Ireland, a district council within the meaning of the Local Government Act (Northern Ireland) 1972;

"management company" has the meaning given by section 237(2) of the Act;

"managing agent" means a person who is permitted by the Council of Lloyd's in the conduct of his business as an underwriting agent to perform for a member of Lloyd's one or more of the following functions—

(a)   underwriting contracts of insurance at Lloyd's;

(b)   reinsuring such contracts in whole or in part;

(c)   paying claims on such contracts;

"market operator" means—

(a)   a person that manages or operates the business of a UK regulated market (including a person who does so as the UK regulated market itself), or

(b)   a person that would fall within paragraph (a) if the person had its registered office (or, if it does not have one, its head office) in the United Kingdom;

other than a person falling within paragraph (1A);

"markets in financial instruments directive" means Directive 2014/65/EU of the European Parliament and of the Council of 15 May 2014 on markets in financial instruments (recast);

"markets in financial instruments regulation" means Regulation (EU) No. 600/2014 of the European Parliament and of the Council of 15 May 2014 on markets in financial instruments as it forms part of retained EU law;

"multilateral trading facility" or "MTF" means—

(a)   a UK multilateral trading facility (within the meaning of Article 2.1.14A of the markets in financial instruments regulation) operated by an investment firm, a qualifying credit institution or a market operator, or

(b)   a facility which—

(i)   is operated by an investment firm, qualifying credit institution or market operator whose home State is not the United Kingdom, and

(ii)   if its operator's home State was the United Kingdom, would be a UK multilateral trading facility (within the meaning of Article 2.1.14A of the markets in financial instruments regulation);

"occupational pension scheme" has the meaning given by section 1 of the Pension Schemes Act 1993 but with paragraph (b) of the definition omitted;

"operator" has the same meaning as in the trading scheme order;

"organised trading facility" or "OTF" means—

(a)   a UK organised trading facility (within the meaning of Article 2.1.15A of the markets in financial instruments regulation) operated by an investment firm, a qualifying credit institution or a market operator, or

(b)   a facility which—

    (i)   is operated by an investment firm, qualifying credit institution or market operator whose home State is not the United Kingdom, and

    (ii)   if its operator's home State was the United Kingdom, would be a UK organised trading facility (within the meaning of Article 2.1.15A of the markets in financial instruments regulation);

"overseas person" means a person who—

(a)   carries on activities of the kind specified by any of articles 14, 21, 25, 25A, 25B, 25C, 25D, 25DA, 25E, 37, 39A, 40, 45, 51ZA, 51ZB, 51ZC, 51ZD, 51ZE, 52, 53, 53A, 53B, 53C, 53D, 61, 63B, 63F and 63J or, so far as relevant to any of those articles, article 64 (or activities of a kind which would be so specified but for the exclusion in article 72); but

(b)   does not carry on any such activities, or offer to do so, from a permanent place of business maintained by him in the United Kingdom;

"owner", in relation to a hire purchase agreement, has the meaning given by article 60N;

"pension fund management contract" means a contract to manage the investments of pension funds (other than funds solely for the benefit of the officers or employees of the person effecting or carrying out the contract and their dependants or, in the case of a company, partly for the benefit of officers and employees and their dependants of its subsidiary or holding company or a subsidiary of its holding company); and for the purposes of this definition, "subsidiary" and "holding company" are to be construed in accordance with section 1159 of the Companies Act 2006;

"the person's firm", in relation to a person acting as an insolvency practitioner or in reasonable contemplation of that person's appointment as an insolvency practitioner, means—

(a)   the person's employer;

(b)   where the person is a partner in a partnership other than a limited liability partnership, that partnership;

(c)   where the person is a member of a limited liability partnership, that partnership;

"personal pension scheme" means a scheme or arrangement which is not an occupational pension scheme or a stakeholder pension scheme and which is comprised in one or more instruments or agreements, having or capable of having effect so as to provide benefits to or in respect of people—

(a)   on retirement,

(b)   on having reached a particular age, or

(c)   on termination of service in an employment;

"plan provider" has the meaning given by paragraph (3) of article 63B, read with paragraphs (7) and (8) of that article;

"portfolio management" has the meaning given by Article 2.7 of the Commission Regulation;

"property" includes currency of the United Kingdom or any other country or territory;

"qualifying contract of insurance" means a contract of long-term insurance which is not—

(a)   a reinsurance contract; nor

(b)   a contract in respect of which the following conditions are met—

    (i)   the benefits under the contract are payable only on death or in respect of incapacity due to injury, sickness or infirmity;

    (ii)   ...

    (iii) the contract has no surrender value, or the consideration consists of a single premium and the surrender value does not exceed that premium; and

    (iv) the contract makes no provision for its conversion or extension in a manner which would result in it ceasing to comply with any of the above conditions;

"qualifying credit institution" means a credit institution which—

(a) is a person who—

    (i) has Part 4A permission to carry on the regulated activity of accepting deposits, or

    (ii) satisfies the conditions for being given permission under Part 4A to carry on that activity, or

    (iii) is a body corporate incorporated in the United Kingdom and would satisfy those conditions—

        (aa) were its head office in the United Kingdom, or

        (bb) if it has a registered office, were its registered office, or its registered office and its head office, in the United Kingdom,

(b) is not a friendly society,

(c) is not a society registered as a credit union under—

    (i) the Co-operative and Community Benefit Societies Act 2014,

    (ii) the Credit Unions (Northern Ireland) Order 1985, or

    (iii) the Co-operative and Community Benefit Societies Act (Northern Ireland) 1969, and

(d) is not a person excluded from the definition of "investment firm" by Schedule 3, read with the Commission Regulation and with Commission Delegated Regulation (EU) 2017/592 of 1 December 2016 supplementing Directive 2014/65/EU of the European Parliament and the Council with regard to regulatory technical standards for the criteria to establish when an activity is considered to be ancillary to the main business;

"reception", "transmission" and "submission" have the same meaning in relation to a bid at an auction for an investment of the kind specified in article 82A as in the emission allowance auctioning regulation or the UK auctioning regulations;

"regulated consumer hire agreement" has the meaning given by article 60N;

"regulated credit agreement" has the meaning given by article 60B;

"regulated home purchase plan" has the meaning given by article 63F(3);

"regulated home reversion plan" has the meaning given by article 63B(3);

"regulated mortgage contract" has the meaning given by article 61(3);

"regulated sale and rent back agreement" has the meaning given by article 63J(3);

"relevant investment" means—

(a) rights under a qualifying contract of insurance;

(b) rights under any other contract of insurance;

(c) any investment of the kind specified by any of articles 83, 84, 85 and 87; or

(d) any investment of the kind specified by article 89 so far as relevant to an investment falling within (a) or (c);

"relevant recipient of credit" has the meaning given by article 60L;

"restricted-use credit agreement" has the meaning given in article 60L;

"reversion seller" has the meaning given by article 63B(3);

"securitisation repository" means a person registered with the FCA (as the competent authority) under Article 10 of the EU Securitisation Regulation 2017;

"security" means (except where the context otherwise requires) any investment of the kind specified by any of articles 76 to 82 or by article 82B or, so far as relevant to any such investment, article 89;

"selling", in relation to any investment, includes disposing of the investment for valuable consideration, and for these purposes "disposing" includes—

(a) in the case of an investment consisting of rights under a contract—

          (i)   surrendering, assigning or converting those rights; or

          (ii)   assuming the corresponding liabilities under the contract;

     (b)   in the case of an investment consisting of rights under other arrangements, assuming the corresponding liabilities under the arrangements; and

     (c)   in the case of any other investment, issuing or creating the investment or granting the rights or interests of which it consists;

"small registered UK AIFM" has the meaning given by regulation 2(1) of the Alternative Investment Fund Managers Regulations 2013;

"stakeholder pension scheme" has the meaning given by section 1 of the Welfare Reform and Pensions Act 1999 in relation to Great Britain and has the meaning given by article 3 of the Welfare Reform and Pensions (Northern Ireland) Order 1999 in relation to Northern Ireland;

"structured deposit" means a deposit which is fully repayable at maturity on terms under which interest or a premium will be paid or is at risk, according to a formula involving factors such as—

     (a)   an index or combination of indices, excluding variable rate deposits whose return is directly linked to an interest rate index such as Euribor or Libor;

     (b)   a financial instrument or combination of financial instruments;

     (c)   a commodity or combination of commodities or other physical or non-physical non-fungible assets; or

     (d)   a foreign exchange rate or combination of foreign exchange rates;

"syndicate" means one or more persons, to whom a particular syndicate number has been assigned by or under the authority of the Council of Lloyd's, carrying out or effecting contracts of insurance written at Lloyd's;

"trade repository" means—

     (a)   a person registered with the FCA under Article 55 of Regulation (EU) 648/2012 of the European Parliament and of the Council of 4 July 2012 on OTC derivatives, central counterparties and trade repositories or a person recognised by the FCA under Article 77 of that Regulation; or

     (b)   a person registered with the FCA under Article 5 of the SFT regulation or a person recognised by the FCA under Article 19 of that Regulation;

"trading scheme order" means the Greenhouse Gas Emissions Trading Scheme Order 2020;

...

"UK auctioning regulations" means the Greenhouse Gas Emissions Trading Scheme Auctioning Regulations 2021;

"UK regulated market" has the meaning given by Article 2.1.13A of the markets in financial instruments regulation;

"UK UCITS" has the meaning given by section 237(3) of the Act;

"voting shares", in relation to a body corporate, means shares carrying voting rights attributable to share capital which are exercisable in all circumstances at any general meeting of that body corporate.

(1A)   A person falls within this paragraph if—

     (a)   the person is excluded from the definition of "investment firm" by Schedule 3, read with the Commission Regulation and with Commission Delegated Regulation (EU) 2017/592 of 1 December 2016 supplementing Directive 2014/65/EU of the European Parliament and of the Council with regard to regulatory technical standards for the criteria to establish when an activity is considered to be ancillary to the main business, or

     (b)   the person is one whose home State is not the United Kingdom and who would be excluded from that definition by Schedule 3, read with the Commission Regulation and with Commission Delegated Regulation (EU) 2017/592, if the person had its registered office (or, if it does not have one, its head office) in the United Kingdom.

(2)   For the purposes of this Order, a transaction is entered into through a person if he enters into it as agent or arranges, in a manner constituting the carrying on of an activity of the kind specified by article 25(1), 25A(1), 25B(1), 25C(1) or 25E(1), for it to be entered into by another person as agent or principal.

(3)   For the purposes of this Order, a contract of insurance is to be treated as falling within Part II of Schedule 1, notwithstanding the fact that it contains related and subsidiary provisions such that it might also be regarded as falling within Part I of that Schedule, if its principal object is that of a contract falling within Part II and it is effected or carried out by an authorised person who has permission to effect or carry out contracts falling within paragraph I of Part II of Schedule 1.

(4)   In this Order any reference to a sourcebook is to a sourcebook in the Handbook of Rules and Guidance published by the FCA containing rules made by the FCA under the Act, as the sourcebook has effect on IP completion day.

        Note. This article is amended by S.I. 2023/548, art. 2, as from 1 January 2025.

PART II
SPECIFIED ACTIVITIES

CHAPTER I
GENERAL

4.   Specified activities: general

(1)   The following provisions of this Part specify kinds of activity for the purposes of section 22(1) of the Act (and accordingly any activity of one of those kinds, which is carried on by way of business, and relates to an investment of a kind specified by any provision of Part III and applicable to that activity, is a regulated activity for the purposes of the Act).

(2)   The kinds of activity specified by articles 51ZA, 51ZB, 51ZC, 51ZD, 51ZE, 52 and 63N are also specified for the purposes of section 22(1)(b) of the Act (and accordingly any activity of one of those kinds, when carried on by way of business, is a regulated activity when carried on in relation to property of any kind).

(2A)   The kinds of activity specified by Part 3A are specified for the purposes of section 22(1A)(a) of the Act (and accordingly any activity of one of those kinds, when carried on by way of business, is a regulated activity).

(2B)   The kinds of activity specified in Part 3B are specified for the purposes of section 22(1B) of the Act (and accordingly any activity of one of those kinds, when carried on by way of business in Great Britain, is a regulated activity).

(3)   Subject to paragraph (4), each provision specifying a kind of activity is subject to the exclusions applicable to that provision (and accordingly any reference in this Order to an activity of the kind specified by a particular provision is to be read subject to any such exclusions).

(4)   Where an investment firm or qualifying credit institution—

        (a)   provides or performs investment services and activities on a professional basis, and

        (b)   in doing so would be treated as carrying on an activity of a kind specified by a provision of this Part but for an exclusion in any of articles 15, 16, 18, 19, 22, 23, 29, 34, 38, 67, 68, 69, 70 and 72E,

        that exclusion is to be disregarded and, accordingly, the investment firm or qualifying credit institution is to be treated as carrying on an activity of the kind specified by the provision in question.

(4A)   Where a person, other than an ancillary insurance intermediary carrying out insurance distribution activities falling within Article 1.3 of the insurance distribution directive (the text of which is set out in Part 1 of Schedule 4)—

        (a)   for remuneration, takes up or pursues insurance distribution, or reinsurance distribution, in relation to a risk or commitment located in the United Kingdom, and

(b)   in doing so would be treated as carrying on an activity of a specified kind by a provision of this Part but for an exclusion in any of articles 30, 66, 67 and 72AA,

that exclusion is to be disregarded (and accordingly that person is to be treated as carrying on an activity of the kind specified by the provision in question).

(4AA) In its application to any activity relating to a contract of insurance entered into before IP completion day, paragraph (4A)(a) has effect as if "or an EEA State" were inserted after "the United Kingdom.

(4B)   Where—

    (a)   a person is a mortgage creditor or a mortgage intermediary; and

    (b)   in acting as a mortgage creditor or a mortgage intermediary in respect of an agreement entered into, or to be entered into, on or after 21st March 2016, that person would be treated as carrying on an activity of a kind specified by article 25A (arranging regulated mortgage contracts), 36A (credit broking), 53A (advising on regulated mortgage contracts), 53DA (advising on regulated credit agreements for the acquisition of land), 60B (regulated credit agreements) or 61 (entering into and administering regulated mortgage contracts), but for an exclusion or exemption provided for by this Order,

that exclusion or exemption is to be disregarded (and accordingly that person is to be treated as carrying on an activity of the kind specified by the provision in question) to the extent that such exclusion or exemption neither relates to an agreement to which section 423A(3) of the Act applies nor falls within the scope of any of the derogations set out in Article 3(3) of the mortgages directive (as it had effect immediately before IP completion day).

(5)   In this article—

"ancillary insurance intermediary" has the meaning given by Article 2.1(4) of the insurance distribution directive, the text of which is set out in Part 4 of Schedule 4, read with the modifications set out in paragraph 3 of Part 6 of that Schedule;

"insurance distribution" has the meaning given by Articles 2.1(1) and 2.2 of the insurance distribution directive, the text of which is set out in Parts 2 and 5 of Schedule 4, respectively, read with the modification set out in paragraph 4 of Part 6 of that Schedule; and

"reinsurance distribution" has the meaning given by Articles 2.1(2) and 2.2 of the insurance distribution directive, the text of which is set out in Parts 3 and 5 of Schedule 4, respectively, read with the modifications set out in paragraphs 2 and 4 of Part 6 of that Schedule.

CHAPTER II
ACCEPTING DEPOSITS

The activity

5.   Accepting deposits

(1)   Accepting deposits is a specified kind of activity if—

    (a)   money received by way of deposit is lent to others; or

    (b)   any other activity of the person accepting the deposit is financed wholly, or to a material extent, out of the capital of or interest on money received by way of deposit.

(2)   In paragraph (1), "deposit" means a sum of money, other than one excluded by any of articles 6 to 9A, paid on terms—

    (a)   under which it will be repaid, with or without interest or premium, and either on demand or at a time or in circumstances agreed by or on behalf of the person making the payment and the person receiving it; and

    (b)   which are not referable to the provision of property (other than currency) or services or the giving of security.

(3)   For the purposes of paragraph (2), money is paid on terms which are referable to the provision of property or services or the giving of security if, and only if—

(a)   it is paid by way of advance or part payment under a contract for the sale, hire or other provision of property or services, and is repayable only in the event that the property or services is or are not in fact sold, hired or otherwise provided;

(b)   it is paid by way of security for the performance of a contract or by way of security in respect of loss which may result from the non-performance of a contract; or

(c)   without prejudice to sub-paragraph (b), it is paid by way of security for the delivery up or return of any property, whether in a particular state of repair or otherwise.

Exclusions

...

7.   **Sums received by solicitors etc**

(1)   A sum is not a deposit for the purposes of article 5 if it is received by a practising solicitor acting in the course of his profession.

(2)   In paragraph (1), "practising solicitor" means—

     (a)   a solicitor who is qualified to act as such under section 1 of the Solicitors Act 1974, article 4 of the Solicitors (Northern Ireland) Order 1976 or section 4 of the Solicitors (Scotland) Act 1980;

     (b)   a recognised body;

     (c)   a registered foreign lawyer in the course of providing professional services as a member of a multi-national partnership; or

     (d)   a Swiss lawyer who is a registered European lawyer; ...

     (e)   ....

(3)   In this article—

     (a)   "a recognised body" means a body ... recognised by—

         (i)   the Council of the Law Society under section 9 of the Administration of Justice Act 1985;

         (ii)   the Incorporated Law Society of Northern Ireland under article 26A of the Solicitors (Northern Ireland) Order 1976; or

         (iii)   the Council of the Law Society of Scotland under section 34 of the Solicitors (Scotland) Act 1980;

     (b)   "registered foreign lawyer" has the meaning given by section 89 of the Courts and Legal Services Act 1990 or, in Scotland, section 65 of the Solicitors (Scotland) Act 1980;

     (c)   "multi-national partnership" has the meaning given by section 89 of the Courts and Legal Services Act 1990 but, in Scotland, is a reference to a "multi-national practice" within the meaning of section 60A of the Solicitors (Scotland) Act 1980; ...

     (d)   "registered European lawyer" has the meaning given by regulation 2(1) of the European Communities (Lawyer's Practice) Regulations 2000 or regulation 2(1) of the European Communities (Lawyer's Practice) (Scotland) Regulation 2000; and

     (e)   "Swiss lawyer" means a national of the United Kingdom or a Swiss national who—

         (i)   immediately before IP completion day was authorised in Switzerland to pursue professional activities under the professional title of Avocat, Advokat, Rechtsanwalt, Anwalt, Fürsprecher, Fürsprech or Avvocato, or

         (ii)   had started training towards but not yet obtained their professional qualifications before IP completion day in order to be authorised in Switzerland to pursue professional activities under one of the professional titles referred to in paragraph (i) but who completed their qualifications and were so authorised before the end of the period of four years beginning with IP completion day.

8.   **Sums received by persons authorised to deal etc**

A sum is not a deposit for the purposes of article 5 if it is received by a person who is—

     (a)   an authorised person with permission to carry on an activity of the kind specified by any of articles 14, 21, 25, 37, 51ZA, 51ZB, 51ZC, 51ZD, 51ZE and 52, or

(b)   an exempt person in relation to any such activity,

in the course of, or for the purpose of, carrying on any such activity (or any activity which would be such an activity but for any exclusion made by this Part) with or on behalf of the person by or on behalf of whom the sum is paid.

9.   Sums received in consideration for the issue of debt securities

(1)   Subject to paragraph (2), a sum is not a deposit for the purposes of article 5 if it is received by a person as consideration for the issue by him of any investment of the kind specified by article 77 or 78.

(2)   The exclusion in paragraph (1) does not apply to the receipt by a person of a sum as consideration for the issue by him of commercial paper unless—

     (a)   the commercial paper is issued to persons—

         (i)   whose ordinary activities involve them in acquiring, holding, managing or disposing of investments (as principal or agent) for the purposes of their businesses; or

         (ii)   who it is reasonable to expect will acquire, hold, manage or dispose of investments (as principal or agent) for the purposes of their businesses; and

     (b)   the redemption value of the commercial paper is not less than £100,000 (or an amount of equivalent value denominated wholly or partly in a currency other than sterling), and no part of the commercial paper may be transferred unless the redemption value of that part is not less than £100,000 (or such an equivalent amount).

(3)   In paragraph (2), "commercial paper" means an investment of the kind specified by article 77 or 78 having a maturity of less than one year from the date of issue.

...

CHAPTER IV
DEALING IN INVESTMENTS AS PRINCIPAL

The activity

14.   Dealing in investments as principal

(1)   Buying, selling, subscribing for or underwriting securities or contractually based investments (other than investments of the kind specified by article 87, or article 89 so far as relevant to that article) as principal is a specified kind of activity.

(2)   Paragraph (1) does not apply to a kind of activity to which article 25D or 25DA applies.

Exclusions

15.   Absence of holding out etc

(1)   Subject to paragraph (3), a person ("A") does not carry on an activity of the kind specified by article 14 by entering into a transaction which relates to a security or is the assignment (or, in Scotland, the assignation) of a qualifying contract of insurance (or an investment of the kind specified by article 89, so far as relevant to such a contract), unless—

     (a)   A holds himself out as willing, as principal, to buy, sell or subscribe for investments of the kind to which the transaction relates at prices determined by him generally and continuously rather than in respect of each particular transaction;

     (b)   A holds himself out as engaging in the business of buying investments of the kind to which the transaction relates, with a view to selling them;

     (c)   A holds himself out as engaging in the business of underwriting investments of the kind to which the transaction relates; or

     (d)   A regularly solicits members of the public with the purpose of inducing them, as principals or agents, to enter into transactions constituting activities of the kind specified by article 14, and the transaction is entered into as a result of his having solicited members of the public in that manner.

(2)   In paragraph (1)(d), "members of the public" means any persons other than—

   (a)   authorised persons or persons who are exempt persons in relation to activities of the kind specified by article 14;

   (b)   members of the same group as A;

   (c)   persons who are or who propose to become participators with A in a joint enterprise;

   (d)   any person who is solicited by A with a view to the acquisition by A of 20 per cent or more of the voting shares in a body corporate;

   (e)   if A (either alone or with members of the same group as himself) holds more than 20 per cent of the voting shares in a body corporate, any person who is solicited by A with a view to—

      (i)   the acquisition by A of further shares in the body corporate; or

      (ii) the disposal by A of shares in the body corporate to the person solicited or to a member of the same group as the person solicited;

   (f)   any person who—

      (i)   is solicited by A with a view to the disposal by A of shares in a body corporate to the person solicited or to a member of the same group as that person; and

      (ii) either alone or with members of the same group holds 20 per cent or more of the voting shares in the body corporate;

   (g)   any person whose head office is outside the United Kingdom, who is solicited by an approach made or directed to him at a place outside the United Kingdom and whose ordinary business involves him in carrying on activities of the kind specified by any of articles 14, 21, 25, 37, 40, 45, 51ZA, 51ZB, 51ZC, 51ZD, 51ZE, 52 and 53 or (so far as relevant to any of those articles) article 64, or would do so apart from any exclusion from any of those articles made by this Order.

(3)   This article does not apply where A enters into the transaction as bare trustee or, in Scotland, as nominee for another person and is acting on that other person's instructions (but the exclusion in article 66(1) applies if the conditions set out there are met).

(4)   This article is subject to article 4(4).

16.   Dealing in contractually based investments

(1)   A person who is not an authorised person does not carry on an activity of the kind specified by article 14 by entering into a transaction relating to a contractually based investment—

   (a)   with or through an authorised person, or an exempt person acting in the course of a business comprising a regulated activity in relation to which he is exempt; or

   (b)   through an office outside the United Kingdom maintained by a party to the transaction, and with or through a person whose head office is situated outside the United Kingdom and whose ordinary business involves him in carrying on activities of the kind specified by any of articles 14, 21, 25, 37, 40, 45, 51ZA, 51ZB, 51ZC, 51ZD, 51ZE, 52 and 53 or, so far as relevant to any of those articles, article 64 (or would do so apart from any exclusion from any of those articles made by this Order).

(2)   This article is subject to article 4(4).

17.   Acceptance of instruments creating or acknowledging indebtedness

(1)   A person does not carry on an activity of the kind specified by article 14 by accepting an instrument creating or acknowledging indebtedness in respect of any loan, credit, guarantee or other similar financial accommodation or assurance which he has made, granted or provided.

(2)   The reference in paragraph (1) to a person accepting an instrument includes a reference to a person becoming a party to an instrument otherwise than as a debtor or a surety.

18.   Issue by a company of its own shares etc

(1)   There is excluded from article 14 the issue by a company of its own shares or share warrants, and the issue by any person of his own debentures or debenture warrants.

(2)   In this article—

   (a)   "company" means any body corporate other than an open-ended investment company;

    (b)   "shares" and "debentures" include any investment of the kind specified by article 76, 77 or 77A;

    (c)   "share warrants" and "debenture warrants" mean any investment of the kind specified by article 79 which relates to shares in the company concerned or, as the case may be, debentures issued by the person concerned.

(3)   This article is subject to article 4(4).

18A.   Dealing by a company in its own shares

(1)   A company does not carry on an activity of the kind specified by article 14 by purchasing its own shares where section 724 of the Companies Act 2006 (Treasury shares) applies to the shares purchased.

(2)   A company does not carry on an activity of the kind specified by article 14 by dealing in its own shares held as treasury shares, in accordance with section 727 (Treasury shares: disposal) or 729 (Treasury shares: cancellation) of that Act.

(3)   In this article "shares held as treasury shares" has the same meaning as in that Act.

19.   Risk management

(1)   A person ("B") does not carry on an activity of the kind specified by article 14 by entering as principal into a transaction with another person ("C") if—

    (a)   the transaction relates to investments of the kind specified by any of articles 83 to 85 (or article 89 so far as relevant to any of those articles);

    (b)   neither B nor C is an individual;

    (c)   the sole or main purpose for which B enters into the transaction (either by itself or in combination with other such transactions) is that of limiting the extent to which a relevant business will be affected by any identifiable risk arising otherwise than as a result of the carrying on of a regulated activity; and

    (d)   the relevant business consists mainly of activities other than—

        (i)   regulated activities; or

        (ii)   activities which would be regulated activities but for any exclusion made by this Part.

(2)   In paragraph (1), "relevant business" means a business carried on by—

    (a)   B;

    (b)   a member of the same group as B; or

    (c)   where B and another person are, or propose to become, participators in a joint enterprise, that other person.

(3)   This article is subject to article 4(4).

19A.   Transformer vehicles: insurance risk transformation

A transformer vehicle does not carry on an activity of a kind specified by article 14 by assuming a risk from an undertaking, provided the assumption of the risk is a specified kind of activity falling within article 13A (transformer vehicles: insurance risk transformation).

20.   Other exclusions

Article 14 is also subject to the exclusions in articles 66 (trustees etc), 68 (sale of goods and supply of services), 69 (groups and joint enterprises), 70 (sale of body corporate), 71 (employee share schemes), 72 (overseas persons), … 72AA (managers of UK UCITS and AIFs) and 72H (insolvency practitioners).

CHAPTER V
DEALING IN INVESTMENTS AS AGENT

The activity

21.   Dealing in investments as agent

(1)   Buying, selling, subscribing for or underwriting securities, structured deposits or relevant investments … as agent is a specified kind of activity.

(2)   Paragraph (1) does not apply to a kind of activity to which article 25D or 25DA applies.

Exclusions

22. Deals with or through authorised persons

(1) A person who is not an authorised person does not carry on an activity of the kind specified by article 21 by entering into a transaction as agent for another person ("the client") with or through an authorised person if—

(a) the transaction is entered into on advice given to the client by an authorised person; or

(b) it is clear, in all the circumstances, that the client, in his capacity as an investor, is not seeking and has not sought advice from the agent as to the merits of the client's entering into the transaction (or, if the client has sought such advice, the agent has declined to give it but has recommended that the client seek such advice from an authorised person).

(2) But the exclusion in paragraph (1) does not apply if—

(a) the transaction relates to a contract of insurance; or

(b) the agent receives from any person other than the client any pecuniary reward or other advantage, for which he does not account to the client, arising out of his entering into the transaction.

(3) This article is subject to article 4(4).

23. Risk management

(1) A person ("B") does not carry on an activity of the kind specified by article 21 by entering as agent for a relevant person into a transaction with another person ("C") if—

(a) the transaction relates to investments of the kind specified by any of articles 83 to 85 (or article 89 so far as relevant to any of those articles);

(b) neither B nor C is an individual;

(c) the sole or main purpose for which B enters into the transaction (either by itself or in combination with other such transactions) is that of limiting the extent to which a relevant business will be affected by any identifiable risk arising otherwise than as a result of the carrying on of a regulated activity; and

(d) the relevant business consists mainly of activities other than—

(i) regulated activities; or

(ii) activities which would be regulated activities but for any exclusion made by this Part.

(2) In paragraph (1), "relevant person" means—

(a) a member of the same group as B; or

(b) where B and another person are, or propose to become, participators in a joint enterprise, that other person;

and "relevant business" means a business carried on by a relevant person.

(3) This article is subject to article 4(4).

24. Other exclusions

Article 21 is also subject to the exclusions in articles 67 (profession or non-investment business), 68 (sale of goods and supply of services), 69 (groups and joint enterprises), 70 (sale of body corporate), 71 (employee share schemes), 72 (overseas persons), … 72B (activities carried on by a provider of relevant goods or services), 72AA (managers of UK UCITS and AIFs), 72D (large risks contracts where risk situated outside the United Kingdom), 72G (local authorities) and 72H (insolvency practitioners).

…

CHAPTER VI
ARRANGING DEALS IN INVESTMENTS

The activities

25.   **Arranging deals in investments**

(1)   Making arrangements for another person (whether as principal or agent) to buy, sell, subscribe for or underwrite a particular investment which is—

   (a)   a security,

   (b)   a relevant investment, …

   (c)   an investment of the kind specified by article 86, or article 89 so far as relevant to that article, or

   (d)   a structured deposit,

   is a specified kind of activity.

(2)   Making arrangements with a view to a person who participates in the arrangements buying, selling, subscribing for or underwriting investments falling within paragraph (1)(a), (b), (c) or (d) (whether as principal or agent) is also a specified kind of activity.

(3)   Paragraphs (1) and (2) do not apply to a kind of activity to which article 25D or 25DA applies.

Note. This article is amended by S.I. 2024/105, reg. 46(1), (2), as from a day to be appointed (save for certain purposes).

25A.   **Arranging regulated mortgage contracts**

(1)   Making arrangements—

   (a)   for another person to enter into a regulated mortgage contract as borrower; or

   (b)   for another person to vary the terms of a regulated mortgage contract falling within paragraph (1A) entered into by him as borrower …, in such a way as to vary his obligations under that contract,

   is a specified kind of activity.

(1A)   A regulated mortgage contract falls within this paragraph if—

   (a)   the contract was entered into on or after 31st October 2004; or

   (b)   the contract—

     (i)   was entered into before 31st October 2004; and

     (ii)   was a regulated credit agreement immediately before 21st March 2016.

(2)   Making arrangements with a view to a person who participates in the arrangements entering into a regulated mortgage contract as borrower is also a specified kind of activity.

(2A)   Making arrangements to enter into a regulated mortgage contract with a borrower on behalf of a lender is also a specified kind of activity.

(3)   In this article "borrower" and "lender" have the meanings given by article 61(3)(a)(i).

…

Exclusions

26.   **Arrangements not causing a deal**

There are excluded from articles 25(1), 25A(1), 25B(1), 25C(1) and 25E(1) arrangements which do not or would not bring about the transaction to which the arrangements relate.

27.   **Enabling parties to communicate**

A person does not carry on an activity of the kind specified by article 25(2), 25A(2), 25B(2), 25C(2) or 25E(2) merely by providing means by which one party to a transaction (or potential transaction) is able to communicate with other such parties.

Note. This article is amended by S.I. 2024/105, reg. 46(1), (6), as from a day to be appointed (save for certain purposes).

28.   Arranging transactions to which the arranger is a party

(1)   There are excluded from article 25(1) any arrangements for a transaction into which the person making the arrangements enters or is to enter as principal or as agent for some other person.

(2)   There are excluded from article 25(2) any arrangements which a person makes with a view to transactions into which he enters or is to enter as principal or as agent for some other person.

(3)   But the exclusions in paragraphs (1) and (2) do not apply to arrangements made for or with a view to a transaction which relates to a contract of insurance, unless the person making the arrangements either—

(a)   is the only policyholder; or

(b)   as a result of the transaction, would become the only policyholder.

28A.   Arranging contracts, plans or agreements to which the arranger is a party

(1)   There are excluded from articles 25A(1), 25B(1), 25C(1) and 25E(1) any arrangements—

(a)   for a contract, plan or agreement into which the person making the arrangements enters or is to enter; or

(b)   for a variation of a contract, plan or agreement to which that person is (or is to become) a party.

(2)   There are excluded from articles 25A(2), 25B(2), 25C(2) and 25E(2) any arrangements which a person makes with a view to contracts, plans or agreements into which he enters or is to enter.

29.   Arranging deals with or through authorised persons

(1)   There are excluded from articles 25(1) and (2), 25A(1), (2) and (2A), 25B(1) and (2), 25C(1) and (2) and 25E(1) and (2) arrangements made by a person ("A") who is not an authorised person for or with a view to a transaction which is or is to be entered into by a person ("the client") with or though an authorised person if—

(a)   the transaction is or is to be entered into on advice to the client by an authorised person; or

(b)   it is clear, in all the circumstances, that the client, in his capacity as an investor, borrower, reversion seller, plan provider, home purchaser, agreement provider or (as the case may be) agreement seller, is not seeking and has not sought advice from A as to the merits of the client's entering into the transaction (or, if the client has sought such advice, A has declined to give it but has recommended that the client seek such advice from an authorised person).

(2)   But the exclusion in paragraph (1) does not apply if—

(a)   the transaction relates, or would relate, to a contract of insurance; or

(b)   A receives from any person other than the client any pecuniary reward or other advantage, for which he does not account to the client, arising out of his making the arrangements.

(3)   This article is subject to article 4(4) and (4B).

...

31.   Arranging the acceptance of debentures in connection with loans

(1)   There are excluded from article 25(1) and (2) arrangements under which a person accepts or is to accept, whether as principal or agent, an instrument creating or acknowledging indebtedness in respect of any loan, credit, guarantee or other similar financial accommodation or assurance which is, or is to be, made, granted or provided by that person or his principal.

(2)   The reference in paragraph (1) to a person accepting an instrument includes a reference to a person becoming a party to an instrument otherwise than as a debtor or a surety.

32.   Provision of finance

There are excluded from article 25(2) arrangements having as their sole purpose the provision of finance to enable a person to buy, sell, subscribe for or underwrite investments.

33.   Introducing

There are excluded from articles 25(2), 25A(2), 25B(2), 25C(2) and 25E(2) arrangements where—

(a)   they are arrangements under which persons ("clients") will be introduced to another person;

    (b)   the person to whom introductions are to be made is—
- (i) an authorised person;
- (ii) an exempt person acting in the course of a business comprising a regulated activity in relation to which he is exempt; or
- (iii) a person who is not unlawfully carrying on regulated activities in the United Kingdom and whose ordinary business involves him in engaging in an activity of the kind specified by any of articles 14, 21, 25, 25A, 25B, 25C, 25E, 37, 39A, 40, 45, 51ZA, 51ZB, 51ZC, 51ZD, 51ZE, 52, 53, 53A, 53B, 53C and 53D (or, so far as relevant to any of those articles, article 64), or would do so apart from any exclusion from any of those articles made by this Order; ...

    (c)   the introduction is made with a view to the provision of independent advice or the independent exercise of discretion in relation to investments generally or in relation to any class of investments to which the arrangements relate; and

    (d)   The arrangements—
- (i) are made with a view to a person entering into a transaction which does not relate to a contract of insurance, or
- (ii) are of the type specified in article 33B (provision of information—contracts of insurance).

33A. **Introducing to authorised persons etc.**

(1)   There are excluded from article 25A(2) arrangements where—
    (a)   they are arrangements under which a client is introduced to a person ("N") who is—
- (i) an authorised person who has permission to carry on a regulated activity of the kind specified by any of articles 25A, 53A, and 61(1),
- (ii) an appointed representative who may carry on a regulated activity of the kind specified by either of articles 25A and 53A without contravening the general prohibition, or
- (iii) an overseas person who carries on activities specified by any of articles 25A, 53A and 61(1); and

    (b)   the conditions mentioned in paragraph (2) are satisfied.

(1A)   There are excluded from article 25B(2) arrangements where—
    (a)   they are arrangements under which a client is introduced to a person ("N") who is—
- (i) an authorised person who has permission to carry on a regulated activity of the kind specified by any of articles 25B, 53B and 63B(1),
- (ii) an appointed representative who may carry on a regulated activity of the kind specified by either of articles 25B and 53B without contravening the general prohibition, or
- (iii) an overseas person who carries on activities specified by any of articles 25B, 53B and 63B(1); and

    (b)   the conditions mentioned in paragraph (2) are satisfied.

(1B)   There are excluded from article 25C(2) arrangements where—
    (a)   they are arrangements under which a client is introduced to a person ("N") who is—
- (i) an authorised person who has permission to carry on a regulated activity of the kind specified by any of articles 25C, 53C and 63F(1),
- (ii) an appointed representative who may carry on a regulated activity of the kind specified by either of articles 25C and 53C without contravening the general prohibition, or
- (iii) an overseas person who carries on activities specified by any of articles 25C, 53C and 63F(1); and

    (b)   the conditions mentioned in paragraph (2) are satisfied.

(1C)   There are excluded from article 25E(2) arrangements where—
    (a)   they are arrangements under which a client is introduced to a person ("N") who is—

    (i)   an authorised person who has permission to carry on a regulated activity of the kind specified by any of articles 25E, 53D and 63J(1),

    (ii) an appointed representative who may carry on a regulated activity of the kind specified by either of articles 25E or 53D without contravening the general prohibition, or

    (iii) an overseas person who carries on activities specified by any of articles 25E, 53D and 63J(1); and

  (b)   the conditions mentioned in paragraph (2) are satisfied.

(2)   Those conditions are—

  (a)   that the person making the introduction ("P") does not receive any money, other than money payable to P on his own account, paid by the client for or in connection with any transaction which the client enters into with or through N as a result of the introduction; and

  (b)   that before making the introduction P discloses to the client such of the information mentioned in paragraph (3) as applies to P.

(3)   That information is—

  (a)   that P is a member of the same group as N;

  (b)   details of any payment which P will receive from N, by way of fee or commission, for introducing the client to N;

  (c)   an indication of any other reward or advantage received or to be received by P that arises out of his introducing clients to N.

(4)   In this article, "client" means—

  (a)   for the purposes of paragraph (1), a borrower within the meaning given by article 61(3)(a)(i), or a person who is or may be contemplating entering into a regulated mortgage contract as such a borrower;

  (b)   for the purposes of paragraph (1A), a reversion seller, a plan provider or a person who is or may be contemplating entering into a regulated home reversion plan as a reversion seller or as a plan provider;

  (c)   for the purposes of paragraph (1B), a home purchaser or a person who is or may be contemplating entering into a regulated home purchase plan as a home purchaser;

  (d)   for the purposes of paragraph (1C), an agreement provider, an agreement seller or a person who is or may be contemplating entering into a regulated sale and rent back agreement as an agreement provider or agreement seller.

...

34.   Arrangements for the issue of shares etc

(1)   There are excluded from article 25(1) and (2)—

  (a)   arrangements made by a company for the purposes of issuing its own shares or share warrants; and

  (b)   arrangements made by any person for the purposes of issuing his own debentures or debenture warrants;

and for the purposes of article 25(1) and (2), a company is not, by reason of issuing its own shares or share warrants, and a person is not, by reason of issuing his own debentures or debenture warrants, to be treated as selling them.

(2)   In paragraph (1), "company", "shares", "debentures", "share warrants" and "debenture warrants" have the meanings given by article 18(2).

(3)   This article is subject to article 4(4).

...

36.   Other exclusions

(1)   Article 25 is also subject to the exclusions in articles 66 (trustees etc), 67 (profession or non-investment business), 68 (sale of goods and supply of services), 69 (groups and joint enterprises), 70 (sale of body corporate), 71 (employee share schemes), 72 (overseas persons), ... 72AA (managers of UK UCITS and AIFs), 72B (activities carried on by a provider of relevant goods or

services), 72C (provision of information about contracts of insurance on an incidental basis), 72D (large risks contracts where risk situated outside the United Kingdom), 72G (local authorities) and 72H (insolvency practitioners).

(2)   Articles 25A, 25B, 25C and 25E are also subject to the exclusions in articles 66 (trustees etc.), 67 (profession or non-investment business), 72 (overseas persons), ... 72AA (managers of UK UCITS and AIFs) and 72G (local authorities).

(2A)   Article 25A is also subject to the exclusion in article 72I (registered consumer buy-to-let mortgage firms).

(3)   Article 25D is also subject to the exclusions in articles 72 (overseas persons), 72AA (managers of UK UCITS and AIFs) and 72H (insolvency practitioners).

...

CHAPTER VII
MANAGING INVESTMENTS

The activity

37.   Managing investments

Managing assets belonging to another person, in circumstances involving the exercise of discretion, is a specified kind of activity if—

(a)   the assets consist of or include any investment which is a security, structured deposit or a contractually based investment; or

(b)   the arrangements for their management are such that the assets may consist of or include such investments, and either the assets have at any time since 29th April 1988 done so, or the arrangements have at any time (whether before or after that date) been held out as arrangements under which the assets would do so.

Exclusions

38.   Attorneys

(1)   A person does not carry on an activity of the kind specified by article 37 if—

(a)   he is a person appointed to manage the assets in question under a power of attorney; and

(b)   all routine or day-to-day decisions, so far as relating to investments of a kind mentioned in article 37(a), are taken on behalf of that person by—

(i)   an authorised person with permission to carry on activities of the kind specified by article 37; ...

(ii)   a person who is an exempt person in relation to activities of that kind; or

(iii) an overseas person.

This Article is subject to article 4(4).

39.   Other exclusions

Article 37 is also subject to the exclusions in articles 66 (trustees etc), 68 (sale of goods and supply of services), 69 (groups and joint enterprises), ... 72AA (managers of UK UCITS and AIFs), 72C (provision of information about contracts of insurance on an incidental basis) and 72H (insolvency practitioners).

...

CHAPTER VIII
SAFEGUARDING AND ADMINISTERING INVESTMENTS

The activity

40.   Safeguarding and administering investments

(1)   The activity consisting of both—

(a)   the safeguarding of assets belonging to another, and

(b) the administration of those assets,

or arranging for one or more other persons to carry on that activity, is a specified kind of activity if the condition in sub-paragraph (a) or (b) of paragraph (2) is met.

(2) The condition is that—

(a) the assets consist of or include any investment which is a security or a contractually based investment; or

(b) the arrangements for their safeguarding and administration are such that the assets may consist of or include such investments, and either the assets have at any time since 1st June 1997 done so, or the arrangements have at any time (whether before or after that date) been held out as ones under which such investments would be safeguarded and administered.

(3) For the purposes of this article—

(a) it is immaterial that title to the assets safeguarded and administered is held in uncertificated form;

(b) it is immaterial that the assets safeguarded and administered may be transferred to another person, subject to a commitment by the person safeguarding and administering them, or arranging for their safeguarding and administration, that they will be replaced by equivalent assets at some future date or when so requested by the person to whom they belong.

Exclusions

41. Acceptance of responsibility by third party

(1) There are excluded from article 40 any activities which a person carries on pursuant to arrangements which—

(a) are ones under which a qualifying custodian undertakes to the person to whom the assets belong a responsibility in respect of the assets which is no less onerous than the qualifying custodian would have if the qualifying custodian were safeguarding and administering the assets; and

(b) are operated by the qualifying custodian in the course of carrying on in the United Kingdom an activity of the kind specified by article 40.

(2) In paragraph (1), "qualifying custodian" means a person who is—

(a) an authorised person who has permission to carry on an activity of the kind specified by article 40, or

(b) an exempt person acting in the course of a business comprising a regulated activity in relation to which he is exempt.

42. Introduction to qualifying custodians

(1) There are excluded from article 40 any arrangements pursuant to which introductions are made by a person ("P") to a qualifying custodian with a view to the qualifying custodian providing in the United Kingdom a service comprising an activity of the kind specified by article 40, where the qualifying person (or other person who is to safeguard and administer the assets in question) is not connected with P.

(2) For the purposes of paragraph (1)—

(a) "qualifying custodian" has the meaning given by article 41(2); and

(b) a person is connected with P if either he is a member of the same group as P, or P is remunerated by him.

42A. Depositaries of UK UCITS and AIFs

A person does not carry on an activity of the kind specified by article 40 if the person carries on the activity in relation to—

(a) a UK UCITS, and the person has a Part 4A permission to carry on the activity specified in article 51ZB in respect of that UCITS; or

(b) an AIF, and the person has a Part 4A permission to carry on the activity specified in article 51ZD in respect of that AIF.

43.   Activities not constituting administration

The following activities do not constitute the administration of assets for the purposes of article 40—

(a)   providing information as to the number of units or the value of any assets safeguarded;

(b)   converting currency;

(c)   receiving documents relating to an investment solely for the purpose of onward transmission to, from or at the direction of the person to whom the investment belongs.

44.   Other exclusions

Article 40 is also subject to the exclusions in articles 66 (trustees etc), 67 (profession or non-investment business), 68 (sale of goods and supply of services), 69 (groups and joint enterprises), 71 (employee share schemes), ... 72AA (managers of UK UCITS and AIFs), 72C (provisions of information about contracts of insurance on an incidental basis) and 72H (insolvency practition-ers).

...

CHAPTER XII
ADVISING ON INVESTMENTS

The activity

53.   Advising on investments

(1)   Advising a person is a specified kind of activity if the advice is—

(a)   given to the person in his capacity as an investor or potential investor, or in his capacity as agent for an investor or a potential investor; and

(b)   advice on the merits of his doing any of the following (whether as principal or agent)—

(i)   buying, selling, subscribing for, exchanging, redeeming, holding or underwriting a particular investment which is a security, structured deposit or a relevant investment, or

(ii)   exercising or not exercising any right conferred by such an investment to buy, sell, subscribe for, exchange or redeem such an investment.

(1A)   Paragraph (1) does not apply to a person who is appropriately authorised except to the extent that they are providing a personal recommendation.

(1B)   A person is appropriately authorised when they are authorised for the purposes of the Act to carry on an activity of a kind specified by a provision of this Order which is not the activity specified by paragraph (1) and is not the activity of agreeing to carry on the activity specified by paragraph (1).

(1C)   Subject to paragraph (1D), a personal recommendation is a recommendation—

(a)   made to a person in their capacity as an investor or potential investor, or in their capacity as agent for an investor or a potential investor;

(b)   which constitutes a recommendation to them to do any of the following (whether as principal or agent)—

(i)   buy, sell, subscribe for, exchange, redeem, hold or underwrite a particular investment which is a security, structured deposit or a relevant investment; or

(ii)   exercise or not exercise any right conferred by such an investment to buy, sell, sub-scribe for, exchange or redeem such an investment; and

(c)   that is—

(i)   presented as suitable for the person to whom it is made; or

(ii)   based on a consideration of the circumstances of that person.

(1D)   A recommendation is not a personal recommendation if it is issued exclusively to the public.

(2)   Advising a person is a specified kind of activity if the advice is—

(a)   given to the person in that person's capacity as a lender or potential lender under a relevant article 36H agreement, or in that person's capacity as an agent for a lender or potential lender under such an agreement; and

(b)   advice on the merits of that person doing any of the following (whether as principal or agent)—

    (i)   entering into a relevant article 36H agreement as a lender or assuming the rights of a lender under such an agreement by assignment or operation of law,

    (ii)   providing instructions to an operator with a view to entering into a relevant article 36H agreement as a lender or assuming the rights of a lender under such an agreement by assignment or operation of law, where the instructions involve—

        (aa)   accepting particular parameters for the terms of the agreement presented by an operator,

        (bb)   choosing between options governing the parameters of the terms of the agreement presented by an operator, or

        (cc)   specifying the parameters of the terms of the agreement by other means,

    (iii)   enforcing or exercising the lender's rights under a relevant article 36H agreement, or

    (iv)   assigning rights under a relevant article 36H agreement.

(3)   Paragraph (2) does not apply in so far as—

(a)   the advice is given in relation to a relevant article 36H agreement which has been facilitated by the person giving the advice, in the course of carrying on an activity of a kind specified by article 36H and is given by—

    (i)   an authorised person with permission to carry on a regulated activity of the kind specified by article 36H(1) (operating an electronic system in relation to lending),

    (ii)   an appointed representative in relation to that activity,

    (iii)   an exempt person in relation to that activity, or

    (iv)   a person to whom, as a result of Part 20 of the Act, the general prohibition does not apply in relation to that activity;

(b)   the advice is given in the course of carrying on an activity of a kind specified by article 39F (debt-collecting) by a person carrying on that activity not in contravention of the general prohibition; or

(c)   the advice is given in the course of carrying on an activity of a kind specified by article 39G (debt administration) by a person carrying on that activity not in contravention of the general prohibition.

(4)   In this article—

"operator" means a person carrying on an activity of the kind specified by article 36H(1) or (2D), and

"relevant article 36H agreement" means an article 36H agreement (within the meaning of article 36H (operating an electronic system in relation to lending)) which has been, or may be, entered into with the facilitation of a person carrying on an activity of the kind specified by article 36H(1) or (2D).

(5)   For the purposes of the application of section 22(1) of the Act (regulated activities) to an activity of a kind specified by paragraph (2) of this article, article 88D (credit agreement), and article 73 (investments: general) in so far as it relates to that article, have effect as if the reference to a credit agreement in article 88D includes a reference to a relevant article 36H agreement.

53A.   Advising on regulated mortgage contracts

(1)   Advising a person is a specified kind of activity if the advice—

(a)   is given to the person in his capacity as a borrower or potential borrower; and

(b)   is advice on the merits of his doing any of the following—

    (i)   entering into a particular regulated mortgage contract, or

    (ii)   varying the terms of a regulated mortgage contract falling within paragraph (1A) entered into by him … in such a way as to vary his obligations under that contract.

(1A)   A regulated mortgage contract falls within this paragraph if—

(a)   the contract was entered into on or after 31st October 2004; or

(b)   the contract—

      (i)   was entered into before 31st October 2004; and

      (ii) was a regulated credit agreement immediately before 21st March 2016.

(2)   In this article, "borrower" has the meaning given by article 61(3)(a)(i).

...

53DA. Advising on regulated credit agreements for the acquisition of land

(1)   Advising a person ("P") is a specified kind of activity if—

    (a)   the advice is given to P in P's capacity as a recipient of credit, or potential recipient of credit, under a regulated credit agreement;

    (b)   P intends to use the credit to acquire or retain property rights in land or in an existing or projected building; and

    (c)   the advice consists of the provision of personal recommendations to P in respect of one or more transactions relating to regulated credit agreements entered into, or to be entered into, on or after 21st March 2016.

(2)   In this article—

    (a)   a reference to any land or building—

      (i)   in relation to an agreement entered into before IP completion day, is a reference to any land or building in the United Kingdom or within the territory of an EEA State;

      (ii) in relation to an agreement entered into on or after IP completion day, is a reference to any land or building in the United Kingdom;

    (b)   "regulated credit agreement" has the meaning given by article 60B(3).

...

Exclusions

54. Advice given in newspapers etc

(1)   There is excluded from articles 53, 53A, 53B, 53C, 53D, 53DA and 53E the giving of advice in writing or other legible form if the advice is contained in a newspaper, journal, magazine, or other periodical publication, or is given by way of a service comprising regularly updated news or information, if the principal purpose of the publication or service, taken as a whole and including any advertisements or other promotional material contained in it, is neither—

    (a)   that of giving advice of a kind mentioned in article 53, 53A, 53B, 53C or 53D, 53DA or 53E, as the case may be; nor

    (b)   that of leading or enabling persons—

      (i)   to buy, sell, subscribe for or underwrite securities, structured deposits, or contractually based investments, or (as the case may be),

      (ia) to enter into a relevant article 36H agreement (within the meaning of that article) as a lender, to assume the rights of a lender under such an agreement by assignment or operation of law, or to assign rights under such an agreement,

      (ii) to enter as borrower into regulated mortgage contracts, or vary the terms of regulated mortgage contracts entered into by them as borrower,

      (iii) to enter as reversion seller or plan provider into regulated home reversion plans, or vary the terms of regulated home reversion plans entered into by them as reversion seller or plan provider,

      (iv) to enter as home purchaser into regulated home purchase plans, or vary the terms of regulated home purchase plans entered into by them as home purchaser;

      (v) to enter as agreement seller or agreement provider into regulated sale and rent back agreements, or vary the terms of regulated sale and rent back agreements entered into by them as agreement seller or agreement provider;

      (va) to enter as a recipient of credit into a regulated credit agreement the purpose of which is to acquire or retain property rights in land in the United Kingdom or in an existing or projected building in the United Kingdom,

     (vi)   to require the trustee or manager of a pension scheme to take any of the actions referred to in article 53E(1)(c).

(2)   There is also excluded from articles 53, 53A, 53B, 53C, 53D, 53DA and 53E the giving of advice in any service consisting of the broadcast or transmission of television or radio programmes, if the principal purpose of the service, taken as a whole and including any advertisements or other promotional material contained in it, is neither of those mentioned in paragraph (1)(a) and (b).

(2A)   Paragraphs (1) and (2) do not apply to advice which is a personal recommendation falling within article 53(1A).

(3)   The FCA may, on the application of the proprietor of any such publication or service as is mentioned in paragraph (1) or (2), certify that it is of the nature described in that paragraph, and may revoke any such certificate if it considers that it is no longer justified.

(4)   A certificate given under paragraph (3) and not revoked is conclusive evidence of the matters certified.

54A.   **Advice given in the course of administration by authorised person**

(1)   A person who is not an authorised person ("A") does not carry on an activity of the kind specified by article 53A by reason of—

    (a)   anything done by an authorised person ("B") in relation to a regulated mortgage contract which B is administering pursuant to arrangements of the kind mentioned in article 62(a); or

    (b)   anything A does in connection with the administration of a regulated mortgage contract in circumstances falling within article 62(b).

(2)   A person who is not an authorised person ("A") does not carry on an activity of the kind specified by article 53B by reason of—

    (a)   anything done by an authorised person ("B") in relation to a regulated home reversion plan which B is administering pursuant to arrangements of the kind mentioned in article 63C(a); or

    (b)   anything A does in connection with the administration of a regulated home reversion plan in circumstances falling within article 63C(b).

(3)   A person who is not an authorised person ("A") does not carry on an activity of the kind specified by article 53C by reason of—

    (a)   anything done by an authorised person ("B") in relation to a regulated home purchase plan which B is administering pursuant to arrangements of the kind mentioned in article 63G(a); or

    (b)   anything A does in connection with the administration of a regulated home purchase plan in circumstances falling within article 63G(b).

(4)   A person who is not an authorised person ("A") does not carry on an activity of the kind specified by article 53D by reason of—

    (a)   anything done by an authorised person ("B") in relation to a regulated sale and rent back agreement which B is administering pursuant to arrangements of the kind mentioned in article 63K(a); or

    (b)   anything A does in connection with the administration of a regulated sale and rent back agreement in circumstances falling within article 63K(b).

(5)   A person who is not an authorised person ("A") does not carry on an activity of the kind specified by article 53DA by reason of—

    (a)   anything done by an authorised person ("B") in relation to a regulated credit agreement which B is administering pursuant to arrangements of the kind mentioned in article 60I(a) (arranging administration by authorised person); or

    (b)   anything A does in connection with the administration of a regulated credit agreement in circumstances falling within article 60I(b).

...

55.   **Other exclusions**

(1)   Article 53 is also subject to the exclusions in articles 66 (trustees etc), 67, (profession or non-investment business), 68 (sale of goods and supply of services), 69 (groups and joint enterprises),

70 (sale of body corporate), 72 (overseas persons), … 72AA (managers of UK UCITS and AIFs), 72B (activities carried on by a provider of relevant goods or services), 72D (large risks contracts where risk situated outside the United Kingdom), 72G (local authorities) and 72H (insolvency practitioners).

(2)   Articles 53A, 53B, 53C, 53D and 53DA are also subject to the exclusions in articles 66 (trustees etc.), 67 (profession or non-investment business), … 72AA (managers of UK UCITS and AIFs), 72G (local authorities) and 72I (registered consumer buy-to-let mortgage firms).

···

CHAPTER 14A
REGULATED CREDIT AGREEMENTS

The Activities

60B.   Regulated credit agreements

(1)   Entering into a regulated credit agreement as lender is a specified kind of activity.

(2)   It is a specified kind of activity for the lender or another person to exercise, or to have the right to exercise, the lender's rights and duties under a regulated credit agreement.

(3)   In this article—

"credit agreement"—

(a)   in relation to an agreement other than a green deal plan, means an agreement between an individual or relevant recipient of credit ("A") and any other person ("B") under which B provides A with credit of any amount;

(b)   in relation to a green deal plan, has the meaning given by article 60LB;

"exempt agreement" means a credit agreement which is an exempt agreement under articles 60C to 60H, but where only part of a credit agreement falls within a provision of articles 60C to 60H, only that part is an exempt agreement under those articles;

"regulated credit agreement" means—

(a)   in the case of an agreement entered into on or after 1st April 2014, any credit agreement which is not an exempt agreement; or

(b)   in the case of an agreement entered into before 1st April 2014, a credit agreement which—

(i)   was a regulated agreement within the meaning of section 189(1) of the Consumer Credit Act 1974 when the agreement was entered into; or

(ii)   became such a regulated agreement after being varied or supplemented by another agreement before 1st April 2014,

and would not be an exempt agreement pursuant to article 60C(2) on 21st March 2016 if the agreement were entered into on that date.

60C.   Exempt agreements: exemptions relating to the nature of the agreement

(1)   A credit agreement is an exempt agreement for the purposes of this Chapter in the following cases.

(2)   A credit agreement is an exempt agreement if—

(a)   by entering into the agreement as lender, a person is or was carrying on an activity of a kind specified by article 61(1) (entering into regulated mortgage contracts); …

(b)   by entering into the agreement as home purchase provider, a person is or was carrying on an activity of a kind specified by article 63F(1) (entering into regulated home purchase plans); or

(c)   ... by administering the agreement on 21st March 2016 a person is carrying on an activity of a kind specified by article 61(2) (administering regulated mortgage contracts).

(3)   A credit agreement is an exempt agreement if—

(a)   the lender provides the borrower with credit exceeding £25,000, and

(b)   the agreement is entered into by the borrower wholly or predominantly for the purposes of a business carried on, or intended to be carried on, by the borrower.

(4)   A credit agreement is an exempt agreement if—

(a)   the lender provides the borrower with credit of £25,000 or less,

(b)   the agreement is entered into by the borrower wholly for the purposes of a business carried on, or intended to be carried on, by the borrower, and

(c)   the agreement is a green deal plan made in relation to a property that is not a domestic property (as defined by article 60LB).

(4A) A credit agreement is an exempt agreement if—

(a)   the lender provides the borrower with credit of £25,000 or less,

(b)   the agreement is entered into by the borrower wholly for the purposes of a business carried on, or intended to be carried on, by the borrower, and

(c)   the agreement is entered into by the lender and the borrower under the Bounce Back Loan Scheme.

(4B) For the purposes of paragraph (4A), "Bounce Back Loan Scheme" means the scheme of that name operated from 4th May 2020 by the British Business Bank plc on behalf of the Secretary of State.

(4C) An agreement exempt under paragraph (4A) may not also be an article 36H agreement by virtue of paragraph (4) of that article.

(5)   For the purposes of paragraph (3), if an agreement includes a declaration which—

(a)   is made by the borrower,

(b)   provides that the agreement is entered into by the borrower wholly or predominantly for the purposes of a business carried on, or intended to be carried on, by the borrower, and

(c)   complies with rules made by the FCA for the purpose of this article,

the agreement is to be presumed to have been entered into by the borrower wholly or predominantly for the purposes specified in sub-paragraph (b) unless paragraph (6) applies.

(6)   This paragraph applies if, when the agreement is entered into—

(a)   the lender (or, if there is more than one lender, any of the lenders), or

(b)   any person who has acted on behalf of the lender (or, if there is more than one lender, any of the lenders) in connection with the entering into of the agreement,

knows or has reasonable cause to suspect that the agreement is not entered into by the borrower wholly or predominantly for the purposes of a business carried on, or intended to be carried on, by the borrower.

(7)   Paragraphs (5) and (6) also apply for the purposes of paragraph (4) but with the omission of the words "or predominantly".

(8)   A credit agreement is an exempt agreement if it is made in connection with trade in goods or services—

(a)   between the United Kingdom and a country outside the United Kingdom,

(b)   within a country outside the United Kingdom, or

(c)   between countries outside the United Kingdom, and

the credit is provided to the borrower in the course of a business carried on by the borrower.

60D. Exempt agreements: exemption relating to the purchase of land for non-residential purposes

(1)   A credit agreement is an exempt agreement for the purposes of this Chapter if, at the time it is entered into, any sums due under it are secured by a legal or equitable mortgage on land and the condition in paragraph (2) is satisfied.

(2)   The condition is that less than 40% of the land is used, or is intended to be used, as or in connection with a dwelling—

    (a)   by the borrower or a related person of the borrower, or

    (b)   in the case of credit provided to trustees, by an individual who is a beneficiary of the trust or a related person of a beneficiary.

(3)   For the purposes of paragraph (2)—

    (a)   the area of any land which comprises a building or other structure containing two or more storeys is to be taken to be the aggregate of the floor areas of each of those stories;

    (b)   "related person" in relation to a person ("B") who is the borrower or (in the case of credit provided to trustees) a beneficiary of the trust, means—

        (i)   B's spouse or civil partner,

        (ii)   a person (whether or not of the opposite sex) whose relationship with B has the characteristics of the relationship between husband and wife, or

        (iii)   B's parent, brother, sister, child, grandparent or grandchild.

(4)   This article does not apply to an agreement if—

    (a)   the agreement is entered into on or after 21st March 2016,

    (b)   under the agreement a mortgage creditor grants or promises to grant a credit in the form of a deferred payment, loan or other similar financial accommodation,

    (c)   the credit is granted or promised to an individual who is acting for purposes outside those of any trade, business or profession carried on by the individual,

    (d)   the purpose of the agreement is to acquire or retain property rights in land or in an existing or projected building, and

    (e)   the agreement does not meet the conditions in paragraphs (i) to (iii) of article 61(3)(a) (regulated mortgage contracts).

(5)   A reference in paragraph (4)(d) to any land or building—

    (a)   in relation to an agreement entered into before IP completion day, is a reference to any land or building in the United Kingdom or within the territory of an EEA State;

    (b)   in relation to an agreement entered into on or after IP completion day, is a reference to any land or building in the United Kingdom.

60E.   **Exempt agreements: exemptions relating to the nature of the lender**

(1)   A credit agreement is an exempt agreement for the purposes of this Chapter in the following cases.

(2)   Subject to article 60HA, a relevant credit agreement relating to the purchase of land is an exempt agreement if the lender is—

    (a)   specified, or of a description specified, in rules made by the FCA under paragraph (3), or

    (b)   a local authority.

(3)   The FCA may make rules specifying any of the following for the purpose of paragraph (2)—

    (a)   an authorised person with permission to effect or carry out contracts of insurance;

    (b)   a friendly society;

    (c)   an organisation of employers or organisation of workers;

    (d)   a charity;

    (e)   an improvement company (within the meaning given by section 7 of the Improvement of Land Act 1899);

    (f)   a body corporate named or specifically referred to in any public general Act;

    (g)   a body corporate named or specifically referred to in, or in an order made under, a relevant housing provision;

    (h)   a building society (within the meaning of the Building Societies Act 1986);

    (i)   an authorised person with permission to accept deposits.

(4)   Rules under paragraph (3) may—

    (a)   specify a particular person or class of persons;

    (b)   be limited so as to apply only to agreements or classes of agreement specified in the rules.

(5)   Subject to article 60HA, a relevant credit agreement is an exempt agreement if it is—

      (a)   secured by a legal or equitable mortgage on land,

      (b)   that land is used or is intended to be used as or in connection with a dwelling, and

      (c)   the lender is a housing authority.

(6)   A credit agreement is an exempt agreement if—

      (a)   the lender is an investment firm or a qualifying credit institution, and

      (b)   the agreement is entered into for the purpose of allowing the borrower to carry out a transaction relating to one or more financial instruments.

(7)   In this article—

"housing authority" means—

      (a)   in England and Wales, the Homes and Communities Agency, the Welsh Ministers, a company which is a wholly-owned subsidiary of the Welsh Ministers, a registered social landlord within the meaning of Part 1 of the Housing Act 1996, or a private registered provider (within the meaning of Part 2 of the Housing and Regeneration Act 2008);

      (b)   in Scotland, the Scottish Ministers or a registered social landlord (within the meaning of the Housing (Scotland) Act 2010;

      (c)   in Northern Ireland, the Northern Ireland Housing Executive or a housing association within the meaning of Part 2 of the Housing (Northern Ireland) Order 1992;

"relevant credit agreement relating to the purchase of land" means—

      (a)   a borrower-lender-supplier agreement financing—

          (i)   the purchase of land, or

          (ii)   provision of dwellings on land,

      and secured by a legal or equitable mortgage on that land,

      (b)   a borrower-lender agreement secured by a legal or equitable mortgage on land, or

      (c)   a borrower-lender-supplier agreement financing a transaction which is a linked transaction in relation to—

          (i)   an agreement falling within sub-paragraph (a), or

          (ii)   an agreement falling within sub-paragraph (b) financing—

              (aa) the purchase of land,

              (bb) the provision of dwellings on land,

              and secured by a legal or equitable mortgage on the land referred to in sub-paragraph (a) or the land referred to in paragraph (ii);

"relevant housing provision" means any of the following—

      (a)   section 156(4) or 447(2)(a) of the Housing Act 1985,

      (b)   section 156(4) of that Act as it has effect by virtue of section 17 of the Housing Act 1996 (the right to acquire), or

      (c)   article 154(1)(a) of the Housing (Northern Ireland) Order 1981.

(7A)   In paragraph (7), in the definition of "housing authority", in paragraph (a), "wholly-owned subsidiary" has the same meaning as in section 1159 (meaning of "subsidiary" etc) of the Companies Act 2006.

(7B)   For the purpose of paragraph (7A), the Welsh Ministers are to be treated as a body corporate.

(8)   For the purposes of the definition of "relevant credit agreement relating to the purchase of land", a transaction is, unless paragraph (9) applies, a "linked transaction" in relation to a credit agreement ("the principal agreement") if—

      (a)   it is (or will be) entered into by the borrower under the principal agreement or by a relative of the borrower,

      (b)   it does not relate to the provision of security,

      (c)   it does not form part of the principal agreement, and

      (d)   one of the following conditions is satisfied—

          (i)   the transaction is entered into in compliance with a term of the principal agreement;

          (ii)   the principal agreement is a borrower-lender-supplier agreement and the transaction is financed, or to be financed, by the principal agreement;

          (iii) the following conditions are met—

(aa) the other party is a person to whom paragraph (10) applies,

(bb) the other party initiated the transaction by suggesting it to the borrower or the relative of the borrower, and

(cc) the borrower or the relative of the borrower enters into the transaction to induce the lender to enter into the principal agreement or for another purpose related to the principal agreement or to a transaction financed or to be financed by the principal agreement.

(9) This paragraph applies if the transaction is—

(a) a contract of insurance,

(b) a contract which contains a guarantee of goods, or

(c) a transaction which comprises, or is effected under—

(i) an agreement for the operation of an account (including any savings account) for the deposit of money, or

(ii) an agreement for the operation of a current account, under which the customer ("C") may, by means of cheques or similar orders payable to C or to any other person, obtain or have the use of money held or made available by the person with whom the account is kept.

(10) The persons to whom this paragraph applies are—

(a) the lender;

(b) the lender's associate;

(c) a person who, in the negotiation of the transaction, is represented by a person who carries on an activity of the kind specified by article 36A (credit broking) by way of business who is or was also a negotiator in negotiations for the principal agreement;

(d) a person who, at the time the transaction is initiated, knows that the principal agreement has been made or contemplates that it might be made.

60F. Exempt agreements: exemptions relating to number of repayments to be made

(1) A credit agreement is an exempt agreement for the purposes of this Chapter in the following cases.

(2) A credit agreement is an exempt agreement if—

(a) the agreement is a borrower-lender-supplier agreement for fixed-sum credit, other than a green deal plan,

(b) the number of payments to be made by the borrower is not more than twelve,

(c) those payments are required to be made within a period of 12 months or less (beginning on the date of the agreement),

(d) the credit is—

(i) secured on land, or

(ii) provided without interest or other … charges, and

(e) paragraph (7) does not apply to the agreement.

(3) A credit agreement is an exempt agreement if—

(a) the agreement is a borrower-lender-supplier agreement for running-account credit,

(b) the borrower is to make payments in relation to specified periods which must be, unless the agreement is secured on land, of 3 months or less,

(c) the number of payments to be made by the borrower in repayment of the whole amount of credit provided in each such period is not more than one,

(d) the credit is—

(i) secured on land, or

(ii) provided without interest or other significant charges, and

(e) paragraph (7) does not apply to the agreement.

(4) Subject to article 60HA, a credit agreement is an exempt agreement if—

(a) the agreement is a borrower-lender-supplier agreement financing the purchase of land,

(b) the number of payments to be made by the borrower is not more than four, and

(c) the credit is—

           (i)   secured on land, or

           (ii)   provided without interest or other charges.

(5)   A credit agreement is an exempt agreement if—

    (a)   the agreement is a borrower-lender-supplier agreement for fixed-sum credit,

    (b)   the credit is to finance a premium under a contract of insurance relating to land or anything on land,

    (c)   the lender is the lender under a credit agreement secured by a legal or equitable mortgage on that land,

    (d)   the credit is to be repaid within the period (which must be 12 months or less) to which the premium relates,

    (e)   in the case of an agreement secured on land, there is no charge forming part of the total charge for credit under the agreement other than interest at a rate not exceeding the rate of interest from time to time payable under the agreement mentioned at sub-paragraph (c),

    (f)   in the case of an agreement which is not secured on land, the credit is provided without interest or other charges, and

    (g)   the number of payments to be made by the borrower is not more than twelve.

(6)   A credit agreement is an exempt agreement if—

    (a)   the agreement is a borrower-lender-supplier agreement for fixed-sum credit,

    (b)   the lender is the lender under a credit agreement secured by a legal or equitable mortgage on land,

    (c)   the agreement is to finance a premium under a contract of whole life insurance which provides, in the event of the death of the person on whose life the contract is effected before the credit referred to in sub-paragraph (b) has been repaid, for payment of a sum not exceeding the amount sufficient to meet the amount which, immediately after that credit has been advanced, would be payable to the lender in respect of that credit (including interest from time to time payable under that agreement),

    (d)   in the case of an agreement secured on land, there is no charge forming part of the total charge for credit under the agreement other than interest at a rate not exceeding the rate of interest from time to time payable under the agreement mentioned at sub-paragraph (b),

    (e)   in the case of an agreement which is not secured on land, the credit is provided without interest or other charges, and

    (f)   the number of payments to be made by the borrower is not more than twelve.

(7)   This paragraph applies to—

    (a)   agreements financing the purchase of land;

    (b)   agreements which are conditional sale agreements or hire-purchase agreements;

    (c)   agreements secured by a pledge (other than a pledge of documents of title or of bearer bonds).

(8)   In this article, "payment" means any payment which comprises or includes—

    (a)   the repayment of capital, or

    (b)   the payment of interest or any other charge which forms part of the total charge for credit.

60G.   Exempt agreements: exemptions relating to the total charge for credit

(1)   A credit agreement is an exempt agreement for the purposes of this Chapter in the following cases.

(2)   A credit agreement is an exempt agreement if—

    (a)   it is a borrower-lender agreement, …

    (b)   the lender is a credit union and the rate of the total charge for credit does not exceed 42.6 per cent, and

    (c)   paragraph (2A) applies to the agreement.

(2A)   This paragraph applies to the agreement if—

    (a)   the agreement is not one to which subsection (2) of section 423A of the Act applies; …

    (b)   the agreement is one to which that subsection applies and—

           (i)   the agreement is one to which subsection (3) of that section applies,

           (ii)   the agreement is a bridging loan ..., or

           (iii) in relation to the agreement—

                  (aa) the borrower receives timely information on the main features, risks and costs of the agreement at the pre-contractual stage, and

                  (bb) any advertising of the agreement is fair, clear and not misleading; or

   (c)   the agreement was entered into before 21st March 2016.

(3)   Subject to paragraph (8), a credit agreement is an exempt agreement if—

   (a)   it is a borrower-lender agreement,

   (b)   it is an agreement of a kind offered to a particular class of individual or relevant recipient of credit and not offered to the public generally,

   (c)   it provides that the only charge included in the total charge for credit is interest,

   (d)   interest under the agreement may not at any time be more than the sum of one per cent and the highest of the base rates published by the banks specified in paragraph (7) on the date 28 days before the date on which the interest is charged, and

   (e)   paragraph (5) does not apply to the agreement.

(4)   Subject to paragraph (8), a credit agreement is an exempt agreement if—

   (a)   it is a borrower-lender agreement,

   (b)   it is an agreement of a kind offered to a particular class of individual or relevant recipient of credit and not offered to the public generally,

   (c)   it does not provide for or permit an increase in the rate or amount of any item which is included in the total charge for credit,

   (d)   the total charge for credit under the agreement is not more than the sum of one per cent and the highest of the base rates published by the banks specified in paragraph (7) on the date 28 days before the date on which the charge is imposed, and

   (e)   paragraph (5) does not apply to the agreement.

(5)   This paragraph applies to an agreement if—

   (a)   the total amount to be repaid by the borrower to discharge the borrower's indebtedness may vary according to a formula which is specified in the agreement and which has effect by reference to movements in the level of any index or other factor, or

   (b)   the agreement—

           (i)   is not—

                  (aa) secured on land, or

                  (bb) offered by a lender to a borrower as an incident of the borrower's employment with the lender or with an undertaking in the same group as the lender; and

           (ii)   does not meet the general interest test.

(6)   For the purposes of paragraphs (5) and (8), an agreement meets the general interest test if—

   (a)   the agreement is offered under an enactment with a general interest purpose, and

   (b)   the terms on which the credit is provided are more favourable to the borrower than those prevailing on the market, either because the rate of interest is lower than that prevailing on the market, or because the rate of interest is no higher than that prevailing on the market but the other terms on which credit is provided are more favourable to the borrower.

(7)   The banks specified in this paragraph are—

   (a)   the Bank of England;

   (b)   Bank of Scotland;

   (c)   Barclays Bank plc;

   (d)   Clydesdale Bank plc;

   (e)   Co-operative Bank Public Limited Company;

   (f)   Coutts & Co;

   (g)   National Westminster Bank Public Limited Company;

   (h)   the Royal Bank of Scotland plc.

(8)   A credit agreement to which subsection (2) of section 423A of the Act applies which is entered into on or after 21st March 2016 is an exempt agreement pursuant to paragraph (3) or (4) only if—

   (a)   the agreement meets the general interest test;

   (b)   the borrower receives timely information on the main features, risks and costs of the agreement at the pre-contractual stage; and

   (c)   any advertising of the agreement is fair, clear and not misleading.

(9)   In this article "bridging loan" means a mortgage agreement that—

   (a)   is of no fixed duration or is due to be repaid within 12 months, and

   (b)   is used by a consumer, within the meaning given by section 423A(4) of the Act, as a temporary financing solution while transitioning to another financial arrangement for the immovable property concerned.

60H.   Exempt agreements: exemptions relating to the nature of the borrower

(1)   A credit agreement is an exempt agreement for the purposes of this Chapter if—

   (a)   the borrower is an individual,

   (b)   the agreement is either—

      (i)   secured on land, or

      (ii) for credit which exceeds £60,260 and, if entered into on or after 21st March 2016, is for a purpose other than—

         (aa) the renovation of residential property, …

         (bb) …

   (c)   the agreement includes a declaration made by the borrower which provides that the borrower agrees to forgo the protection and remedies that would be available to the borrower if the agreement were a regulated credit agreement and which complies with rules made by the FCA for the purposes of this paragraph,

   (d)   a statement has been made in relation to the income or assets of the borrower which complies with rules made by the FCA for the purposes of this paragraph,

   (e)   the connection between the statement and the agreement complies with any rules made by the FCA for the purposes of this paragraph (including as to the period of time between the making of the statement and the agreement being entered into), and

   (f)   a copy of the statement was provided to the lender before the agreement was entered into.

(1A)   Article 4(4B) does not apply to an agreement which is exempt under paragraph (1), the purpose of which is to acquire or retain property rights in land or in an existing or projected building, and—

   (a)   a declaration has been made by the borrower which either—

      (i)   provides that the borrower is UK resident, or

      (ii) provides that the borrower is treated as present in the United Kingdom,

   (b)   a copy of that declaration was provided to the lender before the agreement was entered into, and

   (c)   the agreement is entered into on or after 21st July 2022.

(1B)   For the purposes of paragraph (1A), a borrower is "UK resident" if—

   (a)   the borrower is present in the United Kingdom on at least 183 days during the continuous period of 365 days ending with the date the agreement is entered into, or

   (b)   the spouse or civil partner of the borrower—

      (i)   is living with the borrower on the date the agreement was entered into, and

      (ii) is present in the United Kingdom on at least 183 days during the continuous period of 365 days ending with the date the agreement is entered into.

(1C)   For the purposes of paragraph (1A), a borrower is treated as present in the United Kingdom if, on the date the agreement was entered into, the borrower—

   (a)   is in Crown employment, and

   (b)   is present in a country or territory outside the United Kingdom for the purpose of performing activities in the course of that employment, or

   (c)   is the spouse or civil partner of an individual who—

(i)   is in Crown employment,

(ii)   is present in a country or territory outside the United Kingdom for the purpose of performing activities in the course of that employment, and

(d)   is living with their spouse or civil partner.

(1D)   References in this article to a borrower being present in the United Kingdom on a day are to the borrower being present in the United Kingdom at the end of that day.

(1E)   Individuals who are married to, or are civil partners of, each other are treated, for the purposes of this article, as living together unless—

(a)   they are separated under an order of a court of competent jurisdiction,

(b)   they are separated by deed of separation, or

(c)   they are in fact separated in circumstances in which the separation is likely to be permanent.

(1F)   For the purposes of this article, "Crown employment" means employment under or for the purposes of a government department or any officer or body exercising on behalf of the Crown functions conferred by a statutory provision.

(2)   ...

60HA. Exempt agreements: provision qualifying articles 60E and 60F

(1)   A credit agreement entered into on or after 21st March 2016 is not an exempt agreement pursuant to article 60E(2) or (5), or 60F(4) if it is a mortgage agreement to which paragraph (2) does not apply, if—

(a)   the agreement is of a type described in Article 3(1) of the mortgages directive, and

(b)   paragraph (2) does not apply.

(2)   This paragraph applies to an agreement if—

(a)   ...

(b)   the agreement is a bridging loan within the meaning given by article 60G(9); or

(c)   the agreement is a restricted public loan in respect of which—

(i)   the borrower receives timely information on the main features, risks and costs at the pre-contractual stage; and

(ii)   any advertising is fair, clear and not misleading.

(3)   In paragraph (2)(c) "restricted public loan" means a credit agreement that is—

(a)   offered to a particular class of borrower and not offered to the public generally;

(b)   offered under an enactment with a general interest purpose; and

(c)   provided on terms which are more favourable to the borrower than those prevailing on the market, because it meets one of the following conditions—

(i)   it is interest free;

(ii)   the rate of interest is lower than that prevailing on the market; or

(iii)   the rate of interest is no higher than that prevailing on the market but the other terms on which credit is provided are more favourable to the borrower.

Exclusions

60I.   Arranging administration by authorised person

A person ("A") who is not an authorised person does not carry on an activity of the kind specified by article 60B(2) in relation to a regulated credit agreement where A—

(a)   arranges for another person, who is an authorised person with permission to carry on an activity of that kind, to exercise or to have the right to exercise the lender's rights and duties under the agreement, or

(b)   exercises or has the right to exercise the lender's rights and duties under the agreement during a period of not more than one month beginning with the day on which any such arrangement comes to an end.

60J.   Administration pursuant to agreement with authorised person

A person who is not an authorised person does not carry on an activity of the kind specified by article 60B(2) in relation to regulated credit agreement if that person exercises or has the right to exercise the lender's rights and duties under the agreement pursuant to an agreement with an authorised person who has permission to carry on an activity of the kind specified by article 60B(2).

60JA, 60JB....

60K.   Other exclusions

Article 60B is also subject to the exclusions in articles ... 72G (local authorities) and 72I (registered consumer buy-to-let mortgage firms).

Supplemental

60L.   Interpretation of Chapter 14A etc

(1)   In this Chapter—

"assignment", in relation to Scotland, means assignation;

"associate" means, in relation to a person ("P")—

(a)   where P is an individual, any person who is or who has been—

  (i)   P's spouse or P's civil partner;

  (ii)   a relative of P, of P's spouse or of P's civil partner;

  (iii) the spouse or civil partner of a relative of P or P's spouse or civil partner;

  (iv)   if P is a member of a partnership, any of P's partners and the spouse or civil partner of any such person;

(b)   where P is a body corporate—

  (i)   any person who is a controller ("C") of P, and

  (ii)   any other person for whom C is a controller;

"borrower" means (except in relation to green deal plans: see instead article 60LB) a person who receives credit under a credit agreement or a person to whom the rights and duties of a borrower under a credit agreement have passed by assignment or operation of law;

"borrower-lender agreement" means—

(a)   a credit agreement—

  (i)   to finance a transaction between the borrower and a person ("the supplier") other than the lender, and

  (ii)   which is not made by the lender under pre-existing arrangements, or in contemplation of future arrangements, between the lender and the supplier,

(b)   a credit agreement to refinance any existing indebtedness of the borrower, whether to the lender or another person, or

(c)   a credit agreement which is—

  (i)   an unrestricted-use credit agreement, and

  (ii)   not made by the lender—

    (aa) under pre-existing arrangements between the lender and a person other than the borrower ("the supplier"), and

    (bb) in the knowledge that the credit is to be used to finance a transaction between the borrower and the supplier;

"borrower-lender-supplier agreement" means—

(a)   a credit agreement to finance a transaction between the borrower and the lender, whether forming part of that agreement or not;

(b)   a credit agreement—

  (i)   to finance a transaction between the borrower and a person ("the supplier") other than the lender, and

  (ii)   which is made by the lender under pre-existing arrangements, or in contemplation of future arrangements, between the lender and the supplier, or

(c)   a credit agreement which is—

  (i)   an unrestricted-use credit agreement, and

        (ii)   made by the lender under pre-existing arrangements between the lender and a person ("the supplier") other than the borrower in the knowledge that the credit is to be used to finance a transaction between the borrower and the supplier;

"conditional sale agreement" means an agreement for the sale of goods or land under which the purchase price or part of it is payable by instalments, and the property in the goods or land is to remain with the seller (notwithstanding that the buyer is to be in possession of the goods or land) until such conditions as to the payment of instalments or otherwise as may be specified in the agreement are fulfilled;

"credit" includes a cash loan and any other form of financial accommodation;

"credit agreement"—

(a)   in relation to an agreement other than a green deal plan, has the meaning given by article 60B;

(b)   in relation to a green deal plan, has the meaning given by article 60LB;

"credit union" means a credit union within the meaning of—

(a)   the Credit Unions Act 1979;

(b)   the Credit Unions (Northern Ireland) Order 1985;

"deposit" (except where specified otherwise) means any sum payable by a borrower by way of deposit or down-payment, or credited or to be credited to the borrower on account of any deposit or down-payment, whether the sum is to be or has been paid to the lender or any other person, or is to be or has been discharged by a payment of money or a transfer or delivery of goods or other means;

"exempt agreement" has the meaning given by article 60B;

"finance" includes financing in whole or in part, and "refinance" is to be read accordingly;

"fixed-sum credit" means a facility under a credit agreement whereby the borrower is enabled to receive credit (whether in one amount or by instalments) but which is not running-account credit;

"hire-purchase agreement" means an agreement—

(a)   which is not a conditional sale agreement,

(b)   under which goods are bailed or (in Scotland) hired to a person ("P") in return for periodical payments by P, and

(c)   the property in the goods will pass to P if the terms of the agreement are complied with and one or more of the following occurs—

        (i)   the exercise by P of an option to purchase the goods;

        (ii)   the doing by any party to the agreement of any other act specified in the agreement;

        (iii)   the happening of any event specified in the agreement;

"legal or equitable mortgage" includes a legal or equitable charge and, in Scotland, a heritable security;

"lender" means (except in relation to green deal plans: see instead article 60LB)—

(a)   the person providing credit under a credit agreement, or

(b)   a person who exercises or has the right to exercise the rights and duties of a person who provided credit under such an agreement;

"payment" (except in article 60F) means a payment comprising or including an amount in respect of credit;

"regulated credit agreement" has the meaning given by article 60B;

"relative" means brother, sister, uncle, aunt, nephew, niece, lineal ancestor or lineal descendent;

"relevant recipient of credit" means—

(a)   a partnership consisting of two or three persons not all of whom are bodies corporate, or

(b)   an unincorporated body of persons which does not consist entirely of bodies corporate and is not a partnership;

"restricted-use credit agreement" means a credit agreement—

(a)   to finance a transaction between the borrower and the lender, whether forming part of that agreement or not,

     (b)   to finance a transaction between the borrower and a person ("the supplier") other than the lender, or

     (c)   to refinance any existing indebtedness of the borrower's, whether to the lender or another person;

"running-account credit" means a facility under a credit agreement under which the borrower or another person is enabled to receive from time to time from the lender or a third party cash, goods or services to an amount or value such that, taking into account payments made by or to the credit of the borrower, the credit limit (if any) is not at any time exceeded;

"security" in relation to a credit agreement, means a mortgage, charge, pledge, bond, debenture, indemnity, guarantee, bill, note or other right provided by the borrower or at the implied or express request of the borrower to secure the carrying out of the obligations of the borrower under the agreement;

"total charge for credit" has the meaning given in rules made by the FCA under article 60M;

"total price" means the total sum payable by the debtor under a hire-purchase agreement, including any sum payable on the exercise of an option to purchase but excluding any sum payable as a penalty or as compensation or damages for a breach of the agreement;

"unrestricted-use credit agreement" means a credit agreement which is not a restricted-use credit agreement.

(1A)   For the purposes of this Chapter, a credit agreement that is a green deal plan is to be treated as—

     (a)   a borrower-lender-supplier agreement falling within paragraph (a) of the definition of "borrower-lender-supplier agreement";

     (b)   a restricted-use credit agreement falling within paragraph (a) of the definition of "restricted-use credit agreement".

(2)   For the purposes of the definition of "restricted-use credit agreement"—

     (a)   a credit agreement does not fall within the definition if the credit is in fact provided in such a way as to leave the borrower free to use it as the borrower chooses, even though certain uses would contravene that or any other agreement; and

     (b)   an agreement may fall within paragraph (b) of the definition even though the identity of the supplier is unknown at the time the agreement is made.

(3)   For the purposes of the definition of "borrower-lender agreement" and the definition of "borrower-lender-supplier agreement", a credit agreement is, subject to paragraph (6), entered into under pre-existing arrangements between a lender and a supplier if it is entered into in accordance with, or in connection with, arrangements previously made between the lender (or the lender's associate) and the supplier (or the supplier's associate) unless the arrangements fall within paragraph (5).

(4)   For the purposes of the definition of "borrower-lender agreement" and the definition of "borrower-lender-supplier agreement", a credit agreement is entered into in contemplation of future arrangements between a lender and a supplier if it is entered into in the expectation that arrangements will subsequently be made between the lender (or the lender's associate) and the supplier (or the supplier's associate) for the supply of cash, goods or services to be financed by the credit agreement unless the arrangements fall within paragraph (5).

(5)   Arrangements fall within this paragraph if they are—

     (a)   for the making, in circumstances specified in the credit agreement, of payments to the supplier by the lender ("L") and L indicates that L is willing to make, in such circumstances, payments of the kind to suppliers generally, or

     (b)   for the electronic transfer of funds from a current account held with an authorised person with permission to accept deposits (within the meaning given by article 3).

(6)   If a lender is an associate of the supplier's, the credit agreement is to be treated as entered into under pre-existing arrangements between the lender and the supplier unless the lender can show that this is not the case.

(7)   For the purposes of the definition of "running-account credit", "credit limit" means, as respects any period, the maximum debit balance which, under a credit agreement, is allowed to stand on

the account during that period, disregarding any term of the agreement allowing that maximum to be exceeded on a temporary basis.

(8)   For the purposes of this Chapter, a person by whom goods are bailed or (in Scotland) hired to an individual or relevant recipient of credit under a hire-purchase agreement is to be taken to be providing that individual or person with fixed-sum credit to finance the transaction of an amount equal to the total price of the goods less the aggregate of the deposit (if any) and the total charge for credit.

(9)   For the purposes of this Chapter, where credit is provided otherwise than in sterling, it is to be treated as provided in sterling of an equivalent amount.

(10)   For the purposes of this Chapter, where a provision specifies an amount of credit, running-account credit shall be taken not to exceed the amount specified in that provision ("the specified amount") if—

(a)   the credit limit does not exceed the specified amount; or

(b)   the credit limit exceeds the specified amount, or there is no credit limit, and—

(i)   the borrower is not enabled to draw at any one time an amount which, so far as it represents credit, exceeds the specified amount; or

(ii)   the agreement provides that, if the debit balance rises above a given amount (not exceeding the specified amount), the rate of the total charge for credit increases or any other condition favouring the lender or the lender's associate comes into operation; or

(iii)   at the time the agreement is made it is probable, having regard to the terms of the agreement and any other relevant considerations, that the debit balance will not at any time rise above the specified amount.

(11)   For the purposes of this Chapter, an item entering into the total charge for credit is not to be treated as credit even though time is allowed for its payment.

60LA.   Meaning of consumer etc

(1)   For the purposes of sections 1G, 404E and 425A of the Act (meaning of "consumer"), in so far as those provisions relate to a person ("A") carrying on a regulated activity of the kind specified by—

(a)   article 60B (regulated credit agreements), or

(b)   article 64 (agreeing to carry on specified kinds of activity) in so far as that article relates to article 60B,

a person who is treated by A as a person who is or has been the borrower under a regulated credit agreement is to be treated as a "consumer".

(2)   For the purposes of section 328(8) of the Act (meaning of "clients") in so far as that provision relates to a person ("A") carrying on a regulated activity of the kind specified by—

(a)   article 60B (regulated credit agreements), or

(b)   article 64 (agreeing to carry on specified kinds of activity) in so far as that article relates to article 60B,

a person who is treated by A as a person who is or has been the borrower under a regulated credit agreement is to be treated as a "client".

(3)   In this article, "borrower" includes (in addition to those persons included in the definition in article 60L or, where the credit agreement is a green deal plan, article 60LB)—

(a)   any person providing a guarantee or indemnity under a regulated credit agreement, and

(b)   a person to whom the rights and duties of a person falling within sub-paragraph (a) have passed by assignment or operation of law.

...

CHAPTER XV
REGULATED MORTGAGE CONTRACTS

The activities

61.   Regulated mortgage contracts

(1)   Entering into a regulated mortgage contract as lender is a specified kind of activity.

(2)   Administering a regulated mortgage contract is also a specified kind of activity where—

    (a)   the contract was entered into by way of business on or after 31st October 2004; or

    (b)   the contract—

       (i)   was entered into by way of business before 31st October 2004, and

       (ii)   was a regulated credit agreement immediately before 21st March 2016.

(3)   In this Chapter—

    (a)   subject to paragraph (5), a contract is a "regulated mortgage contract" if, at the time it is entered into, the following conditions are met—

       (i)   the contract is one under which a person ("the lender") provides credit to an individual or to trustees ("the borrower");

       (ii)   the contract provides for the obligation of the borrower to repay to be secured by a mortgage on land …;

       (iii)   at least 40% of that land is used, or is intended to be used—

          (aa)   in the case of credit provided to an individual, as or in connection with a dwelling; or

          (bb)   in the case of credit provided to a trustee which is not an individual, as or in connection with a dwelling by an individual who is a beneficiary of the trust, or by a related person;

        but such a contract is not a regulated mortgage contract if it falls within article 61A(1) or (2);

    (b)   "administering" a regulated mortgage contract means either or both of—

       (i)   notifying the borrower of changes in interest rates or payments due under the contract, or of other matters of which the contract requires him to be notified; and

       (ii)   taking any necessary steps for the purposes of collecting or recovering payments due under the contract from the borrower;

        but a person is not to be treated as administering a regulated mortgage contract merely because he has, or exercises, a right to take action for the purposes of enforcing the contract (or to require that such action is or is not taken);

    (c)   "credit" includes a cash loan, and any other form of financial accommodation.

(4)   For the purposes of paragraph (3)(a)—

    (a)   "mortgage" includes a charge and (in Scotland) a heritable security;

    (aa)   "land"—

       (i)   in relation to a contract entered into before IP completion day, means land in the United Kingdom or within the territory of an EEA State;

       (ii)   in relation to a contract entered into on or after IP completion day, means land in the United Kingdom;

    (b)   the area of any land which comprises a building or other structure containing two or more storeys is to be taken to be the aggregate of the floor areas of each of those storeys;

    (c)   "related person", in relation to the borrower or (in the case of credit provided to trustees) a beneficiary of the trust, means—

       (i)   that person's spouse or civil partner;

       (ii)   a person (whether or not of the opposite sex) whose relationship with that person has the characteristics of the relationship between husband and wife; or

       (iii)   that person's parent, brother, sister, child, grandparent or grandchild; …

    (d)   …

(5)   In this Chapter, a contract entered into before 21st March 2016 is a "regulated mortgage contract" only if—

    (a)   at the time it was entered into, entering into the contract was an activity of the kind specified by paragraph (1), or

    (b)   the contract is a consumer credit back book mortgage contract within the meaning of article 2 of the Mortgage Credit Directive Order 2015.

61A.   Mortgage contracts which are not regulated mortgage contracts

(1)   A contract falls within this paragraph if it is—

    (a)   a regulated home purchase plan;

    (b)   a limited payment second charge bridging loan;

    (c)   a second charge business loan;

    (d)   an investment property loan; ...

    (e)   an exempt consumer buy-to-let mortgage contract; ...

    (f)   an exempt equitable mortgage bridging loan; or

    (g)   an exempt housing authority loan.

(2)   A contract falls within this paragraph if—

    (a)   it is a limited interest second charge credit union loan;

    (b)   the borrower receives timely information on the main features, risks and costs of the contract at the pre-contractual stage; and

    (c)   any advertising of the contract is fair, clear and not misleading.

(3)   For the purposes of this article, if an agreement includes a declaration which—

    (a)   is made by the borrower, and

    (b)   includes—

        (i)   a statement that the agreement is entered into by the borrower wholly or predominantly for the purposes of a business carried on, or intended to be carried on, by the borrower,

        (ii)   a statement that the borrower understands that the borrower will not have the benefit of the protection and remedies that would be available to the borrower under the Act if the agreement were a regulated mortgage contract under the Act, and

        (iii)   a statement that the borrower is aware that if the borrower is in any doubt as to the consequences of the agreement not being regulated by the Act, then the borrower should seek independent legal advice,

    the agreement is to be presumed to have been entered into by the borrower wholly or predominantly for the purposes specified in sub-paragraph (b)(i) unless paragraph (4) applies.

(4)   This paragraph applies if, when the agreement is entered into—

    (a)   the lender (or, if there is more than one lender, any of the lenders), or

    (b)   any person who has acted on behalf of the lender (or, if there is more than one lender, any of the lenders) in connection with the entering into of the agreement,

    knows or has reasonable cause to suspect that the agreement is not entered into by the borrower wholly or predominantly for the purposes of a business carried on, or intended to be carried on, by the borrower.

(5)   For the purposes of this article a borrower is to be regarded as entering into an agreement for the purposes of a business carried on, or intended to be carried on, by the borrower if the agreement is a buy-to-let mortgage contract and—

    (a)   (i)   the borrower previously purchased, or is entering into the contract in order to finance the purchase by the borrower of, the land subject to the mortgage;

        (ii)   at the time of the purchase the borrower intended that the land would be occupied as a dwelling on the basis of a rental agreement and would not at any time be occupied as a dwelling by the borrower or by a related person, or where the borrower has not yet purchased the land the borrower has such an intention at the time of entering into the contract; and

(iii) where the borrower has purchased the land, since the time of the purchase the land has not at any time been occupied as a dwelling by the borrower or by a related person; or

(b) the borrower is the owner of land, other than the land subject to the mortgage, which is—

(i) occupied as a dwelling on the basis of a rental agreement and is not occupied as a dwelling by the borrower or by a related person; or

(ii) secured by a mortgage under a buy-to-let mortgage contract.

(6) For the purposes of this article—

"borrower" and "lender" have the meaning set out in article 61(3) (regulated mortgage contracts);

"borrower-lender agreement", "borrower-lender-supplier agreement", "credit union" and "total charge for credit" have the meanings set out in article 60L (interpretation of Chapter 14A);

"bridging loan" has the meaning given by article 60G(9);

"buy-to-let mortgage contract" has the meaning given in article 4 of the Mortgage Credit Directive Order 2015 (interpretation of Part 3);

"exempt consumer buy-to-let mortgage contract" is a contract that, at the time it is entered into, is a consumer buy-to-let mortgage contract within the meaning of article 4 of the Mortgage Credit Directive Order 2015 and—

(a) is an agreement to which section 423A(3) of the Act applies; or

(b) is a bridging loan;

"exempt equitable mortgage bridging loan" is a contract that—

(a) is a bridging loan;

(b) is secured by an equitable mortgage on land; and

(c) is an exempt agreement within the meaning of article 60B(3) (regulated credit agreements) by virtue of article 60E(2) (exempt agreements: exemptions relating to the nature of the lender);

"exempt housing authority loan" is a contract that—

(a) provides for credit to be granted by a housing authority within the meaning of article 60E (exempt agreements: exemptions relating to the nature of the lender); and

(b) if it is entered into on or after 21st March 2016—

(i) is an agreement to which section 423A(3) of the Act applies,

(ii) is a bridging loan, or

(iii) is a restricted public loan within the meaning of article 60HA (exempt agreements: provision qualifying articles 60E, 60F and 60H), in respect of which the borrower receives timely information on the main features, risks and costs at the pre-contractual stage, and any advertising is fair, clear and not misleading;

"investment property loan" is a contract that, at the time it is entered into, meets the conditions in paragraphs (i) to (iii) of article 61(3)(a) and the following conditions—

(a) less than 40% of the land subject to the mortgage is used, or intended to be used, as or in connection with a dwelling by the borrower or (in the case of credit provided to trustees) by an individual who is a beneficiary of the trust, or by a related person; and

(b) the agreement is entered into by the borrower wholly or predominantly for the purposes of a business carried on, or intended to be carried on, by the borrower;

"limited payment second charge bridging loan" is a contract that, at the time it is entered into, meets the conditions in paragraphs (i) to (iii) of article 61(3)(a) and the following conditions—

(a) it is a borrower-lender-supplier agreement financing the purchase of land;

(b) it is used by the borrower as a temporary financing solution while transitioning to another financial arrangement for the land subject to the mortgage;

(c) the mortgage ranks in priority behind one or more other mortgages affecting the land in question; and

(d) the number of payments to be made by the borrower under the contract is not more than four;

"limited interest second charge credit union loan" is a contract that, at the time it is entered into, meets the conditions in paragraphs (i) to (iii) of article 61(3)(a) and the following conditions—

(a)   it is a borrower-lender agreement;

(b)   the mortgage ranks in priority behind one or more other mortgages affecting the land in question;

(c)   the lender is a credit union; and

(d)   the rate of the total charge for credit does not exceed 42.6 per cent;

"payment" has the meaning set out in article 60F(8) (exempt agreement: exemptions relating to number of repayments to be made);

"regulated home purchase plan" has the meaning set out in article 63F(3)(a) (entering into and administering regulated home purchase plans);

"related person" in relation to the borrower or (in the case of credit provided to trustees) a beneficiary of the trust, means—

(a)   that person's spouse or civil partner;

(b)   a person (whether or not of the opposite sex) whose relationship with that person has the characteristics of the relationship between husband and wife; or

(c)   that person's parent, brother, sister, child, grandparent or grandchild;

"second charge business loan" is a contract that, at the time it is entered into, meets the conditions in paragraphs (i) to (iii) of article 61(3)(a) and the following conditions—

(a)   the lender provides the borrower with credit exceeding £25,000;

(b)   the mortgage ranks in priority behind one or more other mortgages affecting the land in question; and

(c)   the agreement is entered into by the borrower wholly or predominantly for the purposes of a business carried on, or intended to be carried on, by the borrower.

Exclusions

62.   Arranging administration by authorised person

A person who is not an authorised person does not carry on an activity of the kind specified by article 61(2) in relation to a regulated mortgage contract where he—

(a)   arranges for another person, being an authorised person with permission to carry on an activity of that kind, to administer the contract; or

(b)   administers the contract himself during a period of not more than one month beginning with the day on which any such arrangement comes to an end.

63.   Administration pursuant to agreement with authorised person

A person who is not an authorised person does not carry on an activity of the kind specified by article 61(2) in relation to a regulated mortgage contract where he administers the contract pursuant to an agreement with an authorised person who has permission to carry on an activity of that kind.

63A.   Other exclusions

Article 61 is also subject to the exclusions in articles 66 (trustees etc), 72 (overseas persons), … 72AA (managers of UK UCITS and AIFs), 72G (local authorities) and 72I (registered consumer buy-to-let mortgage firms).

. . .

CHAPTER XVI
AGREEING TO CARRY ON ACTIVITIES

The activity

64.   Agreeing to carry on specified kinds of activity

Agreeing to carry on an activity of the kind specified by any other provision of this Part, Part 3A or Part 3B (other than article 5, 9B, 10, 25D, 25DA, 51ZA, 51ZB, 51ZC, 51ZD, 51ZE, 52, 63N and 63S) is a specified kind of activity.

65.   Overseas persons etc

Article 64 is subject to the exclusions in articles 72 (overseas persons), ... 72G (local authorities) and 72H (insolvency practitioners).

CHAPTER XVII
EXCLUSIONS APPLYING TO
SEVERAL SPECIFIED KINDS OF ACTIVITY

66.   Trustees, nominees and personal representatives

(1)   A person ("X") does not carry on an activity of the kind specified by article 14 where he enters into a transaction as bare trustee or, in Scotland, as nominee for another person ("Y") and—
         (a)   X is acting on Y's instructions; and
         (b)   X does not hold himself out as providing a service of buying and selling securities or contractually based investments.

(2)   Subject to paragraph (7), there are excluded from articles 25(1) and (2), 25A(1), (2) and (2A), 25B(1) and (2), 25C(1) and (2) and 25E(1) and (2) arrangements made by a person acting as trustee or personal representative for or with a view to a transaction which is or is to be entered into—
         (a)   by that person and a fellow trustee or personal representative (acting in their capacity as such); or
         (b)   by a beneficiary under the trust, will or intestacy.

(3)   Subject to paragraph (7), there is excluded from article 37 any activity carried on by a person acting as trustee or personal representative, unless—
         (a)   he holds himself out as providing a service comprising an activity of the kind specified by article 37; or
         (b)   the assets in question are held for the purposes of an occupational pension scheme, and, by virtue of article 4 of the Financial Services and Markets Act 2000 (Carrying on Regulated Activities by Way of Business) Order 2001, he is to be treated as carrying on that activity by way of business.

(3A)   Subject to paragraph (7), there is excluded from article 39A any activity carried on by a person acting as trustee or personal representative, unless he holds himself out as providing a service comprising an activity of the kind specified by article 39A.

(4)   Subject to paragraph (7), there is excluded from article 40 any activity carried on by a person acting as trustee or personal representative, unless he holds himself out as providing a service comprising an activity of the kind specified by article 40.

(4A)   There is excluded from article 40 any activity carried on by a person acting as trustee which consists of arranging for one or more other persons to safeguard and administer trust assets where—
         (a)   that other person is a qualifying custodian; or
         (b)   that safeguarding and administration is also arranged by a qualifying custodian.
         In this paragraph, "qualifying custodian" has the meaning given by article 41(2).

(5)   A person does not, by sending or causing to be sent a dematerialised instruction (within the meaning of article 45), carry on an activity of the kind specified by that article if the instruction relates to an investment which that person holds as trustee or personal representative.

(6)   Subject to paragraph (7), there is excluded from articles 53, 53A, 53B, 53C, 53D and 53DA the giving of advice by a person acting as trustee or personal representative where he gives the advice to—
         (a)   a fellow trustee or personal representative for the purposes of the trust or the estate; or
         (b)   a beneficiary under the trust, will or intestacy concerning his interest in the trust fund or estate.

(6A)   Subject to paragraph (7), a person acting as trustee or personal representative does not carry on an activity of the kind specified by article 61(1) or (2) where the borrower under the regulated mortgage contract in question is a beneficiary under the trust, will or intestacy.

(6B)   Subject to paragraph (7), a person acting as trustee or personal representative does not carry on an activity of the kind specified by article 63B(1) or (2) where the reversion seller under the regulated home reversion plan in question is a beneficiary under the trust, will or intestacy.

(6C)   Subject to paragraph (7), a person acting as trustee or personal representative does not carry on an activity of the kind specified by article 63F(1) or (2) where the home purchaser under the regulated home purchase plan in question is a beneficiary under the trust, will or intestacy.

(6D)   Subject to paragraph (7), a person acting as a trustee or personal representative does not carry on an activity of the kind specified by article 63J(1) or (2) where the agreement seller under the regulated sale and rent back agreement is a beneficiary under the trust, will or intestacy.

(7)   Paragraphs (2), (3), (3A), (4), (6), (6A), (6B), (6C) and (6D) do not apply if the person carrying on the activity is remunerated for what he does in addition to any remuneration he receives as trustee or personal representative, and for these purposes a person is not to be regarded as receiving additional remuneration merely because his remuneration is calculated by reference to time spent.

(8)   This article is subject to article 4(4A) and (4B).

67.   Activities carried on in the course of a profession or non-investment business

(1)   There is excluded from articles 21, 25(1) and (2), 25A, 25B, 25C, 25E, 39A, 40, 53, 53A, 53B, 53C, 53D and 53DA any activity which—
        (a)   is carried on in the course of carrying on any profession or business which does not otherwise consist of the carrying on of regulated activities in the United Kingdom; and
        (b)   may reasonably be regarded as a necessary part of other services provided in the course of that profession or business.

(2)   But the exclusion in paragraph (1) does not apply if the activity in question is remunerated separately from the other services.

(3)   This article is subject to article 4(4), (4A) and (4B).

68.   Activities carried on in connection with the sale of goods or supply of services

(1)   Subject to paragraphs (9), (10) and (11), this article concerns certain activities carried on for the purposes of or in connection with the sale of goods or supply of services by a supplier to a customer, where—
        "supplier" means a person whose main business is to sell goods or supply services and not to carry on any activities of the kind specified by any of articles 14, 21, 25, 37, 39A, 40, 45, 51ZA, 51ZB, 51ZC, 51ZD, 51ZE, 52 and 53 and, where the supplier is a member of a group, also means any other member of that group; and
        "customer" means a person, other than an individual, to whom a supplier sells goods or supplies services, or agrees to do so, and, where the customer is a member of a group, also means any other member of that group;
        and in this article "related sale or supply" means a sale of goods or supply of services to the customer otherwise than by the supplier, but for or in connection with the same purpose as the sale or supply mentioned above.

(2)   There is excluded from article 14 any transaction entered into by a supplier with a customer, if the transaction is entered into for the purposes of or in connection with the sale of goods or supply of services, or a related sale or supply.

(3)   There is excluded from article 21 any transaction entered into by a supplier as agent for a customer, if the transaction is entered into for the purposes of or in connection with the sale of goods or supply of services, or a related sale or supply, and provided that—
        (a)   where the investment to which the transaction relates is a security, the supplier does not hold himself out (other than to the customer) as engaging in the business of buying securities of the kind to which the transaction relates with a view to selling them, and does not regularly

solicit members of the public for the purpose of inducing them (as principals or agents) to buy, sell, subscribe for or underwrite securities;

    (b)   where the investment to which the transaction relates is a contractually based investment, the supplier enters into the transaction—

        (i)   with or through an authorised person, or an exempt person acting in the course of a business comprising a regulated activity in relation to which he is exempt; or

        (ii) through an office outside the United Kingdom maintained by a party to the transaction, and with or through a person whose head office is situated outside the United Kingdom and whose ordinary business involves him in carrying on activities of the kind specified by any of articles 14, 21, 25, 37, 40, 45, 51, 52 and 53 or, so far as relevant to any of those articles, article 64, or would do so apart from any exclusion from any of those articles made by this Order.

(4)   In paragraph (3)(a), "members of the public" has the meaning given by article 15(2), references to "A" being read as references to the supplier.

(5)   There are excluded from article 25(1) and (2) arrangements made by a supplier for, or with a view to, a transaction which is or is to be entered into by a customer for the purposes of or in connection with the sale of goods or supply of services, or a related sale or supply.

(6)   There is excluded from article 37 any activity carried on by a supplier where the assets in question—

    (a)   are those of a customer; and

    (b)   are managed for the purposes of or in connection with the sale of goods or supply of services, or a related sale or supply.

(7)   There is excluded from article 40 any activity carried on by a supplier where the assets in question are or are to be safeguarded and administered for the purposes of or in connection with the sale of goods or supply of services, or a related sale or supply.

(8)   There is excluded from article 53 the giving of advice by a supplier to a customer for the purposes of or in connection with the sale of goods or supply of services, or a related sale or supply, or to a person with whom the customer proposes to enter into a transaction for the purposes of or in connection with such a sale or supply or related sale or supply.

(9)   Paragraphs (2), (3) and (5) do not apply in the case of a transaction for the sale or purchase of a contract of insurance, an investment of the kind specified by article 81, or an investment of the kind specified by article 89 so far as relevant to such a contract or such an investment.

(10)   Paragraph (6) does not apply where the assets managed consist of qualifying contracts of insurance, investments of the kind specified by article 81, or investments of the kind specified by article 89 so far as relevant to such contracts or such investments.

(11)   Paragraph (8) does not apply in the case of advice in relation to an investment which is a contract of insurance, is of the kind specified by article 81, or is of the kind specified by article 89 so far as relevant to such a contract or such an investment.

(12)   This article is subject to article 4(4).

69.   **Groups and joint enterprises**

(1)   There is excluded from article 14 any transaction into which a person enters as principal with another person if that other person is also acting as principal and—

    (a)   they are members of the same group; or

    (b)   they are, or propose to become, participators in a joint enterprise and the transaction is entered into for the purposes of or in connection with that enterprise.

(2)   There is excluded from article 21 any transaction into which a person enters as agent for another person if that other person is acting as principal, and the condition in paragraph (1)(a) or (b) is met, provided that—

    (a)   where the investment to which the transaction relates is a security, the agent does not hold himself out (other than to members of the same group or persons who are or propose to become participators with him in a joint enterprise) as engaging in the business of buying securities of the kind to which the transaction relates with a view to selling them, and does not regularly solicit members of the public for the purpose of inducing them (as principals or agents) to buy, sell, subscribe for or underwrite securities;

    (b)   where the investment to which the transaction relates is a contractually based investment, the agent enters into the transaction—

        (i)   with or through an authorised person, or an exempt person acting in the course of a business comprising a regulated activity in relation to which he is exempt; or

        (ii)   through an office outside the United Kingdom maintained by a party to the transaction, and with or through a person whose head office is situated outside the United Kingdom and whose ordinary business involves him in carrying on activities of the kind specified by any of articles 14, 21, 25, 37, 40, 45, 51ZA, 51ZB, 51ZC, 51ZD, 51ZE, 52 and 53 or, so far as relevant to any of those articles, article 64, or would do so apart from any exclusion from any of those articles made by this Order.

(3)   In paragraph (2)(a), "members of the public" has the meaning given by article 15(2), references to "A" being read as references to the agent.

(4)   There are excluded from article 25(1) and (2) arrangements made by a person if—

    (a)   he is a member of a group and the arrangements in question are for, or with a view to, a transaction which is or is to be entered into, as principal, by another member of the same group; or

    (b)   he is or proposes to become a participator in a joint enterprise, and the arrangements in question are for, or with a view to, a transaction which is or is to be entered into, as principal, by another person who is or proposes to become a participator in that enterprise, for the purposes of or in connection with that enterprise.

(5)   There is excluded from article 37 any activity carried on by a person if—

    (a)   he is a member of a group and the assets in question belong to another member of the same group; or

    (b)   he is or proposes to become a participator in a joint enterprise with the person to whom the assets belong, and the assets are managed for the purposes of or in connection with that enterprise.

(6)   There is excluded from article 40 any activity carried on by a person if—

    (a)   he is a member of a group and the assets in question belong to another member of the same group; or

    (b)   he is or proposes to become a participator in a joint enterprise, and the assets in question—

        (i)   belong to another person who is or proposes to become a participator in that joint enterprise; and

        (ii)   are or are to be safeguarded and administered for the purposes of or in connection with that enterprise.

(7)   A person who is a member of a group does not carry on an activity of the kind specified by article 45 where he sends a dematerialised instruction, or causes one to be sent, on behalf of another member of the same group, if the investment to which the instruction relates is one in respect of which a member of the same group is registered as holder in the appropriate register of securities, or will be so registered as a result of the instruction.

(8)   In paragraph (7), "dematerialised instruction" and "register of securities" have the meaning given by regulation 3 of the Uncertificated Securities Regulations 2001.

(9)   There is excluded from article 53 the giving of advice by a person if—

    (a)   he is a member of a group and gives the advice in question to another member of the same group; or

    (b)   he is, or proposes to become, a participator in a joint enterprise and the advice in question is given to another person who is, or proposes to become, a participator in that enterprise for the purposes of or in connection with that enterprise.

(10)   Paragraph (2) does not apply to a transaction for the sale or purchase of a contract of insurance.

(11)   Paragraph (4) does not apply to arrangements for, or with a view to, a transaction for the sale or purchase of a contract of insurance.

(12) Paragraph (9) does not apply where the advice relates to a transaction for the sale or purchase of a contract of insurance.

(13) This article is subject to article 4(4).

70. Activities carried on in connection with the sale of a body corporate

(1) A person does not carry on an activity of the kind specified by article 14 by entering as principal into a transaction if—

(a) the transaction is one to acquire or dispose of shares in a body corporate other than an open-ended investment company, or is entered into for the purposes of such an acquisition or disposal; and

(b) either—

(i) the conditions set out in paragraph (2) are met; or

(ii) those conditions are not met, but the object of the transaction may nevertheless reasonably be regarded as being the acquisition of day to day control of the affairs of the body corporate.

(2) The conditions mentioned in paragraph (1)(b) are that—

(a) the shares consist of or include 50 per cent or more of the voting shares in the body corporate; or

(b) the shares, together with any already held by the person acquiring them, consist of or include at least that percentage of such shares; and

(c) in either case, the acquisition or disposal is between parties each of whom is a body corporate, a partnership, a single individual or a group of connected individuals.

(3) In paragraph (2)(c), "a group of connected individuals" means—

(a) in relation to a party disposing of shares in a body corporate, a single group of persons each of whom is—

(i) a director or manager of the body corporate;

(ii) a close relative of any such director or manager;

(iii) a person acting as trustee for any person falling within paragraph (i) or (ii); and

(b) in relation to a party acquiring shares in a body corporate, a single group of persons each of whom is—

(i) a person who is or is to be a director or manager of the body corporate;

(ii) a close relative of any such person; or

(iii) a person acting as trustee for any person falling within paragraph (i) or (ii).

(4) A person does not carry on an activity of the kind specified by article 21 by entering as agent into a transaction of the kind described in paragraph (1).

(5) There are excluded from article 25(1) and (2) arrangements made for, or with a view to, a transaction of the kind described in paragraph (1).

(6) There is excluded from article 53 the giving of advice in connection with a transaction (or proposed transaction) of the kind described in paragraph (1).

(7) Paragraphs (4), (5) and (6) do not apply in the case of a transaction for the sale or purchase of a contract of insurance.

(8) This article is subject to article 4(4).

71. Activities carried on in connection with employee share schemes

(1) A person ("C"), a member of the same group as C or a relevant trustee does not carry on an activity of the kind specified by article 14 by entering as principal into a transaction the purpose of which is to enable or facilitate—

(a) transactions in shares in, or debentures issued by, C between, or for the benefit of, any of the persons mentioned in paragraph (2); or

(b) the holding of such shares or debentures by, or for the benefit of, such persons.

(2) The persons referred to in paragraph (1) are—

(a) the bona fide employees or former employees of C or of another member of the same group as C;

(b)   the wives, husbands, widows, widowers, civil partners, surviving civil partners, or children or step-children under the age of eighteen of such employees or former employees.

(3)   C, a member of the same group as C or a relevant trustee does not carry on an activity of the kind specified by article 21 by entering as agent into a transaction of the kind described in paragraph (1).

(4)   There are excluded from article 25(1) or (2) arrangements made by C, a member of the same group as C or a relevant trustee if the arrangements in question are for, or with a view to, a transaction of the kind described in paragraph (1).

(5)   There is excluded from article 40 any activity if the assets in question are, or are to be, safeguarded and administered by C, a member of the same group as C or a relevant trustee for the purpose of enabling or facilitating transactions of the kind described in paragraph (1).

(6)   In this article—

(a)   "shares" and "debentures" include—

(i)   any investment of the kind specified by article 76, 77 or 77A;

(ii)   any investment of the kind specified by article 79 or 80 so far as relevant to articles 76, 77 and 77A; and

(iii)   any investment of the kind specified by article 89 so far as relevant to investments of the kind mentioned in paragraph (i) or (ii);

(b)   "relevant trustee" means a person who, in pursuance of the arrangements made for the purpose mentioned in paragraph (1), holds, as trustee, shares in or debentures issued by C.

72.   Overseas persons

(1)   An overseas person does not carry on an activity of the kind specified by article 14, 25D or 25DA by—

(a)   entering into a transaction as principal with or though an authorised person, or an exempt person acting in the course of a business comprising a regulated activity in relation to which he is exempt; or

(b)   entering into a transaction as principal with a person in the United Kingdom, if the transaction is the result of a legitimate approach.

(2)   An overseas person does not carry on an activity of the kind specified by article 21, 25D or 25DA by—

(a)   entering into a transaction as agent for any person with or through an authorised person or an exempt person acting in the course of a business comprising a regulated activity in relation to which he is exempt; or

(b)   entering into a transaction with another party ("X") as agent for any person ("Y"), other than with or through an authorised person or such an exempt person, unless—

(i)   either X or Y is in the United Kingdom; and

(ii)   the transaction is the result of an approach (other than a legitimate approach) made by or on behalf of, or to, whichever of X or Y is in the United Kingdom.

(3)   There are excluded from article 25(1), 25D or 25DA arrangements made by an overseas person with an authorised person, or an exempt person acting in the course of a business comprising a regulated activity in relation to which he is exempt.

(4)   There are excluded from article 25(2), 25D or 25DA arrangements made by an overseas person with a view to transactions which are, as respects transactions in the United Kingdom, confined to—

(a)   transactions entered into by authorised persons as principal or agent; and

(b)   transactions entered into by exempt persons, as principal or agent, in the course of business comprising regulated activities in relation to which they are exempt.

(5)   There is excluded from article 53 the giving of advice by an overseas person as a result of a legitimate approach.

(5A)   An overseas person does not carry on an activity of the kind specified by article 25A(1)(a), 25A(2A), 25B(1)(a), 25C(1)(a) or 25E(1)(a) if each person who may be contemplating entering into the relevant type of agreement in the relevant capacity is non-resident.

(5B)   There are excluded from articles 25A(1)(b), 25B(1)(b), 25C(1)(b) and 25E(1)(b) arrangements made by an overseas person to vary the terms of a qualifying agreement.

(5C)   There are excluded from articles 25A(2), 25B(2), 25C(2) and 25E(2), arrangements made by an overseas person which are made solely with a view to non-resident persons who participate in those arrangements entering, in the relevant capacity, into the relevant type of agreement.

(5D)   An overseas person does not carry on an activity of the kind specified in article 61(1), 63B(1), 63F(1) or 63J(1) by entering into a qualifying agreement.

(5E)   An overseas person does not carry on an activity of the kind specified in article 61(2), 63B(2), 63F(2) or 63J(2) where he administers a qualifying agreement.

(5F)   In paragraphs (5A) to (5E)—

      (a)   "non-resident" means not normally resident in the United Kingdom;

      (b)   "qualifying agreement" means—

          (i)   in relation to articles 25A and 61, a regulated mortgage contract where the borrower (or each borrower) is non-resident when he enters into it;

          (ii)   in relation to articles 25B and 63B, a regulated home reversion plan where the reversion seller (or each reversion seller) is non-resident when he enters into it;

          (iii)   in relation to articles 25C and 63F, a regulated home purchase plan where the home purchaser (or each home purchaser) is non-resident when he enters into it;

          (iv)   in relation to articles 25E and 63J, a regulated sale and rent back agreement where the agreement seller (or each agreement seller) is non-resident when the agreement seller enters into it;

      (c)   "the relevant capacity" means—

          (i)   in the case of a regulated mortgage contract, as borrower;

          (ii)   in the case of a regulated home reversion plan, as reversion seller or plan provider;

          (iii)   in the case of a regulated home purchase plan, as home purchaser;

          (iv)   in the case of a regulated sale and rent back agreement, as agreement seller or agreement provider;

      (d)   "the relevant type of agreement" means—

          (i)   in relation to article 25A, a regulated mortgage contract;

          (ii)   in relation to article 25B, a regulated home reversion plan;

          (iii)   in relation to article 25C, a regulated home purchase plan;

          (iv)   in relation to article 25E, a regulated sale and rent back agreement.

(6)   There is excluded from article 64 any agreement made by an overseas person to carry on an activity of the kind specified by article 25(1) or (2), 37, 39A, 40 or 45 if the agreement is the result of a legitimate approach.

(7)   In this article, "legitimate approach" means—

      (a)   an approach made to the overseas person which has not been solicited by him in any way, or has been solicited by him in a way which does not contravene section 21 of the Act; or

      (b)   an approach made by or on behalf of the overseas person in a way which does not contravene that section.

(8)   Paragraphs (1) to (5) do not apply where the overseas person is an investment firm or qualifying credit institution—

      (a)   who is providing or performing investment services and activities on a professional basis; and

      (b)   whose home ... State is the United Kingdom.

(9)   Paragraphs (1) to (5) do not apply where the overseas person is providing clearing services as a central counterparty (within the meaning of section 313(1) of the Act).

(9A)   Paragraphs (1) to (5) do not apply—

      (a)   where the overseas person is a central securities depository which provides the services referred to in Article ... 25(2) of the CSD regulation in the United Kingdom (including through a branch in the United Kingdom); ...

      (b)   ...

(10)   Paragraphs (5A) and (5C) do not apply where the overseas person is a mortgage intermediary whose home ... State is the United Kingdom.

(10A)   This article does not apply in the following two cases.

(11)   The first case is where the overseas person is—

    (a)   a third-country firm, as defined by Article 4.1.57 ("definitions") of the markets in financial instruments directive ("third country firm");

    (b)   established in a country subject to an equivalence decision; and

    (c)   carrying on an activity a third country firm established in that third country may carry on by virtue of the equivalence decision under—

        (i)   Article 46.1 of the markets in financial instruments regulation (general provisions) if it is registered by ESMA in the register of third country firms established in accordance with Article 48 of that Regulation (register);

        (ii)   Article 47.3 of the markets in financial instruments regulation (equivalence decision) if it has a branch in an EEA State other than the United Kingdom and is authorised in that State in accordance with Article 39 of the markets in financial instruments directive (establishment of a branch); or

        (iii)   Article 46.5 of the markets in financial instruments regulation.

(11A)   The second case is where the overseas person is—

    (a)   a third-country firm, as defined by Article 2.1.42 of the markets in financial instruments regulation;

    (b)   established in a county that is the subject of an equivalence determination; and

    (c)   carrying on an activity a third country firm established in that third country may carry on, by virtue of the equivalence determination, under—

        (i)   Article 46.1 of the markets in financial instruments regulation, if it is registered by the FCA in the register of third country firms established in accordance with Article 48 of that regulation, or

        (ii)   Article 46.5 of that regulation.

(12)   For the purposes of paragraphs (11) and (11A)—

    (a)   "equivalence decision" means a decision adopted by the Commission before IP completion day in relation to a country under Article 47.1 of the markets in financial instruments regulation which has not been withdrawn by a subsequent decision adopted by the Commission before IP completion day under that Article; ...

    (b)   a country is subject to an equivalence decision if a period of more than three years has elapsed since the adoption of the decision by the Commission, beginning on the day after the date of the adoption of the decision;

    (c)   "equivalence determination" means a determination made by the Treasury—

        (i)   in regulations under Article 47.1 of the markets in financial instruments regulation and not revoked; or

        (ii)   by direction under regulation 2 of the Equivalence Determinations for Financial Services and Miscellaneous Provisions (Amendment etc) (EU Exit) Regulations 2019 and not revoked;

    (d)   a country is the subject of an equivalence determination if a period of more than three years has elapsed since—

        (i)   the date on which the equivalence determination came into force, or

        (ii)   where two or more equivalence determinations have been made in succession in relation to the country concerned, the date on which the first equivalence determination came into force;

    (e)   for the purposes of sub-paragraph (d), an equivalence determination is not made in succession to an earlier determination if the earlier determination ceased to have effect before the later determination came into force.

72A.   ...

72AA. Managers of UK UCITS and AIFs

(1)   This article applies to a person with a Part 4A permission to carry on the activity of the kind specified by article 51ZA or 51ZC.

(2)   Activities carried on by the person in connection with or for the purposes of managing a UK UCITS or, as the case may be, managing an AIF, are excluded from the activities specified by this Part, other than the activities mentioned in paragraph (1).

72B.   **Activities carried on by a provider of relevant goods or services**

(1)   In this article—

"connected contract of insurance" means a contract of insurance which—

    (a)   is not a contract of long-term insurance;

    (b)   ...

    (c)   has a premium of—

        (i)   600 euro or less (calculated on a pro rata annual basis), or

        (ii)   where the insurance is complementary to a service being provided by the provider and the duration of that service is equal to or less than three months, 200 euro or less,

        or equivalent amounts of sterling or another currency;

    (d)   covers the risk of—

        (i)   breakdown, loss of, or damage to, non-motor goods supplied by the provider; ...

        (ia)   the non-use of services supplied by the provider; or

        (ii)   damage to, or loss of, baggage and other risks linked to the travel booked with the provider ("travel risks") in circumstances where—

           (aa)   the travel booked with the provider relates to attendance at an event organised or managed by that provider and the party seeking insurance is not an individual (acting in his private capacity) or a small business; or

           (bb)   the travel booked with the provider is only the hire of an aircraft, vehicle or vessel which does not provide sleeping accommodation;

    (e)   does not cover any liability risks (except, in the case of a contract which covers travel risks, where that cover is ancillary to the main cover provided by the contract); and

    (f)   is complementary to the non-motor goods being supplied or service being provided by the provider; ...

    (g)   ...

"non-motor goods" means goods which are not mechanically propelled road vehicles;

"provider" means a person who supplies non-motor goods or services or provides services related to travel in the course of carrying on a profession or business which does not otherwise consist of the carrying on of regulated activities. For these purposes, the transfer of possession of an aircraft, vehicle or vessel under an agreement for hire which is not—

    (a)   a hire-purchase agreement ..., or

    (b)   any other agreement which contemplates that the property in those goods will also pass at some time in the future,

is the provision of a service related to travel, not a supply of goods;

"small business" means—

    (a)   subject to paragraph (b) a sole trader, body corporate, partnership or an unincorporated association which had a turnover in the last financial year of less than £1,000,000;

    (b)   where the business concerned is a member of a group within the meaning of section 474(1) of the Companies Act 2006, reference to its turnover means the combined turnover of the group;

"turnover" means the amounts derived from the provision of goods and services falling within the business's ordinary activities, after deduction of trade discounts, value added tax and any other taxes based on the amounts so derived.

(2)   There is excluded from article 21 any transaction for the sale or purchase of a connected contract of insurance into which a provider enters as agent.

(3)   There are excluded from article 25(1) and (2) any arrangements made by a provider for, or with a view to, a transaction for the sale or purchase of a connected contract of insurance.

(4)   There is excluded from article 39A any activity carried on by a provider where the contract of insurance in question is a connected contract of insurance.

(5)   There is excluded from article 53 the giving of advice by a provider in relation to a transaction for the sale or purchase of a connected contract of insurance.

(6)   For the purposes of this article, a contract of insurance which covers travel risks is not to be treated as a contract of long-term insurance, notwithstanding the fact that it contains related and subsidiary provisions such that it might be regarded as a contract of long-term insurance, if the cover to which those provisions relate is ancillary to the main cover provided by the contract.

72C.   Provision of information on an incidental basis

(1)   There is excluded from articles 25(1) and (2) the making of arrangements for, or with a view to, a transaction for the sale or purchase of a contract of insurance or an investment of the kind specified by article 89, so far as relevant to such a contract, where that activity meets the conditions specified in paragraph (4).

(2)   There is excluded from articles 37 and 40 any activity—

    (a)   where the assets in question are rights under a contract of insurance or an investment of the kind specified by article 89, so far as relevant to such a contract; and

    (b)   which meets the conditions specified in paragraph (4).

(3)   There is excluded from article 39A any activity which meets the conditions specified in paragraph (4).

(4)   The conditions specified in this paragraph are that the activity—

    (a)   consists of the provision of information to the policyholder or potential policyholder;

    (b)   is carried on by a person in the course of carrying on a profession or business which does not otherwise consist of the carrying on of regulated activities; and

    (c)   may reasonably be regarded as being incidental to that profession or business.

...

72E.   Business Angel-led Enterprise Capital Funds

(1)   A body corporate of a type specified in paragraph (7) does not carry on the activity of the kind specified by article 21 by entering as agent into a transaction on behalf of the participants of a Business Angel-led Enterprise Capital Fund.

(2)   There are excluded from article 25(1) and (2) arrangements, made by a body corporate of a type specified in paragraph (7), for or with a view to a transaction which is or is to be entered into by or on behalf of the participants in a Business Angel-led Enterprise Capital Fund.

(3)   There is excluded from article 37 any activity, carried on by a body corporate of a type specified in paragraph (7), which consists in the managing of assets belonging to the participants in a Business Angel-led Enterprise Capital Fund.

(4)   There is excluded from article 40 any activity, carried on by a body corporate of a type specified in paragraph (7), in respect of assets belonging to the participants in a Business Angel-led Enterprise Capital Fund.

(5)   A body corporate of a type specified in paragraph (7) does not carry on the activity of the kind specified in article 51ZA, 51ZC or 51ZE where it carries on the activity of establishing, operating or winding up a Business Angel-led Enterprise Capital Fund.

(6)   A body corporate of a type specified in paragraph (7) does not carry on the activity of the kind specified in article 53 where it is advising the participants in a Business Angel-led Enterprise Capital Fund on investments to be made by or on behalf of the participants of that Business Angel-led Enterprise Capital Fund.

(7)   The type of body corporate specified is a limited company—

    (i)   which operates a Business Angel-led Enterprise Capital Fund; and

    (ii)   the members of which are participants in the Business Angel-led Enterprise Capital Fund operated by that limited company and between them have invested at least 50 per cent of the total investment in that Business Angel-led Enterprise Capital Fund excluding any investment made by the Secretary of State.

(8)   For the purposes of paragraph (7), "a limited company" means a body corporate with limited liability which is a company or firm formed under the law of any part of the United Kingdom and having its registered office, central administration or principal place of business in the United Kingdom.

(9)   Nothing in this article has the effect of excluding a body corporate from the application of the Money Laundering, Terrorist Financing and Transfer of Funds (Information on the Payer) Regulations 2017, in so far as those Regulations would have applied to it but for this article.

(10)   Nothing in this article has the effect of excluding a body corporate from the application of section 397 of the Act (misleading statements and practices), in so far as that section would have applied to it but for this article.

(11)   This article is subject to article 4(4).

72F.   Interpretation

(1)   For the purposes of this article and of article 72E—

"Business Angel-led Enterprise Capital Fund" means a collective investment scheme which—

    (a)   is established for the purpose of enabling participants to participate in or receive profits or income arising from the acquisition, holding, management or disposal of investments falling within one or more of—

        (i)   article 76, being shares in an unlisted company;

        (ii)   article 77, being instruments creating or acknowledging indebtedness in respect of an unlisted company;

        (iia)   article 77A, being rights under an alternative finance investment bond issued by an unlisted company; and

        (iii)   article 79, being warrants or other instruments entitling the holder to subscribe for shares in an unlisted company;

    (b)   has only the following as its participants—

        (i)   the Secretary of State;

        (ii)   a body corporate of a type specified in article 72E(7); and

        (iii)   one or more persons each of whom at the time they became a participant was—

            (aa)   a sophisticated investor;

            (bb)   a high net worth individual;

            (cc)   a high net worth company;

            (dd)   a high net worth unincorporated association;

            (ee)   a trustee of a high value trust; or

            (ff)   a self-certified sophisticated investor;

    (c)   is prevented, by the arrangements by which it is established, from—

        (i)   acquiring investments, other than those falling within paragraphs (i) to (iii) of sub-paragraph (a); and

        (ii)   acquiring investments falling within paragraphs (i) to (iii) of sub-paragraph (a) in an unlisted company, where the aggregated cost of those investments exceeds £2 million, unless that acquisition is necessary to prevent or reduce the dilution of an existing share-holding in that unlisted company;

"high net worth company" means a body corporate which—

    (a)   falls within article 49(2)(a) of the Financial Services and Markets Act 2000 (Financial Promotion) Order 2005 (high net worth companies, unincorporated associations etc); and

    (b)   has executed a document (in a manner which binds the company) in the following terms:

        "This company is a high net worth company and falls within article 49(2)(a) of the Financial Services and Markets Act 2000 (Financial Promotion) Order 2005. We understand that any Business Angel-led Enterprise Capital Fund (within the meaning of article 72F of the Financial Services and Markets Act 2000 (Regulated Activities) Order 2001), in which this company participates, or any person who operates that Business Angel-led Enterprise Capital Fund, in which this company participates, will not be authorised under the Financial Services and Markets Act 2000 (and so will not have to satisfy the threshold conditions set out in Part I of Schedule 6 to that Act and will not be subject to Financial Conduct Authority rules such as those on holding client money). We understand that this means that redress through the Financial Conduct Authority, the Financial Ombudsman Scheme or the Financial Services Compensation Scheme will not be available. We also understand the risks associated in investing in a Business Angel-led Enterprise Capital Fund and are aware that it is open to us to seek advice from someone who is authorised under the Financial Services and Markets Act 2000 and who specialises in advising on this kind of investment."

"high net worth individual" means an individual who—

(a)   is a "... high net worth individual" within the meaning of article 48(2) of the Financial Services and Markets Act 2000 (Financial Promotion) Order 2005 (... high net worth individuals); and

(b)   has signed a statement in the following terms:

> "I declare that I am a ... high net worth individual within the meaning of article 48(2) of the Financial Services and Markets Act 2000 (Financial Promotion) Order 2005 and that I understand that any Business Angel-led Enterprise Capital Fund (within the meaning of article 72F of the Financial Services and Markets Act 2000 (Regulated Activities) Order 2001), in which I participate, or any person who operates that Business Angel-led Enterprise Capital Fund, in which I participate, will not be authorised under the Financial Services and Markets Act 2000 (and so will not have to satisfy the threshold conditions set out in Part I of Schedule 6 to that Act and will not be subject to Financial Conduct Authority rules such as those on holding client money). I understand that this means that redress through the Financial Conduct Authority, the Financial Ombudsman Scheme or the Financial Services Compensation Scheme will not be available. I also understand the risks associated in investing in a Business Angel-led Enterprise Capital Fund and am aware that it is open to me to seek advice from someone who is authorised under the Financial Services and Markets Act 2000 and who specialises in advising on this kind of investment.";

"high net worth unincorporated association" means an unincorporated association—

(a)   which falls within article 49(2)(b) of the Financial Services and Markets Act 2000 (Financial Promotion) Order 2005; and

(b)   on behalf of which an officer of that association or a member of its governing body has signed a statement in the following terms:

> "This unincorporated association is a high net worth unincorporated association and falls within article 49(2)(b) of the Financial Services and Markets Act 2000 (Financial Promotion) Order 2005. I understand that any Business Angel-led Enterprise Capital Fund (within the meaning of article 72F of the Financial Services and Markets Act 2000 (Regulated Activities) Order 2001), in which this association participates, or any person who operates that Business Angel-led Enterprise Capital Fund, in which this association participates, will not be authorised under the Financial Services and Markets Act 2000 (and so will not have to satisfy the threshold conditions set out in Part I of Schedule 6 to that Act and will not be subject to Financial Conduct Authority rules such as those on holding client money). I understand that this means that redress through the Financial Conduct Authority, the Financial Ombudsman Scheme or the Financial Services Compensation Scheme will not be available. I also understand the risks associated in investing in a Business Angel-led Enterprise Capital Fund and am aware that it is open to the association to seek advice from someone who is authorised

under the Financial Services and Markets Act 2000 and who specialises in advising on this kind of investment.";

"high value trust" means a trust—

(a)   where the aggregate value of the cash and investments which form a part of the trust's assets (before deducting the amount of its liabilities) is £10 million or more;

(b)   on behalf of which a trustee has signed a statement in the following terms:

"This trust is a high value trust. I understand that any Business Angel-led Enterprise Capital Fund (within the meaning of article 72F of the Financial Services and Markets Act 2000 (Regulated Activities) Order 2001), in which this trust participates, or any person who operates that Business Angel-led Enterprise Capital Fund, in which this trust participates, will not be authorised under the Financial Services and Markets Act 2000 (and so will not have to satisfy the threshold conditions set out in Part I of Schedule 6 to that Act and will not be subject to Financial Conduct Authority rules such as those on holding client money). I understand that this means that redress through the Financial Conduct Authority, the Financial Ombudsman Scheme or the Financial Services Compensation Scheme will not be available. I also understand the risks associated in investing in a Business Angel-led Enterprise Capital Fund and am aware that it is open to the trust to seek advice from someone who is authorised under the Financial Services and Markets Act 2000 and who specialises in advising on this kind of investment.";

"self-certified sophisticated investor" means an individual who—

(a)   is a "self-certified sophisticated investor" within the meaning of article 50A of the Financial Services and Markets Act 2000 (Financial Promotion) Order 2005;

(b)   has signed a statement in the following terms:

"I declare that I am a self-certified sophisticated investor within the meaning of article 50A of the Financial Services and Markets Act 2000 (Financial Promotion) Order 2005 and that I understand that any Business Angel-led Enterprise Capital Fund (within the meaning of article 72F of the Financial Services and Markets Act 2000 (Regulated Activities) Order 2001), in which I participate, or any person who operates that Business Angel-led Enterprise Capital Fund, in which I participate, will not be authorised under the Financial Services and Markets Act 2000 (and so will not have to satisfy the threshold conditions set out in Part I of Schedule 6 to that Act and will not be subject to Financial Conduct Authority rules such as those on holding client money). I understand that this means that redress through the Financial Conduct Authority, the Financial Ombudsman Scheme or the Financial Services Compensation Scheme will not be available. I also understand the risks associated in investing in a Business Angel-led Enterprise Capital Fund and am aware that it is open to me to seek advice from someone who is authorised under the Financial Services and Markets Act 2000 and who specialises in advising on this kind of investment.";

"sophisticated investor" means an individual who—

(a)   is a "certified sophisticated investor" within the meaning of article 50(1) of the Financial Services and Markets Act 2000 (Financial Promotion) Order 2005; and

(b)   has signed a statement in the following terms:

"I declare that I am a certified sophisticated investor within the meaning of article 50(1) of the Financial Services and Markets Act 2000 (Financial Promotion) Order 2005 and that I understand that any Business Angel-led Enterprise Capital Fund (within the meaning of article 72F of the Financial Services and Markets Act 2000 (Regulated Activities) Order 2001), in which I participate, or any person who operates that Business Angel-led Enterprise Capital Fund, in which I participate, will not be authorised under the Financial Services and Markets Act 2000 (and so will not have to satisfy the threshold conditions set out in Part I of Schedule 6 to that Act and will not be subject to Financial Conduct Authority rules such as those on holding client money). I understand that this means that redress through the Financial Conduct Authority, the Financial Ombudsman Scheme or the Financial Services Compensation Scheme will not be available. I also understand the risks associated in investing in a Business Angel-led Enterprise Capital Fund and am aware that it is open to me to seek advice from someone who is authorised under the Financial Services and Markets Act 2000 and who specialises in advising on this kind of investment.";

"unlisted company" has the meaning given by article 3 of the Financial Services and Markets Act 2000 (Financial Promotion) Order 2005.

(2)   References in this Article and in Article 72E to a participant in a Business Angel-led Enterprise Capital Fund, doing things on behalf of such a participant and property belonging to such a participant are, respectively, references to that participant in that capacity, to doing things on behalf of that participant in that capacity or to the property of that participant held in that capacity.

...

72H.   Insolvency practitioners

(1)   There is excluded from the provisions listed in paragraph (2) any activity carried on by a person acting as an insolvency practitioner.

(2)   The provisions are—
   (a)   article 14 (dealing in investments as principal);
   (b)   article 21 (dealing in investments as agent);
   (c)   article 25 (arranging deals in investments);
   (d)   article 25D (operating a multilateral trading facility);
   (da)   article 25DA (operating an organised trading facility);
   (e)   article 37 (managing investments);
   (f)   article 39A (assisting in the administration and performance of a contract of insurance);
   (g)   article 39D (debt adjusting);
   (h)   article 39E (debt-counselling);
   (i)   article 39F (debt-collecting);
   (j)   article 39G (debt administration);
   (k)   article 40 (safeguarding and administering investments);
   (l)   article 45 (sending dematerialised instructions);
   (m)   article 51ZA (managing a UK UCITS);
   (n)   article 51ZB (acting as trustee or depositary of a UK UCITS);
   (o)   article 51ZC (managing an AIF);
   (p)   article 51ZD (acting as trustee or depositary of an AIF);
   (q)   article 51ZE (establishing etc a collective investment scheme);
   (r)   article 52 (establishing etc a pension scheme);
   (s)   article 53 (advising on investments);
   (sa)   article 59(1A) (carrying out a funeral plan contract as provider);
   (t)   article 89A (providing credit information services).

(3)   There is excluded from articles 39D, 39E and 89A any activity carried on by a person acting in reasonable contemplation of that person's appointment as an insolvency practitioner.

(4)   There is excluded from article 64 any agreement made by a person acting as an insolvency practitioner to carry on an activity of the kind excluded by paragraph (1).

(5)   There is excluded from article 64 any agreement made by a person acting in reasonable contemplation of that person's appointment as an insolvency practitioner to carry on an activity of the kind excluded by paragraph (3).

...

PART III
SPECIFIED INVESTMENTS

73.   **Investments: general**

The following kinds of investment are specified for the purposes of section 22 of the Act.

74.   **Deposits**

A deposit.

74A.   **Electronic money**

Electronic money.

75.   **Contracts of insurance**

Rights under a contract of insurance.

76.   **Shares etc**

(1)   Shares or stock in the share capital of—

     (a)   any body corporate (wherever incorporated), and

     (b)   any unincorporated body constituted under the law of a country or territory outside the United Kingdom.

(2)   Paragraph (1) includes—

     (a)   any shares of a class defined as deferred shares for the purposes of section 119 of the Building Societies Act 1986 or section 31A of the Credit Unions Act 1979; and

     (b)   any transferable shares in a body incorporated under the law of, or any part of, the United Kingdom relating to co-operative and community benefit societies, industrial and provident societies or credit unions, or in a body constituted under the law of another EEA State for purposes equivalent to those of such a body.

(3)   But subject to paragraph (2) there are excluded from paragraph (1) shares or stock in the share capital of—

     (a)   an open-ended investment company;

     (b)   a building society incorporated under the law of, or any part of, the United Kingdom;

     (c)   a body incorporated under the law of, or any part of, the United Kingdom relating to co-operative and community benefit societies, industrial and provident societies or credit unions;

     (d)   any body constituted under the law of an EEA State for purposes equivalent to those of a body falling within sub-paragraph (b) or (c).

77.   **Instruments creating or acknowledging indebtedness**

(1)   Subject to paragraph (2), such of the following as do not fall within article … 78—

     (a)   debentures;

     (b)   debenture stock;

     (c)   loan stock;

     (d)   bonds;

     (e)   certificates of deposit;

     (f)   any other instrument creating or acknowledging indebtedness.

(2)   If and to the extent that they would otherwise fall within paragraph (1), there are excluded from that paragraph—

     (a)   an instrument acknowledging or creating indebtedness for, or for money borrowed to defray, the consideration payable under a contract for the supply of goods or services;

     (b)   a cheque or other bill of exchange, a banker's draft or a letter of credit (but not a bill of exchange accepted by a banker);

     (c)   a banknote, a statement showing a balance on a current, deposit or savings account, a lease or other disposition of property, or a heritable security;

     (d)   a contract of insurance;

(e)   ...

(3)   An instrument excluded from paragraph (1) of article 78 by paragraph (2)(b) of that article is not thereby to be taken to fall within paragraph (1) of this article.

77A.   Alternative finance investment bonds

(1)   Rights under an alternative finance investment bond, to the extent that they do not fall within article 77 or 78.

(2)   For the purposes of this article, arrangements constitute an alternative finance investment bond if—

(a)   the arrangements provide for a person ("the bond-holder") to pay a sum of money ("the capital") to another ("the bond-issuer");

(b)   the arrangements identify assets, or a class of assets, which the bond-issuer will acquire for the purpose of generating income or gains directly or indirectly ("the bond assets");

(c)   the arrangements specify a period at the end of which they cease to have effect ("the bond term");

(d)   the bond-issuer undertakes under the arrangements—

(i)   to make a repayment in respect of the capital ("the redemption payment") to the bond-holder during or at the end of the bond term (whether or not in instalments); and

(ii)   to pay to the bond-holder other payments on one or more occasions during or at the end of the bond term ("the additional payments");

(e)   the amount of the additional payments does not exceed an amount which would, at the time at which the bond is issued, be a reasonable commercial return on a loan of the capital; and

(f)   the arrangements are—

(i)   a security that is admitted to the official list in accordance with Part 6 of the Act,

(ii)   a security that is admitted to an official list in the EEA (in accordance with the provisions of Directive 2001/34/EC of the European Parliament and of the Council on the admission of securities to official stock exchange listing and on information to be published on those securities) and has been so admitted since before IP completion day,

(iii) a security that is admitted to trading on a recognised investment exchange or a UK trading venue, or

(iv) a security that is admitted to trading on an EU trading venue and has been so admitted since before IP completion day.

(3)   For the purposes of paragraph (2)—

(a)   the bond-issuer may acquire the bond assets before or after the arrangements take effect;

(b)   the bond assets may be property of any kind, including rights in relation to property owned by someone other than the bond-issuer;

(c)   the identification of the bond assets mentioned in paragraph (2)(b) and the undertakings mentioned in paragraph (2)(d) may (but need not) be described as, or accompanied by a document described as, a declaration of trust;

(d)   the reference to a period in paragraph (2)(c) includes any period specified to end upon the redemption of the bond by the bond-issuer;

(e)   the bond-holder may (but need not) be entitled under the arrangements to terminate them, or participate in terminating them, before the end of the bond term;

(f)   the amount of the additional payments may be—

(i)   fixed at the beginning of the bond term;

(ii)   determined wholly or partly by reference to the value of or income generated by the bond assets; or

(iii) determined in some other way;

(g)   if the amount of the additional payments is not fixed at the beginning of the bond term, the reference in paragraph (2)(e) to the amount of the additional payments is a reference to the maximum amount of the additional payments;

(h)   the amount of the redemption payment may (but need not) be subject to reduction in the event of a fall in the value of the bond assets or in the rate of income generated by them; and

(i)   entitlement to the redemption payment may (but need not) be capable of being satisfied (whether or not at the option of the bond-issuer or the bond-holder) by the issue or transfer of shares or other securities.

(3A)   In sub-paragraph (2)(f)—

"EU trading venue" has the meaning given by Article 2.1.16B of the markets in financial instruments regulation;

"UK trading venue" has the meaning given by Article 2.1.16A of that regulation.

(4)   An instrument excluded from paragraph (1) of article 78 by paragraph (2)(b) of that article is not thereby taken to fall within paragraph (1) of this article.

78.   Government and public securities

(1)   Subject to paragraph (2), loan stock, bonds and other instruments creating or acknowledging indebtedness, issued by or on behalf of any of the following—

(a)   the government of the United Kingdom;

(b)   the Scottish Administration;

(c)   the Executive Committee of the Northern Ireland Assembly;

(d)   the National Assembly for Wales;

(e)   the government of any country or territory outside the United Kingdom;

(f)   a local authority in the United Kingdom or elsewhere; or

(g)   a body the members of which comprise—

(i)   states including the United Kingdom ...; or

(ii)   bodies whose members comprise states including the United Kingdom ....

(2)   Subject to paragraph (3), there are excluded from paragraph (1)—

(a)   so far as applicable, the instruments mentioned in article 77(2)(a) to (d);

(b)   any instrument creating or acknowledging indebtedness in respect of—

(i)   money received by the Director of Savings as deposits or otherwise in connection with the business of the National Savings Bank;

(ii)   money raised under the National Loans Act 1968 under the auspices of the Director of Savings or treated as so raised by virtue of section 11(3) of the National Debt Act 1972.

(3)   Paragraph (2)(a) does not exclude an instrument which meets the requirements set out in sub-paragraphs (a) to (e) of article 77A(2).

79.   Instruments giving entitlements to investments

(1)   Warrants and other instruments entitling the holder to subscribe for any investment of the kind specified by article 76, 77, 77A or 78.

(2)   It is immaterial whether the investment to which the entitlement relates is in existence or identifiable.

(3)   An investment of the kind specified by this article is not to be regarded as falling within article 83, 84 or 85.

80.   Certificates representing certain securities

(1)   Subject to paragraph (2), certificates or other instruments which confer contractual or property rights (other than rights consisting of an investment of the kind specified by article 83)—

(a)   in respect of any investment of the kind specified by any of articles 76 to 79, being an investment held by a person other than the person on whom the rights are conferred by the certificate or instrument; and

(b)   the transfer of which may be effected without the consent of that person.

(2)   There is excluded from paragraph (1) any certificate or other instrument which confers rights in respect of two or more investments issued by different persons, or in respect of two or more different investments of the kind specified by article 78 and issued by the same person.

...

83.   Options

(1)   Options to acquire or dispose of—

    (a)   a security or contractually based investment (other than one of a kind specified by this article);

    (b)   currency of the United Kingdom or any other country or territory;

    (c)   palladium, platinum, gold or silver; ...

    (d)   an option to acquire or dispose of an investment of the kind specified by this article by virtue of paragraph (a), (b) or (c);

    (e)   subject to paragraph (4), an option to acquire or dispose of an option to which paragraph 5, 6, 7 or 10 of Part 1 of Schedule 2 (read with Articles 5, 6, 7, and 8 of the Commission Regulation) applies.

(2)   Subject to paragraph (4), options—

    (a)   to which paragraph (1) does not apply;

    (b)   which relate to commodities;

    (c)   which may be settled physically; and

    (d)   either—

        (i)   to which paragraph 5 or 6 of ... Part 1 of Schedule 2 (read with Articles 5 and 6 of the Commission Regulation), applies, or

        (ii)   which in accordance with Article 7 of the Commission Regulation (the text of which is set out in Part 2 of Schedule 2) are to be considered as having the characteristics of other derivative financial instruments and not being for commercial purposes, and to which paragraph 7 of Part 1 of that Schedule applies.

(3)   Subject to paragraph (4), options—

    (a)   to which paragraph (1) does not apply;

    (b)   which may be settled physically; and

    (c)   to which paragraph 10 of Part 1 of Schedule 2 (read with Articles 7 and 8 of the Commission Regulation) applies.

(4)   Paragraphs (1)(e), (2) and (3) only apply to options in relation to which—

    (a)   an investment firm or qualifying credit institution is providing or performing investment services and activities on a professional basis,

    (b)   a management company which has a Part 4A permission to do so is providing the investment service specified in paragraph 4 or 5 of Part 3 of Schedule 2 or the ancillary service specified in paragraph 1 of Part 3A of that Schedule,

    (c)   a market operator is providing the investment service specified in paragraph 8 or 9 of Part 3 of that Schedule, or

    (d)   a full-scope UK AIFM which has a Part 4A permission to do so is providing the investment service specified in paragraph 1, 4 or 5 of Part 3 of that Schedule or the ancillary service specified in paragraph 1 of Part 3A of that Schedule.

(5)   ...

84.   Futures

(1)   Subject to paragraph (2), rights under a contract for the sale of a commodity or property of any other description under which delivery is to be made at a future date and at a price agreed on when the contract is made.

(1A)   Subject to paragraph (1D), futures—

    (a)   to which paragraph (1) does not apply;

    (b)   which relate to commodities;

    (c)   which may be settled physically; and

    (d)   to which paragraph 5 or 6 of Part 1 of Schedule 2 (read with Articles 5 and 6 of the Commission Regulation) applies.

(1B)   Subject to paragraph (1D), futures and forwards—

    (a)   to which paragraph (1) does not apply;

    (b)   which relate to commodities;

(c)   which may be settled physically;

(d)   which in accordance with Article 7 of the Commission Regulation (the text of which is set out in Part 2 of Schedule 2) are to be considered as having the characteristics of other derivative financial instruments and not being for commercial purposes; and

(e)   to which paragraph 7 of Part 1 of Schedule 2 applies.

(1C)   Subject to paragraph (1D), futures—

(a)   to which paragraph (1) does not apply;

(b)   which may be settled physically; and

(c)   to which paragraph 10 of Part 1 of Schedule 2 (read with Articles 7 and 8 of the Commission Regulation) applies.

(1CA)   Subject to paragraph (1D), any other derivative contract, relating to currencies to which paragraph 4 of Part 1 of Schedule 2 read with Article 10 of the Commission Regulation (the text of which is set out in Part 2 of Schedule 2) applies.

(1D)   Paragraph (1A), (1B), (1C) and (1CA) only apply to futures, forwards or derivative contracts in relation to which—

(a)   an investment firm or qualifying credit institution is providing or performing investment services and activities on a professional basis,

(b)   a management company which has a Part 4A permission to do so is providing the investment service specified in paragraph 4 or 5 of Part 3 of Schedule 2 or the ancillary service specified in paragraph 1 of Part 3A of that Schedule,

(c)   a market operator is providing the investment service specified in paragraph 8 or 9 of Part 3 of that Schedule, or

(d)   a full-scope UK AIFM which has a Part 4A permission to do so is providing the investment service specified in paragraph 1, 4 or 5 of Part 3 of that Schedule or the ancillary service specified in paragraph 1 of Part 3A of that Schedule.

(1E)   ...

(2)   There are excluded from paragraph (1) rights under any contract which is made for commercial and not investment purposes.

(3)   A contract is to be regarded as made for investment purposes if it is made or traded on a recognised investment exchange, or is made otherwise than on a recognised investment exchange but is expressed to be as traded on such an exchange or on the same terms as those on which an equivalent contract would be made on such an exchange.

(4)   A contract not falling within paragraph (3) is to be regarded as made for commercial purposes if under the terms of the contract delivery is to be made within seven days, unless it can be shown that there existed an understanding that (notwithstanding the express terms of the contract) delivery would not be made within seven days.

(5)   The following are indications that a contract not falling within paragraph (3) or (4) is made for commercial purposes and the absence of them is an indication that it is made for investment purposes—

(a)   one or more of the parties is a producer of the commodity or other property, or uses it in his business;

(b)   the seller delivers or intends to deliver the property or the purchaser takes or intends to take delivery of it.

(6)   It is an indication that a contract is made for commercial purposes that the prices, the lot, the delivery date or other terms are determined by the parties for the purposes of the particular contract and not by reference (or not solely by reference) to regularly published prices, to standard lots or delivery dates or to standard terms.

(7)   The following are indications that a contract is made for investment purposes—

(a)   it is expressed to be as traded on an investment exchange;

(b)   performance of the contract is ensured by an investment exchange or a clearing house;

(c)   there are arrangements for the payment or provision of margin.

(8)   For the purposes of paragraph (1), a price is to be taken to be agreed on when a contract is made—

    (a)   notwithstanding that it is left to be determined by reference to the price at which a contract is to be entered into on a market or exchange or could be entered into at a time and place specified in the contract; or

    (b)   in a case where the contract is expressed to be by reference to a standard lot and quality, notwithstanding that provision is made for a variation in the price to take account of any variation in quantity or quality on delivery.

85.   Contracts for differences etc

(1)   Subject to paragraph (2), rights under—

    (a)   a contract for differences; or

    (b)   any other contract the purpose or pretended purpose of which is to secure a profit or avoid a loss by reference to fluctuations in—

        (i)   the value or price of property of any description; or

        (ii)   an index or other factor designated for that purpose in the contract.

(2)   There are excluded from paragraph (1)—

    (a)   rights under a contract if the parties intend that the profit is to be secured or the loss is to be avoided by one or more of the parties taking delivery of any property to which the contract relates;

    (b)   rights under a contract under which money is received by way of deposit on terms that any interest or other return to be paid on the sum deposited will be calculated by reference to fluctuations in an index or other factor;

    (c)   rights under any contract under which—

        (i)   money is received by the Director of Savings as deposits or otherwise in connection with the business of the National Savings Bank; or

        (ii)   money is raised under the National Loans Act 1968 under the auspices of the Director of Savings or treated as so raised by virtue of section 11(3) of the National Debt Act 1972;

    (d)   rights under a qualifying contract of insurance.

(3)   Subject to paragraph (4), derivative instruments for the transfer of credit risk—

    (a)   to which neither article 83 nor paragraph (1) applies; and

    (b)   to which paragraph 8 of Part 1 of Schedule 2 applies.

(4)   Paragraph (3) only applies to derivatives in relation to which—

    (a)   an investment firm or qualifying credit institution is providing or performing investment services and activities on a professional basis,

    (b)   a management company which has a Part 4A permission to do so is providing the investment service specified in paragraph 4 or 5 of Part 3 of Schedule 2 or the ancillary service specified in paragraph 1 of Part 3A of that Schedule,

    (c)   a market operator is providing the investment service specified in paragraph 8 or 9 of Part 3 of that Schedule,

    (d)   a full-scope UK AIFM which has a Part 4A permission to do so is providing the investment service specified in paragraph 1, 4 or 5 of Part 3 of that Schedule or the ancillary service specified in paragraph 1 of Part 3A of that Schedule.

(4A)   Subject to paragraph (4B), a derivative contract of a binary or other fixed outcomes nature—

    (a)   to which paragraph (1) does not apply;

    (b)   which is settled in cash; and

    (c)   which is a financial instrument to which paragraph 4, 5, 6, 7 or 10 of Part 1 of Schedule 2 read with Articles 5 to 8 and 10 of the Commission Regulation (the text of which is set out in Part 2 of Schedule 2) applies.

(4B)   Paragraph (4A) only applies to derivatives in relation to which—

    (a)   an investment firm or qualifying credit institution is providing or performing investment services and activities on a professional basis,

(b)   a management company which has a Part 4A permission to do so is providing the investment service specified in paragraph 4 or 5 of Part 3 of Schedule 2 or the ancillary service specified in paragraph 1 of Part 3A of that Schedule,

(c)   a market operator is providing the investment service specified in paragraph 8 or 9 of Part 3 of that Schedule,

(d)   a full-scope UK AIFM which has a Part 4A permission to do so is providing the investment service specified in paragraph 1, 4 or 5 of Part 3 of that Schedule or the ancillary service specified in paragraph 1 of Part 3A of that Schedule, or

(e)   a person is carrying on the activity specified by article 25(2).

(5)   ...

...

88.   Regulated mortgage contracts

Rights under a regulated mortgage contract.

...

88D.   Credit agreement

Rights under a credit agreement.

88E.   Consumer hire agreement

Rights under a consumer hire agreement.

89.   Rights to or interests in investments

(1)   Subject to paragraphs (2) to (4), any right to or interest in anything which is specified by any other provision of this Part (other than article 88, 88A, 88B or 88C).

(2)   Paragraph (1) does not include interests under the trusts of an occupational pension scheme.

(2A)   Paragraph (2) does not apply where the kind of activity specified in article 53E (advising on conversion or transfer of pension benefits) or article 89BA (operating a pensions dashboard service) is carried on by way of business in relation to the interests under the trusts of an occupational pension scheme.

(3)   Paragraph (1) does not include any right or interest acquired as a result of entering into a funeral plan contract.

(4)   Paragraph (1) does not include anything which is specified by any other provision of this Part.

PART 3A

SPECIFIED ACTIVITIES IN RELATION TO INFORMATION

The Activities

89A.   Providing credit information services

(1)   Taking any of the steps in paragraph (3) on behalf of an individual or relevant recipient of credit is a specified kind of activity.

(2)   Giving advice to an individual or relevant recipient of credit in relation to the taking of any of the steps specified in paragraph (3) is a specified kind of activity.

(3)   Subject to paragraph (4), the steps specified in this paragraph are steps taken with a view to—

(a)   ascertaining whether a credit information agency holds information relevant to the financial standing of an individual or relevant recipient of credit;

(b)   ascertaining the contents of such information;

(c)   securing the correction of, the omission of anything from, or the making of any other kind of modification of, such information;

(d)   securing that a credit information agency which holds such information—

(i)   stops holding the information, or

(ii)   does not provide it to any other person.

(4)   Steps taken by a credit information agency in relation to information held by that agency are not steps specified in paragraph (3).

(5)   Paragraphs (1) and (2) do not apply to an activity of the kind specified by article 36H (operating an electronic system in relation to lending).

(6)   "Credit information agency" means a person who carries on by way of business an activity of the kind specified by any of the following—

(a)   article 36A (credit broking);

(b)   article 39D (debt adjusting);

(c)   article 39E (debt-counselling);

(d)   article 39F (debt-collecting);

(e)   article 39G (debt administration);

(f)   article 60B (regulated credit agreements) disregarding the effect of article 60F;

(g)   article 60N (regulated consumer hire agreements) disregarding the effect of article 60P;

(h)   article 89B (providing credit references).

89B.   Providing credit references

(1)   Furnishing of persons with information relevant to the financial standing of individuals or relevant recipients of credit is a specified kind of activity if the person has collected the information for that purpose.

(2)   There are excluded from paragraph (1) activities carried on in the course of a business which does not primarily consist of activities of the kind specified by paragraph (1).

(3)   Paragraph (1) does not apply to an activity of the kind specified by article 36H (operating an electronic system in relation to lending).

89BA.   Operating a pensions dashboard service

(1)   Operating a pensions dashboard service which connects to the Money and Pensions Service dashboards digital architecture is a specified kind of activity.

(2)   This article does not apply to the Money and Pensions Service.

(3)   In this Order—

"connect to the Money and Pensions Service dashboards digital architecture" means connect to the information technology systems delivered by or on behalf of the Money and Pensions Service that enable the interconnected system comprised of the following elements to work—

(a)   the Money and Pensions Service dashboards digital architecture,

(b)   the pensions dashboard services that connect to the Money and Pensions Service dashboards digital architecture,

(c)   the interfaces of pension schemes that connect to the Money and Pensions Service dashboards digital architecture,

(d)   the interfaces of pension schemes that connect to pensions dashboard services, and

(e)   any other party or service that needs to be connected in order for the system to work;

"pensions dashboard service" has the same meaning as in section 238A(1) of the Pensions Act 2004.

Exclusions

89C.   Activities carried on by members of the legal profession etc

(1)   There are excluded from articles 89A and 89B activities carried on by—

(a)   a barrister or advocate acting in that capacity;

(b)   a solicitor (within the meaning of the Solicitors Act 1974) in the course of providing advocacy services or litigation services;

(c)   a solicitor (within the meaning of the Solicitors (Scotland) Act 1980) in the course of providing advocacy services or litigation services;

(d)   a solicitor (within the meaning of the Solicitors (Northern Ireland) Order 1976) in the course of providing advocacy services or litigation services;

     (e)   a relevant person (other than a person falling within sub-paragraph (a) to (d)) in the course of providing advocacy services or litigation services.

(2)   In paragraph (1)—

"advocacy services" means any services which it would be reasonable to expect a person who is exercising, or contemplating exercising, a right of audience in relation to any proceedings, or contemplated proceedings, to provide for the purpose of those proceedings or contemplated proceedings;

"litigation services" means any services which it would be reasonable to expect a person who is exercising, or contemplating exercising, a right to conduct litigation in relation to any proceedings, or contemplated proceedings, to provide for the purpose of those proceedings or contemplated proceedings;

"relevant person" means a person who, for the purposes of the Legal Services Act 2007, is an authorised person in relation to an activity which constitutes the exercise of a right of audience or the conduct of litigation (within the meaning of that Act).

89D.   Other exclusions

(1)   ...

(2)   Article 89A is ... subject to the exclusions in articles 72G (local authorities) and 72H (insolvency practitioners).

Supplemental

89E.   Meaning of "consumer" etc

(1)   For the purposes of sections 1G, 404E and 425A of the Act (meaning of "consumer")—

    (a)   an individual or a relevant recipient of credit who is, may be, has been or may have been the subject of the information referred to in article 89A, and

    (b)   an individual or a relevant recipient of credit who is, may be, has been or may have been the subject of information furnished in the course of a person carrying on an activity of the kind specified by article 89B, or article 64 (agreeing to carry on specified kinds of activity) in so far as that article relates to article 89B,

is to be treated as a "consumer".

(2)   For the purposes of section 328(8) of the Act (meaning of "clients")—

    (a)   an individual or a relevant recipient of credit who is, may be, has been or may have been the subject of the information referred to in article 89A, and

    (b)   an individual or a relevant recipient of credit who is, may be, has been or may have been the subject of information furnished in the course of a person carrying on an activity of the kind specified by article 89B, or article 64 (agreeing to carry on specified kinds of activity) in so far as that article relates to article 89B,

is to be treated as a "client".

PART 3B
CLAIMS MANAGEMENT ACTIVITIES IN GREAT BRITAIN

The activities

89F.   Specified kinds of claims management activity

(1)   A claims management activity is a specified kind of activity when it is an activity specified in any of articles 89G to 89M.

(2)   For the purposes of this Part—

    (a)   "claimant" includes, in civil proceedings in Scotland, a pursuer;

    (b)   "defendant" includes, in civil proceedings in Scotland, a defender;

    (c)   "personal injury claim" means a claim for personal injury within the meaning of the Civil Procedure Rules 1998 in England and Wales and an action for damages for, or arising from, personal injuries within the meaning set out in section 8(7) of the Civil Litigation (Expenses and Group Proceedings) (Scotland) Act 2018 in Scotland;

(d) "financial services or financial product claim" includes a claim made under section 75 of the Consumer Credit Act 1974;

(e) "housing disrepair claim" means a claim under section 11 of the Landlord and Tenant Act 1985 or section 4 of the Defective Premises Act 1972 in England and Wales or an application in respect of the repairing standard under section 22 of the Housing (Scotland) Act 2006, or claims in relation to the disrepair of premises under a term of a tenancy agreement or lease or under the common law relating to nuisance or negligence, but does not include claims for statutory nuisance under section 82 of the Environmental Protection Act 1990;

(f) "a claim for a specified benefit" means a claim for one of the following benefits—

    (i) industrial injuries benefit, within the meaning given by section 94 of the Social Security Contributions and Benefits Act 1992;

    (ii) any supplement or additional allowance, or increase of benefit or allowance to which a recipient of an industrial injuries benefit may be entitled under that Act or any other Act;

    (iii) a benefit under a scheme referred to in paragraph 2 or 4 of Schedule 8 to that Act; or

    (iv) a benefit under the Pneumoconiosis etc (Workers' Compensation) Act 1979.

(g) "criminal injury claim" means a claim under the Criminal Injuries Compensation Scheme established under the Criminal Injuries Compensation Act 1995;

(h) "employment related claim" includes a claim in relation to wages and salaries and other employment related payments and claims in relation to wrongful or unfair dismissal, redundancy, discrimination and harassment;

(i) "investigating" means carrying out an investigation into, or commissioning the investigation of, the circumstances, merits or foundation of a claim; and

(j) "representing" means representation in writing or orally, regardless of the tribunal, body or person before which or to whom the representation is made.

(3) A person is to be treated as carrying on a regulated claims management activity in Great Britain when the activity is carried on—

(a) by a person who is—

    (i) an individual who is ordinarily resident in Great Britain; or

    (ii) a person, other than an individual, who is constituted under the law of England and Wales or Scotland; or

(b) in respect of a claimant or potential claimant who is—

    (i) an individual who is ordinarily resident in Great Britain; or

    (ii) a person, other than an individual, who is constituted under the law of England and Wales or Scotland.

(4) For the purposes of this article—

(a) a person is "ordinarily resident" in Great Britain if that person satisfies the requirements of the Statutory Residence Test as set out in Schedule 45 to the Finance Act 2013 either—

    (i) at the time of the facts giving rise to the claim or potential claim; or

    (ii) at the time when the regulated claims management activity is carried out in respect of that claimant or potential claimant;

(b) the references to the "UK" in the Statutory Residence Test in Schedule 45 are to be read as if they were expressed as references to "Great Britain".

89G.   Seeking out, referrals and identification of claims or potential claims

(1) Each of the following is a specified kind of activity when carried on in relation to a claim of a kind specified in paragraph (2)—

(a) seeking out persons who may have a claim, unless that activity constitutes the communication of an invitation or inducement to engagement in claims management activity within the meaning of section 21 (restrictions on financial promotion) of the Act;

(b) referring details of—

    (i) a claim or potential claim; or

           (ii)   a claimant or potential claimant

        to another person (including to a person having the right to conduct litigation); and

    (c)   identifying—

           (i)   a claim or potential claim; or

           (ii)   a claimant or potential claimant.

(2)   The kinds of claim are—

    (a)   a personal injury claim;

    (b)   a financial services or financial product claim;

    (c)   a housing disrepair claim;

    (d)   a claim for a specified benefit;

    (e)   a criminal injury claim; and

    (f)   an employment related claim.

89H.   **Advice, investigation or representation in relation to a personal injury claim**

Each of the following activities is a specified kind of activity when carried on in relation to a personal injury claim—

    (a)   advising a claimant or potential claimant;

    (b)   investigating a claim; and

    (c)   representing a claimant.

89I.   **Advice, investigation or representation in relation to a financial services or financial product claim**

Each of the following activities is a specified kind of activity when carried on in relation to a financial services or financial product claim—

    (a)   advising a claimant or potential claimant;

    (b)   investigating a claim; and

    (c)   representing a claimant.

89J.   **Advice, investigation or representation in relation to a housing disrepair claim**

Each of the following activities is a specified kind of activity when carried on in relation to a housing disrepair claim—

    (a)   advising a claimant or potential claimant;

    (b)   investigating a claim; and

    (c)   representing a claimant.

89K.   **Advice, investigation or representation in relation to a claim for a specified benefit**

Each of the following activities is a specified kind of activity when carried on in relation to a claim for a specified benefit—

    (a)   advising a claimant or potential claimant;

    (b)   investigating a claim; and

    (c)   representing a claimant.

89L.   **Advice, investigation or representation in relation to a criminal injury claim**

Each of the following activities is a specified kind of activity when carried on in relation to a criminal injury claim—

    (a)   advising a claimant or potential claimant;

    (b)   investigating a claim; and

    (c)   representing a claimant.

89M.   **Advice, investigation or representation in relation to an employment related claim**

Each of the following activities is a specified kind of activity when carried on in relation to an employment related claim—

    (a)   advising a claimant or potential claimant;

    (b)   investigating a claim; and

    (c)   representing a claimant.

Exclusions

89N.   Claims management activity conducted by legal professionals

(1)   There is excluded from articles 89G to 89M any activity which is carried on in England and Wales by—

(a)   a legal practitioner;

(b)   a firm, organisation or body corporate that carries on the claims management activity through a legal practitioner; or

(c)   an individual who carries on the claims management activity at the direction of, and under the supervision of, a legal practitioner who is—

(i)   that individual's employer or fellow employee; or

(ii)   a director of a company, or a member of a limited liability partnership, that provides the service and is that individual's employer.

(2)   For the purposes of paragraph (1) "legal practitioner" means—

(a)   a solicitor or barrister of any part of England and Wales or Northern Ireland;

(b)   a Fellow of the Chartered Institute of Legal Executives;

(c)   a European lawyer, as defined in the European Communities (Services of Lawyers) Order 1978 or the European Communities (Lawyer's Practice) Regulations 2000;

(d)   a registered foreign lawyer, as defined in section 89(9) of the Courts and Legal Services Act 1990;

(e)   any other member of a legal profession, of a jurisdiction other than England and Wales, that is recognised by the Law Society of England and Wales or the General Council of the Bar as a regulated legal profession.

(3)   There is excluded from articles 89G to 89M any activity which is carried on in Scotland by—

(a)   a legal practitioner;

(b)   a firm, organisation or body corporate that carries on the claims management activity through or under the supervision of a legal practitioner where that firm, organisation or body corporate is—

(i)   a firm of solicitors;

(ii)   an incorporated practice; or

(iii)   a licensed legal services provider and the activity is a legal service as defined within section 3 of the Legal Services (Scotland) Act 2010.

(4)   For the purposes of paragraph (3) "legal practitioner" means—

(a)   a person who is qualified to practise as a solicitor under section 4 of the Solicitors (Scotland) Act 1980;

(b)   an advocate who is a member of the Faculty of Advocates;

(c)   a European lawyer as defined in the European Communities (Services of Lawyers) Order 1978 or the European Communities (Lawyer's Practice) (Scotland) Regulations 2000; or

(d)   a registered foreign lawyer within the meaning of section 65 of the Solicitors (Scotland) Act 1980.

(5)   But an activity mentioned in paragraph (1) or (3) is only excluded from articles 89G to 89M if the legal practitioner concerned carries on the claims management activity in the ordinary course of legal practice pursuant to the professional rules to which that legal practitioner is subject.

(6)   The exclusions in this article are to be read as if they were expressed as exemptions for the purposes of the following provisions of the Financial Guidance and Claims Act 2018—

(a)   section 32(5)(b) (PPI claims: interim restriction on charges imposed by legal practitioners after transfer of regulation to the FCA); and

(b)   section 33(11) (legal services regulators' rules: charges for claims management services).

...

89V.   Certain providers of referrals

(1)   There is excluded from article 89G the activity of referring details of a potential claim or potential claimant to another person if—

(a)   the person who refers those details ("the introducer") carries on no other regulated claims management activity;

(b)   the activity is incidental to the introducer's main business;

(c)   the details are only referred to authorised persons, legal practitioners, or a firm, organisation or body corporate that provides the service through legal practitioners;

(d)   of the claims that the introducer refers to such persons, that introducer is paid, in money or money's worth, for no more than 25 claims per calendar quarter; and

(e)   the introducer, in obtaining and referring those details, has complied with the provisions of the Data Protection Act 2018, the Privacy and Electronic Communications (EC Directive) Regulations 2003, the General Data Protection Regulation (EU) of the European Parliament and of the Council 2016/679 and the Consumer Protection from Unfair Trading Regulations 2008.

(2)   Paragraph (1)(e) does not apply in the case of a referral to a legal practitioner or firm, organisation or body corporate that carries on the activity through legal practitioners.

(3)   In this article "legal practitioner" has the meaning given by article 89N(2) or (4).

89W.   Services in connection with counterclaims and claims against third parties

There is excluded from articles 89G to 89M any activity carried on in circumstances where—

(a)   a claim has been made by a person ("the claimant") against another person ("the defendant"); and

(b)   the activity being carried on consists of the provision of a service to the defendant in connection with—

(i)   the making of a counterclaim against the claimant arising out of the same set of facts as the claim referred to in sub-paragraph (a); or

(ii)   the making of a claim against a third party (whether for contribution, as a subrogated claim, or otherwise) which is incidental to, or consequent on, the claim referred to in sub-paragraph (a).

PART IV
CONSEQUENTIAL PROVISIONS

Regulated mortgage contracts: consequential provisions

90, 91. ...

...

SCHEDULE 2
FINANCIAL INSTRUMENTS AND INVESTMENT SERVICES AND ACTIVITIES

Article 3(1)

PART 1

...

Financial Instruments

1.   Transferable securities;

2.   Money-market instruments;

3.   Units in collective investment undertakings;

4.   Options, futures, swaps, forward rate agreements and any other derivative contracts relating to securities, currencies, interest rates or yields, emission allowances or other derivatives instruments, financial indices or financial measures which may be settled physically or in cash;

5.   Options, futures, swaps, forwards and any other derivative contracts relating to commodities that must be settled in cash or may be settled in cash at the option of one of the parties (other than by reason of a default or other termination event);

6.   Options, futures, swaps, and any other derivative contract relating to commodities that can be physically settled provided that they are traded on a UK regulated market, a UK MTF or a UK OTF (as defined by Article 2(1)(13A), (14A) and (15A) respectively of the markets in financial instruments regulation), except for wholesale energy products traded on a UK OTF that must be physically settled;

7.   Option, futures, swaps, forwards and any other derivative contracts relating to commodities, that can be physically settled not otherwise mentioned in point 6 of this Section and not being for commercial purposes or wholesale energy products traded on an EU OTF (as defined by Article 2(1)(15B) of the markets in financial instruments regulation) that must be physically settled, which have the characteristics of other derivative financial instruments;

8.   Derivative instruments for the transfer of credit risk;

9.   Financial contracts for differences;

10. Options, futures, swaps, forward rate agreements and any other derivative contracts relating to climatic variables, freight rates or inflation rates or other official economic statistics that must be settled in cash or may be settled in cash at the option of one of the parties other than by reason of default or other termination event, as well as any other derivative contracts relating to assets, rights, obligations, indices and measures not otherwise mentioned in this Section, which have the characteristics of other derivative financial instruments, having regard to whether, inter alia, they are traded on a UK regulated market, a UK OTF, or a UK MTF (as defined by Article 2(1)(13A), (15A) and (14A) respectively of the markets in financial instruments regulation);

11. Emission allowances consisting of any units recognised for compliance with the requirements of Directive 2003/87/EC (Emissions Trading Scheme) or allowances created under article 18 of the trading scheme order.

...

SCHEDULE 3
EXEMPTIONS FROM THE DEFINITION OF "INVESTMENT FIRM"

Article 3(1)

PART 1
ARTICLE 2 OF THE MARKETS IN FINANCIAL INSTRUMENTS DIRECTIVE

1.   The following persons are excluded from the definition of "investment firm"—

(a)   the society incorporated by Lloyd's Act 1871 known by the name of Lloyd's;

(b)   an authorised person with a Part 4A permission to carry on the regulated activity of—

(i)   effecting or carrying out contracts of insurance under article 10;

      (ii)   insurance risk transformation under article 13A;

      (iii)   managing the underwriting capacity of a Lloyd's syndicate under article 57,

when carrying on those activities (and any other activities permitted by rules made by the FCA or the PRA under the Act);

(ba)   a person which is a third country insurance or reinsurance undertaking (as defined by regulation 2(1) of the Solvency 2 Regulations 2015, as those regulations have been amended under the European Union (Withdrawal) Act 2018) where the undertaking is transferring risk to a transformer vehicle, provided that the assumption of risk by that vehicle is a specified kind of activity within Article 13A of this Order;

(c)   a person ("P") providing investment services exclusively for P's parent undertakings, for P's subsidiaries or for other subsidiaries of P's parent undertakings;

(d)   a person providing an investment service where that service is provided in an incidental manner in the course of a professional activity and that activity is regulated by legal or regulatory provisions or a code of ethics governing the profession which do not exclude the provision of that service;

(e)   a person dealing on own account in financial instruments other than commodity derivatives or emission allowances or derivatives thereof and not providing any other investment services or performing any other investment activities in financial instruments other than commodity derivatives or emission allowances or derivatives thereof unless such persons—

      (i)   are market makers;

      (ii)   are members of or participants in a regulated market or an MTF, on the one hand, or have direct electronic access to a trading venue, on the other hand, except for non-financial entities who execute transactions on a trading venue which are objectively measurable as reducing risks directly relating to the commercial activity or treasury financing activity of those non-financial entities or their groups;

      (iii)   apply a high-frequency algorithmic trading technique; or

      (iv)   deal on own account when executing client orders;

(f)   an operator (within the meaning of regulation 3(2) of the Greenhouse Gas Emissions Trading Scheme Regulations 2012), subject to compliance obligations under those Regulations who, when dealing in emission allowances, does not execute client orders and does not provide any investment services or perform any investment activities other than dealing on own account, provided that the operator does not apply a high-frequency algorithmic trading technique;

(g)   a person providing investment services consisting exclusively in the administration of employee-participation schemes;

(h)   a person ("P") providing investment services which only involve both the administration of employee-participation schemes and the provision of investment services exclusively for P's parent undertakings, for P's subsidiaries or for other subsidiaries of P's parent undertakings;

(i)   the Treasury, the Bank of England and other public bodies charged with or intervening in the management of the public debt in the United Kingdom or members of the European System of Central Banks;

(j)   a collective investment undertaking, pension fund or a depositary or manager of such an under-taking or fund;

(k)   a person ("P")—

      (i)   dealing on own account, including a market maker, in commodity derivatives or emission allowances or derivatives thereof, excluding a person who deals on own account when executing client orders; or

      (ii)   providing investment services, other than dealing on own account, in commodity derivatives or emission allowances or derivatives thereof to the customers or suppliers of P's main business, provided that in each case the activity in (i) or (ii), considered both individually and on an aggregate basis, is an ancillary activity to P's main business, when considered on a group basis, and where paragraph 2 applies;

(l) a person who provides investment advice in the course of providing another professional activity which is not an investment service or activity provided that the provision of such advice is not specifically remunerated;

(m) associations set up by Danish and Finnish pension funds with the sole aim of managing the assets of pension funds that are members of those associations;

(n) agenti di cambio whose activities and functions are governed by Article 201 of Italian Legislative Decree No 58 of 24 February 1998;

(o) subject to paragraph 3, transmission system operators within the meaning of Article 2(4) of Directive 2009/72/EC and Article 2(4) of Directive 2009/73/EC when carrying out their tasks under the law of the United Kingdom or part of the United Kingdom relied on by the United Kingdom immediately before IP completion day to implement Directive 2009/72/EC or 2009/73/EC, under Regulation (EC) No 714/2009, under Regulation (EC) No 715/2009 or under network codes or guidelines adopted pursuant to those Regulations, any persons acting as service providers on their behalf to carry out their task under those legislative acts or under network codes or guidelines adopted pursuant to those Regulations, and any operator or administrator of an energy balancing mechanism, pipeline network or system to keep in balance the supplies and uses of energy when carrying out such tasks;

(p) central securities depositories as defined in point (1) of Article 2(1) of Regulation (EU) 909/2014 on the European Parliament and of the Council on improving securities settlement in the European Union and on central securities depositories, except as provided for in Article 73 of that Regulation.

2. This paragraph applies if—

(a) P's main business is not—

(i) the provision of investment services;

(ii) banking activities requiring permission under Part 4A of the Act (or banking activities which would require such permission if they were carried on in the United Kingdom); or

(iii) acting as a market-maker in relation to commodity derivatives;

(b) P does not apply a high-frequency algorithmic trading technique; and

(c) P notifies the FCA under regulation 47 of the Financial Services and Markets Act 2000 (Markets in Financial Instruments) Regulations 2017 that P makes use of this exemption and re-ports to the FCA, upon request, the basis on which P considers that P's activity under points (i) and (ii) is ancillary to P's main business.

3. The exemption in paragraph 1(p)—

(a) only applies to the persons engaged in the activities set out in that sub-paragraph where they perform investment activities or provide investment services relating to commodity derivatives in order to carry out those activities;

(b) does not apply with regard to the operation of a secondary market, including a platform for secondary trading in financial transmission rights.

4. References in this Schedule to "regulated markets", "MTFs" and "trading venues" are to "UK regulated markets", "UK MTFs" and "UK trading venues" within the meaning of Article 2(1)(13A), (14A) and (16A) respectively of the markets in financial instruments regulation.

5. Any expression used in this Part of this Schedule which is used in the markets in financial instruments regulation (as amended by the Markets in Financial Instruments (Amendment) (EU Exit) Regulations 2018) has the same meaning as in the regulation.

Note. This Schedule is amended by S.I. 2023/548, art. 2(1), (5), as from 1 January 2025.

PART 2
PROVISION OF INVESTMENT SERVICE IN AN INCIDENTAL MANNER

6.   For the purpose of the exemption in paragraph 1(d), an investment service shall be deemed to be
         provided in an incidental manner in the course of a professional activity where the following
         conditions are satisfied—

   (a)   a close and factual connection exists between the professional activity and the provision of
         the investment service to the same client, such that the investment service can be regarded
         as accessory to the main professional activity;

   (b)   the provision of investment services to the clients of the main professional activity does not
         aim to provide a systematic source of income to the person providing the professional
         activity; and

   (c)   the persons providing the professional activity do not market or otherwise promote their
         ability to provide investment services, except where these are disclosed to clients as being
         accessory to the main professional activity.

...

Financial Services and Markets Act 2000 (Professions) (Non-Exempt Activities) Order 2001

S.I. 2001/1227

1.   Citation and Commencement

(1)   This Order may be cited as the Financial Services and Markets Act 2000 (Professions) (Non-Exempt Activities) Order 2001.

(2)   Subject to paragraph (3), this Order comes into force on the day on which section 19 of the Act comes into force.

(3)   This Order comes into force—

(a)   for the purposes of article 4(g), on 1st January 2002; and

(b)   for the purposes of article 6A, on such a day as the Treasury may specify.

(4)   Any day specified under paragraph (3)(b) must be caused to be notified in the London, Edinburgh and Belfast Gazettes published not later than one week before that day.

2.   Interpretation

(1)   In this Order—

"the Act" means the Financial Services and Markets Act 2000;

"agreement provider" has the meaning given by paragraph (3) of article 63J of the Regulated Activities Order, read with paragraphs (6) and (7) of that article;

"agreement seller" has the meaning given by article 63J(3) of the Regulated Activities Order;

"home purchase provider" has the meaning given by article 63F(3) of the Regulated Activities Order;

"home purchaser" has the meaning given by article 63F(3) of the Regulated Activities Order;

"contract of insurance" has the meaning given by article 3(1) of the Regulated Activities Order;

"contractually based investment" has the meaning given by article 3(1) of the Regulated Activities Order;

"occupational pension scheme" and "personal pension scheme" have the meaning given by section 1 of the Pension Schemes Act 1993;

"plan provider" has the meaning given by paragraph (3) of article 63B of the Regulated Activities Order, read with paragraphs (7) and (8) of that article;

"record of insurance intermediaries" means the record maintained by the FCA under section 347 of the Act (the public record) by virtue of article 93 of the Regulated Activities Order (recorded insurance intermediaries);

"the Regulated Activities Order" means the Financial Services and Markets Act 2000 (Regulated Activities) Order 2001;

"regulated home purchase plan" has the meaning given by article 63F(3) of the Regulated Activities Order;

"regulated home reversion plan" has the meaning given by article 63B(3) of the Regulated Activities Order;

"regulated mortgage contract" has the meaning given by article 61 of the Regulated Activities Order;

"regulated sale and rent back agreement" has the meaning given by article 63J(3) of the Regulated Activities Order;

"relevant investment" has the meaning given by article 3(1) of the Regulated Activities Order;

"reversion seller" has the meaning given by article 63B(3) of the Regulated Activities Order;

"security" has the meaning given by article 3(1) of the Regulated Activities Order;

"structured deposit" has the meaning given by article 3(1) of the Regulated Activities Order;

"syndicate" has the meaning given by article 3(1) of the Regulated Activities Order.

(2)   For the purposes of this Order, a person is a member of a personal pension scheme if he is a person to or in respect of whom benefits are or may become payable under the scheme.

3.   Activities to which exemption from the general prohibition does not apply

The activities in articles 4 to 8 are specified for the purposes of section 327(6) of the Act.

4.

An activity of the kind specified by any of the following provisions of the Regulated Activities Order—

(a)   article 5 (accepting deposits);

(aa)   article 9B (issuing electronic money);

(b)   article 10 (effecting and carrying out contracts of insurance);

(c)   article 14 (dealing in investments as principal);

(ca)   article 24A (bidding in emissions auctions);

(da)   article 51ZA (managing a UCITS);

(db)   article 51ZB (acting as a trustee or depositary of a UCITS);

(dc)   article 51ZC (managing an AIF);

(dd)   article 51ZD (acting as a trustee or depositary of an AIF);

(de)   article 51ZE (establishing etc a collective investment scheme);

(e)   article 52 (establishing etc. a ... pension scheme);

(ea)   article 52B (providing basic advice on stakeholder products);

(f)   article 57 (managing the underwriting capacity of a Lloyd's syndicate);

(g)   article 59 (funeral plan contracts);

(h)   ...

(i)   article 63S (administering a benchmark).

4A.

An activity of the kind specified by article 21 or 25 of the Regulated Activities Order (dealing in investments as agent or arranging deals in investments) in so far as it—

(a)   relates to a transaction for the sale or purchase of rights under a contract of insurance; and

(b)   is carried on by a person who is not included in the record of insurance intermediaries.

5.

(1)   An activity of the kind specified by article 37 of the Regulated Activities Order (managing investments) in so far as it consists of buying or subscribing for a security, contractually based investment or structured deposit.

(2)   Paragraph (1) does not apply—

(a)   if all routine or day to day decisions, so far as relating to that activity, are taken by an authorised person with permission to carry on that activity or by a person who is an exempt person in relation to such an activity; or

(b)   to an activity undertaken in accordance with the advice of an authorised person with permission to give advice in relation to such an activity or a person who is an exempt person in relation to the giving of such advice.

5A.

An activity of the kind specified by article 39A of the Regulated Activities Order (assisting in the administration and performance of a contract of insurance) if it is carried on by a person who is not included in the record of insurance intermediaries.

6.

(1)   An activity of the kind specified by article 53 of the Regulated Activities Order (advising on investments) where the advice in question falls within paragraph (2), (3) or (5).

(2)   Subject to paragraph (4), advice falls within this paragraph in so far as—

   (a)   it is given to an individual (or his agent) other than where the individual acts—

      (i)   in connection with the carrying on of a business of any kind by himself or by an undertaking of which he is, or would become as a result of the transaction to which the advice relates, a controller; or

      (ii)   in his capacity as a trustee of an occupational pension scheme;

   (b)   it consists of a recommendation to buy or subscribe for a particular security, contractually based investment or structured deposit; and

   (c)   the transaction to which the advice relates would be made—

      (i)   with a person acting in the course of carrying on the business of buying, selling, subscribing for or underwriting the security, contractually based investment or structured deposit, whether as principal or agent;

      (ii)   on an investment exchange or any other market to which that investment is admitted for dealing; or

      (iii)   in response to an invitation to subscribe for such an investment which is, or is to be, admitted for dealing on an investment exchange or any other market.

(3)   Subject to paragraph (4), advice falls within this paragraph in so far as it consists of a recommendation to a member of a personal pension scheme (or his agent) to dispose of any rights or interests which the member has in or under the scheme.

(4)   Advice does not fall within paragraph (2) or (3) if it endorses a corresponding recommendation given to the individual (or, as the case may be, the member) by an authorised person with permission to give advice in relation to the proposed transaction or a person who is an exempt person in relation to the giving of such advice.

(5)   Advice falls within this paragraph in so far as—

   (a)   it relates to a transaction for the sale or purchase of rights under a contract of insurance; and

   (b)   it is given by a person who is not included in the record of insurance intermediaries.

6A.

(1)   An activity of the kind specified by article 53A of the Regulated Activities Order (advising on regulated mortgage contracts) where the advice in question falls within paragraph (2).

(2)   Subject to paragraph (3), advice falls within this paragraph in so far as—

   (a)   it consists of a recommendation, given to an individual, to enter as borrower into a regulated mortgage contract with a particular person; and

   (b)   in entering into a regulated mortgage contract that person would be carrying on an activity of the kind specified by article 61(1) of the Regulated Activities Order (regulated mortgage contracts).

(3)   Advice does not fall within paragraph (2) if it endorses a corresponding recommendation given to the individual by an authorised person with permission to carry on an activity of the kind specified by article 53A of the Regulated Activities Order or a person who is an exempt person in relation to an activity of that kind.

6B.

(1)   An activity of the kind specified by article 61(1) or (2) of the Regulated Activities Order (regulated mortgage contracts).

(2)   Paragraph (1) does not apply to an activity carried on by a person in his capacity as a trustee or personal representative where the borrower under the regulated mortgage contract in question is a beneficiary under the trust, will or intestacy.

6C.

(1)   An activity of the kind specified by article 53B of the Regulated Activities Order (advising on regulated home reversion plans) where the advice in question falls within paragraph (2).

(2)   Subject to paragraph (3), advice falls within this paragraph in so far as—

    (a)   it consists of a recommendation, given to an individual to enter as reversion seller or plan provider into a regulated home reversion plan with a particular person; and

    (b)   in entering into a regulated home reversion plan that person would be carrying on an activity of the kind specified by article 63B(1) of the Regulated Activities Order (regulated home reversion plans).

(3)   Advice does not fall within paragraph (2) if it endorses a corresponding recommendation given to the individual by an authorised person with permission to carry on an activity of the kind specified by article 53B of the Regulated Activities Order or a person who is an exempt person in relation to an activity of that kind.

6D.

(1)   An activity of the kind specified by article 63B(1) or (2) of the Regulated Activities Order (regulated home reversion plans).

(2)   Paragraph (1) does not apply to an activity carried on by a person in his capacity as a trustee or personal representative where the reversion seller under the regulated home reversion plan in question is a beneficiary under the trust, will or intestacy.

6E.

(1)   An activity of the kind specified by article 53C of the Regulated Activities Order (advising on regulated home purchase plans) where the advice in question falls within paragraph (2).

(2)   Subject to paragraph (3), advice falls within this paragraph in so far as—

    (a)   it consists of a recommendation, given to an individual to enter as home purchaser into a regulated home purchase plan with a particular person; and

    (b)   in entering into a regulated home purchase plan that person would be carrying on an activity of the kind specified by article 63F(1) of the Regulated Activities Order (regulated home purchase plans).

(3)   Advice does not fall within paragraph (2) if it endorses a corresponding recommendation given to the individual by an authorised person with permission to carry on an activity of the kind specified by article 53C of the Regulated Activities Order or a person who is an exempt person in relation to an activity of that kind.

6F.

(1)   An activity of the kind specified by article 63F(1) or (2) of the Regulated Activities Order (regulated home purchase plans).

(2)   Paragraph (1) does not apply to an activity carried on by a person in his capacity as a trustee or personal representative where the home purchaser under the regulated home purchase plan in question is a beneficiary under the trust, will or intestacy.

6G.

(1)   An activity of the kind specified by article 53D of the Regulated Activities Order (advising on regulated sale and rent back agreements) where the advice in question falls within paragraph (2).

(2)   Subject to paragraph (3), advice falls within this paragraph in so far as—

    (a)   it consists of a recommendation, given to an individual to enter as agreement seller or agreement provider into a regulated sale and rent back agreement with a particular person; and

    (b)   in entering into a regulated sale and rent back agreement that person would be carrying on an activity of the kind specified by article 63J(1) of the Regulated Activities Order (regulated sale and rent back agreements).

(3)   Advice does not fall within paragraph (2) if it endorses a corresponding recommendation given to the individual by an authorised person with permission to carry on an activity of the kind

specified by article 53D of the Regulated Activities Order or a person who is an exempt person in relation to an activity of that kind.

6H.

(1)   An activity of the kind specified by article 63J(or (2) of the Regulated Activities Order (regulated sale and rent back agreements).
An activity of the kind specified by article 63J(1) or (2) of the Regulated Activities Order (regulated sale and rent back agreements).

(2)   Paragraph (1) does not apply to an activity carried on by a person in his capacity as a trustee or personal representative where the agreement seller under the regulated sale and rent back agreement in question is a beneficiary under the trust, will or intestacy.

7.

(1)   Advising a person to become a member of a particular Lloyd's syndicate.

(2)   Paragraph (1) does not apply to advice which endorses that of an authorised person with permission to give such advice or a person who is an exempt person in relation to the giving of such advice.

8.

Agreeing to carry on any of the activities mentioned in articles 4 to 7 other than the activities mentioned in article 4(a), (aa), (b), (da) to (de) and (e).

Financial Services and Markets Act 2000 (Financial Promotion) Order 2005

S.I. 2005/1529

PART I

Citation, Commencement and Interpretation

1.   Citation and commencement

This Order may be cited as the Financial Services and Markets Act 2000 (Financial Promotion) Order 2005 and comes into force on 1st July 2005.

2.   Interpretation: general

(1)   In this Order, except where the context otherwise requires—

…

"the 2006 Act" means the Companies Act 2006;

"the Act" means the Financial Services and Markets Act 2000;

"close relative" in relation to a person means—

(a)   his spouse or civil partner;

(b)   his children and step-children, his parents and step-parents, his brothers and sisters and his step-brothers and step-sisters; and

(c)   the spouse or civil partner of any person within sub-paragraph (b);

"controlled claims management activity" has the meaning given in article 4(3);

"controlled activity" has the meaning given by article 4 and Schedule 1;

"controlled investment" has the meaning given by article 4 and Schedule 1;

"deposit" means a sum of money which is a deposit for the purposes of article 5 of the Regulated Activities Order;

"direct financial benefit" includes any commission, discount, remuneration or reduction in premium;

"equity share capital" has the meaning given in the 2006 Act (see section 548);

"financial promotion restriction" has the meaning given by article 5;

"Full name", in relation to a person, means the name under which that person carries on business and, if different, that person's corporate name;

"government" means the government of the United Kingdom, the Scottish Administration, the Executive Committee of the Northern Ireland Assembly, the National Assembly for Wales and any government of any country or territory outside the United Kingdom;

"information society service" is to be read in accordance with the definition of "information society services" in regulation 2 of the Electronic Commerce (EC Directive) Regulations 2002;

"instrument" includes any record whether or not in the form of a document;

"international organisation" means any body the members of which comprise—

(a)   states including the United Kingdom …; or

(b)   bodies whose members comprise states including the United Kingdom …;

"overseas communicator" has the meaning given by article 30;

"previously overseas customer" has the meaning given by article 31;

"publication" means—

(a)   a newspaper, journal, magazine or other periodical publication;

(b)   a web site or similar system for the electronic display of information;

(c)   any programme forming part of a service consisting of the broadcast or transmission of television or radio programmes;

(d)   any teletext service, that — is to say a service consisting of television transmissions consisting of a succession of visual displays (with or without accompanying sound) capable of being selected and held for separate viewing or other use;

"qualifying contract of insurance" has the meaning given in the Regulated Activities Order;

"qualifying credit" has the meaning given by paragraph 10 of Schedule 1;

"qualifying cryptoasset" has the meaning given by paragraph 26F of Schedule 1;

"registered person" has the meaning given by article 73ZA;

"the Regulated Activities Order" means the Financial Services and Markets Act 2000 (Regulated Activities) Order 2001;

"relevant insurance activity" has the meaning given by article 21;

"relevant investment activities" has the meaning given by article 30;

"relevant UK market" means a market that meets the criteria specified in Part A1 of Schedule 3;

"solicited real time communication" has the meaning given by article 8;

"structured deposit" means a deposit which is fully repayable at maturity on terms under which interest or a premium will be paid or is at risk, according to a formula involving factors such as—

(a)   an index or combination of indices excluding variable rate deposits whose return is directly linked to an interest rate index such as Euribor or Libor;

(b)   a financial instrument or combination of financial instruments;

(c)   a commodity or combination of commodities or other physical or non-physical non-fungible assets; or

(d)   a foreign exchange rate or combination of foreign exchange rates;

"units", in a collective investment scheme, has the meaning given by Part XVII of the Act;

"unsolicited real time communication" has the meaning given by article 8.

(2)   References to a person engaging in investment activity are to be construed in accordance with subsection (8) of section 21 of the Act; and for these purposes, "controlled activity" and "controlled investment" in that subsection have the meaning given in this Order.

Note. This article is amended by S.I. 2024/105, reg. 47(b), Sch. 3, Pt. 2, paras. 27, 28, as from a day to be appointed (save for certain purposes).

3.   Interpretation: unlisted companies

(1)   In this Order, an "unlisted company" means a body corporate the shares in which are not—

(a)   listed or quoted on an investment exchange whether in the United Kingdom or elsewhere;

(b)   shares in respect of which information is, with the agreement or approval of any officer of the company, published for the purpose of facilitating deals in the shares indicating prices at which persons have dealt or are willing to deal in them other than persons who, at the time the information is published, are existing members of a relevant class; or

(c)   subject to a marketing arrangement which accords to the company the facilities referred to in section 693(3)(b) of the 2006 Act.

(2)   For the purpose of paragraph (1)(b), a person is to be regarded as a member of a relevant class if he was, at the relevant time—

(a)   an existing member or debenture holder of the company;

(b)   an existing employee of the company;

(c)   a close relative of such a member or employee; or

(d)   a trustee (acting in his capacity as such) of a trust, the principal beneficiary of which is a person within any of sub-paragraphs (a), (b) and (c).

(3)   In this Order references to shares in and debentures of an unlisted company are references to—

(a)   in the case of a body corporate which is a company within the meaning of the 2006 Act (see section 1), shares and debentures within the meaning of that Act (see sections 540(1) and (4) and 738);

(b)   ...

(c)   in the case of any other body corporate, investments falling within paragraph 14, 15 or 15A of Schedule 1 to this Order.

PART II

Controlled Activities and Controlled Investments

4.   **Definition of controlled activities, controlled claims management activities and controlled investments**

(1)   For the purposes of section 21(9) of the Act, a controlled activity is an activity which falls within any of paragraphs 1 to 11 of Schedule 1.

(2)   For the purposes of section 21(10) of the Act, a controlled investment is an investment which falls within any of paragraphs 12 to 27 of Schedule 1.

(3)   For the purposes of section 21(10B) of the Act, a controlled claims management activity is an activity carried on in Great Britain of a kind specified in paragraph 11A of Schedule 1.

PART III

Exemptions: Interpretation and Application

5.   **Interpretation: financial promotion restriction**

In this Order, any reference to the financial promotion restriction is a reference to the restriction in section 21(1) of the Act.

6.   **Interpretation: communications**

In this Order—

(a)   any reference to a communication is a reference to the communication, in the course of business, of an invitation or inducement to engage in investment activity;

(b)   any reference to a communication being made to another person is a reference to a communication being addressed, whether orally or in legible form, to a particular person or persons (for example where it is contained in a telephone call or letter);

(c)   any reference to a communication being directed at persons is a reference to a communication being addressed to persons generally (for example where it is contained in a television broadcast or web site);

(d)   "communicate" includes causing a communication to be made or directed;

(e)   a "recipient" of a communication is the person to whom the communication is made or, in the case of a non-real time communication which is directed at persons generally, any person who reads or hears the communication;

(f)   "electronic commerce communication" means a communication, the making of which constitutes the provision of an information society service;

(g), (h) …

7.   **Interpretation: real time communications**

(1)   In this Order, references to a real time communication are references to any communication made in the course of a personal visit, telephone conversation or other interactive dialogue.

(2)   A non-real time communication is a communication not falling within paragraph (1).

(3)   For the purposes of this Order, non-real time communications include communications made by letter or e-mail or contained in a publication.

(4)   For the purposes of this Order, the factors in paragraph (5) are to be treated as indications that a communication is a non-real time communication.

(5)   The factors are that—

(a)   the communication is made to or directed at more than one recipient in identical terms (save for details of the recipient's identity);

(b)   the communication is made or directed by way of a system which in the normal course constitutes or creates a record of the communication which is available to the recipient to refer to at a later time;

(c)   the communication is made or directed by way of a system which in the normal course does not enable or require the recipient to respond immediately to it.

8. Interpretation: solicited and unsolicited real time communications

(1)   A real time communication is solicited where it is made in the course of a personal visit, telephone call or other interactive dialogue if that call, visit or dialogue—

(a)   was initiated by the recipient of the communication; or

(b)   takes place in response to an express request from the recipient of the communication.

(2)   A real time communication is unsolicited where it is made otherwise than as described in paragraph (1).

(3)   For the purposes of paragraph (1)—

(a)   a person is not to be treated as expressly requesting a call, visit or dialogue—

(i)   because he omits to indicate that he does not wish to receive any or any further visits or calls or to engage in any or any further dialogue;

(ii)   because he agrees to standard terms that state that such visits, calls or dialogue will take place, unless he has signified clearly that, in addition to agreeing to the terms, he is willing for them to take place;

(b)   a communication is solicited only if it is clear from all the circumstances when the call, visit or dialogue is initiated or requested that during the course of the visit, call or dialogue communications will be made concerning the kind of controlled activities or investments or controlled claims management activities to which the communications in fact made relate;

(c)   it is immaterial whether the express request was made before or after this article comes into force.

(4)   Where a real time communication is solicited by a recipient ("R"), it is treated as having also been solicited by any other person to whom it is made at the same time as it is made to R if that other recipient is—

(a)   a close relative of R; or

(b)   expected to engage in any investment activity or any claims management activity jointly with R.

8A–11. ...

PART IV

Exempt Communications: All Controlled Activities

12–14. ...

15. Introductions

(1)   If the requirements of paragraph (2) are met, the financial promotion restriction does not apply to any communication which is made with a view to or for the purposes of introducing the recipient to—

(a)   an authorised person who carries on the controlled activity to which the communication relates; or

(b)   an exempt person where the communication relates to a controlled activity or controlled claims management activity which is also a regulated activity in relation to which he is an exempt person.

(1A)   But paragraph (1) does not apply to any communication made with a view to or for the purpose of an introduction to a person who carries on an activity of the kind specified by—

(a)   paragraph 4B of Schedule 1;

(b)   paragraph 4C of that Schedule;

(c)   paragraph 11 of that Schedule, to the extent that it relates to that paragraph 4B or that paragraph 4C;

(d)   paragraph 11A of that Schedule.

(2)   The requirements of this paragraph are that—

(a)   the maker of the communication ("A") is not a close relative of, nor a member of the same group as, the person to whom the introduction is, or is to be, made;

(b)   A does not receive from any person other than the recipient any pecuniary reward or other advantage arising out of his making the introduction; and

(c)   it is clear in all the circumstances that the recipient, in his capacity as an investor, is not seeking and has not sought advice from A as to the merits of the recipient engaging in investment activity (or, if the client has sought such advice, A has declined to give it, but has recommended that the recipient seek such advice from an authorised person).

16.   Exempt persons

(1)   The financial promotion restriction does not apply to any communication which—

(a)   is a non-real time communication or a solicited real time communication;

(b)   is made or directed by an exempt person; and

(c)   is for the purposes of that exempt person's business of carrying on a controlled activity or controlled claims management activity which is also a regulated activity in relation to which he is an exempt person.

(1A)   The financial promotion restriction also does not apply to any communication which is—

(a)   a non-real time communication or a solicited real time communication;

(b)   made by a person who is an appointed representative (within the meaning of section 39(2) of the Act) and is carrying on an activity to which sections 20(1) and (1A) and 23(1A) of the Act do not apply by virtue of section 39(1D); and

(c)   made for the purposes of that person's business of carrying on a controlled activity which is also a regulated activity to which sections 20(1) and (1A) and 23(1A) of the Act do not apply by virtue of section 39(1D).

(2)   The financial promotion restriction does not apply to any unsolicited real time communication made by a person ("AR") who is an appointed representative (within the meaning of section 39(2) of the Act) where—

(a)   the communication is made by AR in carrying on the business—

(i)   for which his principal ("P") has accepted responsibility for the purposes of section 39 of the Act; and

(ii)   in relation to which AR is exempt from the general prohibition by virtue of that section or in relation to which sections 20(1) and (1A) and 23(1A) of the Act do not apply by virtue of that section; and

(b)   the communication is one which, if it were made by P, would comply with any rules made by the FCA under section 137R of the Act (financial promotion rules) which are relevant to a communication of that kind.

17.   Generic promotions

The financial promotion restriction does not apply to any communication which—

(a)   does not identify (directly or indirectly) a person who provides the controlled investment to which the communication relates; …

(b)   does not identify (directly or indirectly) any person as a person who carries on a controlled activity in relation to that investment; and

(c)   does not identify (directly or indirectly) any person as a person who carries on a controlled claims management activity.

17A.   Communications caused to be made or directed by unauthorised persons

(1)   If a condition in paragraph (2) is met, the financial promotion restriction does not apply to a communication caused to be made or directed by an unauthorised person which is made or directed by an authorised person.

(2)   The conditions in this paragraph are that—

(a)   the authorised person prepared the content of the communication; or

(b)   it is a real-time communication.

18.   Mere conduits

(1)   Subject to paragraph (4), the financial promotion restriction does not apply to any communication which is made or directed by a person who acts as a mere conduit for it.

(2)   A person acts as a mere conduit for a communication if—

(a)   he communicates it in the course of an activity carried on by him, the principal purpose of which is transmitting or receiving material provided to him by others;

(b)   the content of the communication is wholly devised by another person; and

(c)   the nature of the service provided by him in relation to the communication is such that he does not select, modify or otherwise exercise control over its content prior to its transmission or receipt.

(3)   For the purposes of paragraph (2)(c) a person does not select, modify or otherwise exercise control over the content of a communication merely by removing or having the power to remove material—

(a)   which is, or is alleged to be, illegal, defamatory or in breach of copyright;

(b)   in response to a request to a body which is empowered by or under any enactment to make such a request; or

(c)   when otherwise required to do so by law.

(4)   Nothing in paragraph (1) prevents the application of the financial promotion restriction in so far as it relates to the person who has caused the communication to be made or directed.

(5)   This article does not apply to an electronic commerce communication.

18A.   ...

19.   Investment professionals

(1)   The financial promotion restriction does not apply to any communication which—

(a)   is made only to recipients whom the person making the communication believes on reasonable grounds to be investment professionals; or

(b)   may reasonably be regarded as directed only at such recipients.

(2)   For the purposes of paragraph (1)(b), if all the conditions set out in paragraph (4)(a) to (c) are met in relation to the communication, it is to be regarded as directed only at investment professionals.

(3)   In any other case in which one or more of the conditions set out in paragraph (4)(a) to (c) are met, that fact is to be taken into account in determining whether the communication is directed only at investment professionals (but a communication may still be regarded as so directed even if none of the conditions in paragraph (4) is met).

(4)   The conditions are that—

(a)   the communication is accompanied by an indication that it is directed at persons having professional experience in matters relating to investments and that any investment or investment activity to which it relates is available only to such persons or will be engaged in only with such persons;

(b)   the communication is accompanied by an indication that persons who do not have professional experience in matters relating to investments should not rely on it;

(c)   there are in place proper systems and procedures to prevent recipients other than investment professionals engaging in the investment activity to which the communication relates with the person directing the communication, a close relative of his or a member of the same group.

(5)   "Investment professionals" means—

(a)   an authorised person;

(b)   an exempt person where the communication relates to a controlled activity which is a regulated activity in relation to which the person is exempt;

(c)   any other person—

(i)   whose ordinary activities involve him in carrying on the controlled activity to which the communication relates for the purpose of a business carried on by him; or

    (ii)   who it is reasonable to expect will carry on such activity for the purposes of a business
           carried on by him;

(d)   a government, local authority (whether in the United Kingdom or elsewhere) or an
      international organisation;

(e)   a person ("A") who is a director, officer or employee of a person ("B") falling within any of
      sub-paragraphs (a) to (d) where the communication is made to A in that capacity and where
      A's responsibilities when acting in that capacity involve him in the carrying on by B of
      controlled activities.

(6)   For the purposes of paragraph (1), a communication may be treated as made only to or directed
      only at investment professionals even if it is also made to or directed at other persons to whom it
      may lawfully be communicated.

(7)   Paragraph (1) does not apply to any communication in respect of a controlled claims management
      activity.

20., 20A–20C. ...

PART V

...

PART VI

Exempt Communications: Certain Controlled Activities

27.   Application of exemptions in this Part

Except where otherwise stated, the exemptions in this Part apply to communications which relate
to—

(a)   a controlled activity falling within paragraph 2 of Schedule 1 carried on in relation to a
      qualifying contract of insurance;

(b)   controlled activities falling within any of paragraphs 3 to 11 of Schedule 1;

(c)   a controlled claims management activity.

28.   One off non-real time communications and solicited real time communications

(1)   The financial promotion restriction does not apply to a one off communication which is either a
      non-real time communication or a solicited real time communication.

(2)   If all the conditions set out in paragraph (3) are met in relation to a communication it is to be
      regarded as a one off communication. In any other case in which one or more of those conditions
      are met, that fact is to be taken into account in determining whether the communication is a one
      off communication (but a communication may still be regarded as a one off communication even
      if none of the conditions in paragraph (3) is met).

(3)   The conditions are that—

(a)   the communication is made only to one recipient or only to one group of recipients in the
      expectation that they would engage in any investment activity or controlled claims
      management activity jointly;

(b)   the identity of the product or service to which the communication relates has been
      determined having regard to the particular circumstances of the recipient;

(c)   the communication is not part of an organised marketing campaign.

28A.   One off unsolicited real time communications

(1)   The financial promotion restriction does not apply to an unsolicited real time communication if
      the conditions in paragraph (2) are met.

(2)   The conditions in this paragraph are that—

(a)   the communication is a one off communication;

(b)   the communicator believes on reasonable grounds that the recipient understands the risks
      associated with engaging in the investment activity to which the communication relates;

(c)   at the time that the communication is made, the communicator believes on reasonable grounds that the recipient would expect to be contacted by him in relation to the investment activity to which the communication relates.

(3)   Paragraphs (2) and (3) of article 28 apply in determining whether a communication is a one off communication for the purposes of this article as they apply for the purposes of article 28.

(4)   Paragraph (1) does not apply to any communication in respect of a controlled claims management activity.

28B–37. ...

38.   **Persons in the business of placing promotional material**

The financial promotion restriction does not apply to any communication which is made to a person whose business it is to place, or arrange for the placing of, promotional material provided that it is communicated so that he can place or arrange for placing it.

39–44. ...

45.   **Group companies**

The financial promotion restriction does not apply to any communication made by one body corporate in a group to another body corporate in the same group.

46–47. ...

48.   **... high net worth individuals**

(1)   If the requirements of paragraphs (4) and (7) are met, the financial promotion restriction does not apply to any communication which—

    (a)   is a non-real time communication or a solicited real time communication;

    (b)   is made to an individual whom the person making the communication believes on reasonable grounds to be a ... high net worth individual, and

    (c)   relates only to one or more investments falling within paragraph (8).

(2)   "High net worth individual" means an individual—

    (a)   who has completed and signed, within the period of twelve months ending with the day on which the communication is made, a statement complying with Part 1 of Schedule 5; and

    (b)   whose completion of that statement indicates that they satisfy the conditions set out in the statement to be classified as a high net worth individual.

(3)   The validity of a statement completed and signed for the purposes of paragraph (2) is not affected by a defect in the form or wording of the statement, provided that the defect does not alter the statement's meaning and that the words shown in bold type in Part I of Schedule 5 are so shown in the statement.

(4)   The requirements of this paragraph are that either the communication is accompanied by the giving of a warning and information in accordance with paragraphs (5), (5A) and (6) or where, because of the nature of the communication, this is not reasonably practicable,—

    (a)   a warning in accordance with paragraph (5) is given to the recipient orally at the beginning of the communication together with an indication that he will receive the warning in legible form and that, before receipt of that warning, he should consider carefully any decision to engage in investment activity to which the communication relates; and

    (b)   a warning and information in accordance with paragraphs (5), (5A) and (6) (d) to (h) is sent to the recipient of the communication within two business days of the day on which the communication is made.

(5)   The warning must be in the following terms—

    " The content of this promotion has not been approved by an authorised person within the meaning of the Financial Services and Markets Act 2000. Reliance on this promotion for the purpose of engaging in any investment activity may expose an individual to a significant risk of losing all of the property or other assets invested.".

But where a warning is sent pursuant to paragraph (4)(b), for the words "this promotion" in both places where they occur there must be substituted wording which clearly identifies the promotion which is the subject of the warning.

(5A) The warning must be accompanied by the following information—

    (a) the full name of the person making the communication, or on whose behalf the communication is made;

    (b) a postal or electronic address to which a person should send requests for further information or any other enquiry regarding the matters to which the communication relates; and

    (c) if applicable—

        (i) the country or territory in which the person making the communication, or on whose behalf the communication is made, is incorporated;

        (ii) where different from the information provided under (b), the address of the registered office of the person making the communication, or on whose behalf the communication is made; and

        (iii) the company number, or unique identification equivalent to a registered number required by the law of the state in which it is incorporated, of the person making the communication, or on whose behalf the communication is made.

(6) The warning and information must—

    (a) be given at the beginning of the communication;

    (b) precede any other written or pictorial matter;

    (c) be in a font size consistent with the text forming the remainder of the communication;

    (d) be indelible;

    (e) be legible;

    (f) be printed in black, bold type;

    (g) be surrounded by a black border which does not interfere with the text of the warning; and

    (h) not be hidden, obscured or interrupted by any other written or pictorial matter.

(7) The requirements of this paragraph are that the communication is accompanied by an indication—

    (a) that it is exempt from the general restriction (in section 21 of the Act) on the communication of invitations or inducements to engage in investment activity on the ground that it is made to a … high net worth individual;

    (b) of the requirements that must be met for an individual to qualify as a … high net worth individual; and

    (c) that any individual who is in any doubt about the investment to which the communication relates should consult an authorised person specialising in advising on investments of the kind in question.

(8) An investment falls within this paragraph if—

    (a) it is an investment falling within paragraph 14 of Schedule 1 being stock or shares in an unlisted company;

    (b) it is an investment falling within paragraph 15 of Schedule 1 being an investment acknowledging the indebtedness of an unlisted company;

    (ba) it is an investment falling within paragraph 15A of Schedule 1 being an investment constituting an alternative finance investment bond issued by an unlisted company;

    (c) it is an investment falling within paragraph 17 or 18 of Schedule 1 conferring entitlement or rights with respect to investments falling within sub-paragraph (a) or (b);

    (d) it comprises units in a collective investment scheme being a scheme which invests wholly or predominantly in investments falling within sub-paragraph (a) or (b);

    (e) it is an investment falling within paragraph 21 of Schedule 1 being an option to acquire or dispose of an investment falling within sub-paragraph (a), (b) or (c);

    (f) it is an investment falling within paragraph 22 of Schedule 1 being rights under a contract for the sale of an investment falling within sub-paragraph (a), (b) or (c);

(g) it is an investment falling within paragraph 23 of Schedule 1 being a contract relating to, or to fluctuations in value or price of, an investment falling within sub-paragraph (a), (b) or (c), provided in each case that it is an investment under the terms of which the investor cannot incur a liability or obligation to pay or contribute more than he commits by way of investment.

(9) "Business day" means any day except a Saturday, a Sunday, Christmas Day, Good Friday or a day which is a bank holiday under the Banking and Financial Dealings Act 1971 in any part of the United Kingdom.

49. High net worth companies, unincorporated associations etc.

(1) The financial promotion restriction does not apply to any communication which—
    (a) is made only to recipients whom the person making the communication believes on reasonable grounds to be persons to whom paragraph (2) applies; or
    (b) may reasonably be regarded as directed only at persons to whom paragraph (2) applies.

(2) This paragraph applies to—
    (a) any body corporate which has, or which is a member of the same group as an undertaking which has, a called-up share capital or net assets of not less than—
        (i) if the body corporate has more than 20 members or is a subsidiary undertaking of an undertaking which has more than 20 members, £500,000;
        (ii) otherwise, £5 million;
    (b) any unincorporated association or partnership which has net assets of not less than £5 million;
    (c) the trustee of a high value trust;
    (d) any person ("A") whilst acting in the capacity of director, officer or employee of a person ("B") falling within any of sub-paragraphs (a) to (c) where A's responsibilities, when acting in that capacity, involve him in B's engaging in investment activity;
    (e) any person to whom the communication may otherwise lawfully be made.

(3) For the purposes of paragraph (1)(b)—
    (a) if all the conditions set out in paragraph (4)(a) to (c) are met, the communication is to be regarded as directed at persons to whom paragraph (2) applies;
    (b) in any other case in which one or more of those conditions are met, that fact is to be taken into account in determining whether the communication is directed at persons to whom paragraph (2) applies (but a communication may still be regarded as so directed even if none of the conditions in paragraph (4) is met).

(4) The conditions are that—
    (a) the communication includes an indication of the description of persons to whom it is directed and an indication of the fact that the controlled investment or controlled activity to which it relates is available only to such persons;
    (b) the communication includes an indication that persons of any other description should not act upon it;
    (c) there are in place proper systems and procedures to prevent recipients other than persons to whom paragraph (2) applies engaging in the investment activity to which the communication relates with the person directing the communication, a close relative of his or a member of the same group.

(5) "Called-up share capital" has the meaning given in the 2006 Act (see section 547).

(6) "High value trust" means a trust where the aggregate value of the cash and investments which form part of the trust's assets (before deducting the amount of its liabilities)—
    (a) is £10 million or more; or
    (b) has been £10 million or more at anytime during the year immediately preceding the date on which the communication in question was first made or directed.

(7) "Net assets" has the meaning given by section 831 of the 2006 Act.

(8) Paragraph (1) does not apply to any communication in respect of a controlled claims management activity.

50.   Sophisticated investors

(1)   "Certified sophisticated investor", in relation to any description of investment, means a person—

   (a)   who has a current certificate in writing or other legible form signed by an authorised person to the effect that he is sufficiently knowledgeable to understand the risks associated with that description of investment; and

   (b)   who has signed, within the period of twelve months ending with the day on which the communication is made, a statement in the following terms:

         "I make this statement so that I am able to receive promotions which are exempt from the restrictions on financial promotion in the Financial Services and Markets Act 2000. The exemption relates to certified sophisticated investors and I declare that I qualify as such in relation to investments of the following kind [list them]. I accept that the contents of promotions and other material that I receive may not have been approved by an authorised person and that their content may not therefore be subject to controls which would apply if the promotion were made or approved by an authorised person. I am aware that it is open to me to seek advice from someone who specialises in advising on this kind of investment.".

(1A)   The validity of a statement signed in accordance with paragraph (1)(b) is not affected by a defect in the wording of the statement, provided that the defect does not alter the statement's meaning.

(2)   If the requirements of paragraph (3) are met, the financial promotion restriction does not apply to any communication which—

   (a)   is made to a certified sophisticated investor;

   (b)   does not invite or induce the recipient to engage in investment activity with the person who has signed the certificate referred to in paragraph (1)(a); and

   (c)   relates only to a description of investment in respect of which that investor is certified.

(3)   The requirements of this paragraph are that the communication is accompanied by an indication—

   (a)   that it is exempt from the general restriction (in section 21 of the Act) on the communication of invitations or inducements to engage in investment activity on the ground that it is made to a certified sophisticated investor;

   (b)   of the requirements that must be met for a person to qualify as a certified sophisticated investor;

   (c)   that the content of the communication has not been approved by an authorised person and that such approval is, unless this exemption or any other exemption applies, required by section 21 of the Act;

   (d)   that reliance on the communication for the purpose of engaging in any investment activity may expose the individual to a significant risk of losing all of the property invested or of incurring additional liability;

   (e)   that any person who is in any doubt about the investment to which the communication relates should consult an authorised person specialising in advising on investments of the kind in question.

(4)   For the purposes of paragraph (1)(a), a certificate is current if it is signed and dated not more than three years before the date on which the communication is made.

50A–52. ...

53.   Settlors, trustees and personal representatives

The financial promotion restriction does not apply to any communication which is made between—

   (a)   a person when acting as a settlor or grantor of a trust, a trustee or a personal representative; and

   (b)   a trustee of the trust, a fellow trustee or a fellow personal representative (as the case may be),

if the communication is made for the purposes of the trust or estate.

54.   Beneficiaries of trust, will or intestacy

The financial promotion restriction does not apply to any communication which is made—

(a)   between a person when acting as a settlor or grantor of a trust, trustee or personal representative and a beneficiary under the trust, will or intestacy; or

(b)   between a beneficiary under a trust, will or intestacy and another beneficiary under the same trust, will or intestacy,

if the communication relates to the management or distribution of that trust fund or estate.

55.   Communications by members of professions

(1)   The financial promotion restriction does not apply to a real time communication (whether solicited or unsolicited) which—

(a)   is made by a person ("P") who carries on a regulated activity to which the general prohibition does not apply by virtue of section 327 of the Act; and

(b)   is made to a recipient who has, prior to the communication being made, engaged P to provide professional services,

where the controlled activity to which the communication relates is an excluded activity which would be undertaken by P for the purposes of, and incidental to, the provision by him of professional services to or at the request of the recipient.

(2)   "Professional services" has the meaning given in section 327 of the Act.

(3)   An "excluded activity" is an activity to which the general prohibition would apply but for the application of—

(a)   section 327 of the Act; or

(b)   article 67 of the Regulated Activities Order.

55A.   Non-real time communication by members of professions

(1)   The financial promotion restriction does not apply to a non-real time communication which is—

(a)   made by a person ("P") who carries on Part XX activities; and

(b)   limited to what is required or permitted by paragraphs (2) and (3).

(2)   The communication must be in the following terms—

"This [firm/company] is not authorised under the Financial Services and Markets Act 2000 but we are able in certain circumstances to offer a limited range of investment and consumer credit-related and claims management-related   services to clients because we are members of [relevant designated professional body]. We can provide these investment and consumer credit-related and claims management-related services if they are an incidental part of the professional services we have been engaged to provide."

(3)   The communication may in addition set out the Part XX activities which P is able to offer to his clients, provided it is clear that these are the investment and consumer credit-related and claims management-related services to which the statement in paragraph (2) relates.

(4)   The validity of a communication made in accordance with paragraph (2) is not affected by a defect in the wording of it provided that the defect does not alter the communication's meaning.

(5)   "Part XX activities" means the regulated activities to which the general prohibition does not apply when they are carried on by P by virtue of section 327 of the Act.

55B.   Insolvency practitioners

The financial promotion restriction does not apply to any non-real time communication or solicited real time communication by a person acting as an insolvency practitioner (within the meaning of the Regulated Activities Order) in the course of carrying on an activity which would be a regulated activity but for article 72H of the Regulated Activities Order (insolvency practitioners).

56–58. ...

59.   Annual accounts and directors' report

(1)   If the requirements in paragraphs (2) to (5) are met, the financial promotion restriction does not apply to any communication by a body corporate (other than an open-ended investment company) which—

    (a)   consists of, or is accompanied by, the whole or any part of the annual accounts of a body corporate (other than an open-ended investment company); or

    (b)   is accompanied by any report which is prepared and approved by the directors of such a body corporate under—

        (ai)   sections 414A and 414D of the 2006 Act; or

        (i)   sections 415 and 419 of the 2006 Act; ...

        (ii), (iii) ...

(2)   The requirements of this paragraph are that the communication—

    (a)   does not contain any invitation to persons to underwrite, subscribe for, or otherwise acquire or dispose of, a controlled investment; and

    (b)   does not advise persons to engage in any of the activities within sub-paragraph (a).

(3)   The requirements of this paragraph are that the communication does not contain any invitation to persons to—

    (a)   effect any transaction with the body corporate (or with any named person) in the course of that body's (or person's) carrying on of any activity falling within any of paragraphs 3 to 11A of Schedule 1; or

    (b)   make use of any services provided by that body corporate (or by any named person) in the course of carrying on such activity.

(4)   The requirements of this paragraph are that the communication does not contain any inducement relating to an investment other than one issued, or to be issued, by the body corporate (or another body corporate in the same group) which falls within—

    (a)   paragraph 14, 15 or 15A of Schedule 1; or

    (b)   paragraph 17 or 18 of that Schedule, so far as relating to any investments within sub-paragraph (a).

(5)   The requirements of this paragraph are that the communication does not contain any reference to—

    (a)   the price at which investments issued by the body corporate have in the past been bought or sold; or

    (b)   the yield on such investments,

unless it is also accompanied by an indication that past performance cannot be relied on as a guide to future performance.

(6)   For the purposes of paragraph (5)(b), a reference, in relation to an investment, to earnings, dividend or nominal rate of interest payable shall not be taken to be a reference to the yield on the investment.

(7)   "Annual accounts" means—

    (a)   accounts produced by virtue of Part 15 of the 2006 Act (or of that Part as applied by virtue of any other enactment);

    (b)   ...

    (c)   a summary financial statement prepared under section 426 of the 2006 Act;

    (d)   accounts produced in accordance with Chapter 3 of Part 5 of the Overseas Companies Regulations 2009 and filed with the registrar under section 441 of the 2006 Act as applied and modified by regulation 40 of those Regulations;

    (e)   ...

60–61. ...

62.   Sale of body corporate

(1)   The financial promotion restriction does not apply to any communication by, or on behalf of, a body corporate, a partnership, a single individual or a group of connected individuals which relates to a transaction falling within paragraph (2).

(2)   A transaction falls within this paragraph if—

    (a)   it is one to acquire or dispose of shares in a body corporate other than an open-ended investment company, or is entered into for the purposes of such an acquisition or disposal; and

    (b)   either—

        (i)   the conditions set out in paragraph (3) are met; or

        (ii)   those conditions are not met, but the object of the transaction may nevertheless reasonably be regarded as being the acquisition of day to day control of the affairs of the body corporate.

(3)   The conditions mentioned in paragraph (2)(b) are that—

    (a)   the shares consist of or include 50 per cent or more of the voting shares in the body corporate; or

    (b)   the shares, together with any already held by the person acquiring them, consist of or include at least that percentage of such shares; and

    (c)   in either case, the acquisition or disposal is, or is to be, between parties each of whom is a body corporate, a partnership, a single individual or a group of connected individuals.

(4)   "A group of connected individuals" means—

    (a)   in relation to a party disposing of shares in a body corporate, a single group of persons each of whom is—

        (i)   a director or manager of the body corporate;

        (ii)   a close relative of any such director or manager; or

        (iii)   a person acting as trustee for, or nominee of, any person falling within paragraph (i) or (ii); and

    (b)   in relation to a party acquiring shares in a body corporate, a single group of of persons each of whom is—

        (i)   a person who is or is to be a director or manager of the body corporate;

        (ii)   a close relative of any such person; or

        (iii)   a person acting as trustee for or nominee of any person falling within paragraph (i) or (ii).

(5)   "Voting shares" in relation to a body corporate, means shares carrying voting rights attributable to share capital which are exercisable in all circumstances at any general meeting of that body corporate.

63.   Takeovers of relevant unlisted companies: interpretation

(1)   In this article and in articles 64, 65 and 66, a "relevant unlisted company", in relation to a takeover offer, means a company which is an unlisted company at the time that the offer is made and which has been an unlisted company throughout the period of ten years immediately preceding the date of the offer.

(2)   In this article and in articles 64, 65 and 66, references to a takeover offer for a relevant unlisted company are references to an offer which meets the requirements of Part I of Schedule 4 and which is an offer—

    (a)   for all the shares in, or all the shares comprised in the equity or non-equity share capital of, a relevant unlisted company (other than any shares already held by or on behalf of the person making the offer); or

    (b)   for all the debentures of such a company (other than debentures already held by or on behalf of the person making the offer).

(3)   Shares in or debentures of an unlisted company are to be regarded as being held by or on behalf of the person making the offer if the person who holds them, or on whose behalf they are held, has agreed that an offer should not be made in respect of them.

64.   Takeovers of relevant unlisted companies

(1)   If the requirements of paragraphs (2) and (3) are met, the financial promotion restriction does not apply to any communication which is communicated in connection with a takeover offer for a relevant unlisted company.

(2)   The requirements of this paragraph are that the communication is accompanied by the material listed in Part II of Schedule 4.

(3)   The requirements of this paragraph are that the material listed in Part III of Schedule 4 is available at a place in the United Kingdom at all times during normal office hours for inspection free of charge.

65.   Takeovers of relevant unlisted companies: warrants etc.

The financial promotion restriction does not apply to any communication which—

(a)   is communicated at the same time as, or after, a takeover offer for a relevant unlisted company is made; and

(b)   relates to investments falling within paragraph 17 or 18 of Schedule 1 so far as relating to the shares in or debentures of the unlisted company which are the subject of the offer.

66.   Takeovers of relevant unlisted companies: application forms

The financial promotion restriction does not apply to any communication made in connection with a takeover offer for a relevant unlisted company which is a form of application for—

(a)   shares in or debentures of the unlisted company; or

(b)   investments falling within paragraphs 17 or 18 of Schedule 1 so far as relating to the shares in or debentures of the company which are the subject of the offer.

67–69. ...

70.   Promotions included in listing particulars etc.

(1)   The financial promotion restriction does not apply to any non-real time communication which is included in—

(a)   listing particulars;

(b)   supplementary listing particulars;

(c)   a prospectus or supplementary prospectus approved—

     (i)   by the FCA in accordance with Part 6 of the Act; ...

     (ii)   ...

     or part of such a prospectus or supplementary prospectus; or

(d)   any other document required or permitted to be published by listing rules or prospectus rules under Part VI of the Act (except an advertisement within the meaning of the prospectus regulation).

(1A)   The financial promotion restriction does not apply to any non-real time communication—

(a)   comprising the final terms of an offer or the final offer price or amount of securities which will be offered to the public; and

(b)   complying with Articles 8(1), 8(4), 8(5), 8(10), ... 17 and 21(2) of the prospectus regulation.

(2)   In this article "listing particulars", "listing rules", "the prospectus regulation" and "prospectus rules" have the meaning given by Part VI of the Act.

Note. This article is amended by S.I. 2024/105, reg. 47(b), Sch. 3, Pt. 2, paras. 27, 30, as from a day to be appointed (save for certain purposes).

71.   Material relating to prospectus for public offer of unlisted securities

(1)   The financial promotion restriction does not apply to any non-real time communication relating to a prospectus or supplementary prospectus where the only reason for considering it to be an invitation or inducement is that it does one or more of the following—

    (a)   it states the name and address of the person by whom the transferable securities to which the prospectus or supplementary prospectus relates are to be offered;

    (b)   it gives other details for contacting that person;

    (c)   it states the nature and the nominal value of the transferable securities to which the prospectus or supplementary prospectus relates, the number offered and the price at which they are offered;

    (d)   it states that a prospectus or supplementary prospectus is or will be available (and, if it is not yet available, when it is expected to be);

    (e)   it gives instructions for obtaining a copy of the prospectus or supplementary prospectus.

(2)   In this article—

    (a)   "transferable securities" has the same meaning as in section 102A(3) of the Act;

    (b)   references to a prospectus or supplementary prospectus are references to a prospectus or supplementary prospectus which is published in accordance with prospectus rules made under Part VI of the Act.

Note. This article is amended by S.I. 2024/105, reg. 47(b), Sch. 3, Pt. 2, paras. 27, 31, as from a day to be appointed (save for certain purposes).

72–73.   ...

PART VIA

Exempt Communications: Controlled Claims Management Activities

73A.   Application of exemptions in this Part

The exemptions in this Part apply to any communication which relates to a controlled claims management activity of a kind specified in paragraph 11A of Schedule 1.

73B.   Communications made by legal professionals

(1)   The financial promotion restriction does not apply to any communication which relates to a controlled claims management activity when that communication is made in England and Wales by—

    (a)   a legal practitioner;

    (b)   a firm, organisation or body corporate that carries on the controlled claims management activity through a legal practitioner; or

    (c)   an individual who carries on the controlled claims management activity at the direction of, and under the supervision of, a legal practitioner who is—

        (i)   that individual's employer or fellow employee; or

        (ii)   a director of a company, or a member of a limited liability partnership, that provides the service and is that individual's employer.

(2)   In paragraph (1) "legal practitioner" means—

    (a)   a solicitor or barrister of any part of England and Wales or Northern Ireland;

    (b)   a Fellow of the Chartered Institute of Legal Executives;

    (c)   a European lawyer, as defined in the European Communities (Services of Lawyers) Order 1978 or the European Communities (Lawyer's Practice) Regulations 2000;

    (d)   a registered foreign lawyer, as defined in section 89(9) of the Courts and Legal Services Act 1990;

    (e)   any other member of a legal profession, of a jurisdiction other than England and Wales, that is recognised by the Law Society of England and Wales or the General Council of the Bar as a regulated legal profession.

(3) The financial promotion restriction does not apply to a communication which relates to a controlled claims management activity when that communication is made in Scotland by—

    (a) a legal practitioner;

    (b) a firm, organisation or body corporate that carries on the controlled claims management activity through or under the supervision of a legal practitioner where that firm, organisation or body corporate is—

        (i) a firm of solicitors;

        (ii) an incorporated practice; or

        (iii) a licensed legal services provider and the activity is a legal service as defined within section 3 of the Legal Services (Scotland) Act 2010.

(4) In paragraph (3) "legal practitioner" means—

    (a) a person who is qualified to practise as a solicitor under section 4 of the Solicitors (Scotland) Act 1980;

    (b) an advocate who is a member of the Faculty of Advocates;

    (c) a European lawyer as defined in the European Communities (Services of Lawyers) Order 1978 or the European Communities (Lawyer's Practice) (Scotland) Regulations 2000; or

    (d) a registered foreign lawyer within the meaning of section 65 of the Solicitors (Scotland) Act 1980.

(5) A communication mentioned in paragraph (1) or (3) is only excluded from the financial promotion restriction if the legal practitioner concerned carries on the controlled claims management activity in the ordinary course of legal practice pursuant to the professional rules to which that legal practitioner is subject.

73C–73J ...

SCHEDULE 1

Article 4

PART I

Controlled Activities

1. Accepting deposits

Accepting deposits is a controlled activity if—

    (a) money received by way of deposit is lent to others; or

    (b) any other activity of the person accepting the deposit is financed wholly, or to a material extent, out of the capital of or interest on money received by way of deposit,

and the person accepting the deposit holds himself out as accepting deposits on a day to day basis.

2. Effecting or carrying out contracts of insurance

(1) Effecting a contract of insurance as principal is a controlled activity.

(2) Carrying out a contract of insurance as principal is a controlled activity.

(3) There is excluded from sub-paragraph (1) or (2) the effecting or carrying out of a contract of insurance of the kind described in article 12 of the Regulated Activities Order by a person who does not otherwise carry on an activity falling within those sub-paragraphs.

3. Dealing in securities, qualifying cryptoassets and contractually based investments

(1) Buying, selling, subscribing for or underwriting securities, structured deposits, qualifying cryptoassets or contractually based investments ... as principal or agent is a controlled activity.

(2) A person does not carry on the activity in sub-paragraph (1) by accepting an instrument creating or acknowledging indebtedness in respect of any loan, credit, guarantee or other similar financial accommodation or assurance which he has made, granted or provided.

(3) The reference in sub-paragraph (2) to a person accepting an instrument includes a reference to a person becoming a party to an instrument otherwise than as a debtor or a surety.

4.   Arranging deals in investments

(1)   Making arrangements for another person (whether as principal or agent) to buy, sell, subscribe for or underwrite a particular investment which is—

(a)   a security;

(aa)   a structured deposit;

(ab)   a qualifying cryptoasset;

(b)   a contractually based investment; or

(c)   an investment of the kind specified by paragraph 24, or paragraph 27 so far as relevant to that paragraph,

is a controlled activity.

(2)   Making arrangements with a view to a person who participates in the arrangements buying, selling, subscribing for or underwriting investments falling within sub-paragraph (1)(a), (aa), (ab), (b) or (c) (whether as principal or agent) is a controlled activity.

(3)   A person does not carry on an activity falling within paragraph (2) merely by providing means by which one party to a transaction (or potential transaction) is able to communicate with other such parties.

4A–4C. ...

5.   Managing investments

Managing assets belonging to another person, in circumstances involving the exercise of discretion, is a controlled activity if—

(a)   the assets consist of or include any investment which is a security, structured deposit, a qualifying cryptoasset or a contractually based investment; or

(b)   the arrangements for their management are such that the assets may consist of or include such investments, and either the assets have at any time since 29th April 1988 done so, or the arrangements have at any time (whether before or after that date) been held out as arrangements under which the assets would do so.

5A.   Debt adjusting

(1)   The following activities are, when carried on in relation to debts due under a relevant credit agreement, controlled activities—

(a)   negotiating with the lender, on behalf of the borrower, terms for the discharge of a debt;

(b)   taking over, in return for payments by the borrower, that person's obligation to discharge a debt;

(c)   any similar activity concerned with the liquidation of a debt.

(2)   The following activities are, when carried on in relation to debts due under a consumer hire agreement, controlled activities—

(a)   negotiating with the owner, on behalf of the hirer, terms for the discharge of a debt;

(b)   taking over, in return for payments by the hirer, that person's obligation to discharge a debt;

(c)   any similar activity concerned with the liquidation of a debt.

5B.   Debt-counselling

(1)   Advising a borrower about the liquidation of a debt due under a relevant credit agreement is a controlled activity.

(2)   Advising a hirer about the liquidation of a debt due under a consumer hire agreement is a controlled activity.

6.   Safeguarding and administering investments

(1)   The activity consisting of both—

(a)   the safeguarding of assets belonging to another; and

(b)   the administration of those assets,

or arranging for one or more other persons to carry on that activity, is a controlled activity if either the condition in paragraph (a) or (b) of sub-paragraph (2) is met.

(2)   The condition is that—
    (a)   the assets consist of or include any investment which is a security or a contractually based investment; or
    (b)   the arrangements for their safeguarding and administration are such that the assets may consist of or include investments of the kind mentioned in sub-paragraph (a) and either the assets have at any time since 1st June 1997 done so, or the arrangements have at any time (whether before or after that date) been held out as ones under which such investments would be safeguarded and administered.

(3)   For the purposes of this article—
    (a)   it is immaterial that title to the assets safeguarded and administered is held in uncertificated form;
    (b)   it is immaterial that the assets safeguarded and administered may be transferred to another person, subject to a commitment by the person safeguarding and administering them, or arranging for their safeguarding and administration, that they will be replaced by equivalent assets at some future date or when so requested by the person to whom they belong.

(4)   For the purposes of this article, the following activities do not constitute the administration of assets—
    (a)   providing information as to the number of units or the value of any assets safeguarded;
    (b)   converting currency;
    (c)   receiving documents relating to an investment solely for the purpose of onward transmission to, from or at the direction of the person to whom the investment belongs.

7.   Advising on investments

(1)   Advising a person is a controlled activity if the advice is—
    (a)   given to the person in his capacity as an investor or potential investor, or in his capacity as agent for an investor or a potential investor; and
    (b)   advice on the merits of his doing any of the following (whether as principal or agent)—
        (i)   buying, selling, subscribing for or underwriting a particular investment which is a security, structured deposit, a qualifying cryptoasset or a contractually based investment; or
        (ii)   exercising any right conferred by such an investment to buy, sell, subscribe for or underwrite such an investment.

(2)   Advising a person is a controlled activity if the advice is—
    (a)   given to the person in that person's capacity as a lender or potential lender under a relevant paragraph 4C agreement, or in that person's capacity as an agent for a lender or potential lender under such an agreement; and
    (b)   advice on the merits of the person doing any of the following (whether as principal or agent)—
        (i)   entering into a relevant paragraph 4C agreement as a lender or assuming the rights of a lender under such an agreement,
        (ii)   providing instructions to an operator with a view to entering into a relevant paragraph 4C agreement as a lender or to assuming the rights of a lender under such an agreement by assignment or operation of law, where the instructions involve—
            (aa)   accepting particular parameters for the terms of the agreement presented by an operator,
            (bb)   choosing between options governing the parameters of the terms of the agreement presented by an operator, or
            (cc)   specifying the parameters of the terms of the agreement by other means,
        (iii)   enforcing or exercising the lender's rights under a relevant paragraph 4C agreement, or
        (iv)   assigning rights under a relevant paragraph 4C agreement.

(3)   In sub-paragraph (2)—

"operator" means a person carrying on a controlled activity of the kind specified by paragraph 4C(1) or (2D), and

"relevant paragraph 4C agreement" means a paragraph 4C agreement (within the meaning of that paragraph) which has been, or is to be, entered into with the facilitation of a person carrying on a controlled activity of the kind specified by paragraph 4C(1) or (2D) not in contravention of the general prohibition.

(4) For the purposes of the application of section 21(9) and (10) of the Act (restrictions on financial promotion) to an activity of a kind specified by sub-paragraph (2), paragraph 26D of this Schedule (relevant credit agreements), and article 4 (definition of controlled activities and controlled investments) in so far as it relates to that paragraph, have effect as if the reference to a relevant credit agreement in paragraph 26D includes a reference to a paragraph 4C agreement.

8. Advising on syndicate participation at Lloyd's

Advising a person to become, or continue or cease to be, a member of a particular Lloyd's syndicate is a controlled activity.

9–11. ...

PART IA

Controlled Claims Management Activity

11A.

(1) A claims management activity carried out in Great Britain is a controlled claims management activity.

(2) For the purposes of this paragraph, a claims management activity is one of the following activities:

    (a) seeking out persons who may have a claim, referring details of a claim or potential claim or a claimant or potential claimant to another person (including a person having the right to conduct litigation), or identifying a claim or potential claim or a claimant or potential claimant in respect of—

        (i) a personal injury claim;

        (ii) a financial services or financial product claim;

        (iii) a housing disrepair claim;

        (iv) a claim for a specified benefit;

        (v) a criminal injury claim; or

        (vi) an employment related claim.

    (b) advising a claimant or potential claimant, investigating a claim or representing a claimant in respect of a personal injury claim;

    (c) advising a claimant or potential claimant, investigating a claim or representing a claimant in respect of a financial services or financial product claim;

    (d) advising a claimant or potential claimant, investigating a claim or representing a claimant in respect of a housing disrepair claim;

    (e) advising a claimant or potential claimant, investigating a claim or representing a claimant in respect of a claim for a specified benefit;

    (f) advising a claimant or potential claimant, investigating a claim or representing a claimant in respect of a criminal injury claim; or

    (g) advising a claimant or potential claimant, investigating a claim or representing a claimant in respect of an employment related claim.

(3) In this paragraph—

    (a) "claimant" includes, in civil proceedings in Scotland, a pursuer;

    (b) "defendant" includes, in civil proceedings in Scotland, a defender;

    (c) "personal injury claim" means a claim for personal injury within the meaning of the Civil Procedure Rules 1998 in England and Wales and an action for damages for, or arising from, personal injuries within the meaning set out in section 8(7) of the Civil Litigation (Expenses and Group Proceedings) (Scotland) Act 2018 in Scotland;

(d)   "financial services or financial product claim" includes a claim made under section 75 of the Consumer Credit Act 1974;

(e)   "housing disrepair claim" means a claim under section 11 of the Landlord and Tenant Act 1985 or section 4 of the Defective Premises Act 1972 in England and Wales or an application in respect of the repairing standard under section 22 of the Housing (Scotland) Act 2006, or claims in relation to the disrepair of premises under a term of a tenancy agreement or lease or under the common law relating to nuisance or negligence but does not include claims for statutory nuisance under section 82 of the Environmental Protection Act 1990;

(f)   "a claim for a specified benefit" means a claim for one of the following benefits—

    (i)   industrial injuries benefit, within the meaning given by section 94 of the Social Security Contributions and Benefits Act 1992;

    (ii)   any supplement or additional allowance, or increase of benefit or allowance to which a recipient of an industrial injuries benefit may be entitled under that Act or any other Act;

    (iii) a benefit under a scheme referred to in paragraph 2 or 4 of Schedule 8 to that Act; or

    (iv)   a benefit under the Pneumoconiosis etc (Workers' Compensation) Act 1979.

(g)   "criminal injury claim" means a claim under the Criminal Injuries Compensation Scheme established under the Criminal Injuries Compensation Act 1995;

(h)   "employment related claim" includes a claim in relation to wages and salaries and other employment related payments and claims in relation to wrongful or unfair dismissal, redundancy, discrimination and harassment;

(i)   "investigating" means carrying out an investigation into, or commissioning the investigation of, the circumstances, merits or foundation of a claim; and

(j)   "representing" means representation in writing or orally, regardless of the tribunal, body or person before which or to whom the representation is made.

(4)   In this paragraph, a person is to be treated as carrying on a controlled claims management activity in Great Britain when the activity is carried on—

(a)   by a person who is—

    (i)   an individual who is ordinarily resident in Great Britain; or

    (ii)   a person, other than an individual, who is constituted under the law of England and Wales or Scotland; or

(b)   in respect of a claimant or potential claimant who is—

    (i)   an individual who is ordinarily resident in Great Britain; or

    (ii)   a person, other than an individual, who is constituted under the law of England and Wales or Scotland.

(5)   For the purposes of sub-paragraph (4) a person is "ordinarily resident" in Great Britain if that person satisfies the requirements of the Statutory Residence Test as set out in Schedule 45 to the Finance Act 2013 either—

(a)   at the time of the facts giving rise to the claim or potential claim; or

(b)   at the time when the controlled claims management activity is carried out in respect of that claimant or potential claimant.

PART II

Controlled Investments

12.   A deposit.

13.   Rights under a contract of insurance.

14.

(1)   Shares or stock in the share capital of—

(a)   any body corporate (wherever incorporated);

(b)   any unincorporated body constituted under the law of a country or territory outside the United Kingdom.

(2)   Sub-paragraph (1) includes—

(a)   any shares of a class defined as deferred shares for the purposes of section 119 of the Building Societies Act 1986;

(b)   any transferable shares in a body incorporated under the law of, or any part of, the United Kingdom relating to co-operative and community benefit societies, industrial and provident societies or credit unions ....

(3)   But subject to sub-paragraph (2) there are excluded from sub-paragraph (1) shares or stock in the share capital of—

(a)   an open-ended investment company;

(b)   a building society incorporated under the law of, or any part of, the United Kingdom;

(c)   any body incorporated under the law of, or any part of, the United Kingdom relating to co-operative and community benefit societies, industrial and provident societies or credit unions;

(d)   ...

15.   Instruments creating or acknowledging indebtedness

(1)   Subject to sub-paragraph (2), such of the following as do not fall within paragraph ... 16—

(a)   debentures;

(b)   debenture stock;

(c)   loan stock;

(d)   bonds;

(e)   certificates of deposit;

(f)   any other instrument creating or acknowledging a present or future indebtedness.

(2)   If and to the extent that they would otherwise fall within sub-paragraph (1), there are excluded from that sub-paragraph—

(a)   any instrument acknowledging or creating indebtedness for, or for money borrowed to defray, the consideration payable under a contract for the supply of goods or services;

(b)   a cheque or other bill of exchange, a banker's draft or a letter of credit (but not a bill of exchange accepted by a banker);

(c)   a banknote, a statement showing a balance on a current, deposit or saving account, a lease or other disposition of property, a heritable security; and

(d)   a contract of insurance;

(e)   ...

(3)   An instrument excluded from sub-paragraph (1) of paragraph 16 by paragraph 16(2)(b) is not thereby to be taken to fall within sub-paragraph (1) of this paragraph.

15A.   Alternative finance investment bonds

(1)   Rights under an alternative finance investment bond, to the extent that they do not fall within paragraph 15 or 16.

(2)   For the purposes of this paragraph, arrangements constitute an alternative finance investment bond if—

(a)   the arrangements provide for a person ("the bond-holder") to pay a sum of money ("the capital") to another ("the bond-issuer");

(b)   the arrangements identify assets, or a class of assets, which the bond-issuer will acquire for the purpose of generating income or gains directly or indirectly ("the bond assets");

(c)   the arrangements specify a period at the end of which they cease to have effect ("the bond term");

(d)   the bond-issuer undertakes under the arrangements—

(i)   to make a repayment in respect of the capital ("the redemption payment") to the bond-holder during or at the end of the bond term (whether or not in instalments); and (ii)　to pay to the bond-holder other payments on one or more occasions during or at the end of the bond term ("the additional payments");

(e)　the amount of the additional payments does not exceed an amount which would, at the time at which the bond is issued, be a reasonable commercial return on a loan of the capital; and

(f)　the arrangements are—

(i)　a security that is admitted to the official list in accordance with Part 6 of the Act,

(ii)　a security that is admitted to an official list in the EEA (in accordance with the provisions of Directive 2001/34/EC of the European Parliament and of the Council on the admission of securities to official stock exchange listing and on information to be published on those securities) and has been so admitted since before IP completion day,

(iii)　a security that is admitted to trading on a recognised investment exchange or a UK trading venue, or

(iv)　a security that is admitted to trading on an EU trading venue and has been so admitted since before IP completion day.

(3)　For the purposes of sub-paragraph (2)—

(a)　the bond-issuer may acquire the bond assets before or after the arrangements take effect;

(b)　the bond assets may be property of any kind, including rights in relation to property owned by someone other than the bond-issuer;

(c)　the identification of the bond assets mentioned in sub-paragraph (2)(b) and the undertakings mentioned in sub-paragraph (2)(d) may (but need not) be described as, or accompanied by a document described as, a declaration of trust;

(d)　the reference to a period in sub-paragraph (2)(c) includes any period specified to end upon the redemption of the bond by the bond-issuer;

(e)　the bond-holder may (but need not) be entitled under the arrangements to terminate them, or participate in terminating them, before the end of the bond term;

(f)　the amount of the additional payments may be—

(i)　fixed at the beginning of the bond term;

(ii)　determined wholly or partly by reference to the value of or income generated by the bond assets; or

(iii)　determined in some other way;

(g)　if the amount of the additional payments is not fixed at the beginning of the bond term, the reference in sub-paragraph (2)(e) to the amount of the additional payments is a reference to the maximum amount of the additional payments;

(h)　the amount of the redemption payment may (but need not) be subject to reduction in the event of a fall in the value of the bond assets or in the rate of income generated by them; and

(i)　entitlement to the redemption payment may (but need not) be capable of being satisfied (whether or not at the option of the bond-issuer or the bond-holder) by the issue or transfer of shares or other securities.

(4)　An instrument excluded from sub-paragraph (1) of paragraph 16 by sub-paragraph (2)(b) of that paragraph is not thereby taken to fall within sub-paragraph (1) of this paragraph.

16–27. ...

28.　Interpretation

In this Schedule—

"agreement provider" has the meaning given in paragraph (3) of article 63J of the Regulated Activities Order, read with paragraphs (6) and (7) of that article;

"agreement seller" has the meaning given in article 63J(3) of the Regulated Activities Order;

"AIFM" has the meaning given in the Regulated Activities Order;

"borrower" has the meaning given by article 60L of the Regulated Activities Order;

"buying" includes acquiring for valuable consideration;

"Commission Regulation" has the meaning given in the Regulated Activities Order;

"consumer hire agreement" has the meaning given by article 60N of the Regulated Activities Order;

"contract of insurance" has the meaning given in the Regulated Activities Order;

"contractually based investment" means—

(a)   rights under a qualifying contract of insurance;

(b)   any investment of the kind specified by any of paragraphs 21, 22, 23 and 25;

(c)   any investment of the kind specified by paragraph 27 so far as relevant to an investment falling within (a) or (b);

...

"EU trading venue" has the meaning given by Article 2.1.16B of the markets in financial instruments regulation;

"hirer" has the meaning given by article 60N of the Regulated Activities Order;

"home purchase provider" and "home purchaser" have the meanings given in article 63F(3) of the Regulated Activities Order;

"investment firm" has the meaning given in the Regulated Activities Order;

"investment services and activities" has the meaning given in the Regulated Activities Order;

"lender" has the meaning given by article 60L of the Regulated Activities Order;

"management company" has the meaning given in the Regulated Activities Order;

"market operator" has the meaning given in the Regulated Activities Order;

"markets in financial instruments directive" means Directive 2014/65/EU of the European Parliament and of the Council of 15 May 2014 on markets in financial instruments (recast);

"MiFID instrument" has the meaning given in article 25D(2) of the Regulated Activities Order;

"multilateral trading facility" has the meaning given in the Regulated Activities Order;

"non-equity MiFID instrument" has the meaning given in article 25DA of the Regulated Activities Order;

"occupational pension scheme" has the meaning given by section 1 of the Pension Schemes Act 1993 but with paragraph (b) of the definition omitted;

"organised trading facility" has the meaning given in the Regulated Activities Order;

"plan provider" has the meaning given by paragraph (3) of article 63B of the Regulated Activities Order, read with paragraphs (7) and (8) of that article;

"property" includes currency of the United Kingdom or any other country or territory;

"qualifying credit institution" has the meaning given in the Regulated Activities Order;

"qualifying funeral plan contract" has the meaning given by paragraph 9;

"regulated consumer hire agreement" has the meaning given by article 60N of the Regulated Activities Order;

"regulated credit agreement" has the meaning given by article 60B of the Regulated Activities Order;

"regulated home purchase plan" has the meaning given in article 63F(3) of the Regulated Activities Order;

"regulated home reversion plan" and "reversion seller" have the meanings given in article 63B(3) of the Regulated Activities Order;

"regulated sale and rent back agreement" has the meaning given in article 63J(3) of the Regulated Activities Order;

"relevant credit agreement" means a credit agreement (within the meaning given by article 60B of the Regulated Activities Order) other than—

(a)   a regulated mortgage contract or a regulated home purchase plan (within the meaning of that Order); or

(b)   a buy-to-let mortgage contract as defined in article 4 of the Mortgage Credit Directive Order 2015;

"relevant recipient of credit" has the meaning given by article 60L of the Regulated Activities Order;

"security" means a controlled investment falling within any of paragraphs 14 to 20 or 23A or, so far as relevant to any such investment, paragraph 27;

"selling", in relation to any investment, includes disposing of the investment for valuable consideration, and for these purposes "disposing" includes—

(a)   in the case of an investment consisting of rights under a contract—

    (i)   surrendering, assigning or converting those rights; or

    (ii)   assuming the corresponding liabilities under the contract;

(b)   in the case of an investment consisting of rights under other arrangements, assuming the corresponding liabilities under the arrangements; and

(c)   in the case of any other investment, issuing or creating the investment or granting the rights or interests of which it consists;

"syndicate" has the meaning given in the Regulated Activities Order.

"UK trading venue" has the meaning given by Article 2.1.16 of the markets in financial instruments regulation.

Note. This Schedule is amended by S.I. 2021/90, art. 5, with effect from 29 July 2022 (save for certain purposes).

SCHEDULES 2 AND 3

…

SCHEDULE 4

Articles 63 and 64

TAKEOVERS OF RELEVANT UNLISTED COMPANIES

PART I

Requirements Relating to the Offer

1.   The terms of the offer must be recommended by all the directors of the company other than any director who is—

    (a)   the person by whom, or on whose behalf, an offer is made ("offeror"); or

    (b)   a director of the offeror.

2.   (1)   This paragraph applies to an offer for debentures or for non-equity share capital.

    (2)   Where, at the date of the offer, shares carrying 50 per cent or less of the voting rights attributable to the equity share capital are held by or on behalf of the offeror, the offer must include or be accompanied by an offer made by the offeror for the rest of the shares comprised in the equity share capital.

3.   (1)   This paragraph applies to an offer for shares comprised in the equity share capital. (2) Where, at the date of the offer, shares which carry 50 per cent or less of the categories of voting rights described in sub-paragraph (3) are held by or on behalf of the offeror, it must be a condition of the offer that sufficient shares will be acquired or agreed to be acquired by the offeror pursuant to or during the offer so as to result in shares carrying more than 50 per cent of one or both categories of relevant voting rights being held by him or on his behalf.

    (3)   The categories of voting rights mentioned in sub-paragraph (2) are—

        (a)   voting rights exercisable in general meetings of the company;

        (b)   voting rights attributable to the equity share capital.

4.   (1)   Subject to sub-paragraph (2), the offer must be open for acceptance by every recipient for the period of at least 21 days beginning with the day after the day on which the invitation or inducement in question was first communicated to recipients of the offer.

(2)   Sub-paragraph (1) does not apply if the offer is totally withdrawn and all persons are released from any obligation incurred under it.

5.   The acquisition of the shares or debentures to which the offer relates must not be conditional upon the recipients approving, or consenting, to any payment or other benefit being made or given to any director or former director of the company in connection with, or as compensation or consideration for—

(a)   his ceasing to be a director;

(b)   his ceasing to hold any office held in conjunction with any directorship; or

(c)   in the case of a former director, his ceasing to hold any office which he held in conjunction with his former directorship and which he continued to hold after ceasing to be a director.

6.   The consideration for the shares or debentures must be—

(a)   cash; or

(b)   in the case of an offeror which is a body corporate other than an open-ended investment company, either cash or shares in, or debentures of, the body corporate or any combination of such cash, shares or debentures.

PART II

Accompanying Material

7.   An indication of the identity of the offeror and, if the offer is being made on behalf of another person, the identity of that person.

8.   An indication of the fact that the terms of the offer are recommended by all directors of the company other than (if that is the case) any director who is the offeror or a director of the offeror.

9.   An indication to the effect that any person who is in any doubt about the invitation or inducement should consult a person authorised under the Act.

10.   An indication that, except insofar as the offer may be totally withdrawn and all persons released from any obligation incurred under it, the offer is open for acceptance by every recipient for the period of at least 21 days beginning with the day after the day on which the invitation or inducement in question was first communicated to recipients of the offer.

11.   An indication of the date on which the invitation or inducement was first communicated to the recipients of the offer.

12.   An indication that the acquisition of the shares or debentures to which the offer relates is not conditional upon the recipients approving, or consenting, to any payment or other benefit being made or given to any director or former director of the company in connection with, or as compensation or consideration for—

(a)   his ceasing to be a director;

(b)   his ceasing to hold any office held in conjunction with any directorship; or

(c)   in the case of a former director, his ceasing to hold any office which he held in conjunction with his former directorship and which he continued to hold after ceasing to be a director.

13.   An indication of the place where additional material listed in Part III may be inspected.

14.   The audited accounts of the company in respect of the latest accounting reference period for which the period for laying and delivering accounts under the 2006 Act has passed or, if accounts in respect of a later accounting reference period have been delivered under the relevant legislation, as shown in those accounts and not the earlier accounts.

15.   Advice to the directors of the company on the financial implications of the offer which is given by a competent person who is independent of and who has no substantial financial interest in the company or the offeror, being advice which gives the opinion of that person in relation to the offer.

16.   An indication by the directors of the company, acting as a board, of the following matters—

     (a)   whether or not there has been any material change in the financial position or prospects of the company since the end of the latest accounting reference period in respect of which audited accounts have been delivered to the relevant registrar of companies under the relevant legislation;

     (b)   if there has been any such change, the particulars of it;

     (c)   any interests, in percentage terms, which any of them have in the shares in or debentures of the company ... ;

     (d)   any interests, in percentage terms, which any of them have in the shares in or debentures of any offeror which is a body corporate ...

17.   An indication of any material interest which any director has in any contract entered into by the offeror and in any contract entered into by any member of any group of which the offeror is a member.

18.   An indication as to whether or not each director intends to accept the offer in respect of his own beneficial holdings in the company.

19.   In the case of an offeror which is a body corporate and the shares in or debentures of which are to be the consideration or any part of the consideration for the offer, an indication by the directors of the offeror that the information concerning the offeror and those shares or debentures contained in the document is correct.

20.   If the offeror is making the offer on behalf of another person—

     (a)   an indication by the offeror as to whether or not he has taken any steps to ascertain whether that person will be in a position to implement the offer;

     (b)   if he has taken any such steps, an indication by him as to what those steps are; and

     (c)   the offeror's opinion as to whether that person will be in a position to implement the offer.

21.   An indication that each of the following—

     (a)   each of the directors of the company;

     (b)   the offeror; and

     (c)   if the offeror is a body corporate, each of the directors of the offeror;

     is responsible for the information required by Part I and this Part of this Schedule insofar as it relates to themselves or their respective bodies corporate and that, to the best of their knowledge and belief (having taken all reasonable care to ensure that such is the case) the information is in accordance with the facts and that no material fact has been omitted.

22.   The particulars of—

     (a)   all shares in or debentures of the company; and

     (b)   all investments falling within paragraph 17, 19 or 21 of Schedule 1 so far as relating to shares in or debentures of the company;

     which are held by or on behalf of the offeror or each offeror, if there is more than one, or if none are so held an appropriate negative statement.

23.   An indication as to whether or not the offer is conditional upon acceptance in respect of a minimum number of shares or debentures being received and, if the offer is so conditional, what the minimum number is.

24.   Where the offer is conditional upon acceptances, an indication of the date which is the latest date on which it can become unconditional.

25.   If the offer is, or has become, unconditional an indication of the fact that it will remain open until further notice and that at least 14 days' notice will be given before it is closed.

26.   An indication as to whether or not, if circumstances arise in which an offeror is able compulsorily to acquire shares of any dissenting minority under Chapter 3 of Part 28 of the Companies Act 2006 (c. 46), that offeror intends to so acquire those shares.

27.   If shares or debentures are to be acquired for cash, an indication of the period within which the payment will be made.

28.   (1)   Subject to sub-paragraph (2), if the consideration or any part of the consideration for the shares or debentures to be acquired is shares in or debentures of an offeror—

        (a)   an indication of the nature and particulars of the offeror's business, its financial and trading prospects and its place of incorporation;

        (b)   the following information, in respect of any offeror which is a body corporate and in respect of the company, for the period of five years immediately preceding the date on which the invitation or inducement in question was first communicated to recipients of the offer—

            (i)   turnover,

            (ii)   profit on ordinary activities before and after tax,

            (iii)   extraordinary items,

            (iv)   profits and loss, and

            (v)   the rate per cent of any dividends paid, adjusted as appropriate to take account of relevant changes over the period and the total amount absorbed thereby.

    (2)   In the case of a body corporate—

        (a)   which was incorporated during the period of five years immediately preceding the date on which the invitation or inducement in question was first communicated to recipients of the offer; or

        (b)   which has, at any time during that period, been exempt from the provisions of Part 15 of the 2006 Act relating to the audit of accounts by virtue of section 477 or 480 of that Act ... ;

    the information described in sub-paragraph (1) with respect to that body corporate need be included only in relation to the period since its incorporation or since it last ceased to be exempt from those provisions of Part 15 of the 2006 Act.

29.   Particulars of the first dividend in which any such shares or debentures will participate and of the rights attaching to them (including in the case of debentures, rights as to interest) and of any restrictions on their transfer.

30.   An indication of the effect of the acceptance on the capital and income position of the holder of the shares in or debentures of the company.

31.   Particulars of all material contracts (not being contracts which were entered into in the ordinary course of business) which were entered into by each of the company and the offeror during the period of two years immediately preceding the date on which the invitation or inducement in question was first communicated to recipients of the offer.

32.   Particulars of the terms on which shares in or debentures of the company acquired in pursuance of the offer will be transferred and any restrictions on their transfer.

33.   An indication as to whether or not it is proposed, in connection with the offer, that any payment or other benefit be made or given to any director or former director of the company in connection with, or as compensation or consideration for—

    (a)   his ceasing to be a director;

    (b)   his ceasing to hold any office held in conjunction with any directorship; or

    (c)   in the case of a former director, his ceasing to hold any office which he held in conjunction with his former directorship and which he continued to hold after ceasing to be a director;

    and, if such payments or benefits are proposed, details of each one.

34.   An indication as to whether or not there exists any agreement or arrangement between—

    (a)   the offeror or any person with whom the offeror has an agreement of the kind described in section 824 of the 2006 Act; and

    (b)   any director or shareholder of the company or any person who has been such a director or shareholder;

at any time during the period of twelve months immediately preceding the date on which the invitation or inducement in question was first communicated to recipients of the offer, being an agreement or arrangement which is connected with or dependent on the offer and, if there is any such agreement or arrangement, particulars of it.

35.   An indication whether or not the offeror has reason to believe that there has been any material change in the financial position or prospects of the company since the end of the accounting reference period to which the accounts referred to in paragraph 14 relate, and if the offeror has reason to believe that there has been such a change, the particulars of it.

36.   An indication as to whether or not there is any agreement or arrangement whereby any shares or debentures acquired by the offeror in pursuance of the offer will or may be transferred to any other person, together with the names of the parties to any such agreement or arrangement and particulars of all shares and debentures in the company held by such persons.

37.   Particulars of any dealings—
      (a)   in the shares in or debentures of the company; and
      (b)   if the offeror is a body corporate, in the shares in or debentures of the offeror;
      which took place during the period of twelve months immediately preceding the date on which the invitation or inducement in question was first communicated to recipients of the offer and which were entered into by every person who was a director of either the company or the offeror during that period; and, if there have been no such dealings, an indication to that effect.

38.   In a case in which the offeror is a body corporate which is required to deliver accounts under the 2006 Act, particulars of the assets and liabilities as shown in its audited accounts in respect of the latest accounting reference period for which the period for laying and delivering accounts under the relevant legislation has passed or, if accounts in respect of a later accounting reference period have been delivered under the relevant legislation, as shown in those accounts and not the earlier accounts.

39.   Where valuations of assets are given in connection with the offer, the basis on which the valuation was made and the names and addresses of the persons who valued them and particulars of any relevant qualifications.

40.   If any profit forecast is given in connection with the offer, an indication of the assumptions on which the forecast is based.

PART III

Additional Material Available for Inspection

41.   The memorandum and articles of association of the company.

42.   If the offeror is a body corporate, the memorandum and articles of association of the offeror or, if there is no such memorandum and articles, any instrument constituting or defining the constitution of the offeror and, in either case, if the relevant document is not written in English, a certified translation in English.

43.   In the case of a company that does not fall within paragraph 45—
      (a)   the audited accounts of the company in respect of the last two accounting reference periods for which the laying and delivering of accounts under the 2006 Act has passed; and
      (b)   if accounts have been delivered to the relevant registrar of companies, in respect of a later accounting reference period, a copy of those accounts.

44.   In the case of an offeror which is required to deliver accounts to the registrar of companies and which does not fall within paragraph 45—
      (a)   the audited accounts of the offeror in respect of the last two accounting reference periods for which the laying and delivering of accounts under the 2006 Act has passed; and

(b) if accounts have been delivered to the relevant registrar of companies in respect of a later accounting reference period, a copy of those accounts.

45. In the case of a company or an offeror—
(a) which was incorporated during the period of three years immediately preceding the date on which the invitation or inducement in question was first communicated to recipients of the offer; or
(b) which has, at any time during that period, been exempt from the provisions of Part 15 of the 2006 Act relating to the audit of accounts by virtue of section 477 or 480 of that Act ... ;
the information described in whichever is relevant of paragraph 43 or 44 with respect to that body corporate need be included only in relation to the period since its incorporation or since it last ceased to be exempt from those provisions of Part 15 of the 2006 Act.

46. All existing contracts of service entered into for a period of more than one year between the company and any of its directors and, if the offeror is a body corporate, between the offeror and any of its directors.

47. Any report, letter, valuation or other document any part of which is exhibited or referred to in the information required to be made available by Part II and this Part of this Schedule.

48. If the offer document contains any statement purporting to have been made by an expert, that expert's written consent to the inclusion of that statement.

49. All material contracts (if any) of the company and of the offeror (not, in either case, being contracts which were entered into in the ordinary course of business) which were entered into during the period of two years immediately preceding the date on which the invitation or inducement in question was first communicated to recipients of the offer.

SCHEDULE 5

...

Financial Services and Markets Act 2000 (Official Listing of Securities) Regulations 2001

S.I. 2001/2956

Note. These regulations are revoked by the Financial Services and Markets Act 2023, s. 1(1), Sch. 1, Pt. 2, as from a day to be appointed.

PART 1
GENERAL

1.   Citation and commencement

These Regulations may be cited as the Financial Services and Markets Act 2000 (Official Listing of Securities) Regulations 2001 and come into force on the day on which section 74(1) comes into force.

2.   Interpretation

(1)   In these Regulations—

"the Act" means the Financial Services and Markets Act 2000;

...

"the Financial Promotion Order" means the Financial Services and Markets Act 2000 (Financial Promotion) Order 2001;

"issuer" has the same meaning as is given, for the purposes of section 103(1), in regulation 4 below;

"non-listing prospectus" has the meaning given in section 87(2); and

"the Regulated Activities Order" means the Financial Services and Markets Act 2000 (Regulated Activities) Order 2001.

(2)   Any reference in these Regulations to a section or Schedule is, unless otherwise stated or unless the context otherwise requires, a reference to that section of or Schedule to the Act.

PART 2
MISCELLANEOUS MATTERS PRESCRIBED
FOR THE PURPOSES OF PART VI OF THE ACT

3.   Bodies whose securities may not be listed

For the purposes of section 75(3) (which provides that no application for listing may be entertained in respect of securities issued by a body of a prescribed kind) there are prescribed the following kinds of body—

(a)   where the securities are securities within the meaning of the Regulated Activities Order, a private company within the meaning of section 4(1) of the Companies Act 2006;

(b)   an old public company within the meaning of section 1 of the Companies Consolidation (Consequential Provisions) Act 1985 or article 3 of the Companies Consolidation (Consequential Provisions) (Northern Ireland) Order 1986.

4.   Meaning of "issuer"

(1)   For the purposes of section 103(1), "issuer" has the meaning given in this regulation.

(2)   In relation to certificates or other instruments falling within article 80 of the Regulated Activities Order (certificates representing certain securities), "issuer" means—

(a)   ...

(b)   for all other purposes, the person who issued or is to issue the securities to which the certificates or instruments relate.

(3)   In relation to any other securities, "issuer" means the person by whom the securities have been or are to be issued.

5.   Meaning of "approved exchange"

For the purposes of paragraph 9 of Schedule 10, "approved exchange" means a recognised investment exchange approved by the Treasury for the purposes of the Public Offers of Securities Regulations 1995 (either generally or in relation to dealings in securities).

PART 3
PERSONS RESPONSIBLE FOR LISTING PARTICULARS, PROSPECTUSES AND NON-LISTING PROSPECTUSES

6.   Responsibility for listing particulars

(1)   Subject to the following provisions of this Part, for the purposes of Part VI of the Act the persons responsible for listing particulars (including supplementary listing particulars) are—

(a)   the issuer of the securities to which the particulars relate;

(b)   where the issuer is a body corporate, each person who is a director of that body at the time when the particulars are submitted to the FCA;

(c)   where the issuer is a body corporate, each person who has authorised himself to be named, and is named, in the particulars as a director or as having agreed to become a director of that body either immediately or at a future time;

(d)   each person who accepts, and is stated in the particulars as accepting, responsibility for the particulars;

(e)   each person not falling within any of the foregoing sub-paragraphs who has authorised the contents of the particulars.

(2)   A person is not to be treated as responsible for any particulars by virtue of paragraph (1)(b) above if they are published without his knowledge or consent and on becoming aware of their publication he forthwith gives reasonable public notice that they were published without his knowledge or consent.

(3)   When accepting responsibility for particulars under paragraph (1)(d) above or authorising their contents under paragraph (1)(e) above, a person may state that he does so only in relation to certain specified parts of the particulars, or only in certain specified respects, and in such a case he is responsible under paragraph (1)(d) or (e) above—

(a)   only to the extent specified; and

(b)   only if the material in question is included in (or substantially in) the form and context to which he has agreed.

(4)   Nothing in this regulation is to be construed as making a person responsible for any particulars by reason of giving advice as to their contents in a professional capacity.

(5)   Where by virtue of this regulation the issuer of any shares pays or is liable to pay compensation under section 90 for loss suffered in respect of shares for which a person has subscribed no account is to be taken of that liability or payment in determining any question as to the amount paid on subscription for those shares or as to the amount paid up or deemed to be paid up on them.

7.   Securities issued in connection with takeovers and mergers

(1)   This regulation applies where—

(a)   listing particulars relate to securities which are to be issued in connection with—

(i)   an offer by the issuer (or by a wholly-owned subsidiary of the issuer) for securities issued by another person ("A");

(ii)   an agreement for the acquisition by the issuer (or by a wholly-owned subsidiary of the issuer) of securities issued by another person ("A"); or

(iii)   any arrangement whereby the whole of the undertaking of another person ("A") is to become the undertaking of the issuer (or of a wholly-owned subsidiary of the issuer, or of a body corporate which will become such a subsidiary by virtue of the arrangement); and

(b)   each of the specified persons is responsible by virtue of regulation 6(1)(d) above for any part ("the relevant part") of the particulars relating to A or to the securities or undertaking to which the offer, agreement or arrangement relates.

(2)   In paragraph (1)(b) above the "specified persons" are—

(a)   A; and

(b)   where A is a body corporate—

(i)   each person who is a director of A at the time when the particulars are submitted to the FCA; and

(ii)   each other person who has authorised himself to be named, and is named, in the particulars as a director of A.

(3)   Where this regulation applies, no person is to be treated as responsible for the relevant part of the particulars under regulation 6(1)(a), (b) or (c) above but without prejudice to his being responsible under regulation 6(1)(d).

(4)   In this regulation—

(a)   "listing particulars" includes supplementary listing particulars; and

(b)   "wholly-owned subsidiary" is to be construed in accordance with section 1159 of the Companies Act 2006 (and, in relation to an issuer which is not a body corporate, means a body corporate which would be a wholly-owned subsidiary of the issuer within the meaning of that section if the issuer were a body corporate).

8.   Successor companies under legislation relating to electricity

(1)   Where—

(a)   the same document contains listing particulars relating to the securities of—

(i)   two or more successor companies within the meaning of Part II of the Electricity Act 1989, or

(ii)   two or more successor companies within the meaning of Part III of the Electricity (Northern Ireland) Order 1992; and

(b)   the responsibility of any person for any information included in the document ("the relevant information") is stated in the document to be confined to its inclusion as part of the particulars relating to the securities of any one of those companies,

that person is not to be treated as responsible, by virtue of regulation 6 above, for the relevant information in so far as it is stated in the document to form part of the particulars relating to the securities of any other of those companies.

(2)   "Listing particulars" includes supplementary listing particulars.

9.   Specialist securities

(1)   This regulation applies where listing particulars relate to securities of a kind specified by listing rules for the purposes of section 82(1)(c), other than securities which are to be issued in the circumstances mentioned in regulation 7(1)(a) above.

(2)   No person is to be treated as responsible for the particulars under regulation 6(1)(a), (b) or (c) above but without prejudice to his being responsible under regulation 6(1)(d).

(3)   "Listing particulars" includes supplementary listing particulars.

10–12. ...

Criminal Justice Act 1993

1996 c. 36

An Act ... to amend and restate the law about insider dealing in securities ...

[27th July 1993]

PART V

INSIDER DEALING

The offence of insider dealing

52.   **The offence**

(1)   An individual who has information as an insider is guilty of insider dealing if, in the circumstances mentioned in subsection (3), he deals in securities that are price-affected securities in relation to the information.

(2)   An individual who has information as an insider is also guilty of insider dealing if—

     (a)   he encourages another person to deal in securities that are (whether or not that other knows it) price-affected securities in relation to the information, knowing or having reasonable cause to believe that the dealing would take place in the circumstances mentioned in subsection (3); or

     (b)   he discloses the information, otherwise than in the proper performance of the functions of his employment, office or profession, to another person.

(3)   The circumstances referred to above are that the acquisition or disposal in question occurs on a regulated market, or that the person dealing relies on a professional intermediary or is himself acting as a professional intermediary.

(4)   This section has effect subject to section 53.

53.   **Defences**

(1)   An individual is not guilty of insider dealing by virtue of dealing in securities if he shows—

     (a)   that he did not at the time expect the dealing to result in a profit attributable to the fact that the information in question was price-sensitive information in relation to the securities, or

     (b)   that at the time he believed on reasonable grounds that the information had been disclosed widely enough to ensure that none of those taking part in the dealing would be prejudiced by not having the information, or

     (c)   that he would have done what he did even if he had not had the information.

(2)   An individual is not guilty of insider dealing by virtue of encouraging another person to deal in securities if he shows—

     (a)   that he did not at the time expect the dealing to result in a profit attributable to the fact that the information in question was price-sensitive information in relation to the securities, or

     (b)   that at the time he believed on reasonable grounds that the information had been or would be disclosed widely enough to ensure that none of those taking part in the dealing would be prejudiced by not having the information, or

     (c)   that he would have done what he did even if he had not had the information.

(3)   An individual is not guilty of insider dealing by virtue of a disclosure of information if he shows—

     (a)   that he did not at the time expect any person, because of the disclosure, to deal in securities in the circumstances mentioned in subsection (3) of section 52; or

     (b)   that, although he had such an expectation at the time, he did not expect the dealing to result in a profit attributable to the fact that the information was price-sensitive information in relation to the securities.

(4)   Schedule 1 (special defences) shall have effect.

(5)   The Treasury may by order amend Schedule 1.

(6)   In this section references to a profit include references to the avoidance of a loss.

Interpretation

54.   **Securities to which Part V applies**

(1)   This Part applies to any security which—

       (a)   falls within any paragraph of Schedule 2; and

       (b)   satisfies any conditions applying to it under an order made by the Treasury for the purposes of this subsection;

     and in the provisions of this Part (other than that Schedule) any reference to a security is a reference to a security to which this Part applies.

(2)   The Treasury may by order amend Schedule 2.

55.   **"Dealing" in securities**

(1)   For the purposes of this Part, a person deals in securities if—

       (a)   he acquires or disposes of the securities (whether as principal or agent); or

       (b)   he procures, directly or indirectly, an acquisition or disposal of the securities by any other person.

(2)   For the purposes of this Part, "acquire", in relation to a security, includes—

       (a)   agreeing to acquire the security; and

       (b)   entering into a contract which creates the security.

(3)   For the purposes of this Part, "dispose", in relation to a security, includes—

       (a)   agreeing to dispose of the security; and

       (b)   bringing to an end a contract which created the security.

(4)   For the purposes of subsection (1), a person procures an acquisition or disposal of a security if the security is acquired or disposed of by a person who is—

       (a)   his agent,

       (b)   his nominee, or

       (c)   a person who is acting at his direction,

     in relation to the acquisition or disposal.

(5)   Subsection (4) is not exhaustive as to the circumstances in which one person may be regarded as procuring an acquisition or disposal of securities by another.

56.   **"Inside information", etc**

(1)   For the purposes of this section and section 57, "inside information" means information which—

       (a)   relates to particular securities or to a particular issuer of securities or to particular issuers of securities and not to securities generally or to issuers of securities generally;

       (b)   is specific or precise;

       (c)   has not been made public; and

       (d)   if it were made public would be likely to have a significant effect on the price of any securities.

(2)   For the purposes of this Part, securities are "price-affected securities" in relation to inside information, and inside information is "price-sensitive information" in relation to securities, if and only if the information would, if made public, be likely to have a significant effect on the price of the securities.

(3)   For the purposes of this section "price" includes value.

57.   **"Insiders"**

(1)   For the purposes of this Part, a person has information as an insider if and only if—

       (a)   it is, and he knows that it is, inside information, and

       (b)   he has it, and knows that he has it, from an inside source.

(2)   For the purposes of subsection (1), a person has information from an inside source if and only if—

       (a)   he has it through—

(i) being a director, employee or shareholder of an issuer of securities; or

(ii) having access to the information by virtue of his employment, office or profession; or

(b) the direct or indirect source of his information is a person within paragraph (a).

58. Information "made public"

(1) For the purposes of section 56, "made public", in relation to information, shall be construed in accordance with the following provisions of this section; but those provisions are not exhaustive as to the meaning of that expression.

(2) Information is made public if—

(a) it is published in accordance with the rules of a regulated market for the purpose of informing investors and their professional advisers;

(b) it is contained in records which by virtue of any enactment are open to inspection by the public;

(c) it can be readily acquired by those likely to deal in any securities—

(i) to which the information relates, or

(ii) of an issuer to which the information relates; or

(d) it is derived from information which has been made public.

(3) Information may be treated as made public even though—

(a) it can be acquired only by persons exercising diligence or expertise;

(b) it is communicated to a section of the public and not to the public at large;

(c) it can be acquired only by observation;

(d) it is communicated only on payment of a fee; or

(e) it is published only outside the United Kingdom.

59. "Professional intermediary"

(1) For the purposes of this Part, a "professional intermediary" is a person—

(a) who carries on a business consisting of an activity mentioned in subsection (2) and who holds himself out to the public or any section of the public (including a section of the public constituted by persons such as himself) as willing to engage in any such business; or

(b) who is employed by a person falling within paragraph (a) to carry out any such activity.

(2) The activities referred to in subsection (1) are—

(a) acquiring or disposing of securities (whether as principal or agent); or

(b) acting as an intermediary between persons taking part in any dealing in securities.

(3) A person is not to be treated as carrying on a business consisting of an activity mentioned in subsection (2)—

(a) if the activity in question is merely incidental to some other activity not falling within subsection (2); or

(b) merely because he occasionally conducts one of those activities.

(4) For the purposes of section 52, a person dealing in securities relies on a professional intermediary if and only if a person who is acting as a professional intermediary carries out an activity mentioned in subsection (2) in relation to that dealing.

60. Other interpretation provisions

(1) For the purposes of this Part, "regulated market" means any market, however operated, which, by an order made by the Treasury, is identified (whether by name or by reference to criteria prescribed by the order) as a regulated market for the purposes of this Part.

(2) For the purposes of this Part an "issuer", in relation to any securities, means any company, public sector body or individual by which or by whom the securities have been or are to be issued.

(3) For the purposes of this Part—

(a) "company" means any body (whether or not incorporated and wherever incorporated or constituted) which is not a public sector body; and

(b) "public sector body" means—

(i) the government of the United Kingdom, of Northern Ireland or of any country or territory outside the United Kingdom;

        (ii)   a local authority in the United Kingdom or elsewhere;

        (iii) any international organisation the members of which include the United Kingdom or another member State;

        (iv) the Bank of England; or

        (v)   the central bank of any sovereign State.

(4)   For the purposes of this Part, information shall be treated as relating to an issuer of securities which is a company not only where it is about the company but also where it may affect the company's business prospects.

Miscellaneous

61.   **Penalties and prosecution**

(1)   An individual guilty of insider dealing shall be liable—

      (a)   on summary conviction, to a fine not exceeding the statutory maximum or imprisonment for a term not exceeding six months or to both; or

      (b)   on conviction on indictment, to a fine or imprisonment for a term not exceeding ten years or to both.

(2)   Proceedings for offences under this Part shall not be instituted in England and Wales except by or with the consent of—

      (a)   the Secretary of State; or

      (b)   the Director of Public Prosecutions.

(3)   In relation to proceedings in Northern Ireland for offences under this Part, subsection (2) shall have effect as if the reference to the Director of Public Prosecutions were a reference to the Director of Public Prosecutions for Northern Ireland.

61A.   **Summary proceedings: venue and time limit for proceedings**

(1)   Summary proceedings for an offence of insider dealing may (without prejudice to any jurisdiction exercisable apart from this subsection) be brought against an individual at any place at which the individual is for the time being.

(2)   An information relating to an offence of insider dealing that is triable by a magistrates' court in England and Wales may be so tried if it is laid—

      (a)   at any time within three years after the commission of the offence, and

      (b)   within twelve months after the date on which evidence sufficient in the opinion of the Director of Public Prosecutions or the Secretary of State (as the case may be) to justify the proceedings comes to that person's knowledge.

(3)   Summary proceedings in Scotland for an offence of insider dealing—

      (a)   must not be commenced after the expiration of three years from the commission of the offence;

      (b)   subject to that, may be commenced at any time—

         (i)   within twelve months after the date on which evidence sufficient in the Lord Advocate's opinion to justify the proceedings came to that person's knowledge, or

         (ii) where such evidence was reported to the Lord Advocate by the Secretary of State, within twelve months after the date on which it came to the knowledge of the latter.

      Section 136(3) of the Criminal Procedure (Scotland) Act 1995 (date when proceedings deemed to be commenced) applies for the purposes of this subsection as for the purposes of that section.

(4)   A magistrates' court in Northern Ireland has jurisdiction to hear and determine a complaint charging the commission of a summary offence of insider dealing provided that the complaint is made—

      (a)   within three years from the time when the offence was committed, and

      (b)   within twelve months from the date on which evidence sufficient in the opinion of the Director of Public Prosecutions for Northern Ireland or the Secretary of State (as the case may be) to justify the proceedings comes to that person's knowledge.

(5)   For the purposes of this section a certificate of the Director of Public Prosecutions, the Lord Advocate, the Director of Public Prosecutions for Northern Ireland or the Secretary of State (as the case may be) as to the date on which such evidence as is referred to above came to that person's notice is conclusive evidence.

62.   Territorial scope of offence of insider dealing

(1)   An individual is not guilty of an offence falling within subsection (1) of section 52 unless—

    (a)   he was within the United Kingdom at the time when he is alleged to have done any act constituting or forming part of the alleged dealing;

    (b)   the regulated market on which the dealing is alleged to have occurred is one which, by an order made by the Treasury, is identified (whether by name or by reference to criteria prescribed by the order) as being, for the purposes of this Part, regulated in the United Kingdom; or

    (c)   the professional intermediary was within the United Kingdom at the time when he is alleged to have done anything by means of which the offence is alleged to have been committed.

(2)   An individual is not guilty of an offence falling within subsection (2) of section 52 unless—

    (a)   he was within the United Kingdom at the time when he is alleged to have disclosed the information or encouraged the dealing; or

    (b)   the alleged recipient of the information or encouragement was within the United Kingdom at the time when he is alleged to have received the information or encouragement.

63.   Limits on section 52

(1)   Section 52 does not apply to anything done by an individual acting on behalf of a public sector body in pursuit of monetary policies or policies with respect to exchange rates or the management of public debt or foreign exchange reserves.

(2)   No contract shall be void or unenforceable by reason only of section 52.

64.   Orders

(1)   Any power under this Part to make an order shall be exercisable by statutory instrument.

(2)   No order shall be made under this Part unless a draft of it has been laid before and approved by a resolution of each House of Parliament.

(3)   An order under this Part—

    (a)   may make different provision for different cases; and

    (b)   may contain such incidental, supplemental and transitional provisions as the Treasury consider expedient.

...

SCHEDULE 1

SPECIAL DEFENCES

Section 53(4)

Market makers

1.—   (1)   An individual is not guilty of insider dealing by virtue of dealing in securities or encouraging another person to deal if he shows that he acted in good faith in the course of—

    (a)   his business as a market maker, or

    (b)   his employment in the business of a market maker.

    (2)   A market maker is a person who—

    (a)   holds himself out at all normal times in compliance with the rules of a regulated market or an approved organisation as willing to acquire or dispose of securities; and

    (b)   is recognised as doing so under those rules.

    (3)   In this paragraph "approved organisation" means an international securities self-regulating organisation approved by the Treasury under any relevant order under section 22 of the Financial Services and Markets Act 2000.

Market information

2.— (1) An individual is not guilty of insider dealing by virtue of dealing in securities or encouraging another person to deal if he shows that—

    (a) the information which he had as an insider was market information; and

    (b) it was reasonable for an individual in his position to have acted as he did despite having that information as an insider at the time.

  (2) In determining whether it is reasonable for an individual to do any act despite having market information at the time, there shall, in particular, be taken into account—

    (a) the content of the information;

    (b) the circumstances in which he first had the information and in what capacity; and

    (c) the capacity in which he now acts.

3. An individual is not guilty of insider dealing by virtue of dealing in securities or encouraging another person to deal if he shows—

    (a) that he acted—

      (i) in connection with an acquisition or disposal which was under consideration or the subject of negotiation, or in the course of a series of such acquisitions or disposals; and

      (ii) with a view to facilitating the accomplishment of the acquisition or disposal or the series of acquisitions or disposals; and

    (b) that the information which he had as an insider was market information arising directly out of his involvement in the acquisition or disposal or series of acquisitions or disposals.

4. For the purposes of paragraphs 2 and 3 market information is information consisting of one or more of the following facts—

    (a) that securities of a particular kind have been or are to be acquired or disposed of, or that their acquisition or disposal is under consideration or the subject of negotiation;

    (b) that securities of a particular kind have not been or are not to be acquired or disposed of;

    (c) the number of securities acquired or disposed of or to be acquired or disposed of or whose acquisition or disposal is under consideration or the subject of negotiation;

    (d) the price (or range of prices) at which securities have been or are to be acquired or disposed of or the price (or range of prices) at which securities whose acquisition or disposal is under consideration or the subject of negotiation may be acquired or disposed of;

    (e) the identity of the persons involved or likely to be involved in any capacity in an acquisition or disposal.

Buy-back programmes and stabilisation

5.— (1) An individual is not guilty of insider dealing by virtue of dealing in securities or encouraging an-other person to deal if he shows that he acted in conformity with—

    (a) Article 5 of Regulation (EU) No 596/2014 of the European Parliament and of the Council of 16 April 2014 on market abuse (market abuse regulation), as that Article has effect at the time mentioned in sub-paragraph (2), and—

      (i) each EU regulation, originally made under that Article before that time, which is assimilated direct legislation; and

      (ii) all subordinate legislation (within the meaning of the Interpretation Act 1978) made under that Article on or after IP completion day;

    (b) rules made under section 137Q(1) of the Financial Services and Markets Act 2000.

  (2) The time is the beginning of the day on which the Market Abuse (Amendment) (EU Exit) Regulations 2019 are made.

6. An individual ("A") is not guilty of insider dealing by virtue of dealing, or encouraging another person to deal, in securities through a trading venue in Gibraltar if A shows that A acted in conformity with—

    (a) the following as they have effect in Gibraltar law—

      (i) Article 5 of Regulation (EU) No 596/2014 of the European Parliament and of the Council of 16 April 2014 on market abuse (market abuse regulation), and

        (ii)   each EU regulation originally made under that Article, and

    (b)   all other applicable Gibraltar law (if any).

7.   An individual ("A") is not guilty of insider dealing by virtue of dealing, or encouraging another person to deal, in securities through a trading venue in an EEA State if A shows that A acted in conformity with—

    (a)   the following as they apply in the EEA State—

        (i)   Article 5 of Regulation (EU) No 596/2014 of the European Parliament and of the Council of 16 April 2014 on market abuse (market abuse regulation), and

        (ii)   each EU regulation made under that Article, and

    (b)   all other applicable law of the EEA State (if any).

8.   For the purposes of paragraphs 6 and 7 "trading venue" has the meaning given by Article 2(1)(16) of Regulation (EU) No 600/2014 of the European Parliament and of the Council of 15 May 2014 on markets in financial instruments and amending Regulation (EU) No 648/2012, as substituted by the Markets in Financial Instruments (Amendment) (EU Exit) Regulations 2018 (S.I. 2018/1403).

SCHEDULE 2

SECURITIES

Section 54

PART I
SECURITIES

1.   Transferable securities.

2.   Money-market instruments.

3.   Units in collective investment undertakings.

4.   Options, futures, swaps, forward rate agreements and any other derivative contracts relating to securities, currencies, interest rates or yields, emission allowances or other derivatives instruments, financial indices or financial measures which may be settled physically or in cash.

5.   Options, futures, swaps, forwards and any other derivative contracts relating to commodities that must be settled in cash or may be settled in cash at the option of one of the parties (other than by reason of a default or other termination event).

6.   Options, futures, swaps, and any other derivative contract relating to commodities that can be physically settled provided they are traded on a UK regulated market, a UK MTF or a UK OTF, except for wholesale energy products traded on a UK OTF that must be physically settled.

7.   Options, futures, swaps, forwards and any other derivative contracts relating to commodities, that can be physically settled not otherwise mentioned in paragraph 6 and not being for commercial purposes or wholesale energy products traded on an EU OTF that must be physically settled, which have the characteristics of other derivative financial instruments.

8.   Derivative instruments for the transfer of credit risk.

9.   Financial contracts for differences.

10.   Options, futures, swaps, forward rate agreements and any other derivative contracts relating to climatic variables, freight rates or inflation rates or other official economic statistics that must be settled in cash or may be settled in cash at the option of one of the parties other than by reason of default or other termination event, as well as any other derivative contracts relating to assets, rights, obligations, indices and measures not otherwise mentioned in this Schedule, which have the characteristics of other derivative financial instruments, having regard to whether, inter alia, they are traded on a UK regulated market, a UK OTF, or a UK MTF.

11.   Emission allowances consisting of any units recognised for compliance with the requirements of Directive 2003/87/EC (Emissions Trading Scheme) or allowances created under article 18 of the Greenhouse Gas Emissions Trading Scheme Order 2020.

PART II
INTERPRETATION

12.   Part 2 of Schedule 2 to the RAO ("the RAO Schedule") (financial instruments and investment services and activities) applies for the purposes of Part 1 of this Schedule as it applies for the purposes of Part 1 of the RAO Schedule but as if references in Part 2 of the RAO Schedule to paragraphs in Part 1 of the RAO Schedule were references to the equivalent paragraphs in Part 1 of this Schedule.

13.   Terms used in this Schedule and in the RAO have the same meaning in this Schedule as in the RAO.

14.   References in paragraphs 12 and 13 to the RAO are to the Financial Services and Markets Act 2000 (Regulated Activities) Order 2001 (S.I. 2001/544) as it had effect on 17th April 2023.

Financial Services Act 2012

2012 c. 21

An Act to amend the Bank of England Act 1998, the Financial Services and Markets Act 2000 and the Banking Act 2009; to make other provision about financial services and markets; to make provision about the exercise of certain statutory functions relating to building societies, friendly societies and other mutual societies; to amend section 785 of the Companies Act 2006; to make provision enabling the Director of Savings to provide services to other public bodies; and for connected purposes.

[19th December 2012]

PART 7
OFFENCES RELATING TO FINANCIAL SERVICES

89. **Misleading statements**

(1) Subsection (2) applies to a person ("P") who—

    (a) makes a statement which P knows to be false or misleading in a material respect,

    (b) makes a statement which is false or misleading in a material respect, being reckless as to whether it is, or

    (c) dishonestly conceals any material facts whether in connection with a statement made by P or otherwise.

(2) P commits an offence if P makes the statement or conceals the facts with the intention of inducing, or is reckless as to whether making it or concealing them may induce, another person (whether or not the person to whom the statement is made)—

    (a) to enter into or offer to enter into, or to refrain from entering or offering to enter into, a relevant agreement, or

    (b) to exercise, or refrain from exercising, any rights conferred by a relevant investment.

(3) In proceedings for an offence under subsection (2) brought against a person to whom that subsection applies as a result of paragraph (a) of subsection (1), it is a defence for the person charged ("D") to show that the statement was made in conformity with—

    (a) price stabilising rules,

    (b) control of information rules, or

    (c) the relevant provisions of Article 5 (exemption for buy-back programmes and stabilisation) of the market abuse regulation.

(4) Subsections (1) and (2) do not apply unless—

    (a) the statement is made in or from, or the facts are concealed in or from, the United Kingdom or arrangements are made in or from the United Kingdom for the statement to be made or the facts to be concealed,

    (b) the person on whom the inducement is intended to or may have effect is in the United Kingdom, or

    (c) the agreement is or would be entered into or the rights are or would be exercised in the United Kingdom.

90. **Misleading impressions**

(1) A person ("P") who does any act or engages in any course of conduct which creates a false or misleading impression as to the market in or the price or value of any relevant investments commits an offence if—

    (a) P intends to create the impression, and

    (b) the case falls within subsection (2) or (3) (or both).

(2) The case falls within this subsection if P intends, by creating the impression, to induce another person to acquire, dispose of, subscribe for or underwrite the investments or to refrain from doing so or to exercise or refrain from exercising any rights conferred by the investments.

(3)   The case falls within this subsection if—

    (a)   P knows that the impression is false or misleading or is reckless as to whether it is, and

    (b)   P intends by creating the impression to produce any of the results in subsection (4) or is aware that creating the impression is likely to produce any of the results in that subsection.

(4)   Those results are—

    (a)   the making of a gain for P or another, or

    (b)   the causing of loss to another person or the exposing of another person to the risk of loss.

(5)   References in subsection (4) to gain or loss are to be read in accordance with subsections (6) to (8).

(6)   "Gain" and "loss"—

    (a)   extend only to gain or loss in money or other property of any kind;

    (b)   include such gain or loss whether temporary or permanent.

(7)   "Gain" includes a gain by keeping what one has, as well as a gain by getting what one does not have.

(8)   "Loss" includes a loss by not getting what one might get, as well as a loss by parting with what one has.

(9)   In proceedings brought against any person ("D") for an offence under subsection (1) it is a defence for D to show—

    (a)   to the extent that the offence results from subsection (2), that D reasonably believed that D's conduct would not create an impression that was false or misleading as to the matters mentioned in subsection (1),

    (b)   that D acted or engaged in the conduct—

        (i)   for the purpose of stabilising the price of investments, and

        (ii)   in conformity with price stabilising rules,

    (c)   that D acted or engaged in the conduct in conformity with control of information rules, or

    (d)   that D acted or engaged in the conduct in conformity with the relevant provisions of Article 5 (exemption for buy-back programmes and stabilisation) of the market abuse regulation.

(10)   This section does not apply unless—

    (a)   the act is done, or the course of conduct is engaged in, in the United Kingdom, or

    (b)   the false or misleading impression is created there.

(11)   See section 137Q(3) of FSMA 2000 regarding the power of the FCA to make rules for the purposes of subsection (9)(d).

91.   Misleading statements etc in relation to benchmarks

(1)   A person ("A") who makes to another person ("B") a false or misleading statement commits an offence if—

    (a)   A makes the statement in the course of arrangements for the setting of a relevant benchmark,

    (b)   A intends that the statement should be used by B for the purpose of the setting of a relevant benchmark, and

    (c)   A knows that the statement is false or misleading or is reckless as to whether it is.

(2)   A person ("C") who does any act or engages in any course of conduct which creates a false or misleading impression as to the price or value of any investment or as to the interest rate appropriate to any transaction commits an offence if—

    (a)   C intends to create the impression,

    (b)   the impression may affect the setting of a relevant benchmark,

    (c)   C knows that the impression is false or misleading or is reckless as to whether it is, and

    (d)   C knows that the impression may affect the setting of a relevant benchmark.

(3)   In proceedings for an offence under subsection (1), it is a defence for the person charged ("D") to show that the statement was made in conformity with—

    (a)   ...

    (b)   control of information rules, or

(c) the relevant provisions of Article 5 (exemption for buy-back programmes and stabilisation) of the market abuse regulation.

(4) In proceedings brought against any person ("D") for an offence under subsection (2) it is a defence for D to show—

    (a) that D acted or engaged in the conduct—

        (i) for the purpose of stabilising the price of investments, and

        (ii) in conformity with price stabilising rules,

    (b) that D acted or engaged in the conduct in conformity with control of information rules, or

    (c) that D acted or engaged in the conduct in conformity with the relevant provisions of Article 5 (exemption for buy-back programmes and stabilisation) of the market abuse regulation.

(5) Subsection (1) does not apply unless the statement is made in or from the United Kingdom or to a person in the United Kingdom.

(6) Subsection (2) does not apply unless—

    (a) the act is done, or the course of conduct is engaged in, in the United Kingdom, or

    (b) the false or misleading impression is created there.

(7) See section 137Q(3) of FSMA 2000 regarding the power of the FCA to make rules for the purposes of subsection (4)(c).

92. Penalties

(1) A person guilty of an offence under this Part is liable—

    (a) on summary conviction, to imprisonment for a term not exceeding the applicable maximum term or a fine not exceeding the statutory maximum, or both;

    (b) on conviction on indictment, to imprisonment for a term not exceeding 10 years or a fine, or both.

(2) For the purpose of subsection (1)(a) "the applicable maximum term" is—

    (a) in England and Wales, the general limit in a magistrates' court (or 6 months, if the offence was committed before 2 May 2022);

    (b) in Scotland, 12 months;

    (c) in Northern Ireland, 6 months.

93. Interpretation of Part 7

(1) This section has effect for the interpretation of this Part.

(2) "Investment" includes any asset, right or interest.

(3) "Relevant agreement" means an agreement—

    (a) the entering into or performance of which by either party constitutes an activity of a kind specified in an order made by the Treasury, and

    (b) which relates to a relevant investment.

(4) "Relevant benchmark" means a benchmark of a kind specified in an order made by the Treasury.

(5) "Relevant investment" means an investment of a kind specified in an order made by the Treasury.

(6) Schedule 2 to FSMA 2000 (except paragraphs 25 and 26) applies for the purposes of subsections (3) and (5) with references to section 22 of that Act being read as references to each of those subsections.

(7) Nothing in Schedule 2 to FSMA 2000, as applied by subsection (6), limits the power conferred by subsection (3) or (5).

(8) "Price stabilising rules" and "control of information rules" have the same meaning as in FSMA 2000.

(8A) "Market abuse regulation" means Regulation (EU) No 596/2014 of the European Parliament and of the Council of 16 April 2014 on market abuse (market abuse regulation) and repealing Directive 2003/6/EC of the European Parliament and of the Council and Commission Directives 2003/124/EC, 2003/125/EC and 2004/72/EC.

(8B) References to Article 5 of the market abuse regulation include—

    (a) any EU regulation, originally made under that Article, which is assimilated direct legislation, and

    (b)   any subordinate legislation (within the meaning of the Interpretation Act 1978) made under that Article on or after IP completion day.

(9)   In this section "benchmark" has the meaning given in section 22(6) of FSMA 2000.

94.   Affirmative procedure for certain orders

(1)   This section applies to the first order made under section 93.

(2)   This section also applies to any subsequent order made under that section which contains a statement by the Treasury that the effect of the proposed order would include one or more of the following—

    (a)   that an activity which is not specified for the purposes of subsection (3)(a) of that section would become one so specified,

    (b)   that an investment which is not a relevant investment would become a relevant investment;

    (c)   that a benchmark which is not a relevant benchmark would become a relevant benchmark.

(3)   A statutory instrument containing (alone or with other provisions) an order to which this section applies may not be made unless a draft of the instrument has been laid before Parliament and approved by a resolution of each House.

95.   Consequential repeal

Section 397 of FSMA 2000 (which relates to misleading statements and practices and is superseded by the provisions of this Part) is repealed.

Regulation (EU) No 596/2014 of the European Parliament and of the Council
of 16 April 2014
on market abuse (market abuse regulation) and repealing Directive 2003/6/EC of the European Parliament and of the Council and Commission Directives 2003/124/EC, 2003/125/EC and 2004/72/EC

(assimilated law)

Note. This Regulation is revoked by the Financial Services and Markets Act 2023, s. 1(1), Sch. 1, Pt. 1, as from a day to be appointed.

CHAPTER 1
GENERAL PROVISIONS

Article 1

Subject matter

This Regulation establishes a ... regulatory framework on insider dealing, the unlawful disclosure of inside information and market manipulation (market abuse) as well as measures to prevent market abuse to ensure the integrity of financial markets in the United Kingdom and to enhance investor protection and confidence in those markets.

Article 2

Scope

1. *This Regulation applies to the following:*
   (a) *financial instruments admitted to trading on a UK regulated market, Gibraltar regulated market or an EU regulated market or for which a request for admission to trading on a UK regulated market, Gibraltar regulated market or an EU regulated market has been made;*
   (b) *financial instruments traded on a UK MTF, Gibraltar MTF or an EU MTF, admitted to trading on a UK MTF, Gibraltar MTF or an EU MTF or for which a request for admission to trading on a UK MTF, Gibraltar MTF or an EU MTF has been made;*
   (c) *financial instruments traded on a UK OTF, Gibraltar OTF or an EU OTF;*
   (d) *financial instruments not covered by point (a), (b) or (c), the price or value of which depends on or has an effect on the price or value of a financial instrument referred to in those points, including, but not limited to, credit default swaps and contracts for difference.*

   This Regulation also applies to behaviour or transactions, including bids, relating to the auctioning on an auction platform in relation to which a recognition order is in force under the Recognised Auction Platforms Regulations 2011 of emission allowances or other auctioned products based thereon ... pursuant to the Greenhouse Gas Emissions Trading Scheme Auctioning Regulations 2021. Without prejudice to any specific provisions referring to bids submitted in the context of an auction, any requirements and prohibitions in this Regulation referring to orders to trade shall apply to such bids.

2. *Articles 12 and 15 also apply to:*
   (a) *spot commodity contracts, which are not wholesale energy products, where the transaction, order or behaviour has or is likely or intended to have an effect on the price or value of a financial instrument referred to in paragraph 1;*

(b) *types of financial instruments, including derivative contracts or derivative instruments for the transfer of credit risk, where the transaction, order, bid or behaviour has or is likely to have an effect on the price or value of a spot commodity contract where the price or value depends on the price or value of those financial instruments; and*

(c) *behaviour in relation to benchmarks.*

3. *This Regulation applies to any transaction, order or behaviour concerning any financial instrument as referred to in paragraphs 1 and 2, irrespective of whether or not such transaction, order or behaviour takes place on a trading venue.*

4. *The prohibitions and requirements in this Regulation shall apply to actions and omissions, wherever those actions and omissions take place, whether in the United Kingdom or another country or territory, concerning the instruments referred to in paragraphs 1 and 2.*

Article 3

Definitions

1. *For the purposes of this Regulation, the following definitions apply:*

(1) *'financial instrument' means those instruments specified in Part 1 of Schedule 2 to the Financial Services and Markets Act 2000 (Regulated Activities) Order 2001, read with Part 2 of that Schedule;*

(2) *'investment firm' means an investment firm as defined in Article 2(1A) of the Markets in Financial Instruments Regulation;*

(3) *'credit institution' means a credit institution as defined in point (1) of Article 4(1) of Regulation (EU) No 575/2013 of the European Parliament and of the Council;*

(4) *'financial institution' means a financial institution as defined in—*

  (a) *Regulation (EU) No 575/2013 as that Regulation forms part of domestic law by virtue of section 3 of the European Union (Withdrawal) Act 2018; or*

  (b) *Regulation (EU) No 575/2013 as that Regulation applies in the European Union;*

(5) *'market operator' means a market operator as defined in Article 2(1)(10) of the Markets in Financial Instruments Regulation;*

(6) *'regulated market' has the meaning given in Article 2(1)(13) of the Markets in Financial Instruments Regulation;*

(6A) *'UK regulated market' has the meaning given in Article 2(1)(13A) of the Markets in Financial Instruments Regulation;*

(6B) *'EU regulated market' has the meaning given in Article 2(1)(13B) of the Markets in Financial Instruments Regulation;*

(6C) *'Gibraltar regulated market' means a regulated market which is authorised and functions regularly and in accordance with Part 3 of the Financial Services (Markets in Financial Instruments) Act 2018 of Gibraltar;*

(7) *'multilateral trading facility' or 'MTF' has the meaning given in Article 2(1)(14) of the Markets in Financial Instruments Regulation;*

(7A) *'UK multilateral trading facility' or 'UK MTF' has the meaning given in Article 2(1)(14A) of the Markets in Financial Instruments Regulation;*

(7B) *'EU multilateral trading facility' or 'EU MTF' has the meaning given in Article 2(1)(14B) of the Markets in Financial Instruments Regulation;*

(7C) *'Gibraltar multilateral trading facility' or 'Gibraltar MTF' means a multilateral system, operated by an investment firm or a market operator, which brings together multiple third-party buying and selling interests in financial instruments (in the system and in accordance with non-discretionary rules) in a way which results in a contract in accordance with Part 2 of the Financial Services (Markets in Financial Instruments) Act 2018 of Gibraltar;*

(8) *'organised trading facility' or 'OTF' has the meaning given in Article 2(1)(15) of the Markets in Financial Instruments Regulation;*

(8A) *'UK organised trading facility' or 'UK OTF' has the meaning given in Article 2(1)(15A) of the Markets in Financial Instruments Regulation;*

(8B) *'EU organised trading facility' or 'EU OTF' has the meaning given in Article 2(1)(15B) of the Markets in Financial Instruments Regulation;*

(8C) *'Gibraltar organised trading facility' or 'Gibraltar OTF' means a multilateral system—*

    (a) *which is not a regulated market or an MTF;*

    (b) *in which multiple third-party buying and selling interests in bonds, structured finance products, emission allowances or derivatives are able to interact in the system in a way that results in a contract, in accordance with Part 2 of the Financial Services (Markets in Financial Instruments) Act 2018 of Gibraltar;*

(9) *'accepted market practice' means a specific market practice that is accepted by the FCA in accordance with Article 13;*

(10) *'trading venue' means a regulated market, an MTF or an OTF;*

(10A) *'UK trading venue' means a UK regulated market, a UK MTF or a UK OTF;*

(10B) *'EU trading venue' means an EU regulated market, an EU MTF or an EU OTF;*

(10C) *'Gibraltar trading venue' means a Gibraltar regulated market, a Gibraltar MTF or a Gibraltar OTF;*

(11) *'SME growth market' means SME growth market as defined in regulation 2(1) of the Financial Services and Markets Act 2000 (Markets in Financial Instruments) Regulations 2017;*

(12) *'competent authority' means—*

    (a) *in relation to an EEA state, the authority which has been designated by that Member State as its competent authority for the purposes of Article 22 of this Regulation as it was in force before IP completion day; and*

    (b) *in relation to a third country which is not an EEA state, the supervisory authority which exercises functions equivalent to those exercised by competent authorities in Member States in accordance with this Regulation as it was in force before IP completion day;*

(13) *'person' means a natural or legal person;*

(14) *'commodity' means a commodity as defined in point (1) of Article 2 of Commission Regulation (EC) No 1287/2006;*

(15) *'spot commodity contract' means a contract for the supply of a commodity traded on a spot market which is promptly delivered when the transaction is settled, and a contract for the supply of a commodity that is not a financial instrument, including a physically settled forward contract;*

(16) *'spot market' means a commodity market in which commodities are sold for cash and promptly delivered when the transaction is settled, and other non-financial markets, such as forward markets for commodities;*

(17) *'buy-back programme' means trading in own shares in accordance with Articles 21 to 27 of Directive 2012/30/EU of the European Parliament and of the Council or the law of the United Kingdom or Gibraltar which was relied on by the United Kingdom or Gibraltar respectively immediately before IP completion day to implement those Articles;*

(18) *'algorithmic trading' means algorithmic trading as defined in regulation 2(1) of the Financial Services and Markets Act 2000 (Markets in Financial Instruments) Regulations 2017;*

(19) *'emission allowance' means emission allowance as described in paragraph 11 of Part 1 of Schedule 2 to the Financial Services and Markets Act 2000 (Regulated Activities) Order 2001;*

(19a) *'UK emission allowance' means an allowance created under the Greenhouse Gas Emissions Trading Scheme Order 2020;*

(19b) *'EU emission allowance' means an emission allowance recognised for compliance with the requirements of Directive 2003/87/EC;*

(19c) *'UK installation', 'UK aviation activities', 'EU installation' and 'EU aviation activities' have the meanings given in Article 7(4);*

(20) *'emission allowance market participant' means—*

    (a)   *a UK emission allowance market participant, and*

    (b)   *any person who would be treated as an emission allowance market participant under Article 3(20) of Regulation (EU) 596/2014 as it applies in the European Union;*

(20A) *'UK emission allowance market participant' means any person who—*

    (a)   *enters directly or indirectly into transactions, including the placing of orders to trade, in UK emission allowances, auctioned products based thereon, or derivatives thereof and*

    (b)   *does not benefit from an exemption based on the second subparagraph of Article 17(2) of this Regulation;*

(21) *'issuer' means a legal entity governed by private or public law, which issues or proposes to issue financial instruments, the issuer being, in case of depository receipts representing financial instruments, the issuer of the financial instrument represented;*

(22) *'wholesale energy product' means wholesale energy product as defined in point (4) of Article 2 of Regulation (EU) No 1227/2011;*

(23) *'national regulatory authority' means national regulatory authority as defined in point (10) of Article 2 of Regulation (EU) No 1227/2011;*

(24) *'commodity derivatives' means commodity derivatives as defined in point (30) of Article 2(1) of Regulation (EU) No 600/2014 of the European Parliament and of the Council;*

(25) *'person discharging managerial responsibilities' means a person within an issuer, a UK emission allowance market participant or another entity referred to in Article 19(10) who is:*

    (a)   *a member of the administrative, management or supervisory body of that entity; or*

    (b)   *a senior executive who is not a member of the bodies referred to in point (a), who has regular access to inside information relating directly or indirectly to that entity and power to take managerial decisions affecting the future developments and business prospects of that entity;*

(26) *'person closely associated' means:*

    (a)   *a spouse, or a partner considered to be equivalent to a spouse in accordance with national law;*

    (b)   *a dependent child, in accordance with national law;*

    (c)   *a relative who has shared the same household for at least one year on the date of the transaction concerned; or*

    (d)   *a legal person, trust or partnership, the managerial responsibilities of which are discharged by a person discharging managerial responsibilities or by a person referred to in point (a), (b) or (c), or which is directly or indirectly controlled by such a person, or which is set up for the benefit of such a person, or the economic interests of which are substantially equivalent to those of such a person;*

(27) *'data traffic records' means records of any data processed for the purpose of the conveyance of a communication on an electronic communications network or for the billing thereof;*

(28) *'person professionally arranging or executing transactions' means a person professionally engaged in the reception and transmission of orders for, or in the execution of transactions in, financial instruments;*

(29) *'benchmark' means any rate, index or figure, made available to the public or published that is periodically or regularly determined by the application of a formula to, or on the basis of the value of one or more underlying assets or prices, including estimated prices, actual or estimated interest rates or other values, or surveys, and by reference to which the amount payable under a financial instrument or the value of a financial instrument is determined;*

(30) *'market maker' means a market maker as defined in Article 2(1)(6) of the Markets in Financial Instruments Regulation;*

(31) 'stake-building' means an acquisition of securities in a company which does not trigger a legal or regulatory obligation to make an announcement of a takeover bid in relation to that company;

(32) 'disclosing market participant' means a person who falls into any of the categories set out in points (a) to (d) of Article 11(1) or of Article 11(2), and discloses information in the course of a market sounding;

(33) 'high-frequency trading' means high-frequency algorithmic trading technique as defined in regulation 2(1) of the Financial Services and Markets Act 2000 (Markets in Financial Instruments) Regulations 2017;

(34) 'information recommending or suggesting an investment strategy' means information:

    (i)   produced by an independent analyst, an investment firm, a credit institution, any other person whose main business is to produce investment recommendations or a natural person working for them under a contract of employment or otherwise, which, directly or indirectly, expresses a particular investment proposal in respect of a financial instrument or an issuer; or

    (ii) produced by persons other than those referred to in point (i), which directly proposes a particular investment decision in respect of a financial instrument;

(35) 'investment recommendations' means information recommending or suggesting an investment strategy, explicitly or implicitly, concerning one or several financial instruments or the issuers, including any opinion as to the present or future value or price of such instruments, intended for distribution channels or for the public.

(36) 'FCA' means the Financial Conduct Authority;

(36A) 'GFSC' means the Financial Services Commission of Gibraltar;

(37) 'the Markets in Financial Instruments Regulation' means Regulation (EU) No 600/2014 of the European Parliament and of the Council of 15 May 2014 on markets in financial instruments and amending Regulation (EU) No 648/2012, as it forms part of domestic law by virtue of section 3 of the EU (Withdrawal) Act 2018, and as it is modified by domestic law from time to time;

(38) 'the EU Market Abuse Regulation' means Regulation (EU) No 596/2014 of the European Parliament and of the Council on market abuse as it has effect in the European Union;

(39) references to a 'third country' (including in expressions including the words 'third country') are to be read as references to a country other than the United Kingdom.

2.   For the purposes of Article 5, the following definitions apply:

    (a) 'securities' means:

        (i)   shares and other securities equivalent to shares;

        (ii) bonds and other forms of securitised debt; or

        (iii) securitised debt convertible or exchangeable into shares or into other securities equivalent to shares.

    (b) 'associated instruments' means the following financial instruments, including those which are not admitted to trading or traded on a UK trading venue, Gibraltar trading venue or an EU trading venue, or for which a request for admission to trading on a UK trading venue, Gibraltar trading venue or an EU trading venue has not been made:

        (i)   contracts or rights to subscribe for, acquire or dispose of securities;

        (ii) financial derivatives of securities;

        (iii) where the securities are convertible or exchangeable debt instruments, the securities into which such convertible or exchangeable debt instruments may be converted or exchanged;

        (iv) instruments which are issued or guaranteed by the issuer or guarantor of the securities and whose market price is likely to materially influence the price of the securities, or vice versa;

        (v) where the securities are securities equivalent to shares, the shares represented by those securities and any other securities equivalent to those shares;

(c)   *'significant distribution' means an initial or secondary offer of securities that is distinct from ordinary trading both in terms of the amount in value of the securities to be offered and the selling method to be employed;*

(d)   *'stabilisation' means a purchase or offer to purchase securities, or a transaction in associated instruments equivalent thereto, which is undertaken by a credit institution or an investment firm in the context of a significant distribution of such securities exclusively for supporting the market price of those securities for a predetermined period of time, due to a selling pressure in such securities.*

Article 4

Notifications and list of financial instruments

1.   *Market operators of UK regulated markets and investment firms and market operators operating a UK MTF or a UK OTF shall, without delay, notify the FCA of any financial instrument for which a request for admission to trading on their trading venue is made, which is admitted to trading, or which is traded for the first time.*

    They shall also notify the FCA when a financial instrument ceases to be traded or to be admitted to trading, unless the date on which the financial instrument ceases to be traded or to be admitted to trading is known and was referred to in the notification made in accordance with the first subparagraph.

    Notifications referred to in this paragraph shall include, as appropriate, the names and identifiers of the financial instruments concerned, and the date and time of the request for admission to trading, admission to trading, and the date and time of the first trade.

    ...

2.   *The FCA shall publish notifications received under paragraph 1 on its website in the form of a list without delay. The FCA shall update that list without delay following receipt of a notification received under paragraph 1. The list shall not limit the scope of this Regulation.*

3.   *The list shall contain the following information:*

    (a)   *the names and identifiers of financial instruments which are the subject of a request for admission to trading, admitted to trading or traded for the first time, on UK regulated markets, UK MTFs and UK OTFs;*

    (b)   *the dates and times of the requests for admission to trading, of the admissions to trading, or of the first trades;*

    (c)   *details of the UK trading venues on which the financial instruments are the subject of a request for admission to trading, admitted to trading or traded for the first time; and*

    (d)   *the date and time at which the financial instruments cease to be traded or to be admitted to trading.*

4.   *The FCA may make technical standards specifying—*

    (a)   *the content of the notifications referred to in paragraph 1;*

    (b)   *the manner and conditions of the compilation, publication and maintenance of the list referred to in paragraph 2.*

5.   *The FCA may make technical standards specifying the timing, format and template of the submission of notifications under paragraph 1.*

Article 5

Exemption for buy-back programmes and stabilisation

1.   *The prohibitions in Articles 14 and 15 of this Regulation do not apply to trading in own shares in buy-back programmes where:*

    (a)   *the full details of the programme are disclosed prior to the start of trading;*

    (b)   *trades are reported as being part of the buy-back programme to the FCA, GFSC or European competent authority in accordance with paragraph 3 and subsequently disclosed to the public;*

    (c)   *adequate limits with regard to price and volume are complied with; and*

(d)   it is carried out in accordance with the objectives referred to in paragraph 2 and the conditions set out in this Article and in the ... technical standards referred to in paragraph 6.

2.   In order to benefit from the exemption provided for in paragraph 1, a buy-back programme shall have as its sole purpose:

(a)   to reduce the capital of an issuer;

(b)   to meet obligations arising from debt financial instruments that are exchangeable into equity instruments; or

(c)   to meet obligations arising from share option programmes, or other allocations of shares, to employees or to members of the administrative, management or supervisory bodies of the issuer or of an associate company.

3.   In order to benefit from the exemption in paragraph 1—

(a)   where shares have been admitted to trading or are traded on a UK trading venue, the issuer must report to the FCA each transaction relating to the buy-back programme including the information specified in Article 25(1) and (2) and Article 26(1), (2) and (3) of the Markets in Financial Instruments Regulation (and for these purposes, Article 26 of that Regulation applies as if the obligation in paragraph (2)(a) only applied to financial instruments which are admitted to trading or traded on a UK trading venue);

(b)   where shares have been admitted to trading or are traded on an EU trading venue, the issuer must make the reports to the competent authority of the trading venue on which the shares have been admitted to trading or are traded which are required in accordance with Article 5(3) of the EU Market Abuse Regulation;

(c)   where shares have been admitted to trading or are traded on a Gibraltar trading venue, the issuer must report to the GFSC each transaction relating to the buy-back programme, including the information referred to in Article 5(3) of Regulation (EU) No 596/2014 of the European Parliament and of the Council on market abuse (as it applies in Gibraltar after exit day).

4.   The prohibitions in Articles 14 and 15 of this Regulation do not apply to trading in securities or associated instruments for the stabilisation of securities where:

(a)   stabilisation is carried out for a limited period;

(b)   relevant information about the stabilisation is disclosed and notified—

(i)   where the securities or associated instruments are traded on a UK trading venue, to the FCA in accordance with paragraph 5;

(ii)   where the securities or associated instruments are traded on an EU trading venue, to the European competent authority of the trading venue in accordance with Article 5(5) of the EU Market Abuse Regulation;

(iii)   where the securities or associated instruments are traded on a Gibraltar trading venue, to the GFSC in accordance with Article 5(5) of Regulation (EU) No 596/2014 of the European Parliament and of the Council on market abuse (as it applies in Gibraltar after exit day);

(c)   adequate limits with regard to price are complied with; and

(d)   such trading complies with the conditions for stabilisation laid down in the ... technical standards referred to in paragraph 6.

5.   ..., the details of all stabilisation transactions shall be notified by issuers, offerors, or entities undertaking the stabilisation, whether or not they act on behalf of such persons, to the FCA (where the securities or associated instruments are traded on a UK trading venue) no later than the end of the seventh daily market session following the date of execution of such transactions.

6.   The technical standards referred to in this paragraph are—

(a)   Commission Delegated Regulation (EU) 2016/1052 of 8 March 2016 supplementing Regulation (EU) 596/2014 of the European Parliament and of the Council with regard to regulatory technical standards for the conditions applicable to buy-back programmes and stabilisation measures—

> > (i)   as that Regulation forms part of domestic law, where the trading takes place on a UK trading venue; or
> >
> > (ii)   as that Regulation applies in the European Union, where the trading takes place on an EU trading venue;
> >
> > (iii) as that Regulation forms part of the law of Gibraltar, where the trading takes place on a Gibraltar trading venue;
>
> (b) any technical standards made by the FCA under paragraph 7, where the trading takes place on a UK trading venue;
>
> (c) any other regulatory technical standards adopted by the Commission under Article 5(6) of Regulation (EU) No 596/2014 of the European Parliament and of the Council on market abuse as it has effect in the European Union, where the trading takes place on an EU trading venue;
>
> (d) any equivalent provisions made by the GFSC which specify the conditions which buy-back programmes and stabilisation measures referred to in paragraphs 1 and 4 must meet, including conditions for trading, restrictions regarding time and volume, disclosure and reporting obligations and price conditions, where the trading takes place on a Gibraltar trading venue.

7. The FCA may make technical standards to specify the conditions that buy-back programmes and stabilisation measures referred to in paragraphs 1 and 4 must meet, including conditions for trading, restrictions regarding time and volume, disclosure and reporting obligations, and price conditions.

8. In this Article, 'European competent authority' means the authority which has been designated by a Member State as its competent authority for the purposes of Article 22 of this Regulation as it had effect before IP completion day.

…

CHAPTER 2
INSIDE INFORMATION, INSIDER DEALING, UNLAWFUL DISCLOSURE OF INSIDE INFORMATION AND MARKET MANIPULATION

Article 7

Inside information

1. For the purposes of this Regulation, inside information shall comprise the following types of information:

> (a) information of a precise nature, which has not been made public, relating, directly or indirectly, to one or more issuers or to one or more financial instruments, and which, if it were made public, would be likely to have a significant effect on the prices of those financial instruments or on the price of related derivative financial instruments;
>
> (b) in relation to commodity derivatives, information of a precise nature, which has not been made public, relating, directly or indirectly to one or more such derivatives or relating directly to the related spot commodity contract, and which, if it were made public, would be likely to have a significant effect on the prices of such derivatives or related spot commodity contracts, and where this is information which is reasonably expected to be disclosed or is required to be disclosed in accordance with legal or regulatory provisions applicable in the United Kingdom, Gibraltar, the European Union or a Member State, market rules, contract, practice or custom, on the relevant commodity derivatives markets or spot markets;
>
> (c) in relation to emission allowances or auctioned products based thereon, information of a precise nature, which has not been made public, relating, directly or indirectly, to one or more such instruments, and which, if it were made public, would be likely to have a significant effect on the prices of such instruments or on the prices of related derivative financial instruments;

(d) for persons charged with the execution of orders concerning financial instruments, it also means information conveyed by a client and relating to the client's pending orders in financial instruments, which is of a precise nature, relating, directly or indirectly, to one or more issuers or to one or more financial instruments, and which, if it were made public, would be likely to have a significant effect on the prices of those financial instruments, the price of related spot commodity contracts, or on the price of related derivative financial instruments.

2. For the purposes of paragraph 1, information shall be deemed to be of a precise nature if it indicates a set of circumstances which exists or which may reasonably be expected to come into existence, or an event which has occurred or which may reasonably be expected to occur, where it is specific enough to enable a conclusion to be drawn as to the possible effect of that set of circumstances or event on the prices of the financial instruments or the related derivative financial instrument, the related spot commodity contracts, or the auctioned products based on the emission allowances. In this respect in the case of a protracted process that is intended to bring about, or that results in, particular circumstances or a particular event, those future circumstances or that future event, and also the intermediate steps of that process which are connected with bringing about or resulting in those future circumstances or that future event, may be deemed to be precise information.

3. An intermediate step in a protracted process shall be deemed to be inside information if, by itself, it satisfies the criteria of inside information as referred to in this Article.

4. For the purposes of paragraph 1, information which, if it were made public, would be likely to have a significant effect on the prices of financial instruments, derivative financial instruments, related spot commodity contracts, or auctioned products based on emission allowances shall mean information a reasonable investor would be likely to use as part of the basis of his or her investment decisions.

In the case of participants in the market for UK emission allowances with aggregate emissions or rated thermal input at or below the threshold set in accordance with the second or fourth subparagraphs of Article 17(2), information about their physical operations relating to UK installations or UK aviation activities shall be deemed not to have a significant effect on the price of emission allowances, of auctioned products based thereon, or of derivative financial instruments.

In the case of participants in the market for EU emission allowances with aggregate emissions or rated thermal input at or below the threshold set in accordance with the second subparagraph of Article 17(2) of Regulation (EU) 596/2014 as that Regulation applies in the European Union, information about their physical operations relating to an EU installation or EU aviation activities shall be deemed not to have a significant effect on the price of emission allowances, or auctioned products based thereon, or of derivative financial instruments.

4A. For the purposes of this Article—

(a) an installation is a "UK installation" if activities at that installation resulting in the emission of carbon dioxide, perfluorocarbons or nitrous oxide ("greenhouse gases") are regulated under the Greenhouse Gas Emissions Trading Scheme Order 2020;

(b) an installation is an "EU installation" if activities at that installation resulting in emissions of greenhouse gases are regulated under the national law of an EEA State which implements Directive 2003/87/EC;

(c) aviation activities are "UK aviation activities" if emissions of greenhouse gases resulting from those activities must be monitored under the Greenhouse Gas Emissions Trading Scheme Order 2020;

(d) aviation activities are "EU aviation activities" if the emissions of greenhouse gases resulting from those activities must be monitored under the national law of an EEA State implementing Directive 2003/87/EC.

5. ...

Article 8

Insider dealing

1.   For the purposes of this Regulation, insider dealing arises where a person possesses inside information and uses that information by acquiring or disposing of, for its own account or for the account of a third party, directly or indirectly, financial instruments to which that information relates. The use of inside information by cancelling or amending an order concerning a financial instrument to which the information relates where the order was placed before the person concerned possessed the inside information, shall also be considered to be insider dealing. In relation to auctions of emission allowances or other auctioned products based thereon that are held pursuant to the Greenhouse Gas Emissions Trading Scheme Auctioning Regulations 2021, the use of inside information shall also comprise submitting, modifying or withdrawing a bid by a person for its own account or for the account of a third party.

2.   For the purposes of this Regulation, recommending that another person engage in insider dealing, or inducing another person to engage in insider dealing, arises where the person possesses inside information and:

   (a)   recommends, on the basis of that information, that another person acquire or dispose of financial instruments to which that information relates, or induces that person to make such an acquisition or disposal, or

   (b)   recommends, on the basis of that information, that another person cancel or amend an order concerning a financial instrument to which that information relates, or induces that person to make such a cancellation or amendment.

3.   The use of the recommendations or inducements referred to in paragraph 2 amounts to insider dealing within the meaning of this Article where the person using the recommendation or inducement knows or ought to know that it is based upon inside information.

4.   This Article applies to any person who possesses inside information as a result of:

   (a)   being a member of the administrative, management or supervisory bodies of the issuer or emission allowance market participant;

   (b)   having a holding in the capital of the issuer or emission allowance market participant;

   (c)   having access to the information through the exercise of an employment, profession or duties; or

   (d)   being involved in criminal activities.

   This Article also applies to any person who possesses inside information under circumstances other than those referred to in the first subparagraph where that person knows or ought to know that it is inside information.

5.   Where the person is a legal person, this Article shall also apply ... to the natural persons who participate in the decision to carry out the acquisition, disposal, cancellation or amendment of an order for the account of the legal person concerned.

Article 9

Legitimate behaviour

1.   For the purposes of Articles 8 and 14, it shall not be deemed from the mere fact that a legal person is or has been in possession of inside information that that person has used that information and has thus engaged in insider dealing on the basis of an acquisition or disposal, where that legal person:

   (a)   has established, implemented and maintained adequate and effective internal arrangements and procedures that effectively ensure that neither the natural person who made the decision on its behalf to acquire or dispose of financial instruments to which the information relates, nor another natural person who may have had an influence on that decision, was in possession of the inside information; and

   (b)   has not encouraged, made a recommendation to, induced or otherwise influenced the natural person who, on behalf of the legal person, acquired or disposed of financial instruments to which the information relates.

2. For the purposes of Articles 8 and 14, it shall not be deemed from the mere fact that a person is in possession of inside information that that person has used that information and has thus engaged in insider dealing on the basis of an acquisition or disposal where that person:

    (a) for the financial instrument to which that information relates, is a market maker or a person authorised to act as a counterparty, and the acquisition or disposal of financial instruments to which that information relates is made legitimately in the normal course of the exercise of its function as a market maker or as a counterparty for that financial instrument; or

    (b) is authorised to execute orders on behalf of third parties, and the acquisition or disposal of financial instruments to which the order relates, is made to carry out such an order legitimately in the normal course of the exercise of that person's employment, profession or duties.

3. For the purposes of Articles 8 and 14, it shall not be deemed from the mere fact that a person is in possession of inside information that that person has used that information and has thus engaged in insider dealing on the basis of an acquisition or disposal where that person conducts a transaction to acquire or dispose of financial instruments and that transaction is carried out in the discharge of an obligation that has become due in good faith and not to circumvent the prohibition against insider dealing and:

    (a) that obligation results from an order placed or an agreement concluded before the person concerned possessed inside information; or

    (b) that transaction is carried out to satisfy a legal or regulatory obligation that arose, before the person concerned possessed inside information.

4. For the purposes of Article 8 and 14, it shall not be deemed from the mere fact that a person is in possession of inside information that that person has used that information and has thus engaged in insider dealing, where such person has obtained that inside information in the conduct of a public takeover or merger with a company and uses that inside information solely for the purpose of proceeding with that merger or public takeover, provided that at the point of approval of the merger or acceptance of the offer by the shareholders of that company, any inside information has been made public or has otherwise ceased to constitute inside information.

    This paragraph shall not apply to stake-building.

5. For the purposes of Articles 8 and 14, the mere fact that a person uses its own knowledge that it has decided to acquire or dispose of financial instruments in the acquisition or disposal of those financial instruments shall not of itself constitute use of inside information.

6. Notwithstanding paragraphs 1 to 5 of this Article, an infringement of the prohibition of insider dealing set out in Article 14 may still be deemed to have occurred if the FCA establishes that there was an illegitimate reason for the orders to trade, transactions or behaviours concerned.

Article 10

Unlawful disclosure of inside information

1. For the purposes of this Regulation, unlawful disclosure of inside information arises where a person possesses inside information and discloses that information to any other person, except where the disclosure is made in the normal exercise of an employment, a profession or duties.

    This paragraph applies to any natural or legal person in the situations or circumstances referred to in Article 8(4).

2. For the purposes of this Regulation the onward disclosure of recommendations or inducements referred to in Article 8(2) amounts to unlawful disclosure of inside information under this Article where the person disclosing the recommendation or inducement knows or ought to know that it was based on inside information.

Article 11

Market soundings

1.   *A market sounding comprises the communication of information, prior to the announcement of a transaction, in order to gauge the interest of potential investors in a possible transaction and the conditions relating to it such as its potential size or pricing, to one or more potential investors by:*

     (a)   an issuer;

     (b)   a secondary offeror of a financial instrument, in such quantity or value that the transaction is distinct from ordinary trading and involves a selling method based on the prior assessment of potential interest from potential investors;

     (c)   an emission allowance market participant; or

     (d)   a third party acting on behalf or on the account of a person referred to in point (a), (b) or (c).

2.   *Without prejudice to Article 23(3), disclosure of inside information by a person intending to make a takeover bid for the securities of a company or a merger with a company to parties entitled to the securities, shall also constitute a market sounding, provided that:*

     (a)   the information is necessary to enable the parties entitled to the securities to form an opinion on their willingness to offer their securities: and

     (b)   the willingness of parties entitled to the securities to offer their securities is reasonably required for the decision to make the takeover bid or merger.

3.   *A disclosing market participant shall, prior to conducting a market sounding, specifically consider whether the market sounding will involve the disclosure of inside information. The disclosing market participant shall make a written record of its conclusion and the reasons therefor. It shall provide such written records to the FCA upon request. This obligation shall apply to each disclosure of information throughout the course of the market sounding. The disclosing market participant shall update the written records referred to in this paragraph accordingly.*

4.   *For the purposes of Article 10(1), disclosure of inside information made in the course of a market sounding shall be deemed to be made in the normal exercise of a person's employment, profession or duties where the disclosing market participant complies with paragraphs 3 and 5 of this Article.*

5.   *For the purposes of paragraph 4, the disclosing market participant shall, before making the disclosure:*

     (a)   obtain the consent of the person receiving the market sounding to receive inside information;

     (b)   inform the person receiving the market sounding that he is prohibited from using that information, or attempting to use that information, by acquiring or disposing of, for his own account or for the account of a third party, directly or indirectly, financial instruments relating to that information;

     (c)   inform the person receiving the market sounding that he is prohibited from using that information, or attempting to use that information, by cancelling or amending an order which has already been placed concerning a financial instrument to which the information relates; and

     (d)   inform the person receiving the market sounding that by agreeing to receive the information he is obliged to keep the information confidential.

     The disclosing market participant shall make and maintain a record of all information given to the person receiving the market sounding, including the information given in accordance with points (a) to (d) of the first subparagraph, and the identity of the potential investors to whom the information has been disclosed, including but not limited to the legal and natural persons acting on behalf of the potential investor, and the date and time of each disclosure. The disclosing market participant shall provide that record to the FCA upon request.

6. *Where information that has been disclosed in the course of a market sounding ceases to be inside information according to the assessment of the disclosing market participant, the disclosing market participant shall inform the recipient accordingly, as soon as possible.*

   The disclosing market participant shall maintain a record of the information given in accordance with this paragraph and shall provide it to the FCA upon request.

7. *Notwithstanding the provisions of this Article, the person receiving the market sounding shall assess for itself whether it is in possession of inside information or when it ceases to be in possession of inside information.*

8. *The disclosing market participant shall keep the records referred to in this Article for a period of at least five years.*

9. *The FCA may make technical standards to determine appropriate arrangements, procedures and record keeping requirements for persons to comply with the requirements laid down in paragraphs 4, 5, 6 and 8.*

10. *The FCA may make technical standards to specify the systems and notification templates to be used by persons to comply with the requirements established by paragraphs 4, 5, 6 and 8, particularly the precise format of the records referred to in paragraphs 4 to 8 and the technical means for appropriate communication of the information referred to in paragraph 6 to the person receiving the market sounding.*

11. ...

Article 12

Market manipulation

1. *For the purposes of this Regulation, market manipulation shall comprise the following activities:*
   (a) *entering into a transaction, placing an order to trade or any other behaviour which:*
       (i) *gives, or is likely to give, false or misleading signals as to the supply of, demand for, or price of, a financial instrument, a related spot commodity contract or an auctioned product based on emission allowances; or*
       (ii) *secures, or is likely to secure, the price of one or several financial instruments, a related spot commodity contract or an auctioned product based on emission allowances at an abnormal or artificial level;*

       unless the person entering into a transaction, placing an order to trade or engaging in any other behaviour establishes that such transaction, order or behaviour have been carried out for legitimate reasons, and conform with an accepted market practice as established in accordance with Article 13;
   (b) *entering into a transaction, placing an order to trade or any other activity or behaviour which affects or is likely to affect the price of one or several financial instruments, a related spot commodity contract or an auctioned product based on emission allowances, which employs a fictitious device or any other form of deception or contrivance;*
   (c) *disseminating information through the media, including the internet, or by any other means, which gives, or is likely to give, false or misleading signals as to the supply of, demand for, or price of, a financial instrument, a related spot commodity contract or an auctioned product based on emission allowances or secures, or is likely to secure, the price of one or several financial instruments, a related spot commodity contract or an auctioned product based on emission allowances at an abnormal or artificial level, including the dissemination of rumours, where the person who made the dissemination knew, or ought to have known, that the information was false or misleading;*
   (d) *transmitting false or misleading information or providing false or misleading inputs in relation to a benchmark where the person who made the transmission or provided the input knew or ought to have known that it was false or misleading, or any other behaviour which manipulates the calculation of a benchmark.*

2. *The following behaviour shall, inter alia, be considered as market manipulation:*

(a)   the conduct by a person, or persons acting in collaboration, to secure a dominant position over the supply of or demand for a financial instrument, related spot commodity contracts or auctioned products based on emission allowances which has, or is likely to have, the effect of fixing, directly or indirectly, purchase or sale prices or creates, or is likely to create, other unfair trading conditions;

(b)   the buying or selling of financial instruments, at the opening or closing of the market, which has or is likely to have the effect of misleading investors acting on the basis of the prices displayed, including the opening or closing prices;

(c)   the placing of orders to a UK trading venue, Gibraltar trading venue or an EU trading venue, including any cancellation or modification thereof, by any available means of trading, including by electronic means, such as algorithmic and high-frequency trading strategies, and which has one of the effects referred to in paragraph 1(a) or (b), by:

   (i)   disrupting or delaying the functioning of the trading system of the UK trading venue or the EU trading venue (as applicable) or being likely to do so;

   (ii)   making it more difficult for other persons to identify genuine orders on the trading system of the UK trading venue or the EU trading venue (as applicable) or being likely to do so, including by entering orders which result in the overloading or destabilisation of the order book; or

   (iii) creating or being likely to create a false or misleading signal about the supply of, or demand for, or price of, a financial instrument, in particular by entering orders to initiate or exacerbate a trend;

(d)   the taking advantage of occasional or regular access to the traditional or electronic media by voicing an opinion about a financial instrument, related spot commodity contract or an auctioned product based on emission allowances (or indirectly about its issuer) while having previously taken positions on that financial instrument, a related spot commodity contract or an auctioned product based on emission allowances and profiting subsequently from the impact of the opinions voiced on the price of that instrument, related spot commodity contract or an auctioned product based on emission allowances, without having simultaneously disclosed that conflict of interest to the public in a proper and effective way;

(e)   the buying or selling on the secondary market of emission allowances or related derivatives prior to the auction of such emission allowances or related derivatives with the effect of fixing the auction clearing price for the auctioned products at an abnormal or artificial level or misleading bidders bidding in the auctions.

3.   For the purposes of applying paragraph 1(a) and (b), and without prejudice to the forms of behaviour set out in paragraph 2, Annex I defines non-exhaustive indicators relating to the employment of a fictitious device or any other form of deception or contrivance, and non-exhaustive indicators related to false or misleading signals and to price securing.

4.   Where the person referred to in this Article is a legal person, this Article shall also apply ... to the natural persons who participate in the decision to carry out activities for the account of the legal person concerned.

5.   The Treasury may by regulations specify the indicators laid down in Annex I, in order to clarify their elements and to take into account technical developments on financial markets.

Article 13

Accepted market practices

1.   The prohibition in Article 15 shall not apply to the activities referred to in Article 12(1)(a), provided that the person entering into a transaction, placing an order to trade or engaging in any other behaviour establishes that such transaction, order or behaviour have been carried out for legitimate reasons, and conform with an accepted market practice as established—

(a)   in relation to a UK market in accordance with this Article;

(b)   in relation to a market in an EEA state, in accordance with Article 13 of the EU Market Abuse Regulation; or

(c)   in relation to a market in Gibraltar, in accordance with Article 13 of Regulation (EU) No 596/2014 of the European Parliament and of the Council on market abuse as it applies in Gibraltar after exit day.

2.   The FCA may establish an accepted market practice, taking into account the following criteria:

(a)   whether the market practice provides for a substantial level of transparency to the UK market;

(b)   whether the market practice ensures a high degree of safeguards to the operation of market forces operating in UK markets and the proper interplay of the forces of supply and demand;

(c)   whether the market practice has a positive impact on UK market liquidity and efficiency;

(d)   whether the market practice takes into account the trading mechanism of the relevant UK market and enables market participants to react properly and in a timely manner to the new market situation created by that practice;

(e)   whether the market practice does not create risks for the integrity of, directly or indirectly, related markets, whether regulated or not, in the relevant financial instrument within the United Kingdom;

(f)   the outcome of any investigation of the relevant market practice by the FCA, in particular whether the relevant market practice infringed rules or regulations designed to prevent market abuse, or codes of conduct, irrespective of whether it concerns the relevant UK market or directly or indirectly related markets within the United Kingdom; and

(g)   the structural characteristics of the relevant UK market, inter alia, whether it is regulated or not, the types of financial instruments traded and the type of market participants, including the extent of retail-investor participation in the relevant UK market.

...

3.–6.   ...

7.   The FCA may make technical standards specifying the criteria, the procedure and the requirements for establishing an accepted market practice under paragraph 2 and the requirements for maintaining it, terminating it, or modifying the conditions for its acceptance.

8.   The FCA shall review regularly, and at least every two years, the accepted market practices that it has established, in particular by taking into account significant changes to the relevant UK market environment, such as changes to trading rules or to market infrastructures, with a view to deciding whether to maintain it, to terminate it, or to modify the conditions for its acceptance.

9.   The FCA shall publish on its website a list of accepted market practices ....

10., 11. ...

Article 14

Prohibition of insider dealing and of unlawful disclosure of inside information

A person shall not:

(a)   engage or attempt to engage in insider dealing;

(b)   recommend that another person engage in insider dealing or induce another person to engage in insider dealing; or

(c)   unlawfully disclose inside information.

Article 15

Prohibition of market manipulation

A person shall not engage in or attempt to engage in market manipulation.

Article 16

Prevention and detection of market abuse

1.   Market operators and investment firms that operate a UK trading venue shall establish and maintain effective arrangements, systems and procedures aimed at preventing and detecting insider dealing, market manipulation and attempted insider dealing and market manipulation, in

accordance with the law of the United Kingdom or any part of the United Kingdom which was relied on immediately before IP completion day to implement Articles 31 and 54 of Directive 2014/65/EU and those Articles' implementing measures—

    (a) as they have effect on IP completion day, in the case of rules made by the Financial Conduct Authority or by the Prudential Regulation Authority under the Financial Services and Markets Act 2000, and

    (b) as amended from time to time, in all other cases.

A person referred to in the first subparagraph shall report orders and transactions, including any cancellation or modification thereof, that could constitute insider dealing, market manipulation or attempted insider dealing or market manipulation to the FCA without delay.

2.   *Any person professionally arranging or executing transactions shall establish and maintain effective arrangements, systems and procedures to detect and report suspicious orders and transactions. Where such a person has a reasonable suspicion that an order or transaction in any financial instrument, whether placed or executed on or outside a UK trading venue, could constitute insider dealing, market manipulation or attempted insider dealing or market manipulation, the person shall notify the FCA without delay.*

3.   *... persons professionally arranging or executing transactions shall be subject to the rules of notification of the United Kingdom where they are registered or have their head office in the United Kingdom or, in the case of a branch, where the branch is situated in the United Kingdom. The notification shall be addressed to the FCA.*

4.   *...*

5.   *The FCA may make technical standards to determine:*

    (a) appropriate arrangements, systems and procedures for persons to comply with the requirements established in paragraphs 1 and 2;

    (b) the notification templates to be used by persons to comply with the requirements established in paragraphs 1 and 2.

CHAPTER 3
DISCLOSURE REQUIREMENTS

Article 17

Public disclosure of inside information

1.   *An issuer shall inform the public as soon as possible of inside information which directly concerns that issuer.*

The issuer shall ensure that the inside information is made public in a manner which enables fast access and complete, correct and timely assessment of the information by the public and, where applicable, in a mechanism referred to in section 89W of the Financial Services and Markets Act 2000. The issuer shall not combine the disclosure of inside information to the public with the marketing of its activities. The issuer shall post and maintain on its website for a period of at least five years, all inside information it is required to disclose publicly.

This Article shall apply to—

    (a) issuers who have requested or approved admission of their financial instruments to trading on a UK regulated market;

    (b) in the case of instruments only traded on a UK MTF or on a UK OTF, issuers who have approved trading of their financial instruments on a UK MTF or a UK OTF or have requested admission to trading of their financial instruments on a UK MTF; and

    (c) UK emission allowance market participants.

1A. *A UK emission allowance market participant is only required to disclose inside information concerning EU emission allowances if that participant enters into transactions, including the placing of orders to trade, directly or indirectly, in EU emission allowances, or in auctioned products based thereon, or derivatives based thereof.*

2.   *A UK emission allowance market participant shall publicly, effectively and in a timely manner disclose inside information concerning emission allowances which it holds in respect of its business, including—*

    (a)   *aviation activities as specified in Annex I to Directive 2003/87/EC or in paragraph 1 of Schedule 1 to the Greenhouse Gas Emissions Trading Scheme Order 2020 ("the Order"), or*

    (b)   *installations within the meaning of Article 3(e) of that Directive or paragraph 2 of Schedule 2 to the Order,*

which the participant concerned, or its parent undertaking or related undertaking, owns or controls, or for the operational matters for which the participant, or its parent undertaking or related undertaking, is responsible, in whole or in part.

With regard to installations, such disclosure shall include information relevant to the capacity and utilisation of installations, including planned or unplanned unavailability of such installations.

The first subparagraph shall not apply to a participant in the emission allowance market where the UK installations or UK aviation activities that it owns, controls or is responsible for, in the preceding year have had emissions not exceeding a minimum threshold of carbon dioxide equivalent and, where they carry out combustion activities, have had a rated thermal input not exceeding a minimum threshold.

For the purposes of the second sub-paragraph—

    (a)   *during the period beginning on the date on which the Recognised Auction Platforms (Amendment and Miscellaneous Provisions) Regulations 2021 come into force and ending with 30th April 2022 ("the initial period"), the "preceding year" means the year ending with 31st December 2020;*

    (b)   *after the initial period, during any period beginning with 1st May and ending with 30th April, "the preceding year" means the year ending with the 31st December which falls before the 1st of May in the period in question.*

The Treasury may make regulations establishing a minimum threshold of carbon dioxide equivalent and a minimum threshold of rated thermal input for the purposes of the application of the exemption provided for in the second subparagraph of this paragraph.

For the purposes of the second subparagraph, "minimum threshold" means—

    (a)   *the thresholds set out in regulations made by the Treasury under this paragraph, or*

    (b)   *if the Treasury have not made such regulations, the thresholds set out in Article 5 of Commission Delegated Regulation (EU) 2016/522 supplementing Regulation (EU) No 596/2014 of the European Parliament and of the Council as regards an exemption for certain third countries public bodies and central banks, the indicators of market manipulation, the disclosure thresholds, the competent authority for notifications of delays, the permission for trading during closed periods and types of notifiable managers' transactions.*

3.   ...

4.   *An issuer or a UK emission allowance market participant, may, on its own responsibility, delay disclosure to the public of inside information provided that all of the following conditions are met:*

    (a)   *immediate disclosure is likely to prejudice the legitimate interests of the issuer or a UK emission allowance market participant;*

    (b)   *delay of disclosure is not likely to mislead the public;*

    (c)   *the issuer or a UK emission allowance market participant is able to ensure the confidentiality of that information.*

In the case of a protracted process that occurs in stages and that is intended to bring about, or that results in, a particular circumstance or a particular event, an issuer or a UK emission allowance market participant may on its own responsibility delay the public disclosure of inside information relating to this process, subject to points (a), (b) and (c) of the first subparagraph.

Where an issuer or a UK emission allowance market participant has delayed the disclosure of inside information under this paragraph, it shall inform the FCA that disclosure of the information was delayed, immediately after the information is disclosed to the public. Upon the request of the FCA, the issuer or a UK emission allowance market participant shall provide a written explanation of how the conditions set out in this paragraph were met.

5.   *In order to preserve the stability of the financial system, an issuer that is a credit institution or a financial institution, may, on its own responsibility, delay the public disclosure of inside information, including information which is related to a temporary liquidity problem and, in particular, the need to receive temporary liquidity assistance from a central bank or lender of last resort, provided that all of the following conditions are met:*

       (a)   the disclosure of the inside information entails a risk of undermining the financial stability of the issuer and of the financial system;

       (b)   it is in the public interest to delay the disclosure;

       (c)   the confidentiality of that information can be ensured; and

       (d)   the FCA has consented to the delay on the basis that the conditions in points (a), (b) and (c) are met.

6.   *For the purposes of points (a) to (d) of paragraph 5, an issuer shall notify the FCA of its intention to delay the disclosure of the inside information and provide evidence that the conditions set out in points (a), (b) and (c) of paragraph 5 are met. The FCA shall consult, as appropriate, the Bank of England, or, alternatively, the following authorities:*

       (a)   where the issuer is a credit institution or an investment firm which is a "PRA-authorised person" within the meaning of section 2B(5) of the Financial Services and Markets Act 2000, the Prudential Regulation Authority;

       (b)   in cases other than those referred to in point (a), any other ... authority in the United Kingdom responsible for the supervision of the issuer.

The FCA shall ensure that disclosure of the inside information is delayed only for a period as is necessary in the public interest. The FCA shall evaluate at least on a weekly basis whether the conditions set out in points (a), (b) and (c) of paragraph 5 are still met.

If the FCA does not consent to the delay of disclosure of the inside information, the issuer shall disclose the inside information immediately.

This paragraph shall apply to cases where the issuer does not decide to delay the disclosure of inside information in accordance with paragraph 4.

       ...

7.   *Where disclosure of inside information has been delayed in accordance with paragraph 4 or 5 and the confidentiality of that inside information is no longer ensured, the issuer or the UK emission allowance market participant shall disclose that inside information to the public as soon as possible.*

This paragraph includes situations where a rumour explicitly relates to inside information the disclosure of which has been delayed in accordance with paragraph 4 or 5, where that rumour is sufficiently accurate to indicate that the confidentiality of that information is no longer ensured.

8.   *Where an issuer or a UK emission allowance market participant, or a person acting on their behalf or for their account, discloses any inside information to any third party in the normal course of the exercise of an employment, profession or duties as referred to in Article 10(1), they must make complete and effective public disclosure of that information, simultaneously in the case of an intentional disclosure, and promptly in the case of a non-intentional disclosure. This paragraph shall not apply if the person receiving the information owes a duty of confidentiality, regardless of whether such duty is based on a law, on regulations, on articles of association, or on a contract.*

9.   *Inside information relating to issuers whose financial instruments are admitted to trading on an SME growth market, may be posted on the UK trading venue's website instead of on the website of the issuer where the UK trading venue chooses to provide this facility for issuers on that market.*

10.   The FCA may make technical standards to determine:

   (a) the technical means for appropriate public disclosure of inside information as referred to in
        paragraphs 1, 2, 8 and 9; and

   (b) the technical means for delaying the public disclosure of inside information as referred to in
        paragraphs 4 and 5.

11.   ...

Article 18

Insider lists

1.   Issuers, and any person acting on their behalf or on their account, shall each:

   (a) draw up a list of all persons who have access to inside information and who are working for
        them under a contract of employment, or otherwise performing tasks through which they
        have access to inside information, such as advisers, accountants or credit rating agencies
        (insider list);

   (b) promptly update the insider list in accordance with paragraph 4; and

   (c) provide the insider list to the FCA as soon as possible upon its request.

2.   Issuers, and any person acting on their behalf or on their account, shall each take all reasonable
        steps to ensure that any person on their insider list acknowledges in writing the legal and
        regulatory duties entailed and is aware of the sanctions applicable to insider dealing and
        unlawful disclosure of inside information.

        Where another person is requested by the issuer to draw up and update the issuer's insider list,
        the issuer shall remain fully responsible for complying with this Article. The issuer shall always
        retain a right of access to the insider list that the other person is drawing up.

3.   The insider list shall include at least:

   (a) the identity of any person having access to inside information;

   (b) the reason for including that person in the insider list;

   (c) the date and time at which that person obtained access to inside information; and

   (d) the date on which the insider list was drawn up.

4.   Issuers, and any person acting on their behalf or on their account, shall each update their insider
        list promptly, including the date of the update, in the following circumstances:

   (a) where there is a change in the reason for including a person already on the insider list;

   (b) where there is a new person who has access to inside information and needs, therefore, to be
        added to the insider list; and

   (c) where a person ceases to have access to inside information.

        Each update shall specify the date and time when the change triggering the update occurred.

5.   Issuers, and any person or any person acting on their behalf or on their account, shall each retain
        their insider list for a period of at least five years after it is drawn up or updated.

6.   Issuers whose financial instruments are admitted to trading on an SME growth market shall be
        exempt from drawing up an insider list, provided that the following conditions are met:

   (a) the issuer takes all reasonable steps to ensure that any person with access to inside
        information acknowledges the legal and regulatory duties entailed and is aware of the
        sanctions applicable to insider dealing and unlawful disclosure of inside information; and

   (b) the issuer is able to provide the FCA, upon request, with an insider list.

7.   This Article shall apply to issuers who have requested or approved admission of their financial
        instruments to trading on a UK regulated market ... or, in the case of an instrument only traded
        on a UK MTF or a UK OTF, have approved trading of their financial instruments on a UK MTF
        or a UK OTF or have requested admission to trading of their financial instruments on a UK MTF
        ....

8.   Paragraphs 1 to 5 of this Article shall also apply to:

   (a) UK emission allowance market participants ... in relation to inside information concerning
        emission allowances that arises in relation to the physical operations of that UK emission
        allowance market participant;

(b)   *any auction platform and auctioneer in relation to auctions of emission allowances or other auctioned products based thereon that are held pursuant to the Greenhouse Gas Emissions Trading Scheme Auctioning Regulations 2021.*

8A.   *A UK emission allowance market participant ("P") is only required to draw up a list of persons who have access to inside information relating to EU emission allowances if—*

    (a)   *P enters into transactions, including the placing of orders to trade, directly or indirectly, in EU emission allowances, auctioned products based thereon or derivatives thereof, and*

    (b)   *the emissions from P's EU installations and EU aviation activities exceed the minimum threshold referred to in the second sub-paragraph of Article 17(2) of Regulation (EU) 596/ 2014 as that Regulation applies in the European Union.*

9.   *The FCA may make technical standards to determine the precise format of insider lists and the format for updating insider lists referred to in this Article.*

Article 19

Managers' transactions

1.   *Persons discharging managerial responsibilities, as well as persons closely associated with them, shall notify the issuer or the UK emission allowance market participant and the FCA:*

    (a)   *in respect of issuers, of every transaction conducted on their own account relating to the shares or debt instruments of that issuer or to derivatives or other financial instruments linked thereto;*

    (b)   *in respect of UK emission allowance market participants ("P"), of every transaction conducted on their own account relating to—*

        (i)   *UK emission allowances, auction products based thereon or derivatives relating thereto, and*

        (ii)   *if the conditions referred to in Article 18(8A) are satisfied by P, EU emission allowances, auction products based thereon or derivatives relating thereto.*

    Such notifications shall be made promptly and no later than three working days after the date of the transaction.

    The first subparagraph applies once the total amount of transactions has reached the threshold set out in paragraph 8 or 9, as applicable, within a calendar year.

1a.   *The notification obligation referred to in paragraph 1 shall not apply to transactions in financial instruments linked to shares or to debt instruments of the issuer referred to in that paragraph where at the time of the transaction any of the following conditions is met:*

    (a)   *the financial instrument is a unit or share in a collective investment undertaking in which the exposure to the issuer's shares or debt instruments does not exceed 20% of the assets held by the collective investment undertaking;*

    (b)   *the financial instrument provides exposure to a portfolio of assets in which the exposure to the issuer's shares or debt instruments does not exceed 20% of the portfolio's assets;*

    (c)   *the financial instrument is a unit or share in a collective investment undertaking or provides exposure to a portfolio of assets and the person discharging managerial responsibilities or person closely associated with such a person does not know, and could not know, the investment composition or exposure of such collective investment undertaking or portfolio of assets in relation to the issuer's shares or debt instruments, and furthermore there is no reason for that person to believe that the issuer's shares or debt instruments exceed the thresholds in point (a) or (b).*

    If information regarding the investment composition of the collective investment undertaking or exposure to the portfolio of assets is available, then the person discharging managerial responsibility or person closely associated with such a person shall make all reasonable efforts to avail themselves of that information.

2.   *For the purposes of paragraph 1, and without prejudice to notification obligations in the law of the United Kingdom other than those referred to in this Article, all transactions conducted on the*

own account of the persons referred to in paragraph 1 shall be notified by those persons to the FCA. Notifications shall be made to the FCA within three working days of the transaction date.

3.   *The issuer or emission allowance market participant must make public the information contained in a notification referred to in paragraph 1 within two working days of receipt of such a notification in a manner which enables fast access to this information on a non-discriminatory basis in accordance with—*

(a)   *Commission Implementing Regulation (EU) 2016/1055 of 29 June 2016 laying down implementing technical standards with regard to the technical means for appropriate public disclosure of inside information and for delaying the public disclosure of inside information in accordance with Regulation (EU) 596/2014 of the European Parliament and of the Council; and*

(b)   *technical standards made by the FCA under Article 17(10)(a).*

The issuer or UK emission allowance market participant shall use such media as may reasonably be relied upon for the effective dissemination of information to the public throughout the United Kingdom, and, where applicable, it shall use a mechanism referred to in section 89W of the Financial Services and Markets Act 2000.

...

4.   *This Article applies to—*

(a)   *issuers who—*

(i)   *have requested or approved admission of their financial instruments to trading on a UK regulated market; or*

(ii)   *in the case of an instrument only traded on a UK MTF or a UK OTF, have approved trading of their financial instruments on a UK MTF or a UK OTF or have requested admission to trading of their financial instruments on a UK MTF;*

(b)   *UK emission allowance market participants ...*

5.   *Issuers and UK emission allowance market participants shall notify the person discharging managerial responsibilities of their obligations under this Article in writing. Issuers and UK emission allowance market participants shall draw up a list of all persons discharging managerial responsibilities and persons closely associated with them.*

Persons discharging managerial responsibilities shall notify the persons closely associated with them of their obligations under this Article in writing and shall keep a copy of this notification.

6.   *A notification of transactions referred to in paragraph 1 shall contain the following information:*

(a)   *the name of the person;*

(b)   *the reason for the notification;*

(c)   *the name of the relevant issuer or UK emission allowance market participant;*

(d)   *a description and the identifier of the financial instrument;*

(e)   *the nature of the transaction(s) (e.g. acquisition or disposal), indicating whether it is linked to the exercise of share option programmes or to the specific examples set out in paragraph 7;*

(f)   *the date and place of the transaction(s); and*

(g)   *the price and volume of the transaction(s). In the case of a pledge whose terms provide for its value to change, this should be disclosed together with its value at the date of the pledge.*

7.   *For the purposes of paragraph 1, transactions that must be notified shall also include:*

(a)   *the pledging or lending of financial instruments by or on behalf of a person discharging managerial responsibilities or a person closely associated with such a person, as referred to in paragraph 1;*

(b)   *transactions undertaken by persons professionally arranging or executing transactions or by another person on behalf of a person discharging managerial responsibilities or a person closely associated with such a person, as referred to in paragraph 1, including where discretion is exercised;*

(c)   *transactions made under a life insurance policy, referred to in Article 2(3)(a) of Directive 2009/138/EC of the European Parliament and of the Council, where:*

       (i)   *the policyholder is a person discharging managerial responsibilities or a person closely associated with such a person, as referred to in paragraph 1,*

       (ii)   *the investment risk is borne by the policyholder, and*

       (iii) *the policyholder has the power or discretion to make investment decisions regarding specific instruments in that life insurance policy or to execute transactions regarding specific instruments for that life insurance policy.*

For the purposes of point (a), a pledge, or a similar security interest, of financial instruments in connection with the depositing of the financial instruments in a custody account does not need to be notified, unless and until such time that such pledge or other security interest is designated to secure a specific credit facility.

For the purposes of point (b), transactions executed in shares or debt instruments of an issuer or derivatives or other financial instruments linked thereto by managers of a collective investment undertaking in which the person discharging managerial responsibilities or a person closely associated with them has invested do not need to be notified where the manager of the collective investment undertaking operates with full discretion, which excludes the manager receiving any instructions or suggestions on portfolio composition directly or indirectly from investors in that collective investment undertaking.

Insofar as a policyholder of an insurance contract is required to notify transactions according to this paragraph, an obligation to notify is not incumbent on the insurance company.

8.   *Paragraph 1 shall apply to any subsequent transaction once a total amount of EUR 5 000 has been reached within a calendar year. The threshold of EUR 5 000 shall be calculated by adding without netting all transactions referred to in paragraph 1.*

9.   *The FCA may increase the threshold set out in paragraph 8 to EUR 20 000 and must inform the Treasury of its decision and the justification for its decision, with specific reference to market conditions, to adopt the higher threshold.*

9A.   *The FCA must publish the thresholds which apply in accordance with this Article and the justification for any decision taken under paragraph 9 on its website.*

10.   *This Article also applies to persons discharging managerial responsibilities within any auction platform or auctioneer involved in the auctions held under the Greenhouse Gas Emissions Trading Scheme Auctioning Regulations 2021 and to persons closely associated with such persons in so far as their transactions involve emission allowances, derivatives thereof or auctioned products based thereon.*

Those persons must notify their transactions to the auction platforms and auctioneer, as applicable, and to the FCA.

The information that is so notified must be made public by the auction platforms and auctioneer in accordance with paragraph 3.

11.   *Without prejudice to Articles 14 and 15, a person discharging managerial responsibilities within an issuer shall not conduct any transactions on its own account or for the account of a third party, directly or indirectly, relating to the shares or debt instruments of the issuer or to derivatives or other financial instruments linked to them during a closed period of 30 calendar days before the announcement of an interim financial report or a year-end report which the issuer is obliged to make public according to:*

      (a)   *the rules of the trading venue where the issuer's shares are admitted to trading; or*

      (b)   *the law of the United Kingdom.*

12.   *Without prejudice to Articles 14 and 15, an issuer may allow a person discharging managerial responsibilities within it to trade on its own account or for the account of a third party during a closed period as referred to in paragraph 11 either:*

      (a)   *on a case-by-case basis due to the existence of exceptional circumstances, such as severe financial difficulty, which require the immediate sale of shares; or*

      (b)   *due to the characteristics of the trading involved for transactions made under, or related to, an employee share or saving scheme, qualification or entitlement of shares, or transactions where the beneficial interest in the relevant security does not change.*

13. The Treasury may by regulations specify the circumstances under which trading during a closed period may be permitted by the issuer, as referred to in paragraph 12, including the circumstances that would be considered as exceptional and the types of transaction that would justify the permission for trading.

14. The Treasury may by regulations specify types of transactions that would trigger the requirement referred to in paragraph 1.

15. The FCA may make technical standards concerning the format and template in which the information referred to in paragraph 1 is to be notified and made public.

...

16. In this Article, "working day" means a day other than—
   (a) Saturday or Sunday,
   (b) Christmas Day or Good Friday, or
   (c) a day which is a bank holiday in England and Wales under the Banking and Financial Dealings Act 1971.

...

Article 21

Disclosure or dissemination of information in the media

For the purposes of Article 10, Article 12(1)(c) and Article 20, where information is disclosed or disseminated and where recommendations are produced or disseminated for the purpose of journalism or other form of expression in the media, such disclosure or dissemination of information shall be assessed taking into account the rules governing the freedom of the press and freedom of expression in other media and the rules or codes governing the journalist profession, unless:

(a) the persons concerned, or persons closely associated with them, derive, directly or indirectly, an advantage or profits from the disclosure or the dissemination of the information in question; or

(b) the disclosure or the dissemination is made with the intention of misleading the market as to the supply of, demand for, or price of financial instruments.

CHAPTER 4
COOPERATION, PROFESSIONAL SECRECY AND DATA PROTECTION

Article 22

Functions of the FCA

...

The FCA shall ensure that the provisions of this Regulation are applied in the United Kingdom, regarding all actions carried out in the United Kingdom, and actions carried out abroad relating to instruments admitted to trading on a regulated market, for which a request for admission to trading on such market has been made, auctioned on an auction platform or which are traded on an MTF or an OTF or for which a request for admission to trading has been made on an MTF operating within the United Kingdom.

Article 23

Interaction with other provisions

1., 2. ...

3. ...

   This Regulation is without prejudice to laws, regulations and administrative provisions adopted in relation to takeover bids, merger transactions and other transactions affecting the ownership or control of companies regulated by the Panel on Takeovers and Mergers that impose requirements in addition to the requirements of this Regulation.

4. A person making information available to the FCA, the GFSC or the competent authority in accordance with this Regulation shall not be considered to be infringing any restriction on disclosure of information imposed by contract or by any legislative, regulatory or administrative

provision, and shall not involve the person notifying in liability of any kind related to such notification.

...

CHAPTER 5
ADMINISTRATIVE MEASURES AND SANCTIONS

...

Article 31

Exercise of supervisory powers and imposition of sanctions

1.   ... *when determining the type and level of administrative sanctions, the FCA must take into account all relevant circumstances, including, where appropriate:*

   (a)   *the gravity and duration of the infringement;*

   (b)   *the degree of responsibility of the person responsible for the infringement;*

   (c)   *the financial strength of the person responsible for the infringement, as indicated, for example, by the total turnover of a legal person or the annual income of a natural person;*

   (d)   *the importance of the profits gained or losses avoided by the person responsible for the infringement, insofar as they can be determined;*

   (e)   *the level of cooperation of the person responsible for the infringement with the FCA, without prejudice to the need to ensure disgorgement of profits gained or losses avoided by that person;*

   (f)   *previous infringements by the person responsible for the infringement; and*

   (g)   *measures taken by the person responsible for the infringement to prevent its repetition.*

2.   ...

...

CHAPTER 7
FINAL PROVISIONS

Article 37

Repeal of Directive 2003/6/EC and its implementing measures

Directive 2003/6/EC and Commission Directives 2004/72/EC, 2003/125/EC and 2003/124/EC and Commission Regulation (EC) No 2273/2003 shall be repealed with effect from 3 July 2016. References to Directive 2003/6/EC shall be construed as references to this Regulation and shall be read in accordance with the correlation table set out in Annex II to this Regulation.

...

Article 39

Entry into force and application

1.   *This Regulation shall enter into force on the twentieth day following that of its publication in the Official Journal of the European Union.*

2.   *It shall apply from 3 July 2016 except for:*

   (a)   *Article 4(2) and (3), which shall apply from 3 January 2018; and*

   (b)   *Article 4(4) and (5), Article 5(6), Article 6(5) and (6), Article 7(5), Article 11(9), (10) and (11), Article 12(5), Article 13(7) and (11), Article 16(5), the third subparagraph of Article 17(2), Article 17(3), (10) and (11), Article 18(9), Article 19(13), (14) and (15), Article 20(3), Article 24(3), Article 25(9), the second, third and fourth subparagraphs of Article 26(2), Article 32(5) and Article 33(5), which shall apply from 2 July 2014.*

3., 4.   ...

...

ANNEX I

A. **Indicators of manipulative behaviour relating to false or misleading signals and to price securing**

For the purposes of applying point (a) of Article 12(1) of this Regulation, and without prejudice to the forms of behaviour set out in paragraph 2 of that Article, the following non-exhaustive indicators, which shall not necessarily be deemed, in themselves, to constitute market manipulation, shall be taken into account when transactions or orders to trade are examined by market participants and the FCA:

(a)   the extent to which orders to trade given or transactions undertaken represent a significant proportion of the daily volume of transactions in the relevant financial instrument, related spot commodity contract, or auctioned product based on emission allowances, in particular when those activities lead to a significant change in their prices;

(b)   the extent to which orders to trade given or transactions undertaken by persons with a significant buying or selling position in a financial instrument, a related spot commodity contract, or an auctioned product based on emission allowances, lead to significant changes in the price of that financial instrument, related spot commodity contract, or auctioned product based on emission allowances;

(c)   whether transactions undertaken lead to no change in beneficial ownership of a financial instrument, a related spot commodity contract, or an auctioned product based on emission allowances;

(d)   the extent to which orders to trade given or transactions undertaken or orders cancelled include position reversals in a short period and represent a significant proportion of the daily volume of transactions in the relevant financial instrument, a related spot commodity contract, or an auctioned product based on emission allowances, and might be associated with significant changes in the price of a financial instrument, a related spot commodity contract, or an auctioned product based on emission allowances;

(e)   the extent to which orders to trade given or transactions undertaken are concentrated within a short time span in the trading session and lead to a price change which is subsequently reversed;

(f)   the extent to which orders to trade given change the representation of the best bid or offer prices in a financial instrument, a related spot commodity contract, or an auctioned product based on emission allowances, or more generally the representation of the order book available to market participants, and are removed before they are executed; and

(g)   the extent to which orders to trade are given or transactions are undertaken at or around a specific time when reference prices, settlement prices and valuations are calculated and lead to price changes which have an effect on such prices and valuations.

B. **Indicators of manipulative behaviour relating to the employment of a fictitious device or any other form of deception or contrivance**

For the purposes of applying point (b) of Article 12(1) of this Regulation, and without prejudice to the forms of behaviour set out in paragraph 2 of that Article thereof, the following non-exhaustive indicators, which shall not necessarily be deemed, in themselves, to constitute market manipulation, shall be taken into account where transactions or orders to trade are examined by market participants and the FCA:

(a)   whether orders to trade given or transactions undertaken by persons are preceded or followed by dissemination of false or misleading information by the same persons or by persons linked to them; and

(b)   whether orders to trade are given or transactions are undertaken by persons before or after the same persons or persons linked to them produce or disseminate investment recommendations which are erroneous, biased, or demonstrably influenced by material interest.

...

Financial Services and Markets Act 2000 (Market Abuse) Regulations 2016

S.I. 2016/680

Note. These regulations are revoked by the Financial Services and Markets Act 2023, s. 1(1), Sch. 1, Pt. 2, as from a day to be appointed.

PART 1
GENERAL

1. **Citation and commencement**
   These Regulations may be cited as the Financial Services and Markets Act 2000 (Market Abuse) Regulations 2016 and come into force on 3rd July 2016.

2. **Interpretation**
   In these Regulations—
   "the 2000 Act" means the Financial Services and Markets Act 2000;
   "the FCA" means the Financial Conduct Authority;
   "the market abuse regulation" means Regulation (EU) No 596/2014 of the European Parliament and of the Council of 16 April 2014 on market abuse (market abuse regulation) and repealing Directive 2003/6/EC of the European Parliament and of the Council and Commission Directives 2003/124/EC, 2003/125/EC and 2004/72/EC, as it forms part of retained EU law; and
   "supplementary market abuse enactment" means—
   (a) any EU regulation made under the market abuse regulation which is retained direct EU legislation;
   (b) any instrument made under the market abuse regulation on or after IP completion day.

3. ...

4. **Delayed public disclosure of inside information**
   (1) Where an issuer or an emission allowance market participant delays the disclosure of inside information under Article 17.4 (public disclosure of inside information) of the market abuse regulation it is required to provide a record of its written explanation of how the conditions set out in Article 17.4 were met to the FCA only upon the FCA's request.
   (2) In this regulation—
   "emission allowance market participant" has the meaning given in Article 3.1 (20) of the market abuse regulation; and
   "issuer" has the meaning given in Article 3.1(21) of the market abuse regulation.

5. **Reporting contraventions of the market abuse regulation**
   The Schedule (reporting of actual or potential contraventions of the market abuse regulation to the FCA) has effect.

6. **Applications under the market abuse regulation**
   (1) Any application to the FCA under the market abuse regulation or a supplementary market abuse enactment must—
   (a) be made in such manner as the FCA may direct; and
   (b) contain or be accompanied by, such other information as the FCA may reasonably require.
   (2) At any time after receiving an application and before determining it, the FCA may require the applicant to provide it with such further information as it reasonably considers necessary to enable it to determine the application.
   (3) Different directions may be given, and different requirements imposed, in relation to different applications or categories of application.

(4)   The FCA may require an applicant to provide information under this regulation in such form, or to verify it in such a way, as the FCA may direct.

(5)   Section 398(3) of the 2000 Act (misleading FCA or PRA: residual cases) applies to a requirement imposed under this regulation as it applies to a requirement imposed by or under the 2000 Act.

7.   Notifications under the market abuse regulation

Any notification to the FCA under the market abuse regulation or a supplementary market abuse enactment must be made in such manner as the FCA may direct.

PARTS 2–4 ...

SCHEDULE
REPORTING OF ACTUAL OR POTENTIAL CONTRAVENTIONS OF THE MARKET ABUSE
REGULATION TO THE FCA

1.   Interpretation

In this Schedule—

"dedicated communication channels" has the meaning given by paragraph 5;

"FCA dedicated staff members" has the meaning given by paragraph 2;

"reported person" means a person who is accused of having committed, or of intending to commit, a contravention of the market abuse regulation by a reporting person;

"reporting person" means a person reporting an actual or potential contravention of the market abuse regulation to the FCA; and

"report of a contravention" means a report submitted by the reporting person to the FCA regarding an actual or potential contravention of the market abuse regulation.

2.   FCA dedicated staff members

(1)   The FCA must have staff members dedicated to handling reports of contraventions ("FCA dedicated staff members").

(2)   FCA dedicated staff members must be trained for the purposes of handling reports of contraventions.

(3)   FCA dedicated staff members must exercise the following functions—

       (a)   providing any interested person with information on the procedures for making reports of contraventions;

       (b)   receiving and following up reports of contraventions; and

       (c)   where the reporting person has provided contact details, maintaining contact with that person except where the reporting person has explicitly requested otherwise or the FCA reasonably believes that maintaining contact would jeopardise the protection of the reporting person's identity.

3.   Information regarding the receipt of reports of contraventions and their follow up

(1)   The FCA must publish on its website in a separate, easily identifiable and accessible section the information regarding the receipt of reports of contraventions set out in sub-paragraph (2).

(2)   The information is—

       (a)   the dedicated communication channels established by the FCA for the purposes of paragraph 5, including—

              (i)   the telephone numbers, indicating whether conversations are recorded or unrecorded when using those telephone lines; and

              (ii)   dedicated electronic and postal addresses, which are secure and ensure confidentiality, to contact FCA dedicated staff members;

       (b)   the procedures applicable to reports of contraventions referred to in paragraph 4;

       (c)   the confidentiality regime applicable to reports of contraventions in accordance with the procedures applicable to reports of contraventions referred to in paragraph 4;

     (d)   *the procedures for the protection of persons working under a contract of employment; and*

     (e)   *a statement clearly explaining that persons making information available to the FCA in accordance with the market abuse regulation are not considered to be infringing any restriction on disclosure of information imposed by contract or by any legislative, regulatory or administrative provision, and do not incur liability of any kind related to such disclosure.*

4.   **Procedures applicable to reports of contraventions**

    (1) *The procedures applicable to reports of contraventions referred to in paragraph 3(2)(b) (information regarding the receipt of reports of contraventions and their follow up) must clearly indicate all of the following information—*

     (a)   *that reports of contraventions can be submitted anonymously;*

     (b)   *the manner in which the FCA may require the reporting person to clarify the information reported or to provide additional information that is available to the reporting person;*

     (c)   *the type, content and timeframe of the response about the outcome of the report of the contravention that the reporting person can expect after the reporting;*

     (d)   *the confidentiality regime applicable to reports of contraventions, including a detailed description of the circumstances under which the confidential data of a reporting person may be disclosed in accordance with Articles 27 (professional secrecy), 28 (data protection) and 29 (disclosure of personal data to third countries) of the market abuse regulation.*

    (2) *The detailed description referred to in sub-paragraph (1)(d) must set out the exceptional cases in which confidentiality of data may not be ensured, including where the disclosure of data is a necessary and proportionate obligation required by ... the law of the United Kingdom—*

     (a)   *in the context of investigations or subsequent judicial proceedings; or*

     (b)   *to safeguard the freedoms of others, including the right of defence of the reported person; in each case subject to appropriate safeguards under such laws.*

5.   **Dedicated communication channels**

    (1) *The FCA must establish independent and autonomous communication channels, which are both secure and ensure confidentiality, for receiving and following up reports of contraventions of the market abuse regulation ("dedicated communication channels").*

    (2) *Dedicated communication channels are considered independent and autonomous provided that they meet all the following criteria—*

     (a)   *they are separated from general communication channels of the FCA, including those through which the FCA communicates internally and with third parties in its ordinary course of business;*

     (b)   *they are designed, set up and operated in a manner that ensures the completeness, integrity and confidentiality of the information and prevents access by non-authorised staff members of the FCA; and*

     (c)   *they enable the storage of durable information in accordance with paragraph 6 to allow for further investigations.*

    (3) *The dedicated communication channels must allow a report of a contravention to be made in one or more of the following ways—*

     (a)   *a written report of a contravention in electronic or paper format;*

     (b)   *an oral report of a contravention through telephone lines, whether recorded or unrecorded; or*

     (c)   *physical meeting with FCA dedicated staff members.*

    (4) *The FCA must provide the information referred to in paragraph 3(2) to the reporting person before or immediately on receipt of the report of a contravention, unless the FCA*

       reasonably believes that providing that information would jeopardise the protection of the reporting person's identity.

(5)   *The FCA must ensure that a report of a contravention received by means other than dedicated communication channels is promptly forwarded without modification to FCA dedicated staff members using the dedicated communication channels.*

6.   **Record-keeping of reports received**

(1)   *The FCA must keep records of every report of a contravention received.*

(2)   *The FCA must promptly acknowledge the receipt of a written report of a contravention to the postal or electronic address indicated by the reporting person, unless the reporting person has explicitly requested otherwise, or the FCA reasonably believes that acknowledging receipt of a written report would jeopardise the protection of the reporting person's identity.*

(3)   *Where a recorded telephone line is used to make a report of a contravention, the FCA may document the oral reporting in the form of—*

    (a)   *an audio recording of the conversation in a durable and retrievable form; or*

    (b)   *a complete and accurate transcript of the conversation prepared by FCA dedicated staff members.*

(4)   *If the FCA prepares a transcript of a report of a contravention for the purposes of sub-paragraph (3)(b) and the reporting person has disclosed his or her identity to the FCA, the FCA must give the reporting person the opportunity to check, rectify and agree the transcript by signing it.*

(5)   *Where an unrecorded telephone line is used to make a report of a contravention, the FCA may document the oral reporting in the form of accurate minutes of the conversation prepared by FCA dedicated staff members.*

(6)   *If the FCA prepares minutes of a report of a contravention for the purposes of sub-paragraph (5) and the reporting person has disclosed his or her identity to the FCA, the FCA must give the reporting person the opportunity to check, rectify and agree the minutes of the call by signing them.*

(7)   *Where a person requests a physical meeting with FCA dedicated staff members to make a report of a contravention under paragraph 5(3)(c) the FCA must ensure that complete and accurate records of the meeting are kept in a durable and retrievable form.*

(8)   *The FCA may document the records of the physical meeting referred to in sub-paragraph (7) in the form of—*

    (a)   *an audio recording of the conversation in a durable and retrievable form; or*

    (b)   *accurate minutes of the meeting prepared by the FCA dedicated staff members.*

(9)   *If the FCA prepares minutes of a report of a contravention for the purposes of paragraph (8)(b) and the reporting person has disclosed his or her identity to the FCA, the FCA must give the reporting person the opportunity to check, rectify and agree the minutes of the meeting by signing them.*

7.   **Protection of persons working under a contract of employment**

(1)   *The FCA must provide reporting persons with access to comprehensive information and advice on the remedies and procedures available under the law of the United Kingdom to protect them against unfair treatment.*

(2)   *The information and advice referred to in sub-paragraph (1) must include information and advice on any relevant procedures under the law of the United Kingdom to claim damages or compensation for unfair treatment.*

8.   **Review of the procedures by FCA**

(1)   *The FCA must review its procedures for receiving and following up reports of contraventions regularly, and in any event at least once every two years.*

(2)   *In reviewing its procedures the FCA must take account of its experience ... and adapt its procedures accordingly and in line with market and technological developments.*

Regulation (EU) No 2017/1129
of the European Parliament and of the Council
of 14 June 2017

on the prospectus to be published when securities are offered to the public or admitted to trading on a regulated market, and repealing Directive 2003/71/EC

(assimilated law)

Note. This Regulation is revoked by the Financial Services and Markets Act 2023, s. 1(1), Sch. 1, Pt. 1, as from a day to be appointed.

CHAPTER I
GENERAL PROVISIONS

Article 1
Subject matter, scope and exemptions

1. *This Regulation lays down requirements for the drawing up, approval and distribution of the prospectus to be published when securities are offered to the public or admitted to trading on a regulated market situated or operating within the United Kingdom.*

2. *This Regulation shall not apply to the following types of securities:*
   (a) *units issued by collective investment undertakings other than the closed-end type;*
   (b) *non-equity securities issued by—*
      (i) *the government of any country or territory,*
      (ii) *a local or regional authority of any country or territory,*
      (iii) *a public international body of which any state is a member,*
      (iv) *the European Central Bank or the central bank of any state;*
   (c) *shares in the capital of central banks of any state;*
   (d) *securities unconditionally and irrevocably guaranteed by the government or a local or regional authority of any country or territory;*
   (e) *securities issued by associations with legal status or non-profit-making bodies, recognised by a state, for the purposes of obtaining the funding necessary to achieve their non-profit-making objectives;*
   (f) *non-fungible shares of capital whose main purpose is to provide the holder with a right to occupy an apartment, or other form of immovable property or a part thereof and where the shares cannot be sold on without that right being given up.*

3. *Without prejudice ... to Article 4, this Regulation shall not apply to an offer of securities to the public with a total consideration in the United Kingdom of less than EUR 1 000 000, which shall be calculated over a period of 12 months.*
   ...

4. *The obligation to publish a prospectus set out in Article 3(1) shall not apply to any of the following types of offers of securities to the public:*
   (a) *an offer of securities addressed solely to qualified investors;*
   (b) *an offer of securities addressed to fewer than 150 natural or legal persons in the United Kingdom, other than qualified investors;*
   (c) *an offer of securities whose denomination per unit amounts to at least EUR 100 000;*
   (d) *an offer of securities addressed to investors who acquire securities for a total consideration of at least EUR 100 000 per investor, for each separate offer;*
   (e) *shares issued in substitution for shares of the same class already issued, if the issuing of such new shares does not involve any increase in the issued capital;*

(f)   subject to paragraph 6a, securities offered in connection with a takeover by means of an exchange offer, provided that a document is made available to the public in accordance with the arrangements set out in Article 21(2), containing information describing the transaction and its impact on the issuer;

(g)   subject to paragraph 6b, securities offered, allotted or to be allotted in connection with a merger or division, provided that a document is made available to the public in accordance with the arrangements set out in Article 21(2), containing information describing the transaction and its impact on the issuer;

(h)   dividends paid out to existing shareholders in the form of shares of the same class as the shares in respect of which such dividends are paid, provided that a document is made available containing information on the number and nature of the shares and the reasons for and details of the offer;

(i)   securities offered, allotted or to be allotted to existing or former directors or employees by their employer or by an affiliated undertaking provided that a document is made available containing information on the number and nature of the securities and the reasons for and details of the offer or allotment;

(j)   non-equity securities issued in a continuous or repeated manner by a credit institution, where the total aggregated consideration in the United Kingdom for the securities offered is less than EUR 75 000 000 per credit institution calculated over a period of 12 months, provided that those securities:

  (i)   are not subordinated, convertible or exchangeable; and

  (ii) do not give a right to subscribe for or acquire other types of securities and are not linked to a derivative instrument.

5.   The obligation to publish a prospectus set out in Article 3(3) shall not apply to the admission to trading on a regulated market of any of the following:

(a)   securities fungible with securities already admitted to trading on the same regulated market, provided that they represent, over a period of 12 months, less than 20 % of the number of securities already admitted to trading on the same regulated market;

(b)   shares resulting from the conversion or exchange of other securities or from the exercise of the rights conferred by other securities, where the resulting shares are of the same class as the shares already admitted to trading on the same regulated market, provided that the resulting shares represent, over a period of 12 months, less than 20 % of the number of shares of the same class already admitted to trading on the same regulated market, subject to the second subparagraph of this paragraph;

(c)   securities resulting from the conversion or exchange of other securities, own funds or eligible liabilities by a resolution authority due to the exercise of a power referred to in the UK law which implemented Article 53(2), 59(2) or Article 63(1) or (2) of Directive 2014/59/EU;

(d)   shares issued in substitution for shares of the same class already admitted to trading on the same regulated market, where the issuing of such shares does not involve any increase in the issued capital;

(e)   subject to paragraph 6a, securities offered in connection with a takeover by means of an exchange offer, provided that a document is made available to the public in accordance with the arrangements set out in Article 21(2), containing information describing the transaction and its impact on the issuer;

(f)   subject to paragraph 6b, securities offered, allotted or to be allotted in connection with a merger or a division, provided that a document is made available to the public in accordance with the arrangements set out in Article 21(2), containing information describing the transaction and its impact on the issuer;

(g)   shares offered, allotted or to be allotted free of charge to existing shareholders, and dividends paid out in the form of shares of the same class as the shares in respect of which such dividends are paid, provided that the said shares are of the same class as the shares *already admitted to trading on the same regulated market and that a document is made available containing information on the number and nature of the shares and the reasons for and details of the offer or allotment;*

(h) *securities offered, allotted or to be allotted to existing or former directors or employees by their employer or an affiliated undertaking, provided that the said securities are of the same class as the securities already admitted to trading on the same regulated market and that a document is made available containing information on the number and nature of the securities and the reasons for and detail of the offer or allotment;*

(i) *non-equity securities issued in a continuous or repeated manner by a credit institution, where the total aggregated consideration in the Union for the securities offered is less than EUR 75 000 000 per credit institution calculated over a period of 12 months, provided that those securities:*

    (i) *are not subordinated, convertible or exchangeable; and*

    (ii) *do not give a right to subscribe for or acquire other types of securities and are not linked to a derivative instrument;*

(j) *securities already admitted to trading on another regulated market, on the following conditions:*

    (i) *that those securities, or securities of the same class, have been admitted to trading on that other regulated market for more than 18 months;*

    (ii) *that, for securities first admitted to trading on a regulated market after 1 July 2005, the admission to trading on that other regulated market was subject to a prospectus approved and published in accordance with Directive 2003/71/EC;*

    (iii) *that, except where point (ii) applies, for securities first admitted to listing after 30 June 1983, listing particulars were approved in accordance with the requirements of Council Directive 80/390/EEC or Directive 2001/34/EC of the European Parliament and of the Council;*

    (iv) *that the ongoing obligations for trading on that other regulated market have been fulfilled;*

    (v) *that the person seeking the admission of a security to trading on a regulated market under the exemption set out in this point (j) makes available to the public ..., in accordance with the arrangements set out in Article 21(2), a document the content of which complies with Article 7, except that the maximum length set out in Article 7(3) shall be extended by two additional sides of A4-sized paper, drawn up in a language accepted by the competent authority ...; and*

    (vi) *that the document referred to in point (v) states where the most recent prospectus can be obtained and where the financial information published by the issuer pursuant to ongoing disclosure obligations is available.*

The requirement that the resulting shares represent, over a period of 12 months, less than 20% of the number of shares of the same class already admitted to trading on the same regulated market as referred to in point (b) of the first subparagraph shall not apply in any of the following cases:

(a) *where a prospectus was drawn up in accordance with—*

    (i) *before IP completion day, either this Regulation as it had effect immediately before IP completion day or Directive 2003/71/EC, or*

    (ii) *on or after IP completion day, this Regulation,*

    upon the offer to the public or admission to trading on a regulated market of the securities giving access to the shares;

(b) *where the securities giving access to the shares were issued before 20 July 2017;*

(c) *where the shares qualify as Common Equity Tier 1 items as laid down in Article 26 of Regulation (EU) No 575/2013 of the European Parliament and of the Council of an institution as defined in point (3) of Article 4(1) of that Regulation and result from the conversion of Additional Tier 1 instruments issued by that institution due to the occurrence of a trigger event as laid down in point (a) of Article 54(1) of that Regulation;*

(ca) where the shares of an FCA investment firm result from the conversion of one class of instrument into another class of instrument because of rules made by the FCA under Part 9C of FSMA;

(d) where the shares qualify as eligible own funds or eligible basic own funds as defined in the UK law which implemented Section 3 of Chapter VI of Title I of Directive 2009/138/EC of the European Parliament and of the Council, and result from the conversion of other securities which was triggered for the purposes of fulfilling the obligations to comply with the UK law which implemented the Solvency Capital Requirement or Minimum Capital Requirement as laid down in Sections 4 and 5 of Chapter VI of Title I of Directive 2009/138/ EC or the UK law which implemented the group solvency requirement as laid down in Title III of Directive 2009/138/EC.

6. The exemptions from the obligation to publish a prospectus that are set out in paragraphs 4 and 5 may be combined together. However, the exemptions in points (a) and (b) of the first subparagraph of paragraph 5 shall not be combined together if such combination could lead to the immediate or deferred admission to trading on a regulated market over a period of 12 months of more than 20 % of the number of shares of the same class already admitted to trading on the same regulated market, without a prospectus being published.

6a. The exemptions set out in point (f) of paragraph 4 and in point (e) of paragraph 5 shall only apply to equity securities, and only in the following cases:

(a) the equity securities offered are fungible with existing securities already admitted to trading on a regulated market prior to the takeover and its related transaction, and the takeover is not considered to be a reverse acquisition transaction within the meaning of paragraph B19 of international financial reporting standard (IFRS) 3, Business Combinations, adopted by Commission Regulation (EC) No 1126/2008; or

(b) the FCA has issued a prior approval, under paragraph 6c of this Article, for the documents referred to in point (f) of paragraph 4 or point (e) of paragraph 5 of this Article.

6b. The exemptions set out in point (g) of paragraph 4 and in point (f) of paragraph 5 shall apply only to equity securities in respect of which the transaction is not considered to be a reverse acquisition transaction within the meaning of paragraph B19 of IFRS 3, Business Combinations, and only in the following cases:

(a) the equity securities of the acquiring entity have already been admitted to trading on a regulated market prior to the transaction; or

(b) the equity securities of the entities subject to the division have already been admitted to trading on a regulated market prior to the transaction.

6c. The FCA may issue prior approval for the documents referred to in point (f) of paragraph 4 or point (e) of paragraph 5 of this Article.

7. The Treasury may by regulations specify the minimum information content of the documents referred to in points (f) and (g) of paragraph 4 and points (e) and (f) of the first subparagraph of paragraph 5 of this Article.

Article 2
Definitions

For the purposes of this Regulation, the following definitions apply:

(za) 'FCA' means the Financial Conduct Authority;

(zb) 'FSMA' means the Financial Services and Markets Act 2000;

(zc) 'markets in financial instruments regulation' means Regulation (EU) No 600/2014 of the European Parliament and of the Council of 15 May 2014 on markets in financial instruments and amending Regulation (EU) No 648/2012;

(zd) references to a 'third country' (including in expressions including the words 'third country') are to be read as references to a country other than the United Kingdom;

(ze) any reference in this Regulation to a sourcebook is to a sourcebook in the Handbook of Rules and Guidance published by the FCA containing rules made by the FCA under FSMA, as the sourcebook has effect on IP completion day;

(zf)   *a reference to the UK law which implemented a Directive, or a provision thereof, is to the law of the United Kingdom which was relied on by the United Kingdom immediately before IP completion day to implement that Directive and its implementing measures—*

       (i)   *as they have effect on IP completion day, in the case of rules made by the FCA under FSMA, and*

       (ii)   *as amended from time to time, in all other cases.*

(zg)   *'FCA investment firm' has the meaning given in section 143A(1) of FSMA.*

(a)   *'securities' means transferable securities as defined in Article 2(1)(24) of the markets in financial instruments regulation, other than money market instruments as defined in Article 2(1)(25A) of that regulation that have a maturity of less than 12 months;*

(b)   *'equity securities' means shares and other transferable securities equivalent to shares in companies, as well as any other type of transferable securities giving the right to acquire any of the aforementioned securities as a consequence of their being converted or the rights conferred by them being exercised, provided that securities of the latter type are issued by the issuer of the underlying shares or by an entity belonging to the group of the said issuer;*

(c)   *'non-equity securities' means all securities that are not equity securities;*

(d)   *'offer of securities to the public' means a communication to persons in any form and by any means, presenting sufficient information on the terms of the offer and the securities to be offered, so as to enable an investor to decide to purchase or subscribe for those securities. This definition also applies to the placing of securities through financial intermediaries;*

(e)   *'qualified investor', in relation to an offer of transferable securities, means—*

       (i)   *a person described in paragraph 3 of Schedule 1 to the markets in financial instruments regulation, other than a person who, before the making of the offer, has agreed in writing with the relevant firm (or each of the relevant firms) to be treated as a non-professional client in accordance with paragraph 4 of that Schedule;*

       (ii)   *a person who has made a request to one or more relevant firms to be treated as a professional client in accordance with paragraphs 5 and 6 of that Schedule and has not subsequently, but before the making of the offer, agreed in writing with that relevant firm (or each of those relevant firms) to be treated as a non-professional client in accordance with paragraph 4 of that Schedule;*

       (iii)   *a person who—*

          (aa)   *is an eligible counterparty for the purposes of Section 6 of Chapter 3 of the Conduct of Business sourcebook, and*

          (bb)   *has not, before the making of the offer, agreed in writing with the relevant firm (or each of the relevant firms) to be treated as a non-professional client in accordance with paragraph 4 of Schedule 1 to the markets in financial instruments regulation; or*

       (iv)   *a person whom—*

          (aa)   *any relevant firm was authorised to continue to treat as a professional client immediately before 3 January 2018 by virtue of Article 71.6 (transitional provisions) of Directive 2004/39/EC on markets in financial instruments; and*

          (bb)   *the firm was entitled immediately before IP completion day to continue to treat as a professional client by virtue of Section II.2 of Annex II to the markets in financial instruments directive,*

    and for the purposes of this definition, 'relevant firm' means an investment firm (within the meaning of section 424A of FSMA) or qualifying credit institution (within the meaning in section 417 of FSMA) acting in connection with the offer;

(f)   *'small and medium-sized enterprises' or 'SMEs' means any of the following:*

       (i)   *companies, which, according to their last annual or consolidated accounts, meet at least two of the following three criteria: an average number of employees during the financial year of less than 250, a total balance sheet not exceeding EUR 43 000 000 and an annual net turnover not exceeding EUR 50 000 000;*

(ii)   *small and medium-sized enterprises as defined in point (13) of Article 4(1) of Directive 2014/65/EU.*

(g)   *'credit institution' has the meaning given in Article 2(1)(19) of the markets in financial instruments regulation;*

(h)   *'issuer' means a legal entity which issues or proposes to issue securities;*

(i)   *'offeror' means a legal entity or individual which offers securities to the public;*

(j)   *'regulated market' means a regulated market as defined in Article 2(1)(13) of the markets in financial instruments regulation;*

(k)   *'advertisement' means a communication with both of the following characteristics:*

(i)   *relating to a specific offer of securities to the public or to an admission to trading on a regulated market;*

(ii)   *aiming to specifically promote the potential subscription or acquisition of securities;*

(l)   *'regulated information' means all information which an issuer, or any other person who has applied for the admission of securities to trading on a regulated market without the issuer's consent, is required to disclose under—*

(i)   *qualifying transparency legislation;*

(ii)   *Articles 17 to 19 of Regulation (EU) No 596/2014 of the European Parliament and of the Council of 16 April 2014 on market abuse (market abuse regulation) and repealing Directive 2003/6/EC of the European Parliament and of the Council and Commission Directives 2003/124/EC, 2003/125/EC and 2004/72/EC;*

(iii) *listing rules,*

and for the purposes of this definition, 'listing rules' and 'qualifying transparency legislation' have the same meaning as in Part 6 of FSMA;

(m), (n) ...

(o)   *'competent authority' means the FCA;*

(p)   *'collective investment undertaking other than the closed-end type' means unit trusts and investment companies with both of the following characteristics:*

(i)   *they raise capital from a number of investors, with a view to investing it in accordance with a defined investment policy for the benefit of those investors;*

(ii)   *their units are, at the holder's request, repurchased or redeemed, directly or indirectly, out of their assets;*

(q)   *'units of a collective investment undertaking' means securities issued by a collective investment undertaking as representing the rights of the participants in such an undertaking over its assets;*

(r)   *'approval' means the positive act at the outcome of the scrutiny by the ... competent authority of the completeness, the consistency and the comprehensibility of the information given in the prospectus;*

(s)   *'base prospectus' means a prospectus that complies with Article 8, and, at the choice of the issuer, the final terms of the offer;*

(t)   *'working day' has the same meaning as in section 103 of FSMA;*

(u)   *'multilateral trading facility' or 'MTF' means a UK multilateral trading facility as defined by Article 2(1)(14A) of the markets in financial instruments regulation;*

(v)   *'organised trading facility' or 'OTF' means a UK organised trading facility as defined by Article 2(1)(15A) of the markets in financial instruments regulation;*

(w)   *'SME growth market' means a multilateral trading facility that is registered as an SME growth market in accordance with Section 10 of Part 5 of the Market Conduct sourcebook;*

(x)   *'third country issuer' means an issuer established in a third country;*

(y)   *'offer period' means the period during which potential investors may purchase or subscribe for the securities concerned;*

(z)   *'durable medium' means any instrument which:*

(i)   *enables a customer to store information addressed personally to that customer in a way accessible for future reference and for a period adequate for the purposes of the information; and*

(ii)   allows the unchanged reproduction of the information stored.

Article 3
Obligation to publish a prospectus and exemption

1.   *Without prejudice to Article 1(4), securities shall only be offered to the public in the United Kingdom after prior publication of a prospectus in accordance with this Regulation.*

2.   ...

3.   *Without prejudice to Article 1(5), securities shall only be admitted to trading on a regulated market situated or operating within the United Kingdom after prior publication of a prospectus in accordance with this Regulation.*

Article 4
Voluntary prospectus

1.   *Where an offer of securities to the public or an admission of securities to trading on a regulated market is outside the scope of this Regulation in accordance with Article 1(3), or exempted from the obligation to publish a prospectus in accordance with Article 1(4), 1(5) or 3(2), an issuer, an offeror or a person asking for admission to trading on a regulated market shall be entitled to voluntarily draw up a prospectus in accordance with this Regulation.*

2.   *Such voluntarily drawn up prospectus approved by the competent authority ... shall entail all the rights and obligations provided for a prospectus required under this Regulation and shall be subject to all provisions of this Regulation, under the supervision of that competent authority.*

Article 5
Subsequent resale of securities

1.   *Any subsequent resale of securities which were previously the subject of one or more of the types of offer of securities to the public listed in points (a) to (d) of Article 1(4) shall be considered as a separate offer and the definition set out in point (d) of Article 2 shall apply for the purpose of determining whether that resale is an offer of securities to the public. The placement of securities through financial intermediaries shall be subject to publication of a prospectus unless one of the exemptions listed in points (a) to (d) of Article 1(4) applies in relation to the final placement.*
No additional prospectus shall be required in any such subsequent resale of securities or final placement of securities through financial intermediaries as long as a valid prospectus is available in accordance with Article 12 and the issuer or the person responsible for drawing up such prospectus consents to its use by means of a written agreement.

2.   *Where a prospectus relates to the admission to trading on a regulated market of non-equity securities that are to be traded only on a regulated market, or a specific segment thereof, to which only qualified investors can have access for the purposes of trading in such securities, the securities shall not be resold to non-qualified investors, unless a prospectus is drawn up in accordance with this Regulation that is appropriate for non-qualified investors.*

CHAPTER II
DRAWING UP OF THE PROSPECTUS

Article 6
The prospectus

1.   *Without prejudice to Article 14(2) and Article 18(1), a prospectus shall contain the necessary information which is material to an investor for making an informed assessment of:*
(a)   the assets and liabilities, profits and losses, financial position, and prospects of the issuer and of any guarantor;
(b)   the rights attaching to the securities; and
(c)   the reasons for the issuance and its impact on the issuer.
That information may vary depending on any of the following:
(a)   the nature of the issuer;
(b)   the type of securities;

       (c)   *the circumstances of the issuer;*

       (d)   *where relevant, whether or not the non-equity securities have a denomination per unit of at least EUR 100 000 or are to be traded only on a regulated market, or a specific segment thereof, to which only qualified investors can have access for the purposes of trading in the securities.*

2.   *The information in a prospectus shall be written and presented in an easily analysable, concise and comprehensible form, taking into account the factors set out in the second subparagraph of paragraph 1.*

3.   *The issuer, offeror or person asking for the admission to trading on a regulated market may draw up the prospectus as a single document or as separate documents.*

       Without prejudice to Article 8(8) and the second subparagraph of Article 7(1), a prospectus composed of separate documents shall divide the required information into a registration document, a securities note and a summary. The registration document shall contain the information relating to the issuer. The securities note shall contain the information concerning the securities offered to the public or to be admitted to trading on a regulated market.

Article 7
The prospectus summary

1.   *The prospectus shall include a summary that provides the key information that investors need in order to understand the nature and the risks of the issuer, the guarantor and the securities that are being offered or admitted to trading on a regulated market, and that is to be read together with the other parts of the prospectus to aid investors when considering whether to invest in such securities.*

       By way of derogation from the first subparagraph, no summary shall be required where the prospectus relates to the admission to trading on a regulated market of non-equity securities provided that:

       (a)   *such securities are to be traded only on a regulated market, or a specific segment thereof, to which only qualified investors can have access for the purposes of trading in such securities; or*

       (b)   *such securities have a denomination per unit of at least EUR 100 000.*

2.   *The content of the summary shall be accurate, fair and clear and shall not be misleading. It is to be read as an introduction to the prospectus and it shall be consistent with the other parts of the prospectus.*

3.   *The summary shall be drawn up as a short document written in a concise manner and of a maximum length of seven sides of A4-sized paper when printed. The summary shall:*

       (a)   *be presented and laid out in a way that is easy to read, using characters of readable size;*

       (b)   *be written in a language and a style that facilitate the understanding of the information, in particular, in language that is clear, non-technical, concise and comprehensible for investors.*

4.   *The summary shall be made up of the following four sections:*

       (a)   *an introduction, containing warnings;*

       (b)   *key information on the issuer;*

       (c)   *key information on the securities;*

       (d)   *key information on the offer of securities to the public and/or the admission to trading on a regulated market.*

5.   *The section referred to in point (a) of paragraph 4 shall contain:*

       (a)   *the name and international securities identification number (ISIN) of the securities;*

       (b)   *the identity and contact details of the issuer, including its legal entity identifier (LEI);*

       (c)   *where applicable, the identity and contact details of the offeror, including its LEI if the offeror has legal personality, or of the person asking for admission to trading on a regulated market;*

(d) the identity and contact details of the competent authority approving the prospectus and, where different, the competent authority that approved the registration document or the universal registration document;

(e) the date of approval of the prospectus;

It shall contain the following warnings:

(a) the summary should be read as an introduction to the prospectus;

(b) any decision to invest in the securities should be based on a consideration of the prospectus as a whole by the investor;

(c) where applicable, that the investor could lose all or part of the invested capital and, where the investor's liability is not limited to the amount of the investment, a warning that the investor could lose more than the invested capital and the extent of such potential loss;

(d) ...

(e) civil liability attaches only to those persons who have tabled the summary including any translation thereof, but only where the summary is misleading, inaccurate or inconsistent, when read together with the other parts of the prospectus, or where it does not provide, when read together with the other parts of the prospectus, key information in order to aid investors when considering whether to invest in such securities;

(f) where applicable, the comprehension alert required in accordance with point (b) of Article 8(3) of Regulation (EU) No 1286/2014.

6.   The section referred to in point (b) of paragraph 4 shall contain the following information:

(a) under a sub-section entitled 'Who is the issuer of the securities?', a brief description of the issuer of the securities, including at least the following:

   (i)   its domicile and legal form, its LEI, the law under which it operates and its country of incorporation;

   (ii) its principal activities;

   (iii) its major shareholders, including whether it is directly or indirectly owned or controlled and by whom;

   (iv) the identity of its key managing directors;

   (v)   the identity of its statutory auditors;

(b) under a sub-section entitled 'What is the key financial information regarding the issuer?' a selection of historical key financial information presented for each financial year of the period covered by the historical financial information, and any subsequent interim financial period accompanied by comparative data from the same period in the prior financial year. The requirement for comparative balance sheet information shall be satisfied by presenting the year-end balance sheet information. Key financial information shall, where applicable, include:

   (i)   pro forma financial information;

   (ii) a brief description of any qualifications in the audit report relating to the historical financial information;

(c) under a sub-section entitled 'What are the key risks that are specific to the issuer?' a brief description of the most material risk factors specific to the issuer contained in the prospectus, while not exceeding the total number of risk factors set out in paragraph 10.

7.   The section referred to in point (c) of paragraph 4 shall contain the following information:

(a) under a sub-section entitled 'What are the main features of the securities?', a brief description of the securities being offered to the public and/or admitted to trading on a regulated market including at least:

   (i)   their type, class and ISIN;

   (ii) where applicable, their currency, denomination, par value, the number of securities issued and the term of the securities;

   (iii) the rights attached to the securities;

   (iv) the relative seniority of the securities in the issuer's capital structure in the event of insolvency, including, where applicable, information on the level of subordination of *the securities and the potential impact on the investment in the event of a resolution under the UK law which implemented Directive 2014/59/EU;*

      (v)   *any restrictions on the free transferability of the securities;*

      (vi) *where applicable, the dividend or payout policy;*

(b)   *under a sub-section entitled 'Where will the securities be traded?', an indication as to whether the securities are or will be subject to an application for admission to trading on a regulated market or for trading on an MTF and the identity of all the markets where the securities are or are to be traded;*

(c)   *where there is a guarantee attached to the securities, under a sub-section entitled 'Is there a guarantee attached to the securities?', the following information:*

      (i)   *a brief description of the nature and scope of the guarantee;*

      (ii) *a brief description of the guarantor, including its LEI;*

      (iii) *the relevant key financial information for the purpose of assessing the guarantor's ability to fulfil its commitments under the guarantee; and*

      (iv) *a brief description of the most material risk factors pertaining to the guarantor contained in the prospectus in accordance with Article 16(3), while not exceeding the total number of risk factors set out in paragraph 10;*

(d)   *under a sub-section entitled 'What are the key risks that are specific to the securities?', a brief description of the most material risk factors specific to the securities contained in the prospectus, while not exceeding the total number of risk factors set out in paragraph 10.*

Where a key information document is required to be prepared under Regulation (EU) No 1286/2014, the issuer, the offeror or the person asking for admission to trading on a regulated market may substitute the content set out in this paragraph with the information set out in points (c) to (i) of Article 8(3) of Regulation (EU) No 1286/2014. ...

Where there is a substitution of content pursuant to the second subparagraph, the maximum length set out in paragraph 3 shall be extended by three additional sides of A4-sized paper. The content of the key information document shall be included as a distinct section of the summary. The page layout of that section shall clearly identify it as the content of the key information document as set out in points (c) to (i) of Article 8(3) of Regulation (EU) No 1286/2014.

Where, in accordance with the third subparagraph of Article 8(9), a single summary covers several securities which differ only in some very limited details, such as the issue price or maturity date, the maximum length set out in paragraph 3 shall be extended by two additional sides of A4-sized paper. However, in the event that a key information document is required to be prepared for those securities under Regulation (EU) No 1286/2014 and the issuer, the offeror or the person asking for admission to trading on a regulated market proceeds with the substitution of content referred to in the second subparagraph of this paragraph, the maximum length shall be extended by three additional sides of A4-sized paper for each additional security.

Where the summary contains the information referred to in point (c) of the first subparagraph, the maximum length set out in paragraph 3 shall be extended by one additional side of A4-sized paper.

8.   *The section referred to in point (d) of paragraph 4 shall contain the following information:*

(a)   *under a sub-section entitled 'Under which conditions and timetable can I invest in this security?', where applicable, the general terms, conditions and expected timetable of the offer, the details of the admission to trading on a regulated market, the plan for distribution, the amount and percentage of immediate dilution resulting from the offer and an estimate of the total expenses of the issue and/or offer, including estimated expenses charged to the investor by the issuer or the offeror;*

(b)   *if different from the issuer, under a sub-section entitled 'Who is the offeror and/or the person asking for admission to trading?', a brief description of the offeror of the securities and/or the person asking for admission to trading on a regulated market, including its domicile and legal form, the law under which it operates and its country of incorporation;*

(c) under a sub-section entitled 'Why is this prospectus being produced?', a brief description of the reasons for the offer or for the admission to trading on a regulated market, as well as, where applicable:

    (i) the use and estimated net amount of the proceeds;

    (ii) an indication of whether the offer is subject to an underwriting agreement on a firm commitment basis, stating any portion not covered;

    (iii) an indication of the most material conflicts of interest pertaining to the offer or the admission to trading.

9.   Under each of the sections described in paragraphs 6, 7 and 8, the issuer may add sub-headings where deemed necessary.

10.   The total number of risk factors included in the sections of the summary referred to in point (c) of paragraph 6 and point (c)(iv) and point (d) of the first subparagraph of paragraph 7 shall not exceed 15.

11.   The summary shall not contain cross-references to other parts of the prospectus or incorporate information by reference.

12   ...

13.   The FCA may make technical standards to specify the content and format of presentation of the key financial information referred to in point (b) of paragraph 6, and the relevant key financial information referred to in point (c)(iii) of paragraph 7, taking into account the various types of securities and issuers and ensuring that the information produced is concise and understandable.

    ...

Article 8
The base prospectus

1.   For non-equity securities, including warrants in any form, the prospectus may, at the choice of the issuer, offeror or person asking for the admission to trading on a regulated market, consist of a base prospectus containing the necessary information concerning the issuer and the securities offered to the public or to be admitted to trading on a regulated market.

2.   A base prospectus shall include the following information:

    (a) a template, entitled 'form of the final terms', to be filled out for each individual issue and indicating the available options with regard to the information to be determined in the final terms of the offer;

    (b) the address of the website where the final terms will be published.

3.   Where a base prospectus contains options with regard to the information required by the relevant securities note, the final terms shall determine which of the options is applicable to the individual issue by referring to the relevant sections of the base prospectus or by replicating such information.

4.   The final terms shall be presented in the form of a separate document or shall be included in the base prospectus or in any supplement thereto. The final terms shall be prepared in an easily analysable and comprehensible form.

    The final terms shall only contain information that relates to the securities note and shall not be used to supplement the base prospectus. Point (b) of Article 17(1) shall apply in such cases.

5.   Where the final terms are neither included in the base prospectus, nor in a supplement, the issuer shall make them available to the public in accordance with the arrangements set out in Article 21 and file them with the competent authority ..., as soon as practicable upon offering securities to the public and, where possible, before the beginning of the offer of securities to the public or admission to trading on a regulated market.

    A clear and prominent statement shall be inserted in the final terms indicating:

    (a) that the final terms have been prepared for the purpose of this Regulation and must be read in conjunction with the base prospectus and any supplement thereto in order to obtain all the relevant information;

    (b) where the base prospectus and any supplement thereto are published in accordance with the arrangements set out in Article 21;

(c)   that a summary of the individual issue is annexed to the final terms.

6.   A base prospectus may be drawn up as a single document or as separate documents.

Where the issuer, the offeror or the person asking for admission to trading on a regulated market has filed a registration document for non-equity securities, or a universal registration document in accordance with Article 9, and chooses to draw up a base prospectus, the base prospectus shall consist of the following:

(a)   the information contained in the registration document, or in the universal registration document;

(b)   the information which would otherwise be contained in the relevant securities note, with the exception of the final terms where the final terms are not included in the base prospectus.

7.   The specific information on each of the different securities included in a base prospectus shall be clearly segregated.

8.   A summary shall only be drawn up once the final terms are included in the base prospectus, or in a supplement, or are filed, and that summary shall be specific to the individual issue.

9.   The summary of the individual issue shall be subject to the same requirements as the final terms, as set out in this Article, and shall be annexed to them.

The summary of the individual issue shall comply with Article 7 and shall provide the following:

(a)   the key information in the base prospectus, including the key information on the issuer;

(b)   the key information in the appropriate final terms, including the key information which was not included in the base prospectus.

Where the final terms relate to several securities which differ only in some very limited details, such as the issue price or maturity date, a single summary of the individual issue may be attached for all those securities, provided the information referring to the different securities is clearly segregated.

10.   The information contained in the base prospectus shall, where necessary, be supplemented in accordance with Article 23.

11.   An offer of securities to the public may continue after the expiration of the base prospectus under which it was commenced provided that a succeeding base prospectus is approved and published no later than the last day of validity of the previous base prospectus. The final terms of such an offer shall contain a prominent warning on their first page indicating the last day of validity of the previous base prospectus and where the succeeding base prospectus will be published. The succeeding base prospectus shall include or incorporate by reference the form of the final terms from the initial base prospectus and refer to the final terms that are relevant for the continuing offer.

A right of withdrawal pursuant to Article 23(2) shall also apply to investors who have agreed to purchase or subscribe for the securities during the validity period of the previous base prospectus, unless the securities have already been delivered to them.

Article 9
The universal registration document

1.   Any issuer whose securities are admitted to trading on a regulated market or an MTF may draw up every financial year a registration document in the form of a universal registration document describing the company's organisation, business, financial position, earnings and prospects, governance and shareholding structure.

2.   Any issuer that chooses to draw up a universal registration document every financial year shall submit it for approval to the competent authority ... in accordance with the procedure set out in Article 20(2) and (4).

After the issuer has had a universal registration document approved by the competent authority for two consecutive financial years, subsequent universal registration documents may be filed with the competent authority without prior approval.

Where the issuer thereafter fails to file a universal registration document for one financial year, the benefit of filing without prior approval shall be lost and all subsequent universal registration *documents shall be submitted to the competent authority for approval until the condition set out in the second subparagraph is met again.*

The issuer shall indicate in its application to the competent authority whether the universal registration document is submitted for approval or filed without prior approval.

...

3.   *Issuers which, prior to 21 July 2019, have had a registration document, drawn up in accordance with Annex I to Commission Regulation (EC) No 809/2004, approved by the competent authority for at least two consecutive financial years and have thereafter filed, in accordance with Article 12(3) of Directive 2003/71/EC, or got approved such a registration document every year, shall be allowed to file a universal registration document without prior approval in accordance with the second subparagraph of paragraph 2 of this Article from 21 July 2019. This paragraph does not apply in relation to a registration document forming part of a prospectus deemed to be approved by the competent authority in accordance with regulation 73 of the Official Listing of Securities, Prospectus and Transparency (Amendment etc.) (EU Exit) Regulations 2019.*

4.   *Once approved or filed without prior approval, the universal registration document, as well as the amendments thereto referred to in paragraphs 7 and 9 of this Article, shall be made available to the public without undue delay, in accordance with the arrangements set out in Article 21.*

5.   *...*

6.   *Information may be incorporated by reference into a universal registration document under the conditions set out in Article 19.*

7.   *Following the filing or approval of a universal registration document, the issuer may at any time update the information it contains by filing an amendment thereto with the competent authority. Subject to the first and second subparagraphs of Article 10(3), the filing of the amendment with the competent authority shall not require approval.*

8.   *The competent authority may at any time review the content of any universal registration document which has been filed without prior approval, as well as the content of any amendments thereto.*

The review by the competent authority shall consist in scrutinising the completeness, the consistency and the comprehensibility of the information given in the universal registration document and any amendments thereto.

9.   *Where the competent authority, in the course of the review, finds that the universal registration document does not meet the standards of completeness, comprehensibility and consistency, or that amendments or supplementary information are needed, it shall notify it to the issuer.*

A request for amendment or supplementary information addressed by the competent authority to the issuer needs only be taken into account by the issuer in the next universal registration document filed for the following financial year, except where the issuer wishes to use the universal registration document as a constituent part of a prospectus submitted for approval. In that case, the issuer shall file an amendment to the universal registration document at the latest upon submission of the application referred to in Article 20(6).

By way of derogation from the second subparagraph, where the competent authority notifies the issuer that its request for amendment or supplementary information concerns a material omission or a material mistake or material inaccuracy, which is likely to mislead the public with regard to facts and circumstances essential for an informed assessment of the issuer, the issuer shall file an amendment to the universal registration document without undue delay.

The competent authority may request that the issuer produces a consolidated version of the amended universal registration document, where such a consolidated version is necessary to ensure comprehensibility of the information provided in that document. An issuer may voluntarily include a consolidated version of its amended universal registration document in an annex to the amendment.

10.   *Paragraphs 7 and 9 shall only apply where the universal registration document is not in use as a constituent part of a prospectus. Whenever a universal registration document is in use as a constituent part of a prospectus, only Article 23 on supplementing the prospectus shall apply*

between the time when the prospectus is approved and the final closing of the offer of securities to the public or, as the case may be, the time when trading on a regulated market begins, whichever occurs later.

11. *An issuer fulfilling the conditions set out in the first or second subparagraph of paragraph 2 or in paragraph 3 of this Article shall have the status of frequent issuer and shall benefit from the faster approval process in accordance with Article 20(6), provided that:*

  (a) *upon the filing or submission for approval of each universal registration document, the issuer provides written confirmation to the competent authority that, to the best of its knowledge, all regulated information which it was required to disclose under the UK law which implemented Directive 2004/109/EC, if applicable, and under Regulation (EU) No 596/2014 has been filed and published in accordance with those acts over the last 18 months or over the period since the obligation to disclose regulated information commenced, whichever is the shorter; and*

  (b) *where the competent authority has undertaken a review as referred to in paragraph 8, the issuer has amended its universal registration document in accordance with paragraph 9.*

  Where any of the above conditions is not fulfilled by the issuer, the status of frequent issuer shall be lost.

12. *Where the universal registration document filed with or approved by the competent authority is made public at the latest four months after the end of the financial year, and contains the information required to be disclosed in the annual financial report referred to in Section 1 of Chapter 4 of the Disclosure Guidance and Transparency Rules Sourcebook, the issuer shall be deemed to have fulfilled its obligation to publish the annual financial report required under that Article.*

  Where the universal registration document, or an amendment thereto, is filed or approved by the competent authority and made public at the latest three months after the end of the first six months of the financial year, and contains the information required to be disclosed in the half-yearly financial report referred to in Section 2 of Chapter 4 of the Disclosure Guidance and Transparency Rules Sourcebook, the issuer shall be deemed to have fulfilled its obligation to publish the half-yearly financial report required under that Article.

  In the cases referred to in the first and second subparagraph, the issuer:

  (a) *shall include in the universal registration document a cross reference list identifying where each item required in the annual and half-yearly financial reports can be found in the universal registration document;*

  (b) *shall file the universal registration document in accordance with Article 19(1) of Directive 2004/109/EC and make it available to the officially appointed mechanism referred to in Article 21(2) of that Directive;*

  (c) *shall include in the universal registration document a responsibility statement using the terms required under point (c) of Article 4(2) and point (c) of Article 5(2) of Directive 2004/109/EC.*

13. *...*

14. *The Treasury may make regulations to supplement this Regulation by specifying the criteria for the scrutiny and review of the universal registration document and any amendments thereto, and the procedures for the approval and filing of those documents as well as the conditions under which the status of frequent issuer is lost.*

Article 10
Prospectuses consisting of separate documents

1. *An issuer that has already had a registration document approved by the competent authority shall be required to draw up only the securities note and the summary, where applicable, when securities are offered to the public or admitted to trading on a regulated market. In that case, the securities note and the summary shall be subject to a separate approval.*

  Where, since the approval of the registration document, there has been a significant new factor, material mistake or material inaccuracy relating to the information included in the registration document which is capable of affecting the assessment of the securities, a supplement to the registration document shall be submitted for approval, at the latest at the same time as the securities note and the summary. The right to withdraw acceptances in accordance with Article 23(2) shall not apply in that case.

The registration document and its supplement, where applicable, accompanied by the securities note and the summary shall constitute a prospectus, once approved by the competent authority.

2.   *Once approved, the registration document shall be made available to the public without undue delay and in accordance with the arrangements set out in Article 21.*

3.   *An issuer that has already had a universal registration document approved by the competent authority, or that has filed a universal registration document without prior approval pursuant to the second subparagraph of Article 9(2), shall be required to draw up only the securities note and the summary when securities are offered to the public or admitted to trading on a regulated market.*

Where the universal registration document has already been approved, the securities note, the summary and all amendments to the universal registration document filed since the approval of the universal registration document shall be subject to a separate approval.

Where an issuer has filed a universal registration document without prior approval, the entire documentation, including amendments to the universal registration document, shall be subject to approval, notwithstanding the fact that those documents remain separate.

The universal registration document, amended in accordance with Article 9(7) or (9), accompanied by the securities note and the summary shall constitute a prospectus, once approved by the competent authority.

Article 11

...

Article 12
Validity of a prospectus, registration document and universal registration document

1.   *A prospectus, whether a single document or consisting of separate documents, shall be valid for 12 months after its approval for offers to the public or admissions to trading on a regulated market, provided that it is completed by any supplement required pursuant to Article 23.*

Where a prospectus consists of separate documents, the period of validity shall begin upon approval of the securities note.

2.   *A registration document which has been previously approved shall be valid for use as a constituent part of a prospectus for 12 months after its approval.*

The end of the validity of such a registration document shall not affect the validity of a prospectus of which it is a constituent part.

3.   *A universal registration document shall be valid for use as a constituent part of a prospectus for 12 months after its approval as referred to in the first subparagraph of Article 9(2) or after its filing as referred to in the second subparagraph of Article 9(2).*

The end of the validity of such a universal registration document shall not affect the validity of a prospectus of which it is a constituent part.

CHAPTER III
THE CONTENT AND FORMAT OF THE PROSPECTUS

Article 13
Minimum information and format

1.   *The Treasury may by regulations supplement this Regulation regarding the format of the prospectus, the base prospectus and the final terms, and the schedules defining the specific information to be included in a prospectus, including LEIs and ISINs, avoiding duplication of information when a prospectus is composed of separate documents.*

In particular, when setting out the various prospectus schedules, account shall be taken of the following:

    (a)   *the various types of information needed by investors relating to equity securities as compared with non-equity securities; a consistent approach shall be taken with regard to information required in a prospectus for securities which have a similar economic rationale, notably derivative securities;*

    (b)   *the various types and characteristics of offers and admissions to trading on a regulated market of non-equity securities;*

    (c)   *the format used and the information required in base prospectuses relating to non-equity securities, including warrants in any form;*

    (d)   *where applicable, the public nature of the issuer;*

    (e)   *where applicable, the specific nature of the activities of the issuer.*

For the purposes of point (b) of the second subparagraph, when setting out the various prospectus schedules, the Treasury shall set out specific information requirements for prospectuses that relate to the admission to trading on a regulated market of non-equity securities which:

    (a)   *are to be traded only on a regulated market, or a specific segment thereof, to which only qualified investors can have access for the purposes of trading in such securities; or*

    (b)   *have a denomination per unit of at least EUR 100 000.*

Those information requirements shall be appropriate, taking into account the information needs of the investors concerned.

2.   *The Treasury may by regulations supplement this Regulation by setting out the schedule defining the minimum information to be included in the universal registration document.*

    Such a schedule shall ensure that the universal registration document contains all the necessary information on the issuer so that the same universal registration document can be used equally for the subsequent offer to the public or admission to trading on a regulated market of equity or non-equity securities. With regard to the financial information, the operating and financial review and prospects and the corporate governance, such information shall be aligned as much as possible with the information required to be disclosed in the annual and half-yearly financial reports referred to in Articles 4 and 5 of Directive 2004/109/EC, including the management report and the corporate governance statement.

3.   *Regulations referred to in paragraphs 1 and 2 shall be based on the standards in the field of financial and nonfinancial information set out by international securities commission organisations, in particular by the International Organisation of Securities Commissions (IOSCO), and on Annexes I, II and III to this Regulation.*

Article 14
Simplified disclosure regime for secondary issuances

1.   *The following persons may choose to draw up a simplified prospectus under the simplified disclosure regime for secondary issuances, in the case of an offer of securities to the public or of an admission to trading of securities on a regulated market:*

    (a)   *issuers whose securities have been admitted to trading on a regulated market or an SME growth market continuously for at least the last 18 months and who issue securities fungible with existing securities which have been previously issued;*

    (b)   *without prejudice to Article 1(5), issuers whose equity securities have been admitted to trading on a regulated market or an SME growth market continuously for at least the last 18 months and who issue non-equity securities or securities giving access to equity securities fungible with the existing equity securities of the issuer already admitted to trading;*

    (c)   *offerors of securities admitted to trading on a regulated market or an SME growth market continuously for at least the last 18 months;*

    (d)   *issuers whose securities have been offered to the public and admitted to trading on an SME growth market continuously for at least two years, and who have fully complied with reporting and disclosure obligations throughout the period of being admitted to trading, and who seek admission to trading on a regulated market of securities fungible with existing securities which have been previously issued.*

The simplified prospectus shall consist of a summary in accordance with Article 7, a specific registration document which may be used by persons referred to in points (a), (b) and (c) of the first subparagraph of this paragraph and a specific securities note which may be used by persons referred to in points (a) and (c) of that subparagraph.

2. *By way of derogation from Article 6(1), and without prejudice to Article 18(1), the simplified prospectus shall contain the relevant reduced information which is necessary to enable investors to understand—*

(a) *the prospects of the issuer and the significant changes in the business and the financial position of the issuer and the guarantor that have occurred since the end of the last financial year, if any;*

(b) *the rights attaching to the securities;*

(c) *the reasons for the issuance and its impact on the issuer, including on its overall capital structure, and the use of the proceeds.*

The information contained in the simplified prospectus shall be written and presented in an easily analysable, concise and comprehensible form and shall enable investors to make an informed investment decision. It shall also take account the regulated information that has already been disclosed to the public pursuant to—

(a) *provisions of the law of the United Kingdom relied on at the time of the disclosure in question to implement Directive 2004/109/EC, where applicable, in relation to disclosures made before IP completion day,*

(b) *the UK law which implemented Directive 2004/109/EC, where applicable, in relation to disclosures after IP completion day, and*

(c) *Regulation (EU) No 596/2014.*

Those issuers referred to in point (d) of the first subparagraph of paragraph 1 of this Article that are or are not required to prepare consolidated accounts in line with section 399 of the Companies Act 2006 after their securities' admission to trading on a regulated market shall compile the most recent financial information pursuant to point (a) of the second subparagraph of paragraph 3 of this Article, containing comparative information for the previous year included in the simplified prospectus, in accordance with Article 23a of Regulation (EU) 2019/980.

Third country issuers whose securities have been admitted to trading on an SME growth market shall compile the most recent financial information pursuant to point (a) of the second subparagraph of paragraph 3 of this Article, containing comparative information for the previous year included in the simplified prospectus in accordance with Article 23a of Regulation (EU) 2019/980.

3. *The Treasury may by regulations supplement this Regulation by setting out the schedules specifying the reduced information to be included under the simplified disclosure regime referred to in paragraph 1.*

The schedules shall include in particular:

(a) *the annual and half-yearly financial information published over the 12 months prior to the approval of the prospectus;*

(b) *where applicable, profit forecasts and estimates;*

(c) *a concise summary of the relevant information disclosed under Regulation (EU) No 596/ 2014 over the 12 months prior to the approval of the prospectus;*

(d) *risk factors;*

(e) *for equity securities, including securities giving access to equity securities, the working capital statement, the statement of capitalisation and indebtedness, a disclosure of relevant conflicts of interest and related-party transactions, major shareholders and, where applicable, pro forma financial information.*

When specifying the reduced information to be included under the simplified disclosure regime, the Treasury shall take into account the need to facilitate fundraising on capital markets and the importance of reducing the cost of capital. In order to avoid imposing unnecessary burdens on issuers, when specifying the reduced information, the Treasury shall also take into account the information which an issuer is already required to disclose under the provisions referred to in the second sentence of paragraph 2 of this Article. The Treasury shall also calibrate the reduced information so that it focusses on the information that is relevant for secondary issuances and is proportionate.

Article 15
UK Growth prospectus

1. *The following persons may choose to draw up a UK Growth prospectus under the proportionate disclosure regime set out in this Article in the case of an offer of securities to the public provided that they have no securities admitted to trading on a regulated market:*

    (a) *SMEs;*

    (b) *issuers, other than SMEs, whose securities are traded or are to be traded on an SME growth market, provided that those issuers had an average market capitalisation of less than EUR 500 000 000 on the basis of end-year quotes for the previous three calendar years;*

    (c) *issuers, other than those referred to in points (a) and (b), where the offer of securities to the public is of a total consideration in the United Kingdom that does not exceed EUR 20 000 000 calculated over a period of 12 months, and provided that such issuers have no securities traded on an MTF and have an average number of employees during the previous financial year of up to 499;*

    (ca) *issuers, other than SMEs, offering shares to the public at the same time as seeking admission of those shares to trading on an SME growth market, provided that such issuers have no shares already admitted to trading on an SME growth market and the combined value of the following two items is less than EUR 200 000 000:*

        (i)   *the final offer price, or the maximum price in the case referred to in point (b)(i) of Article 17(1);*

        (ii) *the total number of shares outstanding immediately after the share offer to the public, calculated either on the basis of the amount of shares offered to the public or, in the case referred to in point (b)(i) of Article 17(1), on the basis of the maximum amount of shares offered to the public.*

    (d) *offerors of securities issued by issuers referred to in points (a) and (b).*

    A UK Growth prospectus under the proportionate disclosure regime shall be a document of a standardised format, written in a simple language and which is easy for issuers to complete. It shall consist of a specific summary based on Article 7, a specific registration document and a specific securities note. The information in the UK Growth prospectus shall be presented in a standardised sequence in accordance with the regulations referred to in paragraph 2.

2. *The Treasury may by regulations supplement this Regulation by specifying the reduced content and the standardised format and sequence for the UK Growth prospectus, as well as the reduced content and the standardised format of the specific summary.*

    The specific summary shall not impose any additional burdens or costs on issuers insofar as it shall only require the relevant information already included in the UK Growth prospectus. When specifying the standardised format of the specific summary, the Treasury shall calibrate the requirements to ensure that it is shorter than the summary provided for in Article 7.

    When specifying the reduced content and standardised format and sequence of the UK Growth prospectus, the Treasury shall calibrate the requirements to focus on:

    (a) *the information that is material and relevant for investors when making an investment decision;*

    (b) *the need to ensure proportionality between the size of the company and the cost of producing a prospectus.*

    In doing so, the Treasury shall take into account the following:

    (a) *the need to ensure that the UK Growth prospectus is significantly lighter than the standard prospectus, in terms of administrative burdens and costs to issuers;*

(b)   the need to facilitate access to capital markets for SMEs and minimise costs for SMEs while ensuring investor confidence in investing in such companies;

(c)   the various types of information relating to equity and non-equity securities needed by investors.

Those regulations shall be based on Annexes IV and V.

Article 16
Risk factors

1.   The risk factors featured in a prospectus shall be limited to risks which are specific to the issuer and/or to the securities and which are material for taking an informed investment decision, as corroborated by the content of the registration document and the securities note.

When drawing up the prospectus, the issuer, the offeror or the person asking for admission to trading on a regulated market shall assess the materiality of the risk factors based on the probability of their occurrence and the expected magnitude of their negative impact.

Each risk factor shall be adequately described, explaining how it affects the issuer or the securities being offered or to be admitted to trading. The assessment of the materiality of the risk factors provided for in the second subparagraph may also be disclosed by using a qualitative scale of low, medium or high.

The risk factors shall be presented in a limited number of categories depending on their nature. In each category the most material risk factors shall be mentioned first according to the assessment provided for in the second subparagraph.

2.   Risk factors shall also include those resulting from the level of subordination of a security and the impact on the expected size or timing of payments to holders of the securities in the event of bankruptcy, or any other similar procedure, including, where relevant, the insolvency of a credit institution or its resolution or restructuring in accordance with the UK law which implemented Directive 2014/59/EU.

3.   Where there is a guarantee attached to the securities, the prospectus shall contain the specific and material risk factors pertaining to the guarantor to the extent that they are relevant to the guarantor's ability to fulfil its commitment under the guarantee.

4.   ...

5.   The Treasury may by regulations supplement this Regulation by specifying criteria for the assessment of the specificity and materiality of risk factors and for the presentation of risk factors across categories depending on their nature.

Article 17
Final offer price and amount of securities

1.   Where the final offer price and/or amount of securities to be offered to the public, whether expressed in number of securities or as an aggregate nominal amount, cannot be included in the prospectus:

(a)   the acceptances of the purchase or subscription of securities may be withdrawn for not less than two working days after the final offer price and/or amount of securities to be offered to the public has been filed; or

(b)   the following shall be disclosed in the prospectus:

   (i)   the maximum price and/or the maximum amount of securities, as far as they are available; or

   (ii)   the valuation methods and criteria, and/or conditions, in accordance with which the final offer price is to be determined and an explanation of any valuation methods used.

2.   The final offer price and amount of securities shall be filed with the competent authority ... and made available to the public in accordance with the arrangements set out in Article 21(2).

Article 18
Omission of information

1. The competent authority ... may authorise the omission from the prospectus, or constituent parts thereof, of certain information to be included therein, where it considers that any of the following conditions is met:

    (a) disclosure of such information would be contrary to the public interest;

    (b) disclosure of such information would be seriously detrimental to the issuer or to the guarantor, if any, provided that the omission of such information would not be likely to mislead the public with regard to facts and circumstances essential for an informed assessment of the issuer or guarantor, if any, and of the rights attached to the securities to which the prospectus relates;

    (c) such information is of minor importance in relation to a specific offer or admission to trading on a regulated market and would not influence the assessment of the financial position and prospects of the issuer or guarantor, if any.

    ...

2. Subject to adequate information being provided to investors, where, exceptionally, certain information required to be included in a prospectus, or constituent parts thereof, is inappropriate to the sphere of activity or to the legal form of the issuer or of the guarantor, if any, or to the securities to which the prospectus relates, the prospectus, or constituent parts thereof, shall contain information equivalent to the required information, unless no such information exists.

3. Where securities are guaranteed by a state, an issuer, an offeror or a person asking for admission to trading on a regulated market, when drawing up a prospectus in accordance with Article 4, shall be entitled to omit information pertaining to that state.

4. The FCA may make technical standards to specify the cases where information may be omitted in accordance with paragraph 1.

Article 19
Incorporation by reference

1. Information may be incorporated by reference in a prospectus where it has been previously or simultaneously published electronically, drawn up in a language fulfilling the requirements of Article 27 as it had effect immediately before IP completion day where the information was published before IP completion day, and where it is contained in one of the following documents:

    (a) a document which has—

        (i)   before IP completion day, been approved by or filed with a competent authority (as defined in this Regulation as it had effect immediately before IP completion day) in accordance with this Regulation (as it had effect immediately before IP completion day), or a competent authority (as defined in Directive 2003/71/EC) in accordance with that Directive; or

        (ii) on or after IP completion day, been approved by or filed with the competent authority in accordance with this Regulation or the UK law implementing Directive 2003/71/EC;

    (b) documents referred to in points (f) to (i) of Article 1(4) and points (e) to (h) and point (j)(v) of the first subparagraph of Article 1(5);

    (c) regulated information;

    (d) annual and interim financial information;

    (e) audit reports and financial statements;

    (f) management reports as referred to in Chapter 5 of Directive 2013/34/EU of the European Parliament and of the Council;

    (g) corporate governance statements as referred to in Article 20 of Directive 2013/34/EU;

    (h) reports on the determination of the value of an asset or a company;

    (i) remuneration reports as referred to in Article 9b of Directive 2007/36/EC of the European Parliament and of the Council;

(j) annual reports or any disclosure of information required under—

- provisions of the law of the United Kingdom relied on at the time of the disclosure in question to implement Articles 22 and 23 of Directive 2011/61/EU, in relation to disclosures made before IP completion day,

- the UK law which implemented Articles 22 and 23 of Directive 2011/61/EC, in relation to disclosures after IP completion day.

(k) memorandum and articles of association.

Such information shall be the most recent available to the issuer.

Where only certain parts of a document are incorporated by reference, a statement shall be included in the prospectus that the non-incorporated parts are either not relevant for the investor or covered elsewhere in the prospectus.

2.   When incorporating information by reference, issuers, offerors or persons asking for admission to trading on a regulated market shall ensure accessibility of the information. In particular, a cross-reference list shall be provided in the prospectus in order to enable investors to identify easily specific items of information, and the prospectus shall contain hyperlinks to all documents containing information which is incorporated by reference.

3.   Where possible alongside the first draft of the prospectus submitted to the competent authority, and in any case during the prospectus review process, the issuer, the offeror or the person asking for admission to trading on a regulated market shall submit in searchable electronic format any information which is incorporated by reference into the prospectus, unless such information has already been approved by or filed with the competent authority approving the prospectus.

4.   The FCA may make technical standards to update the list of documents set out in paragraph 1 of this Article by including additional types of documents required under the law of the United Kingdom to be filed with or approved by a public authority.

...

CHAPTER IV
ARRANGEMENTS FOR APPROVAL AND PUBLICATION OF THE PROSPECTUS

Article 20
Scrutiny and approval of the prospectus

1.   A prospectus shall not be published unless the ... competent authority has approved it, or all of its constituent parts in accordance with Article 10.

2.   The competent authority shall notify the issuer, the offeror or the person asking for admission to trading on a regulated market of its decision regarding the approval of the prospectus within 10 working days of the submission of the draft prospectus.

Where the competent authority fails to take a decision on the prospectus within the time limits laid down in the first subparagraph of this paragraph and paragraphs 3 and 6, such failure shall not be deemed to constitute approval of the application.

...

3.   The time limit set out in the first subparagraph of paragraph 2 shall be extended to 20 working days where the offer to the public involves securities issued by an issuer that does not have any securities admitted to trading on a regulated market and that has not previously offered securities to the public.

The time limit of 20 working days shall only be applicable for the initial submission of the draft prospectus. Where subsequent submissions are necessary in accordance with paragraph 4, the time limit set out in the first subparagraph of paragraph 2 shall apply.

4.   Where the competent authority finds that the draft prospectus does not meet the standards of completeness, comprehensibility and consistency necessary for its approval and/or that changes or supplementary information are needed:

(a) it shall inform the issuer, the offeror or the person asking for admission to trading on a regulated market of that fact promptly and at the latest within the time limits set out in the *first subparagraph of paragraph 2 or, as applicable, paragraph 3, as calculated from the submission of the draft prospectus and/or the supplementary information; and*

(b)   *it shall clearly specify the changes or supplementary information that are needed.*

In such cases, the time limit set out in the first subparagraph of paragraph 2 shall then apply only from the date on which a revised draft prospectus or the supplementary information requested are submitted to the competent authority.

5.   *Where the issuer, the offeror or the person asking for admission to trading on a regulated market is unable or unwilling to make the necessary changes or to provide the supplementary information requested in accordance with paragraph 4, the competent authority shall be entitled to refuse the approval of the prospectus and terminate the review process. In such case, the competent authority shall notify the issuer, the offeror or the person asking for admission to trading on a regulated market of its decision and indicate the reasons for such refusal.*

6.   *By way of derogation from paragraphs 2 and 4, the time limits set out in the first subparagraph of paragraph 2 and paragraph 4 shall be reduced to five working days for a prospectus consisting of separate documents drawn up by frequent issuers referred to in Article 9(11) .... The frequent issuer shall inform the competent authority at least five working days before the date envisaged for the submission of an application for approval.*

A frequent issuer shall submit an application to the competent authority containing the necessary amendments to the universal registration document, where applicable, the securities note and the summary submitted for approval.

7.   *The competent authority must provide on its website guidance on the scrutiny and approval process in order to facilitate efficient and timely approval of prospectuses. Such guidance shall include contact details for the purposes of approvals. The issuer, the offeror, the person asking for admission to trading on a regulated market or the person responsible for drawing up the prospectus shall have the possibility to directly communicate and interact with the staff of the competent authority throughout the process of approval of the prospectus.*

8., 9.   ...

10.   *The level of fees charged by the competent authority ... for the approval of prospectuses, of documents that are intended to become constituent parts of prospectuses in accordance with Article 10 or of supplements to prospectuses as well as for the filing of universal registration documents, amendments thereto and final terms, shall be reasonable and proportionate and shall be disclosed to the public at least on the website of the competent authority.*

11.   *The Treasury may by regulations supplement this Regulation by specifying the criteria for the scrutiny of prospectuses, in particular the completeness, comprehensibility and consistency of the information contained therein, and the procedures for the approval of the prospectus.*

12., 13.   ...

Article 21
Publication of the prospectus

1.   *Once approved, the prospectus shall be made available to the public by the issuer, the offeror or the person asking for admission to trading on a regulated market at a reasonable time in advance of, and at the latest at the beginning of, the offer to the public or the admission to trading of the securities involved.*

In the case of an initial offer to the public of a class of shares that is admitted to trading on a regulated market for the first time, the prospectus shall be made available to the public at least six working days before the end of the offer.

2.   *The prospectus, whether a single document or consisting of separate documents, shall be deemed available to the public when published in electronic form on any of the following websites:*

(a)   *the website of the issuer, the offeror or the person asking for admission to trading on a regulated market;*

(b)   *the website of the financial intermediaries placing or selling the securities, including paying agents;*

(c)   the website of the regulated market where the admission to trading is sought, or where no admission to trading on a regulated market is sought, the website of the operator of the MTF.

3.   The prospectus shall be published on a dedicated section of the website which is easily accessible when entering the website. It shall be downloadable, printable and in searchable electronic format that cannot be modified.

The documents containing information incorporated by reference in the prospectus, the supplements and/or final terms related to the prospectus and a separate copy of the summary shall be accessible under the same section alongside the prospectus, including by way of hyperlinks where necessary.

The separate copy of the summary shall clearly indicate the prospectus to which it relates.

4.   Access to the prospectus shall not be subject to the completion of a registration process, the acceptance of a disclaimer limiting legal liability or the payment of a fee. Warnings specifying the jurisdiction(s) in which an offer or an admission to trading is being made shall not be considered to be disclaimers limiting legal liability.

5.   The competent authority ... shall publish on its website all the prospectuses approved or at least the list of prospectuses approved, including a hyperlink to the dedicated website sections referred to in paragraph 3 of this Article .... The published list, including the hyperlinks, shall be kept up-to-date and each item shall remain on the website at least for the period referred to in paragraph 7 of this Article.

...

6.   ...

7.   All prospectuses approved shall remain publicly available in electronic form for at least 10 years after their publication on the websites referred to in paragraph 2.

Where hyperlinks are used for information incorporated by reference in the prospectus, and the supplements and/or final terms related to the prospectus, such hyperlinks shall be functional for the period referred to in the first subparagraph.

8.   An approved prospectus shall contain a prominent warning stating when the validity of the prospectus will expire. The warning shall also state that the obligation to supplement a prospectus in the event of significant new factors, material mistakes or material inaccuracies does not apply when a prospectus is no longer valid.

9.   In the case of a prospectus comprising several documents and/or incorporating information by reference, the documents and information that constitute the prospectus may be published and distributed separately provided that those documents are made available to the public in accordance with paragraph 2. Where a prospectus consists of separate documents in accordance with Article 10, each of those constituent documents, except for documents incorporated by reference, shall indicate that it is only one part of the prospectus and where the other constituent documents may be obtained.

10.   The text and the format of the prospectus, and any supplement to the prospectus made available to the public, shall at all times be identical to the original version approved by the competent authority ....

11.   A copy of the prospectus on a durable medium shall be delivered to any potential investor, upon request and free of charge, by the issuer, the offeror, the person asking for admission to trading on a regulated market or the financial intermediaries placing or selling the securities. In the event that a potential investor makes a specific demand for a paper copy, the issuer, the offeror, the person asking for admission to trading on a regulated market or a financial intermediary placing or selling the securities shall deliver a printed version of the prospectus. Delivery shall be limited to jurisdictions in which the offer of securities to the public is made ....

12.   The FCA may make technical standards to specify further the requirements relating to the publication of the prospectus.

...

13.   *The FCA may make technical standards to specify the data necessary for the classification of prospectuses referred to in paragraph 5 and the practical arrangements to ensure that such data, including the ISINs of the securities and the LEIs of the issuers, offerors and guarantors, is machine readable.*

        ...

Article 22
Advertisements

1.   *Any advertisement relating either to an offer of securities to the public or to an admission to trading on a regulated market shall comply with the principles contained in paragraphs 2 to 5. Paragraphs 2 to 4 and point (b) of paragraph 5 shall apply only to cases where the issuer, the offeror or the person asking for admission to trading on a regulated market is subject to the obligation to draw up a prospectus.*

2.   *Advertisements shall state that a prospectus has been or will be published and indicate where investors are or will be able to obtain it.*

3.   *Advertisements shall be clearly recognisable as such. The information contained in an advertisement shall not be inaccurate or misleading and shall be consistent with the information contained in the prospectus, where already published, or with the information required to be in the prospectus, where the prospectus is yet to be published.*

4.   *All information disclosed in an oral or written form concerning the offer of securities to the public or the admission to trading on a regulated market, even where not for advertising purposes, shall be consistent with the information contained in the prospectus.*

5.   *In the event that material information is disclosed by an issuer or an offeror and addressed to one or more selected investors in oral or written form, such information shall, as applicable, either:*

        (a)   be disclosed to all other investors to whom the offer is addressed, in the event that a prospectus is not required to be published in accordance with Article 1(4) or (5); or

        (b)   be included in the prospectus or in a supplement to the prospectus in accordance with Article 23(1), in the event that a prospectus is required to be published.

6.   *The competent authority ... shall have the power to exercise control over the compliance of advertising activity, relating to an offer of securities to the public or an admission to trading on a regulated market, with paragraphs 2 to 4.*

        ...

        Without prejudice to Article 32(1), scrutiny of the advertisements by the competent authority shall not constitute a precondition for the offer of securities to the public or the admission to trading to a regulated market to take place in the United Kingdom.

        ...

7., 8.   ...

9.   *The FCA may make technical standards to specify further the provisions concerning advertisements laid down in paragraphs 2 to 4, including to specify the provisions concerning the dissemination of advertisements.*

10.   ...

11.   *This Article is without prejudice to other applicable provisions of the law of the United Kingdom.*

Article 23
Supplements to the prospectus

1.   *Every significant new factor, material mistake or material inaccuracy relating to the information included in a prospectus which may affect the assessment of the securities and which arises or is noted between the time when the prospectus is approved and the closing of the offer period or the time when trading on a regulated market begins, whichever occurs later, shall be mentioned in a supplement to the prospectus without undue delay.*

        Such a supplement shall be approved in the same way as a prospectus in a maximum of five working days and published in accordance with at least the same arrangements as were applied when the original prospectus was published in accordance with Article 21. The summary ... shall also be supplemented, where necessary, to take into account the new information included in the supplement.

2. *Where the prospectus relates to an offer of securities to the public, investors who have already agreed to purchase or subscribe for the securities before the supplement is published shall have the right, exercisable within two working days after the publication of the supplement, to withdraw their acceptances, provided that the significant new factor, material mistake or material inaccuracy referred to in paragraph 1 arose or was noted before the closing of the offer period or the delivery of the securities, whichever occurs first. That period may be extended by the issuer or the offeror. The final date of the right of withdrawal shall be stated in the supplement.*

The supplement shall contain a prominent statement concerning the right of withdrawal, which clearly states:

(a) *that a right of withdrawal is only granted to those investors who had already agreed to purchase or subscribe for the securities before the supplement was published and where the securities had not yet been delivered to the investors at the time when the significant new factor, material mistake or material inaccuracy arose or was noted;*

(b) *the period in which investors can exercise their right of withdrawal; and*

(c) *whom investors may contact should they wish to exercise the right of withdrawal.*

3. *Where the securities are purchased or subscribed through a financial intermediary, that financial intermediary shall inform investors of the possibility of a supplement being published, where and when it would be published and that the financial intermediary would assist them in exercising their right to withdraw acceptances in such case.*

The financial intermediary shall contact investors on the day when the supplement is published. Where the securities are purchased or subscribed directly from the issuer, that issuer shall inform investors of the possibility of a supplement being published and where it would be published and that in such case, they could have a right to withdraw the acceptance.

4. *Where the issuer prepares a supplement concerning information in the base prospectus that relates to only one or several individual issues, the right of investors to withdraw their acceptances pursuant to paragraph 2 shall only apply to the relevant issue(s) and not to any other issue of securities under the base prospectus.*

5. *In the event that the significant new factor, material mistake or material inaccuracy referred to in paragraph 1 concerns only the information contained in a registration document or a universal registration document and that registration document or universal registration document is simultaneously used as a constituent part of several prospectuses, only one supplement shall be drawn up and approved. In that case, the supplement shall mention all the prospectuses to which it relates.*

6. *When scrutinising a supplement before approval, the competent authority may request that the supplement contains a consolidated version of the supplemented prospectus, registration document or universal registration document in an annex, where such consolidated version is necessary to ensure comprehensibility of the information given in the prospectus. Such a request shall be deemed to be a request for supplementary information under Article 20(4). An issuer may in any event voluntarily include a consolidated version of the supplemented prospectus, registration document or universal registration document in an annex to the supplement.*

7. *The FCA may make technical standards to specify situations where a significant new factor, material mistake or material inaccuracy relating to the information included in the prospectus requires a supplement to the prospectus to be published.*

...

CHAPTER V

...

CHAPTER VI
SPECIFIC RULES IN RELATION TO ISSUERS ESTABLISHED IN THIRD COUNTRIES

Article 28
Offer of securities to the public or admission to trading on a regulated market made under a prospectus drawn up in accordance with this Regulation

Where a third country issuer intends to offer securities to the public in the United Kingdom or to seek admission to trading of securities on a regulated market established in the United Kingdom under a prospectus drawn up in accordance with this Regulation, it shall obtain approval of its prospectus, in accordance with Article 20, from the competent authority ....

Once a prospectus is approved in accordance with the first subparagraph, it shall entail all the rights and obligations provided for a prospectus under this Regulation and the prospectus and the third country issuer shall be subject to all of the provisions of this Regulation under the supervision of the competent authority ....

Article 29
Offer of securities to the public or admission to trading on a regulated market made under a prospectus drawn up in accordance with the laws of a third country

1. The competent authority ... may approve a prospectus for an offer of securities to the public or for admission to trading on a regulated market, drawn up in accordance with, and which is subject to, the national laws of the third country issuer, provided that:

    (a) the information requirements imposed by those third country laws are equivalent to the requirements under this Regulation; and

    (b) the competent authority ... has concluded cooperation arrangements with the relevant supervisory authorities of the third country issuer in accordance with Article 30.

2. ...

3. The Treasury may by regulations supplement this Regulation by establishing general equivalence criteria, based on the requirements laid down in Articles 6, 7, 8 and 13.

    On the basis of the above criteria, the Treasury may by regulations state that the information requirements imposed by the national law of a third country are equivalent to the requirements under this Regulation. ...

Article 30
Cooperation with third countries

1. For the purpose of Article 29 and, where deemed necessary, for the purpose of Article 28, the competent authority shall conclude cooperation arrangements with supervisory authorities of third countries concerning the exchange of information with supervisory authorities in third countries and the enforcement of obligations arising under this Regulation in third countries unless that third country is a high-risk third country within the meaning of regulation 33 of the Money Laundering, Terrorist Financing and Transfer of Funds (Information on the Payer) Regulations 2017. Those cooperation arrangements shall at least ensure an efficient exchange of information that allows the competent authority to carry out its duties under this Regulation.

2. ...

3. The competent authority shall conclude cooperation arrangements on exchange of information with the supervisory authorities of third countries only where the information disclosed is subject to guarantees of professional secrecy which are at least equivalent to those set out in Article 35. Such exchange of information must be intended for the performance of the tasks of the competent authority.

4. The FCA may make technical standards to determine the minimum content of the cooperation arrangements referred to in paragraph 1 and the template document to be used therefor.

    ...

CHAPTER VII
THE COMPETENT AUTHORITY

Article 31

...

Article 32
Powers of the competent authority

1.–3.   ...

4.   This Regulation is without prejudice to the law of the United Kingdom on takeover bids, merger transactions and other transactions affecting the ownership or control of companies which implemented Directive 2004/25/EC and that impose requirements in addition to the requirements of this Regulation.

5.   A person making information available to the competent authority in accordance with this Regulation shall not be considered to be infringing any restriction on disclosure of information imposed by contract or by any legislative, regulatory or administrative provision, and shall not be subject to liability of any kind related to such notification.

6.   ...

Articles 33, 34

...

Article 35
Professional secrecy

1.   All information exchanged between the competent authority, the Treasury and any other authority (including a third country authority), or received by the competent authority, the Treasury or any other authority (including a third country authority) from another authority under this Regulation that concerns business or operational conditions and other economic or personal affairs shall be considered to be confidential and shall be subject to the requirements of professional secrecy, except where the authority from which the information is received states at the time of communication that such information may be disclosed or such disclosure is necessary for legal proceedings.

2.   The obligation of professional secrecy shall apply to all persons who work or who have worked for the competent authority or for any third party to whom the competent authority has delegated its powers. Information covered by professional secrecy may not be disclosed to any other person or authority except by virtue of provisions laid down by the law of the United Kingdom or any part of the United Kingdom.

Article 36
Data protection

With regard to the processing of personal data within the framework of this Regulation, the competent authority shall carry out its tasks for the purposes of this Regulation in accordance with Regulation (EU) 2016/679 and the Data Protection Act 2018.

...

Article 37

...

CHAPTER VIII
ADMINISTRATIVE SANCTIONS AND OTHER ADMINISTRATIVE MEASURES

Articles 38–41

...

Article 42
Publication of decisions

1.–3. ...

4. The competent authority shall ensure that any information about an infringement of this Regulation which the authority publishes under section 391(4) of FSMA is published on its website (whether or not also published in any other way) and then remains on that website for a period of at least five years after its publication. Personal data contained in the publication shall be kept on the official website of the competent authority only for the period which is necessary in accordance with the applicable data protection rules.

Article 43

...

CHAPTER IX
TREASURY REGULATIONS

Articles 44, 45

...

Article 45a
Treasury regulations

1. Any power to make regulations conferred on the Treasury by this Regulation is exercisable by statutory instrument.

2. Such regulations may—
    (a) contain incidental, supplemental, consequential, transitional and saving provision; and
    (b) make different provision for different purposes.

3. A statutory instrument containing regulations under this Regulation is subject to annulment in pursuance of a resolution of either House of Parliament.

CHAPTER X
FINAL PROVISIONS

Article 46
Repeal

1. Directive 2003/71/EC is repealed with effect from 21 July 2019, except for:
    (a) points (a) and (g) of Article 4(2) of Directive 2003/71/EC, which are repealed with effect from 20 July 2017; and
    (b) point (h) of Article 1(2) and point (e) of the first subparagraph of Article 3(2) of Directive 2003/71/EC, which are repealed with effect from 21 July 2018.

2. References to Directive 2003/71/EC shall be construed as references to this Regulation and shall be read in accordance with the correlation table in Annex VI to this Regulation.

3. Prospectuses approved in accordance with the national laws transposing Directive 2003/71/EC before 21 July 2019 shall continue to be governed by that national law until the end of their validity, or until twelve months have elapsed after 21 July 2019, whichever occurs first.

Articles 47, 48

...

Article 49
Entry into force and application

1.   This Regulation shall enter into force on the twentieth day following that of its publication in the Official Journal of the European Union.

2.   Without prejudice to Article 44(2), this Regulation shall apply from 21 July 2019, except for Article 1(3) and Article 3(2) which shall apply from 21 July 2018 and points (a), (b) and (c) of the first subparagraph of Article 1(5) and the second subparagraph of Article 1(5) which shall apply from 20 July 2017.

3.   ...

...

ANNEX I
PROSPECTUS

I.   Summary

II.   Identity of directors, senior management, advisers and auditors

The purpose is to identify the company representatives and other individuals involved in the company's offer or admission to trading; these are the persons responsible for drawing up the prospectus and those responsible for auditing the financial statements.

III.   Offer statistics and expected timetable

The purpose is to provide essential information regarding the conduct of any offer and the identification of important dates relating to that offer.

    A.   Offer statistics

    B.   Method and expected timetable

IV.   Essential information

The purpose is to summarise essential information about the company's financial condition, capitalisation and risk factors. If the financial statements included in the document are restated to reflect material changes in the company's group structure or accounting policies, the selected financial data must also be restated.

    A.   Selected financial data

    B.   Capitalisation and indebtedness (for equity securities only)

    C.   Reasons for the offer and use of proceeds

    D.   Risk factors

V.   Information on the company

The purpose is to provide information about the company's business operations, the products it makes or the services it provides, and the factors which affect the business. It is also intended to provide information regarding the adequacy and suitability of the company's properties, plant and equipment, as well as its plans for future capacity increases or decreases.

    A.   History and development of the company

    B.   Business overview

    C.   Organisational structure

    D.   Property, plant and equipment

VI.   Operating and financial review and prospects

The purpose is to provide the management's explanation of factors that have affected the company's financial condition and results of operations for the historical periods covered by the financial statements, and management's assessment of factors and trends which are expected to have a material effect on the company's financial condition and results of operations in future periods.

    A.   Operating results

    B.   Liquidity and capital resources

    C.   Research and development, patents and licences, etc.

    D.   Trends

VII.   *Directors, senior management and employees*
       The purpose is to provide information concerning the company's directors and managers that will allow investors to assess their experience, qualifications and levels of remuneration, as well as their relationship with the company
       A.   Directors and senior management
       B.   Remuneration
       C.   Board practices
       D.   Employees
       E.   Share ownership

VIII. *Major shareholders and related-party transactions*
       The purpose is to provide information regarding the major shareholders and others that may control or have an influence on the company. It also provides information regarding the transactions the company has entered into with persons affiliated with the company and whether the terms of such transactions are fair to the company.
       A.   Major shareholders
       B.   Related-party transactions
       C.   Interests of experts and advisers

IX.   *Financial information*
       The purpose is to specify which financial statements must be included in the document, as well as the periods to be covered, the age of the financial statements and other information of a financial nature. The accounting and auditing principles that will be accepted for use in preparation and audit of the financial statements will be determined in accordance with international accounting and auditing standards.
       A.   Consolidated statements and other financial information
       B.   Significant changes

X.   *Details of the offer and admission to trading details*
       The purpose is to provide information regarding the offer and the admission to trading of securities, the plan for distribution of the securities and related matters.
       A. Offer and admission to trading
       B. Plan for distribution
       C. Markets
       D. Holders of securities who are selling
       E. Dilution (for equity securities only)
       F. Expenses of the issue

XI.   *Additional information*
       The purpose is to provide information, most of which is of a statutory nature, that is not covered elsewhere in the prospectus.
       A.   Share capital
       B.   Memorandum and articles of association
       C.   Material contracts
       D.   Exchange controls
       E.   Warning on tax consequences
       F.   Dividends and paying agents
       G.   Statement by experts
       H.   Documents on display
       I.   Subsidiary information

ANNEX II
REGISTRATION DOCUMENT

I.   *Identity of directors, senior management, advisers and auditors*

The purpose is to identify the company representatives and other individuals involved in the company's offer or admission to trading; these are the persons responsible for drawing up the prospectus and those responsible for auditing the financial statements.

II.   Essential information about the issuer

The purpose is to summarise essential information about the company's financial condition, capitalisation and risk factors. If the financial statements included in the document are restated to reflect material changes in the company's group structure or accounting policies, the selected financial data must also be restated.

    A.   Selected financial data

    B.   Capitalisation and indebtedness (for equity securities only)

    C.   Risk factors relating to the issuer

III.   Information on the company

The purpose is to provide information about the company's business operations, the products it makes or the services it provides and the factors which affect the business. It is also intended to provide information regarding the adequacy and suitability of the company's properties, plants and equipment, as well as its plans for future capacity increases or decreases.

    A.   History and development of the company

    B.   Business overview

    C.   Organisational structure

    D.   Property, plants and equipment

IV.   Operating and financial review and prospects

The purpose is to provide the management's explanation of factors that have affected the company's financial condition and results of operations for the historical periods covered by the financial statements, and management's assessment of factors and trends which are expected to have a material effect on the company's financial condition and results of operations in future periods.

    A.   Operating results

    B.   Liquidity and capital resources

    C.   Research and development, patents and licences, etc.

    D.   Trends

V.   Directors, senior management and employees

The purpose is to provide information concerning the company's directors and managers that will allow investors to assess their experience, qualifications and levels of remuneration, as well as their relationship with the company.

    A.   Directors and senior management

    B.   Remuneration

    C.   Board practices

    D.   Employees

    E.   Share ownership

VI.   Major shareholders and related-party transactions

The purpose is to provide information regarding the major shareholders and others that may control or have an influence on the company. It also provides information regarding the transactions the company has entered into with persons affiliated with the company and whether the terms of such transactions are fair to the company.

    A.   Major shareholders

    B.   Related-party transactions

    C.   Interests of experts and advisers

VII.   Financial information

The purpose is to specify which financial statements must be included in the document, as well as the periods to be covered, the age of the financial statements and other information of a financial nature. The accounting and auditing principles that will be accepted for use in preparation and audit of the financial statements will be determined in accordance with international accounting and auditing standards.

    A.   *Consolidated statements and other financial information*

    B.   *Significant changes*

VIII.   *Additional information*

The purpose is to provide information, most of which is of a statutory nature, that is not covered elsewhere in the prospectus.

    A.   *Share capital*

    B.   *Memorandum and articles of association*

    C.   *Material contracts*

    D.   *Statement by experts*

    E.   *Documents on display*

    F.   *Subsidiary information*

ANNEX III
SECURITIES NOTE

I.   *Identity of directors, senior management, advisers and auditors*

The purpose is to identify the company representatives and other individuals involved in the company's offer or admission to trading; these are the persons responsible for drawing up the prospectus and those responsible for auditing the financial statements.

II.   *Offer statistics and expected timetable*

The purpose is to provide essential information regarding the conduct of any offer and the identification of important dates relating to that offer.

    A.   *Offer statistics*

    B.   *Method and expected timetable*

III.   *Essential information about the issuer*

The purpose is to summarise essential information about the company's financial condition, capitalisation and risk factors. If the financial statements included in the document are restated to reflect material changes in the company's group structure or accounting policies, the selected financial data must also be restated.

    A.   *Capitalisation and indebtedness (for equity securities only)*

    B.   *Information concerning working capital (for equity securities only)*

    C.   *Reasons for the offer and use of proceeds*

    D.   *Risk factors*

IV.   *Essential information about the securities*

The purpose is to provide essential information about the securities to be offered to the public and/or admitted to trading.

    A.   *A description of the type and class of the securities being offered to the public and/or admitted to trading*

    B.   *Currency of the securities issued*

    C.   *The relative seniority of the securities in the issuer's capital structure in the event of the issuer's insolvency, including, where applicable, information on the level of subordination of the securities and the potential impact on the investment in the event of a resolution under the UK law which implemented Directive 2014/59/EU*

    D.   *The dividend payout policy, provisions relating to interest payable or a description of the underlying, including the method used to relate the underlying and the rate, and an indication where information about the past and future performance of the underlying and its volatility can be obtained*

    E.   *A description of any rights attached to the securities, including any limitations of those rights, and the procedure for the exercise of those rights*

V.   *Interests of experts*
       The purpose is to provide information regarding transactions the company has entered into with experts or advisers employed on a contingent basis.
VI.   *Details of the offer and admission to trading*
       The purpose is to provide information regarding the offer and the admission to trading of securities, the plan for distribution of the securities and related matters.
       A.   *Offer and admission to trading*
       B.   *Plan for distribution*
       C.   *Markets*
       D.   *Selling securities holders*
       E.   *Dilution (for equity securities only)*
       F.   *Expenses of the issue*
VII.   *Additional information*
       The purpose is to provide information, most of which is of a statutory nature, that is not covered elsewhere in the prospectus.
       A.   *Exchange controls*
       B.   *Warning on tax consequences*
       C.   *Dividends and paying agents*
       D.   *Statement by experts*
       E.   *Documents on display*

ANNEX IV
REGISTRATION DOCUMENT FOR THE UK GROWTH PROSPECTUS

I.   *Responsibility for the registration document*
       The purpose is to identify the issuer and its representatives and other individuals involved in the company's offer; these are the persons responsible for drawing up the registration document.
II.   *Strategy, performance and business environment*
       The purpose is to inform about the company's strategy and objectives related to development and future performance and to provide information about the company's business operations, the products it makes or the services it provides, its investments and the factors which affect the business. Furthermore, the risk factors specific to the company and relevant trend information must be included.
III.   *Corporate governance*
       The purpose is to provide information concerning the company's directors and managers that will allow investors to assess their experience, qualifications and levels of remuneration, as well as their relationship with the company.
IV.   *Financial statements and key performance indicators*
       The purpose is to specify which financial statements and key performance indicators must be included in the document covering the two latest financial years (for equity securities) or the last financial year (for non-equity securities) or such shorter period during which the issuer has been in operation.
V.   *Operating and financial review (only for equity securities issued by companies with market capitalisation above EUR 200 000 000).*
       The purpose is to provide information about the financial condition and operating results if the reports, presented and prepared in accordance with rules 4.1.8 and 4.1.11 of the Disclosure Guidance and Transparency Rules Sourcebook for the periods covered by the historical financial information, are not included in the UK Growth prospectus.
VI.   *Shareholders' information*
       The purpose is to provide information about legal and arbitration proceedings, conflicts of interest and related-party transactions as well as information on the share capital.

ANNEX V
SECURITIES NOTE FOR THE UK GROWTH PROSPECTUS

I.   *Responsibility for the securities note*
The purpose is to identify the issuer and its representatives and other individuals involved in the company's offer or admission to trading; these are the persons responsible for drawing up the prospectus.

II.   *Working capital statement and statement of capitalisation and indebtedness (only for equity securities issued by companies with market capitalisation above EUR 200 000 000).*
Statement of capitalisation and indebtedness (only for equity securities issued by companies with market capitalisation above EUR 200 000 000) and working capital statement (only for equity securities). The purpose is to provide information on the issuer's capitalisation and indebtedness and information as to whether the working capital is sufficient to meet the issuer's present requirements or, if not, how the issuer proposes to provide the additional working capital needed.

III.   *Terms and conditions of the securities*
The purpose is to provide essential information regarding the terms and conditions of the securities and a description of any rights attached to the securities. Furthermore, the risk factors specific to the securities must be included.

IV.   *Details of the offer and expected timetable*
The purpose is to provide information regarding the offer and, where applicable, the admission to trading on an MTF, including the final offer price and amount of securities (whether in number of securities or aggregate nominal amount) which will be offered, the reasons for the offer, the plan for distribution of the securities, the use of proceeds of the offer, the expenses of the issuance and offer, and dilution (for equity securities only).

V.   *Information on the guarantor*
The purpose is to provide information on the guarantor of the securities where applicable, including essential information about the guarantee attached to the securities, the risk factors and financial information specific to the guarantor.

...

Commission Delegated Regulation (EU) 2019/980
of 14 March 2019

supplementing Regulation (EU) 2017/1129 of the European Parliament and of the Council as regards the format, content, scrutiny and approval of the prospectus to be published when securities are offered to the public or admitted to trading on a regulated market, and repealing Commission Regulation (EC) No 809/2004

(assimilated law)

Note. This Regulation is revoked by the Financial Services and Markets Act 2023, s. 1(1), Sch. 1, Pt. 1, as from a day to be appointed.

CHAPTER I
DEFINITIONS

Article 1
Definitions

For the purposes of this Regulation, the following definitions shall apply:

(a)   'asset-backed securities' means non-equity securities which either:

    (i)   represent an interest in assets, including any rights intended to ensure the servicing of those assets, the receipt or the timely receipt by holders of those assets of the amounts payable under those assets;

    (ii)   are secured by assets and the terms of the securities provide for payments calculated by reference to those assets;

(b)   'equivalent third country market' means a third country market which has been—

    •   deemed equivalent to a regulated market by the Commission, in accordance with the third and fourth subparagraphs of Article 25(4) of Directive 2014/65/EU of the European Parliament and of the Council of 15 May 2014 on markets in financial instruments and amending Directive 2002/92/EC and Directive 2011/61/EU, before IP completion day in retained EU law, or

    •   specified as equivalent to a regulated market in regulations made by the Treasury under paragraph 8 of Schedule 3 to Regulation (EU) No 600/2014 of the European Parliament and of the Council of 15 May 2014 on markets in financial instruments and amending Regulation (EU) No 648/2012;

(c)   'profit estimate' means a profit forecast for a financial period which has expired and for which results have not yet been published;

(d)   'profit forecast' means a statement that expressly or by implication indicates a figure or a minimum or maximum figure for the likely level of profits or losses for current or future financial periods, or contains data from which a calculation of such a figure for future profits or losses can be made, even if no particular figure is mentioned and the word 'profit' is not used;

(e)   'significant gross change' means a variation of more than 25% to one or more indicators of the size of the issuer's business,

(f)   'competent authority' means the Financial Conduct Authority;

(g)   'UK accounting standards' means accounting standards as defined by section 464 of the Companies Act 2006;

(h)   'UK-adopted international accounting standards' has the meaning given by section 474(1) of the Companies Act 2006;

(i)   a reference to the United Kingdom law which implemented a Directive, or a provision thereof, is to the law of the United Kingdom which was relied on by the United Kingdom immediately before IP completion day to implement that Directive and its implementing measures—

(i)   *as they have effect on IP completion day, in the case of rules made by the Financial Conduct Authority under the Financial Services and Markets Act 2000, and*

(ii)   *as amended from time to time, in all other cases.*

CHAPTER II
CONTENT OF THE PROSPECTUS

SECTION 1
MINIMUM INFORMATION TO BE INCLUDED IN THE REGISTRATION DOCUMENTS

Article 2
Registration document for equity securities

1.   *For equity securities, the registration document shall contain the information referred to in Annex 1 to this Regulation, unless it is drawn up in accordance with Articles 9, 14 or 15 of Regulation (EU) 2017/1129.*

2.   *By way of derogation from paragraph 1, the registration document for the following securities, where those securities are not shares or other transferrable securities equivalent to shares, may be drawn up in accordance with Article 7 of this Regulation for retail securities or Article 8 of this Regulation for wholesale securities:*

     (a)   *the securities referred to in Articles 19(1) and 20(1) of this Regulation;*

     (b)   *the securities referred to in Article 19(2) of this Regulation, where those securities are exchangeable for or convertible into shares that are or will be issued by an entity belonging to the issuer's group and that are not admitted to trading on a regulated market;*

     (c)   *the securities referred to in Article 20(2) of this Regulation, where those securities give the right to subscribe or acquire shares that are or will be issued by an entity belonging to the issuer's group and that are not admitted to trading on a regulated market.*

Article 3
Universal registration document

A registration document that is drawn up in accordance with Article 9 of Regulation (EU) 2017/1129 shall contain the information referred to in Annex 2 to this Regulation.

Article 4
Registration document for secondary issuances of equity securities

1.   *A specific registration document for equity securities that is drawn up in accordance with Article 14 of Regulation (EU) 2017/1129 shall contain the information referred to in Annex 3 to this Regulation.*

2.   *By way of derogation from paragraph 1, the registration document for the following securities, where those securities are not shares or other transferrable securities equivalent to shares, may be drawn up in accordance with Article 9:*

     (a)   *the securities referred to in Articles 19(1) and 20(1) of this Regulation;*

     (b)   *the securities referred to in Article 19(2) of this Regulation, where those securities are exchangeable for or convertible into shares that are or will be issued by an entity belonging to the issuer's group and that are not admitted to trading on a regulated market;*

     (c)   *the securities referred to in Article 20(2) of this Regulation, where those securities give the right to subscribe or acquire shares that are or will be issued by an entity belonging to the issuer's group and that are not admitted to trading on a regulated market.*

Article 5
Registration document for units of closed-end collective investment undertakings

For units issued by collective investment undertakings of the closed-end type, the registration document shall contain the information referred to in Annex 4.

Article 6
Registration document for depository receipts issued over shares

For depository receipts issued over shares, the registration document shall contain the information referred to in Annex 5.

Article 7
Registration document for retail non-equity securities

For non-equity securities other than those referred to in Article 8(2) of this Regulation, the registration document shall contain the information referred to in Annex 6 to this Regulation, unless it is drawn up in accordance with Articles 9, 14 or 15 of Regulation (EU) 2017/1129 or contains the information referred to in Annex 1 to this Regulation.

Article 8
Registration document for wholesale non-equity securities

1. For non-equity securities as referred to in paragraph 2, the registration document shall contain the information referred to in Annex 7 to this Regulation, unless the registration document is drawn up in accordance with Articles 9, 14 or 15 of Regulation (EU) 2017/1129 or contains the information referred to in Annexes 1 or 6 to this Regulation.
2. The requirement referred to in paragraph 1 shall apply to non-equity securities that comply with one of the following conditions:
    (a) they are to be traded only on a regulated market, or a specific segment thereof, to which only qualified investors can have access for the purposes of trading in such securities;
    (b) they have a denomination per unit of at least than EUR 100 000 or, where there is no individual denomination, can only be acquired on issue for at least EUR 100 000 per security.

Article 9
Registration document for secondary issuances of non-equity securities

A specific registration document for non-equity securities that is drawn up in accordance with Article 14 of Regulation (EU) 2017/1129 shall contain the information referred to in Annex 8 to this Regulation, unless it contains the information referred to in Annex 3 to this Regulation.

Article 10
Registration document for asset-backed securities

By way of derogation from Articles 7 and 8, a registration document that is drawn up for asset-backed securities, shall contain the information referred to in Annex 9.

Article 11
...

SECTION 2
MINIMUM INFORMATION TO BE INCLUDED IN THE SECURITIES NOTES

Article 12

Securities note for equity securities or units issued by collective investment undertakings
of the closed-end type

1. For equity securities or units issued by collective investment undertakings of the closed-end type, the securities note shall contain the information referred to in Annex 11 to this Regulation, unless it is drawn up in accordance with Articles 14 or 15 of Regulation (EU) 2017/1129.
2. By way of derogation from paragraph 1, the securities note for the securities referred to in paragraphs 1 and 2 of Article 19 and paragraphs 1 and 2 of Article 20 of this Regulation, where those securities are not shares or other transferrable securities equivalent to shares, shall be

drawn up in accordance with Article 15 of this Regulation for retail securities or Article 16 of this Regulation for wholesale securities.

Article 13

Securities note for secondary issuances of equity securities or of units issued by collective investment undertakings of the closed-end type

1.   *A specific securities note for equity securities or units issued by collective investment undertakings of the closed-end type that is drawn up in accordance with Article 14 of Regulation (EU) 2017/1129 shall contain the information referred to in Annex 12 to this Regulation.*

2.   *By way of derogation from paragraph 1, the specific securities note for the securities referred to in paragraphs 1 and 2 of Article 19 and paragraphs 1 and 2 of Article 20 of this Regulation, where those securities are not shares or other transferrable securities equivalent to shares, shall be drawn up in accordance with Article 17 of this Regulation.*

Article 14

Securities note for depository receipts issued over shares

For depository receipts issued over shares, the securities note shall contain the information referred to in Annex 13.

Article 15

Securities note for retail non-equity securities

For non-equity securities other than those referred to in Article 8(2) of this Regulation, the securities note shall contain the information referred to in Annex 14 to this Regulation, unless a specific securities note is drawn up in accordance with Articles 14 or 15 of Regulation (EU) 2017/1129.

Article 16

Securities note for wholesale non-equity securities

For non-equity securities as referred to in Article 8(2) of this Regulation, the securities note shall contain the information referred to in Annex 15 to this Regulation, unless it contains the information referred to in Annex 14 to this Regulation or unless a specific securities note is drawn up in accordance with Articles 14 or 15 of Regulation (EU) 2017/1129.

Article 17

Securities note for secondary issuances of non-equity securities

A specific securities note for non-equity securities that is drawn up in accordance with Article 14 of Regulation (EU) 2017/1129 shall contain the information referred to in Annex 16 to this Regulation.

SECTION 3
ADDITIONAL INFORMATION TO BE INCLUDED IN THE PROSPECTUS

Article 18

Complex financial history and significant financial commitment of issuers of equity securities

1.   *Where the issuer of an equity security has a complex financial history, or has made a significant financial commitment, additional information with respect to an entity other than the issuer shall be included in the prospectus, as referred to in paragraph 2.*

2.   *With respect to an entity, other than the issuer, additional information shall be all information referred to in Annexes 1 and 20 to this Regulation that investors need to make an informed assessment as referred to in Article 6(1) and Article 14(2) of Regulation (EU) 2017/1129, as if that entity were the issuer of the equity security.*

   Such additional information shall be preceded by a clear explanation of why that information is needed for investors to make an informed assessment and shall specify the effects of the complex financial history or of the significant financial commitment on the issuer or on the issuer's business.

3.   *For the purposes of paragraph 1, an issuer shall be considered as having a complex financial history where all of the following conditions are fulfilled:*

    (a)   *at the time of drawing up the prospectus, the information referred to in the relevant Annexes does not represent the issuer's undertaking accurately;*

    (b)   *the inaccuracy referred to in point (a) affects the ability of investors to make an informed assessment as referred to in Article 6(1) and Article 14(2) of Regulation (EU) 2017/1129;*

    (c)   *additional information relating to an entity other than the issuer is needed for investors to make an informed assessment as referred to in Article 6(1) and Article 14(2) of Regulation (EU) 2017/1129.*

4.   *For the purposes of paragraph 1, a significant financial commitment is a binding agreement to undertake a transaction that is likely to give rise to a variation of more than 25% relative to one or more indicators of the size of the issuer's business.*

Article 19
Securities that are exchangeable for or convertible into shares

1.   *Where securities are exchangeable for or convertible into shares that are admitted to trading on a regulated market, the securities note shall contain as additional information the information referred to in item 2.2.2 of Annex 17.*

2.   *Where securities are exchangeable for or convertible into shares that are or will be issued by the issuer or by an entity belonging to that issuer's group and that are not admitted to trading on a regulated market, the securities note shall also contain the following additional information:*

    (a)   *the information referred to in items 3.1 and 3.2 of Annex 11 in respect of that issuer or of that entity belonging to the issuer's group;*

    (b)   *the information referred to in Annex 18 in respect of the underlying share.*

3.   *Where securities are exchangeable for or convertible into shares that are or will be issued by a third party issuer and that are not admitted to trading on a regulated market, the securities note shall contain as additional information the information referred to in Annex 18.*

Article 20
Securities giving rise to payment or delivery obligations linked to an underlying asset

1.   *For securities other than those referred to in Article 19 that give the right to subscribe or to acquire shares that are or will be issued by the issuer or by an entity belonging to that issuer's group and that are admitted to trading on a regulated market, the securities note shall contain as additional information the information referred to in Annex 17.*

2.   *For securities other than those referred to in Article 19 that give the right to subscribe or acquire shares that are or will be issued by the issuer or by an entity belonging to that issuer's group and that are not admitted to trading on a regulated market, the securities note shall also contain the following additional information:*

    (a)   *the information referred to in Annex 17 except for the information referred to in item 2.2.2 of that Annex;*

    (b)   *the information referred to in Annex 18 in respect of the underlying share.*

3.   *For securities other than those referred to in Article 19 that are linked to an underlying other than shares referred to in paragraphs 1 and 2 of this Article, the securities note shall contain as additional information the information referred to in Annex 17.*

Article 21
Asset backed securities

For asset-backed securities, the securities notes shall also contain the additional information referred to in Annex 19.

Article 22
Guarantees

For non-equity securities that include guarantees, the securities notes shall also contain the additional information referred to in Annex 21.

Article 23
Consent

Where the issuer or the person responsible for drawing up a prospectus consents to its use as referred to in the second subparagraph of Article 5(1) of Regulation (EU) 2017/1129, the prospectus shall contain the following additional information:
(a)   the information referred to in items 1 and 2A of Annex 22 to this Regulation where the consent is provided to one or more specified financial intermediaries;
(b)   the information referred to in items 1 and 2B of Annex 22 to this Regulation where the consent is given to all financial intermediaries.

Article 23a
Historical financial information

1.   In relation to any financial year beginning on or before the day on which IP completion day falls, issuers established in the United Kingdom must present their historical financial information in accordance with—
    (a)   International Financial Reporting Standards adopted pursuant to Regulation (EC) No 1606/2002 as it applies in the European Union;
    (b)   if those standards are not applicable, UK accounting standards.

2.   In relation to any financial year beginning on or before the day on which IP completion day falls, issuers established in an EEA State must present their historical financial information in accordance with—
    (a)   International Financial Reporting Standards adopted pursuant to Regulation (EC) No 1606/2002 as it applies in the European Union; or
    (b)   if not applicable, national accounting standards of that EEA State.

3.   In relation to any financial year beginning on or before the day on which IP completion day falls, issuers established outside the United Kingdom and the EEA States must present their historical financial information in accordance with one of the following accounting standards—
    (a)   International Financial Reporting Standards adopted pursuant to Regulation (EC) No 1606/2002 as it applies in the European Union;
    (b)   International Financial Reporting Standards provided that the notes to the audited financial statements that form part of the historical financial information contain an explicit and unreserved statement that these financial statements comply with International Financial Reporting Standards in accordance with IAS 1 Presentation of Financial Statements;
    (c)   Generally Accepted Accounting Principles of Japan;
    (d)   Generally Accepted Accounting Principles of the United States of America.
    (e)   Generally Accepted Accounting Principles of the People's Republic of China;
    (f)   Generally Accepted Accounting Principles of Canada;
    (g)   Generally Accepted Accounting Principles of the Republic of Korea.

4.   In relation to a financial year beginning after the day on which IP completion day falls, issuers established in the United Kingdom, must present their historical financial information in accordance with—
    (a)   UK-adopted international accounting standards; or
    (b)   if those standards are not applicable, UK accounting standards.

5.   In relation to a financial year beginning after the day on which IP completion day falls, issuers established in a country outside the United Kingdom must present their historical financial information in accordance with—
    (a)   UK-adopted international accounting standards;

(b)   one of the accounting standards referred to in Article 23a(3); or

(c)   national accounting standards of a country that are equivalent to UK-adopted international accounting standards in accordance with a determination made by the Treasury in regulations under Commission Regulation (EC) No 1569/2007 of 21 December 2007 establishing a mechanism for the determination of equivalence of accounting standards applied by third country issuers of securities pursuant to Directives 2003/71/EC and 2004/109/EC of the European Parliament and of the Council.

6.   For an issuer established in a country outside the United Kingdom, if such financial information is not prepared in accordance with the required standards, the financial statements must be restated in compliance with UK-adopted international accounting standards.

CHAPTER III
FORMAT OF THE PROSPECTUS

Article 24
Format of a prospectus

1.   Where a prospectus is drawn up as a single document, it shall be composed of the following elements set out in the following order:

(a)   a table of contents;

(b)   a summary, where required by Article 7 of Regulation (EU) 2017/1129;

(c)   the risk factors referred to in Article 16 of Regulation (EU) 2017/1129;

(d)   any other information referred to in the Annexes to this Regulation that is to be included in that prospectus.

The issuer, offeror or person asking for admission to trading on a regulated market may decide the order in which the information referred to in the Annexes to this Regulation is set out in the prospectus.

2.   Where a prospectus is drawn up as separate documents, the registration document and the securities note shall be composed of the following elements set out in the following order:

(a)   a table of contents;

(b)   the risk factors referred to in Article 16 of Regulation (EU) 2017/1129;

(c)   any other information referred to in the Annexes to this Regulation that is to be included in that registration document or that securities note.

The issuer, offeror or person asking for admission to trading on a regulated market may decide the order in which the information referred to in the Annexes to this Regulation is set out in the registration document and the securities note.

3.   Where the registration document is drawn up in the form of a universal registration document, the issuer may include the risks factors referred to in point (b) of paragraph 2 amongst the information referred to in point (c) of that paragraph provided that those risk factors remain identifiable as a single section.

4.   Where a universal registration document is used for the purposes of Article 9(12) of Regulation (EU) 2017/1129, the information referred to in that Article shall be presented in accordance with Commission Delegated Regulation (EU) 2019/815.

5.   Where the order of the information referred to in point (d) of paragraph 1 and in point (c) of paragraph 2 is different from the order in which that information is presented in the Annexes to this Regulation, the competent authority may request to provide a list of cross references indicating the items of those Annexes to which that information corresponds.

The list of cross references referred to in the first subparagraph shall identify any items set out in the Annexes to this Regulation that have not been included in the draft prospectus due to the nature or type of issuer, securities, offer or admission to trading.

6.   Where no list of cross-references is requested in accordance with paragraph 5 or is not voluntarily submitted by the issuer, offeror or person asking for admission to trading on a regulated market, it shall be indicated in the margin of the draft prospectus to which information

in the draft prospectus the relevant information items set out in the Annexes to this Regulation correspond.

Article 25
Format of a base prospectus

1. *A base prospectus drawn up as a single document shall be composed of the following elements set out in the following order:*
    (a) *a table of contents;*
    (b) *a general description of the offering programme;*
    (c) *the risk factors referred to in Article 16 of Regulation (EU) 2017/1129;*
    (d) *any other information referred to in the Annexes to this Regulation that is to be included in the base prospectus.*

    The issuer, offeror or person asking for admission to trading on a regulated market may decide the order in which the information referred to in the Annexes to this Regulation is set out in the base prospectus.
2. *Where a base prospectus is drawn up as separate documents, the registration document and the securities note shall be composed of the following elements set out in the following order:*
    (a) *a table of contents;*
    (b) *in the securities note, a general description of the offering programme;*
    (c) *the risk factors referred to in Article 16 of Regulation (EU) 2017/1129;*
    (d) *any other information referred to in the Annexes to this Regulation that is to be included in the registration document and the securities note.*

    The issuer, offeror or person asking for admission to trading on a regulated market may decide the order in which the information referred to in the Annexes to this Regulation is set out in the registration document and the securities note.
3. *An issuer, offeror or person asking for admission to trading on a regulated market may compile in one single document two or more base prospectuses.*
4. *Where the registration document is drawn up in the form of a universal registration document, the issuer may include the risks factors referred to in point (c) of paragraph 2 amongst the information referred to in point (d) of that paragraph provided that those risk factors remain identifiable as a single section.*
5. *Where a universal registration document is used for the purposes of Article 9(12) of Regulation (EU) 2017/1129, the information referred to in that Article shall be presented in accordance with Delegated Regulation (EU) 2019/815.*
6. *Where the order of the information referred to in point (d) of paragraphs 1 and 2 is different from the order in which that information is presented in the Annexes to this Regulation, the competent authority may request to provide a list of cross references indicating the items of those Annexes to which that information corresponds.*

    The list of cross references referred to in the first subparagraph shall identify any items set out in the Annexes to this Regulation that have not been included in the draft base prospectus due to the nature or type of issuer, securities, offer or admission to trading.
7. *Where no list of cross-references is requested in accordance with paragraph 6 or is not voluntarily submitted by the issuer, offeror or person asking for admission to trading on a regulated market, it shall be indicated in the margin of the draft base prospectus to which information in the draft base prospectus the relevant information items set out in the Annexes to this Regulation correspond.*

Article 26
Information to be included in the base prospectus and the final terms

1. *The information referred to as 'Category A' in Annexes 14 to 19 and 27 to this Regulation shall be included in the base prospectus.*

2.   The information referred to as 'Category B' in Annexes 14 to 19 and 27 to this Regulation shall be included in the base prospectus except for details of that information that are not known at the time of approval of that base prospectus. Such details shall be inserted in the final terms.

3.   The information referred to as 'Category C' in Annexes 14 to 19 and 27 to this Regulation shall be inserted in the final terms, unless it is known at the time of approval of the base prospectus, in which case it may be inserted in that base prospectus instead.

4.   In addition to the information referred to in paragraphs 2 and 3 of this Article, the final terms may only contain the information referred to in Annex 28 to this Regulation. The form of the final terms referred to in Article 8(2)(a) of Regulation (EU) 2017/1129 shall indicate which of the information referred to in Annex 28 to this Regulation is to be determined in the final terms.

5.   The final terms shall not contradict the information included in the base prospectus.

Article 27
Prospectus summary

1.   An overview section of a prospectus shall only use the term 'summary' if it complies with the requirements laid down in Article 7 of Regulation (EU) 2017/1129.

2.   Where the summary of a prospectus is to be supplemented in accordance with Article 23 of Regulation (EU) 2017/1129, the new information shall be integrated in the summary of that prospectus in a way that enables investors to easily identify the changes. The new information shall be integrated in the summary of the prospectus either by producing a new summary or by supplementing the original summary.

...

ANNEX 1

SECTION 1	PERSONS RESPONSIBLE, THIRD PARTY INFORMATION, EXPERTS' REPORTS AND COMPETENT AUTHORITY APPROVAL
Item 1.1	Identify all persons responsible for the information or any parts of it, given in the registration document with, in the latter case, an indication of such parts. In the case of natural persons, including members of the issuer's administrative, management or supervisory bodies, indicate the name and function of the person; in the case of legal persons indicate the name and registered office.
Item 1.2	A declaration by those responsible for the registration document that to the best of their knowledge, the information contained in the registration document is in accordance with the facts and that the registration document makes no omission likely to affect its import. Where applicable, a declaration by those responsible for certain parts of the registration document that, to the best of their knowledge, the information contained in those parts of the registration document for which they are responsible is in accordance with the facts and that those parts of the registration document make no omission likely to affect their import.
Item 1.3	Where a statement or report attributed to a person as an expert, is included in the registration document, provide the following details for that person: (a) name; (b) business address; (c) qualifications; (d) material interest if any in the issuer. If the statement or report has been produced at the issuer's request, state that such statement or report has been included in the registration document with the consent of the person who has authorised the contents of that part of the registration document for the purpose of the prospectus.
Item 1.4	Where information has been sourced from a third party, provide a confirmation that this information has been accurately reproduced and that as far as the issuer is aware and is able to ascertain from information published by that third party, no facts have been omitted which would render the reproduced information inaccurate or misleading. In addition, identify the source(s) of the information.
Item 1.5	A statement that: (a) the [registration document/prospectus] has been approved by the [name of the competent authority], as competent authority under Regulation (EU) 2017/1129; (b) the [name of competent authority] only approves this [registration document/prospectus] as meeting the standards of completeness, comprehensibility and consistency imposed by Regulation (EU) 2017/1129; (c) such approval should not be considered as an endorsement of the issuer that is the subject of this [registration document/prospectus].
SECTION 2	STATUTORY AUDITORS
Item 2.1	Names and addresses of the issuer's auditors for the period covered by the historical financial information (together with their membership in a professional body).
Item 2.2	If auditors have resigned, been removed or have not been re-appointed during the period covered by the historical financial information, indicate details if material.

SECTION 3	RISK FACTORS
Item 3.1	A description of the material risks that are specific to the issuer, in a limited number of categories, in a section headed 'Risk Factors'. In each category, the most material risks, in the assessment undertaken by the issuer, offeror or person asking for admission to trading on a regulated market, taking into account the negative impact on the issuer and the probability of their occurrence shall be set out first. The risks shall be corroborated by the content of the registration document.
SECTION 4	INFORMATION ABOUT THE ISSUER
Item 4.1	The legal and commercial name of the issuer.
Item 4.2	The place of registration of the issuer, its registration number and legal entity identifier ('LEI').
Item 4.3	The date of incorporation and the length of life of the issuer, except where the period is indefinite.
Item 4.4	The domicile and legal form of the issuer, the legislation under which the issuer operates, its country of incorporation, the address, telephone number of its registered office (or principal place of business if different from its registered office) and website of the issuer, if any, with a disclaimer that the information on the website does not form part of the prospectus unless that information is incorporated by reference into the prospectus.
SECTION 5	BUSINESS OVERVIEW
Item 5.1	Principal activities
Item 5.1.1	A description of, and key factors relating to, the nature of the issuer's operations and its principal activities, stating the main categories of products sold and/or services performed for each financial year for the period covered by the historical financial information;
Item 5.1.2	An indication of any significant new products and/or services that have been introduced and, to the extent the development of new products or services has been publicly disclosed, give the status of their development.
Item 5.2	Principal markets A description of the principal markets in which the issuer competes, including a breakdown of total revenues by operating segment and geographic market for each financial year for the period covered by the historical financial information.
Item 5.3	The important events in the development of the issuer's business.
Item 5.4	Strategy and objectives A description of the issuer's business strategy and objectives, both financial and non-financial (if any). This description shall take into account the issuer's future challenges and prospects.
Item 5.5	If material to the issuer's business or profitability, summary information regarding the extent to which the issuer is dependent, on patents or licences, industrial, commercial or financial contracts or new manufacturing processes.
Item 5.6	The basis for any statements made by the issuer regarding its competitive position.
Item 5.7	Investments
Item 5.7.1	A description, (including the amount) of the issuer's material investments for each financial year for the period covered by the historical financial information up to the date of the registration document.

Item 5.7.2	A description of any material investments of the issuer that are in progress or for which firm commitments have already been made, including the geographic distribution of these investments (home and abroad) and the method of financing (internal or external).
Item 5.7.3	Information relating to the joint ventures and undertakings in which the issuer holds a proportion of the capital likely to have a significant effect on the assessment of its own assets and liabilities, financial position or profits and losses.
Item 5.7.4	A description of any environmental issues that may affect the issuer's utilisation of the tangible fixed assets.
SECTION 6	ORGANISATIONAL STRUCTURE
Item 6.1	If the issuer is part of a group, a brief description of the group and the issuer's position within the group. This may be in the form of, or accompanied by, a diagram of the organisational structure if this helps to clarify the structure.
Item 6.2	A list of the issuer's significant subsidiaries, including name, country of incorporation or residence, the proportion of ownership interest held and, if different, the proportion of voting power held.
SECTION 7	OPERATING AND FINANCIAL REVIEW
Item 7.1	Financial condition
Item 7.1.1	To the extent not covered elsewhere in the registration document and to the extent necessary for an understanding of the issuer's business as a whole, a fair review of the development and performance of the issuer's business and of its position for each year and interim period for which historical financial information is required, including the causes of material changes. The review shall be a balanced and comprehensive analysis of the development and performance of the issuer's business and of its position, consistent with the size and complexity of the business. To the extent necessary for an understanding of the issuer's development, performance or position, the analysis shall include both financial and, where appropriate, non-financial Key Performance Indicators relevant to the particular business. The analysis shall, where appropriate, include references to, and additional explanations of, amounts reported in the annual financial statements.
Item 7.1.2	To the extent not covered elsewhere in the registration document and to the extent necessary for an understanding of the issuer's business as a whole, the review shall also give an indication of: (a) the issuer's likely future development; (b) activities in the field of research and development. The requirements set out in item 7.1 may be satisfied by the inclusion of the directors' report required by section 415 of the Companies Act 2006.
Item 7.2	Operating results
Item 7.2.1	Information regarding significant factors, including unusual or infrequent events or new developments, materially affecting the issuer's income from operations and indicate the extent to which income was so affected.
Item 7.2.2	Where the historical financial information discloses material changes in net sales or revenues, provide a narrative discussion of the reasons for such changes.
SECTION 8	CAPITAL RESOURCES
Item 8.1	Information concerning the issuer's capital resources (both short term and long term).

Item 8.2	An explanation of the sources and amounts of and a narrative description of the issuer's cash flows.
Item 8.3	Information on the borrowing requirements and funding structure of the issuer.
Item 8.4	Information regarding any restrictions on the use of capital resources that have materially affected, or could materially affect, directly or indirectly, the issuer's operations.
Item 8.5	Information regarding the anticipated sources of funds needed to fulfil commitments referred to in item 5.7.2
SECTION 9	REGULATORY ENVIRONMENT
Item 9.1	A description of the regulatory environment that the issuer operates in and that may materially affect its business, together with information regarding any governmental, economic, fiscal, monetary or political policies or factors that have materially affected, or could materially affect, directly or indirectly, the issuer's operations.
SECTION 10	TREND INFORMATION
Item 10.1	A description of: (a) the most significant recent trends in production, sales and inventory, and costs and selling prices since the end of the last financial year to the date of the registration document; (b) any significant change in the financial performance of the group since the end of the last financial period for which financial information has been published to the date of the registration document, or provide an appropriate negative statement.
Item 10.2	Information on any known trends, uncertainties, demands, commitments or events that are reasonably likely to have a material effect on the issuer's prospects for at least the current financial year.
SECTION 11	PROFIT FORECASTS OR ESTIMATES
Item 11.1	Where an issuer has published a profit forecast or a profit estimate (which is still outstanding and valid) that forecast or estimate shall be included in the registration document. If a profit forecast or profit estimate has been published and is still outstanding, but no longer valid, then provide a statement to that effect and an explanation of why such forecast or estimate is no longer valid. Such an invalid forecast or estimate is not subject to the requirements in items 11.2 and 11.3.
Item 11.2	Where an issuer chooses to include a new profit forecast or a new profit estimate, or a previously published profit forecast or a previously published profit estimate pursuant to item 11.1, the profit forecast or estimate shall be clear and unambiguous and contain a statement setting out the principal assumptions upon which the issuer has based its forecast, or estimate. The forecast or estimate shall comply with the following principles: (a) there must be a clear distinction between assumptions about factors which the members of the administrative, management or supervisory bodies can influence and assumptions about factors which are exclusively outside the influence of the members of the administrative, management or supervisory bodies; (b) the assumptions must be reasonable, readily understandable by investors, specific and precise and not relate to the general accuracy of the estimates underlying the forecast;

	(c) in the case of a forecast, the assumptions shall draw the investor's attention to those uncertain factors which could materially change the outcome of the forecast.
Item 11.3	The prospectus shall include a statement that the profit forecast or estimate has been compiled and prepared on a basis which is both: (a) comparable with the historical financial information; (b) consistent with the issuer's accounting policies.
SECTION 12	ADMINISTRATIVE, MANAGEMENT AND SUPERVISORY BODIES AND SENIOR MANAGEMENT
Item 12.1	Names, business addresses and functions within the issuer of the following persons and an indication of the principal activities performed by them outside of that issuer where these are significant with respect to that issuer: (a) members of the administrative, management or supervisory bodies; (b) partners with unlimited liability, in the case of a limited partnership with a share capital; (c) founders, if the issuer has been established for fewer than five years; (d) any senior manager who is relevant to establishing that the issuer has the appropriate expertise and experience for the management of the issuer's business. Details of the nature of any family relationship between any of the persons referred to in points (a) to (d). In the case of each member of the administrative, management or supervisory bodies of the issuer and of each person referred to in points (b) and (d) of the first subparagraph, details of that person's relevant management expertise and experience and the following information: (a) the names of all companies and partnerships where those persons have been a member of the administrative, management or supervisory bodies or partner at any time in the previous five years, indicating whether or not the individual is still a member of the administrative, management or supervisory bodies or partner. It is not necessary to list all the subsidiaries of an issuer of which the person is also a member of the administrative, management or supervisory bodies; (b) details of any convictions in relation to fraudulent offences for at least the previous five years; (c) details of any bankruptcies, receiverships, liquidations or companies put into administration in respect of those persons described in points (a) and (d) of the first subparagraph who acted in one or more of those capacities for at least the previous five years; (d) details of any official public incrimination and/or sanctions involving such persons by statutory or regulatory authorities (including designated professional bodies) and whether they have ever been disqualified by a court from acting as a member of the administrative, management or supervisory bodies of an issuer or from acting in the management or conduct of the affairs of any issuer for at least the previous five years. If there is no such information required to be disclosed, a statement to that effect is to be made.

Item 12.2	Administrative, management and supervisory bodies and senior management conflicts of interests.
	Potential conflicts of interests between any duties to the issuer, of the persons referred to in item 12.1, and their private interests and or other duties must be clearly stated. In the event that there are no such conflicts, a statement to that effect must be made.
	Any arrangement or understanding with major shareholders, customers, suppliers or others, pursuant to which any person referred to in item 12.1 was selected as a member of the administrative, management or supervisory bodies or member of senior management.
	Details of any restrictions agreed by the persons referred to in item 12.1 on the disposal within a certain period of time of their holdings in the issuer's securities.
SECTION 13	REMUNERATION AND BENEFITS
	In relation to the last full financial year for those persons referred to in points (a) and (d) of the first subparagraph of item 12.1:
Item 13.1	The amount of remuneration paid (including any contingent or deferred compensation), and benefits in kind granted to such persons by the issuer and its subsidiaries for services in all capacities to the issuer and its subsidiaries by any person.
	That information must be provided on an individual basis unless individual disclosure is not required in the issuer's home country and is not otherwise publicly disclosed by the issuer.
Item 13.2	The total amounts set aside or accrued by the issuer or its subsidiaries to provide for pension, retirement or similar benefits.
SECTION 14	BOARD PRACTICES
	In relation to the issuer's last completed financial year, and unless otherwise specified, with respect to those persons referred to in point (a) of the first subparagraph of item 12.1.
Item 14.1	Date of expiration of the current term of office, if applicable, and the period during which the person has served in that office.
Item 14.2	Information about members of the administrative, management or supervisory bodies' service contracts with the issuer or any of its subsidiaries providing for benefits upon termination of employment, or an appropriate statement to the effect that no such benefits exist.
Item 14.3	Information about the issuer's audit committee and remuneration committee, including the names of committee members and a summary of the terms of reference under which the committee operates.
Item 14.4	A statement as to whether or not the issuer complies with the corporate governance regime(s) applicable to the issuer. In the event that the issuer does not comply with such a regime, a statement to that effect must be included together with an explanation regarding why the issuer does not comply with such regime.
Item 14.5	Potential material impacts on the corporate governance, including future changes in the board and committees composition (in so far as this has been already decided by the board and/or shareholders meeting).

SECTION 15	EMPLOYEES
Item 15.1	Either the number of employees at the end of the period or the average for each financial year for the period covered by the historical financial information up to the date of the registration document (and changes in such numbers, if material) and, if possible and material, a breakdown of persons employed by main category of activity and geographic location. If the issuer employs a significant number of temporary employees, include disclosure of the number of temporary employees on average during the most recent financial year.
Item 15.2	Shareholdings and stock options With respect to each person referred to in points (a) and (d) of the first subparagraph of item 12.1 provide information as to their share ownership and any options over such shares in the issuer as of the most recent practicable date.
Item 15.3	Description of any arrangements for involving the employees in the capital of the issuer.
SECTION 16	MAJOR SHAREHOLDERS
Item 16.1	In so far as is known to the issuer, the name of any person other than a member of the administrative, management or supervisory bodies who, directly or indirectly, has an interest in the issuer's capital or voting rights which is notifiable under the issuer's national law, together with the amount of each such person's interest, as at the date of the registration document or, if there are no such persons, an appropriate statement to that that effect that no such person exists.
Item 16.2	Whether the issuer's major shareholders have different voting rights, or an appropriate statement to the effect that no such voting rights exist.
Item 16.3	To the extent known to the issuer, state whether the issuer is directly or indirectly owned or controlled and by whom and describe the nature of such control and describe the measures in place to ensure that such control is not abused.
Item 16.4	A description of any arrangements, known to the issuer, the operation of which may at a subsequent date result in a change in control of the issuer.
SECTION 17	RELATED PARTY TRANSACTIONS
Item 17.1	Details of related party transactions (which for these purposes are those set out in UK-adopted international accounting standards, that the issuer has entered into during the period covered by the historical financial information and up to the date of the registration document, must be disclosed in accordance with the UK-adopted international accounting standards if applicable. If such standards do not apply to the issuer the following information must be disclosed: (a) the nature and extent of any transactions which are, as a single transaction or in their entirety, material to the issuer. Where such related party transactions are not concluded at arm's length provide an explanation of why these transactions were not concluded at arm's length. In the case of outstanding loans including guarantees of any kind indicate the amount outstanding; (b) the amount or the percentage to which related party transactions form part of the turnover of the issuer.
SECTION 18	FINANCIAL INFORMATION CONCERNING THE ISSUER'S ASSETS AND LIABILITIES, FINANCIAL POSITION AND PROFITS AND LOSSES
Item 18.1	Historical financial information

Item 18.1.1	Audited historical financial information covering the latest three financial years (or such shorter period as the issuer has been in operation) and the audit report in respect of each year.
Item 18.1.2	Change of accounting reference date If the issuer has changed its accounting reference date during the period for which historical financial information is required, the audited historical information shall cover at least 36 months, or the entire period for which the issuer has been in operation, whichever is shorter.
Item 18.1.3	Accounting standards The financial information must be prepared in accordance with Article 23a.
Item 18.1.4	Change of accounting framework The last audited historical financial information, containing comparative information for the previous year, must be presented and prepared in a form consistent with the accounting standards framework that will be adopted in the issuer's next published annual financial statements having regard to accounting standards and policies and legislation applicable to such annual financial statements. Changes within the accounting framework applicable to an issuer do not require the audited financial statements to be restated solely for the purposes of the prospectus. However, if the issuer intends to adopt a new accounting standards framework in its next published financial statements, at least one complete set of financial statements (as defined by IAS 1 Presentation of Financial Statements as set out in UK-adopted international accounting standards), including comparatives, must be presented in a form consistent with that which will be adopted in the issuer's next published annual financial statements, having regard to accounting standards and policies and legislation applicable to such annual financial statements.
Item 18.1.5	Where the audited financial information is prepared according to national accounting standards, it must include at least the following: (a) the balance sheet; (b) the income statement; (c) a statement showing either all changes in equity or changes in equity other than those arising from capital transactions with owners and distributions to owners; (d) the cash flow statement; (e) the accounting policies and explanatory notes.
Item 18.1.6	Consolidated financial statements If the issuer prepares both stand-alone and consolidated financial statements, include at least the consolidated financial statements in the registration document.
Item 18.1.7	Age of financial information The balance sheet date of the last year of audited financial information may not be older than one of the following: (a) 18 months from the date of the registration document if the issuer includes audited interim financial statements in the registration document; (b) 16 months from the date of the registration document if the issuer includes unaudited interim financial statements in the registration document.
Item 18.2	Interim and other financial information

Item 18.2.1	*If the issuer has published quarterly or half-yearly financial information since the date of its last audited financial statements, these must be included in the registration document. If the quarterly or half-yearly financial information has been audited or reviewed, the audit or review report must also be included. If the quarterly or half-yearly financial information is not audited or has not been reviewed, state that fact. If the registration document is dated more than nine months after the date of the last audited financial statements, it must contain interim financial information, which may be unaudited (in which case that fact must be stated) covering at least the first six months of the financial year.* *Interim financial information prepared in accordance with the requirements of section 403 of the Companies Act 2006.* *For issuers not subject to section 403 of the Companies Act 2006, the interim financial information must include comparative statements for the same period in the prior financial year, except that the requirement for comparative balance sheet information may be satisfied by presenting the year's end balance sheet in accordance with the applicable financial reporting framework.*
Item 18.3	*Auditing of historical annual financial information*
Item 18.3.1	*The historical annual financial information must be independently audited. The audit report shall be prepared in accordance with the UK law which implemented Directive 2006/43/EC of the European Parliament and of the Council and Regulation (EU) No 537/2014 of the European Parliament and of the Council.* *Where the UK law which implemented Directive 2006/43/EC and Regulation (EU) No 537/2014 do not apply, the historical annual financial information must be audited or reported on as to whether or not, for the purposes of the registration document, it gives a true and fair view in accordance with auditing standards applicable in the United Kingdom or an equivalent standard.*
Item 18.3.1a	*Where audit reports on the historical financial information have been refused by the statutory auditors or where they contain qualifications, modifications of opinion, disclaimers or an emphasis of matter, the reason must be given, and such qualifications, modifications, disclaimers or emphasis of matter must be reproduced in full.*
Item 18.3.2	*Indication of other information in the registration document that has been audited by the auditors.*
Item 18.3.3	*Where financial information in the registration document is not extracted from the issuer's audited financial statements state the source of the information and state that the information is not audited.*
Item 18.4	*Pro forma financial information*
Item 18.4.1	*In the case of a significant gross change, a description of how the transaction might have affected the assets, liabilities and earnings of the issuer, had the transaction been undertaken at the commencement of the period being reported on or at the date reported.* *This requirement will normally be satisfied by the inclusion of pro forma financial information. This pro forma financial information is to be presented as set out in Annex 20 and must include the information indicated therein.* *Pro forma financial information must be accompanied by a report prepared by independent accountants or auditors.*
Item 18.5	*Dividend policy*
Item 18.5.1	*A description of the issuer's policy on dividend distributions and any restrictions thereon. If the issuer has no such policy, include an appropriate negative statement.*

Item 18.5.2	The amount of the dividend per share for each financial year for the period covered by the historical financial information adjusted, where the number of shares in the issuer has changed, to make it comparable.
Item 18.6	Legal and arbitration proceedings
Item 18.6.1	Information on any governmental, legal or arbitration proceedings (including any such proceedings which are pending or threatened of which the issuer is aware), during a period covering at least the previous 12 months which may have, or have had in the recent past significant effects on the issuer and/or group's financial position or profitability, or provide an appropriate negative statement.
Item 18.7	Significant change in the issuer's financial position
Item 18.7.1	A description of any significant change in the financial position of the group which has occurred since the end of the last financial period for which either audited financial statements or interim financial information have been published, or provide an appropriate negative statement.
SECTION 19	ADDITIONAL INFORMATION
Item 19.1	Share capital The information in items 19.1.1 to 19.1.7 in the historical financial information as of the date of the most recent balance sheet:
Item 19.1.1	The amount of issued capital, and for each class of share capital: (a) the total of the issuer's authorised share capital; (b) the number of shares issued and fully paid and issued but not fully paid; (c) the par value per share, or that the shares have no par value; and (d) a reconciliation of the number of shares outstanding at the beginning and end of the year. If more than 10% of capital has been paid for with assets other than cash within the period covered by the historical financial information, state that fact.
Item 19.1.2	If there are shares not representing capital, state the number and main characteristics of such shares.
Item 19.1.3	The number, book value and face value of shares in the issuer held by or on behalf of the issuer itself or by subsidiaries of the issuer.
Item 19.1.4	The amount of any convertible securities, exchangeable securities or securities with warrants, with an indication of the conditions governing and the procedures for conversion, exchange or subscription.
Item 19.1.5	Information about and terms of any acquisition rights and or obligations over authorised but unissued capital or an undertaking to increase the capital.
Item 19.1.6	Information about any capital of any member of the group which is under option or agreed conditionally or unconditionally to be put under option and details of such options including those persons to whom such options relate.
Item 19.1.7	A history of share capital, highlighting information about any changes, for the period covered by the historical financial information.
Item 19.2	Memorandum and Articles of Association
Item 19.2.1	The register and the entry number therein, if applicable, and a brief description of the issuer's objects and purposes and where they can be found in the up to date memorandum and articles of association.
Item 19.2.2	Where there is more than one class of existing shares, a description of the rights, preferences and restrictions attaching to each class.

Item 19.2.3	*A brief description of any provision of the issuer's articles of association, statutes, charter or bylaws that would have an effect of delaying, deferring or preventing a change in control of the issuer.*
SECTION 20	*MATERIAL CONTRACTS*
Item 20.1	*A summary of each material contract, other than contracts entered into in the ordinary course of business, to which the issuer or any member of the group is a party, for the two years immediately preceding publication of the registration document.* *A summary of any other contract (not being a contract entered into in the ordinary course of business) entered into by any member of the group which contains any provision under which any member of the group has any obligation or entitlement which is material to the group as at the date of the registration document.*
SECTION 21	*DOCUMENTS AVAILABLE*
Item 21.1	*A statement that for the term of the registration document the following documents, where applicable, can be inspected:* *(a) the up to date memorandum and articles of association of the issuer;* *(b) all reports, letters, and other documents, valuations and statements prepared by any expert at the issuer's request any part of which is included or referred to in the registration document.* *An indication of the website on which the documents may be inspected.*

...

ANNEX 11

SECTION 1	PERSONS RESPONSIBLE, THIRD PARTY INFORMATION, EXPERTS' REPORTS AND COMPETENT AUTHORITY APPROVAL
Item 1.1	Identify all persons responsible for the information or any parts of it, given in the securities note with, in the latter case, an indication of such parts. In the case of natural persons, including members of the issuer's administrative, management or supervisory bodies, indicate the name and function of the person; in the case of legal persons indicate the name and registered office.
Item 1.2	A declaration by those responsible for the securities note that to the best of their knowledge, the information contained in the securities note is in accordance with the facts and that the securities note makes no omission likely to affect its import. Where applicable, a declaration by those responsible for certain parts of the securities note that, to the best of their knowledge, the information contained in those parts of the securities note for which they are responsible is in accordance with the facts and that those parts of the securities note make no omission likely to affect their import.
Item 1.3	Where a statement or report attributed to a person as an expert, is included in the securities note, provide the following in relation to that person: (a) name; (b) business address; (c) qualifications; (d) material interest, if any, in the issuer. If the statement or report has been produced at the issuer's request, state that such statement or report has been included in the securities note with the consent of the person who has authorised the contents of that part of the securities note for the purpose of the prospectus.
Item 1.4	Where information has been sourced from a third party, provide a confirmation that this information has been accurately reproduced and that as far as the issuer is aware and is able to ascertain from information published by that third party, no facts have been omitted which would render the reproduced information inaccurate or misleading. In addition, identify the source(s) of the information.
Item 1.5	A statement that: (a) this [securities note/prospectus] has been approved by the name of competent authority], as competent authority under Regulation (EU) 2017/1129; (b) the [name of competent authority] only approves this [securities note/prospectus] as meeting the standards of completeness, comprehensibility and consistency imposed by Regulation (EU) 2017/1129; (c) such approval should not be considered as an endorsement of [the quality of the securities that are the subject of this [securities note/prospectus]; (d) investors should make their own assessment as to the suitability of investing in the securities.

SECTION 2	RISK FACTORS
Item 2.1	A description of the material risks that are specific to the securities being offered and/or admitted to trading in a limited number of categories, in a section headed 'Risk Factors'. In each category the most material risks, in the assessment of the issuer, offeror or person asking for admission to trading on a regulated market, taking into account the negative impact on the issuer and the securities and the probability of their occurrence, shall be set out first. The risks shall be corroborated by the content of the securities note.
SECTION 3	ESSENTIAL INFORMATION
Item 3.1	Working capital statement
Item 3.2	Capitalisation and indebtedness In the case of material changes in the capitalisation and indebtedness position of the issuer within the 90 day period, additional information shall be given through the presentation of a narrative description of such changes or through the updating of those figures.
Item 3.3	Interest of natural and legal persons involved in the issue/offer
Item 3.4	Reasons for the offer and use of proceeds
SECTION 4	INFORMATION CONCERNING THE SECURITIES TO BE OFFERED/ADMITTED TO TRADING
Item 4.1	A description of the type and the class of the securities being offered and/or admitted to trading, including the international security identification number ('ISIN').
Item 4.2	Legislation under which the securities have been created.
Item 4.3	An indication whether the securities are in registered form or bearer form and whether the securities are in certificated form or book-entry form. In the latter case, name and address of the entity in charge of keeping the records.
Item 4.4	Currency of the securities issue.
Item 4.5	A description of the rights attached to the securities, including any limitations of those rights and procedure for the exercise of those rights: (a) dividend rights: fixed date(s) on which entitlement arises;time limit after which entitlement to dividend lapses and an indication of the person in whose favour the lapse operates;dividend restrictions and procedures for non-resident holders;rate of dividend or method of its calculation, periodicity and cumulative or non-cumulative nature of payments; (b) voting rights; (c) pre-emption rights in offers for subscription of securities of the same class; (d) right to share in the issuer's profits; (e) rights to share in any surplus in the event of liquidation; (f) redemption provisions; (g) conversion provisions.
Item 4.6	In the case of new issues, a statement of the resolutions, authorisations and approvals by virtue of which the securities have been or will be created and/or issued.
Item 4.7	In the case of new issues, the expected issue date of the securities.

Item 4.8	A description of any restrictions on the transferability of the securities.
Item 4.9	Statement on the existence of any national legislation on takeovers applicable to the issuer which may frustrate such takeovers if any. A brief description of the shareholders' rights and obligations in case of mandatory takeover bids and/or squeeze-out or sell-out rules in relation to the securities.
Item 4.10	An indication of public takeover bids by third parties in respect of the issuer's equity, which have occurred during the last financial year and the current financial year. The price or exchange terms attaching to such offers and the outcome thereof must be stated.
Item 4.11	A warning that the tax legislation of the investor's home country and of the issuer's country of incorporation may have an impact on the income received from the securities. Information on the taxation treatment of the securities where the proposed investment attracts a tax regime specific to that type of investment.
Item 4.12	Where applicable, the potential impact on the investment in the event of resolution under the UK law which implemented Directive 2014/59/EU of the European Parliament and of the Council.
Item 4.13	If different from the issuer, the identity and contact details of the offeror of the securities and/or the person asking for admission to trading, including the legal entity identifier ('LEI') where the offeror has legal personality.
SECTION 5	TERMS AND CONDITIONS OF THE OFFER OF SECURITIES TO THE PUBLIC
Item 5.1	Conditions, offer statistics, expected timetable and action required to apply for the offer.
Item 5.1.1	Conditions to which the offer is subject.
Item 5.1.2	Total amount of the issue/offer, distinguishing the securities offered for sale and those offered for subscription; if the amount is not fixed, an indication of the maximum amount of securities to be offered (if available) and a description of the arrangements and the time period for announcing to the public the definitive amount of the offer. Where the maximum amount of securities cannot be provided in the prospectus, the prospectus shall specify that acceptances of the purchase or subscription of securities may be withdrawn for not less than two working days after the amount of securities to be offered to the public has been filed.
Item 5.1.3	The time period, including any possible amendments, during which the offer will be open and description of the application process.
Item 5.1.4	An indication of when, and under which circumstances, the offer may be revoked or suspended and whether revocation can occur after dealing has begun.
Item 5.1.5	A description of any possibility to reduce subscriptions and the manner for refunding amounts paid in excess by applicants.
Item 5.1.6	Details of the minimum and/or maximum amount of application (whether in number of securities or aggregate amount to invest).
Item 5.1.7	An indication of the period during which an application may be withdrawn, provided that investors are allowed to withdraw their subscription.

Item 5.1.8	Method and time limits for paying up the securities and for delivery of the securities.
Item 5.1.9	A full description of the manner and date in which results of the offer are to be made public.
Item 5.1.10	The procedure for the exercise of any right of pre-emption, the negotiability of subscription rights and the treatment of subscription rights not exercised.
Item 5.2	Plan of distribution and allotment.
Item 5.2.1	The various categories of potential investors to which the securities are offered. If the offer is being made simultaneously in the markets of two or more countries and if a tranche has been or is being reserved for certain of these, indicate any such tranche.
Item 5.2.2	To the extent known to the issuer, an indication of whether major shareholders or members of the issuer's management, supervisory or administrative bodies intend to subscribe in the offer, or whether any person intends to subscribe for more than five per cent of the offer.
Item 5.2.3	Pre-allotment Disclosure: (a) the division into tranches of the offer including the institutional, retail and issuer's employee tranches and any other tranches; (b) the conditions under which the claw-back may be used, the maximum size of such claw-back and any applicable minimum percentages for individual tranches; (c) the allotment method or methods to be used for the retail and issuer's employee tranche in the event of an over-subscription of these tranches; (d) a description of any pre-determined preferential treatment to be accorded to certain classes of investors or certain affinity groups (including friends and family programmes) in the allotment, the percentage of the offer reserved for such preferential treatment and the criteria for inclusion in such classes or groups; (e) whether the treatment of subscriptions or bids to subscribe in the allotment may be determined on the basis of which firm they are made through or by; (f) a target minimum individual allotment if any within the retail tranche; (g) the conditions for the closing of the offer as well as the date on which the offer may be closed at the earliest; (h) whether or not multiple subscriptions are admitted, and where they are not, how any multiple subscriptions will be handled.
Item 5.2.4	Process for notifying applicants of the amount allotted and an indication whether dealing may begin before notification is made.
Item 5.3	Pricing

Item 5.3.1	An indication of the price at which the securities will be offered and the amount of any expenses and taxes charged to the subscriber or purchaser. If the price is not known, then pursuant to Article 17 of Regulation (EU) 2017/1129 indicate either: (a) the maximum price as far as it is available; (b) the valuation methods and criteria, and/or conditions, in accordance with which the final offer price has been or will be determined and an explanation of any valuation methods used. Where neither point (a) nor (b) can be provided in the securities note, the securities note shall specify that acceptances of the purchase or subscription of securities may be withdrawn up to two working days after the final offer price of securities to be offered to the public has been filed.
Item 5.3.2	Process for the disclosure of the offer price.
Item 5.3.3	If the issuer's equity holders have pre-emptive purchase rights and this right is restricted or withdrawn, an indication of the basis for the issue price if the issue is for cash, together with the reasons for and beneficiaries of such restriction or withdrawal.
Item 5.3.4	Where there is or could be a material disparity between the public offer price and the effective cash cost to members of the administrative, management or supervisory bodies or senior management, or affiliated persons, of securities acquired by them in transactions during the past year, or which they have the right to acquire, include a comparison of the public contribution in the proposed public offer and the effective cash contributions of such persons.
Item 5.4	Placing and underwriting
Item 5.4.1	Name and address of the coordinator(s) of the global offer and of single parts of the offer and, to the extent known to the issuer or to the offeror, of the placers in the various countries where the offer takes place.
Item 5.4.2	Name and address of any paying agents and depository agents in each country.
Item 5.4.3	Name and address of the entities agreeing to underwrite the issue on a firm commitment basis, and name and address of the entities agreeing to place the issue without a firm commitment or under best 'efforts' arrangements. Indication of the material features of the agreements, including the quotas. Where not all of the issue is underwritten, a statement of the portion not covered. Indication of the overall amount of the underwriting commission and of the placing commission.
Item 5.4.4	When the underwriting agreement has been or will be reached.
SECTION 6	ADMISSION TO TRADING AND DEALING ARRANGEMENTS
Item 6.1	An indication as to whether the securities offered are or will be the object of an application for admission to trading, with a view to their distribution in a regulated market or third country market, SME Growth Market or MTF with an indication of the markets in question. This circumstance must be set out, without creating the impression that the admission to trading will necessarily be approved. If known, the earliest dates on which the securities will be admitted to trading.
Item 6.2	All the regulated markets, third country markets, SME Growth Market or MTFs on which, to the knowledge of the issuer, securities of the same class of the securities to be offered or admitted to trading are already admitted to trading.

Item 6.3	If simultaneously or almost simultaneously with the application for the admission of the securities to a regulated market, securities of the same class are subscribed for or placed privately or if securities of other classes are created for public or private placing, give details of the nature of such operations and of the number, characteristics and price of the securities to which they relate.
Item 6.4	In case of an admission to trading on a regulated market, details of the entities which have given a firm commitment to act as intermediaries in secondary trading, providing liquidity through bid and offer rates and a description of the main terms of their commitment.
Item 6.5	Details of any stabilisation in line with items 6.5.1 to 6.6 in case of an admission to trading on a regulated market, third country market, SME Growth Market or MTF, where an issuer or a selling shareholder has granted an over-allotment option or it is otherwise proposed that price stabilising activities may be entered into in connection with an offer:
Item 6.5.1	The fact that stabilisation may be undertaken, that there is no assurance that it will be undertaken and that it may be stopped at any time;
Item 6.5.1.1	The fact that stabilisation transactions aim at supporting the market price of the securities during the stabilisation period;
Item 6.5.2	The beginning and the end of the period during which stabilisation may occur;
Item 6.5.3	The identity of the stabilisation manager for each relevant jurisdiction unless this is not known at the time of publication;
Item 6.5.4	The fact that stabilisation transactions may result in a market price that is higher than would otherwise prevail;
Item 6.5.5	The place where the stabilisation may be undertaken including, where relevant, the name of the trading venue(s).
Item 6.6	Over-allotment and 'green shoe': In case of an admission to trading on a regulated market, SME Growth Market or an MTF: (a) the existence and size of any over-allotment facility and/or 'green shoe'; (b) the existence period of the over-allotment facility and/or 'green shoe'; (c) any conditions for the use of the over-allotment facility or exercise of the 'green shoe'.
SECTION 7	SELLING SECURITIES HOLDERS
Item 7.1	Name and business address of the person or entity offering to sell the securities, the nature of any position office or other material relationship that the selling persons has had within the past three years with the issuer or any of its predecessors or affiliates.
Item 7.2	The number and class of securities being offered by each of the selling security holders.
Item 7.3	Where a major shareholder is selling the securities, the size of its shareholding both before and immediately after the issuance.
Item 7.4	In relation to lock-up agreements, provide details of the following: (a) the parties involved; (b) the content and exceptions of the agreement; (c) an indication of the period of the lock up.

SECTION 8	EXPENSE OF THE ISSUE/OFFER
Item 8.1	The total net proceeds and an estimate of the total expenses of the issue/offer.
SECTION 9	DILUTION
Item 9.1	A comparison of: (a) participation in share capital and voting rights for existing shareholders before and after the capital increase resulting from the public offer, with the assumption that existing shareholders do not subscribe for the new shares; (b) the net asset value per share as of the date of the latest balance sheet before the public offer (selling offer and/or capital increase) and the offering price per share within that public offer.
Item 9.2	Where existing shareholders will be diluted regardless of whether they subscribe for their entitlement, because a part of the relevant share issue is reserved only for certain investors (e.g. an institutional placing coupled with an offer to shareholders), an indication of the dilution existing shareholders will experience shall also be presented on the basis that they do take up their entitlement (in addition to the situation in item 9.1 where they do not).
SECTION 10	ADDITIONAL INFORMATION
Item 10.1	If advisors connected with an issue are referred to in the Securities Note, a statement of the capacity in which the advisors have acted.
Item 10.2	An indication of other information in the securities note which has been audited or reviewed by statutory auditors and where auditors have produced a report. Reproduction of the report or, with permission of the competent authority, a summary of the report.

...

Index